# The American Civil War

# THE AMERICAN CIVIL WAR

Peter J. Parish

HOLMES & MEIER
New York • London

Published in the United States of America 1975
by Holmes & Meier Publishers, Inc.
30 Irving Place, New York, New York 10003

LIBRARY OF CONGRESS CATALOGING IN PUBLICATION DATA

Parish, Peter, J.
The American Civil War.

Bibliography: p.
Includes index.
1. United States—History—Civil War, 1861–1865.
I. Title
E468.P27      973.7      74-84660
ISBN 0-8419-0176-7
ISBN 0-8419-0197-X pbk.

PRINTED IN THE UNITED STATES OF AMERICA

Reprinted 1976, 1986

*FOR NORMA*

# Contents

# Contents

# Maps

TABLE

All the maps were drawn from the author's roughs by Douglas London.

# Preface

The Civil War was once described by Abraham Lincoln as a 'fiery trial' through which America must pass. It was indeed the sternest test which the United States has faced from the achievement of independence down to the present generation – a test of the meaning and the very survival of the great American experiment. The institution of slavery and the problem of race posed fundamental questions about American freedom and equality; sectional rivalry and the competing claims of majority rule and minority rights posed equally basic questions about the principles of American democracy and the practice of American federalism. The history of the United States has witnessed a constant struggle to reconcile the consequences of a swift rate of economic and social change with a set of ideals and beliefs, assumed to have been part of the great experiment from the beginning, deeply cherished and constantly invoked, but often easier to proclaim than to practise. Only in the last decade, perhaps, though in a very different way, has that struggle been as agonising and divisive as in the era of the Civil War; the 1970s may offer an appropriate vantage-point from which to take a broad, critical but sympathetic view of the divided Union of the 1860s. Then as now, the American crisis was a matter of vital concern not merely for the United States but for the world.

Few historical events have produced a literature so remarkable alike for its quantity and (at its highest levels) for its quality. On top of the accumulated wisdom of older generations of historians, there has been in the last twenty years a massive output of specialist work on the war, some of it opening up new aspects of the period, some of it reassessing the judgments of earlier historians, much of it reflecting the concerns of Americans a century after the conflict,

One justification for yet another book about the Civil War may be, paradoxically, that there are already so many. The spate of recent studies of particular facets of the subject has not been matched by comparable attempts to offer an overview of the central drama of American history in the light of modern reinterpretations. There have been, on the one hand, a number of helpful, brief surveys of the period; there has been, on the other hand, the completion of the eight-volume history of the Ordeal of the Union by Allan Nevins – one of the great pieces of historical writing of modern times. Between these two extremes lies a wide middle ground in which the present work seeks to find a place as an attempt to offer not just an introduction, but an all-round view and assessment of the conflict within the confines of a single volume.

A few brief words of explanation may be in order. First, I have chosen to concentrate mainly on the period of the war itself because it is in those years that all the varied and complex themes of the wider period are woven together most tightly. I have tried to use the war years as a lens through which to focus on the longer-term changes taking place in mid-nineteenth-century America. The second point concerns the problem which is one justification for this book – the attempt to keep abreast of the tide of new work on the subject. If the specialist reader discovers that my interpretation of a particular issue does not conform to the latest model, he may wish to regard that as evidence of ignorance, and he may of course be right. But it could also be because I have taken as my text some words of no less a Civil War authority than Abraham Lincoln himself: 'I shall adopt new views so fast as they shall appear to be true views.' This may of course offend those who prefer the opposite principle of adopting true views insofar as they appear to be new views.

One further problem concerns the proportion of military history to be included in a general work of this kind. It would be inappropriate (and unappealing to the author) to indulge in that blend of minute detail and relentless enthusiasm which might be described as the what-did-Robert E. Lee-have-for-breakfast-on-the-third-day-at-Gettysburg school of military history. On the other hand, I reject that opposing school of thought which is prepared to discuss the history of a war without mentioning anything so unpleasant as the actual fighting. I hope to avoid the criticism levelled at Charles Sumner that he regarded the war itself as 'an unfortunate and most annoying, though trifling, disturbance, as if a fire-engine had passed by'. I have therefore tried to use the history of the major campaigns to provide the narrative thread along which discussion of other topics may be strung at appropriate intervals, and I have always sought to relate military affairs to political developments, civilian morale, and the wider concerns of a society at war.

My aim has been to set the story of the actual fighting in the context of the society and the times in which it happened, and the times in the wider context of America's nineteenth-century history. I have sought to convey the extraordinary variety of issues and people which were caught up in the struggle, and to suggest the wide ramifications and complex meaning of the Civil War as the central event of American history.

In one sense, this book has been in the making ever since I first began to teach a course on the Civil War, in this University, fifteen years ago, and I owe a great debt to my students who, over the years, have greatly stimulated and enriched my own study of the subject by their enthusiasm, interest, curiosity, scepticism, and refusal to be satisfied with easy answers. I owe more than I can say to the authors of that vast and rich treasury of Civil War literature which alone makes a general work of this kind possible, and I hope that the notes and bibliography will furnish some more specific acknowledgement of my debts. Like so many other scholars, I have benefited from the generosity of the American Council of Learned Societies, through a one-year Fellowship at Johns Hopkins University at a time before this project finally took shape, when I had the privilege of working under the guidance of Professor David Donald.

I should like to express my deep gratitude to friends and colleagues here at Glasgow. Dr Alan Smith and Dr Patricia Lucie read virtually the whole manuscript with great care, and offered an abundance of helpful comment and shrewd criticism. Mrs Maureen Clark read the earlier chapters, and gave me much-valued advice and encouragement. Miss Patricia Ferguson typed the manuscript with almost infallible skill, and constantly performed the near-miracle of transforming my scribble into something which looked as if it might conceivably become a book.

Miss Christine Pevitt of John Farquharson Ltd, and Mr Christopher Stafford of Eyre Methuen have helped me by their encouragement, enthusiasm, constructive criticism, and genuine friendship, to an extent which has gone far beyond their professional obligations.

Above all, I wish to make some ackowledgement, however inadequate, of what I owe to the two women in my home life. My daughter, Helen, made herself into the best possible omen for this whole enterprise by contriving to be born, one month ahead of expert medical prediction, on the one hundred and tenth anniversary of the outbreak of the Civil War. If her tender age has restricted her role as critic or adviser, she has been invaluable in helping me to preserve a proper sense of proportion, by her constant reminder that there are things in this world more important than books, even books about the American Civil War. To my wife, Norma, I owe most of all. She has created the environment in which I could work contentedly and with a minimum of distraction, and she has nobly borne the many extra burdens and inconveniences which fell to her lot. She has helped in a score of ways, but above all simply by being there and being herself.

When a man has received so much help, it only remains to claim as entirely his own all the errors and shortcomings of what follows.

*University of Glasgow*  P.J.P.
*August 1974*

*'The tempest bursting from the waste of Time*
*On the world's fairest hope linked with man's foulest crime.'*

HERMAN MELVILLE

# Part One : Fission

# Chapter I : Danger Signals

To the twentieth-century eye, the map of the United States looks neat and finite, with its straight lines, rectangular patterns and clear-cut geographical features. In the mid-nineteenth century, however, the picture was very different. American boundaries were indefinite, if not infinite, flexible rather than fixed, expanding rather than exact. Man-made boundaries petered out in the vastness of the west; lines turned into question-marks; the frontier was a process rather than a fixed point. In the 1840s vast new territories had been acquired by a mixture of annexation, conquest, purchase and negotiation. Stimulated by the California gold rush, settlement had leap-frogged across to the Pacific coast, leaving a great void between unsettled, and in parts still virtually unexplored. What was wilderness one day called itself a city the next. Back in the east, men looked at the growing west with fear, envy, admiration or exhilaration, while they exploited the opportunities and pondered the problems presented on their own doorstep by mills and factories and mushrooming cities.

1. If the country's geographical limits were vague and undefined, its political prospects and its future destiny were equally a matter for conjecture. Growth, expansion and change were the dominant themes of the age – and growth and change at an incredible rate and in a wide variety of directions. This was a society and a continent in motion; people moved not just from east to west, but farm to factory, from village to city, and, increasingly, from Ireland and Germany and Scandinavia, to Boston, New York, Philadelphia and sometimes on to the frontier settlements of Wisconsin or Minnesota. But in a world in which everything seemed to be changing, there remained some fixed points,

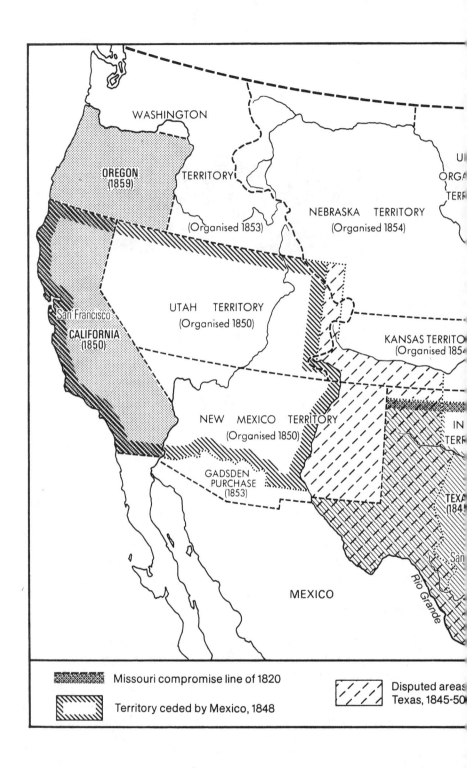

WASHINGTON

OREGON
(1859)

TERRITORY

U

ORGA

TERR

OREGON (1859)

TERRITORY
(Organised 1853)

NEBRASKA    TERRITORY
(Organised 1854)

San Francisco

UTAH    TERRITORY
(Organised 1850)

KANSAS TERRITO
(Organised 185

CALIFORNIA
(1850)

NEW    MEXICO    TERRITORY
(Organised 1850)

IN
TERR

GADSDEN
PURCHASE
(1853)

TEXA
(184

San

MEXICO

Rio Grande

Missouri compromise line of 1820

Territory ceded by Mexico, 1848

Disputed areas
Texas, 1845-50

# IE UNITED STATES IN 1860

1 MASSACHUSETTS
2 RHODE ISLAND
3 CONNECTICUT
4 VERMONT (1791)
5 NEW HAMPSHIRE
6 MARYLAND

MAINE
(1820)

Portland

Boston

SOTA
8)

aul.

WISCONSIN
(1848)

MICHIGAN
(1837)

NEW YORK

Buffalo

Providence

New York

NEW
JERSEY

Detroit

IOWA
(1846)

es Moines

Chicago

Cleveland

PENNSYLVANIA

Philadelphia

INDIANA
(1816)

OHIO
(1803)

Pittsburgh  Baltimore

DELAWARE

ILLINOIS
(1818)

Indianapolis

Cincinnati

Washington

6

Louisville

VIRGINIA

Richmond

St. Louis

MISSOURI
(1821)

KENTUCKY
(1792)

Raleigh

Nashville

NORTH CAROLINA

ARKANSAS
(1836)

TENNESSEE
(1796)

Memphis

Little
Rock

SOUTH
CAROLINA

Wilmington

Atlanta

MISSISSIPPI
(1817)

ALABAMA
(1819)

GEORGIA

Charleston

Vicksburg

Montgomery

Savannah

Mobile

LOUISIANA
(1812)

New Orleans

Pensacola

alveston

FLORIDA
(1845)

s R.

0       500 km
0       300 miles

Free states
Slave states

} with dates of admission as states
(except for original 13 states)

notably in the idea and the ideal of America itself. For, if America was still an unfinished country, it had a very definite beginning and still a not too distant one. A man born in the year of the Declaration of Independence would have been only in his seventies by the middle of the nineteenth century. James Madison, the father of the constitution, if any one man can claim that title, had died only in 1836. John Quincy Adams, son of one of the Revolutionary heroes, and like his father a president of the United States, had served as minister to the Netherlands during Washington's presidency in the 1790s, and yet died only in 1848. As a young man he had lived through the American Revolution, and he gave his dying breath to the struggle against slavery which was to lead to Civil War and emancipation in the next decade and a half. Their country's clear and well-remembered beginning helped to fix a whole cluster of ideas and emotions in the minds and hearts of Americans of the Civil War era. The Declaration of Independence enshrined the high ideals for which America stood, and defined the object of the great experiment. The constitution, with its marvellous blend of precision and ambiguity, had succeeded in becoming both a working instrument of government and a sacred national symbol. George Washington, Thomas Jefferson, and Benjamin Franklin dominated the pantheon of national heroes, and gave individual human form to the national character. In the eyes of many Americans, the United States had been immaculately conceived and born in a state of perfect grace; the problem of the mid-nineteenth century was how to accommodate economic progress, territorial expansion, and constant social change with the ideals and the unique blessings with which the Union had been born. Just as every legal and constitutional problem resolved itself ultimately into interpretation of the original wording of the constitution, so every political development had to justify itself in terms of Jeffersonian principles, and every social change had to be reconciled with the simple virtues of the age of the Founding Fathers. Historians have defined and analysed in various ways this tension between a dynamic social order and fixed principles built into the very foundations of the society. One may see it as a conflict between the agrarian virtue of Jeffersonian America and the ambitions of new men on the make, or as the problem of reconciling a belief in progress with a desire to be faithful to the original American design. Certainly, many of the men who were changing the face of America by their contributions to industrial, technological, and social change were among those most concerned to conserve and protect old values and ideals.[1]

   Whatever tensions they created, expansion and change were real enough in the middle decades of the nineteenth century. The four million Americans who had first tasted independence had become seventeen million by 1840, and that number had almost trebled to fifty million by 1880. Much of the increase came from large families, but a growing contribution was made by immigrants. Some four million came into the United States in the twenty years before the Civil War, and settled mainly in the northern states, and above all in the north-eastern cities. While they thus contributed to the growing imbalance between north and south, they also aroused fears and suspicions in the minds of many native Americans about jobs, wages, housing, and economic opportunity and about their effect on social equilibrium and the essential character of American life. Anti-immigrant feeling in the United States has always tended to intensify at times of crisis, and the pre-Civil War period was no exception.

Within the spectacular overall rate of growth in the population, certain special features stand out. One is the westward shift of population. By 1860 almost half the total population of thirty-one million lived west of the Allegheny–Appalachian mountain chain, the bulk of them in the great central basin of the Mississippi and the Great Lakes. The Atlantic seaboard region, where the United States was born, was now about to be overshadowed by the young giant in the west. Equally striking is the way in which northern population had outstripped that of the southern states. When the war came in 1861, the North had a numerical advantage of much more than two to one: twenty-two million to nine million in round figures. This is linked to another highly significant population trend in the rapid growth of towns and cities. While the United States was still preponderantly a society of farms, villages and small towns, large cities were thrusting themselves into positions of prominence, and proving a powerful magnet to European immigrants and rural and small-town Americans alike. When the American colonies rebelled against Britain, Philadelphia, with forty-two thousand inhabitants, was the largest city in North America. By 1850, New York had passed the half-million mark, well ahead of sturdy challengers like Philadelphia, Boston and Baltimore on the Atlantic seaboard, and rising western cities, like Cincinnati, St Louis and Chicago. In 1830 Chicago did not exist; by 1860, as a booming city of a hundred thousand inhabitants, it played host to the Republican party convention which nominated Abraham Lincoln for president. Not merely the size of the population, but its ethnic make-up, regional distribution and urban concentration posed problems for a country nurtured on Jeffersonian principles of agrarian simplicity and decentralised government.

Settlement flowed freely into the Mississippi valley, particularly during the land booms of the 1830s and 1850s. The great American heartland was filling out, if scarcely filling up, in this period which was in many ways the heyday of the American frontier, both in terms of numbers involved in settlement, and in the impact of the frontier experience on American life. If the frontier ever did exercise a formative influence on American nationalism and democracy, and on the national character as a whole, it was surely in the half-century before the Civil War, when it was an essential part of the pattern of American life rather than the spectacular side-show which it became in the later era of the cowboy, the gunfighter and the transcontinental railroad.[2] By 1861, the original thirteen states had become thirty-three, and most of the new states were west of the Appalachians. The federal government, the creation of the original thirteen states, was now the creator of a majority of the states of the Union. The whole balance of federal-state relations was drastically altered by the growth of the west, and the west became the arena in which the sectional competition of North and South was to be played out.

But expansion in the pre-Civil War decades was not just a question of settlement in territories held since 1783 or since the Louisiana Purchase of 1803. Inspired by a potent mixture of agrarian cupidity, commercial ambition, fear of foreign competition, domestic rivalries and a confident belief in their country's 'manifest destiny', Americans exulted in spectacular new acquisitions which carried the boundaries of the United States to the Pacific Ocean, took over vast tracts of Mexican territory, and pushed British claims in the far north-west back north of the 49th parallel. Texas, which had broken away from Mexico in 1836, ended its independent existence in 1845 when its wish for annexation by the United States was finally gratified. The Mexican War of 1846–8 ended not merely in the confirmation of the American hold on Texas but in the acquisition of the great prize of California, and vast tracts of land in New Mexico and Arizona. Apart from the minor adjustment of the Gadsden Purchase in 1853, and the purchase of Alaska after the Civil War, the continental United States was now complete, but few people realised this at the time, while the air was full of talk of Cuba and Canada, Nicaragua and the rest of Mexico. Moreover, while the newly acquired territories raised acute problems of sectional rivalry at home, they created the temptation to seek sectional advantage by yet further annexations in the years ahead.

American growth in the mid-nineteenth century was not to be measured simply by counting heads or calculating additional thousands of square miles. It was also a question of road, canal and railroad mileage, numbers of cotton mills and ironworks, production figures, export figures, new industrial techniques and processes, and the proliferation of all the commercial, professional and financial services which industrial growth demanded. As a symbol of American progress, the frontiersman's axe was in danger of being superseded by the steam locomotive, the telegraph, or the cotton spindle. Indeed, new territories and a rapidly spreading population could have been more of a liability than an asset without the means to bind the country together, to make New England textile workers, New York merchants, Southern planters and western farmers all part of one economic system. The western pioneer became a significant factor in American economic life not so much when he first hacked a clearing in the virgin forest, as when he abandoned primitive pioneer self-sufficiency, and became linked to the American market economy. Transportation was one of the keys to American development, and by mid-century the railroad was carrying on the process, begun by roads and canals, of replacing the pattern of natural lines of communication, and overcoming the natural obstacles, by a new man-made network linking the far-flung regions of the country. For, if the movement of people and of goods ran increasingly between east and west, the natural lines of communication – the Atlantic coast, and the Mississippi and its tributaries – ran from north to south. So, too, did the greatest barrier to communication, the Appalachian mountain-chain. When the century began, it was easier and cheaper to ship goods in any bulk from, say, Pittsburgh to New York or Philadelphia, by way of the Ohio and Mississippi rivers to New Orleans, and thence by sea, rather than by the direct overland route of less than three hundred miles. If the completion of the Erie Canal in 1825, linking the Hudson River with Lake Erie (and therefore New York with the whole Great Lakes region) was one landmark in the realignment of east–west communications, then the completion in 1852 of the first through rail link between New York city and Chicago was surely another and perhaps even more significant indication of the shape of things to come. If in 1840 it took two weeks or more to travel from New York to St Louis or Chicago, in 1860 it took two days. The effects of this transportation revolution are almost incalculable, both in terms of economic growth and sectional alignments. However much political dissension was threatening to dismember the Union, it was being tied together tighter than ever by the iron rail. Railroad growth was both cause and effect of industrial growth. Economic historians may argue about which decade witnessed the vital industrial breakthrough, or the take-off into economic growth, but it certainly happened in the half-century before the Civil War. In the early years of the United States, manufacturing had been mainly on a small domestic scale, meeting local needs, and based on local raw materials. In the pre-Civil War decades, industrial enterprises developed on a larger scale, mainly but not exclusively in the north-eastern states; industrial workers became a distinct, if still relatively small, section of the community; the whole apparatus of clerical, professional, commercial, financial and distributive services developed in the wake of manufacturing itself; the products of New England textile mills, or boot and shoe factories, Pennsylvania iron foundries, western flour mills and a growing variety of other manufacturing enterprises, were carried to every corner of the Union by river, canal or railroad. A new kind of American society, and a new economic system, was rapidly growing up, and no section of the Union, and no cherished values or traditions, could escape its consequences.

2. This was the great challenge of American life in mid-century – the challenge of rapid growth, and especially rapid industrialisation, to prevailing ideas and accepted ideals. For most Americans shared similar attitudes on basic questions concerning government and society, and, when the Civil War came, both sides believed they were fighting to defend the American ark of the covenant. Strongly held, if not always clearly articulated, beliefs in American democracy, individualism, liberty, equality, morality, and national purpose all contributed to a belief in American destiny, in the distinctiveness of American society. All these basic dogmas of the American faith rested on assumptions built into the United States from the outset. They were firmly rooted in an America of farms and small towns, of simplicity, and self-sufficiency, a loose collection of small communities with limited horizons, but a confidence in the future which was unquestioning and generally unquestioned. How seriously was all this

threatened by vast new territories, burgeoning cities, and proliferating factories
and mills? Was the world of Thomas Jefferson doomed to extinction in the age
of the machine, the railroad, the metropolis, and the national market economy?
The minds of Americans were divided or even confused in their reactions to
rapid change and their attempts to reconcile breathtaking progress with un-
swerving faith in America as it was. Confidence in the future was tinged with
anxiety about old ideals and values. Such mixed feelings were common to all
sections of opinion. If Jacksonian Democrats were anxious both to exploit new
economic opportunities and to preserve the Jeffersonian heritage, a conservative
nationalist, like Daniel Webster from New England, could exult in his country's
industrial achievements and in the growth of a greater New England in the
west, while being disturbed by the implications of yet further, and more remote,
acquisitions of territory. Southern spokesmen, like John C. Calhoun, while
anxious to gain all possible benefits from better communications and the
opening up of new lands, were determined above all to resist the challenge of
industrialisation to their own institutions and way of life. Westerners gloried
in the conquest of the frontier, and welcomed the railroads that brought them
the products of eastern industry and carried away their own surplus crops, but
feared that their section would become no more than a satellite of the industrial
and commercial power of the north-east.

However, amid swift and accelerating change there still seemed to be powerful
elements making for stability in the United States. The political and constitutional
system was now well established and apparently in good working order,
especially after the emergence of a new two-party system, of Democrats and
Whigs, in the 1830s. There was no visible threat to the country's external
security, no powerful neighbour to menace the United States by land or sea.
Prosperity, expanding opportunity, and material well-being were a highly
effective serum against many forms of possible discontent. During the earlier
decades of the century the intricate and shifting sectional balance between north,
south and west had generally worked quite successfully and harmoniously.
Whether or not the frontier did act as a safety valve, many Americans believed
that it performed that function. Above all, the vast majority of Americans
shared a common heritage, a common experience, and a common set of ideas
about the society in which they lived and the government which ruled over
them – and which generally left them very much to their own devices.

But even these stabilising elements were less secure than they appeared at
first sight. The system of government rested on a wide measure of agreement
both among the rulers and the ruled. What if an issue arose which destroyed
that consensus or which undermined the party system, the lubricant of the
complex constitutional machinery? Party politics and sectional bargaining
might be unable to cope with a really intractable issue of the kind which called
into question the basic assumptions and values of the American tradition. In such
a situation, too, isolation from the threat of outside attack might make internal
disruption less dangerous to those who contemplated it.

More serious elements of instability, actual or potential, in American life have become obvious enough in retrospect. The sheer speed of growth and change was frightening enough in itself but it was taking place in a very young country, with unfixed frontiers, an uncertain future, and a destiny which it was easier to celebrate than to predict. The population was extraordinarily mobile, geographically even more than socially, and, however exciting it might be, such constant movement scarcely made for stability. This, too, was a society without the full network of established institutions, the traditional and clearly understood distribution of power, status and prestige, the focal points of authority and leadership which older societies might expect to possess.[3] A hierarchy of classes, a focus of religious authority, an educational élite, a political establishment – none of these was as rigid or as clearly defined, if it existed at all, as in most European societies. American government and society were an impressive edifice, rapidly built on solid foundations, but its structural weakness lay in the shortage of cement to bind the fabric together, or of durable mortar to hold the bricks in position in face of stormy weather or human wear and tear. Within this sprawling edifice each individual was determined to stand on his own feet, but he was not quite sure where he stood – and in any case, he was unlikely to stand there for long. In such a loosely-structured system, where the pressures and restraints from above were so few, other forms of pressure, other kinds of stimuli, could send shock waves rapidly through the community. The mid-nineteenth century was an era of emotionalism, of romanticism, of fervent nationalism, of heady enthusiasms and powerful hatreds. It was, for example, a period when religious revivalism swept across great areas of the United States. Closely related to this was the surge of reforming zeal which prompted an attack on a variety of problems from the treatment of the insane and the physically handicapped, through the temperance and feminist movements, to penal and educational reform. These crusades, like the utopian communities which sprouted across the land, reflected a belief in progress, and in human perfectibility, and a confidence in the individual and his capacity to work out his own salvation, which were very much a part of the spirit of the age. But there was an uglier side, too, to the high emotional temperature of the time. It revealed itself in some of the harsher or more extravagant manifestations of revivalism, and it was most clearly demonstrated in mid-century by the hysterical wave of nativism which swept across the land. A heady brew of super-patriotism, religious bigotry, a sense of insecurity, and a fear of the unfamiliar, nativism latched on to the immigrant, and especially the Catholic immigrant, as the scapegoat for America's problems. It was not a new phenomenon – after all, back in the 1830s, for example, Lyman Beecher had made his 'Plea for the West' on the basis of the urgent need to forestall a giant conspiracy hatched by the papacy and the Habsburg emperor to flood the Mississippi Valley with Catholic immigrants.[4] But nativist feeling reached one of its peaks in the 1850s; the 'Know Nothing' party won control briefly in a number of states, and for a short time it was an open question whether the immigrant or the slave was to provide the issue around which American politics were to achieve a new polarity.

Here was an indication of the real danger. In a society which had inadequate built-in stabilisers, and at a time of rapid change, when emotional excitement was high and reforming zeal was in the air, there was almost no limit to what might happen if a sufficiently large and fundamental issue thrust itself forward. Slavery was just such an issue; it aroused the fiercest moral passions on all sides; it became the focus of attention for reform groups throughout the northern and western states; it revealed the most hideous flaw in the whole American system; its implications, moral, racial, social, political, constitutional and economic, were such that few Americans could escape them. This was the structural weakness which had, unavoidably perhaps, been built into the foundations of the American federal edifice. That edifice had risen to spectacular heights with incredible speed; the question now was whether the flawed foundations could stand the strain.

The political leaders of mid-century America were ill-equipped to face so formidable a problem. The normal pattern of American politics, to be sure, was firmly established, and had generally worked well enough. Everyday politics centred around practical issues, especially those concerned with the role of government in promoting expansion and economic development. Banks, tariffs, the public lands, internal improvements, and the like, these were the stuff of congressional politics. Shifting alignments on such issues reflected a criss-crossing pattern of economic, class, and sectional divisions. Bargains could usually be struck over such issues either between different interest groups – town and country, manufactures, commerce and agriculture – or different regions – a subtle and shifting triangular balance between north-east, west and south generally operated here. The party system of Democrats and Whigs contributed to the same pattern. The parties were loose, ill-defined, often illogical, coalitions of diverse interests, not confined to any one section, but national in scope. They divided from each other on the issues of the day, but, equally important, they united a multiplicity of local and special interests to provide the machinery which enabled the system of government to work at all. The spectrum of opinion covered by the two parties was limited because the normal political issues were practical and specific; underlying disagreements on such issues was a broad area of agreement on what basic American ideals and values should be.

3. The slavery issue burst through this effective but limited piece of political machinery. It blew to pieces the party system, and the normal pattern of bargain and compromise. It destroyed the Whig party, split the Democratic party wide open, and created a new party, the Republicans, sectional rather than national, and rather more ideologically orientated than its predecessors. As things happened, the collapse of the party system followed hard upon the departure from the scene of the old generation of congressional giants; Calhoun, Clay, Webster and John Quincy Adams all died between 1848 and 1852. The new

generation of leaders were either men who were more committed to a cause – Chase and Sumner in the North, Jefferson Davis, Rhett and Yancey in the South – or, if they belonged to the tradition of flexibility and compromise, like Stephen A. Douglas, they lacked the authority of their predecessors, and they found the political climate less congenial. As for the presidents of this period, the politics of bargain and compromise demanded that they be political pygmies, and they were selected as such. It came as a great surprise when one of them – James K. Polk perhaps, or, above all, Abraham Lincoln – proved, once in the White House, to be something very much more.

The normally narrow spectrum of congressional and presidential politics was threatened on both flanks by an issue such as slavery. On the one hand were those who put some moral ideal or ideological commitment ahead of commitment to the constitution and the Union as they were, and to American democracy as already practised. The appeal of men like William H. Seward to a 'higher law' put orthodox practical politics in jeopardy. On the other hand, there were those, in the South, who were determined to defend at all costs a particular way of life, and a particular set of institutions against the onslaughts of political, social and economic change.

Why did the slavery question hold within itself such destructive power? Slavery clearly defined the boundary between North and South, but past experience suggested that clearly defined regions within the framework of the Union need not be a source of fatal weakness. Distinct Northern, Southern and Western sections, and various subdivisions within them had posed problems, but not insuperable ones, and had frequently determined political alignments but scarcely threatened civil war. However, the slaveholding South was becoming increasingly the odd man out, partly because of slavery, partly too because it was not changing in step with other regions of the country. The South became more and more distinct and different simply by remaining the same, or at least by not changing at the same rate or in the same direction as the North. Developments in the northern states were doing much to make the South and the institution of slavery increasingly anachronistic in mid-nineteenth-century America.

Urban-industrial growth had been most marked in the north-eastern states. New York, Pennsylvania and Massachusetts were easily the leading manufacturing states; New York city, Philadelphia and Boston were the leading American cities. Here was an area of opportunity and material progress to rival and, indeed, outstrip the frontier. New interests, new groups, new classes were rising fast – not merely an industrial working class, but an important urban middle class, providing the commercial, financial and professional services which industry required, and still finding time to take up a variety of political, moral and social causes. The middle-class conscience and middle-class moral fervour were to be no less important than middle-class acquisitiveness or ambition in their impact on the America of the Civil War era. In the increasingly urban and industrial north-east, both democracy and nationalism took on a new face and a new meaning. The urban working class was now added to the small farmers in providing the solid numerical foundation of the democratic system. In such a highly mobile, egalitarian society, too, democracy meant more than the right to vote; it meant individual freedom, abounding opportunity, a suspicion of all authority, and a confidence that tomorrow would be better than today. Northern democracy became more and more a matter of the power of King Numbers, a belief in the sovereign power of the majority will, especially as that majority itself became more and more predominantly northern. A new sense of American nationalism went hand in hand with the new democratic spirit. The variety and complexity of northern interests and enterprises now spread far and wide across the country, in a manner which reduced state boundaries almost to irrelevance. The products of northern industry reached every state in the land, and southern cotton and western grain flowed back along the same channels. Northern businessmen thought increasingly in terms of a national market, a national economy, bound together by the railroads and waterways, the banking and credit facilities, and the whole structure of corporate enterprise, which the north-east largely controlled. The sons and daughters, brothers and cousins of New Englanders and New Yorkers were peopling vast areas of the west, adding ties of kinship to the ties of the iron rail. Economic progress and widening horizons engendered a new confidence in national strength and national destiny, and gave a new reality to the Union itself. For more and more people in the north-east, the Union was not just an idea or an ideal, but a going concern. It was both an emotional symbol and a common-sense proposition in terms of their daily lives.

It was against this background of spectacular growth and change that the South felt itself becoming more distinctively Southern, and its peculiar institution of slavery becoming more undeniably peculiar. Cotton and slavery were the twin pillars upon which rested the Southern economy and the Southern way of life. At the end of the eighteenth century, cotton had been a comparatively minor Southern crop, and slavery an institution with a large question-mark over its future. To many Southerners, including large slave-owners like Thomas Jefferson, slavery was a burden which the South should put down, if and when it could. But a cotton crop of 70,000 bales in 1800 had become a crop of almost 4,000,000 bales in 1860. The emergence of cotton as the great staple crop of the South was the result of several factors: the invention of the cotton gin in the 1790s, which removed the main bottleneck in the process of producing cotton; the opening up of the rich new lands of the 'black belt' in Alabama, Mississippi and Louisiana (so called because of the colour of the soil, and not of the skin of the labour force); the development of new strains of 'short staple' cotton, suitable for cultivation over a wider area; and the massive demand for cotton from the expanding textile industries of New England, and, above all, of Great Britain. This concentration on cotton growing gave a new lease of life to slavery, as the most suitable and available source of labour for the cotton-fields of the deep South. Cotton and slavery became interdependent, and the South became dependent on both, and dangerously so in a manner reminiscent of the dependence of the addict on his drugs.

Huge vested interests developed in slavery as both an economic and a social institution. The South was stuck with slavery; its capital was tied up in it, its system of agriculture was based upon it, and its social system was founded upon it. Only if it was shown to be hideously unprofitable, utterly unworkable, or fatally disruptive to the Southern way of life was it likely to be abandoned. As the years passed, new interests became involved; slave-holders in the Atlantic states, like Virginia, where the exhausted soil could no longer compete with the lands of the south-west, turned to the business of selling crops of slaves instead of cotton or tobacco. But behind the economic function of slavery loomed its role as a yardstick of social status and a system of racial adjustment and control. In 1860, out of a white population of 9,000,000 in the slave states, only 383,000 owned slaves, and half of those owned fewer than five. This is still a sizeable proportion of the adult male population, and at the top of the social pyramid were the 48,000 who owned twenty slaves or more. If the characteristic Southern white was a yeoman farmer owning at most two or three slaves and quite probably none at all, there is no doubt that the whole tone of Southern society was set by the large slave-owning planters. They dominated the communities in which they lived and slave ownership was the status symbol of the old South. It also fixed unmistakably the positions and the relationship of the two races. In a situation where there were four million Negroes among eight million whites[5] (and the proportion of Negroes was very much higher in some parts of the deep South), the dominant white community demanded this above all, perhaps, from its peculiar institution. Within the rigid framework of slavery, a good deal of informal, casual (and sometimes very intimate) contact between the races was permissible but only because the lines that mattered were very clearly drawn. Consequently, even the poorest white was assured of a place in Southern society, simply by the colour of his skin; however wretched his circumstances or hopeless his prospects, he could comfort himself by contemplating his social superiority to the Negro slave. Slavery thus provided a floor below which no white man could fall, just as slave ownership offered a ladder by which he might climb higher in his own community. This goes far towards explaining why the non-slave-owning majority of Southern whites was willing to follow the lead of the plantation aristocracy down the road which led to civil war.

Cotton and slavery, then, set the South more and more apart from the rest of the United States. It remained agrarian in outlook, but the concentration of its agriculture on one staple crop also made it heavily dependent on foreign markets, and, in return, on foreign imports, and hence at loggerheads with northern champions of the protective tariff. It was dependent, too, on other sections of the United States – on the north-east for some of its manufactured goods, and even on the north-west for some of its food because its own agriculture was insufficiently diversified. It even depended on New York merchants to handle its own cotton trade (and reap a large share of the profits). Increasingly an odd man out economically, the South was more and more conspicuously set apart by its adherence to slavery. This bred a defensive mentality, which could turn a blind eye to outside realities and replace them by comforting myths. The South tended to build a defensive perimeter around itself, within which developed powerful sanctions against dissent. Elaborate defences of slavery as a positive good, by George Fitzhugh and others, were part of the aggressive defence of the Southern way of life. Southern sectionalism blossomed into Southern nationalism, and an increasing sense of distinctiveness carried clear implications of Southern superiority. By the eve of the Civil War the South had become a distinct society with a distinct culture – agrarian, aristocratic, inward-looking, conservative, resting on assumptions of racial superiority and confident in its own superiority to the materialist, selfish, turbulent, unstable, harshly competitive society of the North.

Of all the differences between North and South, slavery was the most obvious, inescapable, deep rooted and controversial – and the most wide-ranging in its implications. It provided the symbol of North–South differentiation, and it provided the element of moral passion, prejudice and idealism in the sectional argument which led to the ultimate refusal to compromise. Slavery then was the focal point of the whole controversy; it stood for something much wider and more general, and at the same time it created a narrower and more specific political issue. The broader question was one of two distinct societies, two economies, two cultures; the narrow political issue was not concerned with slavery where it already existed but with its extension into new territories in the west. This was the central political issue of the 1840s and 1850s, and even when Abraham Lincoln took office as the first Republican president in 1861, he and his party were committed to the prevention of any further extension of slavery but certainly not to the abolition of slavery itself.

4. Given this picture of two increasingly divergent societies, why should this difference provoke a great crisis, and eventually a civil war in the mid-nineteenth century? Clearly, in the pre-Civil War decades there emerged a much deeper commitment to positions on the slavery issue in both North and South. The economic revival of slavery, and its increasing importance as an instrument of racial control, as the number of slaves increased, and they spread to new lands, transformed it from a cause for shame into a blessing to be celebrated. The defence of slavery as a positive good developed steadily from the comparative moderation of Thomas R. Dew in 1832, through John C. Calhoun, to the fiercely aggressive arguments of Fitzhugh in the 1850s, in his books *Sociology for the South, or the Failure of Free Society* and *Cannibals All! or Slaves without Masters*. The pro-slavery case rested on a variety of arguments and precedents, scriptural and scientific, philosophical and philanthropic, historical and political. But it became markedly more confident, defiant, and ready to counter-attack; indeed Fitzhugh's writings are largely a condemnation

of the *laissez-faire*, capitalist, industrial society of the North. The evils, injustice and degradation of Northern capitalist society are contrasted with the harmony and stability of the slave-holding South. The final stimulus to this uncompromising defence of slavery was provided by the outside attack upon it mounted by the abolitionists in the North. That assault derived much of its strength from the surge of reform activity on many fronts at this time, from new bursts of religious revivalism, from the new aggressive democratic spirit of the Jacksonian era, and possibly from economic and social change, unleashing middle-class energies into crusades against a variety of evils, among which slavery had the comforting advantage of being remote from one's own doorstep. The anti-slavery movement was ill-coordinated and riven by internal dissensions, but William Lloyd Garrison, Wendell Phillips and others in New England, Theodore Weld, James G. Birney and the Tappan brothers in New York, Ohio and points west, kept up an unrelenting attack. They encountered bitter hostility in their own home states, as trouble-makers, fanatics, disturbers of the peace – and perhaps above all as a painful embarrassment to Northern whites no more well-disposed to the Negro than their Southern counterparts. But whatever their impact on Northern opinion, some of the abolitionists, notably Garrison, aroused Southern fears as never before.

On both sides, then, the lines were being drawn in the moral debate on slavery itself. In political terms, the explosive mixture was provided by the connection between slavery and territorial expansion. Many northerners were persuaded by the proposition that the Founding Fathers had accepted or tolerated slavery as something which existed, a fact of American life which could not simply be wished into oblivion, but also as something which would and should die out. They had, after all, made provision for the abolition of the slave trade, and they had surely not seen slavery as an institution which might spread rapidly and indefinitely into new areas. All these calculations were upset by the new lease of life which cotton culture gave to slavery, and by the competition between North and South in the settlement of the west. Controversy flared again with the new burst of expansionism in the 1840s; indeed, the Mexican war and the territorial gains which followed it led in a straight line to the Civil War. Was slavery to spread into yet more territory, and to be protected and fostered there by the federal government? Was slavery to be permitted not merely to continue where it already existed, nor simply to grow within fixed national boundaries, but to extend indefinitely in an ever-expanding Union? That very Manifest Destiny which had been partly inspired by a sense of national mission was to create bitter sectional contention, as pro-slavery expansionists looked for fresh fields to conquer, and anti-slavery men sought to pen slavery within its existing limits. Above all, the linking of slavery and expansion raised new doubts about the future. This was no longer a finite problem within a clearly defined area; it was a competition to be played out bitterly and unrelentingly on a field which extended indefinitely over the western horizon. Far from providing a safety valve for sectional frustration, expansion created an atmosphere of frenzied competition (in an area where the constitution failed to provide any clear rules) and in which extravagant dreams of a new slave empire on the one side were balanced on the other by growing anxieties about the unlimited spread of slavery, even into areas where climate, geography and political reality would surely render it impracticable.

The bitterness of this competition was greatly aggravated by the widening imbalance in the distribution of political power and economic and numerical strength within the United States. The North now far outstripped the South in wealth, strength and numbers, and yet the South remained very strong in all branches of the federal government. This was due partly to the structure of the federal system itself, partly to Southern influence in the Democratic party, and to Southern political skill and experience, and partly to divisions within Northern opinion which militated against the emergence of a solid Northern sectional position. On the whole, the South did very well out of the political system in the 1840s and 1850s, especially as the countless opportunities for obstruction and delay offered by the constitution usually made it possible at least to prevent the passage of uncongenial or unfriendly legislation on, for example, such matters as the tariff or the public lands, and even on slavery itself. In such a situation, it was inevitable that the North should try to assert its numerical and economic strength in political terms, as the power of the majority, and that the South should cling desperately to the political power and influence it had used so effectively, and to the constitutional defences of states rights and minority rights on which it rested its case. For a combination of political, economic and social reasons, the Northern majority was becoming more nationally minded, and for the same reasons, the Southern minority was becoming more sectionally minded. Frustration on one side was matched by anxiety on the other.

Tension mounted, too, because no section of the country could now escape attention from any other for very long. While the United States remained a patchwork of small local communities scattered over a huge area, and strung together only very loosely by economic or political ties, it was not too difficult to live with the problems of regional diversity. But now the revolution in transportation, communications and technology was binding the sections together; freer movement of goods and of people, and all the pressures and opportunities of a national market economy, were creating new contacts and a new state of interdependence just at the time when North and South were becoming more self-consciously distinct from each other than ever before.[6] It was much more difficult for two separate cultures to dwell peaceably within one political entity when they were thrust into such close and constant contact with each other. Distance might not lend enchantment to the view which North had taken of South, or vice versa, but it had created a haze of unconcern, unawareness, even of complacency which could no longer survive.

In the midst of deepening moral commitment, and mounting emotional involvement, of fierce sectional rivalry over westward expansion, of a growing disparity between political and economic power, and of a tightening web of communications and commercial contact, a policy of live and let live gradually became untenable.

The middle ground had been steadily eroded by earlier crises and compromises. The cumulative effects of at least half a century of rivalry, bargain and compromise had, by 1860, left ominously little room for manoeuvre.

5. At mid-century, an issue had emerged which began to look too big and too intractable for the normal processes of compromise, for the political system as it had hitherto worked, or for the leaders who had hitherto worked it. Growth and change in nineteenth-century America had given this issue a new and acute form, and had at the same time weakened the capacity of American government and society to cope with it. As it moved to the centre of the stage, the issue of slavery, and of its further extension, revealed a tragic gap between the promise of American life and its actual performance; it searched out the weak spots in the constitution, and in the political machinery which had grown up around it; it excited radical protest on the one hand, and reactionary defensiveness on the other; it summed up all that distinguished North from South, and all that northerners found objectionable in the South; it converted westward expansion from an affirmation of triumphant nationalism into a confession of sectional incompatibility; it injected a note of passionate disagreement into a system which rested on a wide degree of harmony on fundamental questions. Ultimately, it became a test not merely of the meaning of the American Union but of its very existence.

# Chapter II: How the War Came

The Declaration of Independence affirmed the self-evident truth of the proposition that 'all men are created equal, that they are endowed by their Creator with certain unalienable rights, that among these are life, liberty and the pursuit of happiness'. More than eighty years later, in the course of their great debates in 1858, Abraham Lincoln and Stephen A. Douglas discussed on several occasions the question of whether that declaration did or did not include the Negro. Lincoln insisted that it did and pointed to the danger of allowing any exceptions to it. 'If one man says it does not mean a negro, why not another say it does not mean some other man? If that Declaration is not the truth, let us get the statute book in which we find it and tear it out.' He agreed with Douglas that the Negro was far from being the white man's equal in every respect, but that was no justification for his exclusion from the Declaration.

Anything that argues me into . . . [the] idea of perfect social and political equality with the negro is but a specious and fantastical arrangement of words by which a man can prove a horse-chestnut to be a chestnut horse.

But Lincoln continued:

I hold that . . . there is no reason in the world why the negro is not entitled to all the rights enumerated in the Declaration of Independence – the right of life, liberty and the pursuit of happiness. I hold that he is as much entitled to these as the white man. I agree with Judge Douglas that he is not my equal in many respects, certainly not in color – perhaps not in intellectual and moral endowments; but in the right to eat the bread without leave of anybody else which his own hand earns, he is my equal and the equal of Judge Douglas, and the equal of every other man.

Douglas's answer to this line of argument probably had historical accuracy and political expediency on its side, but it suggested the limitations of his vision and understanding:

> The signers of the Declaration of Independence never dreamed of the negro when they were writing that document. They referred to white men, to men of European birth and European descent, when they declared the equality of all men. . . . When Thomas Jefferson wrote that document he was the owner, and so continued until his death, of a large number of slaves. . . . Now, do you believe – are you willing to have it said – that every man who signed the Declaration of Independence declared the negro his equal, and then was hypocrite enough to continue to hold him as a slave. . . . And yet, when you say that the Declaration of Independence includes the negro, you charge the signers of it with hypocrisy.
> I say to you, frankly, that in my opinion this government was made by our fathers on the white basis. It was made by white men for the benefit of white men and their posterity for ever.

It was right and proper that inferior beings should be given every right and privilege possible 'consistent with the safety of society', but each state must decide for itself what was to be done.[1]

Lincoln and Douglas, like almost all their white contemporaries, agreed on the natural inferiority of the Negro, but drew very different conclusions from that basic premise. Each arrived at a different answer to that recurring problem of American politics and politicians – the reconciliation of the principles which were part of the birthright of the United States with the consequences of rapid change. But America's birthright also included a substantial black population, and the well-entrenched institution of slavery. Negro slavery was America's original sin, and the baptismal waters of the Declaration of Independence failed to wash it away.

The first Negroes were landed in Virginia in 1619, a mere twelve years after the establishment of the first settlement at Jamestown. By the later decades of the seventeenth century, slavery was a legally established institution, mainly but not exclusively confined to the Southern colonies. The highly organised and lucrative slave trade was largely in the hands of New England merchants. By the time of the Revolution, Negroes made up almost one-sixth of the population of the thirteen colonies, and the first federal census in 1790 found almost 700,000 slaves and 60,000 free Negroes in a total population of 4,000,000. During and just after the War of Independence, slavery was abolished in all the Northern states, and the Ordinance of 1787 excluded it from the great Northwest Territory, embracing the modern states of Ohio, Indiana, Illinois, Michigan and Wisconsin.

But, if slavery thus became a Southern sectional institution, it still received national recognition in the federal constitution of 1787 (although the document carefully avoided use of the words 'slave' and 'slavery'). In apportioning seats in the House of Representatives on the basis of population, the constitution provided that a slave should count as three-fifths of a person, although he was clearly not a citizen, and certainly not a voter. In return for this concession which gave it some additional political strength, the South was obliged to accept that the slave trade could be abolished at any time from 1808 – a provision which was acted upon in that very year.

Negro slavery not merely survived the baptismal rites of the new Union, but received confirmation in its permanent constitution.

1. The pious hope that slavery might die a natural death, not too long delayed, was shattered by its economic revival in the early nineteenth century, as King Cotton came into his own, and as expansion into new areas in the south-west underlined its importance as an instrument of social control. In 1819–21 the fatal connection between slavery and westward expansion provoked its first major sectional crisis over the admission of Missouri as a slave state. Missouri was carved out of the vast Louisiana Purchase of 1803, and it straddled what had hitherto been the *ad hoc* dividing line between slave and free states. Its application for statehood raised the whole question of whether slavery should be allowed to take another giant step westward and of what powers Congress did or did not possess to impose restrictions on its spread. It also threatened the delicate balance of free and slave states in the Union. In 1819 they were evenly matched at eleven each, and the parity which this gave to the South in the Senate (where each state has equal representation) was a prized possession at a time when Northern numerical superiority was already giving the non-slave states a clear majority in the House of Representatives. Northern opposition to the admission of Missouri as a slave state was inspired less by moral concern about the institution of slavery than by political calculation and manoeuvre on the part of an uneasy coalition of Northern congressmen, but it generated fierce and protracted debate, and seemed to pose the most direct challenge yet heard in Congress, at least, to the future of slavery itself. Ultimately, the first of the great sectional compromises solved the immediate problems and shelved the basic ones. Missouri's admission as a slave state was balanced by the admission of Maine, in northern New England, as a free state, and slavery was to be excluded from that part of the Louisiana Purchase north of the 36° 30′ line of latitude, with the sole exception of Missouri itself. This last provision in fact confined the future extension of slavery to only a small part of the remaining territory of the United States as it then existed.

The two decades which followed the Missouri Compromise witnessed several further ominous developments in the North–South confrontation over slavery. Within the South, the defence of slavery developed into one of the basic dogmas of the Southern mind. Emancipation societies in the Southern states withered away, voices of dissent about slavery were silenced, and new 'black codes' in most states imposed further restrictions on the slave population. The Vesey plot in Charleston in 1822, and the Nat Turner revolt in Virginia in 1831, aroused lurking fears of large-scale servile insurrection, although neither was a major threat in itself, and both were remarkable mainly for being so untypical of the normal pattern of events.

In the North, in these same years, the anti-slavery movement launched into its great crusade, and sustained it down through the years to the Civil War, in face of fierce and sometimes violent opposition and a stolid mass of indifference. William Lloyd Garrison founded his abolitionist paper *The Liberator* in Boston in 1831, and he and his New England followers joined New Yorkers led by Arthur and Lewis Tappan in founding the American Antislavery Society in 1833. Further west, Theodore Weld turned Oberlin College in Ohio into another centre of the abolitionist crusade, and a successful training ground for workers in the field. In 1837 the death of the abolitionist editor, Elijah P. Lovejoy, at the hands of a mob in Alton, Illinois, gave the cause a martyr. In speeches, sermons, meetings, pamphlets, newspapers, leaflets, petitions, the abolitionists kept up an unrelenting pressure which aroused the fury of many people in the North, and almost all in the South, where great efforts were made to keep out all kinds of anti-slavery propaganda. Abolitionists were abused and mocked, shouted down and beaten up, stoned, mobbed and run out of town, but they were never silenced, and they would not let the issue die. The movement was split by internal disputes and rivalries, over organisation and tactics, and over fundamental matters of policy and principle; it was always a motley collection of diverse groups and societies, often closely linked with other reform causes, rather than a centralised movement waging a coordinated campaign. There were gradualists and immediatists, Garrisonians and anti-Garrisonians, supporters and opponents of political action, believers in passive resistance and supporters of militant action, those who were inspired by religious zeal and Christian ideals, and those like Garrison who could describe one Christian denomination as a 'cage of unclean birds and a synagogue of Satan' and another as controlled by 'blackhearted clergy, conniving with slavery'. But, for all the bitter opposition which they aroused, and for all their feuds and their muddles, they were heard throughout the North – and even in the South, too. They disturbed the consciences of increasing numbers of people throughout Northern society and they profoundly affected the image which each section had of the other. They made the moral issue of slavery harder and harder to escape, so that when slavery became the dominant political issue, it could never be just a political issue to be handled like banks, or tariffs or land grants. For all the backlash effects, for all their rejection as fanatics, extremists, eccentrics, trouble-makers, agitators or whatever, abolitionists took up a basic moral issue, forced it into the forefront of public attention, and at least ensured that things could never quite be the same again.

The anti-slavery movement made its first real impact on Congressional politics in the later 1830s. Theodore Weld and his followers helped to organise a flood of petitions to Congress on various matters concerning slavery and were so successful that the petitions threatened to interfere seriously with the normal business of the House of Representatives. Between 1837 and 1840 the House passed a series of 'gag rules' to limit the use or abuse of the right of petition, and thus enabled the anti-slavery cause to link itself with the defence of one of the cherished and traditional rights of the American citizen. This brought to their aid the formidable figure of John Quincy Adams, ex-President of the United States, now back as a member of the House, who was to earn himself the title of 'Old Man Eloquent' by his championship of this new cause. The petition campaign, and the Congressional battles over the right of petition, including attempts to censure Adams and Joshua Giddings in 1842–3, brought new publicity to the anti-slavery movement, and new support in the country, and created an anti-slavery nucleus in the halls of Congress itself. In 1840, in a more direct move towards political action, the anti-slavery Liberty Party contested the presidential election, with James G. Birney as its candidate, but polled only a handful of votes.

Slavery, North–South tension, and national politics had already been stirred into a potent brew by other events in the decade of the thirties. In 1830 the dramatic Webster–Hayne debate in the Senate had been in part a contest between North and South for the support and friendship of the growing West, and in part a definition of rival theories about the nature of the Union and the rights of the individual states. Then, in 1832–3, this constitutional dispute was given concrete political form in the nullification crisis. Ever since the passage of the high protective tariff of 1828, the so-called 'Tariff of Abominations', the southern states had been protesting against the injustice and illegality of a measure so detrimental to their regional economic interests. South Carolina took the lead, and its most distinguished son, John C. Calhoun, elaborated the constitutional defence of his state's interests. The new tariff of 1832, though it lowered some duties, was still clearly protective in intent, and South Carolina now deployed its new weapon of nullification, that is, the notion that an individual state, as a party to the original compact which created the Union, had the right to declare null and void within its own boundaries a federal law which it deemed unconstitutional and unjust. A special state convention nullified the tariff acts of 1828 and 1832, banned the collection of duties within the state, and declared that any use of force by the federal government would justify secession. President Andrew Jackson reacted vigorously to the challenge from South Carolina in a proclamation which asserted the supremacy of the federal government. Early in 1833 Congress passed the Force Bill giving the president power to collect the revenues by use of military force if necessary, but it was heading towards a compromise on the tariff question, largely the work of Henry Clay, already the architect of one major sectional compromise over Missouri. The passage of the compromise tariff encouraged the South Carolina convention to rescind its ordinance of nullification, but in a final defiant assertion of its constitutional doctrine, it declared the Force Bill null and void. The immediate crisis was over, and all the protagonists believed that they had won something from it. Federal authority had been asserted, but Calhoun and those who thought like him were encouraged to continue their labours on the constitutional defences of the South. The politics of compromise had worked on this occasion, but it was an open question whether they would do so if the Southern states *en bloc*, instead of a single one, took a stand on an issue which they all regarded as a matter of life and death.[2] Each succeeding crisis narrowed the middle ground a little further.

Later in the same decade, territorial expansion added a fresh ingredient to an already dangerous mixture. In 1836 the American settlers in Texas, having avenged the massacre at the Alamo by their victory at the battle of San Jacinto, declared their independence from Mexico, and installed Sam Houston as president of the republic of Texas. There was no doubt that the majority of Texans desired annexation to the United States and they formally requested it in 1837. There was no doubt, either, that Southerners were casting covetous eyes on Texas as a vast new territory open to slavery, out of which not just one but several slave states might be carved. Southern ambitions and Northern suspicions made Texas such a politically sensitive issue that, although the Texans remained willing, annexation was delayed for eight years until 1845.

By the early 1840s, in fact, all the ingredients of the highly combustible compound which finally produced civil war were already being stirred into the pot: a widening disparity in numbers and strength between North and South; the consequent concern of the South to maintain at least a position of equality in the Senate, where each state had two voices, by keeping the balance between slave and non-slave states; the entanglement of the slavery issue with the expansion of the United States; the intensifying debate on the constitutional clash between the will of the majority and the rights of minorities, between federal power and states' rights; the South's sharpening awareness of its own distinctiveness; the Southern commitment to the defence of its peculiar institution matched by a mounting Northern attack on the injustice and inhumanity of Negro slavery; the complicating factor of anti-Negro prejudice and assumptions of Negro inferiority which were common to most white men in North and South; the sheer inescapability and intractability within the existing social and political framework of the issues of slavery and its further extension. In the next two decades, everything was going to depend on whether the South could find a way of safeguarding its special interests which would be acceptable to the North, and whether the Northern majority was willing to live and let live, rather than demand that slavery be put on the road to extinction.

2. What policies were open to the South in its confrontation with the Northern states? The most obvious and potentially fruitful recourse for the South was to avoid just such a confrontation, to prevent the North–South division from becoming the normal pattern within the Union, by creating and consolidating

an alliance either with some geographical part of the north or with some group of political, social and economic interests there. The South had in fact been pursuing just this method quite successfully for many years in the earlier nineteenth century. This past experience suggested two main possibilities. The first was an alliance with the north-western states which in many ways appeared to have more in common with the South than with the North Atlantic states. Nature had clearly decreed that the great central basin of the Mississippi was one geographical region, separated from the north-east by formidable mountain barriers, and with natural lines of communication which flowed south rather than east. South-west and north-west had much else in common, too, including various aspects of the frontier experience, and the whole south shared with the whole west a predominantly rural way of life and a predominantly agricultural set of interests. Moreover, much of the earlier settlement of Ohio, Indiana and Illinois had come from the South Atlantic states by way of Kentucky and Tennessee; Abraham Lincoln's family, for example, had moved from North Carolina to Kentucky, on to Indiana, and finally to Illinois. Many of these Southern settlers in the old north-west were not unhappy to leave slavery behind them, but their ties with the South remained close, and few of them were ever renowned for their sympathetic attitude towards the Negro.

An informal political alliance between West and South had operated for most of the first half-century of United States history. New Englanders and New Yorkers had feared its consequences, and some had resigned themselves to a permanent minority status for their section in a Union dominated by South and West. But the old alliance declined and fell in the pre-Civil War decades. Northern, and particularly New England, settlement gradually came to dominate large areas of the north-west, especially after the opening of the Erie Canal, and other improvements in east–west communications. An energetic missionary effort in the religious and educational fields backed up changing patterns of settlement and trade in the process of 'New-Englandising' the west.[3] A new and fruitful economic relationship developed, as the economies of north-east and north-west increasingly complemented one another, and as the farmers of the north-west were drawn increasingly into the national market economy. Each section provided a market for the other, and each provided what the other needed, although westerners became increasingly convinced that the system operated mainly in favour of eastern business and industry.

Sentiment consolidated the bonds created by trade and settlement. The north-western states, carved out of the great national domain organised by the Ordinance of 1787, were the home of a special kind of American nationalism; by its very existence and rapid growth the region demonstrated the reality and the success of American nationhood. This emotional commitment to the Union was bound to encourage resistance to any threat to dismember it by secession, and so it proved in 1861. Again, most citizens of the north-western states, whatever their origins, had a considerable antipathy to slavery, and especially to its further expansion, even if they may have had little sympathy for either the abolitionists or the slaves themselves. They wanted the continuing westward movement of the frontier to provide new opportunities for themselves and for the system of free labour, and not for the slave-owning planters of the South. Changing political alignments reflected all these developments, and in the fifteen or twenty years before the Civil War there was increasing political cooperation between north-east and north-west on land policy, internal improvements, promotion of railroads, and, of course, in opposition to the extension of slavery. The Republican party was the clearest political expression of the new alignment, and an issue like the homestead bill which granted 160 acres of the public lands free to genuine settlers, demonstrated it in action as clearly as the slavery question itself. Where once the Atlantic seaboard states, north and south, had combined to vote down such pro-settler legislation, by the 1850s, if not earlier, New England, New York and Pennsylvania gave growing support to homestead bills, while the South still voted heavily against them. The beneficiary of a homestead law would be the small farmer, the characteristic settler in the north-west; parcels of 160 acres of land were of no use to Southern planters. In the election of 1860 the Republican party's success in the north-west may have owed more to the homestead plank in its platform than to any other single factor. In a wider sense, that same electoral triumph signified that the North had won the battle for control of the west, and therefore done much to ensure victory in the coming war against the South. Unlike the South, the north-east had been able to use the west, while meeting some western demands in return.

The alternative alliance which beckoned Southern leaders was with the conservative property interests of the Northern states. At first glance there would seem to have been considerable logic on the side of such an alignment of the Southern plantation aristocracy and the Northern mercantile and manufacturing élite in defence of stability and order in an age of turbulence and uncertainty. Calhoun had certainly seen the advantages which it would have offered, and there were times when it seemed near enough to fruition to produce anti-slavery condemnations of an alliance between the lords of the lash and the lords of the loom, as Charles Sumner called them. Indeed, great sectional compromises, like that of 1850, won acceptance largely because they were supported by the conservative and large-propertied interests on either side. Even in 1860–1, New York cotton merchants were to be among the staunchest supporters of compromise, and the sternest critics of coercion of the South.

However, if the preservation of the Union was to depend on collaboration between conservative defenders of the established order in North and South, its prospects were dim indeed, for those conservative interests were bent on conserving very different things. The conservatism of Daniel Webster was poles apart from the reactionary philosophy of John C. Calhoun. Their views of what America should be like were quite irreconcilable. The social order which Calhoun championed and idealised was threatened by the very commercial and industrial interests for which Daniel Webster spoke – for political 'conservatives' in the North were also the agents and promoters of rapid economic and social change. Their philosophies of government had nothing more in common. Webster's confident affirmations of national power contrasted starkly with Calhoun's elaborate defence of states rights. To Webster and others who thought like him, the federal government was to be the active promoter of economic development, and the focal point of a more closely integrated Union. For Calhoun and his Southern followers, the federal government was to be confined to a bare minimum of functions, to be hedged about by constitutional restraints, and at all costs to be prevented from interference with the South's peculiar institution. Northern and Southern conservatives therefore clashed on most of the major politico-economic issues of the day: the tariff, federal internal improvements, the national bank, the public lands. For some decades, it is true, Northern and Southern conservatives did enjoy some considerable success in keeping the slavery problem within bounds, but a law of diminishing returns operated here, especially as Northern conservatives and compromisers faced increasing fire from the rear, from the anti-slavery forces of the North – as Daniel Webster, for example, found to his cost in 1850.[4]

Foiled of their conservative alliance, Southern leaders were thrown back on that illogical liaison with Northern liberals, and with the emergent industrial working class in the North, which has constituted the basis of the Democratic party through much of its history, from Thomas Jefferson to Lyndon Johnson. Such an arrangement worked reasonably well when it was an agreement to do nothing, or a defensive alliance against a common enemy in the commercial and industrial élite, or against the threat of increasing federal power. Its chances of survival were much reduced when one party to the arrangement became obsessed with the protection of one peculiar interest, to which the other was indifferent or even hostile. The slavery issue was to wreck this arrangement, as it wrecked so much else in mid-century, and, in the process, it came close to destroying the Democratic party.

If the normal processes of political bargain, compromise and alliance failed the South, there still remained at least three other means of protection: expansion, constitutional rights, or secession. The first two of these were deployed concurrently with other political processes, and have already been discussed. Whether within the existing territories of the United States, or beyond them, expansion might be used to strengthen and consolidate the position of slavery in the Union, and to maintain parity at least with the non-slave states. The prospect of new slave territory was both cause and effect of the ardent expansionism of the 1840s. The annexation of Texas whetted the appetite for more Mexican territory; when the fruits of the Mexican war turned sour in Southern mouths, interest shifted further afield to small central American republics like Nicaragua, and to Cuba, the most tempting target of all. The annexation of Cuba would offer not merely fertile land, and the removal of an unwelcome Spanish presence so close to American shores, but a valuable new reservoir of slave labour. During heated congressional debates in 1854 when the homestead bill and the acquisition of Cuba jostled for pride of place, Ben Wade of Ohio could jibe that it was simply a matter of priorities between 'land for the landless' and 'niggers for the niggerless'.[5] In the 1840s and 1850s, for Southerners and Northerners alike, expansion was a continuing process with no self-evident limits; it was natural on the one side to see it as a means of sectional salvation and on the other as an opportunity for national development, not to be perverted into an insurance policy for slavery. Thus it was that the question of the further extension of slavery remained the crucial political issue until the coming of war itself, and so it was, too, that any settlement based on the extension of the Missouri Compromise line across the western territories to the Pacific was ruled out by many Northerners as an open invitation to the South to seek additional territory on its side of the line. Moreover, prospects of slavery extension within the existing boundaries of the United States were declining by mid-century, not only because of mounting Northern objections and rapid Northern growth, but also of the harsh facts of climate and geography which seemed to make the south-western territories an unpromising home for the plantation system and the employment of slave labour.

If expansion failed to maintain the South's relative position in the Union, there remained the defences provided by the constitution. By a strict interpretation of the constitution, by a firm defence of the rights of the states, by a resourceful exploitation of all constitutional means of obstructing undesirable legislation, the Southern minority might protect its special interests, and fend off outside interference. It was not Southerners alone who nursed suspicions of any growth of federal power, and the theory of states rights had a considerable weight of history behind it. It may have been a rationalisation of Southern needs, but it was elevated to the status of a dogma, to be revered as much as slavery and the Southern way of life itself. It raised the whole sectional dispute to a higher plane, and cloaked with the respectability of subtle legal argument and solemn legal precedent all manner of special pleading, and defence of vested interests. The South enjoyed no little success in manning the constitutional barricades for many years, but they became harder to defend as affirmation of constitutional rights diverged increasingly from political and economic realities. The will of the Northern majority gradually asserted itself, and the victory of a Northern sectional Republican party in 1860 posed a threat which many Southerners felt could no longer be met by reliance on the constitution, nor even by adherence to the Union itself.

If all else failed, the southern states were left to contemplate secession, the ultimate weapon of a state in a federal system of government. Many Southerners came to believe in secession not as a revolutionary step but as the constitutional right of individual states to withdraw from the compact which they had made. There was a growing feeling too that the Southern identity could best be expressed and Southern interests best defended in a separate Southern polity. However, as with other ultimate weapons, the value of secession lay perhaps not in its use but in the threat of its use. By 1860, Northerners had heard the threat so often that they had begun to question its seriousness. When the threat became a reality, they were shocked, but the South was soon to learn that secession was a dangerous and indiscriminate weapon, ultimately more destructive of its users than its intended victims.

3. In the twenty years before war finally came, the South deployed, or threatened to deploy, all the weapons in its armoury, but neither singly nor in combination did they produce the desired effect. As the crisis deepened, the surviving moderates in the South were increasingly exposed to the danger of being over-taken on the right by secessionist 'fire-eaters'. In the North there was a stiffening determination both to defend the Union and to assert Northern power within it, and, even if there was little sign of a rising sympathy for the Negro himself, there was certainly a more stern and impatient disapproval of the institution of slavery.

The raw fibres of sectional conflict stretched far back into American history, but from the mid-1840s the threads were rapidly drawn together into one tightly woven and apparently unbreakable pattern. There is indeed a remarkably regular chronological progression discernible in the events of these years. At four-yearly intervals, from 1844 to 1860, the demands of a presidential election produced a closing of the party ranks, a blurring if not a total submergence of the great issues, an attempt to maintain stability and to adhere to the normal political processes, and the election of apparently safe and anonymous men – Polk, Taylor, Pierce, Buchanan, Lincoln. But, with equal regularity, in the mid-term years between elections, from 1846 to 1858, a major crisis erupted and threatened the whole political and social fabric – the Mexican war and the Wilmot Proviso in 1846; the great crisis and the last great sectional compromise of 1850; the bitter and disruptive struggle over the Kansas–Nebraska bill in 1854; and then in 1857–9 a whole series of explosive events – the Supreme Court's Dred Scott decision, the furious Congressional battles over Kansas, the Lincoln–Douglas debates in Illinois, and John Brown's lunatic raid on Harper's Ferry. This symmetrical pattern of events was finally shattered when the search for stability failed during the election of 1860, and Lincoln's victory was followed within weeks by secession and within months by war.

The narrative of events moves in a straight line from the Mexican War to the Civil War, with the election of 1844 as an ominous curtain-raiser. A mood of expansionist enthusiasm summed up in the phrase 'Manifest Destiny' dominated that election. Texas and Oregon were the main targets, and lukewarmness in the Texan cause cost Martin Van Buren the Democratic nomination and probably cost that hardy quadrennial Whig candidate, Henry Clay, the election. It was ironical, too, that Clay lost New York and with it the election partly at least because of the few thousand votes taken from him by James G. Birney, candidate of the anti-slavery Liberty Party. The victor in 1844 was the 'dark-horse' Democrat, James K. Polk of Tennessee. 'Who is James K. Polk?' his opponents had scornfully asked, and they were very soon to get their answer. Polk had championed the cause of both Texas and Oregon, and here were the makings of a renewed alliance of South and West, united in expansionist fervour and satisfied with the prospect of a slave Texas balanced by a free Oregon. But it was not to be, or at least it was not to endure. An unspectacular man, with spectacular achievements to his credit as president, Polk was unable to cement that alliance; indeed some of his very achievements did much to destroy it.

The annexation of Texas was completed by a resolution of both houses of Congress even before Polk assumed office. But this by no means disposed of the Texas issue. Texan boundaries were uncertain and the territory now annexed to the United States included parts of other Mexican provinces. To the Mexicans, this was far more than a border dispute, for they still regarded the whole of Texas as a Mexican province. Polk fully supported Texan claims to a frontier on the Rio Grande, rather than on the Nueces river further north, and, like many other Americans, he was now casting covetous eyes on other Mexican territories further west, and above all on California, a province which now had only the most tenuous links with the central Mexican government, and which like Texas had been attracting both American settlers and unwelcome attentions from the British. In the first year of his presidency, Polk attempted by negotiation to settle the Rio Grande frontier and to purchase New Mexico and California. Under pressure from militant opinion at home, successive Mexican governments refused to deal with the Slidell mission sent by Polk. Meanwhile Polk had backed up diplomatic and financial inducements with a show of strength on the Texan frontier. A force under General Zachary Taylor established itself south of the Nueces and in the spring of 1846 moved forward to the Rio Grande. Polk's cabinet was already discussing a war message when news came of a skirmish north of the Rio Grande between the Mexicans and Taylor's force. Swallowing his sabbatarian principles, Polk drafted his war message on Sunday 10 May, and Congress voted for war against Mexico. Polk had declared that the Mexicans had shed American blood on American soil, and, although American claims to this soil were disputable, to say the least, there were few to question such assertions in the first flush of enthusiasm for the war. Among later protesters was an obscure young Congressman from Illinois, Abraham Lincoln, who introduced resolutions demanding clarification of American claims to jurisdiction over the spot where the first blood was shed. Enthusiasm for the war did not endure for long in all parts of the country. Always strongest in the south-western states nearest the area of conflict, the tide of support ebbed quite rapidly the further to the north or east that one cared to look. Northern fears of the designs of Southern pro-slavery expansionists were mingled with Whig reservations about Polk's war. In the north-west there was mounting discontent at the marked contrast between Polk's vehemently aggressive policy against Mexico and his willingness to accept a compromise with Britain over Oregon. Indeed, at the point of embarking on war with Mexico, Polk was anxious for a peaceful settlement with Britain in the north-west. In the 1844 campaign he had supported the claim for the whole of Oregon – '54° 40' or fight' was the expansionist slogan – and early in 1846 he had served notice of the termination of joint rule in the area, and rejected British proposals for a compromise on the 49th parallel. But in June 1846 he accepted a similar proposal, and the Senate ratified the treaty with Britain.

Other grievances aggravated Northern and north-western resentment at Polk's double standard in dealing with Mexico and Britain. The Walker tariff of 1846 upset protectionists in Pennsylvania and other northern states, and wool-growers in the north-west; Polk's veto of a rivers and harbours bill much prized in the north-west was even more unpopular; many Democrats in New York were still unhappy at the shabby treatment meted out to Van Buren in 1844. Northern and north-western Democrats felt that they had been cheated; the promises of 1844 were very different from the performance of 1846. But the reopening gap between North and South was something far bigger than a Democratic intra-party dispute over harbours on the Great Lakes or boundary lines in the distant north-west. From the moment that blood was shed north of the Rio Grande, the real question was the fate of the territories which the United States would assuredly acquire out of the war. The course of the war requires no discussion here; the triumph of American arms culminated in Winfield Scott's capture of Mexico City itself in September 1847. New Mexico and California had already been occupied, and there seemed no limit to possibilities of further conquest. Indeed, Polk's decision to move for peace stemmed partly from his anxiety about those enthusiasts who now clamoured for the annexation of the whole of Mexico. Peace came in the Treaty of Guadalupe Hidalgo in February 1848, which was accepted by Polk and ratified by the Senate despite the extra-ordinary circumstances surrounding its negotiation. The famous jibe of the New York diarist Philip Hone – ' a peace negotiated by an unauthorised agent with an unacknowledged government, submitted by an accidental president to a dissatisfied Senate' – is a pardonable piece of partisan exaggeration.[6] Under the treaty, the United States secured the Rio Grande frontier for Texas, and the whole of California and New Mexico (which included the modern states of Arizona, Utah, and Nevada and parts of Colorado and Wyoming) in return for a financial settlement which totalled just over $18 million.

Thus was lit the fuse which was to set off the explosion in 1861, although that is not to say that it was inevitable that the fuse should burn its full length. What was to be the position of slavery in this huge new domain, all of it in the south-west, but little of it in fact very congenial to slavery in practice? Northerners who had been unhappy about the war from the start, or who saw it as a Southern pro-slavery conspiracy, could join with north-westerners embittered by the administration's failure to fight for 54° 40′ in Oregon in a campaign to prevent slavery from invading the new territories in the south-west. The majority of Northerners whose revulsion against slavery was not strong enough to spur them into an abolitionist crusade against slavery where it already existed might yet be mobilised for a battle against its extension into these vast new areas. For their part, Southerners, having inextricably and fatally entwined the issue of slavery with America's manifest destiny, were determined that they should not now be robbed of the fruits of victory over Mexico, and that there must be no restriction on slavery in the new territories – even if most of those territories were in fact unsuitable for it.

The mere prospect of the acquisition of new territory was enough to produce a clear definition of the basic issue. As early as the summer of 1846 a Democratic Congressman from Pennsylvania, David Wilmot, introduced as an amendment to an appropriations bill his famous 'proviso' that 'neither slavery nor involuntary servitude shall ever exist in any part of said territory' – that is, the territory to be acquired from Mexico. The Wilmot Proviso was passed by the House several times in various forms during the Mexican war, but it never passed the Senate. What it did above all else was to state unequivocally the issue which dominated American politics from 1846 to 1861. The lines were clearly drawn, the legal justifications or rationalisations of the position of each side fully worked out. Northern supporters of the Proviso argued that the territories of the United States not yet organised into states were the responsibility of Congress, which could make all necessary laws for them, including laws concerning slavery – and therefore including laws to keep slavery out. The Southern counter-argument (which had some Northern supporters too) was expressed, for example, in Calhoun's Senate resolutions in 1847. The territories, it was claimed, were the joint property and concern of all the states; as Congress recognised and protected slavery in some of the existing states it must do so in the territories; failure to do so would amount to discrimination against the property rights of citizens of slave states, and would deprive them of a fair chance in the territories. Between these sternly defended positions there was still some room for compromise, perhaps by an extension of the Missouri Compromise line of 1820 across to the Pacific, perhaps by adopting the more novel idea of allowing the settlers in each territory to decide the issue for themselves. There could be little doubt that resourcefulness in achieving compromise was going to be required very soon.

4. In 1848 the two main political parties, still anxious to draw support from all sections of the country, strove once again to smother the slavery controversy. The Whigs paraded as their candidate Zachary Taylor, 'Old Rough and Ready', a hero of the Mexican war which many of them had bitterly opposed, a Southerner, a slave-owner, and a man of no known political views. They solved the problem of drafting an acceptable platform by dispensing with one altogether. Taylor defeated the ageing and uninspiring Democratic candidate, Lewis Cass of Michigan, who ran on a party platform which made no mention of the issue of slavery in the territories. The conspiracy of silence on this burning question was broken by a third party, the Free Soil party, compounded of dissident Democrats, especially in New York, 'conscience' Whigs, mainly from New England, along with survivors of the Liberty party. (One of the confusions in the political language of the period is that 'free soil' and 'free land' meant entirely different things, the former referring to the exclusion of slavery from the territories, and the latter to the homestead policy of granting portions of the public lands free

to genuine settlers.) The Free Soilers produced a strong ticket in 1848, ex-President Martin Van Buren having Charles Francis Adams as his running mate, and Van Buren polled nearly 300,000 votes, a tremendous advance on the record of earlier anti-slavery candidates. In its firm stand against the further extension of slavery, backed by the material inducements of a homestead law and internal improvements, the Free Soil party was moving towards the formula which was to carry its successor, the Republican party, to victory in 1860.

The new president, Zachary Taylor, and the new Congress (in which the parties were so evenly matched that a handful of Free Soilers could hold the balance in the House) were soon confronted with a major sectional crisis. The fate of the territory so recently acquired from Mexico was the main point at issue. If much of New Mexico offered a discouraging prospect for the plantation system and slave labour, this scarcely lessened Southern determination to assert the rights of slavery in that territory. It was vital both to establish the principle and to continue the now desperate struggle to maintain the balance, exactly even in 1850, between slave and non-slave states, for, in the north, Minnesota and Oregon would soon be claiming statehood. One tactic open to the South was to support Texan claims to a large slice of New Mexico, for Texas was already established as a slave state, and there was always the possibility of subdividing it into a number of slave states. Above all there was the question of California, much the most coveted prize among the United States's new possessions, which straddled any putative extension of the old Missouri Compromise line to the Pacific, and which could have a dramatic effect on the sectional balance of power. Sensational developments in California itself soon made the whole problem urgent and immediate. Early in 1848 gold was discovered at Sutter's Mill, and in the following months news of the discovery spread at a speed only exceeded by rumours, hopes, dreams and wild flights of fancy. Within a year at least 80,000 optimistic settlers had arrived by the Cape Horn route, or by way of the central American isthmus, or by covered wagon across the plains and the Rockies. Faced with a rapidly-growing, unstable and heterogeneous population, with more than its fair share of violence and lawlessness, California clearly needed an established civil authority without delay. A convention at Monterey in September 1849 drew up a constitution which prohibited slavery; and early in 1850 a delegation arrived in Washington to seek admission of California as a non-slave state. In the complex manoeuvres and bitter debates of the next eight months, two further issues, this time involving slavery where it already existed, were sucked into the controversy: Southern grievances about the mounting numbers of runaway slaves, aided by the 'Underground Railroad' in the North, and Northern objections to the continued and embarrassing presence of slavery (and an active slave market) in the District of Columbia, that is, in the national capital itself.

The compromise which emerged from months of debate owed much to the old senatorial guard, led by Henry Clay, whose career as the great compromiser had started thirty years earlier, and supported by Daniel Webster in his speech of 7 March, which outraged anti-slavery feelings in New England. However, the final passage of the five separate bills which replaced the earlier omnibus measure probably owed most to a senator of the new generation, Stephen A. Douglas of Illinois, who worked energetically to piece together a majority for each separate bill. Only four Senators in fact voted for all five bills. Supporters of compromise faced a challenge from both sides. A Northerner like William H. Seward of New York argued that the issue was basically a moral one, and whatever the constitutional difficulties there was a law higher than the constitution. This invocation of a higher law set a dangerous precedent which could be exploited in defence of all kinds of causes, good and bad. On the other hand, the dying Calhoun made his last stand in defence of Southern rights and institutions, and younger Southerners like Jefferson Davis of Mississippi were no more disposed to yield anything to the North.

Calhoun's death on 31 March eased the path of compromise; he was determined, Frank Blair jibed later, to die in giving birth to the Southern Confederacy. In July, death removed another obstacle in the person of President Taylor, who had never recovered from some injudicious 4 July celebrations. Much influenced by Seward, he had opposed the compromise package and favoured the immediate admission of California as a free state. His successor, Millard Fillmore, scarcely one of the more lustrous names in the roll of American presidents, shared the outlook of Clay and Webster – indeed he made Webster his secretary of state – and smoothed the path of compromise.

The final compromise was a neat balancing act. The admission of California as a free state was a major Northern gain. The South was compensated by the organisation of the territories of New Mexico and Utah with no conditions for or against slavery; the settlers in the territories could decide the issue for themselves, at the time of elevation to statehood. The Texan boundary was restricted, but the United States government assumed $10 million of Texan debts. The slave trade, but not slavery itself, was abolished in the District of Columbia (the one area where federal authority was direct and unchallenged). The South gained one more major concession in the passage of a very much more severe Fugitive Slave Act; no feature of the settlement did more to ensure that the post-compromise calm would be neither complete nor enduring.

The compromise met with condemnation in some quarters but came as a welcome relief to most people, North and South. Even that relief, however, was tinged from the beginning with doubts, reservations and varying interpretations, and hindsight only strengthens the view that this intricate and ingenious patchwork of measures provided no clear and positive pattern for peaceful development in the future, unless the idea of leaving the crucial decision on slavery to the inhabitants of each territory were to be accepted by all parties. In the northern states acceptance of the compromise and a desire not to push sectional rivalry or moral scruples about slavery to uncomfortable lengths were backed by simple calculations of economic interest on the part of merchants and manufacturers who wanted to keep their national market intact. But anti-slavery voices were anything but silenced by the compromise. They denounced its architects as corrupt bargainers with the forces of evil, and they hammered remorselessly at the inescapable moral issue. As the political and emotional temperature rose again during the 1850s, they evoked a more active response. The fugitive slave law embodied in the compromise itself gave them a ready-made weapon, as one incident involving attempts to help or rescue runaway slaves was followed by another and another in New York, Boston, and further west. If such episodes were sometimes dismissed as mob violence, it has to be admitted that the mobs contained some eminently respectable and distinguished names. Several northern states passed personal liberty laws to counteract the federal measure, and the Chicago Common Council denounced supporters of the hated law as traitors of the stamp of Benedict Arnold and Judas Iscariot. (A whole dictionary of American insults could scarcely offer any more violent denunciation than that.) Harriet Beecher Stowe's best-seller *Uncle Tom's Cabin*, published in 1852, broadened the popular appeal of the anti-slavery cause. To millions of Northerners who, like Mrs Stowe, had never been in the South, slavery was as she described it. Sentimental, ignorant, hostile to the slave-owners but profoundly racist in her assumptions, concerned but curiously blind, perhaps Mrs Stowe was by no means an unrepresentative Northern figure of her day.

Southern reactions to the compromise of 1850 followed much the same pattern as Northern: relief and acceptance predominated for a time, as local and state elections in 1850-1 demonstrated, but from the outset acceptance was cautious and conditional, and insistent that this must be a final settlement. The mood of moderation was fostered by a period of prosperity for much of the South - and by the need to rally round the party flags in the presidential election year of 1852. But more extreme and less accommodating voices were soon re-asserting themselves, and urging reinforcement of Southern defences against the next threat. Indeed, during the fifties, Southern regional self-consciousness rapidly matured into Southern nationalism. The quest for definition of the Southern identity and the assertion of the superior virtue of the Southern way of life had their practical equivalents in attempts to diversify Southern agriculture, or to encourage the growth of manufactures, in the interests of greater economic self-sufficiency. Southern ranks and Southern minds were closing against the threat of Northern aggression or of more subtle and insidious Yankee influences. New leaders like William L. Yancey of Alabama and Robert Barnwell Rhett of South Carolina were more frank and more fiery in their statement of the Southern case and more reckless in their use of the threat of secession. Moderates found it ever more difficult to keep open a window to the North without fanning the flames of extremism in their own hearth.

On both sides, then, men feared for the future even if they accepted the compromise package. Sectional peace had been patched up, and a little time bought at the price of further erosion of the middle ground. Though no one could know it in 1850, the time was to be only a decade; what proved to be a ten-year postponement of secession and civil war inevitably worked in favour of the section which was to grow faster in population, wealth and power in that period. It has indeed been argued that the completion in the 1850s of trunk rail routes linking north-eastern cities with the middle west would alone have been enough to justify the ten-year breathing space for the North.[7]

The election of 1852 took place while the post-compromise lull still prevailed. Whigs and Democrats once again put party loyalties first, although this campaign was to be the last straight fight between these two contestants. The Whigs put their faith yet again in a military hero, General Winfield Scott, while the Democratic choice was the little-known Franklin Pierce of New Hampshire. Both parties professed support for the compromise of 1850, but the Whigs were already going to pieces under its stresses and strains, and Pierce won easily. The Free Soil ticket, headed by John P. Hale, attracted only half the support it had enjoyed in 1848.

Franklin Pierce was never likely to seize the initiative on the slavery question; indeed his backers had never intended that he should. Though a New Englander himself, he was generally controlled by the Southern wing of his party. He hoped to foster national unity and sectional harmony by an expansionist policy which revived Southern ambitions in the Caribbean. Cuba was the main prize; Polk had tried to purchase it in 1848, and while the unsympathetic Whig administration controlled the federal government, private enterprise had taken over in the shape of 'filibustering' expeditions of Cuban refugees and Southern annexationists led by Narciso Lopez, the last of which ended in disaster in 1851. Pierce appointed Pierre Soulé as United States minister to Spain with instructions to renew the bid to purchase Cuba (at a price of up to $130 million). After a spectacularly undiplomatic career in Madrid – 'we wanted an ambassador there; we have sent a matador' was the comment of the New York *Herald* – Soulé met the American ministers to London and Paris in 1854 to discuss policy on Cuba. Their final recommendation is known to history as the Ostend Manifesto, although it was in fact a confidential despatch finally drawn up at Aix-la-Chapelle! It proposed a renewed attempt to buy Cuba, which was deemed essential to the security of slavery; if that failed, Cuba was to be wrested from Spain. Though disavowed by the administration in Washington, this statement caused a furore on both sides of the Atlantic when it became public in 1855. Northern alarm was such that annexation of Cuba became a political impossibility, and even though it remained an objective of the Pierce and Buchanan administrations, one more Southern escape hatch was closed.

5. Even at its peak of excitement the Cuban affair could never steal the limelight for long from the irrepressible question of the western territories. The normal processes of western settlement and expansion ensured that any compromise would soon be overtaken by events. The four-yearly pattern of crises recurred once again in 1854 when Stephen A. Douglas of Illinois introduced into the Senate a bill for the organisation of the territories of Kansas and Nebraska, which included all that remained of the Louisiana Purchase, and a great deal more than

the states which now bear those two names. The crucial feature of Douglas's bill was that it specifically applied to these territories (all of them north of slavery under the old Missouri Compromise line) the principle of squatter sovereignty, or popular sovereignty, that is, the policy of leaving the settlers in the territories to decide the question of slavery for themselves. However much Douglas and others might argue that geography would ensure that these territories would remain free soil, many Northerners leapt to the conclusion that the slave power was now invading the whole of the west. In North as well as South the principle had become more important than its local application, and each side felt that it was defending itself against an insidious attack on its vital interests.

The motivation which inspired the Kansas–Nebraska bill was a complex mixture of personal ambition, political manoeuvre, financial interest and genuine desire to promote sectional harmony. Squatter sovereignty had the appeal of being the proper democratic way of dealing with a thorny problem, and such an exercise of frontier democracy at the grass roots might, it was hoped, also remove a dangerous and disruptive source of conflict from the arena of national politics. Later events in Kansas made a mockery of those pious hopes, and from the outset the bill had other, less lofty, purposes. It was involved in North–South rivalries over the route of the projected transcontinental railroad, and Douglas, anxious to make Chicago its eastern terminal, was in a hurry to organise and settle the territory through which the railroad would pass. The bill was also very much a part of the game of Democratic party politics. Not merely the road to the Pacific but the road to the White House was at stake. Young, dynamic, and burning with presidential ambition, Douglas had scarcely endeared himself to some of the older leaders of the Democratic party, especially in the south. Now he sought an issue which would protect his power base in the north-west and at the same time win him vital support in the south itself. Popular sovereignty as embodied in the Kansas–Nebraska bill seemed just such an issue, and it is ironical, to say the least, that this vehicle of Douglas's ambition was eventually to carry him into a losing battle with Abraham Lincoln for control of the north-west and of the nation, and into a presidential nomination which shattered the Democratic party.[8]

Douglas had not expected his measure to cause a major crisis and yet it ultimately passed only after a titanic struggle in both houses, and at the cost of widespread political devastation. The passage of the bill is a case study in the tactics of political escalation and the processes of party disintegration. Many Southerners were indifferent towards the bill at the outset, fearing perhaps that the advantages which it offered would prove illusory. But Senator Atchison of Missouri, the state which bordered on Kansas territory, was determined to have slavery admitted to the territory, and, acting with a number of Southern senators, forced Douglas to write into his bill a provision that the old Missouri Compromise was void, and that Congress imposed no restriction on slavery in the territories. Southerners in general were aroused by Northern accusations that the bill was the instrument of the aggressive slave conspiracy, and early indifference gave way to firm commitment. As Southern support for the bill solidified, Northern opinion was increasingly aroused against it. As sectional lines hardened, party loyalties no longer proved strong enough to counteract them. The Kansas–Nebraska bill brought the shaky structure of the Whig party tumbling down. Southern Whigs became more self-consciously Southern, while Northern Whigs were bitterly divided between committed anti-slavery men like Seward and supporters of the compromise of 1850. The Democratic party was in little better order, but then as so often in American history it showed a remarkable capacity for survival. Split North and South, and within each section, and riven by endemic feuds over patronage and local issues, the Democrats continued to hold together most of their strength, although they came under withering fire from the small but pugnacious group of free-soil Democrats who had been elected by local coalitions in some Northern states in the preceding years. Men like Salmon P. Chase, Charles Sumner and John P. Hale were formidable antagonists by any standard. Of all the dire consequences of the Kansas–Nebraska Act, its destruction of the old party system was possibly the most serious. For American parties have generally played the role of unifying agents, drawing together all kinds of local and regional interests for the practical purposes of making the system of government work. Now parties had split into factions, and amid general uncertainty and insecurity, men looked for new alignments and new commitments which might create some order out of chaos. In place of the party system, which it had destroyed, the Kansas–Nebraska Act offered the prospect of a new polarity, but a highly dangerous one, sectional and bitterly divisive, and quite incapable of playing the old role of national unification. When the old party system collapsed, the prospect of civil war came nearer by a giant step.

The South had voted almost solidly for the Kansas–Nebraska Act, and although sufficient Northern Democratic votes were mustered to ensure its passage, the Northern outcry against the measure led to the formation of 'anti-Nebraska' coalitions in many states to fight the mid-term elections in the autumn of 1854. Within a year or two of the introduction of Douglas's bill, an increasingly solid South faced a new Northern sectional party dedicated to resisting the further extension of slavery.

If the Republican party was not an overnight growth, it was just about the nearest thing to it in the evolution of political parties. The anti-Nebraska groups which did remarkably well in the elections of 1854 had developed by 1856 into a party fully capable of mounting a major challenge in a presidential election, and already in control of several state governments. Hostility to the Kansas–Nebraska Act was the seed-bed of the party, and the continuing troubles in Kansas proved a most effective stimulant to rapid growth. So, too, did a variety of local issues and grievances, economic or social, ethnic or religious, moral or personal, in states and cities across the North. Numerically, the new party drew its greatest strength from ex-Whigs, some of whom moved directly into the new fold while others found a temporary home in the American or 'Know-Nothing' party which flourished briefly but spectacularly in the mid-fifties. The outburst of anti-immigrant feeling which found political expression in the Know-Nothing party was a symptom of the political confusion and social tension of the day. The party had enjoyed some astonishing successes at local and state level, in Massachusetts for example, and when the old party system finally fell apart in 1854 there was more than a slim chance that hostility to the immigrant, rather than antipathy to slavery, would provide the rallying point for a new major party alignment. A nativist party could claim one big advantage over an anti-slavery party in that its appeal could be national rather than sectional. On the other hand, its cause tended to induce occasional bouts of high fever rather than the chronic malaise which would provide the basis for a durable new party. The sheer excitement of events in Kansas in particular ensured that the slavery issue would remain paramount, and most of the nativists in the North drifted into the Republican party where they were a source of no little embarrassment when it came to appealing for immigrant votes.

If ex-Whigs provided the main numerical strength of the new party, they were also generally its most cautious and conservative element. The other constituent groups in the party may be listed in descending order of numbers but probably in ascending order of commitment to the anti-slavery cause. The anti-Nebraska Democrats were those Northern Democrats who could not stomach the Kansas–Nebraska Act and who subsequently moved into the Republican ranks with varying degrees of celerity and enthusiasm. They followed a path already trodden by free-soil Democrats who had given up their old allegiance before 1854, and by the survivors and heirs of the Free Soil and Liberty parties. These groups provided many of the activists in the early days of the Republican party, the leaven without which the ex-Whig lump might never have risen to oppose the further extension of slavery. The new party also attracted the support of some abolitionists, warriors in the moral crusade against slavery, but most abolitionists opposed involvement in political action, fearing that it would inevitably dilute their basic principles, and obscure the real goal of destroying slavery by concentrating on opposition to its further extension. The Republican party was not in any sense an abolitionist party. At the outset it fixed its attention firmly on the question of excluding slavery from the territories; if on the one hand it had moved towards a policy of abolition, it would have lost the great bulk of its moderate support, while if, on the other hand, it had dwelt too long on other issues of the day, like tariffs or public lands, it would have reopened old wounds sustained in earlier party battles in which its members had been on opposite sides.[9]

Concentration on this one issue was encouraged, if not indeed compelled, by events in Kansas itself. Far from de-fusing a dangerous issue, popular sovereignty in action was rapidly turning Kansas into a battleground. Leaving the decision on slavery to the settlers in the territories produced a fierce competition, and a hectic race against time, between free and slave-owning settlers. Nebraska was too far north to give the pro-slavery cause any real hope, but Kansas, with the slave state of Missouri on its eastern border, was a different matter. Pro-slavery settlers from Missouri had an early advantage but soon met stiff competition from free settlers, many of them sponsored by emigrant aid societies in various parts of the north; the New England Emigrant Aid Society, backed by many prominent figures in Boston, was the most highly organised and best known of them. The turbulence and disorder which were part and parcel of frontier history soon turned the competition into a violent one, and disputed land claims and personal feuds were caught up in the wider struggle. (The line between a crusader against slavery and a horse thief was not always easy to draw on the Kansas frontier.) A pro-slavery raid on Lawrence was followed by the attack on Potawatomie led by John Brown. Kansas was in a state of virtual civil war, and newspapers across the land turned every minor skirmish into a bloody battle. Meanwhile, the first elections for a territorial government were won by the pro-slavery forces, with the help of sympathetic Missourians who slipped across the border on election day. The anti-slavery forces replied by calling a convention at Topeka in 1855 to draw up a constitution and apply for admission as a free state. But the work of this convention, boycotted by the pro-slavery side, was regarded as illegal by the Pierce administration in Washington.

Violence in Kansas was paralleled by acrimonious debate in Congress and this in turn produced an act of violence which sent a shudder of horror and excitement across the land. In May 1856, after Senator Charles Sumner of Massachusetts had delivered his 'Crime against Kansas' speech, which included some savage denunciations of the state of South Carolina and one of its Senators, Andrew Butler, he was badly beaten with a heavy cane, in the Senate chamber, by Preston Brooks, a Congressman from South Carolina. The precise nature and extent of Sumner's injuries have been a matter for debate ever since. He did not resume his place in the Senate for three and a half years, and his injuries became a major theme of Republican propaganda. But there is no convincing evidence that he was shamming, although the psychological damage which Sumner sustained was probably more serious and certainly more protracted than the physical injuries. The Sumner–Brooks affair aroused horrified indignation in the North, but it made Brooks into a Southern hero, and brought him consignments of canes, and advice on their future use, from many of his admirers. In a period of deepening crisis, millions of Americans who were confused or indifferent about constitutional theories or congressional debates on slavery in the territories found their attention focused and their emotions engaged by incidents like the attack on Sumner, or the rescue of a captured runaway slave, or the bizarre escapades of John Brown. Hopes and fears, hatreds and loyalties, excitements and anxieties were fed by the sharp definition (and distortion) of the issues which such sensations produced.

6. Amid such feverish excitement, the election of 1856 could not match its predecessors in its evasion of the burning issue of the day, but it did end in a victory for equivocation and appeasement in the person of the Democrat James

Buchanan. The main challenge now came from the Republican party, standing firm against any further extension of slavery. Their diversity of origins and past loyalties encouraged the Republicans to pass over obvious candidates like William H. Seward and Salmon P. Chase, and select a military hero, though one of a different stamp from Zachary Taylor or Winfield Scott. The young, glamorous western pathfinder, John C. Fremont, was unencumbered by any political record, but also sadly unblessed with any political sense: 'He had every attribute of genius except ability', in the words of Josiah Royce. Both the Know-Nothings and the remnants of the Whig party nominated ex-president Millard Fillmore, but he ran a poor third. However, the combined vote for Fillmore and Fremont comfortably exceeded the Buchanan vote. The Republicans did remarkably well in their first presidential contest, winning in eleven of the northern states and serving notice that the accession of two more sizeable states to their ranks could put a Republican in the White House, for all the efforts of a solid Democratic South to prevent it.

In 1856, at least, a Democrat could still win just enough Northern votes, in addition to his Southern strength, to reach the White House. Buchanan's campaign and his inaugural address had affirmed support for the Kansas–Nebraska Act and for popular sovereignty, but it was ever more difficult to paper over the cracks in the interpretation of that doctrine. To Douglas and his Northern supporters it meant a genuine exercise in local democracy: the people of a territory should decide for themselves whether to admit slavery. To Southerners, however, the appeal of the doctrine was more negative but equally important; it was a device for preventing any interference by the federal government with the right to take slaves into the territories. At the territorial stage of development, slave-owners were to have equal rights with other citizens in taking their property wherever they wished. The debate over the interpretation of popular sovereignty hinged on an argument over timing. At what stage in the development of a territory was the principle of popular sovereignty to operate? The Southern view was that the decision must be delayed until the moment of application for statehood; until then, slavery must have an equal chance in the territory, and, by then, it would no doubt be well established and difficult to eradicate if local conditions were the least bit hospitable to it. The opposing view was that popular sovereignty must operate from the earliest stages, and that the territorial legislature could take steps to keep slavery out in the first place. Such an interpretation aggravated growing Southern doubts about popular sovereignty as a means of salvation for slavery. To submit such a fundamental decision to a single exercise of the majority will at the local level had always seemed at odds with the Southern struggle against the sovereign power of the majority will at the national level. In more practical terms, popular sovereignty was not providing the cast-iron guarantees against interference with slavery which the South wanted. It had served its purpose in gaining for slavery a means of entry into territories hitherto closed to it by the Missouri Compromise. But, once established there, the pro-slavery elements were inclined to deny the right of any authority, federal or territorial, to interfere with their slave property. In supporting popular sovereignty, the South was playing with fire; now, when its fingers were burned, it turned to the constitution and the courts in search of some reliable protective clothing.

When James Buchanan became president, the Dred Scott case which was to provide the occasion for a decision on this vital matter had already been before the Supreme Court for some time. Indeed the Court's decision came two days after Buchanan's inaugural address in which he had forecast that the judiciary would put a speedy end to the controversy over slavery in the territories. The background to the Dred Scott case dated back to the 1830s when Scott, a Negro slave in Missouri, was taken by his master first to Illinois, and then to the territory of Wisconsin. Several years after returning to the slave state of Missouri, he was persuaded to sue for his freedom on the grounds of his residence in a free state and a free territory. The law's delays, in which the United States had always excelled, consumed more than a decade before the final judgment was given. The Supreme Court under Chief Justice Roger B. Taney consisted largely of Democratic nominees, and five of the nine justices came from Southern states. Their decision against Dred Scott was certainly what most Southerners wanted to hear. Taney's written opinion declared that Scott, as a Negro slave, was not a citizen and could not therefore sue in a federal court. If that were so, there was no need to proceed any further, but Taney took the opportunity to say his piece on the question of slavery in the territories. He argued that Scott's period of residence in an area north of the Missouri Compromise line gave him no claim to freedom because Congress had no power to forbid slavery in that territory. Slaves were property, and no citizen could be deprived of property without due process of law. To deprive a citizen of a territory of the right to own slave property would therefore be a denial of constitutional rights. Thus, in 1857, a Supreme Court decision sought to remove from Congress the free hand in legislating for the territories which it had enjoyed for seventy years, and declared unconstitutional the compromise arranged thirty-seven years earlier, and now already defunct in practice. The decision also struck another blow at the doctrine of popular sovereignty in the territories, for if Congress had no power to interfere with slavery in the territories, it could scarcely pass on that power to anyone else.

Reactions to the Dred Scott decision were predictable. The jubilation of Southern Democrats was matched by angry Republican denunciations and allegations of a conspiracy between president and Court. Republican criticisms were directed against the political bias of the Court or of individual justices rather than the powers of the Court itself as an institution, but Southerners chose to interpret such attacks as evidence of the new party's lack of respect for the constitution. As Northern Republicans and Southern Democrats glowered at each other across the judicial minefield which Taney had laid, the group trapped most hazardously in the field itself were the Douglas Democrats of the North. They could scarcely challenge the Court head-on, and yet the Dred

Scott decision left popular sovereignty in ruins. Douglas searched anxiously for an argument which could reconcile the two – and also reconcile the various sections of his party. That party now threatened to prove as vulnerable as the Whigs in face of the slavery issue, and Douglas's Kansas–Nebraska Act had widened the breach it was devised to heal.

As Douglas struggled to adjust policies to events, developments in Kansas created further embarrassments for him and new alarms among the Republicans. A new constitutional convention, this time boycotted by the anti-slavery elements, met at Lecompton in 1857, and inevitably produced a pro-slavery constitution for the future state of Kansas. Since the territorial electorate was offered only the choice of accepting the constitution with or without a provision for the further introduction of slavery, slavery as it already existed in Kansas was guaranteed whatever the outcome. Protesting against this 'fraud', the anti-slavery forces boycotted the vote, and the Lecompton constitution was adopted, and submitted to Congress with the application for statehood. However, when the next elections for the territorial legislature were held, the anti-slavery men participated, and their candidates won a large majority. This encouraged them to put the Lecompton constitution to a popular vote again to defeat it. The position of two years earlier was now reversed; the territorial legislature was in anti-slavery hands, but a pro-slavery constitution had been drawn up, and awaited its fate in Washington.

President Buchanan, receptive as usual to Southern advice, recommended to Congress early in 1858 the adoption of the Lecompton constitution. That constitution was very soon discredited in Kansas itself; it could be regarded at best only as the illegitimate offspring of the doctrine of popular sovereignty. The Congressional debates were long and bitter; the Senate could muster a majority for the measure, but it proved acceptable to the House only in a form which provided for another vote in Kansas. That vote consigned the Lecompton constitution to oblivion, and ensured the future of Kansas as a free state. It finally entered the Union as such in 1861.

For four years the Kansas–Nebraska Act and its repercussions in Kansas and in Washington had kept the question of slavery and its further extension at the centre of affairs. They had also provided a highly effective launching-pad for a new political party; by 1858 it had an established orbit in the American political firmament. Ironically, too, those same events had exploded in the face of the man who had set them in train, for in 1858 Stephen A. Douglas was obliged to disown the Lecompton constitution as a travesty of squatter sovereignty in action. The break between Douglas and the Buchanan administration was now complete. Douglas's hopes of winning Southern support for his presidential bid in 1860 were now virtually nil; the Kansas–Nebraska bridge between Democrats of north-west and south which he had so ingeniously constructed was now swept away by the tide of events. The difficulty about popular sovereignty as a basis for a harmonious solution of the territorial problem was that, to most people in north and south, it was a means rather than an end in itself. Its value depended on its ability to deliver the goods which they wanted. For the voters of Illinois and other north-western states it worked if it opened up Kansas and the remaining territories for free settlers and the system of free labour; for those in the south it worked only if it secured an entry for slavery in those territories and guaranteed it permanent protection there. In its inception, the plan attracted quite widespread support (based on a variety of hopes and expectations), but its specific application in one territory was bound to leave one side or the other, or both, dissatisfied and resentful. Popular sovereignty was a device to cover up the real issues rather than to confront them. By arousing false hopes and then dashing them, it left the situation worse than it found it. By destroying old formulas for sectional harmony and arousing new anxieties, it carried the United States nearer to the chasm of disunion.

If Douglas's presidential ambitions suffered in 1858, his stand against the Lecompton constitution restored his popularity in the north-west, and especially in his home state of Illinois, where he faced a battle for re-election to the Senate in November. Indeed, the demonstration that popular sovereignty could make Kansas safe for free labour whatever the Supreme Court might have said persuaded some Republicans to look upon Douglas with new favour. However, any idea of exploiting the break between Douglas and the Democratic administration by supporting Douglas for re-election was scotched by the Illinois Republicans themselves, who were resolved to oppose the old enemy. The candidate whom they selected to challenge Douglas was a prominent enough figure in Illinois politics, but not a conspicuous figure on the national stage. Ex-Whig, one-term congressman in the 1840s, skilled practitioner in the law and politics of a frontier society, Abraham Lincoln had roused the state Republican convention with his declaration that 'a house divided against itself cannot stand. . . . Either the opponents of slavery will arrest the further spread of it, and place it where the public mind shall rest in the belief that it is in the course of ultimate extinction, or its advocates will push it forward till it shall become alike lawful in all the States, old as well as new, North as well as South.'[10] This was the kernel of Lincoln's argument in the election campaign itself. He exploited for all it was worth the unlikely bogy of the nationwide expansion of slavery; more important, and with great skill, he linked the political issue of slavery in the territories with the moral attack on slavery itself. He was increasingly able to mobilise the feelings of antipathy towards slavery which most Northerners felt without moving into the abolitionist position of demanding an immediate end to it where it already existed. If slavery was penned within its existing limits it would ultimately wither and die. At the same time Lincoln could reproach Douglas for his failure to grasp adequately the moral issues behind the political debate over slavery. This was one of Lincoln's constant themes in the series of seven debates to which he challenged Douglas during the campaign. Douglas's agreement to debate on equal terms with a less well-known opponent did not cost him the election, but it was a tactical mistake, the lesson of which mid-twentieth-century candidates have ignored at their peril.

In the debates, Lincoln also sought to pin Douglas down on the conflict between the Dred Scott decision and the doctrine of popular sovereignty in the territories. Douglas had wrestled with this problem for over a year and had already come up with his highly ingenious, if not altogether persuasive, answer. He restated and amplified it in his debate with Lincoln at Freeport. He argued that, even though the Supreme Court had denied the right to exclude slavery from the territories, a territorial legislature could effectively achieve just this end by refusing to enact the 'friendly legislation' which slavery required. In other words, the lack of a slave code of the kind provided in the southern states would keep slavery out of a territory in practice whatever the Supreme Court might ordain concerning its legal right to be there. This so-called Freeport Doctrine committed Douglas again to an interpretation of popular sovereignty which was essentially free-soil in its implications, and which made both the man and his policy quite unacceptable to Southern opinion. Such was the final burden imposed upon Douglas by the cross which he had designed for himself and which he had carried since 1854.[11]

For all that, he was still returned to the Senate. Senators were then elected not by direct popular vote, but by the members of the newly elected state legislature, and, although the Republicans polled a majority of the popular vote, the Democrats had a narrow majority of seats in the legislature. But no loser ever gained more from an election than Abraham Lincoln. Any candidate who could debate so skilfully with a man of Douglas's formidable talents clearly had a potential which extended beyond his home state. The debates had attracted wide publicity across the land, and, by defining the issues in a way which rallied Republican support, Lincoln turned himself into a prominent and attractive figure on the national stage. The Republicans made gains all across the north in the elections of 1858; by 1860, the White House itself could well be theirs.

7. The intervening two years provided no cooling-off period in the sectional conflict. Northern Republicans and Southern Democrats dug themselves more deeply into entrenched positions, and forays by others far beyond the bounds of party politics only served to intensify antagonism and sharpen suspicions. The most emotionally-charged episode occurred in October 1859, when John Brown, fresh from his wild escapades in Kansas, led an attack on the federal arsenal at Harper's Ferry, Virginia. Patriarchal in appearance, puritanical in doctrine, fanatical in outlook, a blend of insanity, dishonesty and chronic failure in his background and earlier life, John Brown aimed to arouse the slave population of the south and strike a fatal blow at the hated institution on its home soil. He led his band of eighteen men, which included five Negroes and three sons out of his family of twenty, across the Potomac and into the undefended arsenal at Harper's Ferry. Militarily the raid was a fiasco; as a call to arms to the slaves, it fell on deaf ears. Brown's little band was surrounded by a small force commanded by Colonel Robert E. Lee, and most of them were killed or captured. Brown was tried for murder and treason against the state of Virginia and he and six of his

followers were executed. Conceived in fantasy, executed with incompetent folly, and ending in horror and disaster, this episode shocked even Americans hardened by the lurid events of the 1850s. It touched the south on its rawest nerve, the fear of servile insurrection. To a society already riddled with anxiety neuroses about its future and paranoid fears of Northern aggression, it was almost beyond endurance. Rumours and alarms about slave revolts swept the southern states, and John Brown was seen not as an unrepresentative and unbalanced fanatic but as a personification of the overwhelming Northern urge to destroy the South. More than a little credence was given to this view by the evidence that Brown's raid had been backed and financed by prominent Northerners, including Theodore Parker, the New England divine, and Samuel Gridley Howe, the noted social reformer. Moreover, although moderate opinion in the north deplored and denounced the raid, its voice was often drowned by the loud cries of excited approval from other Northerners, including such distinguished men of letters as Emerson and Thoreau. Brown was awarded a martyr's crown and his sins were forgiven or forgotten. Small wonder, then, that Southerners' feelings of insecurity were intensified, and small wonder, too, that they saw the raid as the logical consequence of Republican attitudes and policies, for, although the party had no connection at all with Brown, many of its members deplored his action only for the damage which it might do to the anti-slavery cause.

Harper's Ferry was to the South very much what Preston Brooks's attack on Sumner had been to the North. It intensified feelings by focusing them on a single incident and a single man; it confirmed the most deep-rooted suspicions, and nourished the innermost anxieties; it left scars on the Southern psyche which no reassurances could fully heal.[12]

By the 1850s, myths and symbols, fears, anxieties and suspicions were as real a part of the crisis as border raids in Kansas, violence in the Senate chamber, or the shattering of the peace in Harper's Ferry. Those who dismissed John Brown as a madman, a crank or a criminal in 1859 little realised that the Union army would before long be marching to the strains of 'John Brown's Body'. As another election approached in 1860, there was declining hope that the electoral process could produce even a temporary relief in the agony of the Union, let alone a lasting remedy.

# Chapter III: Crisis of the Union

The sequence of events in 1860–1 has a classic simplicity: the election campaign, Lincoln's victory, the secession of several Southern states, the bombardment of Fort Sumter, the outbreak of civil war. But such simplicity would not make good history; events were too complex, issues too confused, choices too numerous, and opinions too varied to fit any single pattern or all-embracing formula. The road which led to Sumter and on eventually to Appomattox was the one which America took, but in 1860 few if any Americans consciously chose it.

The unpredictability of events conspired with the misconceptions and miscalculations of the participants to create any number of unanswerable questions and intriguing might-have-beens in these months of crisis. At the beginning of 1860, who could have predicted that Abraham Lincoln would be the Republican presidential candidate or that two rival Democratic standard-bearers would take the field against him? Who could have foreseen that Lincoln would win a comfortable majority in the electoral college with slightly less than 40 per cent of the popular vote? Who could have guessed that Lincoln's election would be followed by the secession not of all fifteen slave states, nor of just one or two of the more impatient, but of the seven states of the lower south? Who could have been sure that there would be no great sectional compromise of 1861 which would have prevented or at least postponed armed conflict? Who could have dreamt that the *casus belli* would be provided by a federal garrison of seventy men in an unfinished island fort at the entrance to Charleston harbour? Above all, whose grimmest nightmare could have given warning of the four years of blood and horror which ensued? All that is certain is that no one man or group of men controlled the events of 1860-1, and that no one at all chose the kind of war which actually happened.

1. The twelve months of crisis began and ended at Charleston, South Carolina. Anyone looking for straws in the wind in the spring of 1860 might have found them in the Democratic convention in that city. The split in the party was a pilot project for the subsequent division of the Union itself. Within the party in the spring of 1860, as in the country in the spring of 1861, Northern advocates of compromise were no longer able to find a formula which would give to the South the guarantees it demanded without alienating the bulk of Northern and North-western opinion. Douglas and those who thought like him could no longer appease the South while retaining their appeal in the North. Douglas regarded the Democratic nomination in 1860 as no more than his due, and his supporters were strong enough in the convention to block any other nomination. However, in the unfamiliar surroundings and uncongenial political climate of Charleston, they met equally determined opponents from the Southern delegations. Douglas's stand against the Lecompton constitution and his re-definition of popular sovereignty to placate free-soil opinion in the north had effectively robbed slavery of a permanent home on the plains of Kansas and had put him beyond the pale in Southern eyes. Indeed, there had already been moves well before the convention in many southern states, especially in the lower south, to coordinate policies for the defence of Southern interests, and to make contingency plans against the possibility of a Republican victory. The Alabama platform, devised by William Lowndes Yancey, and endorsed by the Democratic state conventions in Alabama and six other states, insisted upon full protection for slavery in the territories and required the delegates of those states to withdraw from the Charleston convention if their demands were not accepted. Jefferson Davis of Mississippi had introduced resolutions in the Senate in February 1860 denying the right of any authority to interfere with slavery in the territories, and insisting on the passage of a federal slave code for the territories. In the weeks and months before the Charleston convention, threats of secession were freely bandied about in the south, though more moderate opinion, especially in the states of the upper south, still clung to the hope of security within the Union.

The convention ran into trouble from the start and when it rejected a platform along Alabaman lines and adopted resolutions reaffirming support for popular sovereignty, the delegates from eight southern states walked out. Under the rules of the convention, a two-thirds majority of the remaining delegates was not sufficient to nominate Douglas, and it was eventually decided to adjourn and reconvene at Baltimore six weeks later. Much was to happen in those six weeks, but it was already clear that the one remaining nation-wide political organisation was irreparably split. Yancey, Rhett, Ruffin and their followers had taken a bold step on the road towards Southern independence but it was far from clear how many Southerners would follow them. Almost certainly only a fairly small minority had consciously chosen that path in May 1860.

Before the Democrats reassembled, two other candidates were already in the field. Early in May, the newly founded Constitutional Union party, predominantly Whig in outlook and support, nominated John Bell of Tennessee for president, and Edward Everett of Massachusetts for vice-president, on a platform which sententiously pronounced in favour of 'the Constitution of the country, the Union of the States, and the enforcement of the laws'. The party had no hope of winning the election; its main priority was to save the Union by preventing the outright victory of a sectional candidate, and throwing the election into the House of Representatives where a compromise might be arranged.

One week later, a vastly more important convention assembled in Chicago. After their remarkable first showing in 1856, and their impressive gains in the mid-term elections of 1858, the Republicans scented victory in 1860, and, indeed, much of the noise and strife at Charleston had been stimulated by anxieties about just such a prospect. Some Southern extremists even welcomed the likelihood of such an outcome, believing that it would swing the mass of Southern opinion behind moves towards independence.

The Republicans had plenty of would-be presidential candidates in 1860, but all had question-marks against them. Salmon P. Chase of Ohio was highly intelligent and even more highly ambitious, but probably too radical to attract moderate support and certainly too lofty and unbending to excite great popular enthusiasm. Simon Cameron of Pennsylvania was a powerful figure in his home state and an expert political manipulator, but his ambition was not matched by his popularity, nor his influence by his integrity. Edward Bates of Missouri was a safe, solid figure, but by no stretch of the imagination an exciting one, too conservative for many tastes, and too much associated with nativism to be a suitable candidate in an election where immigrant votes would matter. The most prominent national figure in the party, and the undoubted front runner for the nomination, was William H. Seward of New York, ex-governor of the state, a Senator since 1848, a powerful figure in the Whig party for twenty years, and one of the early Republican leaders. A politician of skill and resource, backed by the powerful Thurlow Weed organisation in New York, he was clearly a difficult man to beat, but he was far from invulnerable. Like other disappointed presidential aspirants before and since, he was if anything too well known; he had been too long in public life, had too long a record behind him, and had accumulated too many enemies. Above all, he was widely regarded as too radical, an impression borne out by his earlier hostility to the compromise of 1850, and by his penchant for coining memorable phrases. A man who talked of a law higher than the constitution, or who, in 1858, had spoken of an 'irrepressible conflict' between North and South might be too dangerous in the White House in the stormy days ahead. Ironically, Seward was by 1860 a moderate, and, as Lincoln's secretary of state, was to be the most placatory member of the cabinet in his attitude to the southern states during the secession crisis, and a constant target for radical attack during the Civil War as a sinister conservative influence pervading the conduct of the administration's affairs.

What the Republican party needed in 1860 was a candidate moderate enough to reassure the middle-of-the-road voter but still having anti-slavery credentials satisfactory to the more radical elements in the party. The hour produced the man in the person of Abraham Lincoln, the first choice of comparatively few but a satisfactory second choice for many at the convention. He was an ex-Whig in a party which contained more ex-Whigs than anything else; his record combined a cautious conservatism on most issues with a clear denunciation of the moral evil of slavery; his views were clear-cut where clarity mattered and equivocal where equivocation mattered even more; his supporters were able to mobilise energetic and noisy local support in Chicago. Above all, Lincoln offered the ideal prescription for success as a candidate: a high reputation, recently acquired, a wide popularity which had not had time to go stale. He had a well-established base in his home state, and had won wider renown by his debates with Douglas in 1858 and later speeches in the east. As recently as February 1860, at Cooper Institute in New York city, Lincoln had eloquently linked the moral objection to slavery with the need to bar it from the territories:

> If slavery is right, all words, acts, laws, and constitutions against it, are themselves wrong, and should be silenced, and swept away. If it is right we cannot justly object to its nationality – its universality; if it is wrong, they cannot justifiably insist upon its extension – its enlargement. . . . Their thinking it right, and our thinking it wrong, is the precise fact upon which depends the whole controversy. . . . Wrong as we think slavery is, we can yet afford to let it alone where it is because that much is due to the necessity arising from its actual presence in the nation; but can we, while our votes will prevent it, allow it to spread into the National Territories, and to overrun us here in these Free States?[1]

In 1860 Seward was a man with a past, and Lincoln was a man with a future. Lincoln was nominated on the third ballot at the convention, and Hannibal Hamlin of Maine was chosen as his running-mate. The party's platform bolstered its firm stand against the further extension of slavery with pledges to enact a protective tariff, a homestead law, a programme of internal improvements, a measure to aid the construction of a railroad to the Pacific, and liberalised immigration laws. These proposals offered something to almost every major group of voters in the north and west, and some of them, notably the homestead pledge, no doubt contributed significantly to the Republican victory. But the party remained first and foremost an anti-slavery party, though not an abolitionist one; it had grown out of the Kansas–Nebraska controversy of 1854, it had prospered out of the persistent troubles in Kansas, it had made big gains in 1858 in the wake of the Lecompton fiasco. Individuals and groups across the north might rise to the economic bait in the 1860 platform, but above all, the Northern electorate rallied to the Republicans as a vehicle for their resentment and indignation at Southern assertiveness and their growing impatience with Southern demands for the protection of slavery. Although the Republican platform denounced disunion, the party itself was a symbol of the breakdown of national unity. A party based in one section of the country and representing the interests and attitudes of that section was now in a position to capture the presidency.

When the Democrats reassembled at Baltimore in June, they now knew what faced them, but, far from encouraging a united front, this only made the Southerners more determined to have a platform and a candidate to protect their interests. After confused battles about which delegates were to be admitted, the convention became virtually a Douglas rally, and duly nominated him for the presidency. The Southern 'bolters', many of whom had already met in Richmond to concert strategy, now met separately in Baltimore, and nominated John C. Breckinridge of Kentucky (then vice-president under Buchanan) as their presidential candidate, on something very like Yancey's Alabama platform.

With four major candidates in the field, the campaign was confused, bitter, and remarkably varied in character. In the north the battle was effectively between Lincoln and Douglas while in the deep south Breckinridge ran well ahead of Douglas and Bell. In the upper south and border states Bell and Douglas were the front runners, with Breckinridge third, and Lincoln nowhere. Alone among the candidates, Douglas broke with the conventions of the day and campaigned energetically around the country. His efforts were courageous but unavailing. The final result of the election added up to a classic illustration of how the American electoral system can distort the popular vote. Abraham Lincoln received fractionally less than 40 per cent of the votes cast, but he had a comfortable margin over the combined vote for the other three candidates in the electoral college. Indeed, he would still have won even if all the popular votes cast for Bell, Breckinridge and Douglas had been thrown to a single candidate. Such are the possibilities of a system under which all the electoral college votes of a state go to the leader in the popular vote, however narrow his margin may be, or however large the combined vote for his opponents. Lincoln's strength was strategically concentrated in the more heavily populated northern states, and in fact he won all the electoral college votes of the non-slave states apart from three for Douglas in New Jersey, although his popular margin was small in some states, especially in the north-west. His total of 180 electoral college votes compared with 72 for Breckinridge, mainly from the states of the lower south, 39 for Bell from Tennessee, Kentucky and Virginia, and a mere 12 for Douglas, mainly from Missouri, the only state where he won outright. The contrast between this and the distribution of the popular vote is striking;

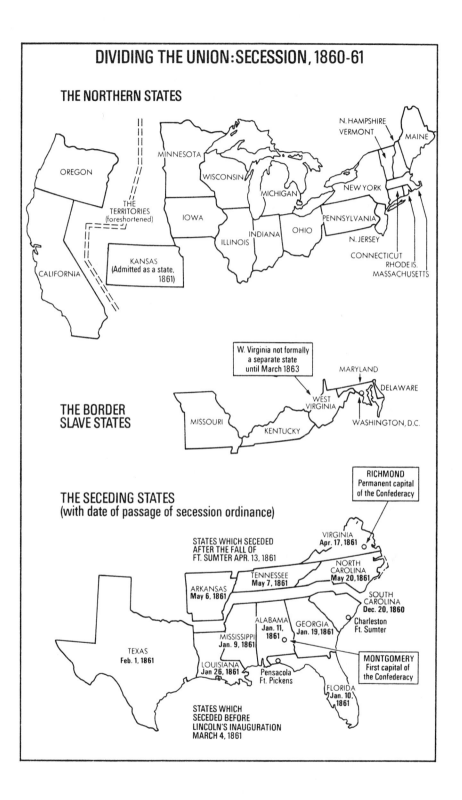

# DIVIDING THE UNION:SECESSION, 1860-61

## THE NORTHERN STATES

N.HAMPSHIRE
VERMONT
MAINE

MINNESOTA

OREGON

WISCONSIN

MICHIGAN

NEW YORK

THE
TERRITORIES
(foreshortened)

IOWA

PENNSYLVANIA

INDIANA OHIO

ILLINOIS

N. JERSEY

KANSAS
(Admitted as a state,
1861)

CONNECTICUT
RHODE IS.
MASSACHUSETTS

CALIFORNIA

W. Virginia not formally
a separate state
until March 1863

MARYLAND

DELAWARE

WEST
VIRGINIA

## THE BORDER
## SLAVE STATES

MISSOURI

WASHINGTON, D.C.

KENTUCKY

RICHMOND
Permanent capital
of the Confederacy

## THE SECEDING STATES
(with date of passage of secession ordinance)

STATES WHICH SECEDED
AFTER THE FALL OF
FT. SUMTER APR. 13, 1861

VIRGINIA
Apr. 17, 1861

NORTH
CAROLINA
May 20,1861

TENNESSEE
May 7, 1861

ARKANSAS
May 6, 1861

SOUTH
CAROLINA
Dec. 20, 1860

ALABAMA
Jan. 11,
1861

GEORGIA
Jan. 19,1861

Charleston
Ft. Sumter

MISSISSIPPI
Jan. 9, 1861

TEXAS
Feb. 1, 1861

LOUISIANA
Jan 26, 1861

Pensacola
Ft. Pickens

MONTGOMERY
First capital of
the Confederacy

FLORIDA
Jan. 10,
1861

STATES WHICH
SECEDED BEFORE
LINCOLN'S INAUGURATION
MARCH 4, 1861

the figures for the latter were Lincoln 1,860,000; Douglas, 1,370,000; Breckinridge 850,000; Bell, 590,000. Douglas piled up his impressive vote by running second to Lincoln all across the north, and running behind Breckinridge or Bell, or both, in the south. The fact remains that Lincoln's victory was perfectly legal and unquestionable, even though his proportion of the popular vote was comparable with, say, Barry Goldwater's in 1964, or George McGovern's in 1972.

The most ominous feature of the 1860 vote was its intensely sectional character. Lincoln's name was not even on the ballot in several southern states, with the result that not a single vote was cast for him in ten states, and even in the border-land, including his native state of Kentucky, he received no more than a handful of votes. The vote for Breckinridge shows the same picture in reverse, though not quite so starkly. More interesting perhaps is Breckinridge's failure to win an overall majority of the vote even in the slave states; the combined totals of Bell and Douglas exceeded his there. Here is one of the clearest pieces of evidence that the south was far from being united, even in 1860, in a Gadarene rush down the slopes of secession. For that matter even Breckinridge had denied during the election that he was a disunionist.

2. Whatever the interpretation of the election returns, and the speculations about the future, the fact remained that, on 4 March 1861, Abraham Lincoln would be duly inaugurated as president of the United States. How was the South to react now that fear had become reality? Threats of secession in the event of a Republican victory had been common currency for some time, and in some states, including South Carolina, commitments and contingency plans had been made. The interests and institutions of the southern states, it was argued, could not be safe under a president elected by the Black Republicans of the north, and dedicated to preventing the further growth of slavery. After all, Lincoln had talked of putting slavery on the road to ultimate extinction, and had made no bones about denouncing it as a moral evil. When Southerners heard other less moderate voices from the Republican ranks, not to mention the fierce blasts of the abolitionists whose influence in the Republican party they wildly exaggerated, many of them were inclined to believe that the threat was immediate rather than remote, and that the extinction of slavery was to be proximate rather than ultimate. Nor were they inclined to pay much heed to the reassurances of the Republican platform, later reinforced by Lincoln himself, that there would be no interference with slavery in the states where it already existed.[2] The real enthusiasts for secession were often impatient with sober calculations about the strategy and tactics best suited to the new situation. They might have done well to take more serious heed of the fact that the new president would not have a Republican majority to support him in either house of Congress – indeed the Republicans had actually lost House seats since 1858 – and that the Supreme Court was still dominated by Democratic appointees, mostly sympathetic to the South. A president elected by less than 40 per cent of the

popular vote, and faced with such handicaps, might find it extremely difficult to slay the monster of slavery, even if he set out to do so. He himself might well be eliminated at the polls in 1864. More moderate and cautious opinion, especially in the upper south, favoured a wait-and-see policy, based on a belief that, once in power, Lincoln and the Republicans would not push matters to extremes, and that the South should wait for some direct and overt act of aggression (if it ever came) before proceeding to the drastic step of secession. In states like Virginia, Kentucky, Tennessee and North Carolina, the majority were as yet unconvinced that they had to make a choice between slavery and the Union.

In the lower south the soft refrain of wait-and-see was less easily heard amid the thundering drumbeats of secession. Predictably, and appropriately, it was South Carolina which led the way, but this was not to be a repeat of the solo performance of thirty years earlier. On hearing the news of Lincoln's election, the South Carolina legislature issued a call for the election of delegates to a special convention to discuss secession. On 20 December 1860 that convention passed a secession ordinance without a dissenting vote. In the weeks and months ahead, South Carolina remained in a fever of secessionist enthusiasm, amid which the handful of Unionists in the state scarcely dared to raise their voices. In April 1861, after the bombardment of Fort Sumter, *The Times* correspondent William Howard Russell found that secession was still all the rage in Charleston: 'Secession is the fashion here. Young ladies sing for it; old ladies pray for it; young men are dying to fight for it; old men are ready to demonstrate it. The founder of the school was St Calhoun. Here his pupils carry out their teaching in thunder and fire.'[3]

Russell found similar zeal for independence in Georgia and other states in April and May, but those states had not taken the plunge with quite the same fervent unanimity as South Carolina. True, they had moved with impressive speed; between 9 January and 1 February 1861, Mississippi, Florida, Alabama, Georgia, Louisiana and Texas had all passed secession ordinances, and, on 4 February, delegates from the seceding states met at Montgomery, Alabama, to discuss a constitution and set up a provisional government for a new Confederacy.[4] However, in most of these states, there had been sizeable minorities opposed to immediate secession. Even in Alabama the vote for delegates to the convention showed only a five-to-four proportion in favour of immediate secession, and in Louisiana the margin was even narrower. Of all those seven states, only Texas actually submitted its secession ordinance to a popular vote, and that only after the fall of Sumter and Lincoln's call to arms. More remarkable still was the fact that, in this first fine careless rapture of secession, only seven out of fifteen slave states had taken themselves out of the Union. It was not too surprising, perhaps, that Delaware and Maryland, small border states with quite small slave populations, should hold their hand, nor even that the larger border states further west, Kentucky and Missouri, should be so reluctant to break the bonds of Union, for Kentucky, in particular, was one of the traditional homes of sectional compromise, and its most famous leader, Henry Clay, 'the Great

Compromiser', now had a worthy heir in John J. Crittenden. But what of Virginia and North Carolina, Tennessee and Arkansas? The Virginia convention rejected secession by a two-to-one margin as late as 4 April, and in the other three states the call for a convention had been rejected by a majority of the voters. Clearly, these states still clung to the hope that both the Union and their own interests could be saved, but, equally clearly, they served notice that any attempt by the federal government to coerce the seceded states would drive them into the arms of their Southern brethren.

The question of Southern Unionism has presented a puzzle both to contemporaries and to later historians. Its extent was exaggerated and its nature misunderstood by many Northerners, including Lincoln and Seward. Its existence was real enough to upset any attempt to depict the South in 1860 as a monolith, solid in its support for secession. But for many people it was conditional upon the new administration's non-interference with the seceded states and it was above all a matter of priorities. Most Southern Unionists wanted to preserve their own way of life and to remain part of the United States. If they became convinced that the two were no longer compatible, how many would put the Union first? Those who were strongly committed to the defence of slavery, from whatever combination of economic, social and racial motives, probably would not. On the other hand, in some areas, where slaves were few and small farmers and the poorer whites predominated, adherence to the Union would be easier to sustain. This was above all true of the Appalachian mountain region which drives a great wedge deep into the heart of the south, through western Virginia and North Carolina and eastern Kentucky and Tennessee, down into northern Georgia and Alabama. Here pro-Union feeling remained strong even during the war; there are even counties in eastern Tennessee whose record of loyalty to the Republican party for over a century after the war can be bettered by no other part of the United States.

3. Northern reactions to the dramatic developments in the south were a mixture of astonishment and fury, complacency and indignation, scepticism and even relief at the departure of such troublesome partners. Some who had always regarded Southern threats as bluff continued to believe that the resort to secession was merely a device to secure better terms in a reunited Union. Some believed that the new Confederacy would quickly collapse out of its own internal weakness, others that a firm stand by the North, with or without some demonstration of force, would soon bring the rebels back to their senses. No doubt many Northerners scarcely knew what to think when precedent and past experience offered little guide, and current leadership none at all.

Opinions about the correct policy to be pursued by the federal government differed just as widely. It is easy enough now to tick off the options open to those in power in Washington: acceptance of peaceful separation, compromise along the lines of earlier sectional bargains, strict adherence to and enforcement of the laws and the constitution, coercion of the seceded states by all necessary means. But in a developing situation, unprecedented and unpredictable, the choices were not clear-cut. What might serve well one day could create new problems the next. Generally it was less easy to decide what to do than to agree on what not to do. In any case, a choice of means depended essentially on a prediction of ends. Peaceful separation, for example, might be accepted either as reluctant recognition of a permanent break or as the means of achieving a smooth restoration of the Union in the short term rather than the long. Support for a new compromise depended very much on its precise terms; terms which might satisfy those who thought the Union worth virtually any price might strike others as a surrender of the very principles on which the Republicans had campaigned in 1860. Coercion might be the chosen policy either of those who were resigned to a full-scale civil conflict, or, more likely, of those who thought that a show of Northern resolution would soon bring the Southern house of cards tumbling down. As the crisis deepened, one option after another was either rejected as unsatisfactory or closed by sheer force of circumstances.

Even if few of the participants in the drama emerge from these events with great credit, they were handicapped by a constitutional system which was generally ill-equipped for such a situation, and which specifically allowed a gap of four months between the election of a new president and his inauguration. In that period seven states had already left the Union which the incoming president would be sworn to defend, and had formed themselves into a new confederacy. In those four months neither the retiring president nor his successor felt able to offer a positive lead, while Congress addressed itself fruitlessly to the possibilities of compromise.

The retiring president, James Buchanan, deserves less censure, perhaps, for his conduct during his last four months in the White House than for what he had done, or more often failed to do, during the whole four years of his presidency. A 'Northern man with Southern principles' in the eyes of many of his opponents in and out of the Democratic party, he had certainly relied heavily on Southern advice and support throughout his term of office. A man who had given full backing to the Lecompton 'fraud' in 1858, and never shown the slightest inclination to take a stand against pro-slavery demands or secessionist threats, was scarcely likely to change his colours now in the last few months of his presidency when his party was divided and already defeated at the polls. When that man was as lacking as James Buchanan in the talent or the will to provide strong leadership, the unlikely became the unthinkable. His main ambition was to avert civil war and final disintegration of the Union until he was safely out of the White House. In his last annual message to Congress in December 1860 he argued against both the right of a state to secede and the power of the federal government to coerce a seceding state. On the specific issue of the federal forts in the southern states, especially those in Charleston harbour which were rapidly becoming a focal point of crisis, Buchanan proceeded with equal caution. He despatched an unarmed relief ship, the *Star of the West*, to Fort Sumter, but the vessel retired after being fired upon by South Carolina shore batteries on

9 January, and for the next two months the administration attempted no further move to Charleston, and tacitly accepted a local truce around Pensacola harbour in Florida where Fort Pickens provided another potential flashpoint.

The retiring president had the power to act but lacked the will. His successor had no power for four months, and his will, too, was far from certain. Busy with cabinet-making and patronage matters, and conscious of the delicacy of the situation and his own lack of authority, Lincoln made no public statements of any consequence before he set out for his inauguration in Washington. This long silence marks one of the least happy phases of Lincoln's career; even if his hands were not yet on the instruments of power, he was certainly not without means of influence and persuasion. But he believed that Southerners would set little store by any reassurances which he could offer and he could scarcely abandon even before his inauguration the platform on which he had been elected. He was far from inactive behind the scenes, taking advice on the possibilities of holding or reoccupying the federal forts in the south, and setting his face against any compromise which would permit the further extension of slavery. Throughout the secession crisis, Lincoln was flexible to a fault on many matters, hesitant and indecisive on others, but he stood unshakably firm on two principles: the integrity of the Union, and the restriction of slavery within its existing limits.

The search for compromise was mainly concentrated in Congress, but, again, under the curious constitutional timetable then in operation, the Congress which met in December was not the one which had been elected in 1860, but its predecessor now embarking on its final 'lame-duck' session. In its hour of direst need the Union was left in the hands of a discredited president, only anxious to lay his burden down, and a Congress already superseded at the polls, but with a three-month session still to complete. In December 1860 two specially selected committees, the Committee of Thirteen in the Senate and the Committee of Thirty-Three in the House, debated a variety of compromise proposals. All kinds of plans from a special national convention to a new version of popular sovereignty dressed up in a series of constitutional amendments were discussed in the Capitol Building and outside. The most persistent one, sponsored by John J. Crittenden, was an extension of the old Missouri Compromise line across to the Pacific, but this was rejected by the majority of Republicans, and by the president-elect himself, partly on the ground that it amounted to an invitation to the South to look for new slave territory beyond existing national boundaries. The only proposal which both houses endorsed, and which Lincoln too was willing to support, was for a constitutional amendment protecting slavery from federal interference in the states where it already existed. But this did not amount to a peace plan in itself, and it was soon dropped. As secession proceeded apace in the lower south in January, Virginia, traditional leader of the South, took the initiative in calling a peace convention which met in Washington on 4 February. Ignored by the states of the deep south busy creating a new government at Montgomery, and attracting only half-hearted support in many northern states, this 'Old Gentlemen's Convention',[5] presided over by John Tyler, who had been president of the United States almost twenty years before, went over familiar ground once again, but lacked the imagination or the status to achieve a breakthrough. Compromise failed because the middle ground had been so worn away that confrontation between the opposing sides was now direct and inescapable. The opponents of compromise in north and south could agree, for opposite reasons, on one thing – namely, that no available formula for compromise was acceptable to both of them.

As southern states seceded, their Senators and representatives left Washington; as compromise plans faltered, all kinds of fantastic future political configurations were taken seriously by one group or another; as Abraham Lincoln left his Illinois home *en route* for Washington, the Montgomery convention formed itself into the provisional Congress of the new Confederate States of America, and Jefferson Davis of Mississippi was sworn in as provisional president. By the time 4 March dawned, there remained little room for manoeuvre. Secession was an accomplished if limited fact; the question now was whether it was to be followed by a rapid reconstruction of the Union, a peaceful but prolonged separation, or a trial by battle.

4. Not the least impressive aspect of Lincoln's inauguration was the fact that it took place at all. Washington was essentially a Southern city, surrounded by the slave states of Virginia and Maryland, and there had been rumours for weeks of a Southern *coup* to take it over and prevent the inauguration of a Republican president. Because of threats against his life, Lincoln himself had been obliged to sneak incognito through Baltimore into Washington only ten days earlier. However, with troops stationed at key points, the inauguration passed off peacefully enough. The new president's inaugural address was a cleverly constructed jigsaw puzzle; those looking among the pieces for clues about future policy found either none at all or so many diverse ones as to be useless. Lincoln tried to reassure the South that there was no threat to slavery where it already existed, but equally he denied both the legality and practicability of secession. 'Plainly,' he said, 'the central ideal of secession is the essence of anarchy', and again, 'Physically speaking we cannot separate. . . . Can aliens make treaties easier than friends can make laws? Can treaties be more faithfully enforced between aliens, than laws can among friends?' He stressed in general terms his sworn duty to uphold the constitution and the laws, but promised uncommon restraint in specific situations:

> Where hostility to the United States, in any interior locality, shall be so great and so universal, as to prevent competent resident citizens from holding the Federal offices, there will be no attempt to force obnoxious strangers among the people for that object. . . . The mails, unless repelled, will continue to be furnished in all parts of the Union. So far as possible, the people everywhere shall have that sense of perfect security which is most favorable to calm thought and reflection.

On the question of the federal forts, he undertook to 'hold, occupy and possess' those still in federal hands, but deleted a reference to retaking those which had been captured.[6] Most of his audience could find in his address what they wanted to find, confirmation of what they wanted to believe. The manysidedness of Lincoln's inaugural was itself a fair guide to his method of handling the crisis during the next six weeks. His policy has been searchingly scrutinised and variously interpreted by generations of historians. One theory has Lincoln manoeuvring deliberately to provoke the South into firing the first shot in a war which offered the only means of rallying Northern support and keeping his party united. Another sees him following a strategy of defence which left the South the choice between submission and aggression, and which ensured that the South would fire the first shot if one was to be fired at all. A third view sees Lincoln pursuing a policy of delay, non-provocation and reduction of tension in the hope that, after a cooling-off period, pro-Union feeling would reassert itself in the south and sectional harmony would be restored. A fourth argues that war was already unavoidable when Lincoln was inaugurated, and that, though sometimes stumbling and uncertain in his tactics, Lincoln was firm and consistent in defence of the Union and rejection of secession.[7]

If none of these explanations is entirely right, only the first perhaps is entirely wrong. Lincoln's preference was to keep open as many options as possible. Like the modern grand designers of nuclear strategy, he sought to interpose as many stages as possible before the ultimate, irreversible decision was reached; when driven to decisions, he preferred those which kept open the widest possible choice of future decisions. If Lincoln himself said that 'my policy is to have no policy', it may be legitimate to interpret that not as a do-nothing attitude but rather as a desire to avoid premature commitment to any one exclusive and irrevocable course of action. Such an approach could make too great a virtue of delay, but at least it kept the possibility of peace with Union open until the last moment.

When Lincoln was sworn in as president, it was rapidly becoming clear that the particular issue of the federal forts would provide the crucial test. As the seceding states severed their ties with the Union, all manner of practical problems arose, from enforcement of law and order to delivery of the mails, but it was possible to live with such difficulties, for a time at least, at the cost of some slight inconvenience. Even the problem of United States forts and arsenals had been resolved in most places by a peaceful take-over of property impossible to defend. But some of the coastal fortifications with access from the sea were a different proposition. The two which really mattered were Fort Pickens off Pensacola on the Gulf coast of Florida, and, above all, Fort Sumter at the entrance to Charleston harbour, where, as self-important Charlestonians were wont to say, the Ashley and Cooper rivers unite to form the Atlantic ocean. If Americans needed a symbolic issue in 1861 what could possibly have served better than an isolated federal garrison marooned on an island fort intended to guard the city which was the very birthplace of secession?

For three weeks and more Lincoln gathered information, listened to advice and avoided major decisions. Hard information was scarce and advice was more plentiful than helpful, spanning the whole range from immediate evacuation to all-out relief and reinforcement. Nor could the new president give his undivided attention to the crisis of the Union and the garrison at Sumter. He was beset with all the pressing decisions concerning appointments, high and low, from minister at the court of St James to postmaster at Geneva, New York, which confront any new administration, and especially the first president of a party which had never before tasted the fruits of federal power. The new cabinet was divided and generally cautious on the great issues of the day, but it contained an immediate problem for Lincoln in the person of Seward, the secretary of state, who was naturally inclined to feel that the presidency should rightfully have been his, and was now quite ready to manage the administration, the cabinet and the president himself. He, too, was the champion of the policy of the cooling-off period, and favoured evacuation of Fort Sumter in the interests of avoiding a showdown. He was closely associated at this time with General Winfield Scott, commander-in-chief of the army, 'Old Fuss and Feathers', an ageing, corpulent veteran of the Mexican War (and even of the war of 1812) who lacked nimbleness of either mind or body.

If Lincoln had some leanings himself towards the policy of delay – and his inaugural could certainly bear that interpretation – he was given distasteful food for thought on the very day after his inauguration. It was then that he read a message from Major Robert Anderson, the commander at Fort Sumter, to the effect that he could not hold out indefinitely and would require relief within approximately six weeks. Military advice was discouraging; Scott estimated that a relief force of 20,000 would be needed, and this at a time when the entire regular army was 16,000 strong, most of it was strung out along the western frontier, and the loyalty of many of its officers was questionable. Amid much bleakly pessimistic advice, the only ray of hope lay in a plan to run fast tugs into Sumter under cover of night, put forward by a retired naval officer, Gustavus Vasa Fox, who happened to be the brother-in-law of the new Postmaster-General, Montgomery Blair. Lincoln's first move was directed at Fort Pickens rather than Fort Sumter; some of his advisers at the time, including Scott and Seward, urged the strengthening of Fort Pickens at Pensacola, which was quite easily accessible and defensible, as a counterweight to the inevitable loss of Sumter. Such a move would reaffirm the government's basic stand on principle and cushion the shock of the evacuation of Sumter to public opinion in the north. Once again Lincoln was intrigued by the possibilities, but not irrevocably committed. On 12 March he sent orders that a relief force lying off Pensacola should reinforce Fort Pickens, but the orders took three long weeks to make their way by sea, and even then the officer commanding the expedition required confirmation that he was to break the truce which prevailed locally. It was 6 April before the president knew that his orders of 12 March had not been executed.

Lincoln's policy moved into a phase of clear-cut decision-making from 28 March onwards. It may be significant that on that day the Senate ended its special session to advise and consent on appointments, thus relieving the president of one serious distraction. It was certainly significant that on that same day General Scott urged evacuation of both Pickens and Sumter on both military and political grounds. Incensed at such advice from such a quarter, Lincoln sounded cabinet opinion next day; whereas, on 15 March, all but two favoured evacuation of Sumter, now only Seward and one other favoured such a course. The rest were either for relief or still uncertain; Attorney-General Bates offered some of the least helpful advice which a president can ever have received: 'I think the time is come when it ought to be either evacuated or relieved.'[8] Orders were sent out for the preparation of a Sumter relief expedition at New York, but Lincoln was of course not yet committed to sending it. The situation was complicated by the simultaneous preparation of another expedition for the further relief of Fort Pickens. This was Seward's brain-child, and so secret that not even the secretaries for War and for the Navy were privy to it. In an administrative muddle, Lincoln signed orders assigning one key vessel, the *Powhatan*, to both expeditions, and the whole affair reveals much about the feverish atmosphere in Washington as March gave way to April, and both sides moved nearer to a collision course.

The man most acutely embarrassed by Lincoln's spurt of decision-making was of course William H. Seward. He had pinned his faith equally on the policy of delay, and evacuation of Sumter, on the re-emergence of pro-Union feeling in the south, and on his own ability to control the administration. A man of vast experience and an enormous range of political contacts, he had kept in close touch with a number of Southerners during the crisis. But he had gone beyond private conversations to sound opinion or gather intelligence. Through intermediaries, the most important of whom was John A. Campbell of Alabama, a Justice of the Supreme Court, he had since mid-March been in touch with three Confederate commissioners who had arrived in Washington ostensibly to arrange the details of a peaceful separation, but no doubt also to play a game of watching and waiting on behalf of the new Confederacy. On 15 March, and again five days later, Seward informed them that Sumter was soon to be evacuated, and this message was relayed to Jefferson Davis in Montgomery. If this statement was intended as a promise it was a shameless piece of deceit; if, as seems more likely, it was a prediction based on confidence in his capacity to control policy, it was still the height of folly. By the end of March the Southern commissioners were becoming impatient, and, once Lincoln had ordered the preparation of a relief expedition, Seward had to face the fact that his gamble had failed. On 1 April he promised the commissioners that no attempt to relieve Fort Sumter would be made without prior notice to the Governor of South Carolina – a quite different and more modest proposition than his earlier assertions. On that same day he made a desperate 'take-over bid' for control of the administration. He submitted 'Some Thoughts for the President's Consideration' which accused the administration of having no policy, advocated a stand against disunion rather than against slavery *per se*, and claimed somewhat mysteriously that this could be achieved by the evacuation of Sumter and the defence of the forts in the Gulf of Mexico. Most remarkable of all, he proposed a foreign war, with Spain or France as the most suitable enemy, as the best means of reuniting the broken Union. If the president would not act someone must do so on his behalf; 'I neither seek to evade nor assume responsibility,' he added, in the least subtle of hints. The reply which Lincoln drafted was cool, courteous and devastating, but it is probable that he never actually sent it and chose instead to convey his message in conversation with the secretary of state.[9] He kept Seward in his cabinet, once and for all established the proper relationship with him, and soon came to regard him as his closest adviser. Seward had fallen into a trap of his own making; Lincoln had generously released him and in the process taught him a lesson.

When Seward reassured the Southern commissioners as late as 7 April with the words, 'Faith as to Sumter fully kept; wait and see', they may be pardoned if they were puzzled and sceptical about the value and precise meaning of that faith. Seward's role in this whole affair is beyond any reasonable explanation; if he was not a knave he was surely a fool. His behaviour on 1 April certainly suggests that he had cracked momentarily under intense nervous strain. The question of Lincoln's possible complicity in the negotiations with the commissioners remains an unsolved mystery. There is no conclusive evidence that he was involved, but his critics question whether a secretary of state could have behaved in such a manner in such a crisis without presidential knowledge or approval. However, Lincoln was much preoccupied elsewhere, and these were no ordinary times, and Seward certainly no ordinary cabinet officer in his conception of his role. Lingering doubts still remain; the commissioners and their activities were well known in Washington; *The Times* correspondent, W. H. Russell, met them as late as 4 April, at a dinner given by Senator Douglas, and attended by two cabinet members, Chase and Smith. The isolation of the man in the White House may or may not have spared him knowledge of such contacts.[10]

Meanwhile, the situation in Charleston harbour waited upon no backstairs intrigues in Washington. With the deadline for the relief of Major Anderson and his men rapidly approaching, Lincoln told Fox on 4 April that he had decided to send the relief expedition, and wrote a message notifying Anderson of his intention. Nothing could better show Lincoln's determination to keep open as many options as possible for as long as possible than his meeting on that very same day with John W. Baldwin, a delegate from the Virginia state convention. He is alleged to have told Baldwin that 'a state for a fort is no bad business', meaning that Fort Sumter would be abandoned if the Virginia convention would immediately adjourn without passing a secession resolution. The 'Old Dominion' of Virginia was a great prize, and Lincoln had certainly considered such a bargain even before his inauguration, but by 4 April it was scarcely feasible, and Baldwin himself later emphasised Lincoln's first words to him: 'You have come too late.'[11]

Two days later, on 6 April, the president at last heard that Fort Pickens had

not been reinforced in accordance with his orders of 12 March. It would probably have been too late now to use the relief of Pickens to offset any projected
evacuation of Sumter, even if this was ever the intention, and Lincoln was
confirmed in the decision already taken to send the Sumter expedition. He
despatched a message to the Governor of South Carolina advising him that an
attempt would be made to relieve the fort with provisions only; men and arms
would be thrown in only if the attempt was resisted or the fort attacked. This
skilfully drafted message placed on Southern shoulders the onus of firing the
first shot but still left open an alternative course of action, though scarcely an
appealing one to those whose every action since the firing on the *Star of the West*
in January suggested its complete rejection. Lincoln can have had small expectation that the peaceful option would be taken, but, if he himself had
consistently sought to provide choices other than war, he could scarcely be
blamed for hoping that his opponents might do the same.

Control of the situation at Charleston had passed some time earlier from the
state authorities to the new government in Montgomery, and, although this
had imposed some restraint on South Carolina hotheads, Jefferson Davis and
his cabinet now moved quickly, partly out of fear of unilateral action by South
Carolina. The military commander at Charleston, Pierre Beauregard, was
instructed to demand the surrender of Sumter before relief could reach it. The
expedition had left New York on 8–9 April and was due to assemble off
Charleston on 11–12 April.[12] On 10 April Major Anderson rejected the surrender
demand, and after the breakdown of a last-minute attempt to settle the matter
on the basis of his admission that he would soon be starved out, he prepared to
offer what reply he could to the batteries which encircled him.

At 4.30 a.m. on 12 April the first shot soared high above the waters of
Charleston harbour. The bombardment of Sumter lasted thirty hours before
Anderson surrendered his battered fort and his tiny garrison, which, astonishingly,
escaped fatal casualties until one soldier died in an accident while firing a last
salute to the flag after the surrender. Some ships of the relief force, scattered and
storm-tossed on the voyage south, witnessed the bombardment from outside
the harbour, but Fox felt unable to intervene.

This almost bloodless encounter at Charleston could scarcely have been a
more misleading or inappropriate prologue to the four years of bloody conflict
which were to come.

5. Whatever the intentions or expectations of those who had guided affairs to
this point, the firing on Sumter at least swept away all manner of doubts and
uncertainties on both sides. Northern opinion rallied to the defence of the
Union now that the secessionists had actually fired upon the flag. Bemused and
bewildered for months by a crisis for which nothing had really prepared them,
Northerners now knew where they stood. Doubts and divisions would reappear
soon enough, but, in the first flush of excitement, Northern unity was impressive
– so impressive indeed that it has probably helped to persuade some historians

that Lincoln's devious policy had provoked the attack on Sumter with precisely this end in mind. In the lower south the bombardment of Sumter raised secessionist fever to a new pitch, confirmed the optimistic view that one Southerner could whip ten Yankees, and destroyed the illusion that independence could be won without a fight. It brought into the Confederacy four states of the upper south – Virginia, North Carolina, Tennessee and Arkansas – which all seceded from the Union soon after the fall of Sumter when it became clear that force was to be used against their departed sister states.

It is fruitless to speculate whether war was inevitable from the moment of Lincoln's election or his inauguration, especially as, in a crisis situation of this kind, how and when an event occurs is often as important as the fact that it occurs at all. The attitudes and the actions of Lincoln, Davis and their respective administrations therefore merit scrutiny and offer striking contrasts. Lincoln's secretaries, Nicolay and Hay, later wrote approvingly of his 'persistent non-committal, his silent hopefulness, his patient and well-considered inaction',[13] but the non-committal is much more characteristic than the alleged inaction. For three weeks, certainly, there were few positive actions, but from 28 March onwards there is plenty of evidence of crisp and effective decision-making. The crucial point is that these decisions were still designed to leave both sides room for manoeuvre, time for reconsideration, and roads back from the brink. The inaugural message, the orders to reinforce Fort Pickens, the exploration of the idea of 'a state for a fort', the preparation of a relief expedition, the delay in the final decision to send it, the 'provisions only' message to Charleston, all have this much in common. Curiously enough the man who did much to obscure this constant theme of Lincoln's policy was Lincoln himself, who, in both private and public justifications of his actions, sought in the months after Sumter to impose a pattern on events which did not exist at the time. Most notably in his message to Congress on 4 July 1861, he described how his plan to soften the blow of evacuating Sumter by reinforcement of Pickens had been wrecked by the delay in carrying out his orders, and how he had thus been obliged to despatch the Sumter relief expedition, lying ready and waiting for just such a contingency. The operation had a peaceful and defensive purpose – 'the giving of bread to the few brave and hungry men of the garrison' who were no threat to the South.[14] It is a brilliant defence of a policy which was in fact only one of several possibilities which Lincoln had kept open, and the chronology of events does not support his later version at some crucial points. Lincoln had eliminated some of these possibilities when they became dead ends; he had adhered to others which kept choices open and hopes of peace alive. As president of the United States, Lincoln could scarcely have done anything less than he did to defend the Union in March and April 1861; as a Republican president, he could scarcely have stood less firmly in opposition to the further extension of slavery; as a man of peace, he could have done more only by sacrificing the Union which it was his duty to protect and disowning the party which had nominated him and the voters who had elected him.

The Southern leadership had to contend with similar pressures, and comparable difficulties. But it is hard to escape the conclusion that Davis and his advisers were more rigid, more stiff-necked, given to more breast-beating and less soul-searching than their Northern counterparts. They were often unable or unwilling to resist the emotional tide which was carrying their new Confederacy into violent collision with the Union. Even when Davis did urge restraint upon the authorities in Charleston, it was only on the grounds that 'the first blow must be successful. . . . A failure would demoralize our people, and injuriously affect us in the eyes of the world as reckless and precipitate.'[15] Even if, as some claim, Lincoln had set a trap to incite the South to fire the first shot, the Southern leadership surely fell headlong into it by bombarding Fort Sumter even before the relief expedition had arrived. There was still a substantial body of moderate opinion in many parts of the south, anxious for peace whether on the basis of separation or a reconstructed Union, which might just have been mobilised by more thoughtful and judicious leadership. This was probably never more than an outside chance, but it was tossed away in the early spring of 1861.

Many secessionists had optimistically believed that they could gain their independence without having to fight for it. Others had been spoiling for a fight for months if not years, and almost all were prepared to fight if necessary. To his credit, Davis had consistently and realistically warned that secession was unlikely to be peacefully accepted and that a long and bitter struggle probably lay ahead. He did not relish the thought, but he did little to restrain the wilder enthusiasts, and he seems to have agonised but little about the steps which might or might not lead to war. Just as Lincoln could not abandon the Union to keep the peace, it never entered Davis's head that secession should be abandoned to prevent a war. A solid majority on either side would have shied away from the thought of war in November 1860, but when the moment of truth came in April 1861, the great mass of people followed a leadership which, on one side, would fight in defence of the Union, and, on the other, would fight for the right to leave it. Few people on either side had expected such a will to fight in the other.

Most Northerners wanted to save the Union, but many had not squarely faced the issue of using force against their separated brethren until the guns in Charleston harbour decided the matter for them. Lincoln had not sought war, but he had rejected two possible means of averting it: a compromise which allowed the possibility of the further extension of slavery, and peaceful acceptance of the dismemberment of the Union. By taking his stand for the Union while delaying a commitment to any one means of defending it until a choice was thrust upon him, he had conditioned the North to accept war when it came. Having first skilfully linked the political issue of slavery in the territories with the moral issue of slavery itself, Lincoln had now forged a link between both and the patriotic feelings of Northerners for the Union. It was no mean achievement, but it was not first and foremost a strategy for peace.

# Chapter IV: Why the War Came

There is no simple or instant explanation of the origins of the American Civil War, as a century of historiography clearly shows. Attempts to work back from the character and consequences of the war to its causes have always been doomed to disaster. Although the war gave a great stimulus, for example, to the mass production of cheap clothing, it would be difficult to maintain that it was embarked upon with that purpose in mind. Attempts by unreconstructed rebels, single-minded idealists and hero-worshippers, dogmatic critics of Northern capitalism, or victims of nostalgia for the old south, to justify one side or vilify the other have obscured rather than clarified the issues, and testified only to the survival of many burning Civil War issues into our own times.

The analysis of the causes of the Civil War, as of any major conflict, involves two closely related and complementary questions, which should provide two stages of a single answer rather than two alternative explanations. One must ask first what were the issues and the circumstances which so deeply divided North and South, and brought them into chronic sectional rivalry, and then, secondly, why these issues and circumstances led to secession and war in 1860–1. For example, to say that slavery was the basic cause of North–South tension may or may not be true; but, if it is true, it still remains to enquire why the problems which it raised were not solved or evaded by peaceful means and why the issue was decided in the 1860s by force of arms. By addressing themselves to one of these questions at the expense of the other, some historians have put the emphasis predominantly or even exclusively on impersonal forces which produced, in Seward's phrase, an 'irrepressible conflict', while others, concentrating on the immediate events leading up to the war, have told a story of human error and failure which allowed a 'needless war' to happen.

1. Changing fashions in the interpretation of the causes of the Civil War have naturally reflected the times through which successive generations of historians have lived.[1] For half a century and more after the conflict itself, the prevailing view was that this was a necessary war fought to save the Union from the threat posed by slavery and its aggressive champions, though there were always Southern voices to dissent from that verdict. In the twentieth century, and more especially after the disillusioning experiences of the First World War and the post-war settlement, notions about a just war or about war as an efficient instrument for any worthwhile purpose were much harder to sustain, and doubts about the necessity of the Civil War and the ostensible aims of the participants were easier to nourish. Some historians, notably Charles A. Beard, argued that economic rivalry between North and South was more fundamental than the moral issue of slavery, which had, indeed, often served as a respectable cloak to cover naked self-interest. A larger group of historians, many of them Southerners, including Avery Craven, Charles Ramsdell and James G. Randall, were inclined to blame the war on the failure of leadership and the irrational behaviour of extremists on both sides. Although they differed considerably among themselves, this group have been collectively labelled the revisionists, and they reached a peak of influence around the time of the outbreak of the Second World War, which, in its early stages, seemed to justify all their anxiety and their scepticism. But in the longer run that war, and American participation in it, renewed faith in the idea of a just war waged against the forces of evil, and stimulated a challenge to the revisionist interpretation. The issue of slavery moved back towards the centre of the picture, and has been kept there more recently, with added emphasis on its racial undertones, by the prominence of the civil rights struggle and the racial crisis of the last two decades. But this trend has not been merely a reversion to the views of seventy or a hundred years ago. If the moral and racial aspects of the slavery question have been emphasised, so too has the factor of power in the sectional equation – hardly surprising in minds conditioned by the world of the mid-twentieth century. New attention has been focused, too, on the flaws and limitations of the American political and social system, rather than of individual leaders, which allowed a sectional argument to degenerate into civil war. New heroes have arisen, and old ones have been removed from the national pantheon or pushed into dark corners. The abolitionist, long condemned as a wild fanatic, has become the prototype of the civil rights worker; abolitionist propaganda, once compared with the outpourings of Dr Goebbels, has become part of the classic literature of American freedom. Stephen A. Douglas, darling of the revisionists, in their view the only statesman who wrestled seriously with the problem of sectional antagonism, has become 'a man of dim moral perceptions', who, on his own admission, did not care much whether slavery was voted up or down.[2] The romantic attachment to the lost cause of the Confederacy has declined almost everywhere but in Dixie itself, where the Stars and Bars still bedecks innumerable flagpoles and car bumpers and windscreens. More important than all this, there is among

serious historians a new sense of the complexity of the issues, less enthusiasm for the apportionment of praise or blame, more determination (or even desperation) to find a formula which will embrace all the factors involved and the subtle interactions between them, and a deepening realisation that no aspect of the American condition in the mid-nineteenth century is totally irrelevant to their analysis or unworthy of their attention.

2. The countless efforts to define what it was which basically divided North and South fall generally into one of four categories. They tend to see that division primarily in terms of social or cultural incompatibility, economic rivalry, constitutional disagreement, or the controversy over Negro slavery. In fact the debate turns essentially upon the relationship between the first three (singly or together) and the fourth. Was the institution of slavery the core of the argument, and were the other factors simply means of conducting it? Or was slavery the surface issue obscuring the real roots of controversy – the clash of cultures or economic interests or constitutional principles? Those who speak of a clash of cultures contend that the relationship between North and South ended in divorce on grounds of the total incompatibility of their respective social systems and sets of values. The two could no longer live at peace under one federal roof. This view has appealed particularly but by no means exclusively to Southern observers, and has often rested on thinly-veiled assumptions about the superiority of the Southern way of life. The agrarian society of the south, enshrining many traditional American values, resting on the economic base of the plantation and the social base of a recognised and accepted caste system, and looking for leadership to the plantation aristocracy, with its sense of responsibility, its elegant style of life, and its pretensions to culture and refinement, offered an example of order, stability and civilised life which the north could not match. On the other hand, the rapidly growing factory system of the north depended on the ruthless exploitation of wage slaves and encouraged a spirit of money-grabbing materialism. The immigrant hordes which it attracted offered a sharp contrast with the Anglo-Saxon purity of the white South, and the way of life which it encouraged struck at the roots of an older-established American social order. So the argument runs, although it is not always couched in such pro-Southern terms. Clearly there was a widening gap between two ways of life, and Southerners in particular were increasingly conscious of their own distinctiveness. This sense of growing apart from the rest of the Union became a source of anxiety as much as a source of pride when it was accompanied by the realisation that, after years of dominance or at least of parity, the South was doomed to a permanent minority status in a Union increasingly dominated by a new kind of society and a new way of life. As the New Englander, James Russell Lowell, saw it, the free states could not help offending the South. 'Their crime is the census of 1860. . . . It would not be enough to please the Southern states that we should stop asking them to abolish slavery – what they demand of us is nothing less than that we should abolish the spirit of the age.'[3]

The picture of two societies or two cultures is clearly an important part of the background of the Civil War drama, and was recognised as such by contemporaries. The difficulty lies in relating this general picture to the way in which the war came. Why should this particular difference lead to civil strife when the whole federal system had been designed to cope with local and regional diversity, and sectional bargaining had been part of the pattern of American politics from the beginning? East and West had their sharp differences, too, and their feelings of jealousy, resentment and superiority about each other, but, despite some earlier talk of the Union dividing at the Appalachians, they had never come anywhere near civil war. The fact is that, by accident or design, the 'two cultures' explanation of the war has involved a serious neglect of the role of Negro slavery. Paradoxically, the case for the incompatibility of North and South has been developed at the cost of soft-pedalling the most conspicuous and controversial of all the differences between them.[4]

The theory of social conflict overlaps in places with the economic interpretation of the causes of the Civil War. The belief that a clash of economic interests was the root cause of conflict has been expressed in a variety of ways, from the grand designs of economic determinism to the spelling out of grievances over the protective tariff. In its crudest form, the Marxist interpretation of the civil war depicts a struggle between capitalism and feudalism in which the former inevitably triumphed. For the most influential non-Marxist American champion of the economic interpretation, Charles A. Beard, the war had much the same character, but he described it in rather different terms. For Beard, it was a clash between Northern business and Southern planters, in which the moral and emotional argument over slavery clouded the real issues. In this struggle, a dynamic new order defeated the static old order, with consequences which Beard, surveying the history of the United States in the post-war Gilded Age, found generally unwelcome. Indeed, both Beard and the Marxists may be found guilty of playing the dangerous game of judging the causes of a conflict by an examination of its consequences, or even by a misreading of them.[5]

There were more modest economic arguments, less cosmic in their implications. After all, concentration on cotton-growing had given the South a very special set of economic interests. In particular, exports of Southern cotton which made up a very large part of total American exports, had contributed much not merely to the international economic relations of the United States but to its rate of domestic economic growth. Southerners felt that they were being cheated of a proper return on their efforts, and exploited by the powerful commercial and manufacturing interests of the north-east. Southerners had fought a long and, surely, often misguided battle against federal schemes of internal improvements; they had battled through the 1850s against a homestead law which would give new advantages to free labour in the west – and with the aid of Buchanan's veto they had hitherto succeeded in preventing its passage; above all, they had resisted for decades the protective tariff desired by Northern manufacturing interests, which placed a costly impediment in the way of the trade with Europe on which they depended. The tariff had precipitated one major crisis over nullification in the 1830s, and there were still men in the south to argue that there was little to choose between abolitionists who wanted to rob the south of its labour force, and Northern protectionists who wanted to rob it of the fruits of that labour. Robert Toombs denounced the tariff bill proposed by the Republicans in 1860 as a 'master stroke of abolition policy' which 'united cupidity to fanaticism. . . . The robber and the incendiary struck hands, and united in a joint raid against the South.'[6]

Such splendid rhetoric somewhat overstated the plight of the South. In the field of legislation, the South had done rather well in the 1840s and 1850s, at least in the negative sense of blocking measures concerning internal improvements, banking and currency, and the public lands which it disliked. On the tariff, the South had done particularly well; the acts of 1846 and 1857 had lowered duties considerably, and in any case many Northern interests were no longer so convinced of the need for tariff protection. The South also prided itself on having proved less vulnerable than many parts of the North to the consequences of the financial panic of 1857. From a wider perspective, it is fair to say that economic grievances, like social differences, had always been a feature of American life, and the political system had generally worked well in striking bargains between competing economic interests. If the South felt impelled to secede on economic grounds in 1860–1, why had the West never seriously threatened to do the same, for it, too, had its special economic interests and its fears and resentments of the power of the north-east? Furthermore, any notion that the war resulted from the aggressive demands of Northern business must overcome the objection that Northern business interests, in New York and elsewhere, were among the most reluctant sections of Northern opinion to accept coercion of the South and, with it, the risk of war. All in all, the generalised economic arguments advanced by many later historical pattern-makers seem to have little in common with what men said and thought and did in the years before 1861. The economic explanation of the coming of the Civil War often leans heavily on the unproved assumption that economic self-interest is somehow more real and basic than ideas, emotions, moral commitments, prejudices, political loyalties or social frustrations. North–South rivalry posed unprecedented problems which proved beyond the capacity of traditional methods to solve or even ultimately to contain, precisely because it centred around an issue like slavery which excited not merely economic anxiety or social concern but a whole host of other deep feelings besides. The narrower economic arguments, like the broader social and cultural arguments, come back inevitably to slavery and all its ramifications, and are devalued if they refuse to face that fact.

Of course economic and social differences remain an essential part of the story. They are part of the scenery against which the drama was enacted; they conditioned much of the action, but they did not dictate the plot, and certainly not the final curtain. The opposite objection is commonly made against any attempt to explain the Civil War as a constitutional conflict; much of the dialogue on both sides was certainly cast in legal and constitutional language, but, it is argued, this was surely no more than a means of articulating (as well as rationalising) more deeply-rooted ideas, emotions and interests. Certainly, constitutional issues have always had an air of unreality about them when studied in isolation; they have assumed significance only as a reflection of political, economic and social factors, and especially of a struggle for power between rival groups. Nowhere is this more true than in the case of states rights which, from the 1790s to the 1970s, have been a convenient resort for minority interests, a handy weapon with which the 'outs' could belabour the 'ins'. 'The group advocating states rights at any period have sought its shelter in much the same spirit that a western pioneer seeks his storm-cellar when a tornado is raging.'[7] From Thomas Jefferson onwards, the staunch champions of states rights have lost some of their zeal for the cause when they have themselves moved into the seats of federal power.

But can one dismiss quite so easily the importance of constitutional arguments in general, and the defence of states rights in particular? Non-Americans probably tend to underestimate the genuine feelings – nay, the burning passions – which such questions can stir in American breasts, especially when their pro- found suspicion of centralised authority is aroused. The constitution, as Sir Denis Brogan has observed, is something like the American equivalent of Magna Carta and the battle of Britain rolled into one. Both sides in the Civil War believed that they were its true guardians and rightful heirs; they were engaged in 'a competition between constitutional orthodoxies'.[8] Nine-tenths of the Confed- erate constitution is a carbon copy of the constitution of 1787. It is hard not to take seriously the devotion of Southerners to states rights when many of them were willing to risk political suicide by clinging so doggedly to the same doctrine even in the darkest hours of the Civil War itself, when the government of their own Confederacy desperately needed greater powers to save itself and to save them.

Within the American constitutional system, the balance between the power of the majority and the rights of minorities has always been a delicate one. Belief in the sovereign will of the majority and respect for the rule of the con- stitution and the law lived side by side, however uneasily, in the minds of many Americans from Jefferson to Lincoln. For Southerners, constitutional theory and political reality virtually became one, as their section became more and more obviously doomed to a minority position in the Union, and as Northern Republicans nailed their colours to the mast of majority rule. (There was not a little irony in the fact that the champions of majority rule in 1860 had mustered only 40 per cent of the popular vote for their successful candidate.) Since they lived under a federal system, it was a reflex action for Southerners to turn for protection to the rights and powers of the states, and the other constitutional checks on the will of the majority. It is plain evidence of the weight which they attached to legal authority, that Southerners justified secession itself not as the as- sertion of a revolutionary right but as the constitutional right of a sovereign state.

In the 1840s and 1850s some sections of Southern opinion became convinced that states rights within the Union could no longer give them the protection they required. But states rights was not the only antidote to the power of an obnoxious and apparently permanent majority, especially now that the state, the basic unit of the federal structure, no longer adequately corresponded to social and economic realities, or political alignments. The alternative was to create a new polity within which a Southern majority would have the power. Majority rule would work more justly in a more homogeneous society, rather than in a situation where one particular majority held sway indefinitely over one particular minority, on the basis of some fundamental and enduring division, regional, ethnic, religious, racial or whatever, within the society itself. This was the rationale, in constitutional terms, of the rising spirit of Southern nationalism. With more enthusiasm than logic, many Southerners maintained their devotion to the doctrine of states rights while responding to the appeal of Southern nationalism, and the Confederacy was to pay dearly for this confusion in its short life. Meanwhile two kinds of nationalism were strengthening their grip in the America of the 1850s: a Northern nationalism (with some Southern supporters, too), predicated upon the Union as it existed, and a Southern nationalism looking to the creation of a separate Southern confederacy. Here was one of those points where constitutional ideas and popular emotions mingled in an explosive mixture.

For all this, it would be difficult to claim that the constitutional dispute was the root cause of the Civil War. It could have had no independent existence without economic and social developments which were dramatically altering the sectional balance of power. On the other hand, it had an enormous bearing on precisely how and when, in what form and under what conditions, the war came, and that in itself has much to do with why it came at all. The mere fact that the United States lived under a federal rather than a unitary system of government made all the difference in the world to the shape of the conflict. This 'configurative role' of constitutional issues, as one historian has called it,[9] had still more specific effects. By its explicit guarantees of property rights against governmental interference, and therefore its implicit guarantees of the right to property in slaves in states which permitted slavery, the constitution ruled out the possibility of a direct attack on the institution of slavery on its home ground. American reverence for the constitution, and acceptance of its rules, is again indicated by the fact that many anti-slavery men in the north, including almost all Republicans and certainly Lincoln himself, willingly adhered to this constitutional provision and even offered to underline it with new guarantees. Only the out-and-out abolitionists like Garrison and Phillips argued that, if the constitution prohibited a frontal assault on slavery, then the constitution must be altered, ignored or destroyed, and, in taking this view, they brought down coals of fire on their heads from North as well as South.

If a direct confrontation was ruled out, then indirect means had to be found, and over the years the slavery issue searched out the weak spots in the work of the Founding Fathers. One such spot was found in the provisions for the return of fugitive slaves, but by far the most important lay in the uncertainty of the constitution on the question of slavery in the territories. Who had the power in this matter – the federal government, the local population, or the several states who could all claim equal rights in the territories? This proved to be the fatal point of controversy; it mattered not just in its own right but because it stood for greater and wider issues. As Professor Arthur Bestor says:

> Thanks to the structure of the American constitutional system itself, the abstruse issue of slavery in the territories was required to carry the burden of well-nigh all the emotional drives, well-nigh all the political and economic tensions, and well-nigh all the moral perplexities that resulted from the existence in the United States of an archaic system of labor and an intolerable policy of racial subjection. To change the metaphor, the constitutional question of legislative authority over the territories became, so to speak, the narrow channel through which surged the torrent of ideas and interests and anxieties that flooded down from every drenched hillside upon which the storm cloud of slavery discharged its rain.[10]

Constitutional disagreements did not cause the war, but they decisively influenced the way in which it came. If economic and social change provided the setting for the Civil War tragedy, the constitution provided the stage directions. The plot was provided by Negro slavery.

3. The *prima facie* case for slavery as the fundamental cause of the Civil War looks unanswerable. If it is asked whether the war could or would have happened without the existence of a large population of Negro slaves in the southern states, the answer can only be no – although there may be some objections to the form of the question. Slavery was at the root of the argument between North and South, slavery was the obvious difference between the two sections, slavery aroused conflicting passions, principles and interests. It presented a moral issue, a political issue, an economic issue, a racial issue, an ideological issue and a highly emotional issue. However, even if an investigation of the origins of the Civil War may start and perhaps end with the proposition that slavery was its prime cause, it must pass through all manner of tests and trials along the way.

Such a proposition can be challenged on the general ground that slavery was but the surface manifestation of a wider and deeper conflict between two cultures, but some of the limitations of that argument have already been suggested. The more serious challenge has been launched at that vulnerable point where any general theory comes up against events as they happened, and ideas as they were articulated by the participants in the conflict. This is the core of the revisionist case: that slavery was not a genuine issue and that there was no need to go to war over it.

A whole battery of arguments has been deployed in support of this case. The political issue of the pre-Civil War years, it is insisted, was not slavery itself, but its further extension into the western territories. Slavery in the states where it already existed was not under direct political attack. The Northern abolitionists who did want to eradicate it were a small, distrusted and untypical minority in the north; actual slave-holders were a fairly small minority in the south. Slavery, long regarded as an anachronism by the rest of the western world, was dying on its feet as an economic institution, especially as it had little or no hope of spreading further into rich, new lands. If the question was merely one of slavery in the territories, then competent political leadership should have been able to cope with it, the more so because this was rapidly becoming a phoney issue. Slavery had almost certainly reached the limits imposed on its expansion by geography and climate, as Kansas, New Mexico and Utah amply showed. The census of 1860 revealed that there were precisely two slaves in Kansas, and only a handful more in all the remaining territories. Even the Congressional Republicans had recognised that slavery posed no real threat in the territories when, early in 1861, they provided for the organisation of the new territories of Colorado, Nevada and Dakota without any ban on slavery. The men of 1860–1 allowed an academic argument about 'an imaginary Negro in an impossible place' to end in a bloody Civil War.[11]

The indictment does not end there but moves on to highlight deeper flaws and inconsistencies in Northern attitudes. For all the talk about the loathsomeness of slavery, many people in the north, and Abraham Lincoln above all, insisted in 1861 that the war was a war for the Union and not a crusade to free the slaves – and the president still insisted on this point in the very act of emancipating the slaves eighteen months later. Slaves were to be freed as a means towards the end of saving the Union, and, after all, several slave states in the borderland had been kept on the Northern side from the start of the war. Final proof of Northern hypocrisy about the Negro slaves was offered by the discrimination against the Negro which was practised, both officially and unofficially, publicly and privately, throughout the northern states. Not merely was the Northern stand against the threat of slavery in the territories a piece of shadow-boxing, but Northern expressions of moral repugnance towards slavery were pharasaical nonsense.

The revisionist historians bolstered their specific arguments with more general observations designed to show that this was a needless war which tragic human failures allowed to happen. They stressed the role of romanticism, emotionalism, fanaticism and hysteria in mid-nineteenth-century America, distorting realities, magnifying difficulties, heightening tensions and clouding real issues. One consequence of this was that the sectional controversy was conducted, not on the basis of facts and realities, but in terms of symbols, slogans and images, and all the trappings of irresponsible and ill-informed propaganda. The North viewed the South through the eyes of Harriet Beecher Stowe, and the South looked North through the distorting lens of George Fitzhugh. Obsessed by such grotesque images of each other, North and South each became convinced that it was the victim of an aggressive, expansionist conspiracy organised by the other. In such a scheme of things, it was not difficult to cast the villains. Two groups stood out: the extremist agitators who created so much of this unnecessary ferment – abolitionists in the North, secessionist fire-eaters in the South (though the former usually received the lion's share of the blame) – and the 'blundering generation' of political leaders who had allowed the disaster to happen – weak and fumbling presidents, and petty and short-sighted Congressional politicians who were unworthy heirs of the giants of the past. In short, there was no problem in the America of the 1850s and 1860s which could not have been solved short of war. The tragedy which came in 1861 was the work of feeble leaders, and dangerous fanatics.

The revisionists performed a great service in focusing attention on precisely how war came, and insisting that explanations couched in terms of generalities about slavery or economic forces or constitutional theories were inadequate and incomplete. But they aimed to prove too much. They in their turn felt obliged to bolster the importance of their half of the story by attempting to devalue the other half. In stressing the circumstances in which war broke out, they turned their backs on the deep-rooted and pervasive forces which had been pushing North and South apart for years, or even for generations. They repeated the mistake made by men like Stephen A. Douglas (the patron saint of revisionism) in the crisis itself, of underrating the moral and ideological issue of slavery, and the high emotions which it aroused; they strove to suppress a central feature of the whole drama, and to fill the gap thus created with a multiplicity of lesser matters.

Some of the specific objections to the case for slavery as the prime cause of the Civil War can be quickly answered. For example, the argument that the North was fighting for the Union and not against slavery is distinctly unrealistic – for whence came the threat to the Union if not from the Southern champions of slavery? It is not necessary to prove that every Northerner was an abolitionist in order to demonstrate the central role of slavery in bringing about the war. It was not essential to believe in immediate emancipation before regarding slavery as a serious menace to the integrity of the Union. Again there is no convincing evidence to support the claim that slavery in the south was on its last legs by 1860. Neither the censure of world opinion nor the pressure of economic forces looked at all likely to deal the institution its deathblow in the foreseeable future. Southerners had insulated themselves over the years against adverse opinion from outside; indeed, partly as a response to the attacks of Northern abolitionists, they had greatly elaborated their defence of slavery as a positive good, and stepped up their claims on its behalf. In the pre-Civil War years there was little indication that slavery would be moderated or reformed, let alone abolished, from within the South itself. Though slave-holders were a minority of the southern population, they held most of the positions of influence and power, and had convinced virtually the whole white south that it had a stake in the continuation of Negro slavery. As for its economic viability, it is true that Southern cotton producers faced problems of rising costs and declining prices by mid-century, and some of the smaller slave-owners, or the less efficient, or those whose lands were exhausted, went to the wall, but cotton produced by slave labour on good land could still reap a healthy profit, and an author like Hinton Rowan Helper, whose book *The Impending Crisis* dwelt on the harmful consequences of slavery, was much abused in the south for his pains. Clearly, slavery had not reached the end of its tether – nor had it even necessarily reached impassable geographical limits. A more flexible and resilient institution than many were willing to admit, it might, with help from technological innovation, have adapted itself to new soils and new situations. In any event, Southerners had certainly not abandoned hope of acquiring new fields for slavery to conquer beyond the existing (but still very elastic) boundaries of the United States. Because of their wastefulness, slavery and the plantation system required a constant supply of new land. The Southern stand on the right of slavery to expand was a deadly serious combination of principle and interest.

At the centre of the revisionist case lies the charge that the question of slavery in the territories was an artificial issue, already outmoded by economic and geographical facts. However, all the plausible arguments about imaginary Negroes in impossible places do not get to the heart of the matter. In the first place, the territorial issue could not be divorced from the existence of slavery itself; it was the particular form of the more general issue, dictated by constitutional and political circumstances. It was the available political issue, but it carried a large share of the ideological and emotional load of the problem of slavery itself. The two cannot be separated; Lincoln himself put it plainly enough in his inaugural address: 'One section of our country believes slavery is right and ought to be extended, while the other believes it is wrong and ought not to be extended. This is the only substantial dispute.'[12] The question of slavery in the territories had become the symbol of all that divided the two sides, a point of principle on which both sides stood firm, however few or however many Negroes the census might find in a particular place at a particular time. This was the breaking point at which Southerners prepared for secession and Northerners prepared to resist in the name of the Union.

To link the future of slavery with the highly emotive question of expansion was to plant a bomb capable of destroying the Union. If a number of slave states and a number of free states had co-existed in a more or less static situation and within fixed boundaries, arrangements on the principle of 'live and let live' might not have proved beyond the wit of political leaders. A stable situation might have been created, with its tensions and its difficulties no doubt, but with a good chance of survival, for a time, at least. But the expansion of slavery within (or beyond) an expanding nation was a very different matter indeed. It introduced an insidious element of uncertainty about the future and an even more ominous element of rivalry in the present. Neither side could allow the other to get ahead; each side constantly raised the stakes for which it was playing. From Texas to Oregon, from Missouri to Kansas, from California to Cuba,

North and South were practising a strategy of escalation a century before the term was invented. What technology is to the nuclear arms race, the frontier was to sectional rivalry over slavery. Far from providing a safety-valve, westward expansion created a dangerous cut-throat competition between North and South. Far from being a scaled-down, synthetic substitute for the dispute about slavery itself, the further extension of slavery was a particularly dynamic and explosive version of it. The translation of the basic issue into territorial terms made conflict harder, and not easier, to resolve.

The repercussions of casting the sectional dispute in this particular form went further still. A vastly greater body of Northern opinion could be mobilised on this issue than could ever have been rallied behind a moral crusade against slavery. For those who disapproved of slavery, but had a distaste for abolitionist bedfellows or for drastic or revolutionary action, prevention of the further extension of slavery appealed as a convenient issue, specific enough to be easily grasped, but general enough to be a vehicle for pent-up resentments against the South. Perhaps, even more important, it attracted support from innumerable Americans who repudiated slavery but who never dreamed of regarding the Negro as an equal, and who felt a deep-rooted prejudice against him. Such opinion could never have been aroused to support emancipation, but could be stirred to resist the claims of the champions of slavery in the west, not in any way in the interests of the Negro, but to keep the territories open for free white labour and the Northern small farmer. In other words, a stand against the further extension of slavery could and did gain support both from those who wanted to express in some way their disapproval of an unjust and inhumane institution, and from those who wanted, on grounds of either racial prejudice or economic self-interest, to keep out of the territories the tragic victims of that institution. Those who hated slavery and those who feared the Negro joined hands to resist the incursions of either into the territories.

There can be no denying that the existence of widespread and deep-rooted racial prejudice in the North is a complicating factor in any explanation of the Civil War. Evidence of it abounds in the legal discrimination against free Negroes in the Northern states, in the social, economic and educational handicaps which hedged them all around, in the fears of an influx of freed Southern Negroes if slavery were abolished. Even the anti-slavery group in the territory of Kansas itself drew up a constitution which banned the entry of any Negro, slave or free, into Kansas. Assumptions of Negro inferiority were almost as little questioned in the north as in the south. To mid-twentieth-century eyes and ears, the following words seem astonishing both in their frankness and in their source:

> I will say then that I am not, nor ever have been in favor of bringing about in any way the social and political equality of the white and black races . . . and I will say in addition to this that there is a physical difference between the white and black races which I believe will for ever forbid the two races living

together on terms of social and political equality. And inasmuch as they cannot so live, while they do remain together there must be the position of superior and inferior, and I as much as any other man am in favor of having the superior position assigned to the white race. . . . I do not understand that because I do not want a negro woman for a slave I must necessarily want her for a wife. My understanding is that I can just let her alone.

These remarks, along with a good deal of ribaldry about the apprehension of his opponents that they could not stop themselves from marrying Negroes unless there was a law to prevent it, were delivered by Abraham Lincoln in his debate with Stephen A. Douglas at Charleston, Illinois, in September 1858.[13]

Anti-Negro prejudice was the great flaw in the moral position of the North during the crisis of the Union, and it cannot be brushed aside. But, equally, it does not invalidate the argument that slavery was, in some form, the prime cause of the Civil War. There are many intermediate stages between prejudice against a group of one's fellow men, or a belief in their inferiority, and a willingness to hold them in bondage. It was all too humanly possible to be against slavery without wanting to grant equality to the Negro, or even without being greatly concerned at all about his fate after emancipation, as long as it did not interfere with the white man's way of life. One favoured solution whose supporters again included Abraham Lincoln was to ship the freed Negroes out of the country – either voluntarily (as Lincoln believed) or compulsorily; another optimistic view was that, once slavery was abolished, even the free Negroes in the north would return to the southern states, their natural habitat within the United States. The final ironical implication for the revisionist argument of this attitude is the possibility that its curious moral ambivalence created feelings of guilt, anxiety, doubt and defensiveness in Northern minds, just as slave-owning and the need to justify it are commonly alleged to have induced similar feelings in Southern minds. The very issue which they sought to play down contributed massively to the emotional unreason, the hysteria, the paranoia, the exaggerations and distortions which the revisionist school of thought blames so heavily for the coming of the war.

Indeed, the internal tensions and ambiguities which troubled both North and South underline rather than undermine the central place of slavery in the total situation. Recent historical work has emphasised the complexities of the position of both sides. If historians' use of the term 'ideology' has occasionally threatened to convert it into an expanding suitcase large enough to hold every conceivable attitude, emotion, ideal or interest, it has also offered an interpretation of the coming of the war immensely more subtle and sophisticated – and credible – than the older, cruder theories of economic determinism or cultural superiority. It has also established slavery more clearly than ever as the key to everything else.

In the north there was a long and honourable tradition of total moral condemnation of slavery, but its active spokesmen had always been a minority, and had often received a rough handling from the majority who found their agitation embarrassing or dangerous. There was a broader popular revulsion against the institution of slavery, but it was often combined with contempt (or at least unconcern) for the Negro. There was a long history of disagreement with the South on specific political and economic issues, from the tariff to the public lands, but there was little reason to think that such disputes would in themselves become unmanageable. There was a widespread confidence in the merits and the blessings of the Northern social system, but that confidence was troubled (though far from undermined) by doubts about the future – as consciousness grew of the threats posed by rapid industrialisation, and by possible restrictions on further territorial expansion into the west. Each of these points was important, but not unambiguous; each on its own was inadequate to consolidate the North into a determined stand against the South and its slave system. If, despite all the nagging doubts and internal conflicts, they could be brought together in one overarching structure of ideas and interests, the strength of Northern anti-slavery would be transformed. The whole would surely be greater than the sum of its parts. It was the achievement of the Republicans in the 1850s to articulate just such a unifying concept. Their 'free labour' ideology and their demonstration of the threat posed to it by Southern slavery and its further expansion at last provided a broad and solid base for action. According to the historian who has explained that set of beliefs so convincingly, the Republicans created

an ideology which blended personal and sectional interest with morality so perfectly that it became the most potent political force in the nation. The free labor assault upon slavery and southern society, coupled with the idea that an aggressive Slave Power was threatening the most fundamental values and interests of the free states, hammered the slavery issue home to the northern public more emphatically than an appeal to morality alone could ever have done.

Foner goes on to list the elements in this powerful ideological compound:

Resentment of southern political power, devotion to the Union, anti-slavery based upon the free labor argument, moral revulsion to the peculiar institution, racial prejudice, a commitment to the northern social order and its development and expansion – all these elements were intertwined in the Republican world view. What they added up to was the conviction that North and South represented two social systems whose values, interests and future prospects were in sharp, perhaps mortal, conflict with one another. The sense of difference, of estrangement, and of growing hostility with which Republicans viewed the South, cannot be overemphasized.[14]

For a wide variety of reasons, slavery had come to be regarded as a menace to the North, and its conception of what American society was and should be.

The Republican party furnished not merely the ideology to define that menace but the political instrument to counter it.

Recent attempts to analyse the precise nature of Southern society and its distinctive ideology have been equally notable for their sophistication, their searching insight into internal tensions and contradictions – and their emphasis on slavery. In the words of Eugene Genovese, 'slavery provided the basis for a special Southern economic and social life, special problems and tensions, and special laws of development'. 'All the essential features of Southern particularity and of Southern backwardness,' he continues, 'can be traced to the relationship of master to slave.'[15] Rejecting the oversimplifications of earlier historians, he treats the South as neither a feudal nor a capitalist society, but as something which was distinct from either, though showing evidence of the impact of both. Its economic relationships with the North and the outside world – especially through the cotton trade – obliged it to develop some capitalist features in the field of commerce and banking. But Southern society was still fundamentally different in both its structure and its values from the business-orientated, highly competitive North. Slave-ownership was the platform which supported an aristocratic planter class, and the measure of the political power, economic position and social status of the members of that class. It gave them a set of attitudes – to labour, to profit, to wealth, to class, to duty, to leadership, to standards of justice and morality and judgments of right and wrong – quite different from those which prevailed in the north. To them, a society based on the cash nexus was as objectionable as was a society based on the ownership of one human being by another to most Northerners. The planters were able to maintain their authority as a ruling class by a network of political, economic, social and racial bonds which tied white Southerners of all ranks and conditions to their leadership. But they paid a heavy price for the slave basis of their society in the economic backwardness which was its inevitable result. Slavery hampered or retarded the diversification of agriculture and the development of industry. The South was trapped by the fact that the foundation of its distinctive way of life and cast of thought was also the reason why it lagged so far behind in economic development. The South and its ruling class were therefore equally affronted by the ideological assumptions and the economic performance of the North. The South was doomed to lose in competition with the North because of the very institution which caused it to compete in the first place.

In such a situation, further territorial expansion seemed to offer the only possible short-term solution – or perhaps it was merely a palliative. If it failed, the only other answer was a bid for independence. Genovese puts it like this:

When we understand that the slave South was neither a strange form of capitalism nor an indefinable agrarianism but a special civilization built on the relationship of master to slave, the root of its conflict with the North is exposed. The internal contradictions in the South and the external conflict with the North placed the slaveholders hopelessly on the defensive with little to look forward to except slow strangulation. The only hope was a bold stroke to complete their political independence and to use it to provide an expansionist solution for their economic and social problems. The ideology and the social psychology of the proud planter class made surrender or resignation to gradual defeat unthinkable, for its entire civilization was at stake.[16]

The prevailing ideologies of North and South, then, made the question of the further extension of slavery a very real issue indeed. They also ensured that the two societies could not indefinitely leave each other alone. They were on a collision course – but their ideologies left them ill-prepared to cope with the consequences of that collision, notably in defining a new place for the Negro in American society. Behind the question of slavery stood the problem of race, but the complexities of racial attitudes – and both the similarities and differences in Northern and Southern attitudes – meant that race was not a clear, direct cause of the war, but rather a lurking presence in the background. The war itself would bring it into the foreground soon enough.

4. Slavery was the focal point of all the differences between North and South; it was the most objectionable and the most vulnerable aspect of Southern society; it aroused moral commitments, deep-rooted prejudices, and ideological conflicts which made this question far more than just another example of sectional rivalry; it proved too much for the tried and tested processes of bargain and compromise, and it smashed the established structure of politics and parties; and, in the constantly recurring problem of the further extension of slavery, it provided the brand which eventually lit the fire.

To say, however, that slavery caused the war is not a complete or final statement. Two other elements in the situation are especially important in explaining why the dispute over slavery ended in war, and why war came in this particular way and at this particular time. The first is simply that, at the very time that slavery was occupying the centre of the stage, the sectional balance of power within the Union was undergoing a crucial change. The South increasingly saw itself as a permanent minority in an ever more tightly integrated Union where a Northern majority held sway. It was this brooding minority self-consciousness which gave substance to Southern arguments about constitutional rights, anxieties about economic prospects, and assertions of social and cultural distinctiveness. On the other hand, the North, conscious of its majority strength, was frustrated at the success of Southerners in holding on to much of their power and influence in the federal government. Northerners resented the apparently widening gap in the distribution of political and economic power. The South was determined to cling to its power, the North determined to assert its own.

At this point a second set of complicating factors increased the likelihood of war. If the sectional dispute was a struggle for power, it was very difficult to contain it because there existed no centre of power strong enough to impose a solution. In other words, the United States in the mid-nineteenth century had unusually weak defences against a serious threat of disunion or disintegration. It was a relatively unorganised and decentralised society with only very limited power residing in the government at Washington. The very federal structure itself, the deep-rooted American antipathy to authority, and especially remote, centralised authority, the lack of any focal point of power to which people would instinctively look in time of crisis, all left the United States unusually vulnerable to threats to its internal stability and cohesion. Americans had never thought or spoken of 'the government' in the same manner as Europeans habitually did. In the past, few people had wanted or expected much of the federal government even for such basic purposes as national defence or the maintenance of law and order. No credible threat to the external security of the United States had existed at least since 1815, and the armed services were minute for a country her size. Americans could thus enjoy the luxury, if that is the appropriate word, of contemplating internal conflict without any grave or immediate threat of external intervention. On the home front, American professions of faith in the rule of law were not always matched by any great respect for its everyday observance or any great efficiency in its regular enforcement. Law and order, in any case, was primarily a matter for state and local authorities, as were most of the matters where government impinged at all on the daily lives of individual citizens. However, as time passed, influential sections of the community were beginning to attach much greater importance to the federal government, and to recognise new possibilities in the exercise of federal power. In the north such groups came to look to the federal government for help in promoting and fostering economic development, by providing tariffs and subsidies, railroad land grants, and banking and currency legislation; in the south men came to look to the federal government for protection of its peculiar institution, whether by more stringent fugitive slave laws, unequivocal Supreme Court decisions, or the enactment of a federal slave code for the territories. As long as the role of the federal government was limited and essentially negative, it was usually possible to reconcile sectional differences or at least to live with them. But it was easier to agree to do nothing than to do something, and when both sides began to look or hope for something more positive from the government at Washington, 'live and let live' gave way to '*sauve qui peut*'. When demands on the federal government were few, it was possible to make the system work on the basis of agreement to disagree; but when that government came to matter more, disagreements mattered more, too, and hardened into clear lines of division. The tensions of the 1850s made it clear that the delicate federal balance, originally designed to cope with one set of interests, needed a drastic redistribution of power to cope with a different set of interests which transcended state boundaries, and demanded a stronger national authority. The political parties had struggled to provide some coherent element amid so much diffusion of power and confusion over issues, but the old parties were themselves shattered in the 1850s, and with them passed one of the few focal points of nationwide loyalties – for both the voters and the men they elected to Congressional and other offices had shown surprising loyalty to their patchwork parties for twenty years. By 1860 those old loyalties had been replaced by new ones, sectional rather than national, and hence incapable of restoring the crumbling political fabric.

Neither the political nor the social structure provided adequate stabilisers for a stormy passage. American society was decentralised, loosely organised, atomistic, highly mobile, not yet settled in its ways. Untrammelled by many of the traditional restraints and restrictions of older societies, highly individualist in outlook and instinctively unwilling to show deference to anyone, the people had nowhere to run for shelter when the tempest came. In a society constantly changing under pressure of westward expansion and urban-industrial growth, and at a time when political excitement, religious enthusiasm, and economic and social aspirations were all running high, Americans had few recognised land-marks, trustworthy charts or reliable pilots to guide them safely through dangerous waters. In a word, the United States lacked an 'establishment'. Of the natural conservative interests in the country, many of the Southern planters were in the van of the movement which was disrupting the Union, and the pleas for peace of Northern commercial and industrial leaders were too obviously based on economic self-interest to provide a rallying cry for the people at large.

Slavery and all its satellite issues had become too much for the American political and social system. They burst through the network of arrangements and processes which had harmonised sections and reconciled interests in the past. Bargain and compromise had postponed a collision but evaded the basic issues. By 1860–1, the future was dark and dangerous, and the past had failed as a guide. Like every really fundamental argument in American history, the dispute over slavery had become a dispute over what America stood for and what America meant. In the unending struggle to reconcile economic and social change with the basic principles with which America had begun, North and South had arrived at incompatible answers. If to many, Negro slavery seemed ludicrously and shamefully out of harmony with the noble ideals of the Declaration of Independence, to others majoritarian democracy and the sover-eignty of King Numbers seemed at odds with the delicate balances of the fed-eral constitution, and teeming cities and grimy factories a far cry from the America of Washington and Jefferson. Champions of moral right confronted defenders of legal rights across a deep chasm of misunderstanding, suspicion and hostility. As long as the main protagonists were on the one side uncompromising crusaders of the Garrisonian stamp and, on the other, tortuous logicians of the school of Calhoun, everyday political and social life could go on its way, disturbed and irritated perhaps, but not fully comprehending the danger, nor fully aroused to it. But the time came when the men who talked of a law higher than the constitution or who warned that a house divided against itself could not stand, were no longer to be dismissed as extremist agitators or irresponsible fanatics. The time came, too, when not merely the theoretical right of secession but its immediate expediency became the common talk of politicians and propagandists all across the south. Moral wrongs and legal rights were caught up in a struggle for power, and the crucial link between them was forged by the issue of slavery in the territories. The great American experiment, launched more than eighty years before, now faced its severest test. Slavery, which had complicated that experiment at its inception, and corrupted it as it developed, now threatened to confound it at its moment of crisis. Now, with all its ramifications, slavery confronted the United States with a problem which ultimately placed an intolerable strain on its constitutional framework, political traditions, social equilibrium, economic growth, cherished ideals and future prospects. Slavery was not an abstraction existing in a vacuum, but a concrete problem in a peculiarly American context, which created unique difficulties for the political and social system at a crucial stage of its development. In 1865 Abraham Lincoln summed it all up in a few words. The Negro slaves in the southern states, he said, 'constituted a peculiar and powerful interest. All knew that this interest was somehow the cause of the war.'[17] That single word 'somehow' has kept the historians busy for over a century.

# Part Two: Explosion

# Chapter V : Preparations, Predictions and Prospects

Most Americans were astonished to find themselves involved in civil war in the spring of 1861. Even the leading protagonists on each side had only the vaguest ideas of how they were to wage and win the war, once they found themselves caught up in it. This was a peculiar kind of civil conflict in that the geographical division between the two sides was fairly clear from the outset. Most people in most communities knew on which side they stood simply because of their place on the map. For the great majority of Americans this was not a war which divided each town or village or family against itself, which set brother against brother or neighbour against neighbour. Only in the borderland between North and South was this a brothers' war. The would-be architect of compromise, John J. Crittenden of Kentucky, had one son who became a general in the Confederate army, and another who became a general in the Union army. Abraham Lincoln's wife Mary, like her husband a Kentuckian by birth, had close relatives wearing the Confederate grey. But, for the citizen of Massachusetts or South Carolina, Michigan or Mississippi, the enemy was distant, impersonal and unfamiliar. This helps to explain why each side had underrated the determination of the other during the secession crisis and continued to do so even after the bombardment of Sumter, and why men on both sides were surprised at the predicament in which they found themselves, and confused and bewildered about the shape of things to come. It took time before North and South could sort out where and how and in what strength they would come to grips with one another.

1. The gunfire in Charleston harbour and the surrender of Fort Sumter removed old uncertainties, but created new ones. In both North and South men rallied quickly, almost instinctively, to their respective causes. In the North, the firing on the flag at Fort Sumter converted latent and hitherto unaroused feeling for the Union into a tidal wave of patriotic emotion. Stephen A. Douglas set aside his disagreements with the Republican administration and devoted the last few weeks of his life to rallying support for the Union cause. The New York diarist, George Templeton Strong, noted within a few days of the fall of Sumter that 'the attitude of New York and the whole North at this time is magnificent. Perfect unanimity, earnestness and readiness to make every sacrifice for the support of law and national life.' A week later he recorded, with a note of congratulatory self-sacrifice, the cancellation of a musical party. 'This is no time for parties,' he said, and continued:

> There are signs of amazement at the South at our general rally in support of law and order and national life. . . . They have counted on the support of Northern capital and on a strong revolutionary 'Democratic' party here. Their miscalculation is natural enough. Twenty days ago – no longer – I thought as they have thought, that the North would be divided and paralyzed whenever the struggle should begin.[1]

Away in Illinois, an obscure ex-army officer, Ulysses S. Grant, wrote to his father that he did not wish to act hastily in rushing to answer the call to arms, but:

> Whatever may have been my political opinions before, I have but one sentiment now. That is, we have a Government, and laws and a flag, and they must all be sustained. There are but two parties now, traitors and patriots, and I want hereafter to be ranked with the latter, and I trust, the stronger party.[2]

Faction, discord and dissension would return soon enough, but in the first flush of excitement most Northerners felt that the issue was as clear as Grant's simple definition of it, and the path of duty much as he described it.

In the South, the enthusiasm generated by the capture of Sumter was given a more steely ring by angry reactions to Lincoln's call for militia to suppress the rebellion. Southern ranks closed tighter than ever to meet the threat of Northern coercion. It was this threat, above all, which brought Virginia, North Carolina, Tennessee and Arkansas hastily on to the Confederate side. 'Tennessee will not furnish a single man for purpose of coercion,' wrote Governor Isham G. Harris, in answer to Lincoln's call, 'but 50,000 if necessary, for the defence of our rights and those of our Southern brethren.'[3] Watching raw recruits drilling at New Orleans, William Howard Russell wrote:

As one looks at the resolute, quick, angry faces around him, and hears but the single theme, he must feel the South will never yield to the North, unless as a nation which is beaten beneath the feet of a victorious enemy. In every state there is only one voice audible.

With undue scepticism, perhaps, Russell added that such remarkable unanimity was aided and abetted by 'the moral suasion of the lasso, of tarring and feathering, head-shaving, ducking and horseponds, deportation on rails and similar ethical processes'.[4]

For some individuals, of course, the decision was more agonising than for others, and this was especially true of Southerners serving in the United States armed forces who faced the cruel dilemma between sworn loyalty to their service and emotional attachment to their homeland. Robert E. Lee, who could have had a high command in the Union army, resigned his commission after deciding that he must go with his beloved native state of Virginia. But other Virginians, like Winfield Scott himself, and George H. Thomas, remained firm for the Union. On the other hand, there were even a few Northern officers who threw in their lot with the Confederacy – like the Philadelphian, John C. Pemberton, who followed the lead of his Virginian wife, and who, two years later, faced malicious accusations of disloyalty to the Confederacy when he surrendered to Grant at Vicksburg.

These were exceptional cases, and the outbreak of war left most men quite certain where their loyalties lay. But it also left them quite uncertain about what would happen next. To the question of what kind of war this was to be, Americans in the spring of 1861 offered almost every conceivable answer except the right one. Enthusiasts and hotheads on either side confidently expected that one battle would produce the inevitable triumph of their cause, rather as if one formal and symbolic duel would settle this sectional affair of honour. Southerners derided the fighting qualities of the Northerner, and joked that the proper riposte to a Yankee who levelled a gun at them was to enquire what price he wanted for it. Even more sober and realistic Southerners, like the diarist Mrs Chesnut, who perceived that 'there is enough and to spare of pluck and dash among us; the do-and-dare style', had no conception of what the future held in store. When Jefferson Davis warned her in June, before any serious fighting had occurred, that the war would be a long and bitter one, 'that floored me at once. It has been too long for me already.'[5] In the North the volatile George Templeton Strong boxed the compass of military prediction, but was more often than not pessimistic. As early as February 1861 he had forecast 'war in earnest' in which the North would have to resort to desperate measures like recruiting slave regiments and breaching the levées of the Mississippi to flood New Orleans, for 'the savages of the South will give no quarter and ignore the amenities of civilised warfare'. Most forecasters on both sides were aggressively confident of success, to be achieved in the short run rather than the long, but Strong, like some other Northern and neutral observers, despaired of crushing the rebellion. The North, he thought, 'can never subjugate these savage millions of the South. It must make peace at last with the barbarous communities off its Southern frontier.'[6]

For three months, from the fall of Sumter to the battle of Bull Run, Americans lived in a twilight world upon which the black horror of war had not yet settled. Frenzied preparations created chaos around Washington, and impatience and frustration around the country. The panic of one day was the anti-climax of the next. Great expectations lived uneasily with minor military skirmishes and major administrative confusion. An air of unreality pervaded North and South, as men adjusted their minds to the unfamiliar fact of war. Old habits and ingrained attitudes lived on in the face of new realities. Peace and war overlapped. The normal peace-time contacts and communications between citizens of North and South lingered on for weeks and months afterwards – after all, even as late as 1863 a Union general could complain that he had no fresh information about the enemy because they had refused to pass on the newspapers on that day.[7] Jefferson Davis complained bitterly about 'the wanton destruction of public property'[8] when Union troops set fire to the armoury at Harper's Ferry in April before abandoning it to the Confederates. Minor incidents were magnified out of all proportion. When, on 24 May, the dashing young Elmer Ellsworth of the New York Fire Zouaves cut down the rebel flag flying over a hotel in Alexandria, just across the Potomac from Washington, he was shot dead by the proprietor of the hotel. This minor affray, a mere pin-prick in comparison with the blood-bath to come, gave the North a martyred hero and outraged popular feelings in North and South alike. The real horrors of war would come soon enough, and endure all too long; meanwhile, men groped for an understanding of their new situation.

2. Even with the mixed blessings of hindsight, it is not easy to make any realistic evaluation of the prospects of North and South as the lines of battle were being drawn in 1861. At this juncture there were still too many imponderables in a highly complex and unstable situation. First and foremost, estimates of the eventual outcome depended very much on the character, duration and scope of the conflict itself. Past American experience of warfare gave no hint of the ordeal to come. The Mexican War, the War of 1812, the War of Independence itself, had been fought by small armies, at a relatively low cost in human lives, and, in the case of the more recent examples at least, with comparatively little disruption of everyday life. Winfield Scott's force of around 14,000 men, which marched on Mexico City in 1847, was the largest force hitherto commanded by any American general. In a war which was limited in numbers, duration, and community involvement, as such precedents would have suggested, Southerners could scarcely be blamed for optimistic assessment of their prospects of victory. The War of American Independence provided an inspiring model for the war of Southern independence.

Other, more immediate, uncertainties clouded calculations in 1861. Would the conflict remain an exclusively domestic American affair? Civil wars are apt to become international conflicts, and one side in this war placed great reliance on foreign aid and recognition, if not active intervention. Even if it did remain a domestic dispute, where precisely would the lines of battle be drawn? The allegiance of most of the states was clear from the start, but the fate of the border states – Maryland, Delaware, Missouri and, above all, Kentucky – could drastically alter the balance between the two sides. If these four states (and the whole of Virginia) had been securely joined to the Confederacy at the beginning of the war, not merely would the Southern manpower deficiency have been greatly relieved, but the whole strategic situation would have been transformed. Confederate control of Maryland and Delaware would have cut Washington off from the North. Confederate prospects were considerably better in Missouri, the most populous state west of the Mississippi, and in Kentucky – and control of the latter would have provided an imposing first line of defence along the Ohio River, and greatly reduced the vulnerability to invasion which was always a weakness of the Confederate western front.

Each side justified its confidence about the outcome on grounds quite different from the other. The case for Union victory was essentially the argument that God favoured the big battalions, and it could be buttressed by any amount of hard facts and figures. The Confederacy, on the other hand, put its faith in the intangible and incalculable advantages of superior morale, more limited objectives, and outside support. The census of 1860 provided ample evidence of Northern strength, but it was not, for Southerners at least, the last word on the prospects for the war.

The North's massive advantages are easily demonstrated. If Kentucky and Missouri are omitted from the calculation, because they were so deeply divided in their allegiance, then the population of the North was well over the 20 million mark, as against 9 million in the eleven states of the Confederacy. But even that two-to-one ratio understates the effective Northern superiority. The Southern population included over $3\frac{1}{2}$ million Negro slaves who, although far from a deadweight on the Confederate war effort, were not regarded as potential soldiers, and whose very presence raised the spectre of servile insurrection at a time when the young white manhood of the South was heavily committed on the battlefront. In the second half of the war, as Northern armies penetrated deep into the South, thousands of these Negroes were to be recruited to fight for the Union cause. The large slave population in the South, together with the influx of immigrants into the North in the pre-war years, meant that, in terms of white men of fighting age (those who were between fifteen and forty in 1860), the Northern preponderance was nearly four to one: 4,000,000 against 1,100,000 according to one estimate.[9]

Northern economic and industrial power was even more impressive than Northern manpower. The Southern states had had but a meagre share in the industrial development of the pre-Civil War decades. When every allowance is made for Southern attempts to expand industrial production during the war,

POPULATION (All figures based on U.S. Census of 1860).

The charts below show separately the population of the Northern non-slave states, the border slave states, and the Southern slave states. Overall estimates of the population of the Union and the Confederacy depend on the division of the border state population between the respective sides. Throughout the war, most of that population was under Union control, whether willingly or not.

### TOTAL POPULATION

| | |
|---|---:|
| Northern non-slave states | 18,907,753 |
| Western territories | 220,195 |
| Border states (inc. District of Columbia) | 3,588,729 |
| Southern states | 8,726,644 |
| | |
| *Total* | 31,443,321 |

*Notes:* 1. *Slave population:* 3,953,760, of whom 450,957 were inhabitants of the border states (including the District of Columbia and West Virginia).
  2. *Free Negro population:* approximately 476,000 of whom 225,000 lived in the free states and 251,000 in the slave states and the District of Columbia.

## THE NORTHERN STATES
(including Kansas which achieved statehood in 1861)

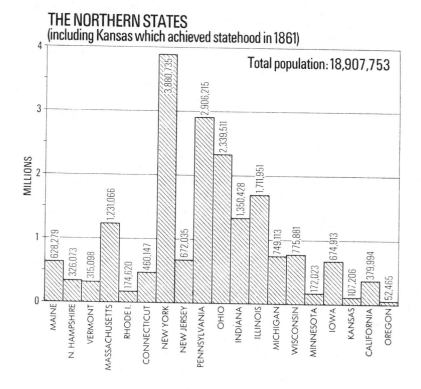

Total population: 18,907,753

## THE BORDER SLAVE STATES
(including District of Columbia)
Total population: 3,588,729

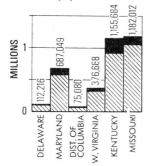

*Notes:* 1. Black sections represent slave population. Number of slaves too small to be shown in Delaware (1,798) District of Columbia (3,185), and West Virginia (18,371).
2. West Virginia is treated as a separate state although it did not finally achieve statehood until 1863.

## THE CONFEDERATE STATES
(excluding all population of the border slave states)
Total population: 8,726,644

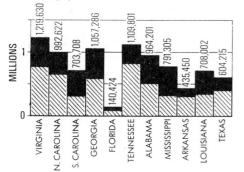

*Notes:* 1. Black sections represent slave population.
2. Figures for Virginia do *not* include West Virginia which became a separate state in 1863. West Virginia is included among the border states. (See above.)

the prodigious efforts of the Tredegar Ironworks at Richmond, or of more modest industrial enterprises in Atlanta and other cities, the ingenious improvisations, the imports from Europe, and the capture of Northern arms, the fact remains that the disparity between Union and Confederacy was enormous, in terms of the industrial war effort, and the availability of the tools of war. The two sides simply lived in different worlds. The Tredegar Ironworks is automatically cited in all accounts of the Confederate industrial effort for the simple reason that it was unique; no one Northern industrial concern can be singled out in the same way because there were so many. In 1860 the states of New York and Pennsylvania each produced manufactured goods to a value more than twice as great as the total production of the Southern states; even a smaller state like Massachusetts easily outproduced the whole South.

The means of communication and transportation, on both land and water, reflect Northern economic superiority. Of the 31,000 miles of railroad in the United States in 1860, only 9,000 were in the states which became part of the Confederacy. In the North the railroads bound together the Atlantic seaboard and the great north-west, and mitigated the problems of deploying resources and waging war over vast distances. In the South the railroads formed a less effective network, with a number of damaging and serious gaps in it. Southern industrial weakness made it impossible to get the best use out of even its limited mileage; a pointer to what happened during the war may be found in the fact that the South produced only nineteen out of the 470 locomotives built in the United States in the year ending 1 June 1860. In a war where the railroad was to play a crucial and unprecedented role, these were serious handicaps indeed. Similarly, in a situation where the South pinned such high hopes on foreign aid, the almost complete lack of either merchant shipping or naval vessels was a paralysing weakness. The naval strength of the United States was made to look more impressive than it really was by the lack of any significant opposition; the remarkable success of commerce raiders like the *Alabama*, built in Britain for the Confederacy, suggests what might have been achieved if the imbalance had not been quite so great. As things were, the slowly tightening Union blockade was an essential part of Northern strategy – and the Union control of the great rivers of the west was no negligible factor in military victory in that theatre.

In 1861 Southerners were undaunted by these seemingly overwhelming disadvantages, and, even a century later, this confidence cannot be dismissed as sheer bravado. Israel and North Vietnam stand as living reminders that numbers, whether of men or weapons, are not necessarily the decisive factor in war. Skill and speed in the deployment of available resources, courageous and enterprising leadership, backed by faithful and dedicated support, were expected to redress the unfavourable balance presented by census returns and production figures. There was surely more to this argument than the confident assertion that one Southerner could whip ten Yankees. As for Northern industrial power, it remained to be seen how effectively it could be applied to the task of waging and winning a war. Northern industry was still an agglomeration of small-scale units, and neither its structure nor its methods were geared to the task which now faced it. The very speed of industrial development, and the novelty of the industrial society which it had created, might make it vulnerable to this new and unexpected test. A new and unstable social order might crack or even collapse under the stresses and strains of civil conflict. At the very least, the fragmented and complex structure of Northern industry might become clogged and choked by the new and unfamiliar demands placed upon it. However impressive the productive capacity of the North was, could it deliver the goods when and where they were needed?

Confident in the superiority of their own agrarian way of life, Southerners could well believe that their society, in its comparative simplicity and its long-established stability, was more resilient in times of crisis, more capable of absorbing punishment, than the rapidly industrialising North. (It was just one more irony in the Southern situation that the Confederacy would in fact have to imitate some of the ways of the industrial North in order to wage effective war at all.) The South could at the very least feed and clothe itself, by adapting its agriculture to new needs, and its long tradition of localism and decentralisation meant that life could probably go on at the local community level even if control from the centre was impossible or communications were disrupted. The Southerner, it has been said, was unlikely to have to tighten his belt in face of invasion and dislocation, though he might have no belt to tighten.[10] Southerners also put their faith in one more economic argument which reflected their high opinion of their own importance but which the events of 1861–5 did little or nothing to substantiate. It was confidently believed that the South, and, above all, Southern cotton, mattered so much to the economic health of the North that the termination of normal economic relations would have a disastrous effect in New York, New England and elsewhere. The South was a valuable market for Northern industry, the supplier of a vital raw material, which fed Northern factories and supplied the basis of American overseas trade. It is true that New York cotton merchants and other interested parties did indeed fear just such a body blow as a result of secession and civil war, but, if Southerners thought that economic separation would bring the North to its knees, they were to be sadly disappointed.

Southern optimism, however, rested less on the rebuttal of Northern claims and assertions than on a positive faith in quite different arguments and assumptions. It might be accepted that a long war, fought to the death, between two sides with similar objectives, would inevitably end in favour of the North, but Southerners did not see the struggle in these terms. In the first place, the Southern objective was more limited than the Northern, and could be achieved by something a good deal less than total military victory. The Confederacy simply wanted recognition of its independence and it would be prepared to end the war as soon as this was conceded. It had no designs on the Northern states, and had no need to conquer and occupy them. Southerners may have been unduly optimistic in believing that a fairly brief and limited war would suffice to achieve this purpose. But they can scarcely be blamed for arguing that, if the North was really determined to maintain the Union, it would have to conquer the whole South, and assert and maintain its control over it – and it was not Southerners alone who believed that such a task was impossible. After all, the Confederate states covered a vast area, which, with Texas in their ranks, even exceeded the area of the states of the North. Was it possible to subjugate several million people scattered over thousands of square miles, and force them back into the Union fold? Many Northerners doubted it, and many outside observers ruled out the possibility. Anthony Trollope, for one, on a visit to North America in 1860–1, forecast that the North might have the better of the war militarily, but that it could never restore the Union as it was.[11] However logical and realistic such calculations seemed to be, many Southerners drew dubious conclusions from them. Limited objectives suggested a defensive war – to Jefferson Davis among others – whereas hindsight may suggest that a quick, bold, aggressive strike, if practicable, might have been a more effective means of persuading the North to recognise Southern independence as a fact.

Closely related to the question of war aims and the means of achieving them was the elusive but important question of morale, both military and civilian. The Confederacy was fighting for its survival; for the individual Southerner, the struggle for independence was inextricably bound up with the defence of Southern institutions and the Southern way of life, and, beyond that, the defence of home and family. Men in the North lacked the same urgent, direct personal stake in the struggle; their hearths and homes were rarely threatened. However strong their loyalty to the Union, they might well harbour doubts about maintaining it by coercion and conquest, or about forcing back into the Union people who plainly desired to leave it, whom they often hated and despised, and who had been an unconscionable nuisance within the Union for several decades. It was not too much for Southerners to hope that Northern will to fight might crack if the war could be kept going, and if the Confederacy could win one or two impressive victories. This hope, so it proved, rested on an underestimation of Northern will and determination, but it was not altogether an unreasonable one, and certainly the greater intensity and immediacy of Southern motivation seemed to suggest that Confederate morale would prove the stronger and more durable. The South was fighting for its life; the North was not.

Political divisions might be expected to reflect, and to aggravate, weaknesses in the Northern will to fight. Southerners were well aware that there existed in the North in 1861, and there persisted throughout the war, a strong and vocal opposition to the Lincoln administration, to the Republican party, and, among some of its members, to the idea of maintaining the Union by force. If the war dragged on indefinitely, or if it went very badly for the North, such opposition might well flourish mightily – and there were, indeed, times when the position of the Lincoln administration was anything but secure. At such times Southerners might be pardoned for hoping that the ballot box might complete the task begun on the battlefield. The mid-term elections of 1862 were a stinging blow to the Republican party, and, in the mid-summer of 1864, Lincoln himself believed that he would not be re-elected for a second term. It may not be too fanciful to suggest that, even in its desperate plight of 1864, the Confederacy had one last chance to snatch, if not victory, at least a tolerable compromise, from the jaws of defeat, in the presidential election in the Northern states in the autumn of that year. If Lincoln had been defeated – and a shift of not many thousands of votes would have done just that – who can tell what might have followed, for war-weariness, frustration and disillusionment were not the monopoly of the South at the end of 1864.

The weapon which carried the most confident Southern hopes in 1861 was neither a military nor a psychological one. Its launching pad was the simple fact that the Southern states supplied more than four-fifths of the raw cotton which fed the mills of Britain and Western Europe. On this fact rested the virtually unquestioned assumption that the European powers, and Britain above all, could not stand idly by and see the South isolated, devastated and subjugated. Despite all the efforts of the North to prevent it, the war would surely become more than a domestic American affair, and it was commonly believed that the mere achievement of European, and especially British, diplomatic recognition of the Southern Confederacy would guarantee permanent independence. Faith in King Cotton diplomacy was already in 1861 a Southern dogma almost to rank alongside the defence of slavery and states rights. So rarely challenged was this fundamental faith indeed that there had been too little practical consideration of exactly how King Cotton would establish his sway and work his royal magic.

This contrast between optimistic general assumptions and inadequate or misleading practical calculations runs right through Southern thinking in the early days of the war. Because Southern objectives did not require the subjugation of the North, there was support for a defensive strategy which might well lead to the kind of protracted war of attrition which the Confederacy could scarcely hope to win. Because the Southern stake in the conflict was more a matter of life and death than the Northern, expectations of a crack in Northern morale were accompanied neither by any sophisticated strategy to exploit such a weakness, nor by sufficient attention to fostering and sustaining support for the war at home. Because a powerful and organised opposition to the administration flourished in the North, Southerners waited for this fatal weakness to destroy their enemy from within while the seeds of political division were allowed to grow unchecked within the Confederacy and a bitter, negative and destructive opposition crippled the Confederate war effort. Because cotton was king by the divine right of the laws of supply and demand, it was not supported by a specific and practical policy to sustain its authority. Because the South was confident that it could win a war which followed the precedents of past American experience, it was ill-prepared for the different kind of war which soon developed. Southern grounds for confidence in 1861 were not altogether unrealistic, but the practical policies for converting assumptions into achievement often were, if indeed they existed at all.

3. In the three months from mid-April to mid-July 1861 there was little time for such cool assessment of comparative prospects. Such plans as were made seldom encompassed the wider horizons, and preparations on both sides partook more of frantic improvisation than sober calculation. Two problems dominated these early days of the war: the hasty mobilisation and organisation of men and arms, and the clarification of the line of demarcation between North and South in the wide borderland stretching from Chesapeake Bay to the plains of Kansas. By the time that the rival armies met in their first major clash at Bull Run on 21 July the fate of the border states was becoming clear, and the shortcomings of hurried military improvisation were about to be exposed. Although the North was to be jolted back on its heels by the blow of Bull Run, it had already won vital if unspectacular successes in the struggle for control in the borderland.

The bombardment of Sumter, and Lincoln's response to it, had stretched the border states – Maryland, Delaware, Missouri, Kentucky – on the rack more painfully than ever. Their immediate neighbours to the south – Arkansas, Tennessee and North Carolina – met the crisis by seceding and joining the Southern Confederacy, although, in the case of Tennessee in particular, the move was fiercely opposed by Unionists in the eastern part of the state. These three states had followed the lead provided by Virginia herself in the days after Sumter, and many Southerners hoped that Kentucky, Missouri and even Maryland might go the same way. After all, Virginia was itself a border state as well as being a traditional leader of the South. But Virginia, like Tennessee, was to face opposition from its Appalachian mountain region – opposition which culminated in the somewhat irregular creation of the new state of West Virginia.

The border states were faced with the agonising choice between their American loyalties and their Southern affiliations. The choice was one which they had desperately sought to avoid. They wished to remain in the Union but they rejected coercion of the seceded states. Their economic prosperity was closely linked with their neighbours to the north; their social system followed the pattern of their fellow slave states to the south. They detested abolitionists while they deplored secessionist fire-eaters. Now, as war stared them in the face, they found one more very good reason for standing aside or offering mediation, for where would the lines of battle be drawn but across their own farms and fields and hills and valleys? They, the most reluctant of belligerents, would provide the first arena of war, and its first victims too. They realised that a Union divided against itself would mean for them states, communities and families divided against themselves. Border state men would volunteer in their thousands on both sides, and three years later, for example, the 4th Kentucky regiment of the Union army was to come face to face with the 4th Kentucky regiment of the Confederate army on Missionary Ridge.

However, if all the border states faced the same basic dilemma, each of them had its own peculiar set of circumstances, and each suffered a rather different fate. In the east the Union government could scarcely allow the states of Delaware and Maryland any choice in the matter if it was to ensure its own survival. Delaware and its slave population were too small to pose a serious problem, and while there were bitter divisions of opinion, secession was never really on the cards and pro-Union feeling steadily gained strength. Maryland was a different proposition, and its geographical situation made it a matter of immediate and direct concern to the authorities in Washington. The federal government could scarcely ignore the threat of disaffection at its own back door. Maryland had always created a Southern image for itself, and the city of Baltimore prided itself (and for that matter still does) on its intense Southernness. The Maryland counties on the Eastern Shore, too, were like a northern outpost of the deep South. As hastily organised regiments were despatched towards Washington in the first days of war, tension mounted, and on 19 April a Baltimore mob attacked the 6th Massachusetts regiment as it moved through the city from one station to another. Several lives were lost, disorders in the city lasted for several days, bridges to the north were blown up, and further troop movements delayed. For almost a week no more regiments reached Washington, while Lincoln negotiated anxiously with Mayor Brown of Baltimore and state governor Hicks, the latter, fortunately, not sharing the pro-Southern sympathies of the Baltimore mob. For a moment the national capital seemed like an isolated Union island in a secessionist sea, and, although the danger from an unprepared South was never very real, there was more than a little relief in Washington when more troops arrived on 25 April. Ben Butler, so often to be a source of trouble as the war went on, had saved the day on this occasion, bringing his men by boat down Chesapeake Bay to Annapolis, and thence to Washington, to avoid the Baltimore trouble spot. Soon the trickle of regiments became a flood – so much so indeed that it threatened to overwhelm the limited capacity of the War Department to absorb them. But at least the build-up of Union strength rapidly improved the position in Maryland. Pro-Union feeling asserted itself, and when the legislature met at the end of April any dangerous notions which it may have entertained were inhibited by a display of military strength. In June elections to Congress were won by Union candidates, and in the autumn election for governor, the Union candidate was successful, with the help of close military supervision, the arrest of nineteen members of the state legislature, and the votes of Union soldiers sent home on leave. Although its citizens were still deeply divided, Maryland was now secure, and Washington could concentrate on the main enemy at its front door.

The security of the capital had been further enhanced by political and military developments in western Virginia. Here was an area of great strategic importance to both eastern and western fronts, and protection of communications between them, and here was an area, too, with a long history of grudges and grievances against the rest of the Old Dominion. The people of the mountain country of western Virginia were in many ways set apart from other Virginians. They looked to the west and to the Ohio river rather than east to the Atlantic seaboard; they had little in common with the plantation aristocracy which dominated state politics; they owned few slaves and resented the disruption of

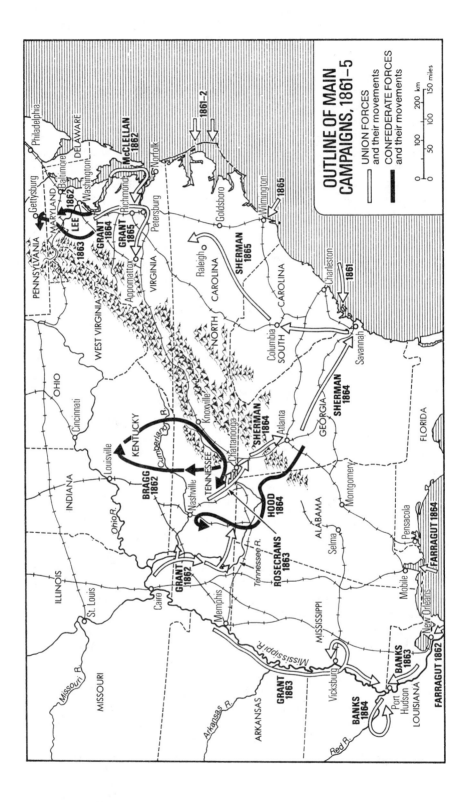

OUTLINE OF MAIN
CAMPAIGNS, 1861–5

UNION FORCES
and their movements
CONFEDERATE FORCES
and their movements

0   50   100   150 miles
0   100   200 km

the Union to save slavery; they felt that they were over-taxed, under-represented and generally neglected in the affairs of the state. Old resentments were revived in the crisis of April 1861; the Virginia ordinance of secession sparked off protest meetings and rallies in the western counties. While forces under George B. McClellan cleared the Confederates from much of the area in some of the war's earliest engagements, a series of conventions at Wheeling, initiated by irregular means and sustained by a very limited vote, formulated two main proposals, one for a reorganised loyal government of the whole state of Virginia, and the other for a new state of Kanawha, or later, West Virginia. Under the first proposal the 'reorganised legislature' of Virginia was established, two senators were sent to Washington, and accepted there, elections were held in which loyalty to the Union was the essential qualification for the vote, and Francis H. Pierpoint became 'governor of Virginia', though his 'government' was still based at Wheeling, and much the greater part of the state was in different hands altogether.

The second proposal took a little longer to mature, and created some knotty legal problems when it did. A convention elected on a very low poll in the fifty counties already designated as belonging to the new state met in the autumn of 1861 to draw up its constitution, and its work was ratified by a similar vote in April 1862. The credentials of such a new state were extremely dubious, especially as individual counties had never had an opportunity to say yea or nay on inclusion within its boundaries. Moreover, the embryo state of West Virginia still confronted two formidable obstacles to its safe delivery into the Union. The constitution provided that no new state could be formed within the jurisdiction of an existing state without the latter's consent. Since it denied the right of a state to secede, prevailing Northern opinion adhered to the view that Virginia was still within the Union, but what authority in Virginia might be persuaded to give its blessing to the creation of the new state in its western counties? The answer was provided by the 'restored' government set up by the earlier proceedings, which gave its consent on 13 May 1862. By doing so, this régime virtually cut the ground from under its own feet, for it, too, was rooted almost entirely in the same western counties which would now form the new state. However, Governor Pierpoint and his régime soldiered on; they transferred the seat of their government to Alexandria, just across the Potomac from Washington, and from that bridgehead maintained until the end of the war the pretence that they were the government of Virginia, whatever the Confederate army and the rebel authorities in Richmond might do or say to the contrary.

The final obstacle to the achievement of statehood for West Virginia was approval by the federal government. Congress voted for admission of the new state, even though many of its supporters had grave doubts about its legal credentials, and one of them, Thaddeus Stevens, candidly admitted that the constitution provided no warrant for such a proceeding. Finally allowing expediency to triumph over constitutional scruple, Lincoln signed the bill on

31 December 1862, and issued a formal proclamation admitting West Virginia to the Union on 20 April 1863.

In Maryland, Delaware and West Virginia, neither legal niceties nor democratic respect for the wishes of the local majority had greatly inhibited Union efforts to assert and maintain control, by force where necessary. Further west beyond the mountains, in Kentucky, the Lincoln administration played a very different game, relying rather on patience, backstage manoeuvre and ostentatious public respect for the integrity of the state and the wishes of its citizens. Kentucky's hand was eagerly sought by two rival suitors, and she seemed likely to reject whichever proved the more pressing and the more ardent. Kentucky was the classic border state, intensely Southern but equally intensely loyal to the Union, unwilling to secede but unwilling to coerce the seceded states, tied by kinship, sympathy and commerce with its neighbours both north and south, and conscious that war would bitterly divide its citizens and ravage its lands. Kentucky was the home of Henry Clay and John J. Crittenden, and the birthplace of both Abraham Lincoln and Jefferson Davis. Even geographically it stood at the very heart of the United States.

Before and even after Sumter, Kentuckians toiled and pleaded for compromise, and when compromise failed they aspired to the status of neutrality. Governor Beriah Magoffin leaned towards the Southern cause, but was restrained by Union sentiment inside and outside the state legislature. He rejected calls for recruits from both Lincoln and Jefferson Davis, warned both governments to keep off Kentucky soil, and worked for mediation, perhaps by means of a convention of the border states. At elections in May and June for such a convention, and to fill congressional vacancies, the Unionists won resounding victories, and in May too, the governor, backed by the legislature, proclaimed the state's neutrality. Such a status could never endure if the war endured, but it did survive through the summer until September, while trade flowed north and south (as long as Lincoln and his administration turned a blind eye to it), while young Kentuckians joined the ranks of both armies, and while Union and Confederate agents and supporters organised recruiting and gathered arms and supplies within the state itself. The state's fragile neutrality was finally cracked on 3 September when Confederate forces occupied Columbus, on the Mississippi, and, within a few days, Brigadier General Ulysses S. Grant ordered Union forces into Paducah at the junction of the Ohio and Tennessee rivers. The state legislature demanded the withdrawal of the Confederates, but the latter were now busy organising a long, thin and vulnerable defensive line across the southern part of the state, and setting up a rebel state government which maintained a precarious existence throughout the war.

Neutrality was now dead and buried in Kentucky. The situation had always slightly favoured the Union side, but the balance was much further tipped in that direction by Confederate impatience and insensitivity to local feelings and by Lincoln's skill, tact and forbearance. He had played his waiting game and tolerated Kentucky's hesitation and equivocation, in the face of sustained

Northern pressure for more drastic and decisive action. He was never one to underestimate the importance of his native state. 'I think to lose Kentucky is nearly the same as to lose the whole game,' he wrote. 'Kentucky gone, we cannot hold Missouri, nor, as I think, Maryland. These all against us, and the job on our hands is too large for us. We would as well consent to separation at once, including the surrender of this capitol [sic].'[12] By September 1861 he had landed his prize catch. It was still to give him no end of trouble throughout the war, but, to Lincoln, Kentucky was worth it all. Success in Kentucky was perhaps the biggest step taken in 1861 towards salvation of the Union, although many Kentuckians were never reconciled to their fate – so much so that, emotionally at least, Kentucky is often said to have joined the Confederacy after the war was over.

Most westerly and most turbulent of the border states was Missouri. The most heavily populated state west of the Mississippi, including within its boundaries one of the great cities of the Union – St Louis – Missouri was a slavery wedge, driven into the free states and free territory which surrounded it on three sides. On its fate depended the future of much of the remoter west, and Confederate prospects in the whole Mississippi valley. Around St Louis and along the rich lands on either side of the Missouri river, pro-slavery and pro-Southern sentiment was strong, but, over the state as a whole, the Union cause certainly had the numerical advantage. In 1860 Douglas had carried the state by the narrowest of margins over the Constitutional Union candidate Bell, and in February 1861 elections for a special convention had gone heavily against disunion candidates. The convention itself voted 89 to 1 against dissolution of the state's ties with the Union. But, in Missouri as elsewhere in the borderland, Union sympathy dwelt side by side with opposition to coercion of the seceded states. The pro-slavery governor, Claiborne F. Jackson, was in close touch with Confederate leaders and ready to exploit anti-coercion feeling whenever the opportunity presented itself. If Jackson represented one extreme, the impetuous Nathaniel Lyon and the intemperate Frank Blair represented the other on the Republican side. Both sides had been making military preparations before the fall of Sumter, and even before Lincoln's inauguration, and both had their sights trained on the United States arsenal at St Louis. Never inclined to shirk a challenge, or to agonise over the consequences of his actions, Lyon had the contents of the arsenal smuggled across the Mississippi to Alton, Illinois, on 25 April, and, early in May, disarmed the state militia at 'Camp Jackson'. During subsequent demonstrations in St Louis his men opened fire indiscriminately on the crowds, and twenty-eight people died.

Lyon and Blair claimed to have saved Missouri for the Union, but it would be nearer the truth to say that they had imperilled the good work being done by time, caution and moderation which were the Union's best allies in Missouri as in Kentucky. Again, by their later actions in May and June, they succeeded in wrecking a truce arranged between the moderate commander of the Union troops in Missouri, General Harney, and the commander of Jackson's secessionist forces, Sterling Price. Frank Blair, son of one of the most powerful political families in American history, carried the internal disputes of Missouri Unionists to the cabinet table in Washington, where his brother Montgomery Blair, the postmaster-general, championed his cause, and the Missourian Edward Bates, the attorney-general, defended the moderate position. Acting on (and beyond) discretionary orders wrung from a reluctant Lincoln, Blair removed Harney and placed Lyon in command. That such a thing could happen was clear evidence of the neglect of Missouri's problems by the administration in Washington, as it struggled frantically to organise the war effort, and fumbled with its order of priorities. Not until 3 July did it establish the military Department of the West and place in command of it John C. Fremont. Explorer, adventurer, and first presidential candidate of the Republican party, he lacked both the experience and the capacity to cope with the military confusion and political intrigue which awaited him in Missouri. He did not arrive in St Louis until 25 July, and while he worked feverishly on makeshift solutions to pressing problems, Lyon's recklessness brought on an engagement in south-west Missouri which proved damaging to the Union cause and fatal to Lyon himself. Refusing to retreat in face of a Confederate concentration more than twice the size of his own force, Lyon attacked instead at Wilson's Creek on 10 August. Lyon himself was killed and his force obliged to retreat. Frank Blair and his tribe were not slow to infer that Lyon had met disaster through Fremont's failure to support him, and thus a new rift was opened in the Union's military and political leadership in Missouri.

By August 1861 the pattern for the next four years in Missouri was well set, although it remained a crude, confused and jagged collection of ill-fitting pieces. Among those pieces were not merely union and disunion, slavery and anti-slavery, but many more besides: native American against immigrant (for the large German population, especially in St Louis, was almost solidly anti-slavery and Republican); faction and discord in the Unionist ranks, moderates against extremists, Harney against Lyon, and later the Blairs against Fremont, and their respective followers, the conservative 'Claybanks' against the more radical 'Charcoals'; a good measure of routine frontier lawlessness, land squabbles, local jealousy, and personal vendetta; frequent incursions from neighbouring states, notably from Kansas 'Jayhawkers', eager to avenge raids from Missouri in the days of 'Bleeding Kansas'; inadequate leadership, and problems of long distance, remoteness and faulty communication, which meant that law and order were at best intermittent, at worst non-existent. Over all, the Union cause held the ascendancy in Missouri; the state, for example, provided over 100,000 men for the Union forces and only 30,000 for the Confederacy. The state government set up in the summer of 1861, under Governor Hamilton R. Gamble, was steadily and discreetly supported by the Lincoln administration; Claiborne Jackson's régime was officially recognised by the Confederacy, but functioned on paper rather than in practice. But for most Missourians the real story of the Civil War was of internal strife and neighbourhood feuds, disorder and violence, raids and ambushes, burning and killing, and all the terrors of guerrilla warfare.

The struggle for the border was a clear but incomplete victory for the North, a crucial success but not an unqualified blessing. If Missouri, Kentucky, western Virginia and Maryland had made a clear choice for the Confederacy, the strategic balance would have shifted dramatically in favour of the South. The Union government would have found Washington untenable; the Confederate army would have stood on the south bank of the Ohio, instead of stretching a thin, grey line across southern Kentucky where no natural defensive line existed; the trans-Mississippi west would have offered the Confederacy boundless opportunities instead of limitless problems. Indeed, for reasons of politics and morale as much as strategy, the departure of the border states would have broken the Union beyond repair. Lincoln was not alone in believing that as the border states went so would almost certainly go the Union itself. By a remarkable and partly fortuitous blend of decision and delay, force and forbearance, legal fiction and extra-legal action, the Union government mastered Maryland, welcomed West Virginia to the fold, saved Kentucky, and rescued something from the Missouri muddle. It made blunders and missed opportunities, but the Confederate government made and missed more. Jefferson Davis and his advisers seem to have been less sensitive to the situation in the border states, and less skilful in handling it. For the North, success brought new problems and new complications. It was often as difficult to maintain control as it had been to achieve it, and large areas of the border states lived in a twilight world for the rest of the war, in which the regular processes of law and order and political and social life were often interrupted by highly irregular and abnormal proceedings. The final irony of Northern success in the borderland was that the line between Union and Confederacy did not correspond to the line between free states and slave states. This was one more difficulty added to the complex relationship between the issues of slavery and union, and no one was more aware than Abraham Lincoln that when the pressure for emancipation mounted, the interests and the loyalties of the border states would have to be weighed in the balance. But the aches and pains created by the border states as members of the Union were a small price to pay for being spared the agonies of amputation.

In the struggle for the western border in 1861 the military leadership on either side was able to achieve little beyond attempting to establish a coherent front line. The situation within Kentucky and, even more, within Missouri precluded any possibility of ambitious Union moves further south. In the east the position was a little clearer, at least in the sense that the Confederate line nowhere ran north of the Potomac, while the Union forces had only small footholds on Virginia soil. But the picture was far from clear behind the lines on either side, where speculations about strategy bore little relation to the immediate realities of administrative muddle and military unpreparedness. On the Confederate side most opinion favoured a defensive policy, and state and local loyalties demanded that every square mile of territory should be defended. There were, however, bolder spirits like General Beauregard who favoured an attacking strategy and a quick strike north of the Potomac. On the Union side the veteran commander-in-chief, Winfield Scott, outlined his 'Anaconda' plan designed to seal off the Confederacy by a naval blockade and an advance down the length of the Mississippi, and then to wait for steady pressure on the South from all sides to do its work. The Anaconda plan contained many of the basic ingredients of the ultimately successful recipe for Union victory, but it could scarcely be called exciting or aggressive, and it put too much faith in a resurgence of Union feeling in the South and in the durability of Northern morale, civilian as well as military. Some other Northern strategists were even more cautious than Scott, and some, including, strangely, Lincoln himself, were inclined to neglect the west in their calculations. Others still looked for the one, quick, decisive blow which would obviate the need for 'Anaconda' and the like. Certainly, the more restive sections of Northern opinion, encouraged by impatient newspaper editors like Horace Greeley, were demanding action, and raising the cry of 'Forward to Richmond'.

From the time in May when, with Virginia safely in the fold, the Confederate Congress voted to make its capital into the capital of the Confederacy, it took no great military insight to deduce that the area between Richmond and Washington would be the main area of concentration for both armies. Those two capital cities, only some 120 miles apart, dictated and sadly restricted strategic thinking on both sides for the next four years. As hastily organised and ill-prepared volunteer regiments descended on Washington and Richmond, each side had by June arrived at a similar disposition of its forces: a main concentration in the area south-west of Washington, flanked to the west by smaller forces in the Shenandoah Valley, and to the east by smaller forces still in the coastal area of Virginia. On the Northern side the troops around Alexandria just across the Potomac from Washington numbered nearly 35,000 by early July. Their commander was Major-General Irvin McDowell, a major in the regular army before the fall of Sumter, a sharp, serious, earnest man, alert but aloof, fond of the pleasures of the table, but not, like so many of his fellow-officers, of the pleasures of the bottle. He was almost as little prepared to lead an army of 30,000 men into battle as most of them were to be led. Up in the Shenandoah region, around Harper's Ferry (which had already changed hands twice), were some 18,000 men commanded by the sixty-nine-year-old Robert Patterson, old friend of Winfield Scott, and like him a veteran of 1812 and the Mexican War, but no longer up to the task which confronted him. Away to the south-east, at the tip of the James Peninsula, some seventy miles from Richmond, Ben Butler held Fortress Monroe with some 15,000 men.

In eastern Virginia the Confederates had small forces under Generals John B. Magruder and Benjamin Huger to keep an eye on Butler. In the centre their main force of 22,000 men under General Beauregard was concentrated around Manassas Junction, some twenty-five miles south-west of Washington, while some 12,000 men under Joseph E. Johnston shadowed Patterson at the northern end of the Shenandoah Valley. The Confederates hoped to compensate for inferior numbers by mobility, particularly by using the railroad which ran westward from Manassas to enable either Johnston or Beauregard to come to the aid of the other, if and when attacked. Cooperation between the two men was unlikely to be smooth and untroubled. Both had been regular officers in the United States army and both aspired to the highest military command in the Confederacy. Johnston, a Virginian and the senior of the two, was inclined to be fussy, over-sensitive and self-righteous, destined to prove himself a skilful commander but one over-addicted to a Fabian policy of delay and strategic withdrawal. Pierre Gustave Toutant Beauregard, a Louisiana Creole, the hero of Charleston harbour, was vain, argumentative and indiscreet, more imaginative but more rash than Johnston in his strategic thinking. The one thing which both men had in common was their inability to get on with President Jefferson Davis, and here the events of mid-summer 1861 set the pattern for the rest of the war, and the battle of the books which followed it. Lacking an overall military commander, but made all too aware of the proximity of the political capital of the Confederacy, Johnston and Beauregard plagued Richmond with their competing demands, and were plagued in return by Davis's intrusive zeal in military matters.

For all Beauregard's aggressive ambitions, it was soon clear that the first attacking move was more likely to come from the North – not that McDowell or Patterson or commander-in-chief Winfield Scott were impatient for action while they were still preoccupied with the desperate task of moulding raw recruits into something recognisable as an army, but the logic of the situation, the numerical advantage, and the public clamour put the onus squarely upon their shoulders. Lincoln himself joined the pressure group urging action; like others, he was not unmindful of the fact that many of the Union troops were three-months men who had answered the first hasty call after the fall of Sumter, and whose term of service would end in the second half of July. If they were still raw and unprepared, there was no time to allow them to mature, and, in any case, their adversaries had the same problems, as well as the weakness of inferior numbers. Winfield Scott, 'Old Fuss and Feathers', laboured hard at the daunting tasks of organisation and preparation, but his strategic notions meant that his heart was not in the idea of an early advance in Virginia, and in any case he was now seventy-five years old, plagued by illness, and almost immobilised by his physical bulk. 'In case of an action,' wrote W. H. Russell, 'it is his intention to proceed to the field in a light carriage, which is always ready for the purpose, with horses and driver; nor is he unprepared with precedents of great military commanders who have successfully conducted engagements under similar circumstances.'[13] Scott was an anachronism in the kind of war which the Civil War was to become, but he had already rendered his greatest service; unlike his fellow-Virginian Robert E. Lee, he had plumped for the Union in its hour of crisis, and as one of the great public figures of mid-century America his example was not unimportant.

Against their better judgment, Scott and McDowell agreed at the end of June on a plan for an advance on Manassas while Patterson was to keep Johnston occupied in the Shenandoah Valley. McDowell's movement began on 16 July, and every step betrayed his army's state of unreadiness. On 18 July it went into position around Centreville, and a reconnaissance in force was sharply rebuffed. McDowell did not launch his attack on the Confederate position until Sunday 21 July, by which time the cream of Washington society, female as well as male, had driven out to take grandstand seats for what many still thought would be not merely the first battle but the only battle of the war. By this time, too, Johnston, helped by Patterson's lamentable errors, and his own excellent intelligence, had been able to move the bulk of his force to join Beauregard at Manassas. The railroad had made the first of its crucial contributions to the war, and the junction of Beauregard and Johnston may well have decided the outcome before the battle began.

The first battle of Bull Run (or Manassas, in Confederate parlance) was an old-fashioned engagement which offered little positive guidance for future campaigns but many lessons in what not to do. It cost 387 Confederate and 481 Union lives, modest totals compared with what was to come. It produced many individual acts of heroism, and many reluctant heroes too, not least among men who did not intend their three months' service to be their last three months on earth. It brought together on one field many who were to be among the greatest names of the Civil War – Sherman, Stuart and Jackson, for example – and Jackson indeed acquired his famous nickname when General Bee sought to inspire his own men with the spirit of Jackson's unyielding defence: 'There stands Jackson like a stone wall.'

McDowell's plan to attack the Confederate left was sensible enough, but too elaborate for untried officers and ill-trained men. It was less difficult for the Confederates to marshal raw recruits for defensive fighting, and Johnston's arrival had produced something like numerical equality. For all that, it was touch-and-go for a time on that Sunday afternoon, and in a battle so confused and ill-coordinated on both sides, it is misleading to talk too certainly of the inevitability of Confederate victory. Fresh Confederate troops under Kirby Smith entered the battle at the crucial stage and turned the tide. Once the Union retreat had begun, it could not be reversed and it was almost impossible to control, especially after retreating soldiers became caught up in the flight of panicking civilian onlookers. Arms, ammunition and other supplies were jettisoned in the headlong rush back to Washington, and mounted officers often outpaced their footsore men in the stampede for safety. Some semblance of a rearguard remained to check the puny Confederate efforts at pursuit. Several hours before the bulk of the fugitives stumbled back across the Potomac, news of the defeat had reached an anxious Lincoln and a dozing Scott in Washington. In the next few days they set about restoring the situation in a capital plunged into a state of alarm and despondency and living in constant fear of a Confederate attack which never came.[14]

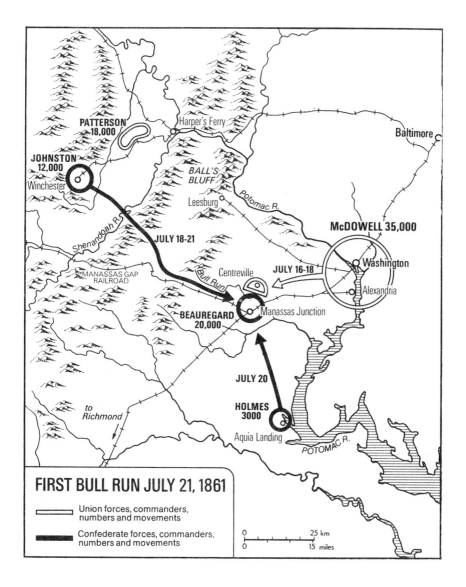

PATTERSON
18,000

Harper's Ferry

Baltimore

JOHNSTON
12,000

Winchester

BALL'S
BLUFF

Leesburg

Potomac R.

McDOWELL 35,000

Shenandoah R.

JULY 18-21

MANASSAS GAP
RAILROAD

Bull Run

Centreville

JULY 16-18

Washington

BEAUREGARD
20,000

Manassas Junction

Alexandria

JULY 20

to
Richmond

HOLMES
3000

Aquia Landing

POTOMAC R.

# FIRST BULL RUN JULY 21, 1861

Union forces, commanders,
numbers and movements

Confederate forces, commanders,
numbers and movements

0          25 km

0          15 miles

Lincoln's opposite number, Jefferson Davis, arrived on the field of Manassas while the battle still raged. Exulted by victory and by evidence of the capture of large quantities of guns, muskets, ammunition, wagons and other supplies, he was anxious to exploit success by immediate pursuit, but Johnston and Beauregard persuaded him that it was not possible, especially after a drenching rain on the night after the battle turned the roads into a quagmire. Johnston, never a man to underrate a difficulty or neglect a reason for caution, believed that his troops were more disorganised by victory than their opponents by defeat. However, nagging doubts remain as to whether the Confederacy missed a great opportunity, if not in the immediate aftermath of Bull Run then in the days and weeks which followed. The road to Washington seemed to lie temptingly open, and, at the end of it, a chance to bring the war to a speedy end. Newspaper editors and armchair strategists in Richmond clamoured for quick action, and Beauregard himself later bitterly condemned Davis for preventing an effective follow-up to the victory at Manassas. He held the president ultimately responsible for the administrative muddle, supply shortages and delays in transportation which, he claimed, ruled out an attack on Washington. The inefficient Commissary-General Lucius B. Northrop was singled out for particular criticism, much of it well-merited. In late September Beauregard managed to persuade the cautious Johnston to support his plan for an invasion of Maryland which would threaten Washington, demoralise the North and favourably impress neutral, and especially British, opinion. But Davis was unable to promise the reinforcements which both deemed essential to the plan, and it came to nothing. Throughout this period Davis and Johnston inclined towards a defensive policy, the latter insisting that Confederate resources were too limited and the Washington defences too strong for a successful attack, and the former asserting that everything possible was being done to supply and strengthen the army. The arguments are delicately balanced; it is essentially a question of whether the badly shaken Union army was even less fit to defend Washington than the poorly-supplied Confederates were to take it and hold it. Lincoln himself once said that, if he were Beauregard, he could take Washington.[15] Attack would have been a gamble, but the South had to gamble to win its independence, and the quavering morale of the North might not have withstood the shock of even the temporary loss of Washington. As things were, Southern elation and wild optimism in July faded away into frustration, dismay and recrimination; such feelings were fed by the unedifying war of words between the Confederate president and General Beauregard which rumbled on through the winter of 1861–2, with Davis accusing the general of 'an attempt to exalt yourself at my expense', and Beauregard replying that 'I have always pitied more than I have envied those in high authority'.[16] The feud became a political issue, and Congress felt obliged to suppress parts of Beauregard's official report on Bull Run, and Davis's comments upon it.

For the South the first sweet taste of victory had turned sour; far from assuring independence, victory had not produced or even promised further victories

For the North, defeat was a shock, and a severe one at that, but, in the slightly longer run, it proved a healthy corrective to complacency. In Washington panic soon passed, and across the Northern states spread a new, more sober, though still impatient, mood of resolution, reflected in another surge of volunteering, the smooth Congressional passage of measures to sustain the war, and an increasing application of Northern resources to the business of war. General George B. McClellan was hurriedly brought to Washington from West Virginia to take command of all the forces around the capital. Hasty improvisation gave way to more orderly preparation. Time might now be a Northern ally, but time had to be used. Both sides had made many mistakes before, during and immediately after Bull Run. The defeated side found it hard enough to learn the lessons; for the victors, it was harder even to see that there were lessons to be learned.

# Chapter VI: Men at Arms

The South had pinned its faith on fighting yesterday's kind of war, but political, social, economic and technological change had conspired to transform warfare by the 1860s. If not a completely new kind of war, the American conflict presented many new and revolutionary features. The old and the new over-lapped; the formal patterns of eighteenth-century strategy and tactics lived side by side with the sledgehammer blows, massive concentrations and rapid movements which heralded the total warfare of the twentieth century. The rifled barrel had already become standard in small arms but the smoothbore cannon lived on; the horse was not rendered obsolete overnight by the iron horse, and the wagon train ran on where the railroad train could not go; the ironclad ship was opening a new age of naval warfare, but the everyday chores of naval blockade were still the job of wooden ships; scientific invention and industrial techniques had multiplied the capacity to inflict pain and death, but medicine had failed to keep in step, so that the chance of surviving a wound was seven-to-one, in comparison with fifty-to-one in the Korean War, and disease killed twice as many Union soldiers as Confederate weapons did. Warfare changed dramatically in the four years from 1861 to 1865. The battle of Bull Run in July 1861 would have been easily recognisable to a veteran of 1846 or 1812, and not totally unrecognisable to a resurrected hero of 1776. The hard slogging-match around Richmond and Petersburg in 1864–5 was a harbinger of the horrors of Flanders fields, while Sherman's march through Georgia to the sea was an early hint of blitzkrieg.

The Civil War, like any other war, reflected the society in which it took place. In particular, it reflected the growth and rapid change which were the dominating themes of American life in the nineteenth century. It reflected American democracy; participation in the American democratic process involved not merely the frequent exercise of the vote, but participation in unprecedented numbers in the fight to preserve the political system or create a new one; opportunity for every citizen implied the expectation that every citizen would take up arms when the situation demanded it. It reflected American nationalism – and Southern nationalism too. Popular feeling for the nation, identification with it and affirmation of its unique destiny now required popular involvement in the struggle to defend an existing nation or establish a new one. The combined forces of democracy and nationalism brought about not only a huge increase in the actual numbers involved in the fighting or in supplying, maintaining and equipping the men at the front – though that was impressive enough in itself by the standards of 1812 or 1846. They also produced a massive increase in commitment to the cause of one side or the other, which made this a people's war as no earlier American war had been – not even the War of Independence itself. The thousands of deserters, draft-dodgers and bounty-jumpers, the legions of critics of the respective administrations and opponents of their war policies, the millions of victims of war-weariness, frustration, disillusionment, despondency and cynicism are powerful reminders that commitment to the cause was never complete, nor unflagging, nor uniform throughout the land. But many millions, in and out of uniform, felt that this was a struggle which concerned them and engaged their emotions, loyalties, interests and beliefs. Through four years of bitter conflict, North and South maintained huge citizen armies of hundreds of thousands of men, the great bulk of whom were volunteers, though, as the war went on, volunteering was backed up by conscription, and there were increasing incentives for those who did volunteer, and discomforts for those who did not. Northern morale, military and civilian, faltered in the face of harsh blows but never broke down; Southern morale collapsed only when the Confederacy itself was falling in ruins. Because this was a civil war, and a people's war, morale was as crucial on the home front as on the battlefront. Public opinion mattered as much as military strategy or political leadership, and the interactions of all three were vital to the fortunes of either side. This could never be a conflict to be fought out by the small professional armies of an earlier age; civil leadership, civilian participation, and citizen-soldiers shaped the conduct of the war at every turn.

The Civil War reflected, too, the impact of industrial growth and technological change on American society – and its differing impact on North and South. The factory and the machine were about to transform warfare but they were also to complicate it, as each new development brought fresh problems. The capacity to produce on a large scale not merely arms and ammunition but clothing, boots, tents, blankets and a hundred other items of equipment alone made it possible to deploy such large armies over such wide distances. Logistics played as large a part in military thinking and planning as more classical considerations of strategy and tactics. It became as important to outproduce the enemy as to outmanoeuvre or outfight him, and it was here that the North had its most overwhelming advantages. Northern victory and its relationship to Northern productive capacity taught a lesson which has influenced the American approach to warfare ever since.

This was the first great war of the railroad age, and it was the railroad (and, to a lesser extent, the steamboat) which made large-scale production applicable to the battlefront. The ability to transport large quantities of both men and material over long distances in a short time gave greater mobility to armies and a new dimension to strategy. Those who predicted in 1861 that it was beyond the power of the North to invade and conquer the South had, among other things, overlooked what the railroad might do. A still more recent development, the telegraph, speeded up communications even more dramatically. It brought commanders into close touch with each other and with their military and political superiors; it made possible a greater measure of direction and control from the centre. This was above all true of the campaigns in northern Virginia, where the armies were always closely linked with their respective capitals in Washington and Richmond.

It was soon clear, however, that the war-making potential of new industrial processes, and new modes of transport and communication, could not be fully realised overnight. New capacity meant new complexity; new methods of making war meant new ways of making mistakes. There were more things to go wrong, more chance of breakdowns, bottlenecks, and bungling. The railroad in America was less than thirty years old when the war came, the first through-routes from New York to the cities of the north-west less than a decade old. The telegraph dated back less than twenty years; when Samuel F. B. Morse tapped out his portentous message 'What hath God wrought' in 1844, he could scarcely have foreseen (even if his Maker could) what the generals and their political masters would make of his invention in his own lifetime. If the railroad and the telegraph revolutionised ideas about speed, distance, mobility and supply, they raised new difficulties and imposed new restraints. A railroad track or a telegraph wire was more vulnerable than the dirt roads – or even the open country – which were good enough for the horse-drawn wagon or the mounted despatch rider. Armies could exploit the advantages which the railroad offered, but if they depended on the iron rail they were tied to its defence. Above all, the railroad and the telegraph were least effective where it mattered most – close to the field of battle. There remained the problem of shifting from railhead to front line the tons of supplies which the trains delivered, and there remained, too, the difficulty for officers in the field of keeping in touch with each other and with their men. The horse and the mule remained essential for the one task, and traditional close-order tactics endured to provide a solution to the other, but a very costly solution in the era of the rifled musket. War in a rapidly industrialising society was clearly going to be a new kind of war, but not a simpler one. It would take time to learn new lessons and master new techniques, and more traditional ideas and practices were not easily discarded.

1. The very weapons with which the war was fought suggest most clearly of all the overlapping of old and new which is so characteristic of the conflict as a whole. The basic infantry weapon on both sides was the rifled musket, which, in its shape and its six-foot length, closely resembled the musket of earlier days but incorporated a number of modifications and refinements which transformed its performance and pointed the way to the modern rifle. Its rifled barrel, replacing the old smoothbore, gave vastly greater range and accuracy. The old musket had an effective killing range of about fifty yards; the rifled musket could kill at five hundred yards or more. It was still a muzzle-loader, but the French officer C. E. Minié had solved the problem of devising a bullet which could be loaded without engaging the rifling in the barrel, but which would engage it on being discharged. His 'Minié ball' (so-called despite its typical bullet shape) had a hollowed base which expanded when the powder exploded, and gripped the spiral grooving inside the barrel. Scores of thousands of dead and wounded on both sides testified to the effectiveness of Minié's small invention; the rifled musket was probably responsible for upwards of four-fifths of battle-field casualties during the war. Reliability in all weathers and an improved rate of fire were added to improved range and accuracy when the percussion cap replaced the old flintlock in the pre-Civil War decades. All the advantages of the rifled musket were multiplied by the newer breech-loading rifles which were available in the 1860s and which could have been produced in large numbers. But here old ideas and old restraints imposed a brake on the application of new inventions, which still needed to be fully tested in battlefield conditions. The rapid rate of fire of such weapons, it was feared, would be extremely wasteful of ammunition, and new methods of transport and supply had not yet under-mined the belief that the individual soldier should carry about him all that he would need on the field of battle. Here, as elsewhere, the Civil War came at the point where innovation was superseding old weapons faster than it was under-mining the conventional military wisdom.

Artillery, even more than small arms, was at a transitional stage. Here the rifled barrel was only just winning acceptance when war began. During the four years of conflict the guns of both armies were fairly evenly divided between smooth and rifled bores, and they fired a mixture of solid shot and explosive shells. In some respects artillery was becoming more mobile; on the other hand the trend towards heavier guns of greater calibre made possible by new methods of reinforcing the barrels, created new problems of movement and supply. On the whole it was the lighter guns which did most of the work, but their effectiveness was limited, especially against an entrenched enemy. The limited range of the old smoothbores made their crews vulnerable even to the infantry-man's rifled musket, while the newer rifled guns lacked sufficient destructive power at longer range. Their explosive shells were often rendered ineffective by the extreme unreliability of their fuses. But, whatever its limitations as an offensive arm, the artillery could wreak havoc among opposing infantry advancing in the open, when the guns fired grape or canister, and showered lead balls or metal pellets into the ranks of the attackers. At close range, canister was almost as lethal as the machine gun of later days. There were plenty of other novel weapons or devices employed at one time or another in the Civil War, from primitive versions of the machine gun to aerial reconnaissance from anchored balloons, but most of them were tentative and experimental. The developments in the standard infantry weapon were what really mattered, and, like the developments in industrial production and transportation, they were to alter the whole shape of the conflict.

2. The men behind the guns mattered too, and new attitudes to manpower and its use evolved much more quickly than any modern concept of firepower. Within weeks of the bombardment of Fort Sumter both sides were busy raising troops on the grand scale, and both were soon thinking in terms of mass armies unprecedented in American experience. The Mexican War, which had ended only thirteen years earlier, had been fought by forces whose total strength had never much exceeded 50,000, and Winfield Scott himself had marched on Mexico City with only 14,000 men. During the Civil War there were well over $2\frac{1}{2}$ million enrolments in the Union army, which, if allowance is made for re-enlistments, means that something like $1\frac{1}{2}$ million different individuals served in the army. The total strength at one time was never much more than 1 million, however, and the number present for duty never reached that figure. Confederate statistics are notoriously inadequate and unreliable, but total enlistments were perhaps around 850,000 to 900,000. In view of the lack of any strong American military tradition, or of a large regular army, and the absence of any contingency planning before April 1861 for large-scale mobilisation, the scale and speed of recruiting in both North and South is quite astonishing and far exceeded the rate of expansion achieved by the United States army in either of the world wars of this century.

The feat is all the more remarkable when it is recalled that both sides relied on volunteers at the outset, and, even after the resort to conscription, volunteers continued to provide the great bulk of the troops throughout the war. There were in fact two main ways in which large armies could have been raised on the voluntary principle. The first was to rely on expansion of existing military organisations – the regular army, the militia, and, to a lesser extent, the volunteer companies which had acquired social standing if not always martial repute in the pre-Civil War years. The second was to raise a new and separate volunteer army on the Mexican War pattern but on a much larger scale. Both Union and Confederate governments put their main faith in the second option, but neither could nor did ignore completely the possibilities of the first.

The regular army of the United States numbered around 16,000 men at the beginning of 1861, most of them scattered over the wide expanses of the western frontier. Of its 1,100 officers, over 300 resigned and went over to the Confederacy, but most of the rank and file remained loyal, partly from inclination, partly from a lack of choice in the matter. The regular army became neither the nucleus of the vastly expanded Union army which fought the Civil War, nor a leaven of experience mixed into the volunteer mass, as much expert opinion then and later recommended, but remained a separate entity commanded by regular officers, and a very small part of the total Union forces. Recruits generally preferred the easier discipline and more attractive terms of service of the new volunteer army, and even ex-regular officers, returning to the colours, saw better prospects of rapid promotion in the new force. The Confederate Congress, for its part, created the regular army of the C.S.A. by an act of 6 March 1861, and fixed its peacetime establishment at 9,000. Jefferson Davis's plea that this is evidence of the modest and peaceable intentions of the Confederacy seems more than a little disingenuous, for on the same day he had been authorised as president to accept up to 100,000 volunteers in a separate force.[1] Throughout the war the Confederate regular army was little more than a paper organisation.

The other established organisational framework for raising large numbers of troops was provided by the militia. This had the appeal of being the true, traditional American way, the free democratic way of maintaining an armed establishment. As the second article of the Bill of Rights put it: 'A well regulated militia, being necessary to the security of a free State, the right of the people to keep and bear arms shall not be infringed.' This somewhat illogical merging of the right of the individual citizen to keep and bear arms, and the universal obligation to serve in the militia perhaps helps to explain the basic paradox which runs right through the history of that organisation. In a society which admired fighting spirit and feats of marksmanship but was profoundly suspicious of military power or pretensions, its political acceptability and its wider popularity rested heavily on its very weakness and inefficiency as a military force. In fact, by the mid-nineteenth century, the militia in most states had fallen into complete decay, and its annual muster was very often little more than a bibulous reunion for the participants, and a laughing stock to everyone else. It remained a state and not a federal force, its officers commissioned and its men trained (if at all) by the state authorities. The constitution gave the federal government the power to call out militia to enforce the law, suppress insurrection or repel invasion, but from the 1790s to the 1860s all attempts to provide some national framework for coordination of the state militia or some cooperation with the regular army had achieved nothing. However, if the militia tradition was more honoured in the breach than in the observance as far as practical utility was concerned, the militia idea still had a strong hold, and in the spring of 1861 even a broken reed seemed to be worth grasping. Lincoln's first reaction to the fall of Sumter had been to call upon the states for 75,000 militia for three months' service to deal with 'combinations too powerful to be suppressed by the ordinary course of judicial proceedings'.[2] (It was these three-months men who were about to set off home at the time of Bull Run.) The more energetic state governors in the North had been busy reactivating the militia ever since the secession crisis had broken, and later in the war they were to use the machinery of the militia to meet the quotas of troops demanded of them from Washington. In emergencies, such as Lee's invasion of the North in 1863, Lincoln was still reduced to calling upon the states immediately threatened for militia for a short period of service – in that particular instance, six months.[3] In the South, recalcitrant state governors were all too willing to exploit the militia system in their struggle to assert their authority against the government in Richmond, and the endless confusion which resulted seriously hampered efforts to make optimum use of the South's limited manpower.

Clearly, then, the militia could not provide the basis for the large, longer-term and centrally directed armies which fought the war. Both Union and Confederacy quickly put their faith in the creation of a new volunteer army. Ideally, a blueprint for the organisation of any such force would have included such features as firm central control and coordination designed to create a truly national army, a careful matching of manpower, weapons and supplies, checks on the medical quality of recruits and the leadership qualities of their officers, and a system designed to maintain regiments at full strength in face of battle losses, sickness, desertion and other wastage. But such priorities fought a losing battle in practice in 1861 against state pride, state loyalties and local initiative, the pitifully inadequate organisation of central government in general and the War Department in particular, the incompetence of many of those in positions of responsibility, a shortage of weapons and supplies, and a formidable combination of political intrigue, personal ambition, and the search for quick profits. Above all, American society and government, North and South, were simply not equipped to prepare any such precise blueprint, let alone follow it in practice. What actually happened on both sides was in the early months haphazard. Only slowly did some tentative and limited central direction develop, and even more slowly still did anything emerge which could be properly regarded as a coherent system. However, what is most remarkable of all is that, by the end of 1861, there had grown out of nothing, through all the chaos and the blunders, men without arms, officers without qualifications, and organisers without organisation, armies running into hundreds of thousands of men, with the prospect of many more to come.

The facts and figures of Northern recruitment are impressive enough and become even more so when related to the story behind them. When Lincoln called for 75,000 militia on 15 April 1861, he also called Congress into special session, but that session was not to start until 4 July. In the interim, the president had not merely provided for an increase in the regular army, but, by the same proclamation of 3 May, had asked for 42,000 volunteers in forty regiments, for a three-year term of service. This was the beginning of the great volunteer army; for all the chaos and confusion which accompanied their recruitment, 208 regiments rather than 40 had been accepted by 1 July, and, together with the three-months men, they took the total strength above 300,000. These recruits had rolled in on the crest of the first wave of enthusiasm for the war to save the Union. By the time Congress assembled it was no longer fanciful to talk in terms not of thousands but of hundreds of thousands, and Lincoln not merely sought retrospective approval of what he had already done, but asked Congress for 400,000 additional men. Congress in fact quickly authorised 500,000, and, in the wake of the Bull Run defeat, added another 500,000 for good measure; the president was to call for these men as and when required. The shock of Bull Run stimulated a new wave of enthusiasm for joining the army, and a new let-them-all-come spirit in the overstretched War Department. It was not until the last few months of the year that an improvement in economic prospects and impatience with the inactivity of the army led to a decline in recruiting. Numbers had passed the half-million mark by the turn of the year; recruiting was deliberately slowed down for a time, and in April 1862 the new secretary for War, Stanton, actually closed down the recruiting service. Although it is now clear that this was always intended as a temporary measure, to give time for the overhaul of the whole system, it had a bad effect at a time when the first flush of enthusiasm had waned, and when the armies were about to launch major campaigns.[4] Recruiting resumed in June, and the government continued to make further large calls for volunteers, but the response showed neither the numbers nor the zeal of the summer of 1861. Ironically, now that the government had learned the lessons and acquired the means, it could no longer attract the men in such abundance as before.

The huge response of 1861 was the product of individual enthusiasm, state action and local initiative, not of War Department management. Lacking machinery of its own, the Department, which had but ninety employees when the war began, relied perforce on the efforts of the states. Lacking any real talent for organisation and administration himself, Simon Cameron, who headed the Department, was quite outshone in energy and efficiency by many of the state governors – in the east, men like Andrew of Massachusetts, Buckingham of Connecticut and Curtin of Pennsylvania; in the west, Morton of Indiana, Blair of Michigan and Yates of Illinois. When a call for volunteers was made, each state was assigned a quota roughly proportional to its population, and it was then the function of the state authorities to raise the appropriate number of regiments. In the early days their efforts ran well ahead of demand; Massachusetts, for example, spurred on by its dynamic Governor Andrew, produced seventeen regiments instead of its allotted six in answer to the first call of May 1861. The efforts of the state governors were backed up by towns and cities, energetic groups of citizens and ambitious individuals all vying with one another to show their dedication to the cause. What was lacking in regularity or orderly procedure was made up in grass-roots enthusiasm and enterprise. A citizen of local prominence or military pretension would organise a regiment or at least a company, in the confident expectation of receiving a commission from the state governor, and winning himself undying military glory in a matter of weeks rather than months. Spurred on by family and friends, motivated by a mixture of patriotism, fear of being thought a coward, and anxiety that it would all be over if he did not hurry, the volunteer joined the company or regiment of his choice. When it had reached minimum strength, it marched off amid much speech-making, cheering and martial music, to be mustered into federal service after a cursory inspection by a regular officer, and an even more cursory inspection of its members by a medical officer. (The number of women, masquerading as men, who successfully enlisted suggests that such medical checks lacked something in rigour and thoroughness.)[5]

In May and June 1861 the Washington authorities, quite overwhelmed by the flood of new regiments which descended on the capital, struggled desperately to find food and shelter for them. The halls of Congress itself became a temporary barracks. Small wonder that Lincoln told Congress on 4 July that 'one of the greatest perplexities of the Government is to avoid receiving troops faster than it can provide for them'.[6] In the latter part of 1861 a better balance was struck between the supply of troops and the supply of weapons and equipment, and between state endeavour and federal organisation. But, even at this stage, Lincoln and Cameron made a confused situation worse by their acceptance of regiments raised by individuals, outside the state-sponsored efforts and often in competition with them. Such glory-hunting private ventures occurred in New York and Pennsylvania, and above all in New England where the independent recruiting efforts of Ben Butler provoked a bitter feud, personal and political as much as military, with Governor Andrew of Massachusetts.

By early 1862, however, the efforts of General McClellan, and then, above all, of Cameron's successor, Edwin M. Stanton, whose arrival transformed the War Department, created a much greater measure of central coordination and control over recruiting. As long as they could point to hordes of eager volunteers demanding acceptance, the state governors had a trump card to play in dealing with Washington. But when the position was reversed, they were left to play a much weaker hand. From being the great organisers of the war effort, and the gadflies of the administration in 1861, they were reduced to the status of recruiting agents for Lincoln and Stanton by the second half of 1862.[7] But whatever the moves towards control from Washington, the ramshackle, decentralised methods of the first year left enduring marks on the organisation and character of the army. It had encouraged extravagance, inefficiency and some corruption in the purchase and distribution of supplies; it had saddled the army with officers with no military aptitude or experience; it had placed obstacles in the way of discipline, military efficiency and a systematic chain of command, especially since officers up to the rank of colonel looked to the state governors for their commissions, while the federal authorities controlled only the higher appointments. These problems will be further discussed later, but one other chronic problem which seriously weakened the efficiency of the army as a fighting force lay in the failure to keep regiments up to full strength. Once a regiment left its home area it often received no more recruits, and local interest switched to new regiments with new opportunities for those who hankered after a commission. Regiments were not divided into battalions, with one battalion based at home to maintain a steady flow of recruits. The result was that many regiments, with an establishment of around 1,000, were reduced to a half or even a third of that size by mid-war, and raw recruits, instead of being fed into existing units alongside battle-hardened veterans, were grouped together in new regiments, often under new and inexperienced officers. The resort to conscription was in large measure an attempt to solve the serious problem of filling up old regiments. In a wider sense, conscription, too, was final proof of the shift of effective control from the states to Washington. The same trend was confirmed by the raising of Negro regiments on the direct authority of the federal government, a step which was to add 186,000 men to the Union army before the war ended.[8] The transfer of power from the states to the central government in this vital field of army recruitment and organisation was very much a sign of the times; the process was not always smooth and not always carefully or even consciously planned, but it was markedly more successful in the North than in the South, and that, too, was a portent of the shape of things to come.

The recruitment of the volunteer or 'provisional' army of the Confederacy shared many of the features of its Union counterpart. The war began with a mass movement to join the ranks in every state across the South. Far more even than in the North, this first phase produced a desperate imbalance between the numbers of men and regiments clamouring for acceptance and the organisation, equipment and weapons available to them. Judah P. Benjamin, Secretary for War at the time, claimed that 600,000 men had offered their services in that year, but that the army numbered only half that total at the end of the year.[9] Having been turned away once for lack of arms above all else. men were less eager to offer their services again later; complacency after Bull Run and then impatience at the lack of further success also discouraged enlistment. However ironically in the light of its political tradition and constitutional principles, the South was forced to accept much earlier than the North that compulsory service should take over where voluntary effort no longer sufficed.

The story of the volunteer army began even before the war itself. In those early days, Jefferson Davis had shown the initiative in military matters which might have been expected of a West Point graduate and one-time Secretary of War, and the Provisional Congress had generally supported him without complaint. Having authorised the president on 28 February 1861 to receive troops offered by the state governors, or volunteers who had their consent, for one year's service, Congress empowered him on 6 March to call for up to 100,000 twelve-month volunteers and to employ state militia for periods of up to six months. Once the war had started, Davis was authorised on 6 May to receive units into service 'without the delay of a formal call upon the respective states', and for a longer term eventually fixed at three years, or the duration of the war, if less. By August over 200,000 men were in the field, and Congress granted Davis the authority to call for up to 400,000 further volunteers. Each of these measures in turn gave more initiative and authority to the president and paid less heed to the rights and powers of the states and the sensibilities of the state governors. But the system on paper did not always reflect the realities of the situation, and the Confederate government patently lacked the organisation and resources to 'go it alone'. Indeed, some of the subsequent bitterness between the administration and the state governors may have stemmed from the tendency of the early legislation to obscure sensitive issues and leave ill-defined the relationship between state-sponsored regiments and a Confederate-controlled army.

Certainly, as in the North, it was state and local efforts which brought forth the men. Governors offered commissions to almost any local figure who would raise a regiment or a company and take responsibility for equipping it, and young men of all stations in society flocked to the colours in a state of excitement better fitted to a short, sharp sprint rather than the gruelling long-distance race which was to come. Some scions of aristocratic families enlisted in the ranks but took the precaution of bringing a slave with them to cushion them against the discomforts of army life. But the great bulk of the rank and file recruits came from the lower ranks of white society, and indeed the appearance in and around Richmond of thousands of unkempt farm boys in uniform aroused even more disquiet and distaste in genteel society there than their Northern counterparts did around Washington. Meanwhile, the state governors were insisting on their rights in return for their recruiting efforts, and asserting their independence in a variety of ways. Some absorbed into their own local defence forces volunteers whom the Confederate authorities were unable to accept in the summer of 1861, and they remained very reluctant to give them up thereafter. Some withheld stocks of arms and other supplies badly needed by the Confederate army, or insisted on their right to supply regiments from their own state in Confederate service. Some even insisted on the right to fill vacancies among the officers in such regiments – a claim which went further than any interference by Northern governors in wrecking effective military discipline and organisation. Control over recruitment of troops and their subsequent deployment became a part of the wider battle between Richmond and the state capitals. Jefferson Davis and successive Secretaries for War were never able to transfer the initiative from the states to the centre as successfully as Lincoln and Stanton in the North. In view of Southern devotion to states rights and resentment of central authority, it is remarkable that they achieved as much as they did in raising a large Confederate army, just as the fighting record of that army becomes all the more impressive in the light of the state interference which plagued it at every turn.

Squabbles with the state governments were one cause of the loss of impetus in the Southern war effort in the winter of 1861–2, and the consequent decline in volunteering. The early months of the new year brought the first real Confederate setbacks on both the eastern and western fronts, and introduced a note of urgency into discussion of manpower problems. However, the immediate danger which drove the Confederate government to drastic action within a year of the outbreak of war was not so much the shortage of new recruits as the fate of men already in the army. Many of the first enthusiastic volunteers in the spring of 1861 had signed on for only twelve months' service. That period was now almost completed, and grievances over bad conditions, poor pay (or no pay at all), and incompetent officers, together with a feeling that others should now take over their burden, made a large number of these men disinclined to re-enlist, despite the incentives in the shape of bounties and furloughs which they were offered. There was a serious possibility that the Confederate army would lose not only thousands of its men, but its most experienced and most valuable men at that.

3. So it was that conscription was adopted by the Confederacy in April 1862, almost a year before the Union moved in the same direction. On paper, at least, the Confederate measure was also much more sweeping and far-reaching than the Union legislation. Conscription was a bitter pill for the South to swallow, and only a critical situation and a sober realisation of the desperate need to compensate for inferior numbers by more effective use of available manpower could have driven the Davis administration to seek it and Congress to authorise it by majorities of more than two-to-one. Except among those who were threatened by it, the initial public response was favourable, and even a veteran secessionist like William L. Yancey came to its defence. In the longer run, however, conscription was to be one of the great bones of contention within the Confederacy, and one of the greatest threats to morale at home and at the front. There were those who always felt that the purity of the Confederate cause was forever sullied by the introduction of compulsory service. The South should not seek its freedom by denying freedom to its citizens, they argued, and the cause of states rights could not be defended by such a formidable assertion of central authority. One Confederate soldier later expressed his feelings very clearly: 'From this time on till the end of the war, a soldier was simply a machine, a conscript. We cussed the war . . . we cussed the Southern Confederacy. All our pride and valor had gone and we were sick of war and the Southern Confederacy. . . . The glory of the war, the glory of the South, the glory and pride of our volunteers had no charms for the conscript.'[10]

The basic provisions of the law of 16 April 1862 were bold and clear enough. All male white citizens between the ages of eighteen and thirty-five were declared members of the Confederate army for three years, or the duration of the war, if less; all soldiers already in the army were required to complete three years' service. By volunteering, a man could still escape the odium of conscription and gain the privilege of choosing his own company in both the military and social sense of the term; thirty days' grace was allowed for the creation of new volunteer units, and a volunteer could join an existing unit at any time before enrolment under the Conscription Act caught up with him. Conscripts were to be used to fill the depleted ranks of existing units from their home states. The War Department quickly drew up instructions for the enrolment, training and disposition of conscripts, but the machinery moved into action only slowly and fitfully during 1862, owing to the shortcomings of Confederate administration, but also in order to give every encouragement to possible volunteers. In September 1862 the upper age limit for conscription was raised to forty-five, and in February 1864 the age limits were extended to cover those from seventeen to fifty, although the seventeen-year-olds and those over forty-five were reserved for state defence.

However thorough and comprehensive it may have appeared at first sight, the conscription law was ruined in practice by two gaping loopholes – what one Southern commentator called 'those twin abortions of legislation, the substitute and exemption bills'.[11] The original act allowed a conscript to avoid service by supplying an able-bodied man, not of conscript age, as a substitute. Abuses inevitably followed; the market price of substitutes steadily climbed to several thousand dollars, and the fitness of many of them was very questionable. The system clearly discriminated against the poorer sections of the community, and aroused understandable animosity in many quarters. At last, in December 1863, Congress abolished substitution, but by then the damage had been done. However, if the effects of substitution were bad, exemptions proved far worse. Jefferson Davis later admitted, with massive understatement, that the exemption granted to men engaged in certain occupations had proved unwise.[12] Designed to mitigate hardship and injustice on the home front and to keep key men in their civilian occupations, the system of exemptions became a device for wholesale evasion of military service. The first list of exempted groups in April 1862 was extended and revised by later legislation, and each change merely encouraged greater ingenuity in its exploitation. The exemption of officers of the Confederate and state governments was flagrantly abused by many state governors to cover all kinds of minor officials. Governor Brown of Georgia fought to establish that a commission in the state militia warranted exemption from conscription, and then proceeded to make the Georgia militia a ludicrously top-heavy organisation, crammed with officers performing the most perfunctory duties. Exemptions given to professional men were easily abused when professional qualifications were extremely vague. The inclusion of teachers of twenty pupils in the list, for example, stimulated a rash of new schools all across the South and an interest in education which had not been one of the more conspicuous features of the ante-bellum South. The provision of October 1862 exempting one white man for every plantation with twenty or more slaves was bitterly resented among the non-slave-owning population, and encouraged complaints about 'a rich man's war and a poor man's fight'. As one soldier put it, 'it gave us the blues; we wanted twenty negroes'.[13] The exemption given to whole classes of key workers in industry, agriculture and transport was too much like a blunt instrument; what was needed was a discretionary power in the hands of the administration to deal with particular cases on their merits and in the light of the real needs of the war effort, but Congress was jealous of any such extension of executive power, and engaged in a long wrangle with Davis on the subject, while the Confederacy was falling apart in 1864–5.

If all else failed, a man determined to avoid conscription could always plead medical unfitness, supported perhaps by a sympathetic doctor or a quack, or could take to the road, to exploit the provision that a man could be enrolled only in the state where he was domiciled. Confederate statistics are notoriously patchy and unreliable, but it is quite clear that substitution and exemption made a mockery of conscription. One estimate suggests that 50,000–75,000 substitutes were enlisted in the army; exemptions were very much more numerous, probably amounting to almost as many as the number of conscripts who actually reached the front. An informed guess suggests well over 100,000 in the area east of the Mississippi alone.[14] The longer the war went on, the nearer the whole conscription system came to complete breakdown. The Confederate authorities lacked the administrative capacity and the power of enforcement to make the law consistently effective, especially when, later in the war, armed bands of draft-dodgers and deserters openly defied them in some areas. State governments were at best uncooperative and at worst obstructive, and many state judges protected unwilling conscripts from arrest with writs of habeas corpus. The conscription law saved the immediate situation in 1862, and it added some tens of thousands of men to the army in the next two years, but not so much directly as by encouraging volunteers. But even here the persistence of the volunteer principle alongside conscription had harmful consequences; it enabled some men to avoid or delay conscription by bogus volunteering, and, more seriously, it reduced the conscript to an inferior status in the eyes of his fellow soldiers. Conscription looked like a punishment rather than an obligation. It has frequently been argued that the limited achievements of conscription were gained at too high a cost, and there is no doubt that the system was repellent to Southern hearts and minds in principle, and socially divisive, politically damaging and militarily inefficient in practice. But, for all that, it is hard to see any alternative. There came a point inevitably beyond which volunteer recruiting would not go; state-conducted conscription might have been less unpopular but would have produced political confusion and military chaos. Ideally the South needed an overall manpower policy, covering both the army and production on the home front, but such a policy was beyond the scope of the government. Ultimately, the failure of conscription was a reflection of the basic weaknesses of the Confederacy itself.

Conscription, indeed, may have been just too much for the mid-nineteenth-century American to accept, for in the North, too, not even the friendliest critic could have called the draft law a success. The timing, the procedures and the flaws of the Union measure were all somewhat different, but their result was much the same. Having flirted with the idea of conscription in the Militia Act of July 1862, Congress finally took the plunge in March 1863, to meet the problems caused by a fall in recruiting and a rise in losses due to battlefield casualties, medical unfitness and large-scale desertion. One particular objective, never satisfactorily achieved, was to fill up the ranks of sadly depleted regiments raised early in the war. The new law provided that all men between the ages of twenty and forty-five were to be enrolled and thus become liable to be drafted, and liable to arrest for evasion of the draft. In contrast to the bold declaration of the Confederate law that all men in the relevant age group were members of the armed forces, the Union citizen's chances depended to some extent on the luck of the draw when a draft was carried out. Machinery for the enforcement of the Northern act was established under the Provost-Marshal-General in Washington. The state authorities were ignored, and even enrolment itself was to be carried out not state by state but by congressional districts. However, once again, the effectiveness of the law in practice was severely damaged by the loopholes which it left. Although exemptions as such were to be granted only on medical or compassionate grounds, the law did recognise the principle of substitution, and the related practice of commutation. In other words, a drafted man could avoid enlistment either by providing a substitute or by paying a commutation fee of $300. Both practices were recognised by military (and militia) precedents, and both were perhaps less shockingly unjust to the mind of the 1860s than they appear today. To provide a substitute was not regarded as a cause for shame in many quarters,[15] and commutation was defended by, of all people, President Lincoln, on the unlikely ground that it was essentially democratic. The price of hiring a substitute in a free market, he argued, would rise far above $300, and commutation would therefore bring avoidance of the draft within range not of the poorest citizens, but at least those of fairly modest means. Inequality could only be removed by sweeping away both substitution and commutation, and, 'this being a great innovation, would probably leave the law more distasteful than it now is'.[16] Whatever their advantages to the citizen liable to be drafted, there is no doubt that both practices robbed conscription of much of its military usefulness, and commutation, at least, was belatedly abolished in July 1864.

Even more than in the South, such benefits as the draft produced were often more indirect than direct, in stimulating a revival of the flow of volunteers. Each time a draft was made, each district was allowed to include volunteers in meeting its quota, and then to employ the draft to make up the deficit. New recruiting campaigns were launched, and states, cities, towns and counties vied with each other in offering inducements to the volunteer in the shape of bounties and other benefits. The federal government followed suit, and by 1864 was offering $300 to new recruits and $400 to veterans who re-enlisted. These sums could be as much as doubled by state and local bounties, and such rich pickings encouraged the growth of bounty-jumping whereby men volunteered, collected their bounties, deserted, and turned up in another state or district to begin the whole process again. The Union, like the Confederacy, paid dearly for attempting to encourage volunteering at the same time as it enforced conscription, and the whole story of bounty-jumpers, quack doctors, substitute brokers, and broken-down substitutes constitutes one of the seamier chapters of Civil War history.

The enforcement of the draft in the Northern states was carried out in the face of bitter hostility, widespread grievances over quotas, allegations of political bias or regional discrimination, and open violence in New York city and elsewhere.[17] There were four main drafts, in July 1863 and March, July and

December 1864. A great reservoir of new manpower was tapped by the process of enrolment, but most of it drained away through the leaks and cracks in the system. The direct results were pitiful: 46,000 conscripts, 116,000 substitutes and almost 87,000 who escaped by the commutation safety hatch. A mere 6 per cent of total enlistments in the Union army came directly from the draft; it is impossible to estimate how many volunteers should be ascribed to the stick of conscription rather than the carrot of the bounty system.

The Union had the numbers and the resources to survive the wastefulness and inefficiency of its recruiting system better than the Confederacy. Neither side proved able to cope with the full implications of conscription or to create and administer a fair and workable system. The capacity of American government was not up to the task in the 1860s, and popular assessments of the function of central government did not extend to such drastic and unwelcome interference in the life of the individual citizen. It was in the nature of American society that Civil War armies should be raised in a much more diffuse and makeshift fashion. It was also something of a tribute to the dynamism of that society that, by grass-roots initiative and hasty governmental improvisation, it could create in months rather than years citizen armies of hundreds of thousands where previously only a minuscule regular army of 16,000 had existed.

4. The common soldier in the Civil War remains a familiar, recognisable and essentially human figure down to our own day, in a way which is not true of those who fought in any earlier conflict. This may be ascribed in part to the magnificent photographic record left by Matthew Brady and others, in part to the continuing appeal of the songs he sang, and in part to his reincarnation on large screen and small in the twentieth century. It also owes something to the written record which so many Civil War soldiers left behind them in diaries, letters and memoirs. This was a war fought in a society with new standards in literacy, although those standards, it is true, were still fairly modest. A soldier from Alabama admitted that 'I do the love letter writing for about 20 men in our company. . . . I have engaged three young men of our Co. in the last month. I get to read all the girls' letters of course.' Another Confederate private, after complaining about his mother's illegible hand, boasted that 'I have lurnd to do my one wrading and writing, and it is a grate help to me'.[18]

The soldiers of Union and Confederacy, 'Billy Yank' and 'Johnny Reb', reflected their common American background as much as their distinctive sectional ones. Both armies drew heavily on the farming population for their recruits, the Southern even more than the Northern. In both, native white Americans were predominant, although perhaps a fifth of the Union soldiers were foreign-born, mainly German or Irish, and the Confederate army had much more than a sprinkling of foreign-born in its ranks. The North, too, made increasing use of Negro troops in the second half of the war, and the Confederates organised three brigades of Indians in the far west. Both Reb and Yank were strong individualists, who took unkindly to discipline, showed no undue respect for their officers, and generally cared little for the spit-and-polish favoured by European armies. Both led the kind of life which soldiers in other armies have known all too well: long periods of inactivity and boredom, punctuated by dreary, tiring marches, much pointless effort, and short, sharp bursts of danger and violent action. Both armies included a solid majority of men who took all that the war threw at them with a mixture of resilience and resignation; both, too, had their share of men who ran away in face of the enemy, or who deserted from the army, whether out of cowardice or boredom, despair or disillusion, concern for themselves or concern for the family at home. Both armies, too, had a tragically large minority of men who did not live to tell the tale of what they had done in the war, but fell victim to the bullets of the enemy, or, in much greater numbers, to the ravages of disease or the perilous ministrations of the doctors.

The conditions under which the Civil War soldier lived and fought showed in some respects a significant advance on the experience of earlier wars, but were in others still extremely primitive, uncomfortable and, on occasion, horrific. Some services which would now be taken for granted were in the 1860s provided only sketchily, and some not at all. There was almost nothing of the array of service, supply and administrative units which give twentieth-century armies such an enormous 'tail'. Men from combat units were detailed for many of these duties as and when required. The Civil War soldier looked after many of his own basic needs much more than his modern counterpart, and often it was the man who was not much good for anything else who was left to act as cook, or as a medical orderly, or to assist in procuring and distributing supplies. The individualism of Billy Yank and Johnny Reb was partly inborn, but also partly thrust upon him.

Training of new recruits was brief and grossly inadequate; little attention, for example, was normally devoted to weapons training or target practice. Discipline was often slack, but very unpredictable, and often governed by the whim of the officer concerned. Soldiers' recollections are full of references on the one hand to harsh punishments, and to the shooting of deserters before their assembled comrades (*pour encourager les autres*, no doubt) and on the other hand to examples of the grossest insubordination, including violent reprisals against unpopular officers.[19] Flogging was officially abolished in the United States army in 1861, but other brutal and barbaric punishments remained; for example, the suspension of a man by his thumbs, with his feet barely touching the ground, or the branding of offenders – C for coward, D for deserter, and so on. The private soldier's pay was modest to say the least: $11 per month on both sides at the outset, rising to $16 on the Union side and $18 on the Confederate. But the later figures in particular came nowhere near to keeping pace with galloping inflation, and Southern soldiers must have wryly compared their initial $11 with the $30 per month which was the going rate in Virginia for hiring the services of a slave.[20] Worse than low pay was no pay, and grievances over long arrears had not a little to do with declining morale and rising desertions, especially on the Southern side. The Union soldier was better provided, too, with disablement benefits and schemes for allotment of a portion of his pay to dependants at home.

The Union soldier was better fed, better clad and better shod than the Confederate. Indeed, he was in most situations so amply supplied that he easily became wasteful and extravagant; General McDowell believed that 'a French army of half the size of ours could be supplied with what we waste', and he added perceptively that 'it is a waste that comes out of the country at large'.[21] The only criticism which some British observers could make of the standard army ration was that there was too much of it. The diet of soldiers on both sides was based upon bread and meat – the latter usually salt or pickled beef or pork, the former hard bread or 'hardtack' (flour and water biscuits) for the Union soldier, and cornbread for the Confederate. Hardtack could be 'as solid as an oak board', said one soldier, and the stamp B.C. (for Boston cracker) which it bore was interpreted as authentic proof of its old age.[22] The Southerner's cornbread could be equally rock-like and unappetising. 'It looks like a pile of cow dung baked in the sun,' said one reluctant eater. 'I could nock [*sic*] down a cow with a pone of it.'[23] The Northern soldier was better fed in every way. He received much more food much more regularly; Southerners often went hungry, more often through bad distribution of supplies than actual shortage. The Northerner ate more vegetables, sometimes fresh, and sometimes desiccated or canned; he could supplement his rations by purchases from the sutlers, private traders who haunted the larger camps, and – though this applied to the Southerner too – by foraging in the surrounding country. In camp the men normally cooked and ate their food in small groups of half a dozen or so, known as 'messes', and the short-comings of the cooking often compounded any inadequacies of the basic diet.

Civil war uniforms were often roughly made and ill-fitting, and shoes not always shaped to distinguish between right and left foot, but armies have seldom paid much heed to such niceties. After the first few hectic months, the Union soldier could usually draw on an ample stock of uniforms and footwear, while, as the war progressed, the Confederate soldier was often reduced to rags and tatters, and the shortage of boots and shoes was so desperate as to become a major factor in the success or failure of military operations. When Lee invaded Maryland in September 1862 his army was drastically thinned out by men who could no longer march on hard roads in worn-out shoes, or no shoes at all. In July 1863 the first contact between the armies at Gettysburg came about when a Confederate force set out to capture a consignment of shoes in the town. Although 'the blue and the gray' has become an easy way of labelling the rival armies, it was some time before the colour problem in uniforms sorted itself out. In early engagements, including Bull Run, this caused some confusion, and, even in later years, Johnny Reb was not averse to donning a captured blue uniform. Indeed, the Confederate grey had a struggle to survive at all, for, when stocks of grey dye ran out, a home-produced dye made from walnut shells was used, and this gave uniforms a yellowish-brown or 'butternut' shade.

A shortage of blankets and tents, like the shortage of clothing and footwear, often left the Southern soldier at the mercy of the elements. For most of the year he usually lived and slept in the open, unless he could capture or improvise some shelter for himself, but during the winter the troops built themselves log huts and contrived a certain amount of comparative comfort for themselves. Their Northern counterparts adopted the same kind of winter quarters, but for the rest of the year used a variety of tents, most commonly the simple shelter tent, of which each soldier could carry a half, when the army was on the move. Camp conditions were usually dusty in summer, muddy at other times, and dirty and insanitary all the year round. Even in long periods of inactivity, washing was never a popular way of relieving the tedium. Lice distributed their favours impartially to both armies, and troops even amused themselves with louse races, using plates as racetracks.[24]

Inevitably, disease flourished in both the blue and grey armies; diarrhoea and dysentery were the most prevalent, but typhoid and malaria, fevers of all kinds, and children's diseases like measles, diphtheria and scarlet fever ran through the camps like wildfire, claiming thousands of victims. Epidemics could put whole regiments out of action more effectively than enemy action, and, in both armies, total deaths from disease during the war were at least twice as great as from wounds sustained in battle. In 1861 army medical care was primitive and ill-organised, and the medical profession as a whole had not come to terms with such new-fangled notions as antisepsis and anaesthesia. Desperate improvisation was characteristic of medical services in both North and South; for the latter, things were made far worse by a shortage of doctors and a much more serious shortage of medicines and anaesthetics – whisky often had to take the place of both. The Confederate Medical Corps, under Surgeon-General Samuel Preston Moore, struggled bravely with an impossible task, but conditions in makeshift military hospitals were often appalling, and many a man who had survived the field of battle succumbed to unskilled and inadequate treatment in verminous and germ-ridden hospitals. With more money, better resources, and more powerfully organised outside help, the Union army coped somewhat better with similar problems, especially once the elderly and ineffective C. A. Finley had been replaced as surgeon-general by William Hammond. Jonathan Letterman devised for the Army of the Potomac a system of first-aid stations, field hospitals and base hospitals which provided a workable model for general adoption. From June 1861 women nurses for military hospitals were organised under the eagle eye of Dorothea L. Dix. The most effective and influential non-governmental agency in this field was the United States Sanitary Commission, formed in 1861, which raised large funds for medical supplies, mobilised the efforts of thousands of middle-class women in the North, and both provided services of its own and constantly badgered the War Department into organising better medical care for the troops. It conducted a running feud with Secretary of War Stanton, who resented both the Commission's self-righteous tone and its apparent bid to take over the Medical Bureau, but many a soldier had cause to be grateful for its efforts.

For all the gradual improvements in supplies and organisation, there is no doubt that, whether in coping with disease or wounds, the medical services represent one of the Civil War's most dismal failures. The accounts of soldier life left by many of the participants tell a horrifying tale of the ghastly wounds inflicted by the rifled musket and other weapons, of chronic sickness, filth and dirt, of clumsy, ill-trained doctors, often spurning the use of chloroform and ignorant of the most elementary knowledge of hygiene, of the piles of arms and legs hacked off to counter the dreaded gangrene, of the vermin, the maggots, the sickening stench and the heart-rending sights and sounds of the military hospitals. If the Civil War had its romance and its glory, as it surely did, this was the other side of the story. If the Civil War soldier was a hero, as often he surely was, he was not the dashing hero of romantic legend, but the ragged, unkempt, undisciplined, resilient, battered, humorous, long-suffering, prosaic hero, not merely of a hundred battles, but of a thousand discomforts.

5. Victory or defeat depended not merely on numbers and quality of men, but also on logistics and leadership. The common soldier himself was at the mercy of the supply arrangements which supported him, and the officers of all ranks who commanded him. The Civil War was a long stride in the direction of the mass-production wars of this century but it did not go all the way, and the Confederacy showed what could be done by makeshift methods and ingenuity in the face of basic deficiencies. The war was a test not merely of productive capacity, but of organisational skill, and aptitude for improvisation. It was a struggle on the one side to turn potential strength into actual performance, and on the other to make the most out of very little. In this unexciting but crucial business of supply each side had to build on a slender administrative base, and each had to strike a balance between central direction and state and local effort. Each, too, had its heroes and villains, for bureaucracies, military or civilian, were still small enough to bear the stamp of the individuals at their head. Montgomery Meigs, the Union Quartermaster-General, might well claim a place among the major architects of Northern victory, while Josiah Gorgas, Confederate Chief of Ordnance, proved himself a master of the art of making bricks without straw. (It may not be without significance that Gorgas was a Northerner who threw in his lot with the Confederacy; many Southerners, hot in the pursuit of glory, looked down their noses at such mundane matters as the organisation of supplies.) On the other hand, Gorgas's Union opposite number, James W. Ripley, earned himself the name of Ripley Van Winkle by his inertia and resistance to innovation, while the Confederate Commissary-General, Lucius B. Northrop, proved tactless, inflexible and incompetent in the difficult task of feeding the army, and his retention in office was widely ascribed to presidential favouritism.

Supply problems were inevitable in this as in any war, but they were aggravated by the lack of any pre-war plans for mobilisation, and by divisions of responsibility both within the respective War Departments and between them and the state authorities. The Confederate Department copied the structure of the Department in Washington with its separate bureaux, responsible for weapons, food and other supplies and equipment, under the Chief of Ordnance, the Commissary-General and the Quartermaster-General respectively. During the first rush to arms in 1861 it was the states which took the initiative not only in raising men but in arming and equipping them. As time went on, the War Department in Washington exercised greater coordination and supervision and ultimately gained effective control over the purchase and distribution of supplies. In the Confederacy, the state authorities battled unceasingly with Richmond over weapons and equipment as they had over manpower. In the first days of the war, for example, Virginia challenged the Confederate government for the right to make use of the machinery captured at the United States armoury at Harper's Ferry. Throughout the war, state governors adhered to their claim to supply their own state troops in Confederate service. By doing so, they disrupted the organisation of armies, unnecessarily raised prices by competitive bidding against the Richmond authorities, and created intolerable inequalities between troops of one state and another. In the closing stages of the war, for example, when most of Lee's army was in rags, the state of North Carolina had 92,000 uniforms in stock.

When the war came there was a stock of well over 600,000 small arms in the whole country, with perhaps two-fifths of them in the South. But such a large figure is grossly misleading; a majority of them were quite unserviceable, and all but about 35,000 were old smoothbore muskets. To provide weapons for hundreds of thousands of recruits, both governments had recourse to both foreign purchase and rapidly expanded home production, supplemented on the Southern side by arms captured from the enemy. In the first eighteen months of the war the Union relied heavily on European purchases, especially of the Enfield rifle. Fierce competition not merely with Confederate purchasing agents but with agents of energetic state governors, from North as well as South, made it a confused, costly and hectic business. However, despite opportunities missed in the early days through over-caution (not to mention Secretary Cameron's protectionist prejudice in favour of the home producer), 726,000 small arms had been purchased in Europe by November 1862. This huge total included a good deal of rubbish, but also much that was vitally important at a time when home output had not yet reached 200,000. However, by 1863 the federal government had a firm grip on the situation, and American production – from both the national armoury and private firms such as Colt's – was enough to meet all needs. The Springfield armoury alone was now producing the rifles that bore its name at the rate of more than 200,000 a year – a ten-fold increase on pre-war output – and production of ammunition and powder was comfortably keeping pace with demand. Output of heavier guns showed a similar impressive growth, and Northern foundries altogether cast 7,892 cannon of various kinds during the war. By 1863 the main complaint against Ripley and the Ordnance Bureau concerned not the quantity of arms available but caution and conservatism over new weapons, and, in particular, the breech-loading rifle. Some authorities argue that the adoption of, say, the Sharps carbine and the Spencer repeating rifle as standard weapons for cavalry and infantry respectively in 1863 might even have ended the war in that year. But such single-factor hypotheses are generally suspect; there had been teething-troubles with the new weapons and nagging doubts about their dependability in battle conditions; it took some time to assess the relative merits of the many models offered; and, having just adapted to the rifled musket, which, though a muzzle-loader, was still quite a novel weapon, and distributed it to a huge, new army, only a very bold man would have abandoned it so soon in favour of something even newer.

For the Confederacy, the story of the supply of weapons was a cliff-hanger from first to last. In 1861 the arms scraped together were insufficient to cope with the flow of would-be recruits, and the South's own output of small arms could be measured in hundreds rather than thousands. Priority was given to European purchases, but the valiant efforts of Caleb Huse, the Confederate agent in Europe, were handicapped by insufficient funds, the competition of enemies and of 'friends' from the state governments, and the difficulty of shipping across the Atlantic such purchases as were made. Only 50,000 arms had reached the South from Europe by August 1862, and the quality of these was very uncertain. Smooth-talking French salesmen did their best to convince purchasers that the old smoothbore, flintlock musket was still much the best of the small arms.[25] But things subsequently improved and, before the war ended, the Ordnance Bureau had brought 330,000 arms through the blockade, some of them in vessels which Gorgas had bought for the Bureau itself, and the individual states had imported about a quarter of a million more. During 1862, however, a small arms famine in the South was only averted by the capture of at least 100,000 weapons from the North, mostly Springfields, and it was fortunate for the South that ammunition for captured Springfields and imported Enfields was interchangeable, although the one was of ·57 calibre and the other ·58. Imported and captured weapons were indispensable, but the greatest achievements of Gorgas were in improvising a great expansion in home production, despite apparently insoluble difficulties over materials, machinery and labour. Armouries at Richmond, Fayetteville, Macon and elsewhere were, from 1863 onwards, producing small arms in tens of thousands, and the Tredegar Ironworks at Richmond, along with others like the ordnance centre at Selma, provided the lion's share of the heavier guns for the artillery. But production of weapons was futile unless supplies of ammunition, powder and percussion caps could keep pace. Here Gorgas excelled in the creation of new enterprises or the expansion of older ones: the splendid power mill at Augusta, directed by G. W. Rains, and one of the great success stories of the Confederacy; the production of chemicals for munitions at Macon; the efforts of the Nitre Bureau to provide saltpetre for gunpowder – including the laying down of nitre beds (which provoked a good deal of ribald comment in prose and verse when local ladies were asked to con-serve the contents of their chamber-pots for use on those beds); the desperate eking-out of supplies of sulphur, mercury, copper and lead. It all adds up to a remarkable story, and a success story too, to the extent that from all sources a total of 600,000 small arms were supplied to the Confederate army during the war, the supply of ammunition never dried up, and the soldiers in the field never went seriously short of powder.

The provision of supplies other than weapons to the two armies became very large-scale business indeed. The supply of food, clothing, tents and blankets has already been briefly discussed from the point of view of the common soldier. For the Commissary- and Quartermaster-Generals on both sides it presented an unprecedented challenge to inventiveness and it carried them into activities undreamed of before 1861. Southern quartermaster officers found themselves running textile mills in North Carolina and the Commissary-General took over the direction of various food-processing plants. Both armies went into the business of railroad management and railroad construction,[26] and both controlled the operation of vast fleets of horse-drawn transport. Perhaps the best way to convey something of the scale and scope of the business of supplying a Civil War army is to take the biggest and best of all examples – the operation of the Quartermaster's Bureau of the Union army under Montgomery Meigs.[27]

In the spring of 1861 the Quartermaster-General's office in the War Department had a staff of thirteen clerks, and normally thought in terms of an annual budget of four or five million dollars. No plans existed for the supply of a very much larger army, nor even any assessment of what such a force would need. In the early chaotic months of the war the state governments took a large but wasteful and confusing part in equipping the new regiments; the War Department was quite unable to cope with the new situation; urgent demands overrode normal safeguards in awarding contracts; corruption, extravagance and incompetence were widespread, and the army acquired much worthless or inferior equipment at inflated prices. However, from late 1861 onwards Meigs and his Bureau steadily tightened their grip, and expanded their activities; scarcity gave way to sufficiency or even surplus, irregularity and confusion to order and control. Meigs's three greatest achievements were in organisation and coordination, accountability and scrutiny of contracts, and, above all, in delivering the goods. The longer the war went on, the more the business of supplying the army came under supervision and then control from Washington. Meigs reorganised his own bureau in nine divisions, the varied functions of which give the clearest indication of the range of his activities: the provision of animals for the army; clothing and equipage; ocean and lake transportation; rail and river transport; forage and fuel; construction of barracks and hospitals; wagon transport; inspection; and finance. By the end of the war his Bureau had nearly six hundred civilian employees – about six times the number in the whole War Department six years earlier. Meigs insisted on careful auditing of the accounts of all the quartermasters, and established new rules governing contracts, and a new system of inspection. He could not stamp out all abuses and all corruption in the business of army contracts, but the racketeers' field day of 1861 was never repeated. Meanwhile, his Bureau was running a many-sided business, which, in the fiscal year 1863–4 for example, involved the expenditure of almost $285 million. It maintained huge depots crammed with supplies, it operated a large fleet of transport vessels on sea, lake and river, and it engaged in construction work on a large scale. Two specific examples of its activities must suffice. Partly by purchase from outside suppliers but mainly through its own manufacturing, the Quartermaster's Bureau kept the great multitudes of the Union army amply supplied with uniforms and other clothing, certainly from 1862 onwards. Meigs was always proud of the fact that, when Sherman's army of 70,000 men reached Savannah after the march through Georgia to the sea in 1864, it found a complete new clothing outfit ready and waiting for it there. The second illustration concerns transport and the distribution of supplies. The Bureau was responsible for providing the army with horses and mules and with wagons and other vehicles. Armies so lavishly equipped by any previous standards depended on a massive number of horse-drawn vehicles to carry supplies at least from the nearest railhead, if no further. Napoleon reckoned on twelve wagons per thousand men; McClellan had twenty-six per thousand in 1862, Grant's army thirty-three per thousand in 1864, this last figure representing a total of 4,300 wagons. By this time the army had half as many animals as men, and the supply of forage for them was itself a major transport problem which often threatened to become a vicious circle. The wastage rate among horses was terrifyingly high and their average working life a matter of a few months. There were many early complaints about the quantity and quality of horses, but, after the first year, the Union armies were generally well provided in this as in other respects. By the latter part of the war Meigs found himself running the most elaborate transport system which the United States had yet seen, and this was only one branch of his activities.

Clearly, in the struggle to supply the armies in the field, the North had almost every advantage. It was the problem of the Confederacy that, however skilful the improvisation, there was just never quite enough of everything to go round. In practice, inevitable shortages were often made worse by breakdowns in organisation or wrangles between rival authorities, although the efforts of Gorgas and others were enough to show that this was a war which might not be decided by simple statistical comparisons of basic resources. It was the problem of the Union to turn its superior resources to advantage and make them count where it mattered most. In practice, the sheer size of the undertaking complicated the problems and delayed their solution, but the work of Meigs and others showed what could be achieved. From the outset the North had the greater strength; in the end it also showed greater skill in its application.

6. In the organisation of the Civil War armies, the basic unit was the regiment, commanded by a colonel, and with an authorised strength of about a thousand men, divided into ten companies, each officered by a captain and two lieutenants.

Regiments were themselves organised into larger units – in ascending order, brigades, divisions, corps and armies, each commanded by a brigadier or major-general, or (in the Confederate army) a lieutenant-general. The Union government granted this last rank only to General Grant, who thus became the first man to hold it since George Washington himself. Union armies were normally named after rivers in the area of their command – for example, the Army of the Potomac, the Army of the Tennessee, the Army of the Mississippi. Confederate armies, appropriately enough, more often took the name of a state or part of a state: the Army of Northern Virginia, the Army of Tennessee, the Army of Mississippi and so on, although conventions in this matter were not strictly observed. While the organisation and disposition of units varied greatly from army to army, time to time and place to place, a fairly typical arrangement would have been, for the Union army at least, five regiments to a brigade, three brigades to a division, three divisions to a corps, two, three, four or more corps to an army. As the war continued, and the North in particular failed to maintain the strength of existing regiments in the face of mounting losses, the number of units in an army became a very unreliable guide to actual strength. At the battle of Chancellorsville at the half-way stage in the war, divisions in the Union army averaged 6,200 men, less than half their full paper strength. The average size of Confederate divisions in the same battle, at 8,700, indicated rather greater success in replenishing old regiments.

There was no remotely adequate pool of talent and experience available in 1861 to officer the thousands of companies, hundreds of regiments and scores of higher formations which were being rapidly created. In the North, for example, the army was left with 440 West Point graduates after the Southern defections, and a rather larger number of ex-officers who returned to the regular army or joined the volunteer army after war began. Many of these officers sooner or later found places in the higher ranks of the army, and the very highest positions on both sides were virtually monopolised by West Pointers. On the other hand, almost all the multitude of vacancies for junior officers, and many of the middle-ranking ones too, were inevitably filled by amateurs. In the absence of military qualifications, social standing, political influence and personal popularity and self-confidence were the best passports to a commission in the volunteer army. All officers up to the rank of colonel received their commissions from the state authorities and the colonel of a regiment was initially appointed by the state governor, as an act of political patronage. Partly out of faith in grass-roots democracy, partly for lack of any available alternative, captains and lieutenants were elected by the rank and file of their own company. Election of officers was pernicious nonsense from an orthodox military standpoint, but probably a necessary evil in a situation, a society and a conflict of this kind. It also meant that the permeation of army life by political influence and political considerations extended from top to bottom; even an election for corporal in one Confederate company turned into a lively debate between the two candidates over Unionism and states rights, although the winner was the candidate who had taken the precaution of providing two jugs of whisky 'to treat the boys' – another time-honoured electoral practice.[28]

Any attempt to knock the new volunteer forces into reasonable fighting shape was bound to depend heavily on the calibre of the junior and middle-ranking officers, and, in the first year of war at least, their quality was often scandalously low. As early as July 1861 the Union army set up examining boards to check on the quality and performance of officers, and the Confederates later followed suit. The mere threat of such scrutiny inspired a spate of resignations, and, as the months passed, incompetents, cowards, drunkards and the like were weeded out, and a steady improvement in standards was achieved, with the help of pressure from above, and from the rank and file below.

Appointments to higher command were normally made by the Washington and Richmond governments, and here too political as well as military qualifications came under consideration. The 'political generals' as a group have been widely condemned, and it would certainly be hard to make out a case for the military genius of men like Nathaniel P. Banks, ex-speaker of the House of Representatives, who was humiliated by Stonewall Jackson in the Shenandoah Valley campaign, or the egregious John A. McClernand, who was an embarrassment to Grant at every turn of the Vicksburg campaign, or, on the other side, Gideon J. Pillow and John B. Floyd, who had an inglorious share in the loss of Fort Donelson in 1862. But the active support of a Banks or a Ben Butler was important to the overall war effort, and so too was the stand of a man like Franz Sigel, which consolidated the loyalty of German-Americans to the Union cause. Even McClernand, for all his later follies, had earned the gratitude of the Lincoln administration by his contribution as a prominent Illinois Democrat in 1861 in rallying the north-west to the Union cause. The most suitable reward for such services was not always a high military command, but the dangers of such appointments have to be weighed against the available alternatives, and a number of the political generals did perform creditably during the war. Many politicians, indeed, and not only politicians, were profoundly jealous of the élitist professionals produced by the United States Military Academy at West Point, and suspicious of their pretensions, their capabilities and even of their loyalties. The West Pointers, for their part, were inclined to look down their noses at the volunteers, and often displayed an air of superiority which was not always justified. It was one of the great ironies of the war, too, that while both armies had their internal feuds between West Pointers and non-professionals, the commanders on opposite sides in the great encounters had often known each other well at the Academy and served alongside each other subsequently. If not often a brothers' war, it was very much a war of brother officers. They knew each others' strengths and weaknesses and they had been brought up on the same precepts from the same training manuals, and a commander like Robert E. Lee (who had been Superintendent of West Point for three years in the 1850s) could frequently exploit his intimate knowledge of his opponents. On the other hand, to be the star product of the military establishment implied limitations as well as outstanding merit, and ultimately the war's most successful commander, Ulysses S. Grant, was one who, having never greatly prospered under the old system, found it much easier to break free from its shackles, and learn the lessons of a new kind of war.

It would be quite wrong to deduce from the distinction between political generals and West Pointers that the latter were apolitical. Despite their constant protests at political interference with military organisation and strategy, nothing could be further from the truth. The political attitudes and affiliations of professional officers were common knowledge, and this was even more true of the many West Pointers who had left the army for the richer prizes of business and industry, but who returned to it in 1861. Everyone knew that McClellan was a Democrat whose view of the nature and purpose of the war differed widely from the views of radical Republicans, and therefore of generals like Hooker or Pope who had well-known connections with the radicals. The Congressional Committee on the Conduct of the War sometimes gave its proceedings the air of a witch-hunt, and some of its members had deep prejudices against West Point, and basic doubts about entrusting important commands to Democratic officers who did not share their conception of the war or their anti-slavery convictions. But they were surely not altogether wrong to concern themselves with the political credentials and attitudes of men entrusted with the prosecution of the war. This was, after all, a civil war over very basic issues concerning the Union, slavery, and the relationship between the two. The only really surprising thing about the intermingling of political and military matters during such a war is that so many people have found it remarkable. It was not merely inevitable, it was right and proper – which is not to say that such matters were always conducted in a right and proper way. It is worth remembering that the South too had its politico-military disputes, although, in view of the structure of the Confederacy, these were conducted on personal or sectional, rather than party lines. Generals had their Congressional supporters and lobbyists in Richmond, and there was talk of running Beauregard against Davis in the presidential election in the fall of 1861. Later in the war, officers in the western army were to touch off a debate on the most sensitive of all issues, the possible recruitment of Negro troops.

It was of course at the very highest level of grand strategy that relations between political and military leaders mattered most of all. Here both sides were hampered by the lack of any adequate institutional framework, and the inadequacy of staff work. Indeed, at all levels, weaknesses in military planning and intelligence plagued both sides during the war. Better organisation and the emergence of some very capable staff officers improved the situation in the North in the second half of the war, but not significantly in the Confederate army, where Lee's staff still consisted of only a handful of relatively junior officers, and the general himself wasted many hours on relatively minor matters. At the very top there was no clear or adequate command system at the beginning of the war; the relationship between president, secretary for war, general-in-chief (if any) and commanders of the major armies was vague and ill-defined.

Much depended on how literally the president took the constitutional provision that he was 'Commander in Chief of the Army and Navy'. In the Confederacy, no real command system ever emerged, or rather, from first to last, it consisted largely of Jefferson Davis himself. Successive Secretaries of War were not all mere clerks, but even the best of them, Randolph and Seddon, had to confine themselves within strict limits, or resign. Although Lee in 1862 and Bragg in 1864 were called to Richmond to act as military advisers to the president, there was no real general-in-chief of the Confederate army until the last two months of the war when Congress at last persuaded Davis to appoint Lee to the post. In the North, Lincoln had no intention of abdicating the role of commander-in-chief, and with an earnestness that is half laudable, half laughable, he bent himself to the study of standard works on military strategy. But he had no intention of monopolising the job either. From 1862 onwards he established a fruitful working relationship with Secretary of War Stanton, but it was not until 1864 that a recognisable high command structure emerged. The post of general-in-chief was held in 1861 by the aged Winfield Scott, and then by George McClellan, who was at the same time commander of the Army of the Potomac. This dual responsibility proved unsatisfactory, and from April to July 1862 Lincoln did without a general-in-chief, and he and Stanton did their not very successful best to fill the breach. Then General Henry Halleck was assigned to the post, but his consistent refusal to take responsibility for major decisions reduced him to the role of military adviser-cum-clerk to the president. Finally, in February 1864, Lincoln found the man and the system he needed. Grant became general-in-chief with responsibility for shaping strategy and directing the movements of the armies, and Lincoln gave him wide discretion, without ever relaxing his own overall supervision. Halleck became 'chief of staff', not in the modern sense of the term, but rather to act as a link between Grant and Lincoln and Grant and the army commanders; he also became a skilled interpreter of military language for the politicians and vice versa.

This was still a fairly crude system but it worked, mainly because the right men were in the right jobs. Indeed, it is true of high command throughout the war that because staffs were so small, and the administrative framework so defective, it was personalities and personal relationships which mattered above all. Lincoln and McClellan could not get on with each other, whereas Lincoln and Grant could. Lee's superiority to Beauregard or Joseph E. Johnston lay primarily in military skill, but also in the ability to humour the prickly personality of Jefferson Davis. The correspondence between Lincoln and his generals always impresses the reader by its intensely personal tone. If one single example can illustrate this point, what better than Lincoln's famous letter to 'Fighting Joe' Hooker on appointing him to succeed Burnside as commander of the Army of the Potomac in January 1863:

I have placed you at the head of the Army of the Potomac. Of course I have done this upon what appear to me to be sufficient reasons. And yet I think it best for you to know that there are some things in regard to which, I am not quite satisfied with you. I believe you to be a brave and skilful soldier, which, of course, I like. I also believe you do not mix politics with your profession, in which you are right. You have confidence in yourself, which is a valuable, if not an indispensable quality. You are ambitious, which, within reasonable bounds, does good rather than harm. But I think that during Gen. Burnside's command of the Army, you have taken counsel of your ambition, and thwarted him as much as you could, in which you did a great wrong to the country, and to a most meritorious and honorable brother officer. I have heard, in such a way as to believe it, of your recently saying that both the Army and the Government needed a Dictator. Of course it was not *for* this, but in spite of it, that I have given you the command. Only those generals who gain successes, can set up dictators. What I now ask of you is military success, and I will risk the dictatorship.[29]

If indeed politico-military relations were so crucially a matter of personal relations, it is not insignificant that Lincoln could write such letters while Davis never did or could. As for the generals, it is surely significant, and ironical, that the ones who best appreciated political considerations, and had the smoothest relations with their political masters, were those like Grant and Lee who had no great political commitments to defend, or political axes to grind.

All in all, few generalisations about the quality of military leadership in the Civil War can be regarded as safe. The Southern generals, almost without notable exception, came from the planter class, and the Confederate army at all levels clearly mirrored the stratification of Southern society. Many of the generals on both sides were surprisingly young. McClellan was only thirty-four when he assumed command of the Army of the Potomac, Stonewall Jackson only thirty-nine when he died in 1863. The great Confederate cavalry leader Jeb Stuart became a Brigadier-General in 1861 at twenty-eight (and died at thirty-one), and the legendary George A. Custer attained the rank of Brigadier-General in the Union calvalry at the age of twenty-three. Men like Grant and Sherman in their forties and Lee and Johnston in their mid-fifties seem quite venerable by comparison. A remarkable number of generals, especially in the Confederate army, were killed or wounded in action, a fact which suggests at least that there was little inclination to lead from behind. Arguments about the merits of individual generals and the comparative quality of Northern and Southern generalship rage on interminably. The common assertion of Confederate superiority in this field at least in the first half of the war has some force behind it, but Confederate superiority really means two men: Robert E. Lee and Stonewall Jackson. Later in the war the North had the greater strength in depth headed by Grant, Sherman, Sheridan and Thomas, all able practitioners of new ways of waging war. Clearly a conflict which could produce not merely a Grant and a Lee, but a Sherman and a Jackson, was not lacking in great commanders by any standards. At the other end of the scale it also threw up more than its share of incompetents, or worse, on both sides. Most revealingly, it also found wanting many capable men who failed to fulfil their promise, or to measure up to the demands of this kind of war: McClellan, Rosecrans, Buell, Hooker, Beauregard, Joseph E. Johnston and Pemberton were some of the prominent names among them. The successful generals were mostly those who proved flexible and adaptable, on the one hand responsive to the political climate of a civil war and on the other capable of learning new methods and discarding old ones.

7. Whether the professional soldiers liked it or not, this was not to be the kind of war they had been brought up to understand. Huge citizen-armies, armed with new weapons, trailing an enormous supply system in their wake, and connected by the iron rail to the centres of industrial power, demanded a new kind of military thinking. But West Point training, insofar as it covered military strategy at all, was based, predictably, on the past and especially on Napoleonic models. Its guiding light was Henri Jomini, the outstanding military theorist of the Napoleonic age, whose *Précis de l'art de guerre* was the sacred text on the subject. When the future General Halleck published his *Elements of Military Art and Science* in 1846, it was, as he admitted, little more than a straight translation of Jomini. Unfortunately, Jominian theories, for all their elegance and precision, were often irrelevant and misleading in the context of the Civil War. In a few decades, changes in weapons and in societies which produced them had over-taken his basic principles. In both strategy and tactics Jomini urged the impor-tance of concentration at the decisive point, stressed the advantages of the offensive and belittled the need for fortifications. His strategy gave high priority to the occupation of enemy territory and the capture of the enemy capital, and his tactics on the battlefield were as elaborate and as precise as moves on a chessboard. All this thinking was based on the premise that war was a matter for the professional soldiers, in which politics, ideology or public opinion really had no place.

With every passing month, the gap between Jominian theories and Civil War realities grew wider.[30] If the war taught one tactical lesson (though the learning of it cost the lives of scores of thousands) it was the advantage of the defensive side of the field of battle. The rifled musket was the crucial factor; its killing range of several hundred yards, its slightly improved rate of fire, and its greater reliability than the old musket meant that the defending side had many more shots at opponents advancing over open ground than had been possible before. Persistence in old infantry tactics of advancing in close formation led to the piles of Union dead at Fredericksburg and of Confederate dead on Cemetery Ridge at Gettysburg. As late as June 1864 Grant lost 7,000 men in a few minutes in a frontal assault at Coldharbor. Defenders multiplied their new advantages by overcoming traditional contempt for trenches and earthworks and digging in to such an extent that the spade became one of the infantryman's best friends. Against such defensive positions, and against the range of the rifled musket, the artillery lost much of its destructive power, and it too became most effective in defence, smashing up infantry advances by showering them with lead or cast-iron balls fired from canister. Even the cavalry, the epitome of the attacking spirit in days of yore, was now reduced to auxiliary though still important roles – reconnaissance, attacking communications and guarding the army's flanks – and when actually engaged in battle they often dismounted and fought as infantry, a far cry indeed from the old days of the bold, sabre-slashing cavalry charge. All these developments made the odds in favour of the defensive side so great that, according to Liddell Hart's estimate, whereas 20,000 men per mile was normal in a defensive position in the days of Napoleon and Wellington, 12,000 came to be regarded as ample quite early in the Civil War, and in the later stages Lee held on successfully with under 5,000.[31] Clearly, new tactics, more flexible and more open, were needed if the attacker was to have any real chance of success, but these were not easy to devise, especially as more open formations made it difficult for officers to maintain contact with their men, and in fact it took another revolution in weapons in the twentieth century to alter the balance once again.

It was still possible to think strategically in attacking terms, but it was important to get priorities right. There were those, including President Lincoln, whose thinking was not conditioned by a West Point education, who insisted that the Jominian emphasis on capturing enemy territory and the enemy capital, as ends in themselves, was quite mistaken, and that the main objective must be the destruction of the enemy army. This emphasis was surely correct, but its implementation was far from easy, in view of the difficulty of forcing a clear-cut decision on the field of battle. The combination of strategic offensive and tactical defensive was a prescription easier to define than to achieve. The answer, in the Lincolnian view, was to abandon another of Jomini's principles – concentration at key points – and exploit the greater numbers and resources of the North by applying pressure all along the line. The president outlined this policy clearly, as early as January 1862, in a letter to General Buell:

> I state my general idea of this war to be that we have the *greater* numbers, and the enemy has the *greater* facility of concentrating forces upon points of collision; that we must fail, unless we can find some way of making *our* advantage an over-match for *his*; and that this can only be done by menacing him with superior forces at *different* points, at the *same* time; so that we can safely attack, one, or both, if he makes no change; and if he *weakens* one to *strengthen* the other, forbear to attack the strengthened one, but seize, and hold the weakened one, gaining so much.[32]

This was in fact very like the final recipe for victory prescribed by Grant in 1864–5, and sanctioned by Lincoln in the homely phrase: 'those not skinning can hold a leg'.[33] A policy of all-out, sustained pressure upon a weaker enemy logically required that war must also be carried to the civilian population, and that their will to resist must be crushed by military strength, economic hardship and political propaganda. This, again, was a far cry from war as the exclusive concern of the professionals, but Grant and Sherman accepted the ruthless logic of the argument. 'We are not only fighting hostile armies,' said Sherman, 'but a hostile people, and must make old and young, rich and poor, feel the hard hand of war, as well as the organized armies.'[34]

For its part, the Confederacy succumbed to the temptation – some would say the necessity – of a defensive strategy which seemed to suit both its ultimate objective and its limited resources. Some opinion in the South favoured a quick dash for victory and looked for a decisive success won by an invasion of the North. This was Beauregard's plan in 1861, and, in more modest form, it was Lee's in his invasions of the North in 1862 and 1863. But Davis would concede nothing more than a strategy which has been called 'offensive-defensive', that is, a policy of defence and careful husbanding of resources, punctuated by aggressive countermoves when the opportunity arose. Such a policy was largely dictated by the obvious weaknesses of the Confederacy. 'The South,' says one of its modern historians, 'would have to compromise between the hopes of strategy and the limits of logistics.'[35] A stout defence might win victory in the end, simply by avoiding defeat.

There was a great paradox implicit in the kind of war which the Civil War became. Both sides were fighting for all-or-nothing ends: one to build a new Confederacy, the other to destroy it, one to save the Union, the other to wreck it. Yet, at this very time, warfare was becoming more complex and less immediately decisive. In particular, the pitched battle was becoming inconclusive; the defensive advantage was too great, the victorious side was usually too exhausted to follow up its success, logistical expertise was not yet sufficient to replenish an army on the morrow of a major battle. Gettysburg and Vicksburg are commonly regarded as the 'decisive' engagements of the Civil War; they both took place in July 1863, but the war did not end until April 1865. What happened on the field of battle had become more than ever the tip of the military iceberg. The great submerged mass was a matter of equipment, supply, transport and communications, of industrial power, and technical skill, and also of public opinion, civilian morale, and sheer will to resist. War had become a matter of management and organisation more than individual heroism or feats of derring-do. A policy of attrition by the stronger side ultimately wore down and wore out the weaker. This was now the way of reaching a military decision, less spectacular and dramatic than the old, but ultimately more relentless and inescapable. It was all summed up in a few words written in 1863 by one of the organisation men of the new warfare, Quartermaster-General Meigs: 'It is exhaustion of men and money that finally terminates all modern wars.'[36]

# Chapter VII: Campaigns of 1862

When General Halleck turned his thoughts to planning military operations in the west during the winter of 1861–2, he had to rely on maps bought from the local bookstore.[1] When General McClellan moved the Army of the Potomac to the James Peninsula in the spring of 1862, he was not a little taken aback to find that neither rivers nor roads always followed the lines laid down on his maps. These examples demonstrate how even experienced regular officers were ill prepared for the contingency of making war in the heartland of the United States itself. This was no small handicap, and generals on both sides needed some hasty geography lessons, for the configuration of the land set the pattern of all the major campaigns of the Civil War. Sheer distance was itself a major factor which aggravated the problems of manipulating unprecedentedly large armies. It remained to be seen whether the leaders in Washington and Richmond could manage and coordinate military operations which stretched from the familiar waters of Chesapeake Bay across two thousand miles to the empty expanse of New Mexico. The Southern problem of defending a huge territory over a wide front, with inferior numbers, was matched by the Northern problem of turning tentative invasion of the South into deep penetration, and temporary capture into permanent conquest.

The two main theatres of war were east and west of the great Appalachian spine which divides the Atlantic seaboard from the American interior. The two faces which the war presented could scarcely have differed more. The eastern theatre offered almost every conceivable advantage to the defensive side. It provided a narrow, constricted, overcrowded field of operations, hemmed in by the geographical barriers of the mountains to the west and the ocean to the east, and the political and psychological barrier of the compulsive need to defend the capital cities of Washington and Richmond, little more than a hundred miles apart, north and south. Across this narrow front, from the Potomac in the north to the James in the south, ran a series of rivers which look modest enough on the map in comparison with the mighty western waters, but which offered rich opportunities for stout defence by the weaker side against the stronger. The direct route from Washington to Richmond looked virtually impassable, and, for four years, the largest armies of North and South moved back and forth over quite a small area of northern Virginia, until the front door of the Confederacy gave way only when most of the house had already been occupied by intruders who had gained admission at side or back entrances. However, the campaigns in the east were not just a series of face-to-face slogging matches; each side varied the direct approach by moves against its opponent's right flank. In 1862 and again in 1864–5, the Northern army sought to exploit the advantage of a safe line of supply by water down Chesapeake Bay, by attacking the Richmond area from a base on the James Peninsula. In 1862 and 1863 the Southern army tried to use the Shenandoah Valley to create a diversion or to assist an invasion of the North. Running from south-west to north-east between the Blue Ridge mountains and the main mountain chain further west, that beautiful valley offered an inviting route for an invading army aspiring to get behind Washington and threaten other northern cities, and, equally important, it offered a safe line of retreat from any such venture. But, whatever the temptations and the dangers of such movements on the flank, the war in Virginia remained basically a protracted struggle between the geographical advantages of the defending side and the numerical superiority of the attacker.

Geography distributed its favours very differently in the area between the Appalachian mountains and the Mississippi river. Here successive Confederate commanders faced the problem of defending a wide-open front of three hundred miles or more with forces which were never large enough for the task. But the difficulty was not only one of too few men and too many miles. From the mountains of east Tennessee to the Mississippi and beyond, geography offered no natural lines of defence. If the rivers of the east slammed a series of doors in the face of the invader, the great rivers of the west gave him an open invitation. The Mississippi itself was a major factor in Northern strategic planning from the outset. Scott's Anaconda plan set great store by reassertion of Union control of the river all the way to the delta, as a contribution to squeezing the life out of the main body of the Confederacy. The Tennessee and Cumberland rivers, tributaries of the Ohio, were avenues sweeping in great half-circles deep into the interior of the south, and slicing through any projected defensive position. In order to exploit the opportunities offered by the western rivers, the Union forces would need to learn new techniques in amphibious warfare, but the western theatre as a whole offered scope for swift movement, bold attack and deep penetration. In a war where the weaker side sought to defend as much of its territory as possible, and the stronger side to apply mounting pressure all along

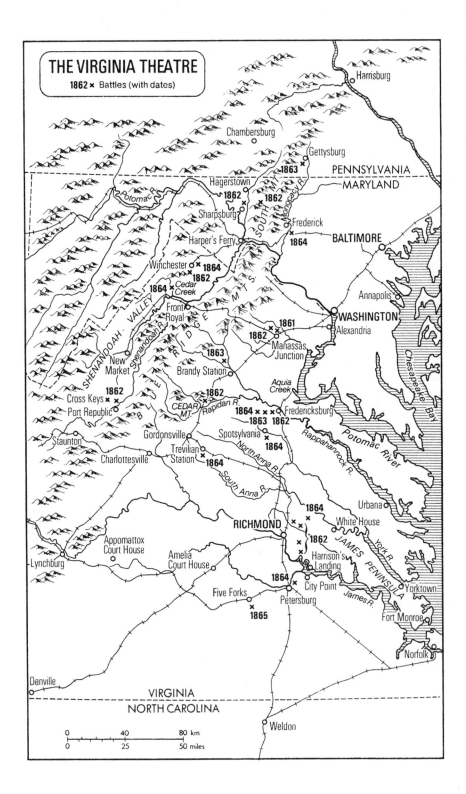

**THE VIRGINIA THEATRE**

1862 ✕ Battles (with dates)

Harrisburg

Chambersburg

Gettysburg
**1863** ✕

PENNSYLVANIA
MARYLAND

Hagerstown
**1862** ✕ **1862**

Sharpsburg

Harper's Ferry

Frederick
✕ **1864**

BALTIMORE

Winchester ✕ **1864**
**1862**
**1864** ✕ Cedar Creek

Annapolis

Front Royal
New Market

SHENANDOAH VALLEY

SOUTH MT.

BLUE RIDGE MTS.

**1861** ✕ WASHINGTON
Alexandria

**1862**
**1863** Manassas Junction

Brandy Station

Aquia Creek

Cross Keys ✕ ✕ **1862**
Port Republic

CEDAR MT. ✕ **1862**
Rapidan R.

**1864** ✕ ✕ ✕ Fredericksburg
**1863** **1862**

Staunton

Gordonsville
Charlottesville

Trevilian Station ✕ **1864**

Spotsylvania
**1864**

North Anna R.

South Anna R.

Potomac River
Rappahannock R.
Chesapeake Bay

Urbana

RICHMOND ✕ **1864**
White House

Appomattox Court House

Amelia Court House

Lynchburg

Harrison's Landing
**1862** ✕

**1864** ✕ City Point

JAMES PENINSULA
York R.

Five Forks
Petersburg
**1865** ✕

James R.

Yorktown
Fort Monroe

Norfolk

Danville

VIRGINIA
NORTH CAROLINA

Weldon

0        40        80 km
0    25        50 miles

the line, it was the western front which proved more dangerous to the one and more profitable to the other.

The need to wage war on other far-flung fronts stretched still further the limited resources of the Confederacy. Operations in the states beyond the Mississippi – Missouri, Arkansas, Texas, western Louisiana – were almost a separate war within a war, especially after July 1863 when Union control of the great river cut the Confederacy in two. Further west still, small forces battled for supremacy in the south-western territories in the first year of the war. All round the long and vulnerable Southern coast-line, Union forces with naval support gained useful footholds and tied down Confederate units desperately needed elsewhere. In January 1863, 32 per cent of the Southern armies were allotted to these peripheral but still significant areas, as compared with less than 20 per cent of the much larger Union forces.[2] This was partly the result of state and local pressures, but it also suggests that, if geography had ever been a neutral force in the conflict, it had by this time been converted into a Union ally. From the very beginning, the generals ignored its demands at their peril.

1. For almost six months after Bull Run there were no major battles in either east or west. This was the period when both sides caught their second wind after the first hectic, breathless rush had reached its climax at Bull Run. Many illusions faded and died, as both sides made a more sober assessment of the massive tasks which lay ahead. These were months of intensive preparation of men and weapons, and slow clarification of lines of battle, but they were also months of frustration and disappointment as confidence that it would all be over in a few weeks gave way to impatience at the lack of any dramatic action at all.

Military preparation on the Union side was in the hands of two of the war's most controversial figures, George B. McClellan in the east, and John C. Fremont in the west. Fremont showed himself to be neither idle nor dilatory but he was never equal to the herculean tasks which faced him. Misled by his own exuberance and the sycophancy of the showy but inept staff officers who surrounded him, bewildered by the intricacy and the intrigues of Missouri politics, distracted by the chaos and lawlessness which spread across the state, Fremont could never master his immediate problems, let alone embark on any ambitious plan to march down the Mississippi. With considerable justification he blamed the Washington government for many of his troubles. Certainly it neglected the west while it concentrated on the situation at its own front door, and the western army was plagued by severe shortages of arms, equipment and transport – and of hard cash to procure them. Such difficulties were exploited by dishonest contractors and aggravated by Fremont's lack of business acumen and administrative ability. Lashing out at the problems which beset him on all sides, the general issued a proclamation on 30 August declaring martial law throughout Missouri, confiscating the property of those who actively aided the rebellion, and setting their slaves free. Lincoln insisted on drastic modification of the proclamation, despite protests from Fremont himself, from his wife who travelled all the way to Washington to plead her husband's cause angrily but unsuccessfully in a midnight interview with the president, and also from vocal sections of press and public opinion. Relations between government and general were now soured, and Fremont's position was undermined by the steady stream of emissaries from Washington who arrived to make all too obvious inspections of his activities. One of them, Secretary of War Cameron, even showed Fremont a presidential order for his removal, but withheld it because the army was moving towards an engagement with the enemy. For all his shortcomings, Fremont had organised a force of 30,000 men and was advancing upon the Confederates in south-western Missouri, and ironically it was at this juncture that the final order for his removal was delivered to him on 2 November. The contrast between his forward movement and McClellan's inactivity along the Potomac had failed to save him, but in view of his deficiences, both military and political, his fate was inevitable and not undeserved. He was replaced temporarily by General David Hunter, one of the watchdogs who had been despatched earlier to keep an eye on him, and then by General Halleck who on 19 November took over the Department of the West, now extended to take in western Kentucky. The Department of the Ohio, including the rest of Kentucky and Tennessee, was entrusted to Don Carlos Buell, rather than the man on the spot, William Tecumseh Sherman, who was showing such signs of strain that gossip about his insanity was widespread in the army and even reached the columns of the press. As 1861 drew to its close, new Union commanders were establishing themselves in the west, and already showing signs of their reluctance to help each other, but action against the enemy was confined to minor affrays like the one at Belmont on the Mississippi on 7 November, which had first brought the name of Ulysses S. Grant briefly to the public notice.

In the east the situation around Washington was even more static, and even more taxing to the patience of politicians, press and public. General McClellan was proving himself to be active and energetic in every way except engaging the enemy, and was already establishing the reputation which kept him in the eye of a storm of controversy for the next twelve months. A West Pointer who had served in the Mexican War and seen something of the Crimean War, he left the army in 1857 but responded to the call to arms in 1861 and quickly made a name for himself in minor operations in West Virginia. His claim to have 'annihilated two armies' there was more than a little extravagant, but in the wake of Bull Run the North turned gladly to any general with victories to his credit, and McClellan was hurried to Washington to take command of the forces around the capital. The next few weeks and months showed him at his best. The immediate priorities of securing the safety of Washington and shaping the jumbled mass of volunteer regiments into something recognisable as an army suited perfectly his remarkable talents both for defensive measures and meticulous organisation. By the autumn Washington was fortified far beyond the capacity of the Confederate army to threaten it directly, and the Army of the Potomac had emerged both in name and in fact as a disciplined, trained and organised force. McClellan had swept idlers, stragglers and pleasure-seekers of all ranks from the streets, bars and brothels of the capital, he had drilled his men until drill seemed to be an end in itself, he had gathered an enlarged and effective staff around him, and he had paid close attention to the myriad problems of equipment and supply. By mid-October he had 150,000 men on his rolls, two-thirds of them ready for active campaigning, but, although the fine autumn weather invited some positive action, he contented himself with elaborate parades and reviews to show off his new army. One brief foray across the Potomac by a small force led to a humiliating fiasco at Ball's Bluff on 21 October, but on the whole the impression grew that McClellan was more interested in displaying his army than using it. Appreciation of his hard work gave way to impatience at his army's inactivity, and both were well deserved.

The military responsibility was his alone, for, to McClellan's satisfaction and largely at his instigation, Winfield Scott had stepped down from the position of general-in-chief on 1 November. 'I can do it all,' McClellan had confidently replied when Lincoln expressed doubts about his new dual role as general-in-chief and commander of the Army of the Potomac. But what did he propose to do? There was an ever-widening gap between the ambitious plan he had outlined in August to crush the rebellion in a series of attacks on Richmond and other Southern cities, and the stagnation of the next few months. The figure of 273,000 men, which, he estimated, his plan would require, suggests the characteristic McClellan blend of precise detail and sheer fantasy. He could make strategic plans, and he could master the practicalities of organisation and supply, but he could not weave the two into one pattern. If the realities of the situation did not fit the plans, then that was the fault of the former, not the latter. Clearly, McClellan would not move until he was ready, and many people began to doubt whether, by his own standards, he would ever in fact be ready. Certainly, he was not to be swayed by the public clamour for action, or by political pressure. He had an ill-concealed contempt for the politicians, and, as a Democrat, a deep suspicion of Republican politicians in particular. When the new session of Congress began in December, the political pressures intensified. The new Committee on the Conduct of the War fastened on to the Ball's Bluff defeat, persecuted Brigadier General Charles P. Stone for his part in it, and began to cast its net more widely in search of larger fish. Although, month after month, Lincoln stood as a shield between McClellan and his fiercest critics in and out of Congress, the general had little respect for the president, and none for his views on military matters. But impatience with McClellan spread eventually to the president and his cabinet, and things came to a climax at the turn of the year when the general fell ill with typhoid fever. Between 10 and 13 January, Lincoln held four meetings with some members of the cabinet and two of McClellan's subordinate commanders, McDowell and Franklin, to discuss what, if anything, could be done. Lincoln's exasperation showed in his remark that, if McClellan was not intending to use the army he would like to borrow it for a while. Warned of these irregular meetings and suspecting the worst, McClellan rose from his sick bed to appear at the last of them but sullenly refused to divulge his plans before, so he implied, such an untrustworthy audience.[3] Mutual confidence between president and general was fast disappearing, and at the end of January Lincoln made a desperate and naïve attempt to prod McClellan into action. He ordered a general movement of all the land and naval forces, to begin on 22 February, and followed this up by ordering the Army of the Potomac to advance on the railroad south-west of Manassas on the same day.[4] The choice of 22 February, George Washington's birthday, suggests that these curious orders were a political and public-relations exercise rather than a serious military move. They certainly reflected the widespread dismay at what had happened, and even more at what had not happened in the preceding six months.

The Southern armies spent this same period not so much in initiating fresh action as in reacting to events and to Northern preparations. After the rejection of Beauregard's swashbuckling plans for attacking Washington, the Confederate forces settled into a defensive posture while they faced the fact of inferior numbers and wrestled with the desperate difficulty of arming and supplying the men they had. In northern Virginia Joseph E. Johnston, with 50,000 men, felt able to do no more than sit out the autumn and winter at Centreville near Manassas, in constant expectation of Northern attack, and as soon as the winter weather eased, he prepared to withdraw even from that position which he now felt was too exposed. But his problems were modest and manageable in comparison with those which faced his namesake Albert Sidney Johnston in the west. With some 40,000 men he had the responsibility of defending a three-hundred-mile front from Cumberland Gap in south-eastern Kentucky to Columbus on the Mississippi, against much greater numbers and with no natural defences to help him. It was a daunting task and, if Johnston sometimes gave the impression of sitting at his headquarters at Bowling Green and waiting for his line to be broken at some point or other, it is hard to see what more positive alternative was open to him. The victory of Union forces under George H. Thomas at the minor battle of Mill Springs (or Logan's Cross-Roads) in eastern Kentucky on 19 January 1862 was not in itself very significant, but it was an ominous sign of what was to come.

The mood of resignation in which the two Johnstons awaited the enemy's moves typified the Confederate situation. At the turn of the year, indeed, gloom predominated in both North and South. On the one side, impatience at the lack of military initiative, irritation with McClellan, and ill-feeling over Fremont's removal were not the only causes of pessimism and disillusion. The raising of the armies had left a stream of grievances, arguments, blunders and scandals in its wake; the Treasury's first efforts at financing the war effort were running into deep trouble; even the apparent triumph of snatching the Confederate emissaries to Europe, Mason and Slidell, off the *Trent* on the high seas had turned into the threat of war with Britain, and ended humiliatingly in the release of the two captives. No matter where one looked, it was hard to see any sign of the war coming to an end, or even of any coherent policy to bring it to an end. In the South an equally bleak diet was relieved by even fewer crumbs of comfort. The Confederacy too had its financial problems and its recruiting headaches – with the fearful prospect early in the new year of a mass departure from the army of the twelve-month volunteers. Southerners were both impressed and depressed by the mounting evidence of massive, solid, serious Northern preparation for a major war effort. The early successes, and Bull Run in particular, had not provided a short cut to independence and recognition; no major battles had been lost, and yet the Confederacy was already losing ground alarmingly.

The balance of despondency, North and South, was in fact an illusion. The South had already lost much of the borderland: Maryland, western Virginia, most of Kentucky and much of Missouri. Wide stretches of the coast of the Carolinas were now under Union control as a result of amphibious operations at Hatteras Inlet in August and Port Royal in November. Another strip of North Carolina coast, including Roanoke Island, was to fall to General Burnside in February 1862. The blockade of the Southern coast, though still as leaky as a colander, was beginning to have some effect.[5] All around its thinly-manned periphery, the Confederacy was giving way to mounting pressure. Without yet having won a major battle or deployed its main strength in the field, the North was gaining ground steadily. Southern resources were already over-stretched and Southern defences undermanned. The new year was still young when the first great Union offensive, in both east and west, would put matters to the test.

2. In the west the Union forces were paying the penalty of divided command while Halleck and Buell haggled over who was to cooperate with whom and which army's movement was to have the first priority. They were spoilt for choice of attacking opportunities between the Mississippi itself, or the Tennessee and Cumberland rivers in the centre, or the invasion of east Tennessee. This latter project was strongly backed by Lincoln on political grounds, for east Tennessee was the most important pocket of pro-Union feeling in the south, but its political appeal was at odds with its military inaccessibility from the north because of the high mountain ridges which protected it. On the Confederate side, Albert Sidney Johnston had a unified command, but his forces were thinly spread between General Leonidas Polk (erstwhile bishop of Louisiana) on his Mississippi flank, and General Hardee, and Johnston himself in eastern Kentucky, with only a small force of 5,000 guarding the two great river approaches in the centre.

At the beginning of February 1862 one of Halleck's subordinates, General Grant, took the initiative himself, with Halleck's tacit approval, and the eager cooperation of Flag Officer Andrew Foote, commander of the motley flotilla of Union river gunboats.[6] His target were Forts Henry and Donelson, which, at a distance of about ten miles from each other, guarded the Tennessee and

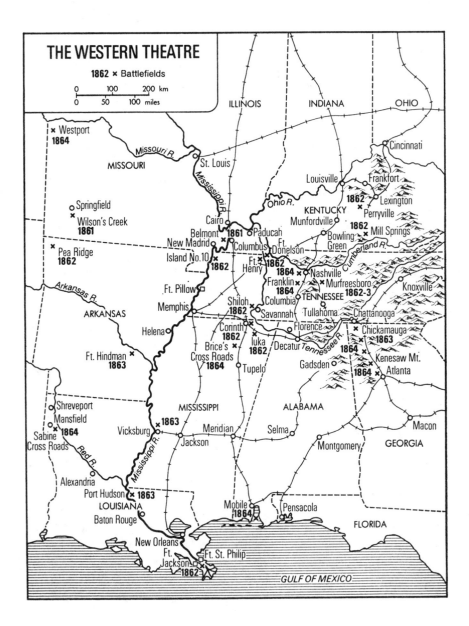

# THE WESTERN THEATRE

1862 × Battlefields

```
0      100      200 km
0    50    100 miles
```

ILLINOIS    INDIANA    OHIO

× Westport
1864

Cincinnati

Missouri R.

St. Louis

MISSOURI

Louisville    Frankfort

Ohio R.

1862    Lexington

○ Springfield    KENTUCKY    × Perryville

× Wilson's Creek    Cairo    Munfordville    1862
1861    Belmont    1861    ○ Paducah    Bowling    × Mill Springs
New Madrid    Columbus    Ft.    Green
× Pea Ridge    Island No.10    ×    Donelson    Cumberland R.
1862    Ft. ×    1862
Henry    1864    × Nashville
Franklin ×    × Murfreesboro    Knoxville
Ft. Pillow    1864    TENNESSEE    1862-3
Shiloh    ○ Columbia
Memphis    1862    × Savannah    Tullahoma    Chattanooga
ARKANSAS    Corinth    Florence    × Chickamauga
Helena    1862    Iuka    ×1863
Brice's ×    1862    Decatur    Tennessee R.    1864 ×
Ft. Hindman ×    Cross Roads    Gadsden    × Kenesaw Mt.
1863    1864    ○ Tupelo    1864 ×    Atlanta

○ Shreveport    MISSISSIPPI    ALABAMA
Mansfield
× 1864    × 1863    Macon
Sabine    Vicksburg    Meridian    Selma
Cross Roads    Jackson    Montgomery    GEORGIA

Red R.

Alexandria
Port Hudson × 1863
LOUISIANA    Mobile    Pensacola
Baton Rouge    1864    FLORIDA

New Orleans
Ft.    Ft. St. Philip
Jackson
1862    GULF OF MEXICO

Arkansas R.
Mississippi R.
```
```

Cumberland rivers respectively, close to the Kentucky–Tennessee state boundary. Although it was intended to defend much the more important river of the two, Fort Henry was an ill-conceived, ill-sited and ill-defended position on low, marshy ground, vulnerable to bombardment from the river. It fell very quickly to naval bombardment before Grant's encircling troops moved upon it on 6 February. Most of its garrison escaped eastward to Fort Donelson, and Grant's army plodded in the same direction over muddy roads in drenching rain. Donelson was a much stronger position, and its defenders soon administered a rebuff to Foote's gunboats, over-confident after their first easy success. The quick and unexpected loss of the deplorably weak Fort Henry had placed Johnston in a quandary. With his defensive line broken, was it worth attempting to restore the position by pushing reinforcements into Donelson to defeat Grant there, or was he to withdraw to a new defensive line much further south, and abandon much of Tennessee in the process? A clear-cut decision between the two was essential, but, in trying to do something of each, Johnston ended with the worst of both worlds. While starting a withdrawal southwards, he sent 12,000 men under John B. Floyd to Fort Donelson, thus bringing its garrison to 20,000 before Grant invested it on 12 February. The fort was strong enough to withstand attack for some time, but its unhappy trio of commanders, Floyd, Gideon J. Pillow and Simon Bolivar Buckner, decided on a bid to fight their way out. On 15 February the attempt was on the point of success when Floyd and Pillow, losing their nerve, ordered the whole force back into the fort. Having closed the trap door on their own troops, they decided that night on surrender, and then escaped themselves, leaving the unfortunate Buckner and the bulk of their men to their fate. Buckner, a friend (and creditor) of Grant's in the pre-war army asked for terms, and Grant's insistence on unconditional and immediate surrender gave him a national reputation and a nickname almost overnight. (Not even the most brazen of public relations men would surely have dared to invent such a coincidence as that between the unconditional surrender phrase and the initials which Ulysses Simpson Grant already shared with Uncle Sam himself.)

Some 14,000 men and large quantities of arms and equipment were surrendered at Fort Donelson, but this was only the beginning of Johnston's troubles. Any chance he had of escaping the consequences of his fatal strategic compromise had been destroyed by the folly and the shame of Floyd and Pillow. The centre of his defensive cordon had been smashed, and Union gunboats ranged far up the Tennessee and Cumberland rivers. Obliged to abandon Nashville, the capital of Tennessee, to Buell's army, Johnston strove to reunite the divided wings of his own army on a new line far to the south. Meanwhile Union forces under John Pope, with vigorous assistance from the navy, captured New Madrid on the Mississippi on 13 March and the heavily defended Island No. 10 on 8 April. In a few weeks the Confederacy had lost much of Tennessee, a long stretch of the Mississippi, and a good deal of confidence in its ability to defend its western front.

The situation might have grown far worse had not the Union advance down the Tennessee river now lost its impetus. Despite his successes, or perhaps indeed because of them, Grant fell foul of Halleck, and on 4 March he was actually removed from command, amid complaints that he had not been submitting despatches and reports as requested, and mutterings that he was hitting the bottle – or resuming 'his former bad habits' as Halleck put it.[7] The misunderstandings were soon cleared up, and Lincoln himself made it clear that he was reluctant to dispense with a general who had proved that he could fight and win. On 13 March Grant was restored to his command by a satisfied Halleck, who had two days earlier achieved his objective of overall command of the western armies, thus bringing Buell as well as Grant and Pope under his control. But Halleck was now more concerned over the problems of a further advance into the south than impressed by the need for urgency. Grant was ordered to keep his army at Savannah and Pittsburgh Landing on the Tennessee, about eighty miles south of Fort Henry, until joined by Buell's force, at which point Halleck would take direct command of the next decisive move. The Confederates were meanwhile making good use of this unexpected breathing-space, and by the beginning of April Johnston had gathered almost 50,000 men at Corinth, a vital junction on the Memphis and Charleston Railroad in northern Mississippi, and a mere twenty miles from Grant's encampment on the Tennessee river. If Johnston was to launch an attack, he had to do so quickly before Grant's 42,000 men were joined by Buell's army. Johnston's inclination to seize the initiative was reinforced by his new second-in-command, Beauregard, who had been transferred to the west in February and who was soon expounding heady plans for a bold counter-offensive which would sweep north to threaten even St Louis itself.

Johnston moved his army forward on 3 April, and after delays which cost vital time launched it against Grant's army early on 6 April. The resulting battle of Shiloh was the biggest and bloodiest encounter of the war so far, and its incoherence, disorder and lack of unified direction were strangely at odds with its crucial importance in determining whether one great Confederate effort could roll back the Union invasion which had already gobbled up so much territory in the west. Grant was caught napping at Shiloh, his army was not entrenched or even drawn up in position to meet such an attack, and Grant himself was at his headquarters several miles away downstream when the fighting began. As the day wore on, the Union forces were pushed back until they stood perilously close to the Tennessee river, its banks swarming with thousands of runaways and skulkers who had found their first taste of battle too much for them. But Grant refused to admit defeat, and he gained invaluable time from the heroic stand of Benjamin Prentiss's division at the 'Hornet's Nest'. Here, General Johnston, urging his men on to renewed attacks, received a bullet wound in the leg which severed an artery, and he died within a matter of minutes. Beauregard took over command and pressed the attack for a while, but he had no more reserves, and his men were nearing exhaustion. The Union army, so near to defeat and destruction, survived to fight again. Buell's troops were now at hand, and on the next morning a revived and reinforced Union army grasped the initiative, and shortly after noon the weary and outnumbered Confederates were driven from the field. They in turn might now have been destroyed if the victors had not been too exhausted to pursue (and too relieved at having won the day). Each side had lost over 1,700 men killed in the battle, and the combined casualties on both sides approached 25,000. If in its confused combat between inexperienced troops Shiloh was 'the Bull Run of the West', its sustained ferocity and appalling casualty lists were stark evidence of the way in which the war had grown in the intervening nine months. Grant had won another victory but his performance was clearly open to criticism and strengthened the view of those who thought his luck greater than his skill. But it was still hard to challenge his willingness to fight. The loss of Albert Sidney Johnston was a blow to the South and especially to Jefferson Davis who valued him so highly. 'In his fall the great pillar of the Southern Confederacy was crushed,' wrote Davis in his memoirs, 'and beneath its fragments the best hope of the Southwest lay buried.'[8] From a longer distance the loss of Johnston may be more soberly assessed; he was a brave soldier and an honourable man, but very much the kind of commander of the old school who would almost certainly have been outdated by the rapid changes of the Civil War.

Shiloh consolidated all that the Union armies had thus far gained in the west, and it opened up rich new opportunities. However, Halleck was determined that those opportunities should be his, not Grant's, and he quickly arrived to assume direct command of the combined forces of Grant and Buell. He spent the rest of April pondering and preparing his next move, and allowing his native caution to prevail, despite good news from other western battlefronts. It had come first from across the Mississippi. Back in early March a new Confederate commander in the trans-Mississippi area, Earl Van Dorn, was talking of a bold counter-offensive which would sweep from northern Arkansas through Missouri to St Louis, and threaten the whole Union advance in the west from the rear. But, unfortunately for Van Dorn, his brave plan fell at the first hurdle. On 7 March he attacked the Union forces under Samuel R. Curtis at the battle of Pea Ridge (or Elkhorn Tavern) in north-west Arkansas. He came within an ace of victory, but Curtis held out and on the next day his tired troops forced Van Dorn's even wearier men to retreat. In the ensuing weeks it became clear that Curtis's narrow, unspectacular victory had in fact firmly established the Union position in Missouri and northern Arkansas, and ruled out any serious threat to Halleck and Grant from that direction. In mid-April came the good news from much further west that E. R. S. Canby had eliminated the Confederate threat in New Mexico.

Later in April came the best news of all, and the most spectacular achievement of the war so far. Plans had been laid for some time for a combined military and naval attack on New Orleans from the Mississippi delta. Now they were brilliantly executed by Flag Officer David Farragut. On 25 April, the greatest port and the greatest city of the Confederacy surrendered, and a week later was occupied by Union troops under Ben Butler. Farragut's dramatic success now laid the Mississippi open to Union advances from south as well as north, and his gunboats were soon ranging far up river.[9]

Halleck, still lingering around the field of Shiloh, could scarcely have been given a greater boost. Whatever its failings and setbacks, the Union offensive in the west was now riding high, and nothing seemed impossible. Yet, at this very moment, things began to go awry, and the momentum so powerfully built up in the past three months was allowed to die away. First Halleck spent the whole of May inching his large army forward towards Corinth only twenty miles away. On 29–30 May Beauregard abandoned the city and retreated south to Tupelo. Despite the snail's pace which he had set, Halleck's prospects were still good. He was now astride the Memphis and Charleston Railroad, one of the great east–west links of the Confederacy, and his capture of Corinth led to the Confederate abandonment of Fort Pillow on the Mississippi, and then of Memphis itself, which, following Nashville and New Orleans, became the third major Southern city to fall in four months. Further rich prizes were there for the taking, but Halleck failed to make a clear choice between them. A move eastward along the railroad to Chattanooga was one obvious possibility which would commend itself to a president always anxious about east Tennessee. One alternative was to strike southward towards Mobile and the Gulf coast. Another closer and more tempting target was Vicksburg, the last Confederate stronghold on the Mississippi. For a brief spell in early summer the Confederates controlled only the two or three miles of the river around Vicksburg while Union gunboats ranged up and down to north and south. But while the navy could run its ships perilously past Vicksburg's batteries, neither they nor the small contingent of troops who accompanied them could take the city itself. Farragut sailed south again towards New Orleans and the Confederates regained control of the river from Vicksburg south to Baton Rouge. What Halleck might easily have taken in the summer of 1862 was to be won twelve months later only after much costly effort, and one of the war's most brilliant campaigns.

The rich harvest of new opportunities yielded by the spring campaign proved too much for Halleck's modest appetite. He nibbled at some of the proffered fruit, and allowed the rest to rot. Instead of concentrating on one major objective, he dispersed his forces, leaving his most aggressive general, Grant, to defend the whole area around Corinth and Memphis, and entrusting his one positive move to the unenterprising and slow-moving Buell, who was to advance eastward along the railroad to Chattanooga. Although long stretches of that line were already controlled by a Union division under Ormsby Mitchel, whose troops had earlier got close enough to shell Chattanooga itself, Buell set a very leisurely pace, and his anxieties about his lines of supply were ably exploited by Confederate cavalry under John Hunt Morgan and Nathan Bedford Forrest. While Buell frittered away his chances by his sluggishness, Halleck, who, from the distance of Washington, looked like the architect of western victory, was called to the capital in July as general-in-chief of all the Union armies. There he faced a problem created by another general, who, like Buell, suffered from what the president called 'the slows'.

3. These same months from February to July 1862 had seen the rise and fall of the first great Union bid for victory in east as well as west. At the end of January General McClellan had at last unfurled his plans before the presidential gaze. Believing that the area around Manassas offered little room for manoeuvre and that even a victory there would pay no worthwhile dividend, McClellan wanted to transfer the army down Chesapeake Bay (which would provide a secure supply line) and attack Richmond from that direction. He claimed that the terrain and the better spring weather in that area would offer much greater attacking possibilities at a point close to the enemy capital, and that Washington itself would meanwhile be safe, because Joseph E. Johnston would have to move his army south to defend Richmond. Many of the advantages which McClellan claimed for his plan were genuine enough, and other observers, including W. H. Russell of *The Times*, had for some time considered that such a strategy was the North's best hope. But there were objections to the plan, both military and political. It seemed to make places, and Richmond in particular, more important than the opposing army, and Lincoln thought this a mistaken order of priorities. The president also feared for the security of Washington; public confidence and political reality required that the capital must not merely be safe but must be seen to be safe. Rightly or wrongly, the suspicion lurked in many minds that McClellan's adoption of the indirect approach was one more piece of procrastination, one more excuse to avoid a challenge to the opposing army. As for more strictly military considerations, McClellan's confident forecast of better weather and better roads in his chosen theatre of operations was to be sadly mocked by subsequent events, and no less an authority than Robert E. Lee thought that the James Peninsula, where McClellan eventually landed, was well-suited to defensive fighting by a smaller force against a larger one.[10]

Lincoln was not happy about the plan, but on 8 March he gave it his grudging and conditional approval. Some indication of his misgivings is given by his orders of the same day, which, against McClellan's wishes, divided the Army of the Potomac into four corps and appointed to their command officers who were not of his choice, and whose political sympathies veered much more to the radical Republican side. Confidence between president and general, never very substantial, was reduced almost to vanishing point three days later when McClellan was relieved of his duties as general-in-chief of all the armies on the ground that he was about to take the field with his own Army of the Potomac. This made good enough sense, but McClellan was not a man to appreciate the point, and it hardly helped when he read of the change in the newspapers before he had been officially notified.

In these same few days in March Johnston's Confederate army also took a hand in embarrassing both McClellan and his plan. On 9 March Johnston

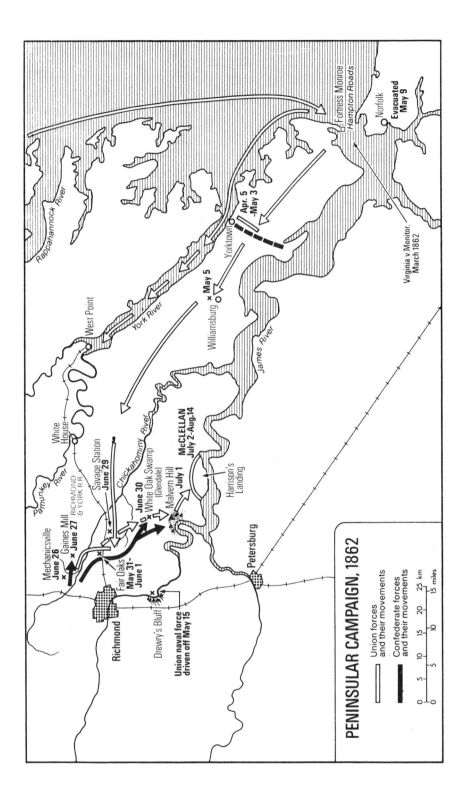

# PENINSULAR CAMPAIGN, 1862

Union forces
and their movements

Confederate forces
and their movements

0   5   10   15   20   25 km
0       5       10      15 miles

Richmond

Petersburg

Drewry's Bluff

Union naval force
driven off May 15

Mechanicsville
June 26
×

Gaines Mill
June 27
×

Fair Oaks
May 31-
June 1
×

Savage Station
June 29

June 30
White Oak Swamp
(Glendale)

Malvern Hill
July 1

McCLELLAN
July 2-Aug.14

Harrison's
Landing

RICHMOND
& YORK R R

Chickahominy River

Pamunkey River

White
House

West Point

York River

Williamsburg × May 5
○

Yorktown ○

Apr. 5
-May 3

James River

Rappahannock River

□ Fortress Monroe
Hampton Roads

Norfolk
Evacuated
May 9

Virginia v Monitor,
March 1862

withdrew southwards from his position around Centreville and Manassas. McClellan marched his army out to the abandoned Southern position where it was soon painfully obvious that the enemy army and its defences had been much weaker than McClellan had believed. Mockery about the logs painted to resemble heavy guns which had kept the Army of the Potomac at bay since the autumn was hard enough for the general to take, but the strategic consequences of Johnston's retreat were even more unwelcome. The new Confederate position was too close for comfort to McClellan's first choice of a landing place for his army, at Urbana, on the south bank of the Rappahannock, and he was obliged to switch to an alternative plan – a landing at Fortress Monroe, and an advance up the James Peninsula, which he regarded as 'a certain, tho' less brilliant movement than that from Urbana'.[11]

After the unpleasant shocks of the first half of March, McClellan turned with relief to a task which he could do well – the organisation of the move to the peninsula. In the second half of the month an armada of some four hundred vessels of all shapes and sizes conveyed men and supplies to Fortress Monroe. McClellan himself followed at the beginning of April, and at once found new anxieties and fears to plague him. It was soon clear that the naval cooperation upon which he had insisted, but which he had not worked out in detail, was not to be forthcoming during the campaign. Moreover, the powerful Confederate ironclad *Virginia* (formerly the Merrimack) was still lying at Norfolk, just across Hampton Roads from Fortress Monroe, after its inconclusive battle with the *Monitor* on 8–9 March.[12] It remained a threat to all Northern shipping and blocked access to the James river on the south side of the peninsula. But McClellan's great concern, as always, was over the question of numbers, both his own and the enemy's. Always ready to believe he was outnumbered, and always demanding new reinforcements, McClellan believed that, when the Washington authorities did not meet his demands, they were conspiring to bring about his downfall. The general's anxiety over numbers was intimately connected with Lincoln's most serious reservation about the whole operation. The president feared that the move to the peninsula had left Washington vulnerable to attack, and he was not convinced by McClellan's assurances that Washington could best be defended on the banks of the James. When James Wadsworth, commander of the capital's defences, reported that he had less than 20,000 men instead of the 70,000 whom McClellan claimed to be available, Lincoln decided that the conditions upon which he had accepted the Peninsular plan had not been fulfilled. This dispute over the numbers available to defend the capital depended very much on which troops were included and which were not. McClellan on the one side and his political enemies (who now included Secretary of War Stanton) on the other juggled with the figures to support their rival views. Lincoln did not adequately grasp McClellan's strategic arguments, and the general did not bother to explain them clearly. The results of the dispute were serious. Lincoln ordered one corps of the Army of the Potomac to be withheld for the defence of Washington, and the corps thus lost to

McClellan was McDowell's, the largest and perhaps the best in the army, numbering some 35,000–40,000 men. The Peninsular campaign thus began with McClellan more than ever convinced that he was betrayed by his political masters, and with his neurosis over numbers more firmly established than ever, although, with a force approaching 100,000 strong, he had an overwhelming advantage over any foe in sight. At the outset he faced only about 13,000 men under the command of John B. Magruder, a dashing, colourful showman of a general whose forte lay in bluffing his opponents into exaggeration of his strength. He was about to find a most receptive audience.

McClellan's chosen field of operations lay between the James river to the south and the York and its tributary the Pamunkey to the north. Fortress Monroe at the eastern tip of the peninsula, which the Union had held since war began, was some seventy miles from Richmond, the Confederate capital. There seemed a certain historical appropriateness in the choice of this battle-ground. Here, in 1607, the original Virginian settlement had been established at Jamestown. Here, in 1781, the surrender of Cornwallis at Yorktown had made American independence a certainty. Here now in 1862, in what might justly be called America's birthplace, General McClellan hoped to destroy the most serious threat ever faced by the young giant which had sprung from this soil.

Yorktown was the first objective, and finding that Magruder's defences were stronger at this point than he expected, McClellan settled down without reluctance on 5 April to besiege it. The month's delay which followed may well have decided the fate of the whole campaign. After a brief look at Magruder's thinly-manned defences, Johnston had advised a complete withdrawal from the peninsula. He was overruled by Jefferson Davis and Lee, and his army was set in motion to meet the new threat. But it would take weeks rather than days to complete the move to the peninsula, and meanwhile the Union army sat in front of Yorktown, facing an incomparably weaker force and in a situation where, Johnston thought, nobody but McClellan would have hesitated to attack. Just when even he was at last ready for his elaborately planned assault, the Confederates withdrew on the night of 3 May. Two days later their rearguard, under James Longstreet, turned to fight a sharp action at Williamsburg, later described by McClellan, in terms which amount to a reproach to his men for moving too fast, as 'an accident brought about by the rapid pursuit of our troops'.[13] Johnston's retreat did not stop until he was almost back in Richmond itself, and, over roads turned to thick mud by heavy rains, McClellan's army plodded after him. By late May McClellan was outside Richmond with a rein-forced army, and facing an enemy none too confident that he could hold the city's still inadequate defences. Moreover, the Confederates had now lost Norfolk, and with it the mighty *Virginia*, thus leaving the James river open. On 15 May, indeed, only desperate efforts enabled the Southern batteries at Drewry's Bluff, a mere seven miles from Richmond, to drive off a Union naval force.

McClellan, however, had established his base at White House on the Pamunkey river, where he could use the Richmond and York railroad to bring up his heavy siege artillery upon which he expected to depend so much in the task that lay ahead. But between his base and Richmond itself flowed the Chickahominy river, a hitherto neglected feature of peninsular topography. From a point north of Richmond it flowed south-eastwards through marshland and swamps before emptying itself into the James. The heavy spring rains had transformed it from an unimportant line on the map into a major natural barrier. McClellan felt obliged to divide his army, with two of its five corps beyond the Chickahominy. With the swollen river at their backs, they offered a tempting target to Johnston, and he launched an attack against them on 31 May. The resulting battle of Fair Oaks, or Seven Pines, was a story of good plans badly executed, and of much bloodshed and slaughter which gained no significant advantage for either side. In this, it was to be typical of many of the war's pitched battles, but it did have important consequences which were personal and accidental. Surveying the battlefield on 1 June, McClellan was appalled at the bloodshed and the carnage, and revealed that sensitivity to the suffering of his men which did him credit as a man but impaired his judgment as a soldier. The impact of the battle on the Southern command was more direct and dramatic. Johnston was seriously wounded and was replaced by Robert E. Lee, who thus began the three years' association with the Army of Northern Virginia which made it and him immortal.

McClellan professed to be unworried by his new opponent, but he was concerned at the still dangerous division of his army, north and south of the Chickahominy. Although he had freely chosen to site his base on the Pamunkey rather than on the James, he later insisted that the decision had been forced upon him by the government's actions, especially its use of McDowell's corps, and he asserted that 'herein lay the failure of the campaign'.[14] Lincoln and Stanton had indeed largely wasted McDowell's corps in their anxiety to protect Washington, but, curiously, out of this situation had grown a new opportunity. McDowell had been pushed forward to the Rappahannock, and on 18 May Lincoln had decided that, from there, he should make an overland march towards Richmond which would enable him to link with McClellan's right wing. McClellan disliked the plan in principle, quibbled over every detail, and complained then and later that the need to link up with McDowell had dictated his unhappy choice of base, divided his army and wrecked his campaign. In fact, having made a plan, McClellan was adhering to it rigidly and inflexibly and refusing to recognise the new opportunities created by changing circumstances not covered by his original design.

The great irony in this situation was that the Southern leadership, and Lee in particular, had been greatly disturbed by the very prospect of a two-pronged attack on Richmond by McClellan from the east and McDowell from the north. It was, in fact, in a daring attempt to ward off this danger that Lee launched the counterstroke which altered the balance of the whole campaign. He sought to create a diversion which would delay and sap the strength of the expected attack on Richmond, and he chose the right place, the Shenandoah Valley, and the

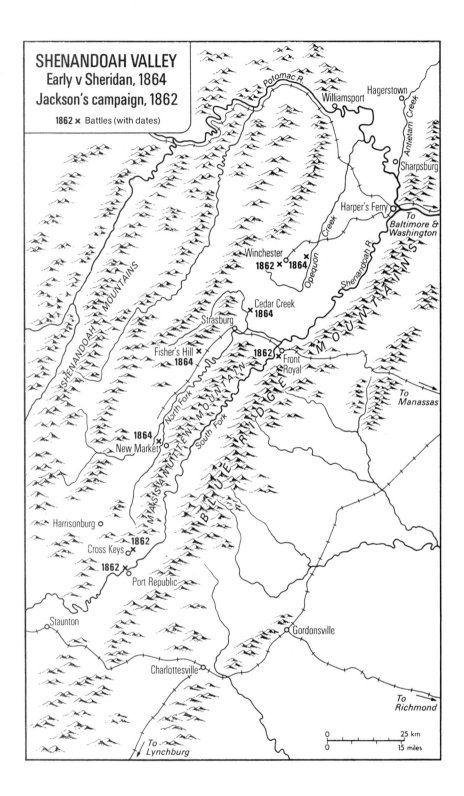

# SHENANDOAH VALLEY
### Early v Sheridan, 1864
### Jackson's campaign, 1862

1862 ✕ Battles (with dates)

Potomac R.

Williamsport   Hagerstown

Antietam Creek

Sharpsburg

Harper's Ferry

To Baltimore & Washington

Winchester
1862 ✕ ✕ 1864

Opequon Creek

Shenandoah R.

Cedar Creek
✕ 1864

Strasburg

Fisher's Hill ✕
1864

1862 ✕ Front Royal

SHENANDOAH MOUNTAINS

North Fork

South Fork

MASSANUTTEN MOUNTAIN

BLUE RIDGE MOUNTAINS

To Manassas

1864
New Market

Harrisonburg ○

Cross Keys ○ ✕
1862

1862 ✕ ○
Port Republic

Staunton ○

Gordonsville ○

Charlottesville ○

To Richmond

To Lynchburg

| 0 | | 25 km |
| 0 | | 15 miles |

right man, Thomas Jonathan 'Stonewall' Jackson. (Few men have ever been burdened with a less appropriate cognomen than the hard-hitting and fast-moving Jackson.) There was no obvious hint of his future glory in his pre-war career, or in his reputation as a religious fanatic, a total abstainer, and a food faddist who enthusiastically sucked lemons but denied himself pepper on the ground that it made his left leg weak. But the Valley campaign was soon to make him a hero to his men and to the whole South, and mark his emergence as one of the great soldiers of the war. It was the kind of operation which suited him perfectly – a small, independent command, wide freedom of action, ample scope for rapid movement and for confusing a divided enemy. With a total force of around 15,000 men he had to contend with much larger but divided Union forces: Nathaniel P. Banks in the Shenandoah Valley itself, the unhappy Fremont now in West Virginia on his left flank, and McDowell away to the east on his right.

Having set Fremont back on his heels early in May, Jackson raced down the valley later in the month, bemusing the unfortunate Banks, pouncing on a detachment of his troops at Front Royal on 21 May, routing his rearguard at Winchester, and putting the rest of his force to headlong flight across the Potomac. It seemed that Jackson, whose numbers were wildly exaggerated, was threatening Washington itself. People in the capital who should have known better were considerably alarmed. McClellan was amused: 'a scare will do them good,' he said.[15] With more energy than efficacy, Lincoln and Stanton strove to organise by telegraph from Washington moves by three separate commands to counter Jackson's threat. To their credit, they aimed not merely to drive him away but to trap him between Fremont advancing from the west and McDowell from the east. But the net failed to close in time, and Jackson slipped away south, turning back to give a bloody nose in turn to the advance guards of Fremont and McDowell at Cross Keys (8 June) and Port Republic (9 June).

The Valley campaign was over. Its month of long, punishing marches and lightning thrusts against detachments of the larger enemy forces made it a model for operations of this kind. It was a remarkable application in practice of the principles which Jackson had laid down early in the war:

Always mystify, mislead, and surprise the enemy, if possible; and when you strike and overcome him, never let up in the pursuit so long as your men have strength to follow; for an army routed, if hotly pursued, becomes panic-stricken, and can then be destroyed by half their number. The other rule is, never fight against heavy odds, if by any possible manoeuvring you can hurl your own force on only a part, and that the weakest part, of your enemy and crush it. Such tactics will win every time, and a small army may thus destroy a large one in detail, and repeated victory will make it invincible.[16]

The Shenandoah campaign had also achieved all that Lee had hoped. Jackson had given Northern morale a sharp jolt and he had brought about a major redisposition of the enemy forces in northern Virginia. His greatest success was in drawing off McDowell's powerful corps on the very eve of its march towards Richmond. This alone would have justified the whole operation and it gave Lee the room for manoeuvre which he needed.

Meanwhile, through most of June McClellan stood before Richmond, not so much missing opportunities as failing to create them, and often less interested in attacking the enemy capital than in complaining to his own. Estimating Lee's strength at 200,000, he believed that he was heavily outnumbered. Although Lee in fact had 85,000 men to pit against his opponent's 100,000 or more, he was now about to seize the initiative which McClellan seemed so willing to concede. Lee believed that his army could not afford to stand still against a more powerful enemy who, however slowly, would steadily wear him down in a long siege. He was ready to gamble by concentrating the bulk of his forces for a counter-attack, and when his cavalry commander, Jeb Stuart, reported that McClellan's line was weakest on its right flank, north of the Chickahominy, he decided to strike there, in the hope of cutting McClellan off from his White House base. He brought Jackson back from the Shenandoah for a key role in this operation, and he meanwhile relied on Magruder's play-acting and McClellan's caution to keep Richmond safe from an attack south of the Chickahominy.

It was on 26 June that Lee began his first major operation as a field commander, and the Seven Days battles which followed brought about an astonishing reversal of the positions of the two armies in the peninsula. Lee scored a major triumph in a week of sustained and furious fighting, but it was not the complete and decisive success to which he had aspired. Day by day, things never quite went according to plan, and the big catch slipped through the net. On 26 June at Mechanicsville (or Beaver Dam Creek) and on 27 June at Gaines Mill, Lee's army was drawn into a battle which he had not really intended, because of Jackson's confusion and delay in carrying out the planned turning-movement on the left. McClellan now gathered his whole army south of the Chickahominy, and Lee lost a valuable day on 28 June in trying to fathom this latest move. Still believing the Union base to be at White House, Lee could not understand McClellan's withdrawal in the other direction, to the south. The latter had in fact decided to change his base to the James river; this was a major undertaking, though a sensible enough step, and it was quite efficiently carried out. But it surely did not necessitate a retreat by the whole Army of the Potomac right back to its new base. So far only one of its five corps had been fully engaged, and it had fought well. The army could and should have been ready to stand and fight, but the slaughter at Gaines Mill had unnerved McClellan, and, that night, he wrote his hysterical Savage Station despatch to Secretary Stanton. It reveals all too clearly his state of mind:

> I have lost this battle because my force was too small. . . . I again repeat that I am not responsible for this. . . . I have seen too many dead and wounded comrades to feel otherwise than that the government has not sustained this

army. If you do not do so now the game is lost. If I save this army now, I tell you plainly that I owe no thanks to you or to any other persons in Washington. You have done your best to sacrifice this army.[17]

A discreet officer in the telegraph office in Washington deleted the last two sentences, and may thus, for good or ill, have saved McClellan from dismissal. Meanwhile the retreat to the James went on, if indeed retreat is the right word, for, years later, McClellan could write that 'Porter's corps was to move *forward* to the James River'.[18] Lee's army took up the pursuit, and missed an opportunity at Savage Station on 29 June, and a much more crucial one next day at the battle variously known as White Oak Swamp, Glendale or Frayser's Farm. Frustrated at his failure to make the most of good opportunities to trap the Union army, Lee allowed himself to be tempted on 1 July into one last rash assault on a very strong position at Malvern Hill. Heroic Confederate infantry assaults ended in disaster, but McClellan declined to consider a counter-attack and withdrew to his new base at Harrison's Landing. Lee, too, drew back and the Seven Days battles were over. So, too, it later transpired, was the Peninsular campaign.

Strangely, it was the general who had thrown his enemy back from the gates of Richmond who was somewhat dissatisfied at the outcome of the campaign, while the general who had retreated to his new base congratulated himself on saving his army against heavy odds. 'This movement was now successfully accomplished,' McClellan wrote later, 'and the Army of the Potomac was at last in a position on its true line of operations';[19] but he could have transferred his base to the James a month earlier, and without retreating from the outskirts of Richmond. He had, it is true, kept his army intact, but that was hardly the object of going to the peninsula in the first place. For his part, Lee had aimed at nothing less than the destruction of the Army of the Potomac, but his excellent plan of campaign had not been matched by its ill-coordinated execution in detail. Intelligence and staff work had been poor, and Lee was already showing that reluctance to keep his subordinates on a tight rein which was later to cost him dearly. Among those subordinates, Jackson had surprisingly been the most disappointing of all, whether through sheer fatigue and loss of sleep or difficulty in adjusting himself to a subordinate role in a large-scale operation in unfamiliar country. Lee also knew only too well that he could ill afford the 20,000 casualties of the Seven Days (as against Union losses of 16,000). But the fact remained that he had saved Richmond, turned the tables on McClellan, and put the Confederacy in a position to strike the next blow.

4. At mid-summer 1862 the war was entering a new stage. The first sharp Northern thrusts on both fronts had been blunted, and a quick end to the war was further out of sight than ever before. The conflict was relentlessly growing in scale and violence, and in its impact on every American. In these circumstances, McClellan's Harrison's Landing letter, delivered to Lincoln when he visited

the army on 7 July, was a sad anachronism. It is a cry from the heart of a general who desperately wanted to keep the war within recognised and manageable limits and conduct it, in his own words, 'upon the highest principles known to Christian civilization'. He protested against confiscation of private property, infringement of individual rights and forcible abolition of slavery. 'It should not be a war looking to the subjugation of the people of any state in any event. It should not be at all a war upon a population, but against armed forces and political organizations.'[20] McClellan and the many who thought like him wanted to restore the familiar America of the pre-Sumter era, but somewhere along the road from Yorktown to Richmond and back to Harrison's Landing the old landmarks had disappeared from view while the outlook ahead was still obscured by the thickening gloom of an unremitting conflict.

A new chapter in the war brought new commanders on both sides. Already, on 26 June, all the Union forces in West Virginia and the Shenandoah Valley, along with McDowell's corps, had been merged into the new Army of Virginia and placed under the command of John Pope, who had acquired a reputation as a bold fighter in the west. By his brave talk and his sympathy with radical views on the conduct of the war he quickly made friends in Washington, but he quickly lost them in the army. His address to the Army of Virginia, issued on 14 July, was a masterpiece of tactlessness. Its main theme was that Pope had come from the west 'where we have always seen the backs of our enemies', and that he intended to introduce the same aggressive approach in Virginia.[21] He followed this with orders (in which Stanton may have had a hand) laying down a tough policy towards the civilian population in Virginia and instructing the army to live off the country as far as possible. His orders outraged Southern opinion and incurred even Lee's contempt, and along with his radical politics and his boastfulness, they confirmed McClellan in his cordial hatred of his new colleague. Pope, it soon appeared, was more adept at making enemies than at fighting them. On 11 July Lincoln filled the post of general-in-chief, vacant since March, by the appointment of another, more eminent, general from the west, Henry Wager Halleck. If Lincoln wanted a man who would and could take responsibility for major decisions, he was to be sorely disappointed. Halleck was a sound administrator and an intelligent, well-informed soldier, but he did not have the look of a man of decision, and his looks did not deceive. With a manner that was both abrasive and evasive, he could not make up by good management and diplomacy what he lacked in force of character. He became a valuable military adviser but he had been selected for a larger role. Halleck's departure from the west ended the period of unified command there, and Grant and Buell were once again independent of each other. They now faced a new opponent, for, shortly after the retreat from Corinth, Beauregard absented himself on sick leave and was replaced by Braxton Bragg, trusted friend of Jefferson Davis, a good organiser and a stern disciplinarian whose firmness was to fail him in critical situations.

Halleck's first task as general-in-chief was to help Lincoln decide the future role of McClellan's army. Its position on the James Peninsula seemed secure, and still offered a promising springboard for a new offensive. But the North could only afford to keep its two main armies in Virginia widely separated if they were going to act quickly and in conjunction with each other. Speed was not to be expected from McClellan, and his relationship with Pope was so poisoned by jealousy and distrust on both sides that collaboration in a giant pincers move on Richmond and Lee's army was almost unthinkable. McClellan propounded various attacking plans, always with the rider that he would need large reinforcements, to match his grossly inflated estimate of Lee's strength. Indeed, his own past record and his fixation about numbers had now undermined the credibility of any such plans. Halleck finally recommended withdrawal from the James Peninsula, and orders to this effect were issued on 3 August. The actual evacuation did not take place until the second half of August, for McClellan's native caution and deliberation were reinforced by his resentment at the decision and his suspicion that he was the victim of a conspiracy. It was true that more than the military merits of the case had been involved. Attacks by radicals (and not only radicals) on the conduct of the war in general and on McClellan in particular had reached fever pitch in July, in Congress, in the press and even in the cabinet. Depressed by the slump in the war effort, and preoccupied with the complexities of the emancipation question, Lincoln longed for a great victory, but he did not share the view of some members of his own party who were so eager for Pope to win that victory that they wished to ensure that McClellan had no chance to do so first.

While the Army of the Potomac was in transit back to the area south of Washington, the North was in some danger and Lee had an opportunity. He would have to seize his chance quickly, for, once McClellan's and Pope's armies were united, they would have a daunting numerical superiority. In any race against time between Lee and McClellan there was only one likely winner. Having reorganised his army and strengthened Richmond's defences, Lee began to send more and more of his troops north to face Pope, even before McClellan's evacuation had begun. As early as 9 August Jackson fought a sharp engagement with Pope's vanguard at Cedar Mountain, and Lee was now looking for the time and the opportunity to strike Pope hard.

After the mid-summer regrouping, the Confederacy was about to launch a major counter-offensive in west as well as east. While Buell dawdled during July, Bragg succeeded in transferring the bulk of his army, some 35,000 men, from Tupelo in Mississippi to save Chattanooga. His troops arrived there well ahead of Buell, although to use the available railroads they had to make an enormous detour by way of Mobile on the Gulf coast. Once in Chattanooga, Bragg decided to strike north into Kentucky, supported by Kirby Smith's small force further east, thus menacing not merely Union supply lines but the whole Union position in the west. In mid-August both Lee and Bragg were poised on the edge of great enterprises which might dramatically reverse the whole trend of the year's campaigns, and decide the outcome of the war itself. Their twin threats were confidently expected to arouse the border states to throw off the shackles of Northern domination and rally to the flag of their liberators, and also to impress neutral opinion in Europe, and above all in Britain, with the need to recognise the fact of Southern independence. Faced with such pressures at home and abroad, and with an invading army on its doorstep, the North would lose heart, abandon its meddling with slavery, and reluctantly accept the fact that the Union was irreparably divided. As the Confederate armies swung north, nothing seemed impossible, except perhaps to the men who actually led them and who knew how great were the hazards and how small their resources. As August gave way to September, the war moved towards one of its great moments of decision.

5. When Lee faced Pope across the Rappahannock on 24 August, his immediate aims were modest enough. He was planning to avoid a major battle in view of growing enemy numbers, and resort instead to a war of manoeuvre, aimed at occupying much of northern Virginia, replenishing his supplies and disrupting his opponent's, and hampering the link-up between Pope and McClellan. Ironically the move which he now launched was to lead within a week to a great battle and a great victory, which in turn encouraged still bolder action. Time was pressing and Pope's army would soon be too large for Lee to risk a direct assault; because of this fact and yet at the same time in defiance of it, Lee divided his army, sending Jackson off on a long march round Pope's right to attack his main line of communication, the railroad which ran back through Manassas to Washington. Lee calmly accepted the risks of ignoring the conventional wisdom about concentration in the face of the enemy, and his audacity was rewarded. Jackson's 25,000 men swept round to the rear of Pope's position, and, descending through Thoroughfare Gap, cut the railroad on 26 August. That same night they fell upon the great Union supply depot at Manassas, and, having helped themselves liberally to unaccustomed luxuries – and many necessities too – they put the rest to the torch. With a force three times the size of Jackson's, Pope set off to find and destroy his troublesome opponent. But, bewildered by what had already happened, he lost control of the situation. The various divisions of his army, marching to and fro, could not even find Jackson, and, more seriously, they failed miserably to prevent the rest of Lee's army from breaking through Thoroughfare Gap to join him. Having at last come upon Jackson, who had taken up a good defensive position at Groveton, north-west of Manassas, Pope pitched into him on 29 August. Second Bull Run (or Second Manassas), fought almost on the site of the first major battle of the war, was another bitter pill for the North to swallow. Pope clung much too long to the belief that he faced only Jackson and that Jackson was intent only on making good his escape. His disjointed and ill-directed attacks failed to break stern Confederate resistance, and left his troops exposed on the second day to a crushing counter-attack from Longstreet's corps which drove them from the field. In the next few days Pope's army hurried north to shelter in the

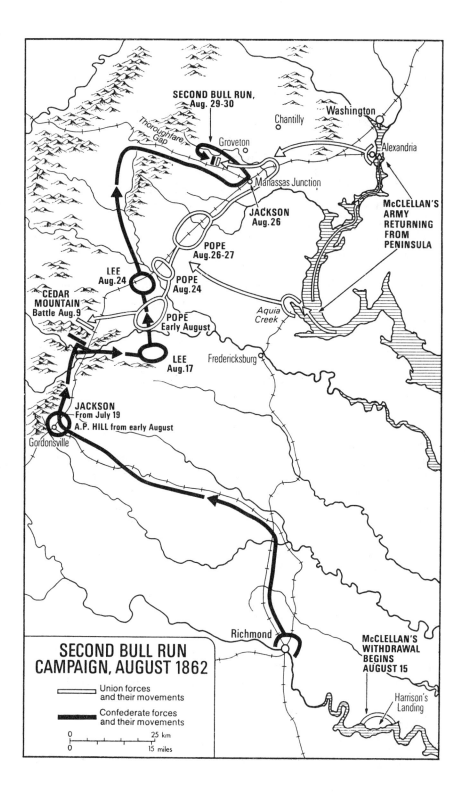

SECOND BULL RUN,
Aug. 29-30

Chantilly

Washington

Thoroughfare Gap

Groveton

Alexandria

Manassas Junction

JACKSON
Aug. 26

McCLELLAN'S
ARMY
RETURNING
FROM
PENINSULA

POPE
Aug. 26-27

LEE
Aug. 24

POPE
Aug. 24

CEDAR
MOUNTAIN
Battle Aug. 9

POPE
Early August

Aquia
Creek

LEE
Aug. 17

Fredericksburg

JACKSON
From July 19
A.P. HILL from early August

Gordonsville

Richmond

McCLELLAN'S
WITHDRAWAL
BEGINS
AUGUST 15

## SECOND BULL RUN
## CAMPAIGN, AUGUST 1862

Union forces
and their movements

Confederate forces
and their movements

Harrison's
Landing

0                25 km
0          15 miles

fortifications of Washington itself, but Jackson gave up the pursuit after a reverse at Chantilly, or Ox Hill, on 1 September.

In two months Lee and Jackson had driven one opposing army away from the gates of Richmond and another back into the defences of Washington. Lee now made the bold decision to invade Maryland; as always he was willing to take great risks for great stakes. He planned to continue his war of manoeuvre, open up new areas for desperately needed food and other supplies, and remove the seat of war from his beloved Virginia. But Lee, whose thoughts did not often stray beyond strictly military matters, was aiming at something more this time. He planned to appeal to the people of Maryland for support, and he even suggested to Davis that the Confederacy might make proposals for a peaceful separation of North and South from the position of strength which his invasion would create. If he could actually win a victory north of the Potomac, Britain and France could surely delay recognition of the Confederacy no longer, and Northern gloom might degenerate into a complete collapse.

While Lee planned his move across the Potomac, Washington plunged into a crisis, compounded of fear and despair, political intrigue, anxiety about the real danger of foreign intervention, and confusion and recrimination in the military high command. Pope blamed McClellan for his defeat at Bull Run, and many people in Washington believed, and Lincoln himself at least suspected, that McClellan had wanted to see Pope defeated. Certainly the withdrawal from the James Peninsula had been sluggish, and McClellan spent much time quibbling about the command arrangements when the two armies were combined, and fabricating excuses for delaying the movement of his various corps to reinforce Pope. He shocked Lincoln by his suggestion on 29 August that one course of action was 'to leave Pope to get out of this scrape'.[22] Two of his corps had reached Pope by the time of the Bull Run battle, and the commander of one of them, Fitzjohn Porter, was later court-martialled and cashiered on charges brought by Pope concerning his conduct there. This episode ensured that the recriminations on both sides would not easily fade; on the wider issue, the feeling lingered that, if McClellan had pushed forward more troops more quickly, the Bull Run disaster might just have been averted.

While the storm raged in the army and outside, Lincoln had to choose a general to defend Washington. Halleck was a broken reed, Pope a willing fighter but an incompetent one – and neither he nor McClellan would ever agree to serve under the other. The man for this particular job was surely McClellan, and the Army of the Potomac would scarcely have accepted anyone else, so closely identified had it become with its commander. Swallowing his distaste at the general's recent behaviour, Lincoln appointed him to the task, and in the next few days he showed once again what he could do in a situation suited to his talents for organisation and defensive preparation as he reintegrated weary and demoralised troops into an effective fighting force.

McClellan's appointment was a military necessity, but it was also political dynamite. His critics were baying for his blood, and even within the cabinet itself Chase and Stanton were collecting signatures to a memorandum demanding his dismissal at the very moment when Lincoln disclosed his decision to them. But the president did not waver. McClellan would have to be used and Pope would have to be sacrificed. (He was in fact sent west to fight the Indians.) A few days later, when the army marched out of Washington to meet the threat from Lee, McClellan remained in command, despite Lincoln's uneasiness about his fitness for the next task ahead.

Lee had crossed the Potomac north-west of Washington on 4–6 September, and concentrated at Frederick in Maryland. He now made the fateful decision to divide his army once again, sending three separate contingents (one of them Jackson's corps) by three different routes to deal with the Union garrison at Harper's Ferry, while Longstreet pushed north to Hagerstown and only D. H. Hill and Stuart remained directly in front of McClellan's likely advance. Both Jackson and Longstreet later insisted that this was the crucial error of the whole campaign.[23] Certainly, at this point things began to go seriously wrong. It took longer than planned to overwhelm the Harper's Ferry garrison. The number of stragglers rose to a quarter of the army's strength as men wearied by months of fighting and marching found the hard, unyielding roads of Maryland too much for their ill-shod feet. Sore feet and flagging hearts could spoil the bravest plans – and then, on 9 September, by a freakish accident, those very plans fell into the enemy's hands. A Union soldier found, wrapped round some cigars in an abandoned Confederate camp, a copy of Lee's orders describing in detail the spreadeagled position of his army in Maryland. This information was in McClellan's hands by 13 September, and gave him a unique opportunity to punish Lee for his audacity. For a day or two Lee was puzzled by McClellan's unusually rapid movements, although, given his knowledge of the situation, he might well have moved much faster still. After hard fighting on 14 September, Union forces burst through the barrier of South Mountain, and, although they failed to exploit their advantage quickly enough, Lee's scattered army was now in great peril. His first inclination was to withdraw south of the Potomac at once, but on 15 September he heard that Harper's Ferry had fallen at last, and he ordered Jackson's corps and all other units of his army to join him at Sharpsburg.

Here, along the line of Antietam Creek, Lee chose to make his stand, and here, with the Potomac and only one worthwhile ford across it at his back, he waited on 16 September, with only 25,000 men on hand to meet an army three times that size. Even when all his army was reunited he would have barely 40,000 men. Caution would surely have dictated a withdrawal into Virginia without giving battle, but Lee believed that the South could not win by caution and delay, and he was reluctant to abandon all the goals which he had set himself in his invasion of Maryland. In one sense, at least, he had provided himself with the best prescription for Civil War success: his invasion had put him strategically on the offensive, but now at Antietam Creek he was tactically

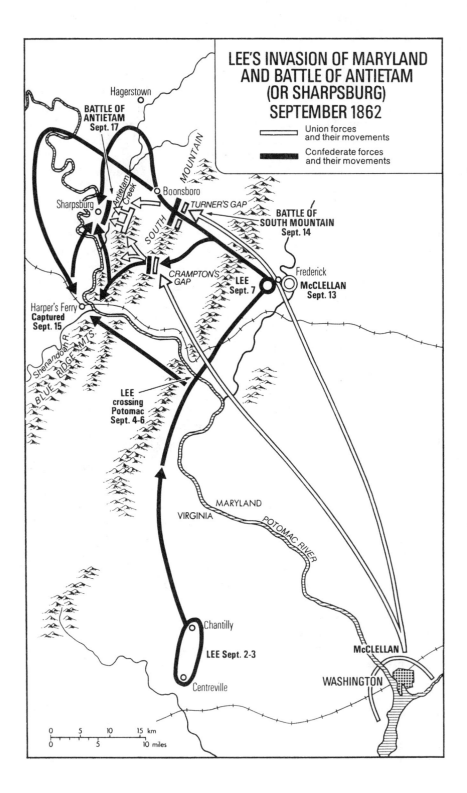

LEE'S INVASION OF MARYLAND AND BATTLE OF ANTIETAM (OR SHARPSBURG) SEPTEMBER 1862

Union forces and their movements

Confederate forces and their movements

Hagerstown

BATTLE OF ANTIETAM
Sept. 17

MOUNTAIN

Antietam Creek

Boonsboro

Sharpsburg

TURNER'S GAP

SOUTH

BATTLE OF SOUTH MOUNTAIN
Sept. 14

CRAMPTON'S GAP

Frederick

LEE
Sept. 7

McCLELLAN
Sept. 13

Harper's Ferry
Captured
Sept. 15

Shenandoah R.

BLUE RIDGE MTS.

LEE
crossing
Potomac
Sept. 4-6

MARYLAND

VIRGINIA

POTOMAC RIVER

Chantilly

LEE Sept. 2-3

McCLELLAN

WASHINGTON

Centreville

0    5    10    15 km
0         5         10 miles

on the defensive, and the Union army would have to attack him. He also relied on McClellan's caution to save him from an attack on 16 September; McClellan duly obliged, and gave him vital time.

The battle of Antietam, or Sharpsburg, on 17 September was, like many another Civil War battle, fiercely contested, confused and chaotic, and, in itself, inconclusive and unsatisfactory to both sides. But Antietam was also unique, not merely in being the bloodiest single day of the whole war, but also in the dramatic consequences which flowed from its apparent stalemate. McClellan's huge numerical advantage was frittered away in a series of unsynchronised and disjointed attacks, and Lee was able to rush men from one part of the line to another to plug gaps in the nick of time. While two of McClellan's corps never got into the battle at all, when their extra weight must surely have made the decisive breakthrough, Lee's troops were holding on by the slenderest of margins. At the end of the day, Burnside's belated attack on the southern end of the Confederate line was finally thrown back at the last possible moment by A. P. Hill's men who were sent straight into action after racing breathlessly up from Harper's Ferry. This day of carnage cost the Confederate army 13,000 in killed, wounded and missing, and the Union army 12,000. Such equality of slaughter was deceptive, for Southern losses were proportionately far higher and were well-nigh irreparable. Incredibly, Lee stood his ground next day and even contemplated a counter-attack. Even more incredibly, with his massive superiority, McClellan did nothing. On the night of 18 September the Confederates withdrew quietly south of the Potomac, and in the next few days and weeks, as stragglers returned, Lee was able to rest, regroup, feed and supply his battered army. McClellan's attempts at pursuit were feeble and his cast of mind still utterly defensive. 'I look upon this campaign as substantially ended,' he wrote on 22 September.[24] Neither commander could be really satisfied with the outcome. Lee had finally asked too much of his army; it had responded heroically, and it had escaped to fight again, but the odds had been too great, and were likely to become greater still in the future. McClellan had rallied the army after the Bull Run disaster and he had now forced Lee to abandon his invasion of Maryland. But he had not made full use of the opportunity offered by the captured orders, he had failed to exploit the advantage of superior numbers at Antietam (he still believed himself to be outnumbered, in fact), and he had allowed Lee to make good his escape. Success had beckoned him and he had shied away from it.

But Antietam was inconclusive only in a very restricted sense. Paradoxically, this mismanaged battle, this half-success for the North where complete victory was possible, profoundly changed the course, the nature and the issues of the whole war. It rescued Northern morale from a dark period of frustration and despondency, and it gave the North time to bring its full weight to bear on a weaker enemy. It removed the very real danger of European mediation or intervention at a time when the British government was awaiting the outcome of the next battle before deciding whether or not to abandon its policy of neutrality and non-involvement. Above all, it had enough of the appearance of a victory to enable Lincoln to issue his Emancipation Proclamation five days later, after he had waited two months to declare his new policy from a position of strength rather than as a panic measure. In short, after Antietam, the North still had the will to fight and the strength to win, the South was condemned to fight alone, without outside help, and the war to save the Union had become also a war to free the slaves. Like the Peninsular campaign, Antietam had pushed the war still further in the direction which McClellan had feared and resisted from the beginning. 'I feel that I have done all that can be asked in twice saving the country,' McClellan wrote,[25] unhampered by false modesty, after Antietam, but in the weeks and months that followed he must have wondered what exactly it was that he had saved.

6. The hinge of fate was turning in the west as well as the east in the autumn of 1862. Lee's invasion of Maryland had appeared all the more full of promise to the one side and menace to the other because it marched very closely in step with Bragg's invasion of Kentucky. Like Lee, Bragg had more than purely military objectives in mind. He hoped to arouse the people of Kentucky, win thousands of new recruits for the army, and throw the region north of the Ohio river into a panic. But, even more than Lee, he was to find that it was much easier to strike deep into enemy-occupied territory than to secure such gains by decisive defeat of the opposing army. Morgan's cavalry indeed had already ranged far and wide in Kentucky ahead of the main advance, and before Bragg moved north from Chattanooga in the second half of August, Kirby Smith's smaller force, moving from its base at Knoxville, was already a step ahead of him on a path further to the east and north. But neither general was in a position to give orders to the other, and the whole invasion of Kentucky suffered from being a two-pronged affair in which the prongs moved often in parallel but seldom in conjunction. By the end of August, on the very day when, in the east, Pope was retreating from Bull Run to Washington, Kirby Smith reached as far north as Lexington and was causing more than a little alarm to the citizens of Louisville and Cincinnati on the Ohio, who thought that the war had long since moved away from their front yards. Early in September (while Lee was crossing the Potomac into Maryland) Bragg was also leading his army into Kentucky, and, by the 17th, had captured Munfordville in the centre of the state. So far the invasion had met no serious challenge. Always inclined to set himself a gentle pace, Buell, the commander of the Union army, was confused by the enemy's rapid movements, and dithered and fretted over his response. Although steadily reinforced by divisions from Grant's army, he postponed any direct move against Bragg, and retreated back north to Nashville and then to Bowling Green in Kentucky. He declined to accept Bragg's challenge to attack him at Munfordville – a correct decision perhaps, but made for the wrong, over-cautious reasons. When Bragg advanced still further north, Buell hastened all the way back to Louisville on the Ohio river. At this point he

would have lost his command had not George H. Thomas, the successor designated by an impatient administration, refused to take over.

Up to the end of September all was seemingly well with Bragg and Kirby Smith, but the success of their invasion, which looked so spectacular, was more apparent than real. Their forces were now quite widely scattered and their supply situation somewhat uncertain. Their numbers were simply not large enough to consolidate the gains made by their sweeping advance, unless perhaps they could tempt the enemy into an attack in conditions which favoured them. Their greatest disappointment was the reaction of the Kentuckians themselves to their liberation. A few cheers were no substitute for a mass uprising, and there was more willingness to wave flags than to join the colours. Even the modest quantity of precious arms which the invading army had carried with it for distribution to new recruits found too few takers among young Kentuckians. Perhaps it was in an effort to stir some greater enthusiasm that Bragg wasted valuable time and effort in a diversion to Frankfort, the state capital of Kentucky, to attend the meaningless ritual of the installation of a Confederate governor of the state. By the beginning of October Bragg's nerve was weakening and his invasion was running out of steam. At last, Buell was making a move against the invading army, and in a situation where neither side was very clear about the other's movements or dispositions, a battle developed on 8 October at Perryville, some fifty miles south-east of Louisville. Only a part of Bragg's forces were engaged, and they emerged creditably from a drawn battle. But Perryville was yet another of those inconclusive engagements which were followed by a Confederate withdrawal. It was enough to snap the frail stem of Bragg's resolution, and, although within a day or two his army and Kirby Smith's were at last brought together at Harrodsburg in a strong concentration, Bragg was not to be dissuaded from abandoning Kentucky and retreating through Cumberland Gap all the way to Chattanooga, before finally establishing himself at Murfreesboro. Buell attempted no pursuit, ignored the opportunity to invade eastern Tennessee and prepared to take his army back to Nashville.

In both east and west, the Confederate counter-offensive was over, and after weeks of bold and rapid movement the armies were back more or less where they had started. While Buell and McClellan had met the Southern challenge in their slow and fumbling way, Grant had been left kicking his heels in the Mississippi theatre, his army weakened by the need to reinforce Buell, his role necessarily defensive. He and Rosecrans had won a half-success at Iuka on 19 September and a more important defensive victory at Corinth on 3–4 October which finally secured the Union gains in this area earlier in the year, but they had been unable to do more than that. As leaders on both sides looked back over the ebb and flow of the year's campaigns, they must have regretted their missed opportunities and noted ruefully that, at the end of October, they stood very much where they had been six months, many battles and countless lives ago.

7. But 1862 still had a sting in its tail. The convulsions of its last two months plunged the North into one of its darkest periods of the war, and yet also depressed the South with setbacks which underlined its perilous situation, and victories which gained no fresh advantage. As in mid-summer, a new phase was heralded by changes in command, and this time some eminent heads rolled. In late October the axe finally fell on both McClellan and Buell; both had warranted dismissal for their military shortcomings, but both also felt, not surprisingly, that they were being hounded out because of their Democratic affiliations. Buell was replaced by William S. Rosecrans, one of the most colourful personalities among Union generals, but one of many whose fighting reputation, won in subordinate positions, was not to be borne out by performance in high command.

The removal of McClellan marked the end of an era. He had managed to survive earlier crises, but after Antietam his slowness in pursuit of Lee and then in preparing his next move finally proved his undoing. Lincoln's correspondence took on an unusually harsh tone as he chided the general for his professed inability to do with his army what Lee seemed willing and able to do with his. At last, on 7 November, McClellan was instructed to hand over command of the Army of the Potomac to Ambrose E. Burnside. He bade his army an emotional farewell, amid much wild talk that he should lead his men on Washington to rout out the nest of vipers there. He never received another military command. In building his army into a fine fighting machine, he had served the Union cause well, and in caring for that army he had won such loyalty from his men that Lincoln was once moved to refer to it as General McClellan's bodyguard. But beyond that his achievements had been negative. He had avoided complete disaster and he had kept his army intact, but the North could not hope to win the war by such means alone. With his complex combination of qualities and defects, McClellan might be regarded as a man of paradox, but in fact he was all of a piece. His defects were his virtues carried to excess. His confidence became arrogance, or mere vanity. His thoroughness led him into over-caution, procrastination and a perfectionism to which the hard and swiftly-changing realities of war could seldom conform. His flair for organisation and planning betrayed him into inflexibility, a tendency to assume that the facts must inevitably fit his plans, and an inability to improvise or seize an unexpected opportunity. His military professionalism degenerated into a narrow exclusiveness, an ill-disguised contempt for his political masters, and a wilful blindness to the non-military considerations which vitally affected grand strategy. His sense of mission caused him to see all who crossed him as conspirators and himself as a martyr. He had most of the talents, except the ability to put them to the greatest use.

The chronic exaggeration of enemy numbers was perhaps the most revealing of McClellan's vices. Here he was aided and abetted by his chief of intelligence, Allan Pinkerton, Glasgow-born founder of the Pinkerton detective agency, who made it his business in peace and war to provide his clients with the kind of information they wanted. More accurate estimates were available, but the general believed what he wanted to believe. His skill in combating these reputedly vast enemy hordes elevated him in his own estimation and in the eyes of his army. Inflated estimates of enemy strength excused his delays and glorified his successes. They also seemed to demonstrate the folly of the administration in failing to support him fully. It is indeed true that the government had not always treated him as fairly or as tactfully as it might have done; there has always been a tendency for enthusiastic partisans of either McClellan or Lincoln in this controversy to fall upon the unfortunate and unpopular Stanton as a convenient scapegoat for the failings of both sides. It is also true that McClellan was the victim of savage attacks from radicals who accused him not only of incompetence but of treachery, or who were fearful that he might win a major victory before they could hunt him down; but no one had done more than the general himself to turn the Army of the Potomac into a political football. Under severe political pressure, Lincoln had stood by him for over a year. But the war proved too formidable a test for him, as for so many others. At last, in November 1862, he departed from the stage, one of the earliest casualties of modern, total war.

McClellan had at least provided the tools, but neither he nor his immediate successors could finish the job. General Burnside, who reluctantly took over the command in November, was a large, handsome, honest and likeable man, a loyal lieutenant of McClellan's, and a courageous officer with a creditable record behind him. But, if he remains one of the most sympathetic and appealing figures among Civil War generals, he was also one of the most disastrous failures. He doubted his capacity for high command, and his modesty was amply justified. Like so many other officers, he performed bravely and effectively up to a certain level of responsibility, but the overall command of an army many times larger than anything for which training and experience had prepared him proved far beyond his capacity. From the outset, too, he was operating under the extremely critical eyes both of the McClellan faction, who believed that Burnside could do nothing which their hero could not have done ten times better, and of those who expected the removal of McClellan's dead hand to produce immediate and decisive victories.

Against the wishes of Lincoln and Halleck, Burnside insisted on transferring the army eastward to the area around Fredericksburg on the Rappahannock, with the intention of moving on Richmond from there. The president rightly insisted that the only hope for this plan lay in rapid movement which would enable the army to get across to the south bank of the Rappahannock before Lee had had time to prevent it. But precious time was sadly wasted in the second half of November, largely owing to inexcusable delay, mainly attributable to Halleck, in bringing up the pontoons which Burnside needed to cross the river, which was some 150 yards wide at this point. While the huge Union army remained north of the river around Falmouth, Lee's army steadily moved into position on the low ridges a mile or two back from the south bank, and behind the town of Fredericksburg itself. This immensely strong Confederate position controlled the plain between the ridge and the river; according to E.P. Alexander, commanding the artillery on Marye's Heights, 'a chicken could not live on that field when we open on it'.[26] To the dismay of many of his subordinates, and the amazement of his opponents, Burnside decided to cross the river in the face of the enemy, and make a direct frontal assault on the heights beyond. The plan itself was as simple and obvious as the reasons for its rapid and total failure. The crossing of the river was accomplished on 11 and 12 December, at two points, one directly opposite Fredericksburg and the other two miles downstream. On the next day Burnside launched his men into suicidal attacks on an impregnable position; as the afternoon wore on, wave after wave of men were shattered by pitiless small arms and artillery fire, and when nightfall came 12,500 Union soldiers lay dead or wounded in front of the Confederate defences. Burnside fluctuated between deep despair and an insane desire to take the lead personally in a renewed bid on the morrow to storm Marye's Heights. He was dissuaded from any such madcap scheme, and he withdrew back across the Rappahannock on the night of 15 December. Lee launched no pursuit or counter-attack, for it could only have laid his army open to the fate suffered by Burnside's. Jackson had argued against giving battle at Fredericksburg for this very reason: 'we will whip the enemy, but gain no fruits of victory'.[27] Lee had taken the opportunity with which Burnside had presented him to win a crushing victory, but the armies were now in the same position as before, and once the first euphoria of another victory had subsided, Southerners faced the sad truth that even success could have its serious frustrations.

For the North, Fredericksburg was perhaps the most humiliating and inexcusable defeat of the war, and its shock waves reverberated through the army, through the capital and across the whole country. Army morale plummeted, and thousands of men absented themselves without leave in the weeks that followed. Lincoln went to the length of having a leaflet distributed to the troops congratulating them on their courage and offering them the thanks of the nation. 'Although you were not successful, the attempt was not an error nor the failure other than an accident,'[28] he wrote in words which made a frontal and unavailing assault on the facts, fit to rank with the army's attack on Marye's Heights. Discord among the officers of the army reached a state of near mutiny, and when members of the Congressional Committee on the Conduct of the War descended upon them to investigate the defeat, some generals like Joseph Hooker poured out their tale of woe into receptive ears. Generals Franklin and Smith wrote direct to Lincoln suggesting a return to the peninsular strategy, and two Brigadier Generals, John Newton and John Cochrane, actually went to Washington to tell Lincoln directly of the demoralised condition of the army. Lincoln was impressed enough to send a telegram to Burnside on 30 December, saying that 'I have good reason for saying you must not make a general movement of the army without letting me know'.[29] As the new year came in, the president was to be confronted with Burnside's resignation, and a continuing crisis of command, and of confidence, in the Army of the Potomac.

But the crisis had spread far beyond the army. For many Northerners, the Fredericksburg disaster was the last straw in a mounting burden of war-weariness, frustration, and dissatisfaction with the administration's conduct of affairs. This mood had already produced a serious Republican setback in the mid-term elections in November, and now it opened new rifts within that party itself. It was the news from Fredericksburg which finally touched off the political crisis in December when Republican senators confronted Lincoln with demands for the reconstruction of his cabinet along more radical lines, and for a more vigorous prosecution of the war.[30] Whether in cabinet office or military command, the argument ran, leadership should only be entrusted to those who were thoroughgoing supporters of all-out war and acknowledged champions of freedom for the slaves. Lincoln foiled the senatorial demands, but, as the year ended, he was well aware that Northern morale had descended to one of its lowest troughs as the casualty lists grew longer than ever, and Robert E. Lee looked more unbeatable than ever. He waited to put the Emancipation Proclamation into force on 1 January, but that was sure to meet a mixed reception, and it was unlikely, in the short run at least, to revive enthusiasm for the war. The crying need was for a clear-cut victory, but where and when would it come?

Not from the west, it seemed, if the events of November and December were any indication. Grant was at last in a position, or so he thought, to move on Vicksburg, and in November he began the long advance along the line of the Mississippi Central railroad. But the further he went, the more vulnerable his supply line became to the cavalry raids of Forrest and Van Dorn, and on 20 December the latter wrecked his supply base at Holly Springs. Grant abandoned his overland march and withdrew north, having already decided to switch the main effort to the Mississippi River approach to Vicksburg. He had entrusted Sherman with this operation, but Sherman's exact status was complicated by the independent activities of John A. McClernand, who had been authorised by Lincoln and Stanton to organise his own Mississippi expedition. Sherman's force sailed down the river, turned up the Yazoo just north of Vicksburg, and tried to storm Chickasaw Bluffs on 27-9 December. His attacks were beaten off with heavy losses by Confederates occupying a strong defensive position, and Vicksburg remained secure for the time being.[31] There was news, too, that the Confederates had created another powerful defensive position at Port Hudson further south to obstruct Union moves upstream from New Orleans. On the Mississippi, the year thus ended in frustration for the North as the Confederates hung grimly on to a vital stretch of the great river. But the South could ill afford complacency, for nothing was more certain than that Grant would renew the attack in the new year, and it remained to be seen whether the South had the resources to withstand his relentless pressure.

On the other main western front in middle Tennessee, Buell's successor Rosecrans had concentrated his army at Nashville and showed no great inclination to move. His opponent, Braxton Bragg, was encamped at Murfreesboro, thirty miles to the south-east, and looked happy enough to settle down there for the winter, after his hectic autumn campaign. But Rosecrans had not been put in command simply to behave like another Buell, and, under considerable pressure to act, he finally marched south on 26 December. His advance, like almost every other Union move in this theatre, was harassed by the energetic Confederate cavalry, but by 30 December the two armies faced each other near Murfreesboro, and here, on the last day of the year, began another of the war's stubborn, hard-fought, costly and indecisive battles. The shape of the battle of Murfreesboro (or Stones River) was confused from the start because each commander had made a similar plan, to envelop his adversary's right flank. Bragg delivered his blow first, and the battle on 31 December developed into a stern defensive fight on the part of the Union army, which emerged battered but still intact. Rosecrans stood firm, and, after more manoeuvring and fighting over the next three days, it was Bragg who broke off the engagement and headed south to Tullahoma. After Antietam and Perryville, this was the third time in just over four months that an inconclusive battle had been turned into a Union victory of a kind by the subsequent retreat of the Southern army. This was an ominous sign of the way in which Southern resources were being stretched to the limit, and Southern manpower was now feeling the strain.

At the end of 1862, as at its beginning, neither side could find easy comfort in the state of the war. Each faced mounting problems on the home front, and each government was under heavy fire from its political opponents. The prospect of a long, grinding war stretched as far ahead as ever. The North's great offensive in the first half of the year had made gains in the west at least, but they had not been followed up. The Southern counter-offensive had promised much but achieved little. It had not set the border states alight, or destroyed the Northern will to fight, or won the international recognition on which the Confederacy counted so much. As the year waned, the North had driven out the invaders but failed to destroy them. In the west it had not yet freed the Mississippi and in the east it had suffered the appalling shock of Fredericksburg. For the South, victory had too often brought no substantial benefit in its wake, and a drawn battle had too often been achieved at irreparable cost and followed by the yielding of hard-won gains. But once again the situation of the two sides was not strictly comparable. The North had missed the greater opportunities but the South still faced the greater dangers. The Confederacy was winning dramatic victories in battles like Bull Run and Fredericksburg, but unceasing Union pressure looked more likely to win the war. Anyone looking for straws in the wind at the end of the year would have done well to note one feature of each of the last two major battles of 1862. At Fredericksburg, the Army of the Potomac had met shattering defeat, and in the whole year it had never won a convincing victory, but it remained a powerful, well-equipped fighting force, needing only the right opportunity and the right leadership to prove its worth. At Murfreesboro, days of dour fighting had produced no clear decision on the field of battle, but in the end it was the Northern army which held its ground and the Southern which fell back. The South had achieved a draw where only victory could suffice. Whatever the surface ripples might indicate, the deeper under-currents of the war were running in favour of the North. But there was still a long way to go, and on one side or the other good or bad leadership, internal dissension or a weakening will to sustain the fight could still divert those currents in a new direction.

# Chapter VIII: Two Governments at War, 1861–1863

Fighting the Civil War was a political as much as a military operation; politics shaped the course of the war and were shaped by it. The governments of both Union and Confederacy struggled to define their objectives, mobilise their resources, satisfy their supporters, and answer their critics, and all in a situation without parallel in earlier American experience. Just as no one could have foreseen the scale of the war or its cost in blood and toil, so no one could have forecast the administrative problems and political complexities which it would create. In the nature of things, neither government could have been prepared for such a contingency. The leaders of North and South faced remarkably similar problems and remarkably similar criticisms during the war. Both were attempting to operate a system of government ill-suited to such a situation. Inspired by a distrust of power wherever it was lodged, the constitution makers of 1787 had devised a system which enshrined the fragmentation of power. To fight the Civil War, strong central direction was essential. In the middle of the nineteenth century the challenge of a major war demanded organisation, executive authority, and government interference in the lives of individual citizens on a scale undreamed-of in the days of Washington or Jefferson or Jackson. In meeting this challenge, the administrations of Abraham Lincoln and Jefferson Davis both faced charges of executive tyranny, abuse of the constitution, meddling and inefficiency, and injustice to particular individuals, groups or regions.

But if the similarities between the Northern and Southern situations

were striking, the differences were perhaps more revealing. Lincoln and the
Republicans took over a going concern in Washington. However limited in size
and inadequate in performance, the executive departments, together with the
two houses of Congress and, not least, the party system, provided a recognisable
framework for organising wartime government. They represented a focus of
loyalty and a basis for action. Washington itself may have been little more than
an overgrown and uncomfortable village, but it was the established federal
capital. The Capitol building, with its uncompleted dome, was almost too
painfully appropriate as the symbol of an imperfect Union. The Confederacy,
on the other hand, was starting from scratch, and indeed had first to decide
where to set up house – and what kind of house it was to be. The Southern
leaders had no precedents to guide them – or, rather, they had only precedents
drawn from the experience of the Union. Their constitution was almost a
replica of the United States constitution – they claimed indeed to be the true
guardians of the American ark of the covenant. Their political habits had been
formed in the halls of Congress and in state houses and court houses and
governors' mansions across the land.

There could conceivably have been advantages in a fresh start, in devising a
government tailor-made for the twin purposes of protecting Southern rights
and institutions and waging a successful war of independence. But, alas for the
South, these twins were not identical – they were not even compatible. The
motives which had inspired secession militated against a successful prosecution
of the war. States rights had been a Southern rallying cry for decades, and however much constitutional tradition might handicap operational efficiency, many
in the South would not or could not cast aside their profound suspicion of
centralised authority, even temporarily until independence was safely won.
Lincoln, too, had his difficulties with state governors and his intractable constitutional problems, but Davis's were of a quite different order, and they grew
steadily worse as the war dragged on, month after month.

The greater fragmentation of Southern politics was not just a matter of states
rights. It affected government and administration at every level – not least at the
level of political controversy and electoral rivalry. Throughout the war,
Confederate politics remained unorganised, shapeless and undeveloped, a
confusing mixture of personal feuds, factional jealousies, local grievances,
constitutional hair-splitting, and chronic obstructionism. Opposition to the
government abounded but it lacked cohesion as much as the government itself.
The Davis administration was desperately short of the political tools to do the
job which faced it. Organised parties were conspicuous by their absence,
although the old political affiliations of ex-Whigs and ex-Democrats were not
completely without significance in the Confederacy. Clearly it was not possible
to fashion an 'instant' two-party system for the independent South, and few
Southerners would probably have thought it desirable, but the lack of it was
surely very harmful.

The North was ill-organised, too, but it did have a two-party system in working order, and party politics proved to be one of the most telling, if unappreciated, weapons in the Union armoury. Lincoln himself was nothing if he was not a party man, and even at the bleakest moments of the war he devoted a remarkable amount of time and energy to questions of patronage and jobs, party organisation and political tactics. He needed to build up and operate a party machine as well as a war machine, and the two tasks were not unrelated. His Democratic opponents, too, operated within a recognised party structure; election campaigns, congressional proceedings and local disputes were all conducted within a party framework. True, some of Lincoln's fiercest critics were members of his own party, but they too accepted the party as part of their political way of life. They might blame Lincoln for the slow progress of the war, or deplore his cautious approach to the emancipation of the slaves; they might even try to dictate a reconstruction of his cabinet or drop him as a candidate for re-election. But they never forgot that they were Republicans, and that their political interests, like the president's, were tied to the party by a complex web of patronage, organisation, calculation, principle and electoral necessity. Nor were they unaware that if their party saved the Union, it might stand as the party of patriotism and loyalty for generations to come. Above all, for Republicans and Democrats alike, party provided a channel through which the various political currents could flow; by comparison, Jefferson Davis, his supporters and his critics sailed upon treacherous and uncharted waters.

1. One of Lincoln's most important priorities was to establish himself, with his cabinet, with his party, with Congress, and with the mass of the people. The Lincoln legend has obscured our view of the man as his contemporaries may have seen him. Even his friends and supporters were inclined to doubt his capacity for the tasks he faced, and thought him well-intentioned and sensible, but weak and irresolute. 'The President is an excellent man, and in the main wise,' wrote his Attorney-General, Edward Bates, at the end of 1861, 'but he lacks *will* and *purpose*, and, I greatly fear, he has not the *power to command*.'[1] Harsher critics and political opponents saw him as a backwoods politician, quite unfit to occupy the White House, especially in such a time of crisis. Moreover, the notion that Lincoln, the champion of the common man, was also and always the hero of the common man, is not easily substantiated. Most important of all, he was still in 1861 a comparatively little-known figure on the national scene. Following the custom of the day, he had not campaigned actively on his own behalf in 1860. As president, his apparent lack of concern with press relations, and his reluctance to leave Washington, or to make speeches – the Gettysburg address is one of the very rare exceptions to the general rule – severely restricted opportunities for image-building in the modern fashion. His physical appearance inspired more ridicule than respect, and his predilection for humorous stories was regarded as unseemly flippancy in a time of agonising crisis. And yet he did make an impact on the American people in the war years, not so much sudden and dramatic as gradual and profound.

Somehow, in his relations with Congress and with the cabinet, as well as with the masses, Lincoln contrived to be both detached and yet intimately involved. The paradox may be explained by his preference for dealing with men rather than institutions, individuals rather than groups, the specific rather than the general. His hold on the mass of the people grew only slowly, but he made a profound impression on the thousands of people who swarmed the White House corridors, or who wrote to him, to ask favours or offer advice. He clearly thought it worthwhile to spend a remarkable amount of his time on them. He had less direct influence over Congress than any other 'strong' American president, but he was in close contact with many individual congressmen and not only those who were his loyal supporters. He bothered little with his cabinet as such, but he knew exactly where he stood with each of its individual members, and he used them more effectively for his own purposes than even they often realised. He granted favours, issued pardons, distributed jobs, begged support, gave or listened to advice, accepted or rejected proposals, exerted or responded to pressure, on thousands of separate and individual occasions. He preferred it that way – it gave him greater freedom, more flexibility, fewer commitments. 'My policy is to have no policy,' he sometimes said, but no policy did not mean no politics. Nor did it mean no decisions. Rather, Lincoln made hundreds of small individual decisions, sometimes as a substitute for major decisions on policy, sometimes to prepare the ground for them.

Lincoln's treatment of his cabinet reflects clearly his own very personal political style. Its composition represented a very delicate balance of regional, political and personal interests. It contained four ex-Democrats and three ex-Whigs – an important factor in a party still only a few years old – and the President himself, another ex-Whig, made the balance perfectly even. The balance is further indicated by the contrast between its two leading members, William H. Seward at the State Department, Salmon P. Chase at the Treasury, both highly ambitious, both unsuccessful aspirants for the place which Lincoln now occupied – on the one hand, Seward, from New York, ex-Whig, now on the conservative flank and busy living down his earlier radical image, and on the other hand, Chase, from Ohio, ex-Democrat, a dedicated and consistent anti-slavery man of radical sympathies, who was as stiff and formal as Seward was flexible and relaxed. It was widely believed in 1861 that Seward would dominate the administration as a kind of prime minister manipulating the weak-willed constitutional monarch in the White House. Seward saw himself playing such a role, but he had the sense quickly to recast himself in a more modest part as he took the measure of the president. Chase's presidential ambitions were un-quenchable, and he ran the Treasury Department partly as a base from which to launch a bid for the nomination in 1864. The administration included two more men who had been among Lincoln's rivals for the Republican nomination in 1860. Simon Cameron, ex-Democrat and a great power in Pennsylvania politics, served as secretary of war during 1861 but was replaced by Edwin M. Stanton in January 1862. Edward Bates, ex-Whig, from the border slave state of

Missouri, became attorney-general, and was among the most conservative of the president's advisers. Another border-state man, Montgomery Blair from Maryland, became postmaster-general, adding another conservative voice, especially on the slavery issue, and ranking second only to Seward as a target for Radical attack. The cabinet also included Gideon Welles, ex-Democrat, from Connecticut, who was appointed secretary of the navy. A shrewd, crusty, reticent New Englander, he looked the part of Father Neptune and acted it faithfully.

The American constitution mentions no cabinet and provides for no system of collective cabinet responsibility; executive power is vested in the president alone. Certainly few cabinets in American history have shown less sense of corporate unity and common responsibility than Abraham Lincoln's. It met irregularly and seldom transacted really important business. Lincoln sometimes presented it with a major decision – as with the Emancipation Proclamation, for example – and sought advice only on points of detail. This method of operation suited the president, who, by temperament and inclination, was never a precise or orderly administrator, and who preferred to consult individual members of the cabinet as and when he saw fit. His system was to have no system. The secretaries generally ran their own departments – and Seward, Chase, Stanton, Welles, and Blair did so with considerable distinction. 'In truth,' wrote Bates, 'it is not an administration, but the separate and disjointed action of seven independent officers, each one ignorant of what his colleagues are doing.'[2] The cabinet was racked, and almost wrecked, by animosities, jealousies and in-compatibilities among its members. The Seward–Chase rivalry was only one of several; a Seward–Welles feud dated back years before the Civil War, and Seward was thought by most of his colleagues to exercise an undue and unhealthy influence over the president. Stanton was as much distrusted inside the cabinet as outside it. Montgomery Blair was regarded with suspicion as the representative of the powerful border-state Blair family. Lincoln himself had no need to divide such a cabinet before he could rule it. Among such a contentious group, co-existence without much cooperation may have been the only possible working arrangement.

For all its tensions and dissensions, Lincoln's cabinet retained a notable stability in personnel. Seward and Welles served throughout the war; Chase, Bates and Blair all remained until 1864. In the first half of the war, indeed, only two changes took place, and one of those a minor one – the replacement of the colourless Caleb B. Smith by John P. Usher at the Department of the Interior. The other change was immensely important. In January 1862 Simon Cameron was replaced at the War Department by his fellow Pennsylvanian, Edwin M. Stanton. The original appointment of Cameron, a politician of dubious reputation but also of influence and resource, had been largely a payment of a political debt, but as the months passed in 1861 he demonstrated ever more clearly his inadequacy in such a crucial post. Stanton, on the other hand, took to the job as if it were made for him. An extraordinary and erratic man, who had served in Buchanan's cabinet in its dying months, who had actually voted for Breckinridge in 1860, and yet who was to become one of the more radical members of the cabinet, he brought order out of chaos, a sense of urgency out of bewilderment, and a ruthless sense of priorities out of bureaucratic indecision. He became one of the great architects of Northern victory, though he made few friends in the process. It is no mean tribute to Lincoln's skill in the management of men that he could work with Stanton and get the best out of him for more than three years.

The president's relations with Congress demanded similar qualities of endurance and flexibility. The Congress which Lincoln faced in 1861 had been depleted by the departure of most of the Southern members, which left the Republicans in command. It is hard to classify all the members, but one estimate of party strength in the House of Representatives gives figures of 106 Republicans, 42 Democrats and 28 'Unionists'. This, the Thirty-Seventh Congress, held three sessions. The first was the special session of July–August 1861, which, meeting before an atmosphere of crisis had come to be taken for granted, was probably the most cooperative session which Lincoln experienced. It ratified his actions thus far with a minimum of jealous protest at the extension of executive power, and it gave him the means and the authority to continue the war. The first regular Congressional session lasted from December 1861 to July 1862, and the 'lame-duck' session, meeting according to the curious political timetable of the period, after the new Congress had already been elected, sat from December 1862 to March 1863. These sessions showed far less inclination towards docile cooperation with the president.

In his relations with Congress, Lincoln was no Woodrow Wilson or Franklin Roosevelt or Lyndon Johnson. He did not attempt to exercise strong, positive leadership over the legislative body; he presented to it no legislative programme; he accepted from it, with apparent meekness, various unwelcome acts and decisions; he vetoed only one important bill in four years. He showed remarkable deference to Congress but he showed equally remarkable independence of it. He allowed Congress to go its way in the optimistic hope that Congress would allow him to go his. The results could be confusing, as when president and Congress pursued separate and conflicting policies on the question of slavery. In any formal sense, as two separate branches of the federal government, the executive and the legislature were far apart in the Civil War years, but at the personal and practical level there were few barriers, and the White House doors were open to a large number of Senators and Representatives. Such close contact did not yield much reward in the shape of legislation, but Lincoln seldom expected or asked that it should. It did not save him from bitter attack in Congress, even from leaders of his own party, but it helped him to survive such attacks and to get on with the vital business at hand.

Tension between president and Congress is of course built into the foundations of the American system of government. It was inevitably heightened by the unique Civil War situation. To fight that war, the federal government would have to extend its authority as never before, and conflict between president and Congress over the exercise and control of such powers was natural and even healthy. Lincoln firmly believed in the doctrine of the separation of powers; but he took a very comprehensive view of the war powers of the president, and was determined to keep the crucial matters – conduct of the war, slavery and reconstruction – under presidential control. He was a strong president in those fields which he believed to be essentially his concern, but a modest one elsewhere, notably respectful of Congressional rights in the field of legislation. He regarded executive and legislature as being each supreme in its own field; his major battles with Congress were fought over the boundary between them.

2. Many of those battles were fought with members of his own party. The wartime Republicans were, even by the standards of American political parties, a remarkable mixture of varied and seemingly incompatible ingredients. The party was after all still less than a decade old, and its unity in opposition to the further extension of slavery stood in contrast to wide disagreements, both on other aspects of the slavery question and on a variety of separate issues. It embraced ex-Whigs and ex-Democrats, former nativists and recent immigrants, protectionists and free traders, representatives of small-town and rural America along with spokesmen for the rising industrial and business interests, pioneers of the abolitionist crusade and cautious conservatives from the border states. Some historians see a hard-and-fast distinction between conservatives and radicals in the party, with the latter forming an identifiable and coherent bloc working in unison towards common ends. But this view achieves clarity at the expense of reality; no political party could ever aspire to such pristine simplicity in its internal make-up. It also leads to a facile identification of heroes and villains, for, if the radicals gave Lincoln so much trouble, then the implication is clear, they were not on the side of the angels. On the other hand, some historians have so blurred the lines of division in the party that the radicals have been completely lost in a historiographical fog, even though the term 'radical' was freely used and understood during the war itself. Again, one view has long seen Lincoln as locked in irreconcilable conflict with the radicals in his own party, while another sees the relationship as one of normal intra-party in-fighting, with the usual amount of give-and-take on both sides. Indeed, one recent interpretation regards Lincoln as basically sympathetic to the radicals, but intent, too, on coaxing or dragging moderates and conservatives into support for more radical measures.[3] Such varied accounts suggest the subtleties of Lincoln's management of his party, but they also suggest the need for an overall picture of some complexity, with plenty of variations of light and shadow. It should be a moving picture, too, to allow for changing attitudes and shifting align-ments. Clearly the radicals were not a solid phalanx, presenting a united front on every issue. Even the men to whom the label can be most confidently applied were a varied and disparate group, and their motives – idealism, vengeance, malice, personal or party advantage – were as mixed as their personalities.

Thaddeus Stevens of Pennsylvania, the most powerful man in the House of Representatives, domineering, dogmatic, acid-tongued and fiercely independent; in the Senate, Ben Wade of Ohio, and Zach Chandler of Michigan, the one rough, unpolished, with a hot temper and a cruel wit, the other boastful, aggressive, with a strong taste for liquor and for intrigue; and Charles Sumner of Massachusetts, elegant, aloof, intolerant, and insufferably condescending: such men as these were scarcely likely to work in close and constant harmony, even if they did share a similar attitude on some major issues. Only their most conservative opponents could have classified as members of a radical bloc senators like Lyman Trumbull of Illinois, or William Pitt Fessenden of Maine, who frequently advocated and supported radical measures, but were essentially too moderate to be comfortably bracketed with men of the stamp of Wade, Chandler and Stevens.

But the radicals cannot be eliminated, nor should the term 'radical' be discarded. It may be safer to apply it, however, to measures rather than men, to attitudes rather than to a bloc. One useful distinction which gets close to the heart of the matter is that the radical position tended to be more doctrinaire on most issues, and the moderate more pragmatic and flexible.[4] The difference between them was often a matter of temperament and timing, as much as priorities or principle. Slavery, with all its ramifications, was the dominant political issue, and, naturally, divisions over slavery were the most prominent of all. But even here the intra-party fight was less like static trench warfare than a free-for-all in which the line dividing the contestants frequently became confused. Men often changed positions or deviated from their regular course. Senator Pomeroy of Kansas, normally regarded as a radical, could yet work actively in the movement to colonise freed Negroes in Central America. Charles Sumner, surely a Radical if such people existed at all, gave his tacit consent to Lincoln's own moderate plan for gradual emancipation in 1862.

The conservatives and moderates in the party also embraced a wide variety of views on emancipation and other issues, and they had significant numerical strength in both houses of Congress. In practice, the Republicans in both houses generally maintained a high degree of party solidarity in votes on major issues, although, at least from 1862 onwards, the division between radical and conservative positions was usually clear and widely recognised. The cabinet was a markedly conservative body – Seward, Blair, Bates and Welles were more conservative and often less flexible on many issues than the president himself. Lincoln stood, not at the opposite end of the political spectrum from the Radical position, but generally in the middle. Even when the rival party factions took to entrenched positions, Lincoln himself was generally left in no man's land, and that was usually where he preferred to be. It could be a most uncomfortable place, but at least it was within hailing distance of both sides. If, by temperament and inclination, Lincoln took his stand in the middle, even this was far from a static position; the middle ground, like so much else, was shifted, sometimes gradually, sometimes suddenly, by the powerful forces of war and the explosive issue of slavery.

If the radical–conservative division is to retain any real meaning, it must be restricted to a few basic issues – the nature, purpose and conduct of the war, the proper attitude to the South and its future restoration to the Union, and the overriding question of slavery and emancipation. It cannot be applied with any consistency to the everyday economic issues of the mid-nineteenth century – the tariff, banking and currency questions, government aid to industry and railroads, and the like. Some 'radical' Republicans were not noticeably radical in their overall view of American society and politics, and votes in Congress showed no significant correlation between anti-slavery radicalism and a particular stance on such questions.[5]

Any attempt to define the nature and purpose of the war was complicated from the outset by the relative priority assigned to the defence of the Union as against the destruction of slavery. For most people in the North, the war began simply as a war for the Union; it was a war to achieve restoration, not revolution. This view, which Lincoln shared, was plainly expressed in July 1861 by the Crittenden Resolution which was almost unanimously accepted by Congress. It affirmed that:

> this war is not waged . . . in any spirit of oppression, or for any purpose of conquest or subjugation, or . . . of overthrowing or interfering with the rights or institutions of those seceded States, but to defend and maintain the supremacy of the Constitution, and to preserve the Union . . . and that as soon as these objects are accomplished the war ought to cease.[6]

Such a modest war aim was too fragile to survive in a long, bitter struggle, and within five months, indeed, the House of Representatives refused, in a close vote, to reaffirm its support for the resolution. The conservative view which it expressed based its hopes on wide support from all parties and sections of opinion in the North, on expectations of a short, limited war, waged with a minimum of bitterness and a maximum of restraint, and on restoring the Southern states to the Union, presumably with slavery still intact, but doomed to ultimate extinction. In contrast, the full-blown radical view favoured all-out war, waged not merely with vigour but with severity, for the purpose of destroying slavery, punishing the South, and remaking it in a new image. 'Free every slave – slay every traitor – burn every rebel mansion,' cried Thaddeus Stevens, 'if these things be necessary to preserve this temple of freedom.' Such purposes might well demand a long war, and such a struggle could be effectively waged only by leaders imbued with a proper zeal for the task – hence the constant radical attack on the conduct of the war, and, in particular, their campaign against Democrats and other undesirables, occupying high places in the army and navy, or any other position crucial to the war effort. This war was indeed too serious a matter to be left to the generals, especially Democratic generals, and generals were too politically important to be left alone to run the war.

Disagreements about the scope and purpose of the war were reflected, as time passed, in disagreements about the issues of slavery and reconstruction.[7] Always, the radicals and those who sounded like radicals had one advantage. Within the Republican party they could claim to be super-Republicans, the activists, the staunchest party men; before the people they could claim to be the super-patriots, the true zealots in the Northern cause, who charted the course which those with fainter hearts would sooner or later have to follow. And, as the war dragged on, it increasingly resembled their conception of it.

However, what was meat for the radicals was poison for the party in opposition, the Democrats. The pressures of the war were extremely damaging to a party already shorn of much of its numerical strength by the secession of the Southern states, and found guilty, in the eyes of many Northerners, by its long-standing Southern associations. The Democratic dilemma was that of any opposition party in wartime, but aggravated by the nature of this particular Civil War. How far could opposition be carried before it became disloyalty or treason? One possible way to achieve the status of an honourable and loyal opposition was to express criticism in constitutional terms, and to warn against the dangers of executive tyranny and arbitrary rule. In 1861 most Democrats and many moderate Republicans saw themselves as defenders of the *status quo*, but Democrats put the emphasis more on defence of the constitution, and Republicans more on defence of the Union. The problem of the Democrats can also be more bluntly defined in terms of party interest. To oppose the administration in time of Civil War might be regarded as playing party politics in a period of supreme national crisis, but to give full support to the administration would be equally unprofitable for the party, since the Republicans would – and did – gain all the political credit for a successful prosecution of the war.

'There can be no neutrals in this war, only patriots and traitors,' said Stephen A. Douglas shortly before his death in June 1861.[8] But even the most patriotic of Democrats faced difficult choices, and they reacted in diverse ways. The so-called 'War Democrats', giving unreserved support to the Union cause, allied themselves with the Republican administration, and often merged with the Republicans in 'Union' parties in various Northern states. The War Democrats brought an important accession of strength to the Republicans, and enabled them to make a closer identification of partisanship and patriotism – and War Democrats, put up as Union candidates, were valuable vote-catchers in crucial elections. The War Democrats included men like Andrew Johnson of Tennessee, Lincoln's running-mate in 1864, and his successor in 1865; Edwin Stanton, secretary of war from 1862 to the end of the war; Benjamin Butler of Massachusetts, who, like Stanton, had voted for the Southern Democrat, Breckinridge, in 1860, but who in the course of an erratic military career during the war moved into a strong radical position; and many others in Congress, in the army, and in every Northern state.

Not perhaps the most conspicuous Democrats, but almost certainly much the largest group among them, were the moderates who loyally supported a war to save the Union, but who were critical of the actual policies pursued by the administration. Their war aim was limited to restoration of the Union, and they attacked Lincoln and the Republicans on the actual conduct of the war, the slavery issue, the question of arbitrary rule and abuse of the constitution, and other specific matters. They came to believe that the war could not be satisfactorily concluded by the Republican administration, and in the election of 1864 they found their champion in General McClellan. Beyond this centre group were the Peace Democrats who believed that some kind of negotiated settlement with the South was both feasible and eminently desirable. Some insisted on the permanence of the Union, but, on the assumption that some compromise embracing peace and union could be arranged, saw no need for continuation of the war. Others, more extreme, were prepared for peace at almost any price – even a price which included recognition of Southern independence. Although few even of the Peace Democrats were clearly and blatantly disloyal, they were numerous enough, and noisy enough, to enable Republicans to pin the disloyalty tag on Democrats in general, and they included some conspicuous, or notorious, figures, like Jesse D. Bright of Indiana, who was expelled from the Senate on charges of disloyalty, and Clement L. Vallandigham of Ohio, who was to play a leading part in a *cause célèbre*, and a crucial election, in 1863. If Northern Democrats responded in various ways to the wartime situation, it should never be forgotten that, for many, party affiliation remained much as it had always been – a matter of tradition, habit, and geography, economic, ethnic or sectional interest. For the party as a whole, the war created grave embarrassment, but, as time went on, it also provided countervailing opportunities, as war weariness, frustration, disillusion, inflation, high taxation, and governmental interference took their toll on the electorate.[9]

3. Always, both parties were conscious that they must answer to the inexorable electoral timetable prescribed by the constitution. One of the wonders of the Civil War years is that it scarcely occurred to anyone that the regular electoral process should be abandoned or postponed. To hold Congressional, state and local elections in 1862 and 1864, and a presidential election, too, in the latter year, in the midst of a terrible civil conflict, was a truly astonishing testimonial to American political attitudes and institutions. The first major test at the ballot box came with the mid-term elections in the autumn of 1862. It took place at an unfavourable time for the Republicans. The war seemed nowhere near a victorious conclusion, and the discarding of McClellan and Buell, the army commanders in east and west, scarcely inspired confidence. Discontent and hostility towards the administration were heightened in September by the unpopularity in some quarters of the Emancipation Proclamation, and of another proclamation making sweeping extensions of the application of martial law and the suspension of the writ of habeas corpus. The election results were a

near disaster for the Republicans. In the key state of New York, the Democrat Horatio Seymour was elected governor; more serious still, the Democrats won a majority of House seats in five great states stretching across the North: New York, Pennsylvania, Ohio, Indiana and Illinois. Republicans may have found some consolation in the slender Democratic margin in the popular vote in most states – the split in Illinois, for example, was 53–47 per cent – and in the salvation of the Republican majorities in both houses of Congress by the results in New England, Michigan, Kansas and California, and by the election of some fifteen Union members in the border states, in contests held under strict military supervision. The new House of Representatives would have, according to one count, 102 Republicans and 'Unconditional Unionists', 75 Democrats and 9 others. If the Emancipation Proclamation had helped the Republicans in some areas it had hurt them in others, and Negrophobia was no doubt a factor, particularly in areas close to the South. But the result was due more to the accumulated stresses and strains, hardships and disappointments of the war, above all the lack of military success. The administration seemed to have no idea how to win the war, and many of the enthusiasts of April 1861 were now among the disillusioned of November 1862.

His party's rebuff at the polls was only the first of a series of blows which struck Lincoln in the closing weeks of 1862. In December, Congress reassembled in truculent mood, and then came news of Burnside's ignominious defeat at Fredericksburg on 12 December. Military and civilian morale fell into one of the deepest troughs of the whole war period; radicals, and not only radicals, felt that only a drastic shake-up in the administration could restore the situation. In attempting to achieve it, they provoked a battle for the control of the government, and a constitutional crisis.

The Republican Senators met in caucus on 16 and 17 December to discuss ways of putting new drive and purpose into the conduct of the war. It was even suggested that Lincoln be asked to resign, but the attack was mainly directed against his conservative cabinet advisers, and, above all, Seward, 'the evil genius', the 'unseen hand', whose unhealthy influence weakened the will of an already over-cautious president. The caucus eventually agreed unanimously to send a delegation of nine Senators to the President. It included Sumner, Wade, Fessenden and Trumbull, but chose the moderate Jacob Collamer as its spokesman. On 18 December the group met Lincoln, and Collamer read a statement demanding a 'vigorous and successful prosecution of the war', a unified and resolute cabinet which would be consulted on all issues, and cabinet changes to secure 'unity of purpose and action'. Other Senators openly and bluntly attacked Seward; Lincoln answered politely, even blandly, and committed himself to nothing. Seward had in fact already tendered his resignation, on hearing of the caucus, but on 19 December Lincoln asked the rest of the cabinet for their support and shrewdly suggested that they attend a second meeting with the delegation of Senators that same evening. The Senators were surprised and embarrassed by the presence of the cabinet officers – but less embarrassed than was Secretary of the Treasury Chase, who was in close touch with the Radicals and was widely believed to be involved in their schemes. In the discussion, Lincoln called for the opinions of cabinet members, and Blair and Bates supported him. So in effect did Chase himself, who offered a little modest criticism, but said there had been no want of unity in the cabinet, and even had a few words in praise of Seward. Baffled and angry, the Senators withdrew, having accomplished nothing, and next morning Chase himself, embarrassed and humiliated, offered his resignation. Lincoln took the letter from him with undisguised glee, exclaiming that 'this cuts the Gordian knot'. Not to be outdone, Stanton too offered to resign, only to be told: 'You may go to your Department, I don't want yours.' Lincoln had all he wanted. He could now make it plain that he would have both Seward and Chase in his cabinet, or he would have neither. In fact, he kept both. He also kept control over his own administration in what had been a crucial test of his will and power, and a unique confrontation between the executive and legislative branches of the government. His flair for managing individuals and coping with crises saved him in a situation which was in truth partly his own fault. When the crisis first broke, Lincoln had told Orville H. Browning: 'They wish to get rid of me, and I am sometimes half disposed to gratify them.' Five days later, when it was all over, Browning reported Lincoln as saying 'with a great deal of emphasis that he was the master'. Now he would go ahead and put the Emancipation Proclamation into force on 1 January 1863, and stand ready to meet future crises and challenges with added assurance.[10]

Lincoln, like his party and the Union itself, was showing an impressive talent for survival. Amid all the vicissitudes of the first two years of war, president and congress, state governors and legislators, Republicans and Democrats, continued to play something akin to the normal roles assigned to them by the political system. In so doing, they made a vital contribution to stability in the North. The war had not been won, but the North had the political, as well as the military and material, resources to achieve victory. It would be difficult to say the same of the South on any or all of these counts.

4. In the creation of their new government, Southerners displayed a harmony and a decisiveness which were happy but misleading auguries for their future. They had rapidly come to the conclusion that the consequences of secession were too serious a matter to be left to the more hotheaded secessionists, and the Montgomery Convention which wrote the new constitution and established the new government was dominated by moderates; indeed something like two delegates in five had originally opposed the secession of their own states. While a zealot like William L. Yancey could not gain a place in the Alabama delegation, Alexander H. Stephens of Georgia, who had opposed secession, and accepted his state's decision only reluctantly, could become one of the chief architects of the constitution and eventually vice-president of the Confederacy itself. The moderation of the convention is all the more remarkable in view of the absence of the states of the upper south which had still not seceded, but if

their restraining hand was not actually present in Montgomery, the delegates were anxious to do nothing which would deter them from joining the Confederate fold.

The Convention, made up of delegates from the six states of the deep south, later joined by Texas, opened its proceedings on 4 February 1861. Four days later it agreed upon a provisional constitution, based broadly upon the constitution of the United States, and intended to last only until a permanent constitution had been devised, ratified and inaugurated. The Convention then formed itself into the provisional Congress and got down to urgent business. Its first task was the election of a provisional president and vice-president. There were a number of candidates with significant support and even more who fancied their own chances. Fire-eaters like Yancey or Rhett found little favour in such a moderate assembly. Georgia had two strong contenders in Howell Cobb and Robert Toombs, but each tended to neutralise the prospects of the other, and many delegates found the one too bland and the other too bold. Some feared that Cobb was not dynamic or exciting enough to inspire the South, others that Toombs's energy and zeal owed too much to alchoholic stimulation. More and more of the state delegations turned their thoughts to another prominent candidate, Jefferson Davis of Mississippi, who enjoyed a high reputation both as a champion of Southern rights and as a man of moderation, dignity, and integrity. On 9 February Davis was unanimously elected president, and Georgia, whose two favourite sons had been denied the leading prize, was rewarded with the vice-presidency, which went, however, neither to Cobb nor Toombs, but to Alexander Stephens. Davis was not a member of the Montgomery Convention, and he was pottering in the rose garden of Brierfield, his Mississippi plantation, when he received official notification of his election. He had consistently forecast that the South would have to fight for its independence, and he aspired to military command rather than civil leadership in the Confederacy. But he was never a man to shirk a duty thrust upon him, and after some parting words to his family and his slaves, he left the tranquillity of Brierfield for the turmoil of Montgomery, and the years of nerve-racking toil which were to come.

Meanwhile, the delegates at Montgomery were hammering out a permanent constitution for the Confederacy. They saved time and preserved their claim to be the true interpreters of the principles of 1787 by taking the existing constitution of the United States as their model. But there were divergent views on how far that document needed to be rewritten. Here again, the more radical secessionists came off second best. Most of the alterations and amendments which were made were limited and very specific, and the alterations which were not made constituted an even greater victory for caution and restraint. The right of a state to secede was not spelt out in the new constitution, for fear that such a change might be interpreted as an admission of the doubtful legal basis of the secession which had already taken place. On 11 March the Montgomery convention completed five weeks of high-speed decision-making by accepting the permanent constitution and submitting it to the state conventions for ratification. One of the most remarkable features of all its work was that at no stage was the electorate asked for its opinion. The delegates had been chosen by the state conventions; they had then taken it upon themselves to become the legislative body under the provisional constitution – much to the consternation of states which had arranged or actually held congressional elections; they had then proceeded to choose a provisional president and vice-president, and to draft a permanent constitution, which, in its turn, was not put to the popular vote. The need for quick action in a crisis was the best justification for such a course; indeed, it was unfortunate for the South that the readiness to take political and constitutional short cuts proved so short-lived. Never again would Confederate leaders get away with so much so easily.

The great bulk of the permanent Confederate constitution was a carbon copy of the work of the Founding Fathers of 1787. This makes all the more interesting and revealing those articles and clauses which it was felt necessary to amend, delete or add. Predictably, these were mainly concerned with the protection of slavery, the bolstering of states rights, and the limitation of the powers of the central government, in the interests of economy and accountability, as well as the defence of the rights of states and individual citizens. The Confederate constitution used the words 'slave' and 'slavery' freely in place of the ponderous circumlocutions by which the men of 1787 had avoided it. It ruled out any law denying or impairing the right of property in Negro slaves, and guaranteed the protection of slavery in any territories of the Confederacy. It retained the old three-fifths ratio as the basis of representation in the lower house of Congress, but it explicitly banned the foreign slave trade, partly as a sop to world opinion. For all its silence on the right of secession, the constitution buttressed state rights in other important ways. In the very first sentence of its preamble, it qualifies the words 'We, the People of the Confederate States' with the phrase 'each State acting in its sovereign and independent character'. The powers which the United States constitution 'granted' to Congress were merely 'delegated' to that body in the Confederate document. A state legislature was given the power to impeach certain federal officers acting solely within the limits of the state concerned. The other side of the coin of states rights was restriction of the authority of the central government. Here the Montgomery constitution was very specific. It eliminated the power of Congress to provide for the general welfare, which had been one of the great agents of the growth of federal authority in the decades before 1860. It banned the imposition of a protective tariff and the appropriation of funds for all but the most minor internal improvements. It put the initiative in amending the constitution entirely in the hands of the states. A number of new provisions were designed to cut out waste and extravagance in the operations of the government and to keep a tighter control on expenditure. The executive branch was affected by other changes, too, notably the restriction of the president to one six-year term. One interesting innovation – and a small step towards a parliamentary system – (never in fact applied in practice) was the provision that the head of each executive department might be granted by Congress a seat in either house to discuss measures relating to his department.[11]

All in all, the new constitution reflected past experience rather than future needs. It erected a framework for a government of Jeffersonian frugality and strictly circumscribed authority; it was emphatically not an instrument for the effective direction and coordination of a struggle for survival. This may have derived from the innocent belief that independence could be won without bloodshed but a much more convincing explanation is that the delegates at Montgomery were more interested in settling old scores than waging new wars. The one great practical advantage of the new constitutional skeleton was that it could be immediately covered with the flesh of existing legal, institutional and personal resources. The state governments and courts were already going concerns, and the Confederacy simply took over the whole corpus of United States law lock, stock and barrel, with the exception of any acts explicitly repealed or held to be in conflict with the new constitution. (Although the constitution provided for a supreme court, Southern fears and memories of past experience prevented its actual establishment.) Most government offices and officers simply exchanged the old allegiance for the new. The most remarkable case was that of the Post Office, where the United States maintained its service until the end of May. On 1 June the same men carried on with the same tasks in the Post Office of the Confederate States of America.

At the end of May the new administration took the long train journey from Montgomery to Richmond, to establish its permanent home amid the more adequate but still hard-pressed amenities of the Virginian capital. The provisional Congress reconvened at Richmond in July, and the provisional gave way to the permanent régime when Davis and Stephens were elected unopposed in November 1861 as president and vice-president, and when they and the two houses of Congress elected at the same time began their terms of office under the new constitution in February 1862.

5. The Confederate government took its structure from the men who drafted its constitution, but its character from the men who ran it. All the evidence in 1861 suggested that Jefferson Davis was splendidly equipped to preside over the new régime. His West Point training and his gallant Mexican War record apparently fitted him for the leadership of a people at arms. His service in both houses of Congress in Washington amply testified to his stout defence of Southern interests, and his right of apostolic succession to the pope of Southern rights, John C. Calhoun. His four years as secretary for war under Franklin Pierce served to demonstrate his administrative capacity and underline his military expertise. His undoubted courage, dedication, rectitude, industry and determination seemed to offer a combination of qualities at least as good as those of any other Southern leader, and much better than most. But the expectations of early 1861 were only partly fulfilled in the months and years which

followed. No fair critic ever doubted his devotion to the cause, although malicious tongues sometimes labelled him a 'reconstructionist' or even a traitor. No one could have decried his prodigious labours, even if they were rewarded all too often with charges of weakness and imbecility on the one hand, or dictatorship on the other. In a comparison with the general run of nineteenth-century presidents and what was expected of them, he might well have emerged with honour, but such a criterion had little meaning in 1861. The real faults and shortcomings of Davis were revealed as he measured himself against the mountainous problems which confronted him. Whereas Lincoln, against all expectation, grew with the terrible responsibilities which he bore, Davis struggled to maintain his old, not inconsiderable, stature under even more crushing burdens. He was admirably stoical, but stoicism was not enough.

His bearing, manner and air of *gravitas* ensured that Davis always looked the part of president, but he lacked the magnetism to make himself the inspiring personal symbol of the Confederate cause. For all the warmth of his family life, and the charm which he exerted over close friends, Jefferson Davis the public figure lacked both humour and humanity. He inspired respect rather than affection, and attacks on him were more often sharpened by bitterness than softened by laughter. He was mercilessly assailed by some sections of the press, notably the Richmond *Examiner* and the Charleston *Mercury*, which vied with one another in vitriolic excess. More revealing and more serious perhaps was the fact that Davis inspired no editorial comment at all in many papers for months on end.[12] The *Southern Illustrated News* printed numerous cartoons depicting the Baboon Abe, but not a single one in which Davis appeared. No publicity was worse than bad publicity in facing one of the major tasks of the first president of the Confederacy: to rally popular support for a new government and a new nation, to create a new focus of loyalty, and to encourage Southerners to look beyond the county seat and the state capital for leadership and a sense of common identity. To the man in the street or on the farm (or in uniform) Davis too often seemed a remote, eminently respectable, earnest, sometimes tedious, sometimes irritating figure, and his deep human feelings remained masked by a natural reserve, an air of aloofness and a strong sense of the dignity of his office and himself.

These same qualities marred his personal relations with cabinet officers and state governors, generals and legislators. As a politician he was deficient in tact and flexibility, and over-endowed with pride and sensitivity. He was too often more concerned to prove the logic, and the legal and moral right of his case than to solve the problem under discussion by bargain and compromise. One critic thought that he prized consistency too highly,[13] and many felt that he took criticism too personally. His judgments of men were often too black or white – and unshakable once made – with the result that he found it hard to work with men who enjoyed less than his full approval, and he showed undying loyalty to those who found favour with him, even when, like Bragg or Northrop, they had become millstones round his neck. He lived on his nerves, and paid the price in the neuralgia, blinding headaches, dyspepsia, insomnia, and bouts of irritation and petulance which punctuated his years as president.

As an administrator, he was diligent and thorough, and more orderly and systematic than his counterpart in Washington. But he was also fussy and meddlesome, and constantly bogged down in endless consultations and a welter of detail. Delegation of responsibility did not come easily to him, especially in matters which he found interesting or deemed important, and he plodded through mountains of paper work, much of it 'little trash which ought to be dispatched by clerks', according to one War Department official. 'Napoleon gave attention to details,' wrote the same observer. 'But he dispatched them; he touched and the work was done. . . . Mr Davis is a slow, very slow worker.'[14] He lacked a proper sense of priorities, the ability so crucial in a chief executive to distinguish what really mattered from what did not.

The Confederate cabinet too often magnified rather than mitigated the president's shortcomings. Its membership did not remotely compare with Lincoln's cabinet in quality and prestige; it drew but little upon the front rank of Southern political leadership. This was not because Davis chose to surround himself with pygmies (although he would never have relished such weighty and strong-minded counsellors as Chase, Stanton and Seward) but rather because many leading Southerners saw little future in cabinet office, and preferred to seek glory on the field of battle or a more independent position in Congress. Only one of Davis's original choices actually filled the office for which he was selected. Choice was dictated not merely by presidential preference or the willingness of the chosen to serve, but by the need to satisfy state pride. Later changes in personnel resulted from a mixture of individual frustration, congressional attacks, and inability to get on with the president. The alleged instability of the Confederate cabinet is, however, only a half-truth. Two men held on to the same posts throughout: John H. Reagan, the postmaster-general, and Stephen R. Mallory, secretary of the navy. Reagan was a bluff, down-to-earth Texan who spoke his mind but still contrived to get along with Davis. He fully accepted the constitutional requirement that the postal service should be financially self-supporting by March 1863, and he made it pay by dispensing with large parts of the service altogether – a technique which has its twentieth-century disciples. Mallory faced an impossible task but made the best of it, and showed something of the inventiveness and flair for the unorthodox which most of his colleagues so conspicuously lacked. The Treasury Department had only one change during the war, and that not until 1864, when Christopher Memminger gave way to his fellow South Carolinian, George A. Trenholm. The German-born Memminger was better versed in financial matters than most of his fellow Confederates, but he was too orthodox and conventional for such an extraordinary situation, and he had no talent for public relations or liaison with Congress.

There was a much more rapid turnover in the three remaining departments. Out of sixteen cabinet appointments in all, twelve were in the War, State and

Justice Departments. The office of Attorney-General was little coveted and offered little scope. Its first holder, Judah P. Benjamin, moved on to higher things, and was succeeded in turn by Thomas Bragg, Thomas H. Watts and George Davis. The State Department offered almost equal frustration, for, as long as foreign countries refused the Confederacy diplomatic recognition, it had little business to transact and little foreign policy of the conventional kind to pursue. 'The busy idleness of the State Department'[15] had few attractions for its first secretary, Robert Toombs, who resigned in July 1861 to join the army. His successor, R. M. T. Hunter of Virginia, lasted a little longer, but preferred the role of Senator when the permanent constitution came into force in February 1862. For the rest of the war, the office was held by Judah P. Benjamin, and it suited him perfectly in that the very nature and limitation of his departmental duties enabled him to play the role of presidential adviser and confidant over the whole field of government business. Benjamin was probably the ablest member of the cabinet and certainly the most untypical. Born in the British West Indies, he came to the United States as a boy, made his fortune through his law practice in New Orleans and served as a Senator from Louisiana in the 1850s. In three different cabinet posts he won Davis's confidence, and exerted increasing influence over him. He had many of the qualities which the president lacked – flexibility, astuteness, tact, subtlety, humour, and bargaining skill. He solved some of the president's more delicate problems, and shielded him from others. To some people his influence seemed sinister and unhealthy; his widespread unpopularity was inspired by distrust and jealousy – and by antisemitism. In the words of T. C. DeLeon, 'the map of the Holy City was traced all over his small, refined face'.[16] When Davis was confirmed in the Episcopal Church, J. B. Jones expressed relief in his diary that the president might thus be saved from unchristian influences.[17]

The frustrations of cabinet office arose partly from the small scale of many departments and their inability to make any real impact on affairs. The State Department in Richmond had a staff of seven at full strength, the Justice Department fourteen, even the Navy Department only sixteen.[18] It was small wonder that ambitious and status-conscious public figures sought employment elsewhere. The War Department on the other hand presented a very different picture. Its civilian staff in Richmond rose to over 250, and its various bureaux and agencies eventually employed over 50,000 workers. It was never likely to be plagued by a sense of insignificance, but its successive heads had any number of other headaches, deriving from the scale and intractability of their problems, and their awkward relationship with the president. Davis allowed many of his cabinet officers a fairly free hand, and was perhaps too willing not to bother himself with tedious but crucial problems like those of the Treasury. But, convinced of his military abilities, he interfered constantly in the detailed affairs of the War Department, and consequently ran through five secretaries of war in four years. The first, Leroy P. Walker of Alabama, like Simon Cameron in the North, knew little of warfare and its problems, and simply lacked the dynamism and administrative ability which the situation demanded. According to one of Mrs Chesnut's sharp-tongued friends, if Heaven had sent the South Napoleon, Walker would have refused to grant him a commission.[19] In September 1861 Benjamin took over from Walker, and created some semblance of order, but he too 'knew as much about war as an Arab knows of the Sermon on the Mount'.[20] His despatches upset a number of generals, for he was much less tactful on paper than in person, and the defeats of early 1862 made him so unpopular that Davis removed him to the shelter of the State Department. His successor was George W. Randolph, grandson of Thomas Jefferson, who boasted not merely impeccable lineage but some military knowledge. He handled the early enforcement of conscription with some success, and remained on good terms with Davis for a while largely by submitting to his wishes. The president's reaction to his first show of independence in November 1862 led to his resignation. He was replaced by another Virginian, James A. Seddon, who, like both Walker and Randolph, was plagued by ill-health. But his frail appearance was deceptive, and he was the longest-serving and most successful holder of his office, and, for a year at least, had a distinct influence on the president's military thinking. He finally resigned early in 1865, and was followed by John C. Breckinridge, ex-vice-president of the United States, and presidential candidate in 1860, who soon decided that, with the Confederacy collapsing all around him, it was futile to remain at his desk, and took himself off to the front line.

The sorry story of the Confederate War Department revealed all the worst features of the administration and of the man who headed it. There was no adequate coordination between departments and agencies, and Davis's own constant involvement was no substitute for a proper system. There was a narrowness of outlook and a lack of vision and imagination at all levels from top to bottom. With but few exceptions, the administration was filled by conventional men, set in their ways, ill-prepared to find unorthodox solutions to unprecedented problems. There was a great deal of confusion and red tape, and 'cumbrous inefficiency', in Eggleston's phrase.[21] Perhaps the Southern way of life had set too little store by business methods and produced too few organisation men. Certainly the men just below the departmental heads were no match for their Northern opposite numbers. There was too little of the right kind of leadership, inspiring, positive, dynamic and daring. With excessive harshness, perhaps, J.B. Jones recorded that 'never before did such little men rule such a great people. Our rulers are like children or drunken men riding docile horses, that absolutely keep the riders from falling off by swaying to the right and left, and preserving an equilibrium.'[22] It was ironic that the South, which had long prided itself on its tradition of statesmanship, should thus be found wanting. But Southern political leaders were trained in the skills of legislative debate and legal hairsplitting, in the tactics of obstruction rather than the tasks of construction, in preventing rather than initiating positive action. They were obsessed with questions of pride and punctilio and honour; throughout the government, said Eggleston, 'there was everywhere a morbid sensitiveness on the subject of personal dignity, and an exaggerated regard for routine'.[23] While faces were being saved, lives were being lost. This may have been a new government in a novel situation, but its leaders were still desperately clinging to old familiar ways, although sheer necessity steadily drove them to adopt new ones. Jefferson Davis and most of his advisers were too conventionally and characteristically Southern to meet the new and urgent needs of the South.

6. In Congress, too, ingrained habits of independence, obstruction and suspicion died hard, and the legislative branch of the government reflected all too faithfully some of the internal weaknesses of the Confederacy. The provisional Congress which was the continuation in a new guise of the Montgomery convention lasted for a year. It held several short sessions in Montgomery and then in Richmond, and grew steadily in size as delegations arrived from the states of the upper south. Its membership was of distinctly higher calibre than its successors, and it showed a sense of urgency and responsibility which they did not always match. In the autumn of 1861, when elections for the first permanent Congress were held, campaigning was in a low key, and polling generally light. There were no clear-cut party lines, and most districts conformed to their pre-secession voting habits. In choosing senators, some state legislatures scrupulously selected one ex-Democrat and one ex-Whig. (In the remarkable elections in Tennessee, it was left to the winners to decide whether to head for Richmond or Washington.) By the time that elections came round again in autumn 1863, there were still no organised parties, but there was a clear-cut issue – the record of the Davis administration – and the president received a rebuff to match the one inflicted on his Union counterpart in the mid-term elections of 1862.

The members of the various Confederate congresses were men of political experience, if not always of distinction.[24] Almost two-thirds had served in their state legislatures, almost one-third in the United States Congress. There were more ex-Democrats than ex-Whigs, and a clear majority of all congressmen had been supporters of secession in 1860–1, although well over a third had not. The planter class was strongly represented; 40 per cent of members owned twenty slaves or more while only a handful owned none at all. Common social background, and ties of kinship, friendship, and business and political experience among many members might well have created a sense of solidarity and camaraderie, but the remarkably high turnover of members worked in the opposite direction. Only 46 out of 146 members of the first permanent Congress had served in the provisional legislature, and in the second Congress, almost 40 per cent of members were newcomers. Apart from the normal casualties at the polls, many politicians found congressional life frustrating, depressing or unrewarding, many hankered after military glory, and some preferred to stay at home rather than face two more years in overcrowded, expensive, uncomfortable Richmond. Only twenty-seven men served in the Confederate Congress from start to finish.

Neither Congress nor congressmen enjoyed any great prestige, and their own behaviour was partly to blame. There was a great deal of procrastination, procedural wrangling, ponderous oratory and preoccupation with trifles while the enemy was almost at the gate. There was not a little disorder and ruffianism, some of it inspired by wounded pride, some by rancorous personal feuds, some by excessive consumption of alcohol. In a famous Senate incident, Benjamin H. Hill of Georgia hit William L. Yancey on the head with a well-aimed inkstand, and was restrained by colleagues before he could follow up with a chair. The lower house was disfigured by several violent incidents, more than one of which involved the truculent Henry S. Foote of Tennessee, who was once attacked by a colleague with a bowie knife. The Senate was scarcely edified by the spectacle of an outraged lady horsewhipping Senator George Vest of Missouri in the lobby, before addressing a few words to the assembled legislators on the nature of her grievance. The inevitable crowd of lobbyists, job-hunters and speculators did little to improve the tone, and the high level of absenteeism among the members was a revealing comment on both Congress and themselves. The popular image of Congress was not helped by the frequent resort to secret sessions which suggested that both legislature and executive had much to hide.

For all its faults, however, the Confederate Congress had a legislative record which is not so black as it is sometimes painted. In the first two years of the war, at least, it gave the administration most of what it wanted, on the important issues, although often so grudgingly and slowly and with so many quibbles over detail as to destroy any idea of harmonious cooperation. It did enact a mass of legislation, some of it unpopular, much of it totally out of step with Southern (or American) tradition. A Congress which passed the conscription act by large majorities, or which accepted, however belatedly, the need for an impressment law, cannot be dismissed as completely obstructive or negative. In the provisional Congress, and in the first elected House of Representatives, only about one-fifth of the members had a consistent anti-administration voting record. There was some sniping at Davis from the start, but it was only during 1862, as the effects of the war really began to bite, and tougher measures were demanded, that administration policy became the clear dividing line between members. But relations between the two branches of the government were never cordial or close. Davis was inclined to adopt a rather lofty tone towards Congress, and some members of his cabinet showed it little respect, and became favourite targets for attack in its halls. The administration had its loyal and consistent champions – Benjamin H. Hill, Howell Cobb, Clement C. Clay, and James Phelan in the Senate, Ethelbert Barksdale and J. L. M. Curry in the House – but the difficulties of their task were often aggravated by the attitude of Davis himself, and Curry, for one, suffered for his loyalty at the polls in 1863. At the other extreme were the constant critics, including neurotic Davis-haters like Foote in the House, and the president's erstwhile supporter, the fiery Louis T. Wigfall of Texas, in the Senate. There were always members willing to make mischief, whether by investigations of military defeats, adoption of the claims or the grievances of particular generals (there was a strong Joseph E. Johnston clique in Congress, for example) or attacks on alleged presidential favourites like Commissary-General Northrop. There was always the temptation, too, to play to the gallery at home by unyielding defence of state and local interests. There is even a suspicion that some members gave their votes to plainly irresponsible but popular measures, and relied on a presidential veto to save them from the consequences. Davis obliged on over thirty occasions.

After a visit to Richmond, Howell Cobb wrote: 'What is wanting in Richmond is "*brains*". I did not find the temper and disposition of Congress as bad as I expected, but there is a lamentable want of brains and good, sound common sense.'[25] Also lacking was any machinery which could give 'brains' and common sense a chance to take over. This applied not merely to Congress but to every level of Confederate politics. It was not so much the structure of Confederate politics which was wrong, as the infrastructure. The differences between the constitutional systems of South and North were marginal, but the one was no more than a skeleton while the other had flesh and muscle, a nervous system and a circulatory system which gave it strength and life, purpose and coordination. What the South desperately needed, but could not create in the feverish atmosphere of war, was some kind of organisation, whether of parties or some substitute for them, which could make the various limbs of government move together, which could keep open lines of communication, supplement formal structures with informal contacts, and massage the stiff joints of the whole system. Davis and his administration lacked a solid political base, and did not fully perceive the need to create one. Their policies became the touchstone of congressional debate and electoral rivalry, but they had no machinery to build up, consolidate and mobilise their strength either in Congress or in the country. Their opponents suffered in the same way – and the administration and the whole Confederacy suffered from the incoherent and unorganised state of the opposition. Critics have sometimes sniped at Lincoln for the time he spent in making minor appointments or worrying about local elections. The Confederacy might have been a sturdier growth, if Jefferson Davis had had the opportunity, and seen the necessity, to do the same.

7. Opposition to the Davis administration was the product of a corrosive blend of principles, personalities and parochialism. In the first two years of the war, the wounds which it inflicted on the Confederate war effort were painful but rarely more than skin deep; later it was to gnaw at the very vitals of its battered and weakened victim. It found nourishment in every region of the Confederacy, and infected every level of society. Indeed, one of its most influential leaders was the vice-president of the Confederacy, Alexander H. Stephens. A tiny, sickly, neurotic but extremely gifted man, Stephens matched Davis in pride, sensitivity, self-righteousness and lack of humour, but had little in common with him in political background and outlook. He was a Whig who had shrunk from the brink of secession as long as he could and accepted it when there was no alternative. A somewhat surprising choice as vice-president, he devoted

most of his energies during the war to the elaborate and unflagging defence of states rights against the encroachments of the central government in which he held the second place. He was for long periods an absentee vice-president; in the two years from October 1862, he made only two brief visits to Richmond. He preferred to remain at home in Georgia, at the centre of a group of states-rights critics of the government, which included Robert Toombs, Joseph E. Brown, and his brother Linton Stephens who declared in 1862 that 'I would as soon undertake to guard the chastity of a whore as to save the consciences of our rulers'.[26]

It is significant that Stephens chose to operate not from Richmond but from his home base. Neither the vice-president nor the Davis-baiters and haters in Congress could coordinate and unify the forces which opposed the adminis-tration's policies. There were plenty of critics of the government in the capital but they were not woven into the pattern of normal political life in the way that was second nature to the political society of Washington. In such a situation, leadership of the opposition devolved upon men in various parts of the country who had a secure political base and firm roots in the local community. The state governors were perhaps best placed of all to seize the initiative. Their office put them in a position to be a real help or a serious hindrance to the Confederate government, but in the nature of things effective cooperation between them could only be a response to a positive lead from the centre, and opposition from them was likely to be negative and divisive, and dictated by local interests and particular grievances. The great strength of the state governor was that he occupied a familiar office at the head of an established government which had long been a focal point of loyalty and political activity – and the very process of secession had given a new boost to state prestige as well as state sovereignty. When war came, the state authorities gained a new awareness of their own importance as they took the lead in raising, organising and equipping troops. As the war went on, both governors and legislatures found themselves taking on new functions, and invading more and more areas of the daily life of their citizens. They raised troops, restricted crops, promoted new industries and regulated old ones, ran blockade-running enterprises, and provided for the relief of the families of the men in grey. Legislatures roused themselves from their old lethargic routine of infrequent and short-lived sessions, and governors were less and less inclined to bow to the demands or even the polite requests of outside authority.

All this wartime development rested on the firm foundation of traditional Southern devotion to states rights. It was remarkable how such dry constitutional principle had become charged with a popular emotion verging on fanaticism. Many a Southern town had its States Rights Street, and many a Southern child was burdened by his fervent parents with the handicap of bearing the name States Rights through life. The doctrine had become a trusty weapon forged in the fires of decades of sectional controversy, and many Southerners refused to cast it aside in the hour of crisis, even though they now had their own

Southern government, and they were engaged in a fight for common survival. The doctrine also reflected many of the realities of Southern life. In most areas, Southern society was still extremely localised, and decentralised; the population was widely scattered, communications were often poor, and horizons were narrow. For some, daily life was lived within the confines of the plantation and one or two of its neighbours; for others, it was limited to the farm, and the local community of small farmers. First-hand knowledge and experience might stretch no further than the local court house, the nearest market or wharf or church. For such people, even the state government might seem distant, but it still had some meaning, some relevance to daily life. A remote authority, whether in Washington or Richmond, was viewed with indifference as long as it left individual citizens alone, and with suspicion and hostility when it did not. In such a society, states rights was more than an abstract theory; it was a congenital condition.

Confronted with the choice between cherished principles and the imperatives of wartime emergency, many Southerners either plumped for the former, or refused to recognise any conflict between the two. In the words of Governor Joseph E. Brown of Georgia,

> I am satisfied that my position is the position of the old State Rights leaders from the days of 1798 to the present time, and I am willing to stand or fall by these doctrines. I entered into this revolution to contribute my humble mite to sustain the rights of the states and prevent the consolidation of the Government, and I am still a rebel till this object is accomplished, no matter who may be in power.[27]

Those who took a more practical view (or a view from Richmond) of wartime needs were banging their heads against a wall of dogma. Ideally, the Richmond government should have mobilised these huge reserves of state loyalty and pride to serve the common cause, but the task called for a measure of tact and discretion, and political skill, far beyond Davis and his administration – and probably anyone else. The president's irritability and his insistence on standing on the precarious pedestal of his own dignity did not help matters, but personal foibles were not the root of the matter. For their part, the state governors presented a varied picture, and compiled a mixed record. There is no need to doubt the loyalty of any of them to the cause of Southern independence, but some wanted to enjoy the fruits of freedom before the crop was safely harvested, some were obsessed to the exclusion of all else by state and local interests as they saw them, a few perhaps were swayed by their vested interest in preserving their own power and position. The story is really eleven different stories of eleven different states, but a few generalisations are possible. Cooperation with Richmond was at its best in the earlier stages of the war, and broke down later as pressures intensified and grievances mounted. States which stood in the front line of battle – Virginia above all – were more likely to be cooperative than those relatively untroubled, at least in the earlier years of the war. States which included parts of the Appalachian region and produced governors hailing from that area were in the vanguard of protest against the despotism of the Davis administration. All the states had their grievances against Richmond, but the majority learned to live with them, and to maintain a measure of cooperation with the central authority. No governor was Davis's yes-man, but, to varying degrees, men like John Milton of Florida, J. J. Pettus and Charles Clark of Mississippi, Thomas O. Moore and Henry W. Allen of Louisiana, and Milledge Bonham of South Carolina managed to achieve a reasonable working relationship with the Richmond government.

The most troublesome states by far were Georgia and North Carolina, joined later in the war by South Carolina when its early enthusiastic devotion to the Confederate cause had waned. It is no coincidence that, apart from their coastal areas, these were the three states remotest from the war during its first two years and more, and safest from Union invasion. States rights were a luxury which they could still afford. Georgia was probably safest of all until the end of 1863, and it had the strongest group of states rights champions. Its governor throughout the war, Joseph E. Brown, came from the poor hill country of northern Georgia, had a flair for stump speaking, and many of the attributes of the successful demagogue. He had been an ardent secessionist, and had welcomed the choice of Jefferson Davis as president. He had his brushes with Davis from the moment the first Georgia regiments were raised, but it is also true that no governor worked more enthusiastically for the cause in the early months. However, his vision seldom extended far beyond his native state, and the coming of conscription in 1862 permanently soured his relations with Richmond. He engaged in a long, acrimonious correspondence with Davis (in which, it must be said, the president was reduced to using constitutional justifications of central authority which he and other Southerners had condemned before 1861).[28] He combined mastery of the arts of obstruction and non-cooperation with skill in preserving his political base in Georgia.

North Carolina had always been something of an odd-man-out in the roll call of Southern states – a society mainly of small farmers with fewer large plantations than its neighbours, and with a large area of hill and mountain country in the western half of the state. It suffered from something of an inferiority complex and made much during the war of the unduly small number of senior army officers from the state, or the appointment of officers from other states to command North Carolina troops. In 1862 the youthful Zebulon B. Vance was elected governor. Initially a supporter of conscription, he turned increasingly against it as grievances over its enforcement accumulated. Vance managed to combine a real devotion to the Confederate cause with a passionate concern for the rights and interests of North Carolina (and a somewhat blinkered view of strategy and military priorities). His very energy and skill in caring for the needs of his state and its troops were eventually to make him a grave embarrassment to the Confederate cause as a whole. He is an excellent example of the capacity of many Southerners to combine ardour for states rights with a sense of Southern identity, without thinking out the conflicting implications of the two causes.

States rights, in fact, was both a treasured principle in itself and a convenient vehicle for articulating opposition to particular policies of the administration. With or without states rights dogma, and obstreperous state governors, the basic wartime issues would have been there just the same. Conscription, impressment of supplies, suspension of habeas corpus, control of blockade-running, these would have been highly sensitive political issues in any case. But defence of states rights proved to be an effective means by which the aggrieved and discontented could present their case. It attracted sympathy, and gave sometimes dubious arguments the imprimatur of hallowed Southern tradition. From the standpoint of the government and the Confederacy as a whole, it was an unfortunate and dangerous way to conduct an argument. It encouraged people to take entrenched positions, it reinforced tendencies towards parochialism, and it made the Richmond government appear 'un-Southern' in resisting such honoured principles. Above all, it tended to convert any petty grievance or trifling complaint into a matter of principle. After all, protests over conscription or impressment often concerned some specific injustice or abuse in the manner of their enforcement, rather than the principle underlying the law itself, but a Vance or a Brown or a Stephens could quickly turn such problems into a sinister threat to basic Southern rights by the despot Davis.

Davis and his administration faced one dilemma after another. They needed to attract popular support to a new and unfamiliar government, and make themselves the symbol of the spirit of Southern nationalism, while still respecting sacred states rights principles and the deeply-rooted loyalties of citizens to their own states. The task of promoting Southern nationalism was the kind of propaganda and public relations exercise which did not come naturally to Davis, but it was none the less important for that. State loyalty was an old and com-fortable habit; Southern nationalism was a new fashion which needed every encouragement from its designers and promoters. Such tasks were often over-ridden by the more obviously urgent priorities of making war. But making war brought the administration back to the delicate issue of states rights. Inevitably, perhaps, Davis often found himself talking states rights while acting like the head of a centralised national government engaged in a desperate conflict. By any standard of earlier experience and tradition, the Confederacy made astonishing strides towards central control, and government regulation and intervention, during the war. But the political cost was heavy, and there always remained the lurking suspicion that even these giant steps were too little and too late – and that authority on paper was not always matched by capacity to use it effectively, or popular willingness to accept it. A people for whom governmental interference in their daily lives had never been a reality was by mid-war faced with a government which touched their lives more and more, and in ways almost without exception unpleasant. To many Southerners, the Confederate government meant in fact the men who conscripted their menfolk, rounded up deserters, impressed their supplies, and collected their taxes. When the war began to go badly, and Union armies penetrated deep into the South, internal stresses and strains would grow too. Then, the Confederate government would face a crisis of confidence and authority at home as well as one of survival on the field of battle.

8. There were clear parallels in the emerging shape and pattern of Northern and Southern politics in the first half of the war. Both administrations faced fierce criticism, and both might be fairly depicted as pragmatists fighting off the onslaughts of doctrinaires. Lincoln followed a complicated route between radical demands on the one hand, and the arguments of constitutional purists on the other. Davis attended to the practical business of war while paying his respects to traditional principles of states rights. But if, in both North and South, there was conflict between the pragmatism of those in government and the dogmatism of those in opposition, the development and ultimate resolution of the problem were very different in each case. In the first place, the strongest and most influential Northern critics were goading the president into a tougher, all-out prosecution of the war; Davis faced men who obstructed the war effort in crucial ways. Lincoln's critics made life uncomfortable, Davis's made it impossible. Secondly, opposition to Lincoln was regulated by the mechanism of party which, if it did not solve conflict, at least made it manageable. Opposition to Davis, if it was channelled at all, flowed through the divergent streams of states rights which did not solve problems and often made then insoluble. Then, too, the North had a president who cared little for his own dignity, who was a master of the political arts and who believed that the practice of those arts was one of his vital contributions to the war effort. The South had a president excessively concerned with matters of status and honour, not flexible enough in his political ways, and too often unmindful of the necessity (and dubious of the propriety) of behaving like a politician at such a time. Lincoln, moreover, was defending an established government, Davis struggling to establish a new one.

By mid-war, in the North, defence of the Union and emancipation of the slaves had each become a means towards the achievement of the other. No such profitable relationship existed in the Confederacy. The movement for Southern independence had been launched in protest against overbearing central authority, but the fight for independence demanded a strong new central authority. The ultimate goal had to be compromised to provide the means to achieve it, or the most effective means had to be sacrificed to preserve the purity of the goal. The North was achieving a harmony of means and ends which the South could not match.

# Chapter IX : Emancipation

In August 1862 a group of free Negroes found themselves face to face with the president of the United States inside the White House. Such a meeting was striking enough in itself but more remarkable still was the tone of Lincoln's words to his somewhat bewildered audience. With more frankness than tact, he pointed to 'our present condition – the country engaged in war! – our white men cutting one another's throats, none knowing how far it will extend; and then consider what we know to be the truth. But for your race among us there could not be war, although many men engaged on either side do not care for you one way or the other. Nevertheless, I repeat, without the institution of Slavery and the colored race as a basis, the war could not have an existence.'[1] Frederick Douglass later commented that Lincoln's argument was like a horse thief pleading the existence of the horse as an apology for his theft.[2] The starkness of Lincoln's language no doubt merited the rebuke, but, if read as a statement of fact and not as an attempt to apportion blame, his words were no more than the sad truth. Even those like the president himself who had hitherto found it convincing, or at least convenient, to argue that the Union and not slavery was the nub of the matter, knew full well that the two questions could not indefinitely be treated in neat, separate compartments, and that the war for the Union could scarcely leave slavery untouched.

There was no shortage of Northern voices (mainly from his own party) to remind the president that an attack on slavery was both a logical means of waging war against the South and a highly desirable end in itself. Within days of Lincoln's address to the free Negroes, Horace Greeley, editor of the *New York Tribune*, warned him publicly that 'all attempts to put down the rebellion and at the same time uphold its inciting cause are preposterous and futile'.[3] The part played by the Negro slaves inside the Confederacy provided ample evidence to back up Greeley's assertion. They constituted almost 40 per cent of the population and were an essential part of the Southern war effort. The United States census of 1860 had counted a total of almost four million slaves, the great majority of whom, a year later, were to be found within the Confederacy – over 2,300,000 in the seven states of the deep south alone. Over half the population of South Carolina and Mississippi consisted of Negro slaves, and over two-fifths in Louisiana, Alabama, Florida and Georgia. (In the border states retained within the Union, by contrast, the slaves were a much smaller proportion of the population: 20 per cent in Kentucky, 13 per cent in Maryland, 10 per cent in Missouri, a mere 1·5 per cent in Delaware.) The slave contribution to the Confederate cause was more crucial than many white Southerners cared to admit, and it was small wonder that many in the North condemned the Lincoln administration for fighting with one hand tied behind its back, as long as it made no move to touch the South's peculiar institution.

Free the slaves and recruit them into the Union army, add to your own strength whilst weakening the enemy's, put new heart into your own cause while obliging him to look constantly over his shoulder for the first sign of servile unrest – it was a tempting prospect and it seemed to make good sense. So it did up to a point, but the matter was not nearly so simple. Emancipation of the slaves was not just a means of attacking the South, or even an act of long overdue justice to an oppressed and exploited race; it was also a highly sensitive political and social issue within those states which still supported the Union. It threatened to divide the North as much as it disturbed the South.

1. The war redefined and intensified the slavery issue as viewed from the North – and as viewed, in particular, by Lincoln, his administration and his party. It shifted the spotlight from slavery where it might exist, in the territories, to slavery where it already existed in the Southern states. No longer could those who hated slavery and those who disliked the Negro (not to mention those who managed to combine both sentiments) shelter under the common umbrella of opposition to the further expansion of both into the west. Emancipation offered no such comfortable refuge from awkward choices, for while it would dispose of the problem of slavery, it seemed bound to aggravate the problem of race. Whoever took up the cause of emancipation, at whatever juncture, and for whatever reason – be he abolitionist or radical, agitator or politician, legislator, soldier or president – had to reckon with the anxiety, the resentment, the naked prejudice and the determined opposition of millions of loyal citizens of the Northern states.

Anti-Negro feeling in the North took many forms and sprang from many sources.[4] The free Negroes of the Northern states could tell countless tales of segregation in schools, churches and public transport, discrimination in jobs and housing, inequality before the law and exclusion from the polls. The situation varied from state to state and city to city; New England generally had the best record, while at the other end of the scale were some of the middle western states (which actually tightened their black laws in the pre-Civil War years) or New York city, scene of the worst outbreak of anti-Negro violence during the war. Some causes of hostility towards the Negro were peculiar to particular groups or areas, some were more general. Cynics could argue that enthusiasm for emancipation was a luxury to be enjoyed at a safe distance from slavery; certainly those parts of the North closest to the border were gripped by fears of an influx of freed Negroes in the wake of emancipation. Many people in those same areas – southern Ohio, Indiana and Illinois in particular – were themselves of Southern stock, and had brought inherited attitudes with them when they left slavery itself behind. In 1862 voters in Lincoln's home state of Illinois voted down a new state constitution but ran up a 100,000 majority in favour of an article forbidding the further settlement of Negroes or mulattoes in the state. Many of the poorer, unskilled workers of the Northern towns and cities, including Irish and other immigrants, lived in dread of free Negro competition which might imperil their precarious foothold even on the lowest rungs of the economic ladder. Anti-Negro riots in Toledo and Cincinnati in July 1862 were both triggered off by attempts to employ Negroes to replace striking Irish workers. It is dangerous of course to classify opinions too simply, and personality, individual experience, education, religion and other factors cut across such broad categories. After all, while the two great Illinois rivals of the 1850s both freely admitted their belief in Negro inferiority, it was Abraham Lincoln, son of Southern parents, born in the slave state of Kentucky, who denounced the immorality of slavery and opposed its further extension, and Stephen A. Douglas, born in northern New England, of impeccable Yankee stock, who viewed it, if not with indulgence, at least with indifference.

In fact, Northern prejudice against the Negro went right across the board, and affected or infected people in every walk of life, at every level of society, and in every village, town or city from Maine to Kansas. It rested on the almost universal and unquestioned assumption of the inferiority of the black race, backed by the scientific wisdom of the day, and now stimulated by fears of an influx of freed Negroes into the North, and concern for the future of free white labour and Northern white society. Fear of emancipation was above all fear of its consequences in the North. Prejudice was not the monopoly of any one political party. While girls carried banners at a Democratic rally in Indiana in the 1860 election demanding: 'Fathers, save us from Nigger husbands', banners at a Republican rally in Springfield, Illinois (Lincoln's home town), in the same year proclaimed: 'No Negro equality in the North'. A Democratic congressman from Illinois, William A. Richardson, smugly announced in 1862 that: 'God made the white man superior to the black, and no legislation will undo or change the decrees of Heaven . . . and unlike the abolitionist equal-izationalists I find no fault and utter no complaint against the wisdom of our Creator.' More surprisingly, perhaps, Republican Senator Jacob Howard of

Michigan, generally accounted a member of the radical wing of the party, suggested a no-nonsense solution to the problem of ridding his state of free Negroes: 'Canada is very near us, and affords a fine market for wool.' In the closing stages of the war a Democratic newspaper in Iowa greeted Congressional approval of the Thirteenth Amendment which finally abolished slavery, with a bitter blend of sarcasm and racism:

EXCELSIOR, SAMBO!
At last the abolition millennium is about to dawn. The incubus of slavery which weighed down our country for over eighty years, and which was foisted upon us by those slave-driving nabobs, Washington, Jefferson, Jackson, and others of their ilk, is about to be removed, and our disenthralled country, with one huge bound will spring into the fore rank of civilized progress, amid the shouts and songs of the freed, the twang of banjo, the clatter of the 'fantastic heel and toe', and 'a most palpable odor'.

But, eighteen months earlier, a Republican paper in the same state, in denouncing its Democratic opponents, could itself offer the following back-handed compliment to the Negro:

It is true that the Negro belongs to a degraded race; but it is equally true that the devils who malignantly abuse them, and deride the government, are more degraded by far than the greasiest, dirtiest Ethiopian whose body finds a resting place in the 'Lincum Hotel'.[5]

It would be a mistake to conclude, however, that there was nothing to choose between the two parties in their attitudes to slavery and to the Negro. Almost all members of both parties accepted Negro inferiority as a fact, and most recognised the depth and pervasiveness of Northern racial prejudice. But, whereas many Democrats surrendered to such prejudice, pandered to it, and exploited it, often successfully for electoral purposes, the Republican party wrestled painfully with the problem which it posed and many of its members took a brave stand against it. Because of the state of feeling in the North, the race issue was a heavy liability to the Republican party during the war, and its opponents knew it. In face of such a handicap the Republican record was uneven. The party's credentials on racial matters were far from simon pure, but not wholly without honour. The existence of Northern white racism does not justify a blanket condemnation of all Northerners. On the contrary, it enhances the reputation of those who defied it.

Emancipation posed one of the fundamental dilemmas of leadership in a democratic or representative form of government: how to achieve what its sponsors regarded as a morally desirable goal in the face of popular fear, prejudice and hostility, how, in a word, to reconcile a sense of what is right with a sense of obligation to the voters (not to mention a sense of insecurity about the next election). Then, as always, certain clear-cut answers presented themselves: the idealist answer of the moral crusaders who would have no truck with compromise, and who would tolerate no dilution of principle; the 'populist' answer which would meet the wishes of the majority, even to the extent of pandering to prejudice; the conservative answer which, blaming agitators and extremists for making trouble, would hope to cool feelings, and wait for the issue to subside. All these views had their adherents during the war, but there were other responses too, more subtle, more complex. Such answers found favour among those who bore the main burden of responsibility, and above all in the mind of Abraham Lincoln himself. It was surely possible to put slavery on the road to extinction while at the same time dispelling some of the more nightmarish visions of the consequences of emancipation. Whether demanding immediate emancipation or moving more cautiously towards it, most Republicans attempted to assuage the fears, resolve the doubts, and soften the hostility of their fellow Northern whites. Freedom for the slave, they argued, was compatible with protection of white interests. It would hit the South where it hurt, shorten the war, and, if Negro troops were recruited, reduce its cost in white lives. As for the fear of a Negro influx into the North, emancipation would in fact have quite the reverse effect. The Southern states were the natural habitat of the American Negro and only the evils of slavery had driven him to seek refuge in the North. The advent of freedom would not merely keep the former slaves happily in the South but would entice back many of the free Negroes from the North. If further reassurance were needed, many Republicans talked of schemes for colonising the freed slaves outside the United States. Colonisation, though widely regarded as impracticable on any large scale, had always had its Republican supporters; there had even been a move to write it into the party platform in 1860, and now it was a useful anodyne to Negrophobia, if nothing more. Even some of the more idealistic champions of emancipation found themselves, in 1861–2, justifying their goal not so much in terms of racial justice, Christian morality or the principles of American liberty, but rather with arguments from military necessity, the saving of white skins, and the interests of free white labour. It was a matter of covering idealism in a cloak of self-interest rather than the reverse. There were times when good intentions could be more of a political liability than shabby ones.

If racial prejudice was the most embarrassing roadblock on the way to emancipation, it was far from being the only one. There were still serious and honest doubts about the constitutional authority for interference with slavery; no doubt legal arguments were often a rationalisation of interest or prejudice, but they were more than that, too, particularly since so many public figures had taken up clear positions on this knotty problem before the outbreak of war. The conventional view had always been that slavery was a domestic institution of the individual states, and, as such, beyond the reach of the federal government in those states where it already existed. But how was the constitutional position affected by secession and civil war? Abolitionists argued, as they always had done, that, if the constitution protected slavery, then the constitution itself must be amended or abandoned (although William Lloyd Garrison, who had denounced the constitution as 'a covenant with death and an agreement with hell', admitted in 1861 that 'I had no idea that I should live to see death and hell secede').[6] Some radical Republicans, like Thaddeus Stevens, argued that the constitution was not fully operative in time of war and must be allowed no longer to save slavery from destruction. Another radical, Charles Sumner, devised a theory of state suicide, under which the seceded states would revert to territorial status. On the other flank, most Democrats and some conservative Republicans fully and willingly accepted the constitutional *status quo* ante bellum; those who had no wish to interfere with slavery in the Southern states adhered to the view that there was no right to do so either.

Those most troubled by the constitutional issue were the moderates in the centre – and most notably the president himself. Lincoln was enmeshed in a network of constitutional scruple, reinforced by public pledges and commitments. He had always accepted that slavery where it already existed was beyond federal control; the Republican platform of 1860 and his own inaugural address in March 1861 explicitly confirmed this view. Even the coming of war did not release Lincoln from the constitutional trap, for the official view of the nature of the war was always that there was no right of secession, that the government faced a rebellion not of the South, but in the South, and that the Southern states were still within the Union. In such a situation, to use the war as a pretext for interfering with slavery in the Southern states was to undermine the accepted constitutional argument and tacitly to recognise secession. There was only one way out of the net which satisfied Lincoln at all, and that was the argument from military necessity which, in addition to its usefulness in reassuring doubters on other grounds, found a constitutional basis in the exercise of the war powers of the president, particularly in his capacity as commander-in-chief. Interference with slavery could be legally justified as a means of waging war against the Southern enemy. This was not the view of Lincoln alone. Long before the Civil War, John Quincy Adams had foreseen such a use of the president's war powers, and during the war itself even abolitionists and radicals found military necessity a convenient weapon, useful alike for beating off conservative critics and goading a cautious president into action. The argument had one further major attraction for Lincoln himself in that it put the question of emancipation precisely where he wanted it, in the hands of the president rather than of Congress. But reliance on the war power also raised an important danger signal, especially as the theory itself did not find universal acceptance. What would be the standing after the war was over of decisions made through the exercise of such powers? What if the process of emancipation was incomplete when the fighting stopped? Anxieties on this score were one reason, among many others, why, in the later years of the war, there was growing support for the idea of an amendment to the constitution itself which would wipe out slavery once and for all throughout the United States.

Freeing the slaves was more than a matter of either moral right or legal rights. Its political ramifications might have daunted the most earnest friend of emancipation. In the first eighteen months of the war a subtle and complex balance of forces was at work on either side of the slavery issue, and no one showed greater sensitivity to any shift in the balance than Lincoln himself. Among the forces ranged against emancipation were the great bulk of Northern Democrats, loyal to the Union, supporting the struggle to defend it, but recognising neither need nor right to tamper with slavery in the South. Although some members of his own party dismissed these partisan objections as of no consequence, Lincoln was anxious to maintain as long as he could the broadest possible coalition in support of the war. He also knew full well that conservative Republicans shared similar views to those of the Democrats, and spoke up for them in the press, in Congress, and in the cabinet itself, where Seward, Welles, Bates and Blair ensured that caution and restraint always had their say. (Montgomery Blair, for example, offered Governor Andrew of Massachusetts some pithy advice on how to improve his prospects of re-election in 1862: 'drop the nigger'.)[7] The border states were among the most powerful brakes on any move towards emancipation, and Lincoln attached a degree of importance to them which irritated his more radical critics. 'We think you are unduly influenced by the counsels . . . of certain fossil politicians hailing from the Border Slave States,' wrote Horace Greeley in August 1862.[8] But after the struggle to hold on to Missouri, Kentucky, Maryland and Delaware, would it be wise – and would it be fair – to test their fragile loyalty by any interference with their slave property? How could emancipation as a 'military necessity' be defended, if it was followed by the loss of Kentucky? There was concern, too, for the feelings of Union sympathisers within the Confederacy itself. A policy of emancipation might drive them reluctantly into the arms of the Richmond government, and produce the ironic effect of consolidating support for the enemy cause, especially by stimulating fears of servile insurrection.

Pressures against emancipation were at their strongest early in the war, and were almost inevitably weakened by the development of the conflict itself. As it became clear during 1862 that this was no longer a war of manoeuvre to achieve the best bargaining position for a compromise peace, but was becoming a struggle to the death, pressures for emancipation correspondingly intensified. As Northern armies penetrated into Southern territory, the incidents of the war itself pointed in the same direction. As slaves deserted their masters (or were deserted by them) and came through the Union lines, they converted the question from a matter for general debate into a matter of immediate human and practical concern. As generals in the field took matters into their own hands and declared slaves free or proposed to recruit them into the army, they cheered the hearts of supporters of emancipation, and embarrassed an administration still picking its way cautiously through the political minefield. Whether motivated by concern for the Negro, distaste for slavery or animosity towards the white South, those who had favoured emancipation from the outset, gathered strength and heart (and lost patience) as the war moved into its second year.

In the vanguard were the abolitionists, hardened by three decades of campaigning, and contemptuous of cautious calculations about the balance of political forces. Some refused to endanger their political virginity at all by giving any support to the administration; some, like Garrison, were prepared to grant the government the benefit of the doubt, for a time at least; some contrived both to preserve the one and concede the other, by piously accepting the mysterious ways of the Almighty, like Lydia Maria Child who confessed that 'Providence sometimes uses men as instruments whom I would not touch with a ten-foot pole'.[9] Many of the more radical Republicans, like many abolitionists, saw the war as a great opportunity to achieve long-standing objectives and were determined to make the most of it, by all-out attack on both the South and slavery. The radical call to action came in increasing volume from Congress, from state governors and legislatures, from influential newspapers, and even from some generals in the field. By midsummer 1862, although Republicans in Congress were still voting quite solidly together on major issues, radical and conservative positions were emerging more clearly,[10] as the former lost patience with the president, and sought to seize the initiative themselves. Less numerous and powerful, but still audible amid the general clamour, were the voices of the free Negroes of the North, led by Frederick Douglass, and backed by the knowledge of the thousands of Southern slaves now running to seek safety and freedom within the Union lines. Still other voices made themselves heard from across the Atlantic Ocean. Nothing had done more to tarnish the image of the Union cause in Europe than the realisation (aided and abetted by Lincoln's own insistence that the war was simply to save the Union) that the difference between South and North was not a simple distinction between slavery and anti-slavery. The ever-lurking threat of foreign intervention in the war produced serious crises in 1861 and 1862; nothing would do more to eliminate that danger and win European sympathy than a clear commitment to emancipation – and this applied above all to Britain, the neutral power which mattered most of all.

2. The power, the opportunity, or the inescapable necessity to take action on the question of slavery rested in the hands of three main agencies: the generals, the Congress, and the president. There was tension along all the lines of this triangle, but for the most part it was the president who was under pressure from the other two. This situation was largely of Lincoln's own making, even of his own choice, for he preferred not to commit himself in support of any of the unilateral actions of the generals, and he was content generally to let Congress go its own way, while quietly following his own course, confident in the knowledge that he was the man who had the power that really mattered, in the war powers of his office.

The generals were men who had the slavery problem thrust upon them, though David Hunter, and possibly others, welcomed the challenge. From the early weeks of the war, slaves presented themselves at Union army camps, seeking protection, sustenance, and, they hoped, freedom. They presented one kind of fairly limited problem in Virginia, another more complicated one in Kentucky and Missouri where their 'loyal' owners (or at least owners resident in loyal states) were also demanding that the army protect their property; another problem again, on a larger scale, on the sea islands of South Carolina when occupying Union forces in late 1861 found themselves confronted with thousands of slaves who had run to them, or belonging to masters who had fled from them.

It was Ben Butler, in command at Fortress Monroe on the tip of the James Peninsula in Virginia, who made the first positive move in May 1861. Faced with a handful of runaway slaves who had been working on Confederate fortifications, he declared them 'contraband of war' – and the name 'contraband' subsequently stuck. A steady stream of runaways followed, almost a thousand by the end of July. Butler put the men to work, some of them on his own fortifications, and secured the approval of the War Department for his action. His 'contraband' policy attracted much attention, but as it did not involve any decision on the emancipation of the slaves concerned, the administration was able to remain non-committal. Other generals, left with so much discretion, were acting very differently, turning fugitives away from their camps, or even returning them to their owners, if the latter were loyal.

It was predictable, perhaps, that at some point, whether out of desperation, determination, or dedication to the anti-slavery cause, some general would overstep the mark. From the president's point of view it was unfortunate that the first general to do so was a man with the prestige and glamour of John C. Fremont, commander of the Department of the West. His proclamation of 30 August, decreeing martial law in Missouri, also declared free the slaves of all who actively aided the enemies of the United States. Fremont's action was acclaimed not merely by abolitionists and radicals, but by many others hungry for drama and decision at a time when the Union war effort was notably lacking in both. But Lincoln could not let it pass unchallenged. He objected to the proclamation on principle because the general had arrogated to himself the right to make a decision which was 'purely political', and which Lincoln reserved to himself; he objected on policy grounds because of the effect of the proclamation on conservative opinion, and especially on border-state opinion – and above all on Kentucky which, patiently and carefully cultivated by Lincoln, was about to fall like a ripe fruit into the lap of the Union.[11] He requested and then ordered that Fremont modify the proclamation to conform to the provision of the Confiscation Act passed by Congress three weeks earlier which limited itself to the declaration that slaves engaged in hostile military service were to be forfeited by their owners. Lincoln bore the brunt of the wrath, scorn and disgust of all those who had cheered, or been cheered by, Fremont's bold step, but he remained convinced that this was neither the time nor the way to move towards emancipation. If there had ever been a honeymoon period between the president and his radical and abolitionist critics it was now definitely over. The critics were further outraged when Fremont's successor, Halleck, ordered that no fugitive slaves be admitted to his army's camps, and that those already there should be removed. The president did not revoke his order.

Practice continued to vary significantly from one military commander to another, but no one, not even Fremont, matched the sweeping gesture of Major-General Hunter in May 1862. David Hunter, a personal acquaintance of both Lincoln and Chase, was a regular army officer, earnest, unsubtle, genuine in his anti-slavery convictions, and a man whose lack of tact and political sense sometimes made him more of an embarrassment to causes which he espoused than a danger to those he opposed. Since March 1862 he had commanded the Department of the South, which in theory covered the whole of South Carolina, Georgia and Florida but was confined in fact to the Union footholds, mainly on the sea islands, along the Atlantic coast. The thousands of Negroes on those islands presented a variety of problems which drove him on 9 May to the extraordinary step of issuing an order freeing all the slaves throughout the three states in his Department. Predictably, his action was cheered by some sections of Northern opinion, deplored by others, and declared void by Lincoln, in a proclamation ten days later, which reserved to the president alone the right to make such a decision. Again, Lincoln was much abused for his pains, and still the pressures upon him mounted.

They came from many quarters now – and most consistently of all from the Republican majority in Congress. Ever since the two houses had reassembled in December 1861 they had been bombarding the more accessible and vulnerable outposts of slavery with a variety of legislative artillery, and were by mid-summer prepared to attack the citadel itself. It was the radicals who led the onslaught, Stevens and Owen Lovejoy in the House, Sumner, Henry Wilson, Wade and Chandler in the Senate, but the great majority of the Republican members gave them steady voting support. The reverberations of their barrage of bills, acts and resolutions were clearly audible at the other end of Pennsylvania Avenue. They invited the president to join them in the final assault, or demanded that, at least, he should not obstruct it. For his part, Lincoln had so far allowed them to go their own way. 'I do not talk to members of Congress on the subject, except when they ask me,' he wrote of one bill.[12] In effect, in the first half of 1862 the Republican majority in Congress attacked slavery at every point where the constitution gave them any sanction to touch it. It passed an act abolishing slavery in the District of Columbia, which Lincoln signed after some delay (partly, it is said, to allow a Kentucky congressman to remove from Washington two ailing slaves unable to fend for themselves!).[13] Another act abolished slavery in all the territories of the United States, in defiance of what the Southern-dominated Supreme Court had decreed in the Dred Scott case five years before. Yet another measure provided that the army should no longer actively assist in the return of fugitive slaves to their owners, although, curiously, the obnoxious Fugitive Slave Act of 1850 remained on the statute book until 1864. Congress also enthusiastically endorsed two presidential proposals: the one to exchange diplomatic representatives with the Negro republics of Haiti and Liberia, the other a treaty with Britain to achieve closer cooperation in suppressing the slave trade. There were those who threw up their hands in horror at the prospect of black diplomats mingling in Washington society, but the president was unperturbed: 'You can tell the President of Haiti that I shan't tear my shirt if he does send a nigger here,' Lincoln is reported to have said.[14]

While these measures chipped away at the perimeter of slavery's defences, Congress had been intermittently debating a bill which attacked its main stronghold. This bill, which was finally passed on 17 July 1862, as the Second Confiscation Act, was much more stringent and sweeping than the First Confiscation Act of August 1861. It covered much else besides slavery, but one of its clauses declared free the slaves of all who committed treason or who supported the rebellion. In fact, this provision was highly unsatisfactory even to enthusiastic champions of emancipation. It did not free all the Southern slaves at a stroke, but only in dribs and drabs as they came into the Union lines, and it relied upon the inadequate machinery of the federal courts to carry out the well-nigh impossible task of establishing whether the owner of each slave had or had not been engaged in the rebellion. Emancipation as an incidental part of a confiscation measure scarcely met the demands of the abolitionists or the needs of the slaves. On paper, it may be said, this act did at least as much as Lincoln's subsequent proclamations to free the slaves, but it would have to be rigorously applied, and, as radicals feared, Lincoln showed little inclination to enforce it. He disliked the whole bill, for its harshness, its shaky constitutional basis, its likely political effects, and its bid to assert Congressional control over slavery policy. The conservative Orville H. Browning warned him that 'his course upon this bill was to determine whether he was to control the abolitionists and radicals, or whether they were to control him'.[15] The president sought no such showdown. He threatened a veto and the infuriated supporters of the bill passed a resolution meeting some of his constitutional objections; he then signed the bill – but still sent his intended veto message to Congress.[16] The radicals were not amused, and the slaves were still not freed. Another measure, the Militia Act, passed on the same day as the Confiscation Act, did seem to offer a means by which some slaves at least could establish their claim to freedom. It provided that rebel-owned slaves who joined the Union armed forces were to be freed, along with their immediate families. But its immediate effect was slight, for, at this juncture, the administration was still refusing to commit itself to the use of Negro troops.

By the time that Congress adjourned in July, it had put together an impressive legislative record, but a frustrating one, for it had made only a marginal difference where it really mattered. It had freed only a few slaves and it was still a matter for conjecture how far, if at all, congressional pressure had influenced the man in the White House. Was it just a coincidence that he moved towards his great moment of decision once the legislators had dispersed to their homes?

3. Beset from all sides by warnings, threats, entreaties and conflicting advice, where did Lincoln stand? And, more important, where was he going?

Alexander K. McClure begins his discussion of 'Lincoln and Emancipation with the words: 'Abraham Lincoln was not a sentimental abolitionist. Indeed he was not a sentimentalist on any subject.' Elsewhere, McClure, like many others, describes him as a 'master politician'.[17] Here are two useful clues to Lincoln's approach to the slavery issue, but only if it is accepted that a man may show political skill and shun sentimentality, without necessarily being either shamelessly opportunist or morally insensitive. Much has been made – too much perhaps – of the equivocations on slavery in Lincoln's earlier career. But his understanding of the problem steadily matured, and by the late 1850s his position included all the important elements which characterised his presidential performance: profound moral conviction of the evil of slavery, frank condemnation of it, and firm resistance to its further extension; genuine reservations about the power of the federal government to touch it where it already existed; sympathy for the South and recognition of a national responsibility for the burden and the guilt of slavery; keen awareness of the interests of free white labour; belief in the impossibility of Negro equality inside the United States, and consequent interest in Negro colonisation abroad; a preference for a gradual approach to abolition combined with an underlying conviction that slavery was doomed. In short, he condemned slavery but did not demand its immediate extinction; he wanted the slaves to have their liberty, but did not believe they could gain equality.

Totally convinced that his first sworn duty as president was to save the Union, he insisted that the question of freedom for the slaves must be fitted into the context of the nation's life-and-death struggle. If emancipation were to be achieved, it must be done with maximum benefit to the war effort and minimum damage to Northern morale. His war powers as president gave him power to act, but also dictated the manner and limited the scope of that action. His sensitivity to all shades of Northern opinion made him as much concerned with the style, the justification and, above all, the timing of emancipation as with the deed itself. Even Horace Greeley admitted that Lincoln was well ahead of the bulk of Northern opinion, and that there was probably a majority in the North against emancipation until mid-1863.[18] In fact, Lincoln was the arch exponent of the indirect approach to the slavery issue, the strategy of the 'soft sell'. In deference to the fears and prejudices of many, perhaps most, Northerners, he played down moral principle and high ideals, and denied himself grand gestures or outbursts of righteous indignation. Aware that many people could never be convinced by the simple argument that emancipation was right and just, he preferred to rest his case on appeals to practical necessity, and shrewd calculations

of interest. He sought to convince Northerners that their welfare could be
protected, or indeed fostered, their anxieties allayed, their prejudices respected,
while he moved step by step towards freeing the slaves. He took the low road to
emancipation rather than the high. It was slower and more circuitous, but it
was safer and it led to the same place. Lincoln the emancipator was neither the
legendary hero-cum-saint who struck the shackles of slavery from four million
Negroes in one sublime act nor the fallen idol who shirked the real issue, and
failed to overcome his racist instincts, whose Emancipation Proclamation, wrung
from him grudgingly, applied only where it could not be enforced, and effectively
freed few slaves. The former view ignores the facts, the latter accepts at face
value deeds and words designed to forestall criticism and calm fears. Lincoln
knew where he was going, although his intentions were frequently obscured by
the fog of war or a smokescreen of his own making. He was the Great
Emancipator, but the road to emancipation was paved with equivocation.

In December 1862 John Murray Forbes, Bostonian businessman and wartime
convert to emancipation, wrote to Charles Sumner about the president's
forthcoming proclamation. His shrewd words might almost have been the
script for Lincoln's whole performance in the preceding year:

> It seems to me very important that the ground of 'military necessity'
> should be even more squarely taken than it was on 22d September. Many of
> our strongest Republicans, some even of our Lincoln electors, have constitu-
> tional scruples in regard to emancipation upon any other ground, and with
> them must be joined a large class of Democrats, and self-styled 'Conservatives,'
> whose support is highly desirable, and ought to be secured where it can be
> done without any sacrifice of principle.
>
> I know that you and many others would like to have it done upon higher
> ground, but the main thing is to have it done strongly, and to have it so backed
> up by public opinion that it will strike the telling blow, at the rebellion and
> at slavery together, which we so much need.
>
> I buy and eat my bread made from the flour raised by the hard-working
> farmer; it is certainly satisfactory that in so doing I am helping the farmer
> clothe his children, but my motive is self-preservation, not philanthropy or
> justice. Let the President free the slaves upon the same principle, and so
> state it that the masses of our people can easily understand it.
>
> He will thus remove constitutional scruples from some, and will draw to
> himself the support of a very large class who do not want to expend their
> brothers and sons and money for the benefit of the negro, but who will be
> very glad to see Northern life and treasure saved by any practical measure,
> even if it does incidentally an act of justice and benevolence.
>
> Now I would not by any means disclaim the higher motives, but where
> so much prejudice exists, I would eat my bread to sustain my life; I would
> take the one short, sure method of preserving the national life, – and say
> little about any other motive.[19]

Two years after the event, Lincoln himself used a different metaphor to explain his approach to George Thompson, the British anti-slavery leader:

Many of my strongest supporters urged *Emancipation* before I thought it indispensable, and, I may say, before I thought the country ready for it. It is my conviction that, had the proclamation been issued even six months earlier than it was, the public sentiment would not have sustained it. . . . A man watches his pear-tree day after day, impatient for the ripening of the fruit. Let him attempt to *force* the process, and he may spoil both fruit and tree. But let him patiently *wait*, and the ripe pear at length falls into his lap! We have seen this great revolution in public sentiment slowly but surely progressing, so that, when final action came, the opposition was not strong enough to defeat the purpose.[20]

In the early months of the war there was certainly more patient waiting than positive action about Lincoln's policy. Out of genuine conviction, as well as for tactical reasons, he continued to stress the primacy of the issue of Union, to resist pressure from all sides, and to avoid commitment wherever possible. However, during the winter of 1861–2 he matured his first emancipation plan. It went through various revisions, but its main features changed little. Under it, emancipation would be gradual – it might be completed as early as 1865, or, in one version, as late as 1900. The initiative was to come from the states, and the plan was directed primarily (though not exclusively) at the border slave states. The slave-holders would be compensated and the federal government would share the financial burden. Running parallel with this plan for gradual, voluntary, compensated emancipation was the idea of voluntary colonisation of the freed Negroes in West Africa or Central America. The plan sought to circumvent the objection to federal interference by leaving the initiative to the states. Its gradualism, provision for compensation, and proposal of colonisation were intended to sweeten the pill for the slave-owners, reassure white opinion generally, and smooth the transition from slavery to freedom.

Throughout 1862 Lincoln constantly but fruitlessly pressed his plans for gradual emancipation and colonisation. First, he had hoped to persuade Delaware, with fewer than 1,800 slaves, to give a lead. But such was the opposition that supporters of the Lincoln plan in the state legislature did not dare even to bring it to a vote. In March 1862 the president sent a message to Congress with a draft resolution outlining his plan. It was generally well received, even by many abolitionists and radicals, as a step in the right direction. Although Thaddeus Stevens thought it 'the most diluted, milk-and-water gruel proposition that was ever given the American nation',[21] Owen Lovejoy, always better disposed towards Lincoln, took a different view:

The Executive rail splitter . . . knows the thin end of the wedge must first enter the wood. . . . So the Executive has taken the Abolition wedge, and struck it into the log of slavery. . . . In very ugly and cross grained or frozen wood the blows have to be a little easy at first or the wedge flies out.[22]

The resolution easily passed both houses of Congress, but the border states would have nothing to do with it, then or later, despite Lincoln's efforts to persuade them. He set much store by an ingenious, if rather naïve, financial calculation which showed that eighty-seven days' cost of the war, at two million dollars per day, would pay compensation for all the slaves in the border states, at $400 apiece, and he claimed that his plan would shorten the war by much more than that by depriving the Confederacy of the hope of attracting wider support.[23] But the border-state leaders were sceptical about the financial provisions of the plan, fearful that even this measure would be an infringement of the rights of the states, and basically unprepared yet to face the consequences of emancipation, even by instalments. As Congress was about to adjourn in July, Lincoln called the border-state members to a final meeting. He repeated old arguments about how his plan would have cut short the war, but there was also a more ominous note in what he said now:

> If the war continue long . . . the institution in your states will be extinguished by mere friction and abrasion – by the mere incidents of war. It will be gone and you will have nothing valuable in lieu of it. Much of its value is gone already.

He spoke too of the mounting pressure upon him for more sweeping measures, and he reminded them of Hunter's proclamation in May, and its popular reception, to reinforce the point. 'I do not speak of emancipation *at once*, but of a *decision* at once to emancipate gradually,' Lincoln said, but the implications of even this request were too much, and a majority of the border-state congressmen turned it down.[24] Congress soon adjourned, and the president switched to more drastic measures, but he did not completely drop his plan for gradual, compensated emancipation. He returned to it in the Emancipation Proclamation itself, and, at great length, in his message to Congress in December.

Lincoln had no more success with his colonisation proposals, but he showed almost equal reluctance to abandon those, too. Indeed, on this subject, his enthusiasm betrayed his judgment, and he listened all too gullibly to the promoters of the highly dubious Chiriqui project in central America – and later to the sponsors of the expedition to Ile à Vache, off the coast of Haiti – but he was saved from the worst consequences of his zeal by the intervention of Seward and Welles. (The Ile à Vache project was actually launched, but turned into a fiasco, and the administration had to send a ship to bring home the wretched survivors.) When Lincoln talked to the free Negroes on 14 August 1862, his object was to persuade them to give a lead on colonisation, but they were generally unimpressed. The president's blunt words to them reveal something of his motivation, and of his concern over the future of the free Negro in the United States:

Your race are suffering, in my judgment, the greatest wrong inflicted on any people. But even when you cease to be slaves, you are yet far removed from being placed on an equality with the white race. . . . The aspiration of men is to enjoy equality with the best when free, but, on this broad continent, not a single man of your race is made the equal of a single man of ours. . . . I do not propose to discuss this, but to present it as a fact with which we have to deal. I cannot alter it if I would.[25]

From the standpoint of a century later, it is easy to deplore the proposed remedy, but hard to dispute the prognosis.

His interest in colonisation persisted even after the Emancipation Proclamation, but he always insisted that it must be entirely voluntary on the part of the blacks – unlike at least one of his cabinet officers, Edward Bates, who favoured compulsory deportation! The colonisation idea eventually died a natural death, partly because of the opposition of the central American republics, partly because of the hostility or indifference of the Negroes themselves, who, especially after the Emancipation Proclamation, looked forward optimistically to a better future within the United States itself. The recruitment of Negro troops gave colonisation its final death blow; even Northerners not renowned for friendship towards the Negro deemed it rather less than reasonable to ask men to fight for a country and then to leave it.

Lincoln's loyalty to the notions of gradual emancipation and colonisation has remained something of a puzzle. Both plans were a curious combination of conservatism and innovation, reality and fantasy, the sordid and the visionary. There was never much chance that gradual emancipation would be acceptable or practicable, and, in the light of West Indian experience, many abolitionists now thought it undesirable, even in the interests of the freed slave himself. There was no chance at all that colonisation would work on a large scale, for financial and administrative reasons, apart from anything else. Chiriqui and Ile à Vache were no more than pilot projects, dealing in hundreds at most. The likeliest answer to Lincoln's persistence with such policies may well be that, whether they worked in practice or not, they fulfilled an invaluable political and propaganda purpose. If the gradual plan failed, it might still serve to assure conservatives that all else had been tried before the resort to more drastic measures, and to persuade radicals that the administration was moving in the right direction. If the colonisation schemes failed, as they surely would, they would still serve to show the president's awareness of the fears of a Negro influx into the North, and his concern with the consequences of emancipation. Many Republicans, some more radical than Lincoln, had spoken in favour of colonisation; a correspondent of Ben Wade had applauded his support for the idea: 'I believe practically it is a damn humbug. But it will take with the people.'[26]

Lincoln would never have put it so crudely, but his well-publicised remarks on colonisation, like his financial arguments for gradual emancipation, were surely calculated appeals to particular interests and deep-rooted feelings. What other motive can so satisfactorily account for his decision to devote so much of his message to the new session of Congress on 1 December 1862 to the proposal to embody his colonisation and gradual emancipation schemes in constitutional amendments? The country was awaiting his second Emancipation Proclamation just a month later, and Lincoln and everyone else knew that the laborious process of amending the constitution would take years rather than months. The message was surely a piece of propaganda, a public relations exercise. His actual words bear out this interpretation. Gradual emancipation, he argued, would not merely smooth the transition for both races, but 'most of those whose habitual course of thought will be disturbed by the measure will have passed away before its consummation. They will never see it.' Some consolation indeed! His elaborate defence of colonisation is even more revealing; it surely implies that he did not really expect it to work, and that his real purpose was to allay white fears. Having argued at length that emancipation, with or even without colonisation, would enhance the wages of white labour, he went on:

But it is dreaded that the freed people will swarm forth, and cover the whole land? Are they not already in the land? Will liberation make them any more numerous? Equally distributed among the whites of the whole country, and there would be but one colored to seven whites. Could the one, in any way, greatly disturb the seven? . . . But why should emancipation south, send the free people north? People, of any color, seldom run, unless there be something to run from. *Heretofore* colored people, to some extent, have fled north from bondage; and *now*, perhaps, from both bondage and destitution. But if gradual emancipation and deportation be adopted, they will have neither to flee from. Their old masters will give them wages at least until new laborers can be procured; and the freed men, in turn, will gladly give their labor for the wages, till new homes can be found for them, in congenial climes, and with people of their own blood and race. This proposition can be trusted on the mutual interests involved. And, in any event, cannot the north decide for itself, whether to receive them?

With characteristic adroitness, Lincoln moved in a few paragraphs from such special pleading to this sublime peroration:

In *giving* freedom to the *slave*, we *assure* freedom to the *free* – honorable alike in what we give and what we preserve. We shall nobly save, or meanly lose, the last, best hope of earth. Other means may succeed; this could not fail.[27]

The cynic might suspect that Lincoln's message had a more humble purpose, as the last, best hope of sugaring the pill of emancipation for those reluctant to swallow it. 'The last, best hope of earth' was now to be saved by 'other means' embodied in the policy which came to fruition in the proclamation of 1 January 1863.

4. That policy dated back at least as far as July 1862, when Lincoln first admitted to some of his advisers that he had been working for some time on the draft of a proclamation. His commitment to the new approach followed hard upon the rejection of his earlier plan by the border states, but the one was not simply a substitute for the other, nor was it simply inspired by a feeling that the border states had had their chance and could no longer be allowed to dictate policy. By July the Union cause badly needed a shot in the arm. The Peninsular campaign had ended in disappointment and there was little movement on the western front. Hopes of a brief war and a smooth restoration of the Union were gone. The international situation was unpromising and the domestic situation discouraging. Morale had sagged, and men and money proved harder to find every day. Congress adjourned, bringing some relief to the harassed president – and more scope for independent action – but, in the Second Confiscation Act, it had staked its claim to initiate and control a policy of emancipation. From the battlefronts, and the home front, pressure for a tougher policy was becoming unbearable, and moderate positions becoming untenable. Lincoln was at his best when appearing to bow to the inevitable while doing very much what he himself wished. His new policy was to be directed at the slaves inside the Confederacy itself rather than in the border states. It was to employ different methods; gradualism and persuasion were giving way to a direct assertion of the war powers of the president.

On 13 July Lincoln told Seward and Welles informally that he had more or less decided on a proclamation, and, nine days later, he read the formal, legal-sounding document to the full cabinet. It first warned all involved in the rebellion of the penalties laid down in the Confiscation Act of 17 July, and this paragraph was published as a separate proclamation three days later. It then made yet another plea for gradual, voluntary, compensated emancipation before announcing the president's intention, on 1 January 1863, to free all the slaves in states still in rebellion. Cabinet reactions were mixed, and rather bewildered, but only Blair was completely hostile. Lincoln did, however, accept Seward's shrewd advice that the proclamation be withheld until some more propitious moment, after a Union victory, when it would convey an air of confidence rather than of panic.[28]

The delay lasted two months, while McClellan's army withdrew from the Peninsula, Pope was routed at Bull Run, Lee invaded Maryland and threatened Washington, and Bragg swept north through Kentucky towards the Ohio river – and while the British government, for the only time in the war, seriously considered mediation or intervention. Meanwhile, Lincoln had to disguise his intentions and ride out a storm of criticism. It must have been an agonising time for the president, but occasionally he seemed to enjoy playing his game of deception. On 14 August he gave the free Negro deputation no hint of what was to come. On 22 August he wrote a reply to Horace Greeley's pretentiously entitled 'Prayer of Twenty Millions' in the *New York Tribune*, which accused Lincoln of treating slavery with kid gloves, and demanded a thorough execution of the laws, including the Confiscation Act. The president's half-candid half-evasive words have been the subject of intensive exegesis ever since:

> My paramount object in this struggle *is* to save the Union, and is *not* either to save or to destroy slavery. If I could save the Union without freeing *any* slave I would do it, and if I could save it by freeing all the slaves I would do it; and if I could save it by freeing some and leaving others alone I would also do that.

After more of the same kind, Lincoln undertook to 'adopt new views so fast as they shall appear to be true views', and ended by distinguishing between his official duty, and his 'oft-expressed personal wish that all men every where could be free'.[29] In such a statement there was something for everybody, and it has certainly been all things to all historians – a verbal smokescreen, a confession of uncertainty, a hint of things to come, a crumb of comfort for radicals or conservatives, or both, or an early warning of the limitations of his proclamation. It is safe to assume that Lincoln said what he meant to say, no more no less. Some radicals and abolitionists were not altogether displeased by the president's letter and they were probably right. After all, it was clear to them that the Union could no longer be saved without freeing any slaves, and no doubt Lincoln thought the same.

On 13 September, as rumours of a proclamation spread, Lincoln spoke at length to a delegation which presented an Emancipation Memorial from a group of Chicago Christians. What he said reads now like a devastating critique of the proclamation which he had prepared but not yet issued. He voiced no moral or legal objections to a proclamation, but professed to doubt its practical advantages. He expressed fears about its effects on the border states and on conservative and moderate opinion in the North, and scepticism about its benefits to the Negro, its impact on international opinion and its power to hurt the Southern war effort.

> What *good* would a proclamation of emancipation from me do, especially as we are now situated? I do not want to issue a document that the whole world will see must necessarily be inoperative, like the Pope's bull against the comet! Would *my word* free the slaves, when I cannot even enforce the Constitution in the rebel states?[30]

With the advantage of hindsight, one may pose a further question: how is it possible to reconcile these remarks with the decision to issue the Emancipation Proclamation just nine days later? The obvious answer lies in the battle of

Antietam on 17 September, which was a Union victory at least in the sense that it was followed by Lee's retreat into Virginia. Here was the opportune moment for which the president, on Seward's advice, had been waiting. True, a more startling explanation of the significance of Antietam has been offered.[31] Lincoln, it is suggested, was still uncommitted to emancipation in August and early September. The limitations of his proclamation indicate that it was intended to head off a more thoroughgoing radical solution, unless a great military victory should boost Northern morale sufficiently to take the heat out of radical demands. 'If military success was thought to render emancipation unnecessary, and defeat to make it unavailing,'[32] in the words of the Chicago delegation, then only a half-success like Antietam made it unavoidable. There can be no real proof of this plausible speculation, and it ignores Lincoln's profound sense of the direction in which the tide of events was running during the war. There remains the question why he should choose to indulge in such a searching criticism of his own as yet undeclared policy. No doubt he was still anxious to mask his real intentions, and perhaps even more anxious to use his audience to test obvious objections to his policy – this was a not uncommon Lincoln habit. Above all, perhaps, as in the reply to Greeley, he wished to make it crystal clear that he had considered every possible objection to a policy of emancipation, and every possible consequence it might have. If he then went ahead with his proclamation, he might hope to retain his credentials as a solid, orthodox, middle-of-the-road defender of the Union. Again, as in his letter to Greeley, he ended his reply to the Chicago delegation on a more promising note:

> Do not misunderstand me because I have mentioned these objections. They indicate the difficulties which have thus far prevented my action in some such way as you desire. I have not decided against a proclamation of liberty to the slaves, but hold the matter under advisement.[33]

In answering the editor of the *Tribune* or conversing with the Chicago churchmen, the pattern was the same: a certain perverse pleasure in laying a verbal smokescreen, great pains to assure conservative opinion that its interests and arguments had been fully considered, and a gentle hint, for those who cared to take it, that emancipation was on the way.

5. In a letter to her husband on 8 August 1862, Mrs Ben Butler wrote: 'The abolitionists will have this a war to free the slaves at once if possible, nothing else is thought of. The Administration will assent to it just as fast and as far as the country will sustain it.'[34] Six weeks later, the president judged that the time had come. On 22 September he called a cabinet meeting, opened it by reading a funny story by Artemus Ward which amused him rather more than them, and then in an extraordinary switch of mood announced his intention to issue the Emancipation Proclamation, which probably amused one or two of them even less. The document had been considerably rewritten and extended since July.

It reaffirmed that the primary war aim was restoration of the Union, repeated proposals for gradual emancipation and colonisation, and drew attention to acts of Congress concerning slavery. But its essential point was the declaration that on 1 January 1863, 'all persons held as slaves within any state, or designated part of a state, the people whereof shall be in rebellion against the United States, shall be then, thenceforward and forever free'. These terms specifically excluded the slaves not only in the border states but also in all other areas under Union control on 1 January; the proclamation, therefore, would not, and did not, wipe out slavery throughout the United States.[35]

Both the limitations written into the proclamation, and its prosaic, impersonal style of legal formality encouraged the widely-held view that it was deliberately ineffective, that it offered freedom only to slaves whom it was beyond the power of the United States government to help, and that it actually freed no one at all. The force of such arguments is more apparent than real. The proclamation was part and parcel of a rapidly developing situation. If the government adhered to the policy it proclaimed, and if the North did not contrive to lose the war, slavery was doomed. Advancing armies, thousands of slaves voting with their feet, and the president's public commitment would see to that. The proclamation assured the freedom of thousands of slaves already within the Union lines and held out the same promise to the many thousands more who would follow. Lincoln's commitment before the nation and the world was irreversible, and he himself acknowledged more than once that he could not avoid it if he would and would not if he could. Its scope broadened rapidly, as many interested parties – abolitionists, foreign sympathisers, and above all the Negroes themselves – chose not to understand, or soon forgot, the specific terms of the proclamation. Negroes in the border states celebrated its announcement, although, legally, they were unaffected by it. 'In a document proclaiming liberty,' writes the Negro historian Benjamin Quarles, 'the unfree never bother to read the fine print,'[36] and they were right, for, if slavery died in South Carolina and Mississippi, how long could it survive in Kentucky or Tennessee? The proclamation soon acquired its own momentum, its own irresistible force, and its author must surely have had a shrewd suspicion that it would. If he was going to launch a revolution, it suited his own temperament and his reading of public opinion and the political situation to launch it quietly and undramatically. If, in the words of Richard Hofstadter, the proclamation had 'all the moral grandeur of a bill of lading',[37] that was because Lincoln chose to have it so, in conformity with his whole cool, calculated strategy of doing good by stealth, of lowering the temperature while raising the stakes.

Inevitably, reactions to the proclamation were mixed; it probably confirmed more people in preconceived ideas and old beliefs than it converted to new ones. Lincoln's strategy was successful up to a point. His proclamation did not satisfy abolitionists and radicals, but they could accept it as a step in the right direction. On the whole, they welcomed it enthusiastically, and Governor Andrew spoke for many when he called it 'a poor document but a mighty act'.[38] It alarmed conservatives and angered the border states, but they could take some comfort in its limitations and in predictions of its ineffectiveness. One newspaper expected it to do no good and hoped that it would do no harm.[39] It gladdened the hearts of Negroes in the North, and the South, too, as the news spread with remarkable speed – in some places, masters were informed by their slaves of Lincoln's edict. There was no prospect that the Confederacy would heed the one hundred days' notice served on it by the proclamation, nor even that Confederate leaders would be adroit or resourceful enough to exploit the opportunity thus offered, to make mischief, if nothing else. Lincoln's statement was generally dismissed in the South as a futile gesture, born of desperation – 'the Government of the United States has shot its bolt,' said one newspaper[40] – but it did heighten fears of slave insurrection and reduce hopes of European support. If, however, the proclamation was addressed in part to a transatlantic audience, its immediate impact was disappointing. Antietam did more than emancipation to avert the immediate threat of British interference in the war. The limitations of the proclamation blunted its moral force in Europe, and provoked a cynical response from governments and press alike. The *Spectator's* famous comment that 'the principle asserted is not that a human being cannot justly own another, but that he cannot own him unless he is loyal to the United States',[41] was a neat jibe, but missed the wider implications. Friends of the Union cause in Europe were heartened by the proclamation, and in the longer run governments were to find it harder than before to justify any intervention on behalf of the South.

The hundred days before 1 January 1863 were a testing time for Lincoln, his party, his cabinet – and the Union cause. News from the battlefronts was generally disappointing and occasionally disastrous. The Republican party suffered a severe jolt in the mid-term elections, and Republican senators challenged the authority of the president himself and brought on a cabinet crisis in mid-December. Many people feared that Lincoln would not go ahead with his second proclamation. He had himself expressed some disappointment at the results of the first: 'The North responds to the proclamation sufficiently in breath; but breath alone kills no rebels.'[42] In his message to the new session of Congress on 1 December, he barely mentioned the proclamation while making his eloquent plea for gradual emancipation and colonisation. Congress and the press were unimpressed by the latter, and the House jogged the president's memory by passing a resolution supporting his proclamation. A Republican congressman thought that Lincoln's determination would be stiffened if he were told that 'the world will pardon his crimes, and his stories even, if he only makes the proclamation a success, and that if he fails he will be gibbeted in history as a great, long-legged, awkward, country pettifogger, without brains or backbone'.[43] But neither he nor anyone else needed to worry; as Lincoln himself said, he might be slow to make up his mind but was hard to move once he had.

On 1 January 1863 he signed the second proclamation, fulfilling the promises of the first.[44] It emphasised that emancipation was justified as 'a fit and necessary war measure', on the basis of the president's war powers. Lincoln's earnestness on this point was indicated by the precision with which the document listed those areas of the South already in Union hands, and therefore excluded from its provisions, because no military necessity applied there. The proclamation also urged the Negroes to 'abstain from all violence, unless in necessary self-defence', and declared that suitable free Negroes 'will be received into the armed service of the United States'. Reactions to the proclamation generally followed the lines of three months earlier. Supporters were a little more elated, opponents a little more resigned, Negro joy a little more unconfined. There was more readiness than ever to overlook the specific terms and subtle distinctions of the proclamation. There could be no going back, and even the cautious Secretary of the Navy, Gideon Welles, wrote that 'passing events are steadily accomplishing what is here proclaimed'.[45] The proclamation produced no sudden dash for freedom by millions of slaves; its results were gradual and cumulative. One observer noted that an earlier Declaration, on 4 July 1776, did not finally become effective for seven years.[46] There remained plenty of unfinished business, which would eventually involve an amendment to the constitution, but, as war measure, political decision, and moral force, the Emancipation Proclamation was justified less by its immediate results than its continuing significance.

Lincoln's public justifications of his policy had all along been an intriguing mixture of genuine beliefs, friendly (and occasionally not so friendly) persuasion and skilful special pleading. The pure white of principle had been well camouflaged in the drab, neutral colours of expediency. One of the greatest social upheavals in American history had been launched on a plea of military necessity. But it would surely be a mistake to conclude that the far-reaching consequences of Lincoln's apparently hesitant policy were unintended or unforeseen. His antipathy towards slavery, and his shrewdness as a politician strengthen the probability that the outcome was what Lincoln expected and what he desired. Two witnesses who could scarcely differ more from each other may be cited in support of this view. Stephen Vincent Benet, in *John Brown's Body*, describes the liberation of the slaves as follows:

> John Brown's raid has gone forward, the definite thing is done,
> Not as we see it done when we read the books,
> A clear light burning suddenly in the sky,
> But dimly, obscurely, a flame half-strangled by smoke,
> A thing come to pass from a victory not a victory,
> A dubious doctrine, dubiously received.
> The papers praise, but the recruiting is slow,
> The bonds sell badly, the grind of the war goes on –
> There is no sudden casting off of a chain,
> Only a slow thought working its way through the ground,

A slow root growing, touching a hundred soils,
A thousand minds – no blossom or flower yet.
It takes a long time to bring a thought into act,
And when it blossoms at last, the gardeners wonder.[47]

Karl Marx, a keen student of the Civil War, wrote to Engels about Lincoln's proclamation in these terms:

> The fury with which Southerners have received Lincoln's Acts proves their importance. All Lincoln's Acts appear like the mean pettifogging conditions which one lawyer puts to his opposing lawyer. But this does not alter their historic content, and indeed it amuses me when I compare them with the drapery in which the Frenchman envelops even the most unimportant point. Of course, like other people, I see the repulsive side of the form the movement takes among the Yankees; but I find the explanation of it in the nature of 'bourgeois' democracy. The events over there are a world upheaval, nevertheless.[48]

His public comment in the columns of the Vienna newspaper *Die Presse* is even more revealing:

> Lincoln is a figure *sui generis* in the annals of history. No pathos, no idealistic flights of eloquence, no posing, no wrapping himself in the toga of history. He always gives the most significant of his acts the most commonplace form. When another man, acting for the sake of so many 'square feet of land' declaims about 'the struggle of an idea,' Lincoln, even when he is acting for the sake of an idea, speaks only in terms of square feet of land.
>
> Indecisively, against his will, he reluctantly performs the *bravura aria* of his role as though asking pardon for the fact that circumstances are forcing him to "play the hero." The most formidable decrees which he hurls against the enemy and which will never lose their historic significance, resemble – as the author intends them to – ordinary summonses sent by one lawyer to another on the opposing side. . . . And this is the character the recent Proclamation bears – the most important document of American history since the founding of the Union.[49]

6. 'Broken eggs can not be mended' was the answer which Lincoln gave more than once to those who suggested or demanded a reversal of the emancipation policy.[50] Such a plea of helplessness came a little disingenuously from the lips of the man who had smashed the eggs in the first place, but it gave some indication of the president's firm adherence to the new policy, once proclaimed. He still justified emancipation mainly on grounds of expediency, but as time passed, and his policy seemed to be working in practice, he exuded a new confidence in both its value and its justice. In his famous letter to James C.

Conkling in August 1863, many of the arguments echoed those of a year
earlier, but the tone was very different:

> You say you will not fight to free negroes. Some of them seem willing to
> fight for you; but no matter. Fight you, then, exclusively to save the Union.
> I issued the proclamation on purpose to aid you in saving the Union.
> Whenever you shall have conquered all resistance to the Union, if I shall urge
> you to continue fighting, it will be an apt time, then, for you to declare you
> will not fight to free negroes.
>
> I thought that in your struggle for the Union, to whatever extent the
> negroes should cease helping the enemy, to that extent it weakened the enemy
> in his resistance to you. Do you think differently? I thought what whatever
> Negroes could be got to do as soldiers, leaves just so much less for white
> soldiers to do, in saving the Union. Does it appear otherwise to you? But
> Negroes, like other people, act upon motives. Why should they do anything
> for us, if we will do nothing for them? If they stake their lives for us, they must
> be prompted by the strongest motive – even the promise of freedom. And the
> promise being made, must be kept.

He forecast that, when victory came:

> there will be some black men who can remember that, with silent tongue, and
> clenched teeth, and steady eye, and well-poised bayonet, they have helped
> mankind on to this great consummation; while, I fear, there will be some
> white ones unable to forget that, with malignant heart, and deceitful speech,
> they have strove [sic] to hinder it.[51]

After a stumbling start in the first few difficult months of 1863, emancipation
steadily won acceptance from more and more Northerners. The process was
greatly helped by mid-summer military success, increasing evidence of the
value of Negro troops, and lack of evidence of any invasion of the North by
ex-slaves. Anti-Negro prejudice abated little if at all, as the New York draft
riots tragically testified in July, but as long as emancipation did not unduly
disturb Northern society, and actually improved the prospects of Northern
victory, many white citizens began to see some merit in it. By 1864 George
Templeton Strong could record that:

> The change of opinion on this slavery question since 1860 is a great historical
> fact, comparable with the early progress of Christianity and of Mahometanism.
> Who could have predicted it? . . . I think this great and blessed revolution is
> due, in no small degree, to A. Lincoln's sagacious policy. But I do wish A.
> Lincoln told fewer dirty stories. What a marvellous change it is! . . . my
> little Louis singing after dinner, Sundays: 'John Brown body's lies a modrin'
> in the grave' just as if it were Star-Spangled Banner.[52]

Supporters of emancipation, and particularly the president himself, knew that there were still many loose ends to tie before the history of slavery in the United States was finished. What of the border states, and the other areas excluded from the proclamations? What of lingering constitutional reservations, and doubts about the durability of wartime measures once the war was over? A constitutional amendment was the safest answer to most of these questions, and the campaign for it gathered strength during 1864. Meanwhile the border states could be coaxed or driven into ridding themselves of slavery, but it was a painful and complicated process. Maryland and Missouri (and Tennessee) had taken the plunge before the war ended, but Kentucky and Delaware had refused. What of the discrimination against Negroes, official and unofficial, institutional and individual which was still practised all across the Northern states? Many abolitionists now turned their attention to the fight for equal rights, and so too did Charles Sumner in the Senate, but their new adversary proved even more formidable and durable – and much more elusive – than slavery itself. The federal government was generally regarded as powerless over much of this field, but, at Sumner's instigation, Congress did pass a law in 1864 prohibiting the exclusion of witnesses from federal courts on grounds of race or colour, and other laws in 1865 repealed Jim Crow regulations on Washington streetcars, and the ban on coloured persons carrying the mails. Lincoln himself contributed little in terms of policy but set an excellent personal example in his relations with Negroes who called at the White House. Such visits were themselves a remarkable precedent, and the president's quiet, unfussy, courteous reception of his guests was final proof of his triumph over his own background. Frederick Douglass testified that of all the prominent men whom he had met, the president was the first who never made him conscious of the colour of his skin. One historian refers to the characteristic Republican mixture of abstract egalitarianism and pragmatic racism.[53] In Abraham Lincoln, the picture was more or less reversed; he could never quite shake off the prevailing abstract assumptions about Negro inferiority, but in practical matters and face-to-face encounters, he had liberated himself from his racist heritage. It is yet one more example of his preference for dealing with the specific, individual case rather than the general, impersonal issue.

Far and away the most pressing item on the agenda left by the Emancipation Proclamations was the question of what to do with the freed slaves in the South. What was the duty of American society, what was the proper role of the federal government, in providing food, shelter, work and land and protecting the rights, safety and welfare of ex-slaves still half-blinded by the unfamiliar glare of freedom? It was precisely in tackling this crucial question that the Lincoln style of emancipation broke down. The cautious, piecemeal approach, the concern to placate Northern opponents, the emphasis on military necessity, the evasions and equivocations, the final act itself which had disguised its revolutionary nature by its surface appearance of futility, all precluded proper discussion of its consequences, or remotely adequate preparation or planning for the day itself. It was not that Lincoln was unaware of the problem or indifferent to the fate of the freedmen. His comments both before and after the proclamations show that, unlike some Northerners, he did not believe that emancipation was the end of the story. It was rather that his energies were so concentrated on the business of war that he gave little attention to the necessary forward planning – and, at the best of times, he was never much inclined to work from blueprints. More culpably, perhaps, his unflagging efforts to soothe the feelings and satisfy the interests of all those concerned about the consequences of emancipation had paid too little heed to the feelings and interests of those most affected of all, the Negroes themselves.

There were many other reasons why emancipation caught everyone so unprepared to cope with its practical results. Abolitionists and wartime emancipationists themselves were torn between their condemnation of the barbarities of slavery and its dehumanising and debilitating effects upon its victims and, on the other hand, their conviction that, once given his liberty, the Negro ex-slave would rapidly prove his worth and his ability to stand on his own feet. While some abolitionists were addressing themselves to practical ways of assisting the adjustment to freedom, others were arguing that the only training for freedom was freedom itself, and that the best form of help was self-help. The free Negro leader, Frederick Douglass, himself inclined to this view, rejecting anything which smacked of paternalism, and insisting that all the freed Negroes asked was to be left alone. If many friends of emancipation tended to minimise the problem, its opponents saw no reason why the government should spend time and money in following up its initial mistake, and asked only that the freedman and his problems should be kept as far away as possible, within the South itself.

The very structure of the federal government itself militated against adequate management of the consequences of emancipation. It had not been designed, and it was still not generally expected, to initiate and carry through the kind of massive social and economic programme which, ideally, was required. Congressional procedures once again proved an instrument more suited to the obstruction of reform legislation than its enactment; for example, the House voted three times at least for the principle of some measure of land confiscation and distribution to the ex-slaves, but it never actually passed into law.[54] The executive branch was totally without the administrative machinery needed to establish and run a properly planned and integrated programme, and could not or would not create it. In any event, its capacity was already stretched by the demands of the war, and victory remained the top priority. Consequently, even when the government did confront the problems of the ex-slaves, its main concern was not always with their welfare. The war came first, and so, very often, did other considerations, like the cotton crop, or the desirability of preventing a large-scale Negro migration into the Northern states – or even into the western territories. Divergence of aims found institutional reflection in the overlapping and competing claims to jurisdiction of various government departments and agencies, notably the army and the War Department on the one hand, and the Treasury Department on the other, with its concern for cotton and confiscated and abandoned lands. The two departments fought many a battle in 1863–4, and the freedman was usually the casualty of their strife. There was inevitable friction, too, between the governmental authorities, military and civil, and the agents and missionaries of the various philanthropic organisations who did invaluable work, but, by their inexperience or their sheer persistence – or even by the simple fact of their defence of Negro rights and interests – incurred the displeasure of officialdom, and the usual jibes and sneers as do-gooders and interfering busybodies.

The story of the Negro during the Civil War is at one level the history of Emancipation (with a capital 'E') followed by the history of Reconstruction (with a capital 'R'). At another level, it is the story, often tragic, almost always painful, seldom untroubled, of the passage of hundreds of thousands of families and individuals from bondage to freedom – and beyond. For most, the lure of liberty proved much stronger than generations of conditioning under slavery, lifelong habits of dependence, and the loyalty which some at least felt to their masters. At the approach of the invading army, slaves became restless and excited, many ran to claim their freedom, many stayed put and waited to see what happened. The slave who had been one day going about his routine tasks in the fields or in the master's house, might the next day be guiding Yankee soldiers to the best road or the nearest ford, or leading them to the hideaway where his departed master had concealed his valuables. Some vowed vengeance against cruel masters, but most viewed their passing without regret but without malice. The very passiveness with which so many slaves accepted the upheaval in their lives – almost as spectators of the drama of their own liberation – was no doubt an asset in the first stage of transition from slavery to freedom. There was no widespread orgy of violence or destructiveness, but a great deal of carefree celebration. Freedom was there to be enjoyed, its present and future blessings not to be questioned. But, if the pull of liberty was strong, the conception of it was vague. The inclination to wait and see what happened next was not often accompanied by any inkling of what that would be. One legacy of slavery was the habit of believing that the individual's life consisted largely of things which were done to him and that he seldom if ever controlled his own destiny. And so the newly freed slave waited to see what befell him, and when it came it was often shocking, humiliating, cruel, bitter and tragic. As more and more Negroes sought safety behind the Union lines, their sheer numbers threatened to clog the machinery of war. Thousands were herded into hastily improvised contraband camps in conditions, unsatisfactory at the outset, which soon degenerated into misery and squalor, for lack of organisation and resources, and sometimes of concern. The most basic requirements of food, shelter, clothing and hygiene were only occasionally met, and very difficult to maintain. Grant, for example, established a huge contraband camp at Grand Junction, Tennessee, in November 1862, under the supervision of John Eaton, but when the army withdrew further north, the camp had to be re-established at Memphis, and the horrors of a mid-winter journey claimed many victims along the way.

The Southern Negroes suffered all the anguish, privation and misery which have been the lot of the refugees, the homeless, and the defenceless victims of war throughout the ages. But to their fate was added the irony and the tragedy that this was the accompaniment to their baptism of freedom. Thousands died before they had tasted real freedom at all; many thousands more were scarred by their first experience of liberty as much as by their long years of slavery. Whether in the contraband camps or in their old homes on the plantations, many were disillusioned, many fearful of a future which seemed to offer only confusion and insecurity. (In its own inhuman way, slavery had at least offered a kind of security.) The ex-slaves were shocked to encounter the racial prejudice of many of their white liberators, and were often ruthlessly cheated, exploited and abused by them. Some of them were more shocked still to find themselves impressed into military service against their will, sometimes without even a chance to say farewell to their families. A great number of ex-slaves soon found themselves back working on the old familiar plantation, perhaps even for their former master. Now they were paid wages – though they did not always in fact receive them – but after the brief, euphoric interlude of liberation and celebration, many must have ruefully reflected that the more things changed the more they were the same. Freedom from slavery did not automatically bring freedom from toil and trouble, or from injustice and discrimination.

Conditions varied widely from area to area, particularly as there was no common government policy for all. The sea islands of South Carolina, occupied in late 1861, had the advantage of being first in the field, and reaped the benefits of the first enthusiastic efforts of the freedmen's aid societies in Boston, Philadelphia and New York. Developments there commanded national attention and, for good or ill, became a test case closely watched alike by friends of the ex-slave and friends of slavery. The experiment in reconstruction carried on in the islands was much more of a planned programme than elsewhere in the South. It achieved its remarkable successes in settling freedmen on their own land, in educating them, and protecting their rights and interests. It also had its share of tension between the military and the missionary, profit and philanthropy, cotton and conscience, paternalism and self-help.[55] In the Mississippi Delta area, where the contraband problem again arose quite early in the war, Butler made arrangements with local planters to employ Negroes on a wage basis. His successor Banks followed a more elaborate policy of arranging contracts under which Negroes worked on the plantations, for wages – or on a sharecropping basis, if they preferred it, which few actually did. The policy was successful to the extent that it made thousands of Negroes economically self-supporting, but it incurred much Northern criticism on the ground that it relegated them to a status akin to serfdom. Undoubtedly some employers abused both the system and their black workers, and tighter regulations were introduced in 1864.

In the Mississippi Valley the contraband problem assumed much greater proportions than elsewhere, and eventually forced the Washington authorities to give more of a lead. The Union advance down the river towards Vicksburg in 1862–3 had given the army responsibility for tens of thousands of Negroes. Grant had coped with the problem in a makeshift way, but he found that any attempt to ship some of the Negroes further north, out of his command, was sternly resisted by a government still highly sensitive to Northern negrophobia. Secretary for War Stanton had already burnt his fingers badly in autumn 1862 when he had to abandon hastily a scheme for distributing black labourers in Illinois. Now, on 25 March 1863, he despatched Lorenzo Thomas, the adjutant-general, on a mission to the west, partly to raise Negro troops, but also, in the process, to tackle the wider problem of putting thousands of contrabands to work. The scheme which Thomas initiated offered the Negro one of a number of choices: military service, military labour, or work for wages on plantations abandoned by their owners which would be leased to former planters or to newcomers from the North. The beauty of Thomas's plan, as the administration saw it, was that it dealt with the problem of the Negro within the South. If it succeeded, it would prove that emancipation could work without detriment to Northern interests, and that the future of the American Negro lay in the Southern states. On the other hand, Northern friends of the Negro had grave doubts about the scheme, and particularly about the arrangements for hiring out black labour to lessees of confiscated and abandoned plantations. Such a system smacked once again of serfdom and was open to serious abuse. With all this land available, would it not be more sensible and just, it was argued, to grant it to the freedmen in small lots of their own? The Thomas scheme went ahead, and under the leadership of John Eaton grew into a very large operation indeed. In July 1864 Eaton reported 113,000 freedmen under his supervision, 41,000 working as military labourers or auxiliaries, 62,000 self-employed or self-supporting as hired labourers, and only 10,000 on subsistence from the government. The aged, the sick and the crippled among these last 10,000 were in special camps, villages or infirmaries – one of which was on Jefferson Davis's plantation. The achievements of the scheme did not answer all the objections of the critics. The hired labourers were frequently exploited, some were brutally treated, and many received little or no pay. The wages were only $7 per month at the outset, and this pittance was subject to deductions for various purposes. One lessee complained that all his workers were in debt to him, although he had never actually paid them any cash at all![56] A clash between the army and the Treasury Department over control of the land led to new regulations bringing better pay and conditions, but, in the process, putting the price of labour beyond the pockets of some lessees. Confederate cavalry and guerrilla raids further damaged the prospects of some plantations and the confidence of employers and labourers alike. On top of all the practical difficulties and flagrant abuses, there remained the basic criticism that, whatever its merits and its successes, the scheme had other objectives than the economic independence of the freedman.

Military necessity, cotton speculation, Treasury pennypinching, and political considerations had too often been accorded a higher priority.

Bitter experience strengthened the case, long argued by abolitionists among others, for a central government department or agency to give some overall direction and coherence to efforts to help the freedmen. In March 1863 the War Department set up the three-man American Freedmen's Inquiry Commission, chaired by Robert Dale Owen. It strongly recommended the establishment of a Freedmen's Bureau to supervise employment and wages, promote a school system, and create courts to adjudicate disputes. At the same time, the Commission warned against paternalism and charity, or federal guardianship, as long-term solutions to the freedman's problems; it preached the virtues of self-reliance, and advocated equal rights under the law as the best guarantee of Negro freedom. Congress had first discussed the creation of a Freedmen's Bureau in 1863, but obstructive tactics by its opponents, and the inflexibility of some of its sponsors, like Charles Sumner, delayed final passage of the measure until March 1865. Until the end of the war therefore, freedmen's aid remained a patchwork of diverse government programmes and valiant philanthropic effort. Private organisations struggled to help the ex-slaves in a variety of ways; if they often lacked the resources and the brutal realism of the army and the Treasury Department, their motives were purer, and their priorities less open to question. They played a notable part in slaking the Negro thirst for education. The Negro schools which operated in many areas under government auspices were actually staffed and run by the freedmen's aid organisations.

7. There remained one other way in which the freed Negro could be provided with both employment and a means of consolidating his new status: recruitment into the army. Such a bold, radical step horrified many conservatives and negrophobes, and for the first twenty months of the war Lincoln circled round the issue as warily as a man examining an unexploded bomb. It was true that, following Butler's early precedent, the army found employment for thousands of contrabands as labourers on fortifications, trenches, roads and railroads, as cooks, servants, teamsters, porters, carpenters and in many other occupations. Wages were poor and irregularly paid, the work often arduous, conditions usually uncomfortable and sometimes dangerous. Negroes generally and understandably hated military labour, and when volunteers were too few, the army impressed the required numbers into service. For the freedman it all added up to one more snare on the path to real liberty. For the army, the Negroes provided a useful pool of auxiliaries, to be used and abused at will. Probably some 200,000 Southern Negroes were employed in this way at some time during the war.

Auxiliary labour was one thing, but regular, uniformed, Negro soldiers were another. Opponents recoiled instinctively from any idea of putting weapons in such hands, and deployed a whole battery of arguments against it. They rejected it as a slur on white Americans, deplored its likely effects in brutalising the war still further, and driving the South to retaliatory measures, cast aspersions on the quality of the Negro as a fighting man, and professed to see in the scheme a device for forcing Negro equality throughout Northern society. There was widespread prejudice against Negro troops in the army itself (which later led to a number of bloody encounters between white and black soldiers who both wore the same blue uniform). Even some prominent Republican politicians ruled the whole idea out of court. When a Negro abolitionist suggested the recruitment of coloured troops in Ohio in 1862, Governor David Tod rebuffed him in no uncertain terms: 'Do you not know, Mr Langston, that this is a white man's government; that white men are able to defend and protect it?'[57] (Incidentally, Governor Tod changed his mind a year later when Negro recruits became a useful device for filling up the state's quota under the Conscription Act.)

Some advocates of black recruitment saw its advantages for the Negro himself in helping to establish his place in American society. But in view of the widespread hostility to the idea they had to proceed warily, and borrow the tactics of those who, from the first, put the case for Negro troops in more down-to-earth terms. The simple numerical addition to the Union forces was the most obvious point of all, backed by the straightforward argument that it was no more than common sense to ask the Negro to contribute towards a struggle which involved him so deeply. General Banks made the point in a crude unvarnished way in an order of 1 May 1863:

> The Government makes use of mules, horses, uneducated and educated white men, in the defence of its institutions. Why should not the negro contribute whatever is in his power for the cause in which he is as deeply interested as other men? We may properly demand from him whatever service he can render.

Other arguments were cruder still. Governor Kirkwood of Iowa said that, before the war was over, he wanted to see 'some dead niggers as well as dead white men', and one army officer declared that 'the Government will be weakened less by the loss of three negroes than it would by the loss of one white man'.[58] When Lorenzo Thomas and others set out to win army support for the idea of Negro troops, they stressed the relief which it would bring to the white soldier, both from death and danger and from dirty and unpleasant tasks, and also the opportunities which it would offer in promotions to provide black regiments with white officers and N.C.O.s. (One ironical result of the organisation of Negro regiments was the creation of a more methodical system of officer selection boards to fill all the new vacancies. It produced some sensational promotions – for example, one from private to colonel.) If the common soldier came to accept his Negro comrade-in-arms, it was very much on the terms of a song popular in the Irish brigade, 'Sambo's right to be kilt', which ended:

> The right to be kilt we'll divide wid him,
> And give him the largest half.[59]

As over emancipation itself, the administration lay low for as long as possible, under the barrage of popular prejudice and outrage. When Secretary of War Cameron began to make sympathetic noises about raising coloured troops, and even mentioned the subject in his report to Congress in December 1861, he was rapped over the knuckles, and his report amended, on the president's insistence. Lincoln avoided the issue when he could, rejected the idea of Negro troops when he was obliged to speak, and publicly expressed doubts about their military value. His first general endorsement of Negro troops came only in the second Emancipation Proclamation on 1 January 1863.[60]

But black regiments had in fact been raised long before this seal of presidential approval, and some had already seen action. Out on the wild western fringe of the war, James H. Lane began to raise coloured troops in Kansas – most of them fugitives from Missouri and Arkansas – as early as autumn 1861, and they were the first to take part in actual fighting, during 1862. In Louisiana, Butler raised three regiments of 'free Negro militia', which included many fugitive slaves, in the latter part of 1862. Most important of all, David Hunter had turned his attention to coloured troops at the same time as he issued his notorious emancipation order in May 1862. He proposed to raise a regiment in the South Carolina sea islands, but his rashness and the government's caution upset his plans. Unable to wait for sufficient volunteers, Hunter resorted to tougher methods. Negroes were dragged off from their homes or their work without warning, and subsequent assurances that they had the option of joining the army or not failed to restore their confidence or satisfy the critics. The government never gave Hunter the authorisation, the uniforms and the money which he sought, and, on 10 August, he disbanded the regiment shortly before leaving his command. Just two weeks later in a sudden reversal of policy which seems to indicate a belief that Hunter was simply not the man for the job, the administration authorised General Rufus Saxton, military governor on the sea islands, to raise up to 5,000 Negro troops. One company of the old regiment survived to provide a link with the new plan, and the work went ahead steadily. As colonel of the first regiment, Saxton secured the services of Thomas Wentworth Higginson, abolitionist, scholar and author of impeccable New England background. His appointment gave respectability to the whole venture, and his leadership self-respect to the whole force. Some of them had already taken part in raids along the coast before the end of the year, and, when he led his troops in New Year celebrations of emancipation, Higginson could reflect that the South Carolina precedent had opened the way to much wider use of Negro troops.

Lincoln's proclamation, however, was not followed by any avalanche of Negro recruits. Characteristically, his administration still approached the matter in a deliberate, piecemeal, unsystematic fashion. Only eight further regiments were authorised before the end of March. One of these was raised by Governor Andrew of Massachusetts whose agent George L. Stearns scoured the North for free Negro recruits, and after a slow start found enough not just for one regiment but for two. By mid-summer the situation had been transformed, and the future of Negro troops assured, by three developments above all. With the war going badly and white recruitment sagging, Lorenzo Thomas set off in April on his mission to the Mississippi Valley. At last the government was making a full-scale effort to raise coloured regiments in the region with the largest concentration of ex-slaves. The very conservatism and stolid orthodoxy of Thomas helped to convince the western army of the merits of his plan. By the end of 1863 he had raised twenty Negro regiments; a year later, thirty more had followed. By the end of the war, Thomas had been instrumental in the recruitment of 76,000 Negro troops, over 40 per cent of the total number raised.[61] The second new development was the creation in May 1863 of the Bureau of Colored Troops, in the War Department, which provided the coordination and central direction so clearly lacking in earlier efforts. The third turning-point was something more dramatic and symbolic. Negro troops had seen action in various engagements in the first half of 1863 – notably at Port Hudson and Milliken's Bend, on the Mississippi – but both they and their critics still felt that they were constantly on trial. On the evening of 18 July the 54th Massachusetts Infantry, the first of Andrew's Negro regiments, commanded by Colonel Robert Gould Shaw, led an almost hopeless assault on Fort Wagner, on Morris Island, just outside Charleston harbour. Militarily, the attack was a failure; Shaw and scores of his men were killed. But the regiment had passed through its fiery trial with great honour, and its deeds, widely publicised throughout the North, won for Negro troops the recognition which they needed, and did more than any words ever could to persuade Northerners that Negro freedom was a right and proper war aim.

By the end of the war, between 180,000 and 200,000 Negroes had served in the Union army, around 10 per cent of the grand total. At least 66 per cent of them had probably been slaves at the outbreak of war. 2,751 were killed in action, but many more died from disease. The pattern of recruiting varied from place to place and time to time. The passive attitude of many ex-slaves made volunteering slow in parts of the South, and low pay (and more remunerative civilian jobs) discouraged some free Negroes in the North. In the Mississippi Valley, and some other areas, impressment was widely used where volunteering was too slow – yet one more rude awakening from the first pleasures of freedom. Elsewhere, George L. Stearns, granted a commission after his successful work in raising Massachusetts regiments, preached and demonstrated in practice the virtues of a system which rejected press-gang methods, and relied on persuasion, encouragement, financial bounties, and specially selected recruiting officers.

The success of Negro recruitment in terms of sheer numbers was marred by some of the methods employed in raising them, and, much more, by the treatment they received after enlistment. They encountered all kinds of discrimination. A quite disproportionate number were assigned to auxiliary roles: garrison duties, guarding fortifications or contraband camps, or, worse still, heavy labour on construction work and fatigue duties of all kinds. Frequent complaints produced only slight and patchy improvement of the lot of the coloured soldier. One reason sometimes adduced for keeping Negroes away from the front line was fear for their fate in Confederate hands if taken prisoner. The fury of Southern reaction to the employment of black troops was predictable, and the Confederate Congress passed a law providing that their captured officers should be charged with servile insurrection, and the men themselves turned over to state law and returned to slavery. Dire threats were not always converted into battlefield realities, but the flames of controversy on this issue were constantly replenished by stories of atrocities against Negro troops. The worst incident followed the capture of Fort Pillow in Tennessee, by Forrest's troops in April 1864, when Negro soldiers were apparently slaughtered in cold blood.[62]

The greatest grievance of the Negro soldier concerned pay. At a time when the white soldier received $13 per month, plus $3.50 clothing allowance, the Negro received $10, out of which a $3 clothing allowance was deducted. This discrimination was first sanctioned by law in the Militia Act of 1862, at a time when Negro troops, if used at all, were expected to perform only an auxiliary role. But it endured for two years, partly out of deference to the interests of white soldiers (and white civilians) who saw equal pay in the army as the thin end of the wedge of Negro equality. The situation was made worse in practice when, for months on end, some regiments received no pay at all. (The 54th and 55th Massachusetts regiments, having been promised equal pay on enlistment, refused to accept any pay for two years until the injustice was put right.) The abolitionists spearheaded the demand for equal pay, and Secretary of War Stanton recommended it at the end of 1863. But Congress was once again slow to act, and unduly influenced by those who considered that equal pay would be an insult to the white soldier. The measure which finally passed in June 1864 made equal pay retroactive only to 1 January 1864 for the great majority of the troops. There were loopholes in the measure, and equal pay backdated for all to the date of enlistment was only achieved in March 1865. Even when grievances over pay were settled, others remained; the Negro soldier did not receive the financial inducements available to white recruits, and his chances of promotion to sergeant were small, to a commission very remote. The wonder is not that volunteering was sometimes slow, but that Negro desertions were not significantly higher than average – and, above all, that so many Negro soldiers served so faithfully and so well.

8. The chequered history of the Negro soldier typifies the whole process of wartime emancipation. The arming of the freedmen, like the act of liberation itself, was a revolutionary step for mid-nineteenth-century America. It not only demonstrated that emancipation as a war measure was no empty legal fiction, but it consolidated the achievement of freedom itself and gave the Negro the best available entry permit into American society. Millions of white Americans, who in 1861 regarded emancipation or the use of black troops as a fantasy or a nightmare, had four years later learned to live with both. Millions

of black Americans gained pride and self-respect from the knowledge that their own menfolk had shared in the fight for freedom. In the words of Frederick Douglass, 'liberty won by white men would lack half its lustre. Who would be free, themselves must strike the blow.'[63]

But, for all that, arming the blacks, like delivering them from slavery, was only a phase in a revolution which remained uncompleted. The crucial questions of land for the freedman, guarantees of his basic rights, and his admission to the franchise, had hardly been confronted, let alone solved. It was one thing to achieve freedom for the Negro, another to achieve equality before the law and before the bar of white opinion. It was one thing to put him in a blue uniform, another thing to put him in the same regiment, with the same pay and the same prospects, as his white counterpart. While abolitionists took up the cause of equal rights and negrophobes dug in their heels to resist it, most Republicans still sought a halfway-house for the black American somewhere between emergence from slavery and complete equality with the white man – and many hoped to find it in some blueprint which would allow equal civil and legal rights, but not full political rights or social integration.

Emancipation and the recruitment of Negro troops were the most dramatic changes wrought by the war, great but flawed monuments to the Northern cause. The flaws were all too obvious, and their origins not far to seek. The shortcomings of emancipation derived from the piecemeal, pragmatic, limited character of a revolution in which morality and justice were cloaked in military uniform, sombre legal robes, or the shabby garments of self-interest. They derived too from the character of the government which initiated the revolution and the society in which it took place. The federal authority was not geared to the huge and complex task of managing the transition of the ex-slave from bondage to liberty and on to a secure place in a society devoted to an individualist creed of self-help, and unrestricted competition. Free enterprise proved a harsh school for the newly freed slave. The limitations of emancipation owed most of all perhaps to the moral ambiguities which clouded the cause for which each side fought in the Civil War. Behind the dogmatic Southern defence of slavery lurked a sense of guilt which might be suppressed but would not die. Behind fierce Northern condemnation of slavery lurked a prejudice against the Negro which some resisted, some denied, but many openly avowed. The price of those ambiguities was a heavy one, and the interest on it is still being paid.

# Part Three: Vortex

# Chapter X: Campaigns of 1863

New Year's day 1863 was anything but a holiday for Abraham Lincoln. The usual White House reception attracted a stream of callers whose eager handshakes left the president's hand so stiff and sore that he had difficulty in grasping the pen for his most important act of this or many another day: putting his signature to the second Emancipation Proclamation (the final version of which he had that very morning written out in his own hand). But before he could play host at a social gathering or inaugurate a social revolution, he had to face another crisis with his generals, in the course of which both the general-in-chief and the commander of the Army of the Potomac would ask to be relieved of their posts. This all added up to a full enough day for any man, and yet Lincoln also found a moment to write a note to Secretary Stanton, supporting a 'piteous appeal' by 'an old lady of genteel appearance' who was threatened with eviction from her Washington house which numbered members of Congress among its boarders.[1]

The arrival of General Burnside at the White House began this day of turmoil. Lincoln was already well aware of the low morale of the Army of the Potomac in the aftermath of Fredericksburg, of the feuds and rivalries among its officers, and of the widespread loss of confidence in its commander. Burnside now complained that not one of his grand division commanders supported his proposal for a new move against the enemy. He offered 'most cheerfully' to give way to another officer, adding for good measure that as both Secretary of War Stanton and general-in-chief Halleck had also lost the confidence of the army and the country, they too should be removed. Halleck and Stanton were themselves brought into the White House discussions on this and subsequent days (and the honest, straightforward Burnside felt obliged to tell them to their faces what he had said to Lincoln behind their backs). Lincoln asked Halleck to examine Burnside's plan for a new attack and give a clear-cut yea or nay to it. 'If in such a difficulty as this you do not help,' he wrote, 'you fail me precisely in the point for which I sought your assistance. . . . Your military skill is useless to me if you will not do this.' Halleck's response was to submit his resignation, but he withdrew it later in the day when Lincoln also withdrew his letter, 'because considered harsh by Gen. Halleck', according to his own endorsement on it. The discussions in the capital and the feuding in the army continued, but Lincoln did not accept Burnside's resignation either on 1 January or when he renewed it a few days later, although the general must surely have read between the lines of Lincoln's reply on this second occasion: 'I do not yet see how I could profit by changing the command of the A.P.'[2]

That change was not long delayed. On 20 January Burnside took the army further up the Rappahannock at the start of a new move against Lee, but the advance became bogged down in heavy rain and thick mud and had to be abandoned. Disaffection among the officers was now degenerating into open disloyalty, and Burnside, driven to desperation, prepared orders dismissing four officers, including Joseph Hooker, from the army and relieving several more from their duties. Inevitably Lincoln refused to sanction such sweeping orders, and reluctantly he chose instead to accept Burnside's resignation on 25 January. He had already decided that the new commander of the Army of the Potomac should be none other than Joseph Hooker, the main target of Burnside's orders. Hooker had earned the name 'Fighting Joe' by his brave and aggressive leadership at all levels up to corps commander, but, in an army riddled with intrigue and faction, he had also earned a reputation as the most inveterate and ambitious intriguer of them all. In the famous letter which Lincoln handed to Hooker on the day after his appointment, he expressed his fear 'that the spirit which you have aided to infuse into the Army, of criticising their commander, and withholding confidence from him, will now turn upon you. I shall assist you as far as I can to put it down.'[3] In fact, in his first few weeks as commander, Hooker worked wonders with the army, and improvements in food, shelter and discipline and in pay and furlough arrangements revived the sagging spirits of officers and men alike. Hooker the fighter had revealed himself as a considerable organiser too. But the real test was still to come: could he manipulate and control his huge army in battle against an adversary of the calibre of Robert E. Lee?

1. The new year brought command problems on the western front as well as in the east. Grant and Rosecrans remained secure in the main commands, although the former still faced sniper fire from his critics and the latter was beginning his sustained bombardment of Washington with a hail of despatches which were as plaintive as they were prolix. (He even asked to have his appointment as major-general backdated so as to make him senior to Grant.)[4] The real trouble came from other sources, above all from the consequences of curious

plans laid and appointments made by the president himself in the autumn of 1862. Very conscious by that time of the importance of regaining control of the whole length of the Mississippi, for political and psychological as much as purely military reasons, he envisaged advances both up-stream from New Orleans and down-stream from Memphis, and he chose two political generals of dubious military repute to command them. For the New Orleans command, he selected Nathaniel P. Banks, whose military record was most notable for the humiliation he had suffered at the hands of Stonewall Jackson in the Shenandoah Valley six months earlier. Now Banks delayed his departure for New Orleans while he accumulated masses of supplies; then, once in Louisiana, he became enmeshed in the problems of governing occupied territory; when he did turn his attention to military objectives, he was so impressed by the strength of the Confederate defences at Port Hudson which blocked his advance up the Mississippi that he turned his thoughts to a tempting foray up the Red River, which could only take him further and further from his true objective.

If Banks's appointment was a mistake, the choice of John A. McClernand to lead the expedition down-river was sheer folly. In a sense, McClernand had chosen himself and persuaded Lincoln to second the nomination. A Democratic politician and former Congressman from Illinois, he had rendered his greatest service to the Union cause in the early days of the war when he had rallied a great deal of support in a vital region, among sections of opinion whose sympathies and loyalties were in the balance. He had been rewarded for his efforts with a commission as major-general of volunteers, and now his military ambition knew no bounds. In the fall of 1862 he came to Washington and convinced Lincoln that, through his political and personal influence, he could raise a new force in the middle West, with which he would then clear the whole of the Mississippi. Lincoln and Stanton drew up orders so deplorably imprecise that Grant was left completely in the dark about his relationship with this new commander operating within his own department; general-in-chief Halleck was neither consulted nor even informed about the whole project.

McClernand's independent force ran into trouble from the start. As he raised his new recruits, they were sent forward to Memphis where, through a confusion of orders in which Grant, Halleck and Lincoln all had a part (whether intentional or not), they were assigned to Sherman's advance down-river in December 1862. By the time McClernand himself arrived in Memphis, his status had been reduced to that of a corps commander in Grant's army, and his own troops had already departed for Vicksburg under Sherman's command. There was nothing left but to leap aboard the nearest available steamboat and hasten down-river in pursuit of his own men. When he finally caught up with them, Sherman had already been repulsed at the battle of Chickasaw Bluffs. As the early date of his commission as major-general gave him seniority over Sherman, McClernand now seized command of everything in sight and headed up the Arkansas river (which joins the Mississippi north of Vicksburg) to attack the Confederate position at Fort Hindman, or Arkansas Post. He took the fort on 11 January, and Grant, who had earlier deplored this 'wild goose chase' up the Arkansas, applauded its success when he found that Sherman had favoured the idea in the first place.

The problem of McClernand remained to plague Grant and Lincoln for the next six months. He pestered both Lincoln and Stanton with complaints about his treatment, blaming most of his troubles on the wretched Halleck, and accusing him of every conceivable kind of incompetence, including even 'want of eminence in any profession or calling, previous to his appointment as Maj. Genl.' Lincoln wearily replied that 'I have too many *family* controversies (so to speak), already on my hands, to voluntarily, or so long as I can avoid it, take up another'.[5] The president may well have realised by now that he was largely to blame for this particular family squabble, and that the whole affair was one of the costlier lessons in his own military education. Grant accepted McClernand as a cross which he had to bear for political as well as military reasons, and he soldiered through the arduous Vicksburg campaign with a senior corps commander whose willingness to fight far exceeded his military skill, whose past political services far outweighed his current military value, and whose thirst for personal glory submerged his small taste for teamwork or cooperation. Grant's decision in January 1863 not to renew the overland march on Vicksburg but to take personal command on the Mississippi itself was amply justified on strategic and tactical grounds; it also had the highly desirable side-effect of confining McClernand to a subordinate role.

In the North there was a widespread feeling that, if Northern superiority in manpower and resources was not yet yielding the expected harvest of victories, there must surely be something radically wrong with the leadership both in Washington and in the field. In the South, expectations and reservations about the generals rested on very different premises. It was an article of faith that Southern generalship should and would always be superior to Northern, and the brilliant feats of Lee and Jackson were living testimony to the truth of this axiom. The Confederacy pinned its faith in the greater genius of its military commanders to offset the Northern numerical and material advantage. Too optimistically, it was assumed that there would be a Robert E. Lee for every occasion.

The Confederate command problem centred on the wide-open western front. It was a question both of personalities and priorities, and it was not helped by the inflexible departmental structure favoured by Jefferson Davis himself. This had already cost him the services of one Secretary of War, George W. Randolph, who resigned in November 1862 after the president had countermanded instructions authorising General Holmes, who was in command west of the Mississippi, to take his army across to the east bank. The western front was the responsibility of at least three different armies with three different commanders: the Army of Tennessee under Braxton Bragg, encamped at Murfreesboro until the end of 1862, and then further south-east at Tullahoma; the Army of Mississippi, under John C. Pemberton, charged with the defence of Vicksburg

and the Mississippi; and the Army of the Trans-Mississippi, under Theophilus
H. Holmes. Cooperation between these three forces was hampered by distance,
the disposition of the enemy's forces, and disagreements over who should come
to whose aid. Grant's army effectively blocked direct east–west communication
between Bragg and Pemberton and spoiled any contingency plans to enable one
to provide speedy reinforcements for the other. Indeed, in terms of travelling
time, Bragg was nearer to Lee in Virginia than to Pemberton in Mississippi.
Each commander was inclined to complain that his numbers were already too
small for the job in hand, without the need to detach men to help out elsewhere.
In the trans-Mississippi area, Holmes was deaf to entreaties from across the river
or even from the president in Richmond that he should join forces with
Pemberton to save Vicksburg. Pemberton, still relatively untried, and distrusted
as a man of Northern birth, concerned himself with the defence of that vital
point to the exclusion of all else. Braxton Bragg presented the greatest headache
of all. He was highly regarded as an organiser and a disciplinarian (except by the
victims of his severity), but his headlong retreat from Kentucky in autumn
1862 and his withdrawal from Murfreesboro after he had aroused hopes of a
great victory, had undermined confidence in him. Early in 1863 he took the
unusual step of asking his subordinate commanders for their candid opinion of
his leadership. Making the most of this unexpected opportunity they left Bragg
in no doubt that a change of command would be welcome. The man charged
by Davis with investigating this sorry mess was Joseph E. Johnston, who, in
November 1862, had been placed in overall command of the whole area between
the Appalachians and the Mississippi in an attempt to devise and execute some
coordinated western strategy. Despite continuing complaints from the army,
Johnston reported in favour of Bragg's retention, and warded off another attempt
to remove him in March and April. It took another crisis of confidence and a
major defeat finally to unseat him at the end of the year.

   Johnston found his wider responsibilities in the west depressing and frustrating.
Never one to make the best of a bad job, he resigned himself to the gloomy
conclusion that the west could not be defended with the available manpower.
His jurisdiction did not extend beyond the Mississippi and he could not therefore
order Holmes or his successor Kirby Smith to collaborate with Pemberton. He
disagreed with Pemberton, and with Davis himself, about the strategy which
which would make optimum use of the available resources. They insisted on
defending as much territory as possible, and above all on defending key fortified
positions like Vicksburg. Johnston, on the other hand, favoured concentration
of his forces and resort to a mobile defence, which might involve the temporary
loss of territory or even of key points but which would keep the army intact,
and save it from being bottled up without means of escape. Above all, Johnston
posed the fundamental question of priorities to which he could never obtain a
satisfactory answer. Which mattered more: Vicksburg and the Mississippi, or
the defence of the line in middle and eastern Tennessee? The answer from
Richmond was that both were vital and both must be saved. Johnston, more

pessimistic (or realistic), believed that 'without some great blunder of the enemy we cannot hold both',[6] and gave top priority to the Tennessee front. Here, he thought, in the middle sector between Virginia and the Mississippi, was the key to the whole strategic position. The collapse of the line at this point would expose the deep interior of the South to Northern invasion, and splinter the whole Confederacy. On the other hand, a concentrated effort here might threaten to drive a wedge into the whole Union position, and put Grant in particular at grave risk; at the very least even the gloomy Johnston might hope that it would force the North to draw off some of its strength from other points to protect the vital centre.[7] Here as elsewhere, the burden on Southern generals was to find the best practical answers to agonising questions of priorities, while the demand on Northern leadership was to maintain constant, unflagging pressure all along the line.

2. All the other high points of the campaigns of 1863 are overshadowed by four soaring peaks: Chancellorsville and Gettysburg in the east, Vicksburg and Chattanooga in the west. At the beginning of the year the most simple-minded armchair strategist could have foreseen the inescapable destiny of three out of the four: Vicksburg, key to the lower Mississippi, Chattanooga, gateway to the Confederate heartland, and Chancellorsville, hard by Fredericksburg where Lee had already thrown back one attempt to dislodge him. But the fates had not yet marked out the fourth; in January 1863 Gettysburg was still just a quiet little Pennsylvania college town, untouched by the war, unconsidered by the military planners and apparently safely remote from the front line.

The new year's campaigning got off to a stuttering start. Indeed, in the middle sector, Rosecrans and Bragg sat looking at each other and doing little or nothing for the first half of the year in what was one of the longest lulls on any major front in the whole war. In the east, Hooker needed time to revive the Army of the Potomac before he dared to throw down a new challenge to Lee. On the Mississippi, in contrast, there was plenty of activity in the late winter and early spring, though it seemed for a long time to be so unproductive that the critics and rumour-mongers raised their voices in chorus once again to cast slurs on Grant's military capacity and personal behaviour. Single-minded and purposeful as ever, the general was preparing his next move on Vicksburg.

Geography wrote the stage directions for the Vicksburg campaign. Grant's problem was as simple to state as it was difficult to solve. Having abandoned the overland approach from the north-east, he was committed to the river approach from the north and west. But Vicksburg's imposing defences were at their most formidable against an attack from precisely this direction and looked powerful enough to interdict any attempt to pass down-river and tackle the city from the more vulnerable south and east. Grant understood the problem, but refused to run away from it. In his own words, 'the problem then became, how to secure a landing on high ground east of the Mississippi without an apparent retreat'.[8] For most of its course through the Southern states, the Mississippi is a wide and

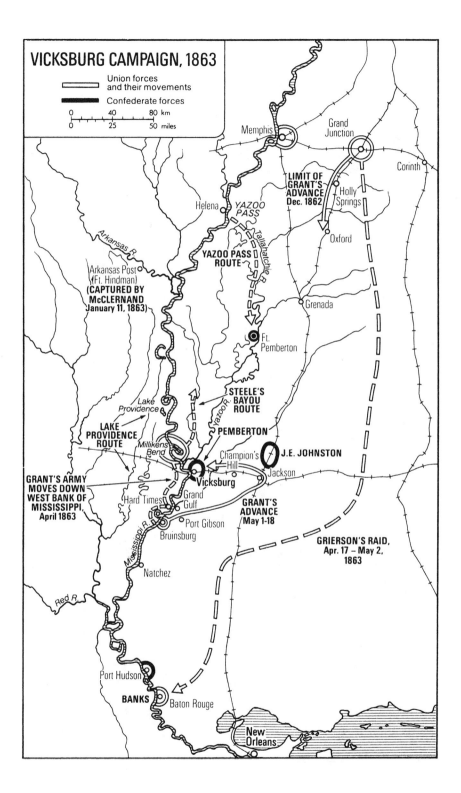

## VICKSBURG CAMPAIGN, 1863

Union forces and their movements

Confederate forces

| 0 | 40 | 80 km |
| 0 | 25 | 50 miles |

Memphis

Grand Junction

Corinth

**LIMIT OF GRANT'S ADVANCE Dec. 1862**

Holly Springs

Helena

*YAZOO PASS*

Oxford

Arkansas R.

**YAZOO PASS ROUTE**

Tallahatchie R.

Arkansas Post (Ft. Hindman) **(CAPTURED BY McCLERNAND January 11, 1863)**

Grenada

Ft. Pemberton

Lake Providence

**STEELE'S BAYOU ROUTE**

Yazoo R.

**LAKE PROVIDENCE ROUTE**

**PEMBERTON**

Milliken's Bend

Champion's Hill

**J.E. JOHNSTON**

Jackson

**GRANT'S ARMY MOVES DOWN WEST BANK OF MISSISSIPPI, April 1863**

Vicksburg

Hard Times

Grand Gulf

**GRANT'S ADVANCE May 1-18**

Port Gibson

Bruinsburg

**GRIERSON'S RAID, Apr. 17 – May 2, 1863**

Mississippi R.

Natchez

Red R.

Port Hudson

**BANKS**

Baton Rouge

New Orleans

tortuous river, winding its way between natural dykes or artificial levées which protect the low-lying land on either bank. For miles on either side, that country was criss-crossed by streams, lakes and bayous (stretches of water which were replenished each time the river overflowed its banks), hemmed in by thick vegetation and overhanging trees. Such country, where streams not infrequently changed course, and the dry land of one day was the swamp of the next, was well-nigh impossible for an advancing army. This was above all true of the area of the Yazoo Delta, on the east bank of the river, north of Vicksburg. If the invaders chose a water-borne advance down the great river itself, geography stepped in again to block the way. There were a few points along the river where the low-lying country gave way to higher ground, or bluffs. Memphis was one such place, and Vicksburg, Grand Gulf and Port Hudson were others. Vicksburg had the most commanding position of all, standing two hundred feet above the river, just below its junction with the Yazoo, and at a point where the river bends sharply (from north-east to south-west). (Since Civil War days, the river has cut a new path further west and by-passed Vicksburg itself.) Back in the summer of 1862, Vicksburg had been inadequately manned and fortified, but now its natural strength was reinforced by elaborate defensive works and its guns commanded a long stretch of river in both directions. One hundred miles to the south (but much further by the winding river route), stood Port Hudson, another strong defensive position which defied attack from the south by General Banks and Admiral Farragut on 14 March 1863. The stretch of the Mississippi between those two points was the remaining link between the main body of the Confederacy and its far western region. Even that link was far from safe, for Union gunboats were already active along much of its length, but while the Confederate army held Vicksburg and Port Hudson it survived, however precariously.

By the end of January the Union army was camped along the levées on the banks of the Mississippi around Milliken's Bend, a mere fifteen miles or so in a straight line from Vicksburg, and Grant had assumed direct personal command. There was no possibility yet of making a major move, especially as the winter was exceptionally wet, and the river running unusually high, but Grant busied himself and his army with a series of 'experiments', as he later described them, in the search for a route, however unlikely or unconventional, which would take his troops round behind the Vicksburg defences. He took up an earlier idea of cutting a canal across the base of the loop in the river on which Vicksburg stood, which would enable ships to by-pass the city's defences. However, the technical and topographical obstacles proved too great, the heavy rain produced conditions which threatened to drown the canal diggers without floating the ships, and Confederate batteries were in any case still within range. At the same time, many miles up-river, Grant instigated exploration of the prospects of a channel from the west bank of the Mississippi to Lake Providence which, it was claimed, would open up a connection with the Red River, and thus facilitate an approach to Vicksburg from the south. But this route involved a detour of several hundred miles along unfamiliar and unnavigable waterways deep in enemy country, and the project was soon abandoned. However, Grant's most serious 'experiments' were concentrated in the area of the Yazoo delta, on the east bank of the Mississippi, where he had hopes of finding a usable route through the maze of streams and bayous which could carry his troops to an advantageous landing-place on the Yazoo river itself, somewhere north-east of Vicksburg. From there they could attack the Confederate stronghold from the more vulnerable landward direction. In this bewildering and unpromising area, two experiments were actually put to the test. The first, the Yazoo pass route, involved blasting a gap in the levée of the Mississippi, far to the north at a point opposite the town of Helena, Arkansas, and sending ships with 20,000 men aboard on a complicated course to reach first the Tallahatchie river and then, it was hoped, the Yazoo itself. Choked and winding waterways, thick and tangled vegetation (and Confederate harassment), made the navy's task appallingly difficult, and the painful Union advance was finally turned back by the hastily prepared Confederate defences at Fort Pemberton, which stood on one of the few patches of firm dry ground in the whole region. Later in March another expedition set out on the Steele's Bayou route, from a point much closer to Vicksburg. Here the Mississippi and the Yazoo were only twenty miles apart, but the route involved a two-hundred-mile detour in conditions even worse than those which ruined the previous venture. Ships found themselves almost going round in circles, and when the Confederates began to fell trees across the narrow streams both ahead and astern of them, it seemed distinctly possible that a Union naval force was about to be cut off and captured by the Confederate army. But some of Sherman's troops were landed to hold off the enemy while the ships beat a clumsy retreat, and the expedition laboured back to its starting-point. As winter gave way to spring, Grant was apparently as far as ever from his objective.

The Northern observer, whether military or civilian, might well have been pardoned for concluding at this point that Grant was a failure. Back in December he had been forced to abandon his overland march through northern Mississippi, and Sherman had been heavily defeated at Chickasaw Bluffs. Now he had apparently wasted three months in futile and fanciful attempts to find the magic key to Vicksburg's defences. It is small wonder that even Lincoln and Stanton were so impressed by the mounting criticism of the general that they sent a special commissioner, Charles A. Dana, to assess Grant and his army at first hand. (Dana, in fact, was very favourably impressed by what he found.) Both then and later Grant maintained that his 'experiments' had been primarily intended to keep his own troops busy and the enemy guessing.[9] It may be doubted whether such activities, beginning in discomfort, continuing in confusion and ending in apparent failure, did much for the morale of his own men, but they were much more successful in achieving their second objective. They kept the puzzled Pemberton under constant pressure, and forced him to disperse his limited forces over a much wider area than he would have wished.

By the end of March, Grant had committed himself to his final solution to the Vicksburg problem. In comparison with earlier plans, it was remarkably simple and direct, but it was also extremely hazardous. It involved no digging, and no detours, but it allowed no halfway house between triumph and disaster. The bulk of the army would be marched south over the difficult terrain on the west bank of the Mississippi, to a point well below Vicksburg. The navy would then run its gunboats, along with transports and supply ships, past the Vicksburg batteries under cover of night, to a point where the army could be ferried across to the east bank. Then at last Grant would be in a position to move on Vicksburg from the south and east. In a dangerous operation of this kind there could be no going back if things went wrong. The poor roads and makeshift bridges over which the army moved south could never ensure either regular supplies or a safe retreat. Once below Vicksburg, Grant could seek to link up with Banks, as Lincoln and Halleck suggested, but he could scarcely be blamed if he found such a prospect unappealing. As for the hazards of the river itself, ships might slip once past the Vicksburg batteries but they could never risk a return journey up-stream against a strong current. Admiral Porter had sent two of his ships past the Vicksburg batteries in February, but their subsequent misadventures scarcely provided the best of omens for further attempts.[10]

During April the bulk of the army, with McClernand's corps in the lead, made its way southwards through appallingly difficult country, west of the Mississippi, and camped on the river bank at Hard Times. On the night of 16–17 April Porter's flotilla of gunboats, transports and barges successfully braved the fire of Vicksburg's guns. The ships suffered heavy punishment, but, with their boilers protected by bales of cotton and hay, or sacks of grain, most of them kept going. A week later more supply ships and barges emerged battered from a similar perilous run, but soon both the ships and their precious supplies were ready to play their part in the next stage of Grant's plan. He had originally hoped to carry the army across the river in the vicinity of Grand Gulf, but, finding the Confederate position there too strong, he chose a landing-place further south at Bruinsburg, on the recommendation of a local Negro informant. On 30 April he was at last able to start disembarking troops on the east bank of the river.

It was a great moment, but Grant was merely exchanging one set of hazards and difficulties for another. As he himself put it:

> I was now in the enemy's country, with a vast river and the stronghold of Vicksburg between me and my base of supplies. But I was on dry ground on the same side of the river with the enemy. All the campaigns, labors, hardships and exposures from the month of December previous to this time that had been made and endured, were for the accomplishment of this one object.[11]

So far, Pemberton had reacted slowly and indecisively. His uncertainty had been nourished by two highly successful diversions instigated by Grant. On

29–30 April, while the crossing at Bruinsburg was taking place, Sherman's corps, which had been left north of Vicksburg for this purpose, was staging an ostentatious demonstration in the area of Chickasaw Bluffs, which left Pemberton still in doubt where the main enemy thrust was to come. His anxieties had also been multiplied by the spectacular Union cavalry raid, led by Colonel Benjamin Grierson, which set out from La Grange, Tennessee, on 18 April, swept through central Mississippi, and joined up with Banks at Baton Rouge, Louisiana, on 2 May. With less than 1,000 men, and in little over two weeks, Grierson covered some six hundred miles, leaving a trail of torn up railroad track, shattered bridges and burning supplies in his wake, and prompting the unhappy Pemberton to commit a whole division to a fruitless pursuit. For all this, Pemberton's position was still one of potential strength, and Grant's one of immediate danger. As long as the Confederates controlled Vicksburg, they stood between Grant and his supply base, and with numbers almost equal to those which he could deploy on the east bank of the river, they could hope to cut off his army and destroy it. Grant could rely for supplies neither on the river, nor on the poor roads to the west of it. He could expect nothing from Banks to the south, for his attention was now diverted to his Red River escapade. This at least gave Grant the excuse he needed to act alone. Having defeated Pemberton's advance guard at Port Gibson on 1 May, Grant pushed inland, apparently intending to extend his precarious supply line still further. But in fact he was about to cap his bold decision to move south of Vicksburg with an even bolder one. He would solve the problem of his vulnerable supply line by dispensing with it altogether. His army would advance deep into Mississippi, carrying its ammunition with it, and living off the country. It was almost as if Grant and his army were disappearing into a dark tunnel, and no one knew when or where, or even whether, they would emerge.

3. While Grant had been probing the Vicksburg defences in February and March, Joseph Hooker had been working hard to reorganise and revitalise the Army of the Potomac, still camped on the north bank of the Rappahannock opposite Fredericksburg. During April, while Grant was at last moving below Vicksburg, Hooker was making plans for a new attack on Lee. At the end of the month, while Grant was crossing the Mississippi and preparing to strike bodly inland, Hooker came face to face with Lee at Chancellorsville. At the first two stages, of preparation and planning, Hooker might well have impressed an impartial observer at least as favourably as Grant, but at the third vital stage, of execution, it was a very different story. While Grant was passing with flying colours, Hooker failed the final stern examination on the field of battle itself.

The arrival of fresh troops and the return of many absentees had carried the strength of the Army of the Potomac over the 130,000 mark – the largest army the war had yet seen. Such numbers gave Hooker a two-to-one advantage over Lee, who had been obliged to detach two divisions under Longstreet for duty further south, in the Virginia–North Carolina coastal area. There was much merit too in Hooker's plan of campaign, which was the complete antithesis of the crude, frontal assault so disastrously attempted by his predecessor. He decided in favour of a move up-stream to get round Lee's left flank, but he left Sedgwick with 40,000 men to create a major diversion by a river crossing a mile or two down-stream from Fredericksburg. The 70,000 men in the main advance were to cross the Rappahannock and its tributary the Rapidan by a number of fords, and then advance from the west through the densely wooded area known as the Wilderness to a point where they could threaten Lee's left and rear. To avoid being cut off, the Confederate army would either have to come out of its powerful defences and fight in the open, or it would have to retreat towards Richmond with the main Union force threatening its flank. Hooker's confidence in his excellent plan was such that he came to regard its promise as self-fulfilling. He was dreaming of the rich harvest to come while the seed was still only half sown and before Lee and Jackson had unleashed their storm upon it.

The flanking move began on 27 April, and all went smoothly enough for three days, although Hooker had already deprived his army of its eyes by sending the bulk of the cavalry on a raid far to the south. By the afternoon of 30 April he had three corps at Chancellorsville near the eastern fringe of the Wilderness, and he chose to halt there rather than push on to more open ground. Lee, well informed of the enemy's movements, decided on that same day to move the bulk of his army against this threat from the west, and left Jubal A. Early with a mere 10,000 men to hold off Sedgwick on the other flank. On 1 May Hooker's army began a three-pronged advance, but after some modest skirmishing with Lee's advance guard, it was unaccountably withdrawn from a promising situation back to its position in the Wilderness around Chancellorsville. At the first minor challenge Hooker had decided against putting his master plan to the test, and surrendered the initiative to an army half the size of his own. Whether this extraordinary error is to be ascribed to loss of nerve or loss of control over a large-scale operation which he could not adequately visualise, no one has ever been able to explain satisfactorily; there are those indeed who ascribe it to loss of the alcoholic stimulation on which Hooker habitually relied, but which he had denied himself since assuming his responsibilities as army commander.

Lee had never contemplated a purely defensive response to Hooker's advance and now he and Jackson planned a counter-stroke which, in its sheer audacity, outshone even the similar decision which had led to Second Bull Run eight months earlier. With his outnumbered forces already divided once, Lee proposed to divide them again, leaving a bare 17,000 men directly facing three times as many Union troops, while Jackson took a force of 26,000 on a long march round the enemy's exposed right flank to attack from the rear. On the morning of 2 May Jackson's men carried out their ten-mile detour round the south of the Union line; neither Hooker nor Howard, the corps commander on that flank,

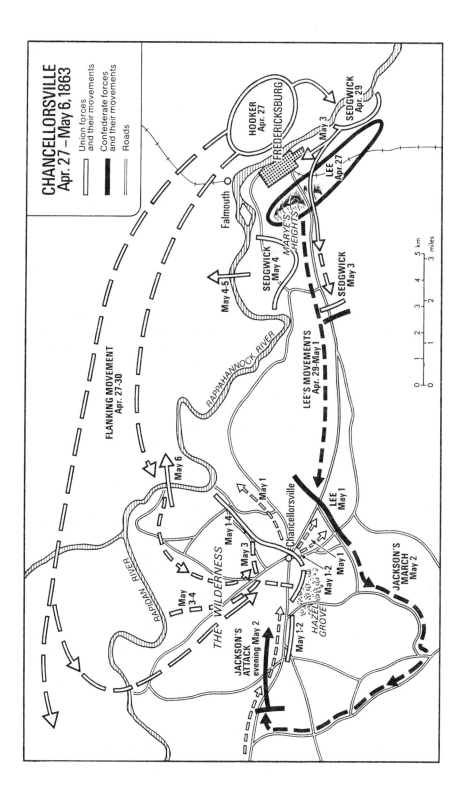

CHANCELLORSVILLE
Apr. 27 – May 6, 1863

Union forces
and their movements
Confederate forces
and their movements
Roads

HOOKER
Apr. 27

FREDERICKSBURG

SEDGWICK
Apr. 29

LEE
Apr. 27

May 3

Falmouth

MARYE'S
HEIGHTS

SEDGWICK
May 4

SEDGWICK
May 3

SEDGWICK
May 3

May 4-5

RAPPAHANNOCK RIVER

LEE'S MOVEMENTS
Apr. 29–May 1

FLANKING MOVEMENT
Apr. 27–30

May 6

May 1

Chancellorsville

LEE
May 1

LEE
May 1

May 1

RAPIDAN RIVER

May 1-4

May 3

THE WILDERNESS

May 3-4

May 1-2

May 1-2

HAZEL
GROVE

JACKSON'S
MARCH
May 2

JACKSON'S
ATTACK
evening May 2

May 1-2

0        1        2        3        4        5 km
0        1        2        3 miles

made any serious or sustained attempt to oppose Jackson's move, although they were well aware of it. (For a time, they even thought that what they were witnessing was a Confederate retreat.) In the early evening Jackson was ready to smash into the rear of the Union position. For a time the attack went well, causing chaos and confusion in the Union ranks, but eventually darkness, the dense undergrowth of the Wilderness and errors by subordinate commanders spread the confusion to the attackers too, and the fighting petered out. The fruits of victory turned sour in Southern mouths when, in the thickening gloom, Stonewall Jackson himself was shot down by troops from his own side, as he returned from a reconnaissance. That night his arm was amputated, and a week later, after a last brave fight, he died.

Despite the humiliating reverses of 2 May, Hooker's position on the following morning was still a strong one. His line now faced south, and as long as his army held the salient in the centre of his position, at Hazel Grove, it kept apart the two halves of Lee's army, the combined strength of which was still less than half his own. But Hooker's mind was not focused on the attacking opportunities thus offered. Instead, he chose to abandon the crucial Hazel Grove position, and then to withdraw still further in the face of a Confederate bombardment in the course of which the last remnants of fighting spirit were knocked out of him by a solid shot which struck the pillar of the Chancellor house against which he was leaning. Badly shaken and partly paralysed for some time, Hooker nevertheless refused to hand over full command to a subordinate. Lee's army, now reunited by the Union withdrawal, kept up the pressure but now had to turn to meet a new threat. Sedgwick had at last broken into Fredericksburg from the east, stormed Marye's Heights at the fourth attempt and was advancing on the rear of Lee's position. Lee flung men hastily into position, and having checked Sedgwick on the afternoon of 3 May, attacked him with a force of 21,000 (against Sedgwick's 19,000) on the next day, while Jeb Stuart with a mere 25,000 men contained the 75,000 in Hooker's main army (which meekly submitted to its own containment). During the following night, Sedgwick withdrew back north of the Rappahannock; Hooker was now intent on doing the same, despite the majority opinion of his corps commanders in favour of an advance, and, on the night of 5–6 May, the main body of the Army of the Potomac retired north of the river once again.

A brief campaign rather than a single battle, Chancellorsville was the high peak of Lee's military career. Placed in real jeopardy by Hooker's clever plan, he had reacted promptly, aggressively and boldly. Seldom if ever can an army have so thoroughly bemused and humiliated an adversary twice its size. By taking stupendous risks, he had contrived to equal or surpass the enemy's strength when and where it really mattered. The brilliance of Lee's victory did not altogether obscure the darker side of Chancellorsville. His total losses, 13,000 as against the Union 17,000, were proportionally much heavier than his opponents'. The death of Jackson was the heaviest blow of all, and Lee was never to be quite the same attacking force again. Chancellorsville was precisely the kind of risky and unorthodox operation which Lee could never undertake with confidence without Jackson to help him. Other doubts lingered in the aftermath of Chancellorsville. Lee had taken the measure of Hooker correctly, but would his matchless audacity and unshakable confidence in his men come to grief against some more steadfast opponent? And did the Chancellorsville triumph offer any better prospect of a successful follow-up than Fredericksburg had done four months earlier? The Army of the Potomac was still there, massive and powerful as ever, painfully hurt rather than permanently damaged by this latest defeat. One-third of the army had scarcely been engaged in the fighting at all, and officers and men alike were inclined to blame the army's disgrace on the loss of nerve and the blunders of its commander. Chancellorsville was a success so dazzling as to be dangerous for the victors, and a defeat so stinging as to arouse rather than demoralise the vanquished.

4. Lee knew what he wished to do next, to exploit his latest success; indeed, even before Chancellorsville, he had been advocating another raid into northern territory. But Lee's wishes were now caught up in a great strategic debate. The Confederacy was under pressure all along the line. Even after his recent triumph, Lee could not afford to stand still in the face of the huge Army of the Potomac; in the west, Grant was penning Pemberton's army within the Vicksburg defences, and Bragg felt able to do no more than await Rosecrans's next move in Tennessee; around the coast, the Union blockade tightened and Union forces strengthened their footholds at one point after another. There were simply not enough men to go around, and the strategic debate was once again essentially a question of priorities. For months, the generals in the west, and Johnston in particular, had been demanding a major effort there to remedy the serious consequences of earlier neglect. Now two other voices were raised in support of the same idea. Longstreet, Lee's senior corps commander, and Beauregard, now back in South Carolina, proposed similar schemes for a major concentration in Tennessee for an attack on Rosecrans which they hoped would liberate Tennessee and Kentucky, threaten Ohio, and thus reduce the pressure on other fronts. In particular, they claimed, it would oblige Grant to call off his operations against Vicksburg. However, a basic condition for the success of any such project was that Bragg's army should be reinforced by troops from other theatres, including a large contingent from Lee's Army of Northern Virginia. Beauregard argued that Lee himself should move west to lead the attack in Tennessee. Lee objected strongly to the whole scheme. He stressed that his army was already heavily outnumbered, and perilously short of food and other supplies. He believed that, owing to the inadequacy of the railroads, the South could shift troops from one theatre to another less rapidly and less effectively than the North. He also firmly believed that Grant's campaign in Mississippi must shortly come to a halt in any case, because Northern soldiers could not work and fight in the stifling heat of a deep south summer. Above all, he insisted that the Confederacy's best hope was to take the offensive in the area where past results offered the best prospect

of future success – and the record of Lee and his army left no doubt where that should be.

In a series of meetings in May, Lee's views won the day. First Longstreet, then Seddon, the Secretary of War, then Davis and the cabinet were won over by Lee's arguments and by the incontrovertible authority of his record and reputation. Initially, he justified another invasion of the North from Virginia in very limited and modest terms. It would free the soil of Virginia from the invader and Richmond from immediate danger; it would open up fresh and urgently needed sources of food and other supplies in the Shenandoah Valley, and, even more, in the rich farmland of Pennsylvania; it would forestall any new aggressive move on the Union side. Basically, Lee argued that, despite past successes, his position was still precarious; he could not afford to stand still and surrender the initiative. Attack was the best form of defence, and, in that sense, an invasion of the North was essentially a defensive operation. As he put it in a letter to Davis during the invasion itself:

> It seems to me that we cannot afford to keep our troops awaiting possible movements of the enemy, but that our true policy is, as far as we can, so to employ our own forces as to give occupation to his at points of our selection.[12]

However, as the idea of an invasion took hold, it acquired grander (or even grandiose) objectives, and inspired thoughts of more valuable prizes, especially if the army could win a great victory on Northern soil. Lee's supreme confidence in his army was matched by the general Southern confidence in them both. It seemed more and more feasible, even to Lee himself, that his invasion might greatly encourage the peace movement in the North which had been growing ever since the winter, and that it might finally destroy Northern morale, already buffeted by one reverse after another. Perhaps even the governments of Britain and France might be forced to reconsider their position and ask themselves whether the Confederates had not after all 'made a nation' and earned recognition.

Knowledge of the eventual outcome of Lee's invasion makes it almost impossible to arrive at a fair assessment of the merits of the strategic argument in May 1863.[13] There can be no certainty that the western strategy would have won all or any of the advantages claimed for it; it is surely hard to imagine that anything short of a major disaster in Tennessee would have caused Grant to relax his hold on Vicksburg. On the other hand, the Confederacy was in serious danger of losing the war in the west, it had never given that theatre an adequate share of its resources, and Lee's invasion of Pennsylvania failed to draw any Union troops away from the western front. Moreover, Lee's contribution to the debate does suggest the limitations of his approach to these wider issues. The price of his single-minded devotion to the job in hand in Virginia was an unwillingness or an inability to take an overall strategic view. He had no first-hand knowledge of the western situation, and the man who had thrown in his lot with the Confederacy because he could not act against his native state still had Virginia at the top of his list of priorities. But, even if his views were rather narrowly based, his authority was beyond challenge from those who could not begin to match his superb record as a commander in the field. The decision in favour of his plan was justified above all by the principle of building on success rather than reinforcing failure. It was all the more to be deplored therefore that his new enterprise was not backed by every man and weapon which could be squeezed out of other commands, and that his offensive thrust remained a virtually independent operation, the sole exception to a general policy of widespread troop deployment in the interests of territorial defence. Lacking the resources to save the situation on all three major fronts at the same time, the Confederate leadership had once again compromised on the vital issue of priorities.

5. While the Confederate strategists wrangled and Lee prepared for his invasion, Grant was rampaging through Mississippi in a campaign which Lincoln described, with pardonable exaggeration, as 'one of the most brilliant in the world'.[14] Having made the momentous decision to abandon his supply line and live off the country, Grant now moved with great speed to get between the two forces opposed to him: Pemberton's army in and around Vicksburg, and the scattered troops whom Johnston was gathering further east, around the town of Jackson. Johnston received orders from Richmond on 9 May to take personal command in Mississippi, but his arrival only served to highlight a fundamental strategic disagreement in the Confederate ranks. Pemberton, backed by urgent messages from Richmond, was determined to defend Vicksburg itself to the last. He was now busy concentrating his troops for that very purpose, and once the Union army began its advance into Mississippi he set out to cut its non-existent supply line. Even after the campaign was over, Pemberton was still insisting that:

> With a moderate cavalry force at my disposal, I am firmly convinced that the Federal army under General Grant would have been unable to maintain its communication with the Mississippi River, and that the attempt to reach Jackson and Vicksburg would have been as signally defeated in May, 1863, as a like attempt from another base had, by the employment of cavalry, been defeated in December, 1862.[15]

Johnston, on the other hand, argued that, if Pemberton's army allowed itself to be besieged in Vicksburg, this could end only in the loss of both the city and the army. Indeed, he claimed that Vicksburg had already lost its usefulness since Union gunboats had passed its batteries and now controlled most of the river down to Port Hudson. It was vital to keep the army intact and in a position where it could link up with Johnston's own forces.

Meanwhile, Grant was bearing down on the town of Jackson itself where

General Johnston had arrived only on 13 May. Next day he was obliged to abandon the town in the face of Union attacks, and withdraw to the north-east. Grant left Sherman to destroy captured supplies and wreck the railroad tracks while the main bulk of the army turned due west towards Vicksburg. The two Confederate forces were still widely separated and Pemberton decided not to obey orders from Johnston to move towards a link-up with him. On 16 May Pemberton's and Grant's armies came face to face at Champion's Hill, where, after a day of confused fighting, the Confederates were forced to retire, although the Union forces were unable to cut off their line of retreat, as Grant had hoped. Neither further messages from Johnston nor any other consideration could now dissuade Pemberton from withdrawing into the Vicksburg defences. On 18 May Grant's army took up positions around the city, and troops under Sherman occupied the high ground to the north-east, overlooking the Yazoo river which Sherman had failed at such cost to take by frontal assault almost five months earlier. The army now once again had a secure supply base on the river; Grant had triumphantly emerged from the 'tunnel' which he had entered two weeks earlier. Since the beginning of the month he had marched his army two hundred miles, and in a series of engagements, large and small, had defeated various detachments of the enemy forces, and inflicted 8,000 casualties at a loss of little more than half that number on his own side. Now he had an enemy army of 30,000 penned inside the Vicksburg fortifications; it was no longer a question of whether Vicksburg would fall but simply when. Sherman was left to hold off any attempt at relief from outside, but Johnston had already convinced himself of the virtual impossibility of any such operation.

All this Grant had accomplished with a force which, though it now numbered over 50,000, had been smaller than the total forces ranged against it for most of the campaign, and which was living and fighting without any line of supply. Grant himself was still not completely satisfied; in particular, he had hoped to trap Pemberton before he could take cover within the Vicksburg defences. Reluctant to settle down to a slow, frustrating siege in steaming summer heat, Grant tried twice, on 19 and 22 May, to take the city by storm, but all to no avail. The end was thus delayed but not altered; Grant's masterly campaign was to finish not with one, quick, fatal blow but with a slow, painful process of strangulation.

While besiegers and besieged sweated through hot early summer days at Vicksburg, the spotlight shifted to the east where the Army of Northern Virginia was sweeping up the Shenandoah Valley and across the Potomac into Maryland and Pennsylvania. In preparation for his invasion, Lee had contrived to bring the strength of his army up to around 75,000 men, and in view of recent losses, and, above all, the death of Jackson, he had carried through a major reorganisation of his army. There were now to be three corps, led by Longstreet, A. P. Hill, and Richard S. Ewell, and many divisions and brigades also acquired new commanders during the reshuffle. This was no longer quite the same army which had made such a brilliant record for itself in the past twelve months, and it would need to be kept on a tighter rein than came naturally to Lee if its component parts were to work smoothly together.[16]

Early in June Lee began moving his army westward from Fredericksburg for an advance up the Shenandoah Valley. A. P. Hill was left behind to keep Hooker occupied as long as possible on the Rappahannock, while Ewell, followed by Longstreet, headed north and began crossing the Potomac on 15 June. The army was now widely spread out, and became more so as the advance drove on into Maryland and Pennsylvania. Hooker's first reaction to Lee's move was to propose that he should cross the Rappahannock and 'pitch into his rear'. Lincoln and Halleck demurred, the latter suggesting that the enemy troops on the move would be a more vulnerable target than those still firmly entrenched, and the former indulging in one of his more vivid figures of speech: 'I would not take any risk of being entangled upon the river, like an ox jumped half over a fence, and liable to be torn by dogs, front and rear, without a fair chance to gore one way or kick the other.' When, five days later, Hooker made the bolder suggestion that he should cross the river and march on Richmond while the approaches to it were so thinly defended, the president reiterated one of his basic strategic themes: 'I think *Lee's* army, and not *Richmond*, is your true objective point.'[17]

On 9 June the Union cavalry under Pleasonton had attacked Jeb Stuart in what proved to be the biggest purely cavalry action of the war, at Brandy Station. They had taken Stuart by surprise and had acquitted themselves well before being forced to withdraw late in the day. If Brandy Station helped to cure the inferiority complex of the Union cavalry, it also hurt the pride of the self-confident Stuart, and left him anxiously searching for an opportunity to refurbish his tarnished image. His men faced further spirited challenges from Pleasonton as they protected the right flank of Lee's advance up the Shenandoah Valley, while Hooker too began to move north, on 13 June, to keep between the Confederate army and Washington. On 15 June, the day on which the president issued a call for 100,000 militia from the states most immediately threatened, Hooker telegraphed Lincoln to announce somewhat belatedly that 'I now feel that invasion is his [Lee's] settled purpose'. Lincoln was anxious that some attempt be made to attack the opposing army while it was so widely strung out: 'the animal must be very slim somewhere. Could you not break him?'[18] By the second half of June any confidence which the authorities in Washington still had in Hooker was rapidly waning. His relations with Halleck had always been bad, his nerves now seemed to be fraying as they had before Chancellorsville, and he was beginning to complain, in the McClellan fashion, that he was outnumbered, although he had at least 90,000 men against Lee's 75,000. On 25 June his army began to cross the Potomac into Maryland, and concentrated around Frederick. Two days later, after a petty dispute over the use of the troops around Harper's Ferry, Hooker submitted his resignation. Its ready acceptance may have surprised him, and may suggest that Lincoln and Halleck had been hoping and possibly even working for just such a conclusion.

In the early hours of 28 June General George G. Meade, who led the Fifth Corps of the Army of the Potomac, was aroused to be told that he was that army's new commander. A month earlier Meade had written to his wife that 'the command of this army is not to be desired or sought for and that it is more likely to destroy one's reputation than to add to it'.[19] He could scarcely have had the command thrust upon him at a less auspicious time. He knew next to nothing of Hooker's plans or of the overall situation, at a time when Lee's army was ranging far and wide into Pennsylvania. His immediate task was to cover Washington and Baltimore whilst moving towards an almost inescapable meeting with his renowned opponent – a meeting which was to come much sooner than Meade probably expected or desired. Meade was a Pennsylvanian who could be expected to fight hard in defence of his home state. He was also a solid, dependable, careful man, lacking the airs and graces which some of his predecessors had given themselves and which might have passed for charisma had they been crowned with success, but also lacking the taste for political intrigue and the propensity for committing egregious mistakes which they had so often displayed. And what the Union cause needed above all in the next few days was a leader who would make no serious blunders. (To a correspondent who urged the recall of McClellan, Lincoln replied with a wry question: 'Do we gain anything by opening one leak to stop another?')[20]

For several days before Meade's appointment, all three corps of Lee's army had been north of the Potomac. By the 28th, Ewell's men were in Carlisle and York, and his advance guard had reached the Susquehanna river opposite Harrisburg, the Pennsylvania state capital. Longstreet's and Hill's corps were in or near Chambersburg, further to the south-west. But the deep penetration and scattered disposition of the Confederate army had become a more dangerous gamble than it need have been because Lee was so ill-informed of the enemy's movements. Committing the error which Hooker had made at Chancellorsville, Lee was moving blindly because his cavalry was raiding miles away, far beyond immediate contact. He had given orders to Stuart which left that dashing cavalryman so much discretion that he was encouraged to go in search of fresh glories which would erase the memory of recent, less happy occasions. Stuart set out to ride right round the Union army on his way north into Pennsylvania. Sweeping well to the east of the main line of the Confederate advance, he crossed the Potomac not far from Washington after almost running into columns of Union troops, reached Hanover on 30 June, and then pressed his weary men – some literally dropping from the saddle with fatigue – on to York, and then on again in a desperate attempt to find his own army. He finally arrived in the vicinity of Gettysburg late on 2 July, when it was too late to make any difference. There were other, smaller detachments of cavalry available to Lee, but these he seems to have overlooked until, again, it was too late.

Deprived of his regular sources of information, Lee did not know until late on 28 June that the Union army was north of the Potomac. Now he quickly ordered his widely dispersed forces to concentrate in the area of Cashtown, where he saw the makings of a good defensive position. Meanwhile, Meade had been advancing north from Frederick, refusing to commit himself either to the offensive or the defensive until he was compelled to do so. He ordered a defensive position prepared at Big Pipe Creek, but half his army was already beyond it to the north-west. The gap between the two armies was closing, and in the middle of that gap stood the small town of Gettysburg. No one on either side made a deliberate decision to stand and fight there. Each army was groping cautiously towards the other, each was hoping to tempt the other to attack. On the first day of July both were sucked into the vortex of a great battle which they could no longer avoid.

It all began modestly and innocently enough. On 30 June Confederate Brigadier-General Pettigrew took his men down the road from Cashtown to Gettysburg to seize a supply of shoes which would have been a valuable prize indeed for Lee's ill-shod, sore-footed infantry. But they were driven back by a Union cavalry force which had occupied the town a few hours earlier. Next day, believing that the main Union army was still far away, the Confederates advanced in greater strength on Gettysburg. The fighting which developed in the area west of the town flared into a major battle, as both sides rushed up more troops to join the fray. On the whole, the Confederates achieved the more rapid concentration which gave them a numerical advantage until late in the day. Just when their attack from the west seemed on the point of failure, one of Ewell's divisions arrived, quite fortuitously, from the north and threatened the flank of the whole Union position. Again, just when this threat appeared to have been met, another of Ewell's divisions arrived by another road further east to create a new danger. The Union forces were driven back through the town of Gettysburg itself, some of them in considerable disarray, until they reached the higher ground on Cemetery Hill. If the Confederates could have seized that higher ground before their opponents had had time to organise their defences and bring up reinforcements, 1 July might have ended in complete Southern victory. Ewell has been widely blamed for failing to act on Lee's discretionary order to seize the hill 'if possible', without bringing on a general engagement. There is no doubt that the burdens of command and of the day's hard fighting had reduced Ewell to a state of weary indecision – and he would never be a Jackson or a Stuart who would jump eagerly at the bait of a chance to use his own initiative. But there is good reason to doubt whether he could have seized Cemetery Hill, and every reason to doubt whether he could have held it, as more and more of the mighty Union army arrived on the scene.

The first day at Gettysburg ended as a qualified success for the Southern army, but ironically that very success had driven the enemy into a stronger defensive position than he had occupied at the outset. That first day had been unplanned, haphazard, and ill-controlled; Lee himself had not arrived on the scene until 2 p.m., and Meade arrived only just before midnight. During the night, more and more troops arrived, especially on the Union side, and took up position alongside those who had borne the brunt of the first day. The second and third

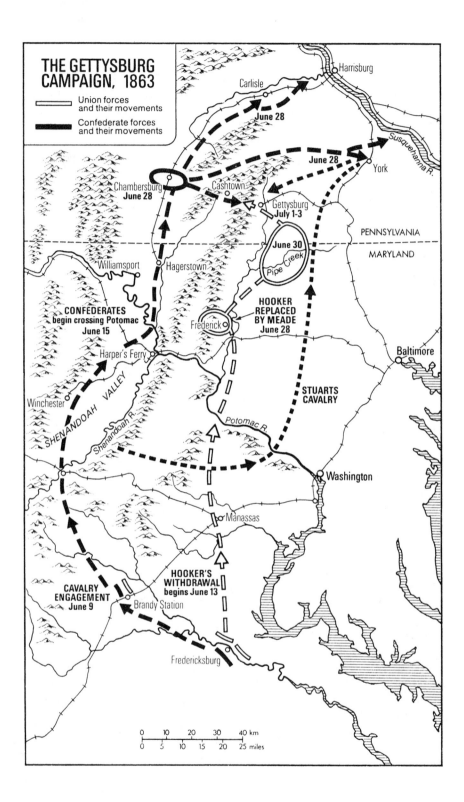

# THE GETTYSBURG CAMPAIGN, 1863

Union forces and their movements

Confederate forces and their movements

Harrisburg

Carlisle

June 28

Chambersburg
June 28

Cashtown

June 28

York

Susquehanna R.

Gettysburg
July 1-3

PENNSYLVANIA

June 30
Pipe Creek

MARYLAND

Williamsport

Hagerstown

HOOKER
REPLACED
BY MEADE
June 28

CONFEDERATES
begin crossing Potomac
June 15

Frederick

Baltimore

Harper's Ferry

Winchester

SHENANDOAH VALLEY

Shenandoah R.

Potomac R.

STUARTS
CAVALRY

Washington

Manassas

HOOKER'S
WITHDRAWAL
begins June 13

CAVALRY
ENGAGEMENT
June 9

Brandy Station

Fredericksburg

0    10    20    30    40 km
0   5    10    15    20    25 miles

days' fighting would be more organised, would follow a clearer pattern and would take place on a static rather than a shifting stage. For two days the opposing armies faced each other in the positions which scores of books and hundreds of sketch maps have depicted: the Union line with its 'fish-hook' shape, centering on Cemetery Hill, running in one direction south along Cemetery Ridge to the two rocky knolls of Round Top and Little Round Top, and, in the other direction, east to thickly wooded Culp's Hill; the Confederate line stretching south to north along Seminary Ridge and then bending round through the town itself and beyond, to face Cemetery Hill and Culp's Hill. (The modern visitor to Gettysburg may be surprised to find that these 'hills' are but modest elevations and that the 'ridges' are often scarcely discernible to the untrained eye amid all the other undulations of the surrounding country.) However it is and was clear enough that the Union line was the tighter, and the more compact, and facilitated the switching of troops from one point to another, while the Confederate line straggled over a much longer distance around and beyond it. The larger army defended the shorter line, and defence was all that Meade had in mind, or needed to have in mind, as he awaited Lee's next move.

Although he had not chosen the place, Lee decided upon attack, with scarcely a second thought. His senior corps commander, Longstreet, urged a flanking move round the southern end of Meade's line, to get between the Union army and Washington, and force Meade to come out into the open and attack, thus yielding the advantage of being tactically on the defensive. Lee believed such a move to be dangerous and impracticable, especially in the absence of the cavalry, and resolved to attack Meade where he stood. The main assault was to be made by Longstreet's corps against Meade's left flank; Ewell was to attack at the other end of the line when he heard the sound of Longstreet's guns. There were long delays in organising and mounting Longstreet's attack, for which Longstreet's reluctance and Lee's loose control were partly to blame, but which owed more to the inevitable hitches in executing hastily devised battle plans. It was almost 4 p.m. when the attack finally started, and in the next few hours there was furious fighting all along the southern half of Meade's position in the area of the wheat field, the peach orchard, Devil's Den and the Round Tops. Amid much confusion, two points stand out. First, in the long delay before the assault, Union corps commander Dan Sickles had advanced his line half a mile forward in a large salient to gain some higher ground. Consequently, what the Confederates intended as a flank attack became a frontal assault on Sickles's line, and, whatever his other errors, Longstreet was surely at fault in stubbornly adhering to the letter of Lee's orders although the situation had drastically changed since they were issued. His fierce attacks gained a good deal of ground but only briefly threatened the main Union line on Cemetery Ridge. Secondly, in reshuffling the forces on the left flank, the Union army had left Little Round Top temporarily unguarded; if the Confederates could have taken it and hauled artillery up to its summit, they would have had the whole Union position on

Cemetery Ridge at their mercy. The contest for Little Round Top became a race, and it was won by Northern troops who arrived just in time to forestall the Confederates who were approaching the summit, and to beat back desperate attempts to dislodge them.

Meade had met the furious asasult on his left flank partly by moving units from other sectors of his compact front, including the extreme right on Culp's Hill. But the weakened Union forces there were not attacked by Ewell until two hours after Longstreet's advance had begun, and, although they yielded some ground, they prevented any major breakthrough. At the end of the day, Lee perhaps overestimated what had in fact been achieved by Longstreet and Ewell on the two flanks, and was sufficiently encouraged to believe that the situation would be ripe next day for a direct assault on the Union centre if only his army could coordinate and synchronise its moves more effectively. His opponent, Meade, having fought a resolute defensive action on 2 July, met his corps commanders that night, and raised the questions of whether to stand or withdraw, whether to attack or await attack. The opinions of his subordinates confirmed his own preference for standing his ground and awaiting developments.

On 3 July Lee again entrusted his main effort to Longstreet, and, again, it took a distressingly long time to get under way. One unfortunate consequence of this was that Ewell, on the left flank, again mistimed his supporting move. Having been too late the day before, he was now too early, and, after hard fighting, he had lost the gains of the previous evening before Longstreet had made any move at all. It was 1 p.m. before a concentration of more than 150 guns opened up in a massive bombardment of the Union centre. The barrage did less damage than had been hoped, partly through overshooting, but when the Union artillery stopped returning fire, in order to conserve ammunition, the Confederates erroneously concluded that they had silenced the enemy guns. By the time the infantry advance at last began, the Confederate artillery was itself perilously short of ammunition. As the 15,000 infantry, led by George E. Pickett, advanced across the open ground which divided Seminary Ridge from Cemetery Ridge, they were torn to pieces, first by renewed artillery fire, and then, as they came within range, by musket fire from the Union infantry. Almost unbelievably, they still came on, and a handful of them actually broke through the stone wall which represented the first Union line of defence, but they were soon engulfed by fire from Union reserves waiting further to the rear. Only fleetingly could Pickett's charge sustain itself at this 'Confederate high-water mark'; the Confederate tide ebbed rapidly and raggedly, as the survivors stumbled back towards their lines, leaving behind them thousands of their dead, wounded and captured comrades. (In the whole battle, the Union army lost 23,000 men, killed, wounded and missing, and the Confederates at least as many – about one-third of their total strength.)

Accepting full responsibility for what had happened, and desperately rallying his depleted forces, Lee braced himself to face the expected counter-attack, but

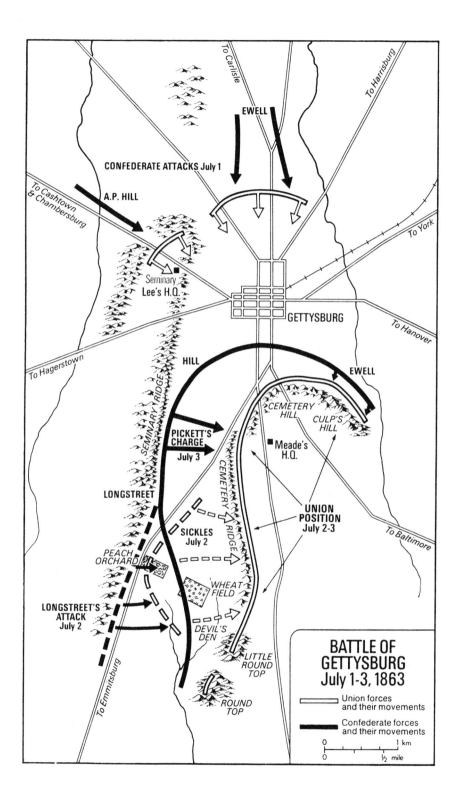

To Carlisle

To Harrisburg

EWELL

CONFEDERATE ATTACKS July 1

To Cashtown & Chambersburg

A.P. HILL

To York

Seminary
Lee's H.Q.

GETTYSBURG

To Hanover

To Hagerstown

HILL

EWELL

CEMETERY HILL

CULP'S HILL

PICKETT'S CHARGE
July 3

Meade's H.Q.

LONGSTREET

CEMETERY RIDGE

UNION POSITION
July 2-3

To Baltimore

SICKLES
July 2

PEACH ORCHARD

WHEAT FIELD

LONGSTREET'S ATTACK
July 2

DEVIL'S DEN

To Emmitsburg

SEMINARY RIDGE

LITTLE ROUND TOP

ROUND TOP

**BATTLE OF
GETTYSBURG
July 1-3, 1863**

Union forces
and their movements

Confederate forces
and their movements

0        1 km

0        ½ mile

it never came. The battle of Gettysburg was over. Next day, Lee stood his ground, as he had at Antietam nine months earlier, and then devoted his full attention to the difficult and depressing business of conducting a safe and orderly retreat back to Virginia. From beginning to end of the battle, Meade had set himself and his army a strictly defensive role. In such a situation, and for a general who had been but a few days in command, such a decision was perfectly proper, perhaps even essential, and Meade played his chosen part coolly, sensibly and courageously. He rightly saw no profit in trading the advantage of a situation where his enemy was willing or was obliged to attack him. The question-marks over Meade's performance concern not the battle itself but its aftermath.

Everyone and everything has been blamed by one critic or another for the Confederate defeat. Lee might with some justice have put much of the responsibility on the shoulders of either his subordinates or his superiors, but he never chose to do so. Unquestionably, Jeb Stuart's irresponsible adventures turned the whole invasion into a shot in the dark. Perhaps A. P. Hill, acting without orders from Lee, should not have allowed troops of his corps to become embroiled in a major engagement on 1 July. Clearly, Ewell's failure to rise to the occasion impaired Confederate prospects on each day of the battle, but he can hardly be blamed for not being another Stonewall Jackson. Arguably, Longstreet delayed too long on both the second and third days in mounting assaults about which he had the gravest misgivings, but there were other reasons, too, why time was lost. On the other hand, the Richmond authorities and Jefferson Davis himself cannot altogether escape censure for the failure to give Lee's invasion the full and wholehearted support in men and supplies which it urgently needed. However, when all is said and done, the personal responsibility belonged first and foremost to Robert E. Lee, and there was much truth as well as great nobility in the words with which he greeted the shattered survivors of Pickett's charge: 'It was all my fault.'[21] Undoubtedly, Lee was far below his superb best at Gettysburg, and the explanation no doubt lay partly in physical weakness brought on by an attack of diarrhoea. He had allowed himself to be enticed into a battle in circumstances not of his own choosing, and his aggressive instincts and his sublime confidence in the invincibility of his men overcame any fleeting inclination to wriggle out of the trap. He consistently failed to impose his personal control on the conduct of the battle; his orders were often imprecise and uncertain and left too much discretion to subordinates who found the luxury of making up their own minds too much for them. He twice entrusted his major attacking moves to Longstreet, a general more renowned for his solid defensive virtues than his speed or élan in attack. By his own high standards, his plans were limited and unimaginative, and, on the third day, simple to the point of crudity. To the modern observer, standing at the stone wall on Cemetery Ridge, it remains hard to credit that the Lee of Chancellorsville could commit 15,000 men to a straightforward frontal assault over wide, open ground on such a strongly held defensive position. This was more like the Lee of Malvern Hill, worried that time and opportunity were running out, and committing himself to one last breathtaking gamble, against all the odds. Perhaps, too, it was the very brilliance of his skating on thin ice at Chancellorsville which emboldened Lee to venture on to even thinner ice in the unfamiliar Gettysburg arena.

But explanations of Confederate defeat at Gettysburg must go beyond the apportionment of individual praise and blame. There was the wastage of men, weapons and supplies from earlier campaigns, and the loss of so many able and trusted lieutenants – Jackson, above all – which had forced Lee to reorganise his army so drastically. There was, too, the sheer strength in men and resources of the Union side; Lee had faced greater numerical odds before, but the circumstances were different, and while Meade's army was amply and efficiently supplied, Lee knew that he could not sustain his invasion much longer, and he could not afford to stand still. The advantages of the waiting game were Meade's monopoly. Confederate defeat cannot be explained in exclusively Confederate terms, although the attempt has often enough been made. As Kenneth P. Williams has observed, the main reason for Lee's defeat was the Army of the Potomac and its commander.[22] Lee had in the past taken merciless toll of the follies and blunders of his opponents and now he missed an adversary like Hooker almost as much as a lieutenant like Jackson. At Gettysburg, the Army of the Potomac had every prospect of victory, unless it lost its nerve or its commander committed some extravagant folly. General Meade had a cool nerve; extravagance was not his style, and he was nobody's fool.

6. On 4 July 1863, the eighty-seventh anniversary of the Declaration of Independence, and the day after Pickett's charge at Gettysburg, John C. Pemberton surrendered Vicksburg to Ulysses S. Grant. For over six weeks the garrison and the inhabitants of the city had endured the mounting hardships and privations of a relentless siege. Slowly and painfully, the attackers edged closer to the city itself, while their guns pounded it from the river as well as from the landward side. Many of the inhabitants were reduced to dwelling in caves and dining off the flesh of mules or even less appetising dishes. By the beginning of July, they and their defenders could stand no more. After some preliminary negotiation, almost 30,000 Confederate troops laid down their arms, before being released on parole rather than shipped to Northern prison camps. In finally taking the prize for which he had so long striven, Grant had also eliminated his immediate enemy completely. (Incidentally, he had already disposed of his most troublesome subordinate, McClernand, who was dismissed during the siege of Vicksburg, after publishing in the press an order congratulating his own troops on winning most of the successes of the campaign, and hinting that only the failings of others had deprived them of even greater glory.) Once Vicksburg had fallen, the fate of the other Confederate bastion on the Mississippi at Port Hudson was finally sealed, and its garrison surrendered on 8 July. The Mississippi River was now in Union hands all the way to New Orleans and the delta; in Lincoln's famous phrase, 'the Father of Waters again goes unvexed to

the sea'.[23] This was the greatest step yet towards crushing the rebellion. The trans-Mississippi region of the Confederacy now became a separate and semi-independent entity, and Jefferson Davis warned the army commander in that theatre, Kirby Smith, that he would now have to look after himself. Not only was the Confederacy geographically split but its morale was profoundly shaken by the loss of Vicksburg and its consequences, and few people from the president downwards were prepared for the shock. The boost which the news gave to Northern morale was felt most strongly in the north-west, where it was most sorely needed. The reopening of the Mississippi outlet was the realisation of the specifically western objective; it reduced, if it did not remove, the suspicion that this was a war being fought by westerners in defence of eastern interests. Vicksburg also finally confirmed Grant's status as a Union hero, and the campaign which preceded its capture remains his strongest claim to fame as a general in the field.

The coincidence of the Union victories at Gettysburg and Vicksburg has helped to create a strong and enduring image of those early July days as the crucial turning-point of the war, the hinge of fate for both North and South. For all the elation on one side and depression on the other, the turn of events may have appeared less dramatic to those who lived through them. Dissemination of news from the battlefronts was less rapid, less certain, and less graphic than in the mid-twentieth century. In any event, Gettysburg seemed to many Northerners an occasion for sighs of relief rather than whoops of joy, and to many Southerners no more than the slightly disappointing but still glorious end to another raid north of the Potomac. (Years later, Jefferson Davis could describe Gettysburg as 'a drawn battle', in which 'it is not admitted that our army was defeated'; the wisdom of the Pennsylvanian campaign was 'justified by the result', and the battle itself merely 'unfortunate'.)[24] The capture of Vicksburg had been so long impending that, however welcome in the North, it was no more than what was expected; to the South admittedly it was a shattering blow, impossible to explain away, but while Lee and the Army of Northern Virginia survived, and Bragg still held Chattanooga, there was no need for despair.

Any Northerners who were optimistic enough to think that the end was in sight in July 1863 were sadly disillusioned by what happened, or failed to happen, in the days, weeks and months which followed. The immediate sequel to Gettysburg and Vicksburg was sad anti-climax, followed in its turn by inactivity on those two fronts and frustration elsewhere. In the west, Grant had aggressive plans for striking at Mobile on the Gulf coast, but, for the second successive year, his early successes were rewarded by the dispersal of his forces on a variety of duties which inhibited any new major campaign. In the east, the maddening scent of missed opportunity hung much more heavily in the air. Having refused to follow Lee's bad example 'in ruining himself attacking a strong position',[25] by a counter-attack at Gettysburg itself, Meade set his army laboriously in motion in pursuit of the defeated enemy on 5 July. Lee had conducted his retreat in bad weather with great skill, but he was held up for several days on the north bank of the Potomac at Williamsport, because the pontoon bridges had been destroyed, and the river was running too high to ford. While awaiting the completion of a makeshift bridge, and a fall in the level of the river, Lee set himself grimly to defend his bridgehead on the north bank. By 11 July Meade's pursuit had caught up with Lee, but he was sufficiently impressed by the strength of the Confederate defences to forgo an immediate assault. He believed that Lee would not and could not withdraw and that, with its back to the river, the Confederate army faced destruction. Meade himself favoured an attack on 13 July but was dissuaded by the majority of his corps commanders. That night the Southern troops began to make their precarious way across the river, and by noon next day the withdrawal was complete. The Army of Northern Virginia was home once again.

In the days after Gettysburg, as after so many of the bruising battles of the Civil War, the victors as well as the vanquished were more aware of their own difficulties than of the enemy's. Meade was so conscious of his army's heavy casualties, of the loss of so many valued senior officers, of the need for fresh supplies, fresh horses and fresh men, and of all the wear and tear of recent long marches and bitter fighting, that he scarcely realised that Lee's plight was far worse. When he came upon Lee's position at Williamsport, he was less inclined to relish a great opportunity than to fear another Fredericksburg if he attacked the impressive-looking Southern defences. In fact, those defences were thinly-manned by a weary, hungry, battered army, reduced by casualties, desertion and straggling to 35,000 men, and critically short of ammunition. Lee's anxiety about his precarious position was exceeded only by his opponent's anxiety about attempting a frontal assault. Meade soon realised what an opportunity had been lost, and it is fair to recall, in his defence, that it was still barely two action-packed weeks since he had been thrust into command. No one was more bitterly disappointed by Lee's escape than President Lincoln himself. He had consistently argued that Lee's invasion was less of a threat than an opportunity for the North. In June he had told Hooker that 'it gives you back the chance that I thought McClellan lost last fall'.[26] In the euphoric days of early July he claimed that 'if General Meade can complete his work, so gloriously prosecuted thus far, by the literal or substantial destruction of Lee's army, the rebellion will be over'. He became so concerned that Meade was intent merely on chasing Lee back into Virginia rather than catching and destroying him that the general proffered his resignation in view of the implied criticism. The resignation was not accepted, but Meade might well have insisted had he ever received the letter which Lincoln drafted but never despatched on 14 July:

> Again, my dear general, I do not believe you appreciate the magnitude of the misfortune involved in Lee's escape. He was within your easy grasp, and to have closed upon him would, in connection with our other late successes, have ended the war. As it is, the war will be prolonged indefinitely. If you

could not safely attack Lee last monday, how can you possibly do so South
of the river, when you can take with you very few more than two thirds of
the force you then had in hand? It would be unreasonable to expect, and I do
not expect you can now effect much. Your golden opportunity is gone, and
I am distressed immeasureably because of it.[27]

This last prognosis was borne out by subsequent events. By the end of July
the two armies were once again facing each other across the Rappahannock in
an area some twenty miles west of where the campaign had started two months
earlier, and there they remained as the summer and autumn days passed quietly.
During October, and again in late November, they came to grips once more
with no significant result, and in December they settled into winter quarters on
either side of the Rapidan, and remained there almost undisturbed for the next
five months. Quite early in the long post-Gettysburg stalemate, Lincoln's
frustration inspired some thoughts on the proper deployment of manpower for
which his twentieth-century compatriots would invent the ungainly word
'de-escalation'.

These two armies confront each other across a small river, substantially
mid-way between the two Capitals, each defending it's own Capital, and
menacing the other. Gen. Meade estimates the enemies infantry in front of
him at not less than forty thousand. Suppose we add fifty per cent to this, for
cavalry, artillery, and extra duty men stretching as far as Richmond, making
the whole force of the enemy sixty thousand. Gen. Meade, as shown by the
returns, has with him, and between him and Washington, of the same classes
of well men, over ninety thousand. Neither can bring the whole of his men
into a battle; but each can bring as large a per centage in as the other. For a
battle, then, Gen. Meade has three men to Gen. Lee's two. Yet, it having been
determined that choosing ground, and standing on the defensive, gives so
great advantage that the three can not safely attack the two, the three are left
simply standing on the defensive also. If the enemies sixty thousand are
sufficient to keep our ninety thousand away from Richmond, why, by the
same rule, may not forty thousand of ours keep their sixty thousand away
from Washington, leaving us fifty thousand to put to some other use?[28]

It was not long before some of those surplus troops did find employment
elsewhere.

7. It was now all quiet on the Virginia front, and all quiet on the Mississippi too.
If Northerners were looking for fresh excitement and new victories, they
would have to look elsewhere, but the outlook was none too promising.
Successes in Arkansas in the autumn were no doubt welcome but scarcely
spectacular or significant enough to kindle great enthusiasm. The continued and
costly failure of amphibious attacks on Charleston in August, September and

October served only to aggravate the mood of frustration and disappointment. There remained one other major front, in Tennessee, but during the long period of inaction from January to June men had lost the habit of looking in that direction for encouraging news. Bragg's Confederate army was content to play a defensive role, broken only by daring cavalry raids. (In one of these, in July, John Hunt Morgan was to penetrate as far north as Ohio and Indiana before finally being captured.) Rosecrans found endless reasons for delay, even to the point of arguing that an advance would only drive Bragg nearer to Vicksburg where he might threaten the success of Grant's operations. At last, after six months' rest, Rosecrans moved out from his base at Murfreesboro on 26 June, and in a series of flanking moves forced Bragg to retreat to Tullahoma, and then all the way back to the area around Chattanooga itself. Rosecrans had demonstrated what everyone knew, that, once he put his mind to it, he could act swiftly and skilfully, and he felt aggrieved that his feats went largely unappreciated because they coincided with the more vivid and dramatic events at Gettysburg and Vicksburg. He tartly asked that 'the War Department may not overlook so great an event because it is not written in letters of blood'.[29]

However, the difficult stage of Rosecrans's advance would be the next one, and he now devoted several more weeks to fastidious preparation for it. Chattanooga was the main target, standing as it did on the Tennessee river where it carved a gap through the formidable mountain barrier. Its capture would finally break that barrier, deliver one more blow at the east–west communications of the Confederacy, open the way into Georgia, and lead to the liberation of the Unionists of eastern Tennessee. But its geographical situation made its capture as difficult as it was desirable. It was well defended against a direct approach along the line of the Tennessee river itself. To the north lay a wasteland of rugged mountainous country with no roads adequate to support the movements of a large army. To the south lay country scarcely less daunting, where a succession of formidable ridges blocked the invader's path, and only one or two country roads pushed through the few widely-separated gaps. Rosecrans chose this southern approach as the least of three evils, and the one which offered the best prospect of trapping Bragg.

At last Rosecrans resumed his advance in mid-August, at the same time as General Burnside, further north, in Kentucky, was leading a small army through Cumberland Gap into east Tennessee. Again, Rosecrans began with considerable dash and skill. He crossed the Tennessee river in early September, and sent one corps to threaten Chattanooga directly while his two remaining corps swept across the ridges to the south, one of them some twenty miles from Chattanooga and the other a further twenty miles beyond that. Bragg decided that his position in Chattanooga was untenable in view of the mounting threat to his rear, and he evacuated the city on 9 September, and headed south to Lafayette in northern Georgia. He was, however, so successful in conveying to his opponent the impression that his retreat was headlong and disorderly that Rosecrans ordered a full-scale pursuit by all three of his corps. In fact, although he had lost

Chattanooga, for the time being at least, Bragg had now put himself in a highly advantageous position, and Rosecrans seemed to be hurrying willingly into a trap. Because of the character of the terrain, and the spacing of the three Union corps at twenty-mile intervals, Bragg now had the chance to attack any one of those corps before the others could come to its aid. But, having created this splendid opening, Bragg now wasted it completely, though the fault was not all his. Between 10 and 13 September he laid plans to attack first the corps of George H. Thomas in the centre, and then Crittenden's corps further north, but the attacks were never carried through, partly through Bragg's lack of firm direction, but much more through the obstructive behaviour of his subordinates, D. H. Hill, Hindman and Polk. Now, as so often before and after, Bragg's authority over his own army was perilously insecure. Having been let off the hook, Rosecrans made frantic efforts to gather his army together, and by 18 September the bulk of his forces faced the Confederate army across Chickamauga Creek, about twelve miles south of Chattanooga. For his part, Bragg, having failed to destroy the Union army while it was scattered far and wide, was desperately anxious to make amends, and the omens were still not unfavourable. He faced an opponent still breathlessly trying to regroup and reorganise, and he enjoyed the rare luxury for a Confederate commander of the numerical advantage. In belated recognition of the vital importance of this front, the Richmond authorities had provided him with reinforcements from various directions, including Longstreet's corps from Lee's army, which, after a prodigious detour over ramshackle Southern railroads, was just arriving as Bragg prepared his battle plans. (Indeed, once he had missed his great opportunity a week earlier, it is hard to see why Bragg did not wait a day or two longer until all of Longstreet's men were present and fit for duty.)

The battle of Chickamauga on 19–20 September was one of those chaotic, scrappy, disjointed (but none the less savage) Civil War encounters, in tangled, difficult country, in which the army commanders, and even corps and division commanders, often lost their grip on exactly what their men were doing or how they were fighting. On the first day Bragg hammered away unavailingly at what he mistakenly took to be the northern end of Rosecrans's position, in an attempt to get between his opponent and Chattanooga itself. On the second day he renewed the assault on the same segment of the Union line, commanded by George H. Thomas, who, steadily reinforced by units from further south, stood his ground uncompromisingly. Then the whole character of this inconclusive slogging match was transformed by a blunder on the Union side and a coincidental piece of remarkable good fortune for the Confederates. Seeking to strengthen the hardest-pressed section of his front, Rosecrans ordered Wood's division to 'close up on Reynolds', whose division he assumed to be next in line. In fact, there was another division, Brannan's, between them, but Wood obstinately adhered to the letter of his orders, and withdrew his troops from the front to march them round behind Brannan to join Reynolds, thus leaving a gap in the line. As luck would have it, Longstreet was just about to launch a heavy attack at this very point, and his troops crashed through the gap, spreading chaos in the Union ranks, and splitting Rosecrans's army in two. Those units which were situated south of Longstreet's breakthrough (fully one-third of the total strength, and including Rosecrans's own headquarters) scrambled their way to the rear, and fled, before it was too late, in the direction of Chattanooga. Apparently quite unnerved by this sudden disaster, Rosecrans made no attempt to return to the battlefield, and left Thomas and the rest of his army to its fate. The remaining hours of the battle belonged to Thomas, the general who was already its hero, and who now earned himself the name 'Rock of Chickamauga', as he and his men, in their horseshoe defensive line, successfully resisted wave after wave of attacks, before retiring in good order as night fell, in the direction of Chattanooga.

Bragg had won a victory, but not the kind of crushing victory which he needed and which had seemed to be within his grasp. His army had not taken full advantage of its astonishingly lucky break on the second day, and, falling prey to the chronic failing of the victors in so many of the war's battles, he had failed to mount an effective pursuit and had allowed his enemy to escape destruction. The reason, as so often, lay in the price which victory itself had exacted. In terms of the proportion of casualties to total numbers engaged, Chickamauga was among the bloodiest of Civil War battles, and the Confederates lost the greater numbers: 18,400 to 16,100. As for Rosecrans, the campaign which he had launched with such style and verve had ended in defeat for his army and humiliation for himself, and his troubles were far from over, for his army was now in grave danger of being locked up inside Chattanooga.

In the weeks that followed Chickamauga, both commanders faced dire problems, the one of threatened starvation, the other of overstretched resources, and both faced crises of confidence in their own authority. Rosecrans remained popular with his troops, but his senior officers found it hard to forgive his flight from Chickamauga, and the general himself seemed stunned into irresolution and apathy. Bragg was no stranger to criticism from his subordinate commanders, and he was not averse to replying in kind to their strictures. The recriminations and the scapegoat-hunting in the army command came to such a pass that President Davis himself felt obliged to make a long and tedious journey to investigate matters on the spot, but his visit achieved nothing except to confirm Bragg in his command. In a situation of this kind, Davis lacked the shrewdness in judging men and the finesse in handling them which characterised his opposite number in Washington. At the meeting on 9 October, one officer after another condemned Bragg's incompetence while the general himself sat listening impassively, but Davis remained loyal to his old friend, and unwilling to contemplate any of the available alternatives, whether from among the complainants, like Longstreet or Hill, or unfavoured outsiders, like Johnston or Beauregard.

Meanwhile, for all the squabbles among its generals, the Confederate army seemed to have a stranglehold on its enemy. Chattanooga lies in a great natural bowl, with rugged, high country to the north, the looming mass of Lookout Mountain to the south, and the long, straight line of Missionary Ridge to the east. Bragg's army occupied much of the rim of this bowl, with its main position on Missionary Ridge, and its flanks stretching in each direction to the Tennessee river, on Lookout Mountain to the left, and on Tunnel Hill to the right. If Rosecrans's army was to be fed, supplied or relieved, only two possibilities were left, and neither looked very promising. The route westward to Bridgeport, either along the river itself, or by the road which hugged its bank, was – or, at least, seemed to be – ruled out by the Confederate forces on the lower slopes of Lookout Mountain. The alternative was a sixty-mile detour to the north over appalling mountain roads which could never have borne the traffic needed to supply a large army. On such a journey, even a packhorse could carry little more than its own fodder. As the October days passed by, and rations were steadily reduced, starvation became a real possibility for Rosecrans's army. There seemed to be no escape at all, as long as Bragg took adequate precautions against it. To make matters worse, Burnside's army, further north, having taken Knoxville, was now in danger of being marooned there through the inadequacies of its supply line.

At this point the administration in Washington took a decisive hand. Always conscious of the strategic and political importance of this area, and alarmed by the situation after Chickamauga, Lincoln urged Rosecrans to hold on: 'If we can hold Chattanooga, and East Tennessee, I think the rebellion must dwindle and die.'[30] But this heavy responsibility was no longer to be left to Rosecrans alone, and the administration took rapid steps to apply on this vital front its crucial advantage in manpower and material. Following the earlier example of the Confederate movement of Longstreet's corps, two corps of the Army of the Potomac were withdrawn from the Virginian front, placed under the command of Joseph Hooker, and packed off to Tennessee in one of the greatest railroad operations of the war. Over 20,000 men, with artillery, horses, and vast quantities of baggage, were carried 1,200 miles in twelve days. But the trains could take them only as far as Bridgeport; they still had to make their way into Chattanooga. Other reinforcements were on their way, too, from the west. Sherman was marching with 17,000 men along the line of the Memphis–Chattanooga railroad, but again there would be no point even in attempting to put these men into the city itself until they could be safely fed and supplied once they were there. On 17 October General Grant was appointed commander of all the western armies, and requested to take direct control of operations at Chattanooga. On authority from Washington, he at once replaced Rosecrans by Thomas and ordered the latter to hold the city at all costs. One more capable and intelligent officer who had flattered only to deceive was thus consigned to the scrapheap.

Grant arrived in Chattanooga on 23 October, and at once things began to move. He brought no magic formula, no bold new plan, but simply the will and the initiative to execute plans which had already been made. Within a week, the army in Chattanooga had a safe, direct supply line, and the men and equipment

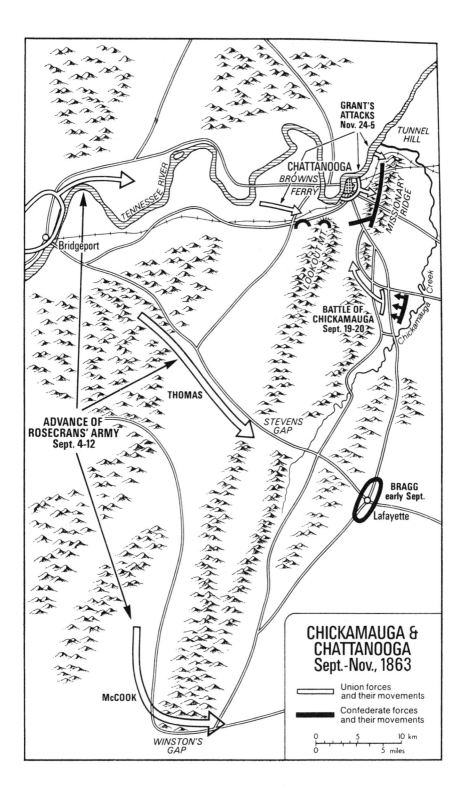

GRANT'S
ATTACKS
Nov. 24-5

TUNNEL
HILL

CHATTANOOGA
BROWNS
FERRY

TENNESSEE RIVER

MISSIONARY RIDGE

Bridgeport

LOOKOUT MT.

BATTLE OF
CHICKAMAUGA
Sept. 19-20

Chickamauga Creek

THOMAS

STEVENS
GAP

ADVANCE OF
ROSECRANS' ARMY
Sept. 4-12

BRAGG
early Sept.

Lafayette

McCOOK

WINSTON'S
GAP

CHICKAMAUGA &
CHATTANOOGA
Sept.-Nov., 1863

Union forces
and their movements

Confederate forces
and their movements

0          5          10 km

0                5 miles

began to roll into the city in impressive strength. Bragg's grip on the vital route westward along the river valley proved so weak that the failure to test it earlier began to look like criminal negligence. The Union army now simply bypassed the loop of the Tennessee river which curves southward to the foot of Lookout Mountain. Troops seized Brown's Ferry, due west of Chattanooga, and floated pontoons down-river to construct a bridge there. Meanwhile, Hooker advanced from Bridgeport, and flushed out the inadequate number of Confederate troops guarding the western approaches to this same position. Seldom can a beleaguered army have been so simply and straightforwardly relieved. Bragg had committed a serious blunder in failing to secure the section of his line which mattered most of all, and he now proceeded to another equally serious mistake in sending Longstreet's corps off towards Knoxville in an attempt to dislodge Burnside there. The move was a response to presidential pressure and a reflection of the strain on Southern resources, but it was still sheer folly, for Knoxville's fate depended on what happened at Chattanooga, and Bragg left himself outnumbered in face of an enemy whose strength and confidence were rising, and whose thoughts were rapidly shifting from defence to attack.

Grant was methodically preparing his plans while he awaited the arrival of his trusted lieutenant, Sherman, whose men would give him something like a three-to-two advantage over Bragg. He would need every bit of that numerical superiority and more, it seemed, for Bragg's main position on Missionary Ridge was as strong a natural defensive position as any commander could have wished. To attack it head-on would be to invite a western Fredericksburg. Grant's plan, in fact, was to hit both flanks of this position while Thomas merely mounted a demonstration in the centre, and, as soon as Sherman arrived on the scene, the plan was put into operation. On 24 November Sherman was to attack Tunnel Hill at the northern end of the line, while Hooker tackled Lookout Mountain. Sherman's furious attacks only slightly dented the Confederate position, stoutly held by Pat Cleburne; even more disappointing was the discovery that Tunnel Hill was not an extension of Missionary Ridge but was separated from it by rock-strewn ravines. On the other flank, Hooker was much more successful in driving the depleted Confederates from the lower slopes of Lookout Mountain and capturing the lofty peak itself, though this latter was more a feat of moun-taineering than of martial valour, and the sight of the Stars and Stripes flying at the summit had more symbolic than strategic significance. Next day, Grant pressed on with the same plan, but again Sherman could make little headway, and Hooker took far longer than expected to sweep down from Lookout Mountain and strike the southern end of Missionary Ridge. By mid-afternoon Grant was so concerned at the lack of progress that he ordered Thomas to attack the first line of enemy trenches in the centre, at the foot of the ridge. He intended no more than a demonstration, or a diversion to relieve the pressure on Sherman. What followed was planned neither by Grant nor by anyone else; it defied every lesson written in blood by the experience of earlier battles, and it continues to defy all generalisations about battlefield tactics during the Civil

War. Thomas's men carried the first line of trenches but found that they could not possibly stay there in face of heavy fire from the ridge itself. Without orders, they began to rush up the slope towards the crest four or five hundred feet above. By all odds, they should have been cut to pieces, and Grant, scanning the ridge through his glasses, was already suggesting that someone would be made to suffer for acting without orders, when it became clear that the charge was carrying the ridge itself. Unable to depress their guns far enough to fire on the attackers, and unnerved by the sight of thousands of men swarming up the hill towards them, the defenders – no green recruits but battle-scarred veterans – panicked and took to their heels. The victors were too elated and too unorganised to pursue, and Cleburne was able to restore some order as he coolly covered the Confederate retreat, but the defeated army did not stop until it was many miles away to the south.

The battles around Chattanooga took place in the most spectacular natural arena provided for any major Civil War engagement, and the climax had come in the shape of a turn of events so unpredictable and unaccountable as to defy the imagination of any dramatist. Bragg could only ascribe his defeat to a 'panic which I have never before witnessed [and which] seemed to have seized upon officers and men',[31] but his own blunders before the battle had fatally weakened his position and finally destroyed his credibility as a commander. Even his friendship with the president could no longer save him, and, still with considerable reluctance, Davis replaced him in December with Joseph E. Johnston. Shortly afterwards, Bragg was kicked upstairs into a post in Richmond as the president's military adviser. On the Union side, Thomas's solid, unspectacular virtues had again been displayed to advantage, and Grant's reputation as a fighter and a winner (and as a friend of Dame Fortune) was enhanced by a performance in which the actors had not always followed his script. Chattanooga led logically to his appointment as commander-in-chief of all the Union armies a few months later. The battle finally secured all the gains which had been expected from the whole campaign, especially as it was followed quickly by the relief of Knoxville and the establishment of a firm hold on East Tennessee. Unlike some other victories, Chattanooga not only closed one chapter of the conflict but opened another. Not merely did it provide a launching platform for Sherman's campaign in Georgia in 1864, but in the combined pressure of units from three great armies, and the combined leadership of the Union's most successful generals, Grant and Sherman, Thomas and Sheridan, it heralded the coordinated and sustained effort which was finally to win the war.

8. Gettysburg, Vicksburg, Chattanooga: these three Union victories on three fronts transformed the war. None had been an unflawed victory nor an unqualified success. The first was a dour, cautious defensive struggle to repel the invader, who had managed to make good his escape; the second, the culmination of a long and often frustrating campaign, ending in a slow, dreary siege, and followed by a dispersal of the victorious army; the third, a victory rescued from

the jaws of disaster with the help of a large measure of good luck. But the combination of the three suggested that Northern power was now being translated into battlefield performance. There was a massive, unrelenting, titanic quality about the Northern war effort now which threatened to overwhelm the desperately overstretched resources of the South. This was no longer a war in which each side could still hope to achieve a decisive military success. It was now a war in which the stronger side was bound to prevail unless the weaker could by its last-ditch resistance undermine its adversary's will and destroy his patient determination. It was now a matter of which would be exhausted first: Southern strength or Northern will, waning Southern resources or wavering Northern resolution. In effect, the North could now only defeat itself. Its leader, at least, showed no sign of flinching. One week before the victory at Chattanooga, Abraham Lincoln, speaking on the battlefield of Gettysburg, had dedicated himself 'to the unfinished work which they who fought here have thus far so nobly advanced'. The completion of that work was still to take many months and countless lives.

# Chapter XI: A Society at War—
# the South

By 1860 the South was a state of mind as much as a place on the map. A definition
of 'Southernness' was and is at least as much a task for the psychologist as for the
geographer. Perhaps it is a task for the historian above all, for out of the experience of the decades before 1860 had grown a sense of Southern self-consciousness
which Washington and Jefferson would scarcely have recognised. But a sense
of identity and a growing solidarity did not betoken uniformity. The South was
a region of many regions. Southerners were a people of many groups, classes and
types, the Southern character was made up of many moods and facets. Within
its vast expanse of territory, the South encompassed plains and swamps, hills and
mountains, the rich, black earth of the cotton belt, and the poor, inhospitable
soil of the pine barrens, the tired, worked-out soils of the Atlantic seaboard and
the bountiful, frontier promise of the south-west, the cosmopolitanism of New
Orleans, the elegance of Charleston, the frontier crudeness of Arkansas, the
hardy self-sufficiency of Appalachia. Problems of distance were aggravated by
indifferent communications, and for the most part Southern society was a
loosely-knit collection of small communities and scattered dwellings, inhabited
by men and women whose preoccupation with immediate problems and local
issues could be disturbed only by exceptional and earth-shaking events.

Yet it still made sense to think and talk of the South as an entity. All the
generalisations (or clichés) about the pre-war South which trip so easily off the
tongue need to be modified or qualified, but not completely abandoned. The
South was predominantly rural and agricultural, says the conventional view –

and that remains true, even after every allowance has been made for the solid evidence of industrial expansion and urban growth in the years before 1860. The Southern economy was heavily committed to the production of staple crops – rice, sugar, indigo, tobacco and above all cotton – and that remains a basic truth even after full acknowledgement that corn was the greatest Southern crop of all and that a whole army of Southern small farmers practised a kind of subsistence agriculture which, if it yielded any surplus, sent it no further than the nearest city market. Southern life, the traditional argument runs, was dominated by a class of large planters and slave-owners. Such a view of the Southern social structure is modified, but not gainsaid, by the frank recognition that there was more to the society than large planters at one end of the scale and wretched poor whites and even more wretched Negro slaves at the other. The large class of yeoman farmers, some owning a few slaves, more owning none at all, was at the very heart of Southern society, but the planters were still at the head. By brandishing the stick of racist fear, and dangling the carrot of social advancement through slave-owning, they still persuaded the farmers to follow their social and political leadership in most parts of the South. There are still other generalisations which may stand but must be kept within bounds. White Southerners were predominantly Anglo-Saxon and Protestant, but there were plenty of exceptions, from the Creole civilisation of Louisiana, to humbler and more recent immigrants in parts of the upper south. Again, the South had closed its ranks politically during the mid-century sectional crisis, but any use of the label 'solid South' would have been premature when Southern Whiggery still showed a remarkable talent for survival, when secession itself enjoyed anything but unanimous support, and when many states had their deep internal divisions – western Virginia against the tidewater, eastern against western Tennessee, for example.

The reality of their distinctiveness and the limits of their diversity became clear enough when Southerners examined the fitness of their society for war in 1861. It was not just that they lacked numbers and certain basic resources in comparison with the Northern states. Many of the distinguishing features of the South marked it as a society ill-equipped for war, in spite of the martial virtues of its people. It had a broad agricultural base, but some of its staple crops, like tobacco, were of dubious advantage to the war effort, and the greatest of them all, cotton, was prized as a diplomatic bargaining counter rather than a means of waging war. The situation demanded a massive adaptation of the South's greatest economic resource, its plantations and farms. It also required the swiftest possible expansion of the narrow Southern industrial base, as far as shortages of skill, techniques and materials would allow. Part of the trouble stemmed from the habits of economic dependence which had developed in earlier decades – dependence on raw materials and skilled workers from the North for Southern industry, dependence on Northern merchants for shipping and selling the cotton crop, and for credit above all, dependence on Northern and European manufactured goods to meet basic needs, and even dependence on north-western farmers to supplement home-grown food supplies. In 1861 there was no solid economic foundation for a bid for political independence. Then again, many Southern economic assets, actual or potential, were peculiarly vulnerable in time of Civil War. A substantial part of such industrial plant and skill as the South possessed was in the border states or the upper south – Virginia, Kentucky and Tennessee above all – and the same states ranked among the leading food-producing areas, and the best sources of supply of the untold thousands of horses on which the army would rely. The Confederacy never gained control of some of these vital areas and soon lost others to Northern invasion. The same story can be told of the main towns and cities of the Confederacy, dotted as they were around its coastal or landward perimeter. The failure to bring Missouri and Kentucky securely into the Confederacy deprived it of one of the great American cities in St Louis, and of several other important ones including Louisville. The first year's fighting in Tennessee brought the loss of Nashville and Memphis, while in Virginia Richmond remained in the front line for four years. Around the coast, Norfolk, Wilmington, Charleston, Savannah, Mobile, New Orleans and Galveston were all vulnerable to enemy attack, and the greatest of them all, New Orleans, four times the size of any other Southern city, fell when the war was scarcely a year old. Not one of the six Confederate cities which boasted more than 20,000 inhabitants in 1860 could have felt really secure at any stage of the war. But the vulnerability of Southern assets was not just a matter of geography. The bulk of Southern capital was tied up in land and slaves, and was singularly difficult to deflect into the business of making war. As the Confederacy set about the business of protecting its assets and concealing or compensating for its deficiencies, it needed all the resources of enthusiasm and enterprise that it could command. It could also remember that the enemy had his problems, too, and he faced the much larger demands of a war of conquest.

1. The switch from cotton and other staple crops to food production was a considerable if uneven achievement in the early years of the war. There is no doubt about the spectacular decline in the cotton crop from 4,500,000 bales in 1860 to 1,000,000 in 1862 and a mere 300,000 in 1864. These drastic reductions were achieved initially by popular demand, patriotic appeals, and voluntary limitation, backed up by vigilance committees and other forms of community pressure. From 1862 onwards, such unofficial action was reinforced by state legislation which imposed severe restrictions on cotton acreage and threatened, but rarely enforced, dire penalties on those who failed to obey them. The Confederate government stayed out of this sensitive area as long as it could, but in the spring of 1863 Davis was authorised by Congress to issue a proclamation urging continued cotton restriction and concentration on food crops. Such a plea was needed because confidence at this time in an early end to the war had encouraged the notion of a switch back to cotton and tobacco. Howell Cobb, commanding the military district of Florida, called a meeting of planters to disabuse them of such fanciful ideas, and he wrote afterwards that:

The delusive idea of an early peace had run the people mad on the subject of planting cotton. It was really becoming an alarming state of things, and I fear that even yet the matter is not properly understood. With all that was done last year, it is difficult to feed the army and support the country. What then is to become of us if instead of planting corn and raising hogs we raise cotton? Starvation and ruin would be upon us.[1]

Planters with an eye to quick profits through blockade-running or trading with the enemy found the restrictions increasingly irksome, but in general they proved effective, perhaps even too effective for the Confederacy's own good, in the latter part of the war. Tobacco production was sharply cut back too, and most state governments also banned or severely limited the distilling of liquor from corn or other grain, more urgently needed to increase food supplies, although such measures were often more honoured in the breach than in the observance.

The more positive side of the change in agricultural priorities was less success-ful. Production of corn, wheat, vegetables, fruit, hogs and cattle was stepped up in many areas, and, though people often went short, there was never any immediate threat of mass starvation. But the difficulties were great, some of them unpredictable acts of God like the drought which afflicted parts of the South in 1862, but many more eminently predictable consequences of human failure. Union invasion cut down the food-producing area significantly from 1862 onwards, and the trampling feet and grasping hands of armies on the move wrought havoc in areas near the front. As farm implements and machinery broke down or wore out, the chances of replacing or repairing them dwindled, and farmers resorted to primitive and long-discarded methods. Shortage of horses brought mules and oxen back into fashion. Shortage of salt made it impossible to preserve meat for very long. The departure of so many farmers and farm workers into the army created a shortage of labour. The old, the lame and the womenfolk did their best to fill the gaps, and struggled to maintain the inexorable routine of the seasons. It was small wonder that so many soldiers took themselves off from their units at harvest-time to help with pressing tasks at home. Planters and farmers who owned slaves faced special problems of organisation and supervision, and there is little doubt that the work-rate of the slave declined during the war, just as the lure of freedom reduced the size of the slave labour force.

In spite of all these difficulties there was no really good reason why Southerners should have gone seriously short of food during the war. In the rural areas, people managed reasonably well, and coped with many local difficulties and petty snags by pooling their resources and their products. But in the towns and in the army it was a different story. The real failure was in distribution rather than production. Transport was never adequate and steadily deteriorated, and organisation was never equal to the task of managing a fair and efficient allocation of limited resources. Where the army was concerned, Commissary-General Northrop did not create its subsistence problems, and could never have solved them completely, but might have done more to mitigate them. Many soldiers were reduced to half or quarter rations at times in the second half of the war. Where the civilian population of the towns was concerned, shortages were accompanied by soaring prices, which caused riots and disturbances in Richmond and other cities, and brought real hardship to workers and their families. Impressment, speculation and hoarding which stemmed from shortage and inflation, were all widely blamed, but they were symptoms rather than root causes of the disease. Four years of war proved the resilience and capacity for survival of a rural society which could meet minimum basic needs at the local community level. But in those same years, the South was becoming somewhat less rural, and it was also turning several hundred thousand producers into consumers in the Confederate army. This created a new problem which, by tradition, temperament and aptitude, the South was ill-equipped to solve.

2. The Confederacy was still less prepared to embark on a crash programme of industrial expansion. Whereas farmers were required to produce one crop instead of another, the industrial problem was to create something out of almost nothing. Southern manufactures in 1860 were worth about one-twelfth of those produced in the North. Out of almost 1,000,000 tons of pig iron produced in the United States in 1860, the South contributed 36,790 tons. The figures for iron ore were 76,000 tons out of a total of 2,500,000.[2] The Southern deficiency in other metals was equally serious; the Southern textile industry had responded to efforts to boost it in the 1850s only to the extent of reaching one-tenth of the size of its Northern counterpart. In every field, the South lagged far behind, and the whole social system, and the values of the more conventional Southerners at least, had put a brake on economic diversification and industrial progress. For all the unflattering comparisons with Northern production, however, the outlook was not entirely bleak. Iron furnaces and forges, foundries and rolling mills did exist, mainly in the states of the upper south and the borderland, and other manufacturing and mining industries had a foothold here and there. Most enterprises were on a small scale, and were often no more than sidelines in a predominantly agricultural community, but they provided a starting-point at least in meeting wartime need. Once again, the loss of the border states was a heavy blow. Kentucky, Missouri, Maryland and western Virginia would have almost trebled Confederate pig-iron production at the outset. Union occupation of large parts of Tennessee in 1862 was another loss of industrial capacity which the South could ill-afford. It was fortunate indeed that Virginia threw in its lot with the Confederacy, for its iron industry was crucial. Richmond was in effect the economic as well as the political capital of the Confederacy and its Tredegar Ironworks was the South's greatest industrial asset. The mineral resources and industrial potential of the deep south, and Alabama in particular, were as yet unrealised, but Selma grew rapidly from almost nothing to become a second home of Southern heavy industry.

Secession and the need to make war spurred Southerners to enthusiastic industrial effort in the early part of the war. A flood of orders from state governments as well as the Confederate authorities flowed into any concern remotely capable of producing weapons and other war material. In January 1861, in the midst of the secession crisis, shells ordered by the federal government in Washington and shells ordered by seceded state governments in the South lay side by side in the Tredegar foundries. Starting from scratch, the Confederate government not merely placed massive orders but increasingly went into the business of armament production itself. The remarkable achievements of Gorgas and the Ordnance Bureau are discussed elsewhere;[3] the armouries at Richmond, Macon, and other places, the Naval Iron Foundry at Selma, the great powder mill at Augusta, the chemicals plant at Macon, the ingenious and wide-ranging efforts of the Nitre and Mining Bureau, these were the direct, government-controlled contribution to the overall industrial effort. But the business of making arms was not altogether in government hands and the whole complex of iron manufacture, engineering and machine-tool industry which underpinned it was largely in private hands, though tied to the government by a spider's web of contracts, regulations, subsidies and controls.

The Tredegar works at Richmond was already by 1860 one of the leading iron foundries and producers of ordnance in the United States. In the early days of the Confederacy it was virtually the sole manufacturer of heavy ordnance, and it continued to be the mainstay of the cause throughout the war. It produced some 1,100 guns altogether, nearly 500 of them heavy siege and seacoast artillery, and, if the quality was not always reliable, this was as much due to faulty materials as bad workmanship. Tredegar did much else besides; it produced vast quantities of ammunition, tools and machinery for government armouries and the powder mill at Augusta, iron plates for the *Virginia* and other warships, and a variety of items for the hard-pressed railroads (though no rails and no loco-motives – ironically it had closed its locomotive shop for lack of orders at the end of 1860). Shortage of raw materials, workers, and transport drove the company into many new ventures. It reactivated the Virginia pig-iron industry to provide its own desperately needed supplies, operated coal mines, ran a small fleet of canal boats, ranged far and wide in search of provisions for its employees, bartering iron goods for bacon and corn, set up a tannery to make shoes and other leather goods, and eventually broke into the blockade-running business in its search for scarce raw materials (and an overseas refuge for some of its profits). Its labour force of 800 in 1860 rose to nearly 2,500 at its 1863 peak.[4] Every one of Tredegar's impressive achievements can be matched by a tale of daunting and often insuperable problems, but all in all, it is small wonder that a Negro employee on a train running out of Richmond, when asked if he worked for the government, could reply: 'No, sah! Fur t'uther consarn!'[5]

Selma, Alabama, was a striking example of new industrial development during the war, with its government arsenal, its powder mill, its iron works, its navy yard, and naval foundry – the latter taken over by the government in mid-war. But Southern industrial growth was more than a matter of armouries and iron foundries. Textile mills, clothing factories, tanneries, shoe factories, flour mills, salt works all increased or expanded as far as shortages of materials and labour would allow. A town like Atlanta enjoyed a wartime boom, as communications centre, supply depot, and industrial complex producing all manner of goods from muskets to matches. Boosters of Southern industry like J. B. D. DeBow exultantly listed the variety of goods produced in small factories in every town from Virginia to Mississippi, from farm implements to stationery, hats to knitting needles, candles to canteens. In 1862, for example, *DeBow's Review* proudly described the industrial enterprise of the small community of Chester Court House:

> Every household has become a manufacturing establishment; the hum of the spinning-wheel may be heard in every hamlet, and the rattle of the loom sings the song of better times to our glorious South. Old and young, rich and poor of our females, are daily discarding the baser fabrics of Yankeedom and are bending their whole energies to keep us supplied with warm clothing raised and made by their own industry.[6]

But euphoria was not enough, and the industrial history of the Confederacy was one incessant struggle against heavy odds. Most crippling of all to the industries which really mattered was the shortage of raw materials. Grossly inadequate supplies of iron (in spite of the Company's own efforts) meant that the Tredegar works operated at only one-third of capacity throughout the war. Transport problems made it impossible to rely on supplies from more distant parts of the Confederacy. Lead, tin and zinc were in desperately short supply, and lack of copper prevented the casting of bronze cannon for months at a time. There was never any hope of realising the considerable industrial potential of the South because of shortage of raw materials, inability to import them, and difficulties in transporting the available supplies over a creaking railroad system. The Confederacy paid a heavy price for its pre-war dependence on vital materials from the North, and, when war came, 'the raw materials base of the Southern economy could not support the industrial superstructure'.[7] The South had also traditionally depended on Northern know-how and technology, and Northern or European skilled workers. With secession and war came a rising demand and a falling supply of skilled labour. Some Northern workers left, some other key workers joined the army, and the system of exemption and detail which followed conscription never worked well enough to keep or put the right men in the right place. The South simply lacked a remotely adequate pool of industrial skill and experience to sustain the required rate of growth, irrespective of any other deficiencies. As Judah P. Benjamin put it in his report of March 1862: 'The difficulty is not in the want of legislation. Laws cannot suddenly convert farmers into gunsmiths. Our people are not artisans, except to a very limited degree.'[8] Southern methods and techniques were often behind the times. Confederate artillery suffered considerably in quality and reliability through the refusal of the Tredegar company to adopt the Rodman method of casting cannon. Again, in 1863, the most serious result of a major fire at the Tredegar works was the loss of machine tools which the South lacked the resources to replace. Basic deficiencies in men and materials were aggravated by a transport system constantly on the verge of breakdown, and also by conflicting priorities between the demands of government and private customers. Manufacturers were disinclined to turn their backs completely on their private customers, whether because they offered higher prices or because they could offer much needed supplies in return for manufactured goods. As government regulation and red tape increased during the war, manufacturers were irked by such restraints, lost their patriotic zeal and looked more directly to their own interests.

In the light of all its overwhelming problems, the performance of Southern industry was in many ways truly remarkable, and must figure largely in any attempt to explain how the Confederacy survived against such odds for four years. But if it was something of a miracle, it was a modest one when the South needed something even more dramatic. What was apparently dead was raised to life, but it could not live for long without further constant miracles to sustain it. The Confederate government overturned every American precedent and went much further than its leaders could ever have imagined a few years earlier in their efforts to stimulate and regulate industrial effort. But paper measures were one thing, and actual performance another. Many regulations and controls simply did not work, and were extremely costly in terms of popularity. The administration began cautiously, and confined its direct control to armouries and the like, where there was ample precedent. In 1861, and again later, it refused offers to turn the whole Tredegar works over to the government, by either lease or purchase, and rejected similar proposals from other companies. But as time passed, the industrial empire of the Ordnance Bureau, the Nitre and Mining Bureau, and the Navy Department steadily expanded. Most of the War Department's 57,000 employees were workers in its arsenals, factories, yards and depots.

The relationship of government to private industry was complex and often abrasive. The Southern and indeed the American tradition was not strictly one of *laissez-faire*, but it thought in terms of aid and subsidy rather than regulation and intervention, and it preferred help from the state governments rather than the central government. The Confederate authorities had to defy such preconceptions. They did offer aid to industry, notably in the form of advances of one-third or one-half on the price of contracts, to help suppliers to extend plant or buy materials. (Jefferson Davis, incidentally, vetoed one such measure early in 1862.) But, increasingly, the government's relationship to industry was one of restriction, regulation and interference. Its great weapons were control of raw materials through its own wide-ranging industrial activities, and control of labour supply through exemptions and details. The latter never managed to put right the indiscriminate mobilisation in the first year of the war, and many generals, including Lee, took a narrow and unsympathetic view of industrial priorities.

In return for releasing key workers to industrial concerns, the government also imposed restrictions on prices and profits which applied to goods sold to all the company's customers. Enforcement of such regulations was never easy, but they were fertile in the production of petty grievances and complaints.

The expanding role of the Confederate government was matched at every stage by the activities of the state governments. They too operated arsenals, powder mills, textile mills, flour mills and a variety of other enterprises. They too handed out large contracts, and made conditions and regulations in return for their custom. They too offered subsidies and incentives to manufacturers. In their search for materials and manpower, they entered into competition with the Richmond authorities, and added more fuel to the flames of states rights controversy. Government itself proved to be one of the most spectacular growth industries of the wartime South. This was a dramatic break with the past, but its practical effect was a good deal less than it appeared at first sight, and it was achieved at heavy political cost. Neither the Southern people nor their leaders could adapt quickly or efficiently enough to the new ways which war thrust upon them.

3. Transport, manpower, inflation, lack of essential supplies – these are the recurring themes of any analysis of Southern economic and industrial problems. Where transport and communications were concerned, the Confederacy had an uphill struggle to make the best of older methods and the most of new ones. There were plenty of roads but no one had ever thought of them as a network for the purpose of conveying large quantities of goods over very long distances. Most roads were no more than tracks, alternating with the seasons between dust and mud. Even if roads had been better, war conditions soon reduced Southern capacity to provide vehicles and motive power to use them. The army's voracious demand for horses, mules and wagons pressed hard upon civilian needs, especially with the increasing resort to impressment. By 1864, farmers were reluctant to take their crops to the nearest market for fear that not merely their products, but their horses and wagons, would be impressed into military service. When wagons broke down, shortages of labour, and of iron tyres or leather goods, often prevented or delayed their replacement or repair. Water transport had played a useful role in the pre-war South, but it provided only a very limited answer to wartime need. Many waterways did not run in the right directions, many of the great natural arteries in the west were soon threatened or actually controlled by Union troops and gunboats, and coastal traffic was inhibited by the fear or the fact of Union blockade. There was a shortage of boats and barges and no chance of overcoming it, in the face of even more urgent claims on overstretched resources.

Railroads were the only possible answer to Southern transport problems. Here the South had some grounds for hope, if it was not too impressed or depressed by comparisons with Northern railroads, and if it made the best of what it had. In 1860 the South had almost 9,000 miles of track out of a United States total of over 30,000. Richmond and the Virginia front were fed by three main lines, one running to Wilmington and with connections to Charleston and Savannah, one running south-west to Chattanooga, with connections to the Mississippi, and a third between these two running through the Carolinas and eventually to Atlanta – but with a crucial gap at the Virginia–North Carolina border. The great east–west artery of the Confederacy ran from Savannah and Charleston through Atlanta and Chattanooga to Memphis, and there were other important east–west links further to the south. Two important lines ran the length of Mississippi from north to south before terminating at New Orleans and Mobile. However, to talk of such long trunk routes is to give a misleading impression of the Confederate railroad system. Indeed there was no system, but a haphazard collection of over one hundred companies, many of them precarious, most of them operating quite short routes. The Southern railroad map was not a neat plan prepared by an expert draughtsman, but a set of graffiti scribbled in an ill-formed hand. Many railroads had been built simply to convey the products of the interior to the nearest river or coastal port. They were often not in the places and not linked together in the manner which strategic considerations would have dictated. Actual gaps at crucial points were bad enough, but things were made much worse by the variations in track gauge between different lines, and, more infuriating still, the fact that termini of different lines in the same city were often unconnected. Hotel-keepers, transfer companies, teamsters and porters had a vested interest in maintaining the inconvenience, labour and delay which this situation entailed. For example, Petersburg, the vital railroad centre south of Richmond, finally gave in to threats and inducements and agreed to a link between termini only on condition that it was to be removed after the war.

Many Southern railroads were lightly constructed, poorly maintained, and, by Northern standards, short of locomotives and rolling stock. Until 1861 they had been heavily dependent on outside sources for engines, rolling stock, rails and other equipment and on skilled labour from the North to operate and maintain their routes. During four years of war the railroads had to exist on their dwindling supply of locomotives and rolling stock with no remotely adequate facilities or labour force to maintain and repair it, and to cope with desperate problems of track shortage and maintenance by tearing up little used or less important branch lines to keep the main routes in usable condition. Not a single rail was produced in the Confederacy during the war, a fact which may reflect both a chronic shortage of materials and a curious sense of priorities. Other needs were neglected, too, but from 1863 onwards the Tredegar company, for example, did contrive to supply wheels, axles, springs and other parts to railroads which were prepared to pay stiff prices or could offer favours in return by delivering materials and provisions which the company urgently needed.

Although totally unaccustomed to cooperation, most railroads did agree, in the first flush of patriotic ardour in 1861, to carry troops and government freight at special rates, but good intentions did not always triumph for long over old rivalries and limited vision. An ever-increasing share of railroad traffic was given over to government business, and normal passenger traffic was constantly disrupted and sometimes virtually abandoned. The railroads did accomplish some impressive troop movements, for example in transporting Bragg's army from Tupelo, Mississippi, to Chattanooga, via Mobile, in 1862, and in transferring Longstreet's corps from Virginia in time to fight at Chickamauga in 1863. They also contrived after a fashion to sustain the Army of Northern Virginia and the Army of Tennessee through thick and thin, almost to the very end. But, living as they were from the outset off their limited capital, the railroads were in a sorry state at least from 1863 onwards. Engines broke down or laboured ever more slowly over track worn out by incessant use; average speeds dropped from over twenty miles per hour to under ten and timetables became meaningless. For passengers, rail travel became first frustrating, as delays grew worse, then uncomfortable, as rickety carriages bumped over deteriorating track, and then dangerous, as derailments multipled, bridges collapsed, and serious accidents increased. In many areas, railroads suffered heavily from the incursions of Union troops, who became experts in the business of wrecking rails beyond hope of repair.

For railroad men as for many others, patriotism wrestled with private interest, and when other customers were prepared to pay freight rates far higher than the government offered, the temptation was often too great to be resisted. The Richmond government, the state governments, vital war industries like the Tredegar company, and more dubious interests, like the blockade-runners, found themselves competing with each other for rail transport, much to the detriment of the common cause. (The state governments were not averse to dabbling in railroad management and regulation, and Georgia, for example, actually took over and ran a railroad formerly in Northern ownership. Several states passed acts during the war providing financial aid for railroads.) But to bemoan the lack of coordinated control of a railroad system is unfair to the men of the 1860s. Railroad men themselves were not yet thinking in such terms, and certainly had no experience of railroad management on the scale now required. 'The conception of the railroad as a public utility with social responsibility is an anachronism for that period,' says one authority.[9] In such circumstances, it is hardly surprising that, as in its industrial policy as a whole, the Confederate government failed to rise to the occasion, although it launched itself once again into an unprecedented and highly complicated programme of aid and regulation. One of its earliest initiatives was an attempt to fill strategic gaps in the railroad map. Davis persuaded Congress in February 1862 to authorise $1 million to aid completion of a line to fill the 48-mile gap between Danville, Virginia, and Greensboro, North Carolina. The measure passed over furious opposition from those who feared such an assertion of national power, but completion of the link was delayed two years, partly through obstruction by the North Carolina government, and objections from a rival railroad fearing loss of business. Some other vital links were completed more quickly, others were proposed but never completed. Another means of government supervision of railroads was through control of the supply of labour and raw materials, but here, whether in granting exemptions or detailing men for vital work, or in allocating precious supplies, the government never gave the railroads the highest priority.

When it came to direct supervision of railroad operations, the Richmond authorities were reluctant to become involved, and the Quartermaster-General, Abraham C. Myers, who was responsible for army transport, was among the most reluctant of all. However, an ex-railroad president, William S. Ashe, became assistant quartermaster in charge of rail transport for the army in Virginia in July 1861. His powers were largely limited to negotiation and persuasion, and after struggling for months to create some measure of co-ordination, he gave up in April 1862. A few months later the very capable William M. Wadley became Military Superintendent of Railroads. He had somewhat wider powers, but his efforts created friction with the railroad companies and received inadequate backing from the government. In 1863 he was replaced by Frederick W. Sims, who was blessed with rather more tact, and enjoyed the support of a new Quartermaster-General, A. R. Lawton, but could achieve only limited success in face of mounting difficulties. At last, in May 1863, Congress had passed a Railroad Act giving the War Department wider authority, including power to commandeer the use of a railroad in an emergency, and to resort to impressment if cooperation were refused. This measure fell far short of full government control, but Davis and his administration were very cautious in using even the powers which they now possessed. In the very last weeks of its life in 1865, the Confederate government was at last authorised by Congress to take complete control of the railroads, but there was no time or opportunity left to use these sweeping powers, even if the will had been present. In its relations with the railroads, the Confederate government found itself suspended between past precedent and present need. It struggled bravely, but it was too inhibited by the one and too slow to appreciate the other.

4. At the heart of Confederate economic difficulties lay the question of finance. Here even more strikingly than elsewhere was a case of gigantic problems tackled by men who were less than giants, wielding puny or double-edged weapons. How could an agrarian society like the South finance a costly war against a far better endowed opponent? It lacked the necessary financial institutions and experience, and its financial attitudes were generally conservative and narrow. It suffered from a desperate shortage of specie, aggravated by the process of secession itself, and it set out upon a war which lasted four years with only between $25 million and $30 million in gold at its disposal. Worst of all, its capital was largely invested in land, slaves and cotton, assets which were unusually difficult to convert to new requirements. There was no Southern class of investors who had the funds, even if they had the confidence, to subscribe in large amounts to government bond issues. Generations of planters

had acquired the habit of living on credit from outside rather than providing credit for others. All in all, this was not a society which was in the habit of handling big sums of money, whether in gold reserves, investments, taxes or the transactions of everyday life.

Next to sheer lack of resources, confidence was the most crucial financial problem. Any revolutionary government struggling to demonstrate that its independence is a fact faces the problem of financial confidence, and, in the case of the Confederacy, doubts about its initial establishment had scarcely had time to subside before doubts about its survival replaced them. Was there any way in which the South could boldly strike for financial stability in the early days of its life, and thus demonstrate both the credibility and the credit-worthiness of the Confederate States of America? There were those, both at the time and later, who thought that the answer lay in one of the South's basic resources – cotton, the 'white gold' which Europe desperately needed and which the South alone could supply. What if the remainder of the 1860 crop and the bulk of the 1861 crop could be shipped across the Atlantic before the Northern blockade tightened its net, and stored there to provide a basis for Confederate credit and for purchases of war supplies? It was a glittering prospect, but less visionary Southerners dismissed it as a mirage. They denied that there were millions of bales of cotton immediately available for such a venture, they asked where was the fleet of ships to carry them across the ocean, and they doubted whether, with such a vast store of cotton known to exist in Europe, the price could be kept up to the expected heights. For its part, the Confederate government lacked the energy and the machinery to manage such a huge enterprise, and in any case it soon tacitly accepted the popular demand for an embargo on cotton exports as a device for forcing European recognition of the South. The question of whether the administration had its cotton priorities right is discussed elsewhere,[10] but the fact remains that, even if only on a much more modest and realistic scale than the original grand design, cotton exports were vital to the finances and the warmaking capacity of the Confederacy. The government tried to use cotton in various ways to boost its finances, but the pursuit of the embargo idea in the first eighteen months of the war fatally delayed a more practical and financially rewarding policy for utilising a major Southern asset.

Not merely in dealing with cotton but in financial matters generally the Confederacy went astray from the start because of the confident expectation that the war would be short and sweet and not too expensive, and the complacent assumption that the inevitable measure of inflation could be fairly comfortably absorbed. In the South as in the North, it was only during 1862, as war costs soared and prospects of an early peace faded, that a new realism began to dawn, more sweeping measures were envisaged, and confidence gave way to crisis.

If Secretary of the Treasury Memminger was unimpressed by flights of cotton fancy or the mania for white gold, he was left with three more orthodox instruments for financing the war effort: taxes, loans, and paper money. His measures in 1861 were both an indication of the widespread misreading of the dimensions of the task, and the first tottering steps down the slippery road to ruin. Memminger believed in principle in the need for heavy taxation, but was never able or willing to insist upon it in face of congressional reluctance and popular antipathy. People who had been lightly taxed under the old government looked askance at a new one which threatened to hit their pockets much harder. There were constitutional difficulties, too; protective tariffs were outlawed, and the permanent constitution provided that direct taxes on property must be apportioned among the states according to a census, which, understandably, in the midst of war, the Confederacy never managed to take. In any case, the Treasury Department lacked the machinery and manpower for large-scale tax assessment and collection. It would take time to organise them and experience verified the doubts of those who said that it could never be done efficiently. The taxes actually imposed in 1861 were minimal, and their results in the first year were virtually nil. An export duty of ⅛ cent per lb on cotton was intended to service the first Confederate loan, but it produced very little. In the summer, import duties, averaging 12½ per cent, were imposed on a variety of goods, but imports were very low. A direct tax (permitted by the provisional constitution) was to be levied on most forms of property at the modest rate of one half of 1 per cent. It was intended to use the assessment and collection facilities of the states, and each state was offered a 10 per cent discount on its quota if it assumed the responsibility. This was an admission of Confederate administrative weakness and it produced chaos. State methods varied widely, the Confederate government had to make reassessments, there was delay in printing forms, and more delay in returning them. Finally and ironically, all but three states claimed their 10 per cent rebate not by collecting taxes, but by floating loans to raise their quota, thus aggravating rather than mitigating the inflationary trend. In two years, the property tax raised only 1·7 per cent of the revenues of the Confederacy.

From the start, Memminger was obliged to put his faith in other methods. In February 1861, Congress voted a $15 million bond issue at 8 per cent, which was enthusiastically promoted and fully subscribed by October despite the prevailing shortage of cash. It was a sound start to Confederate borrowing and brought in some much-needed specie, but it was soon overtaken by bigger and shakier ventures. A $50 million bond issue was authorised in May and the amount doubled in August. To encourage planters to invest, the device of the produce loan was introduced. Lacking cash for immediate purchase, planters could pledge the income from a certain proportion of their next crop to the buying of bonds. Some pledged one quarter, a few pledged the whole crop. But summer enthusiasm for the scheme withered in the cold blasts of autumn and winter, when cotton prices had tumbled owing to the embargo and the blockade, and other prices were rising steadily. Instead of eagerly supporting the Confederate cause by bond purchases, the planters were now looking to the government for relief from their financial straits. Memminger regarded any idea of the government buying up the whole cotton crop as too large an undertaking for his department and too inflationary in its effects on the economy. But both he and Congress agreed in April 1862 that the government should accept actual produce – cotton, grain and other provisions – at a fixed price, instead of the proceeds from selling cotton on the open market. This helped to satisfy the planters but further aroused the critics who had maintained all along that the produce loan was class legislation which gave special benefits to an already privileged group. Memminger hoped to use the cotton thus acquired to obtain vital supplies to sustain the army. His hopes were often disappointed, and only a fraction of the 430,000 cotton bales received ever reached Europe to finance the purchase of war material. By 1863, however, when cotton prices had risen, planters thought that they could handle their crops more lucratively themselves and began to denounce Confederate interference. Produce loans had had their day.

Loans raised far more than taxes in the first year, but between them they met only a third of the rocketing costs of the war. Sheer necessity, therefore, drove the government to resort to the printing press – although it is an interesting sidelight on Confederate problems that shortage of paper and of printers and engravers delayed production for a time. But it was not long before printing paper money became a Southern growth industry. Soon the Confederacy was hopelessly addicted to the drug of fiat money, and every attempted cure was soon followed or even accompanied by further massive injections of the drug itself. The first issue of $1 million in treasury notes in February 1861 was laughable in view of what followed. An issue of $20 million was authorised in May, and $100 million in August, to tide the government over the difficulties with the produce loan. There was no way back now, and as inflation accelerated in 1862, and shortages got worse, the only cure for the evils created by an excess of paper money seemed to be more of the same. Unlike its Northern counterpart, the Confederate Congress refused to make these treasury notes legal tender, and it is hard to say what effect, if any, such a move would have had.

For the rest of the war, the proportions of the cost of the war borne by paper money, bonds and taxes did not vary much: over 66 per cent came from treasury notes, less than 33 per cent from bonds, and between 1 per cent and 5 per cent in taxes. Paper money continued to flood from the presses, as the only means by which the government could pay its bills. In March 1863 an issue of up to $50 million per month was authorised, and by the end of the year, at least $700 million of treasury notes were in circulation, and their worth was down to four cents on the dollar in gold. Attempts in 1862 and 1863 to retire some of the notes from circulation by funding them into bonds proved ineffective. Bond issues followed one another in 1862 and 1863, but they found fewer and fewer takers. As confidence waned and inflation increased, investors found much better opportunities elsewhere, and only patriotism remained as a motive for purchasing bonds. In 1863 the Confederacy negotiated its one significant European loan with Erlanger and Company in Paris. The Confederacy gained more from this $15 million bond issue than the calculations (or mis-calculations) of most historians have allowed. Despite the speculation which accompanied it, the yield from the loan compared not unfavourably with other loans of the period, and was the mainstay of Confederate purchasing in Europe until cotton supplies built up in 1864.[11]

In February 1864 Congress eventually passed new measures in response to Memminger's desperate attempts to restore some order to the finances. They amounted to repudiation of a large part of the currency in circulation. Memminger even hoped to reduce it by two-thirds. Deadlines were set before which the various treasury notes could be funded into bonds, or exchanged for new notes at the rate of two new to three old. After these dates, the old notes were to be taxed at one third of their value, and eventually taxed out of existence. A massive new bond issue of $500 million was floated, but not more than a quarter was ever sold. The measures did not achieve the desired results. They triggered off an immediate orgy of speculation and a sensational price rise, although this was followed after the April deadline by a period of several months in which prices remained on a plateau, albeit a very high one. But old notes continued to circulate with the new, and by the end of the year both were worth only two cents on the dollar in gold. Repudiation was a dangerous game which undermined the last vestiges of confidence, and utter ruin was only delayed and not averted.

High taxation might have helped to shore up the crumbling fabric, and in 1863 and 1864 Memminger extracted from Congress some legislation which moved by cautious steps and a complicated path in this direction. The cumbersome tax law of April 1863 imposed an 8 per cent tax on agricultural products held on 1 July 1863, a 10 per cent profits tax on wholesalers (an intended blow at speculators), licence fees on many occupations, and a graduated income tax starting at 1 per cent on salaries of $1,000. Most interesting of all, it imposed a 10 per cent tax-in-kind on all agricultural products raised in 1863. This last provision, which outraged farmers and planters, was designed as a means of supplying the army and beating inflation at the same time, but it proved very difficult to enforce, and problems in handling perishable items and delays in transport led to enormous wastage. Indeed the whole package of measures yielded indifferent results in practice. The treasury simply could not provide the bureaucratic machine to assess and collect income and other taxes efficiently, and a combination of Northern invasion and Southern evasion meant that many areas contributed little or nothing. All in all, the taxes produced $82 million in a year, a mere pittance by the inflated standards of the time. In February 1864, along with the funding measures already described, Congress approved a new tax law which renewed the income tax and the tax-in-kind, and at last resorted to a tax on property, including those basic sources of Southern wealth, land and slaves, which had hitherto escaped very lightly. It circumvented the constitutional requirement of a census by accepting 1860 property valuations, but the taxes themselves were paid in the depreciated currency of 1864. The tax on the value of land and slaves was at the rate of 5 per cent, but income tax and the tax-in-kind were deductible from it. Evasion was again all too easy, and the yield disappointing – $119 million of hugely depreciated currency by October 1864.

Complaining that Congress would not give him what he needed, Memminger resigned in June 1864 and was succeeded by the wealthy and successful Charleston merchant, George A. Trenholm, a man of greater ability and tact, but one who came to power much too late. In the winter of 1864-5 he proposed swingeing increases in taxation, pleaded for new bond subscriptions and even asked for donations of precious possessions such as jewellery. But it was all to no avail and all too late, and Congress would have little to do with it.

It is easy enough to show that Confederate finance was a colossal failure, and that it finally collapsed into utter chaos. Yet the astonishing fact remains that a nation which went to war with less than $30 million in gold maintained the struggle for four years against a superior foe, and financed it mainly by printing paper money. It suggests that, whatever his errors and shortcomings, Memminger fought a losing battle with considerable doggedness. No doubt he should have taxed more heavily, he should have used cotton more fruitfully as a basis of financial operations, and he should have looked to more drastic and unconventional means of controlling inflation, but he was fighting not merely against the financial weakness of the Confederacy but against its whole political tradition, economic structure and psychological make-up. The Confederacy operated financially on a law of diminishing returns, and it was a question of whether independence could be achieved before diminution became extinction.

The great curse of Confederate finance was of course inflation, and government and people alike were its victims. Paper money and basic shortages, created or aggravated by the blockade, could have no other result. Taxation was never heavy enough to apply a brake, and even those government policies, like impressment and the tax-in-kind, which were intended to combat inflation, often produced the reverse effect by encouraging hoarding and speculation. Altogether, the Treasury churned out over $1½ billion in paper money. In addition, state and city governments poured out their own notes, and railroads, insurance companies and industrial concerns followed suit. 'Shinplasters', or notes of small denominations, flowed out from many sources to swell the volume and add to the confusion. Postage stamps, too, were widely used as currency. Counterfeiting became widespread, and the authorities could generally deal with it only by giving in to it, and bestowing their official blessing upon forged notes. From October 1861 to March 1864, commodity prices rose at an average rate of 10 per cent per month. In January 1864 price levels were twenty-eight times higher than in the early months of 1861. The figure leaped to forty-one times higher in March after the orgy of speculation prompted by the funding measure of February 1864. It then levelled off for the rest of the year, but in the last chaotic months of the life of the Confederacy it soared upwards faster than ever. By April 1865 it was ninety-two times higher than the 1861 figure, but by that time figures had become meaningless and all contact with reality had been lost.

Inflation marched in step all across the South, though perhaps a little faster in the towns than in the country, and in Richmond prices raced ahead of the national average in 1864. There was every incentive not to hold on to money, but feverish spending merely set off the next round of inflation. 'We fell into the habit of paying whatever was asked,' wrote George Cary Eggleston, 'knowing that tomorrow we should have to pay more. . . . Every article of merchandise rose in value every day, and to buy anything this week and sell it next was to make an enormous profit quite as a matter of course.'[12] In such a climate, the line between honest trading and speculation was scarcely discernible to the naked eye. Just as the government resorted to measures like the tax-in-kind, so individuals and companies resorted to barter on an increasing scale. In rural areas most people could supply some of their own needs and had something to barter for other necessities, but many townspeople were defenceless against rising prices, especially when their own wages or salaries lagged far behind. Running like a constantly recurring theme through the diary of J. B. Jones who worked in the War Department at Richmond was his complaint about rising prices, and the sheer impossibility of making ends meet. Already in May 1862 he was quoting such prices as 'meats of all kinds at 50 cts. per pound; butter, 75 cts.; coffee, $1.50; tea, $10; boots, $30 per pair; . . . Houses that rented for $500 last year are $1,000 now.' In January 1863 he was paying a rent of $1,200 for 'a mere robin's nest of four rooms'. Later, he cited a newspaper assessment of the weekly grocery bill for a small family in 1860 and again three years later: $6.55 had become $68.25. At this time, the private soldier was paid $11 per month, and skilled workers from $2 to $5 per day. By March 1864 Jones was busy planting seeds in his own garden, and blessing the kind friend who had given him some fresh pork and cabbage. His family income was now $600 a month, 'but we are still poor, with flour at $300 per barrel; meal, $50 per bushel; and even fresh fish at $5 per pound. A market-woman asked $5 today for a half-pint of snap beans, to plant!' A week later he reported that 'my daughter's cat is staggering today, for want of animal food. Sometimes, I fancy I stagger myself. We do not average two ounces of meat daily.' Next day, he saw $100 demanded in the market for a large wild turkey. By October 1864 he was writing that doctors had agreed to charge $30 per visit; flour was up to $425 per barrel, meal $72 per bushel, bacon $10 per pound.[13]

Such figures drawn from the daily experience of Confederate citizens show that the havoc wrought by inflation was more than purely financial. While it hit the pocket, it also played upon the nerves and depressed the spirits, until it became part and parcel of the final process of demoralisation. In the words of Secretary of War Seddon, inflation 'in its direct, and even more in its indirect, influences, not merely on the market and on the property of citizens, but on their instincts of selfishness, on their sentiments, tastes and aspirations, is a fearful evil, and more demoralizing to our people than the more dire calamities of war'.[14] Perhaps the printing press had to be the main resort of Confederate finance, but it set a time-limit on the struggle for independence, and it unleashed a dangerous and insidious enemy in the rear.

5. Shortages were part of the life of the Confederacy from the outset. Inflation was both a consequence and an aggravation of basic deficiencies, and transport problems, faulty distribution, hoarding and speculation all helped to make a difficult situation worse. As the *Southern Cultivator* put it when war began: 'We are caught unprepared. We have much to sell, nobody to buy, and little to eat and wear.'[15] In the midst of a terrible war no amount of reorganisation, improvisation and re-allocation of resources succeeded in putting things right. It was not just a matter of food shortages, although the experiences of John B. Jones and his family are reminders that the threat and the fact of hunger were very real in Richmond, and sometimes in other towns and cities too. Shortage of a humdrum everyday item like salt posed a threat to the whole Confederate home front because of its essential role as a preservative. Speculators strove to corner the market in what had suddenly become a prized possession, and state governments organised and encouraged desperate efforts to produce it from new sources. North Carolina even appointed a Salt Commissioner. Saltville in south-west Virginia, the main Southern source of supply, suddenly acquired an economic and strategic importance never remotely imagined a few years earlier.

Leather, paper, soap, metal products of all kinds, cloth and clothing of any real quality were all in short supply. 'Broadcloth is worn only by the drones and fireside braves,' wrote one young lady. 'Dyed linsey is now the fashionable material for coats and pants. . . . A gentleman thinks nothing of calling on half a dozen young ladies dressed in home-dyed Negro cloth and blue-checked shirt.' Another girl recalled how 'pins became scarce. People walked about with downcast eyes; they were looking for pins! Thorns were gathered and dried to use as pins.'[16] The womenfolk worked wonders with old dresses or coarse homespun cloth, devised hats, buttons, bracelets, necklaces and furs from unpromising materials, and made their own dyes from bark, walnut shells and various juices. Letters were written on coarse brown paper in home-made ink, and newspapers were even printed on wallpaper. Substitutes for traditional food and beverages seem more ingenious than appetising. Molasses, honey and sorghum replaced sugar for many purposes; substitutes for coffee were concocted from roasted corn, sweet potatoes and peanuts, and 'tea' was made from the leaves of currant bushes and willow trees. One of the South's most serious shortages was in medical supplies, which the North insisted on treating as contraband. Old-fashioned remedies brewed from a variety of plants, herbs, leaves and roots, enjoyed a new vogue, and one of the most valued books to appear during the war years was Dr Francis P. Porcher's six-hundred-page volume on *Resources of the Southern Fields and Forests*, which was a guide to the use of such makeshift medicaments.

Inevitably, shortages became more acute as the war continued. The blockade steadily tightened, and Union armies made deeper and deeper inroads into the South. By 1864 there was evidence on every side, in burnt-out buildings, ripped-up railroad track, devastated fields, and vanishing livestock, of the sheer physical toll of the war on Southern property and resources. The profitable but parasitic activities of speculators and racketeers poured poison into the wounds inflicted by the enemy. And yet, however depleted and diminished, the Confederate home front kept itself going for many a long month in the face of shortages, privations and suffering. The makeshifts and innovations were supplemented by goods run through the blockade,[17] although the benefits of that business were not so evenly spread or judiciously managed as they might have been, and also by the time-honoured if scarcely honourable practice of trading with the enemy, either directly through the lines or indirectly through the blockade.

Like its Union counterpart, the Confederate government had a highly ambivalent attitude towards such trade. Its public face was set against it in the legislation of 1861 banning the export of cotton and other staples except through Mexico or Confederate ports. But behind the public façade was a private awareness that valuable supplies could be acquired by trade through the lines, and that, whether the Richmond authorities said yea or nay, the trade could never be stamped out. Throughout the war, then, the left hand of government did not know what the right hand was doing, or at least preferred not to know. The basis of trade across the lines was simple enough. The South had cotton in abundance and no adequate overseas outlet for it; the North had a hunger for cotton to help its own industry, placate British and European manufacturers, and deprive the Confederacy of the European supplies which cotton might buy. Whether governments smiled or frowned upon the business, there were plenty of operators on both sides eager to exploit it, and plenty of army officers to connive at it or participate in it at the right price. From 1862 onwards, the Mississippi Valley became the most flourishing trading area, and Memphis to the north and New Orleans to the south became its great centres. Two years later a new Union commander at Memphis, determined to sweep out such shady business with his new broom, declared that, since it fell into Northern hands, Memphis had been of more value to the Confederacy than a major blockade-running centre like Nassau.[18] In New Orleans, Ben Butler was heavily involved in a variety of money-making enterprises, and his brother Andrew Jackson Butler made a fortune from the trade. When Butler returned east, he became involved in another version of the same business – the coastal trade between Northern ports and Virginia and North Carolina. Other trade between Northern ports and the Confederacy was conducted indirectly through Nassau or Havana or even Halifax. Here, as elsewhere, incompetence, corruption and collusion nullified attempts to stop the trade, and weapons, ammunition, telegraphic equipment, shoes, blankets, food and medicine reached the Confederacy by this route. Whether on the Atlantic coast or in the Mississippi

Valley, geography and sheer distance were the enemies of any serious effort to stamp out such activities.

Trade with the enemy is inevitably a seamy story, and its cast of characters included any number of greedy speculators, corrupt officers, disloyal sellers and dishonest buyers. But it also included many ordinary Southerners, small farmers or their families, for example, ready to trade a bale of cotton for bacon or salt or other provisions to stave off hunger and hardship, or loyal and conscientious officers willing to obtain desperately needed food and medical supplies for their troops from the only available source. Lee strongly disapproved of trade with the enemy, but in the last year of the war his army was being fed in part by the products of such trade. On the other hand, with the business in private hands, and outside the law, the goods acquired in exchange for cotton were not always those most needed, but those which fetched the highest price. A law of February 1864 virtually gave the War Department power to take over all trade with the enemy, but it could never be properly enforced. For all that, the South could comfort itself that it profited materially from a trade which helped it to prolong the struggle for survival, but it also paid a heavy price in the corruption, demoralisation and disloyalty which followed in its wake.

Supplies from the North as well as from Europe also entered the Confederacy by the Mexican back door. Between August 1861 and June 1864, 152 vessels cleared New York for the Mexican port of Matamoros, carrying cargoes which even included weapons, ammunition, and army wagons, destined for the Confederacy. In return for such supplies, Texans could offer cotton, but speculators moved so eagerly into the trade that government and army priorities were ignored. Resort to impressment of cotton aroused furious denunciations of military dictatorship exercised by a remote authority which had no conception of Texan problems and Texan needs. The trans-Mississippi area of the Confederacy was always something of a region apart, more western than southern in many ways, and its people were always quick to feel slighted or neglected by the Richmond authorities. Early in 1863 the Davis administration made con- cessions to this feeling and to the sheer difficulty of government by remote control when it established a semi-autonomous régime in the area, under the control of General Kirby Smith, who was responsible for tax collection, conscription, transport and supply as well as military operations. Although resented at first as an outsider, he created a good impression by his reorganisation and reinvigoration of the army, recruitment of more men, and improvement in logistics, not to mention his attempt to restore some semblance of law and order to the whole region. In July 1863 his domain – 'Kirbysmithdom' as it was called – was finally sealed off from the rest of the Confederacy by the loss of Vicksburg and Port Hudson. Supplies brought in from Mexico had always been difficult to shift all the way to the east; the task now became impossible. But the supplies were still rolling in, and Smith established a Cotton Bureau to purchase half the crop of each producer, in order to pay for them. Aided and abetted by the governor of Texas, the planters evaded the clutches of the Bureau, and the scheme was abandoned in 1864. Although Arkansas and western Louisiana had been badly scarred by marching armies and guerrilla raids, Texas was little touched by the war, and still produced large quantities of cotton and other crops. Such relative peace and prosperity did not incline Texans to share their blessings with less fortunate parts of the Confederacy, and old grudges against the east did not fade away. Their state survived the war without undergoing conquest or devastation, and its wartime experience was a very different story from that of the Confederacy as a whole. It is an illustration and perhaps in part a cause of the continuing distinctive relationship between Texas and the South: a Southern state, certainly, and yet not completely in or of the South.

6. The manpower problem of the Confederacy is simply stated: there were not enough men. Facing a numerically superior foe, the South altogether put some eight or nine hundred thousand men into the field out of a total white population of five and a half million. If at the same time the war effort at home was to be sustained, two desiderata should have been met: first, a highly organised and selective manpower policy to evaluate military and civilian priorities, and second, maximum use of those sources of labour which were not liable to conscription, namely the women and the Negro slaves. But the very idea of a manpower policy was alien, if not indeed incomprehensible, to the men who led the Confederacy in 1861. The first enthusiastic rush to the colours was eventually restrained, not by considerations of industrial need, but by lack of arms and equipment for would-be recruits. The result was that many key workers, some of them irreplaceable, were lost to the armed forces and never recovered. Some critics have applied the term 'over-mobilisation' to the Confederacy, although it would not have been easy to convince Lee or Johnston that too large a proportion of its limited manpower was at one time or another in uniform. But the real trouble was not the proportion but the lack of discrimination. The let-them-all-come volunteer spirit of 1861-2, and the conscription law which followed, were blunt instruments for what should have been a very delicate operation. The exemption laws often exempted the wrong people, and, in any case, blanket exemptions of whole groups were not the most efficient means of using available resources. What Jefferson Davis wanted, and what he increasingly practised, with or without Congressional authorisation, was a system not of exemptions, but of detail, under which he could allocate men liable to conscription to particular jobs where they were needed. Such a policy caused endless arguments and complaints, and Congress was still wrangling with the president over the rights and wrongs of it until the very end. To the extent that the administration was able to enforce it on an *ad hoc* basis, the detail system was beneficial, but more elaborate machinery, and more careful planning and assessment of priorities, would have been needed to make it the precise and selective instrument which the Confederacy needed.

  Shortcomings in official policy aggravated the basic and chronic deficiency in industrial and agricultural labour, especially skilled labour of all kinds. The consequences of this shortage for industry have already been discussed. Companies made desperate efforts to recruit key workers from Europe, or from the border states, or even from men on parole from prison camps. There was a good deal of poaching from rival concerns, with higher wages as the usual bait. Wages rose fast during the war, but still fell further and further behind the rising cost of living. Wages for Tredegar employees were 80 per cent above pre-war levels by 1863, and rose still faster later, but in order to retain its workers, and maintain even a modest standard of living for them, the company was obliged to feed and clothe them at its own expense in the latter part of the war. In the Confederacy as a whole, it is estimated that wage levels had increased three-fold by September 1863, five-fold just over a year later, and almost ten-fold by March 1865 when finances had finally lost all rhyme or reason.[19] But in real terms, wages had declined to between a third and two-fifths of pre-war levels by March 1865, and many workers needed payment in kind on the Tredegar pattern to survive. Others worked longer hours, or tried to grow some of their own food, and others again put their wives and families to work to supplement the family income.

There had been little or no tradition of labour organisation in the pre-war South, but sensing their importance to the war effort, and dismayed at their falling standard of living, skilled workers in particular staged a number of strikes, walk-outs and protest meetings during the war, in Richmond and elsewhere. Post-office clerks struck for higher wages in 1863, and men working on the ironclad ship *Mississippi* were on strike for five days in November 1861. But labour unrest did not often go to such extremes and the threat of con-scription cooled the militancy of many would-be strikers.

Farms as well as factories felt the effects of shortage of labour, and in the fields, mills, workshops and offices, the women of the Confederacy took over many of the jobs vacated by their menfolk, or created by the demands of war. The wife of the yeoman farmer had always led a life of toil and drudgery, but now she assumed extra burdens not only of actual labour but of responsibility and organisation, buying and selling. The ladies of the large plantations espoused a variety of good causes, and set up societies to foster them. They helped to clothe and equip volunteer regiments, organised medical care for the troops and relief for their families, as well as taking over supervision of much of the activity of the plantation itself. Some women found themselves exciting and romantic jobs as spies or informers; Belle Boyd and Rose O'Neal Greenhow were probably the most renowned. More took on the possibly romantic but more often horrifying task of nursing the sick and wounded in the appalling conditions of the military hospitals. Phoebe Yates Pember, a young widow from Savannah, for example, used a formidable combination of dynamism and charm to overcome entrenched male attitudes, and minister to thousands of victims of war, in the huge Chimborazo Hospital in Richmond. Other women turned to an even older profession which has brought comfort of a kind to the soldier home from the front since time immemorial. Prostitution flourished, especially in a city like Richmond, so close to the front line, and so crammed with a floating population of soldiers, speculators, lobbyists, traders and all who clung to the coat-tails of army and government at such a time.

But for every woman who was a spy or a camp follower there were hundreds more who laboured at much duller tasks. Some took jobs in textile mills, but many more did their own carding, spinning and weaving at home. Others worked in government service, and not merely in office jobs (like the small army of women employed by the Treasury Note Bureau in 1864 to number and sign another mammoth issue of paper currency) but also in ordnance plants and powder mills, sometimes at considerable risk to life and limb. The romantic view of Confederate womanhood has doubly distorted the reality. It has over-emphasised the glamour and the dyed-in-the-wool enthusiasm which they brought to the cause, but it has understated the hard, unpleasant and unremitting labour which was in fact their major contribution. Waving flags was exciting but sewing shirts was more useful.

From the very beginning of the war, the Confederates had argued that they could afford to put a high proportion of their white manpower into the army because the slave labour force could plug many of the gaps on the home front. The great majority of Negro slaves, of course, worked on the plantations and continued to do so during the war. The switch from cotton to food crops, and the absence of many white men, meant that on the plantations some slaves did new work and most probably did less work. Other slaves found new employment elsewhere. Before 1860 the employment of slaves in towns and factories had been steadily growing. Some were bought by urban masters, more were hired out for agreed periods – and a number were even allowed by their masters to hire themselves out. The demand for this kind of slave labour rose rapidly during the war, as other sources of labour supply dried up. The majority of such slaves were used as unskilled labourers, but a significant number came to fill highly skilled and crucial positions, for example in the foundry and the machine shops of the Tredegar Ironworks. By 1864, slaves, mostly hired, comprised well over half of the Tredegar work force.[20] In September 1864 4,300 Negroes and only 2,500 whites were employed in all the iron mines in the Confederacy east of the Mississippi, and in February 1865 over three-quarters of the workers at the Selma naval works were slaves. They were extensively employed on the railroads and waterways, made up probably at least half of the nursing and auxiliary staff in the hospitals, played a vital part in salt works, coal mines, docks, construction work, and many other activities. Most of all they were used to dig trenches, build fortifications, and perform a variety of auxiliary tasks – as cooks, servants, porters, and teamsters, for example – for the Confederate army.

Widespread employment of slaves as military labour was usually justified on the ground that it freed more white men for combat, but it owed much also to the widely held view that digging and other heavy labour were no fit occupation for white men. At first labourers were hired by voluntary contract between the military authorities and the slave-owners. But owners became increasingly reluctant to hire out their precious slaves, and army officers affronted them by impressing slaves when the voluntary system failed. In 1862 the state authorities took a hand, and when the Confederate government resorted to impressment of slaves in March 1863 it did so specifically according to the rules and regulations prescribed by the states. A subsequent law of February 1864 put more power into the hands of the central government but only at the cost of furious arguments with the states, some of which took countermeasures which virtually nullified the Confederate law. Late in 1864, Jefferson Davis proposed that the Confederacy should actually purchase up to 40,000 slaves and form them into a permanent labour corps, but in and out of Congress more hands were raised in horror than voices in support at such a drastic proposal.

Impressment of slaves is a classic example of a Confederate policy conceived and executed in a manner not radical enough to solve a problem, but too radical for the tastes of many Southerners. It did not produce anything like the number of military labourers required by the army, it inflamed states rights arguments yet again, and it proved highly unpopular with slave-owners, and for that matter with the slaves themselves. Slaves engaged on military labour were often overworked on heavy and punishing tasks, inadequately fed, poorly housed, rigorously controlled, and cruelly treated. Owners found that their slaves often returned with their health undermined and attitude soured – and more and more did not return at all, as such unpleasant labour so near the front line encouraged them to make a dash for freedom. Impressment of slaves touched the influential class of slave-owners on a very sore spot, and was one of a whole range of issues which sowed the seeds of doubt about the objectives of the war and the methods of attaining them. If the South had gone to war to protect slavery and to protest at interference by central authority with basic property rights, what were slave-owners to make of a situation where, to further that war effort, a new central government could impress their slaves into arduous and often dangerous work, against their will? There is ironic significance in the story of the planter whose five sons had been taken into the army but who began to lose heart only when the government began to take his slaves.[21] There still remained one more painful twist to this particular knife in the deep wounds of the South: the proposal to use Negroes as troops, which Southerners could no longer put out of their minds completely, but upon which they could bring themselves to act only when it was too late.[22] With or without Negro troops, it was clear enough by mid-war, for those who were able and willing to see, that the Confederacy could continue the struggle only with the help of its Negro slave population. Their contribution was not just useful; it was vital.

But the irony of the situation was not confined to the key role played by slaves in sustaining a war in defence of slavery. The institution of slavery itself changed under wartime conditions. Many slaves enjoyed greater mobility and greater freedom than they had known before. If he worked in the city, a slave might well have made his own terms of employment and he might well live in lodgings which he found for himself. Instead of being constantly under the eye of his master, he worked not for a man but a company, and his daily life was regulated not by his owner but by slave codes and city ordinances enforced by the local police. He was still the victim of discrimination and harassment, but in many ways his daily working routine was not very different from that of the free white worker in the same factory or the same town. On the plantation, too, although slave codes were tightened in theory during the war, many slaves were in practice subject to less discipline than before, either because the only whites in the vicinity were old men, women and children, or because masters feared, with good cause, that strict supervision would merely encourage slaves to run away. Indeed, one aspect of the new mobility of the slave population was the flight to freedom, whether from plantations close to the invading army, military labour camps or front-line cities like Richmond. Not the least of the ironies of Confederate history is that the Richmond household of Jefferson Davis himself suffered a steady drain of runaways during the war. On the other hand, many slaves went quietly about their normal business, giving every appearance of loyalty to their masters, and waiting to see what would happen next.

The white view of slavery during the war was a curious mixture of normality and nervous tension. In the safer areas of the South, the master-slave relationship was subtly modified but not seriously disturbed, except perhaps insofar as owners were increasingly aware of their utter dependence on those whom they owned. The slave trade held up remarkably in the first two or three years of war, both in volume and in price level. On the other hand, there was increasing agitation of the question of slavery reform, led by men like Calvin Wiley of North Carolina and James A. Lyon of Mississippi, who sought to humanise the institution in a variety of ways. Slavery itself was no sin, they argued, but the afflictions of war were God's punishment of the South for the sins which had developed in its actual practice: disregard for marriage and family ties, denial of education, and inadequate concern for the spiritual welfare of slaves.

Northern abolitionists were surprised that the war produced no mass uprising of the slaves against their oppressors. There was, it is true, but little violence, although there was a great deal of disloyalty, insubordination and idleness as the slaves awaited more dramatic developments. Indeed it was the very patience and passiveness, the inscrutability of the slaves, which played most upon the nerves of their owners. War intensified the whole complex of conflicting emotions which generations of slave-owning had left raging in Southern hearts. No one exemplified better than Mary Chesnut the love-hate relationship (laced with fear) of many Southerners with slavery. No event in 1861 inspired more anxious comment in her diary than the murder of a neighbour by her slaves. Her frightened sister did not know how to react when her maid offered to sleep in her room: 'For the life of me, I cannot make up my mind. Does she mean to take care of me or to murder me?' Mrs Chesnut confided to her diary fierce criticisms of slavery, based not on concern for its effects upon the slaves but rather for the burden which it imposed on the whites. 'We are human beings of the nineteenth century and slavery has to go, of course. All that has been gained by it goes to the North and to Negroes. The slave owners, when they are good men and women, are the martyrs. I hate slavery.' Her father-in-law's fortune had gone 'to support a horde of idle, dirty Africans, while he is abused as a cruel slave owner'. She wrote vividly of the anguish of plantation wives who saw their husband's mulatto children as constant reminders of the living lie and the double standards which mocked their basic values. She scorned Northern abolitionists who denounced slavery from a safe distance. 'The Mrs Stowes have the plaudits of crowned heads; we take our chances, doing our duty as best we may among the woolly heads.'[23] Such caustic comments pile one irony on another – slaves put to work in the struggle to defend slavery, while slave-owners professed to hate the institution which bound and burdened them. There is no richer example of the internal tensions and contradictions of the Confederacy, the insoluble conflict between the legacy of the past and the emergency of the present.

7. Four years of turmoil and tragedy shook Southern society to its foundations, but never completely transformed it. The panorama of life in the Confederacy contained scenes of upheaval, turbulence and sudden, violent change but also quieter scenes of continuity and relative calm where life went on, with an adjustment here, an economy there, but still following the well-recognised pattern of earlier days. No community, no citizen escaped the impact of war completely; some were destroyed by it, some came to terms with it, some even profited from it. The war was a time of social disruption, but scarcely of social revolution.

Evidence of disruption abounded on all sides. There were times and places where the whole population seemed to be on the move. At the approach of invading armies, refugees thronged the roads in their wagons, taking with them what possessions they could, including in many cases their slaves, who constituted too valuable a property to be abandoned to the enemy. To a people with such deep roots in the land, and so strong a sense of place, such flight was a special kind of agony. But it was not always the Yankee intruder who drove them to it. Some women abandoned the unequal struggle to keep the farm going in the absence of the menfolk, others travelled to be near husbands or sons at the front or to search for them, tend them (or bury them) when the battle was over. The war took Southern women to new places, put them in new jobs and gave them new responsibilities – and, up to a point, new freedom. It loosened the formalities which had attended the lives of the planter class at least, and broke down some social barriers which had hitherto confined them, but for those in a humbler station in life, it more often simply added new burdens to old. For the menfolk, army life produced some of the same results. It removed the blinkers of parochialism from eyes which had never seen further than the next county; it brought boys from Texas to fight in the Seven Days battles in front of Richmond, and march with Lee into Pennsylvania; even though its regiments were state-orientated, it put men from many states and diverse backgrounds in the same line of battle or the same row of hospital beds. The army was the living symbol of Southern nationhood, and a nationalising influence in Southern life. On the other hand, if it opened the eyes and broadened the minds of some young men, it no doubt confirmed the prejudices and inflamed the animosities of others. But certainly, where an army moved, a whole train followed in its wake – wives and camp followers, nurses and preachers, labourers and teamsters, quartermasters, commissary and impressment agents – and the experience left its mark on them and on the places where they passed.

If the army was one magnet, the towns and cities were another. New industries and new opportunities as well as the compulsion to escape from old surroundings brought an increasing flow of people into the towns. An industrial city like Selma, Alabama, grew up in two or three years from almost nothing; an older city like Atlanta boomed in size, numbers and production; Richmond doubled and trebled in population as its status as capital and front-line city attracted a swarm of soldiers and politicians, speculators and office-seekers, workers and drones. Hotels, bars, shops and offices, hospitals to relieve the suffering, gambling houses and brothels to relieve the hale and hearty of their money, all grew apace in Southern towns and cities. Such movement and upheaval, growth and development, organisation and innovation, thickened the texture and complicated the pattern of Southern life. It certainly changed the face of the South, but it was a moot point how far it altered its real character.

There were other, more subtle, possibly deeper currents of social change in the life of the Confederacy. War demand brought new groups and classes to the fore. Industry and commerce grew not merely in size but in respectability, and men versed in the methods of business and the techniques of production found fresh scope and a greater sense of their own importance. The business of government grew fast, too, and professional men and white-collar workers were needed in unprecedented numbers, not merely in Richmond but in every state and city, to collect taxes, enforce new regulations and staff new agencies. The army promised to open another ladder of social advancement, and election of officers (and the sheer number required) seemed to offer bright prospects to young men blessed with initiative, ambition, an engaging personality and a modicum of talent. The mushroom growth of wartime armies – and their heavy losses, too – have always created the possibility of spectacularly rapid promotion, and the race up the ladder of military rank ran neck and neck with ascent in the social scale. The planter élite had to accommodate the newcomers if it was to retain its own position.

If war widened opportunity, it also inflamed social unrest and class antagonism. Protesting workers and rioting housewives were among the more vivid reminders of such animosities, but much more widespread and pervasive was the feeling among the great class of yeoman farmers that this was 'a rich man's war and a poor man's fight'. In their breasts lurked the suspicion that they had been led down the path to secession, war and ruin by a slave-owning aristocracy which was manipulating them in defence of its own interests. The war itself constantly fed such feelings. Planters were cushioned against some of the harsher realities of war; if the men went into the army, they took positions of privilege and authority within it, while the farmers' sons did most of the fighting, suffering and dying. The exemption of one white man for every twenty slaves on the plantation, and the ability of those with money to avoid conscription, embittered the poor, foot-slogging, ill-fed, ill-clad common soldier – and while he bore the brunt of the fighting, his family and property were suffering at the hands of impressment agents, tax-collectors, guerrillas and marauders. The high rate of desertion, and the rising support for the peace movement in the last eighteen months of the war, had more than a little to do with such grievances. In South and North alike, the enthusiasm of 1861 had merely papered over the cracks in the old society, and they quickly reappeared.

Indeed, for all the signs of change, the elements of continuity in Southern life were stronger still. Changes which could be accommodated or adjusted to old ways were accepted quite readily, but any radical break with the past was bitterly resisted, or accepted either as a temporary emergency measure, or as the dictate of sheer necessity. For all the refugees, and the migrants to the cities, Southerners in much greater numbers stayed at home, or returned after the briefest possible absence, their localism often reinforced by the loneliness and isolation brought about by poor communications, a struggling press and irregular mail. The emergence of Southern women in a new role was significant, but it is grossly exaggerated by a comparison which sets myths about the old South alongside the realities of the war years. In fact the myth of the Southern lady of pre-war days was replaced by the new myth of the Confederate heroine, the inspiration of the men at the front, and the most ardent champion of the cause. Like most myths, both of these contained elements of truth, but the notion that Southern womanhood stepped down from its lofty pedestal to meet the crisis of war is somewhat diminished by the fact that the vast majority of Southern women had never occupied a pedestal in the first place. War simply made their hard life even harder. Similarly, the image of Southern womanhood as the heart and backbone of the cause does not have to be totally discarded, but it must be set against the declining morale and depressing conditions of the second half of the war which prompted many women to write letters to their soldier husbands so heart-rending as to lead them to desert.

The urban and industrial growth of the wartime South is another development all too easy to exaggerate. The very use of the term 'city' was in many cases no more than a cloak of dignity for an overgrown and overcrowded village. New Orleans was the only really large Southern city but it was in Confederate hands for only a year. Richmond was a special case, and it struggled constantly against problems of overcrowding, food and fuel supply, law and order, and inability to provide the basic amenities of city life. The swollen numbers of many towns included a large floating population, which made them more like transit camps than great cities in the making. The scale of Southern industry, too, can easily be overstated, and for all its achievements in improvisation and production, it was still very much a matter of modest factories, small workshops, or home-based enterprise, despite the great exceptions like Tredegar and a few others. The notion of government bureaucracy as an agent of social mobility must also be kept in proportion. Most government departments were still small, and only a minority of the 70,000 government employees were office workers. The very word bureaucracy is an anachronism in this context, and the experience of the 'war clerk' Jones, and many others, testified to the small reward reaped by government servants whether in salary, status or popularity. For its part, the army gave rapid advancement to some, but the plantation aristocracy who monopolised its leadership at the start generally remained in firm control. Nathan Bedford Forrest, the ill-educated slave-driver turned brilliant cavalry general, is often cited as the great example of the rise of the self-made man in the army but in fact he was the great exception to the rule. Almost all the other leading generals were products of the plantation aristocracy or the West Point establishment, or both. In civilian life, the rising professional and business classes were no sudden wartime phenomenon, but simply profited from the acceleration of a steady, unspectacular process in the pre-war South. Merchants and lawyers had long played a part in the affairs of the old South; their interests and attitudes were usually tied closely to those of the planter class, and their aspiration was to set the seal on their own success by joining it.

The Southern 'aristocracy' had never been a tightly closed society and had always shown the capacity to absorb new men and new groups. Many of the pillars of that society were relative newcomers to it; Jefferson Davis himself was not exactly the scion of a long aristocratic line. The slave-owning planters had gone to great lengths to convince poorer whites that slavery was the common interest of all, but if war heightened the tension between classes, that tension was no new creation. The social divisions of the Confederacy were but the divisions of the old South writ somewhat larger. They owed as much to geography as to class, and, insofar as they took on a new dimension, it was less through an upsurge of class hatred than the feelings engendered by secession and the coming of Civil War. As Mrs Chesnut put it in February 1862, referring to her own state of South Carolina:

> The Up Country men were Union men generally, and the Low Country were seceders. The former growl; they never liked those aristocratic boroughs and parishes, they had themselves a good and prosperous country, a good constitution, and were satisfied. But they had to go – to leave all and fight for the others who brought on all the trouble, and who do not show much disposition to fight for themselves.

Three years later, finding refuge in western North Carolina in the last weeks of the war, she commented on the feelings of her hosts:

These people are proud of their heroic dead and their living soldiers, but are prepared to say with truth that they always preferred to remain in the Union, and are ready to assure the first comers of Yankees that they have always hated South Carolina seceders and nullifiers as much as the Yankees do.[24]

For all the upheavals of war, the Confederate South remained a predominantly rural and agricultural society, firmly adhering to its caste system, traditional values and social relationships, profoundly conservative in outlook, and dedicated still, in David Donald's words, to the principles of democracy and the practice of aristocracy. The significant changes which came upon that society were forced upon it. They did not mark the emergence of a new social order but the threatened breakdown of an old and cherished one. The truly abrupt and dramatic impact of the war upon society came from the immediate consequences of fighting, invasion, and conquest: suffering and hardship on a terrible scale, bereaved and broken families, physical devastation over huge areas, the mass desertions from the army, the collapse of law and order, the roving bands of marauders and plunderers, and – the starkest statistic of them all – the death of one-quarter of the able-bodied men of the Confederacy in four years. This was not social revolution but human tragedy on the grand scale.

There was, of course, a more agreeable side to the coin. In areas not too close to the actual fighting, life followed a quiet, not unpleasant course, troubled by shortages and inconveniences, punctuated by news from the front of the loss of loved ones, but retaining a fair measure of normality and routine. The history of a small town like Athens, Georgia, for example, reveals the remarkable extent to which life in many of its aspects moved sedately along familiar paths.[25] In areas well sheltered from the front line, shortages and inconveniences may well have been of a kind not serious enough to depress spirits but rather to encourage ingenuity and cooperation and promote a cheerful defiance. The spirit of business (and pleasure) as usual prevailed as far as local circumstances would allow. Dances, parties, picnics and other social functions continued, lacking only some of the elegance and lavishness of earlier days. Liquor was often of deplorably low quality and sometimes in short supply, but when supplies ran out, 'cold-water' parties became all the rage. In Richmond, a 'society' of some pretensions organised its own round of activities and its own network of friendships, jealousies, feuds and gossip. In her diary, Mrs Chesnut has left a colourful picture of that society in its mixture of fervour and frivolity, high spirits and high prices, political and romantic intrigue, dashing men in uniform and shattered men on crutches. The theatre flourished in the capital and in other cities, and Richmond actually opened a new theatre in 1863 to replace one destroyed by fire. It prospered despite the denunciations of a Baptist minister against such irresponsibility at such a time. 'Away then with the impudent and preposterous plea that the theatre, as it is, is a school of morals. It is what it always has been, a school of immorality and vice. I could as readily conceive of a church in Hell as a theatre in Heaven.'[26] Of all the arts, popular music perhaps drew the greatest inspiration from the war, and the songs of the Confederacy have been one of its most enduring monuments.

The literature of the wartime South was, however, more notable for quantity than quality. The greatest Southern literary figure of the day, William Gilmore Simms, wrote nothing of note during the war. The most popular novel written in these years was Augusta Jane Evans's *Macaria, or Altars of Sacrifice*, with its blend of sentimentality and zeal for the cause. The most notable Confederate poet was Henry Timrod, but his output, like that of Paul Hamilton Hayne, declined greatly in the latter part of the war. Curiously enough, the publishing business survived the toils of war better than might have been expected, and produced numerous school textbooks, and popular editions of Victor Hugo, Charles Dickens and others. The leading Southern periodicals struggled gamely for survival, but *DeBow's Review* ceased publication in 1862 and the *Southern Literary Messenger* in 1864. The newspapers shrank in size and in frequency of publication, but many eked out some kind of makeshift existence for most or all of the war period. A number gave Jefferson Davis and his administration steady, if sometimes lukewarm, support but they were often overshadowed by the strident critics, and the press was not on the whole one of the more useful vehicles for Confederate propaganda. Southern newspapers were subject to remarkably little regulation or censorship, and often published military information useful to the enemy. On the other hand, much of their information was unreliable, and this, added to difficulties of publication and circulation, often created confusion and uncertainty in the minds of readers. The diaries and letters of Confederates suggest that they suffered less anxiety through ignorance than from 'knowing' things which had in fact never happened. Rumours spread like wildfire, whether they related to battlefield triumphs or losses or to stories that Davis was blind or mad, or dead. If rumour could be spiced with horror, it became all the more exciting. The Augusta (Georgia) *Register*, for example, reported Sherman's capture of Milledgeville in December 1864, and dwelt with a subtle sense of social discernment on its consequences: 'We are informed that the incarnate devils ravished some of the nicest ladies in town.'[27]

Southern schools and colleges suffered severely during the war, but those which survived added a propaganda role to their other functions. Textbooks on everything from arithmetic to geography continued to convey a message of Confederate virtue and Yankee iniquity. But schools struggled desperately for funds in competition with more urgent priorities, and, despite the influx of draft-dodgers into the profession, there was an increasing shortage of teachers. Enrolments fell, school sessions shortened, and many schools were closed. Many colleges and universities closed for the duration of the war, and others operated on a drastically reduced scale, as students and their teachers enthusiastically joined the army in 1861-2, and students failed to win exemption from conscription in later years.

The churches of most Southern denominations had broken with their Northern brethren in the pre-war decades, and, in their zeal for the Confederacy, they now sought to turn the conflict into a holy war. They sent chaplains to minister to the troops, and played their part in the religious revivals which swept through the army in the latter part of the war. They were active, too, in organising relief for the soldiers' families, and their good works in this field were something of a new departure for churches hitherto characterised by fundamentalism and the pursuit of personal salvation. Religion was one of the great influences in the lives of the majority of Southerners, and the churches played a key role in stirring enthusiasm for the cause, sustaining morale in bad times, and comforting the bereaved and the suffering. They denounced traitors and deserters, hoarders and speculators, and the evils of drink, gambling, profanity and sexual immorality which both offended God and impaired the war effort. They had an infallible response to both good news and bad; every victory was God's blessing on his chosen people, every defeat a chastisement for their sins. They scrupulously divided the credit for successes between the Almighty and his human agents. One minister was ready 'to give the glory and praise to God' for Southern victories, but thought that 'at the same time honorable mention may properly be made of those by whom they were wrought'.[28]

The role of publicists, educators and churchmen as propagandists presented a sharp contrast with the feebleness of official efforts in this field. Jefferson Davis made speaking tours in various parts of the Confederacy in 1863 and 1864, and proclaimed fast days from time to time. But neither his efforts nor those of other Confederate or state authorities were part of an organised or sustained propaganda campaign. Indeed, neither Davis nor anyone else seriously thought in such terms or saw such a campaign as a high government priority. In the light of their conception of the role of government, and of their preoccupation with other pressing tasks, such a failure was hardly surprising. But for all that, it was a crucial failure in a war where morale on the home front mattered so much, and in a situation where a new government, struggling to establish itself, impinged upon the life of the people in so many other ways, most of them disagreeable and unpopular.

8. The Confederate government was the greatest of all the victims of the two agonising dilemmas which haunted the wartime South: how to reconcile means and ends, and cherished values with urgent need. In struggling to harmonise these divergent trends within the society, the government reflected that society all too accurately. It did not, it could not, opt completely for one thing or the other – either total preservation of a sacred heritage or total commitment to victory in the war. It struggled honourably but unavailingly to achieve something of both. In the name of defending basic Southern rights, it infringed individual freedom by conscription, property rights by impressment, and civil rights by suspension of the writ of habeas corpus. In fighting for survival, it interfered in economic and social life to a degree which would have been unthinkable a year or two before; it ran major industries, dictated to private companies, gave itself priority on the railroads, took over a share of the lucrative

private enterprise of blockade-running, and meddled with the free operation of the labour market. In defence of slavery, it took slaves away from their masters and ultimately decided to recruit them to share in the struggle, perhaps in return for the promise of ending their bondage. These were stupendous strides in a new direction, compelled by sheer necessity, but still they were not enough. The reach of the Confederacy exceeded its grasp, and in reaching so far (but still not far enough) it damaged itself beyond repair. Neither government nor society could sustain the new relationship (almost a shotgun marriage) which war forced upon them. Government could not make its new authority work. Conscription was full of leaks and loopholes; with or without suspension of the writ, the government could not assert its authority over draft-dodgers, deserters and other evaders of the law; impressment of supplies proved cumbersome, inefficient and grossly unjust; manpower policy lacked the sophistication to put enough of the right men in the right places. Regulation of industry and the railroads was fitfully enforced, and very mixed in its results – and the administration shied away from full use of its powers. In matters as divergent as managing the cotton crop, or stimulating civilian morale, the government either refused to acknowledge its responsibility or was obliged to recognise its incompetence. It conspicuously failed to create financial order and stability; indeed, it fell down in the exercise of what is surely one of the fundamental powers of government, the power to tax. None of its major policies worked effectively. Whether in recruiting men, raising money, gathering supplies, fixing fair prices, allocating resources, or bringing lawbreakers to book, its will was widely and increasingly flouted. Failure was not through lack of will. It may have owed something to lack of imagination or intelligence. But most of all it sprang from two roots: lack of ability to carry out such ambitious policies – lack of organisational skills and management techniques, lack of trained men and administrative machinery – and, on the other hand, deep popular (and state) resistance to the exercise of such powers which left the government with the alternatives of abandoning its policies or enforcing them at unbearable political cost. Ultimately, too many people were unwilling to accept the burdens which their new government thrust upon them, while, for its part, that government never had the time or the scope to offer anything but burdens to its people. It was never able to promote policies which suggested concern for individual welfare or the promise of future rewards. While the North endlessly discussed what was to happen after the war, and passed laws to help homesteaders and immigrants, railroads and manufacturers, the South had no time for such luxuries. It was a revealing difference between the two sides.

# Chapter XII: A Society at War— the North

The North acquired a new sense of its own identity in the course of the long contest with the South which culminated in civil war. At first that sense was largely negative; the North was a non-South, that part of the United States where slavery did not exist. But gradually a more positive sense of identity matured, as Northerners exulted in the glories of their 'free labour' system, and pointed to the material blessings as well as the moral superiority which it brought in its train. The war itself completed the merger between the Northern sense of identity and the Northern conception of American nationalism. The whole North from Maine to Minnesota was increasingly bound together by a common resistance to the demands and the pretensions of Southern slave society, by a shared belief in the virtues of its own way of life, and by general participation in a Northern or a national economy which made Illinois farmers, New England mill-workers, New York merchants, Pennsylvania ironmasters, and railroad men everywhere, more and more dependent upon each other. This is not to say that there was uniformity or even harmony; far from it. North-east and north-west had not abandoned their mutual suspicion. The east disparaged the crudity of the west; the west alleged that it was dominated and exploited by the east. New Englanders were reproached for their sharp business practice and ridiculed for their reforming fads and fancies. New York had already become the strange and powerful magnet which attracted even those who were repelled by its turbulence, extravagance and stridency. Ohio, an erstwhile frontier state, was now a crossroads of the Union, peopled half from the south and half from the east, and caught between the older society of the Atlantic seaboard, and a fresh, thrusting frontier society further to the west. The pioneer settler in Iowa required the help but resented the control of city merchants, railroad companies, and governments, local or remote. Within each section and each state of the North were further divisions of interest and outlook: town and country, merchant and manufacturer, employer and employee, craftsman and factory worker, native American and immigrant, Protestant and Catholic, those who welcomed change and those who regretted it. But, if Northern society was a mosaic of many multi-coloured pieces, those pieces were falling more and more into one pattern. Local issues and interests were being drawn into a system which went far beyond one village or city or state or section, and which became something national – or, if the South refused to share it – something Northern.

When war came, the North was a half-developed though rapidly developing society, still bearing many of the marks of its earlier history. It was still very much a land of farms, villages and small towns. Although the forty years before the war saw a percentage rate of urban growth unequalled before or since, the census of 1860 revealed that still slightly less than one in five Americans lived in towns with a population of 2,500 or more. (If the Southern states are excluded, the proportion would of course be a little higher.) The same census revealed that the value of farm lands, livestock, farm machinery and tools was still approximately seven times the capital in manufacturing. If the meeting-place of the North was still the small town rather than the great city, the basic unit of its economic life was the small farm and the small business rather than the great corporation. Most manufacturing was still on a small scale, and still dominated by individual entrepreneurs and small partnerships. Limited liability companies were rare outside such fields as banking and transportation. National organisations of any kind – financial institutions, professional bodies, voluntary associations, governmental agencies – were still the exception rather than the rule. The feeble grip and attenuated functions of federal authority before 1860 suggested that most Americans felt that they had the government which they desired and deserved. Allan Nevins has written eloquently of the unorganised, inchoate, highly individualist society which went to war in 1861; 'invertebrate' is perhaps the most apt of the adjectives which he uses.[1] A government which made a virtue out of inactivity was matched by a society which distrusted regulation, management and expertise. If the backwardness of the postal service bore testimony to the one, the inability of neighbouring cities to agree on a standard time was a symptom of the other. Even the most spectacular achievement of the half-century before 1860 – westward expansion – had been carried out with the barest minimum of regulation, management or control, whether from government or any other source. The settlement of the great West was the apogee of the old unorganised America.

The Civil War did not suddenly create a new America. The signs of change had been there for all to see in the two decades before the war, most notably of all perhaps in the field of transport and communication. In 1848 the first steam packet line between New York and Liverpool had narrowed the great Atlantic divide. A year earlier the telegraph had come into commercial use, and by 1860 the country was stitched together by some 50,000 miles of wire. Most important of all, the railroad had been transformed from the servant into the master of traditional horse-drawn or water-borne transport. Track mileage had trebled in the 1850s, most of it in the north and north-west. Part cause, part symbol of Northern unity and the Northern identity were the trunk rail routes completed in the 1850s, to link the Atlantic seaboard and the mid-west. The railroad, the steamship and the telegraph made the movement of men, goods, and words quicker, easier, more regular and more predictable, and encouraged the growth of a national market, with a more specialised division of labour, a more advanced factory system, and a more ambitious use of machinery.

The cities were the focal point of opportunity and progress. By 1860 the population of New York had passed the half million mark, Philadelphia the quarter million, and among those over 100,000 was a newcomer like Chicago. The cities drew people not merely from the villages and small towns of America but from Europe, too. The foreign-born have never been a higher proportion of the American population than in the years before the Civil War, and almost one quarter of the population increase of the 1850s was through immigration. The north, and especially the northern cities, provided the new home of the great bulk of the immigrants. On every side, then, the northern states in the 1840s and 1850s showed ample evidence of rapid change, giving a new shape (and perhaps a new strength) to a society hitherto invertebrate. The north was well launched into industrial development and economic growth before the war came. War was not their root cause but their first, stern test. Amid so much that was new and almost untried, so much movement of people into and within the country, could Northern society successfully meet a quite different challenge in the shape of civil war? When war came, the South was too much set in many of its ways to meet the challenge effectively; the North faced the opposite danger that it was too little set in its ways, too feverishly preoccupied with novelty and change, too much troubled by the growing pains of industrialisation.

In the early months of the war the signs looked none too promising. Northern business was only just recovering from the financial panic of 1857 when it came face to face with the secession crisis and then the outbreak of war. The unpredictability of the political future in the crisis of 1860–1 sapped a business confidence which was already none too robust; the coming of war darkened the gloom still further. In 1861 there were some 6,000 business failures, half as many again as in the panic year of 1857. The loss of Southern markets, the closure of the Mississippi outlet, and the loss of outstanding Southern debts depressed all those who had important connections with the seceded states: the New York merchants, for example, and the business communities of Baltimore, Cincinnati, St Louis and other cities. Loss of Southern cotton led to closures, short time and unemployment in the New England mills. Many western banks collapsed because they had been issuing large quantities of banknotes on the always shaky and now worthless security of the stocks and bonds of various Southern states. Such misfortunes were not balanced by any optimism about the profits of war. No one foresaw the scale or duration of the conflict or the economic demands and opportunities which it would create. The prevailing mood was one of nervous and gloomy uncertainty, and, as the months passed, confidence was aided by neither the dismal record of Union arms nor the desperate straits of Union finance.

Early in 1862, however, the economic climate improved, as some of the worst fears remained unfulfilled, government contracts warmed more sections of industry into life, and new measures averted financial disaster and put much-needed purchasing power into the economy. But the recovery was led not by manufactures or finance houses, nor by government policy or even war demand. It came rather from the response of American agriculture to an unexpected opportunity beckoning from across the Atlantic.

1. The decade of the 1850s had prepared the agriculture of the north, and especially the north-west, to take new demands in its stride. Its basic unit was still the small family farm, and it had not completely outgrown the tradition of simple subsistence agriculture. But its horizons were expanding rapidly, as Illinois and its mid-western neighbours developed into one of the richest granaries in the world, as the frontier pushed still further into another promised land, and as canals and railroads carried its produce into a wide national market. Beyond lay an international market, fostered by the repeal of the corn laws in Britain and the general trend towards free trade. While western farmers relied more and more upon distant markets, eastern farmers busied themselves with dairy-farming, and vegetable- and fruit-growing for the nearest urban centre. The railroads steadily widened the catchment area for such produce around each major city. To exploit new opportunities, farmers adopted new methods and invested in new machinery. By 1860 the American farmer was breaking free from the narrow, limited, localised way of life that had hitherto been his lot, only to find himself at the mercy of greater and wider forces far beyond his control.

Opportunity came, first, in the shape of three successive poor harvests in 1860, 1861 and 1862, in Britain and some other European countries. With bumper wheat crops in 1860 and 1862 and a healthy one in-between, American farmers were well placed to meet Britain's need. Wheat exports in 1861 were three times as great as in the previous year, and they continued at an exceptional level for two more years at least. Over 200 million bushels of wheat were exported to Europe in 1861-4, and there was also unprecedented European demand for American ham, bacon, pork and lard. The North thus reaped much of the benefit which the South had assumed that it would automatically derive from cotton. The diplomatic implications are discussed elsewhere;[2] the boost to Northern farmers (and to the Union balance of payments) could scarcely have been more timely, and it compensated many times over for the loss of the Southern market for north-western foodstuffs.

The European stimulus to American farming is much easier to measure than the effect of wartime demand at home. An army of several hundred thousand was obviously a voracious consumer, but, on the other hand, almost all the men who belonged to it were already consumers within Northern society before they donned uniforms. When every allowance has been made for military waste and extravagance, the problem was one of adaptation, organisation and distribution rather than of a sudden, spectacular rise in overall demand. From the farming point of view, the problem was less the existence of a new army of consumers than the absence of scores of thousands of producers who left the wheat-fields for the battlefields. But different kinds of farming were affected by the war in diverse ways. The slump in cotton textiles and the consequent demand for woollen goods (spurred on by army demands for clothing) brought a rapid revival in sheep-farming and wool-growing. The sheep population of the Northern states more than doubled between 1860 and 1866, and wool production increased from 90 million lb in 1860 to 165 million lb in 1864. While the sheep population grew, as stock was held off the meat market for wool-growing, numbers of cattle and pigs declined during the war, because of the heavy demand for meat. But the heaviest drain of all on Northern livestock came from the army's demand for horses and mules. The War Department purchased hundreds of thousands of horses, at a time when new machinery was increasing the demand for horses on the farms. In 1864 the Commissioner for Agriculture calculated that, instead of a growth of three-quarters of a million in the horse stock since 1860, which past trends would have indicated, there had actually been a decrease of 150,000.

Over the whole range of agricultural activity, the general wartime picture was one of solid achievement and prosperity, measured not so much by record growth rates or extraordinary advances in productivity as by success in adaptation to new circumstances. The difficulties were obvious enough. Secession and war meant the loss not only of Southern markets, but also of distinctively Southern products, such as cotton, sugar and tobacco, and the closure of the traditional north-western outlet down the Mississippi. Northern attempts to grow cotton and tobacco during the war were little more than token gestures, although tobacco growing made progress in the Connecticut valley: efforts to develop sorghum as a substitute for sugar were generally ill-rewarded. The closing of the Mississippi marked the sudden, dramatic completion of a long-term process of deflecting more and more western trade from the southern outlet to the Great Lakes, the canals and the railroads which provided more direct access to eastern markets. Westerners felt that they were now at the mercy of one set of transport interests, and soaring railroad freight rates in 1861 seemed to justify their worst fears; but those rates declined thereafter, and competition between railroads and canals, and among the railroads themselves, replaced the old rivalry between eastern and southern routes.

The most pressing of wartime agricultural problems concerned manpower. It was the men and boys from the Northern farms who formed the solid mass of the Union armies. It is estimated that 680,000 men joined the army from the five states of the old north-west alone – one-tenth of the total population, and most of them undoubtedly from farming communities. The problem on the farms was met in a variety of ways. As in the south, women took over more of the work than ever before. Boys too young and men too old for military service took up their share of the burden, and immigrant labour helped out here and there. Production was maintained or increased with a smaller labour force, partly by cutting corners, neglecting maintenance and long-term improvements, over-working the soil, and concentrating on immediate priorities. There was a lively interest in new, more scientific methods, and an increasing use of fertilisers. But, above all, the farmer looked to machinery to balance the loss of manpower. The necessary machines did not appear overnight as if by magic. Mechanical reapers and mowers were already widely in use in the 1850s, especially in the west. The real point is that their much more extensive use during the war years enabled fewer Northern hands to grow more. By 1865 farmers probably had three times as many machines as in 1860.[3] The reaper and the mower were by far the most widespread and the most important, but there was increasing interest in other machines too: horse-rakes, threshers, planters, diggers and new kinds of plough.

Machinery increased the capital cost of farming, and added to its complexities. The basic unit, the small farm, did not change greatly during the war, and it continued its spread further into the west, although at a rather slower rate. But it was becoming more and more a link in a long and intricate chain. The increasing use of grain elevators, and the development of improved marketing techniques, centering on the grain exchanges at New York and other cities, greatly facilitated an expanding trade, although they promised to be a mixed blessing to the farmer himself. Chicago became, during the Civil War, the great centre of American meat-packing and processing – the 'Porkopolis of the West'. It almost quadrupled its previous highest output in packing almost a million hogs in its best wartime year. The great Union stockyards in Chicago, opened in 1865, were a direct result of wartime growth. Flour-milling also expanded very rapidly during the war, and so too did the production of canned vegetables and other foods. Gail Borden opened his first large condensed-milk plant in New York in 1861, and found eager customers in the cities and the armies of the north.

The overworked term 'agricultural revolution' is inevitably applied to mid-nineteenth-century American farming, with its soaring production, expanding area, new machinery and methods, and ever-widening markets. Like most such 'revolutions', this was a long-term process, and it would be folly to pretend that the Civil War created it. But, with the help of unusual European demand, it did in many ways accelerate and advance it. The resilience, the resourcefulness and the richness of Northern agriculture were amply demonstrated by its performance under wartime pressure. Moreover, the wartime boom and healthy farm prices continued into the early post-war years; indeed, the farmer enjoyed a prosperity in the mid- and late sixties which he was not to know again for the rest of the century. In the slightly longer run, the American farmer was to face new hazards and new handicaps – or the return of old ones. Foreign demand which had come to the rescue in the early sixties was to encourage the spread of wheat-farming into unsuitable or marginal areas in the 1870s and later. Problems of overproduction, falling prices, fluctuating world markets, competition from new areas, exploitation by middlemen, and a mounting burden of debt, crowded in upon the farmer and put him into the vanguard of protest in the last quarter of the century. American agriculture emerged triumphant from the harsh test of civil war only to face a less dramatic but more searching examination in the generation which followed.

2. American industry, too, was put to the test by domestic conflict, but here, even more than in the case of agriculture, it is desperately difficult to distinguish the impact of war from long-term developments stretching back at least two decades before Sumter and far on into the future beyond Appomattox. No simple statement of the industrial consequences of the war will stand close scrutiny, whether it be the sweeping claim that the war of itself launched the United States into a new era of industrial capitalism and sustained economic growth, or the contemptuous dismissal of the war as a petty and largely irrelevant interruption of the main business of nineteenth-century America. Is the economic significance of the war to be gauged best by twentieth-century notions of economic growth, and the evidence of long runs of decennial statistics, or by bold statements about shifts of economic power or redistribution of income – or by intricate and probably inconclusive examination of the repercussions of war, industry by industry, class by class and group by group? Is the statistical evidence, for all its limitations and unreliability, to be regarded as the supreme arbiter, or must it be merged into the pattern of other evidence, more varied, more elusive, less apparently clear-cut and authoritative? Certainly much of the argument over whether the Civil War was economically an accelerator or a brake has been between those whose motto might be defined as 'if it cannot be quantified, it does not signify', and those more inclined to dwell on institutional, social, political and psychological factors and their bearing on economic change. The mesmeric power of the percentage has compelled one school of thought to treat the absolute increase in production of many items during the war as relatively insignificant beside the decline in the percentage rate of growth. On the other hand, an older school of thought long felt itself competent to talk bravely of industrial expansion stimulated by the war without first checking the detailed facts and figures. It is small wonder perhaps that, when in his exhaustive study of the North at war Allan Nevins faced the question whether the Civil War advanced or retarded industrialisation, he answered it with a yes and a no, and the cautious conclusion that it produced 'mixed results in a very mixed economy'.[4]

Close inspection supports his cautious common sense. The tentative, uncertain response to war in 1861–2 has to be balanced against the roaring boom of 1863–5. The impact of any war – and certainly of this particular war – was bound to be uneven as between industry and industry. The silent cotton mills of New England may be contrasted with the humming activity of the arms factories of the same region. Both offered a sharp contrast to the oil boom in Pennsylvania or the mining boom in the far west which took place during the war but had almost nothing to do with it. There was a pleasing simplicity in the view of the Civil War as the clear watershed between pre-industrial and indus-trial America, but, alas, it never fitted the facts. The rapid growth and change of the pre-war decades had already launched the North upon a new path; indeed, one of the great advantages of the North when war came was precisely that it could work and fight from a significant industrial base, and did not face the Southern task of starting almost from scratch. If pre-war developments blur the notion of the war as dividing line, the experience of the war years obscures it still further. The Civil War was a modern conflict in the sense that industrial capacity and performance mattered enormously, but it is not to be placed on a par with the great wars of the twentieth century. In the words of a historian writing at the end of the First World War:

Half a century ago, war made lighter requisitions upon the productive forces of a country than at present. Man's powers of destruction were comparatively undeveloped, and his powers of creation were correspondingly less exerted.[5]

One estimate suggests that the consumption of iron attributable to small arms production was equal to only 1 per cent of total iron output in 1865 – the equivalent of 650 miles of railroad track.[6] The final stage of demolition of the great economic divide of Civil War is provided by the argument that the great leap forward into the era of the industrial giants came not in the aftermath of war but after the depression of the 1870s. The whole argument receives confirmation with the holy oil of statistics by demonstration of the abnormally low growth rate of the sixties in comparison with any other decade between 1840 and 1900.

But to jump to the conclusion that the Civil War was of little or no economic or industrial importance would be as unwise as to insist that the great divide remains in all its clear and simple grandeur. Man does not live by growth rate alone, and even the economist whose figures are most often cited to show the negative impact of the war has himself suggested that such statistics may fail to bring out changes in the structure of the labour force or in the distribution of income.[7] Other authorities point to reallocation of priorities and resources, changes in the structure of industry, and in its relationship with government, reorganisation of the financial system, resourcefulness in meeting new demands and responding to new situations – all compelled or stimulated by the extra-ordinary circumstances of war. This was a domestic conflict, a *civil* war, and one may well wonder if the proper question is not whether the war retarded the rate of industrial growth, but how did industry, and the economy as a whole, manage to survive so successfully the stress and strain of such an internal upheaval. Those who lived in the north during and after the war – and perhaps, even more, those who visited the country – were constantly struck by the furious economic activity which the war induced. But, of course, such observers of the events of the 1860s had not had the benefit of the statistics of a century later. Even these can be made to talk a different language if the figures for iron and coal production or railroad mileage in the ten years before 1860 are compared with the much higher figures for the ten years after 1865.[8] It is just possible that the Civil War is not unconnected with that development.

The industries of the north may be broadly divided into three categories: those which suffered from the war, those which benefited from it, or found new opportunities, great or small, in responding to its demands, and those which flourished during the war but had little connection with it.

Pre-eminent among the industrial casualties of war was cotton manufacturing. Loss of supplies of Southern cotton forced Northern mills to operate at half – or even quarter – capacity. For a while they survived on existing stocks; later in the war they received a steady trickle of raw cotton from abroad and more substantial relief from the frantic efforts to bring cotton out of the south. Although production figures plummeted, mill-owners were able to make a handsome profit from their reduced output, as they benefited alike from the scarcity of cotton goods and the general inflation of prices. Unemployment in the cotton industry had less serious social consequences than in Lancashire in the same years, as many workers were quickly absorbed into other industries, and many mill-girls returned to their family homes in rural New England. Another serious victim of the war was the American merchant marine which, for reasons which are discussed elsewhere,[9] suffered a drastic acceleration of its pre-war decline. Some historians point also to the decline in the railroad construction during the war years, but the fact that the North still contrived to build several hundred miles of new line in each of those years may well be interpreted rather as evidence of undiminished strength and future confidence.

Among industries given a significant boost by the war, woollen manufacture must take a high place, if only because of its role in substituting for cotton. Not one of the most flourishing of American manufactures before the war, the woollen mills made the most of their new opportunity. The army's heavy demand for uniforms and other clothing handsomely compensated for any decline in the civilian market. In the winter of 1861–2, while soldiers shivered for lack of adequate clothing, the home manufacturers still protested violently against the government's decision to place orders for cloth abroad. Large-scale army demand also came to the aid of the ready-made clothing industry which had developed since the 1840s, and which had found one of its best pre-war markets in the south in providing cheap garments for slaves. It was not difficult to switch from production for slaves to production for soldiers, and the war stepped up the use of sewing machines and the growth of clothing factories at the expense of small-scale workshops. The war encouraged similar trends in the boot and shoe industry. There was the same acceleration in the growth of larger factories, and the same widespread adoption of a pre-war invention, in this case a machine patented by Lyman R. Blake in 1858, which sewed the uppers to the soles, did the work formerly done by many hands, and thus removed the major bottleneck in the manufacturing process. The results of these developments in what was one of the major industries of the North in the 1860s suggest how much care is needed in the analysis of the impact of the Civil War. There was no spectacular climb to a new peak of boot and shoe production; indeed pre-war levels of production were never actually equalled during the war years. But an adequate output was maintained, despite the drain on the labour force, and without a severe rise in prices.

It was in the field of heavy industry that the greatest changes might have been expected, but it has already been suggested that the Civil War did not make the same voracious demands for iron and other metal products as more modern conflicts. Indeed, if figures for pig-iron production are considered in five-year blocs, the years 1860–5 show a rise of only 1 per cent compared with 17 per cent for the preceding period, and 100 per cent for the five years after the war. But such bare figures are misleading – although the implications of the remarkable figure for 1865–70 may be not unimportant. During the war, iron production slumped in 1861–2, the period of recession and uncertainty, climbed back past the 1860 level in 1863, and broke all records with a figure of 1,136,000 tons in 1864. In fact, the American iron industry managed to satisfy military require-ments without depriving the railroads and other civilian customers of what they needed, in spite of the fluctuating economic climate, the labour problems, and the other disruptions of war. There was the same tendency towards consolidation into larger units, the same adoption of new methods – although America still lagged behind in the techniques of steel-making – the same widening interest in new forms of organisation and new processes as in other industries. At one end of the scale, the making of horseshoes moved from the blacksmith's shop to the large factory; at the other, great new rolling mills arose at Allentown and Bethlehem and Pittsburgh. It was no accident that the young Andrew Carnegie, seeing the price of pig-iron climb to new heights in 1864, decided to find the capital to build a blast furnace and a rolling mill at Pittsburgh. The heavy industrial base of the north survived the test of war, emerged with a new strength, and moved confidently into the future. Once again, the Civil War proved to be neither the basic cause of a major development nor a major hindrance to it, but rather a stimulus and an incentive. The war was not the soil in which industrial growth took root, nor a blight which stunted it, but a very effective fertiliser.

Other industries, too, from coal-mining to lumbering, showed notable increases in output during the war. The manufacture of items varying from watches to whisky, wagons to wool carpets showed spectacular advances. Their relationship to the war situation may not in every case be easy to define or even detect. Even more fortuitous in their connection with a state of civil conflict were the oil, gold and silver booms of the early sixties. It was in 1859 that Edward L. Drake struck oil near Titusville in north-west Pennsylvania. In 1861, within weeks of the outbreak of war, oil began to flow more abundantly from other wells in the same vicinity of Oil Creek. A new population swarmed into what had been one of the poorest counties of the state, and the banks of Oil Creek were covered with derricks for miles on end. Most of the new arrivals remained poor, but some did not. The new business slumped for a while when supply outran demand, but by the latter part of the war it was roaring ahead again, and eager prospectors were busy in West Virginia and Ohio as well as Pennsylvania. Refining methods had been greatly improved, the railroads were penetrating into the oil region, and experiments with pipelines had begun. Above all, it had been demonstrated that the new oil was not merely a useful lubricant but the best and cheapest fuel then available for lighting. Demand shot upwards not merely in America but abroad, and prices and profits bounded ahead in consequence. When the war ended, petroleum was already the sixth largest export of the United States. The years of civil strife had seen one of the greatest of American industries through the early stages of infancy – a coincidence which reflects the impact of war not at all, but rather the robust vigour of Northern society, and the rich resources at its disposal.

The same is true of the western mining boom. The gold and silver deposits of the Comstock Lode, in what became Nevada Territory, were discovered in 1859, the Gregory Lode in Colorado in the same year. Gold and other metals were discovered in what became the territories of Montana and Idaho in the early years of the war. The discoveries produced wild excitement and even wilder speculation. They also triggered a large-scale trek westwards from the Mississippi valley across the great plains, which continued throughout the war. Estimates of the numbers involved vary widely, but in 1864 alone they ran into scores of thousands. By mid-war, Virginia City, Nevada, was already the second largest town in the far west; its namesake in Montana, starting from nothing in 1862, had from ten to fifteen thousand inhabitants in 1864. The war stimulated the mining boom in one way, at least; the numbers heading for Montana, Colorado and Nevada were swollen by refugees from conscription or from the chaos of the border states, or from other wartime hardships or difficulties. Even the drama of war could not overshadow the excitement of the mining bonanza, and there were plenty of Northerners who refused to let the hazards of the first rob them of the dreams of the second.

The general picture of Northern industry at war is one of recovery during 1862 from a sluggish start, and emergence into a tremendous boom in the last two years of the struggle, when prices and profits were high, and opportunities almost limitless. Manufacturers were among the great beneficiaries of wartime inflation, for wages did not generally keep pace with prices, debts could be paid off in depreciated currency, and new expansion easily financed. The story of one industry after another shows many of the same features: the trend towards the

factory system and larger units; the growing awareness of the virtues of consolidation, even of some limitation of competition, and of the usefulness of
producers' or traders' associations; the widespread application of recent inventions rather than the sudden development of new ones; flexibility and resource
in the adoption of new methods, the switch to new lines of production, the
exploitation of new opportunities and the improvisation of answers to unusual
problems or shortages. Whether or not this or that industry grew faster under
war conditions, American industry as a whole certainly grew up more quickly.
There was waste and extravagance, folly and failure, but the abiding impression
is one of energy and enterprise, resilience and resource, and a deep strength which
could shoulder the burdens of war and still find time for all manner of other
activity.

3. The transportation and communications system which had done so much to
build the strength of the North before the war now contributed handsomely to
its eventual victory in the struggle. Like other sectors of the Northern economy,
it managed to continue (and even to extend) business as usual while meeting new
demands. In the transmission of news, information, messages, money and small
packages, new agencies which had got off the mark before the war, made rapid
strides during the conflict. Great names in the history of American communications came to the forefront. In the telegraph business, Western Union now
dominated all its rivals and participated in the Atlantic cable project which
achieved success in 1866. In the express delivery business, American Express and
its western subsidiary Wells Fargo now offered a speedy and reliable nationwide
service. As for the large-scale movement of goods and people, for all the advances
of the pre-war decades, it would still have been somewhat premature in 1860 to
talk of a transport system. Most traffic was still local, the scope of most companies was still limited, and long journeys were still a matter of constant
chopping and changing from one mode of transport to another, or at least from
one railroad terminal to another. It was possible to travel from New York to
Chicago in about thirty-six hours, but it was no smooth, uninterrupted ride.

By the 1860s, although the railroads dominated the stage, water-borne traffic
was not yet completely overwhelmed by the competition, certainly where
long-distance freight was concerned. An armada of some 2,000 steamboats and
other vessels plied the waters of the Ohio, the upper Mississippi and their
tributaries, and another armada sailed the wide waters of the Great Lakes. One
of the almost unsung heroes of the Union war effort was Lewis B. Parsons, who
brought order and efficiency to the business of supplying the western armies by
means of the boats and barges of the western rivers. The Erie Canal, much improved by 1860, carried the major share of the western grain sent to the Atlantic
seaboard; in 1861 it carried a greater total tonnage of freight than the two New
York rail trunk lines combined. In the west there was a great campaign for the
improvement of the Illinois and Michigan canal, to provide a free flow of
traffic between the Mississippi and the Great Lakes, and thus break the strangle-

hold of the railroads. A huge convention at Chicago in 1863 pleaded the case for this work and for further improvement of the Erie Canal, but congressional procrastination, local jealousies, and increasing railroad efficiency defeated the plan.

The railroads were not to be denied the leading role. The feverish railroad construction of the 1850s had provided new capacity, hitherto under-used, which was able to absorb the extra traffic of war. Companies which had struggled through the lean years of the late fifties, or even gone into receivership, were paying handsome dividends by the middle of the war. They benefited from military traffic but much more from the overall improvement in business. The east–west trunk routes took over most of the freight traffic of the north-west, and by 1864–5 it was clear even to the most conservative minds that the shift of trade from the Mississippi river route was no temporary wartime diversion but an irreversible change. By 1865 the total tonnage on the Erie Canal was 40 per cent less than the tonnage carried on the two main New York rail routes. Heavy traffic generally brought large profits in spite of spiralling costs, rising wages, and the wear and tear on track and rolling stock. Shortage of labour was often a serious problem, especially as the government would agree to the exemption from the draft only of engine drivers. While wages soared, efficiency suffered through the replacement of skilled workers by those less skilled and less experienced. While railroads in most parts of the country prospered, some were exposed by their geographical situation to the immediate hazards of war. The Baltimore and Ohio, running close to the front line, was particularly vulnerable, and suffered serious disruption through enemy action for some part of each year from 1861 to 1864. Early in the war the B & O actually ran through the lines of both armies, until Stonewall Jackson set an elaborate trap at Harper's Ferry which caught over forty locomotives and nearly four hundred cars. But, for the most part, Northern railroads, unlike their Confederate counterparts, went about their lucrative business undisturbed by fear of the invader.

At the outset, the railroads of the north did share many of the practical difficulties and shortcomings of those in the south. They suffered from a multiplicity of track gauges, from poor terminal facilities, from the irritation and delay of transfer from one terminal to another in the same city, from local monopolies, and all the other hazards of localism, fierce rivalry between companies and between cities, and hasty and skimpy construction of track, bridges, depots and other facilities. But the Northern railroad network was much less fragile and fractured than the Southern, and the North was far less crippled by its deficiencies and far more able to remedy them. During the war there was significant progress in the standardisation of track gauge, or in the temporary alleviation of the problem by adding a third rail or using rolling stock with adjustable axles. Double track was provided on many more lines, and bottlenecks removed by construction of links between terminals, and new bridges to replace old ferries. But there were still numerous complaints about slow speeds, unpunctuality, dirt and discomfort, and the frequency of accidents.

The *New York Sun* claimed that 'we could name half a dozen railroads upon
which a man has less chance for life and limb in a fifty-mile trip than our soldiers
had in the battles of the Wilderness'.[10] The New York–Philadelphia–Baltimore–
Washington route had more than its share of problems. This vital two-hundred-
mile link between the nation's political and business capitals was shared between
at least three different companies. The journey involved frustrating and time-
consuming transfers at Baltimore and Philadelphia, a ferry across the Susquehanna
river and another ferry across the Hudson into New York. The Baltimore and
Ohio claimed a monopoly of the Washington–Baltimore stretch, and, much
more seriously, the Camden and Amboy unyieldingly defended its monopoly,
granted by the state legislature of New Jersey, of routes through New Jersey
between New York and Philadelphia. In 1865 Charles Sumner was still ful-
minating against New Jersey as 'the Valley of Humiliation through which all
travelers north and south from the city of New York to the city of Washington
must pass', and comparing the states rights pretensions of New Jersey to the
'blood-bespattered pretension of South Carolina'.[11] Some improvements were
made during the war, but the journey still took a full twelve hours. The whole
story shows once again that the South had no monopoly of localism, pettifogging
restrictions, and narrowness of outlook. There were times, especially early in
the war, when Washington looked like an offshore island linked to the main
body of the Union by a narrow causeway of iron; there were times, too, when
that causeway was more endangered by the currents of obstructionism from the
north than by the tide rising in the south.

Elsewhere, Northern railroad companies learned to recognise some of the
virtues of consolidation and cooperation (even if they did not always practise
them), especially as the growth of long-distance traffic underlined their dependence upon one another. The east–west trunk routes agreed on union ticket
offices at New York and Boston. All the major railroads entering Chicago
cooperated in promoting the new Union stockyards. Although construction of
new lines declined during the war years, one major new route to the west, the
Atlantic and Great Western, was completed in 1862–4 – no mean achievement in
the midst of civil strife. New lines also spread further into the west, and in 1862
Congress lent its support to the plan for a railroad to the Pacific, although no
significant work was done on that project before the end of the war. The
pressures of heavy wartime traffic stimulated improvements in railroad organisation and management, and hastened the introduction of new techniques and
new equipment – the switch from wood to coal as the main locomotive fuel,
the first use of steel rails on heavily-used stretches of track, the development of
hospital cars, and of railway post office cars.

While carrying a vast amount of government traffic, the wartime railroads
remained essentially a private enterprise. They had a close and sometimes tense
relationship with the federal government, but War Department officials
generally preferred accommodation and negotiation to dictation. It was helpful,
at least, that Tom Scott of the Pennsylvania Railroad served as an Assistant

Secretary of War for a time in 1861-2. Military business caused headaches for railroad managers; it was unpredictable and irregular, it disrupted normal traffic and it caused disagreement over rates. Early attempts to fix rates lacked any power of enforcement, and there were frequent complaints about over-charging and exploitation. Early in 1862 Stanton called a conference of railway officials which made a firmer agreement on schedules for both troop and freight movements. Prosperity smoothed away many points of friction, and the railroads zealously applied the veneer of patriotism to their profit-making activities.

The government had a powerful instrument for control of the railroads in an act passed by Congress in January 1862. It authorised the president to take possession of any or all railroad lines when, in his judgment, the public safety required it, and to place such lines under full military control. But, in the northern states, it was sparingly used, and only a very few railroads, close to the battlefront, were ever seized by the government. However, an infinitely more ambitious and far-reaching exercise in government control developed in the operation of military railroads in the south. The United States Military Railroads, functioning within the War Department, became a large, skilled and complex organisation, building new stretches of line and repairing old, and using them to maintain a constant flow of supplies to the armies in the field. By the end of the war, the Military Railroads were operating over 2,000 miles of track, with over 400 locomotives and 6,000 cars. It had laid 642 miles of track and built 26 miles of bridges. The superintendent and guiding genius of the whole system was Daniel C. McCallum, formerly of the Erie Railroad, and one of the great organisation men of the war. For two years his jurisdiction was confined to the eastern theatre, but in 1864 Grant extended his authority to the west. Here he enjoyed his finest hour, rebuilding, running and constantly repairing the 470 miles of track from Louisville through Nashville and Chattanooga towards Atlanta, which sustained Sherman's campaign against Atlanta – and which, indeed, alone made it possible. Here he applied triumphantly many of the lessons and the techniques learned in Virginia in 1862-3. In Virginia he had owed much to the remarkable talents of another railroad man, Herman Haupt, who took practical charge of railroad construction and transportation for a relatively brief and stormy but vital period. Haupt insisted on adherence to basic principles of railroad operation, and brooked no interference from officers in the field. He organised regular schedules for the Virginian military railroads, and improvised a miraculous rail supply line for Meade's army at Gettysburg in 1863. But his most remarkable feats were even more in the construction than the operation of railroads. His bridge-building achievements were a legend, and his skill in the arts of destruction as well as construction was revealed in his refinement of the technique for destroying the enemy's rails beyond hope of repair. One example of his feats of ingenuity and organisation must suffice. When Burnside moved his army to the north bank of the Rappahannock opposite Fredericksburg in November 1862, Haupt rebuilt the railroad from Aquia

Creek in ten days to form its supply line, improvised a new wharf, and devised a scheme by which freight cars could be run straight on to barges at Alexandria, floated down-stream to Aquia Creek, and run straight off on to the track there to go forward to the army, without any loading or unloading of the contents. This brilliant application of the principle of containerisation a century before its time made enormous savings of time, effort and money.[12]

The history of the railroads during the Civil War has its moments of melodrama, like the great locomotive chase in Georgia and Tennessee in 1862, and its spectacular feats of improvisation, like the transfer of Hooker's troops to the west in 1863, and its impressive feats of engineering, like the 780-ft bridge over the Chattahoochie which McCallum's construction corps put together in five days in 1864. But what counted most of all was the consistent capacity to meet the constant demands placed upon them. For their part, the railroads made it possible to sustain a war waged by large numbers over huge distances – and to sustain it deep into the enemy's territory. The railroad companies played their part, sometimes grudgingly, sometimes wastefully, but with astonishingly little government supervision or control, for the North could afford a slacker rein than the South. For their part the United States Military Railroads were a prime example of enterprise in a traditionally enterprising society, but also of organisation in a hitherto unorganised society. As the war went on, the railroads converted the massively superior potential of the North into a clear and usable military advantage. Having bound the North together in the 1850s, they sustained it in the struggle to defeat the South in the 1860s.

4. The Civil War was preceded and followed by long periods during which the federal government generally had more money than it needed – or at least more than it was thought to need to meet the modest demands placed upon it. It followed therefore that few areas of activity were more shaken by the shock waves of war than public finance. In their turn, questions of currency and banking, debts and taxes affected every interest and ultimately every citizen in the land, and the financial management or mismanagement of the Union war effort left a complex and controversial legacy to the post-war generation. If it did not create an entirely new financial system, the war mercilessly laid bare the deficiencies of the old.

In 1861, as for many years before, federal government expenditure was small because expectations of what that government could and should do were so low. It generally paid its way without difficulty by relying on one or two simple and fairly painless sources of revenue – basically, customs duties and income from sales of the public lands. It had no machinery for the collection of internal revenue – nor even any adequate information on which it could have based assessment of such taxes. In 1862 Justin Morrill, complaining of the difficulty of preparing an adequate tax bill, remarked that 'our public archives, as is well known, are extremely meager in statistical information in all that relates to the industry and resources of the country'.[13] But the federal government was subject to still further limitations, either self-imposed or dictated by political tradition and popular suspicion. It had abdicated from any control over the banking and currency system in the decades before the war. The Jeffersonian–Jacksonian tradition which combined suspicion of centralised government with distrust of banks had reached its climax in the destruction of the Second Bank of the United States in the 1830s and the complete divorce of government and the banks decreed by the Independent Treasury Act of 1846. This measure required all payments to or by the government to be made in gold or its equivalent, and forbade the deposit of the government's funds in any bank. In the words of Bray Hammond:

> To keep relations between the government and the economy 'pure' and wholesome, tons of gold had to be hauled to and fro in dray-loads, with horses and heavers doing by the hour what book keepers could do in a moment.[14]

Financially, such a government could scarcely have been worse prepared for civil war; the financial arrangements and institutions of the mid-nineteenth century all too accurately mirrored the loose, unstructured condition of the society as a whole.

The man who faced the daunting task of financing the war was Secretary of the Treasury, Salmon P. Chase. As an ex-Democrat and a stern moralist in finance as in all else, he subscribed to orthodox hard-money notions, and even continued to plead for cuts in expenditure when the costs of war were shooting up almost by the minute. In fact, Chase was a man of very limited financial experience or expertise; understandably unable, like most of his contemporaries, to foresee the gigantic scale of the conflict, he constantly saw his estimates overtaken by events, but clung to the conventional view that taxation should take care simply of the 'normal' expenditure of government, while loans should pay for the extraordinary expenditure of war. In practice, like his Confederate opposite number, he had to strike a balance between three main ways of paying for the war: loans, taxes and the printing of paper money. Like him, too, he soon found that the answer was not simply a matter of financial calculation, but also of economic buoyancy, administrative capacity, political acceptability and popular mythology. Unlike the unfortunate Memminger, Chase had large resources to tap, and some real foundation, however slender and obscure at times, for confidence. If the problem of Union finance was a persistent, nagging headache, Confederate finance was a constantly ticking time-bomb.

The immediate situation which Chase confronted upon taking office was distinctly discouraging. Unusually, the federal government had been running a deficit for three years in the wake of the panic of 1857. Then the secession crisis had come as a further heavy blow to financial confidence. Chase faced a public debt of $75 million (one-quarter of it incurred since the start of the secession movement), a decline in customs duties and other revenue, and the prospect of mountainous expenditure. In the early weeks of the war he scrambled through only with the help of modest issues of bonds and treasury notes. When Congress assembled in July, he laid before it his longer-term plans. He estimated expenditure for the year ahead at $320 million, and proposed to raise three-quarters of that amount by loans, and one-quarter by taxation. The total figure was to be mocked by subsequent events, but Congress was not disposed to quarrel seriously at this stage either about the amount or the relative proportion of loans and taxes. Both methods were bound to encounter administrative problems and popular reluctance; the tradition of several decades frowned upon internal taxes, and the experience of recent months indicated a sluggish response to government bond issues of comparatively trifling amounts. But, on the whole, borrowing seemed the easier way out, especially while there was still widespread hope that the war would not last long, and Congress quickly authorised loans totalling $250 million. The tax measures, hammered out in lengthier debates, still relied heavily on customs duties (with rates increased once again) but also imposed a diverse, if modest, programme of internal taxes: excise duties on a variety of products, an income tax of 3 per cent on incomes over $800, and a direct tax on property. As with some ill-fated Confederate taxation schemes, it was hoped that the states would use their existing machinery to collect this last tax, in return for 15 per cent of the proceeds, but, in the event, both the property and income taxes were deferred until 1862, and then superseded by later measures.

The deficiencies of the 1861 financial programme were soon revealed. Revenue from taxes proved as disappointing as military expenditures were alarming. Chase was relying mainly on loans for his financial salvation but here, too, he soon met trouble, much of it of his own making. Using the authority granted by Congress, he obtained the support of the banks of New York, Philadelphia and Boston for a loan of $150 million, and the banks agreed on successive $50 million advances to the Treasury in August, October and December. But, adhering to the principles of the Independent Treasury Act of 1846, Chase continued to insist that the bank advances be made in coin. He interpreted a recent amendment apparently relaxing that restriction to mean merely that deliveries of gold from the banks could be made at convenient intervals. In this he may have been right, but the effect of this interpretation on the financial situation was disastrous. The banks had supposed that they were to credit the government of the United States with the sums concerned, and then make payments to the government's creditors by check. Chase's insistence on deliveries of gold put them into great difficulties, and posed a grave threat to their reserves. There was only around $250 million in specie in all the northern states at this time, and the big city banks held but one-third of that amount. Even in the short run, the scheme as interpreted by Chase could only survive on confidence and good luck. Confidence held up remarkably well in the latter part of 1861, and some gold continued to flow back into the banks. Good fortune came to the rescue of the banks in the shape of gold from California, and even more from Europe to pay for unprecendented imports of grain, which helped for a while to disguise the true dimensions of the crisis.

But such luck could not last for ever. Confidence found precious little nourishment towards the end of the year, in the news from the battlefront or from anywhere else. Then came the international crisis resulting from the *Trent* affair, and fears of impending war with Britain. Hoarding of gold increased and bank reserves declined sharply. The government became tardier than ever in paying its suppliers, and its soldiers. Chase's first annual report in December did nothing to restore morale. Chase admitted that expenditure had risen far above estimates a few months earlier but he still proposed to rely mainly on loans for revenue, and showed little inkling of the role which taxation could have played both in financing the war and in restraining inflation. He put most emphasis on proposals for banking reform which offered no immediate relief to urgent problems.

By the last few days of the year, the large city banks concluded that they could take the strain no longer. Their reserves were draining away, and on 30 December 1861 they suspended specie payments; customers could no longer exchange their notes for their value in gold. The Treasury had no real alternative but to follow suit. Already scraping the bottom of the barrel after a mere eight months of war, it might muddle on for a while, improvising here, economising there, delaying payment of its bills everywhere, but sooner rather than later, the Union war effort was faced with its gravest financial crisis. Two main solutions presented themselves. The first was to issue large quantities of non-interest-bearing notes, not redeemable in gold – in other words, to seek solace in the printing press. (This proposal raised the subsidiary issue of whether such notes should be declared legal tender for all purposes.) The alternative was to pour large quantities of government bonds on to the market, to be sold not at face value as the Treasury had hitherto insisted, but at whatever price they would bring. The second option had its champions, among the bankers and elsewhere, but it met stern opposition from those who objected both to putting the government's credit at risk in such a way at such a time, and to granting investors what amounted to a much higher rate of interest. This solution would also fail to provide the circulating medium – a generally accepted currency, usable for all normal purposes – which the North so desperately needed. Paper money, therefore, seemed to be the only answer, but it was a momentous and highly controversial step, which menaced fundamental American values, ethical as well as financial. The moral issue was plain enough to most Americans, bred in the tradition which would lead one of Chase's successors, Hugh McCulloch, to say in 1865 that:

By common consent of the nations, gold and silver are the only true measure of value. They are the necessary regulators of trade. I have myself no more doubt that these metals were prepared by the Almighty for this very purpose, than I have that iron and coal were prepared for the purposes for which they are being used.[15]

Could even the desperate necessities of war justify the abandonment of such sacred standards of value? Would such action be a sensible use of national resources or a shameful confession of national bankruptcy and moral delinquency? Senator Fessenden of Maine could agonise even more exquisitely than most when faced with such a dilemma:

It shocks all my notions of political, moral and national honor. I am beset with letters and telegrams, and told on every hand . . . that without it we shall be utterly bankrupt and cannot carry on the war. I do not believe it, and yet ought I to set up my own judgment as a standard of action? This thing has tormented me day and night for weeks; the thing is wrong in itself, but to leave the government without resources at such a crisis is not to be thought of.[16]

It was Congress which seized the initiative in creating legal tender paper money, and which dragged the reluctant Chase in its wake. (Years later, as chief justice of the Supreme Court, Chase helped to decide that the legal tender act was unconstitutional!) The bill was earnestly debated in both houses of Congress in the early part of 1862. Defenders of the bill argued mainly from necessity, although one or two of its more radical champions rejoiced in the extension of federal power which it implied. Opponents condemned it as unconstitutional and immoral and warned of its dreadful consequences. A radical Republican, Owen Lovejoy, declared that 'there is no precipice, there is no chasm, there is no possible yawning, bottomless gulf before this nation, so terrible, so appalling, so ruinous, as this same bill that is before us'.[17] The Republicans were deeply divided on the issue, and a significant minority voted against it. However, the Legal Tender Act passed both houses and became law on 25 February 1862. It authorised the Secretary of the Treasury to issue up to $150 million of the new legal tender notes, which soon became known as 'greenbacks' because of their colour. They were to be usable for all purposes except payment of import duties, and payment of interest on government bonds and notes.

The greenbacks rescued the Treasury from the dire straits of the winter of 1861–2, and provided the country with a new circulating medium. Chase was soon eagerly paying long-overdue accounts, and investors now had the wherewithal for increased purchases of government bonds. Perhaps most important of all in the long run, the greenbacks were an assertion of the power of the federal government to manage the currency and regulate the whole financial system. The relationship between the government and the money supply would never be the same again. The greenbacks raised problems, of course; they encouraged inflation, although they were far from being its sole cause; they lost value in relation to gold, and led to a rash of gold speculation later in the war;

by leaving open the question of their future redemption, they created one of the great financial and social issues of post-war America. Regarded by many of their sponsors as a temporary wartime expedient, they refused, like so many other such expedients, to die as soon as peace returned.

Once the golden dam had been breached in February 1862, it was inevitable that the flood of greenbacks would soon swell. Lagging revenue, languishing bond sales, and mushrooming expenses prompted Chase to ask for more in July 1862, and Congress authorised the issue of another $150 million. By the end of 1862, the Treasury was facing another crisis, with unpaid bills and soldiers' pay months in arrears. Chase still put his faith in loans, but more greenbacks were urgently needed, and Congress authorised a further $150 million in two stages early in 1863, along with massive new bond issues. The wonder was, indeed, that the torrent of greenbacks ended then and there. The total net issue of greenbacks during the war, allowing for withdrawals, was $431 million, only about one-sixth of the total indebtedness which is generally ascribed to the war. Here lay the crucial difference between the Union and Confederate experience with paper money. In the north the greenbacks tided the government and the country over a severe crisis and helped to pave the way for other financial measures. In the south paper money was an inviting path which soon turned into a slippery slope. The feeling that it had something to lose imposed some restraint upon Union financial policy. The sense that it had nothing to lose encouraged the wrong kind of boldness in the Confederacy. Basically, of course, the North had vastly greater resources upon which to draw, and financial failure would have been far more culpable for the Union than for the Confederate treasury. The greenbacks never became an addictive drug in the way that paper money did in the Confederacy; they were rather a series of massive injections which saved the patient, although they had side-effects which some found distressing. Greenbacks paid for one-sixth of the Union war effort; Confederate treasury notes bore two-thirds of the burden in the south.

5. The inflationary effects of the greenbacks might have been less distressing had their introduction been, as many of their congressional supporters wished, just one element in a tripartite financial programme. The other parts were to be adequate taxation, and the creation of new national banknotes, based on government bonds, which would complement (and eventually replace) the greenbacks. Taxation remained one of the failures of Union finance, although the failure was not so abject as in the Confederacy, and performance improved later in the war. Chase simply never attached sufficient importance to it. For its part, Congress showed surprisingly little resistance to new taxation in principle, but there was endless haggling over the distribution of the burden, and a recurring readiness to postpone or evade the more unpleasant consequences of novel tax proposals. There was never much difficulty about raising tariff levels or extending the tariff to new items. Every year of the war saw significant increases, until the 1864 measure raised the average level of duties to the record level of

47 per cent. Not merely had secession removed Southern critics of the protective tariff, but war had provided a brand new excuse for higher tariffs. It was only fair, the argument ran, to raise import duties to compensate home manufacturers for the internal excise duties levied on their products – and manufacturers' associations and other pressure groups made the most of this point. The protective tariff donned the mantle of patriotism and continued to wear it long after the war was over. The tariff of 1864 was little changed for almost twenty years, although the pretext for its high levels, the excise duties, generally disappeared quite quickly after the war.

During the war such internal taxation affected almost every kind of product – and indeed, every stage of manufacturing, so that one article might pay the 5 per cent duty three or four times over. The virtue of these duties was that they spread the burden widely while raising far more revenue than any other taxes. The government also taxed railroads, banks, insurance companies, advertising and many other businesses, and it imposed licence fees on most professions. The Revenue Act of 1862 which elaborated most of these proposals, also introduced an income tax of 3 per cent on incomes over $600, rising to 5 per cent on incomes over $10,000, and a modest inheritance tax on amounts over $1,000. These major innovations excited remarkably little controversy, except from those who saw an army of federal tax collectors as a dangerous invasion of state rather than individual rights. The income tax did not fall due until 30 June 1863, which reduced its usefulness in raising urgently needed revenue, but provided a breathing-space in which the necessary administrative machinery could be set up. The Act had provided for a Bureau of Internal Revenue, and its first Commissioner, George S. Boutwell, worked hard to prepare the necessary organisation, staff and forms, and set important precedents by his rulings on the implementation of the law. (One interesting feature was that salaries of government employees were taxed at source.) The yield of the income tax was disappointing in 1863, but a new act in June 1864 raised the basic rate to 5 per cent, rising to 10 per cent on incomes over $10,000, and adopted a more sophisticated approach to matters like exemptions, allowances and assessments. A leading radical like Thaddeus Stevens was lukewarm about the income tax because, as a protectionist, he feared that it might become an alternative to high tariffs. He also disliked progressive taxation on higher incomes because it punished the rich man simply for being rich – a curious comment on the 'radicalism' of the most unquestioned of radical Republicans.[18] As late as 1864 the income tax was yielding only $20 million, but there was promise of higher returns to come, and the rates on larger incomes were increased again in March 1865. In that year, income tax produced nearly one quarter of internal revenue, internal taxes as a whole were yielding much more than customs, and total taxation met about one-quarter of government expenditures, compared with one-ninth in 1861–2. For the whole war period, taxation met 21 per cent of expenditure, a modest achievement, but an important one, especially when the 'too little, too late' measures of 1861–2 are compared with later performance.

It was just enough to ward off some of the worst excesses of other wartime expedients and to bolster financial confidence. Wartime taxation also expanded the activities of the federal government, profoundly affected its relationship with the individual citizen, and set important precedents for the future. But that future was distant rather than immediate, for the income tax was repealed in 1872 – and declared unconstitutional when it was next attempted in the 1890s – and most of the excise duties vanished even more quickly.

The modest scale of taxation meant that, as Chase had always proposed, the extraordinary expenses of war were sustained mainly by massive loans. It was a hazardous undertaking for a government which had struggled to raise comparatively minute sums in 1861, and in a country which had no previous experience of such huge issues of government securities. In the past, governments had borrowed on a modest scale by arrangement with the banks. There was no organised and established securities market to handle such business, no army of small investors waiting to snap up every new issue. A society of small farmers and small businessmen would have to be coaxed into investing its savings in government bonds, and there was little in the situation of 1861 to stimulate their enthusiasm. Treasury efforts to promote bond sales met with a poor response, and the new bond issue of $500 million authorised along with the Legal Tender Act went very slowly during the summer of 1862. However, the greenbacks now provided a medium for the purchase of bonds, and the 6 per cent interest on the bonds, payable in gold, grew steadily in real value, as the greenbacks depreciated against gold. Then, in October 1862, Chase put bond sales in the hands of an agent, Jay Cooke, an old Ohio acquaintance whose banking house in Philadelphia undertook to sell securities to the people, in return for a commission. Cooke threw himself into the campaign with energy and zeal; he organised over 2,000 sub-agents all around the country, constantly exhorted them to greater efforts, and bombarded the public with a barrage of newspaper advertisements, posters and handbills which enrolled God, Mammon and love of country in support of bond sales. Cooke's campaign succeeded; by early 1864 the bonds were over-subscribed, though not entirely due to his efforts. But he had made enemies, and his employment as agent was dropped for a time. The summer of 1864 proved to be a lean time for bond sales, partly because of the gloomy state of the war, partly because Chase decided to reduce the interest rate on new issues to 5 per cent. The Treasury was reduced to dire straits once again, and Fessenden, Chase's successor, proposed tough new measures, including higher taxation. Early in 1865 Cooke was again employed as agent for a massive issue of three-year Treasury notes, and his new campaign, even better run than the first, achieved huge sales in the ensuing six months. It is important not to exaggerate Cooke's role in Civil War finance – especially as many government securities were still taken up by banks and other financial institutions – but his success in persuading masses of ordinary citizens to invest in government bonds constituted one of the major advances in mass involvement in the struggle for the Union. It established one more link between the government in Washington and the citizen of Maine or Ohio or Wisconsin who felt that he had enough at stake in the war, and enough faith in the credit of the United States, to invest his small savings in government securities. Those securities proved to be the main financial prop of war; unfortunately, they also left behind an awkward post-war legacy, for the 1862 loan, though specifying that interest was to be paid in coin, did not say in what form the principal was to be repaid – but Jay Cooke, in his promotional zeal, had promised that it too would be paid in gold. The stage was set for a post-war clash between the 'people' and the bond-holders, an ironical end to Cooke's campaign to sell bonds to the man in the street.

All in all, the government resorted to an incredible profusion of different forms of credit during the war, from very short-term notes to bonds running for up to forty years, and offering a variety of rates of interest. In spite of all the difficulties, the confusion, and the fluctuations of confidence, they raised over $2,000 million. By 1865 the national debt was at a level unimaginable a few years earlier; the interest upon it was greater than the debt itself had been when war began.

Chase's preoccupation with bond sales was one of the motives which prompted him to advocate a major reform of the banking system during the war. The new banks which he proposed would be required to use government bonds as security for their issue of notes, and, at one level, the Chase plan was an elaborate device to procure large forced purchases of bonds by the banks. This was one justification of the proposal as a vital war measure, and one answer to critics who complained that the middle of a great civil conflict was no time to undertake a major banking reform. Chase's plan, put forward first in 1861 and again in 1862, and finally enacted into law in 1863 and 1864, certainly envisaged more than bigger and better bond sales. He hoped that the new national banknotes which he proposed would provide a permanent replacement for the temporary (and, to Chase, repugnant) expedient of the greenbacks – and a replacement too for the plethora of state banknotes of all shapes, sizes, values and degrees of reliability, which plagued the country. They were not legal tender, but over $200 million of such notes were in circulation in 1861. The decentralised structure of the banking system, firmly embedded in American tradition, may have been what many people wanted, and may even have helped the rapid economic expansion of earlier years. But if its confusion had been creative, it was confusion none the less. There were some sixteen hundred banks operating under state law, many of them, especially in the west, resting on the shakiest of foundations, while a smaller number, mainly in New England and New York, were thoroughly reputable and stable institutions. It was impossible to keep up with the constant fluctuations in relative value of hundreds of different kinds of banknote. The variegated foliage of all their various note issues was a counterfeiter's paradise. There was much then to be said in favour of the creation of a new national banking system which would create order out of chaos, and issue a new national currency which would have the same value throughout the land.

But such a proposal aroused vigorous opposition, both from those who nursed deep-rooted suspicions of banking 'monopolies', and centralised government control, and from vested interests of all kinds – wildcat western banks for which the new system threatened the day of judgment, stable eastern banks for which note issue was a minor business and which saw few advantages to themselves in federal control, and even inflationists like Thaddeus Stevens who saw the new banknotes as a threat to the greenbacks which, he hoped, would themselves become a permanent national currency. When the bill was at last debated in Congress early in 1863, it squeaked through, by small majorities, only because enough Republicans grudgingly accepted Chase's pressing plea that this was an essential war measure. Its supporters argued, too, that it was a vital contribution to national unity, an antidote to the states rights mania which had produced financial confusion on its way to achieving political disruption of the Union itself.

The National Bank Act of 1863 provided for the organisation of banking corporations or 'associations' which were required to keep certain minimum reserves of specie or greenbacks and which could then issue national banknotes, obtainable from a new government official, the Comptroller of the Currency, when they had deposited with him a slightly larger sum in government bonds. The system of tying note issues to holdings of securities was an application at national level of the New York 'free banking' system, adopted in one form or another by many of the states. The total amount of the new banknotes was to be limited to $300 million, and a fairly crude attempt was made to apportion note issue among the states according to population and business requirements. The keynote of the system was soundness, stability and uniformity – and its immediate benefit was expected to be as a new market for bonds. But the new system met a very mixed reception, and it got under way so slowly that it made little contribution to wartime finance. Westerners who had suffered most from the malpractices of state banks showed the greatest readiness to join the new system. The New York banks, on the other hand, believing that Chase had always treated them shabbily, and little concerned over note issue, were confident that they could prosper outside the system; their attitude was uncooperative to the point of wilful obstruction. Important amendments to the act in 1864 made the plan more attractive, and with steady government pressure many more banks joined – both new institutions and existing state banks which converted to the new national system. At the end of 1863 there were well under 100 national banks; by March 1864 the figure was 469, by mid-1865 almost 1,300, and the state banks were showing a corresponding decline. At the very end of the war the imposition of a 10 per cent tax on state banknotes greatly hastened the process. The plan urged so strongly by Chase as a war measure finally asserted itself just as peace returned. Only the peculiar conditions of civil war made such a banking reform possible, but it remained the foundation of the nation's banking and currency system for fifty years, until the establishment of the Federal Reserve System, although the state banks staged a revival in the later nineteenth century.

The financial map of the United States was redrawn during the Civil War. In this field more almost than any other the war gave the union of the states all the trappings and much of the power of a consolidated national state. States rights were defeated in the banking houses as well as on the battlefields, and government and people entered into a new, more intimate (if not always more agreeable) relationship. The growth in the scale of government finance was significant enough in itself. The national debt rose to unprecedented levels, and, according to one calculation, whereas all federal government expenditures for the whole period 1789–1861 amounted to $1,700 million, expenditures for the four years 1861–5 totalled $3,300 million.[19] The staff of the Treasury Department more than doubled, and the Bureau of Internal Revenue was created. But the character of wartime innovation was even more important than its scale. Reliance on the tariff and land sales gave way to a multiplicity of internal taxes, including the first federal income tax, and the citizen, as earner and as consumer, felt the direct impact of federal financial authority for the first time. The sacred cow (or was it the golden calf?) of specie payments was not slain, but was quarantined for some years. The credit of the United States was staked on legal tender paper money printed and issued by the government itself. A banking system which was the embodiment of the invertebrate society gave way to one more appropriate to the new nation which emerged from the war. Vast quantities of government bonds provided a new broader basis for credit, and the whole financial system a more solid foundation for future growth. Not all the innovations survived for long. In contrast to the longevity of the national banking system was the controversial career of the greenbacks and the short life of the income tax. Nor were they all an unmixed blessing. There is no simple answer to the question who benefited most from the changes, and the men who lived through them were often taken by surprise. New York bankers who had stiffly resisted the new banking system lived to see it confirm and strengthen New York's position as the nation's financial capital. Men who had expressed horror at the coming of the greenbacks lived to fight for their survival after the war. But some consequences of wartime change were clear enough. The pre-1860 financial system was as dead as the dodo. Wartime innovations might be abandoned, but there was no going back to the original point of departure. The federal government might relinquish some of its newly-won authority, but it never lapsed back into the old atrophy. Far from being consigned to oblivion, the financial concerns of the Union at war – the greenbacks, the gold standard, the debt and the banks – were the very stuff of financial, social and political argument in the post-war years.

6. How did wartime finance affect the people who lived through the years of conflict? The creation of money and credit on such an unprecedented scale was closely connected, of course, with wartime prosperity and profits. The very fact that there was so much more money in circulation encouraged a sense of well-being and prosperity, but there was always the nagging doubt about how much

of the wartime prosperity was genuine, and how much of it a mirage created by inflation. For many farmers, traders, manufacturers, bankers, and businessmen, large and small, wartime prosperity was no illusion. On the other hand, inflation took its toll on its habitual victims, those on fixed incomes, and wage-earners whose incomes lagged behind rising prices.

Inflation in the north during the Civil War must be kept in perspective. By the standards of most modern wars, it was scarcely excessive, and in comparison with inflation in the Confederacy it was a flea-bite. By diverting production from consumer goods to military needs (and turning so many civilian producers into military consumers) the war was bound to increase prices, unless the purchasing power of consumers could be soaked up by some other means. Taxation was never heavy enough for this purpose, but the huge bond sales to ordinary citizens did have some mitigating effect. When there was a sudden, large increase in the money supply, inflationary pressure intensified, but the green-backs, a convenient scapegoat for protesters against inflation, were a contributory factor rather than a root cause. The general price level remained fairly steady in the first year of the war, rose about 10 per cent in 1862, increased faster in 1863, and leapt ahead in 1864, before levelling off in 1865. If the figure for 1860 is taken as 100, the figure for the inflationary peak of 1864 is 182. In July 1863 a writer in a labour paper complained about rising prices; beef which had cost 8-10 cents per lb in 1861 was now 15-18 cents; lamb had risen from 8-10 cents to 14-23 cents; coffee from 10-16 cents to 30-50 cents; sugar from 5-10 cents to 12-20 cents. Coal prices were up by a third, wood by a fifth, clothing by a similar amount.[20] If such figures are reasonably accurate, they obviously reflect real pressure on the purses of ordinary citizens – and there was worse to come. On the other hand, a Northerner's complaint would have been a Southerner's delight, as a comparison with the astronomical figures quoted by the Confederate war clerk, J.B. Jones, will readily show.

If, for many a working man, inflation meant an uphill struggle to maintain his standard of living, for the profiteers and speculators it offered rich pickings. The combination of rising prices and considerable uncertainty about the long-term future encouraged the search for quick profits. Shortages of basic commodities and the frantic search for substitute products did not offer the opportunities which were so much exploited in the south, except, of course, in the case of cotton. But that one great exception developed into a business of great proportions and endless ramifications in the second half of the war, as army officers, Treasury agents, traders and speculators went about the business of transferring cotton from the fields of the south to the mills of New England, and old England, too. Fluctuations in supply and demand – and in the currency – encouraged speculation in other commodities from time to time – wool, grain, oil, lumber, salt and many others. Speculation in whisky was positively invited by government announcements of forthcoming increases in the excise duty, and congressional connivance at the practice of feverish production before the deadline, so as to escape the higher duty but enjoy the higher price. The profiteers also enjoyed a field day in the early period of the war, out of government contracts, but the vigilance of Montgomery Meigs and other officers gradually limited such abuses. Nevertheless, the racketeer who sold broken-down horses or shoddy uniforms, or pasteboard shoes or faulty weapons to the army at extravagant prices, became one of the great villains of popular folklore during the war.

The wartime boom encouraged activity in the stock market, and the violent fluctuations in the market produced by news from the front encouraged speculators to play their dangerous game. If hard news did not promise the desired effect, it was always possible to stir excitement by starting a plausible rumour. Speculators even succeeded in 'planting' a spurious Lincoln proclamation in two New York papers in 1864, with the ironic result that publication of the papers, themselves innocent victims of the hoax, was suspended for a few days by presidential order. The flood of government securities pouring on to the market also encouraged speculation of various kinds. Most notorious of all was the speculation in gold itself, which was the direct consequence of the resort to paper money. The suspension of specie payments had made gold a commodity much like any other, and it was still in demand, since the cost of most imports (and all import duties) were paid in it. The coming of the greenbacks almost inevitably led to a premium on gold, which increased, at first gradually, and then more rapidly, until the average price of gold for the whole of 1864 was as high as 203 – that is $203 in greenbacks would buy only $100 in gold. But within the general upward trend in the gold premium, there were frequent and violent fluctuations; in the same year, 1864, the price of gold varied between $151 and $284. The premium would be increased by a new issue of notes, reduced by imports of gold, and affected above all by military victory and defeat. It offered a rich field for speculation, and government efforts to restrain it were totally ineffective. Gold speculators became particularly obnoxious to the public at large, because their attempts to raise the premium were regarded as treason. The gold premium became a thermometer which registered not merely the financial but the military, political and moral condition of the Union cause.

The Civil War, like most wars, provided fertile ground for rackets, cheating and profiteering of many kinds. There was money to be made (and lost) easily and quickly in the wartime boom, and often no excess of scruple about the methods employed. Fortunes were made out of the war, or at least during it, although it would be a mistake to assume that all were made dishonestly or dishonourably. But, in New York and other major cities, new wealth did bring in its train lavish spending, vulgar display, and extravagance of every kind. One recurring theme of protest during the war years was against the selfishness, ruthlessness, and callousness of the 'shoddy aristocracy'. The *New York Herald* gave full vent to such feelings:

The world has seen its iron age, its silver age, its golden age and its brazen age. This is the age of shoddy. . . . Their professions and occupations are pure shoddy. They are shoddy brokers in Wall street, or shoddy manufacturers of shoddy goods, or shoddy contractors for shoddy articles for a shoddy government. Six days a week they are shoddy businessmen. On the seventh day they are shoddy Christians.[21]

7. Protest against the shameless extravagance of the new rich came with particular vehemence from the ranks of American labour. The war, it is true, brought opportunity to Northern workers, but between the wage-earner and his full reward stood the dangers of cheap labour competition, labour-saving machinery, military conscription and, above all, inflation. After the slump of the early months, the war created a new demand for labour – and in a situation where, unlike the Second World War for example, there was no great pool of unemployed workers waiting to be absorbed into the industrial war effort. Yet, in spite of this, the North contrived to man the factories, mills, workshops and farms, while putting hundreds of thousands of young men into uniform. The explanation lies partly in some simple but neglected facts about the American population in the years before 1860. Largely because of immigration (which mainly affected the north), males constituted 58 per cent of the population. Moreover, about two-thirds of the immigrants were between the ages of fifteen and forty on arrival, and thus added to the labour force out of all proportion to their total numbers. Immigrants provided a solid core of labourers and unskilled workers, especially in the large cities where by 1870 they added up to a majority of the labour force. Before the war, too, the growing industrial areas had also attracted workers, male and female, from the villages and farms, particularly in New England, and their intelligence, literacy, resourcefulness and adaptability fitted them well for more skilled work. All in all, the pool from which both workers and soldiers were drawn was significantly larger than population totals would have suggested.

There was little homogeneity or solidarity in the labour force. The contemporary use of the plural form, 'working classes' or 'industrial classes', was an accurate reflection of reality. They were deeply divided by nationality, language and religion – and often by fierce political partisanship. The native American worker had long feared the competition of cheap immigrant labour, although, during the war, native worker and Irish immigrant shared a common anxiety over the threatened influx of Negro ex-slaves after emancipation. There was also great diversity in wages and conditions, fierce rivalry between workers in different trades and occupations, and a high degree of mobility – geographical rather than social – in the labour force as men frequently moved from job to job and town to town. Most of them also shared the competitive outlook and the belief in the merits of the 'free-labour' system, so ardently espoused by businessmen, manufacturers and Republican ideologues. The fragmentation of the labour force was also to a large extent imposed by the pattern of employment. Industry was still composed of small, though growing, units, but growth often meant a work force of eight or ten instead of four or five. For all the magnetic pull of the larger cities, many mills and workshops were still situated in the small towns and villages. Although the old independent craftsman or mechanic was giving way to the factory worker, industrial labour was still too scattered and too varied to feel much sense of unity, or exert much united pressure.

On the other hand, at a time of rapid change, many workers felt already that they had something to lose. European visitors to the United States frequently commented on the independence, intelligence and prosperity of the American worker. Most immigrants in the northern states unhesitatingly supported the struggle for the Union largely because they felt that its social, economic and political system had been beneficial to them and would be even more so to their children. But war itself brought more change and new uncertainties to Northern workers, native and immigrant alike.

The demand for labour was met in predictable ways. There was increasing resort to new methods and new machines, and their introduction sometimes met with stern resistance from workers. The increasing use of grain elevators in New York harbour, for example, led to a long and bitter strike by Irish labourers, who burned two large elevators in Brooklyn. But, in filling new jobs and replacing workers lost to the army, chief reliance was placed on alternative sources of labour, usually unskilled and preferably cheap – women, children, immigrants and Negroes. By 1860 women already made up almost one-quarter of the non-agricultural labour force, but that figure was swollen by the army of domestic servants, and the remainder were heavily concentrated in a few industries, especially textiles. During the war more women were employed in more jobs, in an effort to keep down labour costs. Their wages were low, often scandalously so. The plight of the seamstresses, hired by contractors to make army clothing, was a notorious example. Inflation hit them so hard that they were even worse off, according to one authority, than clerks in offices, and teachers in colleges and universities! Wartime shortage of male teachers encouraged and hastened the trend towards female domination of the schoolteaching profession. Other women followed Dorothea Lynde Dix and Clara Barton into the harrowing work of army nursing. The women of the north have never acquired the romantic aura of their Confederate counterparts, but, if they suffered rather less, they took on many of the same tasks. The apprentice system was abused to provide another source of cheap labour. Free Negroes were also employed, sometimes as strike-breakers, and it was their introduction in this role in the docks of various cities which triggered off a number of riots, and was one cause of the New York draft riots of July 1863. In general, however, the small number of Negro workers made them more of a menace in the minds of white workers than a significant answer to the demand for more labour.

The immigrant made a much weightier contribution. In many ways the Civil War was an exceptional and interesting period in the history of American immigration, and its significance is largely missed by those who simply point out that, over the period 1860–5 as a whole, immigration levelled off at the fairly low level of the previous five-year period, only half that of the peak period of the earlier 1850s. But the early fifties were a truly exceptional period, only equalled for a few years around 1870, until the great tide of immigration in the late nineteenth century. A year-by-year examination of the Civil War period is more revealing. In 1861 and 1862 the number of immigrants slumped to around 90,000, little over half the 1855–60 average – and that is surely unsurprising. But in 1863 it shot up to 176,000, in 1864 to 193,000, in 1865 to 248,000. In the midst of the turmoil and hazards of civil strife, the wonder is surely that the north attracted so many new arrivals rather than so few. Even in the midst of a great conflict, the north remained a magnet for scores of thousands of Europeans.

During the war that appeal was orchestrated in a number of new ways, including the first brief experiment by the federal government in the management of immigration, and some tentative steps by industry itself towards a more organised recruitment of immigrant workers. Government efforts were clouded then and later by suspicion that the main motive was recruitment for the army rather than for industry. Allegations of actual enlistment abroad are unsubstantiated, but obviously the flow of immigrants was always one possible source of replenishment for the army. One of the first sights which confronted the immigrant as he left Castle Garden in New York was an army recruiting station – and bounties and other inducements were not unattractive. (But the notion that the Union fought the war largely with an army of hired foreign mercenaries or forced foreign conscripts is a creation of Confederate propaganda.) Seward, the State Department and the consular service in Europe did make great efforts to encourage immigration, by advertising high wages and job opportunities, publicising the opportunities for free land under the Homestead Act of 1862 (although only a small minority of immigrants ever acquired a homestead) and pressing the shipping companies to reduce fares. An Immigration Bureau, under a Commissioner of Immigration, was established, but its allocation of funds was pitifully small, and its brief life ended in 1868. However, it marked the only attempt by the federal government in the whole of the nineteenth century to place immigrants in suitable jobs. Private enterprise was also lending a hand, and the Boston Foreign Emigrant Aid Society, formed in 1863, and the American Emigrant Company, formed in 1864, were attempts to procure labour from Europe and supply it to manufacturers at home. Many employers had long relied on their own efforts to obtain skilled workers – and sometimes strike-breakers – from Europe, and continued to do so during the war. The arrangement often employed was a contract under which an employer (or one of the new companies) advanced the fare to the immigrant, who undertook to work for the employer for a specified period during which he repaid his fare. The system was a direct descendant of the indentured servitude of colonial days. By 1864 importation of key workers was held up mainly by lack of funds, and the emigrant companies, manufacturers, shipping companies, United States consuls abroad, and aspiring emigrants, were hoping for financial aid from the federal government. But the

contract labour law passed by Congress in July 1864 merely gave a legal blessing
to contracts of the kind already used, and made no provision for government-
assisted passages. The law had little effect, the contract labour system was too
expensive and too vulnerable to dishonest exploitation, the new emigrant
companies faded from the scene, and the federal government soon returned to
its passive role. The law of 1864 was repealed in 1868. Manufacturers relied on
finding the labour they needed from the normal, unorganised influx of
immigrants, and filled specialised jobs by direct negotiation with European
contacts. For all that, the Civil War years stand out as a period of experiment
in both private and public organisation of immigration, and as proof that the
immigrant was now so much a part of the American scene that not even a terrible
domestic upheaval could for long interrupt the flow of new arrivals on American
shores.

The reliance on unskilled men, women and boys to replace skilled workers,
make it hardly surprising that there was no noticeable rise in productivity per
worker during the war. In meeting war demand, it was more important to get
the job done somehow than to worry over the normal criteria of industrial
efficiency. In view of the pressure on labour supply, it is more surprising perhaps
that wages did not keep pace better with rising prices – but, here again, the
wider use of cheaper, unskilled labour provides part of the explanation. The
industrial worker was one of the chief victims of inflation, certainly until the
last eighteen months of the war. During the whole war, average wages rose by
about 50 per cent but most of the rise came in 1864–5, and it was far from evenly
spread. Wages in mid-war lagged far behind the rising cost of living, and the
war period as a whole saw a decline of between 16 per cent and 20 per cent in
real earnings. Some mitigating circumstances did exist; there was an abundance
of jobs, and much greater regularity of employment than before the war;
soldiers' allotments, backed by state and private charity, helped their families to
cope with rising prices; employment of women and children meant that many
families had more than one bread-winner. Such factors may have relieved some
of the financial anxiety of workers but did not remove their sense of grievance.

The marked improvement in wages in the latter part of the war was partly
the result of boom conditions, and partly the reward of labour militancy (which
was itself encouraged by the boom). There was a rash of strikes from 1863
onwards, mainly for higher wages, but also against long hours, introduction of
machines, Negro and immigrant competition, and abuse of the apprenticeship
system. Constant demands for higher wages won concessions from employers
anxious not to lose production during the hectic boom. In April 1864 moulders
at the McCormick reaper factory went on their fourth strike since the previous
autumn and now demanded a 25 per cent increase. There was no collective
bargaining in the modern sense; union members would set a price for their
labour and, after a deadline, would strike against employers who did not meet
it. The union emerged victorious if most of its members obtained the new rate;
if most employers stood firm, and the dispute was long-drawn-out, the union

was frequently broken. But neither employers nor employees were notable for their solidarity in such disputes.

Strikes were usually local and short-lived partly because unions themselves were usually small and local, and often ephemeral. The sympathetic strike was virtually unknown. Most unions had only a very small membership, and their total numbers represented only a tiny minority of the labour force. However, their leadership was tough and ambitious, and they made some progress during the war in organisation at both local and national level. The depression years of the late 1850s had upset earlier fragile attempts at labour organisation. Only three national unions existed when war began, but several more were established during the war, including the Brotherhood of the Footboard and the American Miners' Association. At the end of the war the largest union was probably the Iron Molders, led by William H. Sylvis, the outstanding labour organiser of the day, which probably had 7,000–8,000 members. There were also abortive attempts to create one overall national labour organisation, but a convention, summoned at Louisville in 1864 to establish the International Industrial Assembly of North America, attracted only twelve delegates. More significant in the short run at least were the mixed trades' assemblies which spread to most of the larger cities during the war. They were composed of delegates from local unions, working men's clubs and reform societies, and they concentrated more on propaganda and agitation than industrial action. It was these assemblies which played the leading part in the National Labor Union formed after the war in 1866. All in all, if the unions, like the work force as a whole, were still fragmented and uncoordinated, they were also, like Northern society as a whole, moving in response to wartime pressures in the direction of organisation, nationwide coordination and new and more sophisticated ways of conducting their affairs.

Employers resisted labour demands stubbornly in 1861–2, relented somewhat in 1863–4, and returned to a hard line in 1865 in anticipation of falling prices and declining markets after the war. Disputes were often bitter and sometimes violent, and employers resorted to lock-outs and black-lists, recruited strike-breakers and invoked the aid of state or federal government. In the border states in particular, military commanders forbade strikes and arrested strikers. A strike at the Parrott armaments factory in New York state was smashed by troops, and a strike on the Reading Railroad in Pennsylvania led to its seizure by the military authorities. Some state legislatures debated and a few actually passed anti-strike laws, most notably the sweeping 'LaSalle Black Laws' in Illinois. Indeed the willingness of government to play a repressive role in labour disputes was in strong contrast to its failure to embark on any overall manpower policy. It never contemplated such a task, and, in consequence, like so much else, the mobilisation of labour in support of the war effort was more notable for energy and enterprise than planning and purpose.

For American labour, the Civil War was a profound experience. It accelerated the movement of labour into industry and particularly into heavy industry. It altered the character and make-up of the labour force. It buffeted the industrial wage-earner with inflation, taxation, and conscription, and aroused his fears of the consequences of emancipation and continued immigration. It left him with a sense of grievance, but also with some inkling of his power, and thus helped to shape his role in post-war industrial and political life. It heightened his sense of involvement in national life, and it made him aware of the federal government as a force which affected his life for good or ill. The power that taxed him, drafted him, devalued his wage packet, and menaced his fragile organisations, could also be put to more beneficent purposes. In 1861 labour meetings had called for concession and compromise rather than war and showed little sympathy for the anti-slavery cause. In the next four years, thousands of working men fought and died for the Union, and many more worked for it loyally. In 1865, with the Union saved, they had acquired a new view of its nature, character and potential and some of the labour activists at least looked to the radical Republicans to safeguard the future.[22]

8. The whole community felt the impact of federal power during the war. Indeed there was a growth in governmental activity at all levels, state and local as well as national, starting with the first frantic rush to arms in 1861. However, the heavy wartime responsibilities of the federal government, and the contrast with its torpor in the pre-war decades, made its authority the most far-reaching and conspicuous. But that authority was exercised unevenly, and it still left some surprising gaps. The boldest assertions of power were obviously in matters directly connected with the conduct of the war, and the treatment of the South – the recruitment and organisation of the armed forces, confiscation of enemy property, emancipation of the slaves, and infringement of basic rights in the name of security. By their very nature, they were exceptional exercises of authority in a unique situation; their consequences would endure, but the new powers themselves were not bound to survive. On the other hand, the most remarkable omissions in the assertion of federal power were in the field of the regulation and management of the wartime economy. The economic mobilisation of the North bore little relation to the experience of twentieth-century wars. There was no elaborate apparatus of regulations and restraints, no rationing, no central direction of economic priorities, no attempt to control prices, wages or profits. There was no overall organisation or coordination of industrial production, no conception of a manpower policy, no central control of the transportation system. Government became a huge customer of manufacturing industry, but the manufacturers made their own decisions and controlled their own production. Conscription in the north was an even more random and unselective method of allocating manpower resources than in the south. The government was given sweeping powers to take over the railroads but was extremely abstemious in their use. In the Confederacy the government was obliged, out of sheer desperation and shortage of resources, to plunge into complicated schemes to allocate raw materials, control prices and profits, manipulate manpower through exemption and detail, and regulate the traffic of the railroads.

But the Confederacy was unable to make its elaborate machinery work, and the fumbling attempts to do so were increasingly at odds with the objectives for which the South fought. By comparison, the North was doubly blessed. Drawing upon vastly greater reserves of men, machinery, materials, energy and skill, it was able to put them to use without an intricate apparatus of restrictions and controls. The economic war effort made up in vigour and enterprise what it lacked in order and precision. The stimulus which the war gave to organisation was much more conspicuous at other levels of economic and social activity than in overall direction from the top. If the war put some economic backbone into the invertebrate society, the operation was not performed by the federal government. Again the North did not experience the conflict of means and ends which bedevilled the Confederacy. The free enterprise, free labour society of the North applied itself to the tasks of war, wastefully and clumsily perhaps, but successfully none the less, and it emerged with a renewed faith in its virtue and its strength.

Perhaps the most pervasive influence of the government as regulator was through its financial policy – although, even here, it made only timid use of the power to tax which might have been the strictest control of all. Indeed, most aspects of wartime finance – the greenbacks, the bond issues, the national banking system – have closer connections with the two more positive roles in which the government was cast, as promoter of economic activity and expansion, and as major customer of industry and agriculture. American government in the nineteenth century was much more accustomed to providing aid, subsidy and support than regulation and restriction, and, far from retreating from this role during the war, Congress and the Lincoln administration took advantage of the removal of Southern opposition to step it up to new heights. Changes in the currency and reform of the banking system were one example of this trend, even if they were often inspired less by the desire to stimulate growth than by the government's desperate financial need. The protection given to American industry by successive increases in tariff duties was another example, if a somewhat ironical one, as the protectionist cause was losing support before 1860. In the special circumstances of the Civil War, tariff walls rose to new heights – and there they remained for decades, while Abraham Lincoln was canonised by grateful industrial magnates as patron saint of the protective tariff. The government also took steps to encourage the flow of immigrant labour into American industry, although here its efforts were neither received with conspicuous gratitude nor crowned with spectacular success.

The high-water mark in wartime legislative effort was achieved by the session of Congress which occupied the first half of 1862. On top of all its measures concerning tariffs and internal taxes, greenbacks and bond issues, slavery and confiscation, it found time for three major measures concerning the disposition of the public lands. They covered items which had been on the agenda of national politics for years and which had been obstructed or defeated by Southern resistance. The Homestead Act, passed in May 1862, was the culmination of decades of agitation for the grant of free land to the bona fide settler on the public lands. Under the law, the old minimum price of $1.25 per acre was abolished, and settlers could claim 160 acres of land, and confirm their claim by five years' residence and cultivation. To veterans of the homestead agitation, the act looked like the apotheosis of free-labour America, a land of small, independent property-owners, tilling their own soil, and embodying Jeffersonian virtue. Although by the middle of 1865 almost twenty thousand farms had been settled under the law, it was never to fulfil the hopes and dreams which inspired it. Too much land, and most of the best land, passed into other hands – the railroads, the speculators, the state governments – and the small homestead proved ill-adapted to the conditions of the great plains. Above all, even with free land, the cost of moving west, setting up a home and a farm on virgin land, and surviving until it was able to support a family, was still far beyond most urban workers in the east. But in 1862 such anti-climax lay in the undisclosed future.

Two other measures cut deeply into the land available to the homesteader. The College Land Grant Act of 1862, sponsored by Justin S. Morrill, was the fulfilment of another long-cherished hope. It granted to each state of the Union 30,000 acres of public land for each senator and representative which it sent to Congress. The proceeds were to be used to finance colleges which should give special attention to 'agriculture and the mechanic arts'. There had always been provision for education in the disposal of land to new states, but this huge distribution of land applied to all states, old and new. Some states frittered away the largesse thus bestowed upon them, but most did not. Cornell, Rutgers, Brown and M.I.T. in the east and most of the great state universities of the west were among the main beneficiaries, and remain the great monument to the Morrill Act. The Pacific Railroad Act of 1862 provided massive government aid for a project which had been stoutly championed for years by those who wished to open up the unsettled areas of the far west, link California more closely to the rest of the Union and realise their dreams of dominating the rich commerce of the Pacific. The Civil War gave new meaning to the strategic argument for the railroad; it also silenced the claim for a more southerly route which had bedevilled earlier discussion. The route now chosen was the central one which would link easily with all the major cities of the mid-west. The Union Pacific company was to build westward across the plains and the Rockies, the Central Pacific eastward from Sacramento and San Francisco. Government aid followed the pattern of the railroad land grants of the 1850s, but on an unprecedented scale. The railroad companies received land grants on either side of the route, which totalled some 35 million acres. In addition, because of the enormous scale and special problems of construction, the government agreed to lend the companies government bonds at the rate of $16,000 per mile of track, with more on difficult sections. Hardly any track was laid during the war, but the line was completed four years later in 1869. The spectacular achievement of its construction was matched by the spectacular scandals which characterised its finances. Indeed the 1862 act, and an even more generous land grant to the Northern Pacific in 1864, were the start of an enormous railroad bonanza in the years that followed the war. The financial implications and the economic and social benefits of the transcontinental railroads have been a subject of hot debate, but whatever the consequences, good or bad, it was the Civil War which broke the log jam in their promotion and development.

The influence of the wartime economic and social legislation in setting the pattern for post-war America, or in transferring power into the hands of new economic groups, can easily be exaggerated, but its general importance cannot be ignored. It showed at least that the Union at war had time and energy to spare for more than war. Some measures, already long delayed, might have been delayed for many years more but for the peculiar circumstances of 1861–5; some might never have been passed at all. They were regarded as matters of great moment at the time of their enactment, and, if their consequences were not always foreseen and not infrequently disappointing, that has been a fate shared by much other legislation. They stand as a monument to the confidence and optimism of Northern society at war and they helped to mould the shape of post-Civil War society.[23]

The most obvious and direct influence of the government upon the wartime economy came from its massive orders for weapons, equipment, transport, clothing, food and other supplies. Government contracts were the fuel which stoked much (though by no means all) of the wartime boom. The scale and variety of government business – as, for example, in the work of Montgomery Meigs and the Quartermaster Department – has been discussed elsewhere. But it was of course the task of organising, sustaining and supplying the armies, and maintaining the war effort, which above all stimulated the growth of the federal government itself. The civilian employees of the government rose from 41,000 in 1861 to 195,000 in 1865, and that latter figure was not reached by the federal government in peacetime until the turn of the century.[24] But the growth was very lopsided, most of it in the War Department, and above all within the Quartermaster's organisation. The Navy and Treasury Departments also more than doubled their staffs. A number of new departments and agencies arrived upon the scene, but fewer perhaps than might have been expected. A separate Department of Agriculture was established in 1862, but it remained very small during the war, drew much sceptical comment from the agricultural press, and did not attain cabinet status until 1889. Other new agencies included the offices of the Commissioner of Internal Revenue and the Commissioner of Immigration, the Provost-Marshal-General's Bureau, and the Freedmen's Bureau – and the Government Printing Office, established in 1860, found plenty of new work. But, outside the War Department, the size of administrative units was still generally quite small, and arrangements to meet new responsibilities were usually makeshift and ill-coordinated. Administration became more elaborate, but not more tidy. Meigs's department was exceptional both for the scale of its operations and the skill of its management. But the wartime federal government was blessed with a considerable number of dynamic and effective administrators, both at cabinet level and among the assistant secretaries and bureau chiefs: Tom Scott, Charles A. Dana, Peter H. Watson, James B. Fry and Joseph Holt, among others in the War Department, Gustavus V. Fox in the Navy Department, George Harrington and Hugh McCulloch at the Treasury, to name only a few. Lack of an orderly administrative structure placed an even greater burden on key individuals, and a number, from Secretary of War Stanton downwards, paid for the strain and overwork of the war years with broken health or premature death. In the number and quality of its capable administrators, the Union enjoyed a clear and precious advantage over the Confederacy.

During the war, government grew not only in size and complexity but in impact. It came into the life of every citizen as it had never done before. If its manifestations were often unwelcome and unpleasant – the draft, the taxes, the inflated prices – they were not exclusively so, as was the case with the Confederacy. The government that could free slaves, and offer free land, subsidise higher education, protect high-wage industry, and persuade the man in the street to invest in its securities was a government that mattered. The war did not bring about a complete revolution in government. Not all its new functions survived for long, but it was (or had shown that it could be) a government of the people, and of the nation, in a way that it had never been before.

9. Unlike the South, the North fought the war at a safe distance from home. It was protected by the peculiar character of a civil war in which the protagonists were geographically separated from the start, and by the character of a foe which lacked the means, the ambition or the necessity to attempt all-out invasion and occupation of its soil. With but few exceptions, communities throughout the north were able to go about their daily business undisturbed by threats of invasion or destruction, or even by the minor shortages, inconveniences and disruptions of war. There were times when only the absence of so many young men, and above all, the endless casualty lists, served as reminders of the horrors being perpetrated in Virginia, Tennessee and Mississippi. Posters and local papers advertised the efforts of various societies to help and comfort the boys at the front, but they advertised in much greater profusion new gimmicks and gadgets, new fashions and furnishings, new patent medicines, new processed foods and drinks, new entertainments and diversions. Small-town and country life, from New England to the mid-west, followed its familiar pattern, and local news was only occasionally overshadowed by momentous events far away. In the large cities the war stepped up the already hectic pace of life, but did not upset or overturn the pattern of urban living already fast developing. In many ways the war years confirmed the primacy of New York among the cities of the Atlantic seaboard, and helped to establish the primacy of Chicago among the cities of the middle west. The crowded, filthy, turbulent, malodorous

slums of New York and other cities certainly showed no improvement during the war, while respectable society wrung its hands over the stimulus which the conflict gave to violence, crime and vice of all kinds. The violence of draft riots or labour disputes or Copperhead escapades was a heightened and more conspicuous form of something which was never far below the surface of pre-war society. Some statistics suggest a fall in crime during the war but they may tell less than the whole truth at a time when law enforcement was fitful and the guilty often escaped punishment by joining the army. In all the major cities, prostitution shared in the wartime boom, and temperance reformers fought a losing battle against excessive consumption of alcohol.

The high society of the great cities was joined or gatecrashed by the *parvenus* of the 'shoddy aristocracy', and their gaudy ostentation provoked not very successful protest campaigns in favour of wartime austerity and self-discipline. Cities like New York, Washington and Chicago maintained a hectic social round of parties, dinners, dances, balls, receptions and other functions. A New York paper reported that 'there is a moral heroism in the way some people attend picnics', and a Washington correspondent wrote that 'I have been deeply afflicted over the sufferings of our boys, but have come to the conlusion that a soldier in the Army of the Potomac does not endure a severer strain on his constitution than a women in "society" in Washington'.[25] Fashionable resorts like Saratoga Springs soon won back their visitors after the jitters of the secession crisis, and Newport, Rhode Island, grew in favour as the summer home of the wealthy leaders of New York society. All the favoured forms of popular entertainment continued unabated during the war – theatre of all kinds from grand opera and classics to 'the leg drama' as it was called, concerts, circuses, menageries, horse-races, prize fights, and other sports. Those who thought that some justification was needed for patronage of music, art and drama during such critical times argued that the whole purpose of the struggle was to defend civilisation and culture against the onslaught of barbarism. Others hoped that the war experience would fulfil that long-standing American ambition, the creation of a truly national American art, but the results were disappointing. The war sketches and paintings of Winslow Homer, like the superb photographs of Matthew Brady and Alexander Gardner, were a valuable and enduring record of the conflict. But the inspiration which stirred Julia Ward Howe to write the words of the 'Battle Hymn of the Republic', after a day's visit to the camps of the Army of the Potomac, did not stimulate in others the production of works on a grander scale or a higher plane. Literature of all kinds and all qualities received a more direct boost from the war, although the outstanding best-sellers of the period were still imports from Europe. *Les Miserables* was the most popular book published in the north during the war, followed by the novels of Charles Dickens; the best-selling American work was Edward Everett Hale's *The Man without a Country*. The publishing trade flourished, especially during the second half of the war, and libraries, public as well as private, grew in size and numbers. Civil War poetry is dominated by the giant figure of Walt

Whitman, whose keen awareness of the great issues at stake was matched by his first-hand experience of individual suffering, derived from visits to army camps and hospitals. Among the most sensitive and enduring of other war poems are some of Herman Melville's *Battle Pieces*. At a much lower level of literary endeavour, the war produced a flood of cheap romances and ephemeral verse. Of the latter, one critic was moved to observe that:

> We all know the statement attributed to Beranger, and a hundred other poets, to the effect that if he could make the songs of a nation, he was unconcerned as to who went to the legislature. This is well, perhaps, but if we had power to make the laws, almost our first enactment would be against the writing of such verses as these.[26]

The periodical and newspaper press flourished in the hothouse climate of war. There was of course no national press, although Greeley's New York *Tribune*, with a circulation of 220,000 in 1862 (mainly for its weekly edition), had a readership covering a wide area of the north. The Associated Press helped to supply a steady flow of news, both military and political, and a whole new breed of war correspondents appeared, competing fiercely with one another, running great personal risks, and resisting attempts by the military to censor their despatches. If they drove the keepers of military secrets to distraction, they testified to the astonishing openness of American society at war. Most of the press was fiercely partisan, uninhibited in expressing its views, and full of rumour and speculation as much as hard news. If it was a vehicle of propaganda, it spoke with many voices, moderate and extreme, Copperhead and radical, jingoist and subversive. The pamphlets distributed by the various publication societies were more obvious vehicles for propaganda, and they, along with periodicals like the *North American Review* and the *Atlantic Monthly*, were served by the pens of some of the leading literary figures of the day.

Education at all levels suffered from the loss of teachers (and many college students) to the army, and the departure of many of the older school pupils to work in the fields or factories. But the pressing demands of war did not gravely impair educational development. Most schools were crowded, and a slight fall in college enrolments did not prevent the establishment of new foundations, including M.I.T., Vassar, Cornell and Swarthmore. One possibly surprising gap in the wartime effort was the lack of any attempt to provide any kind of education service for the men in uniform. The Northern churches, like their Southern opposite numbers, staunchly supported the cause of their section, and despatched chaplains of various denominations (and varying quality) to serve with the army. They also made some attempt to turn the occupied south into a mission field and provoked considerable friction with the local churches there. In the first half of the war, church membership and attendance declined a little, but there was some recovery in 1864–5, with revivals sweeping a number of states. In general, the North escaped the suffering and the desperation which drove many Southerners to seek the comforts of religion, and the Northern churches were rather less ardently engaged in converting the struggle into a holy war, partly because their adherents differed so much among themselves over questions like emancipation.

They were, however, heavily involved in the large-scale charity and relief work which was so marked a feature of Northern society at war. Established agencies like the American Tract Society and the American Bible Society turned their attention to the spiritual needs of the soldiers, and a new agency, the United States Christian Commission, established in 1861 as an offshoot of the Y.M.C.A., sent hundreds of 'delegates' into the field to supplement the work of army chaplains, distributed vast quantities of religious literature, provided much-needed supplies to military camps and hospitals, and developed all manner of welfare and relief activities to bring help, comfort and reassurance to wounded, needy and lonely soldiers. The church organisations, along with other private bodies and county, city and state authorities, became part of a complex network of relief for the families and orphans of soldiers. The diverse, haphazard, over-lapping, diffuse character of this particular relief effort is a good illustration both of the energy and of the limitations of the organisational revolution which the war prompted, and of the far from dominating role played by governments in such an enterprise. Charitable organisations to help the freed slaves or white refugees from the south followed the same pattern. There was, however, a move towards national organisation or coordination of such efforts, as, for example, the Christian Commission showed, but again the main impetus came from outside the government. At the apex of such national enterprise stood the United States Sanitary Commission which outshone all other agencies at least in its feats of organisation. Its labours to improve army medical services both by its own efforts and its pressure on the War Department have been described elsewhere.[27] Its organisation had no parallel or precedent in American experience. On the one hand, it ran hospitals, hospital ships, convalescent homes, soldiers' homes in northern cities, and agencies to help soldiers with claims for back-pay, allowances or pensions. On the other, it had an equally elaborate organisation to collect mountains of supplies, mobilise the efforts of hundreds of small, local groups in the north, and mount a huge fund-raising campaign featuring the great 'Sanitary Fairs' in the larger cities. The Sanitary Commission has come under fire recently for the paternalism and élitism of the men who inspired it, for its emphasis on discipline, and order, and for an attitude which at times seemed interested less in the relief of suffering than the education of men to withstand it.[28] There were certainly times when a highly organised body like the Sanitary Commission seemed to give precedence to its own institutional procedures and priorities over the crying needs of suffering soldiers, but the general criticism seems to focus too heavily upon the conservative social philosophy of one or two of the founding fathers of the Commission and to do less than justice to its work in the field. Without the Sanitary Commission, the Northern relief effort might well have been just as energetic and even more well-meaning, but it would surely have been even more disjointed and much less effective.

10. The Sanitary Commission may serve in many ways as a symbol of the wartime North. It represents the trends towards organisation and complexity, national consolidation and massive voluntary effort which the war initiated or accelerated. The American tradition which combined uncompromising individualism with a zeal for voluntary association had long impressed European visitors, none more than De Tocqueville in the 1830s. That tradition survived the test of civil strife, and emerged strengthened but transmuted. Individual enterprise had learned some lessons in cooperation and interdependence, and was working within the framework – and the discipline – of larger units. Manufacturers, merchants, trade associations, unions, reform societies, relief and philanthropic organisations, educational, scientific and professional bodies which had hitherto functioned in the context of the small town, the local community, or at most the big city or the state, were now thinking, working, meeting and organising nationally. If small companies still predominated, they were nevertheless being drawn into a national network, and larger corporations, with wider horizons and greater potential, were looming larger on the industrial scene. Many of the later captains of American industry – Carnegie, Rockefeller, Armour, Weyerhauser, Havemeyer, Marshall Field, Huntington – served as subalterns in the industrial war effort, and never forgot the lessons of those formative years. The war period saw an impressive growth of business and trade associations of all kinds: the National Association of Wool Manufacturers, the New England Cotton Manufacturers Association (which later merged into a national body), the American Iron and Steel Association, the various agricultural producers' associations, the proliferation of boards of trade, chambers of commerce, and other formal and informal meetings of businessmen around the land. The development of nationally organised labour unions was less successful but, in view of the difficulties, equally impressive. Without abandoning their local roots, philanthropy and charity climbed on to the national stage. In 1863 Congress gave its blessing to the creation of a National Academy of Sciences. Consciousness of the nation as a working reality which had been dawning in the 1840s and 1850s now emerged into the clear light of day. Like the Revolutionary war eighty years before, the Civil War created a new national feeling, but it was now more than a sentiment or an ideal. It was also a plain fact of everyday life.

The role of government in this wartime development was important but limited. A new national currency, a swollen national debt, new national taxes, new national measures to protect and promote economic growth, these were all a part of the process of consolidation and integration. Most influential of all, perhaps, among the government's functions was its performance in putting a million and a half citizens from every state into one great federal army. That army began at the grass roots, and owed much initially to state and local effort, but it became the greatest of national organisations, and the focal point and symbol of wartime nationalism. But, for all that, government activity was not so much the generator of nationalising trends as a reflection of them and a response to them. The organised war effort was basically the work of a characteristic American blend of individual initiative, free enterprise and voluntary association, aided and abetted but not ruled and regulated by federal power. It was this approach which converted great potential into actual performance. It was this which enabled so much 'normal' life to continue and to flourish amid the strain and suffering of war, and which allowed westward expansion, oil and mining booms, immigration, social life and leisure activity to proceed with so little restraint or interference. It was this which released sufficient energy to bring defeat to the South and prosperity to the North. In its turn, that prosperity was one of the great props of Union morale – and the spirit of the people of the North was one of the decisive influences on the outcome of the war. People felt that they were living in exceptional times, and, once the excitements and the illusions of the early months of war had faded, they settled into a mood of sober realism which later blossomed into a new self-confidence. That confidence grew with mounting evidence of the strength, resources, capacity, and future prospects of the Union. Whatever the verdict of hindsight (looking through its statistical lens) about the economic performance of the wartime North, those who lived through the experience grasped its true significance. The wonder was not that the economy grew faster or slower than before, but that it grew at all, in the midst of civil strife. Such an achievement reflected credit on the social as well as the economic system. As so often happened, Abraham Lincoln spoke for the commonsense view of his contemporaries. In his message to Congress in December 1864, he dwelt on the fact that the population had continued to grow in spite of the toll taken by the war:

> It is not material to inquire *how* the increase has been produced, or to show that it would have been *greater* but for the war, which is probably true. The important fact remains demonstrated, that we have *more* men *now* than we had when the war *began*; that we are not exhausted, nor in process of exhaustion; that we are *gaining* strength, and may, if need be maintain the contest indefinitely. . . . Material resources are now more complete and abundant than ever.
>
> The national resources, then, are unexhausted, and, as we believe, inexhaustible.[29]

The war was a severe test of strength for both the Union and for the 'free-labour' system which the North so stoutly championed. Both emerged triumphantly from their trial. The future would soon reveal the ironic flaws of that triumph, for the Union preserved proved to be a Union transformed, and the free-labour system, so cherished for the liberty and opportunity which it promised to all, survived the war only to be confronted and confounded by the economic giants of the late nineteenth century. The kind of America which the

North fought to save survived the war, altered but intact, but it could not long survive the peace which followed. In the short run, however, things looked rather different. Not only political and military events but changes in the economic and social order converted the Union of 1861 into the nation of 1865. The very words 'national' and 'nation' more and more replaced 'federal' and 'Union' in common parlance. The power of national government was amply demonstrated during the war but in fields which did not necessarily set patterns and precedents for the 'normal' days of peace. The power which the war unleashed in the social and economic life of the nation proved more enduring, and led after 1865 into new and uncharted paths. The war helped to develop a new national framework for American life, but it did not create a permanent directing force at the centre of it. That mixed legacy did much to shape the American future.

# Chapter XIII : The War and the World

The war between the states never became a war between the nations. Its significance for the world at large belongs in large part to the realm of might-have-beens; its long-term consequences derived less from what did happen than from what did not. No foreign power recognised the Confederacy or intervened on its behalf; the United States was not permanently divided into two or more smaller federations. The American conflict was an exception to the rule that major civil wars tend to become international wars. Americans were permitted to indulge in bloody internecine strife for four years with no outside interference, thanks to the mixed blessing bestowed by the degree of isolation which they enjoyed in the mid-nineteenth century. But to say that the impact of the war was to this extent negative is in no way to belittle its significance as a world event. There was nothing inevitable about the fact that it remained a domestic American affair. It was fought out to the accompaniment of threats and dangers of intervention, and deep-laid schemes to bring it about. It remained a purely American civil war through a combination of good fortune and great skill on the part of those who wished to keep it so, gross errors on the part of those who did not, and canny calculations of national and self interest on the part of those who might have been caught in its toils.

This was after all the greatest war anywhere between 1815 and 1914. It opened amid wild talk of reuniting the disunited states in a common war against a European enemy. It spread its influence to the oceans of the world and the ships, shipyards, ports, mills, factories, press, parliaments, courts and cabinets of foreign countries, great and small. Its last dying embers flickered on amid the whaling fleets in the Bering Sea until June 1865, weeks after Lee surrendered at Appomattox. It raised new questions about the nature and hazards of neutrality in modern war. More important, the prospect of the dissolution of the federal Union forced the European powers to contemplate with an unusual sense of urgency the actual – and, even more, the potential – role of North America in calculations of the balance of power. Palmerston relished the twin prospects of the diminution of a dangerous rival in the Atlantic world, and of French embroilment on the American continent through Napoleon III's Mexican venture. The French Emperor himself saw in the Civil War the best possible safe-conduct for his intervention in Mexico; on the other hand, much expert French opinion regarded the preservation of a strong United States as a crucial counterweight to the power of the British Empire. Prince Gortchakov explained Russian hopes for the salvation of the Union on the ground that Russia and the United States, two rising powers on the fringes of a Europe-centred world, 'appeared called to a natural community of interests and sympathies'.[1]

But it was not merely American power which forced the world to take notice of the conflict. The issues at stake found echoes in Britain and France, Spain and Russia, Canada and Brazil, and many other lands. Karl Marx and Frederick Engels, both keen observers of the struggle in America, never doubted its universal significance. Nor, from a vastly different standpoint, did men like Thomas Carlyle or Lord Acton. But, in spite of (or even because of) the oversimplification of the issues encouraged by ignorance, distance, and condescension, Europeans did not find in the Civil War a simple or reliable test for separating the forces of progress and reaction, liberalism and conservatism. The conflict in America acquired a split personality in Europe. It stirred great issues of slavery and freedom, democracy and privilege, self-determination and imperial ambition, majority rule and minority rights. But the line of division on these issues was often blurred and reactions to them often unpredictable. For those who hated slavery and hailed democracy and liberty, support for the North might have seemed automatic and instinctive, and yet Northern leaders, including Lincoln, were busy denying that the war was a crusade against slavery, and the Confederate cause looked from a distance like a struggle for national independence of the kind which warmed the hearts of European liberals. For those who defended tradition and privilege, and resisted the tide of democracy and equality in Europe, sympathy for the South must surely have seemed natural enough, and yet the Confederates were rebels against a lawfully constituted authority, and posed a threat to order and stability in North America and beyond. When the Czar Alexander II was a firm friend of the Union, and William Gladstone had more than a sneaking sympathy for the Confederacy, there was clearly more to the world impact of the Civil War than first met the eye. In fact, the war posed a series of riddles for the outside world, and the men who suffered least from the strain of trying to answer them were hardened sceptics like Lord Palmerston, who neutralised anti-slavery convictions on the one hand and sympathy for wars of national independence on the other, by concentrating on power politics and pursuit of the national interest. But even the practitioners of *realpolitik* were not spared the muddles or the ironies of a conflict in which Great Britain acted out the role of injured neutral innocent and the United States rode roughshod over the neutral rights which it had defended so earnestly a half century earlier, and was to defend just as earnestly a half century later. The government of the United States, indeed, took the view that this was, in legal terms, no war at all but rather the suppression of an internal disturbance on an unusually large scale, and that foreign powers had no business to recognise the belligerent status of Southern rebels, and no justification for striking dramatic poses of official neutrality.

America's trial by battle was a test of what liberty, democracy, and power meant at many different levels and in many different places. The world-wide repercussions of the Civil War abounded, then, in paradox, irony, ambivalence and confusion. But at least the president of the United States never doubted either that the conflict mattered for the whole world or that its essential and universal meaning concerned not slavery or states rights or nationalism but democracy. The great American experiment was facing its severest trial and the future of popular government not merely in America but beyond, he believed, depended upon the outcome.[2] There were many outside America who believed (and either hoped or feared) that he was right.

1. Britain was the neutral country which mattered most of all. Ties of blood, language, political and legal tradition, commerce and habit reinforced political, diplomatic and strategic interest in American events. Other European powers expected to follow the British lead in reacting to the war, and no other country entertained such a wide range of lively opinions on the subject. Both belligerents confidently expected British sympathy and support, and both became embittered by British attitudes and policy as the struggle unfolded. All the confusing cross-currents which sprang from the war coursed freely through public debate in Britain between 1861 and 1865, and no easy generalisation can summarise the British view of the struggle.

For all that, a fairly simple summary of such views did prevail for a long time, but it was propagated mainly by American historians who knew little more of mid-Victorian Britain than mid-Victorian Britain often knew or understood of the American Civil War. In its simplest form, this analysis identified the 'ruling classes' or the 'aristocracy' as the champions of the South, and the 'working classes' as the friends of the North. The case for such a proposition can be briefly stated, it can be supported by evidence from the debates and propaganda of the 1860s, and it still contains important elements of the truth, but very much less than the whole truth. The sympathy of the upper-class Englishman for the Southern planter was, so the argument ran, the fellow-feeling of one land-owning aristocrat for another. The white South was a society of almost pure British stock in sharp contrast to the polyglot mixture of Irish, Germans,

Scandinavians and others in the north. The vulgarity, coarseness, dishonesty, boastfulness and hypocrisy of the Yankee had been a basic assumption, and a stock joke, of British society for generations. As it happened, the two leading figures of the Northern government, Lincoln and Seward, seemed to personify two popular British stereotypes of the Yankee: the crude, unsophisticated backwoodsman, and the smart and slippery operator. As one staunch British supporter of the Confederacy put it:

> Without relying too much on physiognomy, I appeal to the *carte de visites* of both Lincoln and Davis, and I think all who see them will agree that Jefferson Davis bears out one's idea of what an able administrator and a calm statesman should look like better than Abraham Lincoln, great as he may be as rail-splitter, bargee and country attorney.[3]

Plain snobbery was obviously a real factor, but there were other more substantial grounds for sympathy with the South. Anxiety at the growth of American power (and its manifest destiny pretensions) gave way to rejoicing at its apparent disintegration. Powerful commercial and manufacturing interests found pleasure in the weakening of a dangerous rival, and those interested in cotton – and those more concerned about free trade than free men – were naturally drawn towards the Confederacy. Above all, those who hated and feared the United States as the home of the demon democracy, and therefore as a dangerous example and incitement to others, welcomed what they took to be the total collapse of its political system, and looked with favour upon the stability and order and consciousness of rank and status which they saw in the deferential society of the South. The first eighteen months of the war removed two inhibitions which might have restrained open sympathy for the South; secession was transformed from an idle threat into a going concern, and the Northern government was at pains to emphasise that the abolition of slavery was not its basic war aim. Support for the Confederacy was, it seemed, to be tainted with neither wild impracticality nor embarrassing denial of British anti-slavery tradition.

The sympathy of the British working class for the Northern cause can be even more succinctly explained, according to this same point of view. True, it would require a very optimistic view of human nature to believe that the mass of Lancashire mill workers or London artisans were deeply moved by the plight of Southern Negro slaves. But there was a widespread feeling that the struggle against slavery in the interests of free labour was essentially their struggle. If the United States was for their masters a warning of the dangers of democracy, it was for them the hope of the future, an example to be followed, a model not merely of political democracy, but of social equality and wide economic opportunity. Northern propaganda in Europe harped constantly on such themes, and the address of the working men of Manchester to Abraham Lincoln lauded the free states as 'a singularly happy abode for the working millions where industry is honoured'.[4] If acute awareness of a solidarity of interest with free labour in the northern states may have been confined to the more politically aware and active British workers, there was a more direct emotional link between hundreds of thousands of working men and their sons or brothers or cousins who had emigrated to the United States (almost all to the north and north-west) in the previous half century. It was these personal ties which gave heart and substance to more abstract notions of what was at stake on the battlefields of Virginia.

No such clear-cut classification of attitudes will, however, serve to explain British reactions to a major event with so many conflicting and contradictory implications. In any case, a simple division between the ruling classes and the working classes is much too crude a basis for such an analysis. Does the ruling class include only the landed aristocracy or does it embrace commercial and manufacturing interests who viewed the American war through very different spectacles? When a man of the 1860s attempted a class interpretation of the issues involved in the war, he could reach some surprising conclusions. Monckton Milnes, staunch champion of the North, tried to explain the early successes of the South by a parallel with British society:

> The lower civilization as represented by the South is much braver and cunninger and daringer than the cultivated shopkeepers of the North. It is just as if the younger sons of the Irish and Scotch nobility were turned loose against the bourgeoisie of Leeds. They would kill the men and run away with the women and fire the houses before the respectables knew where they were, or had learned the goosestep.[5]

What of the great force of middle-class opinion which might be impelled by conscience to favour the North or by self-interest to favour one side or the other – or neither? Is it realistic to speak of a working-class view of the conflict, or does this assume a degree of class consciousness and solidarity quite out of keeping with the times? Divisions of opinion on the Civil War may well have run as much on regional as class lines. The war looked different in London and in the provinces. London society tended to be more indulgent to the South and contemptuous of the North, and the press of the capital, headed by The Times, faithfully reflected such feelings. The expanding liberalism of the provinces, finding expression in the increasingly influential provincial press, inclined towards a sturdy, no-nonsense, pro-Northern view. It is more than coincidence, surely, that the great pillars of the Union cause in Britain – men like Bright and Cobden, Forster and Milnes – were men more at home in Lancashire and Yorkshire than in London.

There is some evidence to suggest that the pro-Northern views of political activists among the working men, or of some union leaders, were not always shared by the rank and file, who were often indifferent to remote events, or even inclined to favour the South. Some of the older union leaders found support for the view that, far from being a model to be adopted, Northern society, as it became industrialised, was repeating on a grander scale the mistakes, the miseries, and the injustices of the British experience. At the other end of the social scale, the Union cause had a notable spokesman in the Duke of Argyll, and there were other lesser lights among the nobility on the same side. If the largest bloc of pro-Southern feeling was conservative, the Conservative party generally restrained its feelings carefully. Disraeli steered a cautious and devious course; while willing to score party points off the ministry on American issues, he never made the American question a really divisive issue, and he and his party were embarrassed by ardent pro-Confederates in their ranks, like Lord Robert Cecil (later prime minister as Lord Salisbury). Although cotton manufacturers and merchants may have initially had a vested interest in the Confederate cause, they were rapidly losing it in the second half of the war. More important, most other mercantile and manufacturing interests – the woollen and linen industries, munitions and iron and steel, the shipping business, banks and finance houses – were enjoying the profits of war, were reluctant to imperil their flourishing business with the Northern states, and, if not ardently pro-Northern, were the strongest pressure group working for a continued British neutrality which could only be of help to the North. It was middle-class opinion, too, which jealously guarded the British anti-slavery tradition, and refused to be put off by Northern obfuscation of the slavery issue in the first half of the war. It was, however, among liberals and radicals of middle-class background that the most varied responses were found to the complex political issues posed by the war. For many, faith in the North as the standard bearer of anti-slavery and liberal democracy triumphed over lingering doubts about the rights of minorities, or national self-determination, or Republican protectionism. One of the most doughty champions of the North, William E. Forster, affirmed his passionate belief in free trade, but asked who would say that 'freedom in goods must enter into competition with freedom of men'. John Bright was the most conspicuous and eloquent spokesman for the North as the vanguard of democracy and the nemesis of privilege:

> Privilege thinks it has a great interest in the American contest, and every morning with blatant voice, it comes into our streets and curses the American Republic. Privilege has beheld an afflicting spectacle for many years past. It has beheld thirty million of men happy and prosperous, without emperors – without king – without the surroundings of a court – without nobles, except such as are made by eminence in intellect and virtue . . . and Privilege has shuddered at what might happen to old Europe if this great experiment should succeed.

The United States minister in London, Charles Francis Adams, confessed that 'I never quite appreciated the "moral influence" of American democracy, nor the cause that the privileged classes in Europe have to fear us until I saw how directly it works'.[6]

On the other hand, some liberal and radical opinion was impressed by the constitutional arguments of the South, or inclined to regard the war as a struggle for Southern independence rather than a contest over slavery. Lord Acton saw the South as a bulwark of political liberty; the two most active protagonists of the Confederacy in the House of Commons were William Lindsay, a Liberal, and John A. Roebuck, a Radical. Gladstone himself mingled with his horror of the slaughter an element of admiration for the political and constitutional cause of the Confederacy. All in all, the two faces of the war, and its variations on the theme of liberty, posed endless dilemmas for British liberals who never had any difficulty in discovering at least two sides to every question. Where should liberal priorities lie as between freedom for slaves and freedom of trade, liberal democracy and the liberty of a new nation struggling to be free, the will of the majority expressed through central government and the bulwarks of liberty provided by states rights and constitutional guarantees?

All manner of other influences complicated and confused British reactions to the war. Much of the confusion was caused by sheer ignorance and misunderstanding of America, or by indifference to its domestic squabbles. Any attempt to analyse the repercussions of the Civil War in Britain will almost inevitably exaggerate its impact, by isolating this single topic from all the others which engaged public attention. (Many historians of mid-Victorian Britain have more than compensated for this tendency by paying hardly any attention to the Civil War at all!) Among people who were interested in the American conflict, opinion was by no means static, and not all issues carried the same weight. Fluctuations in the fortunes of war were reflected in the attitudes and enthusiasms of British opinion. Sympathy for the South as an underdog blossomed into admiration for its brave deeds, which in turn faded into disillusion, despair and quiet abandonment of the cause in 1864-5. Among Union sympathisers it is not too cynical to suggest that many finally decided that they had always been pro-Northern, and that the North had right and justice on its side, only after Northern victory was assured, or even after the war was over.[7] Among the key issues, slavery had a special place in British reactions to the war. It is true that cynics brushed the question aside. Carlyle expressed his impatience with people who were 'cutting each other's throats, because one half of them prefer hiring their servants for life, and the other by the hour'.[8] But, for others, Confederate sympathies were a luxury to be enjoyed only as long as there was no clear Northern commitment to emancipation. Lincoln's proclamations were too tardy and too equivocal to satisfy British opinion immediately, but, abroad as at home, they did their work gradually but effectively. The longer they were in force, the more anti-slavery sentiment over-shadowed other feelings, and the less likely it was that some other irritant could goad Britain into the kind of action which would dangerously antagonise the North or significantly help the South. If emancipation scarcely made the popularity of the North unshakable, it made alliance with the South unthinkable.

Attitudes to the war were always shaped, too, by expectations about its outcome. The basic assumption behind much British thinking was that the South could not be bludgeoned back into the Union, and that its eventual independence was assured. At the end of 1861 Palmerston regarded the dissolution of the Union as 'virtually accomplished'. In July 1863 Gladstone could still tell the House of Commons that the war would inevitably end in Southern independence. Even in May 1864 *The Times* could assess Confederate prospects as brighter than ever.[9] Conviction that the war must end in division of the Union stimulated concern to end the horrifying and pointless slaughter as rapidly as possible. Few matters contributed more to Anglo-American misunderstanding during the war than this blend of false calculation and sometimes genuine humanitarianism which, from a distance of 3,000 miles, looked like malicious pleasure in the break-up of the United States.

Misunderstanding and rancour were also increased by the essentially negative character of many British reactions. Often, the decisive influence was not sympathy but hostility, not what a man or group was for, but what he or it was against. British aristocrats hated or feared American democracy more than they loved or respected Southern planters. Spokesmen for British workers abhorred Southern oligarchy and privilege more than they pitied the Negro slave. More generally, what often appeared (especially to Americans) as unwarranted prejudice against one side or the other was in fact the product of a broader, undiscriminating anti-Americanism. Whether inspired by contempt or condescension, disillusion or disgust, Yankee boastfulness or British arrogance, such sentiments were at the root of the British response to America's crisis, and of the bitterness of both North and South at the treatment which they received. For all the crudity of its message, the following anonymous letter received at the American legation in London in October 1863 probably spoke for all too many Britains:

Dam the Federals
Dam the Confederates
Dam you both.
*Kill your damned selves for the next 10 years if you like;* so much the better for the world and for England. Thus thinks every Englishman with any brains. N.B. P.S. We'll cut your throats fast enough afterwards for you if you aint tired of blood, you devils.[10]

For cooler heads and more practical purposes, the most crucial distinction in the British response to the Civil War was between attitude and action, sympathy (or hostility) and policy. It was one thing to make speeches or print editorials or write letters denouncing one belligerent or praising the other. It was quite another to commit Britain to any form of intervention or to risk actual involvement in the conflict. The distinction was clear to most people in Britain, but much less so from the other side of the Atlantic. For all that it included many Southern sympathisers, the Conservative opposition was as anxious as the government to preserve a neutrality which would inevitably favour the North in practice. The Palmerston ministry rested on a rather precarious base, was set mainly on remaining in power, and, to this end, aimed to do as little as possible, and certainly to avoid divisive and explosive issues. Palmerston had no love for the United States and shed no tears over its impending collapse, but for all his reputation for aggression and bluster, he was cautious to a degree in his handling of the war situation. His foreign secretary, Earl Russell, had little more sympathy for Americans in general and the North in particular; his tone was frequently more brusque and truculent than Palmerston's, but his errors were more attributable to weakness, obstinacy or lack of vision than to malice aforethought. Both men were not above exploiting the issues of the war to win popularity at home, with the aid of some modest sabre-rattling. But both were determined to keep out of trouble, and that meant a policy of cautious neutrality. They were acutely aware of the dangers of interference. Palmerston was deeply suspicious of the France of Napoleon III, feared the prospect of a European war, and, from 1863, was more concerned with the problems of Poland and Schleswig-Holstein. It did not come easily to such European-orientated statesmen to put American affairs high on the foreign policy agenda, and, when they did, they worried about the danger to Canada, and the state of the navy during the transition to steam power and iron-clad ships. In a word, there was no basic British interest which would be served by intervention in the war, but several – political, strategic and economic – which might be hurt. In the hands of worldly-wise and somewhat weary statesmen, it was interest and not sentiment which dictated British policy. It was safe rather than spectacular, but it made good sense.

2. Opinion in France and other European countries shared some of the reactions apparent in Britain. There was the same reluctance to translate concern into commitment, interest into interference. Napoleon III was determined to avoid unilateral action which would involve him in a quarrel with the United States, of which Britain was likely to be the only beneficiary. Most other European countries were only remotely likely to become involved in the war, and could afford to view it from a distance and with some detachment. There was in France, as in Britain and elsewhere, a strong presumption that the war was bound to end in the permanent separation of North and South. There was the same widespread ignorance and indifference concerning America, and, in some quarters, the same snobbish condescension which was inclined to wish a plague on both American houses. There was, in diplomatic and political circles, the same instinctive tendency as in Britain to give priority to familiar European problems nearer home.

But France also had its special interests in the American conflict, although those interests pulled in various directions. Traditional friendship for the United States, and abhorrence of slavery, were backed up by the conception of a strong United States as a check to British power. The economic impact of the war was more quickly felt in France than in Britain; the French textile industry, much smaller than the British, proved more immediately vulnerable to the cotton diplomacy of the South. Above all, Napoleon III was developing a very special interest in the western hemisphere. His Mexican expedition was made possible precisely because the United States would be too preoccupied with its domestic upheaval to take a firm stand against it in defence of the Monroe Doctrine. Napoleon saw in the Mexican venture not merely new commercial opportunities for France, but the basis for a new French sphere of influence in the new world, and a check imposed by the Latin nations on the imperial designs of the Anglo-Saxons. (Echoes of more modern French fears of the Anglo-American relationship are even clearer in the opinion of one commentator that eventual Union victory marked the passing of Europe's hegemony in the world, and the dawn of an era of Anglo-Saxon predominance.)[11] In fact, burgeoning French interest in the western hemisphere contrasted with the weakening of the long-standing British concern for the defence of Canada. While Napoleon III eagerly assumed new commitments in Mexico, more and more British opinion sought ways of disengagement from old obligations in Canada.

When the Civil War began, Napoleon III had some leanings towards the North, based partly on his first-hand knowledge of the United States. But his sympathies moved steadily to the other side, through a combination of resentment of the truculent diplomacy of Seward, distaste for the aggressive democracy of the North, a predisposition to support what looked like a nationalist rebellion, and the need to protect his Mexican venture. He was also convinced that the war was bound to end in Southern independence, and that the sooner the end came the better, in order to relieve economic distress and social unrest at home. 'The difficulty,' as Napoleon himself said, 'is to find a way to give effect to my sympathies',[12] and that difficulty was acute when cooperation with Britain was regarded as the *sine qua non* of any intervention. British determination to keep out of trouble, which rarely weakened and never died, was the great stumbling block to the fulfilment of Napoleon's grand designs. Together with awareness of the fragility of his position abroad and at home, this difficulty pushed Napoleon into a policy of drift rather than decision.

Napoleon was acutely conscious of the economic pressures created by the repercussions of the war, and the danger of disorders arising from them. But he had less need than the British government to show any great sensitivity to informed and interested public opinion on the war, as voiced in the press, or by prominent figures in French political and intellectual life. His own court and ministers were predominantly pro-Southern, often much more vehemently so than the Emperor himself, although his cousin, Prince Napoleon, second in line of succession, was one of the strongest French champions of the Union, and his foreign ministers, Thouvenel and Drouyn de Lhuys, seldom allowed sympathy for either side to overrule diplomatic discretion. Support for the Confederacy came mainly from conservative interests – bankers, army officers, many of the clergy, and older and stricter Catholics – and was vigorously expressed by the semi-official press. (One newspaper even saw the struggle as a Northern Puritan crusade against the Catholics of the South.) Generally, the pro-Confederate case rested on the inevitability of Southern victory, the vulgar democracy of the North, scepticism about Northern anti-slavery zeal, and considerable distortion of what was actually happening in America.

Support for the Union cause came mainly from opponents of the Second Empire – Orleanists, Liberal Catholics, Republicans and socialists. The real enthusiasts for the North came from the ranks of the intelligentsia, and found an influential outlet in the *Revue des Deux Mondes* and other journals. The roll-call of prominent Northern sympathisers includes some eminent names: Victor Hugo, Guizot, Montalembert, Lacordaire, Laboulaye, Augustin Cochin and Henri Martin. For them, slavery was a key issue; and so, too, was American democracy as the inspiration of the present and the hope of the future. Some of them mingled praise for the free institutions of the United States with recognition of America's contribution to the balance of power. Laboulaye argued that the dissolution of the Union could only be to the benefit of Britain and not France:

To dismember America is the same thing as restoring the empire of the seas to our rivals; and to maintain the unity of America is to maintain liberty on the ocean and the peace of the world.[13]

Such men espoused the Northern cause out of genuine conviction but they also exploited it skilfully as a vehicle for opposition to the Second Empire. Where direct criticism was difficult or dangerous, the American example or the American analogy could be profitably employed. The cause of the Union, as they interpreted it (and sometimes idealised it) was unmistakably at odds with the cause of the Empire. For this reason perhaps, French liberal and radical opinion was less tortured by the doubts and dilemmas which afflicted liberals in Britain.

Even more than in Britain, too, the debate on America was confined largely to a fairly limited and exclusive group of interested parties who were able and willing to deduce connections between the issues at stake on either side of the Atlantic. The common assertion that the mass of French popular opinion was pro-Northern is very difficult to prove. Insofar as such popular sympathy existed, it ran into conflict with the economic pressure for a quick end to the war, which meant, in effect, permanent separation of North and South. But, even more than in the case of Britain, it is easy to exaggerate the interest which the American war excited among the wider public, and in the French case, such indifference was compounded by the indifference of the Emperor to public opinion on such matters.

Two other lands on the Atlantic perimeter of Europe, Ireland and Spain, had special interests in the American crisis. Because of the large-scale emigration of the preceding twenty years, Ireland had uniquely close links with the United States – and the reduction of immigration in the first half of the war aggravated Ireland's deep economic depression. Predictably, no country felt more acutely than Ireland the contradictions and paradoxes of the war's impact. Most of the

Irish in America were in the north, and many thousands served in the Union army; but few of them were Republicans and few showed much enthusiasm for emancipation. Their kin in Ireland shared the same ambivalent position, and Irish nationalists were painfully torn between emotional ties with the North and awareness of the plausible analogy between the Southern attempt to dissolve the American Union, and their own desire to dissolve the union of Great Britain and Ireland. It was easier, at times, to succumb to the temptation of viewing the American war as some elaborate Anglo-Saxon conspiracy of which the Irish would inevitably be the victims. In Spain, the prospect of the disintegration of the United States revived the dying embers of imperial ambition in the western hemisphere. Bold plans for the recovery of Santo Domingo came to nothing, and dreams of renewed influence in Mexico were overshadowed by Napoleon III's more high-flown ambitions. As for Spanish opinion on the issues involved in the war, even liberals were unenthusiastic about the North, and conservatives ardently admired the social system and values of the Confederacy. Indeed one diatribe from a Spanish newspaper may serve as a summary of what reactionary Europe thought of the Civil War:

This history of this model republic can be summed up in a few words. It came into being by rebellion. It was founded on atheism. It was populated by the dregs of all the nations of the world. It has lived without law of God or man. Within a hundred years, greed has ruined it. Now it is fighting like a cannibal, and it will die in a flood of blood and mire. Such is the real history of the one and only state in the world which has succeeded in constituting itself according to the flaming theories of democracy. The example is too horrible to stir any desire for imitation in Europe.[14]

The shock waves of the war in America were felt much less strongly in other European countries. It caused some economic dislocation in the Low Countries and parts of Germany, but neither there nor elsewhere did it threaten to arouse social disturbances or to involve other European governments directly in the struggle. But interests and sympathies were aroused, and lessons which might have some European relevance were duly noted. Most of the smaller European countries combined an untroubled official neutrality with leanings towards the Northern side. Belgium and Holland fell into this category; Sweden was much more open in its pro-Northern sympathies. The Swiss, having survived a threat to their own confederation a decade earlier, were not disposed to favour the Southern attempt to dissolve the American Union. In Prussia, Austria and the smaller German states, the American conflict generally seemed remote, although German emigration to the north and north-west forged an emotional bond with the Union cause. The rulers of the Habsburg Empire inevitably deplored the separatist example set by the Confederacy. The King of Prussia, and Bismarck, took the view that the war was a simple clash between right and wrong, with right clearly on the side of the properly constituted federal government. Some Prussian army officers and large landowners were inclined to favour the Confederacy, but, on the other hand, Prussian investors subscribed in large amounts to loans floated by the Union government. While the future of the Union was in doubt, federalism on the American pattern fell under a cloud, but after its triumphant restoration, the American example became a more useful precedent for the North German Confederation.

Most shades of opinion in Russia tended to favour the Union. As emancipator of the serfs, the Czar looked with favour upon the emancipation of the slaves. More seriously, he and his ministers valued the United States as a counterweight to British power, and looked unkindly upon any rebellion against established authority. The claims of Southern secessionists and Polish rebels looked too uncomfortably alike to encourage any sympathy for the former. So it was that the archetype of old world autocracy appeared in the guise of firm friend of new world democracy. The Russian Baltic and Pacific fleets visited New York and San Francisco respectively in 1863 and were warmly welcomed. The purpose of their visit, however, was not, as widely rumoured, to make a gesture of solidarity with the Union cause, but to prevent them from being ice-bound in their home bases in the event of the deterioration of the international crisis over Poland. Moderate liberal opinion in Russia sympathised with the North on anti-slavery and wider political grounds, whilst radicals used the United States as a kind of screen on which to project images of their hopes, dreams (and doubts) about the future. They were intensely interested in the great American experiment, but feared that it was already corrupted by materialism and selfishness. They would welcome eventual Northern victory, but were already doubtful about the capacity of the Union which emerged from the war to manage the problems of an industrial society. From their distant and detached position, Russian observers of the war could afford to focus their attention on basic principles and their deeper meaning, without being distracted by the surface cross-currents which affected those who viewed the war from western Europe. But, whether seen from St Petersburg or Paris, Madrid or London, the fundamental importance of the war was that it did raise earth-shaking issues which struck a responsive chord, and created a good deal of discord. No other event in the century from 1815 to 1914 brought America so conspicuously on to the European stage.

3. The neighbours of the United States in the western hemisphere could not afford to view the war with philosophical detachment. They had been living with the growing power and expansionist ambitions of the United States for many years, and now her immediate neighbours feared lest the American war should suck them into its vortex. British North America still consisted of a series of disconnected provinces and colonies stretching from the Maritime Provinces of Nova Scotia, Labrador and Prince Edward Island in the east to Vancouver and British Columbia in the west. The most populous areas were in Canada West and East (the modern Ontario and Quebec), but the total population of British North America was only a little over one-tenth of that of the

United States. All the British provinces were highly sensitive about their relationship with their great neighbour to the south, and the so-called 'unguarded frontier' was a very uneasy frontier throughout the pre-Civil War period. Fears of annexation or absorption into the United States were endemic, and the reciprocity treaty of 1854 was suspected by many Canadians as the first, commercial step in that direction. The coming of the Civil War heightened tension still further, and there were gloomy predictions about its impact on Canada whatever the outcome of the struggle. If the South secured its independence, that would create a new balance of power in north America, possibly to Canada's advantage, but it might turn the attention of the North towards Canada, in the search for compensation for lost territory. If the North won, and the Union was restored, it might unleash its armed might on defenceless Canada, if only to avenge British insults during the war. Even if the whole of British North America was not lost, there seemed a real chance that the vast and almost empty prairie region would be lost to the United States through the north-westward thrust of American settlement from Minnesota.

The question of Canadian security was bedevilled by the conflicting attitudes of Britain and Canada herself. Canada was the Achilles heel of the British government in its relations with the United States. It was a major obstacle to a policy of either complete detachment from the struggle or active interference in it. For years there had been a growing feeling in Britain that Canadians should contribute more to their own defence, and lingering notions of imperial power and responsibility were fighting a losing battle with financial retrenchment. Canada was indefensible, in the opinion of much British liberal opinion; Cobden thought that in a British-American war Britain could no more hold Canada than the United States could defend Yorkshire.[15] The problem of Canadian defence inspired numerous plans and endless discussion, but little action during the Civil War. Those who did not agree that defence was impossible believed that it was easy, and neither view encouraged much serious preparation. In the event of war with the United States, Britain would rely more on naval strength than defence of the long land frontier. Canadians showed marked reluctance to finance or man the forces needed, and washed their hands of any obligation to prepare for a war which would probably arise out of some crisis like the *Trent* incident which would be a British and not a Canadian responsibility. However, if the security problem produced little tangible result during the war, concern over it was one factor which pushed British North America towards confederation a few years later.

The reactions of Canadians to the Civil War showed many of the fluctuations and complexities of British attitudes. Before 1861 most Canadians were strongly anti-slavery, and were therefore inclined to favour the North. But many were soon disabused of naïve notions on this point, and pro-Southern (or at least anti-Northern) feelings gained ground. There was some correlation between conservatism and liberalism on the one hand, and anti- and pro-Northern feeling on the other, but it was far from constant or complete. Conservatives had some admiration for the South, but also some distaste for its rebel image. Liberals admired the democracy of the North, but saw virtue also in the emergent nationalism of the South, and were disillusioned both by Lincoln's ambiguity on slavery, and Seward's bellicose diplomacy. As in Britain, much feeling was negative rather than positive, and a lurking anti-Americanism was already second nature to Canadians – and was skilfully exploited by politicians like John A. Macdonald. As the war went on, there were always incidents and tensions which threatened trouble: the activities of 'crimps' who lured Canadians (or British troops) into the Union army, the draft-dodgers fleeing from the Northern states, and, most serious, the varied activities of Confederate agents in Canada, especially in the second half of the war. Canada's greatest peril was the opportunity which it provided for the Confederacy to embroil Britain in the Civil War. As later events showed, even belated and blundering Confederate attempts in this direction proved too dangerous for comfort.

In Latin America the Civil War years brought the United States some unwonted (and short-lived) popularity. The battle for democracy and against slavery no doubt gave the North a more favourable image in some quarters, but it was fear which gave the main impetus to a change of heart – fear in Latin America that the collapse of the United States would open the way to large-scale European intervention in the western hemisphere. The designs of the French in Mexico and the Spanish in Santo Domingo lent credence to this view, and rumours of a Franco-Spanish plan to re-establish a firm hold on South America gained ground rapidly. There was talk of a French protectorate over Ecuador, and a new European-backed monarchy in Paraguay, but nothing actually happened. Latin America felt that it needed the United States as never before, and Seward assiduously encouraged this trend, as he courted the governments of South America to discourage any notions of recognition of the Confederacy.

Events in Mexico were of course the key to the wider picture. Mexico was the only country which had a land frontier with both belligerents in the Civil War. It still retained fresh memories of the American expansionist drive which had gobbled up Texas, New Mexico and California. (Now, during the Civil War, the North was busy explaining that the Southern states had always posed the threat to Mexico, and the South was equally busy explaining that, with independence, it would no longer need to expand to safeguard its interests.) Be that as it may, Mexico's chronic internal disorders and divisions could always provide a pretext for outside interference. In the years before 1861 the liberals under Juarez had been in the ascendancy, but they did not control the whole country, and a number of provinces, especially near the northern border, were virtually self-governing. Here the key figure was Santiago Vidaurri, governor of Nueva Leon and Coahuila, who extended his control in 1862 to Tamaulipas (and the vital port of Matamoros on the Rio Grande). Vidaurri and the Confederate authorities came to a mutually profitable arrangement which made

Matamoros and the Texan border into a vital back door of the Confederacy beyond the Union blockade.

The European powers had always been interested in Mexico, not least as a buffer against United States expansion. Mexico was to be to its northern neighbour what Turkey was to Russia, a weak power which, with proper backing, could be used to contain the threat of a far stronger one. By 1861 Mexico was so badly in default in its debt payments to European creditors that Britain, France and Spain agreed on joint intervention to secure satisfaction – and placated the United States by an invitation (not accepted) to take part. Britain and Spain soon withdrew when Mexico made a new financial offer, but Napoleon III, determined from the start to convert the joint expedition into the instrument of his own Mexican ambitions, maintained and steadily expanded the French presence. The British government had been well aware from the outset of his ulterior motives, but was far from unhappy to see France heavily engaged in Mexico, doing Britain's dirty work in the new world by checking the power of the United States, and in the process weakening French capacity to threaten or make war in Europe. More and more French troops were brought in to meet tough Mexican resistance. Mexico City was finally captured in 1863, and the throne of Mexico offered to the Archduke Maximilian, younger brother of the Habsburg Emperor, who formally accepted it early in 1864. Maximilian was always totally dependent on Napoleon III and the French army in the face of mounting Mexican opposition. Beset by problems at home and a threatening European situation, Napoleon now found it desperately difficult to extricate himself.

The whole Mexican venture had been feasible only because the United States was preoccupied with its own internal conflict, and was obliged to mix discretion with its objections. It was this situation which led the Confederacy into the delusion that its friendship – rather than the simple fact of the disruption of the Union – was vital to whoever controlled Mexico. The first Confederate mission to Mexico, to the Juarez government, in 1861, was a fiasco, and the highly undiplomatic career of John T. Pickett included thirty days in a Mexican jail. But the later turn of events excited hopes of mutual diplomatic recognition between the Confederacy and the Maximilian government, and, much more important, dreams of a bargain based on Southern support for the new Mexican monarchy in return for French recognition of the Confederacy. But it was precisely at this point that Confederate hopes were blasted by the diplomatic realities so well understood by Napoleon III and Secretary of State Seward. The one thing above all which Napoleon could not afford to do was to provoke the United States beyond endurance by formal recognition of the Confederacy. Civil war or no civil war, Lincoln and Seward would be obliged to retaliate against such a move, by offering arms and other aid to Juarez against the French, or even by threats of direct intervention which might well lead to war with France. Instead, the French stopped short of recognition, and the United States stopped short of confrontation. From 1862 to 1865, Seward and Napoleon

III played out a diplomatic game, based on a version of events in Mexico which both knew to be less than the truth, but which each chose to believe for his own good reasons. As French involvement in Mexico steadily deepened, the Emperor still protested his good intentions and his lack of ulterior motives. On his side, Seward protested regularly that the United States could not tolerate large-scale armed intervention or permanent political interference by a European power in the western hemisphere, and certainly not in the affairs of her immediate neighbour. But he chose to pretend that matters had not come to that (when they surely had), and he confined himself to diplomatic protest, despite congressional and newspaper pressure for tougher action. It would be time enough for toughness when the Civil War was over. Meanwhile, his trump card was the hint, often repeated but never acted upon, that the United States might recognise the Maximilian régime in Mexico provided that it did not recognise the Confederacy. Napoleon III was happy to promote this same idea as the best protection of his increasingly shaky Mexican investment of men, money and prestige.

Of all the ironies of the Civil War as a world event, Mexico was one of the greatest – and one of the cruellest for the Confederacy. To those who peered out at the world from Richmond, it seemed that French recognition of the Confederacy was the one sure way for Napoleon to safeguard his Mexican venture. To those who better understood international politics, in Paris, it eventually seemed the one sure way to destroy it. Seward had only pretended to believe fiction rather than fact. The Confederates had genuinely mistaken dreams for reality. In this respect, and in the hollowness of the foundations upon which policy was based, Mexico was not untypical of the failure of Confederate foreign policy as a whole.

4. In fact, the foreign relations of the Confederacy were based not so much on a policy as on a single idea. For all the rhetoric extolling the ability of the Confederacy to stand on its own feet, the South recognised the need for help from outside, and confidently expected it to come. The need for supplies from abroad to sustain the war was obvious to everyone; the decisive effect of official recognition by the European powers in winning Southern independence was a basic article of faith; actual foreign intervention was not thought likely to be necessary, since the mere threat of it would suffice. The key which would unlock the doors of European factories and treasuries and chancelleries was not military or naval might, nor subtle diplomacy, nor sentimental notions of hands across the sea, but the simple proposition that cotton was king. More than four-fifths of the cotton consumed by the mills of Europe came from the Southern states, and, come what may, Britain and France would have to have that basic raw material. Millions of their citizens depended upon it for their livelihood, and national prosperity and social equilibrium were at risk if it were denied. Britain had as many cotton spindles as the rest of the western world put together – and Britain was the most important neutral. These were the arguments, spread by

propaganda like David Christy's *Cotton is King* in the 1850s, which were almost unquestioned in the South when war came – so much so that *The Times* correspondent, W. H. Russell, protested to Southerners, who constantly proclaimed the power of king cotton, against the assumption that British policy could be dictated wholly by such venal and base motives.[16]

The South was clear in its mind that the cotton weapon would work, but not on precisely how it would work. Was it to be employed primarily to obtain supplies and win independence through military victory, or was its main goal to achieve international recognition and win independence by political and diplomatic pressure? In terms of methods, the choice was between transporting as much cotton to Europe as quickly as possible, and denying cotton to Europe until recognition was granted. Objections to the first course were mainly practical. Certainly brave ideas of the immediate carriage of millions of bales of cotton to Europe by a fleet of steamships, as soon as war began, overlooked Southern deficiencies in shipping, organisation and government capacity, and doubts about the availability of the quantity of cotton involved. What was needed, rather, was the steady despatch of cotton to Europe, to the extent that resources would permit, and what was achieved in the latter part of the war, in face of great difficulties and a tightening blockade, suggests that a crucial opportunity was missed in 1861 and 1862. The policy actually followed in the first half of the war was a cotton embargo. It had the merit of simplicity, and it was supported by the sanction of local public opinion rather than elaborate administrative machinery. It also reflected, in its simple sequence of embargo – recognition – independence, the air of unreality which always pervaded the Confederate attitude to the outside world.

In 1861 the embargo was in fact imposed, not officially by government decree, but unofficially, voluntarily, extra-legally – and, on the whole, very efficiently. Such was the popular faith in King Cotton, backed up by the press, the planters, the cotton factors and merchants, and state governors and legislatures, that the amount of Southern cotton reaching Europe during the first year of the war was about 1 per cent of imports in normal times. If there was any dissent from the embargo policy, it was subdued by the local committees of public safety which policed the ban, and ensured that cotton was kept well away from the ports and other points where it might be vulnerable to Northern raids. Meanwhile the Confederate government played no part in the operation; embargo proposals were frequently discussed in Congress, but never passed into law, largely through pressure from the administration. Davis and his cabinet feared that an official embargo would needlessly antagonise Europe whereas the voluntary policy, while just as effective, enabled the government to pose as the helpless victim of popular pressure. (Davis might have played this role more effectively than he did; he never rivalled Lincoln's skill in protesting that he was controlled by events while continuing to do very much what he pleased.)

Although its operation was almost watertight, the embargo failed to produce the anticipated results in 1861–2. In the second year of the war, the embargo was gradually relaxed and the use of cotton to finance overseas purchases assumed a higher priority. But the King Cotton idea lingered on in other forms. Severe restrictions were imposed on actual cotton-growing, and this time public opinion was backed up by laws passed by several state legislatures. The idea was to restrict the cotton crop to domestic needs and also to make more land available for food production. The cotton crop which had been running at 3,500,000 to 4,500,000 bales in the pre-war years, fell to under 500,000 in 1863, and 300,000 in 1864. The Confederate government made one of its few direct contributions to the policy of cotton restriction by ordering that stocks in areas threatened by Northern armies should be burned, and something like 2,500,000 bales may have been destroyed during the war.

By 1863 King Cotton had conspicuously failed to bring about recognition or intervention. Even when there had been talk of mediation in London and Paris, the cotton shortage had not been the only or even the major question involved. From 1863 onwards, King Cotton quietly abdicated his throne, and such cotton as was available became the effective servant rather than the ineffective tyrant of Confederate policy. Already in 1862 there had been some attempts to use cotton stocks in the South as a means of raising desperately needed funds in Europe. The arrangement with Erlanger & Co. in 1863 was the first major attempt to sell cotton bonds in Europe, and, whatever its limitations, it was crucial to the financing of Confederate purchases in that year. Later in 1863 Colin J. McRae arrived in Paris to coordinate and control all Confederate credit and purchasing operations in Europe, and he achieved considerable success in creating some order and efficiency out of the chaos of competing agents and overlapping programmes which had hitherto enfeebled the Confederate effort. In 1864 the Confederate government at last asserted a measure of control over cotton supplies at home and the vital business of running supplies through the blockade, and these will be discussed in the following chapter.[17] Too late, the Confederacy had at last got its priorities and its policy right: control of the cotton crop, control of its export, and control of its application to the business of sustaining the war. Too late, fantasy had given way to reality.

Explanations for the failure of King Cotton are equally easy to find on both sides of the Atlantic. On the European side the story is a combination of hard facts and hard luck; on the Confederate side it is a case of soft options taken and hard thinking evaded. The Confederates were certainly unlucky in the timing of their embargo. Bumper crops in the two pre-war years meant that British mills had large stocks on hand, and many were in fact facing the problems of over-production and a glutted market before the embargo came to rescue rather than ruin them. For some, Confederate policy was a convenient excuse for closing mills, curtailing production and laying off workers; for others, usually the larger companies, it was an opportunity to hold existing stocks until scarcity raised prices, to continue production of goods to be held until the market improved, and to kill off smaller and more vulnerable rivals. As the war went on, alternative sources of supply were hastily developed in India and Egypt, and, although cotton from these areas posed certain production problems, the industry had adjusted to them by 1864-5. By that time, too, some cotton from Union-occupied parts of the South was finding its way across the Atlantic. All in all, British cotton supplies in the last year of the war were up to three-quarters of pre-war levels, and there were fears of an end to the American war which would bring a flood of cheap cotton, and depress the price of the finished product. So much for the irresistible power of King Cotton!

The cotton famine did have its effect in Britain, but its real impact was delayed until the latter part of 1862, and then its main victims were not the manufacturers who might have had considerable political leverage, but the workers who had very little. Distress in Lancashire and other cotton manufacturing areas reached its peak in the winter of 1862-3, and, although its exact dimensions are hard to gauge, it was real enough for thousands of families. Public and private relief efforts (helped by funds from the United States) and employment in other industries mitigated some of the worst effects of the cotton famine. The picture was a patchy one, with larger mills and their employees coming off best, while some of the smaller pockets of the textile industry – in Scotland for example – were hit so badly that they never recovered from the effects of the Civil War. The hardship caused by the embargo was not severe or protracted or widespread enough to cause major social disturbances, or serious political embarrassment.

The sufferings of the cotton industry and its workers have to be set against economic consequences of the war which were pulling in the opposite direction. Union propaganda made much of the argument that King Wheat had replaced King Cotton – that is, that Britain dared not intervene on behalf of the Confederacy to obtain cotton, for fear of losing huge and vital imports of grain from the north-western states of the United States. It is true that British imports of American grain leaped up in 1861-3 after bad harvests at home, but this was a matter of price and convenience rather than a choice between American wheat and starvation. Protagonists of both belligerents in Britain were not unaware of the importance of grain imports from America, but there is no evidence at all that they became a key factor in the policy deliberations of the government. The real economic counterweight to King Cotton was that so many British industries were prospering handsomely because of (or at least during) the American Civil War, and had no intention of biting the hand which fed them. Lancashire's misery could not outweigh Yorkshire's or Birmingham's prosperity, and cotton from the South was not to be secured at the price of endangering lucrative business with Britain's best customer in the North. But even this point does not get to the heart of the failure of King Cotton diplomacy to deflect British policy from its neutralist course. Men of the stamp of Palmerston and Russell based their policy on national interest, but their conception of national interest was not first and foremost economic, but political and strategic, and, in any case, they were unlikely to react kindly to the kind of threat which the Confederacy was trying to hold over their heads. The cotton embargo brought the wrong kind of pressure on the wrong kind of people in the wrong kind of way, and its impact on British policy was minimal.

French reactions to cotton diplomacy tell a similar story. The French cotton industry was very much smaller than the British, its stocks, though considerable, were exhausted much sooner, and it was therefore hit much harder and much more quickly by the cotton famine. But again the effects were patchy; the more advanced mills of Alsace and Flanders survived better than the smaller-scale, less developed industry of Normandy and Picardy. Unemployment was very high in some areas, and distress acute, and Napoleon III was genuinely fearful of the possibility of riots and disorders. Indeed some of his diplomatic initiatives, proposing mediation or an armistice, may have been designed more to keep the peace at home than make it in America. But the real difficulty of the French textile industry was not the Southern embargo, but its own backwardness in methods and organisation, now exposed to increased competition from British goods as the Cobden Treaty of 1860 came fully into force in the following year. The Civil War was a scapegoat rather than an explanation of the problem. There were other French industries which suffered through the war, particularly those which exported luxury goods – silks, wines, clocks, for example – to both North and South. The blockade, the disruption of shipping, and, in the North, soaring tariff rates, hit them hard, but any policy which might risk war with the North would only make the situation far worse. All in all, the Civil War served to highlight long-term trends and deep-rooted difficulties in French industry and commerce. After 1865, imports of Southern cotton and some other branches of Franco-American trade never recovered to pre-war levels. As for the relationship of economic factors to foreign policy, Napoleon III had his worries about depression and unrest in the textile areas, but his policy was dictated by greater anxieties, and greater ambitions, elsewhere.

The failure of King Cotton diplomacy in Europe strongly suggests that its aims were wrongly formulated and its methods wrongly chosen. It was based on the premise that foreign recognition would bring independence rather than that independence would bring recognition. It therefore neglected the fact that military success was the only sure way to political success, and that European opinion, like so much else in the war, fluctuated with the news from the battlefront. Cotton should therefore have been above all the instrument for achieving military victory through the procurement of essential supplies and weapons from Europe. Instead, it was used in pursuit of a policy which began with a dogma and ended with a mirage. The embargo policy was selected partly because it appeared to demand so little from the Confederate government. But if even this mistaken choice of policy was to have any prospect of success, it needed the active support of an energetic and efficient government, both to channel and coordinate enthusiastic effort at home, and to wage a vigorous and varied diplomatic and propaganda campaign abroad to sweeten this dubious pill for European consumption. The Confederate authorities failed to rise adequately to such a challenge. In any case, a policy of economic sanctions was a strange and unpromising way to win friends. Economic sanctions may be effective as a deterrent or a reprisal against hostile or unwelcome action, but surely not as an inducement to make a public declaration of friendship.

In all its shortcomings King Cotton diplomacy faithfully reflected the blinkered Confederate view of the outside world. In the opinion of Governor Pettus of Mississippi, 'the sovereign state of Mississippi can do a great deal better without England than England can do without her'.[18] The State Department in Richmond remained small-scale and small-minded. With no officially accredited representatives in foreign capitals, it had little of the routine business of international affairs. Its first head, Robert Toombs, carried the Department, he said, in his hat, and doffed that headgear as soon as he could; Judah P. Benjamin, who occupied the post from 1862 to 1865, used it primarily as a base from which to operate as a confidential adviser on all matters to the president. Jefferson Davis himself had little knowledge or understanding of the world at large, and devoted himself mainly to other concerns. The emissaries whom he sent abroad were a curious collection, rarely well-equipped for their task. Of his first trio of emissaries to Europe in 1861, the most prominent was William L. Yancey, outspoken 'fire-eater' of pre-war days, ardent apologist for slavery, and a man unaccustomed to being diplomatic about anything. But even he was a respectable choice in comparison with the egregious John T. Pickett, sent to Mexico in the same year. Later, the vital mission to Britain and France was entrusted to James M. Mason and John Slidell respectively. Slidell was by far the abler and better equipped of the two (although, in his Civil War career, he did not quite live up to his formidable reputation), but he was sent to Paris, when London was the place where the key decisions would be taken. Mason lacked the flexibility of mind and the social sophistication which his task demanded; his tobacco juice was often as ill-directed as his diplomatic moves. Henry Adams thought that Mason and his president had two defects in common: 'Neither could have had much knowledge of the world', and both must have been unconscious of humour.'[19] In the latter stages of the war the long-winded and self-important A. Dudley Mann (one of Yancey's colleagues in 1861) went on a futile mission to the Vatican and sent home an inflated account of papal 'recognition' of the Confederacy. In 1865, when it was much too late, Duncan Kenner, one of the largest slave-owners in Louisiana, was despatched to Europe in a hopeless bid to seek recognition in return for the abolition of slavery. Curiously enough, in contrast to the general ineptitude of its diplomatic representatives abroad, the Confederacy was much better served by some of its agents engaged in other activities in Europe: the resourceful and persevering James D. Bulloch in ship procurement, the efficient Colin J. McRae in purchasing operations, and the ingenious Henry Hotze in the field of propaganda. Hotze's career is one of the success stories of the Confederacy, and his newspaper The Index, published in London, provided copy for many other papers in Britain and elsewhere. Ironically, but characteristically, he was inadequately appreciated and supported in Richmond, and was even criticised for the moderate tone which he adopted in order to appeal to his British audience.

All these examples and others too – like Confederate blunders in Mexico and Canada – illustrate a basic failure in the Southern understanding of the world. For years before the war the South had been building a wall around its perimeter, to protect itself from dangerous agitators and subversive ideas, and now those inside the wall could no longer see over the top, out to what lay beyond. Confederate leaders had no appreciation at all of the context within which European attitudes to the war developed, or the perspective from which European statesmen viewed it. They could not fathom the deep and genuine European antipathy to Negro slavery. British and French notions of national interest or the balance of power were beyond their comprehension, and they simply could not envisage the real connections between domestic pressures and the making of British and French policy. What they could not understand, they resented bitterly, and naïve optimism collapsed into sour disillusionment. Long before secession, the South had begun to close its ranks and close its mind; now it was convinced that all the world was out of step except itself.

The South desperately needed outside aid, but had few realistic ideas on how to get it. The North, in contrast, needed above all to keep foreign powers out of the war, and rapidly developed the skills and stratagems appropriate to the task. Indeed, not the least of the reasons for the failure of King Cotton diplomacy was the success of the more conventional diplomacy practised by the North. Like their adversaries, the Union leaders were firmly convinced that the war was a matter of consequence to the whole world, completely confident that world opinion would be on their side, and deeply shocked when they found that very often it was not. Whilst Lincoln only occasionally intervened decisively on practical issues of foreign policy, he was pre-eminent among his contemporaries in his appreciation of the world-wide significance of the conflict – the salvation or the loss of the last, best hope of earth. His conception of the war as the testing-ground of democracy reached its mature expression in the Gettysburg address, but it was there from the beginning. In his first message to Congress, on 4 July 1861, he described the issue as not merely a trial of political institutions – the necessity of resisting any attempt to appeal from ballots to bullets – but also a test of a social system:

> This is essentially a people's contest. On the side of the Union, it is a struggle for maintaining in the world, that form and substance of government, whose leading object is, to elevate the condition of men – to lift artificial weights from all shoulders – to clear the paths of laudable pursuit for all – to afford all an unfettered start, and a fair chance, in the race of life.[20]

For their part, Seward and the State Department waged a vigorous propaganda campaign in the struggle to appease European opinion. There was no Union equivalent of Hotze to master-mind the campaign in Europe, but Seward sent a stream of visitors to Britain and France in particular to appeal to this pressure group or that special interest. The list included his New York ally, the political operator *par excellence*, Thurlow Weed; the Catholic Archbishop of New York, John Hughes; the eloquent clergyman, Henry Ward Beecher; the Boston businessman, John Murray Forbes; the distinguished lawyer, William M. Evarts; the former Southern Democrat, Robert J. Walker; and a Negro who had once been Jefferson Davis's coachman. The United States consul in Paris, John Bigelow, played a key part, too, in the propaganda war in France. Seward reached a wider public with leaflets extolling the opportunities provided by the Homestead Act, encouraging potential immigrants, or helping public meetings with resolutions endorsing emancipation. The administration's appointments to the main diplomatic posts in Europe were made for the usual, haphazard mixture of reasons. The distinguished historian, John Lothrop Motley, became minister in Vienna; William L. Dayton was a safe, but undistinguished, appointment as minister in Paris; but, as luck and Seward would have it, Charles Francis Adams became minister in London. The son and grandson of American presidents (who had also both been ministers in London), Adams had impeccable credentials for his vital role, and he more than lived up to them. His coldness and austerity may have prevented him from being a great social success or a prominent public figure, but he scarcely put a foot wrong in all the intricate diplomacy of the war years. He moderated the effects of Seward's occasional excesses, but could be stiff and unyielding when the occasion required. He contrived to establish an effective working relationship with the foreign secretary, Earl Russell, and coped successfully with sporadic outbursts from Palmerston. If not much loved, he was widely respected, and eventually emerged, in his son's happy phrase, as 'a kind of leader of Her Majesty's American Opposition'.[21] He was the right man in the right place at the right time, and he did much to preserve British neutrality and therefore to preserve the American Union.

This was the nub of the matter as far as United States foreign policy was concerned – to make sure that the Civil War remained only a civil war, while rigorously maintaining a blockade, and all the other apparatus, so troublesome to neutrals, of a conflict on the high seas. Seward's pursuit of this objective included the propaganda campaign already discussed, exploitation of legal delays and diplomatic evasions, and a combination of solid defence of basic American rights and interests with a soothing response to legitimate neutral grievances. But his basic strategy was simple and unwavering. It consisted of the plain threat that any move by a foreign power to interfere in the war in such a way as to benefit the Confederacy would mean war, or, at least, the grave risk of war with the United States. Such a policy included a large measure of bluff and bluster, but it worked. Seward knew how to make the most of such hostages to fortune as the British interest in Canada and the French in Mexico, and he understood well how neutrality best served British and French national interest, and how embarrassment at the prospect of appearing as the ally of slavery inhibited both countries. Critics thought that Seward's tough talking was unnecessarily offensive and abrasive. At first sight the Seward who talked wildly in April of reuniting the Union by picking a fight with Spain or France looks like the same Seward who in May dashed off a hectoring despatch which Adams was to read to Russell, and which talked menacingly of war with Britain. Up to a point, no doubt it was, and Lincoln saved Seward from his folly by editing the text, and restricting it to Adams's eyes only. But it also marks the birth of a new Seward who quickly learned that controlled truculence could be a diplomatic asset. Those, like Charles Sumner, who dealt more naturally than Seward in moral absolutes, were still bewildered and upset by his aggressive tone and never understood that it was largely assumed to frighten off any power contemplating recognition of the Confederacy (and partly to rally opinion at home behind the administration). It is interesting that Seward, the champion of compromise and pragmatism at home, adopted a stance of uncompromising defiance abroad, while Sumner, reputedly a rigid dogmatist at home, spoke up for moderation and conciliation abroad. Once his basic theme had become familiar through constant reiteration, Seward proved that he could be flexible as well as tough, resourceful as well as assertive. His conduct of foreign affairs was of a kind which Palmerston and Russell could understand if not always appreciate; as one historian has put it, they 'took Northern threats more seriously than Southern assurances'.[22] By keeping the South in quarantine, Seward established an essential pre-condition of ultimate Union victory.

5. During its first year, wartime diplomacy revolved around opposing definitions of the nature of the conflict, and of the rights and obligations of both belligerents and neutrals. The Union insistence that there was in fact no war at all, but merely an internal rebellion, has been discussed elsewhere, but nowhere were its implications more important (or more confusing) than in international relations. It followed logically from this premise that the so-called Confederate government had no standing whatsoever, either at home or abroad, that foreign powers had no right to bestow any kind of recognition or acceptance on such a régime, let alone assist it or intervene actively on its behalf, and that the proper neutral stance was one of sympathetic understanding for the difficulties of the United States in coping with an evil conspiracy within its own domain. Even a well-disposed neutral would have found such a course hard to follow, especially when the conflict grew to the scale of a major war, whatever its theoretical status might be, and, in some respects, as in refraining from executing all prisoners as traitors, the North did not itself adhere strictly to the logic of its own position. For neutrals, the problem would have been acute enough if the war had been fought exclusively on American soil, but once it spread to the high seas it became impossible – and, ironically, it was the Union government which did most to make it so.

In April 1861 neither North nor South was immediately ready to wage a major war on land or sea, but it was easier to make formal declarations of intent regarding maritime rather than land warfare. Within a few days of the fall of Sumter, the Confederate government authorised the issue of letters of marque to privateers who would prey upon Union shipping, and Abraham Lincoln proclaimed a blockade of the Southern ports. The first of these measures produced no significant results at all, and the second took months to become effective. But they immediately confronted neutral nations with awkward questions; whether they liked it or not, blockades and privateers would involve their ships, their goods, their citizens and their interests. Neutral rights on the high seas were an age-old issue. There was a formidable, if inconclusive, body of international law upon the subject, and the major European powers had attempted as recently as the Declaration of Paris of 1856 to agree upon its basic principles. In 1861 Britain was, of course, cast as the major maritime neutral, and what gave a special piquancy to the situation was Britain's past record (and probable future performance), as the great maritime belligerent, trespasser upon neutral rights, and staunch opponent of attempts to extend those rights by law. The result was that, on top of the riddle of when was a war not a war, posed by the North, there came this further confusion caused by the exchange of traditional roles between Britain, the poacher turned gamekeeper, and the United States, the gamekeeper turned poacher. Each could cite against the other precedents which the other had set a half century earlier, when the United States was driven to war with Britain, ostensibly at least in defence of neutral rights. In fact, from 1861 to 1865, each side played a game of bluff and double bluff, and kept in mind both short-term need and long-term interest. The United States sought to defeat the rebels without either fighting Britain or abandoning the long-term American position; Britain sought to protect its citizens and their immediate interests while avoiding involvement in the war, and piling up useful precedents for the future. It was a subtle, intricate and sometimes dangerous game, but the players became very skilful at it, and the delicate balance of short- and long-term interests was one factor among many, on both sides, which helped to prevent constant British–American disputes during 1861–5 from leading to war.

The Northern proclamation of a blockade, and European reactions to it, posed in inescapable form both of these bewildering questions: the legal character of the war, and the ambivalence over neutral rights. A blockade was clearly a weapon of international war between fully-fledged sovereign powers, and it required neutrals to act on that assumption. In other words, from the very beginning, Lincoln and Seward undermined their own legal position. If, as they argued, they were engaged in suppressing a rebellion in states which were still within the Union, they should simply have declared the Southern ports closed. This possibility was considered, and Congress later authorised it, but Seward opposed it and preferred a blockade, on the ground that Britain and France were much less likely to accept the idea of closing the ports, and that a blockade laid down recognised procedures which all neutrals could accept and follow. Seward was, in fact, moving towards the position endorsed by the Supreme Court in 1863, that the conflict had a two-fold character as rebellion and war, and that the

United States government could exercise both sovereign and belligerent rights in dealing with the South. Indeed, Lincoln's proclamation of 19 April 1861 had invoked both 'the laws of the United States and . . . the law of nations'.[23]

The proclamation of a blockade, however, virtually required that neutral countries recognise the belligerent status of both sides in the conflict. Indeed, the logic of the proclamation itself implied that very thing. News of the blockade, and of the Northern intention to treat Southern privateers as pirates, reached Europe hard upon news of the fall of Sumter. The immediate reaction of the British government and parliament was to keep out of trouble, but the blockade and privateering questions needed prompt action. The government moved with almost indecent haste; within a week it had consulted the law officers, despatched naval reinforcements to American waters, concerted action with the French, and decided on a proclamation of neutrality which recognised the belligerent status of the Confederacy (not to be confused of course with full diplomatic recognition). After another week the proclamation was finally published on 14 May, the very day, as it happened, when Charles Francis Adams arrived in London to assume his duties as United States minister. The proclamation acknowledged Southern belligerency, and with it the right to raise loans and supplies abroad, to send out privateers and to exercise all the normal belligerent rights on the high seas. It also recognised the Northern blockade under the usual conditions of international law. France and other powers made similar declarations; to them, as to Britain, this was simply to follow normal procedure, although it was no doubt more than a little disingenuous to expect the United States to accept it cheerfully.

In fact, the American reaction was furious and indignant, a blend, no doubt, of popular misunderstanding of the precise character and meaning of such measures, and confirmation of worst suspicions about British attitudes and intentions. Seward's anger reflected the widespread feeling that the British action was uncalled-for as an interference in a domestic concern of the United States, unwise as an encouragement to Southern rebels to believe that they could achieve an independence impossible without the prospect of foreign aid, and ill-timed both in its undue haste and in the insult which it offered to the newly-arrived American minister. Many Americans professed to believe that this was just the first step towards full diplomatic recognition of the Confederacy. Seward never relaxed his vehement opposition to international (and especially British) recognition of the belligerent status of the Confederacy. He believed that it had been virtually the kiss of life to the Southern cause and that, as long as it lasted, it poisoned relations between Britain, France and the United States. He exploited every opportunity, and used every device, to persuade Britain and France to withdraw their recognition of Southern belligerency at various times during the war, but all to no avail.

As for the Confederacy, although its morale was boosted by the acknowledgement of its belligerent status, it was unhappy about European acceptance of the Union blockade of its ports. International law required that a blockade must be effective in order to be legally acceptable; otherwise a 'paper blockade' could be no more than a cover for virtual piracy. The Confederate government maintained a steady stream of requests to Britain and France to withdraw recognition of the blockade on the grounds of its ineffectiveness. They adduced a variety of evidence to support their contention, and, in the early months of the war at least, they had a real point.[24] Napoleon III was more than once tempted to break the blockade, particularly in order to obtain urgently needed cotton, and, in 1862, Seward hastened to declare open captured Southern ports, including New Orleans, in a not very successful bid to satisfy the French. However, Napoleon III would not act without Britain, and Britain continued to respect the blockade for two reasons in particular. First, the ineffectiveness of the blockade, real or alleged, was being obscured by the Confederate embargo on cotton exports; if, for whatever reason, the South's main export had fallen away to almost nothing, it was not easy to demonstrate that the blockade was a total failure. Ironically, as the cotton embargo was relaxed in 1862-3, the blockade was becoming very much tighter. (This was yet one more example of the confusion of Confederate policy; the efforts of King Cotton's left arm to break the blockade were paralysed by his strong right arm, frantically reaching out for the chimera of full diplomatic recognition.) The second reason for British acceptance of the blockade was more important, and it turned on the double standard of short- and long-term interests by which the British government judged such issues. If a somewhat loose and fallible blockade such as the Union practised in 1861 received international approval, it would set an invaluable precedent which would be of immense advantage to Britain in the future. Nothing could better illustrate the British view than the instructions sent to the ships of the North American squadron to the effect that the Union blockade was to be regarded as effective if there was some kind of force stationed outside the Southern ports which was making some kind of effort to stop vessels passing in and out.

All through 1861 a variety of difficult issues plagued British–American relations. One which greatly aggravated mutual distrust was the attempt of the United States to subscribe to the Declaration of Paris of 1856. That agreement underlined the principle that a blockade must be effective, outlawed privateering, and laid down rules concerning the protection to be afforded to enemy goods under a neutral flag, and neutral goods under an enemy flag. The United States had hitherto refused to accept the Declaration mainly on the ground that it did not go far enough on these latter points. It is possible that Seward – and probable that Adams, in London – was genuine in his desire to subscribe to the Declaration, but it was widely and justifiably suspected that Seward also saw an immediate advantage to be won from such an American change of heart. If the United States accepted all the principles of the Declaration, including the ban on privateering, Britain and France would surely have to withdraw their recognition of Confederate privateers – and, beyond that, Seward hoped, they would have no need to persist in recognising Confederate belligerency. But Seward's ulterior motives did not pass unnoticed in London, and the British government protested that it could scarcely withdraw from a commitment so recently made as the acceptance of Confederate privateering. Earl Russell's conduct of the negotiations was as devious and disingenuous as Seward's. He proposed that both the American belligerents should subscribe to the Declaration, but the United States would have none of that. He suggested that the United States should acknowledge only certain parts of the Declaration, excluding its provisions on blockades and privateers. When Seward insisted on subscribing to the Declaration in full, Russell tacked on a provision that such an agreement in no way affected the situation created by the Civil War. It is hardly surprising that, justifiably or not, the Americans believed that Russell had set a trap for them. The negotiations which dragged on intermittently all summer proved to be as fruitless as they were frustrating, and neither side emerged with much credit or much respect for the other.

Other irritants continued to plague British-American relations. The first Confederate mission to Europe, in search of diplomatic recognition, consisting of William L. Yancey, Pierre Rost, and A. Dudley Mann, was an object of embarrassment to the British government and hawk-like watchfulness on the part of Seward. When they first arrived in May, Russell met them unofficially, but backed down under severe pressure from Seward, and avoided them thereafter. The announcement by the British government that it would refuse to allow either side to bring captured prizes into British ports pleased the North because it hit Southern hopes of privateering. But help for Confederate ships calling at British ports upset the North, although it was quite proper, once belligerent status was granted. The blockade began to cause friction on both sides, despite British willingness to condone it in principle. There was growing resentment in Britain at interference with British ships and normal British trade, and growing American anger at the dominant role of British interests in the business of blockade-running, and the use of British ports in the western hemisphere as bases for such activities. None of these grievances or misunderstandings was enough in itself to pose a serious threat of war between Britain and the United States. But they all maintained a climate in which each side was prepared to believe the worst of the other, and ready to assume that the other was waiting to pick a serious quarrel, if a suitable occasion arose. It came soon enough, not by choice of Lincoln or Seward, Palmerston or Russell, but through the independent action of a cantankerous officer of the United States navy, Charles Wilkes.

6. On 8 November 1861, Wilkes's ship, the *San Jacinto*, fired two shots across the bow of the British mail packet *Trent*, bound from Havana to the Danish West Indian island of St Thomas. After a brief altercation, a boarding party removed from the *Trent* James Mason and John Slidell, two Confederate commissioners bound for Europe. Wilkes had pondered whether he should put a crew aboard the *Trent* herself and bring her into an American port as a prize

for adjudication, but his executive officer, Lieutenant Fairfax, had dissuaded him on the grounds that such a plan would overstretch his own resources, and unduly inconvenience the *Trent*'s passengers. But Wilkes does not seem to have paused long to consider whether he should molest Mason and Slidell at all, although he had no instructions to do so. When the *San Jacinto* arrived back in American waters, Wilkes must have felt confirmed in his judgment by the hero's welcome which he received. The press went wild with delight and even the sober *New York Times* proposed that another Fourth of July be consecrated in honour of Wilkes's deed. The House of Representatives resolved that a special medal be struck for him, and Secretary of the Navy Gideon Welles joined in the general acclaim. Wilkes's action excited such an astonishing popular response because at one stroke it satisfied two deeply felt needs. It slaked the popular thirst for bold, decisive, aggressive action at the end of a dismal year when the Union war effort seemed becalmed and bereft of ideas. It also delighted an audience which was even more eager than usual to applaud anyone who would give a sharp twist to the tail of the British lion. As the days passed, cooler heads began to worry about the consequences, businessmen began to calculate the cost of war with Britain, and the cabinet began to share the anxious second thoughts of the president who feared that Mason and Slidell would prove to be white elephants. There now ensued a tense period of waiting which was bound to last a month or more, while the news of the *Trent* incident travelled to London, and news of the British reaction reached Washington.

In fact, the news reached Britain on 27 November, and it excited as much anger there as jubilation across the Atlantic. No other event of those crowded years aroused quite so much feeling in both countries. In most press and popular reaction it was assumed that the seizure of Mason and Slidell was a deliberate decision of the United States government. It seemed to confirm the worst suspicions of Seward's aggressive policy, and, indeed, to mark the climax of his machinations to provoke a war with Britain. Certainly, it was widely believed in the press, and in Parliament, that war was the almost inevitable outcome. In one respect, at least, the governments in Washington and London shared a common problem: how to reconcile a realistic appraisal of the problem with the clamour of public indignation in their respective countries. It seemed as hard for the one to surrender its captives while saving its face as for the other to demand full satisfaction while preserving the peace. In actual fact, the choices did not prove quite so bleak; this was one of those crises which was solved by decisions which proved more terrible to contemplate than to take.

The British government was not taken completely by surprise by the capture of Mason and Slidell. Indeed, so lacking in secrecy was their departure from Charleston and their presence in Havana, that there is some suspicion (if no more) that their mission was not so much to seek diplomatic recognition in Europe as to embroil Britain in the war by baiting a trap on the high seas. (If so, they could scarcely have hoped for so willing a collaborator as Charles Wilkes.) In any case, Palmerston was so concerned about the possibility of such an incident, especially as a United States warship was lurking in the English Channel, waiting, it was rumoured, to seize the Confederate commissioners, that he sought advice on the matter from the law officers, weeks before he ever heard of Wilkes and the *Trent*. The advice which he received disappointed him, for it suggested that the United States would be perfectly justified in seizing Mason and Slidell, or the ship on which they were travelling. However, when the crisis came, the legal and political position adopted by the British government showed little regard for this unpalatable advice.

The implications of Wilkes's action in international law were complex and confusing. Even among those who condemned his action, there was disagreement on precisely how he had erred. Most modern opinion agrees that Wilkes was wrong to take it upon himself to remove Mason and Slidell from the *Trent* and that, rather than pre-judge the issue in this way, he should have brought the ship itself to a prize court for adjudication. Seward relied heavily on this argument as a face-saving reason for releasing the captives – and yet the legal advice given to Palmerston before the event had made no distinction of this kind. Serious legal doubts hang over other aspects of the incident. It is very uncertain whether persons could ever be treated as contraband, and the prevailing American opinion had always been that civilians certainly could not. Again, the argument that Mason and Slidell were the personification of enemy despatches and therefore liable to seizure conflicted with former American practice which held that despatches were not contraband. More generally, there were grave doubts about any legal right at all to seize anything or anyone from a neutral ship sailing between two neutral ports. The most significant point about the whole legal controversy is that, if Wilkes's action could be justified at all, it was only with the aid of British precedents, while British protests were most strongly supported by the traditional American view. All manner of misleading and irrelevant precedents were quoted in discussion of the case on both sides of the ocean, but some Americans, including Sumner and Lincoln himself, and some Britons, like Cobden and Bright, saw an opportunity to salvage something from the *Trent* affair by trying to commit Britain to a much broader definition of neutral rights than ever before, in return for the release of Mason and Slidell. Lincoln drafted, but never sent, a despatch which proposed settlement of the *Trent* dispute on British terms, provided that 'the determination thus made shall be the law for all future analogous cases, between Great Britain and the United States'.[25] Charles Francis Adams thought that the British were right in principle, but inconsistent with their former views. 'Our mistake is that we are donning ourselves in her cast-off suit, when our own is better worth wearing.'[26] The bifocal lens which both parties used to scrutinise neutral rights during the Civil War were never more in demand than during the *Trent* affair.

Legal technicalities did not detain the British government long in planning its response to news of the seizure of Mason and Slidell. Arrangements were hastily made to send troops to Canada, and naval reinforcements to American waters. Russell penned a set of stiffly-worded instructions to the British minister in Washington, Lord Lyons, but the tone of the despatch was moderated at the suggestion of the Prince Consort, specifically by expressing the hope that Wilkes's action had been unauthorised. (Seward had in fact already made this point clear in a despatch which had not yet reached London.) Russell instructed Lyons to protest against the American violation of international law, and to demand an apology and the release of the prisoners. If those demands were not met, Lyons was to close the legation and withdraw to Canada. However, he was also told to reveal the British demands informally to Seward before presenting them formally and setting a seven-day time limit for an answer. Lyons, who had been stone-walling quietly ever since the crisis first broke in Washington, now played his part well in giving Seward every opportunity to give way gracefully. Seward in fact was already convinced of the need to surrender the two captives, and was looking for ways to persuade the cabinet, and to put the best possible face on things for the benefit of American public opinion. He was greatly helped by the arrival of a French note supporting the British position, which killed any hopes of French support for the United States in the event of war with Great Britain, and removed the possibility, raised in some quarters, of French arbitration of the dispute. The French note also took its stand in defence of neutral rights, in the hope of establishing useful precedents to be quoted against Britain in the future, and this too helped the United States to climb down, without too humiliating a surrender to British pressure.

At crucial cabinet meetings on Christmas Day and the following day, Seward persuaded Lincoln and the cabinet to agree to surrender the captives. Lincoln had invited Charles Sumner to be present, for he set great store by Sumner's advice on foreign policy matters. Sumner had interested the president in the idea of arbitration, but both men now bowed to the necessity of giving up Mason and Slidell, and letters from Sumner's British friends, especially John Bright, helped to push the whole cabinet to the same conclusion. Seward drew up a long despatch which rambled over the various legal issues involved, and which was intended for home consumption rather than to impress Russell and Palmerston. He offered no apology, but the prisoners were freed, and the British government settled for that. Sections of the American press fumed indignantly, but the outcry soon subsided. The British government went to some lengths to discourage a rousing welcome for Mason and Slidell when they at last reached British shores, and in fact their arrival attracted little notice. They may not have known it, but they were never again to come so close to achieving the main diplomatic goals of the Confederacy as they had by languishing in a United States prison. In a sense, their freedom proved to be their greatest failure.

The *Trent* affair was dramatic and highly dangerous in its implications, and it seized the imagination and inflamed the feelings of the public in both Britain and America. But there is a danger of treating it as a uniquely important crisis rather than as one hazardous chapter in a long story – and a danger too of exaggerating the likelihood of war resulting from it. Where both parties talk so much of war, there is a real possibility that it will actually happen. But, in this instance, each side was more intent on frightening rather than fighting the other; each was more ready to believe that the other wanted war than to fire the first shot itself. Each government felt the thunderous protests of its own press and public, but there was little doubt that each could ride out the storm if it chose. As one historian has aptly put it, this was 'a popular, but not necessarily a diplomatic, crisis'.[27] Both governments had very good reasons to avoid war. The United States had not chosen this issue, and at no point did Seward adopt the truculent approach to Britain which he favoured on other occasions. His government had quite enough problems with the war already on its hands. The British government was rightly anxious about the vulnerability of Canada, very conscious of its defence commitments around the world, and deeply suspicious of Napoleon III and the advantage which he might take in Europe or elsewhere of British preoccupation with an American war. The death of the Prince Consort on 14 December had its effect on the public mood; in death as in life, he helped to lower the temperature of the crisis. All in all, the whole affair may have been a little less hazardous than it looked. It is hard to credit that Britain and the United States would ever actually have blundered into war over the unauthorised action of one self-important naval officer, and the fate of two diplomats representing a government which neither power recognised. Perhaps Archbishop Hughes of New York struck just the right note of ambivalence, when he wrote to Seward from Paris while feelings were still running very high. He was praying twice a day, he said, for peace between Britain and the United States, but he also enclosed a plan for making war against Canada.[28] It is often said that slow communications, and the lack of an Atlantic telegraph, helped to prevent a war by giving passions time to cool. But perhaps the reverse is true, and inadequate communications may have caused each government to overestimate the violence of the other's likely reactions. Surprisingly the real loser from the *Trent* incident was the Confederacy. If it could not capitalise on such a golden opportunity, how was the South ever to win the international support it coveted?

7. The *Trent* affair ended on a note of farce. Seward allowed himself the fun of offering transit across Maine for British troops and their supplies, despatched at the height of the crisis to defend Canada, who could not now use the ice-bound St Lawrence. The British took little advantage of Seward's hospitality, and their government was not amused by it. It is often said that the *Trent* incident cleared the air, and ushered in a calmer, less troubled period in British–American relations. This is no more than a half-truth, encouraged by emphasis on the uniqueness of this one event. If there was any change in the diplomatic climate it was probably in making Britain more wary than ever in her dealings (or refusal to deal) with the Confederacy.

But the path of British (or French) neutrality was never easy. There were still numerous hazards which threatened peaceful relations with the United

States. Some of the mines along the road contained as much explosive potential as the *Trent* incident itself, and as the confidence of the United States in its own strength grew, it was less reluctant to detonate some of them. There was, for example, continuing danger in the repercussions of the war upon the immediate neighbours of the belligerents, Canada and Mexico, and that danger was aggravated by Confederate efforts, however unskilful, to exploit it. The most chronic threat came however from the war at sea, where the rights, obligations and interests of neutrals were most directly involved. There were constant problems arising from the blockade and blockade-running, and constant anxiety over further incidents on the high seas. There was the very delicate question of the construction of Confederate warships in British or French yards, and this issue was still capable of creating a major crisis almost two years after the *Trent*. There was also the question of the depredations visited upon American shipping by such vessels built in Britain – and this controversy impaired British– American relations not only during the war but for several years afterwards. Most explosive of all, perhaps, was the possibility that a situation might arise where Britain and France, on their own initiative, might judge that the time was ripe for some kind of mediation or intervention in the conflict.

There were good reasons of self-interest why Britain and France on the one hand and the United States on the other should continue to avoid war with one another. But there was always the chance that folly or anger or pique would upset calculations of interest: that Seward would push the diplomacy of threat and bluff beyond the limit; that Palmerston or Russell or Napoleon III would allow indignation or malice or pride to overcome discretion; that the South would at last succeed in provoking the kind of trouble which would help its cause, or that some new Wilkes would do the job for them. As always, the best real hope of the Confederacy was to achieve such success in the war that Britain and France could not afford *not* to offer recognition. That depended not only on the outcome of battles in Virginia or Mississippi, but on the war at sea. That was the immediate context in which the world saw the war. It is important now to consider the maritime conflict, for it alone can explain the further international ramifications of the struggle.

# Chapter XIV: Oceans, Rivers and Diplomatic Channels

On 8 March 1862 a strange and cumbersome vessel, bearing on its hull what looked like an iron sloping roof, steamed out of the navy yard at Norfolk, Virginia, and bore down upon the wooden ships of the United States blockading fleet in Hampton Roads. The newcomer was the Confederate ironclad *Virginia*, ingeniously and laboriously fashioned out of the United States steam frigate *Merrimack*, scuttled when the Union navy had abandoned Norfolk in the early days of the war. Confederate Secretary of the Navy Mallory had devoted precious labour and materials to the task of creating this new weapon, which, he was not alone in believing, could smash Northern naval superiority, bombard Washington and New York, and virtually win the war. The *Virginia* carried only ten heavy guns, and her other offensive weapon was a cast-iron beak attached to her prow with which she could shatter the wooden walls of her opponents. Her greatest strength lay in the virtual invulnerability to the worst her enemies could do to her, provided by her new shield, consisting of two feet of solid oak, covered by iron plates four inches thick. Her commander was Franklin Buchanan who, like his ship, was a resurrected veteran of the United States Navy, and, as soon as his ship was ready, he took her, and her inexperienced crew, on a trial run in Hampton Roads. If the battle that followed was inconclusive, the trial was, in a broader sense, conclusive beyond a doubt. An era of naval warfare spanning several centuries, and already in its dotage, was finally sentenced to death. Among the early victims of the *Virginia* were ships which Drake and Blake could soon have learned to sail and fight; the *Virginia* herself was one of the heralds of the age of Fisher and Tirpitz.

On the first day of her brief but historic career, the *Virginia* (or *Merrimack*) looked well set to fulfil all the Southern hopes which rode upon her. She steamed through a hail of fire from Union ships and shore batteries, crashed straight into the sailing ship *Cumberland* and sank her with her ram (but lost the ram in the process), and, after pounding another ship, the *Congress*, left her aground and ablaze. Two Union steamships, the *Minnesota* and the *Roanoke*, ran themselves aground in their panicky reactions to the situation. The *Virginia*, intact but not unscathed, and with her commander wounded, returned to base, and prepared to complete her triumph on the morrow. The panic which she had created spread far beyond Hampton Roads. In Washington, Navy Secretary Welles remained calm, but the mercurial Secretary of War Stanton flashed warning messages to New York and Boston to prepare for possible attack, and hastily prepared blockships to be sunk in the Potomac if the *Virginia* chose to threaten Washington. (Later, when the crisis was over, Lincoln referred to these ships as 'Mr Stanton's navy . . . as useless as the paps of a man to a suckling child. There may be some show to amuse the child, but they are good for nothing for service.')[1]

The effective Union answer to the *Virginia* took a very different shape. The North, like the South, had been making frantic if belated preparations to move into the ironclad era. Out of the confusion had so far emerged one new and revolutionary ship, the brainchild of the Swedish-born John Ericsson. Once his strange design was accepted, the vessel was built with incredible speed. Its keel was laid on 25 October 1861; it was launched on 30 January 1862 – and it stayed afloat to the surprise of sceptics among the spectators. Ericsson's *Monitor*, as it was called, was a much smaller vessel than the *Merrimack*. Its ironclad hull was to be almost completely submerged; the only clearly visible features of the ship were a small pilot-house and a revolving gun-turret which carried the *Monitor's* sole armament, two eleven-inch Dahlgren guns. It says much for the bold vision of Welles and Lincoln that they recognised the potential of this bizarre little craft, and gave top priority to its construction. On 6 March Welles ordered the *Monitor* to proceed from New York to Washington. Late in the afternoon of 8 March, as she moved into the entrance to Chesapeake Bay, her crew heard the sound of distant guns, in Hampton Roads, thirty miles away, and she altered course in that direction. Her arrival in the nick of time was an amazing stroke of luck for the Union navy, and brought a totally unexpected end to Confederate euphoria.

When the *Virginia* sallied forth in the early light of 9 March to reap the full rewards of her first day's fighting, she encountered this new, diminutive and extraordinary opponent. For the next four hours, the two ships hammered away at each other, often at very close range, but neither suffered any crippling damage. Their armour plating resisted even direct hits at point blank range; their crews suffered more from the constant din and choking fumes than anything else. Each ship made an unsuccessful attempt to ram the other. The *Virginia* briefly ran aground at one point, and the *Monitor* twice retired to shallow water to bring up more ammunition into her turret. On the second occasion the *Virginia*, perhaps thinking she had won the day, broke off the engagement and retired to Norfolk. The first battle of the ironclads was over. It ended in a stalemate which, like so many drawn battles on land, worked more to the advantage of the North than the South. Neither ship survived this historic encounter for long. Two months later, the *Virginia* was destroyed by the Confederates before they evacuated Norfolk as a result of McClellan's peninsular campaign. Before the year 1862 was out, the *Monitor* sank in a storm off Cape Hatteras. In their premature demise, as in their brief lives, the two ironclads had indicated the problems as well as the possibilities of a new age of naval warfare.

1. The clash between *Virginia* and *Monitor* brought into sharp focus most of the main features of the Civil War at sea. Even more dramatically than on land, the struggle came at a time of rapid transition. Not one but several simultaneous revolutions were taking place, and the techniques and tactics of centuries were being rendered obsolete in a few short years. The transition from sail to steam was already well advanced before 1861, although most steamships could still proceed under sail too – not merely because of doubts about the reliability of steam-power, but also to extend cruising range and reduce costs. By the 1860s the screw propeller was rapidly replacing the old side-wheels, and giving much improved performance. The use of iron plates to protect warships was a more recent development, pioneered by the French in the late 1850s; by 1860 the British were scrambling to catch up. Armour plating was closely connected with – and largely a response to – developments in naval ordnance. The rifled gun, firing explosive shells, transformed the hitting power of warships, and the evolution of the revolving gun turret was now carrying the process a stage further. Defensive armour and new defensive methods were the only possible answer.

The American Civil War, then, came at a time when the oceans were about to be dominated by a new kind of warship, unthinkable a generation earlier, steam-powered, propeller-driven, armour-plated, firing explosive shells from rifled guns mounted in revolving turrets. But the leaders in this naval revolution were the French and the British; the Americans had been left far behind. In 1861 the United States navy did not have a single ironclad ship. Between 1854 and 1858 the United States Congress had authorised nineteen new wooden steam warships (against the opposition only of those who saw no need for new ships at all), and, as late as February 1861, Congress voted funds for seven wooden screw sloops, but no ironclads. Lack of any obvious or credible outside threat had soothed concern over naval preparedness. Moreover, the United States navy lived in a strait-jacket of tradition, conservatism, and the sacred principle of seniority. Younger and abler officers resigned in frustration and despair; the higher ranks were filled by men who were already old and fixed in their ways before new-fangled notions of steam and iron and rifled guns came to plague them. When the Civil War came, the navy was small and ill-prepared for any kind of conflict.

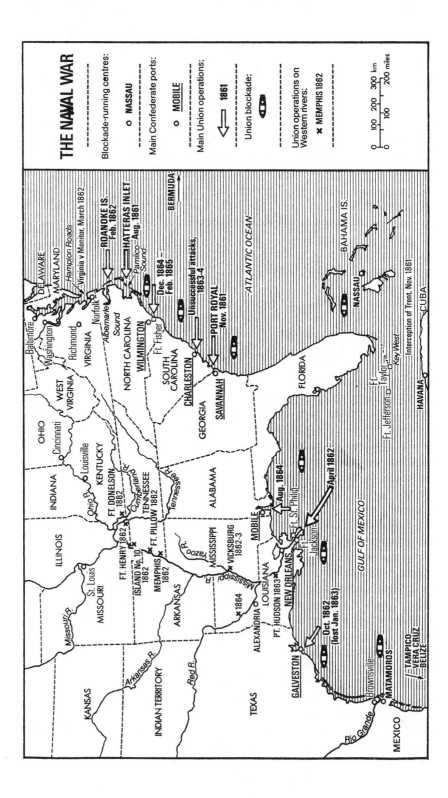

# THE NAVAL WAR

Blockade-running centres: ----

o  NASSAU

Main Confederate ports: ----

o  MOBILE

Main Union operations: ----

⟶ 1861

Union blockade: ----

Union operations on
Western rivers: ----

✕ MEMPHIS 1862

0  100  200  300 km
0   100   200 miles

At a time of rapid transformation there could well be advantages to the side which was unencumbered by tradition and an established, backward-looking service, and which might hope to upset the odds by exploiting new and revolutionary methods.

Such were the thoughts of the men who inspired the Confederate naval effort – and who produced the *Virginia* as one of the first fruits of their resourcefulness and fertile imagination. The Confederate Secretary of the Navy, Stephen Mallory, grasped the essential point from the beginning. He could not compete on level terms with the actual, far less the potential, naval strength of the North. But, when naval warfare was in a state of flux, he could rely on ingenuity, inventiveness, unorthodoxy and bold adoption of new weapons and new methods to outmanoeuvre Northern power. His enemy was not so much the existing naval resources of the North as its productive capacity. Any attempt to out-produce the North was futile; the only available answer to numbers was novelty. Mallory put his faith not only in ironclads, but in specially designed commerce raiders to sweep Northern shipping from the seas. His navy was a pioneer, too, in the use of mines (or 'torpedoes' as they were then called) which proved the most effective defensive weapon at its disposal. Its experiments with submarines began with a series of costly disasters, but eventually scored a major 'first' in naval history, when the tiny submarine *Hunley*, driven by a propeller cranked by hand by its eight-man crew, sank the U.S.S. *Housatonic* with a 'torpedo' outside Charleston harbour on 17 February 1864. The *Hunley*, which had already killed four crews in earlier trials, perished with her victim.

This was but one reminder of the fact that technological advance and innovations in weaponry inevitably brought teething troubles. The submarine was lethal to the men who tried to use it. Mines, like explosive shells, were often unreliable. Steam-power demanded ample coal supplies, and coaling stations at strategic points. New forms of propulsion and new methods of ship construction raised new problems of repair and maintenance. Revolving turrets posed new problems in naval gunnery. There were, simply, more things to go wrong. Makeshift miracles like the *Virginia* and hastily developed new inventions like the *Monitor* had serious flaws which belied both the exuberant hopes of their makers and the exaggerated fears of their opponents. Confidence or anxiety about the ability of the *Virginia* to bombard Washington or New York overlooked simple facts. The ship's engines were unreliable and grossly inadequate for her greatly increased weight. She was ponderous and clumsy and took at least half an hour to turn round. She was quite unseaworthy in the open water she would face on the voyage to New York, and too large to sail up the Potomac to Washington. She was simply not capable of straying far from Hampton Roads. For her part, the *Monitor* had shown in her trip from New York that she was very unstable even in a moderate sea, and the waves which washed over her threatened her crew, if not with drowning, then with asphyxiation through dowsing her fires. The battle between the two ships revealed their limitations as well as their strength. All this was more ominous for the South than the North. Most ominous of all was the fact that, while the Confederacy could never adequately replace the *Virginia*, the Union could build numbers of new, improved *Monitors*. The South might win a head start but it could scarcely retain a monopoly of new weapons. The South might produce one model of some novel device; the North could mass-produce copies of them.

The unconventional methods of the Confederate navy were, however, well-attuned to its distinctive tasks. Since the Confederacy possessed virtually no merchant marine of its own, its navy had no burden of ocean-wide protection or support. Its main tasks were coastal and river defence, the disruption of enemy commerce and the breaking of the enemy blockade. For these purposes novel weapons and a small number of powerful, custom-built ships, might achieve a great deal. If, in the process, they succeeded in dragging important neutrals into the conflict, so much the better. Naval strategy and diplomacy went hand in hand during the Civil War. This applied equally to the North, but in its case the marriage of the two was always more likely to break down. Strategy and diplomacy shared a common objective: to seal the Confederacy off completely from the outside world. The navy's role could be defined with equal simplicity: to enforce an economic blockade of the South and to cooperate with the army in operations on the coasts and rivers of the Confederacy. The difficulty was that the naval power applied to this task threatened the diplomatic objective of political isolation of the enemy – for nothing was more certain than that the imposition of a blockade and all the other manifestations of war on the high seas would create crises with the neutral nations which the politicians were desperately anxious to keep out of the war. It was a paradoxical situation. The naval policy upon which the one belligerent came to rely so heavily constantly threatened to undermine the foreign policy which it pursued so single-mindedly. The other belligerent had to rely on the most slender naval resources to stimulate or provoke the foreign intervention which it sorely needed. The war at sea, and the blockade in particular, revealed another paradox. The North had a strong maritime tradition, and acquired a large navy, but its maritime base was quite restricted; barely half its states had a coast-line. The South had a much weaker maritime tradition, and hardly any navy at all, and yet it had a long ocean front of three and a half thousand miles. Nine of the eleven states of the Confederacy had a coast-line, and all nine were subjected during the war not merely to the blockade but to naval bombardment and amphibious attack. These operations led to the dispersal of already inadequate resources, and the loss of large stretches of territory and one major port after another; they also struck heavy blows at Confederate morale by bringing the war home to people who lived far from the main theatres of land war. Southern improvisation could never completely cover Southern vulnerability.

2. The blockade was the central fact of the war at sea. Its enforcement was the unexciting but vital routine task of the Union navy. In this sense, the duel of *Monitor* and *Virginia* was untypical of the war as a whole, for this was a struggle

of very few, dramatic ship-to-ship encounters. Unless and until Mallory could put some ironclads into service, the blockaders would rarely be molested by enemy warships. The Confederate ships which did put to sea – commerce raiders like the *Alabama* – made it their business to evade the Union navy. One of their objectives, it is true, was to draw enemy ships away from blockading duties, but the strong will and inflexible priorities of Gideon Welles foiled them. He never faltered in his resolve that the blockade must come first. Mallory's attempts to create a diversion and Welles's fixity of purpose both showed good judgment, although both were severely criticised at home, but Welles had strength and time on his side.

When the blockade of Southern ports was first proclaimed in the immediate aftermath of Fort Sumter, it was little more than an act of faith. The navy was required to keep watch on 3,500 miles of coast, riddled with bays and inlets, and much of it protected by an outer line of sea islands and sandbanks which gave ample cover at least to small coastal craft. On the other hand, the number of ports capable of coping with any significant quantity of traffic was very limited: Wilmington, Charleston and Savannah on the Atlantic coast, Mobile, New Orleans and Galveston on the Gulf of Mexico. However, even the task of blockading these widely scattered ports was far beyond the powers of the United States navy in 1861. At that time it had only forty-two vessels in commission, and only a handful of those were in home waters. (One of the problems of fighting a civil war was that American sailors knew the coasts of Mexico or west Africa better than the shores of the Carolinas or Texas.) However, Welles quickly established an Atlantic and a Gulf Blockading Squadron, and soon divided the former into two. Initially, a force of fourteen ships guarded the whole Atlantic coast, and, as its only base was at Hampton Roads, the ships spent much of their time travelling to and fro for supplies and maintenance. It took much longer to organise any kind of blockading force at all in the Gulf. Meanwhile, Welles, aided by his energetic Assistant Secretary, Gustavus V. Fox, embarked on a hectic programme of ship procurement. Orders for new vessels were placed wherever yards could fulfil them, and old naval vessels were recommissioned wherever possible. A motley assortment of merchant ships was commandeered, fitted with a few guns, and pressed into blockading service. In the emergency, quality was sacrificed to quantity, and the North was much more sluggish than the South in addressing itself to the question of ironclads. Not until August 1861 did Welles appoint a board to investigate this issue, or advertise for offers to build ironclad ships.

The blockading force grew rapidly. By the end of 1861 the strength of the navy had risen to 264 ships and 22,000 men. (By the time the war ended, the number of vessels had risen to 670, and men to nearly 60,000.) But many of the difficulties of blockading still remained. Many of the vessels used were quite unsuited to the task, too slow to pursue blockade-runners, too deep in draft to operate in shallow inshore waters, too limited in cruising range to stay on station for long periods. Even the rapidly gowing resources of the navy were still overstretched. Apart from the forces stationed off Confederate ports, it was thought necessary to keep watch on the flourishing centres of the blockade-running business which grew up in the Caribbean. Other ships were from time to time deployed in chasing Confederate raiders across the oceans of the world, and others again lurked off the British and French coasts, waiting to pounce on Confederate ships under construction in foreign yards, or raiders seeking shelter in European ports.

Unquestionably, the blockade became steadily tighter as the war progressed, especially as Union forces captured or sealed off several of the major Southern ports. On the other hand, the business of blockade-running also became more skilful, more organised, and more professional as time passed. The question of the overall effectiveness of the blockade has been endlessly debated, but cannot be definitively answered. Much of the argument turns on questions of definition. A blockade which may not be 'effective' enough to satisfy purist interpretations of international law may yet be 'effective' enough, economically and strategic-ally, to do severe damage to the enemy – and the Union effort of 1861–5 almost certainly falls into this category. If, in order to be effective, a blockade must be completely watertight, the Union navy fell far short of the required standard. On the other hand, it mounted a consistent and cumulative campaign to interdict, or at least impede, the movement of goods in and out of Southern ports.

There is no truly satisfactory criterion for measuring the effectiveness of such a blockade. A count of the number of vessels attempting to pass through it, and the proportion of them which succeeded, is of course useful, but the figures are not always reliable, and they overlook the vital question of the capacity of the ships concerned. Small coastal vessels could slip through the blockade more easily than large ocean-going craft, and the specially-designed fast blockade-runners which took over more and more of the traffic were inevitably of limited capacity. On the other hand, attempts to measure the volume of merchan-dise passing through the blockade are extremely difficult, again because of inadequate statistics, and the difficulty of making meaningful comparison with the pre-war trade of the South. The evidence of many contemporary observers – not only Southerners, but foreign traders, and foreign consuls in the South and in the West Indies – suggests evasion of the blockade on the grand scale. Yet other Southern observers – the diarist Mrs Chesnut, for example – were be-moaning the dire effects of the blockade, even in the first year of the war.[2] One modern historian, straining every nerve to prove the ineffectiveness of the blockade, and the wickedness of the British government in tolerating it, offers the rough estimate that in 1861 not more than one blockade-running vessel in ten was captured; in 1862 not more than one in eight; in 1863 not more than one in four; in 1864 not more than one in three; in 1865 one in two. The average for the whole war, he puts at one in six, and a more recent estimate suggests that 86 per cent of runs through the blockade were successful. If 1,500 blockade-runners were captured, it is argued, there must have been at least seven or eight thousand successful evasions.[3] These estimates, interesting as they are, may prove rather less than their makers intend. Most opinion would agree that in 1861, and even in 1862, the blockade was as leaky as a colander, but these figures suggest that, from mid-war, it was a formidable obstacle, to be challenged only at considerable risk. There can be no figures, either, to show the number of potential cargoes lost to the Confederacy by the deterrent effect of the blockade. Beyond doubt, several hundred thousand bales of cotton were exported through the blockade during the war, and large quantities of desperately needed supplies were brought in – up to 600,000 small arms, nearly two million pounds of saltpetre, 1,500,000 pounds of lead, 600,000 pairs of boots, for example.[4] But such quantities never sufficed, and there were times when the loss of ships to the blockaders created desperate supply crises for the armies at the front. In a society peculiarly vulnerable to economic warfare, even a faulty blockade took a heavy toll, caused or aggravated many shortages and considerable distress, raised prices sky high, sapped civilian morale, absorbed too much of the energy and enterprise of the country, and finally permitted it to survive painfully for four years but not to win its permanent independence. Whether or not it should have satisfied the legal pundits and the interested neutral parties, the blockade proved its worth to those who imposed it. It did not win the war but it established one of the conditions of eventual victory.

Blockade-running grew rapidly during the war from an opportunist attempt to make a quick profit into a sophisticated and lucrative business – and finally and belatedly into an elaborate Confederate government operation. The centres of the business were in places like Nassau, Bermuda, Havana, Belize, Tampico, Vera Cruz, and even Halifax, Nova Scotia, where the goods carried from Europe (or even from the United States) were transferred to the specially built blockade-runners in return for cotton, which they had brought out from Wilmington or Charleston or Galveston. The blockade-runners were low, sleek, fast, quiet ships, drably painted, and burning anthracite which was almost smokeless. The shipyards of Clydeside, for example, made a handsome profit out of producing them, and the men who owned and sailed them could make spectacular fortunes out of their hazardous work. A ship could pay for itself and yield its owners a handsome profit out of, say, two round trips between Wilmington and Nassau. A successful captain could earn up to £1,000 for a month's work, and his crew and the pilot who guided him in and out of port also made large sums, which they supplemented by profiteering in goods which they sold on their own account. The business was dominated by foreign and especially British interests. Many of the ships were British-built, they sailed from British West Indian ports, they supplied the Confederacy with British goods, and they were manned by predominantly British crews and skippered by British masters – some of them officers on leave from the Royal Navy, some scions of noble families, and some, like Tom Taylor from Liverpool, young merchant adventurers, eagerly and successfully in pursuit of a quick fortune. If their exorbitant prices and profits scarcely endeared them to their Confederate customers, their whole business scarcely endeared them to the government of the United States, which accused the British authorities of conniving at the efforts of its citizens to aid and abet America's domestic foes. Some of the blockade-runners made repeated journeys in and out of blockaded ports. The Clyde-built *Robert E. Lee* made twenty trips in less than a year, and the *Ad-Vance*, owned by the government of North Carolina, made over thirty trips altogether. Other vessels, of course, paid the penalty much more quickly for plying their risky trade.

Private enterprise blockade-running was profitable, but the Confederacy was not reaping enough of the reward. Much of the merchandise imported consisted of luxury goods which combined the virtues of small bulk and high price, but watches, jewellery, perfumes and silks were not conspicuously beneficial to the Confederate war machine. But the South was missing out in still more serious ways. A bale of cotton delivered in Europe was worth four or five times the price which it would fetch in the Southern states. As long as the government sold cotton to blockade-running merchants at the lower price, it was denying itself the lion's share of profits which it could have used to buy weapons and supplies abroad. Yet the Confederate authorities were slow to assert any control over blockade-running. In part, their reluctance reflected the modest expectations of their role which they and others shared, and the administrative shortcomings under which they laboured. But it also reflected a much more culpable attitude, stemming like so much else from their unrealistic view of the world. They were so determined to use cotton as a diplomatic weapon that they delayed far too long in mobilising it to exchange for vital supplies. They were, too, so intent on demonstrating that the blockade was totally ineffective, that they shrank from participation in an organised campaign to evade it, for fear that this would be tantamount to recognition of its real impact. Some individual agents of the government took matters into their own hands; for example, Josiah Gorgas, head of the Ordnance Bureau, organised his own blockade-running activities to meet the pressing needs of the army.

At last, in 1863, the Davis administration stepped into the business. The War Department acquired some steamers directly, took a controlling interest in others, and appointed Thomas L. Bayne to coordinate the supply of cotton for export. In August the Confederate authorities took power for the first time to commandeer half the outbound cargo space on blockade-runners, and to take first option on half the incoming cargo. They resisted the temptation to take over the export trade completely, on the ground that the blockade-runners would not work for shipping fees alone. In February 1864 an act of Congress gave the government wide powers over blockade-running and another measure banned the importation of a long list of non-essential goods. The government established a Bureau of Foreign Supplies, under Bayne, to manage the collection and export of cotton. But government regulations created too much red tape in some places and left too many loopholes in others, and neither exports nor imports were sufficient to meet urgent need. The best answer to the problem lay in a larger fleet of government-owned blockade-runners, and new ships were purchased in Europe in the last year of the war. By this time, at last, the Confederacy had the makings of an effective and coordinated policy for foreign supply: Bayne's Bureau to organise cotton exports, McRae's centralised control of purchasing in Europe, and a large measure of government control over the traffic through the blockade. But it had taken an unconscionably long time to arrive at such a scheme, and administrative inadequacy still weakened its operation. It also aroused the bitter hostility of private vested interests, and of state governors who had long engaged profitably in the blockade-running business. Indeed, in the later stages of the war, only Davis's veto saved government regulation of blockade-running from a congressional attempt to quash it. The whole story adds but one more verse to the Confederate theme song of too little and too late – and too much destructive opposition to policies which were dictated by common sense and the common good.

If British companies and British citizens prospered through their efforts to break the blockade, the British government chose not to be impressed by their demonstration that the blockade was less than fully effective. Instead, it cherished the precedent which the United States was setting, and, while putting up more than a token fight in defence of British interests when complex issues of neutral rights arose, it happily stored away for future reference the actions, arguments and decisions of the United States as a maritime belligerent. As always, technological change and new methods of waging war were outmoding the precedents of international law. The Civil War situation was rich in possibilities of new controversy. In pursuit of its prime national interest – the defeat of the Confederacy – the United States was driven to adopt more and more practices which it had wholeheartedly condemned in the good old days of self-righteous neutrality. It exerted control over British ships sailing from United States ports for notorious blockade-running centres like Nassau, with cargoes which, it was suspected, were ultimately destined for the Confederacy. It infringed neutral territorial waters in pursuit of blockade-runners. Its warships waited outside neutral ports to catch their prey, or even waited inside neutral harbours and pursued suspected ships when they left. Its conduct of search and seizure operations inevitably provoked allegations of illegality, undue harshness, or maltreatment of neutral citizens. It interfered with trade by neutral ships between neutral ports, and this caused the most serious difficulties of all.

The problem was to find some legal justification for interference with neutral vessels plying between, for example, Liverpool and Nassau, but carrying cargo which was eventually to be delivered to Wilmington or Charleston. The United States had recourse to the doctrine of continuous voyage, enunciated by Britain in an earlier age, resisted by traditional American arguments, and generally ignored in the pre-Civil War decades. The doctrine rested on the principle that a person had no right to do indirectly what he was forbidden to do directly. A call at an intermediate port did not break the continuity of the voyage, and the vessel and cargo concerned could be seized and taken to a prize court for adjudication. The problem was difficult enough in the case of ports like Nassau and Bermuda, and one case in particular, involving the British ship *Springbok*, caused much ill-feeling in 1863. A New York prize court condemned the captured vessel and its cargo, and, despite some outcry from press and public opinion, the British government eventually accepted this ruling, because it served long-term British interests. Ironically, after the war was over, the United States Supreme Court declared that the ship, though not its cargo, should have been freed.

The whole issue became vastly more complicated and dangerous in the case of trade which passed through the Mexican port of Matamoros, on the south bank of the Rio Grande. Before the Civil War, Matamoros was a sleepy little port where the arrival of a single ship was a notable event. During the war it was a centre of frenzied activity, as ships queued up to unload their cargoes, which were then ferried across the river to Brownsville, Texas, in return for cotton. Many of the ships involved belonged to Britain or other neutrals, but many, too, came from the northern United States. This Mexican back door to the Confederacy threatened to make a farce of the blockade, but it was almost impossible for the United States to close it firmly. The most effective counter, as Seward urged, would have been Union occupation of the Texan side of the Rio Grande frontier, but it was not until October 1863 that General Banks succeeded in taking Brownsville, and the Union garrison had to be withdrawn in June 1864. In any case, its presence had not stopped the traffic across the frontier but merely deflected it further west. However, Grant's Vicksburg campaign of 1863, by splitting the Confederacy, did deprive Matamoros of much of its value to the main eastern part of the Confederacy. Meanwhile, the Union navy had been striving to plug this major leak in the blockade. There was no legal warrant for the formal blockade of a neutral port – and the treaty which had ended the Mexican war of 1848 expressly forbade either the United States or Mexico to blockade the mouth of the Rio Grande. But in fact Union attempts to impede trade with Matamoros amounted to an informal blockade, and awkward legal and diplomatic issues were raised by several seizures of neutral ships.

Most important of these was the case of the British ship *Peterhoff*, carrying a cargo of equipment for the Confederate army, seized by a Union warship in February 1863, and condemned by a prize court in July. Despite the angry protests of British press and public, the Palmerston ministry kept a cool head, and accepted the prize court decision as a valuable precedent, which not merely confirmed the doctrine of continuous voyage but extended it to cover goods which completed their journey, not by sea, but across a land frontier. As in the *Springbok* case, the Supreme Court reversed the prize court decision concerning the ship, but not its cargo, after the war. Indeed, one of Seward's main tactics in handling all disputes of this kind was to rely on the law's delays and confusions, and to avoid clear-cut statements of legal principle, so as to keep neutral traders in doubt about the risks involved in the Matamoros trade. The deterrent effect of such uncertainty was often the best available device to restrict the flow of goods across the Rio Grande, for shippers found it difficult to obtain insurance for their cargoes while the legal issues remained unresolved.[5]

All in all, the emergency of civil war drove the United States to rewrite its interpretation of the international law of the sea. It insisted on the effectiveness of what was, at the outset, a palpably ineffective blockade; it asserted rights of search and seizure in a way which had been anathema half a century earlier; it borrowed hitherto uncongenial theories like the doctrine of continuous voyage, and stretched them to new limits. All these things were done in the name of urgent national interest at a time of exceptional crisis. They were accepted by Britain for equally good reasons of national interest which were much less urgent and in no way exceptional. This was one reason why these highly sensitive questions of neutral rights never seriously threatened to cause a British–American war. The other reason was that both parties were always anxious to avoid serious trouble. Seward used the threat of war as a vital diplomatic weapon, but on these specific issues he was adroit rather than aggressive, inclined to procrastinate rather than to provoke. The British government, too, combined a decent defence of the rights of its citizens with discretion in its playing of the unaccustomed role of innocent neutral. The British naval presence in the Atlantic or the Gulf of Mexico was deployed as an adjunct to diplomacy rather than a harbinger of war. If the blockade of the South became steadily tighter as the war continued, that was partly because the Union navy made it so; it was also because Britain preferred to accept the consequences of Northern attempts to show that it was effective rather than the logic of Southern protests that it was not.

3. There was much tedium and little glory in the job of enforcing the blockade. But there was more opportunity for the Union navy to steal the headlines by its role in combined operations with the army against various points on the Southern coast. These were not of course simply glory-hunting escapades, although they more than once gave Northern morale a boost at a time when news of the land war was distinctly bleak. But the main purpose of these operations was to make the blockade more effective, and to further the war of attrition against Southern capacity and will to resist.

From the outset, the navy was intimately involved in operations on the Virginia front. A hastily assembled collection of river steamers was dubbed the Potomac Flotilla, and given the task of protecting the river approach to the capital, although it could not dislodge the Confederate batteries down-stream near Aquia Creek. The naval squadron in Chesapeake Bay was not merely engaged in blockading Richmond and Norfolk but was also essential to McClellan's peninsular strategy. The navy had to control the York and James rivers, and protect the army's water-borne supplies, but, in fact, cooperation between General McClellan and Flag Officer Goldsborough was never what it should have been. The Confederates had relied heavily on the threat of the

*Virginia* to guard the James river, but even after it had been neutralised and later eliminated, the Union navy did not have its own way entirely. In May 1862 a force including the *Monitor* got within a few miles of Richmond but was beaten back by Confederate guns at Drewry's Bluff. With the abandonment of McClellan's campaign in August 1862, the navy returned to more routine duties in the area until Grant's army closed in on Richmond in 1864.

In the early months of the war the blockade of Richmond and Norfolk was by-passed by small ships using Pamlico and Albemarle Sounds in North Carolina, and the Dismal Swamp canal as a back entrance to those cities. In August 1861 the Union army and navy launched the first of their combined amphibious operations to close this loophole. Their target was Hatteras Inlet, where the Confederates had built fortifications to protect the ocean end of the route. Ben Butler's troops were able to take the enemy positions; a permanent garrison was left there, and Hatteras Inlet became a useful blockading base. In February 1862 a new joint expedition under Flag Officer Goldsborough and General Burnside greatly extended the Union foothold on the North Carolina coast, and captured Roanoke Island. It posed further threats to the rear gateways of Norfolk and Richmond, and the Union command might profitably have launched larger-scale operations in this area, had McClellan not recalled Burnside to take part in the peninsular campaign. Meanwhile, back in November 1861, the most ambitious amphibious operation yet mounted was launched against a target further down the Confederate coast, Port Royal in South Carolina, between Charleston and Savannah. The main object here was to secure a safe and sheltered base for the blockading fleet on the South Atlantic coast, and Port Royal Sound offered an ideal anchorage. Flag Officer Samuel F. DuPont led a force of nine warships and over sixty transport and supply ships, carrying 17,000 troops under Thomas W. Sherman. Once again, the Confederate defences were quite inadequate to beat off such a formidable force. On 7 November DuPont's ships overwhelmed the forts which guarded Port Royal Sound, and the tiny force of Confederate river gunboats could offer no resistance at all. In the months that followed, DuPont's ships occupied islands and other points along the Georgia and Florida coasts. All in all, in the first year of the war, Union amphibious operations had taken over long stretches of the South Atlantic coast, and exposed the vulnerability of the Confederacy's salt-water perimeter.

By spring 1862 the Union navy was ready to reach for a much more spectacular prize, this time on the Gulf coast – nothing less than the largest city and major port of the Confederacy, New Orleans. Plans for such an attack from the Mississippi Delta had been under discussion for some time, but their execution was delayed by respect for the formidable natural obstacles, difficulties of organisation and snags in army–navy cooperation. The Confederates placed an almost blind faith in the natural defences of New Orleans and confidently expected to do to the Yankees in 1862 what Andrew Jackson had done to the British in 1815. The general opinion was that the city was much more open to attack from up-stream than from the delta. But such calculations reckoned without the ingenuity, doggedness and sheer daring which Flag Officer David Glasgow Farragut brought to his task. Having hauled his fleet of seventeen ships over the bars at the delta mouths, the Union naval commander prepared to run past the 115 heavy guns of Forts Jackson and St Philip which guarded the river some ninety miles below New Orleans itself. Schooners carrying mortars were towed into position to bombard the forts, and a gunboat eventually succeeded in breaking the barrier of hulks and logs which barred the river at Fort Jackson. In the early hours of 24 April, Farragut's ships ran past the forts in face of a tremendous pounding, fought off the desperate attacks of Confederate gunboats, rams and fire-rafts, and headed up-stream for New Orleans. Next day, under a pall of smoke from burning cotton bales and blazing ships, Farragut put a landing party ashore to claim the city, and, a week later, Butler's troops took over the task of permanent occupation. Farragut's dramatic success had slammed shut the South's historic gateway to the world, and now opened new prospects of Union penetration up the Mississippi. It was the most resounding Union victory anywhere in the first half of the war.

Indeed, it was to be two years more before the navy (again under Farragut's leadership) was to achieve anything like a comparable success in its assaults on major Confederate ports. In October 1862 a small naval force took Galveston in Texas, but on New Year's Day 1863 a Confederate counter-attack recaptured the town, together with its newly arrived garrison, in one of the more humiliating minor setbacks suffered by Union arms during the war. On the Atlantic coast, the Union navy, urged on from Washington, expended a great deal of effort in unavailing attempts to take Charleston. The understandable craving to smite the Southern rebellion in its birthplace reflected psychological rather than strategic need, and produced only frustration for the North. The rich defensive opportunities offered by Charleston's geographical situation had been ably exploited by the Confederates with forts and batteries, mines and booms, and even makeshift ironclads and highly experimental submarines. Admiral DuPont maintained a tight blockade outside the harbour, although even that task was difficult enough, and two of his ships suffered an embarrassingly rough handling from the Confederate ironclads early in 1863. DuPont insisted on waiting for the ironclads which he had been promised before attempting to enter the harbour itself. At last, on 7 April 1863, DuPont's flotilla of nine ironclads (including seven Monitors) steamed towards the harbour entrance. Held up by the boom across the channel, they milled around in confusion and were pounded by the guns of Sumter and the other forts. After receiving over 400 hits (but suffering only one fatal casualty) they retired in disarray. General Hunter's 12,000 troops on Folly Island, five miles away, were never involved in the engagement. In July DuPont was replaced by John A. Dahlgren, presidential confidant and renowned ordnance expert, and Hunter gave way to Quincy A. Gillmore. The new team settled down to a war of attrition, and hammered away for two months at Fort Wagner on Morris Island. The

Confederates finally abandoned it early in September, but not before the Union forces had suffered hundreds of casualties, among whom were numbered Robert Gould Shaw and many men of his Negro regiment. From their new position, the Union forces could impose a much tighter blockade, bombard the city itself, and reduce Fort Sumter to rubble, although an attempt to capture the latter was a costly failure. But Charleston was to remain a symbol of Southern defiance and Northern frustration until Sherman's army threatened it from the rear in February 1865.

By 1864, Wilmington on the Atlantic coast, and Mobile on the Gulf, were the only major blockade-running ports left to the Confederacy. Farragut had long had his eye fixed on Mobile, but dispersal of his forces on other duties had confined him to maintenance of the blockade of the port rather than direct assault upon it. The city stood at the head of a long, almost landlocked bay, its entrance protected by Forts Morgan and Gaines, as well as mines and other obstructions. Mobile was also defended by a handful of gunboats, and by the mighty ironclad, *Tennessee*, built two hundred miles up the Alabama river at Selma. In the summer of 1864 Farragut prepared his plan of attack. On 5 August his four Monitors led his fourteen wooden ships in the attempt to steam past the forts. The vessels, piling up one behind the other, were caught in a fierce cross-fire. One of the Monitors, the *Tecumseh*, trespassed upon the minefield, hit a mine, and sank almost at once. Farragut met the crisis with the same audacity which he had shown at New Orleans. Shouting his famous order, 'Damn the torpedoes', he drove his flagship, *Hartford*, through the minefield, bumping against mines which, happily for him, proved to be defective. The rest of his squadron now passed safely into the bay, dispersed the enemy gunboats, and finally battered the *Tennessee* into submission. Troops under General Gordon Granger, with naval support, took the forts, and although the city of Mobile remained in Confederate hands for several months longer, it was sealed off from the blockade-runners and the world beyond the bay. Farragut's deeds were not only heroic but timely, for they helped to disperse the black clouds of depression which threatened the North and its president in the high summer of 1864.

Wilmington, the most flourishing of the blockade-running ports, also proved to be the longest-lived. It was nearer to Nassau and Bermuda than other Southern ports, and its communications with Richmond made it vital both to the capital and to Lee's army. Like Mobile and Charleston, the town stood well back from the ocean, in this case some twenty miles up Cape Fear River. The configuration of the river mouth made effective blockade very difficult, and the main channel used by shipping was guarded by the massive Fort Fisher, perhaps the strongest of all Confederate coastal defence works. Only direct attack could completely sever this last lifeline of the Confederacy, but it was not an enterprise to be lightly undertaken, and it demanded close cooperation between powerful land and naval forces. In late summer 1864 David D. Porter was given command of the naval squadron, and by late October he was ready for the assault. But the army was slow to find the men for its part in the operation, and then slow to prepare them for action, and not until December were they finally ready. The first attack on Fort Fisher was a fiasco. The military commander, Ben Butler, set great store by his pet project of exploding a ship laden with powder below the fort, but the defenders scarcely noticed the blast. Much worse, Butler totally failed to cooperate with Porter, put ashore less than a third of his 6,500 troops, and then abandoned this beachhead so hastily that the navy had to rescue 600 of his men. This disgraceful episode at last put an end to Butler's erratic Civil War career. Grant despatched a strengthened force, under a more reliable commander, Alfred H. Terry, and in mid-January he and Porter launched a new and highly coordinated attack. It succeeded, although only after heroic resistance by the outnumbered defenders of Fort Fisher. Wilmington was now sealed off from the ocean, and the town itself finally fell on 22 February 1865. The remnant of the Confederacy no longer had a port worthy of the name.

The United States navy had never expected to operate against its own country's coast and harbours, but between 1861 and 1865 it met the unexpected challenge with energy and ingenuity. Still less had the navy expected to operate on the great rivers of the American interior, and still more did it need those same two qualities in discharging that task. Salt-water veterans found themselves assigned to duty on the Mississippi or the Tennessee rivers, a thousand miles from the nearest ocean, and commanding craft the like of which they had never seen in their lives. The Confederates, too, did their best to improvise some kind of river defence fleet to resist Northern incursions, and, more than once, ironclads which they had managed to construct, despite immense handicaps, threatened to upset Union dominance in the river war. In the western campaigns, rivers – the Mississippi, the Ohio, the Tennessee, the Cumberland, the Red – dictated strategy and provided lines of supply. If they had done nothing else, the Union gunboats would have contributed something vital to final victory by opening up and protecting those lines.

During 1861 there was a scramble to create out of almost nothing some kind of river fleet. James B. Eads, head of a salvage company at St Louis, urged the value of ironclads, and offered his own 1,000-ton vessel, *Benton*, which was converted into the ironclad flagship of the new force. Eads's company also built some of the seven craft which became the main strength of the flotilla, the so-called 'Pook Turtles', designed by Samuel M. Pook. These were flat-bottomed, broad-beamed craft, mounting thirteen guns, and propelled by a single large paddle-wheel, hung amidships. The bow and the engines were protected by iron plates, but not the stern. While the Turtles were under construction, Commander John Rodgers converted three Ohio river packets into scout vessels, and searched the whole north-west for men and materials for his flotilla. But he was operating under army command, and he received little help or understanding from Fremont, who was submerged by demands upon his limited resources. In August, Rodgers was replaced by a tough naval veteran, Andrew H. Foote, who was more successful in his battles with Fremont and his successor, Halleck, even if it did take Lincoln's personal intervention to secure him the guns, the supplies and the men he needed.

By February 1862 Foote was ready to cooperate with Grant in his advance into Tennessee. His Pook Turtles were the first American ironclads ever to go into action. Their first taste of battle was sweet, for their guns soon subdued Fort Henry, on the Tennessee river, and they shrugged off hits from Confederate cannon. But they proved much less effective against the stronger Fort Donelson, on the Cumberland, where their vulnerability to guns on high ground was exposed. However, Foote's little fleet had shared in the glories of these early Union victories in the west; it had opened up the Tennessee and the Cumberland, and now it turned its attention to the great river itself. In contrast to its earlier forays, it would now be attacking down-stream, and Foote worried that a disabled ship, instead of being carried back to safety, would now drift helplessly into enemy hands. After giving vital assistance to General Pope in the capture of the Confederate stronghold on Island No. 10, Foote, who had been wounded at Fort Donelson, gave way to Charles H. Davis, but the river flotilla swept on to new glories. It survived a counter-attack from the Confederate river defence fleet in May, forced the enemy to evacuate Fort Pillow on 5 June, and sailed on to Memphis on 6 June. Here the gunboats were joined by a fleet of seven rams, the creation of Charles Ellet, an experienced river man who combined ingenuity and audacity. Between them, the gunboats and the rams destroyed seven of the eight vessels of the Confederate defence force, while the people of Memphis watched in dismay from the waterfront. Memphis was an important prize, but the flotilla now raced on down-stream towards Vicksburg. In less than half a year a force of new and untried ships, waging a new kind of war, and led by men who were more at home on the wide-open seas, had already made a formidable record of success, and altered the shape of the war in the West.

On the stretch of the Mississippi near Vicksburg they met the ships of Farragut's fleet which had battled up-stream from New Orleans. But here, at the climax of its glorious achievements, the river fleet suffered a period of frustration and lost opportunities. It was as if the navy had overstretched itself in its magnificent exertions in such unfamiliar surroundings. It was also an object lesson in the limitations of what the navy could achieve without proper army support. Progress as far as Memphis had been paralleled by Grant's advance through Tennessee, and had worked in conjunction with Pope's force in the vicinity of the Mississippi itself. But Vicksburg was a very different proposition. The strength of its geographical position, the difficulty of the terrain to the north, and the bad judgment of General Halleck deprived the navy of the military support required to take and hold this last Confederate bastion on the river. Ships could run past Vicksburg without unacceptable risk, but, in the graphic words of Admiral Porter, 'ships . . . cannot crawl up hills 300 feet high, and it is that part of Vicksburg which must be taken by the army'.[6] In the early summer of 1862, when Vicksburg was thinly defended, Halleck would not provide the men to take it; by the end of the year its defenders and its garrison were strong enough to frustrate Grant's best efforts for several months. As for Farragut, his heart had never fully been in the move up-river from New Orleans. Many of his ships were quite unsuited to the river war, but with his lighter vessels he headed up-stream in May 1862. His ships scraped and bumped their way over shallows and sandbars and other snags; his men fell victim to dysentery and malaria, and the small contingent of troops who accompanied the expedition sweated and suffered in foul, overcrowded conditions. Unable to take Vicksburg, he headed back to New Orleans with some relief. But there he found orders from Washington to go back up the Mississippi, and he toiled north again. On 25 June, while his mortars attacked the enemy guns, his ships ran past Vicksburg, but took a considerable battering in the process. He now joined up with Davis's river fleet, with a view to a joint assault on Vicksburg, but Halleck had still not provided the necessary troops. The Union naval force suffered not only from frustration but humiliation when the 1,000-ton Confederate ironclad *Arkansas*, completed despite dire shortages of materials and skilled labour, bulldozed its way down the Yazoo river, smashed through the Northern fleet, and came to rest under the guns of Vicksburg. Farragut could stand no more; he ran down below Vicksburg again (but failed to sink the *Arkansas* as hoped) and soon obeyed with alacrity orders to return to blockading duties in the Gulf of Mexico. Farragut was one sea-dog who was never at home on the inland waters. Later in the year, David D. Porter arrived to breathe new life into the river fleet above Vicksburg, and Grant launched his first strike against the great Confederate stronghold. But Vicksburg itself looked more impregnable than ever. Complete control of the Mississippi still eluded the Union forces, ashore or afloat.

Porter's vital contribution to Grant's ultimate success at Vicksburg in 1863 has already been discussed.[7] But it is worth recalling that, like Grant's army, his flotilla endured frustration and failure before its successful defiance of the Vicksburg batteries in April. In February Porter ordered the ram *Queen of the West* and the ironclad *Indianola* to run below Vicksburg and smash Confederate shipping between there and the Red river. After doing considerable damage, the *Queen of the West* ran aground and was captured. The Confederates converted her to their own use, and employed her in an attack on the *Indianola*, which was now driven aground and captured. Porter salvaged something from this miserable failure by a startlingly successful ruse. A dummy 'Monitor' (in fact made of wood) which he floated down-stream past Vicksburg so panicked the Confederates that they blew up their prize possession, the *Indianola*, to prevent its recapture. In March Farragut returned to the stretch of river below Vicksburg but with only two of his ships, after a severe mauling at the hands of the Confederates at Port Hudson. Meanwhile Porter's ships faced some extremely uncomfortable work in the attempts to find a back door to Vicksburg through the Yazoo pass or Steele's Bayou. Naval vessels can never have operated in more bizarre surroundings, of dense forest, overhanging trees, clinging vegetation, and shallow, twisting, uncharted streams. Porter was eventually relieved to escape from Steele's Bayou without having his ships stranded and captured by the enemy army. But whether in trial and tribulation, or in the final triumph, Porter and Grant achieved a new high level of army–navy cooperation. The dash past the Vicksburg batteries in April was one of the high peaks of the navy's wartime effort, and Porter had his full share in one of the most decisive campaigns of the whole conflict.

But Porter's hectic career on the western waters was not yet over. In the spring of 1864 he took eighteen of his gunboats up the Red river to support General Banks's ill-considered and mismanaged campaign. The level of water in the Red river was notoriously undependable, and Porter suffered more from anxiety on this score, and apprehension about Banks's mistakes, than from the might of the enemy. Relations between army and navy rapidly deteriorated as the campaign continued. Then, after Banks's defeat near Mansfield, Porter was left to make good his escape. When he returned to the rapids above Alexandria, the water level was so low that his ships looked certain to be left high and dry. But an ingenious scheme to dam the river (and frantic labour in executing the plan) raised the water level just enough for the ships to scrape through to safety.[8]

It was an inglorious but typically ingenious end to the major naval operations on the western rivers. The navy had accomplished its main task and had assisted the army to achieve its objectives. There had been many lessons to learn and little time to learn them. Quite clearly, success depended not only on close army-navy cooperation but on a proper appreciation of the respective roles of the two services. Ships could not climb hills or occupy key positions, but troops could not penetrate enemy territory and remain there unless there were ships to take them and sustain them. Grant and Foote, and, later, Grant and Porter, showed what could be done; Farragut, with virtually no military support, or Banks, driving the navy to distraction, showed what could not. The river war was the extreme – at times, almost the absurd – example of the navy's resilience and resource in confronting unfamiliar and unforeseen tasks. There was drama in the story, and occasionally farce, but above all there was solid application to problems for which, by definition, the navy could not have been prepared.

4. The story of the Confederate navy is so different that at times it almost seems to belong to another war. It certainly belongs to a different dimension, for the Southern navy started from nothing and never attained more than a fraction of the size of its increasingly formidable opponent. With rare exceptions, it wisely sought to evade rather than confront its adversary. But two tasks were thrust upon it by hard necessity: the defence of coasts and rivers, and counter-measures against the blockade. Since the army was responsible for coastal fortifications, Secretary of the Navy Mallory saw the main role of his service in the first task as the provision of light-draft gunboats, backed by some heavier, more powerful ironclads, and the resourceful use of mines and other obstacles. Shortage of men, weapons and ships gravely impaired coastal defence, but the weakness was

aggravated by the lamentable state of army–navy relations, as for example at New Orleans in 1862 where there was no coordination in planning at all between the two services. As for a serious challenge to the blockade, Mallory felt obliged to wait until the navy had acquired some powerful ocean-going ironclads. Meanwhile, he turned to the third arm of his strategy, this time a matter of choice rather than necessity. He hoped that a small fleet of commerce raiders would not only create a diversion and thus weaken the blockade but also stage a bold Confederate counter-attack on the high-seas, damage Northern shipping, trade, and industry, extend the horizons of the conflict, and impress world opinion – or at least compel its attention. Despite constant and often unjustified complaints that he was neglecting coastal security in favour of his commerce-raiding toys, he refused to be tied to a negative or exclusively defensive conception of the navy's role. He was, on balance, a better judge than his critics.

The first struggle of the Confederate navy was the struggle to be born at all. The materials were almost non-existent, and the climate was scarcely congenial, for most of the men who led the Confederacy had land-locked minds. Whatever it may have lacked, the new navy soon had a surfeit of officers, for over three hundred resigned their commissions in the United States navy to join the Confederate service. They brought with them their rigid notions of seniority, and, in 1863, Mallory had to create a separate 'provisional' navy mainly as a device to promote young and able officers through its ranks, over the heads of those whose energy had been sapped by years, or decades, of service. If there was an abundance of officers, there was a chronic shortage of men. There were few experienced seamen in the South, and foreign sailors formed a significant part – sometimes a majority – of the crew of many Confederate ships. At no time in the war did the strength of the navy rise much above 5,000 men.

There were many makeshift answers but no satisfactory solution to the shortage of ships. Hopes of large-scale privateering were disappointed; only a handful of small ships were licensed and they took only a few prizes. Britain's decision to close its ports to prizes taken by privateers killed off any more ambitious plans. Meanwhile the navy was procuring its first ships by confiscation or capture of Northern-owned vessels, purchase or commandeering of Southern-owned craft, and hasty conversion of these assorted acquisitions into some semblance of warships. Light craft like revenue cutters and lighthouse tenders, belonging to the federal government, had been taken over when the Southern states seceded. Several of the states created their own navies from these and other sources, but most of their ships were soon transferred to Confederate service. Among the conversions of merchant ships, one of the most successful was the *Habana*, purchased in New Orleans in April 1861, which became the first important commerce raider, the *Sumter*.

In his programme of ship construction, Mallory put the emphasis on ironclads. This made good strategic sense, but it posed enormous practical problems. The Confederacy lacked almost every facility for the construction of ironclad ships. It was short of iron, it had scarcely any foundries, rolling mills or workshops equipped for this kind of work, and it was quite unable to produce the engines to power any vessels which it managed to build. Hasty improvisation wrought some minor miracles; armour plating was made from scrap metal and railroad track, engines were taken from ships captured or bought, new tools and machines were made to enable the ships to be built. Other problems still plagued the whole construction programme. There was a desperate shortage of skilled men and expert management, aggravated by inefficient disposition of the trained manpower which did exist. There was an even more crippling shortage of money, and in finance as in materials and labour, naval needs did not compete very successfully with other urgent priorities. The Navy Department received a smaller appropriation in 1861 than any other government department. As a result, even when materials were available there was no money to buy them and workers went unpaid for weeks on end. Strikes and walk-outs, as well as bottlenecks in supply and transportation, slowed construction when time was of the essence. For example, the two ironclads being built near New Orleans, the *Mississippi* and the *Louisiana*, were held up so long by delays of this kind that they were not ready to resist Farragut's attack in April 1862. Elsewhere, ironclad construction was somewhat more successful. Mallory assigned top priority of course to the *Virginia* at Norfolk, and the loss of the navy yard there in May 1862 was a cruel blow. But as the war went on, ironclads of various kinds were built at Richmond, Charleston, Wilmington, Selma and elsewhere, despite ever-increasing difficulties. Most of them were ponderous, unsophisticated and unseaworthy craft, and they saw little active service. On the other hand, the home-produced ironclads had never really been intended to put out into the open sea or to disperse the blockading squadrons. Their primary function was coastal and river defence, and by their very existence they had some effect, at least as a deterrent to enemy attack. The Navy Department may not have envisaged all the appalling difficulties of building ironclads at home, but its faith in their defensive value was not altogether misplaced. For more spectacular offensive purposes it placed its faith firmly in the ships which it would purchase overseas. This venture involved not only naval strategy and logistics but also the possible internationalisation of the whole conflict.

5. In June 1861, James Dunwoody Bulloch arrived in Liverpool. Ex-officer of the United States navy, more recently a steamship skipper operating from New York, he had now crossed the Atlantic to procure the ships which might assure the independence of his native South. For once, the Confederacy had put the right man in the right place. He had the experience and the expertise, the business sense and the diplomatic skill, the toughness and the smoothness, which his task demanded. He is entitled to a place in any short list of Confederate heroes. If, ultimately, his mission was not a success, the explanation lay in forces beyond his control. From the outset, he faced difficulties which would have daunted a lesser man. His first task was to procure cruisers to raid Northern merchant shipping; later, there was added the search for powerful ironclads capable of

breaking the Union blockade. For neither purpose were ready-made ships likely to be suitable or even available. Britain and France were too busy in adapting their own navies to the ironclad revolution, and, as for the commerce raiders, Bulloch was insistent that these vessels must be specially fitted for their role. They needed to be fast and light, yet durable and capable of staying at sea for very long periods. Bulloch looked for British yards capable of building wooden steamships of high performance which would conserve their fuel and extend their range by being able to proceed also under sail, with the propeller retracted.

Time was of the essence, but Bulloch had to overcome initial doubts about the political prospects and financial standing of the new Confederacy. Inevitably, money became and remained one of his greatest problems. The funds voted for ship procurement were made available through Fraser, Trenholm and Co. of Liverpool, a firm with very close South Carolinian connections, and at times of crisis only their advances sustained Bulloch's programme. Financially and in other ways, he found himself in competition with other Confederate agents, whose missions overlapped or interfered with his own. He also had to compete with much more lavishly supported Union purchasing agents, in bidding for weapons and other equipment. But the Northern agents who bothered Bulloch most of all were not buyers, but spies and informants and untiring observers who frequently penetrated the secrecy in which he tried to cloak his activities. The sharpest eyes and ears among all of these belonged to the United States consul in Liverpool, Thomas H. Dudley, a busy, eager ferret of a man whom nature had fashioned for the pursuits of espionage rather than orthodox diplomacy. The duel of Bulloch and Dudley was one of the most hard-fought engagements of the war. The weapons used were not swords or pistols, but on Bulloch's side secrecy and subterfuge, and, on Dudley's, investigation, bribery, sworn statements and diplomatic pressure.

Bulloch's emphasis on secrecy was not merely intended to throw Dudley and his bloodhounds off the scent. It was also to keep his activities as far as possible from the notice of the British government, and above all to avoid the hazards and uncertainties of the law – both the vaguely defined law of nations and the more explicit but equally confusing law of Great Britain. The generally agreed principle of international law was that neutrality did not require a government to stop its citizens from trading with belligerents. British manufacturers and merchants were soon sending a steady stream of armaments and other supplies to both belligerents, and why, the Confederates were disposed to ask, were warships any different from cannon or rifles? The difference was, of course, that a ship could be activated as a weapon of war from the moment that it left the neutral shore where it was built. To deliver a warship at a belligerent port for subsequent use against a third party was one thing; to allow even the possibility that the ship would proceed directly into action from its neutral place of origin was quite another, and might be construed as participation in the war by allowing a 'neutral' port to be used as a base for a belligerent ship. This was no academic matter when, as in the case of the Confederacy, a belligerent was subjected to a blockade, and, if a ship purchased overseas were delivered to one of its ports, it might be bottled up there for the duration of the war. A number of countries, including Britain and the United States, had, many years earlier, become so concerned about the dangers of selling warships that they had passed their own legislation on the subject.

It was in fact the British law, the Foreign Enlistment Act (passed, as it happened, in 1819, when Spain's American colonies were in revolt), which proved to be the crux of the matter. That measure, largely ignored for several decades, forbade anyone to 'equip, furnish, fit out or arm . . . any ship or vessel with intent or in order that such ship or vessel shall be employed in the service of any foreign prince'. During the Civil War, the application or evasion of the law turned first on the distinction between equipping and actually constructing a ship, and secondly on the question of intent. Bulloch took expert legal advice which assured him that the law allowed him to have ships built in British yards, which he could then arm and equip outside British territorial waters, and this argument was later endorsed by the courts. As for the matter of intent, it was contended that the purpose for which a ship was built could only be satisfactorily proved by its actual performance, by which time of course it was generally too late to do anything about it. By not arming or fitting out his ships before they sailed, and by always placing his orders in the name not of a government but a private citizen, Bulloch made their ultimate intent almost impossible to prove to the satisfaction of the courts, even though the design of the ships made their warlike purpose clear enough. In the case of the *Alabama*, for example, the argument that the actual structure of the ship made its intent obvious was not regarded as conclusive.

Having cleared a path through the legal jungle, Bulloch was ready to push ahead. In fact, he had ordered his first cruiser, later to become the *Florida*, soon after his arrival in Liverpool, and in July he placed a second order, this time with Lairds of Birkenhead, for a second, slightly larger and faster ship, No. 290, which eventually became the *Alabama*. Despite financial problems and other delays, the *Florida* was nearing completion early in 1862, and consul Dudley was already hot on her trail. But she had the advantage of being the first in the field, and Bulloch got her safely away under a British flag and with a British crew in March 1862. The *Florida* sailed to Nassau for a rendezvous with the supply ship (also from Liverpool) bringing her guns and other equipment. But Nassau was of course on British territory, and the *Florida* had sailed into new legal difficulties. Northern agents were soon busy presenting evidence of the ship's purpose, but, after a long delay, the Vice-Admiralty Court ruled that there were no grounds for seizure of the vessel under the Foreign Enlistment Act – a decision which cruelly exposed the practical limitations of the measure. The *Florida*'s commander, John N. Maffitt, now quickly put to sea, but plagued by difficulties over his ship's armament and crew, he was obliged to run into Mobile past the Union blockade, and it was not until January 1863 that the

*Florida* set out upon her commerce-raiding career. She soon made up for lost time.

Meanwhile, the second cruiser, the *Alabama*, had been making a name for herself. By early summer 1862 she was nearing completion at Birkenhead, and Bulloch was increasingly anxious about her safe departure. Learning from the experience of the *Florida*, Dudley had extended his intelligence network, and was accumulating masses of evidence. But much of it came from undisclosed or unreliable sources, and it fell short of the kind of proof which would satisfy the Board of Customs or the courts. Charles Francis Adams took the matter up with the Foreign Office, and, after several unhelpful replies, armed himself with the expert legal opinion of Sir Robert Collier that, if the Foreign Enlistment Act were not enforced in this case, it was virtually a dead letter. This opinion was passed on to the British government on 23 July. The matter was now referred to the law officers, whose reply was delayed for six days because one of them had gone off his head. They recommended seizure of the vessel, but by the time the seizure order reached Liverpool two days later it was too late. Bulloch had got wind of this new danger (from an informant working for Dudley's lawyers!), arranged a trial run for the new ship on 29 July, and invited local worthies to a shipboard party. Amply wined and dined, they were returned to Liverpool by tugboat, while the *Alabama* sailed away. She was in fact still off the coast of North Wales when the seizure order came, but no attempt was made to catch her. She evaded a lurking Union warship, and headed for the Azores, where, as arranged, she met her supply ship, and was fitted out for her serious work.[9]

Not unnaturally, Northern opinion was inclined to attribute the escape of the *Alabama* to the malevolence of Palmerston and Russell. The whole episode seemed to prove just how unneutral was their so-called neutrality. In fact, the failure to detain the ship owed less to any sinister designs of the British government than to more hundrum vices, such as indecision, administrative bungling, and a shortsighted inability to grasp the wider implications of its policy. British neutrality was impaired not by prejudice, but by a misreading of what that neutrality entailed, and by an inertia which too easily took refuge behind an outmoded and unsatisfactory law. The British position also rested on the assumption that Southern independence was the inevitable – and imminent – outcome of the war. (It was, after all, shortly after the escape of the *Alabama* that the British government seriously discussed the idea of mediation in the conflict, for the first and only time.) The fact remained, however, that the British government had eventually decided that the *Alabama* should be detained, and in the next few months it learned several lessons from its failure to enforce that decision. After Antietam, Confederate prospects looked rather less rosy, and the Union government commanded a little more respect. Certainly, the North maintained its pressure on the British government to clamp down on ship-building for the Confederacy. Unwilling to rely exclusively on conventional diplomatic channels, the State Department authorised John Murray Forbes and W. H. Aspinwall to undertake a mission to Britain early in 1863, to spend up to £1 million in buying up vessels intended for the South. Their shopping expedition was a failure, but they threw themselves eagerly into the propaganda war, and worked hard to undermine faith in the Confederacy as a customer and to obstruct and delay work on the ships. Several more ships for the Confederacy were actually on order in British yards, not only from Bulloch but from other agents. There was, for example, the *Canton* under construction on Clydeside, which, after endless delays, was finally forfeited to the Crown in 1864. There were also the two ships ordered by Matthew Fontaine Maury, the *Victor* (later renamed *Rappahannock*) and the *Japan* (later the *Georgia*). Both of these eventually made their escape, but the former got no further than Calais, where she remained laid up for the duration of the war. No other ships ever threatened to match the feats of the *Florida* and the *Alabama*. It was in fact the astonishing impact of those two small cruisers on United States merchant shipping which perhaps did most to provoke second thoughts in London. Their very success probably condemned their successors to failure. More and more the British government was impressed with the danger of the precedent which it was setting. What if, in some future war, the United States or some other neutral were to equip a fleet of *Alabamas* which might drive British merchant shipping from the high seas? When the Confederate agents placed orders for much more formidable ships – powerful ironclad rams – in British yards, the hazards of an over-indulgent neutrality became even more plain. The huge, cumbersome 'Scottish sea-monster', under construction on the Clyde, went eventually to Denmark, and never became a major diplomatic, let alone a naval, threat. But the two smaller but more dangerous Laird rams, on the stocks at Birkenhead, were a very different matter.

It was, however, a much humbler vessel which forced the hand of the British government. The *Alexandra* was a small wooden steamship under construction at Liverpool, and intended for the Confederacy. Dudley had compiled another dossier on her, and, in London, Adams was backing up his protests not merely with this evidence, but with dark, Seward-inspired threats about unleashing a fleet of American privateers on the high seas as a reprisal against British policy. Congress passed a Privateering Act in March 1863 authorising the president to create such a fleet, and the prospect of such ships descending on all vessels (including neutrals) trading with the South, was disturbing to say the least. But there were many other forces at work in shaping British policy. Accepting legal advice that the *Alexandra* should be used to test the Foreign Enlistment Act, Russell ordered the ship to be seized on 5 April. The case was transferred to the Court of Exchequer, and its trial delayed until late June. The long wait left Bulloch uncertain and unhappy about future prospects of completing ships in British yards, but the outcome of the trial cheered him. The decision went against the Crown – and the judge enjoyed the opportunity to quote American precedents which denied the right to seize such a ship. The lodging of an appeal, and the law's delays, still deprived the South of the services of the *Alexandra*, but that seemed a small price to pay for a demonstration of the futility of the

Foreign Enlistment Act. If the British government now chose to prevent the sailing of further ships, in order to avoid a dangerous crisis with the United States, that would be a naked political decision, undraped in legal garb. In marking the end of the road for the legal approach to the problem, the case of the *Alexandra* was something of a turning-point. But it is too much to claim that the seizure of the ship represented a firm and final commitment to a new policy. On the one hand, the British government only succeeded in doing in time what it had attempted to do too late several months earlier in the case of the *Alabama*. On the other hand, it did not predetermine the British response to the looming problem of the Laird rams. The crisis which they provoked a few months later was no mere exhibition of shadow boxing.[10]

Southern dreams and Northern nightmares alike centred on the prospect of powerful ironclads, built in Europe, using their heavy guns and iron rams to crush the wooden blockading ships of the North, and then moving on to hold New York to ransom. Whether such notions were fanciful or not, the mere fact that they were taken seriously on both sides converted the Laird rams into a major storm centre of the war. There had been other, earlier attempts to obtain ironclads in Europe, but the rams, ordered in the spring of 1862, and nearing completion by the summer of 1863, were the first really credible threat to upset the naval odds against the Confederacy. Dudley and his spies had begun surveillance of the ships at Birkenhead early in 1863. Even without guns, an armour-plated ship, equipped with turrets, was hard to disguise as anything but a warship, and Bulloch became increasingly doubtful whether the British government would ever allow the rams to sail into Confederate service. But if their warlike intent could not be easily disguised, their true destination could. Ownership of the vessels was transferred to the obscure French firm of Bravay & Co., which claimed to be acting as agents for the government of Egypt. When Seward and Adams stepped up diplomatic pressure for seizure of the rams, the British government could only prevaricate. Investigations and legal advice yielded no grounds for seizure which seemed likely to satisfy the law – and yet, on political grounds, the case for action was stronger than ever. The successes of the *Alabama* were a constant reminder of past mistakes and embarrassing precedents; the European situation, especially in Poland and Schleswig-Holstein, redoubled Britain's interest in avoiding the risk of war with the United States; news of Gettysburg and Vicksburg raised doubts about the viability of the Confederacy and the advisability of taking risks on its behalf; pressure to seize the ships came not only from Seward and Adams but from sections of the press and the business community at home.

After a lull in August, events came to a rapid climax in the first few days of September 1863. On 1 September Russell wrote to Adams informing him that there was no case against the rams under the Foreign Enlistment Act, but omitting to mention that he was still seeking a way to detain the ships. Before receiving Russell's note, Adams wrote strong protests against British inaction on 3 and 4 September. Having at last received the note, and feeling dismayed by its contents, Adams penned an angry and undiplomatic note on 5 September, ending with the famous words: 'It would be superfluous in me to point out to your Lordship that this is war.' It is perfectly clear from the context of the note that this was not a threat of war, but rather a declaration that a British decision to allow the rams to depart would amount to participation in the conflict on the Confederate side. It is equally clear that both governments were extremely anxious to avoid war. On the day after Adams's last note, the British decision to detain the rams was announced. It looked like a triumph for Adams, but if it was so in any degree, it was more the result of his sustained pressure over several months than his final truculent protest. Russell had decided to detain the rams, pending further investigations, before Adams's final note was written, let alone received. The Solicitor-General had approved the decision grudgingly 'as one of policy though not of strict law', and Palmerston endorsed Russell's action.[11] The decision marked the final triumph of political necessity over legal nicety. For the next month the Royal Navy kept an eye on the rams at Birkenhead, while Russell and Adams engaged in further acrimonious correspondence about the rights and wrongs of the affair. Meanwhile the British government became completely convinced that the rams were destined for the Confederacy, and certainly not for Egypt, and, on 8 October, their temporary detention gave way to formal seizure. After lengthy and complex preparations for a court case, all parties settled for a simpler solution. In May 1864 the British government purchased the rams for £220,000, and they lived out their days as H.M.S. *Scorpion* and H.M.S. *Wivern*.

It is probably true enough to say, with the advantage of hindsight, that the rams episode would never have caused a war between Britain and the United States, but it was still a considerable crisis, for all that. It is also likely that, if the rams had escaped, they would not have lived up to the expectations of the South or the fears of the North. Their seaworthiness was suspect, and, as they could not, like the *Alabama*, remain at sea for months on end, they might soon have been trapped in some Southern port. By 1864, if not earlier, the North had sufficient ironclads of its own to contain any threat which they posed. But no one took that threat lightly in 1863. By its detention of the rams in September, Britain at last served notice that she was no longer to be regarded as the birthplace of a Confederate navy. The South was defeated in the shipyards of Britain as well as the battlefields of America. The Confederate navy met its Gettysburg at Birkenhead.

However, as with Gettysburg itself, a 'decisive' defeat did not bring the story to an immediate end. As late as October 1864 the irrepressible Bulloch engineered the escape of a commerce raider, the *Shenandoah*, which he had purchased to replace the *Alabama*, and, after meeting her supply ship at Madeira, she embarked upon a spectacular career which continued into the summer of 1865. But, from the time when the policy of the British government became distinctly less friendly in early 1863, the main hope of Confederate shipbuilding was transferred to France. On paper, French law looked more discouraging and less equivocal than English, but the Confederates held high hopes that the Emperor's will could brush aside such technical obstacles. Indeed, Napoleon III had himself dropped encouraging hints to Confederate commissioner Slidell in autumn 1862. Early in 1863, the leading French shipbuilder (and an acquaintance of the Emperor), Lucien Arman, approached Slidell, and in the next few months contracts for four corvettes and two ironclads were negotiated by Slidell and Bulloch, always on the understanding that Napoleon and his ministers would turn a blind eye to their construction. But the assurances which they gave were always less than watertight. Secrecy about the purpose and destination of the ships was vital to the enterprise – and so too was sufficient Confederate military success to maintain French confidence. By the second half of 1863, these essential conditions were no longer fulfilled. Gettysburg and Vicksburg took their toll here as elsewhere. Worse still was a disastrous leak of secret information about the ships to Bigelow and Dayton, the United States consul and minister, respectively, in Paris. Northern protests impressed foreign minister Drouyn de Lhuys, who was by this time determined to keep the United States quiet when France was over-extended in Mexico and facing increasing problems in Europe. The French government abandoned its earlier position, put more and more obstacles in the way of ship construction, and finally insisted that the vessels be sold elsewhere, or face government seizure. Ultimately, the French had gone further than the British in denying the right of a private citizen to build (let alone arm or equip) a ship intended for service in the navy of a foreign belligerent. Napoleon's decision to open his blind eye hurt the Confederacy at least as much as Russell's decision to shut his eyes to the loopholes in the British law. Neither Britain nor France was willing to imperil other interests in order to permit the creation of a Confederate navy. For its part, the Confederate government spent too much time chasing the mirage of international recognition before it concentrated on pursuit of real power on land and sea.

There was an ironic footnote to the story of Confederate shipbuilding in Europe. One of the ironclads built in France was sold to Denmark, but, with Bulloch's help, it passed back into Confederate hands. After repairs in Spain, it steamed laboriously across the Atlantic, and arrived off the Southern coast just one month after Lee's surrender at Appomattox. The *Stonewall*, as she was called, was the only Confederate ironclad built in Europe to reach American waters. Her belated arrival was the pathetic anti-climax of a story with an ingenious and complex plot. Like the whole Confederate maritime effort, she was too little and too late.

6. The only Confederate ships which ever sailed the open seas to good purpose were a handful of commerce raiders. Their numbers were few but their effect was dramatic. In an age when sail was still a major means of propulsion and wireless telegraphy still a thing of the future, they worked in favourable conditions. Prevailing winds and currents created crowded shipping lanes and busy ocean crossroads where the raiders could find rich pickings. By the time that the slow

communications of the day had spread word of their whereabouts, they could be away in search of new prey on distant seas.

The first Confederate cruisers were home-produced. On 30 June 1861, Captain Raphael Semmes took the converted merchantman, *Sumter*, out of the Mississippi, evaded the Union watchdogs, and captured eight prizes in the Caribbean in her first week at sea. Altogether, she took eighteen prizes in a career which took her across the Atlantic to Gibraltar in January 1862, where, with Union warships lying in wait for her, Semmes abandoned her. The direct damage which she inflicted on Northern merchant shipping was modest, but she offered a grim warning of what was to come. The *Nashville*, another raider, sailed from Charleston on 30 October 1861, steamed across the Atlantic and back again, but took only two prizes, and was later used as a blockade-runner. It was only when the Confederacy had acquired specially-built ships from British yards that the full possibilities of commerce-raiding became apparent.

The *Florida* and the *Alabama* were in fact responsible for the great bulk of the direct and indirect damage inflicted on Northern shipping, although the first to be completed, the *Florida*, did not embark on her spectacular raiding career until John N. Maffitt took her out of Mobile in January 1863. The next six months were the heyday of the commerce raiders as the *Florida* and the *Alabama* ranged across the oceans of the world. The *Florida* operated mainly in the Caribbean and the South Atlantic, although she once crossed the ocean for a refit at Brest. In all she captured thirty-eight prizes, some of them very rich ones indeed, but she also turned two of her captives into satellite raiders which had brief but exciting careers. Indeed, one of these featured in one of the most fantastic episodes of the whole war. Lieutenant Charles Read, transferring in turn to three captured ships, sailed up the North Atlantic coast in May and June 1863, causing havoc among coastal shipping and then the New England fishing fleet, creating alarm and confusion in Boston and New York, evading the attentions of a fleet of pursuing Union ships, and even capturing a revenue cutter inside Portland harbour, before he was finally caught. The *Florida* herself survived until October 1864 when she was captured by the Union sloop, *Wachusett*, commanded by Napoleon Collins, while she was at anchor in the Brazilian port of Bahia. The United States duly apologised for this flagrant violation of Brazilian neutrality; the *Florida*, after being towed north, sank rather mysteriously in Hampton Roads.

The *Florida* was scarcely less successful than the *Alabama*, but the latter's career has generally commanded more attention. Between August 1862 and July 1864, the *Alabama* sailed 75,000 miles, and captured sixty-four prizes. Her skipper, Raphael Semmes, operated first in the North Atlantic and the Caribbean. In 1863 he reaped a rich harvest in the South Atlantic, but was less successful when he moved on to the Cape of Good Hope and later crossed the Indian Ocean to the East Indies. By 1864 the ship and her crew were tired, and Semmes headed for Europe, picking up a few more prizes on his way. In June she put into Cherbourg, where she was less than cordially welcomed by the French authorities. Soon the U.S.S. *Kearsarge* appeared, to stand guard outside the harbour, and, rather than be trapped indefinitely, Semmes resolved to come out and fight. On Sunday morning, 19 June 1864, large crowds watched from the shore as the two vessels fought out their duel just beyond French territorial waters. On paper they were not unevenly matched, but the *Kearsarge*, her crew, her guns and her ammunition, were in much the better condition. The *Alabama* was battered and finally sunk, though Semmes and most of her crew were saved.

There were, of course, other Confederate raiders. The Clyde-built *Georgia* enjoyed a brief spell of success in 1863 before being holed up in Cherbourg, and finally deemed unfit for further service. The converted blockade-runner *Tallahassee* sailed out of Wilmington in August 1864, and took thirty-three prizes in a month off the coast of the Northern states, and she and a sister ship, the *Chickamauga*, made further forays later in the year. Perhaps the most remarkable of the later raiders was the *Shenandoah*, purchased by Bulloch in 1864 to replace the *Alabama*. Escaping from Britain in October 1864, she sailed to the Cape of Good Hope, then to Australia, picking off some prizes on her way. In 1865 she headed for the North Pacific to attack the Yankee whalers which had long dominated that lucrative trade. By this time, the war had ended, but no news of Appomattox had reached these remote waters close to the Arctic circle. The *Shenandoah* had destroyed thirty whalers before a British ship passed on the news that the Union had been restored. The last red sunset of the Confederacy was lit, not by the flash of gunfire in Virginia but by the flames of burning whalers in the Bering Sea.

A few small ships flying the Stars and Bars certainly made a spectacular haul on the oceans of the world. But the loss of two hundred ships, almost all sailing vessels, a quarter of them whalers, and many of the others small coastal craft, was scarcely crippling to the North. It was embarrassing and at times humiliating, but it never seriously impeded the Union war effort. The most dramatic achievement of the raiders lay not in what they destroyed but what they deterred and what they diverted into new ways. The panic which they caused led to a rapid rise in the extra war risk premiums which insurance companies charged to United States ships. Inevitably, more and more trade was transferred from American to neutral ships. It was the virtual disappearance of the United States flag from the North Atlantic route which drove the commerce raiders further afield, and, by late 1863, the *Florida* and the *Alabama* were hard put to find an American ship even in more distant waters. Hundreds of American ships languished in port and hundreds more were transferred to foreign ownership, first as a kind of subterfuge, but increasingly in genuine sales at bargain prices. More than half of the United States merchant fleet was lost during the war. Barely a ninth of that loss was by direct enemy action; the rest was by sale to foreign owners. This was a disaster for American shipping interests, and one from which there was no post-war recovery, for long-term influences confirmed the changes wrought by the war.

But the commerce raiders were less successful in helping the Southern cause.

They may have swept American merchant shipping from the seas, but the main beneficiary was not the Confederacy, but the maritime rivals of the United States – and Britain above all. They were an irritant to the Union war effort rather than a drain upon it. They were a blow to Northern pride rather than a serious threat to Northern prospects. They failed to draw Union warships away from the blockade or to force a reassessment of Northern naval strategy. Neither in their construction nor their operation did they contrive to embroil Britain or any other neutral in the American conflict. Indeed, their sensational deeds had a deterrent effect by their awful warning of the dangers of condoning the construction of such vessels in neutral yards. The *Alabama* was to become a major bone of contention between Britain and the United States after the war was won – but that was small comfort to defeated Confederates. It is hard to see how two small ships could have achieved more than the *Florida* and the *Alabama*, but it was still not enough.

7. The war on the high seas was most threatening when it impinged on the world of statecraft. Storms on the high seas were most dangerous when they surged into diplomatic channels. But neither the *Trent* nor the *Alabama*, the *Peterhoff* nor the rams, the Union blockade nor Confederate ship purchases could finally provoke Britain, or any other neutral, into actual intervention in the conflict. Not provocation but calculation was the key to the situation, and, as long as calculation of British interests favoured neutrality, Confederate hopes were almost certainly doomed to disappointment. On the other hand, the greatest menace to the Union would arise if Britain and France resolved that the time had come, not to respond to some threat or insult, but to take the initiative in proposing some kind of intervention. Such intervention could take any one of several different forms ranging from rejection of the Union blockade to full recognition of Confederate independence, but the most likely seemed to be some kind of offer of mediation, or proposal for an armistice, which, if refused by the North, might well be followed by recognition of the South. However much it was cloaked in humanitarian concern to end the terrible slaughter, any intervention proposal was bound to work in favour of the Confederacy. Indeed, such proposals usually rested on the assumption that the South was destined to gain its independence, and that further bloodshed would be not merely horrifying but pointless. Interest in intervention therefore waxed and waned with the fortunes of the war itself. In any move which might lead to recognition of the Confederacy, timing was of the essence. A premature commitment was to be avoided, but delay had its dangers, too. There was no profit in backing the winner after it had passed the post. The ideal time for intervention would be when the South was clearly heading for victory but had not finally achieved it. There were times, especially in 1862, when the right moment seemed to be at hand – and when the British and French governments were also sensitive to pressure at home, as the cotton famine tightened its grip. (In September 1862, Gladstone offered a very characteristic argument in favour

of intervention: 'the risk of violent impatience in the cotton towns of Lancashire such as would prejudice the dignity and disinterestedness of the proffered mediation'.)[12]

From the beginning, Napoleon III showed more zeal for intervention than Palmerston and Russell, but he also insisted that he would make no move without British cooperation. In the first year of the war he contemplated a challenge to the blockade, but the British attitude and then Seward's opening of New Orleans and other ports dissuaded him. He dropped unofficial hints to the British government about intervention, but Russell ignored them or pretended not to understand them. In April 1862 William Lindsay, shipowner, and confidant of the Lairds, liberal member of Parliament and political busybody, travelled to Paris, met Napoleon twice, concocted a plan for breaking the blockade and offering recognition to the South, and wrote himself a leading part as Napoleon's go-between with the British government. Russell and Palmerston would have nothing to do with him. In the same month Mercier, the French minister in Washington, felt sufficiently encouraged by talk of mediation in the air – and by Seward's surprise endorsement of his proposed trip – to visit Richmond to sound feelings there. He returned discouraged, and his venture caused consternation – but no action – in Paris and London. In July Lindsay, unabashed by earlier rebuffs, finally initiated a debate in the House of Commons on a motion proposing mediation. It enjoyed no little sympathy but most of its supporters chose not to declare themselves. Palmerston squashed the whole idea, and Lindsay withdrew his motion without a vote.

But July and August brought the Confederacy to its highest peak of achievement: the defeat of the Peninsular campaign, Second Bull Run, the invasions of Maryland and Kentucky – and of course the escape of the *Alabama*. The Southern military offensive was accompanied by a diplomatic offensive, and King Cotton's legions seemed at last to be on the march. On 23 July Slidell presented a formal request for French recognition, and dangled the bait of cotton and free trade – and support for the French in Mexico. He got a friendly reception but an evasive reply. On 24 July, Mason made a similar request in London, but was coolly informed a week later that the time for recognition had not yet arrived. Meanwhile Napoleon III aired the notion of a joint French–British–Russian attempt at conciliation, but Russia would have none of it. Behind the scenes in Britain, Russell was reconsidering his policy of cautious neutrality, and by mid-September, news of Lee's spectacular victory at Bull Run and his invasion of Maryland seemed to have created a new situation. Russell now had in mind an offer of mediation of Britain and France which if rejected by the North would lead to recognition of the South. On 14 September, Palmerston wrote to Russell after receiving news of Second Bull Run, and forecasts of further Union disasters. Even Washington or Baltimore might fall, he said, and 'if this should happen, would it not be time for us to consider whether in such a state of things England and France might not address the contending parties and recommend an arrangement on the basis of separation?' This represented no dramatic change in Palmerston's cautious approach, for, if Washington did fall to Lee, no foreign power could be blamed for contemplating recognition of the victorious Confederacy. But, in his reply three days later, Russell urged that 'whether the Federal army is destroyed or not . . . the time is come for offering mediation to the United States government, with a view to the recognition of the independence of the Confederates'. (The wording leaves no doubt that mediation was little more than a halfway house on the road to recognition.) Palmerston wrote that the mediation was as sure to be accepted by the South 'as the proposal of the Prince of Wales by the Danish Princess, yet, in the one case as in the other, there are certain forms which it is decent and proper to go through'. He suggested, in his letter of 23 September, that any decision should await news of the outcome of the great battle northwest of Washington – which had in fact been fought six days earlier. It was not only the direct effect of that battle on British and European opinion which mattered, but perhaps even more its effect on Northern opinion and morale. If it helped to convince the North that the Union could not be saved, then the government in Washington might be less hostile to peace overtures from Europe. Lee's heroic defence at Antietam was one of his finest hours, but it was inevitably followed by retreat into Virginia, and it confirmed Palmerston in his policy of watchful waiting. On 2 October he wrote to Russell that 'the whole matter is full of difficulty, and can only be cleared up by some more decisive events between the contending armies'.[13]

This might normally have been the end of the matter but now Gladstone, the Chancellor of the Exchequer, took a hand. Fully informed of the mediation proposals in September, he had been away from London and out of touch with his cabinet colleagues for two weeks before he rose to speak at a dinner in Newcastle on 7 October. In what he himself later admitted to be one of the least excusable errors of his long life, Gladstone reaffirmed his belief that the North must eventually acknowledge the dissolution of the Union, and declared that 'Jefferson Davis and other leaders of the South have made an army; they are making, it appears, a navy; and they have made what is more than either, they have made a nation'. Gladstone had committed not one blunder but two. He made public what had hitherto been private, and breathed new life into a proposal which, despite Russell's continuing ministrations, had been ailing since Antietam and the Emancipation Proclamation. (The latter had not made the North popular, but it made the idea of intervention on behalf of the South acutely embarrassing.) A week after Gladstone's Newcastle speech, the Secretary of War, Sir George Cornewall Lewis, spoke out at Hereford against recognition of the South. Other members of the cabinet – and much influential opinion outside – were greatly impressed by the hazards of intervention, and they were supported by the leaders of the Conservative opposition. Russell was still burrowing away behind the scenes, but to no avail. The full cabinet meeting planned for 23 October did not take place, but an informal meeting of some of its members came down against the mediation proposal. On the very same day, Russell calmly assured the alarmed United States minister that the British government adhered to its policy of strict neutrality. The statement was not untrue, but, hardly surprisingly, it left a great deal unsaid.

There was a postscript to the intervention crisis of 1862, written by Napoleon III. During this period of exceptional British interest in mediation, the French government had hitherto been strangely quiet. Southern military success had created rather less of a stir in Paris than in London, and the prevailing French view was that any attempt at mediation would have better prospects after the mid-term elections in the North, which were expected to strengthen the peace movement in Congress and across the country. Foreign minister Thouvenel was a consistent advocate of restraint and delay, and preoccupation with European, and especially Italian, problems took the Emperor's mind off American affairs for the time being. But the Italian question led to Thouvenel's removal and eventual replacement by the more intervention-minded Drouyn de Lhuys. The mounting economic distress caused by the cotton famine made Napoleon III anxious to launch a peace initiative, as a public relations exercise if no more. By the end of October, just when British zeal for mediation was flagging, he turned to the American problem again, decided not to wait until the elections were over, and came up with a mediation plan of his own. He suggested that France, Britain and Russia should jointly propose a six-month armistice, including suspension of the blockade, and he rested his case on the grounds of humanity, friendly neutrality and economic interest. Napoleon's plan was now very close to Russell's current thinking, but `Palmerston was unenthusiastic. Other British cabinet members condemned the proposal as blatantly pro-Southern, and thought intervention at this juncture premature in one sense, because the Confederacy had not done enough to justify recognition, and too late in another sense, because of Antietam and emancipation. When the cabinet discussed the French plan on 11 and 12 November, only Gladstone and Russell gave it any backing, and the latter only half-heartedly. Russia, always well-disposed towards the Union side in the Civil War, rejected the French proposal firmly and promptly. Two months of intense political and diplomatic activity thus ended in anticlimax.[14] But, despite the fact that nothing finally happened, this was the most serious international situation of the whole war. It was not the *Trent* or the Laird rams which brought Britain closest to involvement in the American conflict, but the considered (or ill-considered) judgment of Russell and Gladstone, inspired by the victories of Robert E. Lee, and later reinforced by the restless diplomacy of Napoleon III. In the autumn of 1862 Russell's manoeuvres were an aberration from his normal policy, but Palmerston was a model of consistency in his calculation of British interests. Even at the highest peak of Confederate success, he could see no advantage to Britain in intervention which would offset the risk of war with the United States. Along with Antietam and emancipation, he kept the American conflict in quarantine.

8. Thoughts of European intervention or mediation were not finally killed off in November 1862. Two months later, Napoleon III proposed that commissioners

from the two belligerents should negotiate while fighting continued, but he met with a polite but firm refusal. The first half of 1863 saw another upswing in Confederate fortunes, and a corresponding revival of European confidence in ultimate Southern independence. In May another British member of Parliament, John A. Roebuck, set out on the path followed by Lindsay a year earlier. After discussion with Lindsay and the Confederate commissioner Mason, he put down a motion in favour of recognition of the Confederacy, and then took himself off to Paris for an interview with Napoleon which gave the latter another opportunity to exercise his own dangerous brand of personal diplomacy, and air his ideas on recognition of the South. The efforts of the Emperor's advisers to muffle their master's voice left the British government highly uncertain of the exact French position. When Roebuck's motion was debated in the house on 30 June, he gave a highly coloured and highly indiscreet account of Napoleon's views which, among other things, aroused old resentments about French interference in British affairs. Roebuck's motion was withdrawn after being torn to pieces by John Bright who, in Henry Adams's words, 'caught and shook and tossed Roebuck, as a big mastiff shakes a wiry, ill-conditioned, toothless, bad-tempered Yorkshire terrier'.[15] Another attempt at intervention had ended in a fiasco, but it had had its serious moments, especially on the French side, and it produced a violent American reaction which reduced relations between the United States and France to one of their lowest points of the whole war. News of Gettysburg and Vicksburg proved to be the best of all deterrents to further interventionist ventures, and, by late 1863, the Confederate authorities were so disillusioned about the unhelpful attitude of the British government that they brought Mason's mission to an end.

In the second half of the war there was no possibility of British intervention as a deliberate and calculated decision – and the British attitude was crucial in shaping French policy, too. There still remained the chance that some explosive incident on the high seas or elsewhere might provoke intervention against the cooler judgment of the neutral powers, especially as so much European opinion was so slow to accept that the Confederacy was doomed. In 1864, incidents on the Canadian border created moments of high tension, and angry confrontation. But the British government adhered resolutely to its view that war with the United States was to be avoided, above all for the sound and simple reason that it could serve no basic British interest. Neither wounded pride nor injured dignity, neither Southern sympathy nor chronic anti-Americanism ever quite succeeded in deflecting British policy into a new direction. The Confederacy put its faith in the three weapons of economic sanctions, naval ingenuity, and diplomatic pressure. Misfortune and misguided application defeated the first; American strength and European obstruction overcame the second; Seward's toughness and skill combined with British caution and shrewdness to resist the third. The only sure way to international recognition and support was through success in the war itself, but even the Confederate high tides of 1862 and 1863 were never quite enough to burst the dam of British neutrality and British interest.

# Part Four: Climax

# Chapter XV: Campaigns of 1864

In the eyes of a young New England patrician, he was 'a very ordinary looking man', who 'might pass well enough for a dumpy and slouchy little subaltern, very fond of smoking'.[1] When he descended from the train in Washington on the afternoon of 8 March 1864, there was no one to meet him. But, when he slipped quietly into a White House reception a few hours later, he was mobbed by the excited guests, as he came face to face, for the first time, with his commander-in-chief. The man was General Grant, and his coming opened a new chapter in the history of the war. Congress had just passed a law reviving the rank of lieutenant-general, held previously only by George Washington, and to the surprise of no one, Lincoln conferred this exceptional rank upon Grant, along with an unprecedented responsibility, as commander of all the Union armies. His title of general-in-chief had hitherto belonged to General Halleck, but Grant was to live up to the title in deed as well as in name. Halleck stayed on in Washington in the new post of chief-of-staff, and relieved Grant of a mass of burdensome detail by acting as a channel (and a filter) of communications with the president, and with commanders of more than a dozen armies on several fronts. This role was all the more important because Grant was determined not to make his headquarters in Washington where, as Sherman feared, he might become a military martyr tossed into the political lions' den. He thought first of remaining on his home ground in the west, but soon decided that his presence was needed in the east, and established his headquarters with the Army of the Potomac. Meade had offered to make way for an officer of Grant's choice as commander of that Army, but Grant resolved to keep him, and the two men proved to be successful partners in what was inevitably a delicate and occasionally awkward relationship. To fill the gap which he himself had left in the command of the western armies, Grant had no hesitation in selecting his faithful lieutenant, Sherman; they had now reached an almost intuitive understanding of each other's ideas and intentions.

Lincoln, Stanton and Halleck, Grant, Sherman and Meade, these were the men who now stood at the apex of the Northern command system. After three years of disappointments and bad appointments, there had emerged a command structure which was still quite crude and simple but which at least fitted the system to the best available men rather than the men to the system. In the hands of men who had been tried and tested, it promised a determined and relentless prosecution of the war, and a much better coordination of movements on all fronts. It was a coincidence no doubt, but a revealing one, that all these men save Meade were westerners or had strong western connections. It betokened perhaps a more positive approach to the conflict, confident, aggressive, uninhibited, realistic, resourceful, impatient of detail and delay, unimpressed by precedent and tradition. To Sherman, at least, it meant something more. Begging Grant to make his headquarters in the west, Sherman wrote:

> Come West; take to yourself the whole Mississippi Valley. Let us make it dead-sure, and I tell you the Atlantic slope and Pacific shores will follow its destiny as sure as the limbs of a tree live or die with the main trunk. . . . Here lies the seat of the coming empire; and from the West when our task is done, we will make short work of Charleston and Richmond and the impoverished coast of the Atlantic.[2]

There was more to the Civil War, obviously, than a simple difference between North and South.

1. Before he became general-in-chief, Grant had never been free with advice on overall Union strategy. When, in the winter of 1863–4, his opinions were sounded, he came up with limited and disappointing plans which did not always conform to the realities of the situation. But, in his first few weeks in his new post, Grant hammered out a tough and realistic strategy which put professional military muscle on to the bare bones of Lincoln's long-standing ideas. The exact share of the credit which belongs to each man, the civilian and the military commander, is impossible to decide. Lincoln gave Grant a free hand on many matters, above all on how plans were to be implemented, but he never relinquished his own responsibility in the field of grand strategy. What mattered was that he now had a general who could grasp the significance of his ideas, who shared many of the same views, and who had the ability and the will to carry them out.

Certainly, the two basic points of Grant's plans for 1864 were variations on familiar Lincoln themes. The main target was to be the enemy army, which now meant, in effect, two concentrations of Confederate forces, the one under Lee in Virginia, the other under Joseph E. Johnston, south of Chattanooga. As Sherman later put it, 'he was to go for Lee, and I was to go for Joe Johnston. That was his plan.'[3] The second point concerned the achievement of this goal. The way to 'go for' Lee and Johnston was to apply constant and unremitting pressure against them, and to back it up with pressure on as many other fronts as possible. If the North thus exploited its advantage in men and material to the full, the Southern defences were sure to crack at some vital point. In the spring of 1864 it was impossible to predict when or where the strain would finally tell. What actually happened was always one of the likelier possibilities. Grant and Meade were unable to destroy Lee's army in one campaign of a few weeks or months, but, by pinning that army down, eroding its irreplaceable strength, and destroying its old ability to hit back, they left the way open for Sherman to cut through the heart of the Confederacy, and eventually to turn north through the Carolinas and threaten Lee from the rear. Grant and Meade were at the hub of the struggle, Sherman at the rim, but they all moved together as integral parts of the huge wheel which was destined to crush the life out of the Confederacy.

As Union armies moved deeper into the south, another means of breaking Confederate resistance came increasingly to the fore. Here lay Sherman's special contribution to Northern grand strategy. Citing European precedents, he drew a distinction between international conflicts which were waged between kings and hired armies and not between peoples, and 'insurrectionary wars' in which peoples were inevitably involved.[4] If the Southern people persisted in the folly of rebellion after three years, they must take the consequences. As he swept across their land, he would seize or destroy their crops, their animals, their barns and mills and wagons, not as a wanton act of destruction for its own sake, nor as an act of vengeance, but as a means of destroying the Southern capacity, and above all the Southern will, to make war. Lincoln and Grant were right to attach so much importance to elimination of the opposing armies, but Sherman's mind, like his army, penetrated even more deeply, in its insistence that, in a war of peoples, the prospect of defeat must be brought home to the people themselves. Morale, like so much else in this war, was no longer the concern of the few, whether in or out of uniform.

If a policy of all-out attack and unrelenting pressure was the right choice, it still put a great strain even on the impressive resources of the Union. More recent wars have underlined the difficulty of converting an overwhelming preponderance of power into final and total victory over a determined foe. Every step forward into hostile territory lengthened supply lines while shortening the enemy's, and added to the number of towns to be garrisoned, key points to be defended, and railroads to be patrolled. Both sides were complaining by now about the declining quality of their troops, but raw, reluctant and ill-trained recruits might be expected to serve better behind strong defensive works than in ambitious, elaborate and dangerous offensive operations. Three years' experience had brought such improvements in trenches and other defensive works as to lengthen still further the odds against the attacking side. Although the North now enjoyed a large preponderance of strength, it remained an open question, in view of the task ahead, whether it would be large enough. The attempt to apply pressure all along the line left open the possibility of embarrassing setbacks at the hands of an enemy willing to take risks who, by swift concentration, could launch a counter-stroke at some sensitive point.

Certainly, the news from several fronts in the early months of 1864 was scarcely encouraging for the North. In February a Union raid into Florida was defeated at Olustee. In the same month, in Mississippi, Sherman launched a raid eastward from Vicksburg to Meridian, and destroyed supplies and communications there. But any more ambitious plans were thwarted when the cavalry under W. Sooy Smith, advancing from Memphis to join him, were routed by Nathan Bedford Forrest's much smaller force. This was the first of many occasions in 1864 when Forrest's cavalry in Mississippi and Tennessee was to disturb Northern plans. In March he raided as far north as Paducah, Kentucky, and, on his way back through Tennessee in April, forced the Union garrison at Fort Pillow on the Mississippi to capitulate. (This was the occasion when so many Negro troops among the defenders were slaughtered before and after the surrender.)[5] Worse still for the North was the humiliating failure of Banks's campaign up the Red river in March and April. From a purely military standpoint, this was always a misbegotten venture. Its real purposes were political: to protect Lincoln's fragile experiments in reconstruction in Louisiana and Arkansas, to push a Union army towards Texas as a gentle warning to the French in Mexico, and to lay hands on the rich cotton supplies stored in the region. The expedition was ill-fated from its start in mid-March. Cotton speculation and military discipline could never march in step with each other. Banks did not receive the reinforcements which he had been promised; he failed lamentably in liaison with Porter's naval force, which was constantly threatened by the low level of water in the river;[6] he made enough errors to fulfil amply all his prophecies about the hazards of the whole enterprise. He was badly beaten by Richard Taylor at the battle of Mansfield, or Sabine Cross Roads, on 8 April, although his men recovered some self-respect in an engagement at Pleasant Hill on the following day. The expedition retraced its steps, having achieved nothing. Porter's ships only just made good their escape, Banks's men were needed elsewhere in Grant's grand design, and Banks himself soon lost effective military command in the Gulf area to E. R. S. Canby.

Most of these Union setbacks involved no more than sideshows to the main event. The larger armies had remained generally quiet during the winter of 1863–4, but the lull in Virginia was briefly shattered by an extraordinary and futile Union cavalry action. On 28 February, Brigadier General Judson Kilpatrick led 4,000 horsemen in a raid aimed at Richmond itself with the object of releasing Union prisoners and creating confusion in Lee's rear. The raiders were eventually scattered and put to flight, and the Confederates made political capital out of the affair by producing 'orders' (probably forged) to burn Richmond and kill Davis and his cabinet, which they claimed to have found on the body of Colonel Ulric Dahlgren, who was killed in the raid.

The South could take heart from these various setbacks to Northern arms, but Lee and Johnston nursed no illusions about the prospect ahead. Each had around 60,000 men at his disposal, to face 100,000 or more pitted against him. During the winter, each had struggled to sustain discipline and morale, to mitigate shortages of food, clothing and shelter, to remedy deficiencies in transport, to fill command vacancies with suitable officers, and to fill gaps in the thinning ranks of his regiments. Lee's peerless record and reputation assured him at least of the confidence of his men, of the government and of the people. Johnston, on the other hand, knew that he had been Davis's reluctant choice to replace the discredited Bragg, and that Davis thought as little of him as he thought of the president. He was popular with his men, but much Southern opinion would interpret the first signs of delay or withdrawal as the recurrence of an old Johnston malady. Lee was still full of fight but Johnston instinctively favoured a war of manoeuvre, and would bide his time until his opponent exposed himself to a decisive counter-attack. The Confederacy had no unified command structure, and no one to take clear decisions on grand strategy. Lee, as always, concentrated all his thoughts on Virginia; as Sherman put it, 'Grant's strategy embraced a continent, Lee's a small State'.[7] In his new capacity as the president's military adviser, Bragg was expected by no one, including himself, to fill the vacuum in Confederate strategic planning. In the minds of Lee, Johnston and Davis, there remained the one basic idea of holding on, by a mixture of stubborn defence, delaying tactics, and skilful manoeuvre, varied by diversions and nuisance raids when opportunity presented itself. Despite the military odds against them, it still seemed possible to wear down the Northern titan, undermine his patience and sap his morale, and convince him that he could not conquer and hold a defiant South. (Johnston, for example, urged that the struggle must be sustained throughout 1864, in the hope that the Northern Democrats might win the election in November.)[8] But the Confederate armies had to do more than create frustration in the North; they had to maintain hope in the South. It was a daunting task for a tired, ragged, depleted, underfed, outnumbered army.

2. Grant launched his great offensive, as he meant to continue it, with a co-ordinated movement on all fronts. In the early days of May 1864, not only the great armies of Meade in the east and Sherman in the west but smaller, supporting forces elsewhere, all rolled into action. In Virginia, the Army of the Potomac was to move against Lee's army, encamped south of the Rapidan, some distance to the west of its old stamping ground around Fredericksburg. Grant decided to move round Lee's right flank, although the more open country further west on Lee's left had obvious attractions for an offensive campaign. But Grant was unwilling to rely on a vulnerable railroad to supply his huge army in that area, whereas, in operations further east, he could depend on water-borne supplies. Again, although an advance round Lee's right would encounter more serious obstacles in the shape of the rivers and streams which

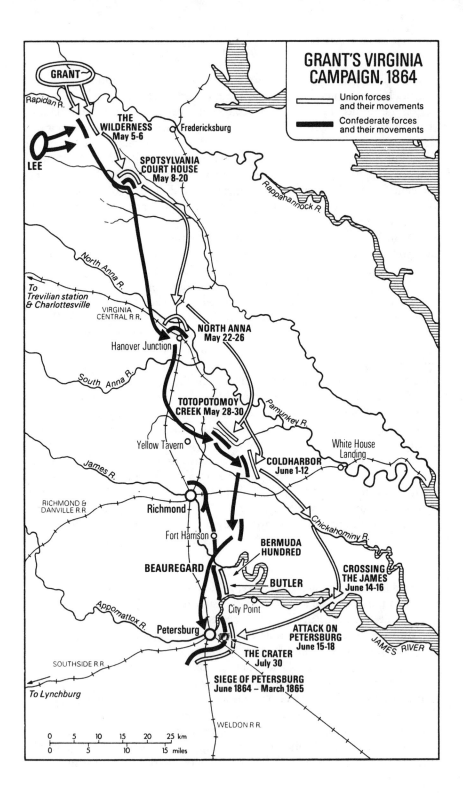

# GRANT'S VIRGINIA CAMPAIGN, 1864

Union forces and their movements

Confederate forces and their movements

GRANT

Rapidan R.

THE WILDERNESS May 5-6

Fredericksburg

LEE

SPOTSYLVANIA COURT HOUSE May 8-20

Rappahannock R.

North Anna R.

To Trevilian station & Charlottesville

VIRGINIA CENTRAL R.R.

NORTH ANNA May 22-26

Hanover Junction

South Anna R.

TOTOPOTOMOY CREEK May 28-30

Pamunkey R.

Yellow Tavern

White House Landing

COLDHARBOR June 1-12

James R.

RICHMOND & DANVILLE R.R.

Richmond

Chickahominy R.

Fort Harrison

BERMUDA HUNDRED

BEAUREGARD

CROSSING THE JAMES June 14-16

BUTLER

Appomattox R.

City Point

Petersburg

ATTACK ON PETERSBURG June 15-18

JAMES RIVER

SOUTHSIDE R.R.

THE CRATER July 30

To Lynchburg

SIEGE OF PETERSBURG June 1864 – March 1865

WELDON R.R.

0   5   10   15   20   25 km

0        5        10        15 miles

emptied into Chesapeake Bay, it also offered the twin possibilities of getting between Lee and Richmond and forcing him to fight in a situation unfavourable to him, or of advancing south-east to the James river and linking with other Union forces already there. From the earliest days of the campaign, Grant had his sights fixed on the south side of the James river, and the railroads south of Richmond which were Lee's lifeline. If he had not shattered Lee's army on his march to the James, he would strangle it once he arrived there.

From the outset, too, he had planned to step up the pressure on Lee by operations both on the James, and in the Shenandoah Valley, the time-honoured areas for alarms and diversions on the Virginian front. Ben Butler was to take 30,000 men up the James from Fortress Monroe, and establish himself at City Point, on the south bank of the river, from which position he could threaten Petersburg or even Richmond itself. In the Valley, Franz Sigel was to advance south with enough energy to prevent the Confederates in that area from going to Lee's aid. Within two weeks both operations ended in dismal failure, and Lee was able to draw small but useful reinforcements from both areas. Sigel advanced from Cedar Creek as far as New Market, but was attacked and defeated there on 15 May by Breckinridge's smaller force, and retreated hastily down the Valley. For his part, Butler forsook City Point for Bermuda Hundred, a wedge of land between the James to the north and the Appomattox river to the south, which offered him a safe defensive position but a poor springboard for attack. The Confederates in the area were ill-prepared and very thin on the ground, but after half-hearted moves against Petersburg and towards Richmond, Butler scurried back to the shelter of Bermuda Hundred. In effect, he had put himself in prison and handed the key to Beauregard, the Confederate commander. A small force manning the fortifications which had been erected between the James and the Appomattox sufficed to keep Butler in confinement, and enabled Beauregard to send some troops to Lee.

Meanwhile, the Army of the Potomac ran into enough trouble of its own. One result of Grant's decision to threaten Lee's right was that, as soon as it crossed the Rapidan, the army entered the dense, confusing undergrowth of the Wilderness where Hooker had come to grief a year earlier. Indeed, Lee, who needed time to concentrate his scattered army, did not contest Grant's crossing of the river because the Union army would be more vulnerable in the Wilderness, where its numerical advantage would be nullified, its formidable artillery would be almost useless, and its commanders would be unable to keep firm control of their units while they were on the move. Fighting in the Wilderness was bound to be a matter of savage encounters between bewildered groups of men, effectively isolated from their fellows only a few hundred yards away by the impenetrable vegetation. The dense smoke of battle added new terrors to the Wilderness, and crackling brush-fires brought further horrors to the wounded and dying.

There was little hope that the huge Army of the Potomac, encumbered with its enormous baggage train, could get clear of the Wilderness in the first day of its advance on 4 May. By the early hours of 5 May, Ewell's and Hill's corps of Lee's army were advancing along the two roads which ran into the Wilderness from the west, to threaten Grant's right flank as he moved laboriously south. Neither side was well-informed about the strength or the dispositions of the other. A Northern attempt to dispose of what was believed to be a minor diversion on its flank developed into a major battle – or rather two major engagements separated by less than a mile of dense thicket. The struggle swayed one way and then the other. At one point the Union army's main road south was seriously threatened, but by the end of the day the Confederates were hard pressed to repel the onslaughts of their stronger foe. Lee was already impressed with the aggressiveness of his new opponent, and he felt it again when Grant ordered a new attack early in the morning of 6 May. Hill's corps was put to flight, but Longstreet's corps, which had had a forty-mile march to reach the scene of the battle, arrived in the nick of time to restore the situation. Later in the day, Longstreet launched a flank attack which began well but lost impetus after Longstreet himself was severely wounded by fire from his own men – not far, by a strange coincidence, from the spot where, a year earlier, Stonewall Jackson had been struck down in much the same way, in the middle of a similar operation at Chancellorsville. There was more furious fighting before the day ended with both armies battered and exhausted, and unable to claim any clear advantage.

For two terrible days the armies had grappled blindly with each other, while their commanders had shown more resolution than resourcefulness. Union casualties had numbered around 17,000, including over 2,000 killed. By this stage of the war Confederate casualties involve a good deal of guesswork, but they can have been only a few thousand less. As a proportion of the total strength they were far higher than on the Northern side, and the men were virtually irreplaceable. But the real significance of the battle of the Wilderness lay in what happened next. Grant's great offensive had suffered a severe jolt, a setback comparable to that which Hooker had suffered in the first two days at Chancellorsville. Unlike all his predecessors, however, Grant did not surrender the initiative or go on to the defensive. He moved his army, not back north of the river, but forward to the south-east, in the direction of Spotsylvania. His decision opened a new chapter in the war. It marked the full implementation of the strategy of relentless pressure on a weaker foe; it served notice that Lee's brilliance in winning (or at least not losing) battles would no longer prevent the North from winning the war.

Spotsylvania Court House lay about twelve miles south-east of the battlefield of the Wilderness. As an important road junction, it was an obvious target for Grant's renewed attempt to pass round the Confederate right flank, and place himself between Lee and Richmond. The race for Spotsylvania became one of several events in the gruelling campaign of 1864, the outcome of which did not decide the war, but did decide how long it would last. With reasonable luck, and against an opponent not blessed with Lee's second sight, the Army of the

Potomac might well have won that race. On the evening of 7 May it began its south-eastward movement, and, despite the delays of a night march, its vanguard was approaching Spotsylvania soon after eight o'clock next morning. But it found Confederate troops blocking the road. These were the men of Longstreet's corps, now commanded by Richard Anderson. Shrewdly reading the earliest signs of Grant's move, Lee had ordered Anderson to rest his men until 3 a.m. and then move rapidly to Spotsylvania. A 3 a.m. start would have given Anderson no hope of blocking the Union thrust, but, finding no suitable resing place, he had pushed on through the night, and his weary men stumbled into position across the road north of Spotsylvania just in time to foil the Union advance. As more troops came up, both sides began to entrench in the practised manner which had now become second nature. Grant's attempted breakthrough had become another face-to-face encounter; having lost the race for Spotsylvania by a couple of hours, he now faced a slogging match which lasted for twelve days.

While he probed Lee's new defences, Grant sent Sheridan's cavalry corps on a raid towards Richmond, to attack the Confederate cavalry, cut railroads and disrupt Lee's supplies. The mission had considerable success in each of these objectives. It caused havoc and confusion in Lee's rear (although the effects of such destructive raids seldom endured for long), it caused some anxiety in the Confederate capital (although it could never have taken Richmond itself) and, on 11 May, it defeated the Southern cavalry at Yellow Tavern, a few miles from Richmond. In this battle the prince of Confederate cavalrymen, Jeb Stuart, was killed. Sheridan rode on to the James and rested for a few days with Butler's command before rejoining Grant on 24 May. The undoubted achievements of his raid have to be measured against its inevitable drawback in depriving the Army of the Potomac of its eyes, as it measured its strength against Lee's formidable defences.

Spotsylvania saw some of the hardest fighting anywhere in the whole war. On 10 May, Grant and Meade forsook a promising manoeuvre on Lee's left flank for a crude and unsuccessful frontal attack. Later in the day Colonel Emory Upton showed what might be done by a carefully prepared and concentrated assault on one stretch of the enemy line, but his initial breakthrough was inadequately supported. After a day's lull, Grant launched a massive assault on the salient in the centre of the Confederate position, which soon came to be called the 'Bloody Angle'. Again, the first attacking waves succeeded in penetrating the Confederate line but were later thrown back. There followed hours of fighting between men sheltering on either side of the parapet which marked the original Confederate position. At the end of the day, the Union forces drew back, and Lee abandoned the salient for a new defensive line. After another lull, Grant now prepared a new move against the Confederate right flank, but drenching rain delayed the movement of his troops, and gave Lee time to counter this new threat. As both armies concentrated in this sector, their whole lines shifted from an east–west to a north–south direction. There was constant contact and intermittent fighting between the two sides, but Grant saw no opportunity for another assault. However, the shift in the positions of the armies had left him well-placed for another move south-east towards Richmond and the James which might force Lee out into a more open and vulnerable position.

Union casualties in the protracted fighting around Spotsylvania totalled more than 17,000; the Confederates, fighting mainly behind defensive works, may have lost little more than half that number. Grant had failed, but it would be wrong to conclude that he had been following a crude policy based on ruthless exploitation of his numerical advantage, of wearing down his opponent by bludgeoning frontal attacks. There had been variety and enterprise and even subtlety, as well as determination, in his tactics, but he was foiled, partly by his own mistakes, but also by bad luck and bad weather, the superb defensive fighting of Lee and his outnumbered army, and perhaps by a still inadequate understanding of the hazards and the cost of direct attacks on prepared defences. Lee emerged successfully from a serious crisis at Spotsylvania. His ranks were already depleted by the casualties of the Wilderness; he had temporarily lost his best corps commanders, Longstreet and A. P. Hill; his supplies were disrupted by Sheridan's raid; he was shocked by Jeb Stuart's death; the Union operations in the Shenandoah Valley and on the James meant that he could expect no reinforcements from elsewhere. But he held on grimly, and his supply situation gradually improved. Then, on 15–16 May, came news of the repulse of Sigel in the Valley and the containment of Butler on the James. Now Lee could expect some modest but valuable reinforcements, and Grant would have to proceed without any expectation of help from his planned diversions.

As after the Wilderness, Grant was still determined to push ahead. He tried but failed to entice Lee into a pursuit of the leading corps of his army which would leave the Confederates vulnerable to attack by his main force. In fact, Lee withdrew in good order some twenty miles south to a strong defensive position behind the North Anna river. Grant felt out the strength of the Confederate defences on 23 and 24 May, and recent experience convinced him that an assault upon them was unlikely to succeed. Yet again he moved south-east around Lee's right flank. The army crossed the Pamunkey river and headed into the area which had been the scene of the Seven Days battles two years earlier. Grant had called up reinforcements in the shape of 12,500 men from Butler's command, led by W. F. Smith, who sailed up the Pamunkey to White House Landing; and, after some delay and confusion, set off to join the Army of the Potomac around Cold Harbor. Meanwhile Lee continued to shadow the Union advance, and moved to a new defensive line along Totopotomoy Creek. He was increasingly concerned at being forced back so close to Richmond. The North Anna was only twenty-three miles from the Confederate capital, his new position much less. He was already convinced that it would be disastrous for his army to be tied to the defence of Richmond in a long siege, but if Grant were allowed to move still further round his flank this would be forced upon him. There developed a race, not unlike the race for Spotsylvania Court House, but this time the prize was the crossroads at Cold Harbor.

It was here that each commander saw a chance to strike a decisive blow. By a swift attack on 1 June, Lee hoped to roll up Grant's left flank, but the attack was mismanaged, and there were just sufficient Union forces in position to throw it back. Now Lee was obliged to extend his line further south to protect his flank, but inevitably his longer line was hastily prepared and thinly manned in places. Grant saw in this situation his best opportunity yet to achieve his elusive goal of winning a good position between Lee and Richmond. He ordered an attack at dawn on 2 June, but delays and mistakes in moving and preparing men for the assault led to a twenty-four-hour postponement. In those twenty-four hours, Lee reinforced the southern end of his line, and his men dug themselves in securely. The opportunity of 2 June became the slaughter of 3 June. In the grey light of early morning, the attacking Northern troops suffered seven thousand casualties in an hour, the defenders only a quarter of that number. Cold Harbor offered one final, terrible proof of the futility of direct, frontal attacks on strong defensive positions. But it also demonstrated that the difference between victory and defeat was not only a matter of men and weapons and positions, but of hours.

For ten days after Grant's bloody failure the two armies maintained a stubborn, bitter trench warfare at Cold Harbor. But the first phase of Grant's 1864 campaign was over. For more than a month the two protagonists had waged a continuous, unrelenting conflict, in constant contact with each other, the like of which had not been seen before. Lee's stubborn defence had nullified Grant's relentless aggression, but, from Spotsylvania to Cold Harbor, there were times when it was a very close-run thing indeed. For all its ferocity and elemental force this was not a simple, crude, blind trial of strength between the battering ram and the brick wall. It was a campaign of thrust and parry, skill and ingenuity, challenge and response, and the endless search to create and exploit a real opportunity. Public opinion on each side found cause for both enthusiasm and alarm in the campaign. The North took heart at Grant's sixty-mile advance to the threshold of Richmond itself, but suffered heartache at the 55,000 casualties which it had cost – over half the combat strength of the army when it first marched into the Wilderness. The South rejoiced at the series of rebuffs which Lee had administered to the invader, but feared for the safety of Richmond, and wept for its 40,000 casualties, almost three-fifths of its initial combat strength. The rival commanders were well aware of past failures and future hazards. Grant had worn down Lee's army but failed to destroy it; proximity to Richmond was no great virtue in itself, but only if it could lead to his true goal. Lee had saved his army and denied Grant the opening which he sought, but that army was weakened to the point where it could no longer launch a major counter-offensive. Lee also knew that the Richmond defences could well be less of a haven than a prison for his weakened army.

It was Grant who still had the advantage and the initiative. Now in mid-June, he launched a new move, brilliant alike in conception and execution, which briefly and tantalisingly restored the vision of a speedy end to the war. From the outset, his eye had been firmly fixed on the James river. He now planned to transfer the Army of the Potomac south of the James and strike at Petersburg and the railroad arteries to Richmond which ran through it. Faced with such a threat, Lee would be obliged either to resign himself to a siege in Richmond, or to come out and risk battle on more open ground. Grant's first problem was to withdraw his huge army quietly from the Cold Harbor position and to keep Lee guesssing about its destination. He mounted a number of diversions to promote this end. Sheridan's cavalry were to strike north and west of Richmond in the direction of Charlottesville, in a bid to link with Union forces in the Shenandoah Valley, now under Hunter, which had advanced as far as Staunton. The cavalry did not fulfil the larger objectives of the mission but they did succeed in drawing off the bulk of Lee's cavalry, and hurting them badly in a tough encounter at Trevilian Station on 11–12 June, and thus depriving Lee of their help in detecting the movement south of the James. (Hunter's progress in the Valley also persuaded Lee to detach Early's corps from his already over-stretched army, to deal with this new threat, just at the time when Grant was planning his new move.) Grant also ordered Butler to make a demonstration against the thinly-held Confederate defences at Petersburg. To cover the actual movement of the Army of the Potomac across the James, one corps was to threaten Richmond from north of the river, so as to strengthen Lee's suspicion that Grant was merely attempting yet another flanking operation, on a limited scale, on the pattern of the previous six weeks.

Aided by this flurry of activity, the crossing of the James was smoothly accomplished. The army quietly abandoned its trenches at Cold Harbor on the night of 12–13 June, and marched south to the James. In the next three days, four corps of the Army of the Potomac crossed to the south bank of the river, the vanguard on transports, the rest on a pontoon bridge over 700 yards long, put together in less than half a day on 14 June. The speed and efficiency of the whole operation cut to a minimum the period of greatest risk when the Union army was divided on either side of a broad river, deep in hostile territory. It also showed the skill, stamina and strength of that army, even after six punishing and disappointing weeks. Grant's brilliant feat left Lee completely in the dark for at least two days, and very uncertain of his opponent's intentions for two or three days more. He had always reckoned with the possibility that Grant would cross the James, but he had to be prepared for other contingencies, such as an attack on Richmond from north of the river, or a simultaneous advance along both its banks. His uncertainty was made worse by poor communications between himself and Beauregard, who commanded the troops around Petersburg and facing Butler at Bermuda Hundred. If he were to cover Richmond, Lee could not move the bulk of his army south of the James until he was quite sure that Grant had done the same. Lee's uncertainty was Grant's great opportunity.

Grant had made plans to exploit precisely this opportunity. W. F. 'Baldy' Smith's troops, which had so recently joined the Army of the Potomac, were to steam back up the James to rejoin Butler's command at Bermuda Hundred, and, from there, launch a quick thrust against Petersburg. The vanguard of the Army of the Potomac, Hancock's corps, would march to join Smith once it was south of the James. The Petersburg defences were massive and formidable, but they were almost denuded of troops, and, until Lee was sure of Grant's movements, they were unlikely to be reinforced. On three successive days, 15, 16 and 17 June, the Union army had wonderful opportunities to take Petersburg, but each time allowed the chance to slip from its grasp. On 15 June Beauregard had only 2,500 men in the Petersburg defences, to face at least 16,000 under Smith; he had less than 5,000 more to contain Butler's 15,000 at Bermuda Hundred just to the north. Smith delayed his attack until the evening; it quickly overran a long stretch of the lightly-held fortifications, but Smith then halted the advance until morning. When Hancock at last arrived, weary, unwell, confused, and angry that he had only just received clear orders to join the attack on Petersburg, he accepted Smith's proposed delay. An easy victory and a priceless opportunity were tossed aside, only to be handed back next day. The Union forces were now more than doubled in strength while Beauregard could bring his Petersburg strength only up to 14,000 – and that partly by the desperate expedient of leaving a mere 1,000 to face Butler's 15,000 at Bermuda Hundred. Butler frittered away his chance to sweep down on Petersburg almost unopposed; Hancock and Smith delayed their assault until evening, again made rapid gains, and again halted prematurely. Beauregard's defence had been tough and resourceful, and it needed to be even more so on the third day, 17 June, as he fought off more sustained attacks. But, by evening, his exhausted men were holding on precariously to a last line of defence and Beauregard was preparing to abandon Petersburg. Yet again, the Union commanders decided to wait until morning to finish the job; by the morning, Lee's troops were filing into the Petersburg defences and the chance was gone.

Beauregard enjoyed his finest hour at Petersburg, but the odds against him were overwhelming, and he was further handicapped (partly through his own imprecise despatches) by Lee's unaccustomed slowness in reading Grant's intentions, and coming to his aid. The blame for the Union failure must lie heavily on many shoulders. But, whatever the failings of others, Smith could and should have taken Petersburg on 15 June, and Smith, Hancock and Butler could and should have taken it next day. Grant and his staff were certainly not blameless; their orders were too vague and confusing, and the army's movements were poorly coordinated. Perhaps Grant's great shortcoming was that not even he could be in two places at once. He could not at the same time supervise the crossing of the James, and direct the assault on Petersburg. The one was a dazzling achievement, the other proved to be a humiliating and disastrous failure, perhaps the most important and inexcusable missed opportunity of a war of missed opportunities. In his days in the west, Grant had seen how Vicksburg, an apple ripe for easy plucking in mid-summer 1862, had been seized a year later only after an arduous campaign and a laborious siege. Now, in the east, Petersburg, which could have been taken in days (if not hours) in June 1864, was to withstand a nine-month siege. And while Petersburg survived, so did Richmond – and so did the Confederacy.

3. In a purely military sense, the failure to take Petersburg postponed but did not alter the almost certain outcome of the war. Lee himself had always acknowledged that, once he was chained to the defence of Richmond and Petersburg, the end could only be a matter of time. But the conversion of the war in Virginia into a dreary and protracted siege put a new strain on the war-making capacity of the North in ways which were not strictly military. It posed new questions about Northern spirit and determination. After three years of war, did the Northern people and their leaders retain the fixity of purpose to endure this further frustration and delay, or would Northern patience fail to match Northern strength in manpower and resources? Discontent and disillusion could find a dangerous political outlet in the presidential election of 1864. The siege of Petersburg and Richmond involved Lincoln's political survival as well as Lee's military survival. It was a test alike of Southern endurance and Northern perseverance.

In the same June days which saw the crossing of the James and the fiasco at Petersburg, Lee launched a diversion which, succeeding beyond his wildest hopes, touched on the tenderest spots of Northern pride and confidence. Once again, the Shenandoah Valley was his chosen field. Lee's spectacular diversion was in fact born out of sheer necessity. The survival of Richmond and Lee's army depedend not only on its railroad lines to the south, but also on its connections with Lynchburg and Charlottesville to the west, and with the rich farmland of the Shenandoah Valley. By early June a Union advance up the Valley, led by David Hunter, threatened this whole area, and, hard pressed though he was, Lee had no hesitation in sending Early's corps to dispose of Hunter. The Union advance was in fact already running out of momentum and losing direction before Early's appearance near Lynchburg unnerved Hunter, and persuaded him to retreat without a fight. Unfortunately for him, he had so positioned himself that the Confederates threatened his line of retreat down the Valley, and, instead, he hastened away westward across the mountains. Hunter's departure left the road down the Valley wide open to Early, and what had begun as a desperate gamble to protect vital supply lines was transformed into a dramatic raid which sped north into Maryland and came to a halt only at the gates of Washington itself. The ghost of Stonewall Jackson had returned to haunt the North.

Early reached Winchester on 2 July, crossed the Potomac into Maryland four days later, headed east towards Washington, and routed a motley Union force under Lew Wallace at the Monocacy river on 9 July. The federal capital was now only forty miles away, and two days later Early reached its outer defences. Those defences were formidable but almost unmanned. There was no unified Northern command to gather together the scratch forces available in the vicinity, and although Halleck, the chief of staff, was on the spot, he was as unwilling as ever to assume responsibility. Early probed the Union defences, and Lincoln himself came under fire when he went to see the action for himself. Just in time, veteran troops of the Army of the Potomac were hurried back to Washington to join the clerks and home guards and invalids manning the defences. Early decided that an assault was now impossible; he retraced his steps, and on 14 July he was once again south of the Potomac. The Union pursuit, like the defence of Washington, was weakened by divided command, and Early was able to linger in the Shenandoah Valley, where he still posed a threat. Indeed, at the end of July he sent his cavalry on a raid into Pennsylvania where they put the town of Chambersburg to the torch.

With no more than 12,000 tired and footsore men, Early could never have occupied Washington, but, if he had penetrated even briefly into the city, the effect on Northern morale, already tottering into depression, might have been disastrous. As things were, he had created an almighty panic in Washington, dealt a humiliating blow to Northern self-respect, and rammed home the uncomfortable lesson that the federal capital itself was still sadly vulnerable. Grant and Lincoln, at least, had not panicked, and both saw in Early's raid a chance – not, alas, taken – to catch and destroy a part of Lee's army. Grant had refused to come to Washington himself on the ground that this would heighten the atmosphere of panic and crisis. He also refused to take the bait which Lee offered, and attack the massive Petersburg defences while Lee's army was weakened by Early's absence. But Grant was now convinced – and Lincoln was insistently reminding him – of the need to create a powerful, unified command to make Washington safe once and for all, and to eliminate the recurring threat from the Shenandoah Valley. Various names, including that of Meade, were proposed for this task, but Grant's final choice was the youthful, pugnacious and determined Sheridan. In the fall of 1864 he proved that he was the right man for the job.

Meanwhile, in the mid-summer heat, the main armies settled down to the grim, tedious business of trench warfare. From mid-June, Lee, with barely 50,000 men, was defending a twenty-five-mile defensive line, from east of Richmond to south-east of Petersburg. Grant had a maximum of 90,000 to oppose him, but that number was soon eroded not merely by casualties, and the detachment of men to deal with Early, but by the departure of thousands of three-year men who had completed their term of service. In truth, both armies were by now suffering a decline in both the quantity and quality of their men, as raw and reluctant recruits inadequately replaced hardened veterans. There was a shortage of competent officers, too, at all levels, and Grant in particular was beset by problems of command involving trouble-makers like Butler and Baldy Smith, and even a general as staunch as Meade himself, whose quick temper meant that things were seldom all quiet in the Army of the Potomac. In an election year, politics permeated the army more than ever and made it impossible, for example, to give the influential Ben Butler what he so richly deserved – dismissal from the army.

The focus of strategic attention was now on the railroads which led into Petersburg – the Weldon Railroad which linked Richmond with the vital port of Wilmington to the south, and the South Side Railroad which ran west from Petersburg to Lynchburg. To cut both of these would be to make Lee's position untenable. But the task was anything but easy, for an extension of Grant's line further to the south and west of Petersburg was an invitation to Lee to cut the Union army in two somewhere east of the town. Grant made one thrust against the much nearer target, the Weldon Railroad, in June, but it was repulsed. A cavalry raid, led by James H. Wilson, wreaked havoc with long stretches of track, but such damage could be repaired in days or weeks at most. The Union army needed to take and hold a significant stretch of these vital lines.

Grant was also probing for a weak spot in the elaborate Petersburg defences, and by forcing Lee to shift his smaller forces to meet threats at various points hoped to find the opening he needed. His best opportunity came in late July. Some Pennsylvanian troops with mining experience proposed to dig a tunnel 500 feet long to reach a point under the Confederate defences east of Petersburg. There they would explode a huge charge of powder, to blow a hole in the line through which Union infantry could charge. The idea was at first not taken very seriously by the generals – nor by the Southern troops who got wind of it – but work went ahead, and by late July Grant and Meade were pinning considerable faith in it. A diversion at the northern end of the line forced Lee to reduce his strength at the vital point. Early on the morning of 30 July the mine exploded with a tremendous roar, throwing guns and men into the air, and burying many of them in a huge crater about 150 feet long and 30 feet deep. Bewildered Confederate troops on either side of the crater ran for their lives. For the best part of an hour, a wide, undefended gap in the line invited a Union advance. But yet again, a rich opportunity degenerated into a fiasco. The assault which followed the explosion of the mine was one of the worst tales of wretched failure in the whole war. It was entrusted to Burnside's corps, and Burnside and failure were acquaintances of long standing. He had not even prepared the ground in front of his own line for a rapid coordinated deployment of his troops; instead, they straggled across to the enemy lines in bits and pieces. A late change of plan (designed to forestall the accusation that Negro troops were being used as cannon fodder) replaced a Black division as the spearhead of the assault with the division of James H. Ledlie, a drunken incompetent who spent the morning of the assault swigging rum in a dug-out behind the Union lines – and found a drinking companion in the white commander of the Negro division. When the troops did reach the crater, they milled around on its rim, or inside it, without purpose and direction, and totally failed to exploit the initial breakthrough. After an hour, the Confederate defences were re-formed, and the men in the crater were exposed to a withering fire, and, before the operation was finally called off, 4,000 were killed, wounded or captured. The ghastly and inexcusable failure of the operation is all the worse in view of the success of the mine itself. The Confederate general Mahone, who rallied the defensive forces after the explosion, believed that, if properly exploited, it could have achieved what was now to take nine weary months longer. It is a little surprising perhaps that the mine idea was not tried again.

The struggle around Petersburg ground on relentlessly, and, at last in August, with the help of another feint at the other end of the line, the Union army was able to cut the Weldon Railroad, and hold its position there. Although supplies still got through to Petersburg by wagon from a railhead to the south, the squeeze on Lee's army was now a little tighter. Grant could see that he was slowly winning the war by constant pressure, but he realised that Northern public opinion might not share his vision. In August he wrote that

We will peg away, however, and end this matter if our people at home will but be true to themselves. . . . The rebellion is now fed by the bickering and differences North. The hope of a counter-revolution over the draft, or the Presidential election, keeps them together.[9]

At a time when Northern morale was sagging into deep gloom and frustration, and Lincoln despaired of re-election, Grant spoke nothing but the truth. Unfortunately, Sherman's campaign in the west, which had begun so brightly, had also lost momentum in the depressing days of August. It was all very well to say that places did not matter, but the people of the North fretted and their spirits flagged as long as Richmond and Atlanta still stood.

4. When Sherman's campaign began in early May, his orders were to break up Johnston's army, penetrate into the interior of the Confederacy, and damage its war-making capacity. No specific geographical target was mentioned, but, willingly or unwillingly, Sherman was drawn towards the magnet of Atlanta, as surely as Grant was drawn to the Richmond–Petersburg area of Virginia. Atlanta was some eighty miles from his starting-point south of Chattanooga, across difficult, rugged hill country, with ridge after ridge offering natural defensive strongholds to his Confederate opponents. Their commander, Joseph E. Johnston, thought naturally in terms of a campaign of flexible defensive manoeuvre, moving back from one position to the next, drawing Sherman deeper into difficulty and danger, and preparing to strike back when Sherman made a false move or was betrayed into a rash, frontal assault. Some of Johnston's more high-spirited subordinates, notably John B. Hood, chafed at such a cautious policy; Hood wrote later of Johnston's 'visions of insuperable difficulties, and vacillations unending'.[10] But Sherman had a healthy respect for his opponent's strategy, and realised only too well that every step forward would increase his supply problems, and narrow his numerical advantage. While his adversary's supply lines were shortened, he would have to commit more of his own men to defence of the railroad which was his lifeline.

Sherman's 100,000-strong force was made up of three armies. Its solid core was the Army of the Cumberland, led by the redoubtable George H. Thomas;

the two smaller components were the Army of the Tennessee, Sherman's old command, now led by the highly promising young James B. McPherson, and the Army of the Ohio, now commanded by John M. Schofield. The western armies had never cared much for spit and polish, and the more pretentious side of military routine, but, for all their intense individualism, and unkempt informality, they were now a tough and experienced fighting force, well-led, and full of confidence in Sherman himself. He was determined to strip any excess weight from the army to enable it to travel fast and hit hard. He reduced his headquarters transport to a single wagon, and abandoned the huge wagon trains which so slowed the movements of an advancing army. 'Soldiering as we have been doing in the past two years with such trains and impediments is a farce,' he wrote, 'and nothing but absolute poverty will cure it.'[11] But at the same time he prepared massive stocks of essential supplies at Nashville and Chattanooga, took over complete control of the vital railroad, and, with the help of Daniel McCallum's railroad expertise, made elaborate preparations for the repair and re-laying of track, the rebuilding or replacement of damaged bridges, and the operation of the line in the immediate wake of his advancing army. His resourcefulness became such a by-word that, when Confederate cavalry destroyed a railway tunnel, pessimists in Johnston's army said that such action was futile for Sherman was sure to carry a spare tunnel with him. He also planned to live off the Georgian countryside as much as possible, and supplemented his first-hand knowledge, based on service in the area as a young lieutenant, with a study of the census reports on every Georgia county. Logistics were, he knew, the key to success in the kind of operation which he now envisaged.

When he moved against Johnston's army early in May 1864, Sherman had no intention of making a direct challenge to the impressive Confederate position on Rocky Face Ridge. Instead, Thomas was merely to demonstrate against that position, while McPherson and Schofield moved round its flanks. McPherson's move against Johnston's left flank was the more important; indeed, in the next few weeks, Sherman's attempts to outflank Johnston's left in Georgia were to be as much of a recurring theme as Grant's attempts to outflank Lee's right in Virginia. This first move, like so many others in both theatres, failed to live up to its early promise. McPherson broke through Snake Creek Gap, but drew back when he might have swept into Resaca, and got astride the railroad in Johnston's rear. Johnston was able to withdraw safely to Resaca, and when his position there was threatened by a new flanking movement, he fell back to Cassville, and then further south again to a strong position at Allatoona Pass, after Hood had bungled an opportunity for a counter-attack against Schofield's force. Sherman had too much respect for the Allatoona Pass position to attack it directly, and took his whole army on another broad sweep round Johnston's left. Johnston moved swiftly to check his advance at New Hope Church after several days of hard fighting. Three weeks of skilful campaigning had brought Sherman a long way towards Atlanta, but Johnston had kept his army intact.

Moreover, with some reinforcements, he now had 70,000 men to face Sherman's reduced combat strength of 90,000.

Sherman now changed his tactics and shifted his line to the left, back to the railroad. Wet weather hampered any further movement in early June, and Sherman worked hard to relieve his growing anxiety about his long and vulnerable supply line, where Wheeler's cavalry was already creating trouble. For three weeks the Union army was held up before the increasingly formidable Confederate line in front of Marietta, its right resting on Kenesaw Mountain. Sherman instinctively thought of another flanking move, but rain, mud and the lie of the land made it difficult. Slowly, he convinced himself that he had now made Johnston so worried about his flanks that he had unduly weakened his force on Kenesaw Mountain itself. There were other reasons, too, why his mind turned to the idea of a frontal assault. There was no point in staying indefinitely where he was, especially with mounting supply problems; some of the men were tired of the war of manoeuvre of recent weeks, while others were all too happy to settle down to protracted, static seige operations. According to Sherman, 'a fresh furrow in a ploughed field' was sufficient obstacle to make the Army of the Cumberland stop and entrench.[12] Rather against his better judgment, then, Sherman ordered a frontal attack on Kenesaw Mountain on 27 June. It was a particularly simple, unsubtle and uncoordinated example of its ill-fated kind. After two hours, and 3,000 casualties, it was abandoned as a failure.

A hard-earned lesson and the return of fine weather persuaded Sherman to return to his previous indirect methods. Another move round the Confederate left was followed by another Johnston withdrawal to a position just north of the Chattahoochee river. But as soon as the Northern army had found suitable crossings of the river near by, Johnston was obliged to fall back yet again, on 9 July, behind Peachtree Creek, only a few miles north of Atlanta. For a week, while Sherman was bringing up supplies, Johnston went through the motions of preparing a counter-attack. But he was never to have the chance to show what he would or could have done. Jefferson Davis had now lost whatever small faith he had ever had in Johnston's will and ability to fight, and on 17 July he ordered him to hand over command of the army to Hood. In view of Johnston's skilful defence and his success in preserving his army in the previous two months, it was a harsh and perhaps foolish decision. But, in the light of Johnston's whole Civil War career, it was understandable if not altogether defensible. Johnston had pursued a Fabian policy so often when it was probably wrong that he was now ousted for pursuing it when it was almost certainly right. The most serious blunder, however, lay not in the removal of Johnston but the choice of his replacement. Hood had a magnificent combat record, and his maimed body bore eloquent testimony to his reckless courage. Broken in body, unbroken in spirit, Hood was, alas, unblessed with much intelligence or discretion. One thing at least was certain: Hood would fight, and sooner rather than later.

Three times in eight days, from 20 July to 28 July, Hood struck at various

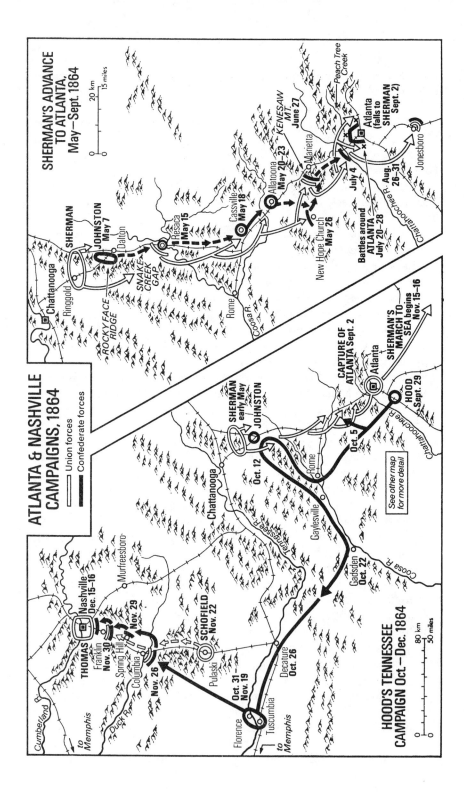

**ATLANTA & NASHVILLE CAMPAIGNS, 1864**

Union forces
Confederate forces

**HOOD'S TENNESSEE CAMPAIGN Oct.–Dec. 1864**

0 — 80 km
0 — 50 miles

to Memphis
Cumberland
Nashville Dec. 15–16
THOMAS
Franklin Nov. 30
Spring Hill Nov. 29
Murfreesboro
Columbia
Nov. 26
SCHOFIELD Nov. 22
Duck Rr.
Pulaski
Decature Oct. 26
Oct. 31–Nov. 19
Florence
Tuscumbia
to Memphis
Memphis
Chattanooga
Tennessee R.
Gaylesville
Gadsden Oct. 22
Rome
Oct. 5
See other map for more detail
Oct. 12
SHERMAN early May
JOHNSTON
CAPTURE OF ATLANTA Sept. 2
Atlanta
HOOD Sept. 29
Chattahoochee R.
SHERMAN'S MARCH TO SEA begins Nov. 15–16
Coosa R.

**SHERMAN'S ADVANCE TO ATLANTA, May–Sept. 1864**

0 — 20 km
0 — 15 miles

Chattanooga
Ringgold
ROCKY FACE RIDGE
SNAKE CREEK GAP
SHERMAN
JOHNSTON May 7
Dalton
Resaca May 15
Cassville May 18 Cassville May 26
Rome
Coosa R.
New Hope Church May 26
Allatoona May 20–23
KENESAW MT. June 27
Marietta
July 4
Peach Tree Creek
Atlanta (falls to SHERMAN Sept. 2)
Battles around ATLANTA July 20–28
Aug. 26–31
Chattahoochee R.
Jonesboro

segments of the opposing army. First, while McPherson and Schofield were swinging round north-east of Atlanta he attacked northwards on part of Thomas's front, at Peachtree Creek itself, but was defeated without much trouble. Hood now withdrew within the Atlanta defences, but only to concentrate his forces for a new challenge. Two days later he struck at McPherson, east of Atlanta, on the extreme left of the Union line. The attack achieved some initial surprise, but its force was soon blunted, and this furious encounter, generally called the battle of Atlanta, brought no gain in return for some 8,000 casualties. The Northern side suffered a cruel blow in the death of McPherson, the dashing young commander of the Army of the Tennessee. Sherman now decided that the attempt to work round Atlanta to the east was too dangerous to his own communications, and he wheeled his army round for a movement to the west of the city. Hood's attempt to counter this thrust, at the battle of Ezra Church on 28 July, ended in another costly rebuff.

Hood's policy of all-out aggression had made his army weaker and his position more vulnerable, but Sherman still faced no easy task. To make Hood's position untenable, he had to cut the remaining links between Atlanta and the rest of the Confederacy, the two railroads running south from the city, the one to Montgomery and the other, more important, running to Macon and on across Georgia to Savannah. This was the object of the movement round to the west of the city, and also of various cavalry raids in late July and August. The latter achieved no lasting success, and one operation which aimed also at the release of Union prisoners at Andersonville ended in the capture of the raiders themselves. The move round to the west and south of Atlanta would take time, and for a while Sherman was reduced to the kind of static warfare which he hated, while he pounded Atlanta with heavy siege guns.

August proved to be a trying month in both east and west. While the war in Virginia settled into dreary and tedious siege, Sherman still found the twin prizes of Atlanta and Hood's army beyond his grasp. Apart from abortive cavalry raids, Sherman was beset with other irritating problems. The replacement of McPherson with the easterner O. O. Howard ruffled feelings among his generals – although it was another easterner, the troublesome Hooker, who took his disappointment worst, and eventually departed, considerably to Sherman's relief. He was always anxious about his long line of communications, but refused to panic when Hood sent Wheeler's cavalry against them. Further west, in Mississippi and Tennessee, was the chronic menace of more Confederate cavalry under the irrepressible Nathan Bedford Forrest. Back in June he had humiliated a force twice the size of his own, under Samuel D. Sturgis, at the battle of Brice's Cross Roads, in northern Mississippi. In July he had come off much worse in an encounter at Tupelo with another force sent by Sherman to destroy him. But by August he was raiding once again through Tennessee, and late in the month he even rode into Memphis and almost captured the Union commander there. While Forrest was still at large, Sherman's supply line all the way back to Nashville could never be completely secure.

As August drew to its close, Sherman was ready to tighten the noose around Atlanta. On 26 August, his forces began to swing south of the city. Two days later they cut the railroad to Montgomery, and three days later they occupied a long stretch of the vital line to Macon. Hood, having at first nursed the illusion that Sherman was abandoning his attempt to take Atlanta, awoke to the real danger too late. He sent half his army along the railroad to Jonesboro, but it could not dislodge the Union forces, and was soon in danger itself. Hood now had no alternative but to abandon Atlanta if he was not to be trapped there himself. Having destroyed his supply dumps on the night of 31 August, he retreated to the south-east, and on 1 September, Atlanta was at last in Sherman's hands.

The capture of Atlanta was even more important as a symbol than a fact. Like Richmond in the east, it had become the obvious target, the simple standard by which success or failure could be measured in the eyes of the general public. Its psychological and political importance was all the greater because of the timing of its capture. It revived Northern spirits at a time when some such boost was desperately needed; it came as a priceless gift to Lincoln and his party, with the election only two months away. In the purely military sense, the taking of Atlanta was a valuable achievement, but not an unqualified success. Sherman had taken the city but not Hood's army, and some critics then and later were inclined to argue that he had come to share the popular fixation about Atlanta, and reversed his proper order of priorities. Certainly, to hold Atlanta was to take an important step towards breaking up the Confederacy, but it was far from certain whether, once taken, the city could in fact be held – or even whether it was worth holding. A prize which demanded half an army to defend it and the other half to protect its long and precarious lifeline was a prize of very dubious value – and seemed likely to remain so while Hood's army was intact. Sherman had fought a brilliant campaign over difficult territory, but its worth depended on how he could now exploit what he had won. Atlanta would be a true prize if it marked not only an end but a new beginning.

5. In retrospect, it is clear that the fall of Atlanta marked the turn of the year's campaigning. For four months before, a massive and costly Union effort had reaped scant reward – or at least little that could be clearly seen and understood as success. In the next four months the walls of the Confederacy came tumbling down. By the end of the year its main army was wasting away in its Virginia stockade; another army had been destroyed in Tennessee; Georgia had watched helplessly as Sherman marched from Atlanta to the sea.

Around Petersburg and Richmond, nothing spectacular happened, but the life and the hope were slowly ebbing out of Lee's army. Grant made some small gains, like the capture of Fort Harrison at the end of September, and suffered some serious disappointments, notably the failure, in late October, of a last attempt to cut the South Side Railroad before the onset of winter. But generally he had to content himself with the maintenance of a steady squeeze on the

Confederate position, while Lee was obliged to spread his men ever more thinly, as the lines were gradually extended south and south-west of Petersburg. By the time that both sides went into winter quarters, the plight of Lee's army was desperate. Sickness and desertion were taking their toll as well as enemy action; the men who stayed at their posts were short of food, warmth and shelter, and running dangerously low in weapons and ammunition.

The most dramatic action in Virginia in the fall was in the Shenandoah Valley. It took Sheridan most of August to organise the motley collection of troops which he had been assigned to command. In all, they numbered almost 50,000, but so many of them were scattered at various points in the West Virginia mountains and elsewhere that Sheridan could never deploy anything like that number in the Valley itself. Against him stood the stalwart Early, with a force now brought up to some 25,000. In addition, constantly threatening the flanks and outposts, supplies and communications of the Union army, were bands of guerrillas and marauders, as elusive as they were destructive. Some, like the audacious John S. Mosby, were fully-fledged members of the Confederate army; others were no more than vultures feeding on the rich pickings from the chaos of war. Sheridan's task was, quite simply, to eliminate the Shenandoah Valley from the war, both as an avenue for Confederate incursions into the North and as an invaluable source of food for Lee's army. The means of achieving these twin goals were first to pursue and eventually destroy Early's force and secondly to lay waste the fertile farmland of the region. In the words of Grant's orders to Sheridan:

In pushing up the Shenandoah Valley . . . it is desirable that nothing should be left to invite the enemy to return. Take all provisions, forage and stock wanted for the use of your command. Such as cannot be consumed, destroy.[13]

In the earlier stages of his campaign, Sheridan found this second task easier than the first. As he advanced up the Valley, he set about the work of devastation with energy and efficiency. But, impressed by the strength of Early's position at Fisher's Hill (and over-impressed by inflated estimates of Confederate strength), he withdrew almost back to his starting-point just south of the Potomac. However, spurred on by a visit from Grant, and encouraged by the return of one of Early's divisions to Petersburg, Sheridan moved south again with a stronger sense of aggressive purpose. He encountered Early at Opequon Creek on 19 September, and after an inauspicious start defeated him soundly. Early retreated to Fisher's Hill, twelve miles to the south, but the position which had deterred Sheridan a few weeks earlier held no terrors for him now. He smashed the Confederate defences on 22 September and drove Early in headlong flight up the Valley. In the next month the work of laying waste the beautiful Shenandoah Valley went ahead relentlessly. On 7 October, for example, Sheridan could report that:

The whole country from the Blue Ridge to the North Mountains has been made untenable for a rebel army. I have destroyed over 2,000 barns filled with wheat, hay and farming implements; over seventy mills filled with flour and wheat; have driven in front of the army over 4,000 head of stock, and have killed and issued to the troops not less than 3,000 sheep.

When the work was completed, he said 'the Valley, from Winchester up to Staunton, ninety-two miles, will have little in it for man or beast'.[14] The rich harvest of 1864 which Early's men had worked frantically to gather was now denied to the hungry men of Lee's army during the winter.

For all that, Sheridan did not believe that his force was strong enough to do what Grant wanted most of all – to break the rail links between the upper Valley, Lynchburg and Charlottesville, and Richmond – and he even talked of returning some of his troops to Grant's army, and limiting himself to a defensive role. But in the event he kept all his troops and it was just as well that he did. After completing his work of destruction, he had retired down the Valley, and the irrepressible Early, reinforced once again, was on the march against his position behind Cedar Creek. Despite being outnumbered at least three to two, Early launched a successful surprise attack in the misty early morning of 19 October. The Union left was routed, and men fled in panic. Disaster seemed imminent, but the Confederate attack was losing momentum, and Early had no reserves to revive it. Sheridan was back in Winchester when the battle began, on the return journey from a conference in Washington. He hastened south, rallying fugitives as he went, helping to restore stability to the Union position, and then launching a powerful counter-attack which brought to a triumphant end a day which had threatened humiliation and ruin. It was a remarkable performance by a general who had no superior in the Civil War in leadership on the field of battle itself. Cedar Creek proved to be the last act of the drama in the Shenandoah Valley. Early retreated southward and was never strong enough to challenge Sheridan again. By the end of the year most of his troops had been sent back to Richmond and Petersburg, and he was left with barely 1,000 cold and hungry men. It was a sad end to six months of heroic battle against the odds. For his part, Sheridan had helped to seal Lee's fate as surely as anything which happened around Richmond and Petersburg.

6. While Sheridan was scorching up and down the Valley in September and October, Sherman, that other apostle of all-out war, remained strangely quiet at Atlanta. Some of his three-year veterans departed, others took a long leave before re-enlisting. Other men were given leave to go home to vote, and some of the political generals went off to fight in the election campaign. Sherman engaged in his own war of words with Hood and others, over his decision to evacuate all the civilians from Atlanta. (The idea was partly to avoid committing large numbers of troops to garrison duty, and thus to enable a smaller number of men to keep a firm hold on the fortified city.) In answer to protests about such high-handed treatment of civilians, Sherman coined some of his most

characteristic phrases about the nature of war: 'War is cruelty, and you cannot refine it', and 'If the people raise a howl against my barbarity and cruelty, I will answer that war is war and not popularity-seeking'.[15]

Although Sherman and Hood were inactive for several weeks after the fall of Atlanta, each knew that he could not, and must not, remain immobile for very much longer. If Sherman remained content to sit in Atlanta, he would find more and more of his men committed to defence of his rail communications (already being raided by Forrest's and Wheeler's cavalry) and he would surrender the initiative which he had held since May. In any case, he was anxious to press on to the next objective; the difficulty was in deciding what that objective should be. Hood's army remained an important target but an elusive one. Mobile on the Gulf coast had figured prominently in earlier planning, but, although the navy had closed Mobile Bay in August, there was no Union army in the area capable of linking up with an advance from Atlanta. Sherman's thoughts turned more and more to the notion of a bold, direct thrust straight across Georgia, to the Atlantic coast, at or near Savannah. But it would take time to mature such an apparently hazardous plan, and more time to convince Grant and Lincoln that it should be tried. Meanwhile, Sherman's adversary Hood was even more aware of the perils of standing still. His 40,000 men were tired and dispirited after the fall of Atlanta, and threatened to melt away through demoralisation, desertion and refusal to re-enlist, unless Hood could breathe new life into them. If a static defence threatened the army with dissolution, a direct attack on Sherman threatened it with destruction. The best prospect seemed to be a war of movement and manoeuvre which would regain the initiative, keep the men busy, and possibly tempt Sherman into rash attack. From September to December Hood proceeded from gamble to gamble, in part because that was his nature, but mainly because the risks of pushing on always seemed less awesome than the dangers of standing still. With Hood determined to push north and Sherman fixing his eye on Savannah, there gradually emerged a unique situation in which each army was to press ahead with its own attacking plan, in defiance of the other, and in exactly opposite directions. The essential difference between the two, however, was that Sherman could leave Thomas to cope with Hood, while Hood left no one to check Sherman.

Jefferson Davis visited Hood's army in late September to discuss strategy and to boost both military and civilian morale in Georgia. He had little success in the latter objective, and his speeches assuring the local people that Hood was about to strike north against the enemy's supply line merely served to confirm Sherman's suspicions about Confederate intentions. Davis also confirmed the appointment of Beauregard as commander of the department of the west. This was the kind of unsatisfactory coordinating role to which Johnston had been assigned two years earlier; it involved Beauregard in hectic dashes from one trouble spot to the next but bestowed on him no real authority. He had grave misgivings about Hood's plans in the next two months, but proved unable or unwilling to restrain him.

On 29 September, Hood began his move north to menace Sherman's long supply line back to Chattanooga and Nashville. By advancing through the country to the west of the railroad, but parallel with it, he could descend upon it as opportunity arose, and perhaps entice Sherman into a battle on terms favourable to himself. In the next two weeks the armies retraced their steps over much of the ground covered in Sherman's advance a few months earlier. Sherman left one corps at Atlanta, and then took up the pursuit on 3 October. But Hood was by now well ahead, and his men were ripping up railroad track at various points. On 5 October, part of Hood's army attacked Allatoona but was foiled by the heroic defence of John M. Corse and his small force. By 12 October, Hood's vanguard was at Resaca and was soon pushing further north, nearer to Chattanooga, but he then veered south-west to Gaylesville and then Gadsden. In fact, although both armies had moved with remarkable speed, neither commander could derive much satisfaction from the turn of events. Hood could cut the railroad almost at will, but the disruption which he caused was only temporary, for Sherman's men were very expert in rapid repairs to the track. More important, there was no sign that Sherman could be tempted into an ill-judged attack somewhere in northern Georgia. Hood's thoughts were turning to a new plan – a march westward, and then a drive north into central Tennessee, which would keep the initiative in his hands and might upset Northern offensive plans for the rest of the year. At the same time, Sherman's distaste for a wild goose chase over the hills of north Georgia convinced him once and for all that he must not be tied to defence of the railroad, and that his right course was to return to Atlanta, and press on to the south. While Hood dreamed of sweeping through Tennessee and Kentucky to the Ohio river, Sherman was determined to march to the Atlantic. 'Let him go north,' said Sherman, 'my business is down South.'[16] Two armies, now only a few miles from each other, were aiming at objectives over five hundred miles apart.

For weeks Sherman had been bombarding Grant with arguments in support of his plan to march to the sea. The only way to solve his problem of defending vulnerable communications, he pleaded, was to abandon them altogether. Then he would be free to do what he chose – to 'make Georgia howl' and carry the war deep into the heart of the Confederacy. More than ever he was convinced that the best way for the North to win the war was to convince the people of the South that they could not win. In a letter to Grant shortly before the march began, he summed up his case:

If we can march a well-appointed army right through his territory, it is a demonstration to the world, foreign and domestic, that we have a power which Davis cannot resist. This may not be war but rather statesmanship, nevertheless it is overwhelming to my mind that there are thousands of people abroad and in the South who reason thus: If the North can march an army right through the South, it is proof positive that the North can prevail.[17]

Grant admired the boldness and aggressiveness of Sherman's plan, but worried about its risks. It left Hood's army at large, and the evidence increasingly suggested that Hood was about to invade Tennessee. It was also vital that the Union navy should be able to link up with Sherman when he reached the coast at or near Savannah, so that he would not be left isolated and out of reach. Perhaps, fundamentally, Grant objected that Sherman's plan seemed to make territory rather than the enemy army its focal point. In fact Sherman's blend of imagination and tough-minded realism had carried him beyond Grant's thinking to the point where it was as important to break the civilian will to fight as the military capacity to fight. Sherman's reassurances and persistence finally won Grant over, and he was authorised to go ahead with his march. In view of the audacity and unorthodoxy of his plan, the eventual willingness of Grant and Lincoln to endorse it compels admiration. It was some consolation to Lincoln that, before this risky venture was actually launched, his own political victory in the election of 1864 was assured.

In early November Sherman prepared his expedition. Thomas had been sent to Nashville earlier to defend Tennessee, and he was now given more troops to add to the varied and somewhat unpromising material with which he was required to work. Quite deliberately, Sherman kept the cream of the army for himself – a force of over 60,000, stripped for quick-moving action and unencumbered by excess baggage. Great quantities of supplies were sent back north before the rail and telegraph links with Chattanooga were cut. In Atlanta itself, factories, warehouses, and railroad installations were destroyed, and the fires started in such places on the night of 15 November inevitably spread to many houses, too. Something like a third of the area of Atlanta was consumed by the blaze, and looters added to the city's woes. Despite all the damage, however, many of its people – and much of its normal life – returned to the city very soon after Sherman's departure.

Sherman's army moved out of Atlanta on 15–16 November in four columns which spread out over a front twenty miles or more in width. Their rate of progress was steady, often less than the modest fifteen miles per day which had been projected. The army was to live largely off the country; each brigade would send out foraging parties every day, which would return in the evening, often groaning under the day's haul of grain, vegetables, meat, and other booty. On the flanks of Sherman's march there moved an irregular army of stragglers, looters, thieves and deserters from both armies who were much less fastidious in their methods, and more wanton in their destruction. Not merely Georgia, but the whole Confederacy, howled in protest as Sherman had predicted, but atrocity stories about the 'Attila of the West', and the rape, butchery and plunder committed by his barbarian horde, were wildly exaggerated. The reality, to be sure, was ugly enough. A corridor, 250 miles long and up to 50 miles wide, from Atlanta to Savannah, was swept almost bare of provisions and livestock, and the systematic destruction of railroads, bridges, mills, workshops and many public buildings left a trail of twisted metal and smoke-blackened ruins behind the marching army. Sherman was certainly making his point to the people of the south.

The white people of Georgia trembled at the approach of Sherman's column, shuddered at the loss of their animals and provisions, but were usually relieved (some perhaps a little disappointed) at being left unmolested themselves, as long as they did not attempt to resist the invader. The black population came out in droves to welcome this new Moses, come to lead them into the promised land of freedom, but were often disappointed by his first edicts. Thousands of Negroes tagged along behind the advancing columns, but Sherman was determined that his military machine should not be clogged with a mass of refugees, and allowed only able-bodied men, useful as labourers, to stay with the army. The rest were asked to stay at home, not to seek revenge against their former masters, and to await the coming of their true and lasting freedom. Whether black or white, all the people in the path of Sherman's army must have been impressed by his demonstration of the power of the Union at arms. One Negro, overwhelmed by the spectacle of 'millions' of marching men, was moved to ask whether there was anyone left in the north.

The march to the sea was virtually unopposed. Wheeler's cavalry and the state militia were powerless to do more than make an occasional nuisance of themselves, and Beauregard, in his new and thankless role, soon resigned himself to the limited but still unpromising task of trying to prepare the defences of Savannah. When Sherman approached those defences on 9 December, he decided that they were too well manned by Hardee's 15,000 troops to permit a direct assault. But he moved on to the mouth of the Ogeechee River, fifteen miles to the south, took Fort McAllister by storm on 13 December, and made contact with Union warships in the sound. Having thus established a secure supply base, he moved upon Savannah. Hardee was determined not to be trapped inside the city and abandoned it on 21 December. On Christmas Eve Lincoln received Sherman's despatch presenting the city of Savannah as a Christmas gift. Sherman's bold and unconventional strategy had been completely vindicated, and he was soon thinking of a new drive northwards through the Carolinas. His march through Georgia had created unparalleled excitement and suspense in the north. During the month when no word came, there was no shortage of armchair critics to pass premature judgment on its inevitable disaster. When the news from Savannah finally arrived, it created that special kind of euphoria which springs partly from relief. As for the South, even the most ardent and loyal Confederate could scarcely mistake the meaning of what Sherman had done. To make December an even blacker month, humiliation in Georgia was matched by disaster in Tennessee.

7. After breaking off his operations against Sherman and his line of communications in mid-October, Hood had marched across northern Alabama to Decatur and then on to Tuscumbia on the Tennessee river. He put a division across the river at Florence, and prepared for his new thrust into Tennessee. The more

desperate Hood's plight, the more grandiose his plans became. He hoped now to advance quickly into Tennessee, defeat Thomas before he could assemble his scattered forces, capture Nashville, and then press on into Kentucky. Like Bragg two years earlier, he had hopes of attracting new recruits in the border states. If Sherman came after him, he would deal with him in Kentucky. Then he would be ready if necessary to cross the mountains and come to the relief of Lee in Virginia. Even if this last far-fetched notion is not taken too seriously, the plan showed too much ambition and too little precision. It never really allowed for the contingency that Sherman would simply ignore it (or leave Thomas to deal with it) and carry on with his march to the sea. When Sherman did precisely that, Hood was too far away to oppose him – and he feared in any case that a hectic rush back into Georgia would lead to the final disintegration of his fragile army.

If Hood was to have any chance of realising even the more modest and immediate objectives of his plan, he would have to move fast. There was a brief period in early November when Thomas was still ill-prepared to meet his advance. Thomas had some 60,000 men all told, but they were widely scattered, and he was dilatory in bringing them together. The reinforcements from Missouri which he was promised were slow to arrive, and many of the troops on hand at Nashville were raw recruits. James H. Wilson was labouring hard to create a cavalry force out of almost nothing, to face the Confederate cavalry under the legendary Forrest. But Hood delayed for almost three weeks at Tuscumbia, waiting for Forrest to return from a raid, waiting for railroads to be patched up and supplies to arrive, and waiting for a clearer idea of what exactly he should do. That delay was fatal to a plan which had been sickly from birth.

When Forrest arrived, Hood had over 50,000 men, and on 19 November he moved forward at last. Thomas had pushed Schofield with about 34,000 men forward to Pulaski to delay any Confederate advance, and give him more time to organise his forces at Nashville. Hood tried to get between Schofield and his line of retreat back to Nashville, and he very nearly succeeded. Schofield withdrew to Columbia on the Duck River just in time, but he was not safe there for long. Hood crossed the river a few miles east of Columbia and headed for Spring Hill, astride the only good road leading north to Franklin and Nashville. There at Spring Hill, on 29 November, he missed his best and last opportunity. Schofield was extremely slow to react to the danger at his rear; most of his force was still at Columbia and he had only 5,000 men to oppose at least 25,000 Confederates who approached Spring Hill that afternoon. Between then and nightfall, Hood never succeeded in mounting a full-scale attack, through a mixture of uncertainty, imprecise orders, poor coordination, and blunders by both himself and some of his subordinates. That night, Schofield's troops passed along the road through Spring Hill under the noses of Hood's army. They went unmolested and made their way safely north to Franklin.

There, next day, Hood made the mistake which better generals had made before him. Having missed a golden opportunity, he tried to atone for it by a reckless assault in unfavourable conditions. Schofield had taken up a good defensive position with both flanks resting on the Harpeth River. Hood's subordinates recommended another flanking move, but their commander blamed them for the failure at Spring Hill, and was disinclined to heed their counsel. Instead, he ordered a frontal attack against Schofield's position in the late afternoon. It enjoyed some brief initial success, but it was a hopeless cause, and wave after wave of later attacks broke against the Union line. Before the assault was called off, Hood's army had suffered 6,000 casualties, the defenders little more than a third of that number. Several generals, including the redoubtable Pat Cleburne, lost their lives in the assault, in a vain attempt to answer Hood's slurs on the fighting quality of their men. Now the Confederate army was severely depleted in strength and drained of all confidence and hope. But, when Schofield fell back to the Nashville defences, Hood followed him. He had no clear idea what to do next; he could scarcely challenge the full strength of Thomas and Schofield in one of the most strongly fortified cities in America, but he feared that any attempt to withdraw would lead to the final disintegration of his army. He therefore neither attacked nor retreated, but sat and awaited his fate outside Nashville.

He had to wait for two weeks. His opponent, George H. Thomas, was massively thorough and reliable, but he was also unhurried and deliberate in everything he did. He was determined that, when he attacked, his victory should be complete, and he would not attack until he was fully prepared. He knew that Hood now offered no real threat; casualties, sickness and desertion had reduced his strength to under 25,000 cold, hungry and dispirited men. Forrest's cavalry were away on another raid towards Murfreesboro. Thomas outnumbered Hood by at least two to one, and he was creating a situation where that superiority would really tell. While he waited, the main threat to Thomas came not from the enemy in front but from his impatient superiors in the east. The situation in Tennessee looked very different, and much more threatening, when viewed from several hundred miles away. With the campaign in Virginia frozen into winter immobility, and with Sherman 'lost' somewhere in Georgia, there was anxiety about the consequences of a possible setback in Tennessee. It was bad enough that a Confederate army should have returned to central Tennessee at all, and Grant and Lincoln took seriously the possibility that Hood would now by-pass Nashville and rampage through Kentucky. Appreciating neither the enfeebled state of Hood's army nor Thomas's mastery of the situation, they saw only another general offering inadequate excuses for needless delay. Grant thought seriously of replacing Thomas with Schofield, and when freezing weather caused a further delay, he ordered John A. Logan to proceed to Nashville to take command. The choice of Logan, one of the more able and aggressive of the political generals but no match for the man he was to replace, suggests that Grant was less than fair in his judgment of the qualities of Thomas. Within a day or so, Grant decided that he should go in person to direct operations at

Nashville. But before Logan could reach his new command, and while Grant had got no further than Washington, there came news which removed all dangers to Thomas's position whether from front or rear.

On 15 December, he delivered the crushing blow against Hood which he had so meticulously prepared, and which a thaw now permitted. Hood's army reeled and tottered under the onslaught, but it survived to fight one more day on a new line a little further south. On the afternoon of 16 December, Thomas renewed the attack, and by nightfall the tattered remnants of Hood's army were fleeing for their lives. In the battle of Nashville, Thomas achieved the kind of total victory which he had sought; he came nearer than any other general in the Civil War to the complete destruction of an opposing army. Some kind of order was restored among the survivors of Hood's army, as they retreated south to the Tennessee river, although they were pursued and harassed by Wilson's cavalry. They escaped across the river in the last few days of the year, and dragged themselves wearily into northern Mississippi. Utterly demoralised and crippled, the Army of Tennessee was but a shadow of its once formidable self. In January 1865, Hood asked to be relieved, and most of the troops who had any fight left in them were transferred east to the Carolinas to join the hopeless resistance to Sherman's advance. All that was left on the army's old stamping ground, where so much of the war had been decided, was the cavalry of Nathan Bedford Forrest.

8. The whole Confederate western front from the Appalachians to the Mississippi had now collapsed. Beyond the Mississippi, too, large-scale fighting was over. That doughty champion of the western Confederacy, Sterling Price, had led 13,000 men out of Arkansas into Missouri in September and October, in a last desperate bid to turn the tide. Briefly, they had threatened St Louis, and had then veered off westwards across Missouri before being defeated at Westport and forced to retire. In the east, the Confederate army had been powerless to resist Sherman as he swept across what had hitherto been the least vulnerable part of the Southern homeland. Collapse in the west and humiliation in Georgia left Lee and his army as the last line of defence of a shrivelled and debilitated Confederacy. But Lee's army too was depleted if not yet defeated, and the Shenandoah Valley, so often a source of hope and comfort, now offered only despair and desolation. With military collapse came political, social and economic collapse as internal dissensions multiplied, unthinkable remedies like arming the slaves were seriously considered, financial chaos spread, shortages pinched harder, morale plummeted, and law and order broke down. The end was in sight except for those like Jefferson Davis who refused to see it.

Thomas's victory at Nashville and Sherman's arrival at Savannah were proof of the overwhelming power of Northern arms which even the pessimists and the sceptics in the north could not deny. Equally important, Lincoln's victory in the election of 1864 finally robbed the Confederacy of hopes of salvation through political rather than military means. All three successes – Thomas's, Sherman's and Lincoln's – were also fit symbols of the progress of the Union cause in 1864. Thomas's deliberate build-up culminated in sudden and complete victory; Sherman disappeared into his 'tunnel' in Georgia for a long and anxious month before emerging triumphant at Savannah; Lincoln endured periods of doubt and depression before winning re-election. So it was with the whole policy of relentless pressure against Southern arms and Southern will devised and executed by Lincoln, Grant, and Sherman. It, too, had its long, slow build-up, its tunnels of anxiety and gloom, its periods of waning confidence and wavering morale. For months, it worked only stealthily, in scarcely discernible ways – by attrition and erosion, and steady undermining of Confederate strength. Then, at the end of the year, it erupted into brilliant, spectacular and unmistakable achievements. For much of 1864 the people of the North endured an agony of frustration; now the people of the South faced the harsher agony of despair and defeat. On the battlefield and in the ballot box, the North proclaimed in November and December 1864 that it was about to win the war.

# Chapter XVI : The Politics of War, 1863–1864

The year 1863 was a year of crisis on the home front. In both north and south the harsh realities of war were biting more deeply than ever. The cost in lives and money, privation and discomfort mounted ever higher, without any real sign on either side that reward in the shape of final victory was just around the corner. Men in their thousands were killed and maimed, prices spiralled upwards, taxes multiplied, treasured freedoms were circumscribed, normal life was disrupted – and all to what purpose? Both Union and Confederate governments struggled to keep the war going, and bolster sagging popular support. By 1863, opposition voices had grown louder and bolder in both camps. After the setback of the fall elections in 1862, Lincoln faced an upsurge of discontent and a plague of war weariness, especially in the west, in the bleak, early months of 1863. Gettysburg and Vicksburg put new heart into the North, but the rest of the year was one long anti-climax: stalemate in Virginia, near-disaster in Tennessee, and frustration at home. For the Confederacy, the year had begun well at the front, with Fredericksburg and Chancellorsville in the east, and Grant's apparent floundering before Vicksburg in the west. But even then there was ample evidence to show how tightly stretched were Southern manpower and resources, how slender was the margin of Southern survival, how heavy was the price already paid. The defeats of mid-summer rammed these lessons home, and the reaction to disappointment and failure was less often a re-dedication to the cause than a search for scapegoats. By 1864, frustration was the great danger to Northern morale, but despair was gaining ground in the south.

1. Jefferson Davis began and ended the year 1863 with messages to Congress which called for new sacrifices and the passage of tougher war measures to counteract the drain on men, money and supplies. In each case, after an abundance of recrimination, a congressional majority gave him a high proportion of what he asked. But on the second occasion neither he nor they could put from their minds all that had passed in that fateful year. It was not just the military defeats – Gettysburg, Vicksburg and Chattanooga above all – though they were bad enough. It was not only the direct military consequences of those defeats – the splitting of the Confederacy along the line of the Mississippi, the loss of large stretches of valuable territory – although these were disquieting enough, and inevitably meant that mounting burdens were now to be shared by fewer people with scantier resources. There was also inescapable evidence of depression and dissension on the home front, going deeper than the windy protests of congressmen, or the splenetic outbursts of editors, or the endless disputes between Richmond and the state capitals. There was serious grass-roots discontent now, indicated by increasing desertion from the army, evasion of some unpopular laws and open flouting of others, and an insidious sapping of morale, brought on by shortages, rampant inflation, frayed nerves, and shattered bodies. Protest in one of its uglier moods reached the president's own front door in the Richmond bread riot of 2 April 1863, when windows were smashed and shops were looted before Davis himself courageously confronted the mob and persuaded them to disperse. This was no isolated outburst, and other Southern cities felt the rumblings of protest during the year.

It was, to say the least, unfortunate for Davis and his supporters that it was now in the wake of military failure and in the midst of popular unrest that they confronted a major test at the polls. The congressional elections of 1863 straggled on through the late summer and autumn, and they turned more and more on the policies of the administration which now bore not merely the burden of unpopularity but the stigma of failure. It cut little ice with many voters to argue that there were deeper causes of recent setbacks, or that far from being too tough, policies had not been tough enough. Even candidates who were loyal to the administration often found it advisable to adopt the tactic of proclaiming their general support, but making exceptions of measures particularly unpopular in their own locality.

Personalities and local issues affected the outcome of the elections, but the general pattern was clear enough.[1] Whereas about one-fifth of the members of the retiring house had been consistently anti-administration, 41 out of 106 members of the new house were to fall into that category, and 12 out of 28 senators. In themselves these figures did not represent a landslide defeat for Davis and his supporters, but they did not tell the whole story. The elections of 1863 highlighted a situation which was becoming apparent even in the earlier Congress. The strongest support for the administration came from the border and other occupied states, and from those areas actually in the front line. By 1863, many of these constituencies were fiction rather than fact. The pitifully small vote which elected most of their representatives came largely from soldiers and refugees. Between them, Arkansas, Louisiana, Mississippi, Missouri, Kentucky and Tennessee returned only 5 opponents of the administration out of 47 members. The stronghold of the opposition, on the other hand, was in the Carolinas and Georgia, with Alabama, Florida and Texas not far behind. In North Carolina the battle was between varying degrees of hostility to the administration; not one Davis sympathiser was returned, and 8 out of 10 men elected had not served in the previous Congress. There was a similar turnover in Georgia and South Carolina; administration supporters who stood for re-election were swept away in the tide of protest. The six states of North and South Carolina, Georgia, Alabama, Florida and Texas had 43 seats in the house, and 32 of them were won by anti-administration candidates. Another notable feature of the results was the return of many ex-whigs, and men who had opposed secession in 1860–1. The united front of the early, exciting days of independence had cracked with a vengeance. Davis was left to soldier on, making the best he could of the support of men whose constituencies lay beyond his or their control, behind the Union lines. It was, to put it mildly, an embarrassing position.

2. Opposition flourished, of course, because the war was going badly. Bad news from the front served to reinforce long-standing criticisms of Confederate policy. Some of the opposition was petty and trivial, but still damaging. Personal spite inspired many of the vicious attacks on Davis in papers like the Richmond *Examiner* and the Charleston *Mercury*, and some of the president's civilian and military advisers – Benjamin and Memminger, Bragg and Pemberton, for example – were targets for similar abuse. There were constant complaints about presidential favouritism, or about the undue influence of West Point-trained officers. There were denunciations of administrative slackness in security matters – in the treatment of spies, traitors, Union sympathisers, applicants for permission to pass through the lines – or, conversely, protests about red-tape, and the proliferation of forms and passes of all kinds, where a more rigorous policy was enforced. Time after time, however, serious opposition came back to a handful of basic issues, involving the raising of men and supplies for the army, the financing of the war effort, and the assumption of special powers, in particular the suspension of the writ of habeas corpus and the resort to martial law. These questions were fiercely debated not only on their own merits, but as sources of friction between the Confederate government and the states. A closer look at one or two of them may indicate the growing conflict between two priorities: winning the war, and protecting the cause for which the war was being fought.

It is worth recalling that financial policy[2] not only represented one of the great failures of the government and one of the great weaknesses of the whole Confederacy, but also that it pressed hard on almost every citizen on every day of his life. The decline and ultimate collapse of Confederate morale owed as much to the depressing and confidence-sapping effects of wild inflation as any other single cause. Paper money sprouted more noughts after the first digit with increasing regularity, and fantastic prices gave an air of bizarre unreality not merely to large-scale commercial transactions, but to the humblest shopping expedition – the purchase of a loaf of bread or a pair of shoes. Few things, if any, did more to convince the ordinary citizen in the latter part of the war that the world in which he was living was not real and could not last.

Political issues arose from the recruitment of the armies, both before and after conscription.[3] Again, however, the chronic nature of the complaints merits emphasis. Arguments about the command of troops from a particular state never subsided for long. Governor Brown of Georgia was still wrangling with Davis on this question in the wake of the Vicksburg and Gettysburg disasters in 1863. Disputes over a state's right to supply its own troops showed equally few signs of fading away. Governor Vance of North Carolina made much of this issue, and could afford to do so, because of his control over his state's sizable textile industry. But it was of course conscription which did most of all to keep the flames of controversy burning brightly throughout the last three years of the war. Inevitably, the very idea of compulsory service was widely regarded as an affront to the rights of states and individual citizens alike. But once again, passage of a law by comfortable congressional majorities did not decide the matter; it merely opened a new and stormier chapter. Every subsequent session of Congress had its debates over extension or reform of the conscription act or the exemption laws. There was endless tinkering with the latter, but while the legislators closed loopholes with one hand they opened fresh ones with the other. Conscription and exemption are classic examples of laws where objections in principle were constantly nourished by protests about actual practice. State governments and their citizens drew on all the resources of obstruction, evasion, and downright defiance at their command, and the central government lacked the machinery to enforce the law consistently and effectively. Conscription did work unfairly, and the actions of its critics aggravated that unfairness. It aroused not merely individual grievances but discontent which ran along sectional and class lines, as well as through states rights channels. It also failed to deliver the goods in rebuilding the waning strength of the army. Ineffectiveness in results and injustice in execution fed upon each other, and opposition fed on both. The administration, the army, and popular morale were the victims.

Two different points of view expressed in the summer of 1863 on conscription and exemption may suggest the passions aroused by both their principle and their practice. Robert Toombs, by now completely disenchanted with the administration, deplored the demoralising effects of compulsory service:

The morale of the army is now pretty much gone. We never had a desertion until we had conscription, for the very good reason that there were thousands outside who wanted to take the places of those inside, and besides men who felt an interest in the cause stepped forward full of energy and enthusiasm for its defence. Conscription and conscription alone destroyed all that feeling. When we began to hunt up men with dogs like the Mexicans, they necessarily became as worthless as Mexicans, and every day has seen a deterioration of the troops brought in as conscripts.[4]

Both the facts and the assumptions underlying Toombs's argument were shaky, but the feeling was genuine enough. The situation looked rather different to the group of generals in the Army of Tennessee who complained to Richmond at much the same time about the operation of conscription in general and exemptions in particular. It was vital, they said, 'to take prompt measures to recruit our wasted armies by fresh levies at home'. Popular illusions on the subject had to be destroyed:

> It is assumed that none of the machinery of society, necessary for its comfort and convenience in a state of peace, is to be disturbed amidst the mighty upheaval of a great revolution. . . . We have been pained to notice that all those vocations are crowded which afford exemption, while the ranks of the army are daily becoming thinner. To their lasting reproach upon their manhood, hearty vigorous young men, rather than take the field, eagerly seek fancy duty which could be performed by women or disabled soldiers.[5]

Such views illustrate the dilemma between the virtue and the viability of their cause, with which Southerners wrestled from first to last.

Financial failure and recruiting difficulties had much to do with two more highly controversial government policies. The first of these concerned supplies for the men recruited, the second was in part a device for putting them in uniform and keeping them there. Basic shortages, and problems of transport and distribution, would have made logistics an unenviable problem at the best of times. Rapidly rising prices made the problem many times worse. Farmers held on to their crops in the confident expectation of a higher price and a greater profit. Speculators bought up supplies and held them for a while for the same reasons. In this situation, army officers began to impress needed supplies from farms in their vicinity, offering in return notes on the Treasury for what they deemed a fair price. The practice spread steadily during 1862, and so did abuses arising from it. It was often carried out with scant regard for justice, honesty or the well-being of the farmer, and it hit hard those who lived within easy reach of large concentrations of troops. Up to this point, the practice had the sanction of no specific Confederate law, and relied on conventional military usage. By 1863, however, with market prices rising to ever giddier heights, and the army's supply problems growing steadily more acute, Congress responded to administration prompting with a measure intended to regularise the position and redress accumulated grievances. The Impressment Act of 26 March 1863 was a complex measure which always looked better on paper than it proved in practice.

Impressment was to be exclusively in the hands of Quartermaster and Commissary officers. If they could not agree a fair price with the farmer or other supplier, there was an elaborate system of appeals, first to local appraisers, then to state commissioners (one appointed by the president, one by the state governor). The commissioners were also to fix schedules of impressment prices, to be published every two months. Only an owner's surplus goods were liable to impressment; he was to be left enough to support himself and his family, and carry on his farm or business.

Congressional and popular support for such a far-reaching measure indicated some awareness of crying need. After all, such a law touched one of the most sensitive spots in the make-up of the Southerner (or for that matter of any American) – the sanctity of private property in general, and his own property in particular. Impressment was a notable congressional triumph over excessive constitutional scruple, but, alas for the South, this victory for common sense was ruined by its operation in practice. Legislation failed to remove the evils of impressment as it had operated before March 1863. Impressment prices remained far below market prices – this was after all one purpose of the law – and the gap widened as inflation went wild in the later stages of the war. Interference with the operations of the market in fact reduced the quantity of supplies upon which the authorities could draw. Farmers still tried to hoard their grain and their livestock, and hide them from the impressment officers. Disinclination to sell, prompted by the low price offered, was further enhanced by doubts about the prospect of ever being paid at all, as confidence waned in the capacity of the Confederate government to meet its obligations. There was still gross unfairness between one area and another, and even between farmers living a few miles apart. Proximity to the battlefront was a terrible misfortune for the farmer, and Virginia, above all, suffered constantly at the hands of impressment officers both genuine and spurious. Proximity to a railroad, a valuable asset in time of peace, became a curse during the war; to the army, the best supplies were those most easily delivered. The army's enforcement of impressment too often satisfied neither the letter nor the spirit of the law. Even honest officers were often too lazy to go far afield in search of available supplies and preferred to strip bare farms near at hand. The less scrupulous officers found an abundance of loopholes in the law or simply ignored its complex provisions. Impressment was often carried out by officers not qualified under the act – and their methods were ruthlessly imitated by marauders masquerading as impressment officers, who presented the owner with 'certificates' which were of course worthless. In its later sessions, Congress made only tentative efforts to reform the system, until in the dying days of the Confederacy it gave up the ghost, and defined the just price for goods as the prevailing market price.

Impressment was a necessary evil, but its operation in practice made its victims aware of the evils to the exclusion of the necessity. Like inflation and conscription, it brought the Confederate government into the life of the people in a highly unpleasant and deeply resented manner. It outraged thousands of decent, loyal citizens more than it upset the speculators and profiteers. It also provided more grist to the mill of the states rights champions. Indeed, even some of the most cooperative governors, Milton of Florida for example, were moved to protest. But once more it was Georgia and the Carolinas where impressment, like conscription, could be most rigorously enforced, which were loudest in their complaints. In Georgia, Governor Brown, backed by decisions of the state supreme court, did his best to sabotage the act; in North Carolina, Governor Vance conducted a long correspondence of charge and counter-charge with the Richmond authorities, during which he had recourse to the Old Testament to reinforce his point:

> If God Almighty had yet in store another plague worse than all others which he had intended to have let loose on the Egyptians in case Pharaoh still hardened his heart, I am sure it must have been a regiment or so of half-armed, half-disciplined Confederate cavalry. Had they been turned loose among Pharaoh's subjects, with or without an impressment law, he would have been so sensible of the anger of God that he would never have followed the children of Israel to the Red Sea. No sir! Not an inch![6]

Just as impressment was an invasion of basic property rights, so another assertion of government authority, the suspension of the writ of habeas corpus, was an invasion of cherished civil rights and liberties. It is hard to imagine a more sensitive issue, at least for the more politically conscious and legally minded Southerners. If necessity was the mother of this kind of infringement of basic rights, as well as of conscription and impressment, there were plenty of Southerners who doubted the legitimacy of the offspring or suspected that it was sired by the despotic ambitions of Jefferson Davis. Very much the same issue arose in the north, although with less of the states rights connotation which it acquired in the south. Lincoln grasped this particular nettle more firmly than Davis, but he stood slightly less chance of being fatally stung by it. In time of war, and especially in places and situations where the normal processes of law and government lapsed, it was inevitable that the two governments should look to those special powers for which some justification could be found in their respective constitutions. Suspension of the writ of habeas corpus was specifically mentioned in both documents, though hedged about with appropriate limitations. Imposition of martial law was another matter, and found no specific warrant in the constitution. Some people argued that the one power was implicit in the other, but more inclined to the view, surely correct, that there was a real distinction between allowing detention without trial, and, on the other hand, suspending the civil courts completely and putting civilians at the mercy of military tribunals. The Confederate Congress, having blurred this distinction at first, realised its importance later in 1862.

Early in that year, suspension of the writ already seemed amply justified, at least in the eyes of the executive, as a practical response to immediate problems.

Various parts of the south were invaded or immediately threatened by invasion, there was no effective civil government in large parts of several states in the west, and law and order in some Southern cities were very precarious. On 27 February Congress passed a law authorising the president to suspend the writ and declare martial law in cities and districts threatened by the enemy. Davis used this power sparingly – but not sparingly enough to suit the tastes of critics in Congress and in the states. The imposition of martial law in Richmond itself brought home to congressmen the implications of these sweeping powers, especially when they were exercised with the energy and relish shown by General John H. Winder, the military governor, who forbade the sale of liquor, demanded the surrender of firearms, set up an elaborate passport system, ordered a number of arbitrary arrests, and even dabbled in the difficult business of price-fixing. Impressed by what was happening on its own doorstep, and by complaints from New Orleans and other places under martial law, Congress modified its earlier measure on 19 April. Suspension of the writ was now limited to arrests made by the authority of the Confederacy and for offences against it – this was clearly a sop to the states. The act itself was to expire thirty days after the opening of the next session of Congress, and it made no mention of martial law. This left the position very vague, and uncertainty bred trouble. Davis himself continued his very cautious use of the powers granted by the law, but some of his generals took it upon themselves to use them more widely. Braxton Bragg placed Atlanta under martial law in August 1862, much to the indignation of vice-president Stephens and his Georgian allies. With more obvious and urgent need, Generals Hébert in Texas, Hindman in Arkansas, and Van Dorn in a large area of Mississippi and Louisiana, proclaimed martial law during the summer of 1862 in situations where normal civil government had broken down. Davis eventually reprimanded the generals and revoked their proclamations, but the damage had been done. There was a swelling chorus of protest, led predictably by men like Joseph E. Brown who solemnly declared that 'we have much more to apprehend from military despotism than from subjugation by the enemy'.[7] When Congress reassembled in August, it debated at length the relationship and the distinction between suspension of the writ and martial law, and came down heavily against the latter. The act which Congress finally passed on 13 October was little more than a re-enactment of the old, but now with the clear understanding that it did not sanction full martial law. Opposition remained so intense that, when the act expired in February 1863, Congress scarcely considered the possibility of renewing it, and for the next twelve months the Davis administration struggled on through military defeats and turmoil at home without the vital power to suspend the writ.

The lack of it was all the more damaging by this time because habeas corpus had become the refuge of draft dodgers and deserters. Sympathetic state judges were issuing writs on the flimsiest pretexts to men intent on evading conscription, to soldiers who had contrived some excuse to get themselves out of the army, or simply to deserters who were anxious to safeguard themselves against recapture.

Justice Pearson of the North Carolina state supreme court was perhaps the most notorious offender, but there were plenty of others, in Virginia and in some of the south-western states. Their behaviour was an open invitation to desertion, and threatened to turn the drain on the army's manpower from a steady stream into an uncontrollable flood. The losses inflicted by Southern writs as well as Northern guns make all the more remarkable the heroic resistance of Lee and his army against overwhelming numbers in the second half of the war. If the sapping of the army's strength was not enough to make the constitutional purists and doctrinaires think twice, some of them may have been impressed by the chaos which reigned over large areas of the Confederacy where the invaders had not yet established their sway, but the civil authority of the Confederate and state governments had broken down. Absence of military government meant no government at all; bands of deserters went unchecked, and trading with the enemy and open disloyalty lost all fear of retribution.

At all events, Congress listened to Davis's plea in February 1864 for renewal of power to suspend the writ, but the act which it passed differed significantly from earlier measures. It suspended the writ throughout the Confederacy in specific cases – treason, conspiracy to overthrow the government, desertion, aiding the enemy, among others – but required prompt investigation of those arrested with a view to a speedy trial or an equally speedy discharge. Again Congress set a time limit; the law was to expire on 1 August 1864. The act clearly gave the administration some help in its hour of need, but it aroused a furore in various states, with North Carolina and Georgia in the van. Vance bombarded Davis with protests, backed by resolutions of the state legislature, and a ruling by the state supreme court which virtually nullified the law in North Carolina. The Georgia states rights forces staged elaborate and well-publicised protests, and a meeting of several state governors in October roundly condemned the use of arbitrary arrests. By that time, of course, the act had lapsed, and such was the mood of Congress that Davis saw no point in seeking its renewal. With the Confederacy collapsing around them, the opposition had deprived the government of one of its few effective powers to meet the crisis. Indeed, with almost its dying breath in 1865, the Senate was to defeat a proposal to restore suspension. Both Civil War presidents had their doctrinaire critics, but a hundred eager radicals were surely less lethal in the one case than a score of such last-ditch defenders of state and individual rights in the other.

What made grass-roots opposition so dangerous was the outlet provided by the state governments and the men who headed them. Many of the state governors enjoyed firm popular support, and the most notorious of them, Brown and Vance, proved it at the polls during the war. From their positions of power, and by their capacity to attract attention and mobilise support, they nourished the popular enthusiasms and grievances which in turn sustained them. Thus, dotted around the country, there were strongholds of protest, concentrations of discontent, which forced the Richmond government, still in its infancy, to fight a political war on many fronts.

3. The names of Brown and Vance, Georgia and North Carolina, constantly recur, not because they were typical or average, but because they were the extreme examples of a wider phenomenon. They, and many like them, refused to admit that there was any inconsistency between unyielding devotion to states rights and loyalty to the Confederacy. Their failure was not basically one of loyalty or honour, but of vision and comprehension. For them, what was good for Georgia or North Carolina was good for the whole Confederacy.

The parochialism and the negativism of this kind of opposition helped to ensure that there was no unanimity, and therefore no effective coalition, among the critics themselves. What was good for Georgia was not necessarily good for North Carolina, and their governors did not always see eye to eye. By the latter part of the war, Vance was declaring Brown to be a humbug. Most observers would probably agree that Vance's states rights motives and his devotion to the Confederacy were less sullied by self-seeking than Brown's. In 1864 he visited North Carolina regiments in Lee's army, and his stout work in rallying their morale was praised by both Lee and Davis. There was something of the opportunist in Brown, although there was more than that to his zeal for states rights and more to Georgia's states rights fervour than the personality of its governor. He was but one of the quartet who led the Georgia states rights group in the second half of the war. Its other members were Robert Toombs, Alexander Stephens and his brother Linton, and in all three, devotion to the principle of states rights was spiced with personal frustration or dissatisfaction, and a good measure of personal spite against the president. Linton Stephens had lost all restraint in his abuse: 'Mr Davis is *mad*, infatuated,' he wrote. 'It seems to me to be a case that calls loudly for a Brutus. . . . He is a *little, conceited, hypocritical, snivelling, canting, malicious, ambitious, dogged* knave and fool.' Alexander Stephens claimed that he resented Davis's defects no more than he resented the infirmities of his old, blind and deaf dog. 'I have regarded him,' he said, 'as a man of good intentions, weak and vacillating, timid, petulant, peevish, obstinate, but not firm.' Toombs denounced 'that scoundrel Jeff Davis' with equal gusto.[8]

In 1864 this group organised a formal protest against administration policy in general and the new habeas corpus law in particular. Brown summoned a special session of the state legislature, and opened it with a message warning against military despotism and airing the question of negotiations with the North. Linton Stephens followed up with resolutions condemning suspension of the writ, and favouring peace negotiations. His brother, the vice-president of the Confederacy, endorsed these proposals (which he had helped to draft) in a long address to the legislature which did much to ensure their final passage. His words were typical of the all-or-nothing doctrinaire position: 'I warn you against that most insidious enemy which approaches with her siren song, "Independence first and liberty afterwards". It is a false delusion. Liberty is the animating spirit, the soul of our system of government, and like the soul of man, when once lost, it is lost forever.'[9] Brown sent a copy of his own address and of the resolutions to the captain of every company of every Georgia regiment in the army, and to the clerk of every county court in what was left of the Confederacy. Copies of Stephens's speech were distributed to the lieutenant of each company, and the sheriff of each county. This was a carefully organised propaganda campaign against the Confederate government, designed to reach the widest possible audience by one route or another. Brown kept unrepentantly to the same course for the rest of the year. He continued to exempt thousands of the Georgia militia from conscription, and in September he withdrew his militia from service with the army after the fall of Atlanta, on the pretext that the campaign was now 'terminated' – this, at a time when the heartland of his state lay wide open to Sherman's advance. In his message to the legislature in November, he was still shouting defiance mingled now with despair: 'Confederate independence with centralised power without State sovereignty and Constitutional and religious liberty, would be very little better than subjugation, as it matters little who our master is, if we are to have one.'[10] Before long, Joe Brown was to be showing his talent for serving new masters, as a supporter of radical reconstruction.

The resolutions of the Georgia legislature in March 1864 are a reminder of how far the peace movement had developed in various parts of the South by this time. There had been rumblings of disaffection from the beginning in such areas as the mountains of east Tennessee, western North Carolina, northern Georgia and Alabama, and the Arkansas hill country. But from these pockets of pro-Union sentiment the peace movement had spread much further and bitten much deeper by the winter of 1863-4. Resentment against the policies of the Confederate government easily spilled over into thoughts of peace and even reunion, especially among those who had not been enthusiasts for secession in the first place. Defeatism about the outcome of the war spurred the desire to end it all as quickly as possible by any available means. Peace societies, with all the trappings of secrecy, attracted support in some areas. Peace proposals were aired from time to time in Congress and Vice-President Stephens was quite anxious to cast himself in the role of peacemaker. Davis always stressed his own pacific intentions but asked what was the point of peace moves while the Northern government insisted on total surrender. He and others feared that an approach which failed would have an adverse effect on morale. The peace advocates argued that the bulk of Northern opinion was also hankering after peace and would force the Lincoln administration to respond to a Southern approach. But they were vague, uncertain and divided both about the method and the goal of peace-making. To talk of reconstruction of the old Union invited the tag of disloyalty, but prospects for negotiating independence looked increasingly dim. During 1864, prominent figures like Brown and Stephens took the matter up more seriously, and convinced themselves that the individual states had the right to take the initiative. They talked of a convention of the states, and the same idea was taken up by a number of congressmen, including William W. Boyce of South Carolina, who hoped to make the most of the prospect of a Democratic victory in the presidential election in the north. But, for all the talk and proposals for action, nothing had been achieved by the end of 1864, and suspicions were growing that Georgia in particular was looking for a way to make a separate peace.

The peace movement had its supporters in every state and in the army, too, but nowhere was it stronger than in North Carolina. Here, William W. Holden, erstwhile friend and ally of Governor Vance, put himself at the head of the movement, and advocated a state peace convention. Equally vague about what the convention could do, and whether peace was to come through reunion or separation, he was nevertheless bold enough to challenge Vance for the governorship in 1864. He was no match for Vance as a campaigner, and the governor was re-elected by a four-to-one majority. The election does, however, put the relationship between Vance and Davis in a different light. Tough and relentless as he was as a critic of the president, Vance confronted opposition in his own state mainly from those who were even more hostile to Davis and disenchanted with the Confederacy. The irony and the tragedy of the Davis–Vance dispute is that each man believed he was taking up a middle-of-the-road position. So in a way he was, but the middle as viewed from Richmond was quite different from the middle as viewed from Raleigh, North Carolina.

By the latter part of 1864 the Confederacy was falling apart, politically as well as militarily. It was now reduced effectively to quite a small area in Virginia, the Carolinas and Georgia, and parts of the Gulf states. There were many districts not yet occupied by the Union army where the Confederate authorities had lost any real control. The great region beyond the Mississippi had been cut off since the middle of 1863, and had become virtually autonomous. There, too, large areas were under the effective control of no authority at all. The territorial break-up of the Confederacy was accompanied by feuds and arguments and rivalries which were tearing its political structure to pieces. The running political battle between Richmond and the state capitals was significant in itself, but it was also a symptom of something deeper in the whole nature of the Southern Confederacy, a contentiousness born of a proud individualism and a blinkered localism, a pride nurtured by a strong tradition of self-reliance and the ingrained habits of a slave society, a deep resentment of distant authority in any shape or form, hardened by generations of political experience, and a talent for obstruction and spoiling, developed in defence of a cherished way of life and refined by decades of sectional controversy. 'No doubt,' as Mrs Chesnut tartly observed, 'the Devil raved of "Devil's Rights" in Paradise.'[11] The South changed dramatically during the war, and the extent of Confederate political innovation and governmental growth should never be belittled. But, not unnaturally, the South could not and would not destroy its old self to save a new self. It is still fair to ask whether the states rights issue, and the whole complex of Confederate political relationships, could have been more smoothly and fruitfully handled. Could zeal for states rights have been more successfully channelled into support for the common cause? The answer is surely yes, though only up to a point. Political skill could have been a palliative but not a cure for a condition with which the South had lived for so long. If Davis had had a thicker skin, and Brown and Vance had had a broader vision; if men like Stephens had used their great talents more constructively and the men around the president had had more talent to use; if only some political structure could have been improvised to produce more answers and fewer arguments; if the Confederate government could have made itself more relevant and more welcome to citizens going about their daily lives – all these things might have made a difference. (They would certainly have meant a different kind of Confederacy.) They would not of themselves necessarily have made the difference between defeat and victory, but they might at least have given the Confederacy the strength and the heart to maintain the struggle even longer. This in turn might have allowed time for sheer frustration to crack Northern morale. After all, even as things stood by the summer of 1864, the best Southern hope of salvaging something from the wreckage lay in the state of feeling in the North, and specifically in the outcome of the election of 1864.

4. There was more than one occasion during 1863 and 1864 when Confederate hopes and Union fears turned less on the battlefields of the south than the ballot boxes of the north. The mid-term elections of autumn 1862 were part cause, part barometer of the crisis of confidence and morale through which the North was to pass in the dark winter of 1862–3. While the Republican party was still licking its electoral wounds, it suffered further self-inflicted damage in the confrontation between the Republican senators and the Lincoln administration in December. Gloom about the military situation turned to bitterness, recrimination and despair in the wake of the Fredericksburg disaster. Events seemed to be justifying those opponents of the party in power who had favoured compromise from the start, and who had condemned as futile and repugnant all efforts to restore the Union by conquest. But those who wanted nothing more nor less than a peaceful restoration of the Union as it was before 1860 were themselves approaching a point of no return as the dawn of a new year approached. Even if they refused to admit that such a deceptively simple objective was already impossible after twenty months of conflict, they were bound to recognise that, once the Emancipation Proclamation came into force in 1863, the old Union was gone beyond recall. Emancipation blocked the road to a compromise peace, and many opponents of that policy now confronted the question whether they could continue to support a war not merely to restore the Union but to remake it, or whether, if they could not reverse the emancipation decision, they must accept the separation of North and South as a fact.

It was small wonder that, at such a time, peace movements – and, above all, rumours of peace movements – should make their presence felt, especially in the states of the north-west. There was more talk than ever before of the creation of a separate north-west Confederacy to safeguard the interests of the region against threats from eastern capital as well as Southern secessionists. There was talk of a peace convention of the western and border states, to be held at Louisville,

Kentucky, and the lower house of the Illinois state legislature even passed a resolution appointing commissioners to attend it. There were clumsy attempts from the South to exploit north-western disaffection by stressing the essential unity of the Mississippi Valley; one such effort was inspired by General Beauregard, another by Southern contacts of General McClernand who himself received short shrift from Lincoln for pointing the finger at emancipation as the main obstacle to peace.[12] If the South had shown more skill and awareness in exploiting the Northern situation, it might have created a great opportunity for itself, and great embarrassment for its adversary, in the winter of 1862–3, before emancipation was firmly enough established to rule out a negotiated peace. But consistently throughout the war, Southern leaders failed to use such opportunities or even to perceive them.

The peace movement was rarely precise in its objectives. A few voices spoke up for peace on the basis of separation, but they were heavily outnumbered by those whose yearning for an end to the horrors of war encouraged the hopeful belief that somehow peace could be made, somehow a compromise could be found, somehow the Union could be restored. The climate of thought and feeling which encouraged talk of peace also presented a great opportunity to the Democratic party, flushed with its 1862 successes, and eager to exploit a favourable situation. But, if opportunity beckoned, danger loomed behind it. The Democrats confronted their recurring problem of how to make the most of partisan advantage without over-stepping into disloyalty, and thus presenting the Republicans with a sitting target. The situation was indeed remarkable, and hindsight only makes it more so. At the most critical phase of a bitter and bloody civil war, the North was still conducting its internal political affairs with an openness, a vigorous enthusiasm, an intense partisanship, and a 'normality' which was converted by its context into something abnormal and indeed phenomenal. The most astonishing feature of Northern politics during the Civil War was not that the normal rules of the game were bent or broken in many places and at many times, but rather that they were so often observed. For all the presidential edicts, the arbitrary arrests, the constitutional evasions, the military presence at the polls, the charges of tyranny and the counter-charges of treason, the political process continued in a fashion and with a regularity which was accepted as normal and taken for granted by the bulk of the citizenry. Elections were held, offices changed hands, parties made gains and losses, and for all the talk of sinister conspiracies and military despotism, politics was still predominantly a matter of business as usual.

In the particular situation of the winter of 1862–3, Democrats differed on the best methods of exploiting their advantage. On the whole, the party leadership in the Atlantic seaboard states was cautious and moderate, and anxious to steer clear of the peace movement in its more dubious forms, although, even here, there were individuals like Thomas H. Seymour of Connecticut, or Fernando Wood of New York, who sometimes let their enthusiasm or their malice run away with them. There were groups, too, at each end of the social scale who sympathised with a more extreme position: wealthy New York merchants with traditionally strong Southern connections, or poor Irish immigrants haunted by fears of Negro competition. The key figure among the eastern Democrats was now Horatio Seymour, who, in the election of 1862, had won the pivotal position of governor of New York. A well-known figure beyond the confines of his own state, Seymour had consistently declared his loyalty to the Union cause and his unyielding opposition to a division of the Union in any circumstances. But, like so many other Democrats, he insisted on a restoration of the Union *as it was*, and argued that the purpose of the war was to crush one revolution, and not to inaugurate another. He had as little affection for abolitionists as for secessionists, and cast the mid-Atlantic and western states in the role of a balance between the extremists of the south and the fanatics of New England. The proper function of the loyal Democratic opposition was to act as a moderating influence on the Lincoln administration, to save it from the clutches of the radicals. Seymour chose a tricky and tortuous path for himself, and he was sometimes so devious in following it that he bewildered his friends and outraged his enemies.[13]

The natural home of the fiercest Democratic opposition was in the north-west, above all in the states of Ohio, Indiana and Illinois. Here, moderate leadership struggled to contain the more extreme views of journalists like 'Brick' Pomeroy of Wisconsin, and Wilbur F. Storey of the Chicago *Times*, and politicians like Daniel Voorhees of Indiana, the 'Tall Sycamore of the Wabash', and, above all, Clement L. Vallandigham of Ohio. Here, their Republican opponents fixed upon them the name of Copperhead to cover a multitude of their political sins, and the name, more properly restricted to peace Democrats, was extended into a smear on the whole party. Here, the mood and the issues of the day served to reinforce long-standing and deep-rooted grievances, of party and culture, class and race, sectional and economic interest. The north-west had been a stronghold of the Democratic party for decades before the Civil War; Republican margins had been narrow in 1860, and many Republicans were recent converts from the Democracy, who might be won back to the fold. Amid all the great issues of the war years, local feuds and quarrels over patronage still affected election results; aggrieved Democrats were inclined to ask why, if the Republicans claimed to be the party of the Union, the patronage was not distributed on a more bipartisan basis. The large population of Southern origin, especially in the Ohio Valley, was stongly Democratic, hostile to emancipation and fearful of its consequences (although they had no monopoly of Negrophobia), and earnestly in favour of a compromise which would restore the Union of North and South which meant so much to them in terms of geography as well as sentiment, commerce as well as kinship. There was also a fairly clear class division between the parties; the Democrats represented the poorer sections of the community – the workers of the towns (where immigrant origins and the Catholic faith often hardened the lines of class demarcation) and the 'butternuts' of the poorer farming areas settled from the south. In the first year and more after Fort Sumter, economic

recession aggravated class and economic grievances. Here again, parts of
the middle west suffered severely through the loss of southern markets and the
traditional outlet down the Mississippi, the decline in farm prices, and the
collapse of banks which had invested heavily in southern state bonds. In their
turn, economic difficulties exacerbated perhaps the most deeply felt of all the
traditional grievances which the Democrats were able to exploit: the sectional
resentment of the west against the east in general, and New England in particular.
From earliest frontier days, westerners had bridled at eastern condescension and
assumptions of cultural superiority; they had fretted against Yankee political
influence and social sophistication; they had protested against economic
exploitation by the merchants and manufacturers of New York, Pennsylvania
and Massachusetts. At least in earlier times of triangular sectional rivalry, they
had been able to play off the north-east against the south, and their Mississippi
outlet had been, psychologically as much as economically, a defence against
Yankee domination. But now the southern exit was blocked, the east–west
railroads were the only available lifeline, and control of those routes was not in
western hands. Of course, mid-western unrest during the Civil War had much
to do with slavery and conscription and other special war issues but it also drew
great strength from old grievances now given a new lease of life. There was a
stream of protests against increased freight rates on the railroads, inflated prices,
big increases in the tariff, allegedly for the benefit of eastern manufacturers at
the expense of western farmers, and the development of a new banking system,
allegedly to suit the interests of the eastern 'money monopoly'. When a
westerner used the common phrase about a rich man's war and a poor man's
fight, he thought of rich and poor virtually as synonyms for east and west.

   In the early months of 1863, traditional grievances were reinforced by the
gloomy state of the war, and by three highly important and highly unpopular
war policies of the Lincoln administration. The coming of emancipation aroused
more fear than favour in the minds of millions of westerners who regarded
abolitionism as a Yankee mania, and the Negro as a threat to free white labour
in the west. Lincoln's first Emancipation Proclamation had been immediately
followed by another edict authorising massive extensions of the use of martial
law and the suspension of the writ of habeas corpus, and Democrats responded
by launching a full-scale attack on military despotism and arbitrary rule, and a
stout defence of basic constitutional rights. Then, in March 1863, came the
Conscription Act, a measure not calculated to win friends anywhere, but
especially obnoxious to those who denied its legality as well as its expediency,
and to those westerners who believed that their states had already provided
more than their fair share of manpower for a war not of their own choosing.

   Protests against both the principle of conscription and such 'undemocratic'
features of the law as substitution and commutation, spread all across the north,
and were aggravated by complaints of unfairness in the allotment of quotas to
various districts. The enrolment of men liable to the draft, and then the first
actual draft in July, threatened to provoke major disorders in both north-east

and north-west; there were disturbances in various western states, and officers attempting to carry out the draft went in peril of their lives in some areas. But the most serious outbreak of violence came not in the west but in New York city, after the first names were drawn on Saturday, 11 July 1863, just a week after the triumphs of Gettysburg and Vicksburg. (Indeed, the violence that followed was given freer rein in a city denuded of troops who had been rushed off to confront Lee in Pennsylvania.) The three days of rioting which took place on 13–15 July cost several hundred lives, and damage to property estimated at $2 million. The looting, burning, pillaging and killing were ended only when veteran troops were rushed back from the battlefront to confront the rampaging mob. Many other issues and grievances apart from the draft were sucked into the vortex in those three terrible days. With its strong Democratic sympathies, its large population of Irish and other immigrants, and its chronic propensity for turbulence and disorder, New York city was never likely to accept the draft calmly. Governor Seymour had aggravated a tense situation by his quibbling and complaining over conscription, and he brought much condemnation upon himself by addressing a noisy crowd from the steps of City Hall as 'my friends', although it is doubtful whether the crowd included many actual rioters. The ugliest feature of the violence was that it turned increasingly into an anti-Negro riot. George Templeton Strong, that most solid of New York citizens, was outraged at the events swirling about him. He reported 'a black man hanged . . . for no offence but that of Nigritude', and he turned his full native American fury upon the Irish immigrants. 'My own theory,' he wrote, 'is that St Patrick's campaign against the snakes is a Popish delusion. They perished of biting the Irish people.'[14] The draft riots revealed much of the seamier side of Northern life during the Civil War: nativist prejudice against the immigrant, immigrant fear of the Negro, class antagonism and narrow partisanship. Not for the first or the last time, the Negro became the scapegoat of a troubled community. And yet, within a few months, New Yorkers were turning out to cheer a newly recruited Negro regiment as it marched through their city on its way to war.[15]

In such feverish times, the flames of controversy needed little fanning, but improved party organisation and propaganda, peculiar local crises in some states and controversial personalities in others, kept the political fires burning brightly. The Republicans and their War Democrat allies were rapidly expanding their Union Leagues or Loyal Leagues across the north, as valuable auxiliaries to the party itself, active propaganda agencies, promoters of the identification of patriotism and party loyalty, and counters to the allegedly sinister secret societies on the other side. Meanwhile, in two key north-western states, an extraordinary political situation kept temperatures constantly high. After the elections of 1862, the Republican governors of Indiana and Illinois, Oliver P. Morton and Richard Yates, each faced a Democratic majority in the state legislature. In the acrimonious struggle between governor and legislature in Indiana, the Democrats made various attempts to clip the governor's powers, Republican legislators absented themselves to prevent a quorum, and the legislative session ended without the passage of the usual appropriation bills to finance the operations of the state government. Governor Morton defied the Democratic opposition, and chose to go it alone. For the next two years he ran the government of Indiana as his own personal empire, assumed extra-legal powers where necessary (while taking care to cloak his every action in patriotic garb), and financed his activities from a variety of unconventional sources, including loans from private individuals and corporations, and funds supplied by the federal government. In Illinois, the Democratic majority in the legislature embarked on a course similar to that of their Indiana neighbours, and were similarly foiled by parliamentary manoeuvres and Republican absenteeism, until Governor Yates finally seized his opportunity to prorogue the legislature altogether.

The unprecedented events in Indiana and Illinois ended in Democratic frustration, and the local elections in various states in the spring of 1863 produced mixed results from which neither party could draw unmixed satisfaction. But, if all these developments helped to keep the political pot boiling, one man did more than anyone or anything else to keep the north-west in ferment through most of 1863. That man was Clement L. Vallandigham, Democratic congressman from Ohio, who had in fact lost his seat amid the general triumph of his party in 1862, largely because of Republican gerrymandering of his district. Vallandigham was a handsome, vain, eloquent, intense man, grimly loyal to his convictions about states rights, personal liberties, and sectional interests, and just as grimly determined in his pursuit of the martyr's crown. In August 1862, he announced his opposition to both rebellions, 'the Secession Rebellion South and the Abolition Rebellion North and West'. On 14 January 1863, in what was virtually his farewell speech to the House of Representatives, he espoused the cause of peace more directly and unequivocally than ever before. Advocating an armistice, and trusting to the healing effects of time to restore the Union, he pronounced the conquest of the South impossible, and warned those who attempted it that their only trophies would be 'defeat, debt, taxation, sepulchers'.[16] In March he returned to his home town of Dayton, Ohio, to a hero's welcome, and the excitement created by his presence added to the worries of the recently appointed army commander of the Department of the Ohio, General Burnside, whose approach to the complex problems of subversion and disloyalty was no more subtle than his direct approach upon Lee's entrenchments at Fredericksburg a few months earlier. He was to cause the Lincoln administration almost as much embarrassment in the one role as in the other. His Order No. 38, issued in April, stated among other things that 'the habit of declaring sympathy for the enemy' would make the individuals concerned liable to arrest and trial before a military tribunal. To Vallandigham, such an order was like preparing the fire for a burning at the stake, and when he addressed a huge crowd at Mount Vernon, Ohio, on 1 May 1863, the sight of a Burnside agent with notebook in hand acted not as a restraint but a goad. Affirming his readiness to spit and stamp upon Order No. 38, Vallandigham declared, somewhat sententiously, that he took his stand on 'General Order No. 1, the Constitution of the United States'. A few nights later, Vallandigham was arrested at Dayton. His outraged Democratic fellow-townsmen responded by putting the offices of the local Republican newspaper to the torch, and Burnside replied by declaring martial law throughout the county. Vallandigham was tried by a military court whose jurisdiction he refused to recognise, was found guilty of violating Order No. 38, and sentenced to imprisonment for the duration of the war. Burnside's action against Vallandigham was as unauthorised by Lincoln as its consequences were unwelcome to him, but he escaped some of the worst repercussions of the general's indiscretion by commuting the sentence to one of banishment to the Confederacy. Thus the eager martyr was snatched from the burning pyre, and found himself instead somewhat ignominiously dumped upon an unsuspecting and unenthusiastic Confederate officer in Tennessee. (If the whole episode encouraged the notion that critics of the administration were pro-Southern fifth columnists, so much the better from Lincoln's point of view.)

Vallandigham made his way to Richmond, and then, by way of Bermuda, to Canada. Meanwhile a chorus of Democratic protest rolled across the north-west, and, in June, the Ohio Democrats nominated the exiled hero as their candidate for the governorship in the autumn elections. If he had not achieved martyrdom, Vallandigham had at least won a nomination which was far beyond his reach until Burnside's soldiers called upon him in the early hours of a May morning. The Ohio election now promised to be a major test of feeling in the north-west and the strength of the Lincoln administration nationwide. The Republicans, campaigning under the 'Union' banner, put up as their candidate a War Democrat, John Brough, a stalwart and highly respected figure in Ohio public life. Even with such a strong candidate, the Republicans might have been in serious trouble if the election had been held in May or June, but by the autumn the situation and the mood had changed. The furore over Vallandigham's arrest and punishment had subsided, and there was a sober realisation of his limitations as a candidate who could not command the middle ground. The military situation, so depressing in the spring, had been transformed by Gettysburg and Vicksburg, and Vallandigham's statement that 'you cannot conquer the South' could no longer be taken as axiomatic. The draft, though scarcely popular, had survived early teething troubles and protests, and become a *fait accompli*. The return of prosperity, stimulated by war, smoothed the rough edges of discontent. The Republicans pulled out all the stops in their campaign to elect Brough; the president himself followed the campaign closely, and could feel satisfaction, tinged with relief, at the news in mid-October that Brough had crushed Vallandigham by a margin of over 100,000 votes. Election returns from other states – Maine, Massachusetts, Iowa, Wisconsin – confirmed the same trend. In Pennsylvania, where the Democrats had erred as in Ohio in nominating an extremist candidate, George W. Woodward, for governor, the Republican incumbent, Andrew Curtin, was comfortably re-elected. The state and local elections of 1863 were, in their way, one of the political watersheds of the

Civil War. The Republicans threw back the Democratic challenge so strongly
mounted a year earlier, and so menacingly sustained in the first half of 1863.
The Peace Democrats in particular suffered severely at the hands of the electorate.
To this extent at least, the elections were a vote of confidence in the war effort
and in those who directed it. They in turn could now look forward to the
presidential campaign of 1864 with confidence and hope – especially if they
could rely once again on military success as the precursor and prerequisite of
victory at the polls.

The mixed record of the Democrats in mid-war prompts a number of
questions. Are they to be regarded as a moderate, responsible, loyal opposition,
or did the party fall into the hands of dangerous and disloyal extremists? The
answer to that question depends on which Democrats are under the microscope.
The great majority fell clearly into the first category, although some, including
even a man like Horatio Seymour, went to the very brink at times. The
Democratic minority in both houses of Congress behaved with some measure
of responsibility, and with a remarkable degree of coherence, in sustaining
financial measures for the support of the war effort, and resisting the easy
temptations to indulge in unlimited procedural obstruction, while abating not
a whit its hostility to emancipation, confiscation, conscription and arbitrary
arrests. A majority of Democrats around the country followed this lead and
in so doing helped to preserve political stability and the subtle balances of the
constitution. On the other hand, there were more than a few Democrats who
could not resist the opportunity to make party capital out of national crisis, who
made a bogey-man out of the tyrant in the White House, who professed to
support the war for the Union but who would have doomed it to failure by their
fastidiousness about methods, and their hypersensitivity to the smallest temporary infringement of constitutional rights and liberties. (It is hard to ignore the
contrast between such scrupulous regard for the protection of constitutional
rights in time of national peril and massive indifference to the most basic human
rights of the Negro slave in his hour of need.) Again, the loyalty of some
Democrats raises the question of loyalty to what? Can those like Vallandigham,
who were willing to contemplate at least a temporary separation, be regarded as
loyal to the Union? Surely not, and yet there had been plenty of men of all
persuasions who in the crisis of 1860–1 had been willing to face such a contingency.
The question of disloyalty carried over from the organised Democratic party to
the secret societies which existed and allegedly flourished in the north-west
during the war – the Knights of the Golden Circle, the Sons of Liberty, the
Organisation of American Knights. The size, the influence, even the existence of
these societies have been a bone of contention among historians for decades. On
the one hand they are seen as a serious and menacing conspiracy, aiming at total
disruption of the war effort; on the other they are treated as largely a figment of
the imagination of Republican propagandists who succeeded in convincing not
merely contemporaries but later students that their fantasies were realities. The
latter view is vitally important in cutting the Knights of the Golden Circle down

to size, but it is doubtful whether they can be written out of existence altogether even when every allowance is made for the inflated estimates which both the organisers and the opponents of the secret societies concocted for their own purposes. One thing is certain: the widely credited existence of the societies enabled the Republicans to set off that chain reaction of alleged treason and disloyalty which spread from the Knights to Copperheads of the Vallandigham stamp inside the Democratic party, and from them to the party as a whole. It was a potent political weapon, and the Republicans used it ruthlessly.

Other questions about the Northern Democrats remain. Were they liberals in the mainstream of nineteenth-century American reform stretching from Jefferson and Jackson to the Populists and the Progressives, or were they conservatives resisting unwelcome social, economic and political change? Were they brave standard-bearers of liberty in face of the usurpations of a despotic government, or narrow-minded reactionaries crying for a lost past? The answer is that they were both. They adopted the classic stance of nineteenth-century American reform, a belief in progress by the re-creation of an idealised version of the past. They represented an America threatened by technology and complexity, by the growth of national power, by a variety of forces which they could not control. Their liberal notions were as limited as their overall political horizons were narrow.

Finally it may be asked whether, simply in terms of party history, the wartime Democrats were by the end of 1863 to be accounted a success or a failure. From one standpoint their achievements in the face of daunting odds were remarkable. In the years before the war the Democratic party had lost much of its progressive strength in the North to the new Republican party. Through secession in 1860–1, it had lost its massive conservative strength in the South. Once the war began, the moderate centre group remaining were liable to erosion as War Democrats moved into alliance with the Republican party. The death of Douglas in 1861 deprived them of their one leader of national repute. And yet the Northern Democrats not merely survived, but they enabled the two-party system to survive in the peculiar wartime situation. In the 1862 elections their impressive gains inspired hopes of recapturing the White House two years later, and, in the months that followed, events and movements of opinion seemed to conspire in their favour. But, at the time of their greatest opportunity, the Democrats, seduced into dangerous paths by men like Vallandigham, and let down by the devious and vacillating leadership of men like Seymour, allowed themselves to stray too far from the solid middle ground. A change in the fortunes of war helped their opponents to regain much lost ground in the autumn of 1863. But such fortunes could change again, and the Democrats were still in a position to launch a major challenge in the election of 1864. In the short run it was no mean achievement, but the long-term cost could yet be heavy.

5. Both genuine conviction and tactical considerations encouraged the Democrats to take up their firmest stand on constitutional rights. In doing so they focused

attention on some of the most fundamental issues of the whole conflict. The very fact that the war had come at all surely represented a failure of the constitution. The question now was whether it could redeem that failure by enabling the Union to save itself, without in the process subverting the rights and liberties which it guaranteed to individual citizens (and to individual states). The political and constitutional precedents of the pre-war decades were not encouraging. The assertions of federal power made by Alexander Hamilton and John Marshall, and even by Thomas Jefferson and Andrew Jackson, in the first half-century of the Republic, had faded into the background since the 1830s. The business of federal government had gone into a long recession, and presidents like Fillmore, Pierce and Buchanan suffered from under-employment rather than vaulting ambition. They were to be despised as office-boys rather than feared as bureaucrats, dismissed as puppets rather than condemned as autocrats. In that same period, Democrats, Northern as well as Southern, had more than ever cribbed and confined the federal authority within the tightening network of states rights. Now, after 1861, in the face of an unprecedented challenge, defenders of the Union had either to resurrect the older nationalist tradition of Hamilton, Marshall, Clay and Webster, or to invent a new legal basis for the exercise of national power. To an old Whig, and disciple of Clay and Webster, like Abraham Lincoln, the former was the natural, almost instinctive, reaction. Here, as elsewhere, such an approach put Lincoln squarely in the middle between the advocates of more drastic action and the unyielding defenders of state and individual rights.

What provision did the constitution make for the extension of federal power to cope with such an emergency? The brevity of the document of 1787 and the non-committal caution of its makers meant that it offered little specific guidance on this point, and, even where it did, as on the suspension of the writ of habeas corpus, its oracular language could be interpreted in various ways. The constitutional history of the United States since 1787 offered few precedents relevant to the situation of 1861–5, and there were few, if any, legal experts to offer guidance on matters such as the use of martial law or the confiscation of rebel property. Broadly, there were three main views in the North on the question of the war powers of the federal government. The most radical view was that the constitution was not fully operative at such a time, and must certainly not be allowed to impede or prevent progress towards the key objectives, whether of winning the war, freeing the slaves, or reconstructing the South. Although Thaddeus Stevens and some others sometimes espoused, or at least flirted with, this view, it is striking how even 'radical' Republicans preferred to find some warrant in the wording of the constitution for all their proposed measures, even if it meant asking some inconspicuous lines in that document to bear more traffic than had ever been intended or imagined.

The second, diametrically opposed, conservative view, adopted by most Democrats, demanded strict adherence to the letter and spirit of the constitution, even in such a crisis. It was vital, as, for example, Horatio Seymour said, to prove that the constitution was not 'a fair-weather thing', but that it must and could be preserved intact whatever the emergency which confronted the Union. Between these radical and conservative views lay a wide and varied expanse of moderate legal ground, and those who dwelt upon it, including the president, argued that the constitution retained its validity during the war, but that, both explicitly and implicitly, it sanctioned special powers in such a contingency. Any constitution, it was argued, must provide the means of its own survival. Legal pundits hastened to devise elaborate theories to show that the American constitution furnished adequate powers to preserve the existence of the Union and of itself. Lincoln reduced such theories to a basic commonsense formulation in his first message to Congress in July 1861: 'are all the laws, but one, to go unexecuted,' he asked, 'and the government itself go to pieces, lest that one be violated?'[17]

But even among those who agreed on the existence of special war powers, opinions differed on a further awkward question: which branch of the government – the executive or the legislative – was to have the major role in exercising such powers? Congress based its claim on its general legislative authority, and, more specifically, on the argument that the power to declare war, explicitly granted to Congress, must imply the power to prosecute that war by all proper means. During the Civil War, Congress certainly took to itself all manner of special powers in legislation which created new war crimes, confiscated property, offered freedom to slaves and conscripted men into the army. On the other hand, Lincoln and those who thought like him argued that waging war was essentially an executive function, that the whole executive power was granted to the president under the constitution, and that, more specifically, the president was commander-in-chief of the armed forces, and clearly the only man in a position to respond immediately to a national emergency. Lincoln himself took an extremely broad view of the presidential war powers, and used them not merely to raise, organise and direct the armed forces, but to free slaves, arrest citizens without trial, organise new governments and operate special courts in the occupied South. Under the guise of presidential proclamations or edicts, Lincoln initiated a series of measures essentially legislative in character, of which emancipation itself was the outstanding example.

At the very outset, having delayed the special session of Congress until July 1861, Lincoln took it upon himself in the meantime to raise troops beyond existing authorised limits, proclaim a blockade of the southern coast, and suspend the writ of habeas corpus in certain areas. Congress later gave its blessing to these measures, as did the Supreme Court two years later in the Prize Cases, but these early presidential initiatives were but the curtain-raiser to a drama of several acts, in which Lincoln and Congress repeatedly confronted each other. Emancipation and reconstruction, the biggest issues, are discussed elsewhere, but they like a number of others, not merely provided a battleground between two branches of the government but also posed much wider constitutional questions, involving the legal character of the war itself. Confiscation of rebel property was a case in point. The Confiscation Acts, especially the Act of July 1862, have too often been examined exclusively in terms of their provisions on slavery, but they covered other controversial ground as well. The Act of July 1862 dealt with crimes of treason and rebellion, made the property of certain classes of rebels subject to forfeiture and laid down the procedure to be followed in such cases. Lincoln, who had never cared for confiscation, disliked many features of the measure, and almost vetoed it. But, more significant than its role as an episode in the executive-legislative conflict, the Confiscation Act reflected and added to the prevailing confusion over the legal nature of the conflict between North and South. Was it a war between belligerents, to which the rules of international law applied, or was it simply an internal rebellion which the Union government was striving to suppress by a gigantic police action? Different sections of the Confiscation Act classified it as first one and then the other, and treated Southerners first as enemies then as rebels. In this, the Act merely mirrored general uncertainty on a question which may now look like a suitable subject for debate among academic lawyers, but which at the time had enormous implications for policy on emancipation and reconstruction – and for the relations of the United States with the outside world. In the end, common sense and convenience triumphed over logic and legal precision, and, in the Prize Cases in 1863, the Supreme Court gave legal sanction to the widely-held view of the dual nature of the conflict. It was held to be both a rebellion and a war between belligerents. The Union government maintained that it was tackling a rebellion of certain people in states still within the Union, but it accorded them belligerent rights (though not recognition of belligerent status). If this was in some respects an attempt to have the best of both worlds, it also softened logic with humanity in removing the necessity to regard all Southern sailors as pirates or all Confederate prisoners as traitors.[18]

None of the constitutional issues of the war years touched on such basic legal rights (or on such sensitive political nerves) as the question of the suspension of the writ of habeas corpus. In any modern war (and certainly in a civil war) governments are likely to have recourse to arbitrary arrests, and detention without trial, in their efforts to maintain internal security. In the United States in the 1860s it required an almost impossible tightrope act of the federal government if it were to pay adequate attention to internal security without infringing basic civil rights and liberties, and laying itself wide open to charges of subverting the constitution itself in its campaign against alleged subversion. It was quite impracticable to draw a simple line between loyal and disloyal acts, between opposition to the policies of the Lincoln administration and deliberate obstruction of the war effort. Some cases were clear enough; espionage, sabotage, supplying the enemy, fell on one side of the line, while a speech criticising emancipation or conscription was clearly on the other. But activities like encouraging desertion or stealing military supplies or intimidating loyal voters fell into the large grey area in between. It was difficult to arraign the perpetrators of such offences as traitors, and in any case, in an atmosphere thick with wild rumours and wilder accusations, talk of conspiracies, and allegations of treachery on the one side and tyranny on the other, the attempt to do so was hardly worth the effort involved. The law's delays and complexities made the courts ill-suited to the government's needs, and the available legislation scarcely met the needs of the situation. Certainly, the treason laws were likely to prove a very blunt instrument, or, worse still, a boomerang more dangerous to the prosecutors than the accused. It would have been difficult to secure convictions, especially in areas where juries were likely to sympathise with the defendant. Worse still, the only penalty prescribed for treason was death. The administration was therefore reluctant to embark upon a complex legal process which, if successful, would create a martyr, and, if unsuccessful, would bring down ridicule upon itself.

What the government needed was some more flexible method which would seek to prevent subversion rather than to punish it. Lincoln found the answer in the suspension of the writ of habeas corpus, a convenient halfway house between the inadequacies of the ordinary courts and the severity of widespread resort to martial law. Lincoln first authorised suspension of the writ in Maryland in the early weeks of the war when the national capital itself seemed to be in peril. Later in the year, further victims of arbitrary arrests in the same state included secessionist members of the state legislature, and other public officials. The numbers arrested not only in Maryland but elsewhere grew from hundreds into thousands. The whole idea of the arrests was not to bring charges or secure convictions, but to detain potentially dangerous people, and teach a lesson to them and to others. Many of those arrested were not detained for long; political influence, the intercession of friends, or, most commonly, willingness to take an oath of future loyalty, could secure a quick release. Arrests were placed, some-what strangely, under the control of the State Department in 1861, and, amid all his other duties, Seward found the time and the energy to create a network of spies, agents and informers to aid him in his task. In February 1862 the War Department took over responsibility, and Stanton brought to the task all his qualities of cold intensity and even colder efficiency. On 24 September 1862 Lincoln issued a proclamation making suspension of the writ applicable any-where in the country to those suspected of a variety of disloyal practices. In March 1863 Congress passed a Habeas Corpus Act which gave legislative sanction to established practice but also provided certain safeguards for the prisoners. In this latter regard, however, the act remained largely a dead letter.

Arbitrary arrests continued throughout the war, and, though no accurate figure of total numbers can be compiled, an estimate of 14,000 may err on the conservative side. Whatever the mitigating circumstances of lenient treatment of prisoners and rapid release, whatever the arguments that such arrests were more moderate, humane and effective than the available alternatives, detention without trial on this scale was a massive interference with the most elementary rights of American citizens. Hardly surprisingly, they were the cause of fierce legal argument, and even fiercer political controversy, especially as the gounds for many arrests seemed slender or frivolous – or were allegedly inspired by a desire to muzzle all opposition. The wording of the constitution on this vital matter has a deceptive simplicity at first sight. Article I, Section 9, paragraph 2 states that 'the privilege of the writ of habeas corpus shall not be suspended, unless when in cases of rebellion or invasion the public safety may require it'. But it does not state which branch of the government is to decide when a state of rebellion exists, and, more importantly, when the threat to the public safety is such as to warrant suspension of the privilege. Silence on this subject could be interpreted as implying a joint or concurrent right shared by president and Congress. The case for an exclusive congressional power to suspend the writ rested mainly on the placing of this paragraph in the first article of the constitution which deals with the legislative branch, but there are other provisions in that article which do not refer exclusively to the legislature. The case for the presidential right to suspend the writ rested largely on the very practical argument that it was the function and the duty of the president to cope with national emergencies and questions of the public safety, and that such emergencies could hardly be expected to wait for the next session of Congress.

Lincoln's action was challenged in the early months of the war by no less a figure than Roger B. Taney, chief justice of the Supreme Court. The *Merryman* case, which arose out of an arrest in Maryland, came before Taney in the circuit court – the case never reached the Supreme Court – and he granted a writ of habeas corpus, but that writ was questioned and a subsequent writ for contempt ignored by the local military commander. Taney bowed before the superior force of the executive power, but placed on record an opinion which was a stinging attack on presidential claims and presidential action in this field. If such usurpations were permitted, Taney said, 'the people of the United States are no longer living under a government of laws', and he bluntly reminded the president of his duty to 'take care that the laws be faithfully executed'.[19] If accepted as the basis of future policy, Taney's opinion would have smashed the whole internal security programme of the administration, but Lincoln had his own ideas on presidential power in this field, and abided by them unrepentantly. He answered Taney briefly and obliquely in his message of 4 July 1861; two years later, in two of his most famous letters, he wrote more fully in his own defence, making the commonsense case for executive responsibility in times of emergency, and stressing that the constitution itself identified certain proceedings, not normally constitutional, which became so when the public safety required it. To reassure those who feared that basic constitutional liberties would be permanently undermined, he resorted to an extraordinary and elaborate medical analogy:

> I can no more be persuaded that the government can constitutionally take no strong measure in time of rebellion, because it can be shown that the same could not be lawfully taken in time of peace, than I can be persuaded that a particular drug is not good medicine for a sick man, because it can be shown

to not be good food for a well one. Nor am I able to appreciate the danger . . . that the American people will, by means of military arrests during the rebellion, lose the right of public discussion, the liberty of speech and the press, the law of evidence, trial by jury, and Habeas corpus, throughout the indefinite peaceful future which I trust lies before them, any more than I am able to believe that a man could contract so strong an appetite for emetics during temporary illness, as to persist in feeding upon them through the remainder of his healthful life.[20]

The Supreme Court itself was never required to give a ruling on the habeas corpus issue during the war, and Congress, too, proved curiously indecisive or evasive on the matter. It was difficult to find a formula which asserted the rights of Congress without challenging what the president had already done, and, even in the Habeas Corpus Act of 1863, the drafters resorted to a form of words which could be interpreted either as a recognition of presidential power or a delegation of a Congressional power to the executive: 'the President is authorised to suspend the privilege of the writ of habeas corpus. . . .'

One of Lincoln's motives in relying so heavily on detention without trial, through suspension of the writ, was to avoid the need for stiffer doses of the more drastic medicine of martial law and the trial of civilians before military tribunals. American legal opinion was vague and uncertain about the scope and applicability of martial law and even its very meaning. During the Civil War there was obvious need for martial law in areas close to the fighting and in parts of the border states where the normal courts were not functioning and where the population included large disloyal elements. But it was a different matter when civilians were tried before military tribunals for offences which could only very loosely be described as military, in areas far from the front line, and free from any immediate danger of invasion or rebellion. Logically, it was hard to see how military and civil courts could function side by side in the same area; in practice, restraint on both sides mitigated some of the worst difficulties. However, one or two exceptional cases, which were as politically sensitive as they were legally doubtful, brought this whole issue to the attention of a wider public, and, eventually, of the Supreme Court. Inevitably, the most controversial case was that of Vallandigham, tried and sentenced by a military tribunal in Ohio in May 1863. Vallandigham had denied the right of the court to try him, and after the trial applied to the United States circuit court for a writ of habeas corpus. This was refused by a judge who held that he had no power to interfere in the decisions of a military tribunal. When the case was carried to the Supreme Court in 1864, it refused to review the proceedings of a military court, on the ground that such a body was not a court within the meaning of the Judiciary Act of 1789 which defined the powers of the Supreme Court. Thus, while the war still raged, the highest tribunal in the land refused to entangle itself in any attempt to question the activities of the military courts, or to undermine the security policy of the administration. Soon after the war, in 1866, the Supreme

Court, reacting rapidly to the changing climate, effectively reversed its earlier position. It reviewed the case of Lambdin P. Milligan, Indiana Copperhead and officer of the Sons of Liberty, who had been tried and sentenced to death by a military court in 1864, for conspiring to overthrow the government, and fomenting insurrection. The Supreme Court ruled that Milligan's trial before a military tribunal was unconstitutional, and that the proceedings had ignored constitutional safeguards which could not be set aside even in time of war. Many sections of opinion, including some radical Republicans (and, for that matter, the president himself), had always found the use of military tribunals to try civilians extremely distasteful, and there was not a little relief that the Supreme Court should take an early opportunity to set the record straight. But the fact remained that, at a time of crisis, the law of the constitution had bowed its knee (or at least averted its eye) in face of the law of necessity.[21]

In pursuit of his belief that the constitution must give the federal government adequate powers to preserve its existence, Lincoln's course had been characterised by sweeping assertions of national, and presidential, power, combined with moderation, restraint, common sense and humanity in their use. This was a typically Lincolnian blend, not so much the mailed fist concealed by the velvet glove, as the mailed fist controlled by a gentle arm. But such an approach had its long-term dangers, for, while bold and far-reaching precedents for government interference with basic rights and liberties had been created, their more menacing or sinister implications had been blurred or concealed by the image – and the reality – of a humane, decent, modest and moderate war leader. In different hands, the use of such precedents might have very different results. It is doubtful whether judgment of the constitutional propriety of the extensions of federal power during the war can be completely divorced from value judgments on the substantive issues involved. Perhaps the attempt is not worth making, for means and ends were so closely connected and so constantly reacting upon each other. Certainly, the Vallandighams and the Seymours, who refused to give an inch in defending the letter of the law as they defined it, showed a curious legal and moral blindness to other matters of rights and right which were at the heart of the American conflict. Certainly, too, there was unflagging ingenuity on all sides in finding and exploiting constitutional justification and legal precedent for whatever course of action was dictated by interest, principle or prejudice. But for all the rationalisations and the verbal gymnastics, the constitutional debates of the war years were much more than a legal sham. The striking feature of the debate was that almost everyone, on every side, argued the pros and cons in constitutional terms; there was hardly any inclination to throw the constitution overboard.[22] Out of the trauma of civil war there emerged at least one promise of future stability in the broad consensus of faith and trust in the constitution, backed up by faith and trust in the ballot-box and the prescribed political and legal processes for the righting of wrongs and the redress of grievances. During and after the war, as before, the constitution demonstrated its configurative role in the political and social life of the Union, and it demonstrated, too, its own capacity for survival. The white heat of civil conflict released powers in the constitutional system hitherto neglected, forgotten, hidden or unused. This latent strength was forced out by the sheer pressure of events. There was no blueprint to redraw the relationship between government and citizen, no conspiracy to undermine the states, no plan to build the foundations of a huge, centralised bureaucracy. Many parts of the constitution had never been put to the test before, and none had been put to so searching an examination. Clauses of the constitution dealing for example with habeas corpus, the president's power as commander-in-chief, and the guarantee of a republican form of government to each state, were stretched to the limit during the war, but the constitution itself never came to breaking-point. While the power of government grew by leaps and bounds, the rights of citizens were sometimes threatened, occasionally violated, but never destroyed. For this considerable achievement, some credit is due to both the administration and its critics. Both acted out the roles written for them by the political and constitutional situation, even if some of the cast could not always resist the temptation to over-play their parts.

6. By 1864 the North had amply demonstrated its capacity for conducting uninhibited political argument without fatally impairing the war effort. Searching and ingenious constitutional argument had served to draw out unsuspected strength in the original document rather than to undermine it. Relations between the federal and state governments had been transformed without shattering the pride and self-respect of state governors or provoking chronic feuds between Washington and the state capitals. Congressional politics had lost none of their keenness, intricacy, or frankness, but had never degenerated into wilful obstructionism. Elections were contested as vigorously as ever, but the party system had kept their divisive tendencies within bounds. New and great issues had been absorbed into the mainstream of politics without completely overshadowing old clashes of sections and interests, or traditional bread-and-butter issues like tariffs and banks and the public lands. A president of gauche manner, unassuming style and deceptive simplicity had also revealed high political skill, unexpected iron determination and a profound understanding of the movement of events. All these were symptoms of a political health which did not immunise the body politic against every ailment or injury, but gave it the strength to overcome them or at least to endure them. All these were attributes which Confederate politics lacked to a greater or lesser degree.

Now, in 1864, the political system of the Union faced two more inescapable challenges, posed by the looming problem of post-war reconstruction and the necessity of conducting a fiercely fought presidential election in the midst of a civil war. These were both severe tests of political strength, but the fact that the North could face such challenges with any confidence at all was in itself a recognition of strength. It was partly fate and partly chance, of course, but it was also partly a true reflection of comparative strength and weakness, that, in the Confederacy, the shape of post-war government and society never had an opportunity to become a major political issue, and there was never a seriously contested presidential election. While the South feuded, the North voted; while the Confederacy defended the past, the Union debated the future.

# Chapter XVII: Reconstruction and Re-election: the Climax of Lincoln's Presidency

Reconstruction would not wait upon the coming of peace. It was not Appomattox but Sumter which made it an overriding issue, for what was the whole Northern war effort but a gigantic and costly endeavour to reconstruct the Union? From the outset, then, the drama of reconstruction was played out against a backdrop of military necessity and wartime politics. In the 1860s there was little or nothing of the sharp distinction between the politics of war and peace which some critics discern in the history of American participation in later conflicts. While the battle still raged, the problem was at one level the very practical one, created by the success of Northern arms, of governing occupied territory in the Southern states. At a very different level it provoked intricate constitutional debate over the nature of the war, the basis of the union of the states, and the rival jurisdictions of president and Congress. Again, it posed fundamental questions about the character of the Union as it was, as it should be, and as it would be in the future. Linking the various aspects of the problem was a criss-crossing network of political interests and alignments. Reconstruction divided the two main parties from each other, and threatened to divide the Republican party against itself. In the last eighteen months of the war it became not merely one issue but the great issue in Northern politics.

But while the politicians wrangled in Washington, the occupied South was in travail. Large parts of Tennessee, Arkansas and Louisiana, and smaller areas of

Virginia and the Carolinas, were in Union hands by the middle of 1862. Parts of other states, like Mississippi, shared the same fate a year later. The inhabitants of these areas endured some of the worst miseries of the war. Their homes were burned or looted, their crops ruined, the day-by-day routine of their lives was shattered. Supplies and amenities – and a sense of stability and security – which had once been taken for granted, were now destroyed or transformed into a matter of daily struggle and nagging uncertainty. Even when the formal lines of battle ceased to ebb and flow across their land, cavalry raids and guerrilla bands continued to plague them. Not surprisingly, many people also went in fear of their ex-slaves in whom the first rapture of freedom might easily curdle into bloody vengeance against their former masters. Even where the shadows of violence and lawlessness were not too heavy, other insidious dangers were at work, sowing doubt and demoralisation – the dilemma posed by the conquerors, offering generous loyalty oaths with one hand, and threatening severe measures against open disloyalty with the other, or the temptation to do business with the cotton speculators or to embark on some other shady or illicit trade which might stave off complete ruin.

The breakdown of normal life, and the collapse of law and order, required firm Union action to bring some measure of control and security to the occupied areas. The government which was provided was essentially military government, sometimes attempting to work through the normal local authorities and courts, sometimes resorting to new agencies and bringing offenders to book before special war courts. As soon as the invading armies and the administration in Washington embarked upon such novel extensions of federal power, however, they came up against problems which were not merely administrative but constitutional, and which turned upon the fundamental question of the legal character of the great American conflict.

1. If the crucial constitutional issue of reconstruction centred on the position of the rebel states, that in turn depended upon whether the conflict was regarded as one between fully-fledged belligerents, as understood in international law, or simply as a domestic matter involving the suppression of large-scale rebellion. Administrative convenience in governing the occupied areas might have favoured the former view, where international law provided ample precedent for full control. But this view created serious embarrassment in other respects. The official view of the administration, and, in 1861, of the great mass of Northern opinion, denied the right of secession, regarded the individual states as indestructible, and claimed that they lived on within the Union, in the persons of their loyal citizens. In its own way such a view had the appeal – and the perils – of simplicity. It reduced the problem to one of restoring loyal governments in the states and restoring them to their proper relationship with the Union. But what if it was thought necessary or desirable to impose conditions for that restoration, or to reconstruct the rebel states in a sense much wider and deeper than mere restoration? Where was the constitutional justification for

interference by the federal government with the structure, institutions and rights of states which had never ceased and could never cease to be states of the Union? Faced with such awkward questions, the administration and particularly the president himself generally adhered to the conventional view of the indestructibility of the states but preferred where possible to avoid elaborate legal argument, or blur the main lines of controversy. The double-status theory of the conflict as both a war and an internal rebellion once again had obvious attractions.

Those who were intent upon a much bolder reconstruction policy were not slow to produce alternative constitutional theories. A few, like Thaddeus Stevens, asserted that, exercising full belligerent powers, the United States could rule the former Southern states as conquered provinces, but even many radicals shrank from this extreme view, and preferred the argument that, while still within the Union, the rebel states had abdicated their rights under the constitution and forfeited their normal powers and functions. In 1862 Charles Sumner talked boldly of 'state suicide', but later muted such over-dramatic language. Much the same idea was couched in less extravagant terms in the theory that the rebel states had reverted to the status of territories, and, like all other territories, were the direct concern of the federal government. The territorial theory had the obvious appeal of relying upon a recognised constitutional and political procedure, while at the same time providing a solid platform from which to launch a major reconstruction of the Southern states, including the final destruction of slavery. But, ironically, there was an embarrassing flaw in this line of argument. The territorial theory, almost as much as the conquered-provinces argument, seemed to go much too far towards recognition of the right of secession, by accepting that a state could virtually destroy its position within the Union. Conservative opinion also resisted the idea that an existing state could revert to territorial status, and argued that no such use of federal control of the territories could possibly have been envisaged by the makers of the constitution. By mid-war, therefore, radicals as well as many moderates were increasingly attracted by yet another constitutional theory which pressed a harmless-looking clause of the constitution into service to meet urgent need. Article IV, Section 4 of the constitution states that 'the United States shall guarantee to every State in this Union a republican form of government'. Here was a justification for federal interference which evaded the question of the standing of the individual states, but there were still snags to be overcome. The application of this clause to such an unprecedented situation stretched the wording of the constitution almost to breaking point, and there was no ready-made or readily agreed definition of 'a republican form of government'. If slavery was incompatible with a republican form of government, where did this leave border slave states like Kentucky and Missouri? And if, later, it was held that equal rights or even Negro suffrage were essential to a republican form of government, where did this leave any one of a dozen or more Northern states which, by law, discriminated against the Negro? But such possible future embarrassments did not outweigh the immediate advantages of the guarantee clause, and, from 1863, it was the basis of most Congressional reconstruction plans, and it met with presidential approval in Lincoln's proclamation of December 1863.

Indeed, one further short-term advantage of the brevity and vagueness of the guarantee clause was that it did not specify which branch of the government was responsible for making good that guarantee. This left open the other great constitutional question involved in reconstruction. As over emancipation, suspension of habeas corpus, and other issues, president and Congress wrestled over their competing claims to power. Congress based its case on its general legislative authority along with its specific control over its own membership. Lincoln relied heavily as always on his generous estimate of his own war powers, backed up by the presidential pardoning power, spelt out in the constitution. He admitted that Congress had certain rights in such a major field of policy, but was determined to keep the initiative and essential control in his own hands. He had one great practical advantage in that Congress was not in continuous session, and for long periods – five months in 1862, nine months in 1863 – he alone was in a position to act. On the other hand, reconstruction was to be bedevilled during the war (and even more so after it) by recurring crises in which executive-legislative rivalry overlapped with serious disagreements on substantive policy issues.

Constitutional arguments about reconstruction were often tortuous and the constitutional debate was often confused, and sometimes riddled with contradiction. Paradoxically, it was the moderate view, insisting that the rebel states were still within the Union, which was most inflexible in its determination to admit nothing which appeared to recognise secession, while some radical views, embracing the territorial or conquered provinces theories, were willing to risk the logical consequences. Again, there was no necessary and consistent correlation between radical constitutional ideas and radical reconstruction policies. In 1862 a moderate measure sponsored by Senator Ira Harris was blocked by conservatives who rejected its 'radical' constitutional basis in the territorial theory. In 1864, on the other hand, Henry Winter Davis based his 'radical' bill on the moderate constitutional theory drawn from the guarantee clause. No one made bolder assertions of unprecedented powers than Abraham Lincoln himself, but the purposes to which he put those powers in practice often caused frustration and anger to radical members of his own party.

Two features of the constitutional controversy stand out. If some provisions of the constitution were draped in heavy shrouds to shield them from the public gaze, while others were decked out in daring new fashions to catch the eye of a wondering audience, it was still remarkable that, on all sides, including almost all those of radical persuasion, the debate was conducted within the framework of the constitution, and with but little inclination to discard it in face of a situation unimagined and unimaginable to its authors. Secondly, the confusions and the contradictions of the debate were often a reflection of the most funda-

mental question of all: the capacity of the constitution and the federal government to find within themselves the power and the resources to cope with such
unprecedented demands. The unflagging search for constitutional justification
for novel exercise of power was itself a token of confidence that the government
and constitution possessed an inner strength adequate to meet the challenge.[1]

Politically, reconstruction was not one single problem, but several, which
overlapped to the extent that a solution to one could hamper or obstruct
solution of another. First was the formal question of restoring loyal governments
in the rebel states and re-establishing them in their proper functions within the
Union. If that had been the full extent of the problem, the answer might have
been relatively simple. But, even if there had been the will to restore the
Southern states as they were to the Union as it was, the facts ruled out the
possibility. The mere fact of civil war ensured that the Union, if restored, would
inevitably be remodelled, and, as the months and then years of conflict passed,
both North and South were being transformed by the changes which it wrought.
Increasingly, Northerners were inclined to attach a variable (but gradually
lengthening) list of conditions to restoration. What kind of treatment was to be
meted out to the defeated white South? Reconstruction on the basis of the loyal
citizens seemed an attractive idea, but, as armies penetrated deeper into the
Confederacy, Southern Unionism looked more and more like an illusion, and
where it existed it was widely misunderstood. In such a situation, for all the
variety of loyalty oaths proffered and taken during and after the war, there
remained the question whether formal allegiance to the federal government and
constitution was enough, or whether loyalty implied acceptance of a new kind
of Union, committed to new ideals and new goals. As the debate over reconstruction developed during the war, there was increasing emphasis on the need
to exclude from power and influence all those who had led the South down the
road to secession, and on into violent resistance to the authority of the federal
government. Such a goal again fitted the convenient assumption that the
rebellion was a conspiracy mounted by evil men who had led astray the mass of
the Southern population. But it also raised all manner of questions about which,
and how many, leaders, civil and military, state and Confederate, were to be
penalised, how severe were to be the handicaps imposed upon them, and whether
their exclusion from political life was to be temporary or permanent. Increasingly,
in their search for a solid base for new state governments, the makers of
reconstruction policy confronted the dilemma that the loyalists had virtue on
their side but lacked numbers, while the alternative white leadership had the
numbers but lacked the will to do penance for its sins.

It was this situation which slowly drove more radical Northern opinion into
the belief that the only viable foundation for loyal state governments rested not
on the white South but upon the blacks. It would take time before this view
became strong enough to shape policy, and it ran the grave risk, of course, of
alienating much Northern opinion as well as almost the entire white population
of the South, loyalists as well as ex-rebels. On the other hand, the general

question of the status of the Negro in the reconstructed South was central to the whole debate from its earliest wartime days. But the field of debate was constantly changing. After all, during the first half of the war emancipation itself was still the focal point of controversy, and Lincoln's proclamations carefully excluded from their provisions not only the border states but areas of the Confederacy already reoccupied. By the second half of 1863 the great divide between radical and conservative approaches to reconstruction was still whether or not complete abolition should be an essential condition of restoration to the Union.[2] Later in the war, when emancipation itself was no longer a point at issue, the debate centred on the guarantees of Negro rights and interests which were to be written into reconstruction policy. By the time that the war ended, serious attention was beginning to shift to the highly sensitive question of Negro suffrage which would safeguard not merely the Negro himself but also the whole notion of loyal state governments in the South. At every stage the dispute revolved around conflicting priorities. On the highest plane, charity to a defeated enemy and justice for the freed slave were both honourable goals in themselves. But each could also be exploited as a device to obstruct the other. Love your ex-enemies could become a euphemism for racial prejudice and discrimination, and justice for the Negro a cloak for vindictiveness against their former masters. Again, to some men, new state governments, exclusion of ex-Confederates, and protection of the ex-slaves were just practical matters to be dealt with piecemeal as they arose. For others, they were all part of the one grand design of restructuring Southern society from top to bottom to bring it into line with the accepted mid-century American model. A truly radical reconstruction would demand not merely new state constitutions and governments, but the destruction of an old ruling class, massive redistribution of property to give the Negro an economic foundation for his freedom, and cast-iron provisions to guarantee his civil and political rights. But few men, and certainly few politicians, had the time, the vision or the daring to think in such terms while war still raged.

The exigencies of war would seldom wait for the maturing of long-term plans. By the summer of 1862 there was no hope left of a quick, smooth restoration of the Union – and, by that same time, Union forces already controlled parts of several rebel states. Thus, as the prospect of an overall reconstruction receded into the more distant future, the immediate, practical necessity to deal with the occupied areas thrust itself into the foreground. Showing once again his predilection for concentrating on the particular rather than the general, Lincoln gave priority to the specific problems of Tennessee, Louisiana and Arkansas, the three main test-beds of reconstruction policy. He was content to allow any long-term overall policy to emerge gradually from these particular situations, and he conceived his short-term policies primarily in terms of undermining the strength and unity of the Confederacy, and thus making a vital contribution to the war effort. In contrast, more radical members of his own party were concerned to lay down general principles and guidelines, to spell out guarantees for the future, and to insist that the various rebel states must conform to the prescribed pattern in the process of reconstruction. In the last year of the war the difference of approach found expression over the question of timing. Lincoln looked to the speediest possible restoration of the states, while radical opinion was more and more impressed by the idea of postponing the main business of reconstruction until after the war.

The politics of reconstruction had still wider implications both for the immediate wartime situation and for post-war developments. As president, Lincoln remained anxious to pursue a course cautious and moderate enough to retain the support of the broadest possible coalition of Republicans and War Democrats in the North, and even to extend that coalition by fostering white Southern support for the Republican party by his conciliatory approach to reconstruction. He never lost sight of his own immediate prospects of re-election in 1864 or the longer-term presidential and congressional prospects of the Republican party. Radical Republicans in Congress had an eye to the political future, too, but their perspective was different. With a safe majority in their home state or district, many of them did not share the president's immediate concern about election prospects, and felt no need to broaden their own base of support. But they were extremely concerned at the prospect of the white South making a rapid recovery from military defeat by regaining its old power and influence in the political life of the Union. Here was one incentive to delay the process of restoration; here was one ground for objection to Lincoln's alleged 'rotten boroughs' in Tennessee, Louisiana and Arkansas; here was one good reason for the exclusion of ex-Confederates from politics, and, later, the promotion of Negro suffrage as the only solid foundation for Republicanism in the south. But all Republicans needed to tread warily on this last point, for too much public enthusiasm for the rights of the Negro, too much zeal for long and costly campaigns on his behalf, would surely arouse the Negrophobia of the North, and expose congressmen to the hazards of any elected representative who devotes too much of his energies to causes which, however worthy, are remote from the interests, or disturbing to the peace of mind, of his constituents. But if Republicans were determined not to have the first political fruits of victory snatched from them by their opponents, the Democrats foresaw the prospect of a rapid resurgence of their party, North and South, after the war. A quick restoration of white government in the South was almost bound to work to their advantage, and thorough exploitation of racial prejudice and anxiety along with other issues like the 'despotism' of the Lincoln administration, seemed likely to pay handsome dividends in the North. Reconstruction involved not merely the restoration of the Union, but a party battle over who would control it once it was restored.

2. The shifting fortunes of war added further complexities. Constitutional arguments, political objectives and moral commitments changed, as the dimensions of the problem grew. Reconstruction became a grim, deadly serious,

and frustrating game, in which not merely the rules, but the tactics, the goals, the rival teams and even the field of play were constantly being changed. In such a contest Lincoln's non-committal, piecemeal approach offered certain advantages, at least in the short run. For the first thirty months of the war his objectives were limited and his approach flexible. He was anxious to create some kind of state governments as quickly as possible as a rallying point for Southern loyalism, and he was loath to impose conditions which might slow down that process. In this period, his main instrument of policy (and his boldest assumption of executive authority) was his appointment of military governors in Tennessee, Arkansas and Louisiana, and also in North Carolina, to fill the void left by the collapse of Confederate authority, until the loyal citizens could form a new state government. The military governor of Tennessee, appointed in March 1862, was Andrew Johnson, the only Southern senator not to abandon his seat when his state seceded. Johnson took a tough, even high-handed, line in Tennessee, resorting to arbitrary arrests, removal of many office-holders, and confiscation of property, in his efforts to punish disloyalty and build up a Unionist political organisation under his own control. He was hampered by divisions in the Unionist ranks (partly of his own making), by the ebb and flow of the battle-front across large parts of the state, and by the misfortune that while Union forces controlled most of west and central Tennessee, the main pro-Union strength of the state was in the mountainous east. Johnson himself seemed to be in no hurry to hold elections and establish a new loyalist state government to take over from his military régime. In Arkansas, the military governor, John S. Phelps, could make little progress until Union forces were in more secure control of a significant area of the state, and in North Carolina Edward Stanley created more embarrassment than enthusiasm in Washington by his extremely conservative policy on slavery and the Negro.

The real test case of Lincolnian reconstruction under the auspices of a military governor was in Louisiana, where, from the spring of 1862, Union forces held New Orleans and the surrounding area. The governor, George F. Shepley, was completely subservient to the departmental military commander, Ben Butler, whose radical views and flamboyant style encouraged a policy designed to create a political machine rather than form a new state government, and likely to antagonise the local conservative leadership of planters and New Orleans merchants. Under presidential pressure, congressional elections were held in two Louisiana districts in December 1862. The size of the poll, about half that in the elections of 1860, was a mildly encouraging sign of loyalist strength, and the two elected members, Michael Hahn and Benjamin Flanders, were admitted to the House of Representatives in Washington in February 1863, and sat through the last month of the life of the thirty-seventh Congress. But, for the rest of 1863, Louisiana brought no further joy to Lincoln. Butler was replaced by the more moderate and conciliatory Nathaniel P. Banks, but he could accomplish little in face of a widening split in the Unionist ranks between a radical anti-slavery group which wanted a new state constitution, including abolition of slavery, and a conservative, planter-dominated group aiming at new elections under the old constitution. When the latter carried their case to Washington, Lincoln came down firmly against them, and in favour of emancipation as a condition of restoration. But the radical group lacked the popular support to carry their proposals for a constitutional convention, and, as 1863 drew to its close, Louisiana reconstruction was stuck fast. Lincoln had clearly endorsed the principle that the rebel states must abolish slavery as a condition of restoration – and that, in 1863, was a radical position – but, in general, his programme of action through military governors had yielded no substantial results.

Meanwhile, in 1862 and 1863, Congress devoted much time and energy to discussion of reconstruction measures, but with equally disappointing tangible results. Lincoln's actions won some congressional support but aroused considerable suspicion of both their allegedly conservative intent and their sweeping assertion of executive authority. In 1862 congressional Republicans sponsored various bills, based mainly on the theory of reversion to territorial status. The most radical of these, promoted by James M. Ashley of Ohio, provided not merely for emancipation, but land redistribution, exclusion of ex-Confederate leaders, and equal rights for Negroes in such matters as jury service, but it was blocked by the votes of Democrats and conservative Republicans. In 1863 Senator Ira Harris of New York introduced a bill, now based on the guarantee clause of the constitution, which foreshadowed later congressional legislation. It aimed to reorganise the Southern state governments on the basis of new constitutions, and it imposed conditions, including abolition of slavery, and disqualification of Confederate office-holders. But, in the short congressional session, it stood no chance of becoming law. In both 1862 and 1863, conservatives in both houses were able to exploit the rich opportunities for obstruction and delay provided by congressional procedure, to block even moderate reconstruction proposals which might have been acceptable to both the president and the Republican majority.

In the latter part of 1863 the pressure of events and of interested parties demanded some more clear-cut, definite statement of policy. The experimental off-the-cuff approach would serve no longer, either to meet the immediate situation in the South or to safeguard the future. Conservatives and radicals had both shifted their ground during the war, and still disagreed among themselves on many points, but the question of abolition of slavery as a condition of restoration was a clear dividing line between them. If disagreement on policy came to coincide with executive-legislative rivalry, the situation would be critical indeed. Lincoln was anxious to avoid such a showdown, and, for all the criticism of his cautious, piecemeal approach, he now stood on the radical side in insisting on abolition. But other vigorous champions stood forth on either side of the dispute. When Charles Sumner published an article in the *Atlantic Monthly* in October 1863, strenuously asserting congressional control over reconstruction, and placing the rebel states completely at the mercy of federal authority, he was met by a blistering attack from no less a person than

Montgomery Blair, the Postmaster-General. Blair compared the abolitionists (with whom he lumped the radical Republicans) to the Southern nullifiers of an earlier day, as potential Union-wreckers, and raised the bogey of miscegenation by declaring that 'they would make the manumission of the slaves the means of infusing their blood into our whole system by blending with it *"amalgamation, equality* and *fraternity"* '.[3] Meanwhile, Lincoln kept his own counsel, and eventually steered his own course in the wide but storm-tossed gulf which so clearly divided a member of his own cabinet from a senator of his own party (with both of whom he was personally on good terms).

Lincoln announced his own new plan – indeed, his first general plan of reconstruction – in a proclamation which accompanied his message to Congress of 8 December 1863. It contained two main sets of provisions: an offer of pardon to individual Southerners, and a scheme for the re-establishment of loyal state governments. Pardon and restoration of property rights (except in slaves) were to be obtained by taking an oath of future loyalty to the United States and obedience to all presidential and congressional measures dealing with slavery, taken during the rebellion. Certain classes of persons were excepted from the benefits of the amnesty; they included the civil and diplomatic officers and agents of 'the so-called confederate government', Confederate army officers above the rank of colonel and naval officers above lieutenant, men who had resigned commissions in the United States forces or left seats in the United States Congress to aid the rebellion, and also anyone who had treated captured Negro troops as anything other than prisoners-of-war. New state governments could be established by persons who had taken the oath, when they amounted to not less than one-tenth of the number of votes cast in the last pre-war election of 1860. Such governments would themselves have to conform to the terms of the oath: that is, they must accept emancipation in the areas where it applied. But the proclamation did permit 'temporary arrangements' for the freedmen provided that their permanent freedom was recognised. In both the proclamation and the message, Lincoln still clung to his precious flexibility and non-commitment by insisting that the endorsement of one method of reconstruction did not preclude other suitable and acceptable schemes.[4]

It has become a commonplace to describe Lincoln's plan as a conservative measure, and it is true that, within a few months, the president was to be at loggerheads with congressional Republicans, especially some of the radicals, over reconstruction policy. But his proclamation was at first generally welcomed by all sections of the party – and probably more by radicals than conservatives. Indeed, one paper referred to 'the President's conversion to the radical programme'.[5] Certainly, the plan had its conservative features – the heavy emphasis on the pardon of individual Southerners, and reliance on the existing framework of the states, for example. But many radicals found these features unexceptionable, and they readily approved of the resort to a loyalty oath required of all citizens, and above all of the insistence on emancipation as a condition of reconstruction. Reliance on such a small minority as 10 per cent of the electorate as the basis of a new government no doubt raised a few eyebrows, but Lincoln and others had learned from bitter experience not to be too optimistic or ambitious about loyalist support in the early stages. For a while, prospects of cooperation between president and Congress looked bright, and James Ashley introduced a bill which, despite some more radical features, looked broadly like a legislative enactment of the Lincoln plan.

But harmony did not prevail for long. Doubts about the president's scheme grew in the minds of those who thought the proposals too generous to ex-rebels, and particularly of those radicals and abolitionists whose thoughts were now turning increasingly to the problem of protecting the rights and interests of the ex-slave. Lincoln's proclamation said little on this latter point, and what it did say could be construed as leaving a loophole through which Southern whites could relegate the freedmen to some twilight, half-and-half zone, in which they might dwell, not exactly in bondage, but certainly not in complete freedom. Such doubts, along with a continuing desire to assert congressional authority, were converted into outright opposition by developments in Louisiana. Early in 1864 Lincoln gave General Banks full powers to bring about the creation of a new state government there as rapidly as possible. The president may well have hoped that Banks would support the radical elements in Louisiana, but such hopes were quickly dashed, and Lincoln felt obliged to support the general when he followed a different course under the old state constitution, which threatened to leave the way open for the planters to recover political power, and to leave the Negroes at the mercy of a labour system apparently little better than slavery. This was one of the most serious political blunders of Lincoln's whole presidency. It endorsed something which was certainly not what radicals understood by reconstruction.

Congressional deliberations on reconstruction were drastically affected by the change of climate. Thaddeus Stevens introduced a bill which treated the rebel states as alien enemies who had forfeited all constitutional rights, and which would have delayed indefinitely the process of their restoration to the Union. The measure stood no chance of being passed, but it encouraged support for the idea of postponing the serious business of reconstruction until the war was over – a far cry from Lincoln's policy designed primarily to help the war effort. Various debates gave members the opportunity to condemn Lincoln's policy in Louisiana; Henry Winter Davis, chairman of the House select committee on reconstruction, ridiculed the attempt of Lincoln and Banks 'to organize another hermaphrodite government, half military, half republican, representing the alligators and the frogs of Louisiana, and to place that upon a footing of a government of a State of the United States'.[6] Banks's policy in Louisiana led to elections for a state government which were won by the moderates under Michael Hahn, and a convention which drew up a constitution abolishing slavery, but which showed little liking for the idea of Negro suffrage, or even of public education for Negro children. Under pressure from Banks, the convention decided to empower the legislature to grant the vote to Negroes but it did not insist upon it, or even recommend it. Similar developments were taking place in Arkansas, but with even more evidence of legal irregularities, military interference, and low voter participation than in Louisiana. Representatives elected in both states, and senators chosen in Arkansas, were refused admission to seats in Congress where suspicion of the Lincoln programme had turned into open hostility. Lincoln's whole policy, including the 10 per cent plan, it was alleged, was designed to create puppet régimes which would support his re-nomination for a second term, and cast electoral votes in his favour in the coming presidential contest. Such a prospect was equally unwelcome to radicals who hoped to replace him with another Republican nominee, and Democrats who saw their chances of victory in the election foiled by the electoral votes of restored Southern states, with governments which represented only a tiny minority of their citizens. Until the end of the war, the new governments of Louisiana and Arkansas lived in a kind of limbo.

In February 1864 Henry Winter Davis introduced a reconstruction bill in the House which became the rallying-point for a congressional challenge to presidential reconstruction. It evoked no great enthusiasm in many quarters; it failed to satisfy extreme hard-liners like Stevens, and it dismayed conservative Republicans and Democrats. But, on its long and hazardous course through Congress, it became the vehicle not merely of congressional jealousy of executive power, but of resentment at the situation in Louisiana, growing determination to give protection to the freedmen and to prevent ex-rebels from regaining power – and also of the attempt to replace Lincoln as the Republican nominee for the presidency in the election of 1864. It finally passed on 2 July, after being rushed through the Senate by Ben Wade, and saved from defeat or emasculation in the final stages by the prodigious efforts of both Wade and Davis.

The Wade–Davis bill based itself on the guarantee clause of the constitution, and was in that sense more moderate than radical measures of earlier vintage. But it was in most respects a much sterner and more radical programme of reconstruction than Lincoln had initiated seven months earlier. It laid down a series of complicated stages in the process of reconstruction, to be supervised by a provisional governor. When military resistance had ended in a state, the white male citizens were to be enrolled, and requested to take an oath of future loyalty to the United States. If more than 50 per cent of those enrolled took the oath, the next step was to elect delegates to a constitutional convention. But in order to vote in that election or to be a delegate, it was necessary to take the much tougher 'ironclad' oath which was a test of past as well as future loyalty. Any person who had held any Confederate or state office, civil or military, during the rebellion or who had voluntarily borne arms against the United States was ineligible either to vote or to be a delegate. The convention was required to write into the new state constitution provisions prohibiting slavery forever, repudiating rebel debts, both Confederate and state, and excluding from the franchise and from office-holding all who had held civil office during the rebellion, or held the rank of colonel or above in the Confederate army. The new constitution would then be submitted to the electorate; if it were accepted, the way was open for presidential recognition of the government thus established. Only then could the state elect members of Congress and participate in presidential elections. The bill also provided certain safeguards of the liberties of the freedmen, and it ended by denying United States citizenship to anyone who thereafter held important civil or military office in the rebel service.[7]

There were of course some features common to the Lincoln and Wade–Davis plans. Both were bold affirmations of federal power, both employed loyalty oaths, both regarded abolition of slavery as an essential condition of reconstruction, both omitted any provision for Negro suffrage. On the other hand, the Wade–Davis bill asserted congressional rather than presidential authority, its oath provisions were far more stringent, it insisted upon the creation of new state constitutions, it imposed other conditions in addition to emancipation, and it made some effort to protect the Negro in his freedom, rather than leave him to the tender mercies of his former masters. It was also far tougher in its attitude to former rebels, and it required 50 per cent rather than 10 per cent of the electorate as the starting-point of the whole operation. (Strangely enough, in its original form, Davis's bill had followed Lincoln's 10 per cent provision.) The greater severity of the Wade–Davis plan, along with its complicated series of stages – and, above all, the 50 per cent requirement – meant that it was in effect a proposal to delay serious reconstruction until after the war. It was an attempt to prepare the ground rules for a systematic post-war reconstruction of the South, while Lincoln on the other hand gave the highest priority to the immediate goal of suppressing the rebellion, and was in any case congenitally ill-disposed towards elaborate blueprints for the future. Even where he accepted the need for radical change, he sought to disguise the boldness of what he did, and to cushion the shock. With reconstruction as with emancipation, he preferred to launch great enterprises with no fanfare of trumpets. The differences between Lincoln and the radicals on the goals of reconstruction were real but often looked greater than in fact they were; the differences in style and tactics were very sharp; the difference was above all perhaps in the perspective from which each side saw the problem and the context in which each made decisions and acted upon them. Lincoln's inclination was to make small decisions which sometimes had large consequences, some good, some bad; others preferred grander gestures and bolder designs which sometimes ended in anti-climax.

The Wade–Davis bill was an embarrassment to Lincoln, but its supporters professed confidence that he would sign it. There was tension in the air on the last day of the congressional session, as the president sat in the Capitol signing last-minute bills, and the promoters of the reconstruction bill watched to see if he would put his name to their handiwork. But the president withheld his signature and took refuge in a little-used provision of the constitution, the so-called 'pocket veto', by which, at the end of a congressional session, if a president took no action on a bill within ten days, it failed to become law. The pocket veto naturally infuriated the bill's supporters, but worse was yet to come.

A few days later, on 8 July, Lincoln issued a curious proclamation explaining his action, although, constitutionally, no explanation was required. If its purpose was to heal the breach with congressional Republicans, its actual effect was just the opposite. The proclamation gave three main reasons for the veto: unwillingness to be committed inflexibly to one plan of restoration, unwillingness to abandon the fragile new governments of Louisiana and Arkansas, which would be ruled out under the Wade–Davis plan, and refusal to recognise 'a constitutional competency in Congress to abolish slavery in States'. This last point was entirely consistent with his position throughout the war that only the war powers of the president could justify such drastic interference with the institutions of states still deemed to be within the Union. But what made this curious document more peculiar still was the sting in its tail. Having refused to allow the bill to become law, Lincoln announced that it nevertheless embodied one proper and acceptable mode of reconstruction, and that he would use the executive power to aid the people of any state who chose to adopt it. In view of the extreme unlikelihood that the people of any Southern state would ever prefer this plan to Lincoln's own much more lenient reconstruction programme, this statement might be classified as a prime example of Lincoln's idiosyncratic sense of humour; but, if so, Wade, Davis and many others failed to appreciate the joke.

Resentment against the president finally burst forth in the Wade–Davis Manifesto, published in the press on 5 August. In contrast to Lincoln's brief, formal proclamation, the manifesto was a long document, full of anger, scorn and threats. It brought out into the open the issue implicit in Lincoln's statement – namely the rival claims of president and Congress to control the processes of emancipation and reconstruction. It made a slashing attack on 'those shadows of governments in Arkansas and Louisiana. . . . They are mere creatures of his will. They are mere oligarchies imposed on the people by military orders under the form of election, at which generals, provost marshals, soldiers and camp-followers were the chief actors, assisted by a handful of resident citizens, and urged on to premature action by private letters from the President.' The manifesto sharply contrasted the strict conditions and firm guarantees which were built into the bill, with the silence of the Lincoln plan on such matters as the rebel debt, the political exclusion of rebel leaders, and protection of the rights and interests of the freedmen. It unmercifully exposed the glaring inconsistency in Lincoln's proclamation:

After this assignment of his reasons for preventing the bill from becoming a law, the President proceeds to declare his purpose to execute it as a law by his plenary dictatorial power. . . .

A more studied outrage on the legislative authority of the people has never been perpetrated.

Congress passed a bill; the President refused to approve it, and then by proclamation puts as much of it in force as he sees fit. . . .

All this was a remarkable enough revelation of the state of feeling between congressmen and a president of the same party. But the manifesto closed with a direct and angry challenge:

> The President has greatly presumed on the forbearance which the supporters of his Administration have so long practised, in view of the arduous conflict in which we are engaged, and the reckless ferocity of our political opponents. But he must understand that our support is of a cause and not of a man; that the authority of Congress is paramount and must be respected; that the whole body of the Union men of Congress will not submit to be impeached by him of rash and unconstitutional legislation; and if he wishes our support, he must confine himself to his Executive duties – to obey and execute, not to make the laws – to suppress by arms armed rebellion, and leave political reorganization to Congress.

The supporters of the government were finally urged to 'consider the remedy of these usurpations, and, having found it, fearlessly execute it'.[8]

This extraordinary outburst revealed the Wade–Davis Manifesto for what it was – a piece of political propaganda, and one of the mid-summer storm clouds of an extraordinary election year. The dispute over the Wade–Davis bill occurred at a time when Lincoln's prospects looked poor, and the radicals were anxious to get rid of him as the party's candidate. The last section of the manifesto was the broadest possible hint to that effect. The situation was indeed exceptional; at such a time, the president's resort to a pocket veto, and the harsh language of the manifesto, show that both sides realised that they were playing for very high stakes. Both felt deeply about the issues of reconstruction, both were well aware of the importance of the coming election – and both realised that the one could not be dissociated from the other. The main item on the agenda of the next president of the United States was bound to be the reconstruction of the Union. The radicals were suspicious of Lincoln's 'rotten boroughs' in the South; Lincoln was determined not to surrender control of reconstruction policy, and equally determined not to surrender the middle ground by committing himself to a plan which would endanger the broad-based coalition upon which his chances of re-election depended. Up to a point, he could afford to risk the ire of the radicals, for they really had nowhere else to turn. If they sought to dislodge Lincoln, they would almost certainly be faced with something and someone far worse – a Democratic victory, and a Democratic president for the next four years. Indeed, there is evidence to suggest that the violent language of the Wade–Davis Manifesto had a boomerang effect on much Republican opinion. From the end of August, developments on the battlefield and elsewhere conspired to persuade the radicals that, for the time being, the better part of valour was discretion. For his part, Lincoln had conducted his side of the argument over reconstruction with pertinacity but with restraint, and his talent for collaborating

with men who disagreed with him or disapproved of him helped those who had
castigated him in high summer to campaign for him in the fall. For the next
few months the politics of reconstruction took second place to the demands of
electioneering.

3. Throughout 1864, reconstruction and the election took turns to occupy the
political limelight. Curiously enough, although each profoundly affected the
other, the clash over the Wade–Davis bill was one of the few occasions when
they shared the spotlight. For the most part, while one took the centre of the
stage, the other confined itself to ominous noises off. But, whatever the other
distractions, the rigid electoral timetable prescribed by the constitution meant
that in 1864 the whole system of government, and the men who ran it, faced
their most severe practical test. As Lincoln among others was always ready to
argue, the ballot box provided the best remedy for grievances, and the best
answer to allegations, about executive usurpation, or infringement of civil
liberties. The constitution would be seriously at risk only if it became impossible
to throw out those who had transgressed against it through elections held at the
appointed times. 1864 was a presidential election year, and no one ever seriously
questioned whether the election should or would take place. Certainly, it
proved in some ways to be an unusual election. Eleven states which had cast
electoral college votes four years earlier did not do so, or were not permitted
to do so in 1864. Military power, including a military presence at the polls,
played an unprecedented role in a number of states. Soldiers in the field voted
in huge numbers for the first time in history. There was a powerful movement
in one party to get rid of the candidate who had been nominated only weeks
earlier at the convention – and who was also the incumbent president. The duly
nominated candidate of the other party virtually set aside the platform on which
he was chosen to run in his letter accepting the nomination. (He was neither the
first nor the last presidential candidate to jettison his party's programme, but
no one else has done so with such indecent haste.) Other questionable or
irregular features of the 1864 election – the pressure on office-holders, the
allegations and the actuality of fraud and cheating at the polls – were very much
a part of the American tradition. If 1864 had its unusual moments and its
unconventional procedures, so too have most other American presidential
elections. The 1864 election was remarkable first in that it took place at all, and
secondly in that it so much resembled other elections before and after.

   At first glance, Republican prospects must have looked good. If the party
had succeeded in 1860 against solid Southern opposition, it could surely triumph
in 1864 when most of the South would play no part. Republican organisation
had had four more years to mature, and it was now backed up by control of the
government and all its patronage. Wartime emergency had provided the
pretext, and military might the instrument, to muzzle dangerous opponents and
frighten their supporters away from the polls. In the crisis atmosphere of war,
the electorate would surely rally behind the existing leadership, and Lincoln

would have all the advantages of an incumbent president. But, if some of these Republican assets were real, some were illusory and others could easily rebound against the party in power. The wear and tear of three years of war threatened to become a severe handicap; assertion of emergency powers could excite rather than silence opposition; emancipation still aroused deeply-rooted fears and prejudices, and successive drafts looked as likely to lose votes as raise men. The appeal of an incumbent president counted for little in the context of the mid-nineteenth century, for no president had served a second term since Andrew Jackson, and the one-term tradition had many adherents. The Democrats had an impressive record of electoral success over the previous thirty years. Only two military heroes had broken their run of victories up to 1860, and it was asking a lot of Abraham Lincoln to perform the feat twice in four years.

Lincoln, indeed, was viewed by his own party as neither an unmixed blessing nor an automatic choice. Those on the radical wing of the party who disagreed with him on policy matters were naturally interested in replacing him as the party's standard-bearer. But doubts about Lincoln were not confined to radicals alone. He was not yet the larger-than-life hero which martyrdom and myth-making were later to create. He had a firm hold on large sections of the electorate of the North but he was also a highly controversial and much-abused public figure. There were those who thought him too weak, vacillating and uncertain of himself, and those, in contrast, who thought him a coarse, vulgar misfit. Others regarded him as a puppet manipulated by a sinister power behind the scenes – Secretary of State Seward, or the deeply distrusted Blair family. Others, again, pointed to the haphazard, unbusinesslike manner in which Lincoln conducted his administration, the notorious feuds and splits among his cabinet advisers, and his recurring disputes with powerful sections of his own party in Congress. For his part, the president made little secret of his desire for re-nomination and he was acutely aware of three currents running steadily in his favour: the quiet, unspectacular but solid build-up of his own standing in the eyes of a mass of Northerners, soldiers and civilians alike, his control of party organisation and government patronage, and the lack of a clear and undisputed challenger for the nomination. His formidable political skill enabled him to make the most of these advantages, and his sober realism told him that he needed one more, highly unpredictable ingredient to complete the recipe for re-nomination and re-election: military success on the right scale and at the right time. Throughout the summer and the autumn, the political weather was influenced above all by the winds of change on the battlefronts.

Those who hoped to replace Lincoln were attracted by the tried and tested formula of nominating a military hero. Their problem was that the available military men in 1864 fell into two categories: generals like Grant who were wreathed in the laurels of victory but who resolutely refused to consider nomination, and those like Fremont or Ben Butler who were willing or anxious to be asked, but whose military record was scarcely untarnished. Fremont, it is true, had some sentimental appeal as the Republican party's first standard-bearer in 1856, and it could plausibly be argued that he had been less than fairly treated by the Lincoln administration. As for Butler, only his ambition, his headline-seeking and his political energy and resource can explain his continued prominence in lists of possible presidential or vice-presidential candidates in 1864. Certainly, for all their radical sympathies, neither Fremont nor Butler looked like the answer to the radicals' prayers. One man who saw himself as the answer to all Republican prayers, including his own, was Salmon P. Chase, secretary of the treasury, the main radical voice in the cabinet, and a man firmly convinced of his presidential destiny. Long before the dawning of the election year, Chase had been using his powerful position to lay the groundwork of his bid for the nomination. By the end of 1863 the Chase machine was ready for action, Chase clubs were springing up around the country, and a national committee was coordinating the Chase campaign. Early in the new year that committee circulated a pamphlet on *The Next Presidential Election*, which pointed in general terms to the need for a new and different kind of leadership for the future. This was followed by a circular issued to prominent figures in the party, over the name of Senator Pomeroy of Kansas, which much more explicitly advocated the nomination of Chase and attacked the record (and the future prospects) of the incumbent president. Although supposed to be strictly private, the Pomeroy Circular was soon leaked to the press. Chase washed his hands of the whole affair in a letter to Lincoln denying any knowledge of the circular or responsibility for it, although other evidence shows quite conclusively that he had been fully consulted about it. Lincoln had been well informed from the start about the development of the 'Chase boom', and his reply showed that he had taken the measure of his man. On 23 February, he sent the briefest acknowledgement of Chase's letter, with a promise to 'answer a little more fully when I can find the leisure to do so'. Six days later he penned one of his best tongue-in-cheek letters. 'Now, on consideration, I find there is really very little to say,' he wrote, adding that, 'in spite of myself', he had known of the circular some days before the press revealed its contents.

> I have not yet read it, and I think I shall not. I was not shocked, or surprised by the appearance of the letter, because I had had knowledge of Mr Pomeroy's Committee, and of secret issues which I supposed came from it, and of secret agents who I supposed were sent out by it, for several weeks. I have known just as little of these things as my own friends have allowed me to know.... I fully concur with you that neither of us can be justly held responsible for what our respective friends may do without our instigation or countenance.

The president ended by brushing aside Chase's half-offer of resignation. He intended to keep his secretary of the treasury chained to his desk, until the waning of his political prospects made it safe to part with him.[9]

Lincoln also knew that the Chase boom was rapidly becoming the Chase boomerang. His campaign had been clumsily managed, and he had been forced out into the open much too soon. The Pomeroy Circular aroused suspicion rather than enthusiasm, and alerted the Lincoln forces to the danger. Chase, in fact, had never been popular enough either with the voters at large or even with many radicals to be a very promising candidate. There was certainly no love lost between him and congressional leaders like Thaddeus Stevens, or Ben Wade, who once declared that Chase's theology was unsound, as he believed there was a fourth person to the Trinity. At all events, on 5 March, Chase asked that no further consideration be given to his name. Few people believed that this withdrawal would be final, if only some better opportunity were to present itself. Meanwhile, the Lincoln camp had been quietly building up its strength, and winning a series of endorsements from state legislatures and Republican state conventions. Indeed, two of the strongest nails in the Chase coffin were the pro-Lincoln votes of the Indiana convention and the Ohio legislature in late February, in the wake of the Pomeroy Circular. If Chase could not rely on his home state of Ohio, and its immediate neighbour, his candidacy looked doomed. The savage attacks on Chase made in the House of Representatives by the vitriolic Frank Blair, brother of the postmaster-general, became superfluous blows aimed at the corpse of his presidential campaign, and owed as much to cabinet feuds, the turbulence of Missouri politics, and the characteristic Blair style, as to the manoeuvres of presidential politics. After the withdrawal of Chase, the radicals continued their frantic but unavailing efforts to find and boost another candidate; they also sought, again unsuccessfully, to postpone the party convention, fixed for the unusually early date of 7 June, to give them more time for their manoeuvres.

Some radicals, though not many, were briefly attracted by the movement to nominate John C. Fremont as a third party candidate, which culminated in a convention which met at Cleveland on 31 May, barely a week before the Republicans gathered at Baltimore. The Fremont movement had started in Missouri, especially among the German element which had always favoured him. It was taken up by some abolitionists, including Wendell Phillips, who were determined to unseat Lincoln, and by that incurable addict of new fads and hopeless causes, Horace Greeley of the New York *Tribune*. Some Democrats encouraged it too, simply to embarrass their opponents, and some War Democrats, with more serious intentions, hoped to use the Cleveland gathering to promote the candidacy of General Grant. Indeed, the delegates who gathered at Cleveland were a hotchpotch of dedicated Fremont supporters, Democratic mischief makers, uncompromising abolitionists, and War Democrats looking for a safe, compromise candidate. They included conspicuously few prominent or influential Republicans. The gathering took for itself the name of the Radical Democracy which offered a clue to the only common ground which united most of those present, apart from their hostility to Lincoln. Both radicals and Democrats could join in denunciation of executive usurpation and arbitrary rule, and the platform which they adopted reflected this theme with its insistence that the rights of free speech, free press and habeas corpus must be inviolate, that the president should be elected by direct popular vote and limited to one term, and that reconstruction was a matter for Congress and not the executive. But the platform also demanded a constitutional amendment to abolish slavery, and the confiscation of the lands of rebels, and some of the Democrats present could not stomach such radical proposals. The convention proceeded to nominate Fremont for the presidency, with John Cochrane as his running-mate. In his letter of acceptance, Fremont attacked Lincoln (against whom he had a strong sense of personal grievance) and stated his willingness to withdraw if the Baltimore convention chose some other candidate. This last offer revealed the only real significance of the Cleveland convention. Its purpose was less to put Fremont in the White House than to put Lincoln out.

Events soon proved just how unrealistic such hopes were. The Baltimore convention revealed Lincoln's mastery over his own party organisation, and the thoroughness with which his friends had prepared the way for his re-nomination. All along, Lincoln had sought to preserve the broadest possible base of support for his re-election; while ensuring that he won the nomination of his party, he had been working to control the vital middle ground of politics as well. The convention itself conformed to this strategy by adopting a label increasingly used since 1862, and calling itself the National Union Convention, to provide an umbrella under which all loyal supporters of the war effort and its leadership could find shelter – and to foster the notion that loyalty to the Union and loyalty to the Republican party were virtually indistinguishable. The Baltimore convention was a noisy, tumultuous affair, but its outcome was too predictable to create much dramatic tension. In a dispute between rival Missouri delegations, it voted to admit the radical delegation in the knowledge that such a concession in no way threatened Lincoln's impregnable position. It adopted a carefully worded platform designed like most such declarations to offend as few people as possible.[10] The platform made no specific mention of the knotty problems of reconstruction, but, partly at Lincoln's instigation, it did declare in favour of a constitutional amendment prohibiting slavery. Those who were expert in the translation into plain English of the full-blown phrases of such documents understood the real meaning of such an apparently innocent resolution as the following:

> Resolved, That we deem it essential to the general welfare that harmony should prevail in the National Councils, and we regard as worthy of public confidence and official trust those only who cordially indorse the principles proclaimed in these resolutions, and which should characterize the administration of the government.

In simple language, the resolution was a request to Lincoln, in return for his re-nomination, to get rid of Montgomery Blair, and possibly other conservative cabinet officers like Bates and Welles.

The convention wasted no time in nominating Abraham Lincoln for the presidency on the first ballot; complete unanimity was spoiled only by the twenty-two radical delegates from Missouri who voted for Grant. The only real excitement or mystery at the convention surrounded the choice of a vice-presidential candidate. The retiring vice-president, Hannibal Hamlin of Maine, had done little to attract attention to himself – a not uncommon state of affairs for holders of that shadowy office – but he had also done nothing which need deny him a second term. On the other hand, he came from a rock-safe Republican state, he carried no great political weight, and he was therefore expendable. There was growing support for the idea of nominating a War Democrat to broaden the appeal of the ticket – and, if that War Democrat were a Southerner, he would also improve the image of the Republicans as a truly national party. Andrew Johnson of Tennessee would fill the bill exactly, but all kinds of party infighting complicated the final choice, including a plan by radical New Yorkers to nominate a War Democrat from their own state, such as Daniel Dickinson, in the hope that Lincoln would be obliged to dispense with their arch-enemy Seward, on the ground that he could not afford to have a secretary of state and a vice-president both from New York. In the event, Andrew Johnson led on the first ballot, and delegation after delegation switched its vote to him, until he was made the unanimous choice. Lincoln was well satisfied with the outcome, as indeed he should have been, for it was final proof of his control of the convention. While protesting a little too strongly that he wished to leave the choice to the delegates, and while not discouraging Hamlin's hopes of a second term, he set several different henchmen to work at Baltimore to procure the nomination of Johnson. Characteristically, he had canvassed a wide field before making his choice; he had even considered Butler, although he had no illusions about him and no great affection for him. (Butler was later to claim that he told Lincoln that he would accept the nomination only if the president would undertake to resign or die within three months of the start of his second term. But the story probably owes something to its author's knowledge of what did happen to Lincoln within six weeks of his second inauguration.)[11] Characteristically, too, Lincoln had his way in the end without seeming to impose his will. The whole episode was typical of his quiet style, his toughness of mind and his political acumen. As Alexander K. McClure put it: 'He rejected Hamlin not because he hated him; he accepted Johnson not because he loved him.'[12] No one dreamed in June 1864 how ominous his choice was to become with a year.

4. The Republican party and its candidate seemed to be riding high after the Baltimore convention, but radical discontent persisted and it soon found new pastures upon which to feed. One of the curiosities of the 1864 election was the exceptionally long gap of almost three months between the conventions of the two main parties. The Democrats had decided to postpone their meeting as long as possible, until the end of August, and, with no rival yet in the field, the Republicans had ample time to fall out among themselves and to lapse into deep

pessimism about their prospects of eventual success. At the end of June, Chase offered his resignation once again over a minor issue, and, possibly to his surprise, it was on this occasion accepted. Lincoln clearly felt free to dispense with him now, and after offering the post of secretary of the treasury to ex-Governor David Tod of Ohio, he eventually appointed William P. Fessenden of Maine, chairman of the Senate Finance Committee. This choice helped to mollify criticism of Chase's departure; as Lincoln confided to his secretary, Fessenden was 'a radical – without the petulant and vicious fretfulness of many radicals'.[13] But the major dispute within the party centred around the Wade–Davis reconstruction bill. Clearly the spectacle of a president and congressional leaders of his own party at daggers drawn over such a vital issue was scarcely calculated to inspire confidence or enthusiasm among the electorate.

Intra-party wrangling was made all the more acrimonious by the general gloom which chilled the mid-summer political climate. In these months the North plumbed new depths of war-weariness and depression as Grant's army, after suffering huge casualties, ground to a halt before Richmond and Petersburg, and Sherman was stalled before Atlanta. Worst of all was the humiliation of the Confederate raid led by Jubal A. Early which penetrated to the outskirts of Washington itself in mid-July.[14] If, after three years of toil and struggle and slaughter, the nation's capital was still so vulnerable, could the North ever force the South into submission? During that summer the North experienced all the agony and frustration of the bigger and stronger contestant who knows that he can and should win, but is somehow unable to land the knockout blow. In this crisis of Northern morale, the administration's popularity, and its prospects, dwindled rapidly. The army cried out for reinforcements to replace its losses and sustain the final push; in July the administration incurred renewed popular displeasure and grave electoral risk by calling for a further 500,000 men and ordering that quotas not filled by volunteers were to be made up by a draft on 5 September. Financial confidence waned, the price of gold soared, and inflation assailed the living standards of workers and their families. Doubts about whether the war could ever be won merged into near-certainty that Lincoln could not be re-elected. From all across the North, Republican party workers and leaders reported that defeat seemed inescapable. The chairman of the Republican National Committee, Henry J. Raymond of the New York Times, became so despondent that he recommended to Lincoln on 22 August that he should make an offer to Jefferson Davis of peace on the sole condition of acknowledgement of the supremacy of the constitution. Raymond's assumption was that Davis would reject the offer and that this would scotch the growing feeling in the North that peace with Union could be arranged but for the insistence on the abolition of slavery. Lincoln took the proposal seriously enough to draft instructions to Raymond himself to act as commissioner, but the plan would have given the impression, at least, that Lincoln was going back on his commitment to emancipation, and he and the cabinet soon decided that it was altogether too risky and too liable to be misunderstood.[15]

The resort of his campaign manager to such desperate remedies may help to explain an extraordinary manifestation of Lincoln's own pessimism about the future. On 23 August he asked the members of his cabinet to sign the back of a memorandum which he had prepared, but which they had not read. Its contents might well have astonished and dismayed them:

> This morning, as for some days past, it seems exceedingly probable that this Administration will not be re-elected. Then it will be my duty to so cooperate with the President elect, as to save the Union between the election and the inauguration; as he will have secured his election on such ground that he can not possibly save it afterwards.[16]

With Lincoln apparently in such despair at his own prospects, it is perhaps a little less surprising that those Republicans who had never enthused over his re-nomination in June were now busily engaged in August in backstage man-oeuvres to get rid of him. Lincoln the alleged conservative was bad enough, but Lincoln the certain loser simply had to go. Letters passed back and forth, and private meetings were arranged, the most important of which were in New York in the second half of August. Horace Greeley was actively at work once again, along with other radical editors, as well as prominent congressional Republicans such as Wade and Davis, state governors including Andrew of Massachusetts, and financial stalwarts of the party – like David Dudley Field and John A. Stevens. They still faced their chronic problem that, even if they could persuade Lincoln (and Fremont) to stand down, they had no agreed or ready-made replacement. A military candidate – Grant, Sherman, even Butler – was still the most widely-favoured choice, but other names were mentioned, including Charles Francis Adams, the minister to London, and a man in whose family the presidency was almost a hereditary office. There was also Salmon P. Chase still lurking in the wings and waiting for his cue. Lacking one obvious candidate, the meeting on 18 August decided in favour of a new convention at Cincinnati at the end of September, which would, if necessary, make a new nomination. The response to their call was mixed, but a second meeting on 30 August decided to go ahead, while in the meantime sounding out the state governors about the election prospects.[17] As things turned out, the plan went no further, but it was remarkable enough that it had progressed so far, and that Lincoln should come so close to an indignity suffered by no other presidential contender of a major party.

In the nick of time, news from the battlefront rescued Republican morale, and the emergence of a definite Democratic enemy helped to rebuild Republican unity. Hitherto the Republicans had monopolised the limelight, but now at last, on 29 August, the Democrats met in convention at Chicago. With their opponents depressed and divided, they had been presented with a great opportunity, but their first priority was to achieve some kind of unity among themselves. On one flank, the party was struggling to prevent too many War

Democrats from succumbing to the siren song of the Republicans in their
National Union party disguise. On the other flank, the party had to satisfy its
peace wing without forfeiting its chances of winning the support of middle-of-
the-road voters. The Peace Democrats were still noisy and active in 1864, and
lengthening casualty lists and military stalemate gave a new impetus to their
propaganda. In the spring, Alexander Long of Ohio had spoken up so bluntly,
in the House of Representatives, for a compromise peace that the Republicans
had sought to expel him, and, failing to raise the required two-thirds majority,
had settled for a vote of censure. Then, in June, the Copperhead revival in the
middle west was given new encouragement by Vallandigham's return from his
Canadian exile. Although he was liable to re-arrest, Lincoln did not lift a finger
against him; he refused to make a martyr again out of a man who, he foresaw,
would soon become a Democratic liability. The Peace Democrats faced problems
similar to those of the radical Republicans; they had no one obvious and attractive
candidate, and they could not persuade their party to desert the vital centre of
Northern politics. For their part, the moderate Democrats desperately needed
a candidate with popular appeal who could draw the various wings of the party
together. They believed that they had found their man in General George B.
McClellan. He could be portrayed as a victim of Lincoln's unfairness, he was
thought to be still extremely popular with the army rank and file, and his almost
complete silence on political issues since his dismissal would help his role as
party unifier. He had solid backing in New York and the east generally; the
mid-western Copperheads had no candidate to match him, and the likeliest
compromise candidate, Horatio Seymour, took himself out of the running.

The Democratic convention at Chicago was preceded and accompanied by
stories of plots and projected uprisings concocted by the secret societies and by
Confederate agents operating from Canada. If such conspiracies were ever much
more than figments of Republican propaganda, they certainly failed to attract
the support even of the many peace Democrats who still believed that they could
achieve their objectives by more orthodox means, within the normal party
political framework. Peace Democrats were certainly very prominent in Chicago
both in the convention and in meetings and demonstrations outside, and they
achieved more success than their numerical strength in the party probably
warranted. They had to resign themselves to the fact that McClellan was
unbeatable, but they had their way over the platform and over the choice of his
running-mate. Vallandigham himself was an influential member of the platform
committee and was largely responsible for the highly controversial peace plank
which was adopted by the convention:

> Resolved, That this convention does explicitly declare, as the sense of the
> American people, that after four years of failure to restore the Union by the
> experiment of war . . . justice, humanity, liberty and the public welfare
> demand that immediate efforts be made for a cessation of hostilities, with a
> view of an ultimate convention of the States or other peaceable means, to the

end that, at the earliest practicable moment, peace may be restored on the basis of the Federal Union of the States.[18]

The remainder of the platform took its stand on defence of the constitution, and condemnation of all the usurpations, arbitrary acts and other excesses of the Lincoln administration. It made no reference to slavery whatsoever. The convention went on to nominate McClellan without serious opposition, and chose as its vice-presidential candidate George H. Pendleton of Ohio, who belonged unmistakably to the peace wing of the party.

There remained some real doubt as to whether McClellan could accept nomination on a platform which dismissed as a failure the war in which he had played so prominent a part. Moreover, the platform offered the Confederacy an armistice, without conditions, and most people believed that once the fighting had ceased in this way it was unlikely to be resumed if the terms of a peaceful restoration of the Union could not be agreed. Could McClellan run on a platform which put peace first and the Union second? In fact, he toiled for a week over his letter of acceptance, listened to copious advice, and struggled for the right form of words. In its final version, McClellan's letter politely disposed of the platform on which he had been chosen to run. No effort would be spared, he said, to secure peace once 'our present adversaries are ready for peace, upon the basis of the Union. . . . The Union is the one condition of peace – we ask no more.'[19] By neatly reversing the order of things, and putting the Union first and peace second, McClellan still disappointed War Democrats who wanted no truck with an armistice in any case, and he infuriated many of the Peace Democrats, especially in the west. A group of them met at Cincinnati and passed resolutions repudiating McClellan, defending slavery and declaring the war to be unconstitutional. But they were powerless to alter the course of events, and not even Alexander Long would accept their nomination as a rival candidate.

The experience of 1864 bears out the view that, in American presidential elections, the struggle within the parties is often at least as important as the struggle between them. In each party, the outcome had been the same where the choice of candidate was concerned; the commonsense requirement of selecting the man with the broadest possible appeal had triumphed over considerations of ideological purity or the temptation to strike dramatic attitudes. But if moderation prevailed in the nominating process, the more extreme elements in each party – radical Republicans and Peace Democrats – had created a considerable stir and diced with electoral death; they still nursed hopes or dreams of taking control of their candidate after victory had been achieved at the polls. However, at a time of grave crisis, and in a volatile political situation, the parties had generally played their stabilising role successfully. In each there were genuine divisions over important issues; each had provided not merely a forum for their discussion but a framework for their management within safe limits. They now confronted the voters with a real choice. It is frequently said that Lincoln and

McClellan had more in common with each other than with many members of
their respective parties. But this is only a half-truth which might equally be
applied to many other rival pairs of presidential candidates. The election was
bound to be a test of public confidence in Lincoln's leadership, but it was more
than just a choice between two men. Party platforms seldom dominate
campaigns, and in 1864 they faded rapidly into the background. But it still
meant a great deal that, while in their verbal gymnastics about peace before
Union or Union before peace, McClellan and Vallandigham both studiously
avoided the awkward word 'slavery' altogether, the Republican platform called
for a constitutional amendment to abolish slavery once and for all, the
Republican candidate was the unrepentant author of the emancipation proclamation, and the Republican party insisted on Union and abolition as conditions of peace. The rivals of 1864 offered the electorate a choice and not an
echo.

The early days of September saw an apparently remarkable change in the
election prospects. The outcome of the Chicago convention drove thousands of
War Democrats and wavering Republicans back into the Lincoln fold. Radicals
who had enjoyed the luxury of plotting to undermine their party's nominee
while they had no other enemy to fight now rapidly decided that, in comparison
with McClellan and the Democratic platform, Lincoln was much the lesser of
two evils. The plan for a new convention was quietly dropped. Far better to
keep the Lincoln bandwagon rolling, and hope to seize the reins after the election
was over, rather than to unseat the driver at once, and risk a crash which would
leave the road open to McClellan and the Democrats. However, what really
brought the scent of electoral victory sweetly back into Republican nostrils was
the news of military victory on several fronts. Admiral Farragut's stirring deeds
at Mobile Bay in August had marked the first turning of the tide. But it was
Sherman's long-awaited capture of Atlanta on 2 September which made the
greatest impact on Northern public opinion and which began to mock the
Democratic platform's assertion that the war was a failure. Later in September
Sheridan's success in the Shenandoah Valley – always an area which acted as a
highly sensitive barometer of popular fears and hopes – carried forward the
revival of Northern spirits and Republican confidence.[20] It may be doubted
whether Republican depression was ever quite so deep and the change of mood
quite so sudden and dramatic as it has often been depicted. But there can be no
doubt that Lincoln's prospects steadily improved from early September and that
by October the result was scarcely in doubt. Lincoln had been doubly fortunate;
his own re-nomination had come too early to be imperilled by the frustration
and pessimism of mid-summer, and his opponent's nomination had come just
too late to profit by it.

In September, too, the Republicans put their house in order for the campaigning season. Wade, Chandler, Davis, Sumner, Greeley and the rest joined
energetically in the campaign, and enthusiastically denounced McClellan, even if
they found less pleasure in singing the praises of Lincoln. The president himself

made a gesture towards party peace, and answered the prayer of the party platform when he secured the resignation of the radicals' arch-enemy, Postmaster-
General Montgomery Blair, on 23 September. His letter to Blair showed that
Lincoln could be as blunt as the next man when the occasion arose: 'You have
generously said to me more than once, that whenever your resignation could
be a relief to me, it was at my disposal. The time has come.'[21] Blair's resignation
followed by one day the removal of another cloud on the Republican horizon
with the withdrawal from the presidential race of John C. Fremont. The two
events were not unconnected, but they were not part of a simple bargain, at
least as far as Fremont was concerned.[22] Zach Chandler, radical senator from
Michigan, was very prominent in the coming and going which preceded the
departure of both Fremont and Blair, and both Lincoln and the radicals clearly
knew what they were doing. But Fremont recognised, without Chandler's
prompting, that his chance was gone, he imposed no conditions on his withdrawal, and he accompanied it with some harsh words about Lincoln. But
whatever its background, Fremont's departure was Lincoln's gain.

5. It is the common fate of election issues to be either broadened and simplified
out of all recognition or totally obscured by clouds of rhetoric and abuse in the
course of the actual campaign, and 1864 was no exception. Lincoln and his
administration were really the basic issue, and the voters faced the decision
whether, on his record as war-maker and emancipator, he was the right man
to achieve speedy and final victory and to rebuild the Union on solid foundations.
In fact, each party spent far more time and energy in attacking the other than in
defending itself. More and more the campaign became a contest between
accusations of tyranny on the one side, and accusations of treason on the other.
Democrats played endless variations on the theme of Abraham Lincoln, the
despot, the destroyer of civil liberties and the wrecker of the constitution. It was
a line of attack to which the president was by no means invulnerable, but his
opponents exploited it with more gusto than skill. They dwelt too on the
repercussions of emancipation which served both as an example of presidential
usurpation and as a stimulus to the far from dormant Negrophobia of the North.
For their part, the Republicans brazened out the charges of executive tyranny,
and played down as far as possible the racial implications of emancipation and
the question of the status of the freedmen in post-war America. The free Negro
leader, Frederick Douglass, stayed out of most of the campaign to avoid
branding the Republicans as 'the nigger party'; 'the Negro,' he wrote, 'is the
deformed child which is put out of the room when company comes'.[23]

But, above all, the Republicans relied on attack as the best form of defence.
They had now brought to a fine art the technique of smearing their Democratic
opponents as traitors, and linking the opposition party to the activities of
disloyal secret societies in the middle west. John P. Sanderson, provost-marshal-
general under Rosecrans in Missouri, and Henry B. Carrington, protégé and
aide of Governor Morton of Indiana, showed unflagging ingenuity and a

talent for exaggeration in producing exposés of the activities of the secret societies. In October, Joseph Holt, judge-advocate-general in the War Department, published a well-timed report on subversive activities which drew heavily on these earlier efforts, and which was grist to the Republican propaganda mill. In the weeks before the election there was endless talk of plots and conspiracies. Both at the time of the Democratic convention and on the eve of election day itself, plans to liberate Confederate prisoners at Camp Douglas, near Chicago, and take over the city, were dramatically exposed in the nick of time. A similar plot to free prisoners on an island camp in Lake Erie was scotched in September. But Indiana was probably the most fertile field for conspiracies and for their sensational exposure; Governor Morton needed all the help he could find in his bid for re-election, after his long struggle to survive without the state legislature, and the Peace Democrats of Indiana had been more embarrassingly involved than elsewhere in the activities of the secret societies. In the pre-election weeks, a number of prominent Democrats were arrested by the military authorities and put on trial before a military tribunal on charges of treason and conspiracy. Three were sentenced to be hanged, but none actually met that fate. They had served their purpose in assisting the election of Morton, and one of them, Lambdin P. Milligan, was to give his name to a highly significant Supreme Court decision in 1866.[24]

The Republicans were often unscrupulous in exploiting the loyalty issue and the technique of establishing guilt by association, and they made the most of the pathetic activities of a handful of dangerous crackpots, inveterate intriguers, and hamfisted Confederate agents operating from Canada. (The futile raid in October on the small town of St Albans, Vermont, was the ill-conceived work of this last group.) The antics of Vallandigham and his friends before, during and after the Chicago convention made a gift of the loyalty issue to the Republicans. Vallandigham had accepted the title of Supreme Commander of the Sons of Liberty, and thus encouraged the notion that the Democratic party and the secret societies were hand in glove; his 'war failure' plank in the party platform became more and more of a liability; his every move attested to the shrewdness of Lincoln's judgment in making him an unwitting ally of the Republican cause rather than a martyr to his own.

Throughout the campaign the Republicans – or, to be precise, the National Union party – were superior to their opponents in organisation, financial support, and propaganda. The official party campaign, managed by Henry J. Raymond, was backed by the many-sided activities of the Union Leagues and Union Clubs around the country, which promised to be as much an asset to the Republican cause as the secret societies threatened to be a liability to the Democratic. The greatest Republican advantage of all lay in control of the power and patronage of the federal government and almost all the Northern state governments. Lincoln and his party had no compunction in following the standard practice of the day in levying campaign contributions from office-holders in all departments, as the price of keeping their jobs, and dropping none too gentle hints to companies and businessmen who had received government contracts or aspired to do so in the future. Workers in the Brooklyn navy yard who were too openly pro-McClellan in their sympathies lost their jobs. A Philadelphia firm, eager for government contracts, drew attention to its 'election expenses' of $5,700.[25] The Democrats had their wealthy backers too, but although no precise estimate of election expenditures can be made, there is no doubt that the Republicans were by far the bigger spenders. This advantage was reflected in the propaganda battle where the avalanche of Republican pamphlets, handbills, newspaper and magazine articles threatened to swamp Democratic efforts – and the latter also faced frequent obstruction in the mails. The Republicans had quality as well as quantity on their side, and enjoyed the support of a pride of literary lions, including James Russell Lowell, John Greenleaf Whittier, Harriet Beecher Stowe and even Emerson and Longfellow. Pamphleteering was now a highly organised business, especially since the emergence in 1863 of the three great propaganda agencies of the war: on the Republican side, the Loyal Publication Society of New York, and the Board of Publications of the Philadelphia Union League, and on the Democratic side, the Society for the Diffusion of Political Knowledge, whose guiding spirit was Samuel F. B. Morse, artist, publicist and inventor of the telegraph and the code which bears his name. The pamphlets which they published often reached a large readership; in a society with a high degree of literacy and political awareness, and at a time before more modern methods of mass communication had developed, the pamphlet, short or long, sophisticated or 'popular', enjoyed something of a heyday.

One new challenge to party organisation and propaganda was provided by the soldier vote. Not the least impressive phenomenon of the 1864 election was the participation of thousands of men in uniform, many of them voting in the field. Earlier in the war, Republicans had feared the consequences of making special arrangements for the soldier vote, but now they were in no doubt that they would reap a rich harvest from it. Eleven states had made provision for voting in the field by 1864. For all the orders of commanders, including Grant, forbidding canvassing among the troops, the army was so completely permeated by politics that it could not be quarantined from election fever. Colonels who owed their commissions to Republican state governors knew what was expected of them, and the governors had state agents who accompanied their regiments in the field, and combined the roles of welfare officer and political propagandist. In bidding for the soldier vote, the Republicans held all the best cards, and opportunities for fraud and intimidation were limitless. Floods of Republican campaign literature poured into army camps, but Democratic material was often lost or blocked *en route*. In a situation where each party printed its own ballot and the voter asked for the one he wanted, the soldier who was inclined to vote the Democratic ticket might easily be dissuaded. For example, the elaborate process of proxy voting prescribed for New Yorkers in uniform required the distribution of ballot forms to the troops who marked them and posted them home to be cast by a neighbour or relative. But Democratic party agents heading south to hand out the forms found themselves arrested on trumped-up charges in Baltimore and Washington, and detained until the voting was over. In states which made no provision for voting in the field, governors made prodigious efforts to have men sent home on leave at election time, and thousands of 'sick' and 'convalescent' soldiers joined the northward trek to the polls. In early November the railroad north from Washington to Philadelphia and New York was choked with eager voters hastening home. No state governor was more zealous in pursuit of the soldier vote than Oliver P. Morton of Indiana, who faced the double problem of state elections in mid-October and the presidential election a few weeks later. Plagued by appeals from Morton, Lincoln refused to postpone the draft in Indiana as the governor wished, but he did write to General Sherman stressing the importance of the October vote, and pleading that 'anything you can safely do to let her [Indiana's] soldiers, or any part of them, go home and vote at the State election, will be greatly in point'. About 9,000 reached home in time to vote. But even after he had been safely re-elected, Morton was not satisfied, and begged Lincoln to extend the soldiers' furlough until after the presidential election, 'for the best interests of the service and the sake of humanity', as they needed a period of rest and recuperation after their long and arduous journey from the front.[26] Lincoln did his best to satisfy both Morton and Sherman; whether or not their presence at home on election day had some magical restorative effect upon the troops, it certainly did Lincoln himself no harm.

For all the allegations and the realities of fraud and malpractice, the soldier vote was in any case overwhelmingly for Lincoln. When every allowance is made, the four-to-one margin in Lincoln's favour among those voting in the field is still impressive. In 1941 some packets of Ohio soldier votes were opened and properly counted for the first time, although they bore on the outside tallies of Lincoln and McClellan votes. The true figures often revealed an even heavier Lincoln majority than the official 'count' in 1864 had estimated.[27] However, if the soldier vote was a valuable weapon in the Lincoln armoury, it is abundantly clear that it did not make the difference between electoral victory and defeat. Only in two or three states at most – New York, Connecticut, Indiana – did it possibly play a decisive part. Indeed, it is sometimes suggested that the more important military influence on the election was the intimidating presence of so many troops on polling day, in some key states including New York, which deterred many a would-be Democratic voter.

6. In the last few weeks of the campaign the tide was running strongly in Lincoln's favour. In the October state elections in Indiana, Ohio and Pennsylvania, the Republicans were uniformly successful. Republican optimism soared, while Democrats took what comfort they could from the close result in Pennsylvania, and charges of massive fraud in Indiana. Lincoln's own calculations were still cautious, although his own estimate on 13 October of victory by the narrowest

of margins has the ring of a man determined to prove to himself that he could win, even after conceding every doubtful state to his opponent.[28] Lincoln was still nervous on election day itself, 8 November, but the results soon set his mind at rest. Only three states – Kentucky, New Jersey and Delaware – ran up majorities for McClellan, and Lincoln had a massive electoral college majority of 212–21. In the congressional elections, the Union party made a net gain of thirty-seven House seats. The state elections left New Jersey as the only Northern state with a Democratic governor. All this added up to a sweeping victory, although this impression was not always confirmed by the details of the popular vote, which produced totals of 2,213,645 for Lincoln, and 1,802,237 for McClellan. In some states, including some of the very largest, the margin had been extremely thin – less than 7,000 in New York in a total poll of over 730,000, 20,000 in Pennsylvania in a poll of over 570,000, less than 2,500 in Connecticut. On the other hand, Lincoln had huge majorities in most of the New England states and very comfortable ones in the middle west, in sharp contrast to the Republican setbacks there in 1862. In an election with a higher turn-out than four years earlier, Lincoln's share of the vote increased by more than 1 per cent in those states which voted in both elections. But while he did considerably better in the west, he actually lost ground in New York, New Jersey and Pennsylvania. A 55–45 per cent split of the total vote can be made to appear a wide or a narrow margin according to the predisposition of the interpreter. It can be shown that a fairly small shift of votes at strategic points would have swung the election to McClellan, but such calculations are the common consolation of the defeated. However, when to this calculation are added the numerous charges of fraud and intimidation, and, above all, the absence of Southern opposition, Lincoln's performance can be made to look puny and unconvincing. On the other hand, a 55 per cent share of the vote was no mean achievement for the minority president of four years earlier – and those four years, moreover, had been filled with crisis and horror inconceivable in 1860. Such a margin was also beyond the wildest dreams of most of Lincoln's predecessors at least since the days of Andrew Jackson, and certainly of his later nineteenth-century successors.

If one of the exceptional features of the election was the size of the winning margin, the pattern of voting still reflected normal electoral behaviour in many ways. The Democratic vote in particular rested on its traditional sources of strength in the North, the urban workers, the immigrants, and the poorer sections of the farming community. Perhaps the most significant Democratic weakness in 1864 was the party's failure, even after the stresses of over three years of war, to win over many disgruntled Republicans, or to attract marginal or floating voters, including those who had voted for the Constitutional Union ticket in 1860. For their part, the Republicans had played the Union party game for all it was worth, and broadened their electoral base as far as possible. However, their greatest strength remained as before in rural and especially small-town America, and also among the middle classes of the larger towns and cities; they still drew heavily on the votes of native-born American citizens both in New England and in that greater New England which had spread across western New York to Ohio, Illinois, Michigan and Iowa. Some controversy surrounds the interpretation of the vote in the largest cities in 1864. It is true that Lincoln's vote in those cities lagged generally somewhat behind his proportion of the vote in the states where they were situated. But, on the other hand, he had a majority in twelve of the nineteen largest cities in 1864 whereas he had carried only eight in 1860, and, while he had lost votes in Detroit and Milwaukee, he had gained ground in several other cities. There is certainly no evidence of a great shift of workingmen's votes to McClellan, and the election of 1864 suggested – as elections later in the century proved – that the great cities were by no means a lost cause for the Republican party.[29]

The outcome of the election guaranteed the continuation of all-out war to save the Union. It is impossible to say what would have happened had McClellan been elected. He himself stood firmly for peace only with reunion, but victory for his party might conceivably have opened the way for some kind of truce or compromise peace on terms which the Republicans would never have accepted and which might have enabled the Southern rebels to snatch something from the jaws of defeat. But now, Northern morale and sense of purpose, though sorely tested, had been triumphantly vindicated. Lincoln's victory sealed the political ring, just as Grant and Sherman were tightening the military ring, around what was left of the Confederacy. It also guaranteed, once and for all, that the war to save the Union would also be the war to end slavery. To Lincoln and many other Republicans not the least satisfying result of the elections was that they had ratified a new state constitution abolishing slavery in Maryland, and ensured that Missouri would now follow the same path. They had also brought a step nearer a congressional vote for a constitutional amendment prohibiting slavery throughout the land. In October, referring to the Maryland constitution, Lincoln had written:

> I wish all men to be free. I wish the material prosperity of the already free which I feel sure the extinction of slavery would bring. I wish to see, in process of disappearing, that only thing which ever could bring this nation to civil war.[30]

Victory at the polls in November soon brought fulfilment of that wish.

The election was also a landmark in party history. Still only a decade old, the Republican party had now won two out of its first three presidential contests. 1864 made the party an enduring feature of the political landscape. Its record of early success far surpassed that of the Whig party a generation earlier, and saved it from the risk of sharing that party's fate, even though the Republicans of the sixties and seventies were as ill-attuned to the social problems of industrial America as the Whigs of the 1850s had been to the sectional problem of slavery. The election of 1864 converted voting Republican from a passing fad into a regular habit. Whereas the Democrats and their forebears had dominated the presidency until 1860, only Cleveland and Wilson were to break the run of Republican success in the seven decades from Lincoln to Hoover. Within the party, the election result was to have unforeseen and ironic consequences. The man who was most responsible for Lincoln's re-nomination and re-election was Abraham Lincoln himself. By his political skill more than by his public image, he had mastered his party and master-minded his victorious campaign, but he was to live only a month into his second term and the presidency was then to pass into the hands of a man who was not really a Republican at all. The men who had searched long and hard for an alternative to Lincoln, who had tried to remove him after his re-nomination, and who had climbed reluctantly and belatedly aboard his campaign train, were to enjoy much more of the fruits of victory over the next four years. Abraham Lincoln was the architect of victory in 1864, but the Radical Republicans were among the chief beneficiaries.

It is proper to describe that victory of 1864 as a Republican triumph, for the National Union device was soon discarded after the election. But the Democratic party showed characteristic resilience in the aftermath of defeat. A defeat it certainly was, but not a total disaster. The party had held on to enough of its regular Northern support to maintain itself as one of the twin pillars of a continuing two-party system, and soon many War Democrats began to drift back into their old party allegiance. For all the blunders and missed opportunities – and handicaps – of the campaign, the party had put up a respectable performance at the polls. Indeed, it could confidently hope that, once the Southern states were restored, it would resume its place as the normal majority party of the United States. As things happened, the Democrats had to wait a further twenty years for victory in a presidential election, but 1864 had not deprived them of the staying power to survive those two decades of frustration in the wilderness.

In broader perspective, the election of 1864 was one of the decisive battles for American democracy. Both the fact that it happened at all, and the nature of the result, were crucial. The holding of such an election, in the midst of a terrible civil war, was a bold affirmation of the strength of American democracy; the outcome was the best guarantee of its future. The contest revealed the robust strength, as well as some of the ugly blemishes, of American party politics. For the immediate future it was a vital step towards winning the war and shaping the peace. But if victory gave the Republican party confidence for the future, the limitations of that same victory, when eleven Southern states cast no electoral votes, troubled the thoughts of those who looked a little further ahead. It made more important than ever the question of political control of the restored Southern states. When the politicians turned their minds again to the problems of reconstruction, it was with a new sense of their urgent importance to the nation, to the Negro and to themselves.

# Chapter XVIII : Victory and Defeat

When, on 4 March 1865, Lincoln delivered his second inaugural address – the most succinct and the most sublime of all such addresses – his tone was modest and reflective, and he showed no inclination to gloat or threaten or condemn. But beneath the humility and the charity lay the confident if unstated assumption that the war was already won. He discussed its meaning as if it already belonged to history, and he sought to make sense of its horror and pain by interpreting them as just retribution exacted from North and South alike for the hideous evil of slavery.

If we shall suppose that American slavery is one of those offenses which, in the providence of God, must needs come, but which, having continued through His appointed time, He now wills to remove, and that He gives to both North and South this terrible war as the woe due to those by whom the offense came, shall we discern therein any departure from those divine attributes which the believers in a living God always ascribe to him?

The president's appeal to the people was no longer a call to arms but a call to the tasks of peace:

With malice toward none; with charity for all; with firmness in the right, as God gives us to see the right, let us strive on to finish the work we are in; to bind up the nation's wounds; to care for him who shall have borne the battle, and for his widow, and his orphan – to do all which may achieve and cherish a just, and a lasting peace, among ourselves, and with all nations.[1]

But, even if victory was certain, the battle had still to be finished, the machinery of peacemaking still to be created, and the future of a reunited America still to be shaped.

1. In the rosy glow of the Republican victory at the polls, there seemed just a chance at the end of 1864 that the party unity forged in the battle against the Democrats might be carried over into a new approach to reconstruction. The issue had been played down for some months, and tempers which had been lost during the controversy over the Wade–Davis bill had had plenty of time to recover. Reconstruction had in fact been something of a submerged issue during the election campaign. The Republican platform had evaded the question, and Republican speakers preferred other topics. For their part, the Democrats chose to concentrate the attack on other, simpler issues, emphasising the sins of the past rather than the hazards of the future. Both the president and the congressional Republicans now had good reasons, up to a point, to favour cooperation. In December the president made both a very fitting appointment and a gesture to party unity in nominating none other than Salmon P. Chase as chief justice of the Supreme Court, in place of Roger B. Taney who had died in October. Lincoln had gained new prestige by his re-election for a second term, and might hope for a more willing and respectful response from congress-men, some of whom had gained their passage into the next Congress by riding on the presidential coat-tails. On the other hand, Lincoln was well aware, as he admitted in his message to Congress on 6 December 1864, that 'the executive power itself would be greatly diminished by the cessation of actual war',[2] which should not now be long delayed. For a president who set so much store by his war powers, there was a strong incentive to win broad support for his policy while he still believed he had the authority to carry it out. For their part, many Republicans in Congress had resigned themselves to acceptance of reconstruction on the Lincoln model in Louisiana, as being virtually a *fait accompli*. Weary of endless arguments over old, familiar ground, some had withdrawn to more moderate positions where they might meet the president in an attempt to settle outstanding questions.

In its final lame-duck session between December and March, the old Congrest showed some signs of the new spirit of harmony and optimism. It finally passed the long-delayed Freedmen's Bureau Act, and, even more significantly, it took up the matter of a constitutional amendment prohibiting slavery throughout the United States. Back in August the Wade–Davis Manifesto had poured scorn upon Lincoln's pious hope that such an amendment might soon be passed. At the time such scepticism, rather than the president's optimism, seemed to have the facts on its side, but Lincoln proved to be the better prophet. Both houses of Congress had debated just such an amendment in the spring of 1864, but while the Senate had passed it easily by 38 votes to 6, the House had failed to muster the required two-thirds majority, voting by a margin of 95–66 in its favour. The Republicans had written a plank supporting the amendment into their election platform, much to Lincoln's satisfaction. By the time the House reassembled, the climate of opinion, helped by the Republican victory in the elections, had changed for the better. Even some conservatives were now ready to accept the Amendment as a convenient method of bowing to the inevitable, while preparing to resist further radical change. Lincoln and Seward contributed to the intense pressure brought to bear on wavering members. Amid scenes of great excitement, and with the help of some Democratic and border-state votes, the amendment passed on 31 January 1865 by 119–56, seven votes more than the required margin. 'This amendment is a King's cure for all the evils,'[3] said Lincoln, somewhat over-optimistically, and he so far forgot himself as to append his signature to the joint resolution, although the procedure for a constitutional amendment requires no such action by the president. He and many others no doubt wryly recalled that the last constitutional amendment seriously mooted four years earlier had been intended to guarantee slavery forever in the states where it already existed. Lincoln did not, of course, live to see the amendment finally ratified by the states; that process was not complete until December 1865. But congressional approval of the Thirteenth Amendment which stated that 'neither slavery nor involuntary servitude . . . shall exist within the United States', consolidated one of the great achievements of the war, and settled one of the basic conditions of post-war reconstruction. But, as so often happened in the tangled history of reconstruction, one item was removed from the agenda only to be replaced by others even more intractable.

If any basis for compromise and collaboration over reconstruction existed, it was at best a fragile one. It was one thing to tidy up old causes of controversy, and another to agree on the way ahead. Not everyone was willing to put the past behind him, and each side still believed that it had a chance to control the future. In such a situation, postponement of a decision looked better than agreement based on too many concessions. If Lincoln knew that the days of his war powers were numbered, he was also well aware that there would be a gap of nine months between the close of this Congress in March and the opening of the new one in December 1865. In that time, a president might carry his own policy beyond the point of no return. Similarly, the appearance of growing moderation among congressional Republicans was somewhat deceptive. The more con-servative, seeing hope for the future in Lincoln's re-election, were hoping to consolidate a coalition of Republicans and War Democrats which would dam the tide of change. But, if their motto was 'so far and no further', their more radical colleagues were anxious to clear up old controversies mainly because they had moved on to new issues and adopted new priorities. More than ever, the centre of the stage was occupied by the question of guarantees for the freedmen, including the possibility of Negro suffrage, and the consolidation of military victory by political means to ensure that control of the post-war south was in safe and loyal hands.

One possible compromise did offer each side tangible gains – and gave each the hope that it would set precedents for the future pattern of reconstruction.[4]

A new bill on the lines of the Wade–Davis bill was introduced in the House, with amendments making some provision for Negro suffrage. The suggestion was that, if Lincoln would accept such a measure, Congress would recognise the Louisiana government created under presidential auspices. The nature of the bargain was clearly understood in both the Capitol and the White House – and it was condemned on the one hand by uncompromising abolitionists and radicals who regarded it as a sell-out, and on the other by conservatives who complained that Lincoln had finally gone over to the radical camp. In fact, the prospects for compromise rapidly faded. In January, Ashley added amendments to the bill which made it much more radical, and imposed strict conditions on the recognition of the Louisiana and Arkansas governments. The House voted to postpone consideration of the bill by a three-to-one margin, including a two-to-one majority of Republican votes, and renewed attempts to pass an amended version of the bill in February were also blocked. There was now a solid, middle-of-the-road group of Republicans who wanted to assert the rights of Congress in this field but who increasingly shared the president's view that it was unwise to be tied inflexibly to one reconstruction formula. The other half of the bargain came to grief in the Senate. There seemed to be a comfortable majority prepared, however unenthusiastically, to recognise the Louisiana régime, but a group of radical senators, including Sumner, Wade and Chandler, launched a filibuster which succeeded in preventing a vote, with the somewhat embarrassing aid of conservative Democratic senators, delighted to make mischief. It was in this debate that Sumner made his much-quoted denunciation of the Louisiana government:

It is a mere seven-months' abortion, begotten by the bayonet in criminal conjunction with the spirit of caste, and born before its time, rickety, un-formed, unfinished – whose continued existence will be a burden, a reproach, and a wrong.[5]

The breakdown of this last bid to bring Lincoln and the congressional majority together on reconstruction policy seemed regrettable enough at the time; hindsight converts it into a major tragedy. In the early months of 1865, Lincoln could still look ahead to the long interval before the new Congress met. Radicals had increasingly held that the crucial questions should be deferred until the war was over, and they were confident that time would still serve to radicalise Northern opinion. Hardly anyone felt that once-for-all decisions had to be taken without further delay. No one could have foreseen the murder of Lincoln, the policy and the tactics of his successor, or even the stiff-necked attitude of the defeated South.

On 11 April, two days after Appomattox, and three days before he was shot, Lincoln gave voice to his last public thoughts on reconstruction. He claimed that he had deliberately avoided the constitutional question – 'a merely pernicious abstraction', he called it – whether the rebel states were in or out of the Union.

All agreed, he said, that they were 'out of their proper practical relation with the Union'. Restoration of that practical relationship was what mattered. 'Finding themselves safely at home, it would be utterly immaterial whether they had ever been abroad,' he added graphically, if ungrammatically. He then dwelt at length on the situation in Louisiana. Admitting his disappointment that the state government rested on a narrow base of only 12,000 votes, he also regretted that there was no Negro suffrage, and expressed his own wish that the franchise be conferred 'on the very intelligent, and on those who serve our cause as soldiers'. But he still argued that it was better to build on existing foundations rather than recklessly to destroy them – better, that is, for all parties, including the Negroes. 'Concede that the new government of Louisiana is only to what it should be as the egg is to the fowl, we shall sooner have the fowl by hatching the egg than by smashing it.' (Charles Sumner's retort gave him the better of this particular battle of the metaphors: 'The eggs of crocodiles can produce only crocodiles; and it is not easy to see how eggs laid by military power can be hatched into an American State.')[6] However, in his concluding remarks, Lincoln gave a characteristic twist to the meaning of his speech. He urged, as always, that each state must be treated according to its own peculiar circumstances, and that an exclusive and inflexible plan would be a needless entanglement for the government. But,

> Important principles may, and must, be inflexible. In the present 'situation' as the phrase goes, it may be my duty to make some new announcement to the people of the South. I am considering, and shall not fail to act, when satisfied that action will be proper.[7]

This last intriguing hint of a new policy has fed speculation ever since, and encouraged fanciful notions about the magic healing formula of which the reunited States were robbed by the assassin's bullet. But genuine clues about Lincoln's intentions are very thin upon the ground. The safest conclusion to draw is no doubt that, in his last word as in all his earlier statements, Lincoln refused to commit himself to any one course of action and that he remained a man not of one policy but of many. His death robbed the nation not of a panacea, but of a flexibility, a political skill, and an instinctive sense of the relationship between basic principles and day-by-day practice that his successor (and few other mortals) could ever match. Perhaps the most explicit clue to what Lincoln envisaged as the next stage was contained in his message to Congress four months before his final words on reconstruction. He pointed out that Southerners had had a full year in which to accept the offer of pardon on generous terms, contained in his proclamation of December 1863. Special pardons had been given with equal generosity to those groups of Confederates excepted from the general amnesty. The door, Lincoln said, was still open to all. 'But the time may come – probably will come – when public duty shall demand that it be closed; and that, in lieu, more rigorous measures than heretofore shall be adopted.'[8]

This was not a statement of policy, but it was at least a signpost pointing the way ahead.

A possible clue to Lincoln's future intentions may be obtained by analogy with his record on the abolition of slavery. What would historians have made of Abraham Lincoln, the Great Emancipator, if his life had ended in the days preceding his first Emancipation Proclamation of 22 September 1862? It is tempting to argue (if impossible to prove) that he stood on reconstruction in April 1865 very much where he stood on emancipation in the late summer of 1862. His last public speech, on 11 April 1865, like some of his earlier pronouncements on reconstruction, has much of the flavour of his reply to Greeley or his conversation with the Chicago Christian delegation in 1862. There is the same elaborate refusal to be committed, the same determination to keep all options open, the same laborious reassurances to conservative opinion, the same searching examination of the dangers and pitfalls of bolder courses of action – and, most striking of all, in each of these statements, the same concluding hint to those who cared to interpret it, of a new policy to come. The Louisiana and Arkansas régimes were perhaps the equivalent of the plans for gradual emancipation and colonisation; the furore over the Wade–Davis bill was a larger model of the dispute over the Second Confiscation Act – even to the quite gratuitous resort to a kind of veto message on each occasion. Would Appomattox in 1865 have played the role of Antietam in 1862 in precipitating a major new pronouncement? In other words, the record of Lincoln's words and deeds up to April 1865 may not be merely unhelpful as a guide to what was to follow; it may be as positively misleading as his record on emancipation before July 1862.

Certainly, both emancipation and reconstruction revealed the same Lincoln style – the preference for the specific and the immediate which never lost sight of fundamental principles; the insistence that everything else must be subordinated to the prosecution of the war, combined with a shrewd awareness of what exceptional war powers and circumstances alone made possible; the inclination to appear conservative while taking over radical positions; the belief that great and even revolutionary changes could be inaugurated by a series of small decisions, and undramatic statements which often seemed cluttered with qualifications, and which disappointed many of their hearers. In the one field as in the other, he showed the same capacity to absorb punishment, ignore snubs, accept rebuffs and survive failures – for, in terms of the actual restoration of ex-rebel states, his policy had certainly been a failure. In reconstruction as in emancipation also, the hazards and shortcomings of the experimental, flexible, step-by-step approach steadily became apparent. The danger of a non-committal attitude was that problems which might have been nipped in the bud were allowed to sprout and spread into a thick undergrowth. The danger of disguising one's real objectives was that intentions were easily misinterpreted or misunderstood. Lincoln was certainly not unaware of the need for conditions and guarantees as part of a policy for reconstruction; indeed he was an early protagonist of the view that emancipation must be just such a condition. But the elusiveness and tentativeness of his statements on Negro civil and political rights created profound misgivings about his whole conception of the scope and purpose of reconstruction. Both emancipation and reconstruction on the Lincoln model were more bold and far-reaching than they appeared at first sight; but, by their concentration on immediate tasks and individual situations, and their weakness in planning ahead, they failed to provide an adequate foundation and a sturdy framework for the difficult transition of the Negro from slavery to freedom. This was not a failure of heart or will or conscience, but a flaw in a style and method which, in other respects, reaped handsome rewards.

The difference between Lincoln and the radicals was essentially over methods of doing business. Lincoln's agenda for reconstruction during the war consisted of one specific item – restoration of state governments – with everything else lumped together under any other business, to be considered as and when the necessity arose. Although, for their part, the radicals were willing to defer much of the practical business of reconstruction until after the war, they insisted on adding more and more specific items to the agenda in the form of principles to be enforced and conditions to be met: complete abolition of slavery, repudiation of the rebel debt, exclusion of leading ex-Confederates, protection for the freedmen, Negro suffrage – with probably more to come, amounting to an elaborate plan for the remaking of Southern society. They had more faith in strong declarations of principle, and more inclination to indulge in detailed planning for the future. But they, like Lincoln, could only look back on a record of frustration and failure when the war came to an end in April 1865. They had no concrete results to show; their most solid achievement was in steadily shifting to wider ground the whole area of debate. In fact, differences in style and tempo, along with the very real dispute over which branch of the government should control the whole process, obscured the very broad area of common ground which was shared by the president, the radicals, and indeed most members of the Republican party. It was surely more than coincidence in this context that, at various times, men as different as Abraham Lincoln, Charles Sumner and Thaddeus Stevens all averred that their basic political ideas, ideals and objectives were derived from the Declaration of Independence. They, and most other Republicans, were convinced that the abolition of slavery was a logical consequence of the principles enshrined in that document. They had come to agree that abolition must be imposed upon the Southern states as a condition of their readmission; from that, it was not a difficult step to accept the need for other conditions. Despite the failure of a compromise on reconstruction in early 1865, the lessons of recent experience were not wholly discouraging. Success in achieving a two-thirds majority for the Thirteenth Amendment, and the passage of legislation like the Freedmen's Bureau Act, showed what could be done when the party pulled together. In the aftermath of the election of 1864, there seemed more clearly than ever to be a solid middle-of-the-road group of Republicans in Congress, who would neither drag their feet nor lose their heads, who wanted to put old, divisive issues behind them, and turn their attention to the pressing questions of the moment. Whatever else they shared, they faced an abundance of common problems.

At fearful cost, the Civil War preserved the Union and destroyed slavery. But it did not clearly determine the shape of the post-war south or its future relationship with the rest of the Union, except to establish that neither would ever be the same as before. Nor, in destroying slavery, did it clarify the status of the Negro in American society or alleviate, let alone solve, the problems of race. The whole country, North and South, had moved a long way since 1860, but now, in order to secure these further goals, the North had to win not only the war but the peace which followed it. High ideals and base self-interest, the health of the Union and the welfare of the Republican party, alike demanded that reconstruction should be a carefully controlled and regulated process, if this second victory was to be won. Without the harsh imperatives and urgent stimuli of war, could the will and the perseverance be found to sustain an unprecedented exercise in the use of federal power? Only as long as Northern ideals and interests continued to work in support of each other was there any prospect at all that they could.

2. As the war approached its end, Lincoln toyed with various peace proposals which apparently threatened to undermine some of the foundations of reconstruction upon which he and most of his party agreed. But these notions reflected above all his immediate desire to end the fighting, and prevent further bloodshed, and his genuine fear that final defeat would bring to the South total disorder, economic disaster, social dislocation and even racial conflict. They did not represent a calculated decision to retrace his steps along the treacherous road to reconstruction.

Peace feelers had been tentatively pushed out at various times during the second half of the war, but without success. The Lincoln administration was reluctant to embark on any negotiation which might imply, however indirectly, some measure of recognition of the Southern Confederacy. Alexander Stephens, vice-president of the Confederacy, encountered this obstacle, among others, when in July 1863 he tried to use a mission to discuss exchange of prisoners to broach wider issues. But, even if this procedural difficulty could have been overcome, there remained until the dying days of the Confederacy an irreconcilable difference over the meaning of peace. For the Southern leaders, peace continued to mean peaceful separation; for the North, reunion was not merely the first essential item of any negotiated settlement, but an essential precondition before negotiations could begin.

Various unofficial go-betweens tried their hand at negotiations during 1864. With Lincoln's consent, but no official backing, James Jaquess, a volatile compound of colonel and Methodist preacher, and J. R. Gilmore passed through the lines in July, and obtained an interview with Jefferson Davis in Richmond. But terms for peace with reunion which they regarded as the mildest that the North could possibly accept looked to Davis like humiliating surrender. Many of the so-called 'peace' manoeuvres in the summer of 1864 were directed at targets other than peace itself. Both governments felt the need to demonstrate to their people – and especially to the disaffected among them – that peace could not be had on terms which were remotely acceptable. The problem was particularly acute in the north where the pressures of an election year and the frustration born of the military situation made Lincoln and his supporters highly sensitive to the accusation that the war was being needlessly prolonged. The Union could be restored, the charge ran, but for stubborn Republican insistence on the complete eradication of slavery in the south. Confederate agents were sent to Canada to stir up trouble in the middle west, encourage the Copperheads, and influence the Democratic convention at Chicago. Through an intermediary, they succeeded in persuading Horace Greeley, the excitable editor of the New York *Tribune*, that they offered a chance of peace, and he urged Lincoln to seize the proffered opportunity. Greeley's indiscriminate enthusiasm for reform of any kind embraced the peace crusade as well as antislavery, but he was taken aback when Lincoln appointed him to conduct the Southerners to Washington. The whole project soon collapsed as it became clear that Greeley had been duped, and the Confederate agents were not empowered to discuss peace terms, but were in fact engaged in a very different kind of mission. Lincoln understood their real purpose clearly enough, but he still had to shoulder an unfair share of the blame for the breakdown of a socalled peace initiative which was in fact nothing of the kind.[9]

The incident did however elicit from him a clear and important statement of the peace terms which he would accept:

> Any proposition which embraces the restoration of peace, the integrity of the whole Union, and the abandonment of slavery, and which comes by and with an authority that can control the armies now at war against the United States will be received and considered by the Executive government of the United States, and will be met by liberal terms on other substantial and collateral points.[10]

A month later, in August, when his re-election prospects were at their blackest, Lincoln flirted with the idea proposed by his campaign manager, Henry J. Raymond, of offering Davis peace on the single condition of reunion. He also drafted but never sent a reply to a Democratic newspaper editor which ended with the remarkable sentence: 'If Jefferson Davis wishes . . . to know what I would do if he were to offer peace and re-union, saying nothing about slavery, let him try me.'[11] But in both cases Lincoln drew back from the brink. There was too much risk that such attempts to demonstrate the intransigeance of the South might add to confusion in the North. Returning confidence, and then electoral victory and military success, brought Lincoln back to the July formula, and the three basic conditions of reunion, the end of slavery, and no temporary truce or armistice before reunion was agreed. If these basic requirements were accepted, Lincoln was ready and anxious to be flexible and generous on all other matters – and even on whether the demise of slavery should be gradual or immediate. There were even hints of a distinction between slaves already freed who could not be returned to bondage, and slaves not yet freed whose fate was negotiable. The difficulty was that, to Southern eyes, the Lincoln formula seemed to combine rigid insistence on certain unacceptable conditions, with vague promises, but no clear guarantees, of leniency or concessions on other matters. It was small wonder that, in his message to Congress in December, Lincoln saw little point in further attempts at negotiation with Davis: 'He would accept nothing short of severance of the Union – precisely what we will not and cannot give.' The issue could now be settled only by 'the victory and defeat following war'.[12]

However, there were still those who, during the harsh winter of 1864–5, hoped for peace without further bloodshed. The peace movement in Georgia and North Carolina, and other parts of the south, still prospered, and there were rumours that, if the Richmond authorities did not take the initiative, some of the individual states might take matters into their own hands. Hopes of a sympathetic Northern response had been upset by the outcome of the election of 1864, but there were still many Southerners, from Vice-President Stephens downwards, who believed that negotiation was the only way to salvage something from the crumbling ruins of the Confederacy. In the north, Peace Democrats – and some Republicans like Horace Greeley – felt that the Confederate leadership might now be willing to discuss peace on the basis of reunion. Greeley helped to persuade Francis P. Blair senior, aged chieftain of the powerful Blair tribe, that he was the man to act as intermediary. With Lincoln's approval, Blair paid two visits to Richmond in January 1865, and had meetings with Jefferson Davis himself. Blair's own plan was for a reunion of North and South in a common struggle to drive the foreign invader out of Mexico. There was little prospect that this idea would be taken seriously in either Washington or Richmond, but out of Blair's travels between the two capitals came a proposal for a more formal peace conference. In a message to be shown to Lincoln, Davis expressed interest in the appointment of commissioners 'with a view to secure peace to the two countries'. Lincoln replied that he was ready to receive any agent whom Davis 'may informally send to me with the view of securing peace to the people of our one common country'. This difference in wording foreshadowed the failure of the meeting which followed.[13]

Davis appointed three commissioners, all of them peace advocates – a fact which suggests that his purpose may have been less to prove to the sceptics that peace was possible than to prove to the enthusiasts that it was not. The commissioners were Vice-President Stephens, R.M.T. Hunter of Virginia, president *pro tem* of the Senate, and John A. Campbell, assistant secretary of war, and negotiator with Seward during the Sumter crisis four years earlier. Lincoln first despatched Seward to meet the Confederate emissaries but soon decided to be present himself at the meeting, which took place on board the steamer *River*

*Queen* in Hampton Roads, on 3 February 1865. From the outset it was clear that, while Lincoln insisted on reunion as a first step, the Confederate commissioners were empowered to discuss peace only on the basis of independence. But this did not prevent a wide-ranging discussion of other issues, notably slavery. In answer to Stephens, Lincoln conceded that, as a war measure, the Emancipation Proclamation could probably free no more slaves once hostilities ceased. Seward referred to the recent congressional resolution in favour of the Thirteenth Amendment to abolish slavery once and for all, but he hinted that, by returning to the Union quickly, the Southern states might delay or even prevent its ratification – and Lincoln hinted that they might at least postpone its implementation for a few years. In fact, out of the Hampton Roads conference came a reiteration of the characteristic Lincoln blend of firmness on the essentials – reunion, no armistice, no retraction of what had already been achieved in emancipation – and extreme flexibility and liberality on other matters. But what looked generous to Lincoln was vague and unsatisfactory to Stephens and Hunter, and totally unacceptable to Jefferson Davis. By what it conceded, it would also have appalled many members of Lincoln's own party.[14]

The Hampton Roads conference failed to produce peace, but neither Davis nor Lincoln had any great expectation that it would. The most that Davis might have hoped to gain was some kind of truce; failing that, it had at least given a sobering lesson to the Southern peace movement, and a powerful argument to support Davis's own brave effort to inspire Southerners to a heroic last-ditch stand. Lincoln, too, gained by the demonstration of the futility of such negotiations, and the failure of the conference spared him the full embarrassment of explaining away to members of his own party the sweeping concessions which he had offered, on slavery and other matters. By this time, in fact, Lincoln was so convinced that slavery was doomed to extinction – and sooner rather than later – that he felt he could afford to be generous and flexible on precisely how and when its end should come. He offered not stimulants to resuscitate a dying patient but analgesics to mitigate its final agony. He also still hankered after the principles of gradualism and compensation which he had espoused three years earlier. Encouraged by the report of another self-important unofficial emissary to Richmond, James W. Singleton, that compensation for loss of slave property might help to smooth the path to peace, he sat down on his return from Hampton Roads to draft a new proposal. It would have offered a payment of $400 million in government bonds to the slave-holding states, if they abandoned resistance to the national authority by 1 April and ratified the Thirteenth Amendment in time for it to become law by 1 July. It also promised generous treatment on all other matters. In defence of the plan, Lincoln offered the same kind of argument that it would save money by shortening the war, as he had used to justify his compensation proposals in 1862.[15] But the cabinet dissuaded him from proceeding with the plan, and the chances were that it would have been unacceptable both to the congressional majority in Washington, and the Confederate leadership in Richmond.

In the last few days of the war, and of his own life, Lincoln would return yet again to the idea of a peace based on firm adherence to a short list of fundamental requirements, and extreme leniency on everything else. The words of his second inaugural were not empty rhetoric; malice toward none, charity for all, firmness in the right, were also a programme, but a programme in which the third item was as important as the first two. If such a policy brought a negotiated peace, so much the better; if it did not, it might serve to weaken final Southern resistance, reduce the cost of military victory in blood and tears, and save the South from chaos and anarchy in the aftermath of war. It mixed idealism and realism in the best Lincoln manner.

3. After Hampton Roads, Jefferson Davis launched himself into a final desperate effort to breathe new life and hope into the Confederate cause. In an impassioned speech before a large crowd on 6 February, he made a special plea to those who had lost heart, and especially those who had deserted from the army, to return to the fold and present a united front in defiance of the invader. But the time had passed when such stirring calls to arms might have saved the day. Desertion, long a debilitating disease of the Confederacy, was now only one symptom of moral and material collapse. Despair and dissension shredded the last remnants of popular morale, just as invading armies were ripping Confederate territory into fragments. The loss of Wilmington early in 1865 deprived the South of the last of its great blockade-running centres, and intensified its sense of isolation, almost of incarceration. It also brought nearer the day when supplies to sustain any kind of resistance would simply run out. Even where, in the short run, there were adequate supplies of food and other materials, it was another matter whether they could any longer be moved to the right place at the right time. Feeble communications and financial chaos were paralysing the truncated body of the Confederacy. Indeed, in these days of actual or impending collapse, many areas of the Confederacy reverted to the ways of primitive society. Local communities were thrown back on their own resources if they were to survive at all, and crude self-sufficiency replaced more complex economic relationships. Chaos in the currency brought an increasing resort to barter as the only practicable way of doing business. Secretary of the Treasury Trenholm called upon the people to contribute their jewellery and other valuables to sustain the war effort.

President and Congress continued to function, and to feud, in Richmond, but it was a moot point how far the writ of the Confederate government ran beyond the capital and its defences. Richmond and Petersburg, and the thin grey lines around them, were almost all that was left of the Confederacy, and Jefferson Davis and Robert E. Lee remained, more than ever, the personal symbols of its continued existence. It took courage and faith of an exceptional kind, which both men shared in abundance, to fight on in defiance of the appalling realities. Of all the Confederate traditions, the one that survived most strongly was the habit of internal strife and dissension. Now it found its happiest home in Congress which, in schizophrenic switches of mood, alternated between recriminations against Davis, and states-rights zeal for clipping the wings of central government, on the one hand, and the grant of sweeping new powers to that same government on the other. Davis was the available scapegoat for all Southern misfortunes, and there was much wild talk of superseding him by the elevation of Lee to some kind of military dictatorship. In early February, Davis at last surrendered to the pressure which he had long resisted, and accepted a measure creating the post of general-in-chief, although he realised that it was intended as a slap in the face to himself. Lee was of course his choice for the post, and at least the president could be certain that the general would give short shrift to any scheme to create a military dictatorship. It was equally certain that it was too late for any general-in-chief to create the kind of effective coordination of military policy which the Confederacy had always lacked – and Lee's preoccupation with the situation on his own doorstep in any case precluded any bold assumption of new powers. Anti-administration forces in Congress were still after more blood. Their sustained campaign to oust Secretary of State Benjamin was unsuccessful, but their carping criticism did lead to the resignation of Secretary of War Seddon and his replacement by John C. Breckinridge. A more welcome consequence of their pressure was the long overdue removal of Commissary-General Lucius B. Northrop, a favourite target alike for his inefficiency and his high esteem in the eyes of the president. His departure gave Lee some hope that his army would be saved from starvation, but with this as with other new appointments, the situation had reached the stage where new hands at the helm might delay but could not alter the inevitable.

A kind of death-wish seemed to seize Congress as it dashed from the presidential grasp many of the powers which he desperately needed at this darkest hour.[16] By the casting-vote of Vice-President Stephens, the Senate refused to renew the presidential authority to suspend the writ of habeas corpus. In a two-hour speech, Stephens denounced the administration of which he was nominally a member, and pleaded that it was still not too late to save the Southern cause if only the government would abandon such tyrannical measures as conscription, impressment and suspension of habeas corpus, and fight for constitutional liberty. Congress did virtually end impressment in March by passing a measure establishing the prevailing market price as the just price for goods impressed. It also abandoned the attempt to regulate blockade-running in the interest of the Confederate government and the war effort, and it denied Davis the extra powers which he sought to detail men for vital jobs and thus eke out the slender manpower resources which remained. There might have been something almost heroic about such breathtaking disdain for the harsh realities if it had been inspired solely by adherence to pure constitutional principle. But it owned at least as much to spite against Davis, and to irresponsibility, fed by demoralisation and despair. There may have been some small comfort for the Davis administration in the knowledge that it now mattered little in most parts of the Confederacy what the legislators in Richmond said or

did. Grant and Sherman were curbing the authority of the Richmond government more effectively than any states rights dogma or legislative pettifogging.
Unfortunately for Davis and his supporters, the same was true when Congress
briefly swung over to one of its more constructive moods. After endless pre-
varication and procrastination, it finally approved in March a drastic increase in
all existing taxes, but even many of the men who voted for the bill realised that
it was little more than an academic exercise. Two weeks earlier, it had granted
the Secretary of War sweeping new powers virtually to take over the railroads
for military purposes. In 1862 or 1863 such a law would have been a real asset,
but now there were only a few railroads left where the Secretary might exert
authority. Another new measure extended the government's powers to impress
Negroes for military labour, but it was too late to make much difference.

Most significant and most startling of all was the congressional change of
heart on that most sensitive of issues, the recruitment of Negro troops.[17] There
was no greater irony in all the efforts of the Confederacy to find adequate means
to match its ambitious goals than the proposal to arm Negroes. A struggle
initiated partly or even largely in defence of the institution of Negro slavery was
to be waged by Negro troops recruited by dangling the bait of liberty before
them. The idea was not new in 1865; a few small voices had proposed it from
the beginning, and the drain on white manpower steadily converted it from
unthinkable heresy to unpleasant necessity. In the winter of 1863–4, General
Pat Cleburne initiated a debate on the subject in the Army of Tennessee, but his
proposals met furious opposition, and, at Jefferson Davis's request, the matter
was dropped, and Cleburne's proposal suppressed. But the issue would not die,
and by late 1864, when the slaves were virtually the only source of manpower
left, sheer necessity gave new urgency to the debate. A meeting of state governors
in October 1864 recommended the use of Negro troops, and Secretary of War
Seddon took the same view. In his message to the new session of Congress in
November 1864, Davis was not prepared to go so far. But he did ask for power
to purchase up to 40,000 slaves to serve as auxiliaries with the army, and he left
no doubt that, if faced with a choice between subjugation and the resort to
Negro troops, the Confederacy should choose the latter.

The debate continued through the dark winter of 1864–5 in the army, in
Congress, in the press and elsewhere. The case against the employment of slaves
as soldiers still stemmed basically from the objection that it was a denial of
everything for which the Confederacy stood. It would abandon at a stroke the
whole Southern defence of slavery, and it would infringe the constitution by
another massive government interference with property rights. The slaves, it was
argued, were more useful and more needed on the home front; they would
make poor soldiers in any case, and many would run away at the first opportunity. Their recruitment would have a devastating effect on morale, both in
the army where white soldiers would object to fighting alongside them, and at
home where slave-owners would resent their loss. In the words of R. G. H. Kean,
the use of Negro troops 'would strike down at a blow the whole productive

power of the country, introduce a thousand domestic questions of amazing intricacy and difficulty, and tear the vitals of society'. The advocates of the new policy built on the foundations of necessity a superstructure of other arguments. By his record in the Union army, the Negro had proved that he could and would fight – and he would fight better for those who knew and understood him in the South. Why should the Confederacy deny itself a source of recruits which its adversary was exploiting so vigorously? The constitutional objections could be met by working with or through the states. It was admitted that slave soldiers would probably have to be promised their freedom when the war was over, but, if the war were lost, they would have their freedom in any case; it was foolish to deny the South its last chance of defending its liberty by denying the slave a chance to obtain his. Kean accepted the force of this argument:

> Men are beginning to say that when the question is between slavery and independence, slavery must go, and this is logical because when independence is lost, slavery is at the same blow destroyed.[18]

There was, in early 1865, a further diplomatic motive behind the proposal to recruit Negro troops with the promise of emancipation. In February, Duncan Kenner was sent to Europe in a last desperate bid to win recognition from Britain and France in return for the promise of emancipation. Predictably, the Kenner mission was a complete failure; only when it was much too late had the Confederate leadership learned the bitter lesson with which Yancey had returned from the first Confederate mission to Europe:

> There is no government in Europe that dares help us in a struggle which can be suspected of having for its result, directly or indirectly, the fortification or perpetuation of slavery. Of this I am certain.[19]

Congress debated the question of Negro troops at length in early 1865, and more and more support built up in its favour. Davis, too, was now a strong advocate of the measure, and Benjamin, his right-hand man, was one of its most active proponents. Governor Smith of Virginia and the state legislature gave Congress a nudge in the new direction by pushing through a law authorising the recruitment of slaves. They had also drawn from no less a person than Lee himself a statement giving reluctant but firm support for the measure, on grounds of inescapable necessity. When Lee also wrote a letter of support for the bill before Congress, his influence was decisive. Hesitations and reservations were pushed aside, and the bill became law on 13 March 1865. It authorised the president to call upon each state for its quota of 300,000 troops, irrespective of colour. The number of slaves recruited from any state was not to exceed 25 per cent of the able-bodied male slaves between the ages of eighteen and forty-five. Freedom was not promised to the slaves recruited but left to the discretion of the states and the slave-owners. After the months of passionate debate, there was no time left for the Confederacy to test the fighting value of its Negro troops. The few companies actually recruited attained no more than curiosity value and never went into action.

Slavery, which had had the first word in the great American conflict, seemed determined to have the last as well. From first to last, its voice was too powerful to be ignored, but too blurred by ironic echoes to deliver a simple and unambiguous message. In the north, Lincoln rejoiced in the progress of the Thirteenth Amendment as a final solution to the slavery problem, but seemed to hint to Southern peace negotiators that it need not be so final after all. In the south, Davis and his henchmen rejected out of hand peace terms which required the abandonment of slavery, and then adopted a scheme for the use of Negro troops which virtually ensured that the days of slavery were numbered. All Americans, North and South, black and white, were still to confront the greatest irony of all that, even after the death of slavery, its evils would live on to poison the future for generations to come.

4. The winter of 1864–5 was the interval before the last act in the tragedy of the Confederacy. It was a harsh winter, too, in Virginia; when it was not freezing hard, there were torrential rains which turned roads and trenches into seas of mud. The guns were seldom silent for long, but there were no significant moves until February when the Union line was pushed a little further south-west of Petersburg, and then nothing more for another month while Grant awaited weather fit for the delivery of the *coup de grâce*. But, during the winter standstill, Lee's army was dying on its feet. The men lived in discomfort and misery, without food to fill their bellies or hope to fill their hearts. At one point in January there were only two days' meagre rations left, and fodder for the horses was equally short. There was neither fuel nor clothing enough to keep out the damp and the cold. Even ammunition was beginning to run dangerously low. In the circumstances, it is less surprising that some men deserted than that so many stayed at their posts. But as conditions grew worse so did the rate of desertion, and in one month from 15 February, nearly 3,000 men left, some heading for home, a few for the enemy lines. The relative comfort of Grant's well-supplied army was almost as hard to resist as its overwhelming power. The Union soldiers were amply fed, and as well protected against the elements as front-line troops could ever expect to be. Evidence alike of their wellbeing and the army's logistical resources was the specially constructed military railroad which ran from the huge base at City Point along the length of the army's line south of Petersburg, bringing vital supplies and creature comforts to the besieging army.

Winter was doing Grant's work by thinning the overstretched line of defenders in front of him to the point where it could be snapped without too much difficulty. While he bided his time in Virginia, the general-in-chief was planning overall strategy with a broad, sweeping confidence which skilfully arranged the movement of pieces across a continental chessboard. When Sherman had reached Savannah in December, Grant intended to transfer most of his army by sea to Virginia to join in the final onslaught upon Lee. But the long delay before transport could be provided for such a move helped Sherman to persuade Grant of the virtues of his own alternative plan. The shattering impact of the march to the sea stimulated Sherman's enthusiasm for a new northward march, through the Carolinas, which would not only bring him to Virginia more quickly than the delayed sea voyage, but would in the process complete the demoralisation of the Confederacy. He was utterly convinced now of the value of such marches:

> I attach more importance to these deep incisions into the enemy's country, because this war differs from European wars in this particular: we are not only fighting hostile armies but a hostile people, and must make old and young, rich and poor, feel the hard hand of war as well as their organised armies.[20]

Grant yielded not unwillingly to the wishes of a general with such an appetite for action, and while Sherman planned his new route, his commander considered how best to help him. He ordered the transfer of Schofield's corps from Thomas's army in Tennessee to join in the operations against Wilmington on the coast of North Carolina, and to prepare a base there to succour Sherman on his progress north. Here was the kind of coordinated strategic planning in the grand manner which had been a pipe dream a few years earlier. In no more than a few weeks, 20,000 men were to be brought from the middle of Tennessee to the Carolina seaboard to provide a link with another army just beginning its advance from a point over 400 miles south of their intended rendezvous. How different from Lee's confinement to a shrinking stage and a dwindling band of players – and how different, too, from Lee's habitual cast of thought. Grant himself was surmising by this time that 'Lee is averse to going out of Virginia, and if the cause of the South is lost, he wants Richmond to be the last place to surrender'.[21]

But Grant had yet more irons in the fire. He ordered an attack on Mobile, and grew impatient with Canby's delays in pressing it home – but Mobile eventually fell in the dying days of the war. He prodded Thomas into organising an advance from Tennessee into Alabama – and into entrusting it to the dynamic young James H. Wilson. With 13,000 men of the cavalry force which Thomas had so carefully prepared before Nashville, Wilson headed south in mid-March. His corps, stripped for speedy action, and equipped with repeating rifles, swept aside Forrest's depleted force, burst into Selma on 2 April, wrecked the town's factories and foundries, and raced eastward in a breathtaking march through Montgomery and on across the border into Georgia before news arrived of the suspension of hostilities. Somewhat over-shadowed at the time by Sherman's deeds, Wilson's expedition was an equally spectacular example – on a smaller scale – of the shape of mobile warfare to come.

Sherman, meanwhile, was sweeping through the Carolinas in a march less

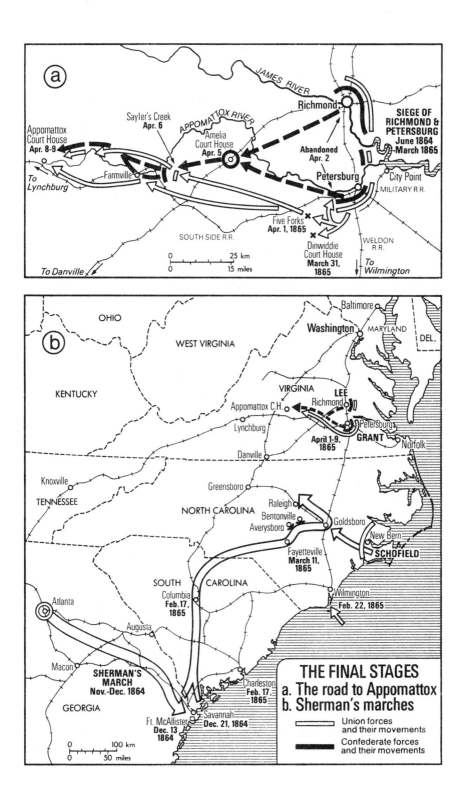

(a)

SIEGE OF
RICHMOND &
PETERSBURG
June 1864
– March 1865

Richmond

JAMES RIVER

APPOMATTOX RIVER

Sayler's Creek
Apr. 6

Appomattox
Court House
Apr. 8-9

Amelia
Court House
Apr. 5

Abandoned
Apr. 2

City Point
MILITARY R.R.

Petersburg

To
Lynchburg

Farmville

Five Forks
Apr. 1, 1865

SOUTH SIDE R.R.

Dinwiddie
Court House
March 31,
1865

WELDON
R.R.

To
Wilmington

0      25 km
0      15 miles

To Danville

(b)

Baltimore

OHIO

Washington      MARYLAND      DEL.

WEST VIRGINIA

KENTUCKY

VIRGINIA      LEE

Appomattox C.H.      Richmond

Lynchburg      Petersburg

April 1-9,
1865      GRANT      Norfolk

Danville

Knoxville      Greensboro

TENNESSEE      NORTH CAROLINA      Raleigh
Bentonville
Averysboro      Goldsboro

New Bern
SCHOFIELD

Fayetteville
March 11,
1865

SOUTH   CAROLINA

Atlanta      Columbia
Feb. 17,
1865      Wilmington
Feb. 22, 1865

Augusta

Macon      SHERMAN'S
MARCH
Nov.-Dec. 1864      Charleston
Feb. 17,
1865

GEORGIA

Ft. McAllister
Dec. 13
1864      Savannah
Dec. 21, 1864

0      100 km
0      50 miles

THE FINAL STAGES
a. The road to Appomattox
b. Sherman's marches

☐ Union forces
and their movements

■ Confederate forces
and their movements

renowned but even more remarkable than his progress from Atlanta to the sea. On this new venture he faced much greater obstacles and the likelihood of much stiffer resistance. In the lowlands of South Carolina he would have to traverse swamps and marshes, crossed by wide rivers, and a network of lesser streams. An exceptionally wet winter had swollen the rivers to double or treble their normal width, and flooded broad tracts of the low-lying countryside. Beyond these natural hazards, his army, 60,000 strong, might have to face up to 40,000 Confederate troops. Many of these were ill-trained militia, or tattered remnants of Hood's army, and their command structure was ramshackle in the extreme, but at least the numerical odds were not unfavourable to a stout defence. But Sherman was not to be deterred or denied. He spent January in preliminary operations, sending his right wing by sea up the coast to Beaufort, and his left north-west, across the Savannah river. At the beginning of February the major advance began, the men building roads and bridges by the mile, or wading waist-deep through flood-waters, finding what shelter they could at night from the sodden ground and the drenching rains, and yet maintaining a rate of progress which would not have disgraced a well-organised army on good roads in dry, summer weather. They were doing with impressive efficiency something which well-informed opponents like Johnston and Hardee had dismissed as impossible in the conditions. They were also bewildering the Confederates about their intended destination. Beauregard, trying to instil some order into his motley command, assigned half of them to block a north-westward advance to Augusta, the other half to check a move north-east to Charleston. Having created precisely the opening he wanted, Sherman drove between them, due north towards Columbia, the state capital of South Carolina, and centre of one of the most productive agricultural areas left to the Confederacy. By mid-month they were within sight of the city.

There was a new, more jagged cutting edge about this deep thrust into South Carolina, the original nest of the secessionist vipers. The march through Georgia had had its moments of carnival as well as carnage, but Sherman's men descended upon South Carolina in a spirit of vengeance and hatred. Both the army itself and the parasites who swarmed upon its flanks were more wanton and ruthless in their destruction, more pitiless in their quest for loot. They fanned out, too, over a wide area on either side of the line of march, and left behind them the smoking remains of mills, factories, stores, railroad depots, barns and bales of cotton. The army marched into Columbia on 17 February; that night half the city was destroyed by fire. For the rest of his life Sherman was plagued by the accusation that he had deliberately put Columbia to the torch, but there is no evidence to support the charge. (The fact that he had set up his headquarters in the middle of the city would also make it improbable, to say the least.) The exceptional devastation at Columbia followed from an unusual concatenation of circumstances: the decision of the Confederate Wade Hampton to set light to the cotton in the city before abandoning it, the abundance of liquor which the occupying troops discovered in the city, the activities of looters and vandals, freed prisoners-of-war and freed slaves, and the strong wind which fanned the flames and spread them uncontrollably. The proportion of the blame to be allocated to these various factors can never be known, but all undoubtedly played their part.[22]

Charleston, like Columbia, was abandoned by the Confederates on 17 February. Sherman's advance through the centre of the state had made it untenable, as he had confidently predicted. He professed to regard it as 'a mere desolated wreck . . . a point of little importance',[23] but, as he also knew, there was a special satisfaction for the people of the north in the recapture of the place where secession had been born and the war had begun. Sherman himself had no time to waste on sentiment or self-congratulation. He was surging ahead again, now turning north-east towards the North Carolina border and Fayetteville on the Cape Fear river. The weather was still appalling, but neither swollen rivers nor seas of mud could delay him for long, and he reached Fayetteville on 11 March. He was now facing a new opponent, or rather an old, familiar one restored to favour, for Lee had placed Johnston in overall command of all forces in the Carolinas. The galaxy of generals pitted against him – Beauregard, Bragg, D. H. Hill, Hardee, as well as Johnston, did not worry Sherman. He was always at least one step ahead of any Confederate plan to thwart him. While his opponents strove to cover first Charlotte then Raleigh, Sherman made enough feints to nourish their mistaken notions, while he pursued his own chosen course. At Fayetteville he made contact with Schofield, who was now firmly established on the coast at Wilmington and New Bern. He fixed upon Goldsboro as the place where his army would link directly with Schofield's, and replenish its supplies. Johnston's only hope – and that a slender one – was to prevent this link from being established. He was also being urged by Lee to keep Sherman out of eastern North Carolina, which was now the main supply area for the army at Richmond and Petersburg. (Lee insisted that supply dumps in North Carolina be reserved for his army, and left Johnston to forage in the countryside for what he could find.)[24] After Hardee had fought a useful delaying action at Averysboro, Johnston challenged Sherman's left at Bentonville on 19–20 March. It was a gallant effort, but Sherman was able to contain it without bringing on a full-scale pitched battle. On 21 March he decided to forgo an unexpected opportunity for a highly promising counter-attack, and press on instead to Goldsboro. There, on 23 March, his junction with Schofield was achieved as planned. With a combined force of almost 90,000, and a secure supply base on the coast, they were invulnerable.

Sherman's second great march covered more than 400 miles in just over seven weeks. Despite all that climate, geography and 40,000 opposing troops could do, he had lost few men through either sickness or enemy action while he tore the heart out of what was left of the Confederacy. It was one of the truly stupendous feats of the war. It seemed to shrink the vast distances and narrow the wide horizons of the north American continent, and it made nonsense of the blithe predictions of 1861 that the territory of the Southern Confederacy was too extensive to be conquered. It brought the west to the east, and men of the armies of the Mississippi, the Tennessee and the Cumberland within striking distance of the James. By its very success, it had driven the two surviving enemy armies into close proximity with each other. It remained to be seen whether they could join and achieve together what was already beyond them separately. The chances were that they were already too late.

5. Lee had long since shed any illusions about the odds which he faced. Even the disparity between the paper strengths of the Northern and Southern armies told only half the story, for on the Confederate side the gap between theoretical and effective strength widened day by day. By March Lee had not much more than 1,000 men per mile to hold his long defensive line. Out of sheer desperation, he wrote to Grant on 2 March to sound him out on the possibility of discussing peace terms, but Lincoln instructed Grant 'to have no conference with General Lee unless it be for the capitulation of Gen. Lee's army', and 'not to decide, discuss, or confer upon any political question'.[25] Out of still deeper despair, Lee now turned to a plan which bordered on fantasy. He proposed to throw Grant off balance by an attack east of Petersburg, and then take the opportunity to slip away south-westwards to join up with Johnston. Their combined force would then defeat Sherman, before returning to Virginia to deal with Grant. It was a dream, of course – which among other things would require Grant and Sherman to cooperate by behaving like men in a trance – but at least it offered more than the inevitable consequences of standing still. On 25 March, he launched the first stage of the plan with a surprise attack on Fort Stedman east of Petersburg. Confederate troops took the fort but could not follow up their initial success. Powerful Union forces contained the threat and then rolled it back, and Lee ended the day in a slightly worse position than at dawn – and with about 4,000 fewer men. All that he could do now was to prepare his escape from Richmond and Petersburg before it was too late. He had only a few days' grace.

Grant's plans for the final assault were ready, and on 27–28 March, he explained them to Sherman and Lincoln, who had both arrived at City Point. (It was at this same meeting that Lincoln spoke of his desire for a generous peace in terms which Sherman was to misinterpret a few weeks later, with embarrassing results.)[26] Sheridan's return to the main army after concluding his business in the Shenandoah Valley helped to convince Grant that the time for action was at hand. The wet weather persisted, but, if he waited for the return of dry conditions, he might give Lee time to slip away. His plan was to build up strength at the western end of his line for a massive left hook against Lee's overstretched position, while Sheridan's cavalry swung still further west to threaten the South Side Railroad. If Lee sought to check the move by extending his line still further, it would become so thin that it could be broken somewhere. If he tried to escape, his army would be vulnerable once it moved out of the shelter of its massive fortifications. Now, after nine months of waiting, the end was to come in little more than nine days.

The offensive began none too well in the last few days of March. On 31

March, Sheridan's cavalry was given a hard fight by Pickett at Dinwiddie Court House, and Warren's infantry were roughly handled by a much smaller Confederate force a few miles to the east. But these fleeting Southern successes were misleading, and achieved only by a risky dispersal of overstretched resources. Next day, Pickett fell back and Warren's infantry came stumbling along muddy tracks to join Sheridan in a devastating attack at Five Forks which virtually eliminated Pickett's force. The last protection for the Confederate right flank was gone, the South Side Railroad was closed, and Lee's days in Petersburg and Richmond were numbered. Grant knew that he had now made the vital breakthrough, and he ordered an all-out attack next day. Lee simply did not have the troops to man his elaborate defences, and, on 2 April, the Union assaults overran the whole Confederate line south-west of Petersburg. The advance stopped short only at the inner ring of the town's defences, where Lee's stout defence and the attackers' disarray enabled the Confederates to survive the day. But Lee was now fighting for no more than a few precious hours to allow for the orderly evacuation of the army and the government from Richmond and Petersburg.

Jefferson Davis was in church on that Sunday morning when the message came that he and his government must abandon the capital. After a hectic day of packing essential documents and the last contents of an almost empty treasury, they escaped by train that night to Danville in south-west Virginia, the first stop on their wretched journey through the wilderness that had been the Southern Confederacy. During the night the military evacuation was smoothly completed, and the army headed for its new rendezvous at Amelia Court House twenty-five miles to the west. But there were scenes of chaos and panic among the inhabitants of Richmond – desperate competition for any kind of transport, a rush to claim money and valuables from the banks, a milling throng fighting over the food supplies which the army was obliged to leave behind. By nightfall, mobs of looters roamed the streets, and when the tobacco warehouses were set alight by order, the flames spread to the surrounding areas. The blowing-up of ammunition dumps, and the warships on the James river, added to the pandemonium, and by morning a pall of thick, black smoke hung over the city, as Union cavalry clattered through the dismal streets and ran up the Stars and Stripes above the Capitol.[27]

On the morning of 3 April, Lincoln came from City Point to meet the victorious Grant in Petersburg. Next day, despite fears for his safety expressed by Stanton from Washington, the president sailed up the James to Richmond itself. In a city which had been the nerve centre of the rebellion two days before, where deserters and looters and released prisoners now moved freely, the president of the United States walked a mile up Main Street, without formality or fuss, and with no more than a token escort. He was followed by a crowd of singing, clapping Negroes who swarmed about him as he paused on his way. Some fell to their knees; 'you must kneel to God only,' said Lincoln modestly, according to one account. He entered the Confederate 'White House' and sat in the presidential chair so recently vacated by Davis. Later, he drove through the Richmond streets, escorted by a troop of Negro cavalry.[28] Their very presence, like his, said all that needed to be said. In its unconcern for protocol or pomp, or even personal safety, as in its blend of the unpretentious and the unprecedented, the performance was characteristic of the man. It remains one of the unforgettable moments of the war.

Lincoln's thoughts that day were all of peace and reconciliation, although neither Lee nor Johnston had yet surrendered his army. He talked about peace with John A. Campbell, whom he had last met at Hampton Roads two months earlier. He began by stressing his basic conditions – union, emancipation, no armistice – but was as flexible as ever on everything else, promising liberal use of the pardoning power and restoration of confiscated property to the people of states which immediately abandoned resistance to federal authority. Prompted by Campbell, he proposed to allow a meeting of the members of the Virginia state legislature in the hope that they would take steps in that direction. In these negotiations, in fact, Lincoln was thinking not only of general peace, but of more immediate and specific objectives: to eliminate Virginia from the war (and with it all the Virginians, from Lee downwards, in the Confederate army) and to create among the leading men of the state some stabilising influence during the dangerous twilight period between war and peace. If he succeeded in the first object, he might end the war without the further costly battle which he still thought likely; if he succeeded in the second, he might ward off the collapse of law and order, the guerrilla raids and mob violence, which he feared might follow the disintegration of Confederate authority.

Events moved so rapidly in the next few days that Lincoln was driven to abandon his plan. Grant was effectively disposing of resistance in Virginia without help from political bargains or manoeuvres, and Lee's surrender on 9 April handsomely achieved Lincoln's first goal. Back in Washington, Lincoln also found his cabinet almost to a man opposed to the idea of granting any kind of recognition to a rebel state legislature, or any other move which might prejudice their own ideas on reconstruction after the war. Lincoln gave way and tried to save his face by pleading that Judge Campbell had misinterpreted him. He had no intention, he wrote on 12 April, of treating the Virginia legislature as the rightful legislature of the state; he had deliberately referred to them as 'the gentlemen who have *acted* as the Legislature of Virginia in support of the rebellion'. On the day before, he had given his last public address on reconstruction, reflecting on the many-sided nature of the problem, and hinting at some new approach to it. Two days later, at his last cabinet meeting, Lincoln seemed to show some sympathy for a tougher reconstruction policy, based on military occupation of the south.[29] Clearly, he still clung to his precious but probably declining assets of flexibility on immediate issues and non-committal on the great long-term questions. As late as 14 April it was still uncertain when he would exchange them for a more explicit policy or what that policy would be. And, that night, he put aside such cares and went to the theatre.

6. The last days of the Army of Northern Virginia were mercifully brief. Lee's superb defensive skill was one of the last Confederate bulwarks to be overwhelmed, and he extricated what remained of his army from Petersburg and Richmond with characteristic coolness and resource. But he now had only about 30,000 troops, and no reliable logistical support for them. When his weary, hungry, bedraggled men gathered at Amelia Court House, they found none of the rations which should have been awaiting them, and lost precious time while the surrounding country was scoured for what little food could be had. Their only possible escape routes were along the railroads either south-west to Danville, or west to Lynchburg – but even escape could only prolong the army's failing life a little further. In fact, Grant was already nearer to Danville than Lee, and was unlikely to waste such an advantage. Rebuffed in an attempt to move south-west, Lee decided to head west up the Appomattox river. If he could get across the river and destroy the bridges, and if supplies could be brought up the railroad from Lynchburg, he might win some brief respite. But it was a forlorn hope, and Grant's pursuit was relentless. Union cavalry raced ahead of Lee's army and nagged constantly at its left flank. Union infantry were snapping at the heels of the retreating Confederates. If Lee halted to fight off the latter, he handicapped himself in the race with the former. On 6 April, his rearguard was routed at Sayler's Creek near Farmville, and 8,000 men were lost (mainly as prisoners) to add to the hundreds who were dropping out every day through hunger, fatigue or despair. At Farmville, many of the survivors were issued with their first rations in four days. After crossing the river and destroying the bridges behind him, Lee headed for Appomattox Station, where trainloads of food and other supplies would await him. But two more blows shattered his last fragile hopes. Union troops, using a bridge further downstream, were already across the river and hotly in pursuit, and Sheridan's cavalry was soon descending upon Appomattox Station and the precious supplies. By the evening of 8 April, the trap was closing around the remnants of the Confederate army, and Grant and Lee had already exchanged messages, but failed to agree, about terms of surrender. Lee ordered one last attack against Sheridan in the early hours of 9 April, but the attackers found themselves confronting not just cavalry but two corps of Union infantry around Appomattox Station. 'Then there is nothing left me to do,' said Lee, 'but to go and see General Grant, and I would rather die a thousand deaths.' With massive dignity and decisiveness, he set his face against a suggestion that his men should scatter and resort to guerrilla war.[30] This was almost the last – but not the least – of his wartime services to his state and to the South.

Lee and Grant met in the house of one Wilmer McLean, who, four years earlier, had given up his farm near Bull Run after the first battle there, and now found himself playing host at the concluding rites of the war in Virginia. The atmosphere was strained but polite, as the two generals chatted briefly about their common experiences in the Mexican War. Grant recalled that, ever since his only previous meeting with Lee during that war, he had never forgotten the

Virginian's impressive appearance, and would have recognised him anywhere; with patrician bluntness and condescension, Lee replied that he could not recall a single feature of Grant's appearance. The main business of the meeting did not take long. Grant proposed quite simply to accept the surrender of the Army of Northern Virginia, to parole all the officers and men and allow them to return to their homes, 'not to be disturbed by United States authority so long as they observe their paroles and the laws in force where they may reside'. In this last provision, Grant had overstepped the letter of the instructions given him by Lincoln, but not the spirit. In effect, it offered an amnesty to every member of the surrendered army from privates to generals; it applied of course only to this one army, but it set a vital precedent and virtually ruled out witch hunts and treason trials involving the Confederate military leadership – for, if Lee was to be immune, who was at risk? Lee gravely accepted the terms, and acknowledged that they would have a good effect upon the men. Without changing the formal terms, Grant acceded to Lee's request that men be allowed to take home horses which they owned, to help with work on their farms. He also promised to send rations across to Lee's camp, and asked if 25,000 would suffice. Lee replied that it would be ample – a last, bleak comment on the depletion of a once mighty army.[31]

At Appomattox, the two great commanders were ill-assorted but appropriate symbols of the causes which they served. Robert E. Lee, still an imposing figure even in defeat, resplendent in fresh uniform, with sash and sword, personified Southern pride and self-respect, concern for honour, and the need to keep up appearances. The way in which something was to be done seemed to matter as much as the thing itself. 'Sam' Grant, smaller in stature, nondescript in appearance, informally dressed in a muddy uniform, almost indistinguishable from that of a private, stood for the plain unvarnished strength of the North, its common sense, its lack of pretension, its concern for the realities. The meaning of what was happening was clear enough, without any need to dress it up. The two men met again next day, and Grant urged Lee to use his influence to bring hostilities to an end throughout the south. Lee still insisted that he must defer to the civil authority, although that authority, in the person of Jefferson Davis, was now a fugitive; according to his own account, he also turned down a suggestion that he should go to Washington to meet Lincoln.[32] When the Army of Northern Virginia formally laid down its arms on 12 April, both commanders had already departed, Lee for his home in Richmond, Grant for City Point and then Washington. They had virtually, though not completely, brought the war to an end, and the note of reconciliation and plain sense which they had struck mellowed the jubilation of the North and softened the anguish of the South. It seemed a good omen, but a thunderbolt was about to shatter this brief interlude of sanity and hope.

There had long been concern about Lincoln's personal safety, but he had brushed aside such fears. Now the president who had survived four years of civil war and who had just walked unscathed through the streets of the rebel capital was to be struck down in the hour of victory, in a Washington theatre, only a few blocks from the White House itself. For many months, John Wilkes Booth had been hatching a plot to kidnap the president and carry him off to the south where he could be used as a bargaining counter to win concessions which the Confederacy could not gain by force of arms. Son and brother of renowned actors, Booth was something of a failed actor himself. Vain, unstable, unquenchable in his thirst for attention and acclaim, he concocted a drama of his own which would satisfy both his personal frustrations and his impassioned zeal for the Confederate cause. From among Confederate sympathisers in Washington and surrounding parts of Maryland, he recruited a supporting cast of drifters, misfits and unfortunates. But the collapse of the Confederacy in the early spring of 1865 undermined his original plan, and he turned swiftly to the idea of assassinating Lincoln, Seward, Vice-President Johnson and other prominent leaders.

It was no accident, surely, but rather the intended fulfilment of the craving for attention which burned in his diseased mind, that he chose the theatre to act out his self-appointed role as avenger. (True to his reputation he was to mar his last appearance by bungling and over-acting.) On the night of Good Friday, 14 April, the president and Mrs Lincoln were watching a performance of *Our American Cousin* at Ford's Theatre; General and Mrs Grant were to have accompanied them but made their excuses. John Wilkes Booth made his way unchallenged into the presidential box, and shot Lincoln in the back of the head. He leaped on to the stage but fell heavily and broke his shin. Shouting 'Sic semper tyrannis' (a phrase which was *inter alia* the motto of the state of Virginia), he hobbled from the theatre and rode out of the city. The mortally wounded president was carried to a house across the street where he lingered through the night. It soon became known that one of Booth's collaborators had gained access to Seward's house where the Secretary of State was already in bed, recovering from a serious carriage accident, and had inflicted further terrible wounds upon him, and his son, in a brutal but clumsy attempt to slash him to death. A third conspirator set out to kill Andrew Johnson, but lost his nerve and got no further than the bar of the hotel where the vice-president stayed. What had actually happened was hideous enough, but on that night of horror wild rumour and hysteria ran through the streets far ahead of hard facts. The euphoria of the days after Appomattox gave way to dread of a new and terrible phase in the history of the conflict.

Shortly before 7.30 on the morning of Saturday 15 April, Abraham Lincoln died, and the tolling of church bells carried the news across the city. The peace which Lincoln had now found threatened the peace which he had sought for the nation. Thoughts of charity for all were swept aside by demands for vengeance and retribution. The president's assassin had been quickly identified but it was to be nearly two weeks before he was tracked down, and shot dead while resisting arrest. Meanwhile, as his wretched collaborators were arrested one by one, popular opinion – and many of those in high places too – shifted from the suspicion to the near certainty that this pathetic band and their deluded leader could not on their own have committed an act of such enormity. Surely some great and sinister conspiracy lurked behind so foul a deed and fevered imaginations produced a crop of theories to explain it. The most widely believed was that Jefferson Davis and his henchmen had resorted to assassination in a last desperate bid to escape the consequences of military defeat. Secretary of War Stanton who had seized the reins of power in the moment of crisis was not above fostering this idea. Ironically, Stanton himself was soon to be cast by others as the lynch-pin of an alleged radical plot to remove Lincoln as the great obstacle to a tough and drastic programme of reconstruction. An even more unlikely candidate for the role of arch fiend was Andrew Johnson, who, dazed and bewildered through he was in the first days of his new and awesome responsibility, was regarded in some quarters as having the most obvious motive for disposing of Lincoln. He was also, of course, a Southerner who could easily be transformed into the leader of a Confederate fifth column in the federal capital. Feeling in the north seemed to demand an explanation which would match the dimensions of both the deed itself and its possible consequences. It regarded as an insult to the dead president and the cause he had led the notion that it was all the work of a second-rate actor determined to strut upon the stage in a role so unique that no one could ignore him.

The wonder was indeed, not that the North was briefly unhinged by so terrible a shock at such a time, but that sanity and stability returned so soon. The orgy of emotion which surrounded the dead president on his last, protracted journey back to Springfield may have had a cathartic effect. Certainly the work so quickly begun by the clergy of transforming a man of ordinary humanity as well as extraordinary gifts into a mixture of martyr, saint and hero, helped to satisfy a deep emotional need. It reached its climax in the elaborate analogies between Lincoln and Christ, in their humble origins, their simplicity, their message of charity and reconciliation – and above all their cruel martyrdom on Good Friday. But if Lincoln was a martyr, his martyrdom was to serve many causes in the months and years to come, from hatred and vengeance against the South to white supremacy and the protective tariff. Perhaps the more realistic analogy between Lincoln and Christ is a much harsher one, between the deeds perpetrated in the names of both by those who claimed to be their followers. Booth's associates were hastily arraigned before a military tribunal, which condemned four to death (including one woman, the widow Surratt, against whom the evidence was sketchy) and others, some of whom were but marginally involved, to long terms of imprisonment.[33]

The American system of government successfully survived its first challenge by presidential assassination. The peace heralded at Appomattox, and imperilled at Ford's Theatre, was in fact concluded in the days that followed – though not without at least one further crisis. On 17 April, as Sherman set out to discuss terms for the surrender of Johnston's army in North Carolina, he heard the news of Lincoln's death, and pondered the possibility of a violent reaction from his men. When Johnston was informed of the assassination, he spoke of it as a calamity for South as well as North. Johnston was in close touch with Jefferson Davis and members of his cabinet, then sheltering at Greensboro, and, largely at their instigation, he proposed to Sherman not the surrender of his army, following the pattern of Appomattox, but the ending of hostilities throughout the south by what amounted to a peace treaty. Sherman, of course, had no authority to negotiate any such thing, but the mutual respect which he and Johnston had long entertained for one another rapidly bloomed into cordiality as the talks continued, and he abandoned his early caution. Sherman had always been an apostle not only of hard war but gentle peace, and now, too, he was probably fired by a desire to carry out the wishes of the dead president as he understood them. Still fresh in his mind was his meeting with Lincoln at City Point just three weeks earlier when the president had talked repeatedly of his wish for a liberal and generous peace, his fear of anarchy and chaos in the south – and, apparently, his willingness to deal with the Southern state legislatures as a *de facto* authority to meet this threat. Sherman was not the only man to see one brief stretch of the flowing (and winding) stream of Lincoln's thoughts on peace and reconstruction, to freeze it into immobility, and then to treat it as the only part which mattered.

It was one thing for Sherman to make his own assessment, right or wrong, of Lincoln's intentions; it was another for him to assume the power to act upon it. He now demonstrated that his oft-professed contempt for politics and politicians was matched by his own naïveté in matters which called for political skill and judgment. At a second meeting on 18 April, Sherman and Johnston drew up and signed a peace convention to be submitted to their respective heads of government. (Meanwhile the contending armies would observe a truce.) It provided that the disbanded Confederate troops should proceed to their state capitals and deposit their arms there, for use in maintaining law and order in the states; it proposed to recognise the existing state governments when their members took an oath of loyalty; it guaranteed the personal, political and property rights of the people of the Southern states, and offered virtually a general amnesty.[34] Jefferson Davis accepted the terms, although his approval meant little. But this new 'treaty' was greeted with outrage by the government in Washington. Apart from Sherman's original sin of exceeding his authority, everything about his agreement was wrong. Its terms were even more unacceptable to the cabinet than they would assuredly have been to Lincoln himself. The convention provided for an armistice which Lincoln had always ruled out; it went much too far towards recognition of the rebel state governments and even the Confederate government itself – after four years' endeavour to avoid any such thing; it dispersed arms throughout the south and thus seemed to invite a resort to guerrilla warfare, or local resistance movements; it had no business to dwell on matters of political and property rights, and, by doing so, it could even be interpreted as resurrecting the right of property in slaves. Stanton, very much the strong man of the cabinet at this time, led his colleagues in delivering a massive rebuke to Sherman and ordered him to give notice of termination of the truce. Grant endorsed the terms of the rebuke, but hastened to Sherman's headquarters at Raleigh to soften the blow as it fell on his most faithful lieutenant. New negotiations were started, and Johnston, bowing to the inevitable, surrendered his army on 26 April on terms similar to those agreed between Grant and Lee. But the storm over Sherman's action was not yet over. Stanton was never a man to let things go easily, and he feared the trouble which Sherman could yet cause, in view of his popularity as the hero of the moment, and the eagerness of the Democrats to 'capture' him if they could. Now, Stanton made public the grounds for rejection of Sherman's agreement, and he did so in unsparing and insulting terms. The general had never been renowned for sweetness of temper, and he replied in kind to all who cared to listen. The first days of victory and peace, then, were disfigured not merely by the foul blot of Lincoln's murder but by smaller blemishes like this feud between two of the major architects of the triumph of the North.

After Johnston's surrender, the organised Confederate forces still scattered across the south were almost bound to follow suit, but the process still took time. Richard Taylor surrendered most of the remaining troops east of the Mississippi at Citronelle, near Mobile, on 4 May. Troops in Florida and Arkansas formally abandoned the struggle in the next two weeks, and Kirby Smith surrendered the trans-Mississippi forces on 26 May, forty-seven days after Appomattox. The war which started six weeks after Lincoln's presidency began, ended six weeks after it was so abruptly terminated.

Jefferson Davis was almost the last Confederate to accept the inevitability of defeat. At Danville, his first stop after the evacuation of Richmond, he issued a stirring call to the people of the South. In North Carolina he tried to instil new fighting spirit into Johnston and his men, and talked of conditions for peace as though he could still negotiate on equal terms. As he moved on, he still dreamed of rousing a new spirit of defiance in the deep south. But Union cavalry were now hot on his trail – although Lincoln had admitted a few weeks earlier that he would feel relieved if Davis made good his escape from the country. On 10 May, the cavalry caught Davis, his wife and a few faithful followers at Irwinville, Georgia. He was removed to Fortress Monroe in Virginia where he was held for the next two years.[35]

In April 1861, Edmund Ruffin, ardent Virginian secessionist, burned with the ambition to fire the first cannon in the bombardment of Fort Sumter. On 17 June 1865, the same Edmund Ruffin wrote a note saying that he preferred death to life under the government of the United States, placed the muzzle of his musket in his mouth, pressed the trigger with the aid of a stick, and blew his brains out. If he did not succeed in firing the first shot in the war for Southern independence, he almost certainly fired the last.

7. The Civil War ended in piecemeal fashion, but the finality of the events of April–May 1865 is none the less impressive. On the Southern side there was no

descent into a period of guerrilla raids, ambushes and savage irregular warfare, and, for that, not a little credit belongs to the wise counsel and dignified example of Robert E. Lee. On the Northern side there was no attempt to wreak vengeance or spread terror, no resort to massacres or mass executions or concentration camps or wholesale trials for treason or war crimes. Even the provocation of Lincoln's murder only momentarily inflamed the North enough for it to entertain such notions. Jefferson Davis was held in custody for two years, but never tried or punished, and eventually released to enjoy a peaceful retirement as a citizen of those United States which he had sought to disrupt. Other Southern leaders, from Vice-President Stephens downwards, were arrested but released much more quickly; others again escaped abroad, like the resilient Judah P. Benjamin who made a new and lucrative career for himself at the bar in London. Four people went to the gallows for their part in the assassination, after a trial which was no great advertisement for American justice. William Wirz, commandant of the Andersonville prisoner-of-war camp, was also hanged after another trial which left something to be desired. Even one execution after a less than fair trial is one too many, but such a tally after four years of bitter strife was astonishingly small. For any war, but above all a civil war, the mildness and restraint of the victors in the hour of triumph was quite exceptional. For this forbearance, much credit belongs to the precedent set by Grant at Appomattox, to the example left by the slain president – and even perhaps to the clumsy efforts of Sherman, the wartime destroyer now anxious to fulfil his promise at Atlanta in 1864:

> When peace does come, you may call on me for anything. Then will I share with you the last cracker, and watch with you to shield your homes and families against danger from every quarter.[36]

Most revealing of all, perhaps, of the prevailing mood was the breathtaking speed of military demobilisation. After the parades and celebrations of May, a volunteer army of 1,000,000 men was dispersed so rapidly that only 200,000 remained by November 1865, only 11,000 a year later. The regular army never dwindled to pre-Sumter levels, but was reduced to 50,000 eighteen months after the fighting ended. This was a modest force to confront the looming problems of peace.

The purpose of war, Sherman had always argued, was to make peace. But he also believed that the struggle should 'inspire respect on which to build up our nation's power'. The mere act of desisting from war did not solve the problem of reconciling these two objectives. Fighting stopped, the Union survived, slavery was dead. But what kind of Union, what kind of peace, what kind of future for the ex-slave was to follow? Sherman might despise the politicians, but politics was the only way to continue the business of war by other means. It would be as false to say that the war had settled everything as that it had settled nothing.

8. So obvious were the advantages of the North and so great the handicaps of the South that the temptation is to ask not why did the Confederacy lose, but how did it endure for four years against such odds. But that temptation should be resisted. The evidence of the massive numerical and material superiority of the North does not require reiteration here. Obvious enough to many observers at the time, it has been thrown into sharper focus by hindsight, and buttressed by an elaborate array of statistics. Because the Northern advantage is both undeniable and quantifiable, it is too easily regarded as irresistible. But wars, and especially wars of rebellion, have been fought and won against equal or greater odds, and a result which may look inevitable in retrospect may well have looked anything but certain in prospect. Indeed, for more than two years after Sumter, it would have taken a brave man to assume that eventual Union victory was beyond doubt. Superiority in manpower and industrial resources should be the starting-point but not the conclusion of the explanation of Northern victory.

It is revealing that, while most later commentators see the balance as heavily weighted in favour of the North from the beginning, the bulk of contemporary opinion in 1861 took the opposite view. Not only Southerners, but many Northerners and the great majority of outside observers, believed that there was little or no chance that the Union could be restored by coercion. History, geography and logic lent support to such a view. The Southern states could surely do in the 1860s what the thirteen colonies had done in the 1770s. In contemporary Europe, empires with more expertise and experience than Lincoln's America in the business of repression, were hard-pressed to resist the forces of separatism, and the emergence of new nations. The huge geographical area of the Confederacy looked like a secure insurance against conquest, as long as the will to resist remained. It stretched credibility to predict that the government and people of the North, having failed to preserve the Union by compromise, would spend their treasure and the lives of hundreds of thousands of young men to hold the recalcitrant South within the Union by superior force. But this was not all; the South had an advantage which, it seemed, could offset or even outweigh the North's greater strength, in that the nature of the task which it faced was far more limited. It had no need to vanquish its foe, but merely to convince him that the South itself could not be vanquished. It was required neither to eject an oppressor from its soil nor to occupy the land of its adversary, but merely to prove that the independence which it had claimed by secession was a reality which had to be accepted.

In such a situation, Northern material and numerical preponderance was a potential, but far from an inevitable, winner. To convert its potential into actual performance required application and perseverance, intelligence and will. Motivation and morale are not separate questions from numbers and resources but the key to their proper and successful deployment. Where morale has been discussed in the context of the eventual outcome of the war, far too much attention has usually been paid to the South to the exclusion of the North. When the conflict began in 1861, Southern motivation seemed clearer and stronger, and yet it was Northern morale which proved more durable. The strength of Northern will was the crucial factor in the war precisely because it was the chief object of Southern attack. The South would win its independence if and when it could break the Northern will to save the Union. That will faltered often, but it never failed, in face of one setback and frustration after another, and the mounting horrors of war on a scale unimaginable in 1861.

Why then did the resolution of the North prevail? It was helped, no doubt, by the ample cushions which protected it against the shock of defeats and disappointments. Among these, prosperity must take a high place. After an uncertain start in the first years of the war, most people in the north – farmers, businessmen, manufacturers and even many workers – were buoyed up by a sense of material well-being, a belief, often but not always sustained by the facts, that they were doing well and had every prospect of doing better. The kind of wartime inflation which affected the north had its dangers, and its victims, but in many ways it was a lubricant of economic and social well-being, in the short run at least – and in the longer run the war was over. In the south, by contrast, runaway inflation ravaged not merely the economic war effort, but the sense of reality and the will to resist. In the north, the cushioning effect of prosperity was matched by the comforting awareness that so much of normal everyday life went on, despite what was happening on the battlefields of Virginia and Tennessee. Only the dreadful casualty lists brought the war home, but, in this respect, of course, the South suffered even more, in proportion to its total population. The quiet routine of small-town life, the gaudier pleasures of the large cities, the excitement of new ventures in oil or gold or silver, were little affected by the war. The North fought the Civil War, as the United States fought its twentieth-century wars, almost at one remove, free, with few exceptions, of danger from shot and shell, invaders or marauders, or even shortages, and sacrifices on the home front. Nothing could have been further from the experience of people in many parts of the Confederacy who bore the full brunt of war and its horrors, the destruction of their homes and the disruption of their lives.

To sustain morale and contain discontent, few things were more important than leadership – in both the individual and institutional senses of the term. Attention has already been drawn to the vastly superior political machinery of the Union – above all in its party system, and its capacity to manage internal conflict. Opposition was vigorous and uninhibited, but it came from men who aspired one day to become the government themselves, and not from men who were against that government on principle and its leaders out of personal spite. In a war where deficiencies of organisation hampered both sides, the North had priceless advantages at least in its political and administrative structure. Whether in raising men, supplying armies, running railroads, raising money, attracting popular support, allaying anxieties, or ordering its priorities, the North wrestled more effectively with tasks which were, admittedly, less unmanageable. For the South, what David Potter says of finance could apply equally to all the other problems: 'While no government could have averted these evils, almost any government could have done more than the Confederacy did.'[37]

At every level of government and political life, the North had a distinct edge in the quality of the men and the machinery involved. There were no Confederate equivalents to Seward, Chase and Stanton at cabinet level, or to the able men who were to be found at lower levels of most government departments in Washington. More surprisingly, perhaps, the personnel of the Confederate Congress never matched up to the formidable and skilful (if contentious) legislators in Washington. Stranger still, the Southern state governors as a group scarcely rivalled the remarkably energetic and resourceful men who occupied the governors' mansions in the Northern state capitals – Morton of Indiana, Andrew of Massachusetts, Curtin of Pennsylvania and several others. At every level, the North, the side which was setting out to conserve an existing system, proved in practice to be the more flexible, dynamic, positive, and at times inventive. The South, setting out to create a new government, proved to be inflexible, traditional, negative and sterile.

This apparent paradox may offer a clue to Southern political weakness and its effect upon morale. The Confederate leaders were men of profound conservatism who found themselves in control of a rebellion, if not a revolution. Their dilemma crippled their leadership and eventually helped to undermine their cause. The most conspicuous example is provided by Jefferson Davis himself, fixed in his ways, conventional in his outlook, reluctant to forgive a critic or forget a grievance, torn between deeply-ingrained beliefs and novel situations demanding unprecedented solutions. Legalistic and self-righteous, passionately devoted to the Confederate cause, he could never finally make up his mind between the purity of that cause and the practical requirements for its survival. In consequence, he was never able to reach out to the whole Southern people, to articulate their war aims in words of genuine inspiration. Plagued by carping critics, he would at least have shamed them, if they were capable of shame, by the devoted way in which he gave all which he had to offer to the service of the Confederacy. It was still not enough, and, in its search for a man to serve as personal symbol of its cause, the South turned more and more to Robert E. Lee.

It has always been Davis's double misfortune to be compared on the one hand with Lee and on the other with Lincoln. But it is worth recalling that the latter comparison would have seemed to most people in 1861 to be strongly in Davis's favour. Like the unsuspected strength of the popular will, Lincoln proved to be another of the unexpected assets of the Union cause – and the two phenomena were not unconnected. Unlike Davis, he proved that he could operate skilfully and flexibly at several different levels, whether dealing with the politicians or the people, principles or priorities. The Lincoln who could speak with such simple grandeur of the last, best hope of earth, who could define the war issues in the inimitable words of the Gettysburg address, and who could promise charity for all and malice toward none, was the same man who could administer stinging rebukes to generals like McClellan and Hooker, who could indulge in sharp horse-trading over the release of Vallandigham, who could wriggle like an eel in the tactical battle over emancipation or reconstruction, and who could collect his pound of flesh from office-holders, and his thousands of votes from the soldiers, to win re-election in 1864. He combined a profound feeling for the deeper currents of his time with ingenuity and resilience in the day-to-day business of presidential politics. Preferring to proceed by small steps, he never forgot his destination, nor willingly restricted his choice of routes. Unlike Davis, he also had a keen appreciation of what really mattered and what did not. Of all democratic leaders of his or any other day, he best preserved the common touch, and was least afflicted with pomposity, self-importance or hypersensitivity. All these qualities went into the make-up of one who has been described by an eminent medieval historian as 'the man who, above all others in modern times, has gone far to solve the deep moral problems underlying the exercise of power over others'.[38] Although no one felt the agony and anguish of war more deeply than Lincoln, he also possessed the iron resolution of a great war leader. He sustained the Union cause in its darkest moments, and freed the slaves in such a way as to underpin rather than undermine it. He became, warts and all, the living embodiment of that cause, whereas Jefferson Davis was more like a marble monument to his.

In military as in political leadership, the North eventually showed a resilience, a flexibility and a breadth of comprehension which the South could not match. Such a judgment would have seemed unthinkable in 1861 or 1862, and the battlefield brilliance of Lee and Jackson was never surpassed. But the North excelled in the seven-eighths of the military iceberg which never surfaced on the field of battle itself – in supply and organisation, and in the relationship of military matters to the grand strategy which embraced much else besides. An organising genius behind the scenes, like Montgomery Meigs, had more value, if less glamour, than a swashbuckling cavalry leader like Jeb Stuart, especially in the kind of conflict which the Civil War became. (It is revealing that the military arm in which the Confederacy most clearly excelled was the cavalry, which was now rapidly losing much of its old glory and its old importance.) Grant and Sherman had a broad conception of the business of war in the 1860s, not merely in its geographical compass, but in its psychological impact, and its relation to non-military considerations. They were prepared to throw overboard conventional but outmoded methods of waging war, and their relentless pursuit of their goals made them, like their president, the personification of Northern resolution.

For all their stunning brilliance and superb courage, Lee and Jackson gradually came to look old-fashioned and narrow by comparison. Their achievements together inspired the South in the first half of the war, and Lee alone kept it alive in the second, as the odds against him, always daunting, became overwhelming. But they were the last great exponents of a dying school; they won the kind of battles which were not to decide this kind of war. The Lee of Second

Manassas and Chancellorsville was also the Lee who belittled the danger to Vicksburg in 1863, who insisted on his own offensive (which ended at Gettysburg) rather than reinforce the vital Tennessee front, and who resisted suggestions that key workers should be spared from the army for absolutely vital jobs in industry or on the railroads. His praise of McClellan as, by all odds, the best of his opponents, is as much a reflection on Lee's conception of the war as a commendation of 'Little Mac's' skill in waging it. By his nobility of character as well as his magnificent record, Lee became a personal symbol of his cause, but one that was almost too appropriate. He was the final embodiment and idealisation of the cause of states rights, rooted in the basic instinct to defend one's hearth and home. He left the Union army not to be the standard bearer of the new Confederacy or the champion of slavery, but to fight for Virginia, in Virginia. His whole system of ideals and loyalties precluded him from the kind of broad strategic approach developed by Grant and Sherman. Lee stood for all that was best in the Confederacy, but he also shared some of its fatal flaws.

There is another paradox about Robert E. Lee which exemplifies a wider dilemma of the whole South. For all his audacity and agility, he excelled above all in defence, or in counter-thrusts launched from defence. He was arguably the best defensive commander on either side in the Civil War, especially on the evidence of his record in 1864. His most brilliant attacking thrusts were swift reactions to enemy plans, as in the moves which led to Second Bull Run in 1862, or his greatest battlefield success at Chancellorsville in 1863. He was, in boxing parlance, a counter-puncher, and he was at his least effective in carrying the fight to the enemy on his own initiative, as in the Gettysburg campaign (or even the Seven Days), or in formulating overall strategy at the highest level. This peculiarity of Lee's personal record closely parallels the Confederate difficulty in deciding whether a war which did not require conquest of the enemy or occupation of his territory was to be most effectively waged by a purely defensive strategy. For all his defensive skill, Lee was reluctant to settle for a wholly defensive war. In this he was probably right, but he was weakest when it came to formulating and executing an alternative policy. Certainly, if the war became a matter of attrition and endurance, the North had all the material advantages, and could only lose through a failure of morale. This was in fact precisely the situation which prevailed in the whole period after Gettysburg and Vicksburg in July 1863.

In political life and in the social order, as in military strategy, the Confederacy faced but never solved this same problem of reconciling means and ends. The efforts to define goals, decide upon methods and relate the one to the other bred contradictions and inconsistencies which, in their turn, corroded Southern morale. In a word, the South helped to defeat itself by the very nature of the things for which it stood, and the impossibility of protecting them intact while prosecuting a war. The seeds of Confederate collapse were present from birth not so much in the shape of inferior resources as through inner tensions and contradictions. Secession was launched on a wave of enthusiasm, but many of its devotees were fair-weather friends, and many more regarded it as a device to win better terms within the Union rather than a proclamation of full independence – and certainly not as a prelude to four years of war and destruction. States rights, elevated from a tactic to a dogma, degenerated into a disease which sapped the strength of the new Confederacy at war. Devotion to a distinctively American (and Southern) brand of democracy, blended of intense individualism, localism, and resentment of any kind of restraint, deprived the South of the bare minimum of regulation and coordination required by a struggle for survival. The idea of Southern nationalism had not put down deep enough roots, and it rubbed too harshly against states rights and individual freedom, to sustain the Confederacy in its time of trial. The superior virtues claimed for the Southern agrarian way of life needed to be compromised, or sacrificed to the ruthless demands of war; to defeat the North, the South would have to become more like the North. The cotton crop which was to be the economic foundation of the new Confederacy, and its passport to world recognition, proved to be an irrelevance to the business of war and a worthless substitute for a proper foreign policy. The barriers against outside influences erected by the ante-bellum South led to fatal misunderstanding of the outside world; the Confederacy which set such store by foreign recognition had no realistic idea how to obtain it.

Above all, slavery, the very cornerstone of the Southern Confederacy, proved to be its severest handicap. It meant that over one-third of Southern manpower was deemed unusable for fighting (until it was too late) while the outnumbered white soldiers of the Confederacy eventually faced almost 200,000 Negroes in the ranks of the enemy. It created fears of servile insurrection and unmentionable horrors at home, while so many white men were away at the front. It deprived the Confederacy of a mass of outside sympathy and support, and blocked the path to European recognition. Perhaps most insidious of all – but hardest to evaluate – was its corrosive effect on Southern morale and self-confidence. If it is accepted that the vehemence of the Southern defence of slavery owed much to feelings of shame and guilt, and suppressed doubts about its defensibility, then clearly the strain and cost of a terrible war must have intensified the questioning, and aggravated uneasy consciences. It was one thing to wreck political parties, constitutional compromises and even the Union itself in order to protect slavery; it was another to destroy the lives of countless young men, and suffer the devastation of much of the homeland in the same unworthy and increasingly hopeless cause. It has even been suggested that many Southerners, unable to rid themselves of the incubus of slavery, secretly welcomed its destruction by an outside agency.[39] Certainly, slavery was central to both the creation and the collapse of the Confederacy. It was the diseased heart of the Southern cause.

The North, too, had its internal tensions, its moral ambiguity over slavery and the Negro, its constitutional wrangles, its critics of excessive centralised authority, its international problems and domestic crises. But their dimensions were more modest, the compensating advantages were greater – and there was the leadership and the machinery to cope with the difficulties. With very few exceptions, the people of the north shared a positive faith in the Union. With rather more exceptions, they came to accept that the abolition of slavery was a vital contribution to both the survival and the quality of that Union. After many blunders and reverses, their political and military leaders evolved a grand strategy to fight the kind of war which the North could win and the South could not – an all-out trial of strength and will, in which outsiders were kept on the sidelines.

The North succeeded in creating the conditions where its superior resources could be effective. It maintained its own commitment to the struggle, through a combination of strong and skilful leadership, the resilience of its society and its institutions, and the successful marriage of means and ends. It excelled the Confederacy on each of these counts. Finally, it has to be said that the level of morale and the strength of a commitment depend upon the quality of the cause – and the North had the better cause, the greater ideological strength, the less damaging moral flaws.

It remained to be seen whether the qualities which won the war could also win the peace which followed.

# Part Five : Aftermath

# Chapter XIX : The Struggle to Win the Peace

In the spring of 1865 the South lay at the feet of the conqueror. One-quarter of its white manhood had perished during the war. Many more, the halt and the lame and the weary, were making their slow way home through the ruin and desolation of broad stretches of their land. The ugly wounds on the corpse of the Confederacy were there for all to see, from the battered ruins of Richmond to the charred remains of Columbia, from the broken bridges and twisted railroad track, to the burnt-out farms and abandoned homes. Hideous though they were, the external scars were but the mark of deeper wounds – the fatherless families, broken lives, and shattered hopes, the collapse of familiar authority and leadership, the plight of the destitute, the refugees, and the homeless, the destruction of a whole way of life. Now white Southerners faced a constant and inescapable reminder of their defeat and its consequences in the presence in their midst of nearly four million black Americans newly delivered from bondage. To the harsh realities of the ruined South was added the nightmare dread of black vengeance. The death of slavery had deprived the South of its basic instrument for the regulation of racial and social relationships. It had also taken from it, without compensation or qualification, a massive investment in 'property', and its traditional labour force. There was, it is fair to add, a less bleak side to the story. If parts of the south had been devastated, larger areas had escaped the ravages of war, and suffered from no more than shortages and neglect. If slave labour was gone, the ex-slaves were still there, and sooner rather than later the freed Negro would need work, and would have to find it not far from his old slave home. If an old pattern of race relations had been destroyed, there were incredibly few signs of black violence or vindictiveness against former masters. The South still retained its traditional basic resources of land and labour, even if the one was scarred and the other was freed; it still retained, too, the will to assert white supremacy. To exploit the first, it needed outsiders to provide capital and expertise and other assistance; to achieve the latter it required no more than that outsiders should turn a blind eye. In the years to come, the white South was to achieve more success than it could have dared to hope in 1865 in re-establishing its old sway and its old ways. But, in the shadow of Appomattox, it could do no more than await the will of the victorious North, and the decisions of those who ruled the restored Union. It had little choice but to accept them.

The Negroes, too, waited to see what came next. If Southern whites accepted the abolition of slavery, they expected emancipation to be the end of that particular story, and hoped that they would be left alone to handle a delicate matter which, they believed, they knew and understood best. If Southern blacks were to make anything real and permanent of their new freedom, they would need sustained intervention on their behalf, and such action would require a whole new conception of federal responsibility in time of peace. In the first days of their liberty, many ex-slaves took to the road, and wandered from their old homes, often with no specific objective in mind, but simply as a demonstration to the world and to themselves of their freedom. But most soon returned, and began to face the enduring and often uncomfortable realities of their new status. The Negroes were far from silent and passive onlookers at the debate over their own future. In organising various Negro conventions during 1865, and formulating declarations of their rights and their needs, black leaders put their case forcefully and at times unanswerably. What convincing reply could there be to the contrast which they pointed out between the early restoration of the vote to white men who had been resisting the Union a few months earlier, and the denial of the franchise to black men who had fought in their scores of thousands on the Union side? It was a cliché of the day, avowed alike by well-disposed whites and many black leaders, that the only way to learn freedom was to be free. But, in practice, the freed Negro desperately needed guarantees of his rights, he desperately craved the opportunity of education, and most desperately of all he needed work and he needed land. The blessings of liberty were nothing without the means of earning a living. As he tested the meaning of his liberation, the freedman, like his former master, looked to the North for the decisions which would shape his future.

1. A mood of uncertainty prevailed in the north. The wartime political battles over reconstruction had been inconclusive and often confusing. The death of Lincoln had added to the sense of doubt and misgiving. In his second inaugural, he had urged the nation 'to finish the work we are in', but the end of the war and the assassination of the president had left more doubt than ever as to what precisely that work was, or should be. Now, while some Northerners retained

the will and the energy to complete the unfinished business of building a new Union, many others were only too anxious to believe that the job was done, and to return to the normal peacetime pursuits of making a living and minding their own business. Millions of Northerners wanted a chance to put first the interests of their families, their local community, and themselves, and were prepared to let the wider world take care of itself. If they bothered their heads about national affairs at all, they were inclined to worry more about tariffs and subsidies, the banks and the currency, rather than disorders in the deep south or the plight of the freed slave. Of course they wanted to enjoy the fruits of victory, but they did not want to labour any longer to bring in the harvest. Those Northerners, on the other hand, who saw the need for further toil before the harvest was safely gathered would have to overcome not merely the sullen obstructionism of the vanquished, but the apathy and indifference of many of the victors.

Amid so much uncertainty, there were some fundamental things which were beyond dispute. The Civil War had exorcised the twin evil spirits of secession and slavery which had plagued the United States throughout its existence. The conclusiveness of the Union victory not merely eliminated this particular attempt to secede but disposed once and for all of secession as a usable weapon in the armoury of the discontented. Although the process of wartime emancipation had been tortuous enough to sadden the idealists and strengthen the sceptics, the Thirteenth Amendment, ratified in 1865, lacked nothing in uncompromising finality. Slavery was dead and the Union was very much alive. But when the question moved on to what kind of Union it should be, and what was to be the place of the South and of the Negro within it, certainty and consensus at once evaporated.

The most obvious question concerned the basis upon which the former rebel states were to be fully restored to the Union. Arguments over whether they had ever been out of the Union, and over their status as territories or conquered provinces or whatever, still continued but became increasingly academic. The practical question concerned the establishment of secure, loyal and acceptable state governments in the south, when it was hardly to be expected that a majority of the white population could be weaned from its rebel sympathies overnight. Upon the answer depended the future prospects of the Union, the Negro and the Republican party. The available solutions were still much as they had been during the war: exclusion of ex-Confederates from the political process, building on the foundations of white loyalism, and creation of a new political structure on the basis of political rights for the Negro freedmen. The choice of weapons was closely related to the objects envisaged, and to the assessment of what conditions in the south made possible, and opinion in the north made tolerable. Should the process of restoration be fast or slow? Should it be made easy or difficult? Was the object to reunite the states with as little upheaval as possible, or was it to destroy the old Southern ruling class, achieve a massive redistribution of property, and elevate the ex-slave to full political and social equality?

Each of the possible courses of action had its dangers and weaknesses. To bar Confederate leaders from voting and office-holding seemed no more than common sense; but how far down the ladder of civil and military leadership should such exclusion go, and would it not deprive the Southern states of the only effective and acknowledged leadership which they had? The protection of Southern white Unionists was surely both a proper reward for past services and a wise provision for the future. But was there still any hope of creating viable régimes in the south on the basis of loyal white support, or had the experience of the war years already demonstrated the futility of such a policy? Lincoln's patient efforts to build up a white Republican or Union party in the south had borne disappointingly meagre fruit. He had combined his efforts in this direction with increasing pressure for at least limited Negro suffrage, but the white Unionists of the South showed little disposition to share their rights and privileges with their newly freed black neighbours. If loyal régimes in the Southern states were to have a substantial numerical base, it seemed necessary, indeed inevitable, that the new governments should rest more on black than on white votes. But could the adoption of such a policy survive the embarrassment which it would create for many of its supporters in the north, and the indignation which it would arouse in its opponents in both north and south? Charles Sumner, purest of radicals, had come round during the war to the view that the only good and true answer lay in the removal of all racial qualifications for the franchise, but even he deemed it wise, in the election year of 1864, not to shout such a proposition from the rooftops. Such was the sensitivity of Northern opinion on the subject that many Republicans, radicals as well as moderates, approached the matter very warily, even in 1865 and 1866.

At this point, the question of the basis of the new state governments merges into the other, even more fundamental, debate over the purposes and methods of reconstruction. How far was the federal government (and the Republican party) to go in the attempt to guarantee the rights of the Negro as citizen and voter, and ensure him a fair opportunity to earn his own livelihood? Most Southerners, allowing the wish, perhaps, to be father to the thought, assumed that matters concerning citizenship, civil rights and the franchise would remain, as they had always been, the concern of the individual states. There were not a few Northerners who agreed with them. Moderate Republican opinion still clung to nice distinctions between the civil rights of the Negro for which the federal government must accept responsibility, the social rights which were beyond the power of any law to enforce or government to protect, and the political rights which lay somewhere between – and presumably still in the province of the states. Conservative and moderate opinion fought shy altogether of the massive interference with property rights which would be entailed in any attempt to provide land for the Negro by confiscation of rebel estates. But such middle-of-the-road views increasingly begged the vital questions, and eventually faced a choice between a new assertion of federal power or acceptance of political defeat at the hands of those who had just been militarily defeated. Even radical

Republican opinion was divided on many of these crucial matters, and certainly not all shared Thaddeus Stevens's belief in confiscation and redistribution of land, or even his conviction that the government of the United States was not a white man's government, but a government of all men alike. But radicals did contemplate the emphatic use of federal power to provide certain basic guarantees for the Negro and to put the old leaders of the South in their place.

Clearly, those who were prepared to fight for equal rights and opportunities for the black American would have to wage a war on two fronts. They faced the serried ranks of the Southern defenders of white supremacy, but they were also threatened from the rear by that Northern Negrophobia which was to complicate and confuse reconstruction as it had earlier bedevilled emancipation. Most Northern, and especially north-western, states still retained their formal and informal barriers against racial equality and integration. When the war ended, all but six of the Northern states still denied the vote to their black citizens, and in the immediate post-war years the electorates of several of them reaffirmed their hostility to Negro suffrage. The 1868 platform of the Republican party demanded Negro suffrage in the south, but left the matter to the individual states in the north. Most white men in the north as in the south took for granted the natural inferiority of the Negro and the *de facto* segregation which had always been woven into the pattern of their lives. The fear of a massive influx of freedmen into the north which had troubled so many minds at the time of emancipation survived into the years after Appomattox. Indeed, one of the grounds on which justice for the freedmen was publicly defended was precisely that, if they were given fair and reasonable treatment in the south they would stay there, and not trouble the good citizens of the north.[1] The evolution of Republican policy in the post-war years can only make sense when it is seen in the context not only of Southern defiance and presidential obstruction, but also of Northern disquiet. Even the most sincere and consistent champions of radical measures ignored this last factor at their peril. It has been plausibly argued, indeed, that there was a more than coincidental relationship between the size of a congressman's majority and his willingness to support radical measures.[2] The safer the seat, the more the man who held it could afford the luxury of radicalism.

The future of the Southern states, and of the Negro freedmen, rested therefore on the capacity of the federal government and the will of those who controlled it, and also on the interplay of diverse sections of opinion, radical and conservative, Northern and Southern, black and white. The American tradition of small and limited government was honoured in north as well as south and it was easy enough to see the wartime growth of national power not as the inauguration of a new era, but as a temporary aberration justified only by a unique crisis. The end of the war was likely to produce a reaction against positive government, and the hasty demobilisation of the army seemed to bear this out. (It certainly suggested that the thought of a long-term, rigorous military occupation of the south was far from anyone's mind.) There was nowhere in the American experience any precedent for the kind of massive, sustained programme of aid and protection for a substantial section of the community which a full-scale and truly radical reconstruction policy would have demanded. It was always unlikely that Northern white society would at enormous expense do for four million Negroes in the south what it had never attempted for any group within its own ranks.

However heated the constitutional debate between radicals and conservatives became, the protagonists, with but few exceptions, evinced the same deep reverence for the American constitution, and respect for the principles of federalism. There was strikingly little talk of setting aside the constitution to make way for a single master plan to be imposed on the defeated South by an uncompromising central authority. The consequence of this constitutional orthodoxy was not merely to be seen in the protracted battle between president and congress, but in the tangled web within which a federal system ensnared all attempts to tackle a problem of this kind. The problem involved a minority within a minority – the substantial black minority within the Southern minority in the United States. In order to reach out to the first of these groups, how could a federal government by-pass the other? Given the necessary will and purpose, the government of a unitary national state could have cut straight to the heart of the matter. In a federal structure, on the other hand, as long as constitutional forms were respected, the problem was immeasurably more complicated, even if the will to solve it was present – and in the case of post-Civil War America, that will, like sovereignty itself, was divided.

Within the federal government, the struggle for power between president and congress assumed overriding importance because it coincided with profound differences over policy. Those differences had already become acute, of course, during the war. At that stage, the presidential side of the argument had enjoyed distinct advantages in the war powers of the executive, and the political skill and flexible, evolutionary approach to reconstruction of Abraham Lincoln himself. Now all that was changed, or about to change. The war was over, Lincoln was dead, and his successor was neither an adroit politician nor a skilful policy-maker.

2. When Andrew Johnson was nominated as Lincoln's running-mate in 1864, no one worried unduly about the possible implications. His job was simply to balance the ticket. (Shortsightedness in the choice of vice-presidential candidates is one of the more enduring – if less endearing – of American political traditions.) When, after fortifying himself too generously from the bottle, Johnson disgraced himself on Inauguration Day in March 1865, the episode seemed embarrassing but no more. But now, by the grace of John Wilkes Booth (and his inefficient accomplice who had never reached the vice-president's hotel room), Andrew Johnson was president of the United States. It was more than an irony; it was a freak. For almost four years to come, the victorious North had a Southern president; the dominant Republican party was saddled with a life-long Democrat

in the White House. Johnson's life story was as near to the log cabin to White House legend as that of Abraham Lincoln himself. Born of humble parents in North Carolina, he had lived most of his adult life in Tennessee. Self-taught and self-made, he had emerged through his dogged determination and aptitude for sturdy, spontaneous, no-nonsense oratory as a spokesman for the Southern yeoman farmer, and an instinctive and pugnacious opponent of the establishment wherever he found it – whether in the plantation aristocracy of the South or the moneyed Yankee aristocracy of the North. Before the war he had served in both houses of Congress, and as governor of Tennessee. When the war came, he was the only senator from a rebel state to remain in the United States senate. His hatred for the plantation aristocracy was matched by his devotion to the Union, and in 1862 Lincoln appointed him military governor of occupied Tennessee. In 1864 his credentials as a War Democrat and a Southern Unionist with a reputation for toughness and apparent leanings towards radicalism made him well-suited, it seemed, to give breadth and balance to the 'National Union' ticket.

Whereas Lincoln's humble origins became a springboard to greatness, Johnson remained a prisoner of his early background. Entering political life in the Jacksonian era, he always adhered to the Jacksonian (and the Jeffersonian) tradition as he had understood it from the beginning. He put faith in small government, states rights, and the superior virtue of an agrarian society of small, independent farmers. His lifelong championship of the small man eventually made Johnson himself small-minded. His reverence for the constitution deepened with the years, and his interpretation of it became both a bone of contention with the congressional majority and a stumbling-block to effective use of his own presidential power. It was not just his Southern origins which made Andrew Johnson an anachronism as president of the United States in 1865. As a politician, he had made his name as a doughty fighter rather than a man of flexibility and resource. As an executive, he was slow and irresolute when forced to make a decision, but almost unshakable once it was made. As a Southerner, he knew very little of the North and Northern opinion, and understood even less. As a champion of the Southern yeoman he detested the slave-owners but had no time for the slaves. He supported emancipation during the war, but shared all the characteristic Southern assumptions about the place of the Negro in a white man's country. In the first days of his presidency, there were radicals who saw in his condemnation of treason and his hatred of the planter class the promise of a harmonious collaboration; there were even some who saw the hand of providence in the removal of the gentle and conciliatory Lincoln at the moment of victory. But they were soon to learn the enormity of their mistake.

In 1865 the people of the North – and indeed the whole Union – sorely needed a president who inspired confidence, who understood their feelings and was himself understood by them, a politician who combined flexibility and firmness, a man with sufficient vision and compassion and authority to lead white Americans towards a measure of justice to the Negroes. Instead, it had as president an honest, courageous and dogged man, who in no sense represented the dominant party, who was an outsider unversed in the ways of the North, and unwilling to learn them, whose political style was more noted for pugnacity than pliability, who held to his own narrow vision of his task, and could not put aside his racist heritage. Rather than giving meaning and dignity to the victory of the Union at arms, Johnson seemed intent on diminishing that victory, or even acting as if it had never happened.

The solid majority of Republicans in Congress were concerned above all that the peace as well as the war must be safely won. For several years after the war, they were to exhibit a solidarity unparalleled in American party history on one crucial vote after another. Their record strongly suggests that they shared certain basic attitudes and objectives – and certain common enemies. On the other hand, they were frequently divided during the earlier stages of debate on major bills, and fought out their internal battles in procedural wrangles, back-stage manoeuvres and party caucuses. There were groups and factions within the party, and many shades of opinion, but, as during the war, positions were not static, lines were not always clearly drawn, and not even 'radicals' or 'moderates' were always united among themselves. Most of the major measures of the reconstruction era were compromises hammered out by rival groups within the party. There was a minority of conservatives who generally adhered to the Johnsonian programme of restoration. There was, from 1865 onwards, a somewhat larger minority of radicals whose honeymoon with the new president was very brief, and who envisaged an entirely different approach to recon-struction. But the balance inside the party, and its greatest numerical strength, lay with the moderates who hoped for cooperation with the president, favoured a rapid restoration of the Union, but believed in the need for certain minimum guarantees of good behaviour as the price of re-admission for the rebel states. They would be swayed by the development of events, by the behaviour of the president, and by the reactions of the conquered white South. Moderation, already sorely tried by four years of war, was to suffer even more in the first years of peace. Radicalism profited from the follies of its enemies in north and south. Measures generally deemed radical were, however, usually passed (and frequently shaped) by the support which moderates gave them. Some moderates changed their minds with the enthusiasm of converts, many more with the reluctance of realists adjusting to events. No doubt some Republicans, reared in the abolitionist tradition, were born radical, and no doubt others achieved radicalism; but many more had radicalism thrust upon them.

The motivation of Republicans in general and the radicals in particular during the reconstruction period has been hotly disputed for a century. The case for the prosecution dismisses all their protestations of idealism, humanitarianism and concern for the Negro as no more than a cloak for more shabby or sinister purposes. The argument is succinctly summarised by one of its leading critics:

The vindictive radical would elevate the Negro to punish the southern white man; the ambitious radical would enfranchise the Negro to use him as a political tool; and the venal radical would mislead the Negro to protect the interests of northern businessmen.[3]

One might add the charge that most Republicans insisted on the Negro's rights in the south, partly to persuade him to stay away from the north, while they continued to restrict and discriminate against the free Negroes in their home states. The case for the defence would admit that radicals, and indeed all Republicans, were not without their share of original sin. The charge of vindictiveness is hard to sustain against all the evidence of astonishing leniency in the treatment of the defeated rebels, the conspicuous absence of purges, executions or witch-hunts, and the extraordinary speed with which rebels, leaders and rank and file alike, regained their full civil and political rights. No more than a few years after the end of a bloody civil war, almost every ex-Confederate, from Robert E. Lee to the humblest private, was allowed to exercise his full rights as an American citizen. Even that handful of radicals – and Thaddeus Stevens above all – who dwelt on the theme of punishment did so often for rhetorical or tactical effect. Stevens's onslaught against the Southern planter class was inspired not simply by malice but by his passionate belief in the need to rebuild Southern society on new, more democratic lines. His zeal for the rights of the freedman was not a cloak for his bid to overthrow their former masters. Both were equally important and genuine parts of his conception of what reconstruction should really be. The truth is that 'vindictiveness' became a code word for one school of reconstruction historians; what they meant by it was any attempt to assert and protect the rights of the Negro.[4]

The political and partisan motives behind reconstruction can scarcely be denied, but need not be condemned. If partisan advantage had been the sole concern of Republican legislators, the indictment might be justified. If it played no part in their calculations, these were rare and eccentric politicians indeed. In the 1864 elections the Republican party had won a handsome victory but the Democratic party was still very much alive in the north. The return of the eleven rebel states to the Union could pose a major threat to Republican supremacy if, as seemed likely, Southern and Northern Democrats quickly picked up the threads of their old alliance. By a strange irony, the abolition of slavery would bring the Southern states back with increased strength, for hitherto the slave had counted as only three-fifths of a person in assessing population for the purpose of apportioning seats in Congress. Now, as a free man, he would count as the equal of the white man for apportionment purposes, even though, if the white South had its way, he would cast no vote. Rebellion, it seemed, was to be awarded, not a punishment, but a prize of some fifteen extra seats in the House of Representatives. It was the threat contained in this situation which did much to explain the solid party voting record of the Republicans in the post-war years. If the chances of building a white Republican party in the South looked increasingly slim, two other counter-measures were still available – a delay in the process of re-admitting the rebel states, and the enfranchisement of the Negro. If many

Republicans made an even closer identification than most good party men are inclined to do between the supremacy of their party and the welfare of the nation, that was scarcely surprising on the morrow of a long and costly civil war. Partisan advantage buttressed principle in Republican policy-making, but never replaced it.

The discreditable economic motives assigned to radical reconstruction also require close scrutiny. Republican politicians were well aware of the economic facts of life; but to portray radical reconstruction as the political arm of a giant conspiracy manipulated by Northern business interests is to create a work of fiction. Northern business was no monolith; sections of it saw great opportunities in the economic reconstruction of the South, but all that they asked from the politicians was the creation of the right conditions for their enterprise. In 1865-6 they were inclined to look with favour upon the Johnsonian programme with its promise of smooth, rapid restoration of the Union, and stability and order in the south, guaranteed by the traditional leadership of Southern society. But when that promise remained unfulfilled, and the south remained in turmoil, they turned more and more to the alternative congressional programme of reconstruction. They hoped that it would produce the conditions which they sought, but they did not dictate it. For its part, neither the Republican party, nor the more radical element within it, was united on matters of economic policy. (Nor is there any discernible correlation between the radical-moderate division in the party, and divisions on economic issues.) The Republican party still included a strong anti-big-business element, anxious to promote opportunities for the small entrepreneur. On specific economic issues it embraced a wide spectrum of opinion – high protectionists and free traders, hard-money and cheap-money supporters, friends and enemies of particular vested interests. But almost all Republicans did have a common economic motive; it grew out of apprehension rather than acquisitiveness. Whatever their special interest – whether in the tariff, the currency, the banking system or the national debt – they had good grounds for anxiety about the revival of Southern opposition and obstruction and the possible resurgence of an agrarian alliance of south and west. The South had a long record of obstruction of Northern-inspired measures to promote economic growth and opportunity, and that record was not forgotten. Insofar as economic motives lay behind congressional reconstruction, they were defensive rather than aggressive. The aim was not to promote a bonanza in the south, but to prevent the South from putting a brake upon the North.

When malice and greed and political self-seeking have been allowed their full part in the making of congressional reconstruction, they still cannot explain the whole story. Like all large political parties, the Republican party contained many groups and types of men, serving many different ends. In the first decade of its existence it had been exceptional among American political parties for its moral fervour and crusading spirit, and there is no evidence to show that that element in its make-up had vanished by 1865. In the long struggle against slavery it had suffered casualties but also won new recruits. Before, during, and after the

Civil War its better nature struggled with uneven success to master its baser elements – the Negrophobes and racists, the opportunists and the cynics. The important point is that it did struggle and it did not surrender to them. If it could not bring itself to make a full, unequivocal commitment to racial equality, it did succeed in writing basic guarantees of equal rights into the constitution. If it challenged Johnsonian reconstruction, and embarked on a difficult and painful alternative course, it did so, no doubt, for many reasons, good and bad, but it is just conceivable that the main reason was simply that it believed it was right. The difference between moderates and radicals in its ranks was not a matter of economic interest or partisan gain, but rather a matter of how far along their chosen path they could and should proceed, what guarantees they could and should offer, what commitments they could and should make.

If the Republicans wrestled with their own ambivalence on matters of race, and rights and justice, they wrestled too with the prejudices and fears of Northern society as a whole. One of the chronic problems of radicals in particular was to persuade a majority of Northerners to support or at least accept the programme which they advocated. If appeals to idealism fell all too often upon stony ground, the alternative was an appeal to interests. They needed to prove that their policies were expedient as well as just – or at least to allay suspicions that they were injurious to Northern white society. Principle was not after all perhaps a cloak to cover the nakedness of self-interest; rather, appeals to self-interest were needed to protect principles from the icy blasts of apathy and hostility. The recurring fear which united Republican moderates and radicals in a concern which blended principle and interest was the fear of losing the peace. The man who above all others stimulated that fear was the man in the White House.

3. The true meaning of the Civil War was only half-settled at Appomattox. The rest depended upon the years which followed. The politics of reconstruction in the second half of the 1860s developed into a three-act play, with moments of melodrama, even of farce, but the predominant note was one of tragedy – the tragedy of missed opportunities. The first act in 1865 saw the attempt of an accidental and anachronistic president to push through his own plan for a swift restoration of the Union, so lenient in its terms that it threatened to make a mockery of the outcome of the Civil War. The second act in 1866 saw the unsuccessful attempt to arrive at an accommodation between the president and the Republican majority in Congress, by adding further specific conditions to the restoration process. It failed for many reasons but not least because of the president's obduracy and its own moderation. The third act, from late 1866 to 1868, saw an all-out battle between president and Congress, and the imposition of a new programme of congressional reconstruction, commonly but questionably dubbed radical. The president lost the battle and barely escaped impeachment; the plan of reconstruction was undermined by the resistance of the South and the flagging spirit of the North. There was irony as well as tragedy in the unfolding of the plot, for at every turn it was Andrew Johnson who drove

moderates into the arms of the radicals, only for the radicals to find that their own proposals were then diluted by their more moderate colleagues on their way to becoming law.

In the spring of 1865, Andrew Johnson had no difficulty in seizing the initiative, for the Congress elected in 1864 would not gather for its first session until December 1865, unless the president himself chose to summon it earlier. (In the aftermath of war, as in its coming four years earlier, the cumbersome timetable prescribed by the constitution made a bad situation very much worse.) Johnson saw an opportunity, in the seven months' grace thus provided, to carry through a smooth restoration of the rebel states to the Union before Congress could make its first move. In two proclamations on 29 May 1865, he established the guidelines of his programme. One offered an amnesty to those Southerners who would take an oath of future loyalty; at a stroke it immunised them against the dangers of confiscation of property or prosecution for treason, and restored their full civil and political rights. There was a long list of exceptions to the provisions of the proclamation, covering the more senior Confederate officers and officials, and also including all those who possessed taxable property valued at $20,000 or more. (This last move was a token of Johnson's bid to deprive the planter class of its traditional power.) But generous use of the pardoning power was promised to those in the excluded categories who cared to apply to the president. The second proclamation laid down for North Carolina the procedure which was soon to be prescribed for the restoration of all rebel states. The president was to appoint a provisional governor in each state who would arrange for the election of a convention to make necessary changes in the state constitution. Only those who had taken the amnesty oath and who qualified under the state laws in operation before secession could take part in this election, as voters or candidates. This latter provision virtually eliminated the Negro from the whole process. The convention – of white Southerners – could then decide the future voting and office-holding qualifications for the state. It needed no great foresight to realise that this in effect deprived the Negro of his political rights for the indefinite future. After the conventions had done their work, elections were to be held to choose state governors and legislatures, and members of Congress. Only then would Congress be able to have its say, for it alone controlled the admission of members to its two houses.[5]

Johnson's plan had the attractions of simplicity and speed, and offered the promise, attractive to many people in North and South alike, of a rapid conclusion to the whole painful business. But it dealt with the deeper issues of reconstruction mainly by ignoring them. To the white South it offered an opportunity beyond its wildest dreams; to the Republicans of the North it threatened to reverse the verdict of the past four years; to the ex-slaves it was the gesture of a Pilate washing his hands of all responsibility. But, if the plan itself was bad enough, what followed from it in the next few months was even worse.

The Southern state conventions made no concessions to the Negro and very few to tact and common sense. The siege mentality which had caused the South to misread Northern opinion and feeling before the war, and to miscalculate world reactions to the conflict itself, now made it blind to the effects of its behaviour in 1865. Some conventions refused to display the Stars and Stripes, others declined to ratify the Thirteenth Amendment or acknowledge the illegality of secession, all poured forth a torrent of words which made very unwelcome music to Northern ears. When the new state governments were elected, they were dominated by ex-Confederate leaders and representatives of the planter class, except in Johnson's home state of Tennessee where Unionists triumphed. The newly elected members of Congress included no less a personage than the ex-vice president of the Confederacy, Alexander H. Stephens. Many of those elected were disqualified under the terms of the amnesty, or earlier measures, but Johnson met this problem by handing out thousands of pardons. Reluctantly or not, he accepted the verdict of the polls that the Southern electorate looked to its traditional leadership, partly no doubt for lack of any alternative. Characteristically, Johnson, having committed himself to a policy, doggedly pursued it even when it did not proceed according to plan.

The behaviour of the new state governments did nothing to reassure the North. There was wild talk of repudiation of the national debt incurred in fighting the war to save the Union, or of a demand for compensation for the emancipation of the slaves. But worst of all were the 'black codes' passed by almost every one of the new state governments in the second half of 1865. Alarmed by the mobility of the ex-slaves, and by their aspirations for land – and, equally unwelcome, for education – the white governments moved fast to put the Negro firmly in the place where they wished to keep him, as an unskilled, uneducated, underpaid labourer, without privileges or prospects, full legal rights or any political rights. The codes varied in severity from state to state, but their general drift was much the same.[6] All that they offered by way of recognition of the Negro's new status were such things as the legalisation of Negro marriages, the right to hold property, and to sue and be sued in the courts. The restrictions which they imposed covered everything from a ban on interracial marriage to the need for special licences to engage in a variety of skilled trades, and severe restrictions on the right to own or rent land. The vagrancy laws which gave a new dimension to the term vagrant were the most notorious of all. Some states provided that Negroes found without legal employment should be arrested as vagrants, and hired off to landowners who would pay their fines. The Louisiana code required all black agricultural labourers to make contracts in January which were binding for the whole year, and which forbade the worker to leave his place of work without permission. It may well be said, of course, that amid the turmoil and instability of the post-war South some kind of codes were needed as a halfway house on the road from slavery to freedom. But the black codes were something very different. If they were a halfway house, they were for travellers being driven in the opposite direction, from freedom back towards a new kind of bondage.

Johnson raised no objections to the black codes, nor indeed to any other of the ugly manifestations of what one historian has called 'reconstruction, Confederate style'.[7] But more and more Northern opinion was moving from anxiety to alarm to anger at the sorry spectacle unfolding in the south. By the time that Congress assembled in December, the North was fully alerted to the danger of the situation. Andrew Johnson and the Confederate-style governments in the south proved to be the best recruiting sergeants which radicalism ever had.

1865 was the crucial year – and the tragic year – in the story of reconstruction. When the war ended in the spring, most Southerners were resigned to accepting whatever settlement the North imposed upon them, for there seemed to be no alternative. For its part, the North was generally in search of reconciliation. If there was ever a chance, however slender, to impose a firm settlement, striking a fair balance between the just rewards of the victor, charity to the vanquished, and a measure of justice to the black American, it was in the weeks and months which immediately followed Appomattox. Andrew Johnson and the white South blighted that hope once and for all. Granted a reprieve when they could have expected none, the leaders of the white South exploited it in a gross and short-sighted manner. By the end of 1865 they seemed to have succeeded in bringing off one of the great escape acts of history. But when, in 1866, they were confronted with new conditions for restoration, and in 1867 with a whole new programme of reconstruction, they felt that they had been cheated, and they bitterly resented what they might have quietly accepted, if it had been offered at the outset. In the years after 1865 the radicals and their allies were to be guilty of many mistakes and lapses from grace but it must be remembered that they were reacting to a situation not of their own making or choosing. There was no satisfactory antidote to the poison which entered the bloodstream of reconstruction during 1865.

In December of that year, Andrew Johnson may have believed that the process of reconstruction was virtually over. In fact, it was only just beginning. The second act of the drama did not open with immediate and inevitable confrontation between president and congress. It is true that, as soon as Congress met, the Republican majorities in both houses moved rapidly to refuse admission to the members elected in the ex-Confederate states. They also set up a Joint Committee on Reconstruction to investigate and make recommendations on the whole problem. Both of these moves were endorsed by radicals and moderates alike, and neither was intended as a direct challenge to the president. If the moderates who held the balance of power in Congress were uneasy about the results of Johnsonian restoration, they also gave short shrift to the radical proposals of Stevens who envisaged a wholesale recasting of Southern society, and Sumner who offered a plan based upon Negro suffrage. The moderates realised that the apparent success of the Johnson programme in binding up the nation's wounds so painlessly still gave it a considerable amount of popular appeal. Although they shared the radical concern that Congress should claim its rights in the field of reconstruction policy, they feared that an open breach with the president would be politically damaging. They saw no reason why some further provisions and conditions should not be grafted on to the Johnson programme to make it acceptable to the North, but still tolerable to the president, and not too unpalatable to the South. Unfortunately, Andrew Johnson did not agree with them, and was ready to see a radical plot behind the mildest of compromise proposals.

At this stage, as so often later, the key men proved to be those who could form a bridge between the moderate and radical positions. One such was William Pitt Fessenden of Maine, who became chairman of the Joint Committee. Another was Lyman Trumbull of Illinois, who sponsored the bills which stated the price of congressional support for the president's policy. The first was a bill to extend the life and strengthen the powers of the Freedmen's Bureau, set up in 1865. The Bureau was the one practical gesture by the federal government in the direction of providing relief and protection for the ex-slave. The new bill not merely expanded its role in the field of welfare and education, but established special courts to offer some judicial protection to the freedman against the violence and intimidation which were all too often his lot. The second measure was a Civil Rights bill which made the first serious legislative attempt to define American citizenship in national terms by basing it simply on birth in the United States, without regard to race or colour. It also affirmed the principle of equal protection under the law for all citizens, and extended the jurisdiction of the federal courts to cases arising under the bill's provisions. These two bills were essentially moderate and cautious, avoiding the sensitive issue of Negro suffrage, and offering the bare minimum of protection to the freedmen, and they passed through Congress by handsome majorities.

Andrew Johnson vetoed them both, and did so on grounds which made the the gulf between the congressional Republicans and himself almost unbridgeable. He questioned both the propriety of passing such bills when the Southern states were unrepresented, and the right to impose further conditions upon a process of restoration which he regarded as complete. He condemned the Civil Rights bill as a serious invasion of the rights of the states. His whole response reflected a refusal to accept any national responsibility for the status and welfare of the freedmen. For lack of one vote in the Senate, the Republicans in Congress failed to find the two-thirds majority necessary to override the veto of the Freedmen's Bureau bill – although they did succeed with a new version of the bill a few months later. They were able to muster the votes to overturn Johnson's veto of the Civil Rights bill – the first occasion in American history when a major piece of legislation was carried against the presidential veto. It set a precedent which was to become a habit in the next two years. It also demonstrated how Johnson, isolated, obstinate, and incapable of understanding the feelings of Northern Republicans, had succeeded in provoking moderates and radicals into an impressive display of solid voting strength. If future measures were also to require a two-thirds majority, as now seemed certain, then the moderates needed the radicals as much as the radicals needed them.

Out of the deliberations of the Joint Committee eventually came the proposal for a Fourteenth Amendment to the constitution which would establish the basic safeguards required to protect the Negro and reassure the Republican party. The Amendment became a hold-all for several different propositions, but its contents were considerably weakened during its passage through Congress. In its final form it had four main provisions. First, it wrote into the constitution something very like the terms of the Civil Rights Act concerning citizenship and equal protection under the law. It expressly forbade any state to abridge the privileges or immunities of citizens of the United States, or to deprive any person of life, liberty or property without due process of law, but its failure to define its terms more precisely has caused countless problems ever since. (Its authors, for example, did not have it in mind to bring about complete desegregation of public facilities.) Secondly, the amendment reduced the representation of a state in the House of Representatives in proportion to the number of its adult male citizens who were denied the vote. This was an ingenious device to prevent the defeated white South from returning to the halls of Congress with increased representation. Instead of a commitment to Negro suffrage, it imposed a penalty upon those states which refused to grant it. The third section of the amendment dealt with the exclusion from office-holding of ex-Confederates – another much-favoured device to clip the wings of the Southern phoenix rising from the ashes of war. But the amendment limited this exclusion to those who, as congressmen or other office-holders, had previously taken an oath to support the constitution, and had then engaged in rebellion. They were not disfranchised, and in any case Congress could remove their disability by a two-thirds vote of each house. The fourth section of the amendment affirmed the validity of the public debt of the United States and completely repudiated the Confederate debt.

The Fourteenth Amendment was vague where it might have been specific, mild where it might have been firm, cautious where it might have been bold, negative where it might have been positive. But it still represents one of the major achievements of the reconstruction era, and its passage was the climax of the work of the first session of the 39th Congress. A constitutional amendment does not require the presidential signature, but Johnson left no doubt of his disapproval, and urged the Southern states not to ratify it. He fastened upon the logical flaw in the constitutional position of the moderate Republicans who still adhered to the view that the Southern states had never been out of the Union, but who were nevertheless willing to pass a constitutional amendment through a Congress in which the South was unrepresented, and remained evasive on whether the eleven rebel states must be included in the ratification process. Thaddeus Stevens's argument that the Southern states should be treated as conquered provinces and therefore excluded from the process of amending the constitution had greater logical consistency on its side, but it was medicine too drastic for most Republicans to swallow.

In the event, then, the Southern states were invited to accept the Amendment, but not obliged to do so. It was at this point that the very moderation of the moderate Republicans became self-defeating. If the Fourteenth Amendment had been more explicit and more positive in its provisions, and if it had been made plain to the South that acceptance of it was the essential ticket of re-admission to the Union, there would have been a fair chance of a speedy end to the formal process of reconstruction. But given a choice, the Southern states reacted by defending their entrenched positions, without serious consideration of whether those positions would be defensible for very much longer. Their governments rejected the amendment out of hand, although they could not prevent its eventual ratification. By failing to accept the terms offered in 1866, the South brought upon itself the stricter terms of 1867. Similarly, by encouraging Southern intransigeance, Andrew Johnson ensured that a new reconstruction programme, much more distasteful to him, would be carried over his head. The attempt to chart a middle course in 1866 foundered while Johnson sailed very close to the Southern shore. In foundering, it muddied the waters for years to come.

When Congress adjourned in July 1866, its most conspicuous failure lay in its inability to enact a general programme of reconstruction. If moderate and radical Republicans were united against the president, they were divided among themselves over the shape and scope of an alternative to Johnsonian restoration. Until Congress reassembled in December, the formal process of reconstruction remained in limbo, but in the intervening months events in both south and north put the problem into clearer, harsher perspective. The Southern attitude to the Fourteenth Amendment had a bad enough effect on Northern opinion, but the constant reports of violence perpetrated against Negroes in the south did even more damage. The outrages reached their peak in the summer of 1866 in riots in Memphis and New Orleans which took scores of Negro lives. In both cases the local police had led the attack upon the blacks, but Johnson took no action.

Meanwhile, the president was heavily involved in a third-party movement designed to give him a solid power base for the future. The National Union movement aimed to create a coalition of Northern Democrats, conservative Republicans and conservative white Southerners on a programme of sectional reconciliation and peace. It took for itself the label under which Lincoln had won re-election in 1864, but it had no chance of emulating that success. By opposing the Fourteenth Amendment, it took its stand too far to the right to attract any Republicans apart from the small minority who were already Johnson supporters. Northern Democrats were unwilling to abandon their traditional allegiance for a new organisation where they would have to share the loaves and fishes with Republicans. The movement faced all the handicaps of a third party in American politics and it fizzled out later in the year. Johnson's talent was for antagonising Republican congressmen and voters rather than attracting them. As early as February, he had virtually branded Stevens and Sumner as traitors; now, in the 'swing-round-the-circle', a speaking tour across the north in August and September, he returned to this and similar themes, and, goaded by his audiences, reverted to the rough, intemperate stump oratory of his early days in Tennessee. In the process, he lost personal dignity and political credibility, and he betrayed his total inability to establish any kind of rapport with the people of the north. The speaking tour was part of the mid-term election campaign – a battle notable for the racist appeals of the Democrats, and Republican counter-blasts which fanned the embers of wartime passions. The outcome of the elections was a landslide victory for the Republicans, who now controlled the governorship and the legislature of every Northern state, and who secured clear two-thirds majorities in both houses of Congress. The elections of 1866 showed just how seriously Andrew Johnson had frightened the North about the danger of losing the peace.

4. Now, as the third act of the drama opened, the onus was upon the congressional Republicans to formulate their own reconstruction programme. It was not of course the newly-elected Congress which assembled in December 1866, but the lame-duck session of the Congress elected two years earlier. If it wished to override presidential objections, its Republican majority would have to keep its ranks tightly closed. Johnson's behaviour was steadily pressing that majority towards tougher measures, and there were other factors, too, working in favour of more radical solutions. Continuing concern over the situation in the south, and the plight of Negroes and Unionists there, was heightened by the Supreme Court decision in the Milligan case in December 1866. In dealing with a case which had arisen in the north during the war,[8] the Court raised new doubts about reconstruction in the south many months after the war was over. In denying the right of military courts to try civilians in areas where the civil courts were open, it seemed to deny the legality of the special courts set up in the south under the Freedmen's Bureau Act. The president certainly lost no time in acting upon that assumption by curtailing the activities of those courts. If Negroes were now to be thrown upon the mercy of the ordinary courts in the south, their need for federal protection was greater than ever. One other development seemed to clear the path for a new, more radical approach to reconstruction. With the mid-term elections safely over, many more Republicans felt free to espouse openly the principle of Negro suffrage, without placing their political lives in immediate jeopardy. Negro suffrage was never a straightforward moderate-versus-radical issue. Men as different as Andrew Johnson and Thaddeus Stevens had earlier shared the view that the Negroes would probably vote for their former masters and thus put more power into the hands of the planter class. But now those Republicans who embraced the idea with enthusiasm were joined by those who accepted it with resignation, whether as an act of justice or from sheer necessity.

There were still powerful brakes upon the possibility of a genuinely radical approach to reconstruction. Moderate Republicans were inclined to see the Fourteenth Amendment as the capstone of a process of reconstruction which now simply had to be enforced by the North and accepted by the South. Radicals on the other hand saw the amendment as the foundation stone of a new and elaborate process, leading, if Stevens had his way, to a massive redistribution of property and power in the south, which amounted to social revolution. The moderate majority was not willing to follow that path, and the outnumbered Democrats in Congress used every tactical and procedural device to exploit any signs of division in the Republican ranks, and to prolong and complicate the legislative process. Time was a real enemy in a short session such as this which had to end in early March, especially when it was vital to pass any law early enough to allow time to override a presidential veto. As recent accounts have clearly shown, what emerged was a Reconstruction Act conceived in obscure debates and manoeuvres, and delivered in a final hectic rush.[9] The measure which finally passed was a somewhat shapeless lump, which its parents were not very proud to claim as their own. The law which was the foundation of radical reconstruction was in truth a compromise from which radicals probably drew less satisfaction than moderates. It disfranchised some of the white leaders of the South, but no one could estimate how many – and, in any event, their disability lasted for a few years at most. Some radicals had wanted harsher penalties (including even loss of citizenship) applied to many more categories of Southern whites. Some also wanted tougher conditions for re-admission, and tighter guarantees of equal rights and privileges under the law. Some indeed thought that the whole process prescribed was too brief and wanted to delay re-admission and keep the South under military rule indefinitely. Perhaps the most fundamental radical objection of all was that the measure took no account whatsoever of the wider economic and social aspects of reconstruction – the need for a new social order in the south, and, specifically, the need for land for the freedmen.

The Reconstruction Act of 2 March 1867 placed the South under military rule. The ten states (Tennessee had been re-admitted in 1866) were grouped in five military districts, and the commander of each district was given wide powers to protect the local population and punish wrong-doers. With law and order thus established, the states could then move towards restoration to the Union by a new and complicated route. Conventions were to amend the state constitutions to bring them fully into line with the constitution of the United States (as amended). These conventions were to be elected on the basis of universal manhood suffrage, including Negroes, but excluding those ex-Confederates barred from office-holding under the Fourteenth Amendment. The state constitutions, which were also to make provision for universal manhood suffrage, required the approval of a majority of the voters and of both houses of Congress. States which had passed through all these stages could then be re-admitted, but only when the Fourteenth Amendment had been finally ratified. (This last provision was an inducement to all the states to approve that amendment.) Until new state governments were established under this procedure, all existing state governments in the south were to be regarded as purely provisional, and subject to the paramount authority of the United States.[10]

The Southern states soon made it plain that they preferred to take their chance with these 'provisional' governments, controlled by white men, rather than embark upon this new and unwelcome experiment which embodied the dreaded notion of Negro suffrage. The new session of Congress acted swiftly to pass further acts which put teeth into the earlier measure, and gave the military governors power to initiate the whole process. Faced with compulsion, the South submitted, and a number of states moved quite briskly towards re-admission. Six of the ten states were re-admitted by 1868, helped on by Republican hunger for their votes in the election of that year, and the other four were re-admitted by 1870. The speed of the process can only increase speculation about what might have been achieved in the first year or eighteen months after the war, if a fair but firm set of terms had been imposed upon the South when it was in much more compliant mood. As things were, from 1867 onwards the Southern whites sullenly accepted the new programme of reconstruction only until they were able to subvert it. They soon found hope both in opportunities to reassert themselves at home, and evidence of failing zeal for Negro rights in the north.

Meanwhile, during 1867 and 1868, the congressional Republicans took a series of unprecedented steps to strip President Johnson of all capacity to obstruct or undermine their reconstruction programme. Their solid two-thirds majority had already nullified his veto of their legislation; now they sought to ensure the full execution of their laws. First, in January 1867, Congress claimed the right (hitherto belonging to the president alone) to call itself into special session, and decreed that the new Congress should meet as soon as the old one ended its term in March. There was to be no long interval until December in which Johnson would enjoy a free hand, as he had in 1865. A provision added to the Army Appropriation Act in March limited the president's authority as commander-in-chief and strengthened the position of the General of the Army – who was of course General Grant. The main object was to protect military rule in the South from presidential sabotage. The Tenure of Office Act, also passed in March, restricted the presidential power over patronage; office-holders appointed with the consent of the Senate could now only be removed with the consent of the Senate, and cabinet members were to hold office during the term of the president who appointed them, unless the Senate consented to their removal. The specific object of this last provision was to protect Secretary of War Stanton, the one cabinet member of any radical sympathies. The wider object of the act was to meet the case of a president, with all his formidable powers of appointment, who was now at daggers drawn with the majority party in Congress.

When Congress also passed a law restricting the appellate jurisdiction of the Supreme Court in certain cases, there seemed to be real grounds for anxiety that the radicals were upsetting the whole balance of the constitution, and setting up a congressional dictatorship. There were radicals who occasionally spoke in terms which might substantiate such fears, and the dubious constitutional propriety of this series of measures remains one of the shadier areas in the record of congressional reconstruction. But for the great majority of Republicans, these were exceptional measures dictated by exceptional circumstances and not the deliberate first steps to rewriting the constitution. They were signs of the extraordinary lengths to which Congress was driven by the provocative behaviour of Andrew Johnson, and the unplumbed depths to which the battle between executive and legislature had descended.

When men had moved so far, it was not difficult to take the final step towards impeachment of the president. The idea had been mooted early in 1867, but eventually dropped. However, later in the year, Johnson's continued efforts to cripple military rule in the south renewed interest in the proposal. Finally, the president attempted to suspend Stanton from office, and replace him by Grant. Using its power under the Tenure of Office Act, the Senate refused its consent to the change. An element of farce entered the affair when Johnson tried to appoint another replacement for Stanton, and the latter barricaded himself in the War Department and refused to budge. The Stanton affair finally persuaded the House of Representatives to vote in February 1868 to impeach the president 'of high crimes and misdemeanours in office'. Of the eleven articles of impeachment, eight referred to the removal of Stanton, but two made a much broader attack on Johnson's conduct as president. The trial took place before the Senate in the spring of 1868. The prosecution was ineptly managed, and its case was anyway extremely dubious. It steadily broadened out from Johnson's alleged offences against the law to the much wider political argument that he was simply unfit to hold the presidential office any longer. A successful impeachment on such grounds might have created an extremely dangerous precedent, but in fact Johnson finally escaped conviction by the narrowest of margins. A two-thirds majority of senators was needed to convict; thirty-five Republican senators found Johnson guilty, but nineteen – twelve Democrats and seven Republicans – voted against conviction. The transfer of one vote to the other side would have changed the verdict. In the light of his record over three years, it may well be thought that, politically, his conduct warranted the harshest censure available, namely impeachment, but that, legally, there was no cast-iron case against him.

As it was, Andrew Johnson served out the remaining months of his term fairly quietly. Later in 1868, the Republicans nominated and elected General Grant as the next president, and Negro votes in the reconstructed states of the south assured him of an overall popular majority – although he would have won a majority in the electoral college without them. With Grant in the White House, the era of confrontation between president and Congress was over, the talk of legislative supremacy faded into the background, and the Tenure of Office Act was quietly repealed.

It soon became obvious that the serious attempt to use federal power to reconstruct the South was almost over, too. But before that happened, the Republicans carried through one last, fitting monument to their reconstruction programme. There had been a move for some time to write impartial suffrage into the constitution, to consolidate the work of the Fourteenth Amendment and the Reconstruction Acts. Now, with the presidential election safely over, the time seemed ripe. In February 1869, Congress approved a Fifteenth Amendment which simply stated that 'the right of citizens of the United States to vote shall not be denied or abridged by the United States or by any state on account of race, color, or previous condition of servitude'. The Amendment in its final form was once again a victory for moderates rather than radicals. The latter had fought for an amendment in the form of a positive national commitment to universal manhood suffrage, backed by firm guarantees. They warned that an amendment in negative form, which merely forbade disfranchisement on grounds of race or colour, was an open invitation to the Southern states to deprive Negroes of the vote on some other ground. The radicals had the foresight but the moderates carried the day. It has been elaborately argued that the real object of the amendment lay not in the South but the North. In the 1868 elections, the margin between the two parties in several Northern states had been minute, and enfranchisement of the Negro, it was thought, would provide a welcome boost to the Republican vote. Undoubtedly, this was a factor in some Republican calculations, but if the Fifteenth Amendment was a bid for votes in the north, the calculation was a very shortsighted one. Negroes made up from one to three per cent of the population of the key states in the north, and it was problematical, to say the least, whether their votes would offset the white backlash against such a measure which Republicans had long feared – and which was one reason for its postponement until after the presidential election. One reason why the amendment had been watered down was precisely the fear that a more strongly-worded version might have difficulty in securing ratification by the states. If the Fifteenth Amendment was likely to be such a mixed blessing to the Republican party in the north, the real driving force behind it surely lay elsewhere. It may have been to strengthen the new régimes in the Southern states, but few Republicans were optimistic on that score. The likeliest answer was that the Republican party now believed it was right to place a commitment to Negro suffrage in the constitution. The limitations of its final form reflected not so much calculations of partisan gain, but recognition of what was possible in the face of prejudice and fear.[11]

As such, it was the last major piece in the complex jigsaw puzzle of the reconstruction programme. It was also a peculiarly apt symbol of the whole process. Its negative wording and limited compass typified the compromises and dilutions of so much of the programme; it was one more step back from the brink of a truly radical policy. On the other hand, the fact that it could be passed at all, even in this form, showed just how far things had moved in a few short years. The Fifteenth Amendment epitomised both the achievement and the ambivalence of 'radical' reconstruction.

The political history of the later 1860s presented a number of extraordinary features without parallel in earlier American history. A spate of presidential vetoes was consistently overridden by a solid two-thirds majority in both houses of Congress. The first assassination of an American president was followed three years later by the first attempt at impeachment of a president – which failed by a single vote. Since the Bill of Rights, only two minor amendments had been added to the constitution, and none at all in sixty years before 1865. Now, in four years, three amendments of shattering significance were added. However justified the criticism of their limitations and shortcomings, they had redefined the meaning of American freedom, equality, democracy – and citizenship itself. They had also imposed severe restrictions on state sovereignty, even if they did not necessarily add greatly in practice to federal power. Vetoes, two-thirds majorities, impeachment proceedings and constitutional amendments, all were signs and portents of truly exceptional times. If some of the more unpleasant aspects of the story were peculiar to the era of reconstruction, it is fair to add that so too were the positive achievements of the three amendments. Only the exceptional circumstances made them possible or even conceivable.

For all the acrimony which accompanied its evolution, the process of reconstruction produced a settlement truly remarkable in its leniency, coming as it did in the wake of a civil war which was also the greatest war of the nineteenth century. The programme which finally emerged was too much of a bundle of compromises to be labelled unequivocally radical in its conception or intent; it remains to be seen whether it made any truly radical impact in the south.

5. The limitations of 'radical' rule in the south are plain enough, but have been frequently ignored. In the first place, the life of the new régimes was extremely brief. Tennessee, Virginia and Georgia were under 'conservative' Southern white control by 1870. In other states the reconstruction governments lasted for periods varying from less than three years to rather less than ten. The notion of the whole south blanketed by 'radical' rule (or misrule) for almost a decade is quite false. The new governments were also restricted by the precarious base upon which they rested – Negroes newly released from slavery, whites newly arrived from the north, and a minority of Southern whites who were ostracised by their fellows for their pains. The strength of these governments was still further sapped by the wavering and then waning support which they received from the North and from the federal authorities. It is not really surprising, then, that the record of the reconstruction governments is often less striking for what they did than for what they were unable to do. Their limited impact is most obvious of all in their failure to do more than scratch the surface of the economic and social problems which demanded attention if any meaningful reconstruction of the South was to take place. The making of reconstruction policy in Washington had concerned itself predominantly with rights, votes and political machinery. The state governments in the south were unable to redress the balance in favour of land, jobs and economic recovery.

In the context of the prevailing mid-nineteenth-century notions on the role of government, it was hardly surprising that there was no economic master plan at the heart of reconstruction policy. The South had to repair the ravages of war, rebuild its old lines of communication and construct new ones, put its land back into full production, and devise a new labour system to replace slavery. It patently lacked the capital and other resources to cope with such problems on its own. But no one contemplated the 1860s equivalent of a Marshall plan. Unlike the defeated enemies of the United States in the twentieth century, the South was to benefit from no economic miracle. Indeed, the confiscation of cotton and other loot in the immediate aftermath of war, and the tax on cotton which took $68 million out of the south between 1865 and 1868, aggravated the economic plight of the whole region. Those few radicals like Thaddeus Stevens who talked of the need for economic and social revolution in the south had social justice rather than economic recovery as their goal. The Northern investment and business activity which did develop in the south after 1865 came from private enterprise and not through government initiative. The policies of the federal government provided a congenial climate for their operations, but little more. The Yankees who came south bought plantations, engaged in trade, or launched new mills and factories. If they made a profit, much of it did not stay in the south. Many did not succeed and left after a few years. The Yankees who came to invest and trade in the south were not all ruthless exploiters, come to steal what the Northern armies had failed to destroy. Some sincerely believed that an injection of the methods of Northern business and industry was the best way to regenerate the south. If they came in search of opportunity and rapid advancement, this was no more than thousands of their contemporaries were seeking in the west. The carpetbagger villain of the south and the pioneer hero of the frontier were brothers under the skin. (One reason, indeed, for the inadequacy of investment and enterprise in the post-war south lay in the richer and easier opportunities which presented themselves elsewhere.)

Southern state governments of all political hues struggled to finance rebuilding programmes or to attract capital for new railroads, but often landed themselves in deep financial waters (and frequent financial scandal) as a result. Southern industry grew steadily from its small base, but even after the promotional efforts of 'New South' enthusiasts later in the century it still contrived to produce a smaller proportion of American manufactured goods in 1900 than the old South had in 1860. The economic prospects of the Southern states after 1865 would stand or fall, as they had always done, by the performance of their agriculture. The first post-war cotton crop of around two million bales was less than 40 per cent of the pre-war peak, and it took over a decade to climb back to pre-war levels. Much the same picture is true of tobacco and other crops. As a producer of staple crops for distant markets, the South was as dependent as ever on forces beyond its control, and those forces were generally hostile in the years after 1865. Because of competition from India and the Middle East, Southern cotton never recovered its old share of world markets, and world cotton prices fell by nearly a half during the 1870s. But the high tariff policy now enshrined in Republican dogma meant that there was no comparable fall in the price of many of the goods which Southerners bought.

Unfavourable market trends, and a desperate shortage of cash and credit, were only half the problem. The other was simply how to come to terms with a new labour situation in the wake of emancipation. The white farmers and planters needed Negro workers, but lacked the cash and often the will to pay wages. Among their other ill-effects, the Black Codes virtually ruled out a free-labour system as the North understood it; where a wages system was tried, it usually functioned badly, as neither employer nor wage-earner really understood its working, the cash often ran out, and wages were simply not paid. For his part, the freedman wanted work, and he hankered most of all after land, as the only real guarantee of both his liberty and his livelihood. But he did not have the money, and he was seldom given the opportunity, to buy or rent land. What the South needed was a system in which the planter would obtain labour without paying wages, and the Negro could obtain land without having to pay cash. The answer was found in sharecropping – but the answer soon created more problems than it solved. Sharecropping was a system by which the planter rented a part of his land to the 'cropper' (black or white) and often supplied seeds, tools and other equipment, in return for a share of the crop. But sharecropping did not normally produce a simple two-way split between cropper and owner. Both parties could only survive on credit until the first crop was safely in, and, in an economy starved of cash and normal forms of credit, they could do so only by borrowing on the strength of that future crop. This 'crop-lien' system, under which the next crop was always mortgaged in advance, was operated by a new breed of country merchants, sometimes Southerners, more often from the north, who provided loans in return for a share – often one-third or more – of the crop. As they in turn borrowed money at high rates of interest from Northern sources, they turned the screw ever more tightly upon both planters and croppers. More and more the merchants came to dominate the lives of their victims, and insisted upon continuing concentration upon the small range of staple crops, cotton above all, upon which the whole system depended.

The twin evils of sharecropping and the crop-lien system played havoc with the lives and the self-respect of its victims, black and white, and put the agricultural economy of the South into a strait-jacket. Crushed by the burdens of debt and increased taxation, planters were obliged over the years to sell off part or all of their land, to the merchants or other 'new men' in the south, who aped all the more disagreeable characteristics of the old plantation aristocracy, but few of the redeeming features of its paternalism. Over the years, too, many white yeoman farmers were sucked into the sharecropping system, and impoverished and degraded by it. Ex-planters and yeoman farmers alike, their social status crumbling in ruins, frequently turned upon the Negro as the scapegoat for their misery as well as the symbol of their defeat in the war. The Negro suffered most of all from the new system. It relegated him to a new status of dependence – indeed of virtual peonage – scarcely better than his old bondage, and often a good deal more insecure. Partly out of sheer force of circumstances, and partly from the design of some and the neglect of others, the years of reconstruction consigned the Negro to his familiar fate, as the supplier of cheap, unskilled, underprivileged, exploited labour for the white South. Worse than all that, he was still in a real sense unfree.

Land was the only key to genuine freedom for the Negro in the south, and the failure even to attempt to provide it by any better means than sharecropping is tragic evidence of the shallowness of the economic roots of radical reconstruction. Even among radical Republicans in the north, there were only a few, like Stevens and Julian, who seriously argued the case for confiscation of large estates in the south, and their distribution in something like forty-acre lots to the freedmen. The coolness or downright hostility which such proposals provoked reflected deep-rooted attitudes in American society. Such a programme offended against two of that society's most cherished principles (or sacred cows): the sanctity of property, and the belief in individual self-help, and advancement as the reward for virtue and hard work. It could have thoroughly unpleasant repercussions far beyond the south, and, by removing a pool of very cheap labour in the south, might raise the price of labour everywhere. It would also have required the federal government to play a role more ambitious and arduous than anything previously contemplated for it in such a field. Emancipation itself, of course, might be quoted as a precedent, but it was not a good one. It had been born of the exigencies of war, and it was precisely because wartime emancipation had not looked to its future consequences that the problem now existed in this dire form. Lacking trust in massive government intervention, the architects of reconstruction put their faith in the law and guarantees of legal rights as instruments of reform – and in this they were part of a great American tradition, not without honour and success. But in this case, legalism was not enough.

Deprived of the land they coveted, the Negroes looked elsewhere for hope. Prospects of employment outside agriculture were dim, partly because Southern industry was still on such a small scale and partly because, in north and south, white workers in and out of the unions were ready to resist Negro competition, particularly at a time when jobs were not easy to find. Large-scale migration to the north was never seriously regarded as a possible answer to the economic problems of the freedmen in the era of reconstruction. Most of them were not anxious to go, and they would certainly not have been made welcome. Aside from the immediate need for work, the Negroes pinned many of their longer-term hopes of advancement on education. While white Americans debated whether Negroes could and should be educated, the Negroes seized eagerly upon every opportunity which they were given, and asked for more. Some whites – and not only in the south – argued that the Negro was simply incapable of profiting from schooling because of his innate inferiority; those who supported Negro education accepted the obligation to make up for the handicaps which generations of slavery had imposed. Opponents thought that it would encourage militancy and arrogance, and fanciful notions of equality; the more cautious among its supporters retorted that it would make the Negro more rather than less 'responsible', and a more useful and stable member of society.

In the war and early post-war years, Negro education in the south was in the hands of the churches, the Freedmen's Aid Societies, and, to some extent, the army. The Freedmen's Bureau was increasingly involved in educational work and by 1870 was running over 4,000 schools with nearly a quarter of a million pupils. From 1868, the new state constitutions and the radical governments made the first real commitment to public education financed by taxation which the South had ever known. They lacked the money, the teachers and the resources to honour that commitment in full, in face of many difficulties, especially from whites who believed that 'education is ruining our Negroes', and only two states, Louisiana and South Carolina, took even the first tentative steps towards integrated education. But their record in education is one of the best monuments to the radical governments in the south.

If land was withheld, and the hunger for education not even half-satisfied, politics seemed to offer the only other avenue for Negro advancement. Black leaders (though not always their followers) and their white friends in the north set so much store by Negro suffrage not merely as a right or an end in itself, but as the means by which the black population could assert its influence and make progress towards its wider goals. The Negroes were a substantial minority of the population of the south; in two states, South Carolina and Mississippi, they actually formed a majority, and in a third, Louisiana, they were just about half of the total population. Especially at a time when some whites were disfranchised and others disinclined to take part in politics, they seemed to have a chance to make their presence strongly felt. Negro members took part in the proceedings of the state conventions which drew up new constitutions in 1867–8; those constitutions were generally the best and most liberal which the Southern states had ever had and they endured for many years after reconstruction. Negroes voted and were elected to state legislatures, to various state offices and to Congress in the years that followed. When a Negro, Hiram Revels, sat in the United States Senate seat occupied a decade earlier by Jefferson Davis as a senator from Mississippi, black political power had surely arrived.

However, like so many symbols and tokens in the history of the American Negro, this one was rather misleading. Black power and influence never reflected Negro numbers in the total electorate throughout this period. Only in the lower house of the South Carolina legislature did Negroes ever have a majority in any house of any state legislature. No Negro was ever elected to a state governorship, although a few did fill other state offices including that of lieutenant governor. Two Negro senators and twenty representatives served in Congress (though never more than seven at any one time). In comparison with what had gone before, this was remarkable enough – and no Negro congressman was elected from a Northern state until 1928 – but it was still but a tiny proportion of a Congress of around 300 members. Lack of experience, education and organisation made it hard to turn potential into actual voting strength. It took time for leadership to emerge, and for effort to arouse many newly-enfranchised voters from inertia. There were divisions of status, class, skin colour, economic interest and political outlook within the Negro community itself. With some Negroes, it was habitual or instinctive to accept white leadership; with others it was regarded as politic. Black legislators and office-holders generally held to a moderate line, doing their best to restrain both the hostility of their white opponents and the militancy of many of their supporters. There remains, too, the simple fact that Negroes were a minority in most of the Southern states. The whites had all the advantages of experience, organisation, leadership and real power, and they exploited them by every available method, legal or not, to cripple and destroy black political strength.

The radical régimes which ruled the Southern states for a few brief years were not, then, black governments. They rested on three very uneven legs, and, if the Negroes supplied the majority of the votes, more of the power was exercised by the two white groups who bear the opprobrious names of 'carpetbaggers' and 'scalawags', bestowed upon them by their enemies. The carpetbaggers from the north were a very mixed group, and only a few arrived in the south with political aspirations or ambitions. Some came as prophets of a new order, others came to make profits out of it, a few managed to combine both roles. Their ranks included hucksters and opportunists but also businessmen of better repute, teachers, missionaries, agents of the Freedmen's Bureau, and veterans of the Union army returning to settle in the land which they had conquered. When they did enter politics, their attitudes and per-formance ran the whole gamut from high idealism to shameless exploitation of the black vote; most conformed to normal patterns of political behaviour between those extremes. The Southern white 'scalawags' were equally varied in their motives and attitudes, and were much stronger in some areas (usually outside the deep south) than in others. Some had always been Unionists, some decided that the time had arrived to come to terms with the realities of defeat and reconstruction. An ex-general like James Longstreet, and a politician with an exceptional instinct for survival, like ex-Governor Joseph E. Brown of Georgia, were examples of this latter group. Some joined the Republicans for partisan political reasons – ex-Whigs, for example, who saw the Republican party as heir to the Whig tradition. Some joined for reasons of economic or class interest – men anxious to develop new business and industrial interests or, at the other end of the scale, poor whites and yeomen who saw the Democrats or 'conservatives' as the party of the planter class. But for all their diversity, the scalawags were never more than a small minority in most Southern states, and their proportion of the Southern white vote in any of the elections of the period was probably never more than one-fifth, at the very best. Few of the scalawags (and not many of the carpetbaggers) were conspicuous for their belief in racial equality. The whites occupied most of the leading positions in the Republican party and the radical governments in the South, and exercised the real control.

6. The image which Southern folklore has given to the radical governments in the South is one of corruption, extravagance, exploitation, scandal and greed –

'a Saturnalia of robbery and jobbery', in Lord Bryce's phrase.[12] This was the picture which the majority of white Southerners expected to see and needed to believe from the moment that the new governments were launched. What else was to be expected from governments controlled and supported by blacks whom they regarded as totally unfitted for self-government, outsiders whom they condemned as trouble-makers and self-seekers, and Southern whites whom they branded as traitors to their race? What is more remarkable is that this propaganda indictment of reconstruction in the south remained enshrined in the historiography of the period for so long. It has been rebutted, but it has taken a long time to die.[13]

Like any effective piece of character assassination, it contained elements of truth. There was fraud and graft and waste – although the most frequently-cited examples are ludicrous rather than sinister, like the vote of the South Carolina legislature to grant its speaker $1,000 as compensation for a wager on a losing horse. State debts multiplied and taxation rose steeply. The state governments made numerous mistakes and had many failures, although they were the result of inexperience, incompetence or even innocence more often than greed and cynicism. There are further pleas of mitigation which need to be entered on their behalf. It is surely right that the corrupt practices of black and white Republicans in the south should be judged in the general context of political and business life in the gilded age. Scandals in Southern state capitals, like the scandals of the Grant era in Washington, were evidence of the widespread corrosive effects of civil war and economic expansion on many areas of American life. More germane to the case of the South perhaps is the fact that Southern white governments before and after the years of radical rule had their full share of scandals and irregularities. Whoever happened to be in power, the rebuilding of the south, which required governments to make loans, provide subsidies, and award contracts, created ample opportunity for both honest and dishonest gain.

These considerations are relevant if scarcely reassuring. The claim that everyone else was cheating cannot exonerate those caught with their hands in the till. But there are more substantial arguments which help to set the record straight. The extent of corruption and extravagance in the years of radical rule has been wildly exaggerated. If government expenditure and indebtedness grew by leaps and bounds, that was largely because there was so much to be done to promote economic recovery, public education and social reform. Southern state governments in the past had done so little for their citizens that they had spent little and borrowed little. Similarly, the increased levels of taxation in the years of radical rule looked exceptional only in comparison with the very modest revenues of pre-war state governments. (It is also true that the tax burden now fell much more heavily on land which had escaped lightly in the days of planter-dominated government.) In other words, the scale of the financial operations of the radical régimes was largely a function of the vastly greater responsibilities which they faced, and of their more positive conception of their role.

During their brief lives those governments had important achievements to their credit. They aided and encouraged the expansion of industry and the railroads, and launched into legislation on child welfare, hospitals for the mentally ill, homes for orphans and other much-needed social reforms. They overhauled and modernised the legal codes and they committed themselves to free public education for all children. They injected a new democratic serum into the body of Southern politics, and broke for a time at least the entrenched power of old oligarchies. The mere fact that Negroes voted and held office and served as judges and jurors is the best indication of the changes which radical government wrought, however briefly, in Southern life. It is that same fact which explains the determination of its white critics to paint in indelible colours a picture of vicious, dishonest, and shameful misgovernment. The most telling contrast is between the record of the radical governments and the miserable record of the years from 1865 to 1868 when the Johnson governments allowed violence, disorder, intimidation, misery and injustice to flourish and grow unchecked, and sought only to turn the clock back to 1860.

The policies of the radical governments were not always successful – nor were they always very radical, for they never grasped the nettle of land re-distribution or other such measures to underpin the liberty of the freedman. In fact, whatever their intentions, the radical régimes never had the strength or the time to turn promise into effective performance. The odds were stacked against them from the very beginning. They lacked a firm political base; Union leagues made an initial effort to mobilise, organise and arouse the new black electorate but their efforts soon flagged in face of tough opposition. The new governments lacked the funds and the administrative machinery to make their economic and social policies a working reality in the lives of citizens, white and black – and, in 1869, Congress voted to bring to an end the activities of the Freedmen's Bureau, the one federal agency which might have backed up their efforts in this field. They lacked the capacity to enforce the law effectively against determined and violent resistance. The military occupation of the South under the Reconstruction Acts of 1867 used the soft pedal more than the iron heel. There were never more than twenty thousand soldiers unevenly spread across the vast territory of the South, and, in the early 1870s, the number dwindled to four or five thousand. Many Southerners never saw a Union soldier at all. As the army withdrew, and violence and defiance of the law persisted, the state governments hastily organised militia, largely but not exclusively Negro in composition. But the militia was quite unequal to the task of establishing law and order, and, instead of taming the lawbreakers, its members were often terrorised by them. As time passed and problems mounted, the uneasy radical coalition in the Southern states came apart at the seams, and factional disputes, ill-feeling between the races, and other divisions were eagerly exploited by the opposition.

That opposition – the implacable, organised and often violent opposition of the majority of Southern whites – was the central fact in the breakdown of radical reconstruction in the south. The Southern white 'conservatives' had the firm power base, the wide support, and the resources which the radicals lacked. In the fight against 'black reconstruction' they could unite whites of all classes and types in the common purpose of doing honour to the Lost Cause of 1865, reasserting white supremacy, and re-establishing a 'proper' order of society. They did not need to arouse or 'educate' their supporters, but simply to appeal to deep-rooted instincts. They worshipped at the shrine of the old South while they worked to build a new South given over to modern ways of business enterprise. They sought to paper over the cracks of class and status within white society by emphasis upon the stake of every white Southerner, from planter and entrepreneur to the most wretched and degraded of the poor, in returning the Negro to his old place at the very bottom of the heap. The only restraints upon their white supremacist campaign were imposed by fear of reopening the blind eye of the North to what was actually happening, and, paradoxically, by hopes of winning the 'deference' vote of some of the blacks.

The conservative strategy to regain control was a blend of propaganda, politics and brute force. They found it not too difficult to convince many people in the north of the barbarism, corruption and generally unsavoury character of the radical régimes in the south. They built bridges of common business interest and common attitudes to the Negro across the great divide between North and South. They exploited every division in the Republican ranks in the south, and won converts from the disillusioned, and the bewildered, both white and black. (Hiram Revels, first Negro to become a United States senator, later went over to the 'conservative' camp.) By their sustained efforts, they persuaded former enemies in north and south to leave them a free hand – or even to support them. By effective use of methods which were perfectly legal if not always wholly admirable, they were able to go a very long way towards the 'redemption' of the south. (Like the words 'carpetbagger' and 'scalawag', 'redeemer' represents another enduring triumph of the Southern whites in the battle of words. Whatever the judgment of the revisionists of a later day, radical reconstruction still bears the stigmata inflicted by those who did it to death.) But in some states – notably Mississippi, Louisiana and South Carolina – the sheer size of the Negro electorate demanded something more. In those states, but not only in those states, terror completed what other methods had begun.

The Ku Klux Klan was born in Tennessee in 1866, and its white-robed and hooded members were pledged to oppose Negro equality and secure a white man's government. In the earlier years of reconstruction, the murders, beatings, burnings and plunder perpetrated by the Klan against Negroes and their white allies helped to smooth the way to rapid restoration of conservative control in states like Tennessee, Virginia, North Carolina and Georgia. In the early 1870s, the Klan was harassed by new federal legislation, and disbanded – in theory but not in practice. It lived on in other guises, and, in any case, it had never been the only white secret society engaged in the work of 'redeeming' the south. From 1874, violence reached a new pitch in those states not yet under conser-vative control, and the so-called 'Mississippi Plan' of massive terror succeeded in deposing the Republicans in the elections in that state in 1875. The basic principle of the plan was succinctly stated by one of its supporters: 'Carry the election peaceably if we can, forcibly if we must.'[14] The same method was applied in South Carolina and Florida in the following year. So obvious had the perils of attempting to vote Republican become that, often, outright violence was unnecessary. Intimidation and ostentatious displays of strength were enough to deter all but the most resolute voter. Economic coercion was a quieter but equally effective method. To threaten the labourer with loss of his job, or the sharecropper with loss of his land, was a persuasive way to keep him from the polls.

The Southern 'redeemers' had a formidable array of weapons to back up their determination. They could invoke past memories and loyalties, present grievances, and fears for the future. They could exploit the one issue which never failed to stimulate a response from the mass of white Southerners. They were fighting on their home ground, with the advantages of political experience, traditional authority, and control of the economic and social levers which regulated the lives of most citizens, black and white. Behind it all lurked their ability and their willingness to resort to force when and where it mattered. They soon won a string of victories and, by 1876, only South Carolina, Louisiana and Florida remained precariously in Republican hands.

The radical régimes in the south simply lacked the strength to defeat such a formidable attempt to overthrow them. If the wealth, the established leadership, the business élite – and, in many states, the numerical majority too – were determined to ride roughshod over Negro liberties and Republican rule, only powerful intervention by the federal government could have stopped them. But as Southern resistance waxed, Northern resolution waned. Congress did make the attempt to protect the Negro (or any other citizen) in his exercise of the right to vote, but the Force Acts of 1870 and 1871, though formidable on paper, were not very effective in practice. They extended the jurisdiction of the federal courts and the law-enforcement powers of the federal troops, but it was still extremely difficult to track down the perpetrators of terror and intimidation, and even harder to get local white juries to convict them. The troops were very thin on the ground in most places – and not always noticeably eager to put themselves out on behalf of the Negro. Neither Congress nor the president kept up the pressure for strict enforcement of the law. Congress failed to vote adequate funds, and more of the money that was allocated was spent in policing elections in the north than in the south. (The Republicans hoped to exploit the Force Acts to curb the power of the Democratic machines in New York city and elsewhere.) President Grant used the Force Acts to some effect in 1871 – in South Carolina, for example – but, by 1875, his administration turned a deaf ear to desperate cries for help from Mississippi where the Republicans were fighting for their lives against mass terror. Already, too, in 1874, the Supreme Court had begun to suggest doubts about the constitutionality of the acts.

The changing congressional climate in matters concerning the reconstruction of the south showed itself in a number of ways. The Amnesty Act of 1872 removed the political disabilities of all but a handful of ex-Confederates, and Grant offered a free hand with pardons for those who still needed them. Congress was increasingly reluctant to contemplate further major legislation to protect the rights and freedom of black citizens, and throughout the earlier 1870s it rejected the pleas of Charles Sumner for a new civil rights measure outlawing segregation and discrimination of all kinds as infringements of the Fourteenth Amendment. In 1875, the year after Sumner's death, a Civil Rights Act was passed as a kind of epitaph to the great radical Senator, but only in a considerably diluted version which excluded schools from its provisions. The Civil Rights Act of 1875, weakened before it became law, generally regarded as a dead letter in the years that followed, was eventually declared unconstitutional by the Supreme Court in 1883. For all that, it did mark the first attempt to legislate in the highly sensitive area of desegregation of public facilities.

By the mid-1870s, the Republican party in the north was running out of ideas, idealism and ideological capital in its dealings with the south and the Negro. No party – and certainly no electorate – can sustain indefinitely an overriding commitment to one cluster of issues, however important. The two decades which the Republican party had devoted to slavery and race, the salvation and reconstruction of the Union, suggest a span of concentration and perseverance to be admired rather than belittled. That concentration had never of course been complete or exclusive. Even at its most highly-charged and critical moments, the era of reconstruction did not concern itself only with the reconstruction of the south. Politicians and many others were much exercised, too, by highly complicated financial questions, or economic policy, or local and ephemeral issues. By the 1870s, as the war faded further into the background, it was these matters – greenbacks and tariffs and subsidies – which became the normal agenda of politics, and the unrewarding toils of reconstruction which came to be regarded as exceptional (or even peripheral) problems. Perhaps the impeachment of Johnson and the election of Grant mark a kind of dividing line in this respect. The melodrama of the one kept the spotlight on the immediate post-war issues; the consequences of the other revealed a considerable shift of emphasis. After all, the scandals of the Grant administration and its squalid business associates were unfolding at the same time as the radical governments in the south were living out their brief and stormy lives. It is the historians who too often insist on putting them into separate watertight compartments.

The financial panic of 1873 and the subsequent depression certainly gave a new cutting edge to concern over economic and financial issues, and relegated to the background the unsolved and apparently insoluble problems in the south. By the mid-1870s, the Republican party was a more conservative, pragmatic, business-orientated party than in its earlier years. Its attitudes and its arteries were beginning to harden. The first generation of its leaders had created the party to serve certain causes; the new generation of 'stalwarts' felt little involvement in the great causes of their predecessors, and were the servants of new and powerful interests. Even some of the older generation were disillusioned by the consequences of reconstruction and the response of the Negro, as they understood (or failed to understand) them. A number of the leading figures had left the stage. Stevens died in 1868, Fessenden in 1869, Sumner in 1874; Wade and Chandler lost their Senate seats. Party strategists were increasingly sceptical of the prospects of winning reliable support in the south through the radical régimes, and pinned more faith in a solid Northern vote as the key to future electoral success. The business interests now so influential in party councils were even firmer advocates of sectional reconciliation as a springboard for new enterprise. The Southern conservatives seemed, if anything, more friendly to business than their opponents, and offered the best guarantee of future stability in the south. While the gap between Northern Republicans and Southern Negroes steadily widened, the bridges between Northern Republicans and Southern conservatives were strengthened, as they discovered common interests and ideas. The pressure to forget the past and its unfinished business grew stronger, and steadily weakened the will and sense of purpose which had inspired the reconstruction programme. That will was vulnerable to pressure and fatigue because the makers of reconstruction had always struggled in vain to disenthral themselves completely from the flaws and ambiguities of the prevailing white American view of the place of the black American in society. Their tragedy lay in their ultimate failure, their glory in that, against great odds, they made the attempt.

In the election of 1872, the writing was already on the wall, when would-be reformers in the Republican ranks, disgusted by the Grant administration, formed the Liberal Republican party. But instead of plans to reconstruct a region or a nation, reform was now attenuated into a concern, understandable enough, with clean, honest, efficient government. When they addressed themselves to the Southern problem, the Liberal Republicans favoured reconciliation and the restoration of state self-government. The party's ticket, headed by Horace Greeley, of all people, and supported by a motley collection of ex-radicals, ex-Copperheads and Southern conservatives, went down to heavy defeat. Its significance lay in the first post-war alliance of 'respectable' white leadership in north and south – an alliance which was able to reconcile the profession of liberal intentions with the abandonment of the Negro to his fate.

In the election of 1876 another north–south alliance rescued the United States from a new and serious crisis, again at the expense of the Negro. The outcome of the election depended upon the hotly-disputed returns from the three still 'unredeemed' Southern states, South Carolina, Florida and Louisiana. The Republican candidate, Hayes, needed the votes of all three states to win a majority in the electoral college. After weeks of tense argument and backstage manoeuvre, he received them. The essential parties to the compromise of 1877 were Northern Republicans and Southern conservatives, and their business friends. The Southerners finally deserted the Northern Democrats and allowed Hayes to be elected. In return, they procured the withdrawal of federal troops from the three unredeemed states and the recognition of the conservative régimes there. The South was also promised a fair share of federal patronage and money for railroad and other developments. Whether or not the compromise of 1877 was the work of a renewed alliance of Northern and Southern Whigs on the pattern of ante-bellum days, it certainly marked the end of the dominance of the issues and alignments of the Civil War era.[15] The North finally abandoned the struggle to win the peace as decisively as it had won the war, and gave its full attention to pursuit of the rewards of an expanding industrial society. The South won acceptance as a respectable participant in national life once again, and was left to manage its own affairs as it wished. White Americans, North and South, finally agreed to bury the hatchet – but they buried it deep in the aspirations of the Negro for real freedom and genuine equality.

7. Two general conclusions about 'radical' reconstruction stand out. First, it failed largely because it was not in fact radical enough – and in some respects not radical at all. Secondly, its failure was tragic but it was not total or unrelieved. Reconstruction was not radical enough partly, of course, because its major enactments were born of compromise with moderates. Men with any real claim to be regarded as radical were always in a minority – and often quite a small one – in the Republican party. They achieved a great deal in shifting the agenda of reconstruction steadily to the left in the later 1860s, but to pass laws they relied upon moderate support. The two constitutional amendments offer the best but by no means the only examples of the results of this process of compromise by dilution.

But this is only part of the explanation. With very few exceptions, even so-called radicals had no radical conception of what reconstruction should be. Most of them fought shy of the drastic economic changes which should have been the foundation of social and political reconstruction; they drew back from confiscation and redistribution of land for essentially conservative reasons of respect for property rights, and fear of creating awkward precedents. As some of them honestly confessed, they had great difficulty in living up to the principles of racial equality which they espoused. If radicals often wavered on the implementation of such a principle, many of the moderates upon whose support they relied never really adhered to it at all. There was great honour in the struggle to master prejudice, and deeply-entrenched assumptions, but there was a great price, too, in the opportunism, pragmatism, indirection and equivocation involved in attempts to win support or appease opponents. Lincoln had paid a similar penalty in securing emancipation, but there was a crucial difference in that case. Lincoln foresaw and probably intended that his proclamations would soon come to mean much more than they actually said. The supporters of the Fourteenth and Fifteenth Amendments, on the other hand, foresaw – and some of them intended – that they would mean much less than they actually appeared to say. The men who shaped reconstruction were often too busy studying white reactions to worry about the black response. They scarcely consulted the Negro about his own future. The 'radical' policy was still a white man's policy for the black American.

However menacing they may have continued to look and sound at times, almost all Republicans were further restrained by their respect for conventional constitutional forms. They consistently sought to find in the constitution the power which they needed, and they never launched a frontal attack on the federal structure which hampered any attempt at a truly radical reconstruction. They clipped the wings of the states but never for a moment considered their complete destruction. They showed a truly remarkable regard for the civil rights and liberties of their defeated enemies (with incredibly few, and short-lived, exceptions). They lacked the element of ruthlessness which true radicalism surely demands. In the words of one constitutional historian, 'they were, in short, not revolutionary radicals at all. Instead they were rather conservative constitutional legitimists, operating well within the Hamiltonian–Marshall tradition.'[16] Their constitutional orthodoxy left them almost as helpless as their predecessors before 1861 in face of the problem of how to impose the will of a national majority upon a well-entrenched local majority (or controlling minority).

Partly because of these constitutional inhibitions, there was a lack of toughness and stamina in the execution of the radical programme in the South. There was inadequate appreciation of the scale and complexity of the task of implementing such a programme in face of highly organised and bitter local resistance. There was no adequate administrative or legal machinery to help the makers of reconstruction, and they scarcely even tried to create it. It was a reflection of the whole character of mid-nineteenth-century government and society in America (and beyond), that there were no institutions, no experts, no precedents, no well-tried methods capable of putting such a programme into fully effective practice. The 'radicals' should not perhaps be blamed for being children of their age and working largely within the limitations of conventional notions on such matters, but such criticism must surely cast doubt upon their claims to radicalism. If their political difficulties caused the dilution of their basic statements concerning the rights and status of the freedmen, their constitutional inhibitions and administrative limitations ensured that those rights would be ill-protected in practice.

Fundamentally, most Republicans, radical and moderate, were inspired by their devotion to the kind of America in which they had grown up – a land of small property owners, small towns and small business where equality meant equality of opportunity, and equality of opportunity meant something real and hopeful because of rapid growth and expansion. If radicals now wished to make the South conform to the same social pattern, that scarcely betokened a radical philosophy or ideology. In order to move towards their goal, the Republicans were driven by force of circumstances in general (and Andrew Johnson in particular) to some desperate and even radical expedients. Georges Clemenceau, surveying the American scene for himself, put his finger on this point:

Most of the radicals of today embarked on the abolitionist sea without any clear idea of where the course would lead; they arrived at their present position only after being forced from one reform to another.[17]

Like most Republicans, the 'radicals' were in fact liberals, occasionally driven (but never for long permitted) to adopt extreme measures in exceptional circumstances. Like most American liberals of the nineteenth century, they were as much as anything conservators of a well-established liberal tradition, striving to reconcile long-held and deeply-cherished beliefs with the consequences of political, economic and social change. Their position was exceptional, and their policy occasionally 'radical' only because the changes through which they had lived amounted to a unique upheaval. In the tradition of American reform, they harked back to the old values of an idealised past, and sought to apply them to a changed and still changing situation. The radical senator Henry Wilson summed up this whole attitude; the task, he said, was to 'accept the living truths of the present, and . . . incorporate into the fundamental law of the land what is necessary to make the country what its founders intended it should be'.[18] The irony of the Republican position was that, while they struggled to impress upon the South a pattern long familiar in their own lives, that very pattern was in the process of being destroyed in its Northern home by the machine, the giant corporation, the great cities and an influx of new population. Faced with this dilemma, more and more Republicans opted for the material promise of the new age at the expense of the ideological commitments of the old. There is a curious parallel between the Confederate leaders during the war, and the Republican leaders during reconstruction. If the first were conservatives trapped in a revolutionary situation, the second were fairly conventional liberals trapped in a situation which demanded unconventional and unmitigated radical solutions.

Were the Republicans then doomed to complete failure? Were those who said in 1861 that the North could not conquer the South proved right by what happened after rather than before Appomattox? There is surely a silver lining to the story, if scarcely a happy ending. Through the turmoil of reconstruction as through the trials of war, the American political system – American democracy, in fact – revealed great resilience, unsuspected strength and a talent for survival. Elections followed their normal timetable, presidents and legislators came and went, the courts continued to function, despite the turbulent drama of vetoes and constitutional amendments, an unsuccessful attempt to impeach a president, and a successful attempt to manipulate the result of a presidential election. The Republican party, too, survived and established itself – if not yet very firmly – as the dominant party for the next sixty years.

More important, for all their limitations, the Fourteenth and Fifteenth Amendments built into the constitution commitments which might cause embarrassment and receive neglect, but which did not die. They planted two time-bombs which ticked away at the heart of the American constitutional system for a century. Like other measures, including the Civil Rights Act and even the Force Acts, they set precedents and taught lessons which could be invoked and applied a century later. Their passage would have been unthinkable outside the context of reconstruction and the political battles which were fought over it. They were deeply flawed, of course, but, in the words of Vann Woodward, 'the laws outlasted the ambiguities of their origins'.[19] For a few brief years, too, Negroes did vote and hold office and take part in the political life of the South, and if that fact left a memory and a bitterness in the minds of the white South, it left a memory and a hope, too, in the minds of black Americans. If reconstruction was a false dawn, it left behind an afterglow that was never quite extinguished. In the reconstruction era, the American nation made only the most tentative and ambiguous commitment to the proposition that the black man was included in the affirmation of the Declaration of Independence that all men are created equal. It made only the most faltering and unconvincing attempt to honour that commitment, and virtually abandoned it in the years that followed. But the ideals behind the commitment proved stronger than the men who made it so uncertainly and lived up to it so dismally. In the 1860s and 1870s, the United States had no examples to guide it in confronting the problems of a society in which large numbers of whites and blacks were both to live as free men. More recent history compels some humility in the critic, and some respect for the Republicans of the post-Civil War era. If the peace was finally lost, it was not lost without trace, nor even without honour.

# Chapter XX : The Enduring Legacy

There is a minor character in Thomas Wolfe's novel *You Can't Go Home Again*, an old man of nearly ninety, a veteran of the Union army, living out his days in a basement room in Brooklyn, in the 1920s, surrounded by his scrapbooks and mementoes of the Civil War.

> Although he was alert and eager towards the life around him, and much too brave and hopeful a spirit to live mournfully in the past, the Civil War had been the great and central event in old man Wakefield's life. Like many of the men of his generation, both North and South, it had never occurred to him that the war was not the central event in everyone's life. Because it was so with him, he believed that people everywhere still lived and thought and talked about the war all the time.[1]

To the popular imagination, the Civil War has always remained 'the great and central event' in American history. Until Vietnam, at least, it was always *the* war, without need of more specific label – and that was even more true in the defeated south than the victorious north. It took far more lives than any other American war, and it left more scars upon the survivors and their environment. It was the time of great decision when the Union was saved, slavery destroyed, and the whole American future determined. It was the crisis which produced the most famous of all Americans, Abraham Lincoln, who typifies and yet transcends the essential American character. It was the birthplace of modern America.

More sophisticated and intellectual opinion has often found this picture overblown, but it too has habitually seen the Civil War as the great divide of

American history, the great watershed where, on one side, the currents run back to the colonial and revolutionary origins of an innocent, pastoral America, and on the other flow forward to the complex, throbbing machinery of the affluent but anguished America of a century later. The war draws the obvious line between the world of Jefferson and Jackson and the world of Theodore and Franklin Roosevelt, between the west of Daniel Boone and the west of Buffalo Bill, between the South of *Gone with the Wind* and the South of *Intruder in the Dust*, between the era of the village store, the small workshop and the family farm, and the age of Rockefeller, Carnegie and J. P. Morgan. Whether as cause or symbol of the transformation of America, the place of the Civil War has seemed beyond challenge. As drama, blending epic with tragedy, it surely remains unique.

1. Yet, for all that, its central place does not go unchallenged. Insistent voices, sometimes small, sometimes strident, have questioned its clarity as a landmark, pointed to the irony and ambiguity of its results, and sought to flatten the great historical divide to the point where it is little more than a bump on the broad, sweeping plain of America's nineteenth-century development. No such reassessment can wish away the cost of the war in lives and suffering; rather, it turns the knife in old wounds by seeking to demonstrate the futility or irrelevance of such sacrifice. The attempts to scale down the significance of the Civil War have applied in most cases to one particular facet of it – its effect on economic growth, the balance of political power, social attitudes or Negro rights. It may be illuminating to put together these various arguments in an attempt to build up a broader case against the traditional view of the Civil War as the hinge of America's fate.

The presentation of the case might begin with those who lost the war. How was it that the defeated South survived, bloody but unbowed, unrepentant about its past and, within a few years, securely in control of its own future? Southern pride and self-consciousness waxed rather than waned, through constant devotion to the memory of the lost cause. The South emerged from its time of trial and defeat not less distinctively Southern, but clearly more so. Its cherished principle of white supremacy survived the military and political onslaughts intact. The black American, on the other hand, whose liberation was, or at least became, a war aim, proved to be the most tragic victim of the struggle. The freedom which he was given with one hand was taken away with the other, and he was betrayed into a new kind of subjection which was slavery in all but name. The war period saw merely the transition from the formal to the informal empire of white over black. America remained a white man's country, its government a white man's government. The whites of North and South eventually shook hands in a gesture of reconciliation across the prostrate body of Negro hopes. In a word, the war had brought little more than a nominal end to the evil of slavery; it had not begun to solve – indeed, it probably exacerbated – the problem of race.

Other charges in the indictment can be made to look just as formidable. The war, it might be argued, produced no great or enduring upheaval in the political and constitutional system. Such innovations as there were in the exercise of presidential power or the shift of authority from the states to the federal government were generally held to be justified only by the wartime emergency – and were as likely to spark a strong reaction as to set powerful precedents in the years that followed. (The record of the late-nineteenth-century presidents from Grant to McKinley, for example, scarcely suggests that Lincoln's extraordinary wartime powers set the pattern for a dynamic, expanded use of presidential authority for the next thirty years.) Almost all the groups engaged in Civil War politics insisted that they were fighting to defend the constitution rather than to rewrite it.

The case against any decisive economic and social impact of the war has been very strongly pressed in recent years. Charles A. Beard's interpretation of the struggle as 'the second American Revolution' has been interred beneath an avalanche of statistics, tables and econometric models.[2] The factors which governed American economic development during the nineteenth century were deep-rooted and operated over a long period, and the Civil War, it is implied, was no more than a surface ripple which scarcely affected the deeper currents of economic change. Where its effects were discernible at all, it slowed rather than speeded the rate of economic growth. The only consequence of the war which bears any of the hallmarks of social revolution is the destruction of slavery – and that, it is often alleged, was bound to happen soon in any case. The other great changes of the later nineteenth century – rapid industrial and urban growth, the emergence of giant corporations and of a large industrial working class, the new influx of immigrants, the decline of old élite groups and the rise of new ones – these all happened after the war but not because of it. Even in the purely military sphere, the greatest war of the century was followed by headlong demobilisation, and a return to the conspicuously non-military society of pre-war days when defence and security had held an uncommonly low priority. Astonishingly in a civil conflict, there was never any serious prospect of a military *coup*, or of army domination of politics and government. For all its scale and its drama, the war had no perceptible effect on European military thinking, which preferred to turn to the lessons offered on its own doorstep in the Austro-Prussian and Franco-Prussian wars. The chancelleries of Europe, too, temporarily roused by some of the wartime diplomatic crises, were happy to see the United States lapse back into what looked like its pre-1860 unconcern with the world beyond the western hemisphere.

In short, the period from the 1840s to the 1870s can be interpreted as the great aberration in American history when ideological issues reigned (but did not always rule) and the normal pattern of political bargain and compromise was abandoned – but only temporarily – and exceptional issues held the stage. Then, in 1877, the old pattern was finally restored in a setting changed no more than was to be expected over the span of a generation. The skin closed over the self-inflicted wounds of civil strife, and society gave itself over to other, more normal, pursuits. If the pain lingered in places below the surface, there was soothing balm, for some at least, in turning the war into a feast of glory, romance and nostalgia, a holiday from the real business of American life.

2. If the traditional picture of the war's importance is oversimplified, and the debunking picture grossly overstated, is it possible to provide a cooler, more balanced estimate of its place in American history? It would be fair to start with the simple fact of the interest which the war has consistently aroused in the century and more since it actually occurred. If history is concerned not merely with what happened but with the thoughts and feelings of men about what happened, it is a historical fact of prime importance that generations of Americans (and not only Americans) have treated the war as a major historical event with consequences which spread far and wide in the years and decades which followed. If the war has been almost universally regarded as the great watershed of American history, that consensus of opinion in itself has helped to shape later developments, at times almost with the power of a self-fulfilling prophecy.

It was only to be expected of course that the immediate post-war decades should be obsessed with the memory of the war. In politics, the South made the most of emotional attachment to the lost cause, and invoked it to win support even for measures designed to create a new kind of South. In the north, Republicans 'waved the bloody shirt' at election times, and assiduously cultivated that close identity between loyalty to the party and to the Union which was one of their most valuable assets. Veterans' organisations, most notably the Grand Army of the Republic, founded in 1866, were not merely social clubs, welfare organisations and outlets for those who wished to relive the excitements of their youth, but powerful political pressure groups which congressmen and even presidents ignored at their peril. The Grand Army of the Republic had over 400,000 members in the mid-eighties, and it held its last 'encampment' as late as 1949. For twenty or thirty years after Appomattox, the stamina (and the digestion) of the war's surviving heroes were tested by an endless round of dinners, reunions, parades and other celebrations. As the years passed, the festivities were punctuated by more solemn ceremonies as dead warriors were carried to their final, honoured rest. On such occasions, reconciliation of former enemies was a prominent theme, and in 1891 it found its perfect symbol in the presence of Joseph E. Johnston as a pall-bearer at Sherman's funeral, a gesture which hastened Johnston's own death a few weeks later. The same post-war period also produced the inevitable spate of memoirs, autobiographies, authorised biographies, recollections and eye-witness accounts which reached their climax in the long series of magazine articles, brought together in 1887 in the four volumes of Battles and Leaders of the Civil War.[3] Much of this output was devoted to elaborate exercises in the art of self-defence, or the settling of old scores – or to the business of making money. But it also included some items of great merit, like Grant's memoirs, and some vivid portrayals of the life of the ordinary soldier. The market for such literature in the later nineteenth century certainly suggests little or no inclination to let the memory of the Civil War fade and die.

What is more remarkable perhaps is the persistence of enthusiastic interest in the war deep into the twentieth century, in spite of the 'competition' provided by American participation in two great world conflicts. The proliferation of Civil War monuments, the preservation and restoration of the battlefields under the care of the National Parks Service, the pilgrims who visit both these and the more questionable Civil War sites (or sights) designed to trap the unwary tourist, all attest to continuing popular, official and commercial interest. It all came to a grand, if somewhat inflated, climax in the extraordinary re-enactments of the great events of the war during the centennial years from 1961 to 1965.[4] The Civil War round tables, and other societies, the Civil War magazines and papers, still flourish. An honoured tradition of popular Civil War history in the grand manner, which includes eminent names from Carl Sandburg to Bruce Catton, still reaches a huge reading public. Among academic historians there was a fashion in the 1940s and 1950s to debate whether the great Civil War themes were now exhausted, but such doubts have been answered in a re-sounding negative as old themes have been revived and new ones explored in the last twenty years. Any historical problem which can inspire the work of a Randall, a Nevins, a Craven and a Nichols in one generation, a Donald, a Current, a Hyman in the next – and a small army of able younger historians following in their wake – is still very much alive and seems likely to remain so.[5] It is clear enough, then, that whether as an escape into nostalgia or a search for true understanding, a retreat from the present or a quest for explanation of it, the interest in the Civil War which has passed its first century is fairly launched into its second.

Much of that interest, of course, lies in the appeal of the excitement and romance of the Civil War. But behind that surely lies a deeper conviction of its enduring and complex meaning for later generations. No single, clear, un-equivocal statement of that meaning is possible; the real significance of the Civil War is subtle, varied, often elusive, but pervasive. A clear distinction needs to be drawn between those developments and changes which may be regarded as the direct achievement of the Civil War, and those where the war had some influence, discernible but not perhaps decisive, whether as a secondary or indirect cause, a catalyst, a stimulus, an accelerator or even a brake. The items in the first category make up a short but impressive list. Those in the second category are more numerous and diverse, and much more difficult to define and evaluate, especially at the point where the contribution of the Civil War to a particular development becomes caught in a tangled web of causation which includes many other strands. In such cases the role of the war may have been less as a generator of entirely new developments than an influence which first protected institutions and structures which already existed and then helped to shape their future or deflect them into new directions. The way in which events happen is as important as the fact that they happen at all, and it is this configurative role[6] of the Civil War in American society and politics, ideology and mythology, which demands further investigation.

First, however, the direct, unmistakable consequences of the war deserve to be underlined. It is stating the obvious to say simply that the war preserved the Union and destroyed slavery, but it still needs to be said, for the obvious is too easily taken for granted. Neither of these major achievements was obvious – or even likely – when the war began in 1861. The South entered the fray to defend its way of life and its 'peculiar institution', and it was widely expected that it would make good its independence. When the war began, the leadership of the North stoutly denied any intention of destroying slavery where it already existed. In the first year of the war, at least, slavery seemed safe whichever side won the advantage, and yet the pressures of war destroyed it once and for all in the next three years. It is hard to conceive of any circumstances in which slavery would have been abolished in the Southern states in the 1860s without the Civil War. An institution with two hundred years' history in north America behind it was swept away by four years of civil conflict. Its passing undermined a whole way of life, and created the opportunity of a new life for four million liberated black Americans. The fact that that opportunity was so tragically lost in so many ways does not deprive the Civil War of its one great destructive achievement.

Its other great result – the salvation of the Union – was in a sense a conservative achievement. It was, however, a considerable surprise to those who had seen in secession final proof of the fatal weakness of American federalism and democracy, and who believed that a Union which could no longer be held together by compromise, could certainly not be saved by coercion. But, of course, the unsuspected power and resilience which had rescued the Union had also changed it. It was no longer the Union as it was in 1860. The war to restore the *status quo* had in fact revised it. The triumph of Northern aims gave an enormous moral and emotional boost to American nationalism. The war had created some precedents and offered some new possibilities for the growth of political and social institutions to match national feeling with commensurate national power. But it was still an open question in 1865 whether the precedents would be followed and the possibilities exploited. The answer depended on the more subtle and indirect ways in which the war might shape the American future.

3. The Civil War did not bring about an economic and social revolution throughout the United States, and even the revolution launched in the south with the abolition of slavery was soon abandoned. It is extremely doubtful whether the war of itself caused any fundamental economic change which would not otherwise have taken place. In the economic history of the United States it was not the great, spectacular watershed between one era and another. Its economic influence was less dramatic but still important, especially

as it helped to shape the way in which long-term developments actually happened – how quickly, through what agencies, at what cost, and to whose advantage.

The economic impact of the Civil War has been discussed in an earlier chapter, and only a few general comments are in order here. The war smoothed the path of industrial capitalism in the United States by the destruction of slavery, and of the power of the slave-owning planter class to obstruct that line of development. Wartime conditions provided a searching test of American industry at a crucial formative stage, and its successful passing of that examination gave it confidence in its power and its future place in American life. Indeed, by its contribution to the salvation of the Union, it acquired an aura of patriotic virtue which could be used, almost like an economic equivalent of 'waving the bloody shirt', to legitimise the whole process of spectacular industrial expansion in the later nineteenth century. The war gave industry much more tangible gains, too, in the mushrooming profits of the boom from 1863 onwards, and in a spate of economic legislation which, however meagre the practical results of some individual measures, provided ample evidence overall of the beneficent intentions of the federal government and the Republican party. The new financial system which emerged from the war years – greenbacks, bonds, taxes, national banking system – was the most conspicuous of those changes, and possibly the most important. Although various economic interests and political groupings spent the post-war years fighting over the implications of that system, it generally helped to promote large-scale industrial enterprise and found its best friends among the industrial entrepreneurs. In general terms, if it is over-dramatic to argue that, in a few short years, the Civil War transferred effective economic and political power into the hands of industrial capitalists, it is fair to say that it gave a vigorous push to a movement which was already under way.

If the statistics do eventually prove that the war slowed rather than accelerated the rate of economic growth in the decade of the 1860s, that is still only one part of the story. It is possible, even probable – but very hard to prove conclusively – that it had other long-term catalytic or configurative effects. It gave a stimulus to new methods of production, organisation and marketing; it forced producers and traders to think more than ever in terms of a national market; it accelerated the shift of labour into industry and especially heavy industry; it may well have brought about a redistribution of income in favour of manufacturing interests and of the north-eastern region of the United States; it encouraged and hastened the replacement of Southern cotton by western grain as the leading element in the American export trade; it helped to make the mid-sixties a period of prosperity the like of which American farmers were not to experience again before the end of the century.

It remains to explore a little further the elements of ambiguity and irony and unpredictability in the economic impact of the war. American business was no single monolithic interest engaged in a giant conspiracy to exploit the sectional crisis for its own ends. It contained a variety of often conflicting interests which disagreed with each other over high or low tariffs, soft or hard money – and the Republican party faithfully reflected those differences during and after the Civil War. Economic policies did not always produce the expected results. The eastern bankers who had fought the new national banking system tooth and nail found after the war that it worked very much in their favour and became a major instrument of their financial hegemony over other sections of the country. Men who had bemoaned the issue of the greenbacks in 1862 as a confession of moral as well as financial delinquency lived to fight for their preservation in the years after 1865. The Fourteenth Amendment, ratified in the mid-sixties as part of the programme to reconstruct the south, acquired within a few years a new and largely unforeseen meaning as a bastion to protect great corporations (in their guise as legal 'persons') from interference by state governments.[7] If the manufacturers proved to be the chief economic beneficiaries of the war, as some historians argue, their victory was an incidental rather than a planned result of the conflict.

The deepest irony lies in the fact that the Northern victors in the war believed for the most part that they had succeeded in protecting an economic and social system with which they had long been familiar and which they greatly cherished – a society of small units, individual enterprise, and open opportunity. In a sense they were right, in spite of the new skeleton of organisation and complexity and interdependence which the war had fitted into its loose-limbed structure. But the world which they had saved was a world which was doomed. Having survived the fiery trial of civil conflict, it succumbed after the panic of 1873 and the subsequent depression to the strength of a new industrial society of complex technology, huge mills and factories, giant corporations and teeming cities. In the economic as in other spheres, the true significance of the Civil War lay not so much in what it altered or initiated as in what it protected and allowed to grow and flourish. (The sceptics who question the economic repercussions of the war all seem to take for granted the fact that the North actually won it; they might stop to consider the social and economic consequences which would have followed from either a Southern victory or a compromise peace arising out of military stalemate.) But, ironically in this instance, the war not merely preserved the free-labour system idealised in the Republican ideology of 1860; it also preserved and fostered the conditions out of which the new urban industrial America could and would soon rise to overshadow it. In the words of William Dean Howells's hero, Silas Lapham, describing his return from the war to pick up the threads of his small business, 'I found that I had got back to another world. The day of small things was past, and I don't suppose it will ever come again in this country.'[8]

Much the same pattern emerges from a consideration of the impact of the war on the working classes of America. Certainly, in the north, it produced no massive upheaval in the social order, but, in protecting the *status quo* it protected too the seeds of future change. It appeared to preserve a system in which one man worked for another only until he acquired the means and the opportunity to work for himself. But it helped to clear the way for a system in which the typical worker was the employee of a huge, impersonal corporation, with little or no prospect of ever achieving the traditional kind of economic independence as a reward for his labours. The members of the trade unions which made important gains during the war generally shared the prevailing 'free labour' ideology. After the war, those unions faced an uphill struggle to hold on to wartime gains in face of the double challenge of a less favourable labour market, and the growing power of large-scale business organisation. The National Labour Union formed in 1866 had no solid union basis and soon became little more than a talking shop. In the post-war era, American labour faced the transition from an age when the phrase 'working classes' included manufacturers as well as workers – indeed all who were engaged in productive labour – to an age in which the industrial working class consisted of a mass of wage-earning, non-property-owning employees.

In January 1865, Karl Marx drafted an address from the International Workingmen's Association to Abraham Lincoln. It declared that the working-men of Europe felt instinctively that 'the star-spangled banner carried the destiny of their class', and it built up to this remarkable conclusion:

The workingmen of Europe feel sure that as the American War of Indepen-dence initiated a new era of ascendancy for the middle class, so the American anti-slavery war will do for the working classes. They consider it an earnest of the epoch to come, that it fell to the lot of Abraham Lincoln, the single-minded son of the working class, to lead his country through the matchless struggle for the rescue of an enchained race and the reconstruction of a social world.[9]

This was a picture which few Americans would have recognised. Less than a year earlier, in a reply to a group of New York workingmen, Lincoln himself had discussed the working-class stake in the war in words which began in apparent agreement with Marx but ended in the exposition of a peculiarly American ideology, as non-Marxian as it is possible to be:

None are so deeply interested to resist the present rebellion as the working people. Let them beware of prejudice, working division and hostility among themselves. The most notable feature of a disturbance in your city last summer was the hanging of some working people by other working people. It should never be so. The strongest bond of human sympathy, outside of the family relation, should be one uniting all working people, of all nations, and tongues, and kindreds. Nor should this lead to a war upon property, or the owners of property. Property is the fruit of labor – property is desirable – is a positive good in the world. That some should be rich, shows that others may become rich, and hence is just encouragement to industry and enterprise. Let not him who is houseless pull down the house of another; but let him labor diligently and build one for himself, thus by example assuring that his own shall be safe from violence when built.[10]

Lincoln provides much the more accurate picture of the America which he knew – but it offered little comfort to the worker in the age which was soon to come.

He also highlighted another feature of American society which the Civil War did not invent, but certainly intensified. This was the stumbling block to working-class solidarity created by the problem of race. It is possible to reverse the judgment of one historian who writes that 'class conflict . . . was the sub-merged shoal on which radical dreams [of equality before the law] foundered',[11] and suggest that race was the submerged shoal upon which hopes of working-class unity foundered. Before, during and after the Civil War, it was above all the poorer, less skilled, less secure white workers who feared the consequences of emancipation of the slaves. It was this which led to 'the hanging of some working people by other working people' during the draft riots in New York City in July 1863. It was the same fear of the influx of freed Negroes into the north, competing for jobs and houses, which drove unions to debar Negroes from membership in the post-war years, and which helped to undermine the prospects of a genuinely radical reconstruction of the south. Labour organisations showed far more interest in the currency question than in guarantees of equal rights for Negroes before the law. The conservatism of white workers on matters such as race widened the gap which separated labour from middle-class 'radical' Republicans, eagerly pursuing the cause of Negro rights but, with few exceptions, totally lacking any conception of a radical economic and social programme to meet working-class demands. When the reconstruction issues no longer held the top priority, the surviving radical Republicans had little or nothing to offer in answer to the problems of the new-model industrial America. While the industrial workers looked elsewhere for guidance, they faced continuing divisions in their own ranks, not merely between black and white, but native American and Italian or Slav immigrant. The whole story offers an excellent example of a recurring pattern in American history when a wide gap grows between middle-class liberals intent upon righting moral or legal wrongs and working-class discontent focused upon more practical matters of bread, jobs, houses and security.

The shattering impact of the Civil War and reconstruction era upon the Negroes themselves has been discussed elsewhere. The shock of liberation was rapidly followed by the shock of its harsh and unpleasant consequences – the loss of political rights, the denial of social equality, the maintenance of segregation, the exploitation and degradation of sharecropping and other devices wielded by those who had economic power. After its death, slavery was seen for what it was – a valuable but not indispensable instrument for the preservation of white supremacy. The broken and unfulfilled promises of the years of war and reconstruction left a trail of bitterness, disillusion, injustice and festering discontent which nothing could wash away. The North, which had freed the slaves in time of war, had no intention of treating the Negro as an equal in time of peace. In its own way of life and its own modes of thought it could not live up to the commitment which it had half-made. In the closing years of the century, the white South fastened upon the Negroes an elaborate legal apparatus of discrimination and segregation which restricted them at every turn in their daily lives. The North turned a blind eye, and the Supreme Court endorsed such laws by accepting that the provision of separate but equal public facilities satisfied the terms of the Fourteenth Amendment. Also in the 1890s, the white leaders of the South, having used the Negro vote as long as it was docile and manageable, moved quickly to eliminate it as soon as it showed signs of becoming unreliable or independent. The attempt to bring Negroes and poor whites together in the Populist party in the Southern states soon led to difficulties and defections in the ranks of the groups concerned. But it also alerted conservative white leadership to the danger, and led to a quick rallying of all whites to the standard of white supremacy, and the swift disfranchisement of the Negro by means of literary tests, the poll tax and all the other devices to exploit the loopholes in the Fifteenth Amendment. Twice in the last quarter of the nineteenth century the rights of the black American were sold to pay the price of compromise between rival groups of white Americans – once in 1877 in order to reconcile North and South, and again, in the 1890s, to reconcile the conservative and the discontented within the South itself.

Against such a bleak background there were some compensations and some hopes left to the Negroes. Nothing could quite undo the simple, revolutionary fact of the abolition of slavery. The Negroes were now freer to develop their own culture, their own institutions, their own capacity to state their case and improve their lot. The Negro churches were a training ground for community leadership and an instrument for fostering a sense of identity and self-respect. Negro schools and colleges provided a ladder for advancement and hope for the future. Some Negroes did prosper in business or the professions – and segregation had the ironic effect of stimulating that development. The long twentieth-century struggle for the advancement of the Negro in American society at least had the inspiration of the memory of a brief period when black men had played an active part in government and politics. There was, too, the knowledge that the promises and the pledges of the Fourteenth and Fifteenth Amendments still stood in the constitution. They represented a national commitment which the nation might yet be brought to honour. When, in the twentieth century, the question of black–white relations in American society was itself 'nationalised' by the mass migration of Negroes to the north, that commitment became harder to ignore or escape. Meanwhile, even after he had shed the fetters of slavery, the Negro remained an odd man out in a white man's country.

The South, too, remained something of an odd man out in the reconstructed Union. In the first shock of defeat, it seemed to accept its humiliation almost abjectly. Pondering the steady flow through Washington of ex-rebels seeking pardon, the New Yorker George Templeton Strong wrote in July 1865:

> The cause these penitent traitors worked and fought for is simply destroyed by force, without any treaty or compromise or concession wherewith to justify their submission or soften its pang, doubly humiliating when they remember their savage swagger and bluster of bygone days. The nation rides roughshod over states rights and abolishes slavery! Cavaliers of 1650, Puritans of ten years later, Jacobites any time after 1688, Tories after our Revolution, Legitimists after the French Revolution, Red Republicans of our own day, have chosen death or civil disabilities or exile before allegiance to the new order against which they had struggled in vain. Our rebels are elbowing each other as they crowd up to the office where the oath is administered.

A month later, Strong was not so sure. He distrusted their apparent resigned acceptance of defeat, and feared that 'Southerners will talk in another tone as soon as their sham humility has restored them to their old places of power'.[12] In fact, the white leadership of the South recovered much of its confidence and the confidence of its supporters remarkably quickly, with the aid of the Johnsonian reconstruction programme. By the time that it was confronted with a tougher set of conditions for full re-admission to the Union, the white South was strong enough to mount a sustained and ultimately successful campaign of resistance against the new radical régimes. Putting behind it any notion of quiet acceptance of defeat – but not the treasured memory of the cause itself – the South recovered control of its own affairs, and even convinced many Northerners that it knew the best way to handle delicate questions of race relations and minority rights. In 1877 an alliance of conservative interests in north and south achieved the kind of sectional compromise which had proved impossible in 1860–1. It was practicable in 1877 because the North rather than the South had exhausted its resolution to stand firm in defence of its basic principles. In the generation after 1877, the South evolved and applied a new instrumentation of white supremacy to replace the one which the war had destroyed.

But the South was still beset with the problem of defining its new place within the United States. Its astonishing political and psychological recovery was not matched by an equally spectacular economic recovery or material advance. At the same time, even the apparent revival of its morale hid an inner turmoil of shame and doubt and guilt. Two of the key factors which still set the South apart and nourished its strong sense of separate identity were its economic and social backwardness, and its experience, unique in America, of failure, defeat and humiliation. The third factor, which obstructed any cure for the first and prevented the exorcism of the second, was its self-torturing obsession with race. After the bitter experiences of war and reconstruction – military defeat, abolition of slavery, economic ruin, black participation in government – the new South fastened upon itself a new strait-jacket as tight as that which slavery had placed around the old South. Once again, the very things which gave the South its separate identity were the things which also made it both backward and backward-looking – a lagging and inefficient economy, the romance of the lost cause, and the unshakable priority of white supremacy. The South could either abandon its past, its memories and its obsessions, and stretch out to grasp the material benefits and share the common values of American society as a whole, or it could remain locked in a prison of its own making. For at least a century after Appomattox, the South faced the agonising problem of how to catch up with the rest of the United States without being swallowed up in the process.

4. The war which saved the Union transformed it into a nation; if George Washington was the father of the Union, Abraham Lincoln was the father of the nation. Ideas such as these have been expressed often enough, and they encapsulate one of the basic truths about the significance of the war. But the nationalising influences of the Civil War worked themselves out in strange and sometimes paradoxical ways, and eventually left the nation strong and secure, but still lacking a political instrument adequate to express its meaning or a governmental system adequate to transmit its power.

The Civil War was the most profound and dramatic experience which millions of Americans had ever known or would ever know in their lives. It was an experience which, at every turn, encouraged or compelled them into a sense of belonging to the nation and of participation in its affairs. The stimulus which the war gave to American nationalism was emotional and practical, popular and coercive, individual and institutional, social and economic, military and political. The final victory of the Union cause was the most emphatic demonstration possible of the power of the nation. The long struggle to achieve that victory – in its blacker as well as its brighter moments – helped to build up a sense of involvement in the nation's affairs such as the bulk of Americans had never known before. Out of involvement grew commitment and loyalty. At least one and a half million men served, eagerly or reluctantly, in the Union army, and they involved not merely themselves but their families, friends and neighbours in their life-and-death struggle on behalf of the nation. The Union army was one of the most potent agencies of American nationalism; it was, apart from anything else, by far the largest national organisation which the United States had ever seen. The men who returned home from the army had seen places and people hitherto remote, but now fixed in their minds as part of the same American nation to which they belonged; they had seen the nation in action as something real and comprehensible (if not always congenial). The men who did not return home contributed to the nation that stock of heroes and memories which a sense of nationality demands. If the Union did not already have an adequate sense of purpose and direction, it would have to be invented to justify their sacrifice.

Soldiers and civilians alike had developed their sense of belonging to the nation not only by their blood, sweat and toil but by the continued exercise of their rights and duties as citizens and voters throughout the war. In that sense, the election of 1864 was as much a triumph for American nationalism as for American democracy, when, at a time of national crisis, farmers, workers, businessmen and even soldiers in the field were able to cast their votes and have their say about their national government. The Civil War created a new sense of national citizenship, and the post-war constitutional amendments simply gave legal definition to a concept of citizenship and its rights which was already fixing itself in the minds of the people themselves.

The nationalism generated by the war had its roots well established among the mass of the people. But its strength was also revealed in the rich foliage of new institutions and organisations which the war produced or fostered in the economic and social life of the country. The process, so eloquently described by Allan Nevins, of transforming an unorganised into an organised society, an invertebrate into an integrated Union, was very much part and parcel of the nationalising influence of the Civil War.[13] The day of the truly giant business organisations was still to come, but, under wartime pressures, industry, business and transport were obliged to think more than ever in national terms. They were brought face to face with the consequences of the interdependence of various interests, sections and groupings within society. They operated in a national market, and they were obliged to realise that what was decided in the banking-houses of New York, authorised by government agencies in Washington, produced in the mills of New England or the blast furnaces of Pennsylvania, or despatched from the freight yards of Chicago, had implications and repercussions which were nationwide. Professional bodies, labour organisations and charitable and voluntary associations, too, saw the need to think and meet and act nationally. This whole web of organisations and institutions was an essential part of the framework of the new American nation. The trend was of course running in this direction before 1860; the Civil War proved such an effective stimulus precisely because it was pouring new and fast-flowing streams into an already existing current.

Government, of course, was part creator, part reflector of the nationalist tide. By resisting and finally crushing the threat of secession, the federal government eliminated a chronic threat to the stability of the Union once and for all. It shattered the notion of state sovereignty, and weakened (but did not destroy) the idea of states rights. If it had done no more, the war would have shifted the whole balance of the federal system in a national direction. But it also took the government of the Union into fields of activity and assertions of power un-imaginable a few years earlier. These have been discussed in earlier chapters, and they cover everything from the top priority of making war and the breathtaking assumption of the authority to destroy slavery, to the restriction of cherished civil liberties and the enactment of an ambitious nationalist programme of economic measures. The significance of the whole process has been clearly expounded by James A. Rawley:

The Civil War . . . created a truly national state, in which distinctions of section and caste were blurred, states were subordinated, and political and economic institutions were placed on a national basis and made to serve national ends. It repudiated the doctrine of secession. . . . It inculcated the doctrine that all citizens owe their first and paramount loyalty to the nation, and it adopted various measures to give effect to this doctrine: conscription of manpower, the income tax, a national banking system, the legal tender acts, national subsidies to education and railroads, a protective tariff, and a new national immigration policy.[14]

As Strong confided to his diary soon after the war ended, 'the people has (I think) just been bringing forth a new American republic – an amazingly large baby – after a terribly protracted and severe labor, without chloroform'.[15] It remained to be seen, in the following years, whether the United States had a government, *in loco parentis*, strong enough to prevent that amazingly large baby from getting out of hand.

As long as the war lasted, its nationalising effects seemed well-nigh irresistible, and in 1865 they were anointed with the holy oil of victory. But what kind of permanent legacy would they bestow upon post-war America? The emotional bonds forged by the war lived on (if not with their wartime intensity) and became a central part of the national heritage, and a vital contribution to the national spirit. As time passed, even the Southern experience became merged into the national heritage and Robert E. Lee emerged as an American as well as a Southern hero. The sense of national belonging and identity engendered by the war was sometimes threatened or weakened, but never lost. The social, economic, and institutional framework of nationalism stimulated by the war, lived on into the peace and spread its tentacles further and wider – largely because it was itself a part of a long-term, virtually irresistible development, in a century of industrial and urban growth.

But the political and governmental legacy of the Civil War was much more mixed and uncertain. So many of the functions assumed by government during the war were clearly exceptional, and justified only by unique circumstances that the functions themselves proved to be ephemeral. They could live only in the hothouse climate of war. The rapid demobilisation of the army in 1865 is the most obvious but not the only example of the hasty abandonment of wartime powers. Along with conscription and all the other apparatus for raising and sustaining a huge army, the government discarded many wartime sources of revenue, including the income tax, scaled down the attempt to manage the whole financial system, slashed its own expenditures and restricted its inter-ference with such basic civil rights and liberties as the writ of habeas corpus to those Southern states which were not yet re-admitted to the Union. Now that the Union was safe, the Supreme Court felt free to resume its role of watchdog on the excesses of government in a series of decisions of the kind which it had studiously avoided while the war still raged.

The cut-back was not of course complete. Federal expenditure and revenue (and the national debt) remained well above pre-war levels; the national banking system survived; even the greenbacks continued a somewhat precarious existence. The wartime legislation on the tariff, the public lands and the railroads was consolidated, not abandoned, in the post-war decades. But the role of the government as promoter and provider of subsidies was not the invention of the Civil War; it had a much longer history in the economic development of the United States. The federal government did not, then, shed all its wartime weight, but within a few years it was closer to its slender figure of 1860 than its bulging frame of 1865.

The same pattern applies to the balance of power between the executive and legislative branches of the government. During the war, Lincoln built upon the imprecise foundation of presidential war powers an elaborate panoply of executive power, and his critics talked darkly of the threat of presidential dictatorship. Within three years of the end of hostilities, after a long and bitter battle with Andrew Johnson, the Republican majority in Congress seemed bent on asserting its supremacy over the executive and the judiciary; its critics deplored the trend towards legislative tyranny. But, ten years later, the balance between president and congress was back very much where it had been before the war. Whatever else they may have been, the presidents from Grant to McKinley were scarcely dictators, and the congressional leaders were more often dismissed as time-servers than condemned as tyrants. In other words, after being tugged violently first one way and then the other, the pendulum settled very close to dead centre.

A more enduring shift in the balance of power did occur in the relationship between the federal government and the states. The exigencies of war brought about a great increase in government activity at all levels, but also a steady shift of real power to the centre – exemplified for example in the story of the recruitment and supply of the Union armies. If the effect of the war was to diminish relatively, but not absolutely, the power of the state governments, at a time of general expansion of government, the effect of peace was to diminish those powers still further, at a time of general contraction of government. The programme of congressional reconstruction asserted the supremacy of the federal government over the states in various ways, imposed stringent conditions on the re-admission of the ex-rebel states, and sought to transfer from the states to the federal government jurisdiction over wide areas, particularly concerning citizenship and civil and voting rights. In practice, the reconstruction measures were far more effective in reducing the power of the states than in expanding the power of the federal government. The constitutional amendments weakened the authority of the states without giving effective power to the federal government or the federal courts to enforce and execute the guarantees which they stated as general principles. Whether in reconstructing the Southern states or, later, in protecting the freedom from legal restraint of business corporations, the Fourteenth Amendment eroded the power of the states without putting anything effective in its place. Up to a point, the constitutional developments of the Civil War and reconstruction era launched the same kind of two-pronged attack upon the states as Marshall's Supreme Court had done almost half a century earlier. The two prongs were, first, the defence of individual and corporate rights and liberties, and, second, the assertion of federal authority. But, in the 1860s, the judicial fork proved stronger in the first prong than the second.

The dismantling of federal power after the Civil War was in some vital respects, therefore, much too effective. It left the federal government without the strength to compensate for the decline of the states, let alone tackle the looming problems of industrial America. Important precedents had of course been set, but when the doctrines of *laissez-faire* and social Darwinism came into their own in the last three decades of the century, they were relegated into the background. The Civil War, then, left the United States with a national government lacking machinery or power commensurate with the needs of the evolving nation. The war had helped to create a nation, but not an effective national government.

There were some contemporary observers who caught glimpses of what was happening. In 1865, Strong poured scorn on those who would stick to the letter of the constitution as it was, even when the whole future of the country was at risk.[16] In his general disillusion with the shape and character of post-war America, Henry Adams condemned the inadequacy of the system of government:

The whole government, from top to bottom, was rotten with the senility of what was antiquated and the instability of what was improvised . . . the whole fabric required reconstruction as much as in 1789, for the Constitution had become as antiquated as the Confederation. Sooner or later a shock must come, the more dangerous the longer postponed. The Civil War had made a new system in fact; the country would have to reorganise the machinery in practice and theory.

He went on to reach characteristically gloomy conclusions:

The political dilemma was as clear in 1870 as it was likely to be in 1970. The system of 1789 had broken down, and with it the eighteenth-century fabric of *a priori*, or moral principles. . . . Such a system, or want of system, might last centuries, if tempered by an occasional revolution or civil war; but as a machine, it was, or soon would be, the poorest in the world – the clumsiest – the most inefficient.[17]

In such a context, the Civil War years look like a great opportunity to reform the system, fleetingly grasped, but ultimately lost. The war revealed the potential scope and strength of national power, and stimulated a remarkable attempt to realise it. Peace reversed the process, and reconstruction soon revealed the severe limitations of available national power. In the later nineteenth century that power was manifest everywhere but in government. One of the most puzzling but pervasive and permanent legacies of the Civil War lies in the consolidation of a uniquely powerful nation, without a powerful national government to match it.

5. The Civil War has every appearance of being a watershed in the history of American political parties. The Democrats, the party of Jefferson and Jackson, had been the dominant force for most of the period from 1800 to 1860. Under various labels, they had controlled the federal government as the normal, natural majority party, although their ascendancy was threatened by the Whigs at times in the 1840s. In the seventy years after 1860, by contrast, only two Democratic presidents occupied the White House, and the Republicans generally held sway. Obviously, the Civil War is fundamental to any explanation of this change. The Republican party lived for decades, if not generations, on its reputation as the party which had saved the Union and freed the slaves, the party of Abraham Lincoln, the national martyr-hero. Its appeal in the later nineteenth century was based upon its exploitation of historic issues – the choice between the loyal men who had preserved the Union, and the traitors who had almost succeeded in destroying it. The election campaign of 1864 set a pattern which lasted for many years.

But the fact remains that that appeal produced only a limited return. From the time that all the Southern states returned to full participation in national politics in the 1870s, the Republican position was anything but secure. A Democratic South, with its Northern allies, was a match for a Republican party which was now once again almost an exclusively Northern sectional organisation. The five presidential elections from 1876 to 1892 were all desperately close-run affairs. Two of them were won by the Democrat, Grover Cleveland, and only one of the three Republican victors, James A. Garfield, had a clear majority of the total vote. In ten congressional elections between 1874 and 1892, the Democrats won a clear and sometimes large majority of seats in the House of Representatives on eight occasions. After the end of formal reconstruction in the 1870s, the Republicans continued their efforts to build up effective support in the south. They fluctuated between bids to attract and organise the Negro vote, and attempts to create a white Republican party in the Southern states. Neither strategy produced any significant success. When, in the 1890s, the Republican party did break through into a period of ascendancy as the national majority party, it did so by making gains not in the south but in the north and west. The serious economic depression beginning in 1893, during a Democratic administration, gave them their opportunity, and they made spectacular gains in the mid-term elections of 1894. Two years later, the Democratic party was 'captured' by its agrarian western and southern wing, and chose William Jennings Bryan as its standard-bearer. The Bryan campaign, based upon the agrarian discontent of the south and west, and supported by the third-party

Populists in those regions, virtually turned its back on urban-industrial America. But increasingly it was urban-industrial America which had the people and therefore the votes and the Republican McKinley won the election by the most decisive margin since 1872. The big city vote for which both parties had fought hard since the Civil War now swung heavily to the Republicans, and stayed there for most of the next thirty years.[18] In that period, Republican supremacy was seriously threatened only by the party's own internal divisions.

The Civil War, then, was but the first step towards Republican ascendancy – a vital step but still a tentative one. It gave the party a good chance to establish itself as one half of a two-party system, with a reasonable expectation of life. But it faced something of a crisis as the generation of its founders passed away, new men of different outlook took over, and its original ideals and objectives receded into the background. Once its attempt to put down roots in the south had failed, and its historic appeal began to fade, it needed a new image and a new approach if it was to become the majority party. With generous help from the mistakes of its opponents, it succeeded in the 1890s in projecting itself to the mass of Northern voters as the party of prosperity and economic growth, the party which was prepared to make some attempt to come to terms with urban-industrial society. While it had the image (well-deserved) of a party of big business and cautious conservatism, it was less negative and backward-looking than its opponents, and it did provide shelter for the newly-emerging progressive movement at the turn of the century. For a very long time, of course, the Republican party continued to derive some benefit from its Civil War record, and it was invoked whenever and wherever it would serve. The fact that the bulk of the Negro vote (largely in the north, of course) went solidly to the Republicans right up to the 1930s almost certainly had more to do with Abraham Lincoln than with whoever happened to be the candidate at the time.

Strangely enough, it was probably the Democrats who, in the long run, depended more upon their Civil War legacy. It is often the losers who have the longer historical memories, and, in the aftermath of defeat and reconstruction, solid support for the Democratic party in the south eventually became more than an expression of defiance or a calculation of interest; it was the political expression of loyalty to one's race. The Democratic party in the south became the political agency of white supremacy. The Democrats in the north who had survived the fierce political battles of the war and reconstruction period, and all the accusations of stabbing the loyal defenders of the Union in the back, were still strong enough to exploit post-war discontent, especially in the depression years after 1873. In both south and north, however, the Democratic party paid a high price for its survival in such strength. It was now an extremely conservative and backward-looking party, clinging desperately to the fading Jeffersonian America of yesteryear, and resisting all the forces which were reshaping American society. It was still the party of states rights and small government, scarcely addressing itself to the real problems of a new and different America, and relying heavily on its appeal to white racism – and not only in the south.

Its strong agrarian tradition always offered the possibility of an alliance of south and west in common protest at their reduction to 'colonial' status by the business empire of the north-east – but the campaign of 1896 showed the limitations of that strategy. Only in the twentieth century would the party once again build up a strong and dynamic liberal wing in the north, and re-create the powerful if illogical coalition of Northern liberalism and Southern conservatism which has usually been its recipe for success.

The configurative role of the Civil War in the history of political parties is particularly clear and long-lasting. The example of the Negro Republican vote down to the 1930s has already been quoted. The paradox of the Democratic party in the last hundred years is inexplicable without reference to the Civil War and reconstruction. In the later nineteenth century the Republicans seized the middle ground in American politics. In the twentieth century the Democrats increasingly sought to attack this position on both flanks, on the one hand from a liberal reforming standpoint concerned with twentieth-century issues, and on the other from a doggedly defended reactionary position stemming from the issues of the 1860s. Alignments on the socio-economic issues of modern America cut across alignments on the historic issues of the past, and created all manner of ironies and contradictions in party politics. In the 1920s many of the members of the revived Ku Klux Klan and most of its bitterest enemies and critics were supporters of the Democratic party. In the 1960s the leading spokesmen and the most diehard opponents of the civil rights movement were members of the Democratic party. The mould into which the Civil War pressed American politics has been very hard to break. It has too often meant that genuine debate on real issues has been obscured by clouds of rhetoric and techniques of obstruction, which are a relic of the stormy past.

6. The salvation of the Union insistently raised the question of salvation for what? The transformation of the old, loosely-structured Union into a new, integrated nation affected far more than constitutional arrangements, party fortunes or business prospects. Many intellectuals, reformers and moral crusaders had endorsed the fight for the Union not so much as an end in itself, but as a means of attaining or at least approaching their own particular objectives. During the war, some became so caught up in the struggle itself that their zeal for reform waned or even disappeared, while others feared what the conflict might do to their cherished ideals of individual freedom, and social progress. The war inevitably put a premium on the more conservative virtues of order, stability, discipline and obedience, and a number of erstwhile reformers were seduced by their fashionable appeal. Those who resisted the charms of a social order disciplined by war waited to see what kind of society and what kind of freedom would emerge in the post-war nation. The value of preserving the Union would depend for them upon the direction which it subsequently took.[19]

The reformers carried their doubts and hesitations into the post-war years. At first many of them hoped, in the words of one historian, that the Civil War had been a creative national experience rather than a sterile national disaster. Through some strange alchemy, the conflict had given Americans at last a sense of purpose, uniting them behind principles of equality and individual freedom, imbuing them with high moral principles, ennobling them with a patriotism that only trial by battle could engender.[20]

But their hopes were soon blighted by the failures of reconstruction, and the increasingly blatant corruption, materialism and acquisitiveness of the 'Gilded Age'. The squalid politics of the Grant era and the unbridled selfishness and ruthlessness of industry and business drove most of the intellectual or patrician reformers from the fray in disgust. They washed their hands of the new industrial society, bemoaned the passing of an earlier, purer, freer America, and blamed the Civil War for all the evils which they saw around them. Those who had abandoned their old individualist, anti-authoritarian position, and pinned their faith in the potential of a strong central government, born of war, to bring about the regeneration of American society, lived to see that governmental power either drastically reduced, or perverted into the tool of the very forces which they sought to resist.

In fact, the old individualism of pre-war America did survive into the post-war era, and received a shot in the arm from the social Darwinist theories which became dominant in the 1870s. It had to learn, it is true, to live with the new spirit of nationalism stimulated by the war – but that nationalism did not embrace after 1865 the kind of strong central government which might have posed a serious threat to individual freedom. That threat in the gilded age came less from government than from huge aggregations of privately controlled power, inadequately restrained by the government acting in the name of the community. What both the old individualism and the new nationalism lacked, and what the Civil War failed to provide, was a social ethic or social concern which would use both individual effort and national power positively in the cause of human welfare, social justice and community interest.

To suggest that such a new ideology of reform could possibly emerge in the America of the sixties and seventies is almost certainly to expect too much. However, the Civil War did occur at a time of transition for liberalism, on both sides of the Atlantic. The classical liberalism of *laissez-faire*, individualism, free enterprise and limited government, although still at the very height of its influence, was increasingly confronted with the inadequacy of its programme to cope with the problems of urban-industrial society. A new kind of liberalism was gradually evolving – more collectivist or interventionist in its approach, and thinking in social as much as traditional political and constitutional terms. If the outcome of the Civil War was some kind of triumph for liberalism, the question remained what kind of liberalism. America was still largely a stronghold of the older, more conventional variety, although some of the bolder spirits among the radical Republicans – and even some of the more flexible moderates, including Lincoln himself – veered towards the newer approach.

In Britain, the new school had advanced rather further by the mid-1860s. The divided reaction of European and especially British liberals to the American Civil War may well reflect the divided state of liberal ideology at this time of transition. On the whole it was the older, classical school of liberals, exemplified by Lord Acton, who supported the South on constitutional grounds, while the newer, more radical school of Bright, Cobden and Forster supported the North because it represented the kind of political and social system in which they passionately believed. The most interesting case is that of Gladstone, whose sympathies were divided but predominantly with the South as the defender of minority rights against arbitrary rule, and as a brave protagonist in a struggle for independence. In a highly suggestive comment, his biographer, Morley, argues that Gladstone made the common British error of treating as a political contest an event which was a social revolution.[21] (It is possible to question the term 'revolution', but still agree with Morley that Gladstone and many others in Britain failed to grasp the wider social implications of the American conflict.) One of the unfulfilled promises of the Civil War was that it might lead the way to a new, broad-based liberal approach, relevant to social and economic, as well as political, problems on both sides of the Atlantic, and combining a concern for both legal rights and social justice.[22]

The Civil War was also an admission of the failure to find a satisfactory answer to one of the basic dilemmas of liberal democracy: how to combine majority rule with proper respect for the rights of a minority, concentrated in one region, or racial or religious community within the larger society. In other words, straightforward majority rule is only fair or even tolerable where the composition of that majority is constantly changing or open to change. Where there is a permanent or hard and fast division between a majority and a minority community, on regional, racial, religious or some such grounds, majority rule is almost bound to become repression of the minority, however mild its actual form. The American federal system failed to solve or at least accommodate this problem in 1860-1. The only effective answer which it was able to produce was coercion of the minority; a liberal régime, heir to a revolutionary tradition, was driven to suppress a revolution by a minority which attempted to secede. On the merits of the substantive issues involved in the dispute, it may be fairly said that such action was justified, in order to save the Union and free the slaves. But it procured the survival of a great experiment in liberal democracy only by resort to essentially illiberal means. It is this paradox which helps to explain the Gladstonian position, if not to excuse its narrowness of vision.

In fact, the problem of majority rule and minority rights was posed in a particularly acute and complex form in nineteenth-century America. Within the territorial minority of the Southern states was a substantial racial minority of Negroes. In that sense, the best modern parallel lies not in Nigeria or the Sudan but in Ulster. The tripartite relationship between the United States (with its Northern majority), the white South and the Negroes is mirrored in the relationship between the United Kingdom (with its overwhelming non-

Irish majority), the Ulster Protestants and the Ulster Catholics. The analogy at least serves to highlight the intractability of the problem, and the desperate difficulty faced by the national majority in any attempt to come to the effective support of a minority community at the mercy of a local majority. The fact that the division within white America was territorial or geographical made it much easier for a local majority to resort to secession and war in the first place, and much harder for the nation to achieve a successful reconstruction in the second.

If, in its origins, the Civil War posed searching questions about American federalism as well as liberalism, its consequences raised equally serious questions about American nationalism. Some of the implications and inhibitions of that nationalism within the American framework have already been discussed. Its wider universal significance may lie principally in the conjunction of nationalism and liberalism which the Civil War achieved. In a characteristically perceptive essay, David Potter writes of the conflict's wider meaning:

The significance lay rather in the fact that the Civil War, more perhaps than any event in Europe, fused the two great forces of the nineteenth century – liberalism and nationalism. It fused them so thoroughly that their potential separateness was lost from view. The fusion gave to nationalism a sanction which, frequently since then, it has failed to deserve, and gave to liberalism a strength which, since then, it has frequently not known how to use.[23]

Potter points out that, before 1860, European liberalism had a depressing record of failure in its attempts to promote national unification, in Germany, Italy and elsewhere. In the year that the Civil War began, Victor Emmanuel was crowned king of an Italy which had only been united when liberalism had been stiffened by a stronger driving force. In the next few years, Bismarck brought about the unification of Germany by replacing pious liberal intentions with a policy of blood and iron. Only in Lincoln's America were liberalism and nationalism fused into a successful compound. Lincoln, too, had to resort to 'blood and iron' to save the great American experiment from collapse, but he never abandoned the goal of freedom.

For a man with no first-hand knowledge or experience of the outside world, Lincoln showed a truly remarkable understanding of the cosmic significance of the great American conflict. He always insisted that the preservation of the Union was not just an end in itself, but a means of protecting the great experiment in liberal democracy and fostering the national mission, not to conquer the world but to lead it by example. In the most oft-quoted of all his speeches, he defined the Civil War as a crucial test of whether a nation conceived in liberty, and dedicated to the proposition that all men are created equal, could endure. He exhorted Americans to ensure that 'government of the people, by the people, for the people', should not perish, not merely from America, but from the earth. His fusion of liberalism and nationalism was successful, perhaps, because its purpose was to defend a going concern and not to create a new nation or a new system of government, as in Germany and Italy. Had Lincoln lived beyond 1865, he might well have been shocked by the direction taken by the great experiment once it had survived its most critical ordeal. James Russell Lowell thought that Lincoln's government of the people, by the people, for the people, had become a 'kakistocracy', a government for the benefit of knaves at the cost of fools.[24] By its necessary concentration upon the threat posed by slavery and secession, the Civil War left the nation which it saved extremely vulnerable to a danger from another direction – the corruption and gross materialism of the Gilded Age. As Thomas Wolfe's hero puts it:

> Sometimes it seems to me . . . that America went off the track somewhere – back round the time of the Civil War, or pretty soon afterwards. Instead of going ahead and developing along the line in which the country started out, it got shunted off in another direction – and now we look round and see we've gone places we didn't mean to go.[25]

In the diatribe which follows, Wolfe distorts and oversimplifies the point, but he does put his finger on the great ironic consequence of the Civil War. It saved the great American experiment, and apparently strengthened its liberalism and its nationalism. But in the process of salvation the experiment began to change, and, within a decade, it was showing different and disappointing results. If the war brought about Lincoln's 'new birth of freedom', it also spawned some unwelcome progeny, and provided a safe home for some even less attractive offspring of other parentage.

European readings of the significance of the Civil War were often confused and unpredictable. The differing interpretations of its liberal message, and the competing claims for sympathy of American and Southern nationhood, no doubt go a long way to explain the broken pattern of European reactions. Certainly the Civil War created some very strange European bedfellows. It is hard to see what else but pro-Northern sympathies could ever have rallied behind one standard such a motley group as Karl Marx, Czar Alexander II, John Bright, Bismarck, Victor Hugo, Robert Browning and John Stuart Mill. In the pro-Southern camp were gathered an almost equally incongruous collection of names, including Napoleon III, King Leopold of the Belgians, Lord Robert Cecil (later prime minister as Lord Salisbury), Sir John A. Macdonald, John Ruskin, Lord Acton and William Ewart Gladstone.

But, of course, outside reactions to the Civil War were dictated as much by international politics as ideological sympathy. The immediate issues of wartime diplomacy have been discussed elsewhere; the long-term implications of the conflict and its outcome were not always immediately obvious. What began as an apparent demonstration of American weakness and instability ended as an impressive demonstration of American might. But the European powers were relieved to find after 1865 that the United States showed little inclination to deploy its newly-proven strength in areas beyond the western hemisphere. Not until the twentieth century would the full implications of the Civil War in international relations become clear. Meanwhile, as the United States resumed its comfortable cloak of relative, if not absolute, isolation, Europe shut its eyes to most of the lessons and portents which the war offered. The general staffs and military academies of Europe took but small notice of what the Civil War had to teach about logistics and mobility, defensive entrenchments and deep penetration of enemy territory, the advantages and the problems of new armaments. The European wars between Prussia and Austria, and Prussia and France, provided all the lessons which Europe wanted to learn, and seemed to suggest that brief, fast-moving, decisive campaigns were the trend of the future rather than the protracted, cumbersome war of attrition waged at such cost by the citizen-armies of America. When British officers rekindled an interest in the Civil War at the turn of the century, they took as their inspiration the Confederate heroes, Lee and Jackson, who had limited value as guides to twentieth-century warfare. Only after the blood-bath of the First World War did military theorists (Liddell Hart above all) began to show the value of the study of the campaigns of Grant and Sherman, and the lessons which they might have taught to the generals of 1914–18, and would certainly teach to the strategists and tacticians of the next conflict.[26] The Civil War obviously had a profound influence on American strategic and tactical thinking, above all in the emphasis on outproducing rather than outfighting the enemy, and in the organisation, management and technology of war, but again the full significance of such ideas for both America and the world would not become clear until well into the twentieth century.

Perhaps only in the western hemisphere itself were the international repercussions of the war immediately obvious. The primacy of the United States in that hemisphere was established beyond a doubt. Europe – and especially Britain – abandoned the attempt to maintain a balance of power in north America and conceded the hegemony of the United States in the area. Britain withdrew from its responsibility for the defence of Canada, and, by the Treaty of Washington in 1871, and the subsequent Geneva arbitration, settled the troublesome *Alabama* claims and removed all the outstanding sources of disagreement with the United States. The treaty was 'a peace settlement between the United States and Britain which concluded a war that wisely had never been fought'.[27] Under heavy American pressure, Napoleon III withdrew all French troops from Mexico in 1867, and left his protégé, the Archduke Maximilian, to be captured and shot later in the same year. In 1867, too, Russia agreed to the sale of Alaska to the United States for just over $7 million. Within a few brief years of the end of the war, Britain, France and Russia had all acknowledged the consequences of the conflict for the whole of north America. The Civil War was also the prime external cause of the creation of the Canadian Confederation in 1867, although its basic roots were to be found in British North America itself. The war did more than stimulate Canadian nationalism, and concern for security through unity. By its exposure of the flaws in American federalism, it persuaded the makers of the Canadian Confederation to create the framework of a stronger, more positive central government than was provided in the American model. Beyond as well as within the boundaries of the United States, the Civil War acted out its configurative role.

The longer-term implications of the Civil War for world history are so far-reaching as to be incalculable. If the war had ended in the achievement of Southern independence, and a permanent division of the once United States, the balance of world power and the shape of world politics in the twentieth century would obviously have been completely different. A whole school of counter-factual historians would be needed to calculate the consequences for the world conflicts of this century, and indeed for the inhabitants of every corner of the globe. Meanwhile such speculations must be more a matter for guesswork than precise historical analysis. Suffice it to say that, if the Civil War had ended differently, it would automatically have been treated as one of the great turning-points of modern history. Because it ended as it did, in the preservation rather than disintegration of the Union, its world significance has frequently been belittled or ignored.

7. The problem of proving the importance of what did not happen goes beyond the international repercussions of the war. For America as for the world, the essential meaning of the Civil War lay not so much in what it achieved as what it prevented, not so much in what it changed as what it enabled to continue, not so much in what it initiated as in what it encouraged or permitted to happen. The greatest upheaval in American history culminated not in a sharp break but a demonstration of continuity. Rather than being itself a revolution, the war crushed a revolution launched by the 'radical right' of the day. To do justice to its unique importance, it is necessary to remember constantly what would or might have happened, had its outcome been different.

Of the two great incontrovertible results of the war, one – the saving of the Union – is the key to this whole theme of continuity. The other – the abolition of slavery – is obviously the great exception to it. It represents the one radical break, the one truly revolutionary act of the war. Like some other revolutions, it was engineered principally by a man of moderate, even conservative, inclina-tions, it was done in the name of conserving something else, and it was not followed up by the kind of further revolutionary acts required to build success-fully upon the ruins of what it had destroyed. It was a revolutionary measure carefully contained within a non-revolutionary process. For the rest, the Civil War years were crowded with change and ferment, but none of it (nor indeed all of it) amounted to a revolution. The war may have created a potentially revolutionary situation, but it failed in the end to give birth to a revolution. It was, rather, the greatest work of maintenance, overhaul, repair and re-modelling which the United States has ever known.

Beyond its two fundamental achievements, the legacy of the Civil War is full of ironies, contradictions and surprises. The line between victors and vanquished, the beneficiaries and the casualties of the war, is not always as sharp and clear as appears at first sight. In some senses, both sides won and both sides lost, and America as a whole both won and lost. The North preserved the Union but found its structure and character much changed; it freed the slaves, but failed to define and guarantee the position of the Negro in American society; it won a battle for American democracy only to see it besmirched by the politics of the next generation; it won a victory for its vision of what America should be, only to see that vision overshadowed if not overwhelmed by galloping social and economic change. The South lost its struggle for independence, but within scarcely a decade regained effective control of its own affairs; it saw the institution of slavery destroyed but soon constructed a new system of white supremacy; it was humbled by defeat but soon found a new pride in the memory of the lost cause, and a new intensified sense of its own identity. There is a streak of moral and ideological ambivalence running right through the history of the war. The South had a defensible political and constitutional case, based on the rights of minorities and of the individual states, but that case was fatally linked to an indefensible social and moral case, resting upon the institution of slavery. By *force majeure*, the North crushed the Southern political and constitutional argument, and not merely restored the Union but made it into a more integrated nation. But, while it also destroyed slavery, it was unable to destroy the whole incubus of racial prejudice, discrimination and injustice which lay behind it, because the North, too, was infected with the same virus. The Negro, perhaps the most obvious beneficiary of the war which freed him from slavery, was also one of its greatest casualties, because of the failure to make that freedom real and complete.

Because the Civil War was significant above all for what it allowed to continue or for what it made possible, its enduring consequences were still very much an open question in 1865. The fertile soil of the Union which it had preserved contained many seeds; those that grew and flourished after the war owed to it not their original existence but rather a congenial environment in which to grow. The economic growth, the industrial giants, the burgeoning cities of the later nineteenth century were not the creation of the Civil War but the beneficiaries of the opportunities which it created or preserved. As in many other conflicts, the consequences often bore little relationship to the causes, or to the objectives of the original parties to the dispute. The Republicans spent a generation wrestling with the gigantic problems of slavery, war and reconstruction, but while they struggled in vain to remake Southern society in the image of their own, their own society was being transformed. Once again, the spectacular rate of economic and social change had outrun the capacity of the politicians and the political system. They now had to come to terms with the new issues of a new age.

The Civil War was above all the supreme test of the strength, meaning and purpose of the American experiment – a test on the one hand of its stability, resilience and capacity for survival and, on the other, of its democracy, freedom, justice and equality. The obvious fact that it failed parts of that test, and passed others with less than distinction, should not obscure the importance of its success in passing the crucial test of survival. If the Union survived, its promise survived – and the enduring promise was at least as important as specific and repeated failures to live up to it. The United States of the 1860s was ahead of its time in confronting the problems of democracy, liberty and equality – that is why its ordeal mattered so much to other nations less advanced along the same road. If it failed to find satisfactory solutions to the problem of reconciling majority rule and minority rights, economic growth and social justice, the rights and liberties of black and white men living in the same society, that should scarcely surprise those who confront the same problems a century later, with far more precedents to guide and resources to help them, but little more success. There is an uncannily modern ring about the great issues of the Civil War era – nationalism, democracy, equality, race, civil and minority rights, central authority and local self-government, the use and abuse of power, the horrors of all-out war. No generation since the Civil War has surely been better equipped than that of the 1960s and 1970s to view the 'fiery trial' of the 1860s with sympathetic understanding. 'We cannot escape history,' wrote Abraham Lincoln in 1862; and over a century later, American history still cannot escape the influence of the Civil War.

# Notes

## CHAPTER I

1. The tension between the consequences and opportunities of rapid change, and the preservation of an idealised version of the past, is one of the recurring themes of Richard Hofstadter's writings, notably *The American Political Tradition and the Men who Made it* (New York, 1948) and *The Age of Reform* (New York, 1955). For a particularly interesting exploration of this theme in the pre-Civil War era, see Marvin Meyers, *The Jacksonian Persuasion: politics and belief* (Stanford, 1957). For an illuminating insight into the conservative forces behind educational reform, for example, see Michael B. Katz, *The Irony of Early School Reform: educational innovation in mid-nineteenth-century Massachusetts* (Cambridge, Mass., 1968).

2. Certainly, the essays of Frederick Jackson Turner, the great apostle of the frontier and its influence on American history, seem at their most persuasive when they are focused on the first half of the nineteenth century. For an excellent sample of Turner's work, see Ray A. Billington (ed.), *Frontier and Section: selected essays of Frederick Jackson Turner* (Englewood Cliffs, N.J., 1961). For a selection of the views of Turner's many critics, see Ray A. Billington (ed.), *Frontier and Section: selected essays of Frederick Jackson Turner.*

3. For a challenging discussion of the sources of instability and vulnerability in pre-Civil War America, see David Donald, 'An excess of democracy: the American Civil War and the social process', reprinted in Donald, *Lincoln Reconsidered: essays on the Civil War era* (2nd edn, New York, 1961).

4. Lyman Beecher, *A Plea for the West* (Cincinnati, 1835). The standard work on nativism in this period, which places heavy emphasis on its anti-Catholic element, is Ray A. Billington, *The Protestant Crusade, 1800–1860: a study of the origins of American nativism* (New York, 1938).

5. These figures refer to all the slave states, and not just to the eleven states which were to form the Southern Confederacy.

6. Avery O. Craven, *Civil War in the Making, 1815–1860* (Baton Rouge, La., 1959), 92–105.

## CHAPTER II

1. Paul M. Angle (ed.), *Created equal? The Complete Lincoln–Douglas Debates of 1858* (Chicago, 1958), 41, 327, 294, 295.
2. For an authoritative account of the nullification crisis, which emphasises the defence of slavery as the fundamental concern of South Carolina, see William W. Freehling, *Prelude to Civil War: the nullification controversy in South Carolina, 1816–1836* (New York, 1966).
3. For one example of the use of this phrase, see Joseph S. Clark, 'New England and the West', *Congregational Quarterly*, III (1861), 20. On this general theme, see Rush Welter, 'The frontier West as image of American society', *Mississippi Valley Historical Review*, XLVI (1960), 593–614.
4. For an interesting discussion of the failure of the North–South conservative alliance, see Barrington Moore, *Social Origins of Dictatorship and Democracy* (London, 1967), 125–32.
5. Quoted in Samuel E. Morison and Henry S. Commager, *The Growth of the American Republic*, 2 vols (5th edn, New York, 1962), I, 665.
6. Bayard Tuckerman (ed.), *The Diary of Philip Hone, 1828–1851* (New York, 1910), II, 347. The treaty was negotiated between Nicholas Trist, after Polk had sent instructions for his recall, and a moderate faction in Mexico whose position was very precarious.
7. On the general question of the consequences, predictable and unpredictable, of the compromise, see Holman Hamilton, *Prologue to Conflict: the crisis and compromise of 1850* (Lexington, Ky., 1964), 166–90.
8. A good historiographical survey of the motivation and making of the Act is provided by Roy F. Nichols, 'The Kansas–Nebraska Act: a century of historiography', *Mississippi Valley Historical Review*, XLIII (September 1956), 187–212.
9. On the varied groups, interests and attitudes in the Republican party, see Eric Foner, *Free Soil, Free Labor, Free Men: the ideology of the Republican party before the Civil War* (New York, 1970). The complex origins of the party in one city are described in Michael F. Holt, *Forging a Majority: the formation of the Republican party in Pittsburgh, 1848–1860* (New Haven, 1969).
10. Roy P. Basler (ed.), *The Collected Works of Abraham Lincoln* (New Brunswick, N.J., 1953), II, 461. (Hereafter cited as Lincoln, *Works*.)
11. Don E. Fehrenbacher, *Prelude to Greatness: Lincoln in the 1850s* (Stanford, 1962), ch. vi, makes it clear that sheer force of circumstances, and not just Lincoln's embarrassing questioning, was responsible for Douglas's dilemma.
12. On the impact of John Brown's raid on the South, see C. Vann Woodward, *The Burden of Southern History* (Baton Rouge, La., 1960), 61–8, and Steven A. Channing, *Crisis of Fear: secession in South Carolina* (New York, 1970), 18–57.

## CHAPTER III

1. Lincoln, *Works*, III, 549–50.
2. Ibid., IV, 262–3.
3. William H. Russell, *My Diary North and South* (London, 1863), I, 153. (Hereafter cited as Russell, *Diary*.)
4. On the Montgomery convention, and the framing of the Confederate constitution, see Chapter VIII, pp. 210–13.
5. Robert G. Gunderson, *Old Gentlemen's Convention: the Washington peace conference of 1861* (Madison, Wisc., 1961), provides a detailed account.

6. The inaugural address is in Lincoln, *Works*, IV, 262–71. The passages quoted are on pp. 268, 269 and 266.

7. The first of these views is expressed in Charles W. Ramsdell, 'Lincoln and Fort Sumter', *Journal of Southern History*, III (1937), 159–88, and, in more extreme terms, in John S. Tilley, *Lincoln Takes Command* (Chapel Hill, N.C., 1941). The second view is taken in Kenneth M. Stampp, 'Lincoln and the strategy of defense in the crisis of 1861', *Journal of Southern History*, XI (1945), 297–323, and the same author's *And the War Came: the North and the secession crisis* (Baton Rouge, La., 1950). The third is the view of David M. Potter, *Lincoln and his Party in the Secession Crisis* (2nd edn, New Haven, 1962). The fourth is put forward in Allan Nevins, *The War for the Union*, Vol. I, *The Improvised War* (New York, 1959), 30–74. Useful summaries of the Fort Sumter question and its various interpretations are to be found in Richard N. Current, *Lincoln and the First Shot* (Philadelphia, 1963), and Peter J. Parish, 'Lincoln and Fort Sumter', *History Today*, XI (April 1961), 262–70.

8. Howard K. Beale (ed.), *The Diary of Edward Bates, 1859–1866* (American Historical Association Annual Report, 1930, Vol. IV, Washington, 1933), 180.

9. Lincoln quite commonly drafted a message or a letter containing sharp criticism or a severe rebuke, and then either conveyed its meaning orally rather than in writing, or never delivered it at all. The text of Seward's memorandum and Lincoln's reply are in Lincoln, *Works*, IV, 316–18.

10. Russell, *Diary*, I, 86–7, 91, 92–3. Much of the correspondence between Seward, the commissioners and their intermediaries, is conveniently brought together in Jefferson Davis, *The Rise and Fall of the Confederate Government* (New York, 1881), I, Appendix L, 675–85. (Hereafter cited as Davis, *Rise and Fall*.)

11. What actually took place at this meeting remains something of a mystery. There are useful discussions in Richard N. Current, *The Lincoln Nobody Knows* (New York, 1958), 120–1, and James G. Randall, *Lincoln the President*, 4 vols (New York, 1945–55), I, 324–7.

12. There is no substance in Jefferson Davis's charge that, but for the delay caused by a severe storm, the relief ships would have arrived off Charleston before the Confederate authorities would have had time to react in any way to Lincoln's message. See Davis, *Rise and Fall*, I, 274.

13. John G. Nicolay and John Hay, *Abraham Lincoln: a History* (New York, 1890). III, 409.

14. Lincoln, *Works*, IV, 423–6.

15. Davis's views are conveyed in a letter from the secretary of war, Leroy P. Walker, to Governor Pickens of South Carolina, 1 March 1861. The letter is quoted in Alfred Roman, *The Military Operations of General Beauregard* (New York, 1884), I, 424.


CHAPTER IV

1. Thomas J. Pressly, *Americans Interpret Their Civil War* (Princeton, 1954), is a valuable study of changing fashions in interpretation in the century from 1860.

2. The Goebbels comparison was made by Frank L. Owsley in a review of Clement Eaton, *Freedom of Thought in the Old South* (Durham, N.C., 1940), in *Journal of Southern History*, VI (1940), 559. The description of Douglas is in Allan Nevins, *Ordeal of the Union* (New York, 1947), II, 108.

3. James R. Lowell, 'The question of the hour', *Atlantic Monthly*, VII (1861), 120–1, quoted in Kenneth M. Stampp (ed.), *The Causes of the Civil War* (Englewood Cliffs, N.J., 1959), 137.

4. This criticism does not apply to more recent studies, written from a very different standpoint. See, for example, the references to the work of Eugene Genovese later in this chapter, pp. 95–6.

5. For an old-fashioned Marxist view, see Algie M. Simons, *Class Struggles in America* (Chicago, 1906). The Beard interpretation is expounded in Charles A. and Mary Beard. *The Rise of American Civilization*, 2 vols (New York, 1927), ch. xviii.

6. Quoted in Stampp, *Causes of the Civil War*, 70.

7. Arthur M. Schlesinger, Sr., *New Viewpoints in American History* (New York, 1922), 243.

8. Denis W. Brogan, *An Introduction to American Politics* (London, 1954), 12; Daniel J. Boorstin, *The Genius of American Politics* (Chicago, 1953), 124.

9. Arthur Bestor, 'The American Civil War as a constitutional crisis', *American Historical Review*, LXIX (January 1964), 329–32. This article is a highly illuminating study of the interaction of constitutional and other issues, and the concept of the 'configurative role' of constitutional questions is a valuable tool for understanding the whole problem of Civil War causation.

10. Ibid., 351–2.

11. This paragraph is an amalgam of the arguments of such revisionist historians as Avery Craven, Frank L. Owsley, James G. Randall and Charles W. Ramsdell.

12. Lincoln, *Works*, IV, 268–9.

13. Ibid., III, 145–6.

14. Eric Foner, *Free Soil, Free Labor, Free Men: the ideology of the Republican party before the Civil War* (New York, 1970), 309, 310. Foner's book is probably the most important contribution towards an understanding of the coming of the war, as viewed from the North, to appear in recent years.

15. Eugene D. Genovese, 'The slave South: an interpretation', *Science and Society*, XXV (December 1961), reprinted in Allen Weinstein and Frank O. Gatell (eds), *American Negro Slavery: a modern reader* (New York, 1968), 288.

16. Ibid., 295–6. Brief quotation from this one essay does less than justice to the range and subtlety of Genovese's argument, which is more fully developed in his books *The Political Economy of Slavery* (New York, 1965), and *In Red and Black: Marxism explorations in Southern and Afro-American history* (New York, 1971).

17. Lincoln, *Works*, VIII, 332.


CHAPTER V


1. Allan Nevins and Milton H. Thomas (eds), *The Diary of George Templeton Strong* (New York, 1952), III, 123–4, 135. (Hereafter cited as Strong, *Diary*.)

2. John Y. Simon (ed.), *The Papers of Ulysses S. Grant* (Carbondale, Ill., 1969), II, 7.

3. Quoted in Paul M. Angle and Earl S. Miers (eds), *Tragic Years, 1860–1865: a documentary history of the American Civil War* (New York, 1960), I, 66.

4. Russell, *Diary*, I, 345–6.

5. Ben A. Williams (ed.), *A Diary from Dixie, by Mary Boykin Chesnut* (Boston, 1949), 50, 69. (Hereafter cited as Chesnut, *Diary*.)

6. Strong, *Diary*, III, 99, 133.

7. Joseph Hooker to Lincoln, 11 April 1863 (Lincoln, *Works*, VI, 169).

8. Davis, *Rise and Fall*, I, 328–9.

9. There is a useful comparison of the resources of the two sides in Allan Nevins, *The War for the Union* (New York, 1959), I, 424–6.

10. Carl R. Fish, *The American Civil War: an interpretation* (New York, 1937), 158.

11. Anthony Trollope, *North America* (London, Penguin edn, 1968), 30–1.

12. Lincoln, *Works*, IV, 532.

13. Russell, *Diary*, II, 149.

14. Ibid., II, 214–66. Russell's caustic account of the Bull Run debacle earned him wide-

spread unpopularity in the North, although, in general, his sympathies in the struggle were too pro-Northern to please his newspaper in London.

15. T. Harry Williams, *Lincoln and his Generals* (London, 1952), 20.
16. T. Harry Williams, *P. G. T. Beauregard: Napoleon in Gray* (Baton Rouge, La., 1955), 139, 140.

## CHAPTER VI

1. Davis, *Rise and Fall*, I, 306.
2. Lincoln, *Works*, IV, 331–2.
3. Ibid., VI, 277–8.
4. Benjamin P. Thomas and Harold M. Hyman, *Stanton: the life and times of Lincoln's secretary of war* (New York, 1962), 200–2.
5. Bell I. Wiley, *The Life of Billy Yank: the common soldier of the Union* (Indianapolis, 1952), 23, 337–9.
6. Lincoln, *Works*, IV, 432.
7. This change is traced in detail in William B. Hesseltine, *Lincoln and the War Governors* (New York, 1948).
8. For a discussion of the recruitment of Negro troops, see Chapter IX, pp. 256–60.
9. Quoted in Frank L. Owsley, *State Rights in the Confederacy* (Chicago, 1925), 22.
10. Sam R. Watkins, '*Co. Aytch': a side show of the big show* (New York, Collier edn, 1962), 46–7.
11. Thomas C. DeLeon, *Four Years in Rebel Capitals: an inside view of life in the Southern Confederacy from birth to death* (New York, 1962), 213.
12. Davis, *Rise and Fall*, I, 515.
13. Watkins, '*Co. Aytch*', 47.
14. Albert B. Moore, *Conscription and Conflict in the Confederacy* (New York, 1924), 40, 107–8.
15. Strong, *Diary*, III, 479–80. Strong reports that he purchased as a substitute 'a big, "Dutch" boy of twenty or thereabouts, for the moderate consideration of $1,100. . . . My *alter ego* could make a good soldier if he tried. Gave him my address, and told him to write to me if he found himself in hospital or in trouble, and that I would try to do what I properly could to help him.'
16. Lincoln, *Works*, VI, 447–8.
17. See Chapter XVI, pp. 500–1.
18. Bell I. Wiley, *Embattled Confederates* (New York, 1964), 78.
19. See, for example, Robert H. Strong, *A Yankee Private's Civil War*, ed. Ashley Halsey (Chicago, 1961), 83–6.
20. Clement Eaton, *A History of the Southern Confederacy* (New York, 1954), 104.
21. Russell F. Weigley, *Quartermaster-General of the Union Army: a biography of M. C. Meigs* (New York, 1959), 205–6.
22. Strong, *Yankee Private*, 102.
23. Wiley, *Embattled Confederates*, 81.
24. Strong, *Yankee Private*, 24; Watkins, '*Co. Aytch*', 55.
25. Earl S. Miers (ed.), *A Rebel War Clerk's Diary [by] John B. Jones* (New York, 1958), 43.
26. For discussion of the railroads of South and North at war, see Chapter XI, pp. 311–14, and Chapter XII, pp. 348–52.
27. The following account is based on Russell F. Weigley's valuable study, *Quartermaster-General of the Union Army*.
28. Watkins, '*Co. Aytch*', 85–8.
29. Lincoln, *Works*, VI, 78–9.
30. For an excellent brief discussion of Jomini's writings and their influence, see David

Donald, *Lincoln Reconsidered: essays on the Civil War era* (2nd edn, New York, 1961), 88–102.
31. B. H. Liddell Hart, *Manchester Guardian Weekly*, 25 June 1959, quoted in Allan Nevins, *The War for the Union* (New York, 1960), II, 466.
32. Lincoln, *Works*, V, 98.
33. T. Harry Williams, *Americans at War: the development of the American military system* (Baton Rouge, La., 1960), 81.
34. William T. Sherman, *Memoirs of General W. T. Sherman* (New York, 1875), II, 227.
35. Frank E. Vandiver, *Their Tattered Flags: the epic of the Confederacy* (New York, 1970), 94.
36. Weigley, *Quartermaster-General of the Union Army*, 284.

## CHAPTER VII

1. T. Harry Williams, *Lincoln and his Generals* (London, 1952), 5.
2. Archer Jones, *Confederate Strategy from Shiloh to Vicksburg* (Baton Rouge, La., 1961), 24–5.
3. Williams, *Lincoln and his Generals*, 46–7, is a good, brief account of the meetings of 10–13 January
4. Lincoln, *Works*, V, 111–12, 115.
5. See Chapter XIV on the war at sea, and especially p. 428 on Hatteras Inlet, Roanoke Island and Port Royal.
6. See Chapter XIV, p. 432, on the naval contribution to the campaign.
7. Bruce Catton, *Grant moves South* (Boston, 1960), 193–7.
8. Davis, *Rise and Fall*, II, 67.
9. See Chapter XIV, pp. 428–9, for a brief account of the capture of New Orleans.
10. Davis, *Rise and Fall*, II, 87.
11. Lincoln, *Works*, V, 124.
12. See Chapter XIV, pp. 415–17, on the historic encounter between *Virginia* and *Monitor*.
13. George B. McClellan, *McClellan's Own Story* (New York, 1886), 324.
14. Ibid., 346.
15. Ibid., 396.
16. Robert U. Johnson and Clarence C. Buel (eds), *Battles and Leaders of the Civil War* (New York, repr., 1956), II, 297. (Hereafter cited as *Battles and Leaders*.)
17. Lincoln, *Works*, V, 290.
18. *McClellan's Own Story*, 428.
19. Ibid., 439.
20. Henry S. Commager (ed.), *Documents of American History* (5th edn, New York, 1949), I, 413–14.
21. Ibid., I, 415.
22. Lincoln, *Works*, V, 399.
23. Hal Bridges, *Lee's Maverick General: Daniel Harvey Hill* (New York, 1961), 160–1, quotes Jackson's opinion. Longstreet gives his own verdict in *Battles and Leaders* II, 663, 673–4.
24. *McClellan's Own Story*, 614.
25. Ibid., 613.
26. *Battles and Leaders*, III, 79.
27. Bridges, *Lee's Maverick General*, 155.
28. Lincoln, *Works*, VI, 13.
29. Ibid., VI, 22.
30. See Chapter VIII, pp. 209–10.
31. See Chapter X, pp. 267–8, on McClernand's role.

## CHAPTER VIII

1. Howard K. Beale (ed.), *The Diary of Edward Bates, 1859–1866* (American Historical Association Annual Report, 1930, Vol. IV, Washington, 1933), 220.
2. Loc. cit.
3. Hans L. Trefousse, *The Radical Republicans: Lincoln's vanguard for racial justice* (New York, 1969).
4. T. Harry Williams, 'Lincoln and the radicals: an essay in Civil War history and historiography', in Grady McWhiney (ed.), *Grant, Lee, Lincoln and the Radicals: essays on Civil War leadership* (Evanston, Ill., 1964), 100–1. The essays by Professors Williams and Donald in this volume are the latest round in their long-running conflict over the radicals and their relationship with Lincoln. See also T. Harry Williams, *Lincoln and the Radicals* (Madison, Wisc., 1941), and David Donald, *Lincoln Reconsidered* (2nd edn, New York, 1961), ch. vi.
5. For further discussion of the radical Republicans, their relations with Lincoln and the limitations of their radicalism, see Chapters IX, XVI, XVII and XIX. For a particularly striking example of the conservative views on some issues of so conspicuous a radical as Thaddeus Stevens, see Chapter XII, p. 358.
6. Henry S. Commager (ed.), *Documents of American History* (5th edn, New York, 1949), 395–6.
7. See Chapters IX and XVII.
8. Damon Wells, *Stephen Douglas: the last years, 1857–1861* (Austin, Tex., 1971), 288.
9. For further discussion of the Democratic party during the Civil War, see Chapters XVI and XVII.
10. Theodore C. Pease and James G. Randall (eds), *The Diary of Orville Hickman Browning* (Springfield, Ill., 1927–33), I, 600, 604. There are good accounts of the cabinet crisis in T. Harry Williams, *Lincoln and the Radicals*, 205–14, and Allan Nevins, *The War for the Union* (New York, 1960), II, 352–65. Extracts from the main first-hand accounts of the affair are conveniently brought together in Charles M. Segal (ed.), *Conversations with Lincoln* (New York, 1961), 220–32.
11. The permanent constitution of the confederacy is set out side by side with the United States constitution in Jefferson Davis, *Rise and Fall*, I, Appendix K, 648–75.
12. Harrison A. Trexler, 'The Davis administration and the Richmond press, 1861–5', *Journal of Southern History*, XVI (1950), 177–8, 193–5.
13. Earl S. Miers (ed.), *A Rebel War Clerk's Diary* [by] *John B. Jones* (New York, 1958), 16. (Hereafter cited as Jones, *Diary*.)
14. Edward Younger (ed.), *Inside the Confederate Government: the diary of Robert Garlick Hill Kean* (New York, 1957), 100–1.
15. Ibid., 205.
16. Thomas C. DeLeon, *Belles, Beaux and Brains of the 60's* (New York, 1909), 91.
17. Jones, *Diary*, 73–4. 'It may,' he wrote, 'place a great gulf between him and the descendant of those who crucified our Saviour.'
18. Paul P. Van Riper and Harry N. Scheiber, 'The Confederate civil service', *Journal of Southern History*, XXV (1959), 448–70.
19. Chesnut, *Diary*, 85.
20. Quoted in Robert D. Meade, *Judah P. Benjamin: Confederate statesman* (New York, 1943).
21. George C. Eggleston, *A Rebel's Recollections*, ed. David Donald (Bloomington, Ind., 1959), 168.
22. Jones, *Diary*, 119.
23. Eggleston, *A Rebel's Recollections*, 168.
24. Richard E. Beringer, 'A profile of the members of the Confederate Congress', *Journal of Southern History*, XXXIII (1967), 518–41, is the source of most of the information in this paragraph.

25. Ulrich B. Phillips (ed.), *The Correspondence of Robert Toombs, Alexander H. Stephens, and Howell Cobb* (American Historical Association Annual Report, 1911, Vol. II, Washington, 1913), 631.
26. James Z. Rabun, 'Alexander H. Stephens and Jefferson Davis', *American Historical Review*, LVIII (1953), 297.
27. Brown to Alexander H. Stephens, 2 July 1862. Ulrich B. Phillips (ed.), *The Correspondence of Robert Toombs, Alexander H. Stephens and Howell Cobb*, 598.
28. Davis, *Rise and Fall*, I, 506–14.

## CHAPTER IX

1. Lincoln, *Works*, V, 372.
2. Philip S. Foner, *The Life and Writings of Frederick Douglass*, 4 vols (New York, 1950–5), III, 268.
3. *New York Tribune*, 20 August 1862.
4. See Leon F. Litwack, *North of Slavery: the Negro in the free states, 1790–1860* (Chicago, 1961), for an authoritative account of such discrimination.
5. The quotations in this paragraph are taken from V. Jacque Voegeli, *Free but not Equal: the Midwest and the Negro during the Civil War* (Chicago, 1967), 15, 18, 154, 124–5.
6. James M. McPherson, *The Struggle for Equality: abolitionists and the Negro in the Civil War and reconstruction* (Princeton, 1964), 100.
7. Ibid., 58.
8. *New York Tribune*, 20 August 1862.
9. Benjamin Quarles, *Lincoln and the Negro* (New York, 1962), 86.
10. David Donald, *Charles Sumner and the Rights of Man* (New York, 1970), 61–4.
11. Lincoln, *Works*, IV, 531–2.
12. Ibid., V, 169.
13. Theodore C. Pease and James G. Randall (eds), *The Diary of Orville Hickman Browning* (Springfield, Ill., 1927–33), I, 541.
14. *Douglass' Monthly*, September 1862, quoted in Quarles, *Lincoln and the Negro*, 100.
15. Browning, *Diary*, I, 558.
16. Lincoln, *Works*, V, 328–31. This strange device of withholding the veto, yet still sending to Congress the message explaining his objections to the bill, suggests that Lincoln remained extremely unhappy about the measure which he now permitted to become law.
17. Alexander K. McClure, *Lincoln and the Men of War Times*, ed. J. S. Torrey (Philadelphia, 1962), 102, 92.
18. Horace Greeley, *The American Conflict*, 2 vols (Hartford, Conn., 1864–6), II, 254–5.
19. Sarah F. Hughes (ed.), *Letters and Recollections of John Murray Forbes*, 2 vols (Boston, 1899), I, 350–1.
20. Frank B. Carpenter, *Six Months at the White House with Abraham Lincoln* (London, 1866), 77.
21. Fawn M. Brodie, *Thaddeus Stevens: scourge of the South* (New York, 1959), 156.
22. Edward Magdol, *Owen Lovejoy: abolitionist in Congress* (New Brunswick, N.J., 1967), 341–2.
23. Lincoln, *Works*, V, 152–3, 160–1.
24. Ibid., V, 317–19.
25. Ibid., V, 371–2.
26. Voegeli, *Free but not Equal*, 45.
27. Lincoln, *Works*, V, 531, 535–6, 537.
28. Ibid., V, 336–7.
29. Ibid., V, 388–9.

30. Ibid., V, 419–25.
31. Richard N. Current, *The Lincoln Nobody Knows* (New York, 1958), 225–7.
32. William W. Patton, *President Lincoln and the Chicago Memorial on Emancipation* (Baltimore, 1888), 17.
33. Lincoln, *Works*, V, 425.
34. Jessie A. Marshall (ed.), *Private and Official Correspondence of General Benjamin F. Butler During the Period of the Civil War*, 5 vols (Norwood, Mass., 1917), II, 164.
35. Lincoln, Works, V, 433–6. There is a good account of the cabinet meeting of 22 September 1862 in David Donald (ed.), *Inside Lincoln's Cabinet: the Civil War diaries of Salmon P. Chase* (New York, 1954), 149–53.
36. Quarles, *Lincoln and the Negro*, 149.
37. Richard Hofstadter, *The American Political Tradition and the Men who made it* (New York, 1948), 132.
38. McPherson, *The Struggle for Equality*, 119.
39. *National Intelligencer*, 23 September 1862, quoted in John H. Franklin, *The Emancipation Proclamation* (New York, 1963), 65.
40. Richmond *Examiner*, 29 September 1862, quoted in Franklin, *The Emancipation Proclamation*, 67.
41. *Spectator*, 11 October 1862.
42. Lincoln, *Works*, V, 444.
43. Charles Sedgwick to John Murray Forbes, 22 December 1862, in Sarah F. Hughes (ed.), *Letters and Recollections of John Murray Forbes*, I, 345–6.
44. Lincoln, *Works*, VI, 28–31.
45. Howard K. Beale (ed.), *Diary of Gideon Welles, Secretary of the Navy under Lincoln and Johnson*, 3 vols (New York, 1960), I, 212.
46. William Robinson, quoted in McPherson, *The Struggle for Equality*, 122.
47. Stephen V. Benet, *John Brown's Body* (New York, 1928), 232–3.
48. Karl Marx to Frederick Engels, 20 October 1862, in Marx and Engels, *The Civil War in the United States* (3rd edn, New York, 1961), 258.
49. *Die Presse*, 12 October 1862, quoted in Belle B. Sideman and Lillian Friedman (eds), *Europe Looks at the Civil War* (New York, Collier edn, 1962), 160.
50. See, for example, Lincoln, *Works*, VI, 48
51. Ibid., VI, 409–10.
52. Strong, *Diary*, III, 408.
53. Voegeli, *Free but not Equal*, 180.
54. McPherson, *The Struggle for Equality*, 255–7.
55. For a sensitive and illuminating account of developments in South Carolina, see Willie Lee Rose, *Rehearsal for Reconstruction: the Port Royal experiment* (Indianapolis, 1964).
56. Bell I. Wiley, *Southern Negroes, 1861–1865* (New Haven, 1938), 231. Much of this paragraph is extracted from the mine of information in Wiley's book.
57. McPherson, *The Struggle for Equality*, 206–7.
58. Dudley T. Cornish, *The Sable Arm: Negro troops in the Union army, 1861–1865* (New York, 1956), 127; William B. Hesseltine, *Lincoln and the War Governors* (New York, 1948), 203; Voegeli, *Free but not Equal*, 102.
59. Cornish, *The Sable Arm*, 229–30. Cornish's thorough and authoritative study is the source of much of the information in this section.
60. Lincoln, *Works*, VI, 30. As late as September 1862 Lincoln expressed serious doubts about the value of ex-slaves as fighting men. Ibid., V, 423.
61. Cornish, *The Sable Arm*, 114.
62. For a good summary of this episode, see Cornish, *The Sable Arm*, 173–6. Controversy, exaggeration, charges and counter-charges have always surrounded this incident, but it is as clear as anything can be in such a situation that a considerable number of Negro troops were slaughtered after the fort had fallen.

63. Philip S. Foner (ed.), *The Life and Writings of Frederick Douglass* (New York, 1950–5), III, 318.

## CHAPTER X

1. Lincoln, *Works*, VI, 33. There is a good description of Lincoln's social and ceremonial duties on this momentous day in John G. Nicolay and John Hay, *Abraham Lincoln: a history*, 10 vols (New York, 1890), VI, 421, 429.
2. Lincoln, *Works*, VI, 31–2, 46–8, 74–5, 77–8. There is a good account of these events in T. Harry Williams, *Lincoln and his Generals* (London, 1952), 165–9.
3. Lincoln, *Works*, VI, 79. For the earlier part of Lincoln's letter to Hooker, see Chapter VI, pp. 155–6.
4. Lincoln, *Works*, VI, 138–40.
5. Ibid., VI, 70–1.
6. Joseph E. Johnston, *Narrative of Military Operations*, ed. F. E. Vandiver (Bloomington, Ind., 1959), 200.
7. For an excellent discussion of Confederate strategic problems on the western front, see Archer Jones, *Confederate Strategy from Shiloh to Vicksburg* (Baton Rouge, La., 1961).
8. Ulysses S. Grant, *Personal Memoirs of U.S. Grant* (Greenwich, Conn., abridged edn, 1962), 158.
9. Ibid., 158–9, 165.
10. For further details on the naval contribution to these operations, see Chapter XIV, pp. 433–4.
11. Grant, *Personal Memoirs*, 177.
12. Lee to Jefferson Davis, 25 June 1863, in Clifford Dowdey (ed.), *The Wartime Papers of R. E. Lee* (Boston, 1961), 532.
13. For an excellent discussion of this strategic debate, see Archer Jones, *Confederate Strategy* 198–218.
14. Lincoln, *Works*, VI, 230.
15. Quoted in Davis, *Rise and Fall*, II, 403.
16. Douglas Southall Freeman, Lee's most authoritative biographer, argues that the consequences of this reorganisation were fatal to the whole Gettysburg campaign. Freeman, *R. E. Lee: a biography*, 4 vols (New York, 1934–5), III, 8–17, 150–3.
17. Lincoln, *Works*, VI, 249–50, 257.
18. Ibid., VI, 276–7, 277–8, 273.
19. Freeman Cleaves, *Meade of Gettysburg* (Norman, Okla., 1960), 118.
20. Lincoln, *Works*, VI, 311.
21. Walter Lord (ed.), *The Fremantle Diary, being the journal of Lieutenant Colonel James Arthur Lyon Fremantle . . . on his Three Months in the Southern States* (London, 1956), 215.
22. Kenneth P. Williams, *Lincoln Finds a General: a military study of the Civil War*, 5 vols (New York, 1949–59), II, 729.
23. Lincoln, *Works*, VI, 409.
24. Davis, *Rise and Fall*, II, 448, 447.
25. Cleaves, *Meade*, 174.
26. Lincoln, *Works*, VI, 281.
27. Ibid., VI, 319, 328.
28. Ibid., VI, 466–7.
29. Quoted in Bruce Catton, *Never Call Retreat* (Centennial History of the Civil War, Vol. III, London, 1966), 210.
30. Lincoln, *Works*, VI, 498.
31. *Battles and Leaders*, III, 727.

## CHAPTER XI

1. Ulrich B. Phillips (ed.), *The Correspondence of Robert Toombs, Alexander H. Stephens, and Howell Cobb*, 613.
2. Charles B. Dew, *Ironmaker to the Confederacy: Joseph R. Anderson and the Tredegar iron works* (New Haven, 1966), 89; Albert D. Kirwan (ed.), *The Confederacy* (New York, 1959), 63–4.
3. See Chapter VI, pp. 149–50.
4. Most of the information in this paragraph is derived from Dew, *Ironmaker to the Confederacy*.
5. Thomas C. DeLeon, *Four Years in Rebel Capitals* (New York, Collier edn, 1962), 111.
6. *De Bow's Review*, XXXII–XXXIII (1862), 333, quoted in Kirwan (ed.), *The Confederacy*, 68.
7. Dew, *Ironmaker to the Confederacy*, 178.
8. Kirwan (ed.), *The Confederacy*, 64.
9. Lester J. Cappon, 'Government and private industry in the Southern Confederacy', *Humanistic Studies in honor of John Calvin Metcalf* (New York, 1941), 187.
10. See Chapter XIII, pp. 397–8, 401–2
11. Judith F. Gentry, 'A Confederate success in Europe: the Erlanger loan', *Journal of Southern History*, XXXVI (1970), 157–88.
12. George C. Eggleston, *A Rebel's Recollections* (Bloomington, Ind., 1959), 96.
13. Jones, *Diary*, 79, 149, 159, 349, 351, 430–1.
14. Kirwan (ed.), *The Confederacy*, 131.
15. Ibid., 55.
16. Ibid., 173, 193.
17. On blockade-running, see Chapter XIV, pp. 422–5.
18. Joseph H. Parks, 'A Confederate trade center under Federal occupation: Memphis, 1862 to 1865', *Journal of Southern History*, VII (1941), 308.
19. Eugene M. Lerner, 'Money, prices and wages in the Confederacy, 1861–65', *Journal of Political Economy*, LXIII (1955), 23–8.
20. Dew, *Ironmaker to the Confederacy*, 250.
21. Frank L. Owsley, *State Rights in the Confederacy* (Chicago, 1952), 264–5.
22. For discussion of the eleventh-hour decision of the Confederacy to raise Negro troops, see Chapter XVIII, pp. 561–3.
23. Chesnut, *Diary*, 140, 164, 21–2, 122, 163.
24. Ibid., 193, 494.
25. Kenneth Coleman, *Confederate Athens* (Athens, Ga., 1968).
26. Kirwan (ed.), *The Confederacy*, 107.
27. *Augusta Register*, 2 December 1864, quoted in James W. Silver, 'Propaganda in the Confederacy', *Journal of Southern History*, XI (1945), 500.
28. James W. Silver, *Confederate Morale and Church Propaganda* (Tuscaloosa, Ala., 1957), 34.

## CHAPTER XII

1. The dominant theme of Nevins's massive four-volume study of the war years is the transition from an unorganised to a more organised society. See in particular Nevins, *The War for the Union*, I, 240–65, and III, 271–7.
2. See Chapter XIII, p. 400.
3. For this information, and a good general discussion of the impact of the war on Northern agriculture, see Wayne D. Rasmussen, 'The Civil War: a catalyst of agricultural revolution', *Agricultural History*, XXXIX (1965), 187–96.
4. Nevins, *The War for the Union*, III, 268. The economic impact of the war has become

one of the major battlegrounds of recent Civil War historiography. The assumption that the war was a great stimulus to (if not indeed a basic cause of) industrialisation and economic growth in America remained almost unchallenged for decades, and the idea that the war brought about a socioeconomic revolution was elaborated by historians such as Charles A. Beard and Louis M. Hacker. The seminal contribution to the opposite thesis, that the war was an economic brake rather than an accelerator, was Thomas C. Cochran's article, 'Did the Civil War retard industrialisation?', *Mississippi Valley Historical Review*, XLVIII (1961), 197–210. Other contributions to the debate are conveniently brought together in Ralph Andreano (ed.), *The Economic Impact of the American Civil War* (Cambridge, Mass., 1962), David T. Gilchrist and W. David Lewis (eds), *Economic Change in the Civil War Era* (Greenville, Del., 1965), and William E. Parrish (ed.), *The Civil War: a second American Revolution?* (New York, 1970).

5. Victor S. Clark, 'Manufacturing development during the Civil War', *Military Historian and Economist*, III (1918), reprinted in Andreano (ed.), *The Economic Impact of the American Civil War*, 45.

6. Stanley L. Engerman, 'The economic impact of the Civil War', *Explorations in Entrepreneurial History*, 2nd series, III (1965–6), 185. Engerman's article is one of the most important 'post-Cochran' contributions to the whole debate.

7. Robert Gallman, in Gilchrist and Lewis (eds), *Economic Change in the Civil War Era*, 161–2, 168–9.

8. Stephen Salsbury, 'The effect of the Civil War on American industrial development', in Andreano (ed.), op. cit., 164–5.

9. See Chapter XIV, pp. 444–5.

10. *New York Sun*, 9 March 1865, quoted in Emerson D. Fite, *Social and Industrial Conditions in the North During the Civil War* (New York, 1910), 74.

11. Thomas Weber, *The Northern Railroads in the Civil War, 1861–1865* (New York, 1952), 124.

12. On this, as on all aspects of railroad operations in the Union war effort, Weber, *The Northern Railroads*, is invaluable. See also Francis A. Lord, *Lincoln's Railroad Man: Herman Haupt* (Rutherford, 1969).

13. *Congressional Globe*, 37 Cong., 2 Sess., 349.

14. Bray Hammond, *Sovereignty and an Empty Purse: banks and politics in the Civil War* (Princeton, 1970), 23.

15. Hugh McCulloch, *Men and Measures of Half a Century* (New York, 1888), 201

16. Francis Fessenden, *Life and Public Services of William Pitt Fessenden*, 2 vols (Boston, 1907), I, 194.

17. *Cong. Globe*, 37 Cong., 2 Sess., 691.

18. Sidney Ratner, *American Taxation, its History as a Social Force in Democracy* (New York, 1942), 84–5.

19. Paul Studenski and Herman E. Krooss, *Financial history of the United States* (New York, 1952), 152, 159, 504–5.

20. *Fincher's Trades Review*, 4 July 1863, quoted in George W. Smith and Charles Judah (eds), *Life in the North During the Civil War: a source history* (Albuquerque, 1966), 201.

21. New York *Herald*, 6 October 1863, quoted ibid., 232–3.

22. This last point is one of the main themes of David Montgomery, *Beyond Equality: labor and the radical Republicans 1862–72* (New York, 1967). The impact of the Civil War upon American labour needs further study, but see Norman J. Ware, *The Labor Movement in the United States, 1860–1895* (New York, 1929), ch. i, for a brief survey. There is an excellent study of one aspect of the subject in Charlotte Erickson, *American Industry and the European Immigrant, 1860–1885* (Cambridge, Mass., 1957).

23. See Leonard P. Curry, *Blueprint for Modern America: nonmilitary legislation of the first Civil War Congress* (Nashville, 1968), for a full discussion of these measures, which, as its title indicates, takes a generous view of their lasting importance.

24. For these figures, and much other useful information on the expansion of government during the war, see Paul P. Van Riper and Keith A. Sutherland, 'The Northern civil service, 1861–1865', *Civil War History*, XI (1965), 351–69.
25. Emerson D. Fite, *Social and Industrial Conditions in the North During the Civil War* (New York, 1910), 270, 268.
26. *The Round Table*, 6 February 1864, quoted in Smith and Judah (eds), op. cit., 306.
27. See Chapter VI, p. 146.
28. George M. Fredrickson, *The Inner Civil War: Northern intellectuals and the crisis of the Union* (New York, 1965), ch. vii.
29. Lincoln, *Works*, VIII, 151.

## CHAPTER XIII

1. Kenneth Bourne, *Britain and the Balance of Power in North America, 1815–1908* (London, 1967), 252–7; Lynn M. Case and Warren F. Spencer, *The United States and France: Civil War diplomacy* (Philadelphia, 1970), 306; Belle B. Sideman and Lillian Friedman (eds), *Europe Looks at the Civil War* (New York, 1960), 71.
2. The Gettysburg address (Lincoln, *Works*, VII, 23) is the most familiar of Lincoln's statements on this theme, but there are a number of others. See, for example, ibid., IV, 426, 438–9, and V, 537.
3. Alexander J. Beresford-Hope, *A Popular View of the American Civil War* (London, 1861), quoted in Sideman and Friedman (eds), *Europe Looks at the Civil War*, 42.
4. Henry S. Commager (ed.), *Documents of American history* (5th edn, New York, 1949), I, 418.
5. Milnes to C. J. McCarthy, 24 October 1862, in T. Wemyss Reid, *The Life, Letters and Friendships of Richard Monckton Milnes, First Lord Houghton*, 2 vols (London, 1891), II, 86.
6. D. G. Wright, 'Bradford and the American Civil War', *Journal of British Studies*, VIII (1969), 78; Henry Adams, *The Education of Henry Adams* (Boston, 1918), 189; Worthington C. Ford (ed.), *A Cycle of Adams Letters, 1861–1865*, 2 vols (Boston, 1920), I, 244–5.
7. Joseph M. Hernon, 'British sympathies in the American Civil War: a reconsideration', *Journal of Southern History*, XXXIII (1967), 367.
8. Donaldson Jordan and Edwin J. Pratt, *Europe and the American Civil War* (Boston, 1931), 73.
9. John Bigelow, *Retrospections of an Active Life*, 3 vols (New York, 1909), I, 405; David Donald, *Charles Sumner and the Rights of Man* (New York, 1970), 116; *The Times*, 3 May 1864.
10. Sarah A. Wallace and Frances E. Gillespie (eds), *The Journal of Benjamin Moran, 1857–1865*, 2 vols (Chicago, 1948–9), II, 1220.
11. David H. Pinkney, 'France and the Civil War', in Harold M. Hyman (ed.), *Heard Round the World: the impact abroad of the Civil War* (New York, 1969), 118.
12. Case and Spencer, *The United States and France*, 301.
13. Quoted in Sideman and Friedman (eds.), *Europe Looks at the Civil War*, 143.
14. *El Pensamiento Espanol*, quoted in Jordan and Pratt, *Europe and the American Civil War*, 251–2.
15. Robin Winks, *Canada and the United States: the Civil War years* (Baltimore, 1960), 281.
16. William H. Russell, *My Diary North and South* (London, 1863), I, 142–3, 362–3, 376.
17. See Chapter XIV, pp. 424–5.
18. Henry Blumenthal, 'Confederate diplomacy: popular notions and international realities', *Journal of Southern History*, XXXII (1966), 153.
19. Henry Adams, *Education*, 185.
20. Lincoln, *Works*, IV, 438.
21. Henry Adams, *Education*, 194.
22. Blumenthal, 'Confederate diplomacy', 167.
23. Lincoln *Works*, IV, 338–9.

24. See Chapter XIV, pp. 421–3.
25. Lincoln, *Works*, V, 63–4.
26. Ford (ed.), *A Cycle of Adams letters*, I, 82.
27. Robin Winks, *Canada and the United States*, 103.
28. Quoted ibid., 96, note 33.

## CHAPTER XIV

1. Howard K. Beale (ed.), *Diary of Gideon Welles*, 3 vols (New York, 1960), I, 67.
2. Chesnut, *Diary*, 92, 105 (27 July, 8 August 1861).
3. Frank L. Owsley, *King Cotton Diplomacy: foreign relations of the Confederate States of America* (2nd edn, Chicago, 1959), 259–67. More elaborate statistical calculations are to be found in a series of articles by Marcus W. Price in *American Neptune*, VIII (1948), 196–241; XI (1951), 262–90; XII (1952), 229–38; XV (1955), 97–131.
4. Frank E. Vandiver, *Their Tattered Flags: the epic of the Confederacy* (New York, 1970), 233–4.
5. On the legal and diplomatic issues raised by the *Peterhoff* and other prize cases, see Stuart L. Bernath, *Squall Across the Atlantic: American Civil War prize cases and diplomacy* (Berkeley, 1970).
6. Richard S. West, *Mr Lincoln's Navy* (New York, 1957), 190.
7. See Chapter X, pp. 273–4.
8. See also Chapter XV, p. 456.
9. See two useful articles by Douglas H. Maynard: 'Plotting the escape of the *Alabama*', *Journal of Southern History*, XX (1954), 197–209, and 'Union efforts to prevent the escape of the *Alabama*', *Mississippi Valley Historical Review*, XLI (1954), 41–60.
10. Ephraim D. Adams, *Great Britain and the American Civil War* (New York, 1925), II, 121–51, takes the view that the seizure of the *Alexandra* marks a decisive shift in British policy, which virtually predetermined the outcome of the crisis over the Laird Rams later in 1863. Wilbur D. Jones, *The Confederate Rams at Birkenhead: a chapter in Anglo-American relations* (Tuscaloosa, Ala., 1961), convincingly reinstates the rams affair as the climax of the whole story. See esp. pp. 52–8.
11. Henry Adams, *Education*, 172–8, offers a dramatic account of the rams crisis, and depicts it as his father's supreme diplomatic triumph. Wilbur D. Jones, *The Confederate Rams at Birkenhead*, 62–80, provides a cooler more judicious, modern appraisal.
12. John Morley, *The Life of William Ewart Gladstone*, 3 vols. (London, 1903), II, 76–7.
13. The correspondence between Palmerston and Russell is conveniently brought together in Belle B. Sideman and Lillian Friedman (eds), *Europe Looks at the Civil War* (New York, 1960), 149–52. For a good, concise, recent account, see Frank J. Merli, *Great Britain and the Confederate Navy* (Bloomington, Ind., 1970), 100–16, and for an interesting evaluation of British motives and policy, see Kinley J. Brauer, 'British mediation and the American Civil War: a reconsideration', *Journal of Southern History*, XXXVIII (1972), 49–64.
14. In addition to Merli, see Lynn M. Case and Warren F. Spencer, *The United States and France: Civil War diplomacy* (Philadelphia, 1970), 333–46. On the whole intervention question, the brilliant if erratic account in Henry Adams, *Education*, 152–66, is still very well worth reading.
15. Henry Adams, *Education*, 187.

## CHAPTER XV

1. Worthington C. Ford (ed.), *A Cycle o Adams Letters, 1861–1865*, 2 vols (Boston, 1920), II, 133.

2. William T. Sherman, *Memoirs of General William T. Sherman*, 2 vols (New York, 1875), I, 400.
3. Lloyd Lewis, *Sherman: fighting prophet* (New York, 1932), 345.
4. Ibid., 334–5.
5. See Chapter IX, p. 260.
6. On the naval contribution to the operation, see Chapter XIV, p. 434.
7. Lewis, *Sherman*, 644.
8. Joseph E. Johnston, *Narrative of military operations* (Bloomington, Ind., 1959), 363.
9. Bruce Catton, *Grant takes command* (Boston, 1968), 355.
10. John B. Hood, *Advance and retreat* (New Orleans, 1880), 95.
11. Lewis, *Sherman*, 353.
12. Ibid., 375.
13. Philip H. Sheridan, *Personal Memoirs of P. H. Sheridan*, 2 vols (New York, 1888), I, 465.
14. Paul M. Angle and Earl S. Miers (eds), *Tragic Years, 1860–1865*, 2 vols (New York, 1960), II, 904–5.
15. Sherman, *Memoirs*, II, 126, 111.
16. Lewis, *Sherman*, 430.
17. Ibid., 431.

## CHAPTER XVI

1. Wilfred B. Yearns, *The Confederate Congress* (Athens, Ga., 1960), 49–59, 224–6, provides an excellent analysis of the elections and the make-up of the new Congress.
2. See Chapter XI, pp. 314–212.
3. See Chapter VI, pp. 137–41.
4. Ulrich B. Phillips (ed.), *The Correspondence of Robert Toombs, Alexander H. Stephens and Howell Cobb* (American Historical Association Annual Report, 1911, Vol. II, Washington, 1913), 629.
5. Braxton Bragg, D. H. Hill and other Confederate generals signed this protest. Quoted in Albert D. Kirwan (ed.), *The Confederacy* (New York, 1959), 205–6.
6. Frank L. Owsley, *State Rights in the Confederacy* (Chicago, 1925), 245.
7. Phillips (ed.), *Correspondence of Toombs, Stephens and Cobb*, 605.
8. James Z. Rabun, 'Alexander H. Stephens and Jefferson Davis', *American Historical Review*, LVIII (1953), 307, 310; Phillips (ed.), *Correspondence of Toombs, Stephens and Cobb*, 608.
9. Henry Cleveland, *Alexander H. Stephens in public and private, with letters and speeches, before, during and since the war* (Philadelphia, 1866), 785.
10. Joseph H. Parks, 'State rights in a crisis: Governor Joseph E. Brown versus President Jefferson Davis', *Journal of Southern History*, XXXII (1966), 23.
11. Chesnut, *Diary*, 456.
12. Lincoln, *Works*, VI, 48–9.
13. Stewart Mitchell, *Horatio Seymour of New York* (Cambridge, Mass., 1938), defends Seymour unwaveringly and almost uncritically. More recently, other historians have taken a more critical view; see, for example, Allan Nevins, *The War for the Union* (New York, 1971), III, 125–6, 170, and Eugene C. Murdock, *Patriotism Limited, 1862–1865: the Civil War draft and the bounty system* (Kent, Ohio, 1967), 63–80.
14. Strong, *Diary*, III, 337, 343. The vividness, and the intemperate language, of Strong's whole account of the riot (pp. 334–44) convey something of the feelings of anger, hate and fear which it excited.
15. Dudley T. Cornish, *The Sable Arm: Negro troops in the Union army, 1861–1865* (New York, 1956), foreword.
16. Henry C. Hubbart, *The Older Middle West, 1840–1880* (New York, 1936), 185, 211.

On Vallandigham's controversial Civil War career, see Frank L. Klement, *The Limits of Dissent: Clement L. Vallandigham and the Civil War* (Lexington, Ky., 1970).

17. Lincoln, *Works*, IV, 430.
18. Any discussion of these constitutional questions must rely heavily upon the standard work on the subject, James G. Randall, *Constitutional Problems under Lincoln* (Revised edn, Urbana, Ill., 1951). For a more recent and challenging discussion of some of the issues, see Harold M. Hyman, 'Reconstruction and political-constitutional institutions: the popular expression', Hyman (ed.), *New Frontiers of the American Reconstruction* (Urbana, Ill., 1966), 1–39.
19. For Taney's opinion, see Henry S. Commager (ed.), *Documents of American History* (5th edn, New York, 1949), I, 398–401.
20. Lincoln, *Works*, VI, 267. For the full text of the two letters in which Lincoln defended the policy of arbitrary arrests in general, and the arrest of Vallandigham in particular, see ibid., VI, 260–9, 300–6.
21. For the Supreme Court decision in the Milligan case, see Commager, *Documents*, II, 22–6. Randall, *Constitutional Problems under Lincoln*, 174–85, provides a lucid summary of both the Vallandigham and Milligan cases. See also Klement, *The Limits of Dissent*, 156–72, 319–21.
22. Both Harold Hyman and Alfred H. Kelly make interesting observations on the adequacy of the constitution in coping with new and unprecedented demands during and after the Civil War, in Hyman (ed.), *New Frontiers of the American Reconstruction*, 1–58, *passim*.

## CHAPTER XVII

1. On the constitutional (and most other) aspects of the problem of wartime reconstruction, Herman Belz, *Reconstructing the Union: theory and policy during the Civil War* (Ithaca, N.Y., 1969) is invaluable.
2. Belz, *Reconstructing the Union*, 138–42, 162–3.
3. William E. Smith, *The Francis Preston Blair Family in Politics*, 2 vols (New York, 1933), II, 238. There is a good discussion of the Sumner–Blair argument in Allan Nevins, *The War for the Union* (New York, 1971), III, 462–5.
4. Lincoln, *Works*, VII, 50–6, contains the text of the proclamation and Lincoln's comments upon it in his message to Congress.
5. Boston *Commonwealth*, 18 December 1863, quoted in Belz, *Reconstructing the Union*, 166,
6. *Congressional Globe*, 38 Cong., 1 Sess., 681–2.
7. For the text of the bill, see Harold M. Hyman (ed.), *The Radical Republicans and Reconstruction, 1861–1870* (Indianapolis, 1967), 128–34.
8. Ibid., 136–47, for Lincoln's proclamation and the Wade–Davis manifesto.
9. Lincoln, *Works*, VII, 200–1, 212–13.
10. For the text of the platform, see Henry S. Commager (ed.), *Documents of American History* (5th edn, New York, 1949), I, 435–6.
11. Benjamin F. Butler, 'Vice-presidential politics in '64', *North American Review*, CXLI (1885), 333.
12. Alexander K. McClure, *Abraham Lincoln and Men of War Times* (Philadelphia, 1892), 104.
13. Tyler Dennett (ed.), *Lincoln and the Civil War in the Diaries and Letters of John Hay* (New York, 1939), 201–2.
14. See Chapter XV, pp. 466–9, 473, on Early's raid, and the general state of the war in mid-summer.
15. Lincoln, *Works*, VII, 517–18.
16. Ibid., VII, 514–15.

17. William F. Zornow, *Lincoln and the Party Divided* (Norman, Okla., 1954), 110–18, gives a good account of these machinations.
18. Ibid., 132–3.
19. Ibid., 136.
20. On Mobile Bay, see Chapter XIV, p. 430; on the successes of Sherman and Sheridan, see Chapter XV, pp. 474, 475–6.
21. Lincoln, *Works*, VIII, 18.
22. The evidence relating to a possible deal concerning Blair and Fremont is discussed in Richard N. Current, *The Lincoln Nobody Knows* (New York, 1958), 207–9.
23. Philip S. Foner, *The Life and Writings of Frederick Douglass*, 4 vols (New York, 1955), III, 424. On the intensely racist element in the Democratic campaign, see Forrest G. Wood, *Black Scare: the racist response to emancipation and reconstruction* (Berkeley, 1968), 53–75.
24. For further details on the Milligan case, see Chapter XVI, pp. 511–12 and Chapter XIX, p. 604.
25. Harry J. Carman and Reinhard H. Luthin, *Lincoln and the Patronage* (New York, 1943), 298, 292.
26. Lincoln, *Works*, VIII, 11–12, 46–7.
27. William B. Hesseltine, *Lincoln's Plan of Reconstruction* (Tuscaloosa, Ala., 1960), 131–2.
28. Lincoln, *Works*, VIII, 46.
29. Zornow, *Lincoln and the Party Divided*, 208–10, emphasises the limitations of Lincoln's appeal to urban workers; David Montgomery, *Beyond Equality: labor and the radical Republicans, 1862–1872* (New York, 1967), 107–11, stresses Lincoln's gains in the cities since 1860.
30. Lincoln, *Works*, VIII, 41.

CHAPTER XVIII

1. Lincoln, *Works*, VIII, 333.
2. Ibid., VIII, 152.
3. Ibid., VIII, 254.
4. The best account of this compromise move is in Herman Belz, *Reconstructing the Union* (Ithaca, N.Y., 1969), ch. ix.
5. David Donald, *Charles Sumner and the Rights of Man* (New York, 1970), 204
6. Lincoln, *Works*, VIII, 403–4; Donald, *Charles Sumner and the Rights of Man*, 207.
7. Lincoln, *Works*, VIII, 405.
8. Ibid., VIII, 152.
9. Ibid., VII, 435–6, 440–2, 443, 459–60, 461. The standard work on all these peace moves is Edward C. Kirkland, *The Peacemakers of 1864* (New York, 1927).
10. Lincoln, *Works*, VII, 451.
11. Ibid., VII, 517–18, 501.
12. Ibid., VIII, 151.
13. Ibid., VIII, 275–6.
14. There is a good, brief account of the Hampton Roads conference in Richard N. Current, *The Lincoln Nobody Knows* (New York, 1958), 243–7. The most elaborate account left by any of the participants in the meeting is Alexander H. Stephens, *A Constitutional View of the Late War between the States*, 2 vols (Chicago, 1868–70), II, 589–622, 791–803.
15. Lincoln, *Works*, VIII, 260–1.
16. Wilfred B. Yearns, *The Confederate Congress* (Athens, Ga., 1960), is useful on this as on all phases of congressional activity (or lack of it). On the refusal to suspend the writ of habeas corpus, see James Z. Rabun, 'Alexander H. Stephens and Jefferson Davis', *American Historical Review*, LVIII (1953), 317–18.
17. On this whole question, see Bell I. Wiley, *Southern Negroes, 1861–1865* (New Haven, 1938), ch. ix, and Yearns, *The Confederate Congress*, 95–9.

18. Edward Younger (ed.), *Inside the Confederate Government: the diary of Robert Garlick Hill Kean* (New York, 1957), 183–4, 182–3.

19. John Bigelow, *Retrospections of an Active Life*, 3 vols (New York, 1909), I, 568–9. On the Kenner mission, see Frank L. Owsley, *King Cotton Diplomacy* (2nd edn, Chicago, 1959), ch. xvii.

20. Sherman to Halleck, 24 December 1864, in William T. Sherman, *Memoirs*, 2 vols (New York, 1875), II, 227.

21. Grant to Sherman, 18 December 1864, in Sherman, *Memoirs*, II, 224.

22. Lloyd Lewis, *Sherman: Fighting Prophet* (New York, 1932), 500–8, puts up a stout and generally convincing defence of Sherman. The general's own report on the affair is quoted in Henry S. Commager (ed.), *Documents of American History* (5th edn, New York, 1949), I, 446.

23. Sherman, *Memoirs*, II, 225.

24. Joseph E. Johnston, *Narrative of Military Operations* (Bloomington, Ind., 1959), 374–5.

25. Clifford Dowdey (ed.), *The Wartime Papers of R. E. Lee* (Boston, 1961), 911–12; Lincoln, *Works*, VIII, 330–1.

26. See below, pp. 574–6.

27. There are vivid accounts of the evacuation of Richmond and its occupation by Union troops in Earl S. Miers (ed.), *A Rebel War Clerk's Diary [by] John B. Jones* (New York, 1958), 526–32, and [Sallie A. Putnam], *Richmond During the War: four years of personal observation. By a Richmond lady* (New York, 1867), 362–7. The latter is quoted in Albert D. Kirwan (ed.), *The Confederacy* (New York, 1959), 284–8.

28. Benjamin Quarles, *Lincoln and the Negro* (New York, 1962), 235–8.

29. Lincoln, *Works*, VIII, 386–7, 389, 405–8; Current, *The Lincoln Nobody Knows*, 250–60.

30. Douglas S. Freeman, *R. E. Lee: a biography*, 4 vols (New York, 1935), IV, 120, 122–3.

31. There are good accounts of the proceedings at Appomattox in Bruce Catton, *Grant Takes Command* (Boston, 1968), 463–8, and Freeman, *Lee*, IV, 134–43. A selection of first-hand accounts may be found in Paul M. Angle and Earl S. Miers (eds), *Tragic Years, 1860–1865* (New York, 1960), II, 1035–40.

32. Catton, *Grant Takes Command*, 471.

33. Lloyd Lewis, *Myths after Lincoln* (New York, 1929), is a colourful account of every aspect of the assassination and its aftermath. See Current, *The Lincoln Nobody Knows*, 272–85, for an interesting discussion of the controversies and unsolved questions which still surround Lincoln's death.

34. For the terms of this convention, see Commager, *Documents*, 5th edn, I, 447–8. Current, *The Lincoln Nobody Knows*, 247–50, 260–5, provides a balanced appraisal of the whole affair.

35. There is a vivid account of the last desperate journeys of Davis and members of his cabinet in Alfred J. Hanna, *Flight into Oblivion* (Richmond, 1938).

36. Sherman, *Memoirs*, II, 127.

37. David M. Potter, 'Jefferson Davis and the political factors in Confederate defeat', David Donald (ed.), *Why the North won the Civil War* (Baton Rouge, La., 1960), 94.

38. David Knowles, *The American Civil War: a brief sketch* (Oxford, 1926), vii.

39. Kenneth M. Stampp, 'The Southern road to Appomattox', *Cotton Memorial Papers*, No. 4 (1969), 3–22. (Reprinted in Lawrence W. Levine and Robert Middlekauff (eds), *The National Temper: readings in American culture and society* (2nd edn, New York, 1972), 210–23.)

CHAPTER XIX

1. C. Vann Woodward, *American Counterpoint: slavery and racism in the North–South dialogue* (Boston, 1971), 169–71.

2. David Donald, *The Politics of Reconstruction, 1863–1867* (Baton Rouge, La., 1965), 26–52.

3. Kenneth M. Stampp. *The Era of Reconstruction, 1865–1877* (New York and London, 1965), 89.

4. The founding father of the long-dominant school of reconstruction history which saw little virtue in the radicals and little merit in any attempt to guarantee the civil and political rights of the Negro, was William A. Dunning. His book, *Reconstruction, Political and Economic, 1865–1877* (New York, 1907), and the studies by his students of individual states during reconstruction stated what remained the conventional view of the period until at least the 1940s. For an excellent discussion of the durability of the Dunning interpretation, and its undermining in the last thirty years, see the introduction by Harold Hyman to his own collection of documents, *The Radical Republicans and Reconstruction, 1861–1870* (Indianapolis, 1967), ix–lxviii.

5. The text of Johnson's proclamations is given in various collections of documents, including Hyman (ed.), *The Radical Republicans and Reconstruction*, 249–56.

6. Examples of the black codes may be found in Henry S. Commager (ed.), *Documents of American History* (5th edn, New York, 1949), II, 2–7.

7. John H. Franklin, *Reconstruction: after the Civil War* (Chicago, 1961), ch. iii.

8. For the circumstances of the Milligan case, see Chapter XVI, pp. 511–12, and Chapter XVII, p. 542.

9. Donald, *The Politics of Reconstruction*, 53–82; William R. Brock, *An American Crisis: Congress and reconstruction, 1865–1867*, 188–98; Woodward, *American Counterpoint*, 172–3.

10. For the precise terms of the act, see Hyman (ed.), *The Radical Republicans and Reconstruction*, 379–82.

11. The argument that the Negro vote in the north was the main objective of the Fifteenth Amendment is put forward in William Gillette, *The Right to Vote: politics and the passage of the Fifteenth Amendment* (Baltimore, 1965). A formidable challenge to this view is presented in an important and persuasive article by LaWanda and John H. Cox, 'Negro suffrage and Republican politics: the problem of motivation in reconstruction historiography', *Journal of Southern History*, XXXIII (1967), 303–30.

12. Such remarks, as Kenneth Stampp points out, show Bryce as a precursor of the Dunning school of reconstruction history. (Stampp, *The Era of Reconstruction*, 155.)

13. In addition to Hyman (ed.), *The Radical Republicans and Reconstruction*, see Stampp, *The Era of Reconstruction*, chs i and vi, for good, brief discussions of the acceptability of the Dunning version of reconstruction, and of the character of the radical régimes in the South.

14. Vernon L. Wharton, *The Negro in Mississippi, 1865–1890* (Chapel Hill, N.C., 1947), 187. See the whole of ch. xiii of Wharton's study for a grimly impressive account of the Mississippi plan in action.

15. C. Vann Woodward, *Reunion and Reaction: the compromise of 1877 and the end of reconstruction* (Boston, 1951), is essential to an understanding of the forces behind the compromise.

16. Alfred H. Kelly, in Harold M. Hyman (ed.), *New Frontiers of the American Reconstruction* (Urbana, Ill., 1966), 57.

17. Georges Clemenceau, *American Reconstruction* (New York, 1928), 278, quoted in Hyman (ed.), *The Radical Republicans and Reconstruction*, lxvii.

18. *Congressional Globe*, 39 Cong., 1 Sess., 114.

19. Woodward, *American Counterpoint*, 183.

## CHAPTER XX

1. Thomas Wolfe, *You Can't Go Home Again* (London, Penguin edn, 1970), 373.

2. See Chapter XII, pp. 343–5, for discussion of this point. For an example of the new

economic history which treats the Civil War as an event of little consequence (except, perhaps, in a negative sense), see Douglass C. North, *Growth and Welfare in the American Past: a new economic history* (Englewood Cliffs, N.J., 1966).

3. Robert U. Johnson and Clarence C. Buel (eds), *Battles and Leaders of the Civil War*, 4 vols (New York, 1887). There is a reprint edition of the full four volumes (New York, 1956) and a useful one-volume abridgement, edited by Ned Bradford (New York, 1956).

4. The authenticity and the interest of the multitude of Civil War monuments, sites, relics and other curiosities varies enormously, but non-American visitors can scarcely fail to be impressed by the scope and quality of the work of the National Parks Service at battlefields now under its control. The *Historical Handbook* series, issued by the Service, is also of great value. For an amusing parody of the kind of exploitation of the war which occurs at the other end of the scale, see T. Lawrence Connelly, *Will Success Spoil Jeff Davis?: the last book about the Civil War* (New York, 1963).

5. Thomas J. Pressly, *Americans interpret their Civil War* (Princeton, 1954), surveys changing interpretations of the war up to the 1940s, but is concerned mainly with the causes of the conflict. In the last ten or twelve years there has been a remarkable output of important new work, much of it on the period of the war, and much on the relationship of the slavery and race questions to the conflict, by an extremely able group of historians of a new generation, including James M. McPherson, Willie Lee Rose, Martin Duberman, V. Jacque Voegeli, Eric Foner, James H. Brewer, George M. Fredrickson.

6. This concept of the 'configurative role' of certain forces and issues is once again borrowed from the work of Arthur Bestor. See Chapter IV, pp. 87–8.

7. Howard J. Graham, 'The "conspiracy theory" of the Fourteenth Amendment', *Yale Law Journal*, XLVII (1938), 371–403, and XLVIII (1938), 171–94.

8. William D. Howells, *The Rise of Silas Lapham* (New York, Collier edn, 1969), 26.

9. Karl Marx and Frederick Engels, *The Civil War in the United States* (3rd edn, New York, 1961), 279, 281.

10. Lincoln, *Works*, VII, 259–60.

11. David Montgomery, *Beyond Equality: labor and the radical Republicans, 1862–1872* (New York, 1967), x.

12. Strong, *Diary*, IV, 23, 29.

13. For further discussion of Nevins's thesis, see Chapter XII, esp. pp. 338, 378–9.

14. James A. Rawley, 'The nationalism of Abraham Lincoln', *Civil War History*, IX (1963), 297–8.

15. Strong, *Diary*, IV, 2.

16. Ibid., IV, 20–1.

17. Henry Adams, *The Education of Henry Adams* (Boston, 1918), 248–9, 280–1.

18. Carl N. Degler, 'American political parties and the rise of the city: an interpretation', *Journal of American History*, LI (1964), 41–59.

19. For an interesting discussion of many of these issues, see George M. Fredrickson, *The Inner Civil War: Northern intellectuals and the crisis of the Union* (New York, 1965).

20. John G. Sproat, '*The Best Men': liberal reformers in the Gilded Age* (New York, 1968), 6.

21. John Morley, *The Life of William Ewart Gladstone*, 3 vols (London, 1903), II, 70.

22. It is a comment on the ambiguous message conveyed across the Atlantic by the war in America that, in the debates leading up to the second Reform Act in 1867, the American example was cited by speakers on both sides, in the one case as a guiding light, in the other as an awful warning. For an interesting discussion, see Harry C. Allen, 'Civil War, reconstruction and Great Britain', in Harold M. Hyman (ed.), *Heard Round the World: the impact abroad of the Civil War* (New York, 1969), 77–96.

23. David Potter, 'Civil War', in C. Vann Woodward (ed.), *The Comparative Approach to American History* (New York, 1968), 144.

24. Lowell to Joel Benton, 19 January 1876, Charles E. Norton (ed.), *Letters of James Russell Lowell*, 2 vols (London, 1894), II, 179.

25. Thomas Wolfe, *You Can't Go Home Again* (London, Penguin ed., 1970), 360.
26. For an interesting discussion of the limited impact of the Civil War on European military thinking, see Jay Luvaas, *The Military Legacy of the Civil War: the European inheritance* (Chicago, 1959), esp. 216–25 on Liddell Hart, and 226–33 for general conclusions.
27. W. L. Morton, 'Canada and reconstruction, 1863–79', in Harold M. Hyman (ed.), *New Frontiers of the American Reconstruction* (Urbana, Ill., 1966), 119.

# Chronology of Events
## November 1860–May 1865

|  | *The War* | *The North* |
|---|---|---|

*1860*

NOV

6 Abraham Lincoln elected president.

DEC

4 James Buchanan's last annual message to Congress.
18 Crittenden's compromise resolution presented to House of Representatives.

*1861*

JAN  9 Failure of the *Star of the West* to relieve Fort Sumter.

FEB

4–27 Washington Peace Convention.

MAR.  29 Lincoln orders preparation of Fort Sumter relief expedition.

4 Inauguration of Abraham Lincoln as president.

APRIL  8 Relief expedition sails from New York.
12–13 Bombardment and surrender of Fort Sumter.
19 Lincoln proclaims blockade of Southern coast.

15 Lincoln declares state of insurrection and calls for 75,000 militia.
19–25 Washington cut off from the North.

MAY

JUNE  June–July Political and military moves to secure Union control of west Virginia.

9 Establishment of United States Sanitary Commission.

676

*13* South Carolina legislature calls special convention to discuss secession.

*20* South Carolina convention votes for secession.

*9–1* Feb. Secession of six more states: Mississippi, Florida, Alabama, Georgia, Louisiana, Texas.

*4* Opening of Montgomery Convention which created Confederate States of America, drew up a constitution and chose Jefferson Davis as provisional president (9 Feb.).

*11* Montgomery Convention approves draft of permanent Confederate constitution.

*17–20* May Secession of Virginia, Arkansas, Tennessee and North Carolina.

*20* Kentucky declares its neutrality.
*29* Richmond becomes capital of Confederacy.

*3–9* Confederate mission, headed by W. L. Yancey, received in London by Lord John Russell, foreign secretary.
*13* British proclamation of neutrality.

*1861*

JULY
*21* Confederate victory at Bull Run (or Manassas).
*25* Fremont assumes command in the West.
*27* McClellan takes command of Union forces around Washington.

AUG.
*10* Confederate victory at Wilson's Creek, Missouri.
*29* Union success at Hatteras Inlet, on North Carolina coast.

*6* First Confiscation Act.
*30* Fremont's proclamation declaring martial law, and freeing slaves, in Missouri.

SEPT.
*3–6* End of Kentucky's 'neutrality'.

OCT.

NOV.
*1* McClellan becomes general-in-chief of all Union armies.
*7* Union capture of Port Royal on South Carolina coast.
*19* Halleck replaces Fremont as Union commander in West.

DEC.

*20* Creation of Joint Committee on the Conduct of the War.
*30* Suspension of specie payments.

*1862*

JAN.

*15* Stanton becomes secretary of war.

FEB.
*6* Union capture of Fort Henry on Tennessee river.
*8* Union success at Roanoke Island, North Carolina.
*16* Confederates surrender Fort Donelson to Grant.
*25* Confederate evacuation of Nashville.

*25* Legal Tender Act, authorising issue of 'greenbacks'.

MAR.
*7–8* Union victory at Pea Ridge (or Elkhorn Tavern), Arkansas.

*6* Lincoln proposes gradual emancipation to Congress.

| The South | The World |
|---|---|
| Oct.–Nov. Elections for president and first permanent Congress. | |
| *6* Jefferson Davis elected to six-year term as president. | *8* Seizure of Confederate commissioners Mason and Slidell from British ship *Trent*. |
| | *26* Lincoln cabinet decides upon release of Mason and Slidell. |
| *22* Inauguration of Jefferson Davis as president.<br>*27* Congress authorises martial law and suspension of habeas corpus. | |
| | *22* Confederate cruiser *Florida* escapes from Mersey. |

*1862*

MAR.  *8–9* *Virginia* v. *Monitor* in Hampton
Roads.
*17–2* April Movement of McClellan's
army to James Peninsula.

APRIL  *5–4* May McClellan besieges Yorktown.
*6–7* Grant turns near-defeat into
Union victory at Shiloh.
*24–25* New Orleans falls to Admiral
Farragut.

MAY  *8–9* June Jackson's Shenandoah
Valley campaign.
*31–1* June Battle of Fair Oaks (or
Seven Pines) near Richmond. Lee
takes command of Army of Northern
Virginia.

*9* General David Hunter issues proclamation freeing slaves in South
Carolina, Georgia and Florida –
revoked by Lincoln.
*20* Homestead Act passed by Congress.

JUNE  *6* Confederate evacuation of
Memphis.
*26* Creation of Army of Virginia
under John Pope.
*26–2* July Lee drives McClellan
back from Richmond in Seven Days
battles.
June–July Failure of Union naval
operations against Vicksburg.

JULY  *11* Halleck appointed general-in-
chief of Union armies.

*1* Congress passes Pacific Railway
Act, and Revenue Act (including
income tax).
*12* Lincoln fails to persuade border
states to accept plan for gradual
emancipation.
*17* Second Confiscation Act.
*22* Lincoln reads draft emancipation proclamation to cabinet.

AUG.  *3* Decision to evacuate McClellan's
army from peninsula.
*27–8* Beginning of Confederate
invasion of Kentucky.

*20–22* Greeley–Lincoln exchange of
letters on emancipation.

*16* Conscription Act passed by
Congress.

*18* Debate in House of Commons
on Lindsay's motion proposing
mediation in Civil War.
*23–4* Formal Confederate requests
for British and French recognition.
*29* Escape of the Confederate
cruiser *Alabama* from the Mersey.

*1862*

AUG.   *29–30* Confederate victory at
Second Bull Run (or Manassas).

SEPT.   *2* McClellan in command of defence          *22* First Emancipation Proclamation.
of Washington                                        *24* Proclamation on suspension of
*4–6* Lee invades Maryland.                          habeas corpus.
*17* Battle of Antietam (or Sharps-
burg), followed by Lee's withdrawal into Virginia.
*19* Union defensive victory at Iuka,
Mississippi.

OCT.   *3–4* Union defensive victory at              Oct.–Nov. Mid-term elections
Corinth, Mississippi.                                produce severe setbacks for Repub-
*8* Battle of Perryville, Kentucky,                  licans.
followed by retreat of Bragg's Con-
federate army.

NOV.   *7* McClellan dismissed; Burnside
assumes command of Army of
Potomac.
Nov.–Dec. Failure of Grant's overland advance towards Vicksburg.

DEC.   *13* Lee routs Burnside at Fredericks-        *16–20* Cabinet crisis; Lincoln retains
burg.                                                both Seward and Chase.
*27–9* Sherman defeated at Chickasaw
Bluffs, near Vicksburg.
*31–3* Jan. Battle of Murfreesboro
(or Stones River), followed by
Bragg's withdrawal.

*1863*

JAN.   *25* Burnside replaced by Hooker as          *1* Second Emancipation Procla-
commander of the Army of the                         mation.
Potomac.

FEB.   Feb.–Apr. Grant's abortive attempts          *25* Congress passes National Bank
to find back door to Vicksburg.                      Act.

*14–2* Oct. Palmerston and Russell
discuss plans for intervention in
Civil War.

*7* Gladstone's Newcastle speech.

*11–12* British government rejects
Napoleon III's plan for joint
British–French–Russian mediation.

*15* The cruiser *Florida* sails from
Mobile to begin commerce-raiding
career.

*13* Expiry of law authorising suspension of habeas corpus.
Feb.–Mar. Trans-Mississippi becomes
a semi-autonomous area under Gen.
Kirby Smith.

*1863*

MAR.                                           *3* Conscription Act, and new
                                               Habeas Corpus Act passed by Con-
                                               gress.

APRIL   *7* Failure of Union attack on Fort
        Sumter.
        *16–17* Porter's ships run past the
        Vicksburg batteries.
        *30–6* May Lee routs Hooker at
        Chancellorsville.

MAY     *1–18* Grant's successful campaign     *5* Arrest of Vallandigham.
        in Mississippi; Pemberton trapped
        in Vicksburg.
        *10* Death of 'Stonewall' Jackson.

JUNE    *3* Start of Lee's advance north.
        *15* Lee's army begins to cross
        Potomac.
        *26–7* July Rosecrans manoeuvres
        Confederates under Bragg back
        towards Chattanooga.
        *28* Hooker replaced by Meade as
        commander of Army of Potomac.

JULY    *1–3* Union victory at Gettysburg.     *13–16* New York draft riots.
        *4* Vicksburg surrendered to Grant.
        *8* Confederates surrender Port
        Hudson, on Mississippi.
        *13–14* Lee retreats across Potomac
        into Virginia.
        *18* Robert Gould Shaw's Negro
        troops in action at Fort Wagner,
        near Charleston.

AUG.    *20* Rosecrans begins movement to
        south of Chattanooga.

SEPT.   *8* Union capture of Fort Wagner,
        near Charleston, after many setbacks.
        *19–20* Rosecrans defeated by Bragg
        at Chickamauga.

*26* Congress passes Impressment Act.

*2* Bread riot in Richmond.
*24* Congress passes new tax law,
including income tax, and tax-in-
kind.

*5* British government orders
seizure of *Alexandra*, under construction on Merseyside for Confederacy.

*1* Railroad Act gives much wider
powers to War Dept.

*7* French forces occupy Mexico
City.
*30* Debate in House of Commons
on Roebuck's motion to recognise
Confederacy.

Sept.–Nov. Congressional elections
produce severe setbacks for Jefferson
Davis.

*1–8* Climax of crisis over building
of Laird Rams for the Confederacy,
at Birkenhead.

*1863*

OCT.   *17* Grant becomes overall Union commander in West.
*28* Relief of Union forces besieged in Chattanooga.

Oct.–Nov. Local and state elections, including defeat of Vallandigham in Ohio, indicate Republican recovery.

NOV.   *24–5* Union victory at Chattanooga.

*19* The Gettysburg address.

DEC.

*8* Lincoln's proclamation of amnesty and proposals for reconstruction

*1864*

JAN.

Jan.–Feb. Widening gap between Lincoln and Congress on reconstruction. End of Chase's presidential 'boom'.

FEB.   *17* Confederate submarine *Hunley* sinks U.S.S. *Housatonic.*

MAR.   *9* Grant becomes general-in-chief.

APRIL   *8* Union defeat at Mansfield (or Sabine Cross Roads), Louisiana, leads to abandonment of Red River expedition.
*12* Forrest captures Fort Pillow, Tennessee; alleged massacre of Negro troops.

MAY   *4* Start of major Union offensive in Virginia and Georgia.
*5–6* Battle of the Wilderness.

Feb. Tough measures passed by
Congress: new tax law (including
property tax), attempt to retire
some paper currency, new law on
impressment of slaves, laws giving
government wide powers over
blockade-running, and renewed
authority to suspend habeas corpus.

*16* Vice-president Stephens's address
to Georgia legislature attacking
despotism of Davis administration.

*31* Nomination of Fremont as          *28* Archduke Maximilian arrives in
presidential candidate of the 'Radical  Mexico.
Democracy'.

*1864*

MAY　*8–21* Battles at Spotsylvania Court
House.
*25–9* Battle between Sherman and
Joseph E. Johnston around New
Hope Church, Georgia.

JUNE　*1–3* Battle of Coldharbor.
*14–16* Grant's army moves south of
James River.
*15–18* Failure of attacks on Petersburg; beginning of nine-month
siege.
*27* Sherman defeated at Kenesaw
Mountain.

*7* Baltimore Convention re-
nominates Lincoln, chooses Andrew
Johnson as running-mate.
*30* Resignation of Secretary of the
Treasury Chase.

JULY　*11* Confederate force led by Jubal
A. Early reaches outskirts of
Washington.
*17* Hood replaces Johnston as Confederate commander at Atlanta.
*20–28* Battles around Atlanta.
*30* Union failure at battle of the
'crater', near Petersburg.

*4* Lincoln's pocket-veto of Wade–
Davis reconstruction bill.

AUG.　*5* Union naval victory at Mobile
Bay.

*5* Wade–Davis manifesto.
*18–30* Moves to ditch Lincoln as
presidential candidate.
*29* Democrats nominate McClellan
as presidential candidate.

SEPT.　*2* Sherman captures Atlanta.
*19–22* Sheridan's victories at Opequon Creek and Fisher's Hill,
in Shenandoah Valley.

OCT.　*19* Union victory at Cedar Creek
ends Confederate threat in
Shenandoah Valley.
*23* Union victory over Sterling
Price at Westport, Missouri, ends
major fighting west of Missi-
sippi.

*19* Sinking of *Alabama* off Cherbourg.

*1* Expiry of law allowing suspension of habeas corpus.

*17* Meeting of state governors protests against suspension of habeas corpus and other government policies.

*7* Confederate cruiser *Florida* captured at Bahia, Brazil.

*1864*

NOV.   *15–16* Beginning of Sherman's          *8* Lincoln re-elected president.
       march from Atlanta to the sea.
       *30* Confederates under Hood
       defeated at Franklin, Tennessee.

DEC.   *15–16* Hood's Confederates routed      *6* Chase becomes Chief Justice of
       by Thomas at Nashville.               Supreme Court.
       *21* Savannah falls to Sherman.

*1865*

JAN.   *15* Union forces capture Fort          *31* Congress passes Thirteenth
       Fisher, North Carolina.               Amendment, abolishing slavery.

FEB.   *1* Start of Sherman's march through
       the Carolinas.
       *17* Burning of Columbia, South
       Carolina. Confederates evacuate
       Charleston.

MAR.   *21–3* Completion of Sherman's          *4* Lincoln's second inauguration.
       march; junction with Schofield's
       forces in North Carolina.
       *30–31* Beginning of Grant's final
       assault in Virginia.

APRIL  *2* Fall of Petersburg.                 *14–15* Lincoln shot by John Wilkes
       *3* Fall of Richmond.                  Booth, dies next morning.
       *9* Lee surrenders to Grant at
       Appomattox Court House.
       *26* Joseph E. Johnston surrenders in
       North Carolina.

MAY    *26* Surrender of Kirby Smith in
       trans-Mississippi region brings war
       formally to an end.

*3* Hampton Roads Conference.
*6* Lee becomes commander-in-chief
of all Confederate armies.

Feb.–March Kenner's abortive
mission to Europe to seek diplomatic recognition for Confederacy,
in return for abolition of slavery.

*13* Congress authorises recruitment
of slaves into army.

*4* Jefferson Davis's last appeal to
people of South.

*10* Jefferson Davis captured at
Irwinville, Georgia.

# Bibliographical Essay

One purpose of this essay is to acknowledge my debt to the numerous and distinguished company of Civil War historians upon whose work I have drawn. But it is above all designed not for show but for use, to help the interested reader and the student who wishes to know where to pursue various aspects of the Civil War in greater detail. Inevitably, my approach is highly selective; I have included primary sources only when they offer some illumination not adequately provided by secondary works, and articles only where they are of quite exceptional importance, and the books on the subject are inadequate. I have paid special attention to areas of historiographical controversy, and to recent books of interest and importance. I am well aware that, such is the extent and variety of the literature on the Civil War, I have been obliged to omit many works of merit and value.

There is an admirable Civil War bibliography in paperback, including books and articles which appeared up to the late 1960s, compiled by David Donald, *The Nation in Crisis, 1861–1877* (New York, 1969). Another useful, slightly older, list published by the Library of Congress, is Donald H. Mugridge (comp.) *The American Civil War: a selected reading list* (Washington, 1960). A Civil War bibliography on the grand scale is provided by Allan Nevins, James I. Robertson and Bell I. Wiley (eds), *Civil War Books: a critical bibliography*, 2 vols (Baton Rouge, La., 1967–9). Many of the books listed below have excellent bibliographies on their own particular aspect of the period. The best way to keep up with new works on the Civil War is through the bibliographies published annually by the periodical *Civil War History*.

## I. GENERAL WORKS

The eight volumes of Allan Nevins's *The Ordeal of the Union* represent a pro-digious achievement. Four volumes deal with the pre-war period: *Ordeal of the Union*, 2 vols (New York, 1947) and *The Emergence of Lincoln*, 2 vols (New York, 1950). Four more volumes cover the war years themselves, under the collective title, *The War for the Union*; they are *The Improvised War, 1861–1862* (New York, 1959), *War Becomes Revolution, 1862–1863* (New York, 1960), *The Organised War, 1863–1864* (New York, 1971) and *Organised War to Victory, 1864–1865* (New York, 1971). The sheer scale of the work creates its own problems; no single, clear interpretation of the causation of the war emerges from the first four volumes, and the volumes on the war years are essentially a history of Northern society at war, in which military and naval matters sometimes receive less than their due, and the Confederacy only occasionally commands attention. But whatever the unevenness of treatment, and occasionally of quality, criticism pales into insignificance beside the overall authority, integrity, and eloquence of the whole work.

There are a number of useful brief surveys of the Civil War era. Roy F. Nichols, *The Stakes of Power, 1845–1877* (New York, 1961), is a condensed account by a historian who has devoted a lifetime of study to the subject. Alan Barker, *The Civil War in America* (London, 1961), is a lucid, brief introduction designed originally for British readers. Bruce Catton, *The Penguin Book of the American Civil War* (London, 1966), originally published in the United States as the *American Heritage Book of the Civil War* (New York, 1960), concentrates largely on the actual fighting. Two recent brief interpretative surveys are Robert Cruden, *The War That Never Ended* (Englewood Cliffs, N.J., 1973), and Emory M. Thomas, *The American War and Peace, 1860–1877* (Englewood Cliffs, N.J., 1973). An interesting new interpretation of the whole mid-nineteenth-century period is provided by William R. Brock, *Conflict and Transformation: the United States, 1844–1877* (Baltimore, 1973), which, unlike my own work, does not focus its attention on the war itself.

In the wide area between such brief introductions and Nevins's multi-volume history, the standard text-book is James G. Randall and David Donald, *The Civil War and Reconstruction* (2nd edn, Boston, 1961; 2nd edn revised, 1969). A work of great authority, with a superb bibliography, this is a skilful revision by Professor Donald of Randall's volume first published in 1937, and still adheres largely to its original format. An older text-book, very uneven in its treatment, but well-written and particularly good on the early stages of the war, is Carl R. Fish, *The American Civil War: an interpretation* (New York, 1937). There is an outstandingly good collection of articles and essays on the Civil War era in Irwin Unger (ed.), *Essays on the Civil War and Reconstruction* (New York, 1970). James A. Rawley, *Turning Points of the Civil War* (Lincoln, Neb., 1965), is also useful.

Reference books of value for the study of this period include *Historical*

*Statistics of the United States: colonial times to 1957* (Washington, 1960) and Richard Morris, *Encyclopedia of American History* (revised edn, New York, 1961). Mark M. Boatner, *The Civil War Dictionary* (New York, 1959), is valuable on military matters. E. B. Long, *The Civil War Day by Day: an almanac, 1861–1865* (Garden City, N.Y., 1971), contains a comprehensive bibliography and a mass of other information in addition to its very readable day-to-day chronology. A simpler month-by-month chronology, together with brief biographies of leading figures and other useful information, is available in Ralph Newman and E. B. Long, *The Civil War Digest* (New York, 1960).

II. PRE-WAR AMERICA

The earlier volumes of Nevins provide the most comprehensive picture. On economic and social developments, George R. Taylor, *The Transportation Revolution, 1815–1860* (New York, 1951), is a lucid straightforward account much broader in scope than its title would indicate. Paul W. Gates, *The Farmer's Age* (New York, 1960), is the standard work on agriculture in this period. Thomas C. Cochran and William Miller, *The Age of Enterprise: a social history of industrial America* (revised edn, New York, 1961), remains a stimulating and attractively written account, while Douglass C. North, *The Economic Growth of the United States, 1790–1860* (Englewood Cliffs, N.J., 1961), offers a challenging interpretation, representing a newer school of economic history.

On the west in this period, the writings of Frederick Jackson Turner are the inevitable and invaluable starting-point. See Ray A. Billington (ed.), *Frontier and Section: selected essays of Frederick Jackson Turner* (Englewood Cliffs, N.J., 1961), for a good sample, and Billington, *Westward Expansion: a history of the American frontier* (3rd edn, New York, 1967), for a comprehensive account of western history. Henry Nash Smith, *Virgin Land: the American west as symbol and myth* (Cambridge, Mass., 1950), is a superb discussion of what the west meant to nineteenth-century America.

Alexis de Tocqueville, *Democracy in America*, 2 vols (New York, 1945 and many other modern editions), remains the classic contemporary account of American politics and society in the earlier nineteenth century. Daniel Boorstin, *The Americans: the national experience* (New York, 1965), is a fascinating exploration of the highways and by-ways of American social history in this period. Irving H. Bartlett, *The American Mind in the Mid-Nineteenth Century* (New York, 1967), is a very brief but useful summary.

There are stimulating discussions of the tension between the consequences of rapid change and the legacy of the past in Marvin Meyers, *The Jacksonian Persuasion: politics and belief* (Stanford, Calif., 1957), Richard Hofstadter, *The American Political Tradition and the Men who Made It* (New York, 1948), and, Fred Somkin, *Unquiet Eagle: memory and desire in the idea of American freedom 1815–1860* (Ithaca, N.Y., 1967).

*The South*

One of the burdens of Southern history is that it has been written almost exclusively by Southerners. Much of it is self-consciously defensive, and, even when its tone is more critical, it is often the savage, self-lacerating criticism of the passionate but embittered partisan, who feels that his unwavering loyalty gives him the exclusive right to find fault.

For all that, the old South has inspired much historical writing of high quality. Clement Eaton's books, including *A History of the Old South* (New York, 1949), and *The Growth of Southern Civilization, 1790–1860* (New York, 1961), are solid, authoritative works by a sympathetic critic. Charles S. Sydnor, *The Development of Southern Sectionalism, 1819–1848* (Baton Rouge, La., 1948), paints a sensitive portrait of the ante-bellum South, while Avery O. Craven, *The Growth of Southern Nationalism, 1848–1861* (Baton Rouge, La., 1953), concentrates more on the Southern view of the mounting sectional crisis. Other useful studies include Jesse T. Carpenter, *The South as a Conscious Minority, 1789–1861* (New York, 1930), John H. Franklin, *The Militant South* (Cambridge, Mass., 1956), David Bertelson, *The Lazy South* (New York, 1967), and William R. Taylor, *Cavalier and Yankee: the old South and American national character* (New York, 1961). Wilbur J. Cash, *The Mind of the South* (New York, 1941), is a powerful evocation of Southern ways of thought and feeling. More subtle and sophisticated – and more searching – are the interpretations offered in the following richly rewarding volumes of essays: Charles G. Sellers (ed.), *The Southerner as American* (Chapel Hill, N.C., 1960), C. Vann Woodward, *The Burden of Southern History* (Baton Rouge, La., 1960), and David M. Potter, *The South and the Sectional Conflict* (Baton Rouge, La., 1968).

*The North*

The North has never been treated separately, in its own right, to anything like the same extent as the South. The student must rely on general works dealing with the whole country in this period, such as those listed above, and on regional, state and local histories. Of the latter, only a few examples can be cited here: Henry C. Hubbart, *The Older Middle West, 1840–1880* (New York, 1936), A. L. Kohlmeier, *The Old Northwest as the Keystone of the Arch of American Federal Union* (Bloomington, Ind., 1938), Edward C. Kirkland, *Men, Cities and Transportation: a study in New England history, 1820–1900*, 2 vols (Cambridge, Mass., 1948), Oscar and Mary F. Handlin, *Commonwealth* (New York, 1947), on Massachusetts, and Louis Hartz, *Economic Policy and Democratic Thought* (Cambridge, Mass., 1948), on Pennsylvania. A good, wide-ranging survey of the ante-bellum North, which treated it as more than just a non-South, would be most welcome.

*Slavery, Anti-Slavery, and Race*

No subject in American history has inspired more controversy – or more fascinating literature – in recent years than Negro slavery. The old sympathetic picture of slavery presented by Ulrich B. Phillips, *American Negro Slavery* (New York, 1918), has given way to a different view, most ably presented by Kenneth M. Stampp, *The Peculiar Institution: slavery in the ante-bellum South* (New York, 1956), which stresses the profitability of slavery for the owner and its harshness for the slave. Since Stampp's book appeared, a steady output of new work has provided fresh insights into many aspects of slavery. Three main focal points of controversy have emerged: the profitability of slavery, comparison with slavery elsewhere, especially in Latin America, and the effect of generations of bondage upon the slave himself. The best approach to these controversies is through three excellent collections of readings. Quite outstanding among them is Allen Weinstein and Frank O. Gatell (eds), *American Negro Slavery: a modern reader* (New York, 1968). On profitability and the wider economic issues, see Harold D. Woodman (ed.), *Slavery and the Southern Economy* (New York, 1966). For the comparative approach, see Laura Foner and Eugene D. Genovese (eds), *Slavery in the New World: a reader in comparative history* (Englewood Cliffs, N.J. 1969). Genovese's own contributions, avowedly but unconventionally Marxist, range widely over the whole subject, and stress the distinctive 'pre-capitalist' character which slavery gave to Southern society. They include *The Political Economy of Slavery* (New York, 1965), *The World the Slaveholders Made* (New York, 1969), and *In Red and Black: Marxian explorations in Southern and Afro-American history* (New York, 1971). On profitability, see also Alfred H. Conrad and John R. Meyer, *The Economics of Slavery and Other Studies in Econometric History* (Chicago, 1964). The comparative approach is ably explored in Carl N. Degler, *Neither Black Nor White: slavery and race relations in Brazil and the United States* (New York, 1971).

The debate over the effect of slavery upon the slave personality centres around the controversial work of Stanley M. Elkins, *Slavery: a problem in American institutional and intellectual life* (Chicago, 1959), which includes the analogy between the slave plantation and the Nazi concentration camp. The most convenient means of following the controversy which Elkins aroused is Anne J. Lane (ed.), *The Debate Over Slavery: Stanley Elkins and his critics* (Urbana, Ill., 1971). There are great difficulties, of course, in obtaining an adequate slave's eye view of slavery, and a picture of slave life, but see the excellent recent study by John W. Blassingame, *The Slave Community: plantation life in the ante-bellum South* (New York, 1972). Important recent works on special aspects of slavery include Richard Wade, *Slavery in the Cities* (New York, 1964), Robert S. Starobin, *Industrial Slavery in the Old South* (New York, 1970), and Ronald T. Takaki, *A Pro-Slavery Crusade: the agitation to reopen the African slave trade* (New York, 1971).

The anti-slavery movement has also attracted a great deal of attention in recent years, and while the prevailing view has been increasingly sympathetic to the abolitionists, voices of dissent have been anything but silenced. One good approach to anti-slavery is through the history of the wider reform movement of the 1830s and 1840s. Charles S. Griffin, *Their Brothers' Keepers: moral stewardship in the United States, 1800–1865* (New Brunswick, N.J., 1960), and the same author's *The Ferment of Reform, 1830–1860* (New York, 1967), are trenchant and sometimes iconoclastic critiques. Alice F. Tyler, *Freedom's Ferment* (Minneapolis, 1944), is an older, more detailed and more sympathetic account. Two useful general histories of the anti-slavery movement are Louis Filler, *The Crusade Against Slavery, 1830–1860* (New York, 1960), and Dwight L. Dumond, *Antislavery: the crusade for freedom in America* (Ann Arbor, Mich., 1961), although the first is bewildering in its lack of organisation, and the second overwhelming in its zeal for the cause. Some valuable contributions to the new, more favourable image of the abolitionists are collected in Martin L. Duberman (ed.), *The Antislavery Vanguard: new essays on the abolitionists* (Princeton, 1965). There are excellent biographies of a number of the leading abolitionists; see, for example, John L. Thomas, *The Liberator: William Lloyd Garrison, a biography* (Boston, 1963); Irving H. Bartlett, *Wendell Phillips: Brahmin radical* (Boston, 1961); Benjamin P. Thomas, *Theodore Weld: crusader for freedom* (New Brunswick, N.J., 1950); Betty Fladeland, *James Gillespie Birney: slaveholder to abolitionist* (Ithaca, N.Y., 1955). Elkins's *Slavery* includes a vigorous critique of the alleged irresponsibility of the abolitionists, and the obstacle which they posed to a gradual, peaceful demise of slavery.

Other important recent works on the character and achievements of abolitionism include Aileen S. Kraditor, *Means and Ends in American Abolitionism* (New York, 1969), Benjamin Quarles, *Black Abolitionists* (New York, 1969), and Larry Gara, *The Liberty Line: the legend of the Underground Railroad* (Lexington, Ky., 1961). Any realistic evaluation of the anti-slavery movement must take into account the political and social climate of the times, and especially the racial attitudes and prejudices of white Americans. For the earlier background, see the masterly Winthrop D. Jordan, *White Over Black: American attitudes towards the Negro, 1550–1812* (Chapel Hill, N.C., 1968). Nineteenth-century attitudes are searchingly investigated in George M. Fredrickson, *The Black Image in the White Mind: the debate on Afro-American character and destiny, 1817–1914* (New York, 1971). See also Thomas F. Gossett, *Race: the history of an idea in America* (Dallas, 1963), and the characteristically wise and shrewd reflections of C. Vann Woodward, *American Counterpoint: slavery and racism in the North–South dialogue* (Boston, 1971). Discrimination against the free Negro in the north is expertly analysed in Leon F. Litwack, *North of Slavery: the Negro in the free states, 1790–1860* (Chicago, 1961). There is a revealing study of violent opposition to the abolitionists in the north in Leonard L. Richards, *'Gentlemen of property and standing': anti-abolition mobs in Jacksonian America* (New York, 1970).

### III. THE ROAD TO WAR

The first four volumes of Nevins provide the fullest and best narrative. Elbert B. Smith, *The Death of Slavery: the United States, 1837–1865* (Chicago, 1967), is a useful brief survey. Between these two extremes of length lies Avery O. Craven, *The Coming of the Civil War* (2nd edn, New York, 1957), old-fashioned in its point of view and pro-Southern in its bias, but providing a beautifully written, lucid narrative of events. Two recent analytical studies, emphasising the importance of party alignments and party loyalties, are Joel H. Silbey, *The Shrine of Party: congressional voting behavior, 1841–1852* (Pittsburgh, 1967), and Thomas B. Alexander, *Sectional Stress and Party Strength: a study of roll-call voting, 1836–1860* (Nashville, Tenn., 1967).

Large-scale biographies of some of the principal political figures are important for an understanding of the developing sectional crisis. See, for example, Claude M. Wiltse, *John C. Calhoun*, 3 vols (Indianapolis, 1944–51), Charles Sellers, *James K. Polk*, 2 vols to date (Princeton, 1957–66), William N. Chambers, *Old Bullion Benton: senator from the new west* (Boston, 1956), Robert W. Johannsen, *Stephen A. Douglas* (New York, 1973), David Donald, *Charles Sumner and the Coming of the Civil War* (New York, 1961), Philip S. Klein, *President James Buchanan* (University Park, Pa., 1962), and Albert D. Kirwan, *John J. Crittenden: the struggle for the Union* (Lexington, Ky., 1962). Those who admire the quality of these works but are daunted by their length may find the following much briefer biographies useful: Richard N. Current, *Daniel Webster and the Rise of National Conservatism* (Boston, 1955), Clement Eaton, *Henry Clay and the Art of American Politics* (Boston, 1957), Gerald M. Capers, *John C. Calhoun, Opportunist: a reappraisal* (Gainesville, Fla., 1960), and Gerald M. Capers, *Stephen A. Douglas, Defender of the Union* (Boston, 1959). Biographies of figures who were important during the years of the war are listed in later sections.

Important monographs deal with each crucial stage of the developing sectional crisis. William W. Freehling, *Prelude to Civil War: the nullification controversy in South Carolina, 1816–1836* (New York, 1966), puts the defence of slavery into its proper central place in the story. Gilbert H. Barnes, *The Antislavery Impulse, 1830–1844* (New York, 1933), includes a good account of the controversy over the right of petition. On the expansionism of the 1840s, see the works of Frederick Merk, especially *Manifest Destiny and Mission in American History* (New York, 1963), and *The Monroe Doctrine and American Expansionism, 1843–1849* (New York, 1966). The second volume of Sellers, *James K. Polk*, cited above, is valuable, and Richard W. Van Alstyne, *The Rising American Empire* (New York, 1960), is a stimulating interpretation. On the Mexican War, Justin H. Smith, *The War with Mexico*, 2 vols (New York, 1919), is the massive standard work, and Otis A. Singletary, *The Mexican War* (Chicago, 1960), a useful, brief, modern account. Two sound monographs deal with the consequences of the Mexican War for sectional rivalry at home: Chaplain W. Morrison, *Democratic Politics and Sectionalism: the Wilmot Proviso controversy* (Chapel Hill, N.C., 1967), and Holman Hamilton, *Prologue to Conflict: the crisis and compromise of 1850* (New York, 1966). There are important insights into varied Northern reactions to the threat of slavery expansion in Joseph G.

Rayback, *Free Soil: the election of 1848* (Lexington, Ky., 1970), Thomas H. O'Connor, *Lords of the Loom: the cotton Whigs and the coming of the Civil War* (New York, 1968), Kinley J. Brauer, *Cotton Versus Conscience: Massachusetts Whig politics and southwestern expansionism, 1843–1848* (Lexington, Ky., 1967), and Philip S. Foner, *Business and Slavery: the New York merchants and the irrepressible conflict* (Chapel Hill, N.C., 1941).

The politics of the 1850s are well covered in many of the biographies and general works listed earlier in this section. The agonies of the Democratic party are exhaustively analysed by Roy F. Nichols in *The Democratic Machine, 1850–1854* (New York, 1923), and *The Disruption of American Democracy* (New York, 1948). Eric Foner, *Free Soil, Free Labor, Free Men: the ideology of the Republican party before the Civil War* (New York, 1970), is a superb study of Republican attitudes and assumptions. Michael F. Holt, *Forging a Majority: the formation of the Republican party in Pittsburgh, 1848–1860* (New Haven, 1969), shows the many-sided character of the party at the grass roots.

On Kansas and Nebraska, James C. Malin, *The Nebraska Question, 1852–1854* (Lawrence, Kansas, 1953), is important. James A. Rawley, *Race and Politics: bleeding Kansas and the coming of the Civil War* (Philadelphia, 1969), heavily underlines the factor of Negrophobia in free soil calculations. Eugene H. Berwanger, *The Frontier Against Slavery* (Urbana, Ill., 1967), conveys a similar message. Vincent C. Hopkins, *Dred Scott's Case* (New York, 1951), is an authoritative account. John Brown's stormy career is well covered in Stephen B. Oates, *To Purge This Land With Blood: a biography of John Brown* (New York, 1970). On the Lincoln–Douglas debates, see Harry V. Jaffa, *Crisis of the House Divided* (Garden City, N.Y., 1959). A wider look at Lincoln in the 1850s, offering many fresh insights and exploding a number of myths, is provided by Don E. Fehrenbacher, *Prelude to Greatness: Lincoln in the 1850's* (Stanford, Calif., 1962).

There are a number of important books on the crisis of 1860–1. On the Southern side, see Dwight L. Dumond, *The Secession Movement, 1860–1861* (New York, 1931), Ralph A. Wooster, *The Secession Conventions of the South* (Princeton, 1962), and Steven A. Channing, *Crisis of Fear: secession in South Carolina* (New York, 1970), an outstanding state study which emphasises fear for the future of slavery as the prime motive. Two works of exceptional merit analyse Northern attitudes and policy: Kenneth M. Stampp, *And the War Came: the North and the secession crisis, 1860–1861* (Baton Rouge, La., 1950) and David M. Potter, *Lincoln and his Party in the Secession Crisis* (2nd edn, New Haven, 1962). Two slim volumes of essays contain fascinating discussions of controversial issues: Norman A. Graebner (ed.), *Politics and the Crisis of 1860* (Urbana, Ill., 1961), and George H. Knoles (ed.), *The Crisis of the Union, 1860–1861* (Baton Rouge, La., 1965). For literature on the Fort Sumter problem, see chapter III, note 7.

IV. CAUSES OF THE CIVIL WAR: INTERPRETATIONS

The literature spawned by this great historiographical debate is vast – and includes, of course, many of the books already listed. The best approach to the many different interpretations of the causes of the war is through one of the collections of readings on the subject. Outstanding among these is Kenneth M. Stampp (ed.), *The Causes of the Civil War* (Englewood Cliffs, N.J., 1959), a carefully chosen and skilfully organised blend of the opinions of both contemporaries and later historians. Other good collections include Edwin C. Rozwenc (ed.), *The Causes of the American Civil War* (2nd edn, Boston, 1972), and Hans L. Trefousse (ed.), *The Causes of the Civil War* (New York, 1971). The fullest account of changing interpretations down to 1950 is Thomas J. Pressly, *Americans interpret their Civil War* (Princeton, 1954). Some of the more important and illuminating briefer analyses are: Howard K. Beale, 'What historians have said about the causes of the Civil War', in *Theory and Practice in Historical Study* (Social Science Research Council Bulletin No. 54, New York, 1946); Thomas N. Bonner, 'Civil War historians and the needless war doctrine', *Journal of the History of Ideas*, XVII (1956), 193–216; Alan Conway, *The Causes of the American Civil War: an historical perspective* (London, 1961); and, above all, David M. Potter, *The South and the Sectional Conflict* (Baton Rouge, La., 1968), a collection of the author's brilliant and penetrating essays on this and related themes.

There is no need here to cite all the major works of older generations of historians of this subject, including the revisionists of the 1930s and 1940s. Full references will be found in many of the books already listed in this section, and books by Avery Craven, James G. Randall, Roy F. Nichols and others have been listed in earlier sections of this essay. See also the notes for Chapter IV. Three articles representative of various revisionist arguments are: Charles W. Ramsdell, 'The changing interpretation of the Civil War', *Journal of Southern History*, III (1937), 3–27; James G. Randall, 'The blundering generation', *Mississippi Valley Historical Review*, XXVII (1940), 3–28; Frank L. Owsley, 'The fundamental cause of the Civil War: egocentric sectionalism', *Journal of Southern History*, VII (1941), 3–18. The later work of one eminent revisionist historian, Avery Craven, shows some shift away from the 'needless war' thesis. See his *Civil War in the Making, 1815–1860* (Baton Rouge, La., 1959), and a collection of his articles and essays, demonstrating clearly the evolution of his views, *An Historian and the Civil War* (Chicago, 1964). The counter-attack against the revisionist school was vigorously led by, among others, Arthur M. Schlesinger, Jr., 'The causes of the Civil War: a note on historical sentimentalism', *Partisan Review*, XVI (1949), 969–81, and Pieter Geyl, 'The, American Civil War and the problem of inevitability', *New England Quarterly* XXIV (1951), 147–68.

In the last twenty years, many historians have contributed towards a more subtle and complex picture of Civil War causation. Slavery has moved back into the centre of the picture, and the question of race, emphasised by Allan Nevins, has loomed ever larger, though more as an inescapable and complicating presence rather than as a direct cause. The fundamental importance and pervasive influence of slavery and its defence in the south is stressed by many of the recent books on slavery cited above, and, most importantly, in relation to the coming of the war, in the writings of Eugene D. Genovese. Steven A. Channing, *Crisis of Fear*, cited above, relates this general theme to the specific circumstances of secession in an extremely convincing fashion. On the Northern side, two different and sometimes contradictory themes have emerged: a new and, on balance, more sympathetic, evaluation of the abolitionists, and, on the other hand, a full-scale exploration of racism in the north, in, for example, the works of Jordan, Fredrickson, Gossett, Woodward, Litwack, Rawley and Berwanger, cited above. If slavery is to be regarded as the fundamental issue, the problem has therefore become one of attempting to explain why a society so riddled with racism as the North should be moved to resist slavery and its further extension to the point of war. Several of the historians cited have said their piece upon this subject, but the question has been most convincingly and brilliantly answered in Eric Foner's *Free Soil, Free Labor, Free Men*, cited above, which shows how the Republicans were moved to defend their own positive conception of what American society was and should be, against the threat posed by slavery.

Another important thrust of recent work on the subject has been towards an exposure of the vulnerability of the American political and social order in this period, in the face of a serious internal crisis. Earlier historians, including Nevins and Nichols, had touched upon this theme, but Stanley Elkins and David Donald gave a sharper edge to the argument and pointed to the lack of traditional, institutional bulwarks against instability and division. See Elkins, *Slavery*, cited above, and David Donald, *An Excess of Democracy* (Oxford, 1960), reprinted in Donald, *Lincoln Reconsidered* (2nd edn, New York, 1961). The stresses and strains which the sectional crisis imposed upon the constitution are brilliantly analysed in Arthur Bestor, 'The American Civil War as a constitutional crisis', *American Historical Review*, LXIX (1964), 327–52. The mixed blessings of isolation and 'free security', and their relation to the coming of the war, are discussed in C. Vann Woodward, 'The age of reinterpretation', *American Historical Review*, LXVI (1960), 1–19, and A. E. Campbell, 'An excess of isolation: isolation and the American Civil War', *Journal of Southern History*, XXIX (1963), 161–74.

There is a stimulating and controversial discussion of the causes and character of the Civil War by one of the gurus of the new left history – Barrington Moore, *Social Origins of Dictatorship and Democracy* (New York, 1966).

V. THE WAR

The literature on the war itself is vast in quantity, extremely variable in quality, and surprisingly uneven in coverage. The innumerable campaign and battle narratives, army and regimental histories, and biographies of generals and lesser military fry, are not matched by a similar array of more analytical studies of mobilisation, organisation, supply, command, strategy and tactics.

*Recruitment and Organisation*
Russell F. Weigley, *History of the United States Army* (New York, 1967), has two informative chapters on the Civil War which make an excellent introduction. Nevins's four volumes on the war years are extremely interesting on this subject. Marcus Cunliffe, *Soldiers and Civilians: the martial spirit in America, 1775–1865* (London, 1969), is a beguiling tour round the by-ways of its subject, which deals with both more and less than its title would indicate. The standard (and sharply critical) work on the Northern Armies is Fred A. Shannon, *The Organization and Administration of the Union Armies, 1861–1865*, 2 vols (Cleveland, 1928), but it is now itself open to criticism on many scores, and was one of numerous targets singled out for attack in the appendices to Kenneth P. Williams, *Lincoln Finds a General*, cited below. See A. H. Meneely, *The War Department, 1861* (New York, 1928), Erwin S. Bradley, *Simon Cameron, Lincoln's Secretary of War* (Philadelphia, 1966), Benjamin P. Thomas and Harold M. Hyman, *Stanton: the life and times of Lincoln's secretary of war* (New York, 1962), and William B. Hesseltine, *Lincoln and the War Governors* (New York, 1948), for various phases of the organisation of the war effort. On recruitment, and especially on the use and abuse of the draft and the bounty system, see two books by Eugene C. Murdock, *Patriotism Limited, 1862–1865: the Civil War draft and the bounty system* (Kent, Ohio, 1967), and *One Million Men: the Civil War draft in the North* (Madison, Wisc., 1971), although both are stronger on colourful detail than searching analysis. Conscription in the Confederacy is given a more sober, conventional treatment in Albert B. Moore, *Conscription and Conflict in the Confederacy* (New York, 1924). Thomas L. Livermore, *Numbers and Losses in the Civil War in America, 1861–1865* (Boston, 1901), must be treated with great caution – as must most statistics on the strength of the armies and the casualties which they suffered.

On problems of supply, Russell F. Weigley, *Quartermaster General of the Union Army: a biography of M. C. Meigs*, is excellent on the Northern side. Robert V. Bruce, *Lincoln and the Tools of War* (Indianapolis, 1956), deals with technical innovation and developments in weaponry. For the Confederate side, see two useful monographs, Richard D. Goff, *Confederate Supply* (Durham, N.C., 1969), and Frank E. Vandiver, *Ploughshares into Swords: Josiah Gorgas and Confederate ordnance* (Austin, Tex., 1952).

The life of the common soldier is a subject which Bell I. Wiley has made very much his own, in two fascinating volumes of social rather than military history, which draw heavily upon the letters and diaries of the men themselves: *The Life of Johnny Reb: the common soldier of the Confederacy* (Indianapolis, 1943), and *The Life of Billy Yank: the common soldier of the Union* (Indianapolis, 1952). There are good accounts for both armies of the medical services and their shortcomings: George W. Adams, *Doctors in Blue: the medical history of the Union army in the Civil War* (New York, 1952), and Horace H. Cunningham, *Doctors in Gray: the Confederate medical service* (Baton Rouge, La., 1958). See also George W. Smith, *Medicines for the Union Army: the United States army laboratories during the Civil War* (Madison, Wisc., 1962). William Q. Maxwell, *Lincoln's Fifth Wheel: the political history of the United States Sanitary Commission* (New York, 1956) is useful, but see also the favourable assessment of the Commission in Nevins, and the very sharp attack in George M. Fredrickson, *The Inner Civil War*, cited below.

Civil War strategy has not always received the overall analysis and examination which it deserves. Quite the best and liveliest brief discussion of the influence of Jomini's ideas is the chapter on 'Re-fighting the Civil War', in David Donald, *Lincoln Reconsidered*. On the effect of new weapons, and social and technological change, on military thinking, Weigley, *A History of the United States Army*, is also useful. Walter Millis, *Arms and Men: a study in military history* (New York, 1956), achieves raciness at the occasional expense of reliability in setting the Civil War in the context of the American military tradition. Theodore Ropp, *War in the Modern World* (revised edn, Durham, N.C., 1962), puts the Civil War in a world context, but is not very illuminating on the war itself. Jay Luvaas, *The Military Legacy of the Civil War: the European inheritance* (Chicago, 1959), is a fascinating attempt to trace the lessons which European military pundits could have learned from the war, but reaches the conclusion that they failed to learn them. Many of the military narratives and biographies contain incidental discussion of strategy, but there have been too few attempts to look at the history of the war in primarily strategic terms. Two honourable and valuable exceptions are Archer Jones, *Confederate Strategy from Shiloh to Vicksburg* (Baton Rouge, La., 1961) and Thomas L. Connelly and Archer Jones, *The Politics of Command: factions and ideas in Confederate strategy* (Baton Rouge, La., 1973).

*Military Narratives*
As a lucid, judicious, well-informed, single-volume, survey of the campaigns, R. Ernest and Trevor N. Dupuy, *A Compact History of the Civil War* (New York, 1960), stands out, although it is less convincing when it occasionally strays from military matters. An invaluable aid to following the campaigns and battles is provided by the maps and commentary in Vincent J. Esposito (ed.), *The West Point Atlas of American Wars* (New York, 1959), Vol. I, although it is curiously uneven in its treatment – fourteen pages of maps, for example, on the battles of the Wilderness and Spotsylvania, but only three

on the whole of Sherman's advance to Atlanta, and almost nothing on his unprecedented marches through Georgia and the Carolinas.

Large-scale narratives of the fighting abound. Kenneth P. Williams, *Lincoln Finds a General*, 5 vols (New York, 1949–59), is a massive piece of work, based on exhaustive research in the *Official Records*, by a professor of mathematics! It is opinionated and contentious – and was left unfinished at the author's death, at a point before Grant, the general whom Lincoln 'found', had reached the supreme command. Another historian who has written at great length on the war as seen from the Northern side, but in much more popular, romantic, colourful vein, is Bruce Catton; if Williams's style is sometimes acid, Catton's prose is often purple. *This Hallowed Ground* (Garden City, N.Y., 1956) is a lively, single-volume account, but Catton has been over the 'hallowed ground' a number of times, notably as author of two separate trilogies. The first, concentrating on the Army of the Potomac, consists of *Mr Lincoln's Army* (Garden City, N.Y., 1951), *Glory Road* (Garden City, N.Y., 1952), and *A Stillness at Appomattox* (Garden City, N.Y., 1953). The second trilogy, *The Centennial History of the Civil War*, 3 vols (Garden City, N.Y., 1961–5), has a broader sweep, but surprisingly crams the last two and a half years of the war into the final volume. Comparably voluminous accounts of the war from the Southern viewpoint are listed in the biographical section below.

No attempt is made here to list even a selection of the innumerable histories of particular battles or campaigns: the literature on Gettysburg alone, for example, is enormous. There are good bibliographies of these works in a number of the books listed in this section and in section I, above.

*The Generals*

Two collective biographies, very useful for reference purposes, are Ezra J. Warner, *Generals in Blue: lives of the Union commanders* (Baton Rouge, La., 1964) and Ezra J. Warner, *Generals in Gray: lives of the Confederate commanders* (Baton Rouge, La., 1959). Warren W. Hassler, *Commanders of the Army of the Potomac* (Baton Rouge, La., 1962), is another interesting collective portrait. On the structure of the high command and its relationship with the political leadership, see two books by T. Harry Williams for the Northern side, *Lincoln and his Generals* (New York, 1952), a lively account of the war years, and *Americans at War: the development of the American military system* (Baton Rouge, La., 1960), a brief book of reflections on the American tradition in such matters. On the Confederate side, Frank E. Vandiver, *Rebel Brass: the Confederate command system* (Baton Rouge, La., 1956), is excellent.

From the countless lives of Civil War generals, there is space here only for a selection of the more scholarly biographies (as opposed to hagiographies) of the more important commanders. On Grant, see the two volumes by Bruce Catton. *Grant Moves South* (Boston, 1960) *and Grant Takes Command* (Boston, 1969), which complete the story begun by Lloyd Lewis in *Captain Sam Grant* (Boston, 1950). J. F. C. Fuller, *The Generalship of Ulysses S. Grant* (London,

1929) and *Grant and Lee: a study in personality and generalship* (London, 1933), make up an older assessment by a British authority, which played its part in the upward swing of Grant's modern reputation as a commander. There are two attractive and vigorous accounts of Sherman's Civil War career: Basil H. Liddell Hart, *Sherman: soldier, realist, American* (New York, 1929) and Lloyd Lewis, *Sherman, Fighting Prophet* (New York, 1932). Each is splendid in its way, but neither is completely satisfactory, the one too didactic, the other too romantic. The best modern study of McClellan is Warren W. Hassler, *George B. McClellan: the man who saved the Union* (Baton Rouge, La., 1957). It offers an interpretation completely different from my own; like his subject, the author is skilled in the arts of defence, but he is defending against overwhelming odds, which, unlike those which faced his subject, are not a figment of his imagination. Other useful biographies of Northern generals include Stephen E. Ambrose, *Halleck: Lincoln's chief of staff* (Baton Rouge, La., 1962), Freeman Cleaves, *Meade of Gettysburg* (Norman, Okla., 1960), Freeman Cleaves, *Rock of Chickamauga: the life of General George H. Thomas* (Norman, Okla., 1948) and Richard O'Connor, *Sheridan the Inevitable* (Indianapolis, 1953). On two of the more controversial political generals, see Fred H. Harrington, *Fighting Politician: Major-General N. P. Banks* (Philadelphia, 1948), a sober, balanced study, and Hans L. Trefousse, *Ben Butler, the South called him beast* (New York, 1957), the best of several accounts.

Among biographies of Confederate commanders, Douglas S. Freeman, *R. E. Lee: a biography*, 4 vols (New York, 1934–5), stands out as one of the masterpieces of Civil War historiography. Predictably sympathetic to his subject, Freeman limits the broader significance of his work by providing the reader only with the information available to Lee at any given stage of a battle or campaign. There is a useful one-volume abridgement of Freeman's *Lee* by Richard Harwell (New York, 1961). After his four volumes on the great Confederate commander, Freeman produced the valuable *Lee's Lieutenants*, 3 vols (New York, 1942–4). Clifford Dowdey, *Lee* (Boston, 1965), is a solid, recent biography, but even more in awe of its subject than Freeman. On Jackson, the older, classic account is by a British authority, G. F. R. Henderson, *Stonewall Jackson and the American Civil War*, 2 vols (London, 1900), and the best modern study is Frank E. Vandiver, *Mighty Stonewall* (New York, 1957). Among the best studies of other Confederate commanders are T. Harry Williams, *P. G. T. Beauregard: Napoleon in gray* (Baton Rouge, La., 1955), Gilbert E. Govan and James W. Livingood, *A Different Valor: the story of General Joseph E. Johnston, C.S.A.* (Indianapolis, 1956), Charles P. Roland, *Albert Sidney Johnston: soldier of three republics* (Austin, Tex., 1964), Grady McWhiney, *Braxton Bragg and Confederate Defeat*, Vol. I (New York, 1969), John W. Thomason, *Jeb Stuart* (New York, 1930), Hal Bridges, *Lee's Maverick General: Daniel Harvey Hill* (New York, 1961), and Albert Castel, *General Sterling Price and the Civil War in the West* (Baton Rouge, La., 1968).

*The War at Sea*
The predominance of long, detailed narrative accounts over critical analysis
and evaluation is even more true of the naval than the military historiography
of the Civil War. A brief list of some of the more recent narrative histories may
be enough to satisfy a variety of tastes.

Virgil C. Jones, *The Civil War at Sea*, 3 vols (New York, 1960–2), is a very
full and authoritative account. More compact and popular treatments of the
subject include Bern Anderson, *By Sea and by River: the naval history of the
Civil War* (New York, 1962), James M. Merrill, *The Rebel Shore: the story of
Union sea power in the Civil War* (Boston, 1957) and Richard S. West, *Mr
Lincoln's Navy* (New York, 1957). The river war has attracted a lot of attention;
see, for example, H. Allen Gosnell, *Guns on the Western Waters: the story of
river gunboats in the Civil War* (Baton Rouge, La., 1949), John D. Milligan,
*Gunboats down the Mississippi* (Annapolis, Md., 1965), and James M. Merrill,
*Battle Flags South: the story of the Civil War navies on western waters* (Rutherford,
N.J., 1970).

Two general works which help to place the Civil War in the context of
naval development are James P. Baxter, *The Introduction of the Ironclad Warship*
(Cambridge, Mass., 1933) and Harold M. and Margaret Sprout, *The Rise of
American Naval Power 1776–1918* (Princeton, 1939). Two valuable studies by
William N. Still, *Confederate Shipbuilding* (Athens, Ga., 1969) and *Iron Afloat:
the story of the Confederate armorclads* (Nashville, 1971), explain much concerning
the problems and the policy of the South in creating a navy out of nothing.
See also Milton F. Perry, *Infernal Machines: the story of Confederate submarine and
mine warfare* (Baton Rouge, La., 1965).

Studies of the secretaries of the navy on the two sides are very helpful on
policy-making and the organisation of the naval war effort; see Richard S.
West, *Gideon Welles: Lincoln's navy department* (New York, 1943) and Joseph
T. Durkin, *Stephen R. Mallory: Confederate navy chief* (Chapel Hill, N.C.,
1954). George W. Dalzell, *The Flight from the Flag: the continuing effect of the
Civil War upon the American carrying trade* (Chapel Hill, N.C., 1940), is mainly
a spirited narrative of the escapades of the *Florida, Alabama* and other Confederate commerce raiders, but does briefly discuss the more enduring consequences. The admirals have attracted many fewer biographers than the
generals, but see Charles L. Lewis, *David Glasgow Farragut*, 2 vols (Annapolis,
Md., 1941–3) and Richard S. West, *The Second Admiral: a life of David Dixon
Porter* (New York, 1937).

Other books which have a bearing on the naval war are listed in Section IX.

*The Photographic Record*
The character of the war – and its horror – were captured for posterity in the
photographs of Mathew Brady, Alexander Gardner and their associates. Their
equipment did not enable them to take action pictures, but they succeeded in
conveying, as no other evidence could, what the battlefields and encamp-

ments – and the devastation – of the war were really like. Francis T. Miller (ed.), *The Photographic History of the Civil War*, 10 vols (New York, 1911, reprinted 1957), is the fullest record, but there are excellent modern photographic histories, with a higher quality of reproduction, and authoritative accompanying text. See, for example, David Donald (ed.), *Divided We Fought: a pictorial history of the war, 1861–1865* (New York, 1952), Bell I. Wiley, *They Who Fought Here* (New York, 1959) and Bell I. Wiley, *Embattled Confederates: an illustrated history of Southerners at war* (New York, 1964). Other collections include Roy Meredith, *An Album of Portraits by Mathew B. Brady* (New York, 1951) and James D. Horan, *Mathew Brady: historian with a camera* (New York, 1955). There is a superb modern reprint of Alexander Gardner, *Gardner's Photographic Sketch Book of the Civil War* (New York, 1959), which contains some of the most unforgettable Civil War pictures.

VI. THE POLITICS OF WAR

There has been surprisingly little comparative study of wartime politics in the Union and the Confederacy. Allan Nevins, *The Statesmanship of the Civil War* (New York, 1953), is a small volume of thoughtful essays. Roy F. Nichols offers some interesting reflections in his article, 'The operation of American democracy, 1861–1865', *Journal of Southern History*, XXV (1959), 31–52, and in his curiously uneven but rewarding book *Blueprint for Leviathan, American Style* (New York, 1963). David Potter offers typically incisive comments in his essay in David Donald (ed.), *Why the North won the Civil War* (Baton Rouge, La., 1960). Much the most stimulating and important recent contribution to the comparative approach is that of Eric L. McKitrick, 'Party politics and the Union and Confederate war efforts', in William N. Chambers and Walter D. Burnham (eds), *The American Party Systems: stages of political development* (New York, 1967), upon which I have relied heavily in chapter viii and elsewhere.

*The North*
The most convenient approach to some of the best recent work on Northern politics is through some excellent collections of readings, articles and essays. James A. Rawley (ed.), *Lincoln and Civil War Politics* (New York, 1969) is extremely useful, especially in its section on the Democrats. Don E. Fehrenbacher (ed.), *The Leadership of Abraham Lincoln* (New York, 1970), Norman A. Graebner (ed.), *The Enduring Lincoln* (Urbana, Ill., 1959) and James G. Randall, *Lincoln the Liberal Statesman* (New York, 1947) focus more directly upon the president himself. Irwin Unger (ed.), *Essays on the Civil War and Reconstruction*, cited in Section I, contains some important items on this subject. Richard Current, *The Lincoln Nobody Knows* (New York, 1958), contains judicious and lucid essays on many points of Civil War controversy, in which the author,

while cannily reserving his own position, summarises opposing views so skilfully that he might be described as an alternating Current. David Donald, *Lincoln Reconsidered: essays on the Civil War era* (2nd edn, New York, 1961), includes some scintillating essays, sharper, more outspoken and partisan than those in Current's book. Current sums up controversies; Donald provokes them.

The make-up, and the divisions, of the wartime Republican party are discussed in all these collections of essays. T. Harry Williams, *Lincoln and the Radicals* (Madison, Wisc., 1941), for a long time the standard work on the subject, depicts a constant dog-fight between the president and his radical critics, in which Lincoln steadily gave ground. In an essay in *Lincoln Reconsidered*, David Donald challenged this bipolar view, and suggested that, like American political parties in all periods, the wartime Republicans revealed a more complex and shifting pattern of groups and factions. Both Williams and Donald offer further thoughts on the subject – and each concedes a minimum of ground – in Grady McWhiney (ed.), *Grant, Lee, Lincoln and the Radicals* (Evanston, Ill., 1964). For a different perspective, see William D. Mallam, 'Lincoln and the conservatives', *Journal of Southern History*, XXVIII (1962), 31–45. Hans L. Trefousse, *The Radical Republicans: Lincoln's vanguard for racial justice* (New York, 1969), contains much useful information, but does not smooth away the controversy either within the party or among the historians. Eric Foner's invaluable *Free Soil, Free Labor, Free Men* does not deal specifically with the years after 1861, but helps to explain a great deal about the wartime Republicans.

The Northern Democrats have also attracted much attention, and controversy, among modern historians. Among older studies, Henry C. Hubbart, *The Older Middle-West, 1840–1880* (New York, 1936), gives a strongly sectionalist emphasis to Democratic discontent, and George F. Milton, *Abraham Lincoln and the Fifth Column* (New York, 1942), is a vigorous, popular history of wartime dissent throughout the North. Wood Gray, *The Hidden Civil War: the story of the Copperheads* (New York, 1942), is more scholarly, but also much more hostile; it questions both the loyalty and the sense of the Copperheads, and takes seriously the menace of the secret societies. Frank L. Klement, *The Copperheads in the Middle West* (Chicago, 1960), challenges this view, treats the Democrats as the loyal opposition, and dismisses the secret societies as largely the figment of Republican propaganda. Klement has also written an important biography of the leading Copperhead: *The Limits of Dissent: Clement L. Vallandigham and the Civil War* (Lexington, Ky., 1970), although the book does not probe very deeply into the problem stated in its title. There is a first-rate discussion of recent work on the Copperheads, written from a generally sympathetic standpoint, in an article by Richard O. Curry, 'The Union as it was: a critique of recent interpretations of the "Copperheads" ', *Civil War History*, XIII (1967), 25–39.

On the wartime constitutional issues, so often a matter of concern to the

Democrats, the standard work has for many years been James G. Randall, *Constitutional Problems under Lincoln* (revised edn, Urbana, Ill., 1951), and it remains a mine of useful information. However, a splendid recent book by Harold M. Hyman, *A More Perfect Union: the impact of the Civil War and reconstruction on the constitution* (New York, 1973), has added a new dimension to this aspect of Civil War history, and contains any number of new insights and ideas. David M. Silver, *Lincoln's Supreme Court* (Urbana, Ill., 1956), is a solid, useful study. Three recent books, mainly concerned with the post-war period, have important implications for the war years: Stanley Kutler, *Judicial Power and Reconstruction Politics* (Chicago, 1968); Charles Fairman, *History of the Supreme Court of the United States. Vol. VI. Reconstruction and reunion, 1864–1888* (New York, 1971); and contributions by Harold Hyman and Alfred H. Kelly in Hyman (ed.), *New Frontiers of the American Reconstruction* (Urbana, Ill., 1966).

Congress during the Civil War has not received the attention which it deserves from historians, although a number of the works listed above and the biographies listed below contain relevant information. Leonard P. Curry, *Blueprint for Modern America: nonmilitary legislation of the first Civil War Congress* (Nashville, 1968), is a valuable study, although not everyone will accept its high estimate of the enduring importance of all the legislation concerned. On the election of 1864, see William F. Zornow, *Lincoln and the Party Divided* (Norman, Okla., 1954), a scholarly account which dwells mainly on the Republican party and its internal dissensions. Edward C. Kirkland, *Peacemakers of 1864* (New York, 1927), remains the standard work on its subject.

On the Lincoln administration, and wartime administrative problems in general, Nevins is once again invaluable. Burton J. Hendrick, *Lincoln's War Cabinet* (Boston, 1946), is readable but superficial. Harry J. Carman and Reinhard H. Luthin, *Lincoln and the Patronage* (New York, 1943), is a fascinating account of how Lincoln lubricated the governmental and political machinery. William B. Hesseltine, *Lincoln and the War Governors* (New York, 1948), skilfully depicts the shift of power from the states to the federal capital, but his view is not universally accepted. Paul P. Van Riper and Keith A. Sutherland, 'The Northern civil service, 1861–1865', *Civil War History*, XI (1965), 351–69, breaks new ground and suggests the uneven growth of wartime bureaucracy.

There have been numerous studies of state and local politics during the Civil War, but few begin to approach the quality of Kenneth M. Stampp, *Indiana Politics During the Civil War* (Indianapolis, 1949). John Niven, *Connecticut for the Union: the role of the state in the Civil War* (New Haven, 1965), is an admirable state history, good on politics as on other matters. Much older studies such as Edith E. Ware, *Political Opinion in Massachusetts During the Civil War and Reconstruction* (New York, 1916), and George H. Porter, *Ohio Politics During the Civil War Period* (New York, 1911), contain useful information. Biographies of prominent local figures are also helpful; see, for example, Henry G. Pearson, *The Life of John A. Andrew, Governor of Massachusetts, 1861–1865*, 2 vols (Boston, 1904), James A. Rawley, *Edwin D. Morgan, 1811–1883* (New York, 1955),

and Stewart Mitchell, *Horatio Seymour of New York* (Cambridge, Mass., 1938).
Biographies also offer vital clues to national poltics. Despite the massive output of Lincoln books, there is, curiously enough, no altogether satisfactory
single-volume modern biography. Benjamin P. Thomas, *Abraham Lincoln: a
biography* (New York, 1952) remains the best of them, but it is now over
twenty years old, and its approach – and its style – now look rather dated.
Reinhard H. Luthin, *The Real Abraham Lincoln* (Englewood Cliffs, N.J., 1960),
is a larger volume, too often neglected, but not always the easiest of reading.
Among Lincoln biographies on the grand scale, three very different works
stand out: John G. Nicolay and John Hay, *Abraham Lincoln: a history*, 10 vols
(New York, 1890), the classic life by the president's secretaries; Carl Sandburg,
*Abraham Lincoln: the war years*, 4 vols (New York, 1939), a colourful, folksy
account, with a poet's rather than a scholar's approach to historical truth; and
James G. Randall and Richard N. Current, *Lincoln the President*, 4 vols (New
York, 1945–55), by far the most thorough scholarly biography. The best work
on Lincoln in recent years has been on particular aspects of his presidency, and
a new synthesis is now needed.

The members of Lincoln's cabinet have been well served by modern bio-
graphers. Glyndon G. Van Deusen, *William Henry Seward* (New York, 1967),
is a solid, meticulous, cautiously defensive study. Benjamin P. Thomas and
Harold M. Hyman, *Stanton: the life and times of Lincoln's secretary of war* (New
York, 1962), is authoritative and illuminating. A good, modern biography of
Salmon P. Chase is badly needed. On lesser members of the cabinet, see Erwin
S. Bradley, *Simon Cameron: Lincoln's secretary of war* (Philadelphia, 1966),
Marvin R. Cain, *Lincoln's Attorney General: Edward Bates of Missouri* (Columbia,
Mo., 1965), and, on Montgomery Blair, the relevant sections of William E.
Smith, *The Francis Preston Blair Family in Politics*, 2 vols (New York, 1933).
See also H. Draper Hunt, *Hannibal Hamlin of Maine* (Syracuse, N.Y., 1969).

Biographies of congressional leaders have been much in vogue in recent
years. Outstanding alike in importance and in quality is David Donald's
superb *Charles Sumner and the Rights of Man* (New York, 1970). Among several
lives of Thaddeus Stevens, the best is probably Fawn M. Brodie, *Thaddeus
Stevens: scourge of the South* (New York, 1959). Other useful biographies include
Charles A. Jellison, *Fessenden of Maine: Civil War senator* (Syracuse, N.Y., 1962),
Patrick W. Riddleberger, *George Washington Julian: radical Republican* (Indianapolis, 1966), Edward Magdol, *Owen Lovejoy: abolitionist in Congress* (New
Brunswick, N.J., 1967), Mark M. Krug, *Lyman Trumbull, conservative radical*
(New York, 1965), Hans L. Trefousse, *Benjamin Franklin Wade: radical Repub-
lican from Ohio* (New York, 1963), and Richard H. Abbott, *Cobbler in Congress,
the Life of Henry Wilson, 1812–1875* (Lexington, Ky., 1972).

*The South*

All the general histories of the Confederacy include extensive coverage of
politics, and all are written from a committed pro-Southern standpoint. In

ascending order both of size and nostalgia for the good old South, are the following: Charles P. Roland, *The Confederacy* (Chicago, 1960), Clement Eaton, *A History of the Southern Confederacy* (New York, 1954), Frank E. Vandiver, *Their Tattered Flags: the epic of the Confederacy* (New York, 1970), and E. Merton Coulter, *The Confederate States of America, 1861–1865* (Baton Rouge, La., 1950). Coulter has the most detail, Eaton the widest range, Roland the keenest perception, and Vandiver the most purple prose.

On the constitutional history of the Confederacy, see Charles R. Lee *The Confederate Constitutions* (Chapel Hill, N.C., 1963), Curtis A. Amlund, *Federalism in the Southern Confederacy* (Washington, 1966), which seeks to show the centralising trends of Confederate government, and William M. Robinson, *Justice in Gray: a history of the judicial system of the Confederate States of America* (Cambridge, Mass., 1941).

The best collective portrait of the Davis administration is Rembert W. Patrick, *Jefferson Davis and his Cabinet* (Baton Rouge, La., 1944), although it is more descriptive than analytical. Burton J. Hendrick, *Statesmen of the Lost Cause: Jefferson Davis and his cabinet* (Boston, 1939), is rambling and diffuse, and devotes as much space to Confederate diplomacy as to administration. Paul P. Van Riper and Harry N. Scheiber, 'The Confederate civil service', *Journal of Southern History*, XXV (1959), 448–70, is extremely illuminating.

The composition and performance of the Confederate Congress has been brought into much sharper focus in recent years, first by Wilfred B. Yearns's excellent study, *The Confederate Congress* (Athens, Ga., 1960), then by Richard E. Beringer's article, 'A profile of the members of the Confederate Congress', *Journal of Southern History*, XXXIII (1967), 518–41, and, most recently, in a formidable study by Thomas B. Alexander and Richard E. Beringer, *The Anatomy of the Confederate Congress: a study of the influence of member characteristics on legislative voting behavior, 1861–1865* (Nashville, 1972).

Because of the very nature of the Confederacy, state and local politics merit serious study. Frank L. Owsley, *State Rights in the Confederacy* (Chicago, 1925), is the standard work, although more recent studies question whether the states rights issue was such a fatal weakness, and treat it as a symptom rather than a cause of discontent and divisiveness. Georgia L. Tatum, *Disloyalty in the Confederacy* (Chapel Hill, N.C., 1934), is essential to an understanding of many deeply felt grievances in various parts of the South. Mary S. Ringold, *The Role of the State Legislatures in the Confederacy* (Athens, Ga.,1966), puts state politics in a more positive light, and shows that increased political and governmental activity was no monopoly of Richmond. Emory M. Thomas, *The Confederacy as a Revolutionary Experience* (Englewood Cliffs, N.J., 1971), stresses the growth of Confederate government as part of that revolution, but overstates his case. See also Frank E. Vandiver, 'The Confederacy and the American tradition', *Journal of Southern History*, XXVIII (1962), 277–86. State histories vary enormously in quality and character; many books with titles which suggest a history of a state during the war prove to be largely narrative accounts of the heroic deeds of troops from the state concerned. Among those which do give serious attention to wartime politics are John K. Bettersworth, *Confederate Mississippi: the people and politics of a cotton state in wartime* (Baton Rouge, La., 1943), Charles E. Cauthen, *South Carolina Goes to War, 1861–1865* (Chapel Hill, N.C., 1950), and T. Conn Bryan, *Confederate Georgia* (Athens, Ga., 1953). On the western part of the Confederacy, Robert L. Kerby, *Kirby Smith's Confederacy: the trans-Mississippi, 1863–1865* (New York, 1972), is absolutely indispensable. Useful studies of state governors include Louise B. Hill, *Joseph E. Brown and the Confederacy* (Chapel Hill, N.C., 1939) and Richard E. Yates, *The Confederacy and Zeb Vance* (Tuscaloosa, Ala., 1958).

Biographies of prominent Confederate political leaders are usually reverential in tone. Numerous lives of Jefferson Davis vie with one another in uncritical admiration of their hero; despite its unflagging adulation, the fullest and most reliable is Hudson Strode, *Jefferson Davis*, 3 vols (New York, 1955–1964). A good, balanced, scholarly single volume biography of the Confederate president would fill a real gap in Civil War literature. See Bell Wiley's introduction to the reprint edition of Davis's own *The Rise and Fall of the Confederate Government*, 2 vols (New York, 1958), for a restrained critical assessment. Vice-president Alexander Stephens also lacks a worthy modern biographer; see Rudolph Von Abele, *Alexander H. Stephens: a biography* (New York, 1946), for an interesting psychological approach. James Z. Rabun, 'Alexander H. Stephens and Jefferson Davis', *American Historical Review*, LVIII (1953), 290–321, says a good deal in a short space. On members of Davis's cabinet, see Robert D. Meade, *Judah P. Benjamin: Confederate statesman* (New York. 1943), Joseph T. Durkin, *Stephen R. Mallory: Confederate navy chief* (Chapel Hill, N.C., 1954), Ben H. Procter, *Not Without Honor: the life of John H. Reagan* (Austin, Tex., 1962), and William Y. Thompson, *Robert Toombs of Georgia* (Baton Rouge, La., 1966). Useful studies of other prominent figures include Alvy L. King, *Louis T. Wigfall: Southern fire-eater* (Baton Rouge, La., 1970), Horace Montgomery, *Howell Cobb's Confederate Career* (Tuscaloosa, Ala., 1959), Laura A. White, *Robert Barnwell Rhett: father of secession* (New York, 1931), and Avery O. Craven, *Edmund Ruffin, Southerner: a study in secession* (New York, 1932).

### The Border States

Edward C. Smith, *The Borderland in the Civil War* (New York, 1927), for long the standard work, is now out of date, but remains useful. Kentucky, in particular, needs further investigation; two studies from rather different viewpoints are E. Merton Coulter, *The Civil War and Readjustment in Kentucky* (Chapel Hill, N.C., 1926), and William H. Townsend, *Lincoln and the Bluegrass: slavery and Civil War in Kentucky* (Lexington, Ky., 1955). Richard O. Curry, *A House Divided: a study of statehood politics and the Copperhead movement in West Virginia* (Pittsburgh, 1964), skilfully unravels that very tangled story. On the even greater complexities of Missouri, William E. Parrish, *Turbulent*

*Partnership: Missouri and the Union, 1861–1865* (Columbia, Mo., 1963), is very helpful. On the smallest of the border states, see Harold B. Hancock, *Delaware During the Civil War: a political history* (Wilmington, Del., 1961).

## VII. TWO SOCIETIES AT WAR

Once again, there has been surprisingly little resort to the comparative approach, and, beyond the level of general surveys, most studies have concentrated on either North or South. Some volumes in the series currently in progress on the impact of the Civil War deal with both sides; two important volumes in this series are: Mary E. Massey, *Bonnet Brigades: American women and the Civil War* (New York, 1966), which is infinitely better than its whimsical title would suggest, and Paul W. Gates, *Agriculture and the Civil War* (New York, 1965). Among older works, Arthur H. Cole, *The Irrepressible Conflict, 1850–1865* (New York, 1934), is still useful.

*The North*

The impact of the war upon the North and the transition from an un-organised to an organised society are the leading themes of Nevins's four volumes on *The War for the Union*. Even those who may not accept his thesis *in toto* will find these volumes a rich mine of information and insight. Emerson D. Fite, *Social and Industrial Conditions in the North During the Civil War* (New York, 1910), is out of date, but has never been superseded, and is packed with valuable information. George W. Smith and Charles Judah (eds), *Life in the North During the Civil War: a source history* (Albuquerque, 1966), is a superb collection which shows just what can be done by a skilfully chosen and edited group of documents.

On the lively controversy over the effect of the war upon American indus-trialisation and economic growth see the references in the notes to chapter xii, especially note 4. General economic histories of nineteenth-century America seldom have much to say on the impact of the war, but see the characteristically shrewd comments scattered through the chapters of Edward C. Kirkland, *Industry Comes of Age, 1860–1897* (New York, 1961). Labour history is another area in which the Civil War has received less than its due, either in general surveys or specialist studies. Even Norman J. Ware, *The Labor Movement in the United States, 1860–1895* (New York, 1929), disposes of the war years in the first few pages. David Montgomery, *Beyond Equality: labour and the radical Republicans, 1862–1872* (New York, 1967), is a stimulating work, full of fascinating information and vigorous argument, although the reader may doubt whether the one always supports the other. Charlotte Erickson, *American Industry and the European Immigrant, 1860–1885* (Cambridge, Mass., 1957), is an admirable study of one aspect. On the contribution of the railroads to the Union war effort, Thomas Weber, *The Northern Railroads in the Civil War*,

*1861–1865* (New York, 1952), is lucid and informative, and F. A. Lord, *Lincoln's Railroad Man: Herman Haupt* (Rutherford, N.J., 1969), is a useful study of a key figure. The relationship of the war to long-term railroad development is traced in George R. Taylor and Irene D. Neu, *The American Railroad Network, 1861–1890* (Cambridge, Mass., 1956). On government aid for the Pacific railroad, see Wallace D. Farnham, 'The weakened spring of government: a study in nineteenth century American history', *American Historical Review*, LXVIII (1963), 662–80, and Robert W. Fogel, *The Union Pacific Railroad: a case study in premature enterprise* (Baltimore, 1960).

There are several important studies of wartime finance. The brief treatment in Margaret G. Myers, *A Financial History of the United States* (New York, 1970), provides a useful introduction. Wesley C. Mitchell, *A History of the Greenbacks* (Chicago, 1903), has become a classic, but needs to be used in conjunction with later works. Bray Hammond, *Sovereignty and an Empty Purse: banks and politics in the Civil War* (Princeton, 1970), the last work of a distinguished financial historian, is in fact mainly a detailed and illuminating account of the adoption of the greenbacks in 1861–2. Its solid virtues are occasionally clouded by polemics about the sinister growth of federal power. Wartime taxation is clearly described in Sidney Ratner, *American Taxation: its history as a social force in democracy* (New York, 1942). On the enduring financial consequences of the war, two books mainly concerned with the post-war era take contrasting views. Robert P. Sharkey, *Money, Class and Party: an economic study in Civil War and reconstruction* (Baltimore, 1959), argues that the Civil War did see a transfer of power to new groups, but defines those groups with more subtlety and precision than the monolithic 'capitalists' of the Beard interpretation. Irwin F. Unger, *The Greenback Era: a social and political history of American finance, 1865–1879* (Princeton, 1964), regards Sharkey's approach as too rigidly economic determinist, and stresses political, social and moral influences on financial developments. See the early pages of Walter T. K. Nugent, *Money and American Society, 1865–1880* (New York, 1968), for a useful summary of some of the issues.

Information on social conditions and social life has to be collected from general works such as Nevins and Fite, and some of the other studies listed above. The source material in Smith and Judah, cited above, offers the best approach of all. Margaret Leech, *Reveille in Washington* (New York, 1941), is an informal and entertaining account of the federal capital at war. State and local histories are often useful. See, for example, John Niven, *Connecticut for the Union*, and Henry C. Hubbart, *The Older Middle West*, both cited in Section VI, and Arthur H. Cole, *The Era of the Civil War, 1848–1870* (Centennial History of Illinois, Vol. III) (Springfield, Ill., 1919). There are several studies of wartime journalism, but all are more interested in reporting what the reporters said than in analysing the structure and character of the press. See, for example, J. Cutler Andrews, *The North Reports the Civil War* (Pittsburgh 1955) and Bernard A. Weisberger, *Reporters for the Union* (Boston, 1953).

One rapidly developing and fascinating field of study concerns the attitudes and ideas of Northerners about the war and the issues which it raised. George M. Fredrickson, *The Inner Civil War: Northern intellectuals and the crisis of the Union* (New York, 1965), breaks new ground in a stimulating fashion, but is less than fair at times to the views of some of his rather small sample of intellectuals. See also the brief references to the impact of the war in John G. Sproat, '*The best men*': *liberal reformers in the Gilded Age* (New York, 1968). Opinion at a less rarefied level is analysed in a modest but revealing study by William Dusinberre, *Civil War Issues in Philadelphia, 1856–1865* (Philadelphia, 1965). Some of the most vigorous debate on the war issues is brought together in a superb collection, edited by Frank Freidel, *Union pamphlets of the Civil War*, 2 vols (Cambridge, Mass., 1967).

*The South*
The general histories of the Confederacy cited in the previous section all deal with economic and social developments; Coulter is particularly full on such matters. Emory M. Thomas, *The Confederacy as a Revolutionary Experience* (Englewood Cliffs, N.J., 1971), extends his thesis to include social and economic as well as political matters, but here too he is more provocative than persuasive. Just as a combination of an old-fashioned factual survey (Fite) and an excellent modern collection of source material (Smith and Judah) can be of great help to a student of Northern society at war, a similar pairing is of great value for the South. John C. Schwab, *The Confederate States of America, 1861–1865: a financial and industrial history of the South during the Civil War* (New York, 1901), contains a mass of information, unexcitingly presented. Albert D. Kirwan (ed.), *The Confederacy* (New York, 1959), arranges its source material to provide a vivid picture of the wartime South. Charles W. Ramsdell, *Behind the Lines in the Southern Confederacy* (Baton Rouge, La., 1944), is a brief but indispensable guide to the domestic problems of the South.

Two specialist studies of Southern industry help to fill out the picture provided by more general works. Lester J. Cappon's essay, 'Government and private industry in the Southern Confederacy', in *Humanistic Studies in Honor of John Calvin Metcalf* (New York, 1941), 151–89, is easily the best study of the subject. Charles B. Dew, *Ironmaker to the Confederacy: Joseph R. Anderson and the Tredegar iron works* (New Haven, 1966), is a splendid, scholarly account of the South's greatest industrial asset. Robert C. Black, *The Railroads of the Confederacy* (Chapel Hill, N.C., 1952), is another first-rate study. The standard work on the dire financial problems of the South is Richard C. Todd, *Confederate Finance* (Athens, Ga., 1954), but see also a series of important articles by Eugene M. Lerner: 'Monetary and fiscal programs of the Confederate government, 1861–65', *Journal of Political Economy*, LXII (1954), 506–22; 'Money, prices and wages in the Confederacy, 1861–65', *Journal of Political Economy*, LXIII (1955), 20–40; and 'Inflation in the Confederacy, 1861–1865', in Milton Friedman (ed.), *Studies in the Quantity Theory of Money* (Chicago, 1956), 163–78.

The social history of the Confederacy has been more amply covered than that of the Union. Bell I. Wiley, *The Plain People of the Confederacy* (Baton Rouge, La., 1943), is a pleasantly written, brief account. Important books on special aspects include: Mary E. Massey, *Ersatz in the Confederacy* (Columbia, S.C., 1952), Mary E. Massey, *Refugee Life in the Confederacy* (Baton Rouge, La., 1964), Ella Lonn, *Salt as a Factor in the Confederacy* (New York, 1933), and Ella Lonn, *Foreigners in the Confederacy* (Chapel Hill, N.C., 1940). Some state histories, including those mentioned in the previous section, help to provide a picture of wartime social conditions. There are two studies of the Confederate capital: Alfred H. Bill, *The Beleaguered City: Richmond, 1861–1865* (New York, 1946), and Emory M. Thomas, *The Confederate State of Richmond: a biography of the capital* (Austin, Tex., 1971). In contrast, a small Southern town is the subject of Kenneth Coleman, *Confederate Athens* (Athens, Ga., 1968). The diaries of Mrs Chesnut, and of J. B. Jones, the 'rebel war clerk', cited in the notes to chapter xi, give vivid pictures of life on the home front. See, too, the rich collection of family letters, shaped by the editor into a fascinating human story, in Robert M. Myers (ed.), *The Children of Pride: a true story of Georgia and the Civil War* (New Haven, 1972). Much of the story of the Union-occupied areas of the south remains untold, but there is a valuable study of the largest Southern city, Gerald M. Capers, *Occupied City: New Orleans under the federals, 1862–1865* (Lexington, Ky., 1965). See also Joseph H. Parks, 'A Confederate trade center under federal occupation: Memphis, 1862 to 1865', *Journal of Southern History*, VII (1941), 289–314.

J. Cutler Andrews, *The South Reports the Civil War* (Princeton, 1970), is a descriptive account of Confederate journalism. Harrison A. Trexler, 'The Davis administration and the Richmond press, 1861–1865', *Journal of Southern History*, XVI (1950), 177–95, makes interesting comments on the political complexion of the press. James W. Silver, 'Propaganda in the Confederacy', *Journal of Southern History*, XI (1945), 487–503, is useful, and the same author's *Confederate Morale and Church Propaganda* (Tuscaloosa, Ala., 1957), is valuable on the churches' support for the war effort. On wider aspects of cultural life in the Confederacy, the best study is Clement Eaton, *The Waning of the Old South Civilization* (Athens, Ga., 1968).

VIII. THE NEGRO: SLAVERY, EMANCIPATION AND WARTIME
RECONSTRUCTION

Recent work has enriched and transformed our understanding of this aspect of the Civil War. It has shown, among other things, the force and complexity of Northern white opinion and prejudice, and the positive contribution of the black American to the process of his own liberation. Many of the books listed in the previous two sections, and especially a number of those on Lincoln and Northern politics, have much of value to offer on this subject, but the specialist literature deserves separate attention. On the evolution of Lincoln's attitude and policy, see the lucid, sensitive and eminently sensible Benjamin Quarles, *Lincoln and the Negro* (New York, 1962). John H. Franklin, *The Emancipation Proclamation* (New York, 1963), is an authoritative, brief account. There is a very useful selection of readings on Lincoln and the Negro in Don E. Fehrenbacher (ed.), *The Leadership of Abraham Lincoln* (New York, 1970). Pressure from within the Republican party is skilfully analysed in Mark Krug, 'The Republican party and the emancipation proclamation', *Journal of Negro History*, XLVIII (1963), 98–114. The surprisingly varied attitudes and responses of the abolitionists are dissected by a sympathetic critic in James M. McPherson's masterly *The Struggle for Equality: abolitionists and the Negro in the Civil War and reconstruction* (Princeton, 1964). Charles L. Wagandt, *The Mightly Revolution: Negro emancipation in Maryland, 1862–1864* (Baltimore, 1964), is an important account of the ending of slavery in a border state. Northern white opposition to, and fear of, emancipation is brilliantly exposed in V. Jacque Voegeli, *Free But Not Equal: the midwest and the Negro during the Civil War* (Chicago, 1967). Another valuable study is Forrest G. Wood, *Black Scare: the racist response to emancipation and reconstruction* (Berkeley, 1968).

On the Negro himself, see Benjamin Quarles, *The Negro in the Civil War* (Boston, 1953), for a sound general survey, and the same author's *Frederick Douglass* (Washington, 1948), for the life of the leading free Negro. Even more valuable are Douglass's own writings in Philip S. Foner (ed.), *The Life and Writings of Frederick Douglass*, 4 vols (New York, 1950–5). Perhaps the best insight of all into the Negro view of the war is offered by the fascinating collection of source material in James M. McPherson (ed.), *The Negro's Civil War: how American Negroes felt and acted during the war for the Union* (New York, 1965). The history of the black soldiers in the Union army is thoroughly examined in the excellent Dudley T. Cornish, *The Sable Arm: Negro troops in the Union army, 1861–1865* (New York, 1956).

Bell I. Wiley, *Southern Negroes, 1861–1865* (New Haven, 1938), is the standard work, supplemented but not supplanted by more recent studies. It deals with the Negro both in the Confederacy and in the Union occupied areas of the South. James H. Brewer, *The Confederate Negro: Virginia's craftsmen and military laborers, 1861–1865* (Durham, N.C., 1969), is a valuable recent study which shows just how vital Negro labour was to the Confederate war effort. Robert F. Durden, *The Gray and the Black: the Confederate debate on emancipation* (Baton Rouge, La., 1972), is a much-needed study of a curious and important subject.

The emergence of reconstruction as a wartime issue in the north is given some attention in a number of the books cited in Section VI, including Trefousse, *The Radical Republicans* and Randall and Current, *Lincoln the President*, Vol. IV. William B. Hesseltine, *Lincoln's Plan of Reconstruction* (Tuscaloosa, Ala., 1960), is a brief, pithy but erratic account. Virtually all earlier work on the subject is superseded by the masterly Herman Belz, *Reconstructing the Union:*

*theory and policy during the Civil War* (Ithaca, N.Y., 1969). The impact of emancipation and reconstruction upon Negroes in the occupied south during the war is a much more elusive subject, although Wiley, *Southern Negroes*, cited above, has some useful information. Joel Williamson, *After Slavery: the Negro in South Carolina during reconstruction, 1861–1877* (Chapel Hill, N.C., 1965), is a sensitive and perceptive study. On the first wartime testing-ground of Northern policy and intentions, see Willie Lee Rose, *Rehearsal for Reconstruction: the Port Royal experiment* (Indianapolis, 1964), a model monograph which, through a combination of scholarship and imagination, brings out the full significance of its subject without ever claiming too much for it.

## IX. THE WAR AND THE WORLD

This is another field in which recent work has helped to produce a more varied, subtle, three-dimensional picture not merely of the diplomatic history of the war, but even more of outside attitudes and reactions to the war issues. A new synthesis is now needed; meanwhile two faithful stand-bys remain required reading. Ephraim D. Adams, *Great Britain and the American Civil War*, 2 vols (New York, 1925), is a meticulous diplomatic history, of the conventional, rather narrow kind. Frank L. Owsley, *King Cotton Diplomacy: foreign relations of the Confederate States of America* (Chicago, 1931; 2nd edn, 1959), is a more vigorous and much more opinionated work by a fierce Confederate partisan. These two basic books were best supplemented, among older studies, by Donaldson Jordan and Edwin J. Pratt, *Europe and the American Civil War* (Boston, 1931), an informative, but largely uncritical survey of public opinion.

Two more recent books survey foreign reactions to the war. Belle B. Sideman and Lillian Friedman (eds), *Europe Looks at the Civil War* (New York, 1960), is a fascinating collection of documents, and Harold M. Hyman (ed.), *Heard Round the World: the impact abroad of the Civil War* (New York, 1969), a group of essays, very uneven in scope and quality. There have been several interesting recent reassessments of British opinion, most notably Joseph M. Hernon, 'British sympathies in the American Civil War: a reconsideration', *Journal of Southern History*, XXXIII (1967), which casts serious doubt on many stock assumptions and stereotypes. See also Max Beloff, 'Great Britain and the American Civil War', *History*, XXXVII (1952), 40–8, Wilbur D. Jones, 'The British conservatives and the American Civil War', *American Historical Review*, LVIII (1953), 527–43, J. R. Pole, *Abraham Lincoln and the Working Classes of Britain* (London, 1959), and an interesting local study, D. G. Wright, 'Bradford and the American Civil War', *Journal of British Studies*, VIII (1969), 69–85. A very recent study has exploded, perhaps almost too destructively, the long-held view, or myth, that Lancashire cotton workers were solid, dedicated supporters of the North: see Mary Ellison, *Support for Secession: Lancashire and the American Civil War* (Chicago, 1972). Most studies of mid-Victorian Britain continue, alas, to neglect or underplay the impact of the Civil War. On French reactions to the conflict, older books such as W. Reed West, *Contemporary French Opinion on the American Civil War* (Baltimore, 1924) and Lynn M. Case, *French Opinion on the United States and Mexico, 1860–1867: extracts from the reports of the Procureurs Generaux* (New York, 1936), may be supplemented by more recent specialised studies such as Serge Gavronsky, *The French Liberal Opposition and the American Civil War* (New York, 1968). On Ireland, there is an illuminating, brief study by Joseph M. Hernon, *Celts, Catholics and Copperheads: Ireland views the American Civil War* (Columbus, Ohio, 1968). The complex and serious implications of the war for Canada are fully explored in a splendidly written and perceptive study by Robin W. Winks, *Canada and the United States: the Civil War years* (Baltimore, 1960).

The diplomacy of the war has also received a good deal of attention in recent years. On British policy, Frank J. Merli, *Great Britain and the Confederate Navy* (Bloomington, Ind., 1970), is a useful and interesting synthesis, though questionable on some points. Eli Ginzberg, 'The economics of British neutrality during the American Civil War', *Agricultural History*, X (1936), 147–56, deflates the more extravagant versions of the 'King Wheat' thesis. Wilbur D. Jones, *The Confederate Rams at Birkenhead* (Tuscaloosa, Ala., 1961), supersedes earlier accounts, and clearly defines the true significance of the dispute. The relevant chapters in Kenneth Bourne, *Britain and the Balance of Power in North America, 1815–1908* (London, 1967), put British policy in a fresh perspective, but inevitably, perhaps, cannot always resist the temptation to overstate the importance of strategic considerations and contingency plans.

On French policy, the massive and authoritative Lynn M. Case and Warren F. Spencer, *The United States and France: Civil War diplomacy* (Philadelphia, 1970), towers above all else, although its style and method are very much those of an old-fashioned, immensely detailed narrative of exchanges between diplomats. A more modest but useful study is Henry Blumenthal, *A Re-appraisal of Franco-American Relations, 1830–1871* (Chapel Hill, N.C., 1959). There is a valuable recent study of the French minister in Washington during the war: Daniel B. Carroll, *Henri Mercier and the American Civil War* (Princeton, 1971). The complex relationship of the Mexican situation to the war is well treated in Alfred J. and Kathryn A. Hanna, *Napoleon III and Mexico: American triumph over monarchy* (Chapel Hill, N.C., 1971). Albert A. Woldman, *Lincoln and the Russians* (Cleveland, 1952), is a readable but fairly superficial account of Russo-American relations during the war.

Owsley's account of the foreign relations of the Confederacy may be supplemented by a number of specialist studies: Samuel B. Thompson, *Confederate Purchasing Operations Abroad* (Chapel Hill, N.C., 1935), Charles S. Davis, *Colin J. McRae: Confederate financial agent* (Tuscaloosa, Ala., 1961) and an interesting account of the work of Henry Hotze and other, less successful, propagandists, Charles P. Cullop, *Confederate Propaganda in Europe, 1861–1865* (Coral Gables, Fla., 1969). There is a devastating critique of the unreality of

Confederate foreign policy in Henry Blumenthal, 'Confederate diplomacy: popular notions and international realities', *Journal of Southern History*, XXXII (1966), 151–71.

A good, modern study of Union foreign policy would be most welcome. Biographies of leading figures are very helpful. The thorough and reliable Glyndon G. Van Deusen, *William Henry Seward* (New York, 1967), offers plenty of information; Martin Duberman, *Charles Francis Adams* (Boston, 1961), provides a sensitive, sympathetic but not uncritical assessment of the American minister in London. David Donald, *Charles Sumner and the Rights of Man* (New York, 1970), is excellent on foreign policy matters. Stuart L. Bernath, *Squall Across the Atlantic: American Civil War prize cases and diplomacy* (Berkeley, 1970), is an excellent monograph on one aspect of policy; more of its quality and type are needed.

Much work remains to be done on the international aspects of the war, not least on its enduring significance as a world event. There is a brilliant and stimulating brief discussion of this last theme by David Potter, 'Civil War', in C. Vann Woodward (ed.), *The Comparative Approach to American History* (New York, 1968).

## X. VICTORY AND DEFEAT

By far the liveliest and most wide-ranging discussion of the reasons for Northern victory and Southern defeat is to be found in the essays by leading historians in David Donald (ed.), *Why the North Won the Civil War* (Baton Rouge, La., 1960). Many other books on the war include their own explicit or implicit explanations of its eventual outcome. More specialist works discuss the problem mainly from the viewpoint of the defeated South. See, for example, Charles H. Wesley, *The Collapse of the Confederacy* (Washington, 1922); Bell I. Wiley, *The Road to Appomattox* (Memphis, 1956); an interesting collection of readings in Henry S. Commager (ed.), *The Defeat of the Confederacy* (Princeton, 1964); and two provocative articles, one by Grady McWhiney, 'Who whipped whom? Confederate defeat re-examined', *Civil War History*, XI (1965), 5–26, and the other by Kenneth M. Stampp, 'The Southern road to Appomattox', *Cotton Memorial Papers*, No. 4 (1969), 3–22. It is noteworthy that most of these analyses stress failure of morale, loss of will, or internal dissension more than economic or numerical deficiencies. Comparable attempts to explain the resilience of Northern morale have never been made on anything like the same scale.

## XI. THE STRUGGLE TO WIN THE PEACE

There is no need here for an extensive bibliography of the reconstruction period. The decisive if belated vicory of the new school (or schools) of reconstruction historiography is clearly demonstrated in three admirable concise surveys: Kenneth M. Stampp, *The Era of Reconstruction, 1865–1877* (New York, 1965), quite the best brief reassessment of the whole problem; John H. Franklin, *Reconstruction after the Civil War* (Chicago, 1961), which is somewhat fuller on reconstruction in the South itself; and Robert Cruden, *The Negro in Reconstruction* (Englewood Cliffs, N.J., 1969). Two recent histories which retain more than a little sympathy with the old school are Rembert W. Patrick, *The Reconstruction of the Nation* (New York, 1967), and Avery O. Craven, *Reconstruction: the ending of the Civil War* (New York, 1969). Many of the earlier revisionist successes were won in essays and articles and a number of the more important ones are collected in Kenneth M. Stampp and Leon F. Litwack (eds), *Reconstruction: an anthology of revisionist writings* (Baton Rouge, La., 1969), and Staughton Lynd (ed.), *Reconstruction* (New York, 1967).

On Johnsonian reconstruction, Howard K. Beale, *The Critical Year: a study of Andrew Johnson and reconstruction* (2nd edn, New York, 1958), might be described as Johnson's last stand, before the onslaughts of a new school, led and exemplified by Eric McKitrick, *Andrew Johnson and Reconstruction* (Chicago, 1960), carried the day. LaWanda and John H. Cox, *Politics, Principle and Prejudice, 1865–1866* (New York, 1963), heavily underlines the importance of the third part of that alliterative trio in the Johnson programme. These works, and especially McKitrick, are also important on congressional reconstruction. William R. Brock, *An American Crisis: Congress and reconstruction, 1865–1867* (London, 1963), makes out a powerful case for the radical Republicans. Harold M. Hyman (ed.), *The Radical Republicans and Reconstruction, 1861–1870* (Indianapolis, 1967), is a superb collection of documents, with a brilliant introduction which carries the rehabilitation of the radicals a stage further. David Donald, *The Politics of Reconstruction, 1863–1867* (Baton Rouge, La., 1965), uses quantitative techniques to show the complex evolution of the so-called radical programme, and belittles the role of ideals or ideology. Hans L. Trefousse, *The Radical Republicans*, and a number of the biographies cited in Section VI, are useful for this period. On the constitutional amendments, see Joseph B. James, *The Framing of the Fourteenth Amendment* (Urbana, Ill., 1956), and William Gillette, *The Right to Vote: politics and the passage of the Fifteenth Amendment* (Baltimore, 1965). The latter's unflattering view of the motives behind the Fifteenth Amendment is effectively countered in an extremely important article, essential to an understanding of the whole question of radical motivation: LaWanda and John H. Cox, 'Negro suffrage and Republican politics: the problem of motivation in Reconstruction historiography', *Journal of Southern History*, XXXIII (1967), 303–30. This article, like some of the essays in C. Vann Woodward, *American Counterpoint*, already cited, highlights the problems posed for the radicals by racist attitudes in the north.

On various aspects of the reconstruction process on the ground in the South, consult the following: Michael Perman, *Reunion Without Compromise: the South and reconstruction, 1865–1868* (Cambridge, 1973), which breaks much new ground; George R. Bentley, *A History of the Freedmen's Bureau* (Philadelphia, 1955); James E. Sefton, *The United States Army and Reconstruction, 1865–1867* (Baton Rouge, La., 1967), and Allen W. Trelease, *White Terror: the Ku Klux Klan conspiracy and Southern reconstruction* (New York, 1971). There are good, modern histories of reconstruction in a number of the Southern states; two outstanding examples, both focusing on the Negro, are Vernon L. Wharton, *The Negro in Mississippi, 1865–1890* (Chapel Hill., N.C., 1947), and Joel Williamson, *After Slavery: the Negro in South Carolina during reconstruction 1861–1877* (Chapel Hill, N.C., 1965).

The basic book on the ending of formal reconstruction is C. Vann Woodward, *Reunion and Reaction: the compromise of 1877 and the end of reconstruction* (Boston, 1951).

XII. THE SIGNIFICANCE OF THE WAR

Many of the books on the war already cited contain some discussion or at least some hints on its enduring legacy. Some, however, are so reticent on the subject that at times the new economic historians who dismiss the conflict as a little temporary disturbance, largely irrelevant to the real business of American history, seem to be winning the argument by default.

Those historians who do take the war seriously as a major event of modern history do not of course agree among themselves about its meaning. Karl Marx and Frederick Engels, *The Civil War in the United States* (3rd edn, New York, 1961), may be compared – or contrasted – with a 'new left' view in Barrington Moore, *Social Origins of Dictatorship and Democracy* (New York, 1966).

Southerners, of course, have been much preoccupied with the special meaning which the war has had for them. See, for example, Wilbur J. Cash, *The Mind of the South* (New York, 1941), and Robert Penn Warren, *The Legacy of the Civil War: meditations on the centennial* (New York, 1961). The consequences of the Southern experience of defeat are brilliantly explored by C. Vann Woodward in *The Burden of Southern History* (Baton Rouge, La., 1960).

From a national rather than a regional standpoint, Allan Nevins, 'A major result of the Civil War', *Civil War History*, V (1959), 237–50, is a convenient, brief statement of some of the major themes which dominate his *magnum opus*.

The treatment of the Civil War in literature has received less attention than might be expected. Edmund Wilson, *Patriotic Gore: studies in the literature of the American Civil War* (New York, 1962), discusses the varied writings of some of those who lived through the struggle itself; the book is more admired, perhaps, among literary critics than historians. Stephen Vincent Benet's epic poem, *John Brown's Body* (New York, 1928), should not be lightly dismissed, either as verse or as history.

### XIII. RECENTLY PUBLISHED WORKS

*The pre-Civil War years*
Frederick J. Blue, *The Free Soilers: third party politics, 1848–54* (Urbana, Ill., 1973)
Jane H. and William W. Pease, *Bound with them in Chains: a biographical history of the antislavery movement* (Westport, Conn., 1972)
Lewis Perry, *Radical Abolitionism: anarchy and the government of God in antislavery thought* (Ithaca, N.Y., 1973)
Gerald Sorin, *Abolitionism: a new perspective* (New York, 1972)
Kenneth M. Stampp, ed., *The Causes of the Civil War*, revised edition (Englewood Cliffs, N.J., 1974)
William C. Wright, *The Secession Movement in the Middle Atlantic States* (Rutherford, N.J., 1973)

*The war years*
Louis S. Gerteis, *From Contraband to Freedman: federal policy towards Southern blacks, 1861–1865* (Westport, Conn., 1973)
Robert H. Jones, *Disrupted Decades: the Civil War and reconstruction years* (New York, 1973)
James L. McDonough, *Schofield: Union general in the Civil War and reconstruction* (Tallahassee, Fla., 1972)
John Niven, *Gideon Welles: Lincoln's secretary of the navy* (New York, 1973)
William E. Parrish, *A History of Missouri, Vol. III, 1860–1875* (Columbia, Mo., 1973)

*The post-war years*
Michael L. Benedict, *The Impeachment and Trial of Andrew Johnson* (New York, 1973)
John W. Blassingame, *Black New Orleans, 1860–1880* (Chicago, 1973)
Martin E. Mantell, *Johnson, Grant and the Politics of Reconstruction* (New York, 1973)
James C. Mohr, *The Radical Republicans and Reform in New York during Reconstruction* (Ithaca, N.Y., 1973)

# Index

N. = North or Northern
S. = South or Southern
C.S.S. = Confederate States ship
U.S.S. = United States ship

742 *Index*

North Carolina, secession of, 69, 70, 79, 104, 114; and opposition to Davis administration, 223, 491, 493–4; and peace movement, 496, 557; Edward Stanley appointed military governor of, 522; Sherman's march into, 567; reconstruction in, 598

Northrop, Lucius B., Confederate commissary-general, blamed for failure to follow up Bull Run victory, 126; shortcomings of, 147, 306–7; attacked in Congress, 220, 560; dismissed, 560

Northwest. *See* West, the

Nueces river, 45

Nullification crisis (1832–3), 38–9, 85

Oberlin college, Ohio, 37

Oil industry, early developments in, 347

Olustee, Florida, battle of, 456

Opequon Creek, Virginia, battle of, 475

Order of American Knights, 504

Ordinance of 1787, 35, 40

Ordnance Bureau, Confederate, 149, 308, 310

Oregon question in 1840s, 44–6

Ostend Manifesto (1854), 51

Owen, Robert Dale, 256

Ox Hill. *See* Chantilly

Pacific railroad, Republicans and, 65; Act passed (1862), 350, 372–3

Paducah, Kentucky, occupied by Grant, 118; raided by Forrest, 456

Palmerston, Viscount, 404, 405, 439; attitude towards Civil War, 382–3, 388–9; and policy of neutrality, 389, 400, 449; and *Trent* affair, 412; and Laird rams, 442; hostile to Lindsay's mediation proposals, 447; and intervention question, autumn 1862, 447–9

Pamphlets, as means of propaganda during Civil War, 543

Panic of 1857, 85, 339, 353

Panic of 1873, 619, 643

Pardon, presidential power of, 518; and Lincoln's proclamation of Dec. 8, 1863, 524, 552; and Johnson's proclamation of May 29, 1865, 598–9

Parker, Theodore, 61

Parsons, Lewis B., 348

Party politics, before the Civil War, 24, 26, 97-8; collapse of old party system, 53; and relation to Northern war effort, 199–200, 210, 220, 225, 498, 513–14, 539, 547, 579; impact of Civil War upon, 642–4

Patterson, Robert, N. general, 122, 123, 124

Pea Ridge, Arkansas, battle of, 171

Peace Democrats (*See also* Democratic party), 208, 498, 502, 504, 557; and Chicago convention (1864), 538–9; in Indiana, 542

Peace movements, in the North, 280, 495, 497–8, 502; in the South, 331, 495–6, 557

Peace proposals (1864–5), 555–9

Peach Tree Creek, Georgia, battle of, 473

Pearson, Richmond M., of North Carolina, and writs of habeas corpus, 493

Pember, Phoebe Yates, 325

Pemberton, John C., 105; and defence of Vicksburg, 268–9, 273, 274–5, 279, 281–2, 291; surrender, 291; target of critics, 487

Pendleton, George H., Democratic vice-presidential candidate (1864), 539

Peninsula, the, Virginia. *See* James peninsula

Perryville, Kentucky, battle of, 191, 196

*Peterhoff* case, 426

Petersburg, Virginia, 128, 459, 464; as railroad centre, 312, 464; failure of Northern attack upon (June 1864), 464–6; siege of, 466, 467–9, 474–5, 476, 559, 563; final stages, 568–9; fall of, 569

Petition, right of, and antislavery movement, 37–8

Pettus, John J., governor of Mississippi, 223, 402

Phelan, James, 219

Phelps, John S., military governor of Arkansas, 522

Phillips, Wendell, 31, 87, 533

Pickett, George E., S. general, at Gettysburg, 288; at Dinwiddie Court House and Five Forks, 569

Pickett, John T., 396, 402

Pierce, Franklin, 44, 51, 55, 506

Pierpoint, Francis H., 117

Pillow, Gideon J., S. general, and loss of Fort Donelson, 153, 169

Pinkerton, Allan, 192–3

Pleasant Hill, Louisiana, battle of, 456

Pleasonton, Alfred, N. general, 283

Political parties. *See* Party politics

Polk, James K., 27, 44–6, 51

Polk, Leonidas, S. general, 167, 296

Pomeroy, Marcus M. 'Brick', 499

Pomeroy, Samuel C., 205; and 'Pomeroy circular', 532–3

Pook, Samuel M., and the 'Pook turtles', 431, 432

Pope, John, N. general, 154, 170; captures New Madrid and Island No. 10, 169; takes command of Army of Virginia, 182–3; defeated at second Bull Run, 183–6; dismissed, 187

Popular sovereignty, 47, 49; and Kansas-Nebraska Act, 52; in Kansas, 54–5; disputes over, 56–60; the South and, 56–7; and Dred Scott decision, 57–8

Population, growth of, 20–1; of North and South (1860), 21, 108–9; mobility of, 25

Populists, 635, 642–3

# Index

743

Porcher, Francis P., *Resources of the Southern fields and forests*, 321

Port Gibson, Mississippi, battle of, 275

Port Hudson, Louisiana, 267, 281; Confederate defences established at, 195; Negro troops engaged at, 259; withstands Union attacks, 272, 433; surrendered to Banks, 291

Port Republic, Virginia, battle of, 179

Port Royal, South Carolina, 167, 428

Porter, David D., and Vicksburg campaign, 274, 432–4; operations against Fort Fisher, 430–1; and Red River campaign, 434, 456

Porter, Fitzjohn, N. general, 186

Potawatomie, Kansas, attacked by John Brown, 55

Potomac flotilla, 427

*Powhatan*, U.S.S., 76

Prentiss, Benjamin, N. general, defends 'Hornet's Nest' at Shiloh, 170

Press, the, in the South, 214, 321, 334; in the North, 376

Price, Sterling, S. general, agreement with Harney, in Missouri, 119–20; campaign in Missouri, ending in defeat at Westport (1864), 483

Prices, in the South, 307, 318, 319, 489–90; in the North, 363

Prince Consort, and the *Trent* affair, 412–13

Privateering Act (1863), 440

Privateers, Confederate, 406–7, 408–9, 435; threat of Northern, 440

Proclamations of Amnesty and Reconstruction, issued by Lincoln, Dec. 8, 1863, 518, 524–5, 552; issued by Johnson, May 29, 1865, 598

Produce loan, 316–17

Propaganda, of antislavery movement, 37–38; and causes of Civil War, 89–90; in the Confederacy, 334–5; in the North, 376; in Europe, by the Confederacy, 402–3; in Europe, by the North, 403–4; of the Republican party, 501, 504–5, 538, 543

Protective tariff. See Tariff

Public lands, 352, 371–2. See also Homestead law

*Queen of the West*, U.S.S., and operations at Vicksburg, 433

Race, and causes of Civil War, 96; and consequences of war, 555, 587–8, 623–4, 626, 634–5. See also Negroes, Negrophobia, Slavery, Emancipation, etc.

Radical Democracy, the, and election of 1864, 533–4

Radical reconstruction, 520, 608, 609; character and limitations of, 621–3. See also Radical Republicans during reconstruction, and Reconstruction

Radical Republicans:
character and identity of, 204–7, 621–3; and crisis of Dec. 1862, 209–10; and emancipation, 231, 233, 235–6, 246; and organised labour, 370; and the constitution, 506, 512, 518, 622; and wartime reconstruction, 520–1, 524–5, 527, 528–30, 550–1, 554; and election of 1864, 529–30, 535–6, 537, 539, 540–1, 547

during reconstruction: and use of federal power, 590–2; high hopes of Johnson in 1865, 593; relationship with moderates, 594, 597–8, 601, 603, 621–2; motives, 594–7; effects of Johnson's programme upon, 600; and Reconstruction Acts, 604–5; and 15th Amendment, 608; and waning of reconstruction in South, 619–620; and industrial working class, 634; as orthodox liberals, 622–3, 645

'Radical' rule, in Southern states, 609, 613, 614–16, 618

Railroads, growth of before Civil War, 22–23, 51; and prospects of both sides in 1861, 110; and first Bull Run, 124; impact on warfare of, 130; and movement of troops from Virginia to Tennessee, 296, 298, 313; in the South during the war, 311–14, 561; and east-west communications, 339, 341, 349; in the North during the war, 349–52, 372–3; and Sherman's advance to Atlanta, 470, 478

Rains, George, W. 149

Ramsdell, Charles W., 82

Randall, James G., 82, 629

Randolph, George W., Confederate secretary of war, 155, 217, 268

*Rappahannock*, the, 440

Raymond, Henry J., recommends peace moves, 536, 556; and election of 1864, 542

Reagan, John H., Confederate postmaster-general, 215

Reconstruction:
during the Civil War, 456, 513, 515, 516–530, 549–55; as a constitutional problem, 516–19, 551–2; Lincoln and, 518, 524–5, 551–4; rivalry between president and Congress over, 518, 523, 525–30, 550–1, 554; political issues concerning, 519–21, 527, 554; Negroes and, 519–20, 552, 554–5; in Tennessee, Louisiana, and Arkansas, 520, 521, 522–3, 525–6, 528, 549–52; and election of 1864, 526, 529–30, 547, 549; Wade-Davis bill and Lincoln's veto, 526–8; situation at end of war, 554–5, 570

after the Civil War, 589–624; problems of, 589–92; federal power and 591–2,